Introduction to Psychology

Christopher Peterson
University of Michigan

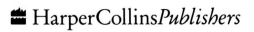
HarperCollins*Publishers*

To my brother Carl with all of my love

Sponsoring Editor: Anne Harvey
Project Coordination, Text and Cover Design: Proof Positive/
    Farrowlyne Associates, Inc.
Cover Illustration: Hans Zander
Photo Research: Cheryl Woike Kucharzak
Production: Michael Weinstein
Compositor: Weimer Typesetting Co., Inc.
Printer and Binder: R. R. Donnelley & Sons Company
Cover Printer: Phoenix Color Corp.

Library of Congress Cataloging-in-Publication Data

Peterson, Christopher.
    Introduction to psychology / Christopher Peterson.
        p.   cm.
    Includes bibliographical references and indexes.
    ISBN 0-673-39807-2
    1. Psychology. I. Title.
    BF121.P44   1990
    150–dc20

91 92 93 9 8 7 6 5 4 3 2

Contents in Brief

Contents

Chapter Twelve

Abnormal Psychology   489

Chapter Thirteen

Therapy   537

Chapter Fourteen

Social Cognition   581

Preface

My goal in this textbook is to introduce students to the major theories, findings, and applications of psychology. In doing so, I have tried to respect both the diversity of psychology as well as its unity. *Introduction to Psychology* is intended to be readable (by students), teachable (by instructors), and understandable (by all). It attempts to go beyond a mere cataloging of facts and findings. It also tries to advance a point of view. I would like students to become critical consumers of psychology, appreciative yet skeptical.

These are laudable goals, to be sure, but how does this book go about achieving them? I thought back on the strategies and techniques that I have found particularly useful in my own study of psychology. I've incorporated these into *Introduction to Psychology*.

Strategies and Techniques

First, I have always learned the most when I could apply abstract ideas to my everyday life. The book thus relies on vivid examples to explicate concepts. Every chapter begins with a vignette from history, literature, or popular culture that pertains to the chapter's subject matter. Other examples are found throughout the chapter.

Second, I have always grasped material best when I had a sense of the bigger picture. Examples are compelling only when one knows the larger ideas that they convey. When I was first introduced to psychology, I had to create the bigger picture for myself. I've tried to help today's students acquire useful frameworks more quickly and efficiently by including after each chapter-opening vignette a section called "Topics of Concern." Here I discuss some of the broad issues that concern psychologists who work within a given area. For example, in what way are people products of evolution (Chapter 2)? How do infants become children (Chapter 9), and how do children become adults (Chapter 10)? Why do some people suffer from emotional problems (Chapter 12)? How do other people affect what we do (Chapter 15)?

Third, psychology became easier for me to grasp when I finally understood how psychologists conduct research. Other textbooks point out that psychology is a science, but then offer conclusions without describing exactly how they were reached. In Chapter 1 of *Introduction to Psychology*, there is an overview of research methods in psychology. But in every subsequent chapter, I also explain how studies are conducted in a given area. Researchers interested in the brain may use lesion and ablation techniques (Chapter 2). Those interested in sensation rely on the procedures of psychophysics (Chapter 3). Developmental psychologists must choose between cross-sectional and longitudinal designs (Chapter 9). Social psychologists often rely on deception experiments (Chapter 13). Consistent with my other strategies in this book, these research discussions are general and accessible, accompanied in each case by carefully chosen examples, both classic and recent studies.

Fourth, psychology made better sense to me when I started to understand how the field evolved. Psychology has a history, and its past can shed light on its present and even hint at its future. *Introduction to Psychology* thus has a historical emphasis, more so than many other textbooks. Like all authors, I have done my best to include current ideas, but I have taken equal care to specify the roots of today's work. In the typical chapter, I discuss the history of people's attempts to understand a given topic, such as the brain (Chapter 2), the mind (Chapter 7), intelligence (Chapter 8), personality (Chapter 11), and human sexuality (Chapter 16). Many of these attempts predate the formal existence of psychology, and I believe it is important for students to know that the broad concerns of psychology are really longstanding human concerns.

Fifth, I have found that humor can facilitate difficult discussions. Psychology abounds with conflicting ideas, and sometimes humor is the best way to capture the apparent paradoxes of the field. Furthermore, because psychology concerns itself with the human condition, aspects of its study can threaten and upset us. Appropriately chosen humor creates bonds and bridges among people, helping us see that psychology is not about them and us, but simply about us. Every chapter opens with a cartoon by Gary Larson. He calls his cartoon strip *The Far Side*, but his humor often examines the human condition "close up."

Text Organization

Instructors will find much about the content and organization of *Introduction to Psychology* that is familiar. The book moves from particular topics such as the nervous system, sensation, and perception to more inclusive and interpersonal topics such as personality, abnormality, and social interaction. This is an effective way of introducing students to psychology.

However, there exist as well organizational innovations in this book. A brief Appendix devoted to statistics appears—not at the end of the entire book—but immediately following the general discussion of research methods in Chapter 1. This Appendix presents the basics of descriptive and inferential statistics. It is quite easy to manage, and it is placed where it actually belongs in an introductory psychology book. Most introductory psychology textbooks have a statistics section, but these are almost always too abstract and too detailed to be of much use to the beginning student.

Another organizational innovation is an Appendix at the end of the book that provides an overview of such prominent fields of applied psychology as industrial psychology, consumer psychology, health psychology, and sports psychology. These applied fields are growing in popularity and importance. By covering them all in one place, and doing so after my introduction to the whole of psychology, I show how they are based in so-called basic psychology as well as how they have their own identities.

Unique Coverage

Within individual chapters, I cover particular topics not mentioned or detailed in other textbooks so that students will fully appreciate the richness of psychology. In Chapter 1, I compare and contrast scientific psychology with the psychology of common sense and casual conversation. Beginning students are curious about how the psychology covered in their introductory course differs from everyday psychology, so I address this question explicitly. This discussion advances the book's goal of encouraging students to be critical consumers.

For another example, in Chapter 2, I discuss the structure and function of the nervous system in relation to the theory of evolution. Also in this chapter, I discuss sociobiology in some detail, because this evolutionary approach to social behavior will attract further attention within psychology in the 1990s. Indeed, an evolutionary perspective is carried through the entire book.

Further examples of innovative content include discussions of contemporary challenges to learning theory (Chapter 5); complex emotions (Chapter 6); the extremes of intelligence (Chapter 8); the psychology of aging (Chapter 10); the resolution of the personality consistency controversy (Chapter 11); psychotherapy research (Chapter 13); and romantic relationships conceived in terms of emotional attachments (Chapter 15).

The last chapter of *Introduction to Psychology* is devoted to human sexuality. Here I cover an important topic while showing the student that psychology is a unified field; all of its seemingly disparate aspects must be brought to bear on complex topics such as sexuality.

Introduction to Psychology contains frequent cross-referencing of material, aiding its integration. Concepts discussed in one chapter—such as the nature-nurture controversy—are linked to discussions in other chapters. I make these connections to underscore one of the important themes of the book: Despite its diversity, psychology is conceptually unified. Another reason for the cross-referencing is to encourage students yet again to be critical. What is a reasonable idea in one context may be less reasonable in another, and I invite them to consider where the boundaries might lie. So, operant conditioning makes perfect sense as an explanation of certain habits (Chapter 5), but does it work as well as an explanation of language acquisition (chapter 9)? Evolutionary considerations certainly explain the nature of our sensory organs (Chapter 3), but are they as helpful in explaining human aggression (Chapter 15) or sexuality (Chapter 16)?

Ancillary Materials

A full set of ancillaries accompanies *Introduction to Psychology*. Included with the textbook is a special issue of *Discover* magazine, containing articles that discuss contemporary theories and findings of psychology. I helped create this issue, but the real credit should go to Scott Hardy, Paula Fitzpatrick, Lisa M. Bossio, and particularly Paul Hoffman, the editor of *Discover*. Glenda Smith of North Harris County College devised both the *Instructor's Manual* and the *Student's Study Guide*, which should go a long way to helping instructors and their students be on the same page—both literally and metaphorically—while covering *Introduction to Psychology*. In addition, there is computer software support for instructor and student. *Supershell* functions as a combination computer study guide and tutorial. *Journey* is a full-color, graphic programmed learning tour of the psychology experiment, the nervous system, learning, development, and psychological assessment. *The Psychology Encyclopedia*, a laser disk program that contains images from transparencies, slides, films, and videotapes, is also available. Finally, I wrote all of the items for the *Test Bank*. An author-written test bank, unusual for an introductory psychology textbook, has the obvious advantage of compatibility with text content and emphases. Available also is a computerized testing system—*Testmaster*—for the IBM and Macintosh computers.

Acknowledgments

Books have histories in which particular people figure prominently, and *Introduction to Psychology* is no exception. My efforts would have amounted to little without the assistance of many other people. Editors Scott Hardy, Donald Hull, Laura Pearson, Leslie Hawke, and Anne Harvey helped me shape this book from its original plan through countless revisions into what you see before you. Guy Huff secured permissions; Ellen Pettengell designed the book; Sandy Schneider and Cheryl Woike Kucharzak chose illustrations; and Dan Weiskopf of Proof Positive/Farrowlyne Associates did the copy-editing.

I express special gratitude to Paula Fitzpatrick. Her official title was Developmental Editor, but perhaps Head Shepherd would have been more descriptive. Books and their authors may often stray, and I am grateful to Paula for getting this book·and this author back on the right path so many times, with humor and encouragement. "We're getting there," she always said to me, and we finally did.

Reviewers galore were consulted while *Introduction to Psychology* was written and revised. I express special gratitude to Myra Heinrich of Mesa College for helping me reorganize several chapters. The comments of all the reviewers, individually and collectively, did much to correct the substance and improve the style. Much thanks to:

Bruce Abbott
Indiana University-Purdue University at Fort Wayne

Tony Albiniak
University of South Carolina

Frank Bagrash
California State University at Fullerton

Lou Bandaret
Northeastern University

Mario Benassi
College of Lake County

William Beneke
Lincoln University

Brenda Bennett
Vincennes University

Nyla Branscombe
University of Kansas

R. Gary Brendel
Walla Walla College

Charles Brewer
Furman University

Thomas Brothen
University of Minnesota

Robert Brown
Jefferson Community College

James B. Buchanan
University of Scranton

Frank Calabrese
Community College of Philadelphia

John Clark
Macomb County Community College

Edward Clemmer
Emerson College

Eric J. Cooley
Western Oregon State College

Keith Davis
University of South Carolina

Bill Dwyer
Memphis State University

Claire Etaugh
Bradley University

John Faust
Parkland College

David Filey
El Paso Community College

Grace Galliano
Kennesaw State College

Josh Gerow
Indiana University-Purdue University at Fort Wayne

Gary Greenberg
Wichita State University

Richard Griggs
University of Florida

Sandra Holmes
University of Wisconsin-Green Bay

William Huitt
Valdosta State College

Chris Jazwinski
St. Cloud State University

Carl Johnson
Central Michigan University

James J. Johnson
Illinois State University

Cindy Kennedy
Sinclair Community College

Andrew Kinney
Mohawk Valley Community College

Ned L. Kirsch
University of Michigan

Terry Knapp
University of Nevada at Las Vegas

Victor Koop
Goshen College

James Korn
St. Louis University

Rosemary Krawczyk
Mankato State University

Patricia Lazar
Bucks County Community College

Donald Lisenby
University of Missouri at St. Louis

Thomas Lombardo
University of Mississippi

Robert Lowder
Bradley University

Gordon Matheson
Worcester State College

James McCaleb
*South Suburban College
of Cook County*

Richard McDouglas
Dean Junior College

Angela McGlynn
Trenton State College

Carolyn Meyer
Lake-Sumter Community College

Eleanor Midkiff
Eastern Illinois University

Karla Miley
Black Hawk College

Joel Morgodsky
Brookdale Community College

Peggy Nash
Broward Community College

Steve Nida
Franklin University

William C. Owen
Virginia Western Community College

Nancy Parker
Embry-Riddle Aeronautical University

Tom Patton
Graceland College

Linda Pierce
Appalachian State University

John Pinto
Morningside College

David B. Porter
United States Air Force Academy

Steven Rosengarten
Middlesex Community College

Michael Ross
St. Louis University

Connie Schick
*Bloomsburg University
of Pennsylvania*

Peggy Skinner
South Plains College

Glenda Smith
*North Harris County
Community College*

William C. Stebbins
University of Michigan

W. Scott Terry
*University of North Carolina
at Greensboro*

Tom Thiemann
College of St. Catherine

J. David Tipton
Gadsden State Community College

Gaston Walker
Tarrant County Junior College

Neff Walker
University of Michigan

Phyllis Walrad
Macomb County Community College

Sean Ward
Le Moyne College

Paul Watson
University of Tennessee at Memphis

Cecelia Yoder
Oklahoma City Community College

Eve Wolf
Kent State University

Stephen J. Zaccaro
George Mason University

Ric Wynn
County College of Morris

Michael Zeller
Mankato State University

Finally, my friends and family have taken great interest in this book, from start to finish. Lisa M. Bossio, in particular, labored mightily on behalf of *Introduction to Psychology*. She certainly knows part of what she did, from researching to editing to organizing. But only I know how much she really helped. Thanks, Lisa, as usual.

A Note to the Student

Here is how I recommend that you read chapters. Look first at the outline that begins each chapter. It is organized in terms of the main headings of the chapter. Then read the summary at the end of each chapter; again, it is organized in terms of the chapter's main headings. Next read the chapter itself, taking time along the way to reflect on what you encounter. Look at the list of important terms and names to be sure that you can identify each one. Glossary terms appear throughout the text in **boldface**, and they are defined in the margin right next to where they first appear as well as in a page-referenced glossary at the end of the book. Try to answer the multiple-choice review questions at the end of the chapter. These cover some of the important concepts in the chapter, and are similar to the questions you will be asked on actual exams. After each review question, I provide a brief explanation of its answer—but not the answer itself. Now do all of this again, until you understand the major ideas and the important details that flesh them out.

Christopher Peterson

Introduction to Psychology

The testing of theories against evidence is what makes
psychology a science.

Chapter One

What Is Psychology?

Topics of Concern
Masters or Victims?
Minds or Bodies?
Nature or Nurture?
Subjectivity or Objectivity?
Past or Present?
Scientific Progress

Scientific Psychology versus Everyday Psychology

The History of Psychology
Wilhelm Wundt and Edward B. Titchener: Structuralism
Max Wertheimer and Kurt Lewin: Gestalt Psychology
William James and John Dewey: Functionalism
John Watson: Behaviorism
Sigmund Freud: Psychoanalysis
Recent Trends in Psychology
Fields of Psychology

Research Methods in Psychology
Basic Concepts
Case Studies
Correlational Investigations
Experiments
Research Ethics

Topics of Concern

On December 23, 1888, artist Vincent Van Gogh cut off part of his left ear, which he then took to a prostitute named Rachel. "Keep this object carefully," he said to her.

Why did Van Gogh cut off his ear? For the past 100 years, many people—including psychologists—have tried to explain this bizarre event. Can psychologists shed any light on the matter? You might at first think not, because this event is too unique and too strange. But, in a provocative essay, William M. Runyan (1981) tackled the question from the viewpoint of psychology. More generally, in this essay he discussed how psychology might explain *any* specific action of a particular person. Van Gogh's action was an unusual occurrence, to be sure, but as you will see, the subject matter of psychology includes both the unusual and the commonplace.

Runyan cataloged more than a dozen possible explanations suggested over the years to account for Van Gogh's action, including the following:

1. Van Gogh was frustrated with the engagement of his brother, to whom he was greatly attached, as well as with his inability to establish a personal and working relationship with artist Paul Gauguin.
2. On a previous visit to Rachel, Van Gogh had been teased by her about having large ears.

Psychologists are concerned with all aspects of human behavior—from the bizarre ("Why did Van Gogh cut off his ear?") to the commonplace.

3. Van Gogh was influenced by the custom in bullfighting of presenting a victorious matador with the severed ear of the bull, which he then would give to the lady of his choice.
4. Van Gogh had read about the exploits of Jack the Ripper, who killed and mutilated prostitutes, in some cases cutting off their ears.
5. Van Gogh was trying to win attention and sympathy from any of a variety of people, including his brother, his mother, and/or his patrons.
6. Van Gogh experienced hallucinations—hearing voices that others did not—and thought his ears were diseased.

Runyan tried to sort through these alternative explanations. Can all of them be true? Are some more reasonable than others? Is there any way to test a given explanation?

Before going on to consider these questions and others like them, let's pause and define the discipline we will be studying. **Psychology** is the scientific study of behavior and mental processes. Often its focus is on the thoughts, feelings, and actions of people. Certainly, Van Gogh's cutting off his ear falls within the scope of psychology. At other times, psychology is concerned with animal behavior.

Psychologists use the term **behavior** to refer to the actions and reactions of a person or animal that can be observed and measured by others. Examples of behavior include an infant babbling, a child working a puzzle, an adult voting in an election, and a rat running through a maze. **Mental processes** refer to occurrences within someone's mind—hopes and dreams, thoughts and beliefs, wishes and fears, which cannot be directly observed by another person. But mental processes become legitimate topics for psychology when we specify how we can draw inferences about them from behaviors that we observe. Therefore, we can conclude that Van Gogh feels frustrated with his brother because when he sees him Van Gogh clenches his jaw, breathes rapidly, and speaks loudly.

To say that psychology is a science means that its investigations of behavior and mental processes are of a special kind: They are based on **hypotheses,** tentative predictions that can be tested against the observable evidence. Hypotheses are derived from more general explanations called **theories.** The various procedures available to scientists for testing hypotheses are together referred to as the **scientific method.** Later in this chapter, we'll discuss some of the important procedures that psychologists use to evaluate their theories. Right now, let's go back to Van Gogh, his ear, and our attempts to explain what happened.

Runyan proposed that the scientific method be used to answer the question, "Why did Van Gogh cut off his ear?" Consider the various explanations in turn. Do we have evidence, for instance, that arguments with his brother, or Gauguin, or anyone else took place immediately prior to the event in which we are interested? Do we know that Van Gogh had been teased about the size of his ears? Was he a bullfight fan? Do we know that he had read about Jack the Ripper? Did he indeed experience hallucinations?

Runyan offered no absolute answer to the question about Van Gogh. However, he did succeed in arguing—in light of available historical records—that some explanations are more plausible than others. On the one hand, there is not a shred of evidence that Van Gogh had ever been teased by Rachel about the size of his ears. On the other hand, there is ample evidence that Van Gogh responded poorly when his close relationship with his brother was threatened. Van Gogh cut off his ear when his brother announced his engagement; and Van Gogh later experienced emotional problems when his brother married, and when his brother's first child was born.

Don't be disappointed that Runyan only narrowed the range of possible explanations. This is the best that any scientist can do. Scientific explanations are hypotheses, and they are not meant to last forever. Psychologists are always questioning and testing their explanations, looking for better ways to account for what people (or animals) are all about. Your classroom instructor and I will do our best to describe

psychology
the scientific study of behavior and mental processes

behavior
actions and reactions of a person or animal that can be observed by others and measured

mental processes
occurrences within someone's mind, like hopes and dreams, thoughts and beliefs, wishes and fears, that are not observable by others

hypotheses
tentative predictions that can be tested against observable evidence

theories
general explanations from which hypotheses are derived

scientific method
the systematic procedures used by scientists to check explanations against evidence

for you what is currently known and accepted in psychology. However, at best, what you will have is a snapshot of an ongoing endeavor.

Psychology as a science changes and grows, and old theories give way to new ones. Nonetheless, basic questions and issues endure. Michael Wertheimer (1972) has identified some of the issues that cut across the whole of psychology, and we will briefly discuss them here. These fundamental concerns show up throughout the rest of this book, in one form or another.

Masters or Victims?

When people think or feel or act, what motivates these behaviors? Some psychologists believe that people respond automatically to environmental or biological events. These psychologists grant no real purpose or intentionality to people, and conceive of them instead as victims of events outside their control (Chapter 5). Other psychologists take an opposite view, proposing that people are masters of their fates: active and purposive (Chapter 7).

Note how this issue becomes concrete in the Van Gogh example. Some explanations propose that he cut off his ear to make a deliberate point (to his brother, to Gauguin, and/or to Rachel). Other explanations suggest that he was out of control during the incident, a victim of emotions triggered by external events.

Minds or Bodies?

In their attempts to explain what people are all about, psychologists face a difficult decision—whether to focus on mental processes, such as thoughts, feelings, and attitudes; or on physical events, such as the operation of the muscles, nerves, and glands. Obviously people have minds and bod-

The nature-nurture debate centers on the relative importance of inherited traits and learning and experience to human development.

ies, but many psychologists emphasize one aspect over the other in their work. Psychology is often organized in terms of relative emphasis, and our textbook follows this organization, starting with topics where biology seems to predominate (Chapters 2, 3, and 4), and then moving to topics where our mental processes seem more critical (Chapters 6, 7, and so on). To explain Van Gogh's actions, we could refer either to some sort of biochemical disruption or to emotional upset.

Nature or Nurture?

Closely related to the mind or body issue is another question of enduring concern: Are people better understood in terms of their inherited characteristics or their learning and experiences? Answering this question involves us in the **nature-nurture controversy,** which we will encounter throughout the book. For example, some psychologists believe that relative intelligence is largely a matter of genetics; others strongly disagree, believing that intelligence is determined more by family upbringing and available educational opportunities (Chapter 8). The issue of differences between men and women is also part of the nature-nurture controversy (Chapter 9). The differences themselves are usually clear enough, but should we explain them in terms of nature ("that's just the way men and women are") or nurture ("that's just the way men and women are raised in our society")? Similarly, in making sense of Van Gogh, should we look for tendencies toward unusual behavior that he may have inherited or for habits brought about by particular experiences during his life?

Subjectivity or Objectivity?

There are other strategies psychologists might follow in developing a better understanding of people. One can describe people from the inside, using their views of the world to get a handle on their behavior. Using this approach, the psychologist must grasp someone's subjective reality. Indeed, as you will see later in this chapter, the first psychologists were interested in consciousness, and many contemporary psychologists are interested in thoughts and beliefs. Conversely, one can opt to describe people only from the outside, stressing objective reality. The influential movement within psychology known as behaviorism started with the explicit goal of describing people in objective terms (Chapter 5). Some psychologists would try to understand Van Gogh by reading his letters and journals, hoping for an insight from his descriptions of his thoughts and feelings. Other psychologists would look instead at external events that were occurring around Van Gogh at a given time.

Past or Present?

When explaining someone's behavior, we can focus on the present or on the past. The relative merits of one strategy or the other represent one more topic of concern to psychologists. Psychoanalysis, the approach to psychology introduced by Sigmund Freud, stresses the influence of early childhood conflicts. Decades later, these events may still influence a person's thoughts, feelings, or actions. Indeed, psychoanalysis proposes that one's adult personality is a product of childhood events (Chapter 11). The opposite point of view argues that people respond chiefly to the influence of immediate events, such as the actions of others nearby (Chapter 15).

One important implication of this issue concerns the nature of people's problems (Chapter 12) and approaches for solving them (Chapter 13). If the causes of behavior are to be found in the distant past, then change in the present is necessarily slow and difficult. If the causes of behavior are more recent, then change is easier, at least in principle. Contemporary therapy might well have helped Van Gogh solve whatever problems he faced, but the approach taken by different therapists would vary according to what each presumed was the source of Van Gogh's problems—something in the there and then, or in the here and now.

Scientific Progress

These and related issues have dominated the study of psychology for the more than 100 years of its existence. There are no answers that all psychologists accept; that's why these are enduring concerns. Does this mean that psychology has made no progress? Not at all. To see this point, consider the notion of scientific progress.

Let us start with a distinction between scientific information and scientific explanations. Scientific information, or **data,** refers to the evidence psychologists use to test hypotheses in an investigation. Data are observable. What was the person's score on that test? How fast did the monkey push the button? How close are those two children standing to one another? In contrast, scientific explanations are hy-

nature-nurture controversy
a long-standing debate central to the field of psychology that concerns whether our development is due to biological inheritance (nature) or learning and experience (nurture)

data
facts obtained through measurement or observation in a scientific study

potheses, that is, tentative attempts to make sense of the data. The defining feature of an explanation is that it can be tested against the evidence, and thus proven right or wrong.

Scientific information accumulates as science progresses, and scientists attempt to explain the information available to them. But explanations do *not* accumulate. Instead, explanations pass in and out of fashion, depending on how useful scientists find them. Thomas Kuhn (1970) is an influential historian and philosopher of science who likens the coming and going of a scientific theory to a revolution: sudden and abrupt. Consider Darwin's theory of evolution (Chapter 2), which proposes that one species evolves from another. This account of the world is profoundly different from those that preceded it. These earlier accounts suggested that different species did not change over time. The overthrown theories did not slowly advance to become Darwin's theory of evolution. Instead, they were weak in precisely those places where Darwin's account was strong. When the time and place were right, a scientific revolution took place.

Absolute truth is not really the goal of science. Scientists grope for better explanations of their subject matter, but "better" reflects a relative judgment made with respect to competing theories. And this relative judgment can be made along a number of dimensions: better with respect to simplicity, better with respect to concrete application, better with respect to prediction, and so on. Think of the concerns of psychology not as signs of the field's lack of progress, but rather of the progress that occurs all the time, as one explanation is discarded in favor of another.

Everyday psychologists believe that some people freely choose to participate in activities that many of us consider dangerous.

determinism
the philosophical assumption, held by psychologists, that all behaviors have causes

Scientific Psychology versus Everyday Psychology

Scientific progress takes place as explanations are checked against the evidence. If we forget that science requires evidence, then we risk confusing the theories of psychology with mere opinion. Surely you have heard psychology criticized as "just" common sense (or worse). But this is an unfair criticism, as it overlooks the critical role that relevant evidence plays in psychology.

We can understand scientific psychology better by contrasting it with a close relative that also tries to explain what people are all about: so-called everyday psychology (Heider, 1958). Everyday psychology is made up of the explanations that we use in the course of daily life to account for our own behavior or that of others. The line between the two can be fuzzy. Indeed, everyday psychology can provide insights into people's behavior. Nonetheless, we can distinguish between the two because psychology is a science, whereas its close relative is not.

Everyday psychology differs from scientific psychology in several ways. First, *scientific psychology attempts to explain everything that people do, whereas everyday psychology attempts to explain behavior that is surprising.* Scientific psychologists take the whole of human activity as their domain: the mundane and the exotic, the good and the bad, the typical and the unusual. Everyday psychologists, however, apply their version of psychology only to thoughts, feelings, or actions that are discrepant with their experience. They have no interest in why brides and grooms kiss at weddings, why the Notre Dame football team wins, or why children like candy. Instead, everyday psychologists want to know why athletes overdose on drugs, why people poison medications in grocery stores, and why teenagers tuck in their trousers but not their shirts (or vice versa).

Sometimes psychology students are disappointed that scientific psychology doesn't focus exclusively on the bizarre things that people are apt to do. Although psychology has something to say about the bizarre (remember Runyan's essay on Vincent Van Gogh), its strategy is to say it in terms of theories about the whole of human behavior. Without getting too philosophical about it all, may I suggest that the real miracles of human behavior are not the activities chronicled on the pages of the *National Enquirer.* Rather, they are topics that most of us take for granted. How do we combine our sensations into coherent perceptions (Chapter 4)? How do we learn language (Chapter 9)? Why are some people happier than others (Chapter 12)? Is prejudice inevitable (Chapter 15)?

Second, *scientific psychology assumes determinism, whereas everyday psychology assumes free will.* Scientific psychologists believe in **determinism,** that is, that all behaviors have causes. Everyday psychologists instead assume that a person's behavior is undertaken freely except in certain special cases, such as hypnosis, brainwashing, lust, and intoxication.

This distinction between scientific psychology and everyday psychology has an important implication: Psychologists probably have less to say in a court of law than one might think. The legal system in the United States works under the same assumption as everyday psychology: that people's behavior is freely chosen, unless there is good reason to believe otherwise. Psychologists are sometimes called to serve as expert witnesses with respect to the "otherwise." Unfortunately, in giving testimony, a psychologist is asked to think in terms that contradict one of the central assumptions of his or her discipline.

This confusion is well illustrated in legal cases where the accused pleads insanity (Coleman, 1984). Perhaps you've noted that both the prosecution and the defense can find psychologists who will support their positions. Such cross-testimony makes psychology look like an arbitrary endeavor. It is not. Rather, the contradictions result from asking individual psychologists to make distinctions alien to their science. Indeed, *insanity* is a legal term, not a psychological one, because it refers specifically to a person's inability to choose freely his or her actions.

Third, *scientific psychology offers tentative explanations, whereas everyday psychology offers ultimate explanations.* Tentativeness is one of the hallmarks of scientific explanation. All scientific explanations are subject to revision or replacement. If not, they are dogma, not science. Yet if we look at the way people in the street explain someone's behavior, we find that they rarely regard their opinion as a hypothesis. Rather, they call it as they see it, and once they decide upon an explanation, they stick with it.

When I first began to teach, I had an interesting encounter with a student who took it upon herself to inform me of the "true" personalities of the other psychology professors. She described one fellow in extremely negative terms. Among his poor qualities were stupidity and sneakiness. I listened to her descriptions for a while, and then decided to argue with her. "Wait a minute," I said. "You describe him as stupid, but I happen to know that he is a respected scholar. He has a great vocabulary. He's witty. And he's explained all sorts of complicated things to me so that I understand them. How can you describe him as stupid?" She smiled triumphantly. "He's fooled you, too, hasn't he?" she said. "I told you he was sneaky."

Explanations that embrace this kind of circular reasoning are called **nonfalsifiable explanations** because there is no way that they can ever be proven wrong. If they can't be proven wrong, then any and all evidence becomes irrelevant. When a psychologist refers to an explanation as nonfalsifiable, that's strong criticism, because it means it is unscientific.

Fourth, *scientific psychology checks its explanations against the facts of the matter, whereas everyday psychology may not.* As already emphasized, scientific psychology evaluates its claims about the human condition against data. If the available data support the explanation, the psychologist stays with his hypothesis for the time being, but continues to evaluate the explanation against other information. If data contradict the explanation, then the psychologist concludes that his explanation was wrong, and he tries to think of a better one.

Perhaps you're familiar with the adage "birds of a feather flock together." We can explain human behavior in a similar fashion, asserting that people like to be with others who are like them. But a scientific psychologist would not accept this explanation on first hearing. Instead, he or she would wonder if the facts supported this claim. It turns out that in many ways they do. Friends tend to resemble each other with respect to various attitudes, values, and interests (Byrne, 1971). Billy Joel and Christie Brinkley notwithstanding, husbands and wives tend to resemble each other as well (Buss, 1984b).

nonfalsifiable explanation
an explanation that cannot be proven wrong by any evidence

Certain relationships are marked by a commonality of interests and values—a rebellious posture, for example. Others are marked by needs that are more complementary.

As researchers in the field kept testing the claim that birds of a feather flock together, they found some evidence that contradicted the claim. Certain friendships are not marked by a similarity of needs, but are complementary (Winch, 1958). Two people will remain friends with each other as long as they satisfy each other. If both need to dominate a conversation, then despite their similarities, they will probably not remain friends for life. If one is a talker and the other is a listener, given that these styles mesh, a continued friendship is likely. We recognize other examples of friends or couples whose relationships work because the needs of one complement the needs of the other: the dependent individual and the nurturant individual, the dreamer and the doer, the sadist and the masochist, Oscar and Felix, Tom and Jerry, George Steinbrenner and his managers.

So, as a scientific explanation of human behavior, "birds of a feather flock together" should be modified in light of the facts to read, less elegantly but more accurately, "birds of a feather flock together, unless their feathers clash." Everyday psychologists would not scrutinize the adage so closely. If called upon to justify this claim, they might rely on evidence, but they might also rely on authority ("Ann Landers said so"), power ("Why? Because I said so, that's why!"), intuition ("It's obvious if you're sensitive to it"), and so on.

Fifth, and finally, *scientific psychology offers explanations in probabilistic terms that refer to people in general, whereas everyday psychology explains particular examples.* Students often have trouble grasping this final aspect of scientific psychology, preferring instead the apparent richness of everyday psychology. They hear statements like "supportive parents tend to have well-adjusted children" or "learning a second language after adolescence is difficult" either as vague generalizations or as altogether incorrect claims, because a counterexample is at hand. "My next-door neighbors are the nicest parents in the world, but their little Freddie terrorizes the entire block." "My mother learned Serbo-Croatian through a correspondence course at age 47, and had no trouble whatsoever."

Scientific hypotheses are generalizations, whether the science in question is chemistry, biology, or psychology. One expects some exceptions to these generalizations; it is impossible to account for every instance. Meteorologists can't predict every rainstorm (as we all know), but they can predict yearly rainfall. Physicians can't predict the course of every illness (again, as we all know), but they do predict typical responses. And psychologists can't predict the exact behavior of particular people, but they are able to predict typical thoughts, feelings, and actions. In attempting to make sense of Van Gogh, for instance, a psychologist draws on explanations that presumably apply to most people. The application of these theories to Van Gogh may work quite well, but the possibility that he is an exception to what are otherwise reasonable accounts must be considered.

One of the goals of science is to reduce the number of exceptions to its claims. But no science can completely eliminate exceptions. Scientific psychology certainly has its share, keeping psychologists busy weighing the validity of any generalization against its exceptions. To this end, a whole host of statistical procedures have been developed for making their judgments precise (see appendix to this chapter). In contrast, everyday psychology focuses on the particular instance to the exclusion of general trends. When the person in the street makes a pronouncement, we find it richer in detail, easier to grasp, and more believable than the qualified generalizations of a psychologist.

Everyday explanations may be so specific that they end up nonfalsifiable. Scientific psychology may give up vividness by offering generalizations, but it thereby gains the ability to apply its claims to people in general, and the ability to say whether the generalization is reasonable or unreasonable. That's what science is all about, and that's why everyday psychology is not quite the same thing.

The History of Psychology

It has been said that psychology has a long past but a short history. In other words, although psychology as a discrete field of scientific work began little more than 100 years ago, the beginning of psychology marked the coming together of various scientific and philosophical trends long in existence (Boring, 1950). In this section, we'll look at the history of psychology. We'll see how, over the last 100 years, it has grown and become specialized as a discipline.

Wilhelm Wundt and Edward B. Titchener: Structuralism

The first individual to identify himself as a psychologist was the German professor Wilhelm Wundt (1832–1920). In 1879, he founded the first psychology laboratory at the University of Leipzig. Wundt's approach to psychology generated controversy, from which there later arose other approaches to psychology. He defined psychology as the science of con-

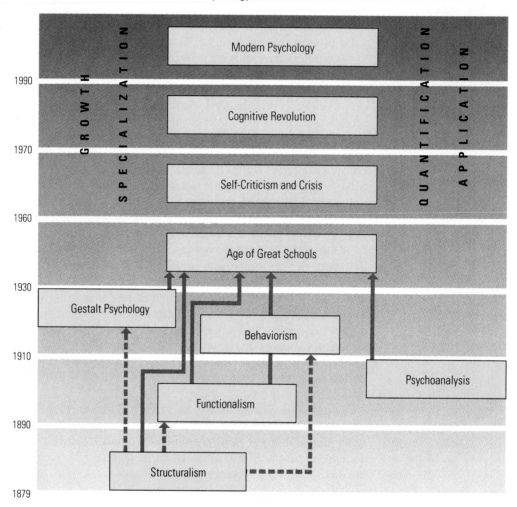

sciousness, and its subject matter as experience. The goal of psychology was to identify the basic building blocks of experience and how they are combined to create a person's complex sensations and perceptions.

In this approach, we can find an explicit parallel with chemistry, which studies how basic elements are combined into complex compounds. Today we refer to this approach to psychology as **structuralism,** the term proposed and popularized by one of Wundt's most loyal followers, Cornell University professor Edward B. Titchener (1867–1927). The term *structuralism* captures the concern with how consciousness is put together—structured—from simple parts.

This approach to psychology relied heavily on the method of **introspection** to identify what was going on in someone's mind. Introspection takes place when someone literally "looks in" at the elements that compose his or her experience, examining mental contents and processes and attempting to discern what is fundamental about them. Thus, introspection

structuralism
the psychological approach which proposes that psychology is the science of consciousness, and experience its subject matter

introspection
a method of identifying the contents of thought through the precise reporting of one's mental experiences

Wilhelm Wundt (on the right) and colleagues in his laboratory.

Edward B. Titchener

gestalt psychology

the psychological approach which suggests that our experiences are best described by focusing on the relationships among the elements of our consciousness, rather than the elements themselves

is not a casual report of what you are thinking: "I like to stick my hand in fans." Rather, it is a disciplined description of one's immediate experience that avoids confusing experience with whatever external events are responsible for it.

Suppose you are watching television and are called upon for an introspective account. You might describe the different sensations and feelings you are experiencing in basic terms like colors and shapes—that would be an acceptable introspection. But if you described what you are doing as watching reruns of *The Honeymooners,* that would be unacceptable. Ralph and Ed are not in your immediate experience.

Introspection of this kind may strike you as complicated and unwieldy, and this is exactly the way history remembers Wundt's research strategy. The biggest problem that the earliest experimental psychologists using introspection encountered was in resolving disagreements. Theoretically, the immediate experience of all individuals is composed of the same elements; theoretically, introspection by different individuals should yield the same results. What happened in practice, however, was disagreement, which called into question Wundt's favored means of conducting psychological research. Introspection as practiced by the very first psychologists could not be validated. Thus, this early approach to psychology was ultimately unscientific. Although hypotheses were checked against evidence, the evidence was not publicly observable.

Do not belittle Wundt because his research method encountered difficulties. He is appropriately honored as the first psychologist. Wundt phrased many of the important issues still addressed by those who study sensation and perception (Chapters 3 and 4), and he showed the value of experimentation for answering questions about mental processes. Many of the important psychologists in the early twentieth century studied with Wundt at Leipzig, including a number of Americans who returned home to establish the first psychology programs at such universities as Berkeley, Catholic, Clark, Columbia, Cornell, Iowa, Minnesota, Nebraska, Pennsylvania, Princeton, Stanford, and Yale.

Wundt's major contribution to psychology was his explicit statement about its purpose, agenda, and method. Subsequent psychologists disagreed with structuralism and championed their own ideas. Yet without structuralism as a point of departure, it is hard to believe that the history of psychology would have followed the same direction. Remember what was said earlier about scientific progress. A science changes when different theories come into conflict. Structuralism provided ample grounds for conflict and hence for progress.

Max Wertheimer and Kurt Lewin: Gestalt Psychology

Gestalt is a German word which, roughly translated, means whole, pattern, or configuration. The notion of a gestalt lies at the center of one of the most important reactions to structuralism: **gestalt psychology.** This approach takes issue with Wundt's goal of isolating the elements of consciousness and only later describing how these elements combine to form complex mental events. Gestalt psychologists argued instead that conscious experience cannot be grasped by describing it in terms of its parts. Instead, experience *as it is given* is patterned. It is not the elements of

Gestalt psychology holds that, like the game of chess, human consciousness can only be understood in terms of the interrelationships among its various elements.

consciousness that are important, but the relationships among these elements.

A transposed melody is a good example of a gestalt. We can recognize a particular tune regardless of its key, which means that the notes per se do not define it. Critical instead is the relationship among the notes. Another example of a gestalt is the pattern of the pieces on a chessboard. Whether these pieces are made of ivory or plastic, whether they are big or small, whether their design is modern or traditional, we can still recognize the same endgame. Checkmate!

German psychologist Max Wertheimer (1880–1943) founded the gestalt approach following his observation that a common visual illusion—apparent movement—contradicted the basic tenet of structuralism. Apparent movement is the phenomenon that makes us experience "motion" pictures as moving. Films are really a series of still pictures. Flashed in rapid enough succession, the pictures seem to move. The point here is that our experience of movement cannot possibly be reduced to the elements that make up this experience, because the elements are static while the experience is not.

Wertheimer concluded that the whole of experience is not the same as the sum of its parts. This simple formula gave rise to a far-reaching approach to psychology that stresses relationships (gestalts) as fundamental. The first gestalt psychologists studied sensation and perception, and were particularly interested in how experience can be at odds with the physical world, as in visual illusions. In these cases, our experiences tend toward what are known as good gestalts, forms characterized by simplicity, balance, and other desirable qualities (Chapter 4). In other words, as we experience the world, we impose an organization upon it. The error of structuralism, according to the gestalt psychologists, was starting with the elements of consciousness, thereby missing the most striking aspect of experience: its organization.

Other psychologists, notably Kurt Lewin (1890–1947), applied the gestalt perspective to social behavior, emphasizing that groups are not simply a collection of members. Instead, the group's mode of organization plays a critical role in understanding the nature of the group. Lewin contrasted different leadership styles, for example, arguing that groups with democratic leaders and those with authoritarian leaders are different entities, because their modes of organization are different.

Many consider Lewin the most important figure in American social psychology (Chapter 14). We can cite numerous reasons for his influence, one being that Lewin came out of the gestalt psychology tradition. The point of view he championed lent itself well to the description and explanation of social behavior. Our interactions with others are structured and not easily reduced to the characteristics of the individuals. We seek out balance in our interactions, just as our perceptions tend toward good gestalts. Did you ever notice that all your friends are good people, and all of your enemies are clods or worse?

William James and John Dewey: Functionalism

functionalism

an approach to psychology which emphasizes the function of thought: how one's mental abilities aid adaptation to the environment

Another important reaction to structuralism was **functionalism,** which developed in the United States. Whereas the structuralists' approach was static, a careful classification of the elements of consciousness, functional-

Max Wertheimer

William James

John Dewey

ists were interested in the consequences of mental processes. Functionalists wanted to know the significance of particular sensations and perceptions to the individual. They believed the proper focus for psychology was not the structure of the mind, but its function. Where Wundt and his followers emphasized content, the functionalists emphasized process.

William James (1842–1910) looms as one of the giant figures in the history of functionalism. The brother of novelist Henry James, William came from a prominent Boston family. He received his medical degree from Harvard, where he later taught physiology, then philosophy, and finally psychology. James is the first *American* psychologist. Indeed, James once said that the first psychology lecture he ever heard was one that he gave.

Psychologists point to his two-volume *Principles of Psychology,* first published in 1890, as a major contribution to the field and as the beginning of functionalism as a discrete point of view. It was a best-selling textbook, but it was really more of a series of essays on far-flung topics in psychology. In contrast to structuralism, which James reportedly found dull and "nasty" (Wertheimer, 1979), the psychology of James explored the everyday significance of consciousness—in short, how our mind is used.

Rather than looking at consciousness as a compound of elements, James likened it to a stream. His characterization of this "stream of consciousness" is sophisticated and still influential (Chapter 4). For example, James believed that consciousness was selective, flowing in one direction and not in another. Personal significance determines the flow of consciousness. We think about food in the refrigerator if we haven't eaten enough, about medication in the bathroom if we have eaten too much, and about other things if we ate just the right amount.

The other giant figure in functionalism is John Dewey (1859–1952), who is honored not just for his contributions to psychology, but also for his contributions to education and philosophy. At the University of Chicago and then at Columbia University, Dewey argued for the functional point of view. He contended that psychology should pay attention to how a person adjusts to the environment. Consciousness cannot be understood except as a tool that individuals use to respond to the environment and to make the environment respond to them.

How different is functionalism from the psychology that Wundt originally proposed? The major contrast is not so much in the details—both approaches were concerned with consciousness and employed introspection as a research approach—but in spirit. Functionalism spoke to the practical and democratic temper of the United States in a way that structuralism did not.

In emphasizing consequences, the functionalists greatly extended the scope of psychology. Psychology was brought into the complex world, resulting in a whole host of approaches that we now refer to as applied psychology. Psychology came to include different types of people as legitimate subjects of investigation. American psychology is still highly functional in its orientation, although psychologists no longer identify themselves as functionalists.

John Watson

John Watson: Behaviorism

Some psychologists today still identify themselves as behaviorists, one more sign of the historical importance of functionalism. The approach to psychology known as behaviorism is the child of functionalism. Although the first behaviorists disavowed the functionalist concern with mind, they continued to emphasize consequences. Let us therefore take a look at behaviorism, starting with its founder, John Watson (1878–1958).

An American psychologist, Watson was trained as a functionalist at the University of Chicago. He was originally interested in how animals learned. The tendency at this time was to interpret animal behavior in mentalistic terms. Sometimes these interpretations became a bit excessive, committing the error of anthropomorphism, treating animals as if they were exactly like people. We may know pet owners who do this, talking about Spot or Puff as fully-functioning human beings with needs and desires, hopes and wishes, plans and schemes.

John Watson preferred to interpret animal behavior in as simple terms as possible. It's unnecessary to say that animals act in a certain way because they have intentions if one can explain their actions by pointing to habits. Habits are simpler than intentions; explaining animal behavior in terms of habits is therefore more plausible than explaining it in terms of intentionality.

So far, Watson's caution is quite understandable. Other students of animal behavior had raised the same objections concerning anthropomorphism. But what made Watson important is that he carried this objection one step further. If it makes no sense to talk about the mental life of animals, then why does it make sense to talk about the mental life of people? Think about it. If the behavior of animals can be explained in terms of simple habits without reference to consciousness, then so too can the behavior of people.

Watson's manifesto was conveyed in a 1913 article entitled "Psychology as the Behaviorist Views It." In this article, he laid out his objections to a psychology of consciousness (that is, to *all* psychology that currently existed) and suggested instead that psychology focus on observable behavior. Watson's suggestions gave rise to the influential approach known as **behaviorism.**

behaviorism
an approach to psychology, originally proposed by John Watson, that focuses on observable behavior

There certainly were problems with introspection, as we've already seen. Watson's criticisms were therefore apt. However, scientific progress does not occur simply because an established theory is flawed. One needs a better alternative, and Watson was able to provide this alternative. He was greatly intrigued by the discoveries of the Russian physiologist Ivan Pavlov, who found that dogs salivated in the presence of those who fed them. This phenomenon was an extremely simple form of learning (Chapter 5), and Watson proposed that it was the basic form of all learning.

Behaviorism became popular for at least two reasons. First, Watson's approach gave psychologists concrete methods for gathering data with which to test theories. All things being equal, research strategies that are simple to carry out usually catch on. Second, Watson's approach was upbeat because it held that the human condition can be changed for the better. If what we do is the result of simple learning, then we can unlearn undesirable behaviors and relearn desirable ones just as simply. Watson dangled this promise in front of American psychologists, and they liked this rendering of the American dream in psychological language. Any individual, no matter how humble his or her original circumstances, can learn how to be a senator, a doctor, or a millionaire.

The rise of behaviorism is perhaps the most important chapter in the history of American psychology. Its emphases on laboratory experimentation (often with animals), learning, the environment, and intervention to improve the human condition still characterize contemporary psychology. One of the best-known of all psychologists today is the behaviorist B. F. Skinner, whose work carries through Watson's original vision (Chapter 5).

Sigmund Freud: Psychoanalysis

psychoanalysis
an approach to psychology, introduced by Sigmund Freud, that stresses the role of unconscious conflict in human behavior

Our history needs one more strand. Sigmund Freud (1856–1939), the Viennese physician, created psychoanalysis, a complex approach to human activity that rivals behaviorism in its influence on contemporary psychology. What is psychoanalysis? Preoccupation with sex, you might think, granted popular conceptions of the theory. Like many popular notions, there is a kernel of truth here, but this characterization falls short of capturing the significance of psychoanalysis. Rather, **psychoanalysis** is an approach to psychology that explains human behavior in terms of unconscious conflicts and their resolutions.

The story of psychoanalysis begins with neurology, the study of the nervous system. Neurology became a medical speciality in the 1800s when knowledge of how the brain and the nervous system worked also made it possible to understand how they malfunctioned. A whole new class of patients was recognized. People with various mental and emotional difficulties were treated by neurologists, under the assumption that their problems stemmed from defects in their nervous systems.

Freud was among the first of these neurologists. Among the patients of the early neurologists were individuals (chiefly women) who experienced puzzling losses of physical functioning, with no clear physical cause. This disorder was termed *hysteria*. Although he approached these patients as a neurologist, Freud's crowning achievement was proposing that psychological factors were responsible for their symptoms. In particular, he stressed the role of unconscious conflict.

Sigmund Freud

Table 1.1

The Early History of Psychology

Approach to Psychology	Important Event
Structuralism	Wilhelm Wundt establishes the first psychology laboratory in Germany.
Gestalt psychology	Max Wertheimer studies the illusion of apparent movement.
Functionalism	William James publishes *Principles of Psychology*.
Behaviorism	John Watson calls on psychology to study only observable behavior.
Psychoanalysis	Sigmund Freud describes his first studies of hysteria.

Many of these conflicts were sexual in nature. Hysterical patients were extremely ambivalent about sexual matters, on the one hand experiencing desires, and on the other hand finding them repugnant. Freud regarded hysterical symptoms as the reaction to this conflict, and the patients were thought to be unconscious of the underlying conflict. Treatment consisted of bringing this unconscious material into their awareness, which caused the symptoms to disappear.

Freud's original interest in hysteria eventually led him to a general theory of abnormality, a strategy of treating emotional difficulties, a view of personality, and finally to a comprehensive approach to the whole of psychology. Psychoanalytic theory regards people as complex energy systems. The energy is generated by instinctive drives, chiefly sexual and aggressive in nature. People seek to discharge energy, but the larger society typically opposes immediate gratification of one's sexual and aggressive instincts. People thus learn indirect means of satisfying themselves. Much of psychoanalytic theory catalogs these indirect means of discharging energy. If this process becomes unbalanced—too strong an instinct or too strong a prohibition against satisfying the instinct—then the person suffers.

Recent Trends in Psychology

Let's take stock of what we've learned to this point (see Table 1.1). Modern psychology took form in nineteenth-century Europe when Wilhelm Wundt defined the field as the science of consciousness, and proposed that its purpose was to identify the basic building blocks of experience. Subsequent psychologists disagreed with aspects of Wundt's structuralism and established rival approaches, most notably gestalt psychology, functionalism, and behaviorism. At the same time, Freud created his own brand of psychology—psychoanalytic theory.

Great Schools. This brings us to psychology in the 1920s and 1930s, often described as "the age of great schools" to emphasize the central role played by the approaches to psychology just described. Theory and research centered on the issues that each approach deemed important. Most psychologists could be readily placed within one school or another, and a more detailed history than this one would document the innumerable skirmishes among them.

Following the 1930s, the importance of the great schools waned, as psychologists became more tolerant of other points of view and more specialized in their own work. Structuralism, gestalt psychology, and functionalism for the most part vanished as discrete approaches, although we still see their respective influence today. Behavioristic and psychoanalytic psychologists maintained their separate identities.

World War II. The Second World War played an important role in stimulating the growth of American psychology. Indeed, the center of psychology moved from Europe to the United States as a direct result of the war. There are several reasons for this. First, the Nazi persecution of European Jews caused leading European scientists and intellectuals to immigrate to the United States. Both academic psychology and psychoanalysis in the United States were enriched as their ranks were joined by such individuals as Wertheimer and Lewin, among many others. Second, the demands of the war spurred on applications of psychology. Remember that psychology in the United States was always a pragmatic undertaking; the war effort capitalized on this problem-solving bent. What resulted were studies in such topics as prejudice, attitude change, group dynamics, and adjustment.

Psychologists who before the war had administered tests to aid in the diagnosis of psychiatric patients were pressed into service as therapists in their own right. Following the war, these psychologists were unwilling to resume their previous role. Instead, they created the field of clinical psychology, which uses the theories and findings of psychology to help people suffering with problems in their daily lives. There are now tens of thousands of clinical psychologists.

Postwar Trends. Psychology following World War II shows a number of clear trends (Gilgen, 1982). Understanding these trends will help you understand the material in the rest of this book. Chief among them is the exponential *growth* of the field of psychology (see Figure 1.2). By any and all criteria, psychology has become increasingly popular during the past few decades. The numbers of psychologists, psychology students, and psychology books increase every year.

Figure 1.2

The Growth of Psychology. The American Psychological Association is the largest professional group to which psychologists belong. The rapid growth of its membership illustrates the growth of psychology as a field.

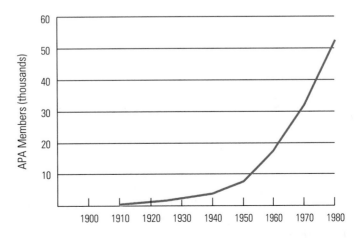

Psychologists have also shown increasing *specialization*. In the era of great schools, someone was simply a psychologist. Theorists aspired to general explanation. Now no one is a psychologist per se. Instead, someone is a developmental psychologist, a clinical psychologist, or a social psychologist. Theorists propose much more narrow accounts. Their intention is to explain particular thoughts, particular feelings, and particular actions. Psychology journals show the same specificity.

In recent years, psychology has seen the development of a paradoxical "speciality" that is actually not a speciality at all: general psychology. The general psychologist tries to become conversant with the entire field of psychology. Granted the growth and specialization of psychology, it is difficult to be a general psychologist. However, if no one tried to be a general psychologist, then no one would be in front of your class trying to introduce you to the whole of psychology.

Psychology has also moved toward increasing *quantification*. Indeed, many contemporary psychologists cannot do their work without using numbers. Theories in most fields of psychology have become so sophisticated that we cannot simply look at research evidence to evaluate them. Instead, researchers use statistics to describe the results of their studies and then to make inferences from these results. You will find a detailed discussion of statistics in the appendix to this chapter.

A trend toward increasing *application* is also unmistakable in the recent history of psychology in the United States. We've already mentioned clinical psychologists who treat individuals with emotional or behavioral difficulties. There are also many other types of applied psychologists, and the number increases all the time. We can find psychologists in a wide variety of settings, including hospitals (health psychologists), schools (educational psychologists), factories (industrial psychologists), Madison Avenue (consumer psychologists), and locker rooms (sports psychologists). Some applied psychologists even work in conjunction with lawyers in choosing jurors for trials, with politicians in mounting campaign strategies, with artists in fine-tuning their creations, and with architects in designing highways and homes. You will find a discussion of applied psychology in the appendix of this book.

Self-Criticism and Crisis. During the late 1960s and early 1970s, the United States as a whole went through a period of turmoil and change. Much of this tumult centered on the unpopular Vietnam War, but every aspect of society was similarly scrutinized and criticized: politics, religion, morality. As you might expect, psychology and psychologists went through a period of self-criticism as well. Long-accepted practices and assumptions were called into question. Here is just a sampling of the issues explored during this time:

- The use of experiments to study complex human behavior is unethical.
- Psychotherapy does not work.
- Psychological testing is biased toward preserving the status quo.
- Psychology in the United States is chauvinistic: Theories and findings have little relevance to people in other cultures.
- Psychology tends to ignore women and minorities; when not ignored, they are depicted as deficient versions of white males.

- Psychological theories have nothing to say about the good and noble side of human beings.
- Results from laboratory studies do not apply to actual behavior in the real world.

These criticisms were not easy to dismiss. Indeed, some of them were raised by the most respected individuals within the profession.

What happened? Well, the United States indeed survived the 1960s and 1970s, but ours is now a different nation. As citizens, we are both more sophisticated and more modest in our expectations. The same seems true of scientific psychology. The criticisms raised in the 1960s and 1970s shook the field, causing contemporary psychologists to approach their science in a different way, expecting complexity and difficulty. Psychology is no longer a young science, full of naive hope and innocence. This is not a cynical conclusion. Indeed, psychology matured during its stormy adolescence, and it is likely that the most exciting chapters in its history have yet to be written.

The Cognitive Revolution.   Perhaps the most important occurrence in the recent history of psychology is the fact that psychology regained its mind. When the great schools of the 1930s waned, behaviorism was the exception that survived, ruling academic psychology well into the 1960s. Learning theories dominated the field, and so too did learning theorists (Chapter 5).

cognition

the various mental processes responsible for how we "know" the world, including perceiving, thinking, and remembering

But something happened in the 1960s. Stimulated in part by the general unrest within psychology, certain theorists and researchers called for psychology to return to the study of **cognition:** the various mental processes responsible for how we "know" the world, such as perceiving, thinking, and remembering. To ignore the mind in explaining what people were all about produced a necessarily incomplete view of human nature. New methods made it possible to study the mind without the pitfalls of introspection as practiced by the structuralists.

In 1967, Ulric Neisser published *Cognitive Psychology,* an influential book describing this "new" psychology of the mind. Since then, psychology has become an increasingly cognitive endeavor. The so-called cognitive revolution has encompassed not just learning and memory (Chapter 7), but also social psychology, clinical psychology, and personality. Virtually every chapter of this book will show the influence of this cognitive revolution.

The development of the computer has given us new techniques and a new language to aid our understanding of mental processes.

Popular among many participants in the cognitive revolution is the computer metaphor (Gardner, 1985; Knapp, 1986). If the notion that science is conducted by real people who live in particular times and places has not yet taken root in your mind, here's yet another example. Computers have affected psychology not just in the obvious way, helping researchers manipulate data, but also in a subtle way, suggesting different ways in which our minds might work. Computers receive information from the world (input), transform it according to rules (programs), and yield results (output). For psychology grappling with the relationships between events in the world and our responses to them (input and output), computer notions provide helpful hints.

The success of the cognitive revolution does not mean theoretical progress in psychology has come to a halt. To say that people are like computers is not to say that they are computers. According to Howard Gardner (1985), future theory and research will probably focus precisely on those aspects of human nature poorly captured by the computer metaphor, like emotion and will.

Fields of Psychology

An understanding of the history of psychology can help you make sense of the many topics you will encounter in the rest of this book. As already mentioned, psychology has become highly specialized, so much so that contemporary psychology is a dazzling array of different fields (see Table 1.2). Some speciality areas have already been discussed, including social

Table 1.2

Specialities within Contemporary Psychology

One way to illustrate the diversity of contemporary psychology is by showing you the various divisions within the American Psychological Association (APA). Each division represents a subgroup of members who share a common interest.

APA Division Number*	Name	APA Division Number	Name
1	General Psychology	26	History of Psychology
2	Teaching of Psychology	27	Society for Community Research and Action: Division of Community Psychology
3	Experimental Psychology		
5	Evaluation, Measurement and Statistics	28	Psychopharmacology
6	Physiological and Comparative Psychology	29	Psychotherapy
7	Developmental Psychology	30	Psychological Hypnosis
8	Society for Personality and Social Psychology	31	State Psychological Association Affairs
9	Society for the Study of Social Issues— SPSSI	32	Humanistic Psychology
		33	Mental Retardation and Developmental Disabilities
10	Psychology and the Arts	34	Population and Environmental Psychology
12	Clinical Psychology	35	Psychology of Women
13	Consulting Psychology	36	Psychologists Interested in Religious Issues—PIRI
14	Society for Industrial and Organizational Psychology	37	Child, Youth, and Family Services
		38	Health Psychology
15	Educational Psychology	39	Psychoanalysis
16	School Psychology	40	Clinical Neuropsychology
17	Counseling Psychology	41	American Psychology-Law Society
18	Psychologists in Public Service	42	Psychologists in Independent Practice
19	Military Psychology	43	Family Psychology
20	Adult Development and Aging	44	Society for the Psychological Study of Lesbian and Gay Issues
21	Applied Experimental and Engineering Psychologists	45	Society for the Psychological Study of Ethnic Minority Issues
22	Rehabilitation Psychology		
23	Society for Consumer Psychology	46	Media Psychology
24	Theoretical and Philosophical Psychology	47	Exercise and Sport Psychology
25	Experimental Analysis of Behavior	48	Peace Psychology

*There are no Divisions 4 or 11.

psychology, cognitive psychology, and clinical psychology. Numerous other specialities exist as well.

One important distinction is between basic and applied fields of psychology. Basic psychologists propose theories and conduct studies for the purpose of better understanding our behavior and mental processes. Applied psychologists use the theories and findings of basic research to help solve people's practical problems. Probably the most familiar example of applied psychology is psychotherapy (Chapter 13), but applications are also made by psychologists who work in business and industry, health care, sports, schools, and the legal system.

An appreciation of psychology's history lets you see its contemporary fields as coherent, sharing a common origin. In this section, we'll take a brief look at some of the major fields of psychology. We'll discuss each of these fields in more detail in later chapters. You can regard this section as an introduction to the rest of the book.

Biological psychologists are interested in how biological processes relate to behavior. They study the brain and nervous system (Chapter 2), how our senses work (Chapters 3 and 4), and the effects of hormones on our motives and emotions (Chapter 6). They may work on a microscopic level, investigating how a particular neuron works, for instance, or they may tackle an extremely broad question, such as whether psychological differences between males and females are due to biology (Chapters 9 and 16).

Experimental psychologists are the direct descendants of the very first psychologists, and are now at the forefront of the cognitive revolution. Experimental psychologists are interested in basic processes of sensation (Chapter 3), perception (Chapter 4), learning (Chapter 5), motivation, emotion (Chapter 6), memory, cognition (Chapter 7), and intelligence (Chapter 8). They almost always use laboratory experiments to study these topics—hence the name of the speciality. However, we should also note that psychologists in all specialities may use experiments in their research, so the term "experimental" to describe one particular speciality of psychology is not strictly accurate.

Developmental psychologists concern themselves with the physical and psychological changes that take place throughout life, from conception to death. Some developmental psychologists look only at infancy or childhood (Chapter 9). Others focus on adolescence, adulthood, or old age (Chapter 10). Developmental psychologists investigate how biological inheritance and particular experiences influence a host of psychological characteristics, including intelligence (Chapter 8), morality, social relationships, cognitive skills (Chapter 7), and sexuality (Chapter 16).

Personality psychologists study differences among people, often focusing on such traits as sociability, moodiness, and impulsivity. These psychologists are interested in how an individual's thoughts, feelings, and actions are related. In short, they take as their topic of concern the whole person (Chapter 11).

Psychopathologists are concerned with describing and explaining severe psychological problems, such as drug abuse, anxiety, depression, and schizophrenia (Chapter 12). Psychopathologists ask what causes these disorders: our environment or biological predispositions? Are these problems stable and pervasive, or do they reflect the influence of time and place?

As already mentioned, *clinical psychologists* diagnose and treat people with psychological disorders (Chapter 13). Granted that people encounter problems in their daily lives, how can these be solved or even prevented in the first place? At the present time, clinical psychologists are extending their procedures to promote physical health and combat disease (Chapter 6). *Counseling psychologists* are similarly concerned with helping people solve problems, usually within a particular domain of life, such as school or the family.

Social psychologists study how people's actions affect others (Chapter 14). These psychologists try to understand the relationship between individuals and the social groups to which they belong. Topics like conformity, obedience, prejudice, altruism, and aggression are typical concerns of social psychology (Chapter 15).

Research Methods in Psychology

Research is the process of checking hypotheses against pertinent evidence. Regardless of the details, all research involves making observations in a systematic way, with the goal of understanding how different concepts relate to one another. In some psychological research, behavior is observed as it naturally occurs. A researcher might study toddlers at a preschool, for instance, noting whether they play by themselves or with others. Here the intent is to disrupt behavior as little as possible in order to describe what actually happens. In other psychological research, a researcher observes behavior as it takes place in a laboratory under deliberately arranged circumstances. For example, a psychologist might see how a college student responds when she finds out that her opinions are very much in a minority.

Granted the importance of research in making psychology a science distinct from everyday opinion, the next section takes a close look at psychologists' research methods. The focus here is on three particular research strategies: case studies, correlational investigations, and experiments. In subsequent chapters, other methods will be discussed as well.

Basic Concepts

Before discussing particular approaches, it is important to mention several matters that concern all psychologists, regardless of their favorite research strategy. When judging a particular investigation as good, bad, or ugly, one pays attention to precisely these matters.

operational definition
a concrete measure of an abstract concept

Operationalization.   In order to do research, a psychologist must measure the concepts that he or she is interested in. The process of devising a concrete measure of an abstract concept is called operationalization, and the resulting measure is an **operational definition.** So, an operational definition of "hunger" might be how quickly someone races through a cafeteria line. An operational definition of "academic achievement" might be one's grade point average.

In everyday life, we are often quite careless in the operational definitions we employ. It may be far from obvious to someone listening to us talk just how we have gone about deciding

- that Pee Wee is a great guy;
- that Louella is a flirt;
- that Fred is an intellectual;
- that Beulah is belligerent;
- that Oscar is curious.

Our listeners know what these descriptions mean on an abstract level, of course, but do they know the concrete rules we have used in identifying great guys or flirts? Probably not. Could they go among the masses and find people that we would agree were intellectual, belligerent or curious? Again, probably not.

The point is that everyday psychologists often fail to operationalize their concepts in an explicit and public way. Scientific psychologists, in contrast, start with clearly specified measures, hoping that questionable ones can thus be headed off at the pass. There is no foolproof measure of anything, so researchers must scrutinize their operational definitions at all points of their research.

I can't resist telling you an old joke about a scientist and a flea. If you've heard it before, bear with me. It illustrates the point I'm trying to make.

A scientist is studying fleas and their renowned jumping ability. He discovers that if he stands right over a flea and yells "Jump" then the flea indeed jumps. He then pulls off one of the flea's legs, and yells "Jump." Again, the flea jumps. He repeats this, pulling off a second leg and yelling "Jump." Once again, the flea jumps. The scientist keeps doing this until the flea is down to its last leg. He removes this leg, yells "Jump" at the flea, and nothing happens. The scientist is impressed.

He carefully repeats this experiment with a number of fleas, and in every case the conclusion is the same. When a flea loses all of its legs, it becomes deaf.

The scientist in this joke misses the point that his operational definition of deafness (i.e., whether the flea jumps when he yells at it) reflects something quite different (i.e., the flea's inability to jump). This "something different" always threatens measures of particular concepts. Scientists refer to it as a **confound:** an irrelevant factor that distorts operationalization.

confound

an irrelevant factor that distorts an operational definition

The people at *Consumer Reports* devise quite clever operational definitions. Their task is to judge whether products are good or bad, and they try to make the basis of their judgments as public as possible. What follows are synopses of some of their testing procedures.

Toothpaste abrasiveness. Extracted teeth are bombarded with radiation and mounted in resin blocks. A brushing machine equipped with a toothbrush of medium hardness is loaded with the toothpaste to be tested and strokes the teeth 2,000 times. The teeth are rinsed in water, and the amount of radiation in the rinse water is detected by a geiger counter; the more radiation, the more abrasive the toothpaste (March 1986).

Charcoal starter speed. Thirty charcoal briquettes are arranged in a standard pile. How long does it take a particular charcoal gimmick to turn each coal thoroughly gray (June 1986)?

Electric mattress pad comfort. This operational definition comes straight out of the fairy tale "The Princess and the Pea"! Each type of mattress pad is sent home with 16 different staff members, who sleep on it and report any discomfort experienced (January 1984).

Chocolate chip cookie goodness. First, the ultimate chocolate chip cookie is created to use as a standard. This is done by having two bakers modify the classic Nestlé recipe in all possible ways, creating a variety of different batches. "Sensory consultants" taste cookies from each batch and vote independently about which is the best. Second, store cookies are compared against the standard by sensory consultants who rate how close each commercial brand is to the ultimate chocolate flavor, texture, and so on (February 1985).

These are excellent operational definitions because they specify explicit measures that seem to get at the abstract concept of concern. In each case, though, there is a possible confound that might distort the particular measure, yielding a high score for a bad product or a low score for a good product.

For example, suppose the oven in which the different batches of chocolate chip cookies are baked becomes progressively more dirty, so that later batches taste more greasy than early batches. If we didn't know this was happening, we would conclude that it was the recipe that made the critical difference, not the grease and grime in the oven.

As you read the rest of this book, you will see that researchers do not study topics in the abstract, but always in the concrete. They use operational definitions. To study memory, a researcher might investigate how many words in a list a person can recall 10 minutes after looking at it (Chapter 7). To study intelligence, a researcher could ask subjects to interpret particular proverbs (Chapter 8). To study aggression, a researcher may measure how many times a child punches a doll (Chapter 15).

reliability

consistency in research results: on each occasion that particular measures are used, they yield the same results

Reliability.   We all know what **reliability** means in everyday life: consistency or stability. In terms of psychological research, reliability has essentially the same meaning. Reliable measures are those that yield the same result on different occasions, thus researchers strive for them. A standard step in psychology research involves checking whether measures are reliable or not. Perhaps you have completed a questionnaire and noted that some questions are repeated in different places. Whether the questionnaire aims at gauging an attitude, an opinion, or a trait, the repeated questions allow the researcher to estimate how reliable a measure is. If the questionnaire is reliable, the vast majority of people should answer the same question in the same way.

Remember that no operational definition is foolproof. One of the potential pitfalls of all measurement is *reactivity:* the alteration of a phenomenon by the mere fact of measuring it. Reactivity becomes a particular problem when researchers measure what people think, feel, or do. Because a research subject knows that the researcher is interested in particular characteristics, he or she may act in a different way in light of this knowledge.

Reactivity can make measures seem either more or less reliable than they actually are. If you are asked the same question three times, you may feel obliged to answer consistently, even if your opinion fluctuates. I've administered questionnaires to people who go back and study their earlier responses in order to make their later responses. "You're checking my memory, aren't you?" some of them ask me. Actually, I'm trying to check reliability, and my estimate is falsely inflated. On the other hand, a subject may resent being asked the same question on repeated occasions. One reaction might well be to give a different answer. This lowers reliability below what it actually is.

For reasons like these, psychology researchers often ascertain reliability in a more subtle way than using the exact measures twice in a row. They devise alternative measures of the same factor and see whether these different versions agree or not. If they do, they will combine them into a composite (by averaging them together) which they justifiably regard as a reliable measure. For example, in measuring the degree to which someone is experiencing a depressed mood, a researcher might ask the person how frequently he feels sad, how frequently he feels gloomy, how frequently he feels down in the dumps, and so on. These different questions presumably all get at the same factor, although in slightly different ways.

validity

the degree to which a research study measures what it purports to measure

Validity. The **validity** of research means that it studies what it purports to study. This may sound strange to you. How could a researcher *not* be studying what she intends to study? Well, there are innumerable ways that this could happen, because no operational definition is foolproof. In some cases, particular measures may be so confounded by unintended factors that they reflect only these factors and not what is intended, invalidating the research.

For instance, psychology researchers sometimes study competition and cooperation with a procedure called the Prisoners' Dilemma Game, which is based on the following scenario:

> Two prisoners have plotted an escape a week from Thursday. The plans are set, but each realizes that he has two alternatives: (a) proceed with escape as planned or (b) speak to the warden and turn in his partner. Further, each realizes that the other guy has the same alternatives. A dilemma is produced because the cost versus the benefit of a particular alternative depends on what the other prisoner does.
>
> Pretend that you are one of the prisoners in this dilemma. If you both opt for escape, you may or may not get away with it. If you try to escape and your partner rats on you, then you'll be severely punished and he'll be rewarded. On the other hand, if he tries to escape and you rat, then he'll be punished and you'll be rewarded. Finally, if you each turn the other guy in, the warden will have a good chuckle and punish you both.

On the face of it, the Prisoners' Dilemma Game provides an elegant operationalization of cooperation versus competition. It is highly suitable for research purposes, because it is simple to set up and to carry out. Once presented with the dilemma, subjects can make dozens of choices in a short period of time. And it is not even necessary to have a "real" partner for the subject. Instead, the researcher often gives the subject phony choices attributed to a partner. In this way, the researcher studies how certain strategies (like consistent cooperation or consistent competition) affect the subject's own choice of strategy.

All prisoners face, to some degree, the difficult choice between cooperation and competition presented in the Prisoner's Dilemma Game.

The Prisoners' Dilemma Game, for all its virtues as a research tool, has nevertheless been criticized on grounds of validity. Stop and think of the differences between this laboratory procedure and "real" competition and cooperation, like that between Burger King and McDonald's, between the United States and the Soviet Union, or between you and your laboratory partner in Organic Chemistry. Are these differences critical in defining what we mean by competition and cooperation?

If the Prisoners' Dilemma Game "operationalizes" competition and cooperation by leaving out a necessary element, then it is not valid. The game usually allows no communication between a subject and his or her partner. In everyday life, those who cooperate or compete are in contact with each other. Is this critical? Also, this game often uses trivial stakes, like pennies or imaginary points. In everyday life, the stakes are high: money, fame, even the survival of humankind. Is this critical?

You can make up your own mind about the validity of the Prisoners' Dilemma Game. Be aware, however, that no procedure is perfectly valid. Further, note that validity is not an all-or-nothing proposition. Particular procedures may be more or less valid than other procedures for given purposes, and they must be judged accordingly. Consider the use of animals in psychology experiments. Is this a valid way to understand human beings? The answer depends on the aspect of human behavior you are interested in. If you want to know how people learn simple habits, studies using animals may be quite informative (Chapter 5). If you are interested in how people learn to play chess, studies using animals are probably not valid.

Generalization.　Researchers study particular animals or people, but they often wish to arrive at general conclusions about animals or people. **Generalization** is therefore a concern to researchers: How far and how well do findings from a given study apply?

A useful distinction here is between samples and populations. A **sample** is the actual group of research subjects investigated in a study: 96 college students from a school in Florida, 27 white rats shipped by express mail from an animal supply house last Tuesday, or 12 toddlers observed at a nursery school down the block. In contrast, a **population** is the larger group to which a researcher wishes to generalize from a study of a particular sample: middle-class children in the United States, young adults, the entire human race, or all living creatures.

It is obvious that the more a given sample resembles the population of interest, the better the generalization of any findings. The ideal way to achieve a sample that resembles the population of concern is to have equal access to all members of the population, and then to select research subjects at random. This ideal proves virtually impossible to accomplish, however, for a host of practical reasons. The "best" samples we see on this score are public opinion polls (Chapter 14). But these are costly, and still end up not fully representing certain groups, such as those without permanent homes.

Recognizing the difficulties involved in generalizing results, some researchers opt for caution and phrase their conclusions in very narrow ways. They protect themselves from criticism, but they also sacrifice applicability of their findings. Deciding just how far to generalize results is a constant challenge for researchers.

generalization
the degree to which the findings from a given study apply to animals or people in general

sample
the actual group of research subjects investigated in a study

population
the larger group to which a researcher wishes to generalize from a study of a particular sample

Case Studies

case study

a research strategy in which a single individual or group is studied intensively

With an appreciation of the concepts of operationalization, reliability, validity, and generalization, let us now turn to the actual methods that psychologists use in doing research. The first important method is the **case study,** an intensive investigation of a single subject or group. Case studies are sometimes dismissed as unscientific, but this criticism is too harsh. When conducted correctly, a case study involves the testing of a hypothesis against evidence, the essence of the scientific method. At the same time, it is worth considering why case studies are open to criticism.

Sigmund Freud (1909a) reported one of the best known case studies decades ago: the case of Little Hans, a five-year-old boy who was afraid of horses. According to Freud's interpretation, Hans was not really afraid of horses per se. Rather, Hans was afraid of his father, in particular that his father planned to castrate him because of the sexual desires Hans harbored for his mother.

Where do horses come into all of this? Freud believed that Little Hans did not consciously acknowledge his fear of castration at the hands of his father—that would be too threatening. So, the boy displaced his fear from Dad onto horses, because his father reminded him of a horse.

Freud's explanation of Hans's fear may or may not strike you as plausible, but it seems possible to test it against evidence. Let's break the explanation down into its major components.

- Little Hans harbors sexual desires for his mother.
- Little Hans fears his father will retaliate.
- Little Hans transforms his fear of his father into fear of horses.

Freud reports evidence in support of each of these components. However, the evidence strikes some readers as a bit tenuous (Wolpe & Rachman, 1960).

Freud obtained information through conversations with the boy's father. Freud (1909a, p. 19) used the following story as evidence for Little Hans's sexual desires.

> This morning Hans was given his usual daily bath by his mother and afterwards dried and powdered. As his mother was powdering round his penis and taking care not to touch it, Hans said: "Why don't you put your finger there?"
>
> Mother: "Because that'd be piggish."
>
> Hans: "What's that? Piggish? Why?"
>
> Mother: "Because it's not proper."
>
> Hans (laughing): "But it's great fun."

Is this incident good evidence for Freud's hypothesis that Little Hans sexually desires his mother? Not exactly. The incident shows that he wanted his mother to touch his penis, and that he thought this would be fun. But it might well have been a spur-of-the-moment comment. Freud's hypothesis requires that this wish be a rather constant one, and so we would want to hear about repeated instances of Little Hans asking his mother to touch him. Instead, Freud gives evidence that Little Hans was preoccupied with his penis and with little girls. However, this evidence is not relevant to the hypothesis.

The case study of Little Hans illustrates some of the weaknesses in this method of research. First, the reliability of information may be highly suspect. Note that Freud obtained evidence secondhand (from Little Hans's father) as well as after the fact. What guarantee was there that inaccuracy did not creep into the process?

Second, the attempt to draw links between potential causes and effects is difficult. Freud presents the case of Little Hans in chronological order, and tries to explain subsequent events as due to earlier events. So, Freud places great emphasis on the birth of a little girl into the family, and Hans's observation that her genitals were different than his own. But how can we be certain that events would have ensued differently had no little girl joined the family? We can't, and this problem plagues all case studies that stress the critical role of singular events.

Third, how does one generalize from a case study? Even if everything Freud reported about Little Hans was perfectly reliable and valid, would we be confident in treating Little Hans as the prototypic little boy? This was Freud's intention, because he used this case study to argue for the universality of these impulses among young children. Obviously, this is unwarranted without further studies of young boys.

We've taken an extremely close look at the case of Little Hans, and we've been critical. However, notice that many of the difficulties mentioned here are *not* inherent problems with case studies. They can be surmounted or sidestepped, leaving this research strategy with certain strengths. For example, case studies don't have to rely on the retrospective memory of the researcher or informants. Current case studies use tape recorders or video cameras to preserve the relevant information (e.g., Luborsky, 1970). Some researchers work from permanent documents like letters, diaries, or newspaper interviews (e.g., Allport, 1942).

A case study can be used to draw conclusions about causes and effects as long as the researcher appreciates the need to test a causal hypothesis repeatedly. For instance, Freud's interpretation of Little Hans's phobia leads to the following prediction:

increased worry about father's revenge → increased fear of horses

In other words, immediately following a rebuke by his father, Little Hans should be more afraid of horses than immediately following a reassurance by his father. A researcher might therefore pay particular attention to how Little Hans acts toward horses following rebukes, as compared to reassurances. If Freud's hypothesis is correct, what pattern of behavior should the researcher observe?

The researcher might even arrange rebukes or reassurances on the part of Hans's father, and then gallop through the living room on a horse to see how afraid the boy becomes. How might you operationalize "fear" in this case? Perhaps the intensity and duration of shrieks by Little Hans could be used to measure his fear.

Finally, although a case study can never establish what is generally true about people, sometimes this is not the psychologist's purpose. One of the best reasons to use a case study is to provide a solid counterexample to a prevailing theory. For example, thinkers for centuries assumed that language was a uniquely human ability. All the evidence was certainly on their side, because they had never encountered a talking animal. But in the 1960s and 1970s, several research groups reported success in teaching

Case studies of transsexuals, such as James/Jan Morris, have provided psychologists with valuable insights into unusual aspects of human behavior.

an ape to use language (Gardner & Gardner, 1969; Patterson, 1978; Premack & Premack, 1972). Although their conclusions continue to be controversial, no one dismisses them because they are based on studies of a single subject. The importance of these case studies is their challenge to conventional wisdom about animals' ability to master language.

Another reason for using a case study is that it may be the only way to investigate a rare phenomenon. Certain individuals or events are so singular that they are encountered only once or a few times in the life of a researcher. Are these individuals or events therefore off-limits for science? We would hope not.

One example of an unusual topic investigated with a case study approach is Harold Garfinkel's (1967) investigation of Agnes.

> She was tall, slim, with a very female shape. Her measurements were 38-25-38. She had long, fine dark-blonde hair, a young face with pretty features, a peaches-and-cream complexion. . . . [S]he was dressed in a tight sweater which marked off her thin shoulders, ample breasts, and narrow waist. (p. 119)

Oh, yes, Agnes also had "the normal external genitalia of a male" (p. 119).

To make a long story short, Agnes was a *transsexual,* an individual whose gender identity is at odds with his or her biological sex (Chapter 16). She was born a male but always regarded herself as a female. At puberty, Agnes secretly took estrogen pills, knowing them to be a "female" medication. She succeeded in producing the secondary sexual characteristics of a female, although the male penis also developed.

As an adult, Agnes had a sex change operation and became a "real" woman. She had to learn, as an adult, how to act like a woman, figuring out then what other women acquire over the course of a lifetime. Accordingly, Agnes was acutely mindful of what stereotypically female behavior involved. She was an excellent source of this information, and Garfinkel queried her extensively on this subject.

Agnes reported, for instance, that a woman on a date did not need to have a history, because the typical man was remarkably uninterested in anything she happened to have done in years past. This of course suited Agnes just fine, because she wished to conceal her history from other people. Her case shows how easily a woman can do this, a conclusion that perhaps would not have been possible from interviews with a more commonplace individual.

In sum, investigations using the case study strategy have notable strengths. First, they provide rich detail about their subject matter. Second, they demonstrate what may or may not be possible. Third, they may be the only way for researchers to study rare phenomena. On the other hand, case studies may lead to problems with fidelity of information, causal inference, and representativeness.

Correlational Investigations

correlational investigation
a study that ascertains the degree of relationship between two variables

What is the relationship between college grades and later income? Is good health associated with happiness? Is divorce harmful to children? Each of these questions can be investigated by gathering data pertaining to these factors and then seeing how these data are associated. A study that proceeds in this way is a **correlational investigation.** The word *correlation*

Figure 1.3

Examples of Correlations. What is the relationship between two variables? In the graph on the left, increases in one variable are associated with increases in the other. In the graph on the right, increases in one variable are associated with decreases in the other. In the middle graph, there is no relationship between the two.

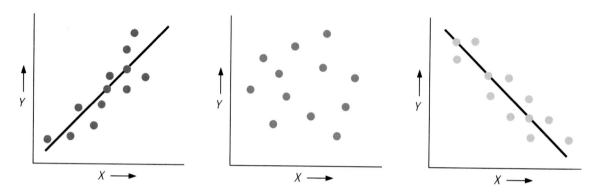

comes from *co-relation:* literally, the relation between two variables (Galton, 1888). Two related questions concern researchers who conduct correlational investigations. Do two factors show any association at all? If so, how strong is this association? A strong relationship allows us to predict one factor from the other with great certainty. A weak relationship makes prediction much more tentative.

A positive correlation describes a relationship in which increases in one variable are associated with increases in the other variable, and vice versa (see Figure 1.3). For a simple example, hat size and shoe size are positively correlated. There may be exceptions, someone with big feet and a small head, like Charlie Chaplin, or small feet and a big head, like Nancy Reagan. But most people who wear large hats also wear large shoes, and most people who wear small hats also wear small shoes.

In contrast, a negative correlation describes a relationship in which increases in one variable are associated with decreases in the other variable, and vice versa (again see Figure 1.3). Consider a group of parents. It's likely that the more children each set of parents has in college at the present time, the fewer expensive vacations each plans for the next year.

Finally, a zero correlation describes a relationship between two variables that have nothing to do with each other (once more see Figure 1.3). Increases or decreases in one tell you nothing about increases or decreases in the other. A student's college grade point average probably has a zero correlation with his or her systolic blood pressure. The amount of spare change in someone's pocket probably has a zero correlation with his or her shoe size (unless the shoe size is 18-EEEE, which may mean that its wearer is a well-paid professional athlete).

Many of the hypotheses that concern psychologists can be answered with information about the correlations between variables. Accordingly, the correlational research strategy is widely used. Here is an example from a study by Anderson and Anderson (1984). These researchers were interested in the possible relationship between external temperature and violent crime. They cited the commonsense belief that uncomfortably hot temperatures produce increased aggression, but they also noted that particularly hot circumstances might lead to decreased aggression, because individuals might be so preoccupied with the heat that they would overlook any stimulus to aggression.

Anderson and Anderson proceeded by finding out the number of criminal assaults (e.g., homicide, rape, battery, and armed robbery) committed each day during the summer of 1977 in Chicago. They also ascertained the temperature in Chicago on each of these days. Consistent with common belief, violent crimes indeed increased as the temperature increased, with no evidence of tailing off even at the highest temperatures. In a second study using crime statistics and weather reports from Houston, Anderson and Anderson obtained the same results.

In their conclusion, they raised a caution that applies to all correlational data.

> We would like to acknowledge that the field studies discussed in this article all are based on correlational data. Thus, causal inferences should be made with great caution. . . . We do not believe . . . that our data conclusively prove that the temperature-aggression link is linear. (p. 96)

In other words, Anderson and Anderson greatly desire to draw the conclusion that high temperatures *cause* violent crimes since their evidence points to that conclusion. However, they pull up short of the strongest possible statement because the correlational research strategy does not allow the researcher to say with absolute certainty that Variable A causes Variable B.

Why not? Because something else might be going on. Despite a correlation between Variable A and Variable B, there may be no necessary link between the two. Another factor, called a third variable, may produce both Variable A and Variable B. You should recognize third variables as a particular type of confound. Psychologists conducting correlational investigations must be alert for possible third variables that threaten the conclusions they wish to draw.

What are some possible third variables in the Anderson and Anderson study? One possibility is that "day of the week" confounds the correlation between temperature and aggression. More violent crimes are committed on Saturdays, Sundays, and Mondays than on other days. If, by chance, weekend days in Chicago and Houston were particularly hot during the period of the research, then there indeed would be a positive correlation between temperature and crime, but not because the two had any meaningful connection. Anderson and Anderson anticipated this possibility and ruled it out in their data.

Another possible confound is that the operational definition of aggression (crime reports) measured not aggression per se but the willingness of victims to complain about crime. And temperature may affect people's willingness to complain. Researchers would still find a positive correlation between temperature and "aggression" as operationalized with crime reports, but the interpretation would be quite different. Again, Anderson and Anderson worried about this third variable, and, in their Houston study, obtained information about reports of nonviolent crime (e.g., burglary and arson). Because temperature was not related to increased reports of nonviolent crime, the confound of biased reporting was ruled out.

If correlational studies limit the researcher's ability to offer conclusions about the links between variables, why does anyone bother conducting these studies in the first place? Remember that all research strategies present a combination of strengths and weaknesses. In stressing that correlational data do not allow strong causal conclusions, we should not obscure the virtues of this approach.

Correlational investigations typically study a large number of individuals (or groups) with the goal of describing naturally occurring relationships among their characteristics. Results can thus be generalized with much more confidence than results from case studies. Even if the nature of the links between variables is unclear, one can still say with confidence that such links exist.

Correlational research also makes it possible to grapple with topics impossible, unwieldy, and/or unethical to investigate with other strategies. Let's suppose that a researcher is concerned with sex differences. Why are men more violent than women? A case study of a particularly violent man doesn't really get at the question of interest. What is needed is a comparison of men and women with respect to violence, that is, a correlational study that looks at the relationship between sex and violence.

Researchers can and do draw conclusions about causes and effects from information about correlations. When doing so, they tease out the role of possible third variables. You saw such an attempt in the Anderson and Anderson (1984) studies on the link between temperature and violence. A researcher can never rule out all third variables, but if the most plausible candidates are examined and shown to be irrelevant, then a causal conclusion can be made. Needless to say, these conclusions—like all conclusions from psychology studies—should be regarded as tentative.

In sum, correlational investigations can be quite useful to the researcher who wishes to describe the naturally occurring characteristics of large numbers of individuals or groups that are difficult or impossible to study otherwise. The drawback to the correlational strategy is the difficulty of offering conclusions about causes and effects.

Experiments

Scientists as well as the general public are duly impressed with "experimental" evidence, although their reasons for being impressed may differ. The general public often thinks of experiments as particularly reliable and valid. However, by now, you should see that reliability and validity do not automatically adhere to one research strategy more than another. Scientists like experimentation for a more specific reason: *All other things being equal, experiments are the best way to identify causes.* Because many scientific hypotheses are phrased in terms of causes and effects, experiments are clearly valuable.

In an **experiment,** the researcher deliberately manipulates certain events and measures the effects of these manipulations on other events. An **independent variable** is the factor manipulated by the researcher. It is the potential cause that she wishes to investigate. It is called the "independent" variable because one hopes it is independent of extraneous variables, which the researcher attempts to hold constant. A **dependent variable** is the factor assessed by the researcher following the manipulation—the potential effect of concern. It is called the "dependent" variable

experiment
a research strategy in which the researcher manipulates certain events and measures the effects of these manipulations on other events

independent variable
in experiments, the factor manipulated by the researcher

dependent variable
in experiments, the factor assessed by the researcher following a particular manipulation

because it presumably depends on the manipulation (and only on the manipulation).

Experiments usually introduce the potential cause to one group of research subjects and withhold it from a second. The former group is often termed the **experimental group,** and the latter the **control group.** Don't be misled by these labels; both experimental and control groups are necessary for an experiment.

In some studies using the experimental strategy, researchers use more than one control group, the reason being that manipulations usually affect more than just the intended cause. So, the operationalization of the independent variable is less than perfectly valid. Additional control groups are therefore used to rule out the role of extraneous variables introduced by a manipulation.

Here's an example. One of the ways that biological psychologists study how the brain works is to selectively destroy a particular part of the brain. They might do this by performing surgery on a rat, opening its skull and making a wound in a given location in the brain. They let the animal recover and then observe its behavior.

One obvious control group in this sort of research is animals whose brains were not destroyed by the experimenter. But stop and think for a minute. In comparing the behavior of animals with and without damage to their brains, aren't you also making another comparison—one between animals with and without surgery? Suppose animals in the experimental group act listlessly, eat excessively, or fall ill. Is this due to the particular wound made by the researcher or to the invasive and traumatic surgery? One cannot tell. For this reason, a second control is probably a good idea as well: a group of animals whose skulls are opened and then closed, without any damage to their brain. Maybe the researcher also feels the need for yet another control group: animals receiving wounds in an altogether different part of the brain.

You can see that the process of adding control groups to an experiment is analogous to the process of ruling out third variables in a correlational study. The extraneous variables that control groups try to eliminate are potential confounds that threaten validity. In both correlational and experimental studies, the researcher intends to sharpen the conclusions, to have confidence that operational definitions are more rather than less valid.

The defining feature of an experiment is the explicit control the researcher exercises over possible causes. He decides which research subjects will brush their teeth with Crest and which subjects will not. He determines who will memorize information in a noisy environment and who will do so in utter quiet. He chooses the rats reared in crowded conditions as well as those who live in splendid solitude.

In an experiment, all research subjects must have an equal chance to be exposed to the different conditions created by the experimenter. In other words, subjects must be assigned to the experimental and control groups on a random basis, in a process called **random assignment.** The goal here is to cancel all possible third variables, so that the only difference between Group One and Group Two is the factor manipulated by the researcher.

Consider what happens to conclusions if the researcher violates random assignment. Does aerobic exercise improve someone's mood, as

experimental group
in experiments, the group of subjects exposed to the independent variable

control group
in experiments, the group of subjects not exposed to the independent variable

random assignment
in experiments, the process of assigning research subjects to different groups on a random basis, so that all subjects have an equal chance to be exposed to the different conditions created by the experimenter

many claim (see Figure 1.4)? A researcher might proceed in answering this question by making up two types of recreational programs, with and without aerobic exercise. "Aerobic exercise or not" is therefore the independent variable in this study. Then the researcher might recruit children in a junior high school as research subjects. They will be placed in one type of program or the other for one school period a day during the next school year. A questionnaire measuring their mood will be given to all subjects at the end of the year, and the researcher will see if the manipulated factor (aerobic exercise) has an effect on their reported mood. "Mood" is the dependent variable in this study.

Now suppose the researcher happens to assign the children to conditions according to their homerooms. Students with homerooms on the first floor are assigned to the aerobic exercise group, and students with homerooms on the second floor are assigned to the control group. But what happens if students in the first floor homerooms, for whatever reason, are mainly females, whereas those in the second floor homerooms are mainly males? The experimenter has dramatically weakened the study, because the aerobic exercise or not conditions are also female versus male conditions. If exercise subjects have better (or worse) moods, does this mean that aerobic exercise is the critical cause, or does it mean that females in the first place are happier (or sadder) than males? One cannot tell, and this is why random assignment of subjects to the manipulated

Figure 1.4
The Parts of an Experiment

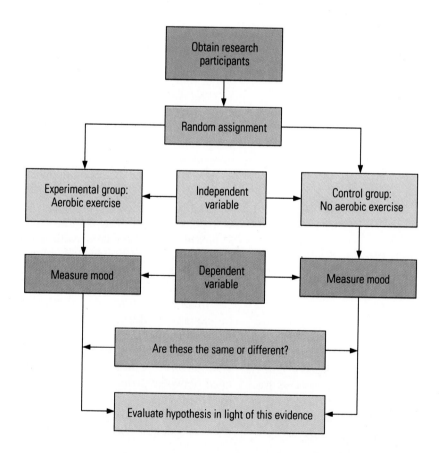

conditions is critical. Otherwise, third variables are introduced, and causal conclusions cannot be readily advanced.

People sometimes have trouble appreciating the importance of randomization in conducting an experiment. Maybe the difficulty stems from common connotations of random: capriciousness and carelessness. In the context of experimentation, though, these connotations are quite misleading. Randomization accomplishes just the opposite in an experiment. Rather than introducing unknown factors into research, randomization eliminates them, by spreading them across conditions so that they have no systematic effect.

This point is important. Experiments require randomization. At the same time, randomization can never cancel out all possible confounds. Subjects—even rats—show some variation. Sometimes just the luck of the draw introduces variation with respect to a critical characteristic. Regardless, experiments remain superior to case studies or correlational investigations for drawing causal conclusions.

To summarize, the experimental research strategy has the ability to draw causal conclusions. At the same time, experiments have drawbacks. As noted in the discussion of the correlational method, the researcher cannot manipulate all variables. Experiments have no value if one is concerned with factors like sex or age or race.

Experiments have another drawback: They may be highly reactive with respect to some topics. Complex social behavior in particular may be altered when it is brought into the experimental laboratory for investigation (Chapter 15). For example, it is difficult to study racial prejudice in an experiment nowadays, not because racial prejudice doesn't exist, but rather because the typical research subject is unwilling to act in a prejudiced way under a psychologist's scrutiny.

Do not confuse this shortcoming of experiments with another common criticism—that experiments are invalid because they oversimplify what they are studying. Indeed, experiments are useful precisely because they make complex phenomena simple, holding constant all factors except one and systematically investigating the consequences of this one factor. Yes, experiments are artificial, but it is their artificiality that allows us to offer causal conclusions.

The reactivity of experiments is a different matter, and the criticism here is more subtle. Because of their very nature, psychology experiments can alter what they intend to study. The problem is not simplification but transformation. Remember the Prisoners' Dilemma Game from earlier in the chapter (p. 25)? Perhaps this research strategy captures not competition and cooperation but rather "fun and games" (Ring, 1967). Maybe the situation presented to subjects virtually demands that they treat the Prisoners' Dilemma Game as something different than real competition or real cooperation. To sum up this section, Table 1.3 compares the strengths and weaknesses of case studies, correlational investigations, and experiments.

Research Ethics

All researchers must eventually confront the ethical implications of what they do. This confrontation usually occurs when research findings are applied in ways that may be harmful to individuals or to society. Sophisti-

Table 1.3

Comparison of Research Methods

Research Method	Strengths	Weaknesses
Case studies	Provide rich details Can demonstrate what is or is not possible Are the only way to study rare phenomena	May rely on secondhand information Cannot identify causes Do not allow generalization
Correlational investigations	Allows generalization Are the only way to study certain topics	Cannot identify causes
Experiments	Can identify causes	Cannot study certain topics May be reactive

cated instruments of war are just one obvious example of how science can enter the ethical arena. What starts out as "basic" science can end up as "applied" science that the world might be better off without.

Psychologists face the same dilemma regarding the eventual use of their findings. However, unlike researchers in many other fields, psychologists additionally face an immediate dilemma when they use human beings in their research. Studies that use animals present their own ethical problems concerning how to treat them in a humane fashion, and we will discuss animal research at the end of this section.

Research with People. Many of the requirements of sound research design run the risk of infringing on the rights of the individual, as in the following cases:

- To have representative research subjects, psychologists must (sometimes) coerce people into participating.
- To have unbiased research subjects, psychologists must (sometimes) deceive people about the real purposes of the study.
- To investigate important behavior, psychologists must (sometimes) expose people to stress.
- To draw causal conclusions, psychologists must (sometimes) manipulate people.
- To evaluate the benefits of an intervention like psychotherapy, psychologists must (sometimes) withhold a potentially helpful treatment from people in need.

One of the most controversial studies ever conducted by a psychologist is Stanley Milgram's (1963) investigation of obedience. This work will be described in detail later in the book (Chapter 15), but let's look at it briefly right now, noting the ethical issues involved. Milgram recruited adult subjects through newspaper ads in New Haven, ostensibly to participate in a study of learning. Upon arriving at the laboratory, each subject encountered another subject who in actuality was working with the experimenter. (The real subject did not know this until the experiment was complete.) The two subjects were told the procedure: One would play the role of a teacher, and the other the role of a student. When the student made a mistake, the teacher was to press a button that would shock him. Each mistake would warrant an increasingly powerful shock.

The "real" subject became the teacher, while the "confederate" became the student. The student went into a different room, and the teacher was seated at a console with buttons and dials controlling the shocks. As the experiment progressed, the student made errors, and the teacher delivered shocks. (Actual shocks were not delivered, but the "real" subject did not know this.) At one point, the student started banging on the wall and yelling about his heart condition! As you might imagine, the teacher became extremely uncomfortable with this state of affairs and turned to the researcher for guidance. He was told, "The experiment requires that you continue."

Here's why the Milgram study is of *substantive* importance. Fully two-thirds of the subjects continued to deliver shocks under these circumstances. Although many subjects were obviously distressed and anxious, they nevertheless continued to obey the experimenter. Only the most cynical person would have expected this result, which may explain why people sometimes perpetrate horrors against their fellow men and women—obedience to authority. When the research was completed, the subject met the confederate and saw that he was alright. The true purpose was then explained in detail to the subject.

Let's step back and discuss how the Milgram procedure raises a number of ethical questions (e.g., Baumrind, 1964). Were the research subjects treated fairly? They were misled about the nature of the experiment. They

Milgram's study of obedience raised questions about the nature of obedience—and the importance of ethics in scientific research.

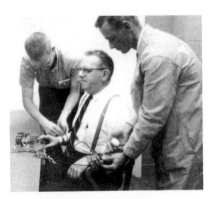

were exposed to something extremely disquieting. Whether the information provided at the end of the study effectively dispelled anxiety and self-doubt is unclear.

On the other hand, one can argue that research benefits society. Certainly, Milgram's investigation of disobedience makes an important contribution to knowledge. The general conflict in doing psychology studies is therefore between the rights of the individual research subject and the rights of the larger society. How can this conflict be resolved?

We can make after-the-fact judgments that a particular study was valuable or not, but hindsight is of no help in planning research. Accordingly, the American Psychological Association has published a code of ethical principles to help researchers with potential dilemmas. These ethical principles are not a cookbook of what thou shall and shall not do. Instead, "the decision to undertake research should rest upon a considered judgment by the individual psychologist about how best to contribute to psychological science and human welfare" (APA, 1981, p. 1).

At the same time, psychologists try to avoid violating individual rights by following certain conventions. If you have ever participated as a subject in a psychology study, these conventions will probably be familiar to you. First, almost all research settings, such as colleges, hospitals, and mental health centers, have a *human subjects committee* composed of psychologists and nonpsychologists that reviews research proposals for possible ethical problems. Second, researchers usually obtain *informed consent* from potential subjects before involving them in a study. They explain the general procedures to be followed (e.g., you will complete questionnaires taking about 45 minutes) and any risks or discomforts the subjects may experience (e.g., the noises you will hear are uncomfortably loud). Then they ask the subjects to consent to participate under these conditions. Third, subjects are told explicitly that they have the *right to withdraw* from the study at any time they choose without penalty. Finally, subjects are entitled to a full *debriefing* concerning the purpose of a study once it has been completed.

Not all psychologists are pleased with these conventions, arguing that important experiments like that of Milgram cannot be conducted if the ethical principles are strictly followed. The APA Ethical Principles allow exceptions to the guidelines, but urge careful deliberation under these circumstances. What do you think? The vast majority of subjects who participate in psychology experiments seem to find them inoffensive, which implies that researchers are sensitive to potential problems. Nevertheless, continued scrutiny of methods and techniques is a good idea.

Research with Animals. The same ethical dilemma faces psychologists conducting research that uses animals, such as rats, mice, dogs, cats, and monkeys. In many of these studies, animals experience stress, pain, and eventually death. The use of animals in research is a subject of growing social and political controversy. On the one hand, researchers point to the methodological benefits of animal research, including experimental control, objectivity, and efficiency, as well as to the contributions animal research makes to human welfare (e.g., Miller, 1985). On the other hand, critics argue that whatever the benefits and contributions, these are outweighed by the unnecessary suffering to which laboratory animals are exposed (e.g, McArdle, 1984).

Animal research has become more controversial in the latter part of the twentieth century.

There is no easy solution to this legitimate debate. Some researchers are trying to devise alternatives to the traditional use of animals in laboratory studies. Gallup and Suarez (1985) have surveyed some of these alternatives. Although these alternatives may not be fully adequate replacements, some possibilities are intriguing:

- naturalistic observation (studying animals in the wild)
- case studies (studying animals one at a time)
- use of "lower" animals (studying cold-blooded animals)
- plants as alternatives (studying the "behavior" of plants)
- tissue cultures (studying parts of animals)
- computer simulations (programming an "animal" on a computer)

Each alternative may be useful, depending on the particular purpose of a researcher.

In conclusion, let's review the material covered in this chapter. We started by defining psychology as the science that describes and explains behavior and mental processes. We then saw that what makes psychology a science is its concern with systematically testing explanations against evidence. Psychology began a little more than 100 years ago, and it now is a large and specialized field. Various research methods exist as well, notably case studies, correlational investigations, and experiments. In subsequent chapters, we will discuss in turn the most important fields of contemporary psychology. Chapter 2 begins this discussion with the field of biological psychology.

Summary

Topics of Concern

- Psychology is the science that describes and explains behavior and mental processes. Often its focus is on the thoughts, feelings, and actions of people, but psychology is also concerned with animals.
- To say that psychology is a science means that its explanations are tentative hypotheses checked against evidence.
- Because psychology as a science changes, old theories give way to new ones. However, certain basic questions endure.
- The most general of psychology's enduring concerns is the view of human nature that a given theory embraces.

Scientific Psychology versus Everyday Psychology

- Psychology is a science because its explanations are tested against evidence from the world. Although this definition of psychology is straightforward, matters become a bit complicated when we consider that an important part of our everyday life is explaining what people do. Not all everyday explanations qualify as scientific psychology, because we do not test them.

The History of Psychology

- Psychology began in 1879 when the German professor Wilhelm Wundt founded the first psychology laboratory at the University of Leipzig. Wundt defined psychology as the science of consciousness and its subject matter as experience. The goal of psychology was to identify the basic building blocks of experience.
- Wundt's psychology came to be known as structuralism because of its interest in the structure of the mind. Structuralism was popularized in the United States by Edward Titchener, one of Wundt's most loyal students.
- The structuralists used introspection to identify the elements of consciousness. Introspection as

a research method was unwieldy, and soon rival approaches to psychology were proposed.
- Gestalt psychology was founded by Max Wertheimer, and started with the premise that experience is inherently organized, not assembled from isolated elements. Kurt Lewin applied the gestalt perspective to social behavior, and is regarded as the founding father of social psychology.
- William James and John Dewey were leaders in the American approach to psychology known as functionalism, which was interested in the consequences of mental processes. They believed that the proper focus of psychology was not the structure of the mind, but its function.
- Behaviorism began in 1913 when John Watson argued that psychology should study not the mind but observable behavior. Behaviorism became extremely popular and influential in the United States, perhaps because of the emphasis it placed on processes of learning.
- The Viennese physician Sigmund Freud created psychoanalysis, a complex approach to human activity that stresses unconscious conflicts and how they are resolved.
- The more recent history of psychology is characterized by great growth of the field, as well as increasing specialization, quantification, and application. The 1960s were a period of self-criticism and doubt in psychology, mirroring larger societal trends, but psychology emerged from this period with greater maturity.
- The most important occurrence in recent history is the cognitive revolution, a widespread return of psychology to the study of cognition, the mental processes responsible for how we know the world.
- Contemporary psychology is a specialized endeavor, and each of the subsequent chapters in this book features a particular speciality, ranging from a focus on the brain and nervous system to an interest in culture and society.
- Uniting these specialities are a concern with describing and explaining what people do, a commitment to evaluating theories by conducting research, and a common history.

Research Methods in Psychology

- Various research methods are available for testing psychological theories. Regardless of the method, a researcher must operationalize the concepts of interest—that is, devise concrete measures of them. A researcher wants measures to be reliable, yielding the same result on different occasions; valid, assessing what they purport to get at; and generalizable.
- Case studies are intensive analyses of single individuals or groups. Correlational investigations describe how variables are associated. Experiments manipulate possible causes and measure the effects of doing so. Each of these methods has its own strengths and weaknesses, and there is no best research method for all purposes.
- Because many studies in psychology investigate people, psychologists need to protect the individual rights of research subjects.
- The ethical use of animals in psychological research is also a topic of great concern to psychologists.

Important Terms and Names

What follows is a list of the core terms and names for this chapter. Your instructor may emphasize other terms as well. Throughout the chapter, glossary terms appear in **boldface** type. They are defined in the text, and each term, along with its definition, is repeated in the margin.

Topics of Concern

psychology/2
behavior/2
mental processes/2
hypotheses/2
theories/2
scientific method/3
nature-nurture controversy/4
data/5

Scientific Psychology versus Everyday Psychology

determinism/6

The History of Psychology

structuralism/10
introspection/10
gestalt psychology/11
functionalism/12
behaviorism/14
psychoanalysis/15
cognition/19

Wilhelm Wundt/9
Edward B. Titchener/10
Max Wertheimer/12
Kurt Lewin/12
William James/13
John Dewey/13
John Watson/14
Sigmund Freud/15

Research Methods in Psychology

operational definition/22
confound/23
reliability/24
validity/25
generalization/26
sample/26
population/26
case study/27
correlational investigation/29
experiment/32
independent variable/32
dependent variable/32
experimental group/33
control group/33
random assignment/33

1. What makes psychology a science?
   a. Psychologists check explanations against evidence.
   b. Psychologists propose theories about human nature.
   c. Psychologists use animals in their work.
   d. Psychologists use statistics.

   The defining characteristic of *any* science is the checking of theories against data. The other answers mention factors that are often associated with science but do not define it./2

2. Scientific progress refers to
   a. the continual revision of scientific theories in light of research findings.
   b. the gradual discovery of truth by scientists.
   c. the greater complexity of scientific theories.
   d. the increasing specialization of scientific fields.

   Scientific progress occurs as theories are modified or discarded in light of evidence. Despite stereotypes about science, there is no necessary movement toward absolute truth, greater complexity, or increased specialization./5

3. In contrast to everyday psychology, scientific psychology
   a. assumes determinism.
   b. attempts to explain everything that people do.
   c. offers explanations in probabilistic terms that refer to people in general.
   d. offers tentative explanations.
   e. all of the above.

   All of these are characteristics of scientific psychology. Everyday psychology usually has the opposite characteristics, which is why it fails to qualify as a science./6

4. The very first psychologists concerned themselves with
   a. the behavior of animals.
   b. the behavior of people.
   c. conscious experience.
   d. emotional and mental problems.

   Wilhelm Wundt was the very first psychologist, and he defined psychology as the scientific study of conscious experience./9

5. Which of these approaches to psychology began by disagreeing with structuralism?
   a. gestalt psychology
   b. functionalism
   c. behaviorism
   d. all of the above

   Although gestalt psychology, functionalism, and behaviorism disagreed with different aspects of structuralism, all took issue with at least part of the agenda of Wundt and Titchener./11

6. In contrast to the other great schools of psychology, psychoanalysis is notable because it relied on _____ for evidence.
   a. animal experiments
   b. clinical case studies
   c. computer simulation
   d. logical arguments

   Psychoanalysis had its origins in observations made by neurologist Sigmund Freud of distressed patients in his clinical practice. The other great schools of psychology occasionally used case studies in their research, but not to the same extent as psychoanalysis./15

7. The most recent occurrence in the history of psychology is the
   a. cognitive revolution.
   b. phenomenal growth of the field.
   c. increased quantification of research.
   d. self-criticism within the field.
   e. specialization of the field.

   All of these answers mention changes in psychology throughout the twentieth century, but the increased attention to people's thoughts and beliefs is the most recent trend in psychology./19

8. Measures of _____ are usually foolproof operationalizations.
   a. consumer product quality
   b. mental states and processes
   c. observable behavior
   d. time, space, and matter
   e. none of the above

   There are *no* foolproof measures of any abstract concepts./23

9. Which of these statements is false?
   a. Measures can be both reliable and valid.
   b. Measures can be reliable but not valid.
   c. Measures can be valid but not reliable.
   d. Measures can be neither reliable nor valid.
   A measure that gives different answers on different occasions cannot possibly be valid. So, there are no valid measures that are unreliable, which means there is only one false statement./24

10. The best psychological research uses
   a. case studies.
   b. correlational investigations.
   c. experiments.
   d. none of the above.
   The best approach to research depends on the investigator's purpose. There is no best research strategy for all purposes./35

Appendix: Statistics

Statistics are usually discussed without mentioning statisticians, the men and women who devise the formulas in the first place. Thus, it is no wonder students sometimes find statistics arbitrary and confusing. We can make statistics a bit more human by describing two central figures in the early history of statistics: Florence Nightingale (1820–1910) and William S. Gossett (1876–1938).

Florence Nightingale—the famous nurse of the Crimean War? You probably never thought of Florence Nightingale as a statistician, but her place in the history of statistics is as secure as her place in the history of medicine. Indeed, they are entwined. Nightingale was a great advocate of hospital reform. In her opinion, the typical hospital of her day killed more people than it saved, due to bad food, poor hygiene, and other deficiencies. To buttress her arguments, Nightingale gathered and compared the facts about mortality rates in and out of hospitals, finding that hospitals indeed were hazardous to one's health! She appreciated the need for uniformity of records as no one before. Once uniform information is available, opinions can be checked against evidence. "We can see the statistical mind at work: formulation of a hypothesis—search for data—measurement operations on the data—derivation of the conclusions" (Kennedy, 1984, p. 43).

The general public does not know William S. Gossett as well as it knows Florence Nightingale. Even statisticians might not recognize his name. He published his numerous contributions under a pseudonym—"Student"—because his employer did not want to publicize the fact that it hired scientifically trained researchers (Tankard, 1984). Gossett was a brewer for Arthur Guiness Sons & Co., Ltd., of Dublin. Now you have an association with Gossett: Guiness stout! (And the *Guiness Book of World Records,* as well, because the same company that makes the beer publishes the book to settle the arguments that occur when people drink the beer.)

The brewing of beer requires the combination of four ingredients: barley, hops, yeast, and water. The Guiness Company tried to make this process less mysterious than it had been for centuries by hiring researchers to analyze the process of brewing and discover optimal ways of combining the ingredients. Gossett and the other "scientific" brewmasters carefully measured characteristics of the different ingredients (e.g., amount, temperature) and experimented with different combinations of them. Which approaches yielded good beer, and which produced bad beer? To answer this question objectively, Gossett devised techniques of inferential statistics. One of these is among the commonly used statistical procedures today, and if you take a statistics course, you'll encounter Student's *t* test for assessing whether the means of two samples are really different. And I'm sure you'll inform your fellow classmates that the original samples were bottles of beer.

In short, statistics are tools. They've been used to save lives, and they've been used to make beer. Contemporary psychologists use statistics to better understand the human condition. One can neither conduct nor understand psychology research without a grasp of basic statistics. This grasp is easy to come by. Many students are put off by statistics, but I suspect they are not seeing that statistics are tools. Hammers, chainsaws, or chisels can hurt you as well if you pick them up with no idea about what you want to do.

In this brief section, we will examine how psychology researchers use statistics. (If we have time, we will also look at the purpose of hammers, chainsaws, and chisels.) First of all, statistics *describe* one's data. Think back over the different investigations I've used as examples in this chapter. Not even for the case studies did we look at every detail, and neither did the original researchers. Rather, they offered an overview of the research results.

Descriptive Statistics

descriptive statistics
statistics that describe the patterns within data

Descriptive statistics are formulas that allow the researcher to get a handle on complex sets of data by describing their general characteristics and patterns. Consider the following statement:

> On the average, people with a pessimistic view of the future live shorter lives.

This statement is easy to understand. Suppose you were presented instead with unsummarized numbers pertaining to pessimism and longevity. Although such a list would be rich in detail, you would probably miss the straightforward generalization lurking within. Descriptive statistics unearth it.

In overviewing data, one can focus on virtually any aspect of the information. A researcher, for instance, could describe the single subject in a correlational study who scores most extremely on the variables of concern. So, I just obtained copies of brief interviews with 102 individuals, compiled for the purpose of studying the relationship of beliefs to physical health. It turns out that one of these folks is 115 years old! This extreme case seems to deserve special note.

Central Tendency

central tendency
the mean or average value of a variable

For the vast majority of studies, however, researchers focus on just a few aspects of their data. First, they are often interested in describing the **central tendency** of variables: their mean or average values. We are constantly concerned with central tendencies in everyday life. How much do meals cost at that restaurant? What's the starting salary with a college degree in this discipline? What kind of grades does the teacher give? With these questions, we're asking for average values. The information proves useful to us.

Averages are often useful in describing research results as well, particularly the results of experiments. Suppose you are interested in the effects of psychotherapy on someone's marital satisfaction. You might investigate this question in an experiment, assigning married subjects at random to two conditions: psychotherapy or no psychotherapy. Later, you might operationalize marital satisfaction as the number of sappy notes each subject wrote to his or her spouse in a 7-day period. (Remember that no operationalization is foolproof.) Does psychotherapy lead to an increase in sappy notes? This question translates to one asking about averages: Is the average number of notes greater for subjects in psychotherapy than for subjects not in psychotherapy?

Variability

variability
the variation in a particular variable

Researchers also focus on the **variability** of their measures. How much variation is there in a particular variable? In everyday life, we may be less attuned to variability than we are to central tendency, but stop and think for a minute, and you'll find that you also have a good feel for variability. If you are a sports fan, you know that some players or teams show a steady level of performance, whereas other players or teams can be very good or very bad. The former show less variability than the latter. We can make the same observation about students. Two of your friends have identical C+ averages, let us say, but Consistent Connie achieves her GPA by getting a C+ grade in every course she takes, while Awesomly Fluctuating Annie-Flo gets only A grades and F grades.

The variability of data interests researchers for several reasons. In a correlational study, one must have a sufficient spread of scores to see which variables go together. For example, researchers have tried to investigate some of the correlates of depressed mood by soliciting volunteers and giving them a questionnaire that measures degree of depression. Sometimes other variables show no correlation whatsoever with depression scores. What gives? Sometimes, the subjects were exclusively cheerful individuals, as you might expect given that they volunteered for the study. One of the symptoms of depression is curtailment of activities, and, of course, voluntary participation in a psychology experiment is an activity! Insufficient variability works against the success of a correlational study.

A more subtle reason for paying attention to variability is that one can best interpret averages in light of variation among the consistent scores. Let's return to your C+ friends. If you were asked to characterize what kinds of students Connie and Annie-Flo were, you would have a lot of confidence in your description of Connie, because her individual grades are so consistent. What could you say about Annie-Flo that wouldn't require hedging and qualification? The variability of her grades precludes you giving a confident answer.

The same reasoning applies to the interpretation of the results of experiments. Let's return to the wedded couples and their sappy notes. Table A.1 presents two sets of hypothetical data. In both cases, individuals in psychotherapy send more notes than people not in therapy. The data are arranged so that the means of the two conditions are identical in both versions of the data. But note that in the top set of scores, there is little variation within the psychotherapy subjects and little variation within the nonpsychotherapy subjects. In contrast, the bottom set of scores are highly

Table A.1
Number of Sappy Love Notes Exchanged by Spouses within a 7-Day Period

Couples in Psychotherapy			Couples Not in Psychotherapy		
Set 1	Couple 1–1	14	Couple 1–6	10	
	Couple 1–2	14	Couple 1–7	11	
	Couple 1–3	15	Couple 1–8	10	
	Couple 1–4	14	Couple 1–9	12	
	Couple 1–5	14	Couple 1–10	10	
	Mean = 14.2		Mean = 10.6		

Couples in Psychotherapy			Couples Not in Psychotherapy		
Set 2	Couple 2–1	21	Couple 2–6	0	
	Couple 2–2	7	Couple 2–7	21	
	Couple 2–3	27	Couple 2–8	2	
	Couple 2–4	12	Couple 2–9	3	
	Couple 2–5	14	Couple 2–10	27	
	Mean = 14.2		Mean = 10.6		

variable. Which sets of scores allow you to make the more confident conclusion about the effects of psychotherapy? The answer is clear, and this is why researchers pay attention to how much or how little scores vary. There are specific formulas to describe the variability of a set of scores.

Correlations

Finally, researchers want to describe the degree to which two variables are correlated. In Chapter 1, correlations were introduced merely as positive, negative, or zero. Researchers in practice make finer distinctions, and they do so by computing a numerical value called a **correlation coefficient.** The exact mathematics need not concern us here. Just be aware that positive correlation coefficients range from 0.00 to 1.00, and that negative correlation coefficients range from 0.00 to –1.00.

The larger the magnitude of the coefficient (that is, the farther the correlation coefficient is from 0.00), the greater the degree of correlation between the two variables. What does it mean to say that two variables are highly correlated? Remember the graphs in Figure 1–3. Highly correlated variables yield a graph in which the data points come very close to being a straight line. Variables correlated to a lesser degree have data points that fall less tightly along a straight line.

Here is an example of variables correlated to different degrees. Let's consider the height of you and your classmates. Suppose we find out the height of everybody's mother, as well as the height of everybody's grandmother. If we compute the correlation between children's height and mother's height and the correlation between children's height and grand-

correlation coefficient

a number between –1.00 and 1.00 reflecting the degree to which two variables are correlated with one another; the further the number is from 0.00, the stronger the correlation—negative or positive, as the case may be mothers' height, both will be positive, because height (or its lack) runs in families. However, the former correlation will be stronger than the latter, because whatever genetic links exist are more direct between child and mother than between child and grandmother.

If you are a skeptical type, good for you; why not test this out? Gather the relevant heights for fifty or sixty families. Your teacher can explain how to compute correlation coefficients. Alternatively, you can simply graph the information and see if the child-parent data result in a better straight line than the child-grandparent data.

Inferential Statistics

Psychologists also use statistics to draw conclusions from their data. In particular, they wish to *infer* whether particular results came about by chance or not. When there is a decent possibility that the study's results represent random fluctuations, a researcher refrains from getting too excited about the results. So, **inferential statistics** are formulas that let the researcher calculate the likelihood that particular research results arose by chance. Thus, he or she can decide whether patterns in obtained data are reliable findings or simply flukes.

Suppose the students in your class who sit in the front of the room get higher examination scores than students who sit in the back. Say the difference is 77 percent correct versus 73 percent correct. Although 77 percent is different than 73 percent, this difference might well be the result of chance. Maybe a few people in the front row happened to guess well, and a few people in the last row happened to guess poorly. If it's just chance, then we wouldn't want to conclude that where students sit has anything to do with their grades. We've got to make a judgment about the possible role of chance in producing results. Inferential statistics provide an explicit way of making this judgment.

To make this judgment, the researcher uses standard formulas that take into account probabilities. These procedures usually start by assuming that all outcomes are equally likely. Let's say you play checkers with your eight-year-old nephew in order to decide the championship of the known universe. You plan to play until one player is clearly superior, until one of the players wins a lot more than 50 percent of the games. But if you both win about half the time, then you are cochampions.

After two games, he is ahead 2–0. Does this mean he is a better checker player? You'd be pretty safe arguing against this conclusion. Hey, he got lucky. Play the best 3 out of 5. After 100 games, he is ahead 97–3. Does *this* mean he is a better checker player? You'd be hooted if you persisted in arguing against this conclusion. Luck could conceivably account for these results, but this seems pretty remote. Do you care to go for the best 98 out of 195 matches?

Results that seem unlikely to have occurred by chance are termed **statistically significant.** There is no further meaning here. Statistically significant results are merely those that seem unlikely to have occurred by chance. Many psychologists use a 1 out of 20 (5 percent or .05) criterion to designate results as statistically significant or not. If results could have arisen from chance no more than 1 time out of 20, then the researcher

inferential statistics
statistics that allow conclusions beyond the immediate results of a particular study, specifically, whether or not results arose by chance

statistically significant results
a pattern of findings unlikely to have occurred by chance

decides the results are worth taking seriously. The so-called .05 level is arbitrary. Some researchers use a more stringent criterion, and others use one that is less stringent.

Do people perform better when rewarded for their successes, or when punished for their failures? Although there is probably no simple answer to this question, imagine you are trying to answer it with respect to playing a video game. In one condition, when players exceed their PR (personal record, to the uninitiated), they gain $1. In a second condition, when players fail to exceed their PR, they lose $1. Fifty players are in each group, and you have each subject play 100 games with rewards or punishments, as the case may be. You operationalize "performance" as the score on the 101st game.

Which group does better? On a descriptive level, you answer this question simply by calculating the average scores in the two groups. Say you find that subjects in one group score 17 points higher on the average than subjects in the other group. You are not done, however, until you decide what this difference really means. Maybe it makes no difference whether you reward or punish video game players. You'd then expect average scores in the two groups to be about the same. Is "17 points higher" about the same? Here is where inferential statistics are brought to bear. Starting with the assumption of no difference, you calculate the probability that a 17 point discrepancy could occur by chance. As you might imagine, the formula you use takes into account the variability of the scores. The more tightly bunched scores are in each group, the less likely the 17 point difference arose by chance.

You don't need to understand the exact mathematics to see the point of inferential statistics, and so we haven't gone into the formulas here. Let's understand two important points: (a) Psychologists use inferential statistics to decide whether their results might have been produced by chance, and (b) statistical significance should not be confused with theoretical significance, practical significance, or validity; it only means that results probably did not arise by a fluke.

Conclusion: Statistics Are Tools with Particular Purposes

What else to add? Oh yes, I promised you information about tools besides statistics. Hammers can be used when you can't locate a screwdriver. Chainsaws can be used as props in B-grade horror movies. And chisels can be used to pry weeds out of your lawn. What's the point? Tools can be used in many ways. Some ways make more sense than others. As a psychology student, you'll do fine if you remember that the best use of statistics is to describe data and to make inferences about whether results arose by chance.

The cerebral cortex organizes information relayed to it by other brain structures.

Chapter Two

Biology and Behavior

Topics of Concern

Charlie Mohr. Benny (Kid) Paret. Davey Moore. Willie Classen. Duk Koo Kim. Do you recognize any of these names? Each was a boxer who died of injuries suffered in the ring. These are the most obvious casualties of boxing, but short of banning boxing altogether, such deaths probably cannot be prevented. There is no way to know if a punch will rupture a blood vessel in a boxer's brain, causing the blood to fill up the narrow space between the hard skull and soft brain, creating tremendous pressure that literally squeezes the brain to death.

But there are less obvious casualties of boxing, much more common than immediate death but also preventable. Chronic brain damage, shown by such symptoms as slurred speech, drooling, memory loss, slow movements, and an unsteady gait, is an all too frequent consequence of a career as a boxer. You can see why we commonly refer to a person with this kind of damage as punch-drunk.

In the 1920s, the boxing press all but ignored brain damage as a danger of boxing, attributing the symptoms to the fact that many boxers of this era were drinkers and drug addicts who ate poorly (Boyle & Ames, 1983). Today we know better, because autopsies have been performed on the brains of former boxers. The brain damage caused by alcoholism does not rival the damage caused by too many punches to the head! Professional boxers are more susceptible to chronic brain damage than amateurs because they sustain so many more punches in a given fight and over their career. Brain damage also tends to afflict sluggers more than stylish fighters, because they are more willing to take a punch in order to land one themselves.

Let's look at Muhammad Ali, perhaps the best known and most charismatic boxer the world has ever seen. Is he punch-drunk, as some observers fear, or is there another reason for his slurred speech and rambling monologues (Boyle & Ames, 1983)? We have no privileged information, but Ali seems a prime candidate for chronic brain damage because he had such a long and active career—61 fights over 21 years in the ring. As far back as 1976, he was warned that he should retire to avoid brain and kidney damage. Tests in 1981 showed that he had certain abnormalities in his brain associated with chronic brain damage.

Others contend that these tests don't prove anything, that they simply reflect processes of normal aging. Indeed, Ali has fared well on many neurological tests. More stringent

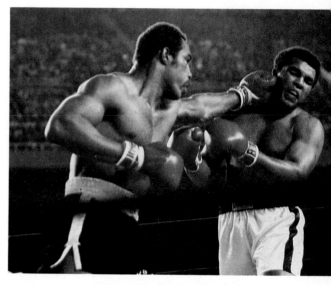

Is brain damage—from countless blows to the head—the cause of Muhammad Ali's loss of his legendary verbal skills?

use of these tests might reduce the long-term risk of brain damage, however, if fighters were banned from boxing after showing early indications.

Tests notwithstanding, Muhammad Ali may have substantial brain damage. It has been reported that he suffers from a form of Parkinson's disease brought about by too many blows to his head (Maugh, 1988). Recently, Ali has considered experimental surgery in which healthy tissue from his adrenal glands will be transplanted to his brain.

The case of Muhammad Ali, whatever its outcome, is evidence of the importance of the brain in our everyday functioning. It also underscores more generally the importance of biology to behavior and mental processes. If we are to fully understand the topics of psychology, we must at the same time appreciate the role played by biology. Let's consider several of the important issues involved here.

Pros and Cons of Using Biology to Explain Behavior

What does it mean to give a biological explanation of behavior? Niko Tinbergen (1968) observed that biologists explain things in one of four ways: by stressing cause, function, development, or evolution. Each explanation is different, but they are also compatible. For example, human sex differences can be explained in all these ways. Indeed, a full account of why men and women differ in the ways that they do (as well as why they are similar in other ways) must encompass all four types of explanations (Daly & Wilson, 1978). Let's consider a particular difference between the sexes—*spatial ability.* Some research implies that men are better at visualizing three-dimensional objects than women (Maccoby & Jacklin, 1974). What might we make of this difference?

We might seek the cognitive or neural mechanism responsible for the difference (its *cause*). We might look for its adaptive significance (its *function*): How has our species benefited by having men with better spatial ability than women? Or we might ask how spatial ability develops in little boys as compared to little girls (its *development*), perhaps suspecting that boys are encouraged by their parents to visualize objects but girls are not. And, finally, we might wonder about primates in the wild, seeking a clue to the human difference by examining the activities of our cousins (its *evolution*). Suppose all of these investigations bear fruit? No problem; these modes of explanation are not incompatible. Indeed, they complement each other nicely.

Biological explanations of behavior are specific cases of biological explanations in general. These explanations can take various forms, stressing cause, function, development, or evolution, as the case may be. Most generally, biological explanations of behavior try to account for the operating principles of our bodies. We can only think or feel or do those things that our bodies allow.

Controversy enters when we ask if biological explanations tell the whole story about people's behavior. Here we can see in a most stark fashion the nature-versus-nurture debate discussed in the previous chapter. There are some psychologists who emphasize nature, as it applies to sensation (Chapter 3), perception (Chapter 4), intelligence (Chapter 8), child development (Chapter 9), emotional disorders (Chapter 12), and human sexuality (Chapter 16). Other psychologists stress nurture, arguing that learning

> If we are to fully understand the topics of psychology, we must at the same time appreciate the role played by biology.
>
> • • •

through interactions with the environment is the most important determinant of what we are all about.

How Does the Brain Work?

The ancient Greeks believed that the mind and soul were located within the heart. They felt that the brain was simply a radiator, a means to cool the blood! Not a bad guess, because they were suitably impressed with the large surface area of the brain relative to its mass. This of course is the principle of a car radiator; the large surface area allows for highly efficient cooling. But the large surface area also allows a great deal of interconnectedness among the parts of the brain, which is the contemporary interpretation of the brain's particular shape. And we now locate mental activity in the brain.

The ancient Greeks weren't the only ones who tried to understand the nature of the brain. Throughout history, scientists and philosophers have attempted to capture the essence of the brain, accounting for both its structure and function. A typical method has been to compare the brain to something else, in the hope that the brain would thus be clarified by the metaphor chosen. Over the years, almost every new technological breakthrough has suggested a new comparison.

For example, let's turn to the theorizing of René Descartes (1596–1650), the French philosopher and mathematician. Among Descartes's many contributions was one of the first models linking the brain with behavior. As a young man in Paris, Descartes was inspired by the mechanized statues found in the Royal Gardens. When visitors walked through the gardens, they would step on hidden plates that activated a hydraulic mechanism, making the statues move and dance.

Descartes speculated that the means by which people moved were analogous to those by which the statues moved. He knew that the brain contained hollow, fluid-filled chambers; that the brain was linked to the parts of the body by nerve cells; and that muscles appeared to enlarge as they were used. So, he theorized that behavior occurred when fluid was conducted through the nerve cells from the brain to the muscles. Like the statues, we move in response to the force of fluid. The brain—metaphorically—is a hydraulic mechanism.

Today, we see Descartes's theory as somewhat on target and somewhat off. The brain indeed is connected to every part of the body through a vast network of individual nerve cells called **neurons.** We refer to the brain and this network collectively as the nervous system. However, the nervous system is not powered by a hydraulic mechanism. Rather, it operates via complex electrical and chemical processes.

When psychologists concern themselves with the brain and nervous system, they want to know how these work and how they influence behavior. Three related roles are attributed to the brain and nervous system. First, they *receive* information from the world. Second, they *coordinate* this information in view of the organism's prevailing state. Third, they *react* on the basis of this coordination.

Like the brain, a computer receives, coordinates, and reacts to information. Thus, a currently popular theory views the brain as a computer because both "process" information (Chapter 7). Like any metaphor, the computer metaphor falls short of capturing the whole of the phenomenon it tries to explain. In the case of the brain, the emotional aspect of our mental life is practically ignored. Psychologists are currently casting about for new metaphors that can preserve the insights of the computer model into our cool, calm, and collected side, while also recognizing our passionate, motivated, and tumultuous one. (Mr. Spock of *Star Trek* faces this dilemma every day in attempting to integrate his Vulcan half [rational] with his human half [emotional].)

Evolution and Behavior

In discussing the biological aspects of behavior, we must take into account ideas concerning **evolution,** the changes

neurons
the basic units of the nervous system, individual nerve cells

evolution
the changes that take place over time in the characteristics of a species

that take place over time in the characteristics of species. Evolution provides the major unifying perspective on the whole of biology and thus on any attempt to use biology to explain behavior. Charles Darwin revolutionized biology in 1859 not just by arguing that species evolve, but also by proposing a persuasive theory explaining why.

According to Darwin, some characteristics of a species prove helpful in allowing its members to live long enough to reproduce. Other characteristics are not helpful. What ends up happening, then, is that the helpful characteristics are passed on to the next generation, whereas the other characteristics are not. Over time, across many generations, the changes introduced in this process can become very large ones. Altogether different species may appear, evolved from earlier species.

All aspects of our physical being are presumably the product of evolution. When we focus on particular body parts—like eyes or ears—there is no argument about the useful insights provided by an evolutionary perspective. But when we discuss complex behaviors, we enter a controversial arena. Do our social tendencies reflect the influence of evolution? How about our sexual orientations?

For that matter, how about boxing? Why does this supposed sport, with its well-documented dangers, flourish in the twentieth century? Some might point to the evolution of our species and the presumed advantage enjoyed by individuals who were physically aggressive. The need to engage in physical combat with another may be deeply rooted within us. The counterargument is that our impulses to violence are encouraged or thwarted by the environment. By this view, explanations in terms of human "nature" are simply wrong and perhaps even dangerous in their implication that we should not bother to attempt reform.

Structure and Function of the Nervous System

Let us turn to a discussion of the structure and function of the nervous system. We begin with an overview of the nervous system as a whole, identifying its major divisions. Then we take a close look at its most basic components, neurons. We close this section by discussing the ways in which the nervous system is organized.

Divisions of the Nervous System

central nervous system
all the neurons in the brain and spinal cord

peripheral nervous system
the part of the nervous system that links the CNS to our senses, glands, and muscles

somatic nervous system
the part of the peripheral nervous system that controls our skeletal muscles and sense organs

autonomic nervous system
the part of the peripheral nervous system that controls our heart, lungs, and digestive organs

The nervous system as a whole is highly complex, as we would expect granted that it allows us to think, feel, and behave. One way to understand the nervous system is by making distinctions among its major parts (see Figure 2.1). First is the distinction between the **central nervous system,** which contains all of the neurons in the brain and spinal cord, and the **peripheral nervous system,** which contains all the neurons in all other parts of the body: legs, arms, face, and so on. The peripheral nervous system carries impulses *from* the central nervous system to our muscles and glands as well as impulses *to* the central nervous system from our various sense organs.

The peripheral nervous system is customarily divided into the **somatic nervous system,** which controls the skeletal muscles and sense organs, and the **autonomic nervous system,** which controls the heart, lungs, and digestive organs. The term *autonomic* should be understood as a synonym for automatic; the intended implication is that the autonomic nervous system operates for the most part automatically, with little influence from the central nervous system.

Figure 2.1
Major Divisions of the Nervous System

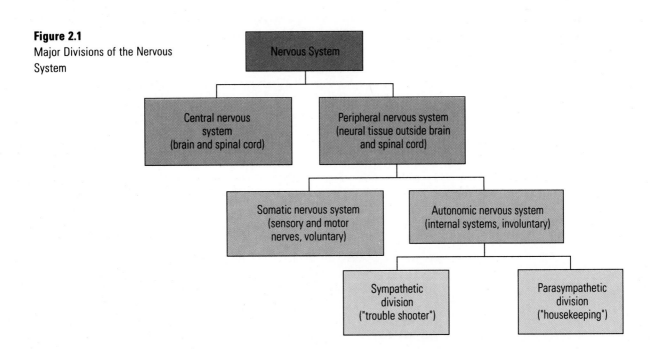

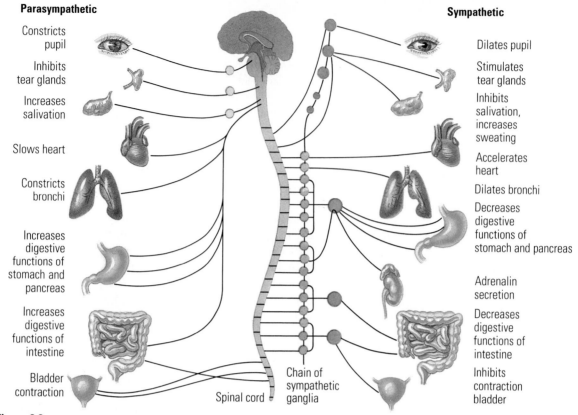

Parasympathetic

Constricts pupil

Inhibits tear glands

Increases salivation

Slows heart

Constricts bronchi

Increases digestive functions of stomach and pancreas

Increases digestive functions of intestine

Bladder contraction

Spinal cord

Chain of sympathetic ganglia

Sympathetic

Dilates pupil

Stimulates tear glands

Inhibits salivation, increases sweating

Accelerates heart

Dilates bronchi

Decreases digestive functions of stomach and pancreas

Adrenalin secretion

Decreases digestive functions of intestine

Inhibits contraction bladder

Figure 2.2

Sympathetic and Parasympathetic Nervous System. These two parts of the autonomic nervous system affect many of the same bodily organs, but usually in opposite ways.

sympathetic nervous system
the part of the autonomic nervous system that serves an excitatory role

parasympathetic nervous system
the part of the autonomic nervous system that serves an inhibitory role

Finally, the autonomic nervous system is made up of two parts. The **sympathetic nervous system** produces arousal. So, when you are threatened, your pupils dilate, your heart rate accelerates, and your perspiration increases. The **parasympathetic nervous system** counteracts arousal, reversing the bodily processes set into operation by the sympathetic nervous system. These two systems usually work in opposition to one another, creating the appropriate balance between excitement and calm (Chapter 6). Figure 2.2 shows the different organs respectively affected by these two divisions of the autonomic nervous system.

Making these divisions within the nervous system helps us understand how it works, but do not forget that the nervous system acts as a whole. A typical thought, feeling, or action reflects the influence of all the divisions of the nervous system. When we identify a given behavior as determined by a particular aspect of the nervous system, we are speaking somewhat imprecisely.

Neurons

As we have seen, all divisions of the nervous system are composed of microscopic cells called *neurons*. Neurons were only discovered about 100 years ago. Though not impressive in size, they are certainly impressive in sheer number. Estimates of the number of neurons in the brain vary, but some who venture a guess place the number at about 100 billion (Hubel, 1979)!

Structure. Figure 2.3 shows a generic neuron. Note that it has four major structures:

- the **cell body,** which is the cell's largest concentration of mass and contains the nucleus of the cell
- **dendrites,** which receive messages from other neurons
- **axons,** which send these messages
- **terminal buttons,** which secrete chemicals that influence other neurons

The neuron depicted here is a generalized one, and different neurons have markedly different shapes.

About half the neurons in an adult's body are covered by a white, fatty substance called **myelin.** Myelin protects the axons and helps neurons send their messages to one another more rapidly. Neurons with myelin may speed a communication along as rapidly as 120 meters per second, whereas neurons without myelin may communicate as slowly as .5 meters per second. Neurons that send messages over a greater distance tend to be the ones covered with myelin.

At birth, the infant's neurons are not covered with myelin to nearly the extent that we see in adults. Myelin develops over the first few years of life, which is one of the reasons why infants cannot move like children or adults (Chapter 9). Their nervous systems simply do not allow highly skilled and coordinated movements.

Function. Neurons are not directly connected to one another, but they "communicate" by secreting chemicals. These chemical secretions are responsible for transmitting *neural impulses* from one part of the nervous system to another. When a neuron transmits a neural impulse, we sometimes say that it has "fired," because a chemical reaction has rapidly taken place within the cell. The trigger for this reaction may well be located outside the organism (stimulus → sense organ → neuron), but we'll look at the simple case of a neuron stimulated by another neuron.

cell body

the neuron's largest concentration of mass, containing the nucleus of the cell

dendrites

the parts of a neuron that receive messages from other neurons

axon

the part of a neuron that sends messages to other neurons

terminal buttons

the end points of an axon where chemicals are secreted that influence other neurons

myelin

a white fatty substance that covers some axons, protecting them and allowing them to send their messages more rapidly

Figure 2.3
A Generic Neuron

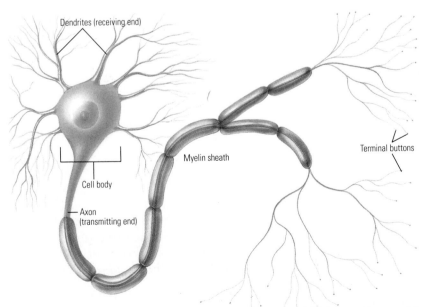

Dendrites (receiving end)

Cell body

Axon
(transmitting end)

Myelin sheath

Terminal buttons

neurotransmitter
chemical secreted by a neuron that affects other neurons

synapse
the gap between the axon of one neuron and the dendrite of another into which neurotransmitters are secreted

resting potential
the difference in electrical charge between the inside and outside of a neuron at rest

action potential
electrical and chemical changes that take place when a neuron fires

refractory period
interval following the firing of a neuron during which it cannot fire again

excitation
process by which one neuron induces a second neuron to fire

inhibition
process by which one neuron induces another neuron not to fire

A chemical called a **neurotransmitter** is secreted by the axon of one neuron into the space between it and a second neuron. This gap between two neurons is known as a **synapse,** and chemical communication usually occurs across the synapse from an axon to a dendrite. (You can keep this straight by telling yourself that an axon "acts on" a dendrite.) The dendrite of the second neuron detects the neurotransmitter. If the neurotransmitter is secreted in sufficient quantity, the second neuron fires.

When not transmitting a neural impulse, the inside and outside of a neuron have different electrical charges, called the **resting potential.** Relative to the outside, the inside is negative. Firing involves a series of electrical and chemical changes collectively termed the **action potential.** When a neuron is stimulated by an adjacent neuron, this produces a chemical change in the permeability of the cell surface, or membrane. The change in membrane permeability in turn leads to a temporary reversal of the inside and outside electrical charges. So, relative to the outside, the inside becomes positive.

This chemical/electrical flip-flop rapidly travels down the length of the axon, sometimes reaching speeds up to several hundred miles per hour! Myelin, as already explained, speeds up the action potential. When a neural impulse reaches the axon, it leads to the secretion of a neurotransmitter, which in turn stimulates adjacent neurons, and the process just described is repeated.

Communication between neurons is not continuous. It occurs in discrete bursts, which is why we speak of neurons firing. Once a neuron has fired, it is unable to fire again until a brief time has passed, an interval typically a few thousandths of a second long. This is the **refractory period,** during which time the resting potential of the neuron is restored.

We've so far discussed neurons that induce other neurons to fire. This process is called **excitation,** because the one neuron leads other neurons to fire. However, another process also exists, called **inhibition.** With inhibition, a neuron may affect other neurons by making it *less* likely that they will fire. The exact mechanism here is again chemical. Inhibition occurs when the insides of these neurons become even more negative in charge relative to their outsides, thereby making excitation all the more difficult. A nervous system guided by checks and balances results. Given behaviors occur or do not occur depending on the relative mix of excitatory or inhibitory processes in the part of the nervous system responsible for them.

Consider the example of strychnine, a highly toxic substance that is sometimes used as rat poison. Strychnine prevents inhibition from taking place at synapses. If an animal or person ingests strychnine, we see uncontrollable activity of the nervous system: twitches, spasms, and eventually convulsions that may result in death. Stated another way, strychnine is fatal because it upsets the nervous system's necessary balance between excitation and inhibition.

When the function of neurons is described, we sometimes speak of a message traveling along a neuron. Nothing physical is sent "down" or "through" the neuron. Instead, the action potential moves along the neuron, from one end to the other.

A neuron either fires or does not, depending on whether enough neurotransmitter is present. And once the action potential is triggered, a neuron fires in the exact same way. We call this phenomenon the **all-or-none principle.** The all-or-none principle might seem a bit puzzling, because it seems to contradict our everyday experiences. Surely we perceive the world in degrees: the volume of a rock-and-roll band, the brightness of a light bulb, the spiciness of chili. If neurons either fire or do not, how are gradations introduced? There are two answers.

First, an intense stimulus registers as intense not because it stimulates an individual neuron to respond more intensely, but because it stimulates a greater number of neurons to fire. Second, an intense stimulus can also cause particular neurons to fire more rapidly. Neural messages can be integrated, across time and across different neurons. So, when a given stimulus repeatedly stimulates multiple neurons, these messages are added together to produce a sensation of greater intensity than a stimulus that either stimulates fewer neurons or does so less frequently.

Neurotransmitters

Because excitation and inhibition are the two processes that are possible when one neuron influences another, one might hypothesize that there are two transmitter substances, one excitatory and the other inhibitory (Carlson, 1986). This is not the case. The nervous system did not evolve with the ultimate goal of easing the burden of introductory psychology students. There are literally dozens of neurotransmitters (Panksepp, 1986). Some indeed are exclusively excitatory, and some exclusively inhibitory, but many others both excite or inhibit, depending on the synapse into which they are secreted.

Norepinephrine (popularly called adrenaline), *acetylcholine, serotonin,* and *dopamine* are among the major neurotransmitters. We'll encounter some of these again in Chapter 12 on psychopathology. Biological theories link particular mental disorders to problems with these important neurotransmitters. Schizophrenia may be produced by too much dopamine, for instance, and depression may be the result of too little norepinephrine (Andreasen, 1984). Medication for these disorders presumably targets the implicated transmitter substance, decreasing it or increasing it, as the case may be.

Neurotransmitters allow yet another classification of neurons, because given cells differ in terms of the transmitter substance to which they are sensitive. So, there are dopamine neurons, serotonin neurons, and so on. One explanation of this specificity proposes that a neurotransmitter affects the permeability of a neuron only if its molecular shape fits the appropriate sites in the membrane—like a key fits a lock (Cooper, Bloom, & Roth, 1986).

Endorphins, naturally secreted neurotransmitters, allow the body to cope with pain that might otherwise be unbearable, whether it is the result of surgery or strenuous exercise.

People have long known that certain chemicals have analgesic properties—they alleviate pain. Among these chemicals are opiates, the family of drugs that includes opium, morphine, and heroin (Chapter 4). These analgesics come from outside our bodies (e.g., from Turkey). But we've recently discovered that under some circumstances, the brain produces its own analgesic chemicals, called **endorphins.**

Endorphins are naturally secreted neurotransmitters chemically similar to the opiates (Hughes et al., 1975). When secreted, they disrupt messages from our pain receptors. These receptors may still be stimulated, but the stimulation is stonewalled. Endorphins are secreted in response to pain, which means that they allow people to endure stimulation that would otherwise seem unbearable. Although the full picture of endorphins is still sketchy, they may be involved in the successful use of acupuncture to alleviate a patient's surgical pain, in the exhilaration sometimes experienced by those who habitually exercise (so-called runner's high), and even in people's acquired taste for spicy foods (Davis, 1984).

Organization of the Nervous System

The nervous system involves a division of labor among its different cells. The simplest case is the **reflex,** where one neuron, the **receptor,** receives stimulation from the environment and automatically leads a second neuron, the **effector,** to initiate some response toward the environment. If your hand touches a hot stove, then you withdraw it. Receptors (saying "it's hot") and effectors (saying "hand, get moving") are both involved here.

Among people, reflexes vary greatly in complexity. Spinal reflexes, for example, resemble the simple reflex just described. The pathway from stimulus to response goes directly to the spinal cord and back, without involving the brain. Many of our immediate reactions to pain are spinal reflexes.

Reflexes are but one example of how the nervous system is organized. Indeed, the nervous system is characterized by multiple modes of organization (Rozin, 1984). Take, for example, the principle of *spatial organization.* Neurons located close to each other are likely to be involved in the same psychological functions. This mode of organization will be particularly obvious when we discuss the different structures of the brain. Each structure is composed of adjacent neurons that perform the same functions.

The nervous system also shows a *biochemical organization.* As explained in our discussion of neurons, different sets of neurons are respectively sensitive to particular neurotransmitters, and their shared sensitivity creates one more basis of structure.

Finally, the nervous system shows *hierarchical organization,* meaning that its parts and functions are arranged in different levels. "Higher" levels moderate "lower" levels. *Higher* and *lower* have several related meanings. They refer quite literally to where in the nervous system these structures are to be found. As we will soon see, structures at the literal top of the brain often direct those at the center and bottom of the brain. The brain itself often directs the rest of the nervous system. The terms *higher* and *lower* also refer to the hypothesized evolutionary history of the brain (pp. 185–87). Lower centers presumably appeared prior to higher centers. Finally, the higher levels of the brain are involved in what we think of as characteristically human abilities: language, reasoning, and problem solving.

Realizing that the nervous system has a multidimensional structure helps us to understand how and why it works as it does. Rozin (1984) offers four generalizations about the functioning of the nervous system.

- *There is a balance between excitation and inhibition.* We encountered this idea already at the level of specific neurons. It also applies to the

---

reflex
automatic reaction in which an external event leads to a response

receptor
neuron that receives stimulation from the environment

effector
neuron that initiates some response toward the environment

nervous system as a whole, a necessary consequence of its structural checks and balances.

- *There is redundancy in the nervous system.* The nervous system can perform its functions in different ways. Although this makes it difficult to offer firm statements about the functioning of the nervous system, it certainly benefits the organism.
- *There is recovery of function following damage to the nervous system.* The major benefit of redundancy is that people often recover from neurological injury or illness. Neurons themselves do not regenerate after infancy. However, other parts of the nervous system can often take over following the loss of particular neurons.
- *There is variation in the vulnerability of neurological functions.* As a rule, the higher functions are more readily disrupted following neurological trauma than the lower functions, because—of necessity—there is more redundancy lower in the hierarchy.

Consider the advantage to human beings and other species in having nervous systems that function in this way. We are capable of reorganizing ourselves following damage or insult. Reorganization occurs more readily among infants and children than adults. So, the equivalent brain damage in an infant and a mature adult has different consequences. An infant can usually recover more fully than an adult.

This makes evolutionary sense. Younger organisms must survive long enough to pass on their characteristics to offspring. Recovery of neurological functioning enhances their ability to do so. A similar argument fails to hold for older organisms. They have already reproduced, and there is no need—biologically speaking—for them to be able to reorganize their nervous system following injury to it.

The Brain

The human brain is about the size of a grapefruit, composed of as many as 100 billion neurons. The number of potential interconnections among these cells is almost beyond comprehension. Ornstein and Thompson (1984) liken the overall structure to a ramshackle house originally built for a small family but then added to as subsequent generations needed accommodations. In the end, you have a layered structure, reflecting the presumed evolution of the brain.

Ornstein and Thompson (1984) provide the following exercise to help us visualize the brain:

> Place your fingers on both sides of your head beneath the ear lobes. In the center of the space between your hands is the oldest part of the brain, the brainstem. Now, form your hands into fists. Each is about the size of one of the brain's hemispheres, and when both fists are joined at the heel of the hand they describe not only the approximate size and shape of the entire brain but also its symmetrical structure. Next, put on a pair of thick gloves—preferably light gray. They represent the cortex . . . the newest part of the brain and the area where functioning results in the most characteristically human creations, such as language and art. (pp. 21–22)

hindbrain

the lowest and oldest layer of our brain, consisting of most of the brain stem

midbrain

the middle layer of our brain, consisting of the upper part of the brain stem

forebrain

the highest and newest layer of our brain

medulla

the part of the brain stem directly connected to the spinal cord that controls respiration and cardiac function

cerebellum

the part of the hindbrain that is involved in maintaining coordination and balance

Figure 2.4 depicts the three major layers of the brain. First is the **hindbrain,** which consists of most of the brain stem. It was the first part of the brain to appear during evolution, and it controls breathing and heart rate. The **midbrain**—the upper part of the brain stem—is next. It plays a coordinating role in sleep and wakefulness. Then we have the **forebrain,** the most recent layer to evolve. Its purpose is to maintain such critical activities as movement, memory, and speech.

Let us now discuss the more specific parts of the brain. In each case, we'll note the types of functions attributed to each particular structure, but don't forget the complexity of the nervous system. It's never so simple that one and only one brain structure controls a particular function.

The Brain Stem

The brain is connected to the spinal cord. Indeed, there is no precise separation between the hindbrain and the spinal cord. The hindbrain itself is composed of three structures (see Figure 2.5). First is the **medulla,** the part of the brain stem directly connected to the spinal cord that controls respiration and cardiac function. Most of the functions of the medulla involve involuntary reflexes. If a mosquito flies toward your eye, you blink without thinking about it. This automatic response is controlled by the medulla.

If we try, we can exert some conscious control over the functions of the medulla, but only within certain limits. The medulla controls breathing rate, for instance, and if we wish, we can hold our breath, thus overriding the medulla. We might even be able to hold our breath long enough to pass out, but we cannot refrain from breathing to the point of death. Once we lose consciousness, the medulla resumes its control of our breathing.

The second structure of the hindbrain is the **cerebellum,** which is involved in coordination and balance. Our intentional movements do not originate in the cerebellum, but here is where they are coordinated and made smooth. Take speaking, for example. In order to say what we intend to say, our lips, mouth, and tongue must be carefully orchestrated. Most people can speak flawlessly, at the rate of several hundred words per minute, and the cerebellum is responsible. Damage to this part of the brain can make one's speech slurred, and a person may also stagger and tremble when moving. Among the types of brain injuries suffered by boxers, damage to the cerebellum is common (Boyle & Ames, 1983).

Figure 2.4

Layers of the Brain

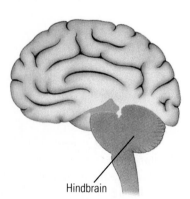

Hindbrain

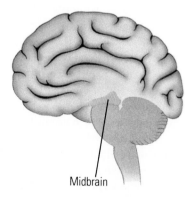

Midbrain

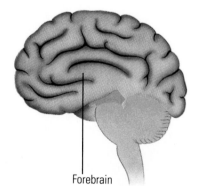

Forebrain

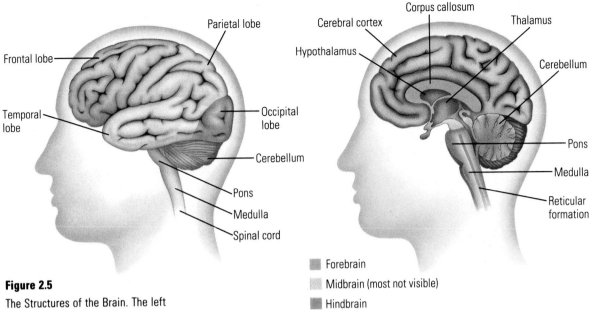

Forebrain

Midbrain (most not visible)

Hindbrain

The third structure of the hindbrain is the **pons,** in effect a bulge in the brain stem. The pons links the hindbrain to the rest of the brain, playing the role of relay station. Indeed, the word *pons* means bridge. The pons sorts out and relays sensory messages from the spinal cord to other parts of the brain, and from these other parts of the brain back to the spinal cord. Also, the pons appears to play some role in sleep and wakefulness (Carlson, 1986).

The Reticular Formation

Notable in the midbrain area is the **reticular formation,** a large structure occupying the core of the brain stem (see Figure 2.5). The reticular formation is a complex network of neurons that reach into all parts of the brain, from bottom to top. The reticular formation is centrally located in the brain, and it is richly connected with other structures. It therefore plays a coordinating role, linking parts of the hindbrain to parts of the forebrain. However, there is still much to be learned about this structure.

We do know that the reticular formation receives sensory information which it then relays to structures in the forebrain. Most importantly, it also controls one's general level of arousal as well as one's mode of consciousness—awake, asleep, and so on (Chapter 4). In animals whose reticular formations have been destroyed, a constant state of sleep may result, suggesting that the reticular system can turn off sensory information altogether, as well as turn it back on.

The Limbic System

The human forebrain plays a particularly complex role. Indeed, the forebrain controls our most characteristic functions. A number of structures are critical. Let's start by discussing the **limbic system,** which is actually

amygdala
part of the limbic system that seems to produce rage and aggression

septum
part of the limbic system that seems to lessen responses of rage and aggression

hippocampus
part of the limbic system that seems to be involved in the processing of memories

hypothalamus
part of the limbic system that links the autonomic nervous system and the endocrine system

thalamus
part of the forebrain that relays input from the senses to higher structures

cerebral cortex
outer layer of the forebrain, responsible for organizing information and initiating responses

cerebral hemispheres
the symmetric halves of the forebrain

corpus callosum
the bundle of neurons that connects the cerebral hemispheres

occipital lobe
cerebral hemisphere region located at the rear of the brain

temporal lobe
cerebral hemisphere region near the temple

frontal lobe
cerebral hemisphere region located right behind the forehead

a collection of related structures. The limbic system is particularly important in nonhuman animals, where it is thought to control behaviors we describe as instinctive. In people, the limbic system is involved in the expression of emotions (Chapter 6).

One structure within the limbic system, the **amygdala,** seems to produce rage and aggression; another structure, the **septum,** seems to lessen these responses (Albert & Walsh, 1984). Again, the limbic system seems vulnerable to damage from boxing. One study comparing boxers and nonboxers found four times as many limbic system abnormalities among boxers (Boyle & Ames, 1983).

Another part of the limbic system is the **hippocampus,** which seems to be involved in the processing of memories (Chapter 7). People with damage to the hippocampus are unable to remember events for much longer than a few seconds, suggesting that no permanent record of their experience has been made (Matthies, 1989).

The limbic system also contains the **hypothalamus,** found at the top of the brain stem (see Figure 2.5). The hypothalamus controls much of the activity of the autonomic nervous system, coordinating activities critical to survival: sex, feeding, and so on. The hypothalamus resembles a thermostat. It monitors the state of our body—for example, its fluid level—and triggers reactions to restore balance as necessary. Too little fluid results in thirst, which motivates us to drink (Chapter 6).

Close by the hypothalamus is the **thalamus.** (*Hypo* means under, so we can deduce, correctly, that the hypothalamus is underneath the thalamus; again see Figure 2.5.) Like the pons, the thalamus is a relay center, sending messages to and from the structures located in the very top of the brain. But the thalamus does more than just relay messages. It also integrates and organizes them, ensuring that specific messages, from our eyes or ears, for example, go to the appropriate part of the forebrain.

The Cerebral Cortex

The outer layer of the forebrain is called the **cerebral cortex.** The cerebral cortex is the most recent addition in the evolution of the brain, appearing perhaps 50 million years ago. As we earlier discussed, the brain and nervous system can be arranged in a hierarchy, with "higher" structures controlling "lower" structures. In these terms, the cortex is the boss, the chief executive, the leader of the band. It has the final say in both organizing information relayed by other structures and initiating the appropriate responses.

A view from the top shows that the forebrain is composed of two structures, more or less symmetric. These are the **cerebral hemispheres** (see Figure 2.6). They are connected by a bundle of nerve fibers called the **corpus callosum.** Looking at the brain from the side, we can divide the cortex into four regions called lobes (again see Figure 2.6). These regions are separated by deep indentations in the brain called fissures. The **occipital lobe** is at the rear of the brain. The **temporal lobe** is near the temple. The **frontal lobe** is located right behind the forehead. And finally, the **parietal lobe** is found behind the frontal lobe and in front of the occipital lobe.

Figure 2.6
The Cerebral Cortex. The cortex is divided into the left and right hemispheres. Each of the hemispheres is divided into four lobes.

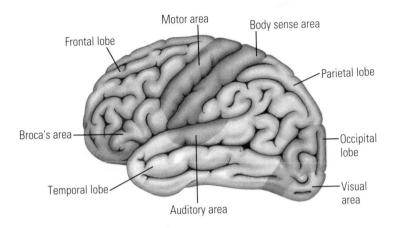

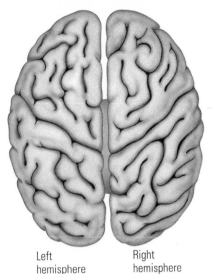

Left hemisphere   Right hemisphere

parietal lobe
cerebral hemisphere region found behind the frontal lobe and in front of the occipital lobe

An important generalization about the cerebral hemispheres is that each controls the opposite half of the body. In other words, the left arm is connected by neurons mainly to the right hemisphere, whereas the right arm is connected mainly to the left hemisphere. So, if a neurologist examines a patient who has recently lost strength or feeling on one side of the body following a blow to the head, there is good reason to suspect that damage has occurred to the *opposite* side of the brain (Lezak, 1976). Because the various activities that people perform (e.g., throwing, kicking, and writing) often involve one side of the body more than the other, we refer to the corresponding brain hemisphere as dominant.

The left cerebral hemisphere is associated with speech and language usage; the right, with visual imagery and spatial relationships.

lateralization
the organization of the brain on a left-right basis

split-brain patients
individuals who have had the connections between the two cerebral hemispheres surgically severed in an attempt to reduce epileptic seizures

Lateralization.   The left-right structure of the brain is referred to as **lateralization.** What is its significance? Roger Sperry and others shed some light on this matter in pioneering studies of **split-brain patients** (Springer & Deutsch, 1985). In an attempt to relieve individuals from severe epileptic seizures, neurosurgeons cut the corpus callosum that connects the two hemispheres. For some patients, this surgery curbed their seizures.

However, there are two important aspects of people who underwent this operation. First, in many ways their behavior was unremarkable. You may find it surprising that such a profound surgical procedure seems to have little effect on behavior. Second, under certain laboratory conditions, researchers discovered that the split-brain patients did behave in a remarkable way.

Suppose visual information is made available to a patient in such a way that only one hemisphere of the brain receives this input. Then the side of the patient controlled by the other hemisphere acts unaware of this information.

> Split-brain patient N. G. . . . sits in front of a screen with a small black dot at the center. She is asked to look directly at the dot. . . . A picture of a cup is flashed briefly to the right of the dot. N. G. reports that she has seen a cup. Again, she is asked to look directly at the dot. This time, a picture of a spoon is flashed to the left of the dot. She is asked what she saw. She replies, "No, nothing." She is then asked to reach under the screen with her left hand and to select, by touch only, from among several objects the one that is the same as the one she has just seen. Her left hand palpates each object and then holds up the spoon. When asked what she is holding, she says, "Pencil." (Springer & Deutsch, 1985, pp. 29–30)

One conclusion from these striking results is that we really have two brains, the left hemisphere and the right hemisphere. The split-brain operation separates the two hemispheres, which typically are connected and work in concert. But if separated, they go about their respective business independently.

Another conclusion is that each brain half performs its functions in different ways. According to one version of this conclusion, the "left" brain is analytical and logical, whereas the "right" brain is intuitive and holistic (see Figure 2.7). These stereotypes are probably overstated, and obscure the fact that the two hemispheres work together. Nevertheless, there is some basis to the distinction between the two hemispheres, and lateralization continues to be a hotly researched topic.

Localization of function.   Because the cortex is the surface of the brain, it is more accessible to researchers than other structures. Accordingly, we know a fair amount about what it does. (Exactly *how* it does these things is another matter.) Investigations of the cortex have helped clarify one of the long-standing debates within psychology about the nature of the brain: whether or not different human capacities (abilities, faculties, functions, and so on) are located within particular parts of the brain.

This issue is referred to as a debate over **localization of function** in the brain. An extreme position in favor of localization can be found in the nineteenth-century practice known as *phrenology.* Phrenologists as-

localization of function
doctrine that particular capacities, like memory or language, are located within specific parts of the brain

Figure 2.7

Functions of the Hemispheres. The left hemisphere controls the right side of the body, and the right hemisphere controls the left side. More controversial is the idea that the left and right hemispheres process information in wholly different ways. This figure shows the presumed functions of the two hemispheres.

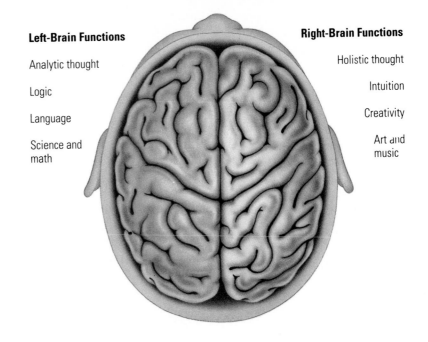

Left-Brain Functions

Analytic thought

Logic

Language

Science and math

Right-Brain Functions

Holistic thought

Intuition

Creativity

Art and music

sumed that the mind was composed of different faculties, that each faculty had a particular location within the brain, and that dominant faculties could be discerned by inspecting one's head for bumps (see Figure 2.8).

The opposing point of view is that the brain acts as an organized whole; its functions are not performed by its separate parts, but rather by the brain as a single entity. Asking which part of the brain is responsible for memory or emotion or motor coordination is like asking which part of a car is responsible for left turns or which player in the infield is responsible for a double play.

Figure 2.8

Phrenology Chart. In the 1800s, phrenologists believed they could discern people's particular skills and traits by mapping the bumps on their heads. Each area of the skull presumably corresponded to a particular faculty.

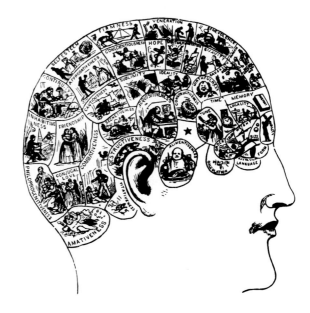

mass action
doctrine that opposes localization of function, holding that the brain acts as a whole

In the 1920s, Karl Lashley performed pioneering experiments with rats showing that their behavior was disrupted to the degree that large amounts of their brains were destroyed (e.g., Lashley, 1929). The sheer amount of damage was more important than the particular location of the damage. Research like this swung psychological opinion away from the phrenologists' position of extreme localization of function toward an assumption of **mass action,** meaning the brain acts as a whole.

In recent years, we find that the pendulum has swung back to a belief in at least a degree of localization of function. For example, psychologists now believe that the four lobes of each hemisphere (Figure 2.6) are involved to varying degrees in different functions. Studies of brain-damaged people support this conclusion, because different functions are lost depending on the location of the damage.

Thus, the occipital lobe is devoted to vision. Researchers have discovered that occipital damage can produce blindness, even when there has been no damage to the eyes. The temporal lobe controls speech comprehension and memory. The frontal lobe is involved in planning and decision making; individuals with frontal lobe damage are incapable of carrying out actions that allow them to adjust to new situations. And finally, the parietal lobe appears to integrate sensory information relayed from lower parts of the brain.

Researchers have also mapped areas of the cortex where information is received or sent out. *Sensory projection areas* are parts of the cortex that receive information from the various senses—vision, hearing, taste, smell, touch, and so on (Chapter 3). *Motor projection areas* send messages to the various muscles. A useful rule of thumb for understanding these areas is that the more complex and important a function is to an organism, the more cortical area is devoted to it (see Figure 2.9).

association areas
locations in the cortex once thought to link sensory and motor projection areas and now believed to be where higher mental activities take place

The cortex also contains **association areas,** so named because theorists once believed that they linked the sensory and motor projection areas. Current opinion holds that the association areas are responsible for higher mental processes like memory, thought, and language. Lesion studies with human beings bolster this conclusion. Studies of brain-damaged people often show disturbances in one or more complex mental activities.

In sum, current opinion about localization of function is hardly as simple as the phrenologists' neat and tidy (and incorrect) vision. Contemporary psychologists prefer a more complex view: The brain works as a whole, although its different parts have respective emphases.

Language. Our discussions of laterality and localization of function would not be complete without mention of the relationship between the brain and language. In trying to understand what makes language possible, researchers have learned a great deal about the structure and function of the brain.

Many questions about the brain and the nervous system are answered through animal studies. However, questions about the neurological basis of language can only be answered through studies with humans, which limits the investigator. Much of what we know comes from studies of people suffering damage to one or more parts of the brain. Researchers look for relationships between particular injuries and particular language deficits, hoping thereby to infer what the process might be like in a neurologically intact individual.

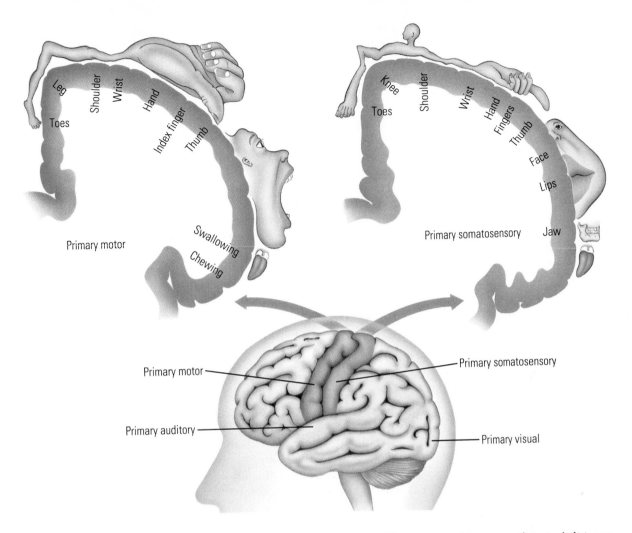

Figure 2.9

Projection Areas. These figures represent motor and sensory projection areas of the cortex by showing the part of the body associated with each. The more cortical area devoted to a function, the more important it is. Note, therefore, the size of the projection areas associated with our hands and our mouth.

Aphasia refers to a group of language problems entailing inabilities to express and/or comprehend speech or writing. Over a century ago, French physician Paul Broca (1861) described the results of his autopsy of a patient who for years had suffered from an inability to produce words. Broca found that this man had damage in a small area of the left frontal lobe that has since been called Broca's area. Broca argued, correctly as it turned out, that this part of the brain translated ideas into words. (Interestingly, damage to Broca's area does *not* impair a person's ability to sing a familiar song, implying that a different part of the brain is involved in singing than in speaking.)

Not long after, German physician Carl Wernicke (1874) argued from similar evidence that a part of the left temporal lobe was responsible for the comprehension of speech. The patients he studied were able to produce words but not to comprehend them. Perhaps as a result of this inability, their speech was faulty, sometimes little more than a jumble of words. The part of the brain implicated in this form of aphasia is called Wernicke's area. Many people with damage to Wernicke's area do not seem to recognize that they have any difficulty with language. They follow social conventions while speaking to others, taking turns in conversation, even though what they say has no apparent meaning.

Findings like these clarify both localization and laterality. They show that many language functions are "located" in one part of the brain, which, for most individuals, is the left central hemisphere. Remember the split-brain patient N. G. whose behavior we described earlier (p. 66). When a picture of a spoon was flashed to the left of where she was looking, visual information went to her right hemisphere. She says she sees nothing because her left hemisphere—the center of language functions—is unaware of the spoon.

We see again that the two halves of the brain are not symmetric in function. A person suffering a stroke in the left side of the brain, for instance, often has difficulty speaking or understanding speech. A person suffering the identical damage in the right side of the brain usually encounters no such language difficulty, although he may encounter problems finding his way around or performing other tasks that require orienting himself.

Experience

One of the most important human characteristics is our ability to learn from experience. On one level, this malleability liberates us from our biology, because we have a far smaller number of fixed reflexes than our animal cousins. But on another level, the human capacity for learning leads us to further emphasize biology's importance to human behavior. Granted that experience does change us, how does this change occur? Experience presumably alters the brain and nervous system and thus our behavior.

Psychologists interested in the brain have long speculated about how experience changes the brain and nervous system (Gould, 1986). This is *not* simply a matter of opening up someone's skull before and after she has learned how to write computer programs in BASIC, for example, and observing where and how programming conventions have been added. Indeed, it is not even clear just what one should look for when investigating how experience alters the brain.

One might look at structural changes in the nervous system. Mark Rosenzweig (1984) followed this strategy in an intriguing research program. He started by raising rats in one of two environments: an *enriched* environment containing numerous objects that the animals could manipulate and explore and an *impoverished* environment that provided minimal variation and stimulation. Think of the difference between Disney World and the dreariest bus station you've ever been stranded in. Obviously, Rosenzweig wanted to manipulate the amount of stimulation and learning that the two groups of rats experienced.

What happened? The brains of the rats reared in the enriched environment indeed differed from those of the rats reared in the impoverished environment (Carlson, 1986). "Enriched" brains were larger, better supplied with blood, and higher in protein content. The neurons in these brains were more richly interconnected. However, these findings are not as detailed as we would like.

Although it is tempting to explain the structural differences in terms of different experiences, they may mirror mundane differences in health. Maybe the rats raised in the enriched environment were healthy, whereas those in the impoverished environment were sickly. Their brains therefore looked different, but learning had nothing to do with it. Further, this line of research might not show the effects of an enriched environment so much as the effects of an impoverished one. In other words, learning may not produce larger brains; lack of learning may produce smaller brains.

Other researchers interested in the effects of experience on the brain look for changes at a molecular level—in terms of the biochemistry of the nervous system, particularly neurotransmitters. Learning may influence the thresholds for secretion of a particular neurotransmitter and/or the amount of the chemical secreted (Farley & Alkon, 1985; Woody, 1986). In either case, certain actions become more or less likely. To date, researchers have investigated this process in extremely simple organisms, like mollusks, capable only of the rudiments of learning (Kandel & Schwartz, 1982). We need further research to see if results hold up for more complex learning by more complicated creatures.

The Endocrine System

endocrine system
the set of glands that secrete hormones into the bloodstream

hormones
chemicals secreted by endocrine glands that are carried through the bloodstream to affect various bodily organs

The **endocrine system** refers to glands that secrete **hormones,** chemicals carried through the bloodstream that affect various bodily organs. Although not part of the nervous system, our glands are intimately linked to the brain and work in concert with it to affect behavior as well as physical processes like reproduction and growth. Figure 2.10 shows the major glands and where they are located.

Figure 2.10
The Endocrine System

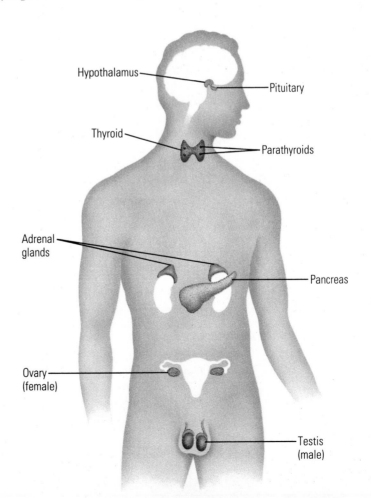

Like the nervous system, the endocrine system communicates among its parts. However, because this communication takes place by means of hormones released into the blood, the endocrine system is not nearly as speedy as the nervous system. This is why some of our reactions to events take a while to occur and then linger long after the event is over.

Imagine merging onto a busy interstate highway. You put your turn signal on, and you find what looks like a reasonable space into which to ease your car. Suddenly someone speeding along in the passing lane swerves right into your chosen space. You slam on the brakes, averting a crash.

You have avoided disaster in a quick and cool way. You hesitated not at all in responding to the careless driver, and you did so skillfully enough that he may have been unaware that he posed any danger in the first place. But as he weaves down the interstate blissfully unaware, your heart starts to pound and your mouth goes dry. Your palms perspire so much it is difficult to grasp your steering wheel. You stay in this state of emotional arousal for miles.

You avoided the careless driver in the first place because this is how your nervous system works—rapidly. You experienced a relatively slow and lingering emotional reaction because this is how your endocrine system works—slowly. To be specific, your emotional reaction to the driver was directed by your **adrenal glands,** which are involved in responses to threat and danger.

For purposes of illustration, the nervous system and the endocrine system have been contrasted. But as we have emphasized throughout our discussion of the nervous system, the body operates as a whole. The nervous system and the endocrine system typically work in conjunction. Hormones affect the functioning of the brain. The brain affects the secretion of hormones.

Indeed, much of the endocrine system is controlled by hormones produced in the hypothalamus, which you recall is part of the brain. Because it produces hormones, the hypothalamus can also be considered part of the endocrine system. Hormones from the hypothalamus in particular influence the **pituitary gland** (see Figure 2.10), which in turn controls the secretions of many of our other glands. Sometimes the pituitary is referred to as the master gland because it is so centrally linked to the rest of the endocrine system. Among its many functions, the pituitary gland controls growth and is responsible for triggering the onset of puberty.

Studying the Brain and Nervous System

So far, our discussion of the brain and nervous system has simply described what is known without explaining how we obtained this knowledge. Let's now turn to some of the research approaches that have been used.

Lesion and Ablation Techniques

Lesion and ablation studies provide an important way to see how damage to the nervous system is linked to subsequent behavior. A **lesion** is a wound or injury to a particular part of the brain or nervous system. An

adrenal glands
endocrine glands located on top of the kidneys that control the body's reaction to threat and danger

pituitary gland
endocrine gland located at the base of the brain that controls the secretions of many other glands

lesion
a cut or incision in the brain

ablation

destruction or removal of part of the brain

Figure 2.11
Phineas Gage. Here is a cast of the head of Phineas Gage and his actual skull. See where the iron bar passed through his head.

ablation is the complete destruction or removal of some structure. We saw examples of this approach to research in the work of Broca and Wernicke, who discovered in autopsies that particular types of damage to the brain were associated with particular types of aphasia.

Another well-known example of this approach is the story of Phineas Gage (Bigelow, 1850). In 1848, as a young man, Gage was working as a foreman on a construction project. An explosion drove an iron bar completely through his head! It entered through his jaw and emerged from the top of his head (see Figure 2.11). Miraculously, he did not die. Within two months, he was up and about, and, in a way, he had recovered from the accident. However, his behavior was markedly changed, as if his entire personality had undergone an alteration. He was now loud and profane, irresponsible, and unable to plan ahead. This was in sharp contrast to his behavior prior to the accident.

The change in Phineas Gage's personality can be traced directly to his brain damage. His frontal lobes were damaged by the iron bar. Their role in controlling the functions of structures lower in the brain was thereby precluded, and Gage acted accordingly. He directly expressed his emotions and his impulses. He lost the ability to think through the consequences of his acts.

Lesions and ablations may be caused by illness or accident, as the example of Phineas Gage shows. A researcher may also create them deliberately in the brains or nervous systems of animals. Let's make sure the logic here is clear. Although researchers who create lesions and ablations are focusing on damaged or destroyed neural tissue, they intend to offer conclusions about normal nervous systems. And quite often, when lesions and ablations and their effects are investigated, we find out information that would be impossible to obtain if we observed a brain that was not damaged.

Consider a new automobile, still under warranty, that works perfectly. Although the owner knows nothing about cars, she is so smitten with her new vehicle that she likes to prop the hood open and watch the engine run. Despite hours of observation, she has no good notion of what's going on. Now consider the same car, one day after its warranty runs out. In keeping with fundamental principles of the universe, the automobile suddenly performs poorly; it overheats and stalls. The owner peers under the hood for the umpteenth time, and sees something different. One of the rubber belts has frayed and ripped. Everything else looks the same.

The car owner has finally learned something about the way her car works. Apparently, the particular rubber belt has something to do with keeping the engine at the correct temperature. If she wants to verify this hypothesis, she can randomly select ten cars in her neighborhood and sever the corresponding belts on each engine. Then she can find out how many of these cars overheat and stall, comparing this number to a control group of other cars in the neighborhood that she left alone. While later serving five to ten for malicious mischief, she can contemplate her findings.

Even though the example is fanciful, it captures the thinking behind the use of lesions to study how the brain and nervous system operate. Abnormality sometimes provides a better window into normality than normality itself provides. Our car owner first conducted a case history, observing that her car "behaved" in an unusual manner when its engine

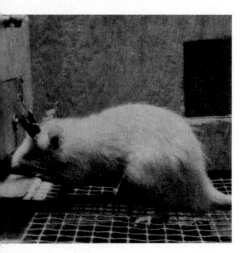

The behavior of this rat has been profoundly affected by electrical stimulation of its brain.

was "lesioned." Broca, Wernicke, and other human neurologists proceed in an analogous fashion. The car owner next conducted an experiment, explicitly producing a "lesion" in some cases but not others, and then seeing if unusual "behavior" resulted from this manipulation. Again, this is strictly analogous to the way that experimentalists proceed.

In destroying the brain tissue of animals, researchers use a host of techniques. Particular parts of the brain are cut, burned, or sucked up with a vacuum pump. Electricity, chemicals, and radio waves can also create lesions. In each case, particular behaviors are measured after lesions have been made, and researchers check to be sure that lesions are in the intended place. Experiments of this type may require numerous comparison groups, because the "manipulation" can have unintended effects.

Lesion studies provide some of the strongest support for the conclusion that brain structures are organized in a hierarchy. As already discussed, higher parts of the brain coordinate lower parts. Recall the three major layers of the brain introduced earlier in the chapter. Psychologists believe that each layer developed at a different stage of evolution, adding on to the already existing layers and taking over command. Consistent with this hypothesis, lesions at different points in the hierarchy disrupt the organism to varying degrees (Gallistel, 1980). Thus, a cat with an intact hindbrain (but nothing above) can make miscellaneous motor movements, but cannot coordinate them into action. A cat with an intact midbrain (but nothing above) can string behaviors together, but does so ineptly.

Electrical Stimulation Techniques

Neurons can be stimulated with electrical pulses, allowing researchers to identify neural connections straightforwardly. Pass a current through one structure in the brain and see what happens to other structures. If the latter structures show an increase in activity, then they must be linked to the structure that was stimulated.

For instance, researcher Jose Delgado (1969) showed that by stimulating different parts of animal and human brains, he could produce full-blown emotions, like fear or rage. Here is Delgado's description of a surgical patient's behavior when a mild electric current stimulated her thalamus.

> Stimulation . . . induced a typical fearful expression and she turned to either side, visually exploring the room behind her. When asked what she was doing, she replied that she felt a threat and thought that something horrible was going to happen. This fearful sensation was perceived as real, and she had a premonition of imminent disaster of unknown cause. . . . The response started with a delay of less than one second, lasted as long as the stimulation, and did not leave observable after effects. The patient remembered her fear but was not upset by the memory. (Delgado, 1969, p. 135)

Remember that the thalamus plays a role in emotion, a function suggested by this example.

Being Spanish, Delgado was inspired to demonstrate in spectacular fashion how electrical brain stimulation affects the behavior of bulls in a bull ring. He surgically implanted electrodes in the brains of "brave" bulls

medial forebrain bundle (MFB)
group of neurons connecting the midbrain and the forebrain, involved in pleasure and reward

(those which will attack a human being on sight), arranging it so that stimulation could be delivered through remote control. As long as the electrodes were placed correctly, a charging bull could be stopped virtually in midstep (see Figure 2.12). There has been disagreement over how to interpret this demonstration. Did Delgado locate a center of the brain that actually inhibits aggression, or did he merely find a way to affect the particular movements associated with a charge (Valenstein, 1973)? Regardless, his results show the link between brain activity and behavior.

Other researchers have located a pleasure center in the brain (Olds & Milner, 1954). Electrically stimulating the **medial forebrain bundle (MFB)**—a group of neurons connecting the midbrain and the forebrain—produces pleasure. If an experimenter arranges matters so that a rat can stimulate its own MFB by pressing a lever, it will do so indefinitely at an extremely high rate. Reportedly, rats given the choice between self-stimulation of the pleasure center and food will starve to death! This is important research because it suggests that parts of the brain mediate reward, and as we will see in Chapter 5, reward proves to be a potent determinant of how we behave.

A final example of how electrical stimulation allows psychologists to study the brain comes from the work of Wilder Penfield. His original interest was in epilepsy and how brain surgery might alleviate the associated seizures. In some of the operations he performed, the patient was conscious. (This is not as strange as it sounds, because the brain itself contains no pain receptors.)

Penfield found that when he stimulated the cerebral cortex, the patient recollected vivid and detailed experiences. Here is an example of what happened as a result of stimulation of a particular location of one patient's cortex called Point 23.

Figure 2.12
Delgado and the Charging Bull. Jose Delgado faces a charging bull with the traditional matador's cape and not-so-traditional radio transmitter that is in contact with electrodes implanted in the bull's brain.

12:30 P.M. . . . 23-repeated. The patient said, "I hear some music." 23-repeated without warning. The patient observed, "I hear the music."

12:45 P.M. 23-repeated again without warning. "I heard the music again; it is like the radio." When asked what tune it was, she said she did not know but that it was familiar. . . . When the electrode was

held in place, the patient hummed the air passing from chorus to verse while all in the operating room waited in silence. Then the operating nurse, Miss Stanley, interrupted. "I know it. It's 'Rolling Along Together.'" "Yes," the patient replied, "those words are in it but I don't know whether that is the name of the song." (Penfield & Jasper, 1954, pp. 130–131)

Even though Penfield found such recollections in fewer than 10 percent of the patients whose brains he stimulated, his results are amazing. Do they imply that past experiences are somehow stored in their entirety somewhere in the brain, waiting to be elicited? As you will see in Chapter 7, this interpretation seems at odds with contemporary theories of memory (Loftus & Loftus, 1980). Nevertheless, Penfield's results must ultimately be explained.

More generally, this sort of stimulation technique has been extensively used to discover the functions of different parts of the brain. For example, an electric current is applied to one part of someone's cortex and a particular feeling or sensation is reported: "I see a flash of light!" Another part of the cortex is stimulated, with an altogether different effect: "My left arm is twitching!" The projection areas described earlier in this chapter (Figure 2.9) were mapped out in exactly this way (Penfield & Rasmussen, 1952).

Electrical Recording Techniques

When neurons generate and transmit impulses, electrical activity occurs, suggesting to researchers that records of this activity might provide yet another glimpse at how the brain and nervous system work. Several different recording techniques exist. For instance, the appropriately named *microelectrode* monitors the activity of a single neuron.

In contrast to microelectrodes, *macroelectrodes* record the activity of an extremely large number of cells. These electrodes can be attached to the scalp and hence do not require surgery to implant them. The **electroencephalogram (EEG)** is a record of brain activity. An EEG is made using a device with macroelectrodes to detect general electrical patterns called brain waves (see Figure 2.13). Scientists and physicians alike have employed this method to examine what goes on in the brain during different states of consciousness (Chapter 4).

electroencephalogram (EEG) device for recording the general electrical patterns of the brain

Figure 2.13
EEG Recording from a Normal Brain

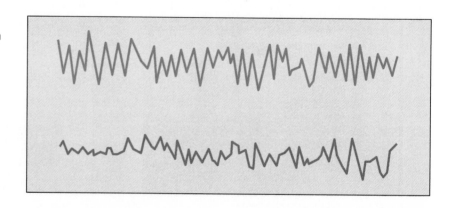

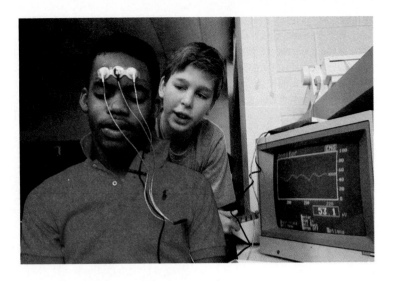

Biofeedback techniques allow therapists to train patients to relax.

EEGs have been made from individuals suffering from *epilepsy,* a group of neurological disorders characterized by seizures. In an extreme form of seizure, which can last up to 5 minutes, the epileptic loses consciousness, falls to the floor, and experiences severe muscular spasms. Seizures apparently result from the brain's temporary electrical instability—a metaphorical short circuit, as it were. EEGs showing abnormal rhythms may flag an impending seizure.

A particular electrical pattern called *alpha waves* seems to be associated with a relaxed mental state. Because some therapists believe that the cultivation of alpha waves can combat anxiety, they monitor and display this pattern to clients in need of relaxation. People can use this information from their brain—called *biofeedback* because it is "fed back" to them—to learn how to relax (Chapter 5).

Imaging Techniques

CAT scan (computerized axial tomography)
a technique for forming an image of the brain by taking many X rays and then assembling them into a three-dimensional picture by computer

PET scan (positron emission tomography)
a technique for forming an image of the brain by ascertaining levels of metabolic activity

Recent years have seen the introduction of yet another set of techniques for studying the brain. These techniques employ X-ray and computer technology. The first of these techniques is called a **CAT scan,** an abbreviation for **computerized axial tomography.** Once a person's brain is x-rayed from various angles, a computer assembles the different pictures into a composite, helping a physician locate particular tumors or lesions in a way that a conventional X ray cannot. CAT scans have also greatly improved a researcher's ability to draw conclusions about what parts of the brain are involved in particular behaviors. Had Broca and Wernicke had CAT scans at their disposal, they would not have needed to wait for their patients to die to interpret their problems with language.

The second technique of this type is called a **PET scan,** for **positron emission tomography.** This technique allows investigators to study metabolic activity in different parts of the brain by having a patient ingest a radioactive version of glucose. Then, as in the CAT scan procedure, the patient's brain is x-rayed from various angles. The X ray pictures show which parts of the brain are metabolically active, because the more active an area of the brain, the more it uses up the radioactive glucose. The

Figure 2.14

PET Scan. This photo shows a series of images of the brain, formed while the individual was doing different activities. Portions of the brain in red are particularly active metabolically.

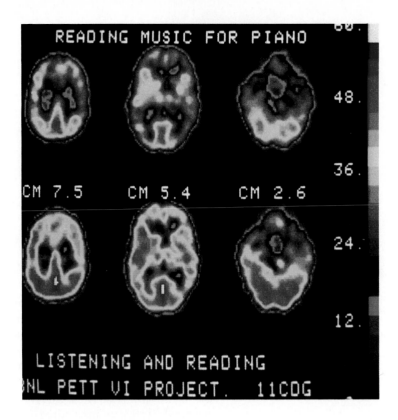

NMR (nuclear magnetic resonance scanning)

a technique for forming an image of the brain by detecting magnetic patterns

NMR technology provides an image of the internal structure of the brain without danger of overexposure to radiation.

resulting composite picture gives an overall view showing which parts of the brain are active, and which are not (see Figure 2.14). Therefore, problems in the brain like tumors or lesions can be identified with a PET scan, because they show abnormal patterns of metabolic activity.

We can expect more techniques like these in the near future. For example, **NMR,** or **nuclear magnetic resonance scanning,** has been recently developed. (NMR is sometimes called MRI, for *magnetic resonance imaging.*) This technique relies not on radiation but on magnetism to provide a glimpse at the structure and function of an intact brain. Although its pictures of the brain are not quite as detailed as those resulting from a PET scan, NMR does not require any exposure to radioactive substances. (For a good summary of how these new imaging techniques are remaking medicine, see the January 1987 *National Geographic* article by Howard Sochurek.)

Biological Explanations of Behavior

The importance of Charles Darwin's theory of evolution to Western thought in general and biology in particular cannot be overestimated. When we explain psychological phenomena in biological terms, we must therefore take into account the theory of evolution. In terms of our earlier discussion of explaining behavior in biological terms (pp. 52–53), the theory of evolution provides a general account of the adaptive significance—the function—of our characteristics. Let us take a closer look at evolution, starting with an important distinction between the *fact* of evolution and the *explanation* of this fact.

The Fact of Evolution

Charles Darwin

Charles Darwin (1809–1882) was an English naturalist with far-ranging interests in biology. Like many scientists in the 1800s, he was intrigued with questions concerning evolution: How do species of animals and plants originate and change? He proposed his own theory of evolution in his 1859 book *The Origin of Species*. In this book, he first argued that species indeed evolve. Then he went on to explain why.

What reasons do we have for believing that species change? If we look at the arguments presented by Darwin, we find several lines of evidence. First, Darwin pointed to domesticated animals and plants to prove the fact of evolution. Cattle, pigs, dogs, sheep, goats, cats, chickens, pigeons, and rock bands have "wild" and "domesticated" versions, as do wheat, corn, barley, cabbage, and peas. Darwin argued that each domesticated version evolved from a particular wild version.

In the case of domestic pigeons, such evolution occurred in the very recent past, under the watchful eye of scientists like Darwin. Indeed, Darwin was an expert on pigeons, so much so that one reviewer of *The Origin of Species* lamented that Darwin didn't focus on pigeon breeding, a much more interesting topic than evolution itself (Leakey, 1979)! At any rate, here is Darwin (1859/1979) on pigeons:

> Believing that it is always best to study some special group, I have taken up domestic pigeons. I have kept every breed which I could purchase or obtain, and have been kindly favoured with skins from several quarters of the world. I have associated with several eminent fanciers, and have been permitted to join two of the London Pigeon Clubs. The diversity of the breeds is something astonishing. (p. 52)

Pigeon fanciers create new breeds that differ strikingly from each other. By breeding increasingly extreme specimens with each other, they can produce fascinating variations in plumage, beak shape, size, and so on. If we see the end product of this breeding, we see wholly different birds. When we know the breeding history, the fact of evolution is clear. Similar examples come from intentionally breeding dogs, cats, roses, and corn.

As a second argument for the fact of evolution, Darwin pointed out that different species have highly similar body parts. For example, the hands of people, the paws of dogs, the wings of bats, the hooves of horses, and the fins of dolphins all contain similar bones arranged in similar patterns. We can presume that different species at some point were related to each other, even though they have since changed.

Further support for this argument comes from research that has documented repeatedly the recurrence across species of basic structures and forms. Consider the similarities of early development among species. The young often resemble each other more than the respective adults. Darwin (1859) discussed this with respect to such species as crustaceans, insects, and cats. For example, both cougar kittens and lion cubs have spotted coats; neither cougars nor lions have spots as adults. Embryos of different mammalian species also look very much alike, particularly in their earliest stages. Most generally, *all* living things develop according to the blueprints found within their cells. Evidence like this points to links among species at earlier times, leading us to conclude that change has occurred.

Darwin pointed to the breeding histories of various domesticated species—each of which had developed from a wild one—to support his theory of evolution.

A third line of evidence for evolution comes from the fossil record. In the decades immediately prior to Darwin's work, great strides were made in the fields of geology and paleontology. So, by Darwin's time it was widely recognized that the earth had existed for an immense period of time. Further, it was widely recognized that eons ago the earth was inhabited by plant and animal species no longer in existence. Putting these two ideas together, people in the 1800s accepted that different species existed at different points in time. On the whole, fossils in earlier geological time resemble modern species less than more recent fossils. Consider the likely evolution of the modern horse. Starting as a relatively small creature without hooves, the horse culminated in the likes of Mr. Ed, Secretariat, and the father of Little Hans (Chapter 1).

Critics sometimes argue that the absence of so-called *missing links* disproves the very idea of evolution. A "missing link" is a form of life intermediate between two different species. Shouldn't some number of these intermediate forms exist if one species evolved from another? The answer to this argument is that the critics seem to be asking for intermediates between contemporary species, like apes and people. Contemporary species are cousins, and they share a common ancestor. Think of the evolution of species as the branching of a tree, not as the addition of rungs to a ladder. With this view, the missing links are no longer seen as missing.

The Theory of Evolution

Granted that species change, how do biologists explain these changes? Darwin's theory was inspired in part by the way pigeon breeders artificially produce a new breed. To create a pigeon with a long neck, let us say, pigeon fanciers choose those birds with longer than average necks and breed them together. Among the offspring are some number of long-necked birds. Now these birds are selected for breeding. After this process is repeated through numerous generations, what results (for the sake of our example) is a pigeon with an ostrichlike neck.

Darwin proposed that this process of selection can also occur without the intentional intervention of pigeon breeders—naturally, as it were. Hence, his theory of evolution emphasizes the role of **natural selection** in producing change. Nature plays the role of the pigeon breeder, although, of course, there is no final goal like a long neck. Necks become increasingly longer only if a longer neck aids survival every step of the way.

Here then are the main assumptions of Darwin's theory:

* The members of particular species have characteristics that vary.
* At least some of these variable characteristics are passed on from parents to offspring.
* Some of these variable characteristics aid survival.
* Species produce more offspring than survive to be adults.

The conclusion thus follows that across time, as one generation begets another generation, those characteristics that aid survival will become more prevalent, whereas those that get in the way of survival will become less prevalent. Given the appropriate period of time, wholly new species can develop. By this view, members of adjacent generations resemble each other to a great degree, but members of distant generations may resemble each other very little. Quantitative differences become qualitative ones.

A critical idea here is that any two species existing today at some point had a common ancestor. For some pairs of species, one need not trace them back too far to find their common ancestor; for other pairs of species, their common ancestor is lost in the dawn of time. When one speaks of human beings as related to the great apes (chimps, gorillas, and orang-utans), one means that these species share a common ancestor in the relatively "recent" past, maybe 15 million years ago. One most definitely does not mean that people descended from the great apes (or vice versa). As already emphasized, evolutionary theory proposes that contemporary species are the *cousins* of human beings, not the ancestors.

Genetics

Darwin devised his theory of natural selection without knowing how the characteristics of parents are passed to their offspring. The mechanisms became clear only when the studies conducted by Austrian monk Gregor Mendel (1822–1884) were later published. Mendel investigated the inheritance of characteristics among pea plants. His work eventually led to modern genetics.

natural selection

Charles Darwin's theory of evolution: species change in the direction of characteristics that lead to successful reproduction

Gregor Mendel

gene

the microscopic mechanism of inheritance, composed of DNA molecules, passed from parents to offspring

chromosomes

sets of genes contained in each cell of the body

germ cell

cell involved in reproduction—egg or sperm—that contains only one pair of chromosomes

genotype

an individual's genetic inheritance; the blueprint for development provided by the genes

phenotype

an individual's actual characteristics, produced by one's genotype in combination with the environment

dominant gene

the member of a pair of genes that determines one's phenotype

recessive gene

the member of a pair of genes that does not determine one's phenotype when a dominant gene is present

Thanks to Mendel, the evolutionary theorists of today regard the **gene** as the mechanism by which inheritance occurs. Genes are microscopic structures found within each cell of the body, composed of complex molecules called *DNA* (deoxyribonucleic acid). Think of genes as blueprints or plans for biological development. Genes determine whether we are human beings, chimpanzees, or petunias. Genes determine whether we are males or females, tall or short, dark haired or fair haired.

Human beings may have as many as 100,000 different genes. They are arranged along **chromosomes,** strands of protein found in each cell of the body. Chromosomes are inherited from one's parents (see Figure 2.15). Each **germ cell,** egg and sperm, contains 23 chromosomes. When germ cells combine, the resulting cell thus has 46 chromosomes, that is, 23 pairs. Reproduction in effect takes half of the chromosomes from each parent and puts them together to form a unique offspring.

An individual's complete set of genes—from both parents—is called the **genotype.** In conjunction with environmental events during development, the genotype determines the characteristics that the individual actually shows, which are called the **phenotype.** One's phenotype does not perfectly reflect one's genotype, because innumerable events occurring during development determine just how the plan contained in the genes is actually carried out. For example, height is determined by one's genes. Tall parents tend to have tall children; short parents tend to have short children. But height is also determined by nutrition and by how the pituitary gland functions. Someone may be taller or shorter than called for in the genetic plan, if his or her pituitary happens to be damaged by illness or accident (see Figure 2.16).

Let's take a closer look at those pairs of genes. In the simplest case, one member of the pair is **dominant** and the other is **recessive,** which means that the former gene determines the phenotype and the latter gene does not. To use a familiar example, brown-eyed genes dominate blue-eyes genes; hence, the gene for brown eyes is considered dominant, and the gene for blue eyes is considered recessive. An individual's phenotype reflects a recessive gene only if both pairs of a gene are recessive. People with blue eyes inherited a blue-eyed gene from both their mother and father.

Figure 2.15

Human Chromosomes. Our chromosomes exist in 23 pairs. A female's chromosomes are shown on the right, and a male's chromosomes on the left.

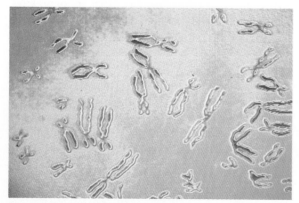 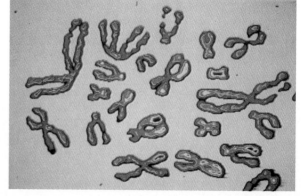

Figure 2.16

Andre the Giant. This well-known professional wrestler attained his great height and weight because his pituitary gland secreted too much growth hormone. And you thought professional wrestling was done entirely with smoke and mirrors!

Although the inheritance of eye color is a familiar example, it turns out to be oversimplified. Several genes are actually involved. Blue-eyed parents can have brown-eyed children. This is called **polygenic inheritance**—the determination of particular characteristics by more than one gene at a time—and it is the rule rather than the exception. Nevertheless, the example of eye color helps introduce some basic ideas about genetics. And you now know more about the mechanics of inheritance than Darwin did.

Darwin nonetheless had some hunches about the means of inheritance, some right and some wrong. He hypothesized that particles akin to genes were created throughout the body and collected in the reproductive organs. From there, they influenced the characteristics of offspring. Borrowing the ideas of another evolutionary theorist, Jean Baptiste de Lamarck (1744–1829), Darwin further speculated that characteristics acquired during the lifetime of an organism influenced these particles and hence the characteristics of offspring. Animals that developed certain characteristics through use or disuse of body parts passed on these acquired characteristics. Giraffes, for example, may have lengthened their necks in the course of stretching for leaves. Lengthened necks were then passed on to the next generation of giraffes.

This view of evolution is no longer accepted. Instead, biologists believe that genes are inherited, not characteristics per se. Necks lengthen in giraffes not because they stretched them out while nibbling leaves but because giraffes with genes for long necks survived better than those with genes for short necks.

Important Evolutionary Concepts

Remember, we are discussing evolution because it is the backbone of biology and hence of a biological perspective on behavior. And to better understand biology and behavior, we need to discuss a few more evolutionary concepts. Then we'll turn our attention to how the theory of evolution has been used to explain human behavior.

polygenic inheritance

the determination of characteristics by several genes working in combination; for people, polygenic inheritance is the rule rather than the exception

fitness

the ability to reproduce successfully

Fitness. Herbert Spencer's (1864) catch-phrase "survival of the fittest" is frequently invoked to summarize Darwin's theory of evolution. However, this idea requires closer examination. **Fitness** refers to successful reproduction, not staying power or longevity. To an evolutionary theorist, an organism is fit if it successfully passes its genes into the next generation. "Survival" thus refers to continuation of genes, *not* individuals.

Take Pacific salmon, for example. They expend all their resources in a single spawning, after which they die (Daly & Wilson, 1983). Although the life history of this fish appears at odds with most usages of the term *survival,* it fits exactly what biologists mean by the term. A pair of salmon produces from 3000 to 5000 eggs, and only a small number of these eggs will result in adults to repeat the process.

To a biologist, Pacific salmon are fit, not because they can swim upstream thousands of miles, but because they can reproduce successfully. A creature that stays at home and passes genes into the next generation may exceed the salmon in fitness, if it reproduces more successfully.

Inclusive Fitness. Some interpretations of evolution see the process as a bitter competition among individual organisms. Strictly speaking, the real competition occurs not among organisms but among their genes. Fitness transcends an individual to encompass all those sharing genes in common.

There are circumstances, therefore, in which laying down your life for the life of another can be evolutionarily advantageous—as long as the two of you share common genes. If the "sacrifice" of your life enhances the reproductive success of your close relative, then your act ends up enhancing the survival of your own genes. So, **inclusive fitness** is the fitness of an individual plus the influence of the individual on the fitness of its kin (Hamilton, 1964).

Inclusive fitness powerfully extends the traditional interpretation of fitness, allowing evolutionary theory to be applied to topics that previously seemed outside its limits. Some animals act "altruistically" toward each other, foregoing their own reproduction for that of others. The social insects (ants, termites, bees), for instance, have a large percentage of sterile members. Without the notion of inclusive fitness, it is difficult to explain how this state of affairs came to be through natural selection. Inclusive fitness explains it readily: The sterile workers share genes with those few insects who do reproduce; hence, the success of the king and queen is the success of the workers as well.

Daly and Wilson (1978) describe a striking example of inclusive fitness. One particular species of ground squirrels stakes out territories in close proximity to each other. When predators threaten, a squirrel gives a loud alarm call, alerting other squirrels while putting itself in danger. This appears altruistic. But research also shows that sometimes a squirrel does not sound an alarm when a predator is near. The critical factor that determines whether or not a squirrel gives an alarm is whether its neighbors happen to be close relatives.

Proximate Causation versus Ultimate Causation. The ground squirrel example is intriguing, but it might be misunderstood. Someone hearing about these squirrels might conclude that the creatures know their relatives like humans know their relatives, perhaps through frequent family reunions and inexpensive long-distance calls, and that they apply this knowledge on a case-by-case basis when predators approach: "Here comes an eagle. Cousin Mildred is scuba diving off Florida, so I guess I'd best keep my mouth shut."

Exaggeration here makes a point. We must distinguish between **proximate causation**—how a characteristic like sounding a distress call occurs in an individual—and **ultimate causation**—how this characteristic contributes to the fitness of a species. Although the alarm calls of ground squirrels seem to have evolved because they contributed to reproductive success (ultimate cause), one should not conclude that considerations of inclusive fitness determine when a particular squirrel squeaks or not (proximate cause). These animals do not have an address book filled with the names of their close relatives that they consult when predators attack. The direct cause is probably more mundane—like smells encountered during infancy. It may do the work of an address book, but it is not the same thing.

inclusive fitness
the fitness of an individual plus the influence of the individual on relatives that share genes in common

proximate causation
the direct mechanism bringing about a biological phenomenon

ultimate causation
the contribution of a biological phenomenon to fitness

ontogeny

changes that take place within the lifetime of an individual

phylogeny

changes that take place within the evolution of a species

Ontogeny and Phylogeny. **Ontogeny** is the course of development of an individual organism within its lifetime, whereas **phylogeny** involves the evolution of a species or a genetically related group of organisms. Perhaps you have heard that "ontogeny recapitulates phylogeny." The phrase suggests that as an organism develops, it undergoes changes similar to those that its ancestors underwent in evolution. At a descriptive level, this is sometimes true. Consider human beings, who at the moment of conception are but a single cell. As embryos, we have gill slits that look like those of a fish. But ontogeny does not recapitulate phylogeny in all cases, which means that we cannot look to individual development for a foolproof notion of species development (Gould, 1977).

Constraints on Evolution. The forms of new species are necessarily constrained by the forms of old species. Evolution does not act on infinite variation in characteristics—only on existing variation. Why do human beings have two eyes? Wouldn't four eyes help us as we traversed the jungle, the interstate highway, or the football field? Perhaps, but we are constrained by our immediate ancestors. And their form was constrained by their immediate ancestors, and so on (Eldredge & Gould, 1972). At this point in evolution, it's impossible for primates to develop four eyes.

phylogenetic scale

arrangement of species from primitive to advanced; not sensible when the species in question are contemporaries

Evolution and Progress. Finally, let us emphasize that the process of evolution has no final destination and follows no preordained plan. If you have read the material in this chapter carefully, you should have no trouble understanding this statement. Yet since Darwin, some thinkers have had trouble grasping the idea that evolution need not imply progress.

For example, consider the **phylogenetic scale,** an arrangement of living species in a presumed order from primitive to advanced.

fish → reptiles → amphibians → birds → mammals

Among mammals, there is a similar rank order, ending with primates. And among primates, the scale culminates in human beings. The phylogenetic scale makes no more sense than an attempt to arrange your cousins from primitive to advanced.

Theorists tend to be drawn to the products of evolution—genes, individuals, species, and so on. They theorize about these products without paying sufficient attention to the environment in which evolution occurs. Evolution, however, is determined by the particular characteristics of the immediate surroundings. Once we remember that organisms live in a particular setting, we realize that we must describe fitness in relation to that setting. We cannot regard organisms per se as primitive or advanced. Are human beings more advanced than houseflies? Are guinea pigs more primitive than baboons? These are wrongheaded questions, because these species live in different environments, or *niches,* to use the technical term.

The Evolution of the Brain

Many of these ideas about evolution can be illustrated by considering the brain and nervous system as products of evolution. What survival value do they offer? Consider how important it is for an organism to react as a whole to events in its environment. An organism composed of connected but uncoordinated parts doesn't stand a chance in competition with one possessing an intact nervous system. For example, a consequence of diabetes in adults is the loss of sensation in one's extremities. The person so afflicted may be unaware of injuries, because the brain doesn't receive a distress "message" from a finger or toe. Serious infection constantly threatens, because a minor cut can easily be overlooked and neglected.

How has the nervous system changed in the course of evolution? Although neurons and brains are not part of the fossil record, some consensus exists about the general process that occurred (e.g., Jerison, 1973; Kaas, 1987). Virtually all multicelled animals have nervous systems that work according to similar principles, suggesting that communication between the parts of an animal probably appeared quite early in evolution, probably before the earliest multicelled creatures differentiated into their major types (like mollusks, insects, and, eventually, vertebrates).

In the course of evolution, neurons began to clump together into groups called *ganglia*. Ganglia themselves became arranged in a hierarchy, so that some ganglia controlled other ganglia. This process did not take place with the aim of evolving into the human brain. Rather, each step of the process occurred because it conferred a reproductive advantage over the immediately preceding step.

For those animals that became elongated, the set of ganglia that ran their entire length took on increased importance. Just as a street running through the length of a town becomes Main Street, these ganglia became the central nervous system. And the "higher" ganglia became the brain. What started out as several extra neurons at one end (or the other) of a primitive animal evolved into the billions of interconnected neurons that make the human condition possible.

The brain evolved through the addition of layers—first the hindbrain, then the midbrain, and finally the forebrain. It is tempting to view this process simply as the addition of new layers that leave intact the original layers. For instance, the human brain stem looks like the entire brain of a reptile and sometimes is called the reptilian brain. Remember, though, that these layers are integrated with each other. Each new layer adds a level to the hierarchy of the nervous system. Functions of the "older" parts of the brain necessarily changed as "newer" parts evolved. Human beings are *not* reptiles with fancy accessories.

The human brain acquired its distinctive structure and function over eons. We can tell stories about the selective advantage resulting from each of these characteristics, but at the same time, we must temper our speculations by understanding that these ultimate explanations may be impossible to verify. As we have already discussed, natural selection can only work on what exists, so that current structures were necessarily constrained by immediately preceding ones. Without a clear picture of the earlier structures, we cannot offer a full evolutionary account of the present structures.

Take brain size, for example. The larger the brain, the more neurons. The more neurons, the more interconnections among them. And the more interconnections among neurons, the more functions the nervous system can perform. So, we might hypothesize that brain size reflects an organism's complexity and flexibility. Mammals, primates, and particularly humans have large brains because large brains make learning possible.

Or maybe not. Remember that natural selection works on particular species in particular environments. Jerison (1973), for instance, speculates that large brains in mammals developed because mammals occupied a particular environment where vision was more important than hearing, taste, or smell. Granted the constraints of existing brains at that time, enhanced vision was possible only through increased brain size. By this argument, brain size did not increase because it allowed the organism to be more flexible. It increased because it allowed the organism to see better. Although a larger brain size then had the side effect of making learning possible, this was not the active factor in evolution. Keep in mind that all of this is speculation. We have no definitive answer as to why people have large brains.

Evolution and Human Behavior

In his 1871 book *The Descent of Man,* Charles Darwin applied his theory of evolution to human beings, concluding that our species evolved from an earlier one, that apes are our close cousins, and that the difference between human beings and apes is less than the difference between apes and other animals. Darwin's conclusions sparked criticism and controversy in some quarters (and still do to this day). However, including human beings under the same evolutionary umbrella with other living creatures has also met with enthusiastic acceptance. The theory of evolution, when applied to human beings, legitimizes a new viewpoint within psychology. People's characteristics—including not just body parts but also thoughts, feelings, and actions—exist as they do because they have had survival value. In this last section of the chapter, we will discuss some of the theoretical attempts that have been made over the years to explain human behavior in evolutionary terms.

This cover from *Punch's Almanack for 1882* satirizes Darwin's theory of evolution.

MAN·IS·BVT·A·WORM.

social Darwinism
the application of the theory of
natural selection to human
societies as a whole

Social Darwinism.   One of the earliest attempts to relate evolutionary ideas to human behavior was **social Darwinism,** the application of the theory of natural selection to human societies as a whole. Here is the logic. Cultures compete for scarce resources. The more fit survive, while the less fit do not. Social Darwinists in the 1800s pointed to the ascendance of European culture, Christian values, and the upper class. Here were clear instances of the survival of the fittest, or at least the social Darwinists thought so.

The social Darwinists ended up defending the status quo as the way it had to be. Those with power and privilege were "fit" and deserved their fate, just as the sick and feeble deserved their lot in life. The problem with social Darwinism was that it was circular. It metaphorically used the theory of evolution to justify whatever happened to exist at the moment (Vining, 1986). It was dragged into political, religious, and moral arenas, and used as a justification by those who wished to promote their particular beliefs. In fact, social Darwinism played a role in Nazi ideology about "pure" and "impure" races. Nazism was so repugnant that few people after World War II were willing to identify themselves as social Darwinists (Bannister, 1979).

comparative psychology
the study of behavioral similarities
and differences among animal
species, usually with the goal of
discerning their evolutionary
history

Comparative Psychology.   Other approaches to psychology inspired by evolutionary thought have been more useful than social Darwinism. **Comparative psychology** is the study of behavioral similarities and differences among animal species, usually with the goal of discerning evolutionary relationships among them (Hall, 1983). Comparative psychologists have typically studied the performance of two or more species at some task requiring intelligence (Bitterman, 1965; Heim, 1954; Romanes, 1882; Thorndike, 1911). Similarities between human beings and other species can be illuminating in view of all the factors that might work against comparable behavior.

Hall (1983) gives an example. Suppose we present people with two stimuli (i.e., disks, buttons, levers, whatever). A reward follows when someone chooses the "larger" stimulus. Think about this task. It requires a relative judgment and therefore demands some subtlety. Some theorists suggest that language allows people to respond appropriately. We tag the stimuli as "larger" or "smaller" and answer accordingly. However, rats and pigeons are also capable of making these relative judgments. They can learn to choose consistently the larger or smaller of two stimuli in order to earn a reward. These animals obviously do not have language to assist them. Any psychologist interested in explaining human judgment must take the animal findings into account, because they suggest that these judgments do not depend on having words to express concepts.

ethology
field that studies animal behavior
from a biological perspective,
usually stressing instincts

fixed-action patterns (instincts)
unlearned behaviors, common to an
entire species, that occur in the
presence of certain stimuli

Ethology.   **Ethology** is the field that studies the behavior of animals in their natural environments. Ethologists bring to bear on their investigations a biological perspective and look in particular at how patterns of behavior may have been inherited in different animal species (Eibl-Eibesfeldt, 1970; Lorenz, 1965; Tinbergen, 1951), including human beings (e.g., Morris, 1967). Ethologists often make use of the notion of **fixed-action patterns** (also known as **instincts**), unlearned behaviors, common to an entire species, that occur in the presence of certain stimuli. For instance, male stickleback fish will automatically attack other males, even if they have never before been exposed to them (Chapter 6). The trigger for this attack is apparently the red belly that characterizes males of this species (Tinbergen, 1951).

Do people show instinctive behavior? One way to demonstrate that a particular instance of animal behavior is unlearned is to isolate an individual at birth from any environmental input that might influence the behavior in question. If the behavior later appears (e.g., the male stickleback attacks), the researcher concludes that it is a fixed-action pattern. But such experiments cannot ethically be conducted with human beings, because we would need to isolate an infant from all contact with other people.

In some unfortunate cases, children grow up under such circumstances (see Chapter 9 for an example). These feral children (literally, wild children) show profound intellectual, emotional, and social poverty (Maclean, 1977). Very little of what we would call "human" behavior spontaneously occurs as they develop. In other words, language typically does not exist, and the ability to form social relationships is gravely impaired. This argues against the possibility that *complex* human behavior is inherited as a whole, but it still leaves room for some genetic influence.

Ethologists interested in human beings sometimes study our close cousins, the primates, as they live in their natural environment (e.g., Smuts, 1985) as well as particular human cultures, such as the !Kung of the Kalahari, the Aborigines of Australia, and the BaMbuti of the Congo, that still exist in much the same way that they have for tens of thousands of years (e.g., Shostak, 1981; Turnbull, 1962). The premise of these investigations is that we can learn something about behavior by studying it in the settings in which people presumably evolved.

Here is what such studies imply about the very first members of our species, who came into existence somewhere between 300,000 and 100,000 years ago. People lived in small groups, and they were nomads. They built only temporary shelters, and they foraged for food. Males in these groups hunted large animals. Females gathered plants. Glantz and Pearce (1989, p. 15) reached the following conclusions regarding such groups:

> The social organization of a . . . hunting and gathering band is a miracle of dynamic balance. Freedom and conformity, self-reliance and cooperation, generosity and envy, sharing and greed, love and anger—all are bound together. . . . Every problematic impulse can be observed . . . and yet it all works: the band swirls through desert and jungle in a tiny tornado of communication and support.
>
> There is no single explanation for this acrobatic triumph of sociality. The band is a product of long years of evolution, an integrated system. . . .
>
> The members of a band are closely related. Helping someone means helping a relative or someone married to a relative. . . . As a result, self-interest and the good of the community are very difficult to separate.
>
> Order is achieved through tradition and conformity. No courts, judges, or prisons are necessary. No one wants to be ostracized from the circle.

Reconstructing the behavior of our ancestors thousands of generations removed is obviously difficult, and firm answers will remain elusive. However, ethologists who concern themselves with human evolution argue that this is the best way to understand people's behavior in the present.

behavior genetics
field that studies how genetic differences within a species are related to behavior differences

Behavior Genetics. Yet another approach to psychology based on evolution is **behavior genetics,** which studies how genetic differences within a species are related to behavior differences (Hirsch, 1967; Wimer & Wimer, 1985). At first glance, this field seems to overlap with ethology, but there are two important differences. First, ethologists are concerned with behaviors that all members of a species show, whereas behavior geneticists focus on differences within a single species. Why do some rats run through a maze rapidly, while other rats amble along in slow motion? Why do some human infants squirm and struggle when held, while others relax and snuggle? Second, ethologists study behaviors minimally influenced by environmental input, whereas behavior geneticists look at behaviors caused by complex interactions between genetic and environmental factors.

Pioneers within behavior genetics showed that animals could be selectively bred to behave in one way or another. For example, Robert Tryon (1940) produced good and bad maze learners among rats this way, just as the pigeon fanciers described earlier produced animals that looked so different from each other. Similarly, dog breeders who intentionally create physical variations sometimes end up creating behavioral variations. You probably know that cocker spaniels are mellow and Irish setters are nervous—these are genetically based differences (Scott & Fuller, 1965).

heritability
the proportion of a trait's variation due to genetic factors

One of the key behavior genetics concepts is **heritability,** the proportion of a trait's variation due to genetic factors. The more a trait's variation in a group of individuals is due to genetic factors, the greater its heritability. You will see in Chapter 8, for example, that people's intelligence shows a fair degree of heritability, meaning that differences among people in intelligence at least in part reflect differences in their genes.

Do not equate heritability with any simple notion of inherited. In the preceding paragraph, it was *not* said that intelligence is inherited, passed directly from parents to children. Heritability is a more abstract concept, referring to a group of people and not to an individual. Also, it refers to the variation in intelligence across these people, not to their intelligence per se. Behavior geneticists seek to link *variation* in traits or behaviors to *variation* in genes. This goal differs from that of ethology, which tries to ascertain which traits or behaviors are inherited as a whole.

The difference between heritability and inherited will become clear when we discuss research on the heritability of intelligence (Chapter 8), personality characteristics (Chapter 11), and psychological disorders (Chapter 12). In each case, evidence supports the heritability of these characteristics, which means that their variation has a genetic basis—not that the characteristics themselves are inherited.

Behavior geneticists who study people usually focus on complex behavior (Loehlin, Willerman, & Horn, 1988). They expect the environment to play a role, in combination with genetic factors, in determining behavior. Because behavior genetics is a young field, much work remains to be done in specifying the mechanisms by which genetic variation influences behavioral variation.

sociobiology
the application of modern evolutionary theory, particularly the notion of inclusive fitness, to social behavior

Sociobiology. The most recent attempt to explain human behavior using biological concepts, called **sociobiology,** is the application of modern evolutionary theory to social behavior (Wilson, 1975, 1978). Complex social interaction invariably proved a stumbling block to evolution theorists, because any society requires cooperation, compromise, and occasional sacrifice on the part of its members. It was not clear to an earlier generation of theorists how natural selection could encourage selfless behaviors.

Sociobiology avoids this pitfall by using the notion of inclusive fitness. As you recall, inclusive fitness allows "altruism" to be explained in biological terms by referring to genes that two organisms share in common. Sociobiologists use this concept to interpret social behavior just as they interpret individual characteristics—as adaptive. We follow certain social conventions because they helped our ancestors pass their genes on to subsequent generations. This is why conclusions about the earliest human beings are so intriguing. Perhaps the practices that proved adaptive to hunter-gatherers have a genetic basis and have been passed on to modern human beings. Although we live in a markedly different environment, we still have the same genetic blueprint as our distant ancestors.

Sociobiologists have applied the concept of inclusive fitness to various types of social behavior, such as aggression, helping, sex roles, and morality (e.g., Alexander, 1979; Barash, 1982; Daly & Wilson, 1983; Freedman, 1979; Lumsden & Wilson, 1981). Many of these applications share the common problem that explanations of behavior are offered *after* the fact. "Predictions" are derived, apparently from evolutionary considerations, about matters that are already well known. For instance, sociobiology explains why males are more aggressive than females by saying that this pattern has been adaptive for the human species. Males usually did the hunting, and so a tendency to be aggressive was adaptive. But the fact of male aggression hardly proves a sociobiological explanation, because the sociobiologist started with knowledge of this fact.

Critics refer to such sociobiological explanations as *just-so stories,* after Rudyard Kipling's fanciful accounts of how animals developed their characteristics, like an elephant's baggy skin or a kangaroo's hop. Evolutionary theorists may be concocting their own just-so stories, starting with some trait or behavior and working backwards to explain how it developed. But such retrospective tales cannot easily be tested, leaving the trait or behavior they are trying to explain as their only "evidence."

One way around such difficulties is to repeat the same study in a variety of societies around the world in an attempt to show that results do not depend on the practices of a given culture. For example, psychologist David Buss (1989) investigated some evolutionary hypotheses about the types of mates preferred by males and females through simultaneous questionnaire studies in 37 different countries, from Australia to Zambia.

He predicted that males would tend to be attracted to young and good-looking women, because these characteristics foreshadow the ability to bear children successfully. And he predicted that females would tend to be attracted to older and industrious men, because these characteristics signify the ability to provide resources for a family. These predictions were supported in the great majority of cultures around the world.

Sociobiology generates controversy for two related reasons. First, it argues that many of our species-typical activities are biologically based and, further, that they must somehow be adaptive. When we suggest that redundancy in the nervous system has functional significance (p. 61), none would disagree. But eyebrows are raised in many quarters when this same argument is applied to rape, infanticide, and war. Some sociobiologists have argued that *these* activities are the product of evolution, thus part of a fixed human nature and indeed an adaptive part. Let us be clear that many sociobiologists would disagree with these particular applications of sociobiological ideas, but the ensuing arguments still color the entire field.

Second, sociobiology generates controversy when used to explain differences within the human species as biologically based. To say that men and women are fundamentally different because of evolutionary reasons is to undercut, at least by implication, social and political movements for equality between the sexes. To say that different ethnic groups are fundamentally different because of evolutionary reasons again implies that attempts to change an inequitable status quo are pointless and perhaps even wrong.

One of the most heated debates about sociobiological ideas followed the publication of several papers by J. Philippe Rushton (1985, 1988), who argued that many behavioral differences among individuals of European, Asian, and African ancestry are based in the different evolutionary histories of these groups. Among the particular behaviors that Rushton discussed were sexual restraint, mental health, respect for the law, and marital stability. He offered sweeping conclusions that certain ethnic groups as a whole exhibit these behaviors in varying degrees relative to other ethnic groups and that the reason for these differences is biological.

Needless to say, these conclusions have been widely criticized. Rushton's evidence and logic are both shaky (Zuckerman & Brody, 1988). His arguments ignore the role of cultural and economic factors in determining differences among groups. Further, he treats the so-called races as if they were defined solely on biological grounds. The more reasonable view treats races as social categories, not biological ones (Chapter 8), which then means that evolutionary theorizing about them is meaningless.

Despite the objectionable extrapolations by some theorists, sociobiology nonetheless has an important place in contemporary psychology, and will have one in the future, as well (Buss, 1984a, 1988). Some previous attempts to explain human behavior in biological terms failed when they became too sweeping, assuming that biology requires no assistance from psychology (Parisi, 1987). If sociobiology can avoid the temptation to explain every aspect of the human condition, it will have greater "fitness" than its predecessors.

In conclusion, biological explanations of behavior reflect the theory of evolution, interpreting what we do in terms of its functional value for our species. Among the most important products of evolution is the nervous system. A biological perspective provides a general explanation regarding the "why" of behavior, and thus supplements other explanations that focus on the "what" and "how" of behavior. It is by studying people's thoughts, feelings, and actions that we can most readily appreciate the importance of biological factors, and this is our task in subsequent chapters.

Summary

Topics of Concern

- Biology is important to psychology, because we can only think, feel, and act in ways made possible by our bodies. Biological explanations of behavior stress either its cause, function, development, or evolution. Controversy arises when biological explanations are proposed to the exclusion of explanations phrased in terms of learning and the environment.
- The brain and nervous system are the center of mental activity. They receive information from the world, coordinate it, and then react. How best to understand the structure and function of the brain has long interested psychologists.
- Any biological explanation of behavior must take into account ideas of evolution. More than 100 years ago, Charles Darwin proposed that species change—evolve—in the direction of characteristics that allow survival and successful reproduction.

Structure and Function of the Nervous System

- The nervous system is an organized whole, with different divisions. The central nervous system is made up of the brain and spinal cord. The peripheral nervous system contains the neurons in all other parts of the body. The peripheral nervous system is divided into the somatic nervous system, which controls the skeletal muscles and sense organs, and the autonomic nervous system, which controls our heart, lungs, and digestive organs. The autonomic nervous system in turn is divided into the sympathetic nervous system, which produces arousal, and the parasympathetic nervous system, which counteracts arousal.
- The nervous system is composed of billions of cells called neurons, which communicate with each other by secreting neurotransmitters that trigger chemical and electrical processes known as the action potential.
- The nervous system is simultaneously organized on a spatial basis, a biochemical basis, and a hierarchical basis. This multiple organization means that the nervous system has considerable redundancy built into it, which may allow recovery of function following damage to a particular part.

The Brain

- The brain has three major structures: the hindbrain, the midbrain, and the forebrain. These correspond to layers of the brain, from bottom to top, respectively. Each of these layers contains its own structures, which may be more or less involved in any particular function. However, the brain also acts as a whole.
- People can and do learn from experience. How does experience change the brain so that learning is possible? No firm answer is yet available, although researchers have looked at structural changes in the nervous system following particular experiences as well as changes in biochemistry.

The Endocrine System

- The endocrine system refers to glands that secrete hormones, chemicals carried through the bloodstream that affect various bodily organs. Although not part of the nervous system, our glands are linked to the brain and work in concert with it to affect behavior as well as physical processes like reproduction and growth.

Studying the Brain and Nervous System

- Researchers have at their disposal various techniques to study the brain and nervous system. With lesion and ablation techniques, they link damage to the nervous system to subsequent behavior. With electrical stimulation techniques, they stimulate parts of the brain with an electric current and observe the effects. With electrical recording techniques, they monitor the electrical activity of neurons, either individually or in groups. Finally, imaging techniques make use of groups. Finally, imaging techniques make use of technological innovations to produce visual representations of the brain and its functioning.

Biological Explanations of Behavior

- When we speak of evolution, we must distinguish the fact of evolution—that species change—from the explanation of this fact that is currently favored: Darwin's theory of natural selection. This theory proposes that the natural environment "selects" for characteristics that allow the individual to survive and reproduce. These adaptive characteristics come to predominate, and with sufficient time, new species may arise from old ones.
- The characteristics of parents are passed on to their offspring through genes, microscopic structures found within each cell of the body that provide plans for biological development. The actual characteristics of any individual reflect the influence of genes on the events that occur during development.
- A key evolutionary concept is fitness, which refers simply to the individual's ability to repro-

duce successfully. Another important concept is inclusive fitness, the fitness of an individual plus the influence of the individual on the fitness of its kin. Inclusive fitness allows evolutionary theory to be applied to social behavior, because in some cases, it may be adaptive for an individual to cooperate with others or even to lay down its life for them, as long as they share genes in common.
- The brain evolved by adding new layers to those that already existed. Higher levels came to control and coordinate lower levels, making possible complex thoughts and actions.
- Ever since Darwin first proposed his theory of evolution, attempts have been made to apply these ideas to human behavior. Social Darwinism, comparative psychology, ethology, and behavior genetics are examples. The most recent attempt to explain human behavior in evolutionary terms is sociobiology, which relies on the idea of inclusive fitness to argue that our social behavior has a biological basis, reflecting tendencies that were adaptive during the evolution of the human species.

Important Terms and Names

What follows is a list of the core terms and names for this chapter. Your instructor may emphasize other terms as well. Throughout the chapter, glossary terms appear in **boldface** type. They are defined in the text, and each term, along with its definition, is repeated in the margin.

Topics of Concern

neuron/54
evolution/54

René Descartes/53
Charles Darwin/54

Structure and Function of the Nervous System

reflex/60
central nervous system/55
peripheral nervous system/55
sympathetic nervous system/56
parasympathetic nervous system/56
dendrite/57
axon/57
neurotransmitter/58
action potential/58
endorphin/59

The Brain

hindbrain/62
midbrain/62
forebrain/62
hypothalamus/64
cerebral hemispheres/64
lateralization/66
localization of function/66

The Endocrine System

endocrine system/71
adrenal glands/72
pituitary gland/72

Studying the Brain and Nervous System

lesion/72
ablation/73
EEG/76
CAT scan/77
PET scan/77
NMR/78

Jose Delgado/74
Wilder Penfield/75

Biological Explanations of Behavior

natural selection/81
gene/82
chromosomes/82
genotype/82
phenotype/82
polygenic inheritance/83
fitness/83
inclusive fitness/84
social Darwinism/88
comparative psychology/
    88
ethology/88
fixed-action patterns
    (instincts)/88
behavior genetics/90
heritability/90
sociobiology/90

Gregor Mendel/81

Review Questions

1. Controversy about the use of biology to explain behavior arises chiefly over the issue of whether these explanations
   a. apply to people.
   b. are circular.
   c. are necessary.
   d. are sufficient.

   Most psychologists believe that biological explanations have something important to add to our understanding of behavior. The controversy about biological explanations has to do with whether they tell the whole story of human behavior./53

2. Arousal is under the control of the _____ nervous system.
   a. autonomic
   b. parasympathetic
   c. peripheral
   d. sympathetic

   The sympathetic nervous system and parasympathetic nervous system are part of the autonomic nervous system, which in turn is part of the peripheral nervous system. The sympathetic nervous system specifically controls arousal./56

3. When we speak of a neuron firing, we in actuality are referring to
   a. communication between different parts of the brain.
   b. electrical and chemical changes taking place within the neuron.
   c. inhibition of the neuron by fatigue.
   d. sparks occurring between one neuron and another.

   The firing of neurons refers to changes inside individual cells./57

4. The most recent addition in the evolution of the brain is the
   a. cerebellum.
   b. cerebral cortex.
   c. hypothalamus.
   d. medulla.
   e. reticular formation.

   "Higher" parts of the brain are thought to have appeared most recently in evolution. The cerebral cortex is the highest part of the brain./64

5. Current research and opinion in psychology supports the idea of
   a. mass action.
   b. phrenology.
   c. localization of function.
   d. a modified version of localization of function.

   Psychologists today believe that different parts of the brain are involved to varying degrees in different functions; this is a modified version of the idea of localization of function./68

6. For most people, language is "located" in the
   a. hindbrain.
   b. midbrain.
   c. left cerebral hemisphere.
   d. right cerebral hemisphere.

   Studies show that damage specifically to the left cerebral hemisphere usually interferes with language production and comprehension./70

7. Evidence for the fact of evolution comes from
   a. the existence of domesticated plants and animals.
   b. the fossil record.
   c. the similarity of body parts across different species.
   d. all of the above.

   The fact of evolution does not depend solely on the fossil record but rather on a number of sources of evidence./79

8. Darwin's theory of evolution proposes that characteristics persist in a species to the degree that they contribute to
   a. longevity.
   b. size.
   c. strength.
   d. successful reproduction.

   According to the theory proposed by Darwin, the persistence of characteristics in a species is determined by how much they add to the fitness of the species, that is, successful reproduction. The other answers involve characteristics that are irrelevant to evolution as Darwin conceived it./83

9. Which is the most advanced species?
   a. American Beauty roses
   b. dolphins
   c. human beings
   d. primates
   e. none of the above
   Contemporary species are cousins of one another, and it is a mistake to think of them as relatively advanced or primitive./85

10. Sociobiology relies most fundamentally on the concept of
    a. evolutionary constraints.
    b. inclusive fitness.
    c. ontogeny recapitulates phylogeny.
    d. proximate causation.
    According to the idea of inclusive fitness, it may be advantageous in an evolutionary sense for an organism to sacrifice its life for that of another, if they share common genes. This idea allows "altruism" and other forms of social behavior to be explained in evolutionary terms./90

The lens of the eye focuses images on the retina, although at times the process is less than perfect.

Chapter Three

Sensation

Topics of Concern
How Do We Know the World?
What Are the Basic Senses and How Do They Work?

Psychophysics
Detection of Stimuli: Absolute Thresholds
Discrimination of Stimuli: Difference Thresholds
Signal Detection
Scaling of Stimuli: Fechner's Law
Adaptation Level Theory

Sensory Systems
Vision
Hearing
Taste
Smell
Cutaneous Senses
Pain
Position Senses

Topics of Concern

One of the characters in Frederick Pohl's (1984) science fiction novel *The Years of the City* is an old man named de Rintelen Feigerman. The story is set in a futuristic New York, where one of the tasks facing those who live in the city is to cover it with a gigantic protective bubble. Feigerman is the builder charged with this task, and so he is an important individual. It is unfortunate, therefore, that in his old age, he has become blind.

Although Feigerman's eyes no longer work, he still is able to "see" his beloved city and plan innovations for it. Every morning upon awakening, he straps a 5-inch by 7-inch plate to his chest. On the plate, against his skin, is a dense array of electrical contacts. Wires lead from these contacts to another device that he wears on the top of his head like a hat. This device emits short beeps at a very high frequency, beyond the hearing of any person. These beeps bounce off nearby objects, and their echoes return to the device on Feigerman's head where they are converted into a pattern of tiny electric shocks that tickle his chest in a characteristic way.

As the objects in Feigerman's environment change, so too do the ultrasonic echoes, and so too does the pattern of electrical shocks that tickle his chest. With practice, Feigerman learns to "read" these patterns. He can recognize specific objects, estimate their sizes, and tell whether or not they are moving. Feigerman's gadget doesn't provide all the information that vision does, because the skin on a person's chest does not contain nearly as many nerve cells as do the eyes. Nonetheless, the device serves many of the same purposes as vision. Indeed, Feigerman's dog Rosalyn, who enthusiastically guided him around the city before the apparatus became available, greatly resents it. She has been put out of her job!

There is an understandable temptation to dismiss science fiction as simply fiction, but the devices that Frederick Pohl describes are based on thoroughly solid science (see White et al., 1970). His story serves to introduce this chapter, which is concerned with sensation. We may take sensory experience for granted, until something goes amiss, as it did for Feigerman. Then we can be grateful that psychologists

Contemporary psychologists who study sensation and perception believe that an infant's understanding of the world is based on a combination of innate and experiential knowledge.

have added greatly to our knowledge about such experiences.

As you learned in the last chapter, the brain integrates and reacts to incoming information from the environment. But how does it get this information? There must be some way for environmental stimulation to be translated into a "language" that the brain can understand. Our sense organs evolved so that they are sensitive to various sources of environmental stimulation. The exact sources differ—these include light, sound, mechanical pressure, and gravity—but each **stimulus** is a form of energy. **Sensation** is the process by which this environmental energy is transformed into neural activity. Thus our sense organs let the physical world speak to the nervous system in biological language (Coren, Porac, & Ward, 1984).

Think of Feigerman in these terms. He was blind, meaning he no longer was sensitive to light energy. However, through the intermediary of technology, some of the information ordinarily provided by light was provided instead by electrical shocks that stimulated his skin.

Perception is the process by which we organize and interpret sensory information. When Feigerman first donned the gadget that allowed him to "see" the world, he had sensations but no perceptions; these took some time to develop. The distinction between sensation and perception can sometimes be fuzzy. We take up the topic of perception in the next chapter.

Let us now turn to some of the major concerns of psychologists interested in sensation. These can seem highly abstract because they pose "large" questions about knowledge. You should understand that these concerns also can become concrete, when they seek to explain how each of us comes to know the particular worlds in which we dwell.

stimulus
any environmental event that produces a response in an organism

sensation
the transformation of environmental stimulation into neural impulses

perception
the transformation of sensory information into psychological terms meaningful to the observer

empiricists
those who support the philosophical doctrine that knowledge is acquired through experience

rationalists
those who support the philosophical doctrine that knowledge is inborn

How Do We Know the World?

We often assume that the information available to us accurately renders the world as it is. When we speak of our sensations, for instance, we locate them in objects "out there" in the world.

- Lights are bright.
- Yogurt is sour.
- Blankets are soft.

In addition, other people understand what we mean when we attribute these characteristics to external objects.

However, none of our sensations is a literal reflection of the outside world. Sensations are actually a part of our neural activity, a series of electrochemical reactions. How do these reactions produce experiences *inside* of us that compel us to believe that they really occur *outside* of us? Explaining this process is a fundamental task for psychologists. Indeed, interest in this topic existed long before the first psychologists.

Over the centuries, philosophers concerned with the origin of knowledge debated whether particular ideas originate through experience or are born within us. Those who emphasize the role of experience in providing us knowledge are called **empiricists,** whereas those who support innate ideas like the notion of God or the postulates of geometry are called **rationalists.**

These two positions, which have been carried from philosophy into psychology, contrast sharply in describing what a newborn infant knows. The empiricists propose that babies know nothing, because they have experienced nothing. Their world is literally a jumble of sights and sounds, tastes and smells, pleasures and pains. Only through experience can they begin to organize knowledge. The rationalists give us a different view of human nature. By virtue of being people, we share certain knowledge at birth, including what to do with our sensations. So, information does not arrive in a miscellaneous heap that we must learn to organize. Rather, people can automatically and without any learning organize their sensations.

This debate between the empiricists and rationalists plays out the larger nature-nurture controversy we have already encountered. As is often the case with these major controversies, available evidence implies that both positions are correct to some degree. Contemporary psychologists who study sensation and perception believe that both of these processes reflect a complex combination of innate and learned influences.

What Are the Basic Senses and How Do They Work?

Many of you have heard that people have "five basic senses." This idea comes from Aristotle, who enumerated vision, hearing, taste, smell, and touch. For centuries his pronouncement was unquestioned, but the era of modern science ushered in a more skeptical attitude. When researchers looked for additional senses, they found them.

psychophysics
the field of psychology concerned with the relationship between physical stimuli and psychological experience

transduction
the process by which external energy produces a neural impulse in a sensory receptor

And a caution was added by the theory of evolution—no sense is inherently basic. Rather, the importance or unimportance of a particular sense depends on the species and the niche that it occupies.

Psychologists interested in sensation want to know the relationship between physical stimuli and our psychological experience of them. We know that there is not a perfect identity between stimuli and what we experience. What then is the relationship? How does a physical object with particular characteristics relate to our psychological experience of it? Psychologists who try to answer basic questions like these work in the field known as **psychophysics,** so named because it concerns itself with both mind (psycho-) and physical reality (physics).

All of our senses share certain characteristics. Each is stimulated by external energy which produces neural impulses in neurons called receptors (Chapter 2), in a process known as **transduction.** These neural impulses give rise to different sensations which are eventually coordinated into perception. To understand sensation, then, psychologists try to characterize the basic properties of external energy as well as the way that particular receptors respond to these properties.

Psychophysics

The first psychophysicist was Gustav Fechner (1801–1887), who named the field and developed research methods for investigating sensation and perception that remain popular to this day (Gescheider, 1988). Fechner was a professor of physics at the University of Leipzig (where Wundt later established the first psychology laboratory) with a strong interest in the workings of the mind. Psychophysics was literally born from his attempt to bridge the material world and the mental world.

Today, psychophysics has several concerns. First, how do we *detect* stimuli in the environment? Second, how do we *discriminate* between two stimuli? Third, how do we ascertain how much of something is present? In other words, how do we *scale* a stimulus and/or experience? What follows is an examination of each of these concerns.

Detection of Stimuli: Absolute Thresholds

We usually take for granted the presence or absence of stimuli. However, there are circumstances where we are much less certain about what did or did not happen. Perhaps we heard our name called. Perhaps not. Perhaps the milk tasted sour. Perhaps not. Perhaps we saw our true love across a crowded room. Perhaps not. These circumstances raise questions about the **absolute threshold** for a particular sensory system—the minimal amount of energy needed to create a sensation that we can detect.

To investigate absolute thresholds, Fechner and other psychophysicists created several simple procedures. One is the *method of constant stimuli*. Here's how it might be used to identify the absolute threshold of a light's intensity. We need some device that can present light at various intensities. Some of these lights should be so dim that an observer never sees them, others so bright that she always sees them, and still others of intermediate intensity. We present these different intensities of light to our observer a number of times, in a random order. We ask her to tell us when she detects a particular light. After a number of trials, we can graph the likelihood of detecting the stimulus as a function of its intensity. The smallest intensity at which the light is detected 50% of the time is considered the absolute threshold.

Studies show that absolute thresholds are never perfectly constant, because identified threshold values vary from test to test. To get around this, researchers measure the same threshold several times and average the results. Perhaps you are surprised that "absolute" values are not absolute, but stop and think about the reasons for this. The stimulus that an observer tries to detect is not the only source of stimulation in her environment. Consider a clock on your desk that ticks away at a regular pace. During the day, with the competing noise provided by traffic, conversation, and television, you may be unable to hear the clock at all, even when you concentrate. At night, with no other sounds, the clock ticks loudly. The sound has stayed the same from day to night, but your absolute threshold for detecting it has changed.

Also, your nervous system is constantly in flux, which affects "absolute" thresholds. Still, we can make some generalizations about thresholds.

absolute threshold
the minimal amount of energy needed to create a psychological experience

Gustav Fechner

Table 3.1

Absolute Thresholds for Familiar Events

Sensory System	Threshold
Vision	On a dark night, a candle flame at 30 miles
Sound	In quiet conditions, a ticking watch at 20 feet
Taste	A teaspoon of sugar in 2 gallons of water
Smell	In a 3-room apartment, one drop of perfume
Touch	From 1 centimeter, the falling of a bee's wing on the cheek

Source: Galanter, 1962.

Table 3.1 presents representative thresholds for the various sensory systems.

Absolute thresholds are important in our everyday lives, and engineers who design products must take into account what psychologists have learned about them (Martin, 1989). How large must letters be on a highway sign in order to be seen by drivers whizzing by at 50 miles per hour? How loud must warning bells and buzzers be in the cockpits of airplanes? How much artificial scent must be added to otherwise odorless natural gas in order for people to be able to detect a leak in their heating system?

Not all individuals have the same absolute thresholds. Research supports several generalizations about the differences observed among people in their sensitivity to various stimuli. First, women tend to have lower absolute thresholds than men for both taste and smell (Money, 1965). The same is true for touch (Weinstein & Sersen, 1961) and hearing (Corso, 1959). Some theorists believe that the greater sensory sensitivity on the part of women is due to the presence of estrogen, because absolute thresholds of women rise and fall during their menstrual cycle (Mair, Bouffard, Engen, & Morton, 1978).

Second, absolute thresholds for many sensory systems change as we age (Chapter 10). For vision and touch, thresholds become higher for older people. Sensitivity to taste also falls off as people age. The elderly may therefore have difficulty distinguishing among foods that look alike, such as blended or pureed dishes (Schiffman, 1977). Interestingly, absolute thresholds for pain show *no* change with age (Harkins & Chapman, 1977).

Third, people who are introverted have lower absolute thresholds than people who are extraverted (Eysenck, 1967). As we will discuss in Chapter 11, whether someone's characteristic style is inwardly or outwardly directed—that is, introverted or extraverted—is an important personality trait. These findings about absolute thresholds support the popular stereotype that introverts are indeed sensitive to the world, in this case literally so.

Discrimination of Stimuli: Difference Thresholds

The second concern of psychophysics is with the degree to which two stimuli must differ in order to be perceived as distinct. Because stimuli

Absolute thresholds for many sensory systems—vision, touch, taste—change as we get older.

can vary along numerous dimensions, like size or shape or color, this
question is usually tackled in experiments that hold all dimensions constant except one. Subjects are asked to make comparisons between two
stimuli that differ along only the varied dimension.

Suppose you are sampling different types of wine, trying to select the
one that is most dry. You sip from different glasses in succession, making
sure that each wine is the same temperature, that each glass has the same
shape, and that each sip contains the same amount of wine. You may treat
one wine as a standard against which the others are evaluated as being
more or less dry.

This procedure becomes formalized when researchers establish what
is known as a **difference threshold,** the minimal distinction between
two stimuli that can be discriminated. As with absolute thresholds, difference thresholds are not perfectly uniform, meaning that they are calculated several times and then averaged. It is conventional to locate the
difference threshold for "greater than" at a point where stimuli greater
than the standard are correctly discriminated at least half the time, and the
difference threshold for "less than" at a point where stimuli less than the
standard are correctly discriminated at least half the time.

A difference threshold is also referred to as a **just noticeable difference (jnd)**. A small jnd is associated with good discrimination, because
two stimuli need not be too different in order to be recognized as different. A large jnd is associated with poor discrimination, because disparate
stimuli are not distinguished. Let's return to our example of tasting wines.
If you cannot distinguish between the taste of two types of wine, then they
fall within a jnd of each other. If they have different prices, good for you!
You can buy the less expensive bottle and never know the difference when
you drink it.

Here's some background on jnds. Ernst Heinrich Weber (1795–1878)
was among the pioneer investigators of sensation. In some of his experiments, subjects were required to judge relative weights, comparing a series of weights in turn against a standard weight. Was a given weight
different than the standard or not? In calculating various jnds, he discovered what is now known as **Weber's law:** the size of the jnd depends
directly on the size of the standard. Indeed, if we graph the jnd against the
weight of the standard, the result is a straight line (see Figure 3.1).

Here is an everyday example. Suppose we have a standard that weighs
10 pounds. For most people, the jnd for this standard is two-tenths of a
pound (approximately 3 ounces), which means that objects weighing less
than 9.8 pounds or more than 10.2 pounds can be discriminated from the
standard. Now suppose we have a standard that weighs 100 pounds. For
most people, the jnd here is 2 pounds, which means that objects weighing
less than 98 pounds or more than 102 pounds can be discriminated from
the standard. But objects weighing 99 pounds or 101 pounds cannot be
discriminated from those that weigh 100 pounds.

The ratio of the jnd to the standard is called a *Weber fraction*. Weber's
law describes all sensory systems reasonably well, failing only at the extremes. We can therefore compare the discrimination abilities of different
senses by comparing their respective Weber fractions (see Table 3.2). Note
that the Weber fraction for electric shock is small, which means that we
can readily detect slight changes. The Weber fraction for brightness is

Ernst Weber

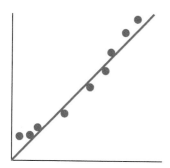

Figure 3.1
Weber's law. As the standard becomes larger, so too does the jnd, and vice versa.

signal detection theory
theory which assumes that people detect stimuli through a process of decision making in which they attempt to separate a stimulus (or signal) from background noise

large, which means that we can't detect changes as easily. It seems plausible to entertain an evolutionary interpretation of these fractions. Variations in pain *should* grab our attention quickly.

Signal Detection

The most sophisticated strategy for studying detection and discrimination is through **signal detection theory,** which assumes that people detect stimuli through a process of decision making in which they attempt to separate a stimulus (or signal) from background noise (Green & Swets, 1966). Signal detection theory surmounts methodological problems inherent in earlier procedures. By definition, threshold investigations concern themselves with stimuli that are difficult to detect and discriminate, and the tasks they pose to research participants can be considered ambiguous. Subjects are often mistaken as to when they detect stimuli. Researchers have a problem, then, when these mistakes are systematic, as they sometimes are.

In studies of absolute thresholds, for example, some subjects tend to say that a stimulus is absent when it is present, and other subjects tend to say that a stimulus is present when it is absent. Averaging across different tests does not necessarily cancel out these systematic mistakes. Here is how signal detection theory attacks this problem. Rather than simply having trials when a stimulus is presented and asking subjects if they detect it or not, signal detection procedures also have trials when no stimulus is presented at all. Because the subject still responds yes or no during these trials, it is possible to separate their bias to respond one way or another from their actual *sensitivity* to the stimulus.

Consider Table 3.3, which reports the results of an experiment where a subject had to detect the presence of a particular odor. One hundred trials were conducted, with the odor present during fifty of them. Note that the particular subject responded liberally, saying yes more frequently than no. If we look merely at her responses to stimuli that were presented, we would conclude that her absolute threshold is low, and she is particu-

Table 3.2
Weber Fractions

For a particular sensory dimension, a Weber fraction is defined as the ratio of the jnd to the standard. The smaller this figure, the more readily one can detect small changes. For instance, two lights must differ in brightness by at least 8 percent for this difference to be detected, whereas two electric shocks need differ in intensity by only 1 percent for this difference to be detected.

Sensory Dimension	Fraction
Brightness	0.08
Taste (salt)	0.08
Loudness	0.05
Heaviness	0.02
Electric shock	0.01

Table 3.3

Detecting the Presence or Absence of an Odor

On some trials, an odor is presented to a subject. On other trials, it is not presented. In all cases, the subject must say if she smells the odor or not. Note that this subject tends to say yes whether or not the odor is actually present, thereby showing considerable response bias.

	Response	
Stimulus (Odor)	Yes	No
Present	42	8
Absent	36	14

larly sensitive to this odor. But if we also look at her responses when no stimuli were presented, we would revise this conclusion and note that she shows considerable response bias. Signal detection thus gives us a more valid estimate of absolute thresholds. Similar procedures also enhance our ability to estimate difference thresholds.

Signal detection has been used to investigate **vigilance:** paying attention to the same stimuli for long periods of time, like an air traffic controller who stares at a radar screen for hours at a stretch. This task can be seen in signal detection terms, because the controller must correctly detect signals indicating planes while ignoring irrelevant signals. The performance of air traffic controllers falls off the longer they stare at the screen, which is hardly surprising.

But what explains this deterioration? One possibility is that the sensory systems begin to show fatigue. The results of signal detection experiments stand against this possibility. Sensitivity stays the same over time. What changes is a person's response bias. A person becomes less willing to say that a stimulus is present (Broadbent & Gregory, 1963, 1965). This is an important distinction, because the person can be instructed regarding this tendency. This knowledge can then lead to improved vigilance.

Signal detection theory reminds us that, in the business of sensation, the entire person is engaged, not simply the sensory organs. Further, signal detection theory gives us a different way of thinking about stimuli. Where traditional psychophysics conceived detection as an all-or-nothing process of determining the presence or absence of a stimulus (hence the term threshold), signal detection theory conceives the process as one that involves probabilities.

Scaling of Stimuli: Fechner's Law

The final concern of psychophysics is the quantitative relationship between physical stimuli and our psychological experience. Our sensations exist in varying degrees. Noises are more or less loud. Tastes are more or less bitter. The intensity of a physical stimulus obviously has something to do with our psychological experience of it, but can we be more precise? Gustav Fechner was the first researcher to systematically investigate the

vigilance

deployment of attention to the same stimuli for long periods of time

According to Fechner's law, our experience of the change in intensity of a stimulus—loud music, for example—depends on the intensity of the original stimulus.

Fechner's law

changes in sensation intensity are a function of changes in stimulus intensity, divided by the magnitude of the stimulus already present

adaptation level theory

an approach to scaling that takes into account not just the stimuli being judged but also other stimuli that we have experienced in the past

quantitative relationship between stimulus intensity and sensation intensity.

He turned to physics for scales to measure stimulus intensity. He had to invent a way to measure the intensity of sensations. His great insight was that he could use Weber's law and the notion of the jnd to measure sensations. Fechner assumed that the subjective sizes of all jnds are the same, which made it possible for him to describe the intensity of any sensation as the number of jnds above the absolute threshold.

What follows from this assumption is **Fechner's law,** which proposes that changes in sensation intensity, measured by the number of jnds, depend on changes in stimulus intensity divided by the magnitude of the stimulus already present. The exact relationship depends on the sensory system being considered. Fechner's law proposes that we experience changes in the intensity of a stimulus not just in terms of how much the stimulus itself increases or decreases, but also in terms of how much of the stimulus is present in the first place. The more intense the original stimulus, the *more* it must change for us to detect any difference in its intensity. The less intense the original stimulus, the *less* it needs to change for us to detect any difference.

Let's use Fechner's law to understand how you experience changes in the volume of your radio while it's playing a song. You perceive changes in loudness as the intensity of sound is increased. But the louder the radio is to begin with, the more the volume knob must be turned for you to notice any difference. When I was in college, I had a friend who always turned up the radio when it played a song he particularly liked. Then he left the volume at that level until his next favorite came on. Fechner's law explains why he had to increase the volume more and more with each song in order to hear any difference. More generally, the significance of Fechner's law is that it explains why we can be sensitive to wide ranges of stimuli—because our sensory systems in effect compress them.

Adaptation Level Theory

Fechner addressed the relationship between stimulus intensity and sensation intensity per se, without reference to context. His focus was only on the stimuli being judged. In contrast, **adaptation level theory** proposes that scaling is additionally affected by other factors (Helson, 1964). Obviously, the stimulus being judged influences magnitude estimates, as Fechner's law proposes. But so too do other stimuli surrounding the stimulus being judged, as do residual stimuli, those which have been experienced in the past.

Background stimuli and residual stimuli create the context (or adaptation level) in which scaling occurs. Height is a typical example. We judge people as short or tall not only in terms of their actual heights, but also in terms of other people in the vicinity and in terms of other people we have known. A common experience is to see some basketball players like Isiah Thomas or John Stockton as quite short, even though they are in fact notably taller than the average American male. We see them as short because their peers are so tall. Another common experience is for Americans who visit foreign countries where people are shorter to feel quite tall. The actual height of these tourists hasn't changed, of course, but their adaptation level makes them feel as if it has.

René Descartes believed that the body was a machine that worked according to certain laws. This woodcut illustrates Descartes' understanding of the nature of vision.

There can never be a simple and invariant relationship between stimulus intensity and sensation intensity. The processes involved in adaptation level theory guarantee that Fechner's law and similar approaches to scaling will be at best mere generalizations. The most accurate thing to say about sensation is that it is not an isolated and simple event. Although we've casually discussed sense organs as if sensations occurred within them, this is not the best way to regard them. Eyes do not see—people see. Tongues do not taste—people taste. Ears do not hear—people hear. And because people are subject to innumerable influences, so too are their activities.

Sensory Systems

With an appreciation of the methods with which psychologists investigate sensation, let us turn to a more detailed discussion of our senses. In this section, we will discuss in detail the major human senses of vision and hearing. We will also describe taste and smell. Finally, we will cover the cutaneous senses of touch and temperature, pain, and senses that help us establish our physical position in the world.

Vision

Vision is the sense that psychologists know the most about. Nevertheless, the complexities involved in explaining how we see are dizzying, so you're getting but a brief "peek" at the topic here. Let's start by discussing light, the external energy that gives rise to vision.

light
radiant energy that travels in an oscillating pattern of waves

amplitude
the height of a wave of light

brightness
the psychological experience of the intensity of light

Light.   What is **light?** Physicists tell us that light is radiant energy that travels in an oscillating pattern of waves. We see objects that emit light themselves or reflect light from other sources. In either case, light waves have a number of physical characteristics that influence vision. Of particular importance are the amplitude, wavelength, and purity of light, because they determine our different visual sensations.

The **amplitude** of light is the height of its wave (see Figure 3.2), and this represents the physical intensity of the light. We psychologically register the amplitude of light as its **brightness.** The difference between a dim light and a bright light is therefore due to the difference in their amplitudes.

Radiant energy includes not only visible light but also X rays, ultraviolet and infrared radiation, microwaves, and radio waves. Each of these types of energy comes in waves, and what distinguishes one from another

Figure 3.2
Light Waves. These representations of light waves differ in amplitude and wavelength.

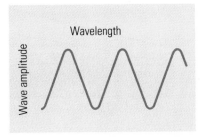

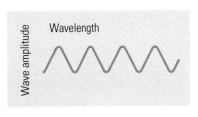

wavelength

the distance between peaks of two successive waves of light

hue

the psychological experience of the wavelength of light

is the **wavelength,** the distance between the peaks of two successive waves (again see Figure 3.2). These wavelengths vary greatly, from distances almost too tiny to imagine in the case of cosmic rays to hundreds of feet in the case of radio waves. Figure 3.3 arranges the types of radiant energy according to their wavelength. The length of a light wave is measured with a unit called a *nanometer,* equal to one billionth of a meter, so you can see that the wavelengths of the light we can see are indeed short, ranging from about 400 nanometers to about 700.

Nevertheless, variations in the wavelengths of visible light are psychologically quite important because they give rise to our experience of **hue,**

Figure 3.3

Radiant Energy. Each form of radiant energy comes in waves. What distinguishes them is their characteristic wavelengths. Visible light represents but a small part of the entire spectrum of radiant energy.

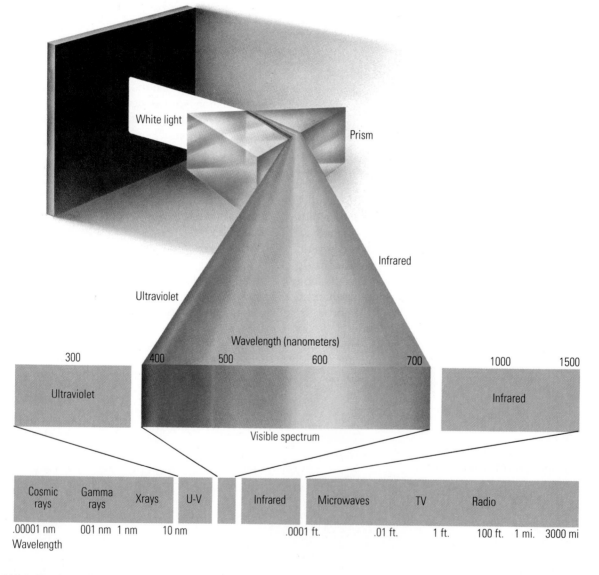

purity
the degree to which light is dominated by a single wavelength

saturation
the psychological experience of the purity of light

vitreous humor
the fluid contained in the eyeball

cornea
the transparent, protective outer covering of the eye

pupil
opening in the iris that changes size in relation to the amount of available light

iris
the colored band around the pupil that responds reflexively to light levels, changing the size of the pupil

lens
the structure in the eye directly behind the iris that changes its shape in order to focus images

retina
the structure at the back of the eye which is lined with nerve cells

photoreceptors
the nerve cells contained in the retina that are sensitive to light

rods
cylinder-shaped photoreceptors responsible for vision in dim light and sensations without color

cones
photoreceptors with a tapered shape responsible for vision in bright light and sensations with color

or color. Wavelengths are why grass is green, apples are red, and the sky is blue. Wavelengths have made KODACHROME a household word. (Paul Simon's song by the same name helped, too.)

So far our discussion of wavelength has sidestepped the fact that the actual light we see is always a mixture of different wavelengths. When we see an apple as red, it is because red wavelengths predominate, but there are other wavelengths mixed in as well. The degree to which light is dominated by a single wavelength of light is its **purity.** The psychological property to which purity gives rise is called **saturation,** which in everyday conversation we often call richness. The more wavelengths mixed into a light, the more pale and washed out it becomes.

Light of the lowest possible saturation is called *white light.* The light bulbs we use in our homes are only able to create an approximation of white light. Fluorescent bulbs tend to produce too many short wavelengths (blues and violets), whereas incandescent bulbs tend to produce too many long wavelengths (reds and oranges). Sunlight comes closer to white light, not because it is pure, but precisely because it is impure, that is, of low saturation.

Our eyes respond to the amplitude, wavelength, and purity of light, changing light energy into neural impulses that we experience as intensity, hue, and saturation. The structures of the eye not only make this transduction possible for light that hits its receptors, they also make sure that light gets to the receptors in the first place.

The Eye.   Let's move from our discussion of light to the sense organ that is sensitive to light. The human eye is a sphere about 1 inch in diameter (see Figure 3.4). It keeps its shape because of internal pressure caused by a fluid called **vitreous humor.** Light enters the eye at its front through the **cornea,** a transparent membrane that protects the eye and refracts the light that hits it, bending it so that it goes through the **pupil.** The pupil is an opening in the colored part of the eye called the **iris.**

Whether green, blue, grey, or brown, the iris controls the size of the pupil. It is the reflexive response of the iris to light levels that changes the size of the pupil. In bright light, the iris contracts, making the pupil small and thus letting in little of the available light. In dim light, the iris dilates, opening the pupil wide and letting in much of the available light. The pupil also reacts to our psychological states, increasing in size when we experience fear, surprise, anger, or other types of heightened emotion (Chapter 6).

Once light passes through the pupil, it encounters the **lens.** The lens changes its shape in order to focus images, just like a zoom lens does on a fancy camera. The lens becomes fatter when focusing on close objects and flatter when focusing on those far away. As many of you eyeglass wearers know, sometimes the ability of the lens to accommodate is less than perfect, and then we suffer from either near- or farsightedness.

The lens then focuses its image onto the **retina,** a structure at the back of the eye which is lined with nerve cells directly sensitive to light, called **photoreceptors.** As early as 1860, we knew of two types of photoreceptors, which suggested that our eyes had two functions. Subsequent research supported this hypothesis. **Rods** are shaped like cylinders and are responsible for vision in dim light. The sensations produced by rods are without color. **Cones** have a more tapered shape and are responsible

Figure 3.4

Structure of the Human Eye

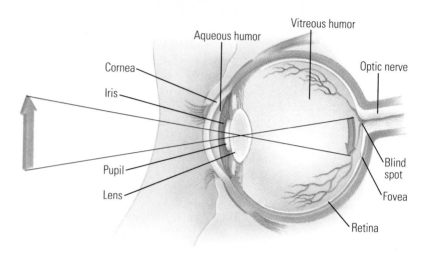

for vision in bright light. Cones require more illumination in order to function, and produce color sensations. In each eye, there are approximately 120 million rods and 6 million cones.

Figure 3.5 is a cross section of the human retina that shows rods and cones. Note that the rods and cones are not on the surface of the retina.

Figure 3.5

Cross Section of the Human Retina Showing Rods and Cones

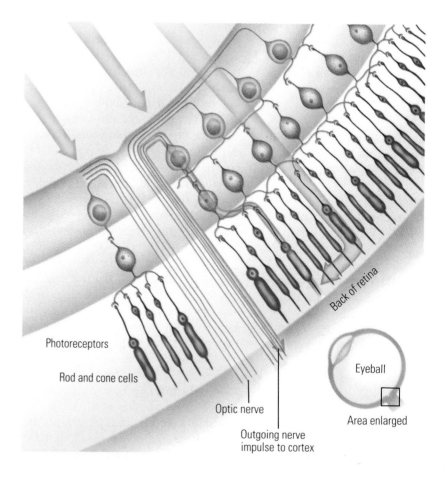

Indeed, they face away from the pupil. Light must pass through several layers of other cells in order to stimulate the photoreceptors. This arrangement reflects the fact that photoreception is a neural process that requires a rich supply of oxygen. Hence, rods and cones are as close to blood vessels as possible, and blood vessels are not to be found on the surface of the retina.

The **fovea** is the central point in the retina where an image is focused. It contains the densest arrangement of the photoreceptors, most of which are cones. Because of the density of cones in the fovea, our ability to make discriminations among objects, called **acuity,** is greatest when light from these objects falls directly on the fovea, as happens when we look directly at them. In contrast, objects seen "from the corner of our eyes" appear less distinct, because their images do not fall on the fovea. Instead, these images fall in an area *peripheral* to the fovea, where rods predominate. So-called peripheral vision is therefore handled mainly by rods.

Photoreceptors contain **visual pigments,** chemicals that are sensitive to light. When exposed to light, these chemicals break down, causing photoreceptors to generate a neural impulse. Other neurons lead away from the photoreceptors and are bundled together in the **optic nerve** (see Figure 3.4), which leads directly to the brain. The area where the optic nerve passes through the retina is without photoreceptors, creating a **blind spot.** Most of us are unaware that we have this blind spot, because we "fill in" the missing information (see Figure 3.6).

Visual pigments can resynthesize by enzyme activity. This means that the photoreceptors can work over and over again. You may have heard that carrots are good for your night vision. Here's the rationale. Carrots contain vitamin A, one of the substances needed to resynthesize the visual pigment found in our rods. What would happen if you had a deficiency of vitamin A? Your rods would not regain their photosensitivity after stimulation, and so your ability to see in dim light would suffer.

Brightness and Adaptation.   Now that you know something about the structure of the eye, let's turn to some of the important visual functions and how they are possible. First there is the sensation of brightness. In very

fovea
the central point in the retina where an image is focused, containing the densest arrangement of nerve cells

acuity
the ability to make fine visual discriminations among stimuli

visual pigments
the chemicals in photoreceptors that change when exposed to light

optic nerve
the nerve leading from the eye directly to the brain

blind spot
the part of the retina through which the optic nerve passes; because there are no photoreceptors in the blind spot, it is incapable of vision

Figure 3.6
Demonstration of Blind Spot. Close your right eye and stare at the cross on the top line. Holding the page about a foot from your eye, move the page slowly forward and backward until the star disappears. It has fallen on your blind spot. Similarly, close your right eye and stare at the cross on the bottom line. With the page about a foot from your eye, move the page slowly forward and backward until the break in the line disappears. Again, it has fallen on your blind spot, and you have filled in the missing information.

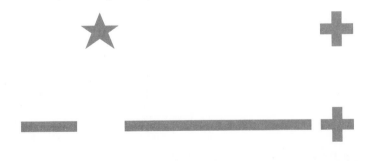

general terms, the experience of brightness is easy to explain; the more intense the light is once it reaches the retina, the more photoreceptors are stimulated, and the more we experience an object as bright. But with closer analysis, the experience of brightness becomes a bit more complex, because other factors prove influential.

One of these factors is the level of background illumination. When you move from a dark room to a well-lit one, or vice versa, you know that it takes a little time before you can see very well. In the one case, everything looks too bright and hence not clear. And in the other, everything looks too dim and just as unclear. These familiar experiences exemplify **adaptation.** When we say that we must "get used" to the illumination in a room, what we really mean is that the visual pigments in our photoreceptors must acclimate to background illumination. In the dark, our rods become more and more sensitive to light, and our cones less and less so. In the light, just the opposite happens.

Acclimation reflects chemical processes involving the pigments as well as changes in the sensitivity of the nervous system (Green & Powers, 1982). In either case, these processes unfold over time, and so adaptation is not instantaneous. Our cones more rapidly acclimate than our rods, which means that it takes less time for us to see clearly after entering a bright room from a dim room than vice versa. Adaptation to the light may take but a few seconds, whereas full adaptation to the dark may take as long as twenty minutes. What is important about adaptation is the range of light intensity to which it allows us to be sensitive. Sunlight gives *one million times* the illumination of moonlight, yet we can see objects at both noon and midnight.

Earlier we discussed how cones sense the wavelengths of light. We now understand that cones work best at levels of high illumination. Rods are not sensitive to wavelength, but they respond better than cones at low illumination. So, images that fall chiefly on the rods—in other words, away from the fovea—are seen as brighter than those that fall chiefly on the cones. An interesting implication here is that we can more readily detect dim objects, like distant stars, if we do not look straight at them. If we look somewhat to the side, we bring into play the rods, which are most sensitive to the amplitude of light.

Color Vision.   Another important visual function is how we experience the sensation of color. Over the years, two different theories of color vision were popular: trichromatic theory and opponent-process theory. More recently, these two theories have been combined, and the integration is now accepted by many psychologists as the best available account (Hilgard, 1987). Let's see how this integrated theory was achieved.

Remember that objects that reflect light of particular wavelengths are seen as having those particular colors. A first step toward explaining how we sense color might be to look for different types of cones for different wavelengths of light. What is the immediate objection to this kind of explanation? There are an *infinite* number of wavelengths, and it is highly unlikely that we have an infinite variety of cones. So, our second step toward explaining the experience of color must be to look for a mechanism by which a finite number of visual elements can produce the thousands of shades of color that people can discriminate.

adaptation
process by which a sensory system becomes more or less sensitive to stimuli

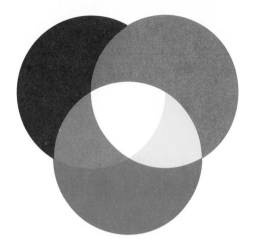

Hermann von Helmholtz

primary colors

red, green, and blue; lights of these colors can be combined to produce all other colors

trichromatic color theory

theory of color vision that proposes there are three types of cones, sensitive respectively to red, green, and blue wavelengths

Following this reasoning, early theorists were intrigued by *color mixture studies,* which showed that any and all shades of colors could be produced by combining various amounts of red, green, and blue lights (see Figure 3.7). Red, green, and blue are therefore called **primary colors,** because it is possible to construct all other colors from them.

Does the existence of primary colors mean that there are three types of cones? If so, then color vision could be explained readily in terms of the relative stimulation of red cones, green cones, and blue cones. Such an explanation was indeed proposed almost two centuries ago by Thomas Young (1773–1829) and later popularized by Hermann von Helmholtz (1821–1894). It is known as **trichromatic color theory.**

The most intriguing support for trichromatic theory comes from various studies of color-blind individuals. Color-blindness is not a single problem, but rather a family of problems. Different forms of color-blindness involve different inabilities. Trichromatic theory predicts that there should be five types of color-blindness.

Let's work through this prediction (Table 3.4). Suppose there are three different types of cones. If a person has none of these cones, he wouldn't be able to make any distinctions among colors. The world would look black and white. Further, vision in bright light would be difficult because the person only has rods. So, that's one form of color-blindness. If a person has one of these types of cones, regardless of which one, he would still not be able to make distinctions among colors. However, he would be able to see in bright light because cones are present. That's a second form of color-blindness. Now suppose a person has only two of these cones; he would therefore be insensitive to the third color—red or green or blue, as the case may be. That's a third, fourth, and fifth form of color-blindness, and no other types are found (Matlin, 1988). In terms of accounting for the forms of color blindness that exist, trichromatic theory holds up.

More direct support for trichromatic theory comes from investigations of a human eye after it has been surgically removed (Bowmaker & Dartnall, 1980). Researchers aimed a narrow beam of pure light at particular cones and then measured how much of the light was absorbed. They found that a given cone was sensitive to light at one of three different wavelengths, which corresponded exactly to red, green, and blue light.

Table 3.4

The Five Types of Color Blindness

Particular Problem with Receptor	Type of Color Blindness
Person has no cones	Insensitivity to all colors; impaired vision in bright light
Person has only one type of cone	Insensitivity to all colors; unimpaired vision in bright light
Person has red and green cones	Insensitivity to blue
Person has red and blue cones	Insensitivity to green
Person has green and blue cones	Insensitivity to red

Although the evidence for three types of cones is persuasive, trichromatic theory has problems explaining certain aspects of color vision. One immediate difficulty is that *psychologically* there are not three primary colors but four. When people are given a large number of color samples and asked to sort them into what look like pure types, they usually come up with the categories of red, green, and blue—as trichromatic theory predicts—but also yellow. Further, these four colors seem to fall into pairs that are psychological opposites—red versus green, blue versus yellow. Note that you have never experienced reddish-green, for instance, or bluish-yellow.

The second popular theory of color vision was originally proposed by Ewald Hering (1834–1918) and is called **opponent-process color theory.** Its strengths and weaknesses are precisely the opposite of trichromatic theory. According to opponent-process theory, two systems are responsible for color vision. Each system is composed of a pair of colors that oppose each other. So, the hue we experience reflects a balance between red and green on the one hand and between blue and yellow on the other.

Opponent-process theory explains the phenomenon of **negative afterimage** (see Figure 3.8). If you stare for a while at a green object and then look quickly away to a white surface, you will see a red spot; if you originally stared at a red object, then you see a green afterimage. Blue and yellow objects respectively produce yellow or blue afterimages. So, in each instance you see an image of the "opposite" color. Afterimages like these imply that our eyes are sensitive to four basic colors, arranged in pairs, and this is at odds with trichromatic theory.

Opponent-process theory nicely explains why there seem to be four primary colors. It accounts well for negative afterimages. However, it does not handle the evidence that most strongly supports trichromatic theory. Specifically, why are there five types of color-blindness? And why do cones show sensitivity to light at one of three different wavelengths?

We do not have to end this discussion with an impasse, because, in an elegant formulation, Leo Hurvich and Dorothea Jameson (1974) combined trichromatic and opponent-process theories. Both theories could be seen as partially right. There are three types of cones that, working together,

opponent-process color theory
theory that proposes two systems for color vision, each composed of a pair of colors that "oppose" each other

negative afterimage
perceptual phenomenon in which one stares at an object of one color, quickly looks away, and sees an image of the "opposite" color

Figure 3.8

Example of Negative Afterimage. Stare at the center of this green, black, and yellow flag for at least 30 seconds. Then look away and focus on the center of a sheet of white paper. Please do not burn your negative afterimage!

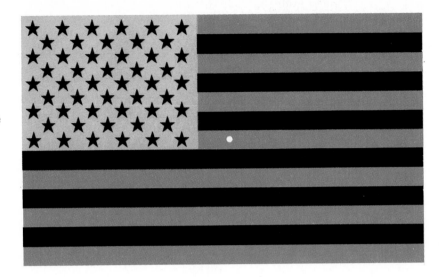

produce four primary colors. This integration was made possible by remembering that neurons can both excite and inhibit other neurons. The particular *pattern* of excitation and inhibition from three types of cones can give rise to the four psychological primary colors as well as to our experience of black and white.

The details of this integrated theory are a bit complicated, to be sure, but perhaps you will find it of interest that color television works in much the same way as Hurvich and Jameson propose our color vision works. A television camera first captures a scene in terms of red, green, and blue. The picture is then transformed into opponent-processes for transmission. Engineers designed color television in this way because it is the most efficient way to transmit information about color. Perhaps evolution hit upon the same strategy.

Hearing

Let's now move from vision to another important sense, hearing. Sound originates when an object vibrates and sets air molecules into motion against the ear. The object can be a tuning fork, vocal cords, a loudspeaker, or a fingernail on the blackboard. Like light, sound comes to us in waves, and we can distinguish several important properties of these waves that determine our different auditory sensations.

loudness
the psychological experience of the intensity of sound

frequency
the number of times that sound waves repeat themselves in a given period of time

pitch
the psychological experience of the frequency of sound

Sound. First, there is *amplitude,* which you remember as the height of waves. In terms of sound, amplitude creates the psychological experience of **loudness.** The greater the amplitude of sound waves, the louder they are. Loudness is measured with units called *decibels,* as shown in Figure 3.9. Note that hearing loss occurs with prolonged exposure to sounds above a certain decibel level. These sounds need not be experienced as painful in order to do damage, and for certain workplaces—such as assembly lines—loss of hearing sensitivity is a potential hazard.

Second, there is **frequency,** the number of times that waves repeat themselves in a given period of time. Frequency affects our psychological experience of **pitch,** whether a sound is experienced as high or low. High

Figure 3.9

Loudness in Decibels of Various Sounds

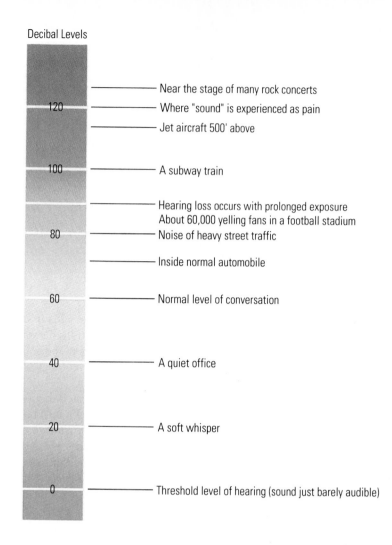

Decibal Levels

120	Near the stage of many rock concerts
	Where "sound" is experienced as pain
	Jet aircraft 500' above
100	A subway train
	Hearing loss occurs with prolonged exposure
	About 60,000 yelling fans in a football stadium
80	Noise of heavy street traffic
	Inside normal automobile
60	Normal level of conversation
40	A quiet office
20	A soft whisper
0	Threshold level of hearing (sound just barely audible)

sounds are those with high frequencies, and low sounds those with low frequencies. The hearing loss that occurs with old age or from repeated exposure to loud noise shows up chiefly in the decreased ability to hear higher frequency sounds.

The frequency of sounds is measured with a unit called a *hertz,* corresponding to one sound wave per second. People are sensitive to frequencies ranging from about 20 hertz up to 20,000 hertz. Some animals, like dogs, can hear sounds with higher frequencies than people can detect.

Other animals, like elephants, are sensitive to sounds lower than those which we can detect. Indeed, despite a popular stereotype that elephants are silent and stately creatures, we now know that they communicate with one another by making sounds too low for people to detect (Payne, 1988). Elephants chatter away all the time. When audio recordings are made with equipment sensitive to low-frequency sound, they reveal a variety of vocalizations. Speeded up, we can hear these vocalizations, and they can be characterized as barks, snorts, roars, grumbles, and growls.

timbre

the sharpness or clarity of a tone; its quality

A third property of sound is its *purity,* the degree to which a sound is dominated by waves of a single frequency. We experience the purity of sound waves as **timbre,** the sharpness or clarity of a tone. Some describe timbre as the quality of a sound. Every musical instrument is characterized by its own timbre, which is why we can distinguish between a violin and a trumpet, even when both are playing the same note at the same volume. Analogous to white light is *white noise,* sound with a random mixture of frequencies.

The Ear. The ears of all mammals have the same structure. Some theorists believe that ears evolved from the organs of touch found in primitive animals (Stebbins, 1980). This organ, the *lateral line,* is a series of nerve endings that stretches the length of a water-dwelling animal. Protruding from these nerves are sensory hairs stimulated by the movement of water. In the course of evolution, part of the lateral line "sunk" into the head of the animal, where it became the specialized organ we now know as the ear. When animals moved from the water to the land, their ears came with them, and these organs proved useful in detecting sound waves propagated through the air.

pinna

the outer ear

auditory canal

connection between the outer ear and the middle ear

Figure 3.10 presents a representative human ear. The outer ear, called the **pinna,** serves to channel sound waves into the **auditory canal.** At

Figure 3.10
Structure of the Human Ear

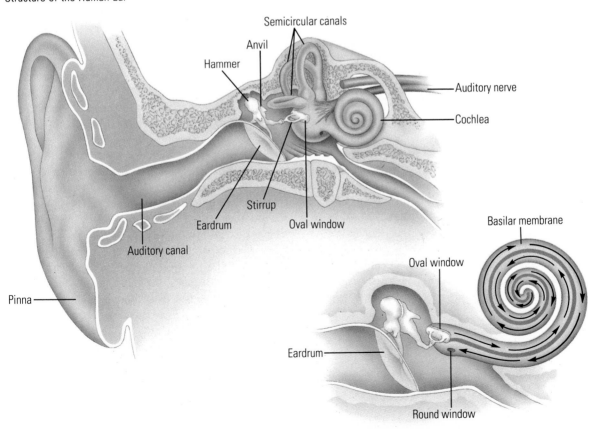

eardrum
membrane between the auditory canal and the middle ear that vibrates when sound waves push against it

malleus, incus, and stapes (hammer, anvil, and stirrup)
three small bones in the middle ear that transmit vibrations from the eardrum to the oval window

oval window
membrane that focuses sound waves and makes the fluid in the cochlea move

cochlea
fluid-filled canals in the inner ear

basilar membrane
structure which runs the length of the cochlea, which when moved by the cochlea's fluid, triggers the movement of hair cells on its surface

hair cells
cells in the cochlea which send neural impulses to the brain

auditory nerve
nerve that runs from the inner ear to the brain

place theory
theory of hearing proposing that sound waves of different frequencies affect different locations along the basilar membrane

frequency theory
theory of hearing proposing that sound waves of different frequencies cause neurons in the ear to fire at different frequencies

the end of the auditory canal is a membrane called the **eardrum.** Sound waves cause the eardrum to vibrate, which in turn transmits the vibrations through three tiny bones that make up the middle ear: the **malleus** (or hammer), the **incus** (or anvil), and the **stapes** (or stirrup). These bones eventually pass the vibrations on to another membrane known as the **oval window.** The oval window is much smaller than the eardrum, which means that the sound waves become more focused and thus amplified as they pass through the middle ear.

The oval window is part of the inner ear, which is composed chiefly of three spiral-shaped fluid-filled canals known collectively as the **cochlea.** Movement of the oval window makes the fluid in these canals move, creating a wave in the cochlea that corresponds to the original sound wave. Inside the cochlea is the **basilar membrane,** which runs the length of the cochlea. The waves in the cochlea's fluid move the basilar membrane, which in turn triggers the movement of the **hair cells** on its surface. The hair cells are the receptors for hearing. Stimulation of the hair cells starts a neural impulse that travels through the **auditory nerve** and then to the brain.

How Do We Hear?   How does stimulation of these hair cells—the auditory receptors—produce what we hear? This is a complicated matter. There is agreement that loudness is reflected in the firing rate of individual nerve cells and also the total neural activity. Pitch proves more complicated to explain.

There are two theories that seek to explain how we hear different pitches or sounds of various frequencies. **Place theory** proposes that sound waves of different frequencies affect different locations along the basilar membrane (Bekesy, 1947). For example, high-frequency sounds tend to move the end of the basilar membrane closest to the oval window, as place theory proposes. Complicating matters for this theory is the fact that low-frequency sounds move the entire basilar membrane. **Frequency theory** suggests that the firing rate of neurons in the ear is determined by the frequency of a sound (Wever, 1949).

Although these theories appear to conflict, it turns out that both are correct, depending on the particular frequencies of sound being considered. Lower frequencies are sensed, as frequency theory hypothesizes, by the rate at which neurons fire. Higher frequencies are sensed, as place theory predicts, by where the neurons are located. Sounds of intermediate frequencies are detected by place and frequency.

Hearing tells us more than simply the loudness and pitch of sounds. It also gives us information about the location of whatever object it is that is producing the sounds (Phillips & Brugge, 1985). Both ears are essential to the task. Is it to our left or right? Below us or above us? Is it far away or—watch out!—right in our face?

We judge the location of a sound by attending to various sources of information concerning it. For example, if a sound originates on one side of our head, it arrives at one ear somewhat sooner than the other, and it will be somewhat louder to that ear as well. It may produce different patterns of echoes depending on where it has originated. In localizing sounds, we often tilt our head one way or another, and these head movements provide still further clues about the origin of sounds.

The "topophone" allowed a ship's captain to determine the direction of a whistle in the fog, just as the human ear enables us to determine not only loudness and pitch but also direction.

chemical sense
sensory system that is stimulated chemically, like taste or smell

taste buds
receptors located on the tongue and elsewhere in the mouth that are responsible for taste

Taste

Life originated in the sea, and so the sense of taste is probably the most primitive and widely represented across species. Taste receptors are stimulated chemically by substances dissolved in water; taste is therefore called a **chemical sense.** The adaptive functions of taste are obvious. Taste can give us clues about what is safe to put into our mouths. Indeed, taste tells us what is spectacular to ingest—chocolate chip cookies, lobster, blueberry pancakes, and M & M's, to name a few of the substances that appeal to my good taste. Taste can also tell us what is dangerous to put into our mouths. Needless to say, taste is not a foolproof guide to the safety of substances we might ingest, which is why parents are careful to keep household cleaners and the like out of the reach of inquisitive youngsters.

Taste buds are the receptors that are sensitive to taste. We have about 10,000 taste buds, mostly located on our tongue (see Figure 3.11), but also elsewhere in our mouth. Taste buds are *not* the bumps we can see on our tongue when we look in the mirror. These are called *papillae,* and taste buds are contained in and around them. Taste buds are much smaller than papillae; each papilla contains about 200 taste buds.

Taste buds are stimulated by water-soluble substances that come into contact with them. This explains why cold foods usually have less taste than hot foods, because they don't dissolve as readily in our saliva. Taste buds die off over time, and parts of them can literally be destroyed by foods that are too hot. However, taste buds regenerate constantly.

There are four primary taste qualities: sweet, salty, sour, and bitter. We have different taste buds that respond primarily to each of these different tastes. However, they are not distributed evenly on the tongue. Receptors most sensitive to sweetness are at the very tip, and those for bitterness are at the very back of the tongue. Our tongues are most sensitive to sour tastes along the sides. Saltiness is detected most readily toward the front of the tongue.

Figure 3.11
Structure of the Human Tongue. Also shown here is an enlarged side view of a taste bud.

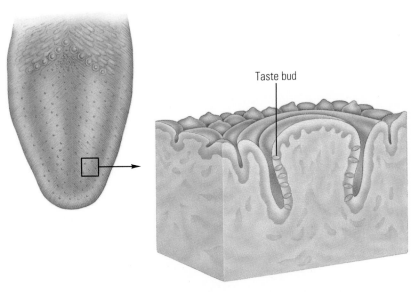

A. Top view of tongue   B. Enlarged side view of papilla

We've made some progress in understanding which substances are associated with which tastes. Organic compounds (those containing carbon, hydrogen, and oxygen) often taste sweet. Substances containing nitrogen often taste bitter. Salty substances are those that form ions. Acidic substances taste sour. As we learn more about the substances that give rise to different tastes, we can use this information to create certain tastes on demand. Commercial sweeteners are a familiar example. Researchers intentionally create them to taste sweet without containing the calories that characterize most other sweet-tasting substances.

Smell

Like taste, smell is a chemical sense. Indeed, taste and smell often work in concert, as you may have noticed the last time your nose was stuffed up due to a cold. Because you could not smell the food you ate, it did not taste the same as it usually does.

We smell substances that are carried through the air to receptors that are located at the top of our nasal cavity (see Figure 3.12). Neurons leading from these receptors bundle together in the *olfactory nerve*. This nerve travels to the *olfactory bulb* at the base of the brain.

The sense of smell probably evolved from the sense of taste when our water-dwelling ancestors long ago moved on to land. Smell is not as important to human beings as it is to other animals. In fact, our sense of smell is not particularly keen (Brown, 1975). Consider that dogs have about 100 million smell receptors as opposed to the 5 million that people have.

Figure 3.12
Human Nasal Cavity

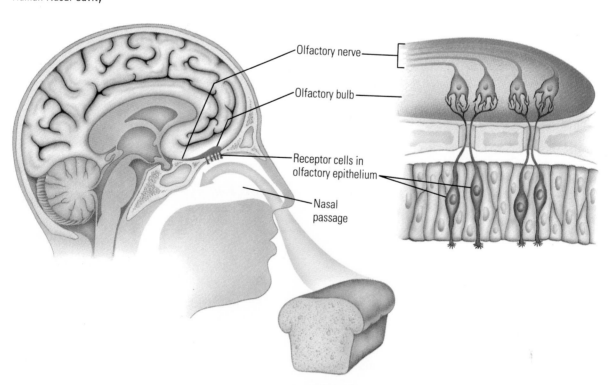

Olfactory nerve

Olfactory bulb

Receptor cells in olfactory epithelium

Nasal passage

Smell is poorly understood. We do know that the neural pathways from smell receptors are directly connected to the brain (Chapter 2), suggesting an important role early in evolution. But we don't know exactly how smell receptors are stimulated by the particular chemicals that reach them. Attempts to discover primary odors, analogous to the primary taste qualities just discussed, have not been successful.

One theory of smell that has been proposed is called the **lock-and-key theory** (Amoore, 1964). According to this theory, different sites on smell receptors have different shapes. Only molecules with compatible shapes can fit into these sites, thereby stimulating the appropriate smell. This theory is similar to the one discussed in Chapter 2 that explains why particular neurons are sensitive to particular neurotransmitters but not others (p. 59).

The lock-and-key theory of smell has a problem, though. It implies that once a molecule has served as the key for a particular lock, it occupies that receptor site, staying there and blocking subsequent smells. If this really happened, then we would eventually lose our ability to smell anything, because all the receptor sites would be occupied. So the lock-and-key theory cannot be complete. At the present time, we just don't have a good explanation for our sensation of smell.

Cutaneous Senses

Because all organisms have a surface (i.e., "skin"), most also have various capacities called **cutaneous senses.** These respond to touch (or pressure) and temperature. Pain is thought by some psychologists to be a cutaneous sense as well, but it is sufficiently different that we will discuss it separately in the next section. The different cutaneous senses combine to produce other sensations like itching and tickling.

Matters would be simple if each of the cutaneous senses had its own special receptor, but so far, researchers have discovered a specialized receptor only for touch: the **pacinian corpuscle** (see Figure 3.13). The skin contains other types of receptor cells, but it appears doubtful that these match up one-to-one with specific cutaneous senses. For instance, we know that the cornea of the eye contains only one type of sensory receptor, yet it is sensitive to touch, cold, *and* pain.

Touch.   The entire surface of our body responds to mechanical pressure, but sensitivity to touch varies greatly, depending on the particular part of the body that is stimulated (see Figure 3.14). Pacinian corpuscles are found in a fatty layer of skin beneath the surface. Each consists of onionlike layers containing dendrites connected to a single axon. When these layers move relative to the axon, the neuron fires. These corpuscles thus respond not to pressure per se but to changes in pressure. Then they fire, telling the brain not only *how much* force has been applied but also *where* it has been applied.

Temperature.   Researchers have long known that there are areas of the skin sensitive to warmth but not to cold, and vice versa (Dallenbach, 1927). This difference in sensitivity means that our sense of temperature is really created from two different processes working in concert. Particular receptors sensitive to warmth or cold have not been located. When exclusively

Figure 3.13

Pacinian Corpuscle

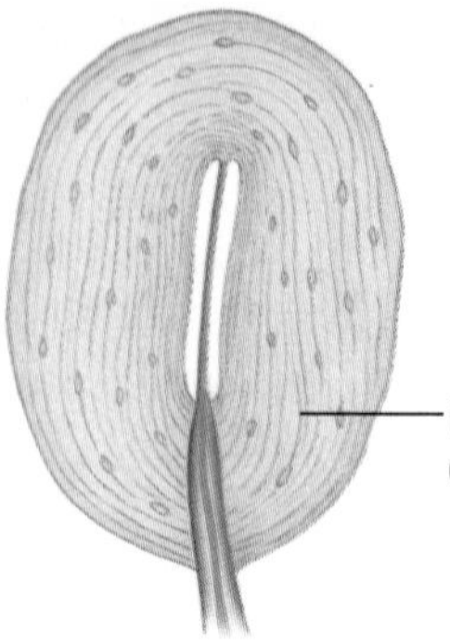

Pacinian corpuscle

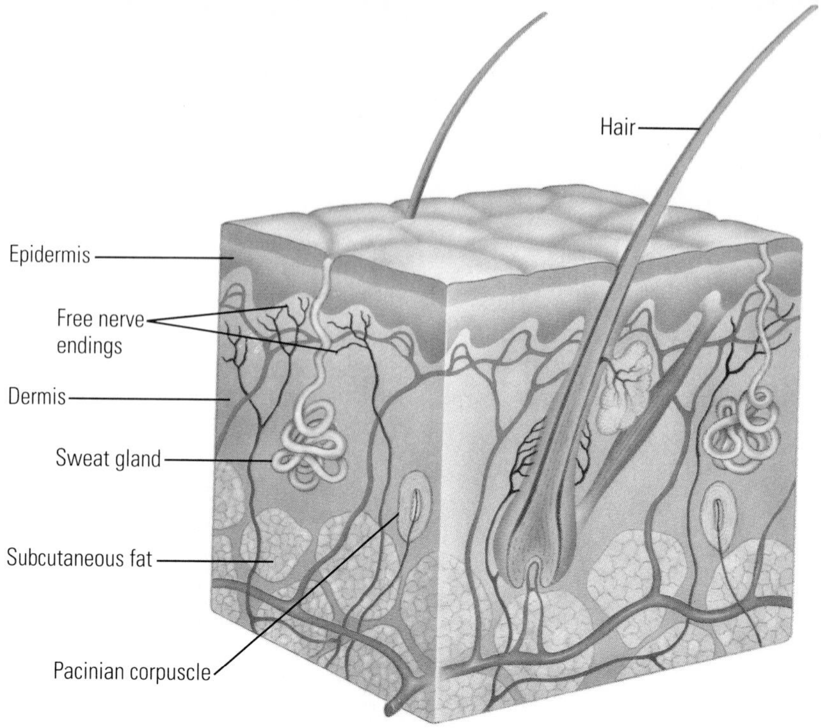

Hair

Epidermis

Free nerve endings

Dermis

Sweat gland

Subcutaneous fat

Pacinian corpuscle

Figure 3.14

Two-point Thresholds for Different Regions of Skin. A *two-point threshold* refers to how far apart two stimuli touching the skin must be before they are felt as separate. This figure shows that considerable variation exists, depending on the region of skin. Fingers show a low two-point threshold; they are highly sensitive. Calves and thighs show a high two-point threshold; they are much less sensitive. This diagram shows the thresholds for an average female. Thresholds for males are similar but on the whole higher (Kenshalo, 1968).

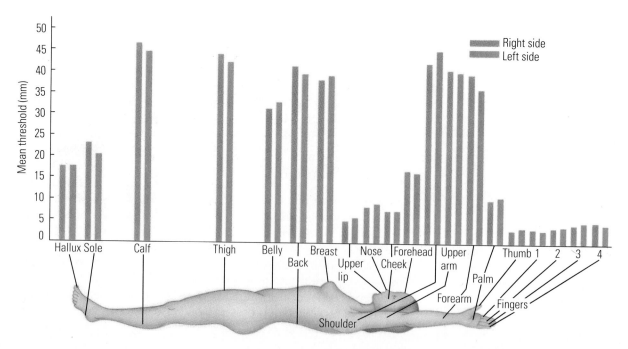

Figure 3.15

A sensation of extreme heat can be produced by the simultaneous sensations of warm and cold. Even when you know that these pipes contain only warm and cold water, you will feel them as quite hot when you take hold of both at the same time.

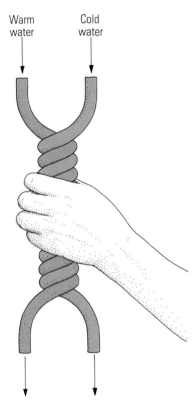

Warm water   Cold water

"warm" or exclusively "cold" parts of the skin are examined, the same sorts of receptors are found, suggesting that it is the *pattern* of stimulation across receptors that is responsible for our sensation of temperature.

Consider the two pipes shown in Figure 3.15. They are wrapped around each other. Through one we can send cold water, and through the other we can send warm water. People asked to take hold of these pipes will give a yell and rapidly withdraw their hand. They experience a sensation of extreme heat, which of course is not the case. But what has happened is that the pipes have simultaneously stimulated sections of the skin sensitive to warmth and to cold, with the net effect being a sensation of great heat.

Pain

You might think that **pain** is classified as a cutaneous sense, what with cut fingers, stubbed toes, and sunburn. Although certain stimuli that touch our skin cause pain, researchers have been unable to find specific pain receptors in the skin. Further, pain can occur via the stimulation of any sensory receptor. Deafening sounds, blinding lights, and overwhelming tastes produce pain just as readily as damaged skin. Although pain usually results from intense stimuli, this is not always true. Compare a pulsating shower with the prick of a pin. The water from the shower produces much more neural activity than the pin, but it is the pin that produces pain, not the shower.

Pain is unpleasant. A *Peanuts* cartoon you may recall has Linus carefully explaining that he dislikes pain because, after all, "it hurts!" But the ability to sense pain can be highly useful. Pain can warn us of danger, both inside and outside of our body, and perhaps we can take steps to remove a threat to our well-being. Sometimes this immediate benefit can backfire in the long run, when it turns into *chronic pain* that lingers in the wake of an injury or illness.

A view of pain that has attracted a great deal of interest is called **gate-control theory** (Melzack, 1973). According to this theory, the nervous system is limited in the amount of sensory information it can handle at a given time. When too much information is present, cells in the spinal cord act as a gate, blocking some signals from going to the brain, while letting others pass. The brain may send messages to the spinal cord to open or close this hypothesized gate, which explains the influence of psychological factors on the experience of pain. Most of us have sustained an injury in the course of an activity in which we were fully engaged, like playing a sport. We didn't even notice the gash in our leg, or our chipped tooth, or our blackened eye until the activity ended. Presumably, the pain gate had been turned off.

Perhaps people troubled by chronic pain have pain gates that stay open too long. Accordingly, we might be able to help them if we can devise a way to close these hypothesized gates. Endorphins, which we discussed in Chapter 2, may be involved in the biological mechanism responsible for the gating (or not) of pain (Basbaum & Fields, 1984). Along these same lines, some psychologists believe that the Chinese practice of acupuncture controls pain because it closes particular gates by stimulating the production of endorphins (Chapman, Wilson, & Gehrig, 1976).

pain
aversive sensation associated with overstimulation of any sensory system

gate-control theory
theory of pain proposing that we experience pain only when hypothesized gates in the spinal cord allow sensory signals to pass to the brain

This Chinese anatomical drawing (ca. 1031) illustrates points of incision for acupuncture.

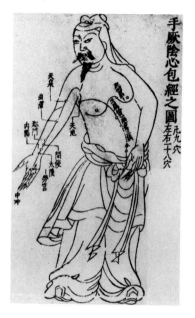

kinesthetic sense
the sensory system that responds to the position and movement of body parts relative to each other

vestibular sense
the sensory system that responds to the position of the body relative to gravity, and is thus responsible for balance

When vestibular organs are overstimulated—for instance, when we spin about—dizziness and nausea may result.

Position Senses

When we move about the world, we need to know more than just the state of the environment. We also need to know what our own bodies are doing. Consider the following:

- Am I moving, or am I stationary?
- Where are my legs in relation to my torso?
- Is my fist clenched or relaxed?

Answers to questions like these are provided by the position senses, of which there are two: the **kinesthetic sense,** which tells us about the movement or position of our muscles and joints, and the **vestibular sense,** which informs us about our balance and just where we are in relationship to gravity.

We may take the kinesthetic sense for granted, but consider the consequences if we didn't have the information it gives us. Oliver Sacks (1984) describes this state of affairs, following an injury to his leg.

> *I had lost my leg.* Again and again I came back to these five words: words which expressed a central truth for me, however preposterous they might sound to anyone else . . . I was now an amputee. And yet not an ordinary amputee. For the leg, objectively, externally, was still there; it had disappeared subjectively, internally. . . . I had lost the inner image, or representation, of the leg. There was a disturbance, an obliteration, of its representation in the brain—of this part of the "body image." (p. 75)

Sacks eventually "regained" his leg, but his account vividly reminds us of the importance of the kinesthetic senses.

Also taken for granted except in its absence is the vestibular sense, which allows us to stay oriented while we move. In people, the vestibular organs are contained in the semicircular canals and vestibular sacs of the inner ear (again see Figure 3.10), which is why ear infections are so disruptive to our balance. The vestibular organs consist of tiny hairs embedded in a jellylike substance. As we begin to move, quickly or slowly, the hairs bend, causing the associated neurons to fire. Once we attain a

particular speed, though, the hairs no longer bend, and the neurons no longer fire. The vestibular organs are stimulated not by speed per se, but by changes in speed or bodily orientation.

When we spin about, we may overstimulate our vestibular organs, resulting in feelings of dizziness and nausea. Our susceptibility to this type of overstimulation varies with age, with children much less likely than adults to get sick from too much spinning. Indeed, many children seem to enjoy the sensations resulting from overstimulation of the vestibular organs, which may be why roller coaster rides are so much more popular with children than adults.

In this chapter, we have discussed the basic processes of sensation, looking at how our sensory receptors translate physical stimulation into biological language that makes sense to our brain. The only way we know the world is through our sensations, and these do not exactly replicate external reality. We continue our discussion of how we come to know the world in the next chapter, which concerns the psychological processes of perception and consciousness.

Summary

Topics of Concern

- Sensation is the process by which environmental energy is transformed into neural impulses sent to the brain. Perception is the process by which we organize and interpret this sensory information.
- Sensation and perception are the first steps involved in gaining knowledge of the world. A long-standing debate concerns whether experience provides all of our knowledge—a position called empiricism, or whether there exist inborn ideas—a position called rationalism.
- Although we may casually speak of sensations as if they exist in the external world, their actual basis is within electrochemical events in our nervous systems. Each sense is stimulated by external energy which produces a neural impulse in a receptor. These impulses give rise to the different qualities of a particular sensory experience.
- A central task of psychologists who study sensation is to identify and explain our various senses.

Psychophysics

- The field of psychophysics attempts to specify the relationship between physical stimuli and psychological experience.
- The minimal amount of external energy needed to create a psychological experience is called the absolute threshold of a sensory system.
- The minimal physical distinction between two stimuli that can be discriminated is called the difference threshold.
- In scaling, psychophysicists determine the mathematical relationship between the amount of a physical stimulus which is present and our psychological experience of it.

Sensory Systems

- The sense of vision responds to the energy contained in light. Light is a wave of radiant energy, and we experience the various properties of these waves as brightness, hue, and saturation.
- The human eye is a complex structure that gathers light and focuses it on nerve cells called photoreceptors. There are two types of photoreceptors. Rods are responsible for vision in dim light. Cones are responsible for vision in bright light.
- Brightness is obviously determined by the intensity of light but also by the level of background illumination and our adaptation to it.
- The sensation of color has been explained over the years by two competing theories. The trichromatic color theory proposes that there are three different types of cones sensitive to red, green, and blue light. The opponent-process color theory proposes that color vision is created by two different systems that detect the balance between red and green light on the one hand and blue and yellow light on the other. Both theories have strong and weak points, and in 1974, Hurvich and Jameson were able to combine the two into a sophisticated and widely accepted account of color vision.
- The sense of hearing responds to the energy contained in sound. Sound comes in waves, and the properties of sound waves produce our experiences of loudness, pitch, and timbre.
- Our ears gather and channel sound waves so that they stimulate sensitive nerve cells in a structure called the cochlea.
- Taste is called a chemical sense, because it responds to chemicals dissolved in water. Taste buds are the receptors sensitive to taste, and these are located mostly on the tongue, but also elsewhere in the mouth. There are four basic tastes: sweet, salty, sour, and bitter. Different taste buds respond primarily to each of these different tastes.
- Smell is also a chemical sense. We smell substances that are carried through the air to receptors located at the top of our nasal cavity. The sense of smell is not well understood. Psychologists have been unable to identify basic categories of odors.
- The cutaneous senses allow us to detect pressure, warmth, and cold on our skin. A pacinian corpuscle is a specialized receptor that detects touch, but the other receptors in our skin do not match up one-to-one with specific sensations.

- Pain is sometimes classified as a cutaneous sense, but it is sufficiently different to warrant its own category. Pain can occur via the stimulation of any sensory receptor. A currently popular view of pain is called gate-control theory. According to this account, the nervous system is limited in the amount of sensory information it can handle. We experience pain only when hypothesized "gates" allow pain signals to go from the spinal cord to the brain.
- The kinesthetic sense tells us about the movement and position of our muscles and joints. The vestibular sense informs us about our balance and our position relative to gravity.

Important Terms and Names

What follows is a list of the core terms and names for this chapter. Your instructor may emphasize other terms as well. Throughout the chapter, glossary terms appear in **boldface** type. They are defined in the text, and each term, along with its definition, is repeated in the margin.

Topics of Concern

sensation/101
empiricism/101
rationalism/101
psychophysics/102
transduction/102

Psychophysics

absolute threshold/103
difference threshold/105   Gustav Fechner/103
just noticeable   Ernst Weber/105
    difference/105
Weber's law/105
signal detection theory/106
Fechner's law/108
adaptation level theory/108

Sensory Systems

light/109
rods and cones/111
trichromatic color
    theory/115
opponent-process color
    theory/116
place theory
    (of hearing)/120
frequency theory (of hearing)/120
chemical senses/121
lock-and-key theory
    (of smell)/123
cutaneous senses/123
pain/125
gate-control theory
    (of pain)/125
kinesthetic sense/126
vestibular sense/126

Thomas Young/115
Hermann von
    Helmholtz/115
Ewald Hering/116
Leo Hurvich and
    Dorothea Jameson/116

Review Questions

1. Sensation translates _____ into neural activity.
   a. consciousness
   b. environmental energy
   c. hormonal messages
   d. perception
   Common to all sensory systems is sensitivity to a particular source of environmental energy—light, sound, pressure, and so on./101

2. If someone believes that newborn babies must learn how to organize their sensations into meaningful perceptions, we can describe her as a(n)
   a. developmentalist.
   b. empiricist.
   c. psychophysicist.
   d. rationalist.
   Rationalists believe that people are born with innate ideas, including knowledge of how to organize sensory experience. Empiricists, in contrast, believe that at birth people's minds are blank slates./101

3. A jnd is another term for a(n)
   a. absolute threshold.
   b. difference threshold.
   c. juvenile delinquent.
   d. signal detection.
   e. Weber fraction.
   A difference threshold is the minimal distinction between two stimuli that can be discriminated. It is sometimes called a "just noticeable difference."/105

4. Signal detection procedures correct for
   a. motivational differences.
   b. random error.
   c. response biases.
   d. stimulus fluctuations.
   Using signal detection procedures, researchers can separate a subject's actual sensitivity to a stimulus from his bias to respond one way or another./106

5. According to Fechner's law, we notice changes in stimulus intensity in accordance with
   a. how much the stimulus actually changes.
   b. how much of the stimulus is present in the first place.
   c. our attention to the stimulus.
   d. a and b.
   Attention is an important factor, to be sure, but Fechner's law specifically proposes that changes in stimulus intensity are jointly determined by how much the stimulus actually changes and by how much of the stimulus is initially present. The more intense a stimulus, the more it must change for us to notice any difference./108

6. We experience the amplitude of light as _____, the wavelength of light as _____, and the purity of light as _____.
   a. brightness; hue (color); saturation
   b. brightness; saturation; hue (color)
   c. hue (color); saturation; brightness
   d. saturation; brightness; hue (color)
   e. saturation; hue (color); brightness
   Vision is the sensory system that responds to light energy. Different characteristics of light waves determine different aspects of visual experience: the height of light waves registers psychologically as brightness, the distance between peaks of successive waves registers as color, and the degree to which light is dominated by a single wavelength registers as purity./109

7. The photoreceptors responsible for color vision are _____. They work best in _____ light.
   a. cones; bright
   b. cones; dim
   c. Pacinian corpuscles; constant
   d. rods; bright
   e. rods; dim
   Cones—not rods—are responsible for color vision. And Pacinian corpuscles are involved in touch! Cones require more illumination to function than do rods, and hence work best in bright light./112

8. Currently favored as an explanation of color vision is
   a. trichromatic theory.
   b. opponent-process theory.
   c. neither a nor b.
   d. a and b in combination.
   Over the centuries, two competing theories of color vision existed, each with its own strengths and weaknesses as explanations. In 1974, Hurvich and Jameson elegantly combined the two into what is now the most generally accepted theory./116.

9. The chemical senses include _____ and _____ .
   a. hearing; vision
   b. perception; altered consciousness
   c. taste; smell
   d. touch; temperature
   Chemical senses respond to substances dissolved in water, and so they include taste and smell, which often work in concert./121

10. For which of these senses have no specialized receptors been discovered?
    a. hearing
    b. pain
    c. smell
    d. taste
    e. vision
    Pain can occur via the stimulation of any sensory receptor. Usually pain results from intense stimulation, although this is not always true./125

Psychologists value illusions for what they reveal about
everyday perceptions.

Chapter Four

Perception and Consciousness

Topics of Concern

With some frequency, we hear the tragic stories of people who became blind through illness or accident. Although less frequent, there are also stories of individuals who were born without sight but then as adults gained the ability to see. These latter individuals have intrigued psychologists because they allow a unique glimpse, so to speak, at how people first come to see the world. Obviously every infant goes through this process, but infants cannot tell us what they are seeing. An adult seeing for the first time can inform a researcher whether the ability to see is present from the very first or whether it develops slowly.

S. B. was one such individual who was extensively studied by psychologists interested in vision (Gregory, 1966). Up until age fifty-two, S. B. was not able to see at all. However, he was active and fearless in his approach to the world. He bicycled. He built things. He always tried to imagine how the objects that he touched might look.

At age fifty-two, a corneal graft operation was performed, allowing S. B. to see for the first time in his life. He initially saw only blurs. Objects did not take form for him. But in a few days, he was able to see objects as discrete shapes. He explored the world with great interest. He soon had little difficulty recognizing objects by sight, as long as he had previously touched them. For example, he could readily tell time, because while blind, he had developed the habit of carrying a pocket watch with no crystal; he would feel where the hands were.

Other visual tasks proved more difficult. He had particular trouble perceiving distance. Looking down from a window some 30 or 40 feet above the ground, he thought he could lower himself down by his hands! He never learned to read by sight, although he almost immediately recognized capital letters and numbers. Again, the crucial factor seemed to be his previous experience with these symbols via touch. In the school for the blind that he had attended, prior to learning to read Braille, he had learned to recognize by touch the shapes of capital letters and numbers.

You might think that S. B. was ecstatic about his new eyesight, but this was not the case. Shortly after the operation, S. B. became depressed and much less active, and he stayed this way until his death 3 years later. Depression can be a common reaction among those who gain sight as adults, perhaps because they begin to appreciate how many experiences and opportunities had heretofore been denied them (Gregory, 1966). Some individuals even revert to living in the dark. S. B. would often sit alone in the shadows of the evening, not turning on a light even though one was available.

The story of S. B. provides an introduction to this chapter. As you learned in the last chapter, our sensory organs react to incoming energy, translating it into information that is then passed on to the brain. But what organizes this information into a coherent whole? What allows us to be aware of our sensory experience? Answers to these questions are the subject of this chapter.

The process by which we organize and interpret sensory information is called **perception.** Where psychologists interested in sensation ask, "How bright is that object?" those interested in perception ask a slightly different question: "And what was that object anyway?" (Coren, Porac, & Ward, 1984)

Consciousness is often defined as awareness of our environment and our mental processes. Precise definition can be elusive, but consciousness includes our awareness of particular sensations and perceptions, as well as hopes, fears, and dreams, to name but a few other entities that dance through the mind. Without consciousness, S. B. would not have *known* what he was or was not seeing. He would not be able to comment on discrepancies between what he saw and what he thought. For instance, when S. B. first saw the moon in the sky, he said that it did not look right! He had always imagined that the quarter moon, which is what he happened to see, would look like a quarter piece of cake. The fact that it did not have this shape bothered him, illustrating the role of consciousness in detecting discrepancies in experience.

Our experience and knowledge of the world are in large part shaped by our sensory perceptions. How would you describe a sunset to a blind person?

The Structure of Perception

Remember the discussion of the disagreement between rationalists and empiricists concerning how we come to know the world (Chapter 3). Despite this disagreement, both agree that our conscious experience has a structure to it. We perceive forms, detect movement, and discern patterns. When and how does structure come into the sensation → perception process? Wilhelm Wundt, the first psychologist, assumed that consciousness is composed of elements: particular sensations, feelings, and the like (Chapter 1). These elements are first apprehended individually and only later put together. Gestalt psychologists disagreed, arguing that experience is inherently organized. The meaningfulness of our perceptions is not something imposed upon sensory experience. Rather, organization is present all along.

Obviously, this debate can become quite complex. It's difficult to state unequivocally the way in which we organize our conscious experience. Consider the example of S. B. He was able to make immediate sense of visual sensations if he had previously touched the objects in question. If not, he seemed unable to merge his sensations into a coherent whole. In one instance, he was shown a woodworking tool in a glass case at a museum. He didn't understand what he saw. Then it was taken out of the case. He closed his eyes, touched it, and then exclaimed, "Now . . . I can see." The way we perceive the world reflects a complex interaction among environmental stimulation, the nervous system, and past experiences.

How Can We Distinguish Sensation, Perception, and Consciousness?

Psychologists interested in sensation, perception, and consciousness puzzle over how to distinguish these important

perception
the process by which we organize and interpret sensory information

consciousness
our awareness of our environment and our mental processes

information processing
an approach to sensation, perception, and consciousness that stresses the sequence by which information is transformed ("processed") from environmental stimuli into psychological terms

activities from one another, and at the same time to explain how they are related. Is an overall theory possible?

Various metaphors have been entertained over the years, in the hope that these comparisons would clarify these mental activities. Philosopher John Locke (1632–1704), for instance, proposed that our mind is a blank tablet upon which experience writes. Sensation and perception are the means by which this writing occurs. Consciousness, according to Locke's metaphor, is the monitor who stares over our shoulder and inspects what has been written. Other comparisons suggest a camera, a boat captain, a photocopier, an expert jury, a filter, a detective, a novelist, and of course a computer. Note that some of these metaphors, specifically those with an executive who oversees matters, can accommodate consciousness better than others.

Sensation, perception, and consciousness can be difficult to distinguish. When does sensation end and perception begin? And when does perception stop and consciousness start? These questions may not make sense because they divide mental activity into discrete events. Many psychologists therefore dispense altogether with firm distinctions among sensation, perception, and consciousness, grouping them together as **information processing** (Cutting, 1987). This approach stresses the sequence by which information is transformed or "processed" from environmental stimuli into psychological terms. The key term is *process,* an ongoing sequence. One may describe mental activity in terms of its relative place in the sequence, but one does not divide the sequence into separate stages. However, for the sake of simplicity, we will first discuss perception and then later consciousness.

Perception

Chapter 3 dealt with sensation and sensory organs, so let's now turn to how sensations are organized into meaningful experiences. How do we organize certain sensations so that we perceive the poster that hangs on our wall, or others so that we perceive a symphony? The term *perception* is sometimes used to describe the *process* by which sensations are organized. It is sometimes used as well to refer to the *product* of this organization, to the creation of an internal representation of some external stimulus. Research by psychologists interested in perception converges to a particular characterization of the process and product, stressing that perception is selective, coherent, creative, and personal. Let us see what each of these means.

Perception Is Selective

attention
processes responsible for the selectiveness of perception

orientation
the process by which we position our sense organs so that they can best receive stimulation

divided attention
ability to attend to different stimuli at the same time

To say that our perception is selective means that we cannot simultaneously attend to all the stimuli occurring around us. In a crowded restaurant, you listen carefully to what your friend across the table is saying, and you listen not at all to conversations at other tables. On a bus, you look out the window to see how close you are to your intended stop; you do not notice the clothing or cologne that your fellow bus passengers might be wearing. In a library, you stare at the notes you have taken for tomorrow's exam, and you concern yourself not at all with the other books and papers you have brought with you. In all of these examples, you accord some stimuli more weight than other stimuli. The selectiveness of perception is one of its fundamental characteristics, and the processes responsible for this selectiveness are collectively called **attention.**

Among the phenomena of attention that psychologists have studied is **orientation.** Orientation refers to the positioning of our sense organs so they can best receive environmental stimulation. We stare at those objects we want to see. We stick our nose over objects we wish to smell. We place our ears close to objects we wish to hear. These are all examples of overt orientation. Psychologists who study perception are also concerned with covert orientation. This phenomenon occurs when we direct our attention to particular stimuli without physically moving our sense organs (Posner, 1978). "Don't be obvious, but check out who just walked in the room." Covert orientation implies that attention does not occur solely through our senses, but also involves cognitive processes.

Divided attention describes another familiar phenomenon—our ability to attend to different stimuli at the same time. As we learn to perform a particular task, we need to attend to its details less and less. Performance becomes automatized, and our attention can be deployed elsewhere. Consider driving a car. When you first slid behind the wheel of an automobile, the amount of stimulation overwhelmed you. So many things competed for your attention: steering wheel, brakes, accelerator, turn signal, speedometer, pedestrians, school crossings, other cars. Is it surprising that a novice driver may overlook the gas gauge? With experience, we can do all sorts of things while driving, including listening to the radio, carrying on a conversation, watching a child in the back seat, even watching the gas gauge.

Selective perception allows us to give some stimuli more weight than others, whether we are having an animated conversation or studying quietly in the library.

As a task becomes more routine—driving an automobile, for example—we are better able to sort out the different stimuli involved that require our attention.

selective attention
ignoring some information while paying attention to other information

bottleneck model
theory of attention that proposes a biological restriction on the amount of sensory stimulation that can be noticed

capacity model
theory of attention that proposes a psychological limit, determined by available effort, on the amount of sensory stimulation that can be noticed

Another topic of interest concerns **selective attention** (Johnston & Dark, 1986). We can tune in some information while tuning out other information. "Tuned in" information is obviously front and center in our conscious experience, but what about the "tuned out" information? One way researchers answer this question is through studies of *shadowing*. They place headphones on a subject and deliver one message to the right ear and another message to the left ear. The subject is asked to repeat one of the messages out loud (i.e., to "shadow" the message), under the assumption that he will therefore pay more attention to it. The typical finding is that subjects completely shut out the nonshadowed message. When asked later to recall its content, a subject can report nothing. He may not even know what language was spoken (Cherry, 1953). However, other studies suggest that selective attention is more complex than this demonstration implies. If the nonshadowed message contains the subject's name, the subject indeed notices it at least some of the time (Moray, 1959).

Currently, there are two different, yet equally popular, explanations of attention. First of all, there is the **bottleneck model,** so named because it hypothesizes a biological restriction on the amount of sensory stimulation that we can attend to (Broadbent, 1958). Like cars in a traffic jam, sensory information piles up. Only a small amount can make it through the bottleneck at any one time. In paying attention to a conversation, then, you allow only words from your friend to come through the bottleneck. Unlike cars in a traffic jam, though, sensory information that does not get through the bottleneck quickly enough is lost, forgotten, or replaced.

Second, there is the **capacity model** of attention, which attributes the selectivity of perception not to biological restrictions but to psychological ones (Kahneman, 1973). According to this model, attention requires effort, and we have only so much effort to give. Once this limit is reached, we can no longer attend to other stimuli. However, if we learn more efficient strategies for processing information, we can attend to an increasing number of stimuli. To return once more to you and your friend in the restaurant, the capacity model implies that with practice, you will be able to attend both to what your friend is saying and to what is going on at adjacent tables. The bottleneck model, in contrast, argues for a necessary limitation on the amount of information to which you can attend.

Investigations of orientation, divided attention, and selective attention suggest that neither the bottleneck model nor the capacity model fully accounts for all aspects of attention. Some combination of the two is needed, one that recognizes both structural and processing limitations. Here we see the complexity of perception and its dependence on both biological and psychological factors—on the processes proposed by the rationalists *and* the empiricists. Again, we encounter another facet of the nature—nurture controversy, which, as always, requires a complex resolution.

Perception Is Coherent

figure-ground relationship
the tendency to organize perception in terms of a coherent object—the figure—within a context—the ground

To say that our perception is coherent is to say that conscious experiences are meaningful wholes. Remember S. B., whose story began this chapter? When he first gained sight, all he saw were blurs. But he quickly came to see the world in terms of discrete (coherent) objects. The exact means of achieving coherence of perception was at the center of the debate between the structuralists and the gestalt psychologists (Chapter 1).

According to the structuralists, experience is composed of separate elements combined into larger wholes. The gestalt psychologists argued instead that experience is inherently structured. Remember that the word *gestalt* itself means pattern or whole (p. 11). Yet both the structuralists and gestalt psychologists agreed that everyday experience is indeed coherent. Let's discuss in this section several examples of the coherence of perception, starting with our perception of forms.

Form Perception.　To recognize an object, we use the principle of the **figure-ground relationship.** We group stimuli together into a unified form called a figure and distinguish the figure from the other stimuli present, referred to as the ground. All perception of forms entails the organization of figures against grounds, a fact strikingly illustrated by ambiguous pic-

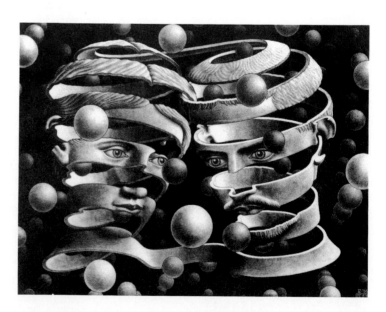

The principles of form perception play a vital role in the viewer's experience of the work of artists such as M. C. Escher.

Figure 4.1
Figure-Ground Reversal. You can see this picture either as an old woman or as a young woman, but at any given moment, you see but one of them.

tures like the one in Figure 4.1. You can see this either as an old woman or as a young woman. Your perception may flip back and forth rapidly, but regardless, at any given moment you see only one figure against one ground.

Psychologists have specified a number of principles that describe how we organize stimuli into coherent forms. Because these principles were first proposed by the early gestalt psychologists, they are called **gestalt organizational principles** of form perception. Examples are shown in Figure 4.2. These come from the realm of our visual perception, but analogous principles hold for other senses as well.

Proximity is our tendency to group together stimuli that are near each other. In the upper left of Figure 4.2, we see not six lines but three pairs of lines, organized by the principle of proximity. *Similarity* refers to our tendency to group together stimuli that are similar in size, shape, color, or form. Moving to the right in Figure 4.2, we next see not vertical columns or varied shapes, but horizontal rows of dots and dashes, organized by the principle of similarity. When an object has gaps, like the one in the lower left of the figure, we fill them in, according to the principle of *closure*. What results in this case is a tiger. The tendency to smooth out irregularities in an object also shows *continuity,* as shown in the lower right of the figure. These and similar principles work together to create good gestalts (Chapter 1).

Distance Perception. In everyday life, we judge distances all the time, usually with great accuracy. How far away is that approaching truck? How far away is that fork wrapped in spaghetti? How far away is that wastebasket at which we are tossing wads of paper? Explaining just how people go about perceiving distance has been a major concern of psychologists (Gibson, 1988). Therefore, let's discuss distance perception as an important example of the coherence of perception.

Remember that vision involves the projection of images onto the retina, where they stimulate neurons leading to the brain. These images contain no information about distance or depth. Indeed, the projections of objects at differing distances might well look exactly the same, if the objects are of appropriately different sizes (see Figure 4.3). Why, then, do we have no trouble telling how far away an object is, whether it is under our nose, just beyond our reach, or somewhere over the rainbow?

Figure 4.2
Gestalt Principles of Form Perception. These exemplify the principles of proximity, similarity, closure, and continuity.

Proximity

Similarity

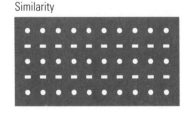

Closure

Continuity

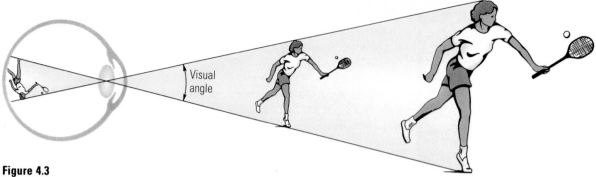

Figure 4.3
Retinal Size. Objects of different size may have the same retinal image, depending on their distance.

ecological approach
Gibson's theory of visual perception that stresses the role of the actual environment in determining what is seen

Psychologist James Gibson (1979) believes that the answer partly lies within our very makeup: Depth perception is innate. His theory, called the **ecological approach,** emphasizes the actual environment that people perceive. So, we perceive not just an object but also its background, which contains a wealth of information, including clues about depth. Backgrounds may be composed of elements that produce a particular texture. Because the texture of an environment becomes denser with distance, the *texture gradient* provides us with direct information about distance. Figure 4.4 shows sand in the desert, and you can see how the ridges appear closer together as distance increases. According to Gibson, someone does not have to learn to perceive distance in the desert. The relevant information is present all along, and our perceptual apparatus is sensitive to it.

At the beginning of the chapter, we learned that S. B. had difficulty perceiving distances. Does this mean that Gibson is wrong? Not necessarily, because we would want to test S. B. in situations where appropriate distance clues were present. Perhaps S. B. misjudged the distance to the ground when looking straight down from an upstairs window because he saw no texture gradient.

Supporting Gibson's view of distance perception are studies using what is known as a *visual cliff* (Gibson & Walk, 1960). Here a transparent surface has underneath it two patterns, one suggesting greater distance than the other (Figure 4.5). Very young infants and animals show extreme reluctance to crawl from the "shallow" to the "deep" side of the surface, suggesting that depth perception has an innate component.

Gibson's approach to perception, with its emphasis on the structured environment, stands in sharp contrast to approaches that emphasize the role of experience in distance perception. Perhaps depth perception is a gradually acquired ability that results from learned associations. When we see people, we see retinal images of various sizes. We learn that in some cases we can reach out and touch them, whereas in other cases we cannot. In the former cases, they are close; in the latter, they are far away. For our visual world to make sense, we need to take into account factors other than retinal images. Here, it is touch. Needless to say, this is a simplified example, because our different senses can and do provide many possible clues that we can learn to associate with distance (Chapter 3).

In sum, our visual perceptions typically have depth to them, and different explanations of depth perception emphasize nature or nurture as responsible. Some combination of these explanations is probably the most

Figure 4.4
Texture Gradient. Ridges of sand in the desert appear closer
together the farther away they are from the viewer.

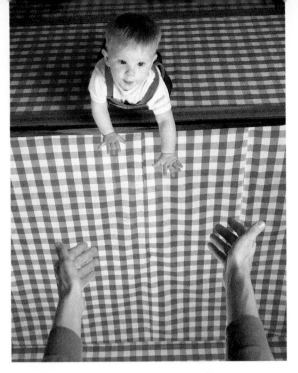

Figure 4.5
Visual Cliff. Under the transparent surface are two patterns,
one suggesting greater distance than the other. Very young
infants and animals are reluctant to crawl from the "shallow"
to the "deep" side.

reasonable. But whatever the correct account, depth perception is a good
example of the more general point that perception has a structure to it; it
is coherent.

Perception Is Creative

To say that our perception is creative means that it is not a literal version
of reality but rather is something we create. Among the raw ingredients of
perception are of course our sensations, which as we have seen bear a
sensible relationship to external stimuli (Chapter 3). However, perception
is also determined by the habits, tendencies, and styles we bring to bear
on our sensations.

Visual Constancies.   Consider the following familiar experiences:

- You see a friend at the top of a staircase. As he walks down the stairs,
  his size remains constant. This becomes intriguing when you appreciate that the light stimulating your retina is constantly changing. In
  particular, the size of the retinal image constantly changes. Why don't
  you experience a change in your friend's size?
- You are reading this book while slouching in a chair. Although the
  book tilts away from you, it still maintains its rectangular shape. Again,
  this is intriguing. The retinal image changes from rectangular to trap-
  ezoidal as the book tilts. Why don't you experience a change in the
  book's shape?

Because we learn to use distance in judging the size of familiar objects, we fail to see that the two smaller men in this photograph are exactly the same size.

- You have switched to a new laundry detergent, and your pleasure knows no bounds because your clothes have never looked so bright! You walk down the street admiring the brightness of the sleeve of your favorite shirt. You pass beneath a large tree that shades the entire sidewalk, you, and your sleeve. You continue to admire how bright your clothes have become. Yet the intensity of light reflected by your shirt was greatly reduced when you walked under the tree. The amount of light stimulating your retina has changed. Why don't you experience a change in your shirt's brightness?

visual constancies

the tendencies for our perception of the size, shape, and brightness of objects to stay the same even as the moment-to-moment stimulation from the environment changes

These examples illustrate **visual constancies** of size, shape, and brightness, respectively.

Visual constancies illustrate what we mean when we say that perception is creative. As physical stimulation changes, our perceptual experiences remain constant. This is certainly useful for us, because the world appears stable, even though our moment-to-moment stimulation fluctuates wildly. We somehow take into account factors besides the size or shape or intensity of retinal stimulation, but what does "take into account" mean (Wallach, 1987)?

The answer depends on the particular type of constancy. For instance, brightness constancy appears built-in, produced by the physiological phenomenon of *brightness contrast*. Our eyes are particularly sensitive to the edges of objects, which makes evolutionary sense. Edges mark the boundaries of things—good, bad, or ugly—and thereby make it possible for us to detect them. Indeed, research with infants shows that they are particularly likely to examine the edges of objects, ignoring the interior (Maurer & Salapatek, 1976).

Sensitivity to edges is produced by the fact that nerve cells in the retina, when stimulated, also inhibit adjacent nerve cells. Bright objects thus seem brighter than adjacent objects (because the nerve cells stimulated by the adjacent objects have been inhibited), while dim objects seem dimmer.

Do you see how brightness contrast explains brightness constancy? Remember the example of walking under a shady tree and seeing your bright shirt sleeve stay bright. The light reflected by your sleeve indeed decreased as you walked under the tree, but so did the light reflected by everything else—your hand, the sidewalk, and so on. Absolute levels of retinal excitation and inhibition changed as you walked into the shade, but their particular balance stayed the same. As a result, brightness remained constant.

Size constancy and shape constancy, however, may be produced in part by learning (Coren et al., 1984). We saw in the previous section how people can learn to use the apparent size of objects to judge their distance. They can also learn to use the apparent distance of objects to judge their size.

The instructions given to subjects in experiments can actually affect how they experience stimuli. They can be told either to report the size and shape of objects or to report the size and shape of the retinal image produced by these objects. In the latter case, size and shape constancy is reduced! Although a subject cannot completely eliminate these constancies, the fact that one can exert some control over them suggests a degree of learning.

illusions

phenomena in which our perceptions of objects are at odds with their actual characteristics

Illusions. Perception psychologists have always been particularly interested in **illusions,** phenomena where our perception of an object is at odds with its actual characteristics. The value of illusions is what they reveal about everyday perceptions, where the role of our creative tendencies may be much less obvious. Let's discuss some of the illusions described by perception psychologists and see the lessons they have to teach.

If you recall from Chapter 1, gestalt psychology began with a particular illusion—apparent movement of objects that were in reality stationary— that was not readily accommodated within Wundt's system of psychology. Apparent movement takes various forms. The *phi phenomenon,* for example, refers to the fact that stationary objects in different locations are seen to move if they flash at the appropriate interval (about four to five times per second). Figure 4.6 illustrates how the phi phenomenon was originally demonstrated by Max Wertheimer (1912).

Another type of apparent movement is the *autokinetic effect,* the tendency of a single point of light in a darkened room to appear to move, even when it is stationary. The autokinetic effect is caused by slight movements of our eyes while we fixate on the point of light (Matin & MacKinnon, 1964). Because we lack a context in which to locate the light, we are not aware that our eyes are moving. Instead, we attribute the movement to the light itself. The significance of apparent movement is its demonstration of the gestalt truism that the whole (perception) is not the same as its parts (sensations). That is, perception is creative.

Figure 4.6
The Phi Phenomenon

Line flashes on and off at left

Darkness lasting 50 msec

Line flashes on and off at right

Movement perceived from left to right

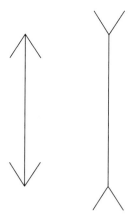

Figure 4.7
The Müller-Lyer Illusion. The two lines above are actually the same length. One possible explanation of this illusion is that the left line looks like the outside corner of a room and that the right line looks like the inside corner. We treat the "outside" as closer than the "inside" and hence see it as shorter.

Look at Figure 4.7. Which line is longer? Most people will say the one on the right, although in fact both lines are the same length. Be skeptical and measure them for yourself. This is the *Müller-Lyer illusion.* One explanation for this illusion is that it is a carryover from our attempts in everyday life to perceive the size of objects while taking into account their distance from us (Gregory, 1966). So, the left line looks like the outside corner of a room, whereas the right line looks like the inside corner of a room (see photos above). Because inside corners tend to be further away from us than outside corners, we compensate in the Müller-Lyer illusion by perceiving the right line as longer than it really is. By the way, this particular explanation has been challenged by some researchers, and no fully acceptable account of the Müller-Lyer illusion yet exists (Robinson, 1972). Regardless, it remains a good example of how we create our perceptions.

One of the more striking illusions was first devised by researcher Adelbert Ames (1951), and so it is called the *Ames room* (see top of Figure 4.8). Although we see its walls, floors, and ceiling as if they were rectangularly shaped, they are not. Accordingly, the sizes of objects in the room appear greatly distorted because we overlook the distortion of the room itself, which serves as their background (see bottom of Figure 4.8). Even though we *know* that the people standing in the Ames room cannot be of such discrepant heights, our tendency to see the room itself as rectangular leads us into this illusion. The Ames room shows that our perception of objects is determined not simply by the objects themselves, but also by the context in which they appear. Further, we try to make objects fit sensibly within this context.

Among the illusions studied by perception psychologists are what can be called *impossible figures* (see Figure 4.9). We perceive these as coherent wholes at first, but when we later trace out the patterns involved,

Figure 4.8
The Ames Room

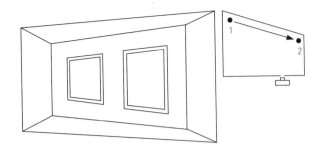

we see that they defy reality. These illusions apparently stem from our habit of treating two-dimensional pictures as representations of three-dimensional objects, using what seem to be distance cues but really are not (Gregory, 1986). Our tendencies to do this are so ingrained that we persist even when we know that our perceptions are impossible. Most people enjoy the discrepancy inherent in such illusions, as shown by the continued popularity of the artist M. C. Escher, whose prints abound with impossible figures.

The illusions just described are visual ones, because they are well-documented and easy to present in a book. However, we also experience illusions with our other senses (Gregory, 1986), as shown previously in Figure 3.15 (p. 124), where warm and cold sensations combine to create the experience of great heat. One obvious lesson from all these illusions is that perception is not a passive process. We actively perceive, bringing to bear on our sensations various habits, tendencies, and styles that create a coherent experience. These may be inherited or learned. Most of the time, our resulting perceptions allow us to navigate the real world with no difficulty. Illusions represent exceptions and thus have been instructive to psychologists interested in perception.

Figure 4.9
Impossible Figures

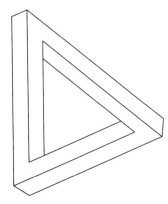

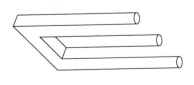

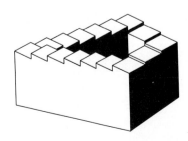

Perception is influenced by our personal experiences as well as our state of mind.

Perception Is Personal

To say that our perception is personal is to say that we see the world from our own point of view. In the obvious sense, this is trivial. Of course we see with our own eyes, hear with our own ears, and so on. But there are two less obvious ways in which perception is personal, and these are worth discussing.

First, perceptual habits and styles develop over time (Aslin & Smith, 1988). Certain ways of structuring sensations are indeed built into our nervous system (Hubel & Wiesel, 1962, 1979), but others show the influence of experience. This means that perception reflects the life history of the perceiver. For example, as children get older, they become increasingly able to recognize patterns. Figure 4.10 is an arrangement of fruits and vegetables in the shape of a bird (Elkind, 1978b). Four-year-old children describe this figure only in terms of its parts: carrots, cherries, a pear, and a tomato. Seven-year-old children see both the parts and the whole: fruits and carrots and a bird. Nine-year-old children give the most integrated response: a bird made of fruits and vegetables. Stop and imagine, if you can, a world of parts but not wholes. We all once lived in such a world, where partridges and pear trees both exist yet have no relationship to one another.

Another example of how perception changes in accord with one's personal experiences comes from the field of sports psychology. Optometrist William Harrison describes the following case:

> Jim Simons, the PGA golfer, came to me in 1977 with a concentration problem. His vision was fine when he was sitting in an exam chair, but it was disturbed when he was slightly off-balance—standing on a sidehill lie or even putting in a strong wind.
>
> My drills taught his visual system to function while he was off-balance. He read an eye chart while bouncing on a trampoline. He shifted focus among different targets while balancing . . . on a beam. (Schechter, 1987, p. 15)

Figure 4.10
Vegetable-Fruit-Bird

There was nothing wrong with this golfer's eyes. His problem was with how he made sense of his visual sensations. Dr. Harrison's other clients have included baseball player George Brett and race car driver Roberto Guerrero. In these and many other cases, he taught them to perceive differently . . . and better. Perhaps someday perceptual training will be commonplace, yet another way, along with eyeglasses, contact lenses, and surgery, for people to correct their vision problems.

The second way in which perception is personal is that our various psychological states influence what and how we perceive. Our motives and personality characteristics may influence what we perceive. And we often perceive simply what we expect to perceive. For example, a **perceptual set** (or **mental set**) is a predisposition to perceive a particular stimulus in a particular context. Perceptual sets can be created in different ways. Simple instructions are effective, for instance. If someone told you to look at the "young woman" in Figure 4.1, you would be much more likely to see her instead of the "old woman" also present. Perceptual sets may result from habitual experiences, prevailing needs like hunger or thirst, personality characteristics, or social pressures. Regardless, we perceive the world in ways that have meaning to us.

We've discussed perception in terms of four important characteristics. Perception is selective, coherent, creative, and personal. It is usually distinguished from sensation on the basis of such characteristics, all of which underscore the organization and meaning inherent in perception. In the final section of this chapter, we will consider yet another important mental activity, consciousness.

Consciousness

As mentioned in the beginning of the chapter, we can define consciousness as our awareness of our environment and our mental processes. One of the most obvious characteristics of consciousness is that it is experienced in different forms. These are usually called **states of consciousness** because we experience them as qualitatively different. Indeed, within any given day, all of us show dramatic changes in our states of consciousness. In the morning, we may linger in bed and daydream. Our fantasies are interrupted when we happen to glance at the clock and remember that we have an important appointment in just 1 hour. Then we jump out of bed and start to get ready. We have a mental checklist that we consult. What do we need to take with us this morning?

Right before we leave, we stop to heat up yesterday's coffee. We quickly drink a large cup, and soon we experience the familiar results of caffeine. Not the least of these is feeling more awake and alert. We'll be sharp during our appointment, that's for sure. The only problem will be to keep from talking too much!

At the end of the day, we return home, tired and drained. This is no way to feel. The day went well, and there is the evening in front of us. Some coffee is still left over. Is it worth heating up again? We decide not, knowing from experience that a cup of coffee at this time means we won't sleep well at night. Instead, we decide to sit still and breathe deeply and slowly. We clear our minds. In 10 minutes, we feel differently, alert yet calm. We spend the evening writing letters to several old friends. That night we sleep well, and we dream about these friends.

perceptual set (mental set)
a predisposition to perceive a particular stimulus in a particular context

states of consciousness
forms of consciousness experienced as qualitatively different from one another

Some states of consciousness are commonplace, as in our example, and others may be quite exotic. In this section, we will discuss various types of consciousness of interest to psychologists. Then we will explore the ways that people deliberately alter consciousness, using meditation, hypnosis, or drugs.

Normal Waking Consciousness

Ornstein (1988) calls consciousness the front page of the mind. His newspaper metaphor is useful, because we represent in consciousness what is new, surprising, and important to us. Consciousness is *our* front page, not that of anyone else. In the consciousness that characterizes normal wakefulness, we monitor our ongoing experience. When something notable occurs, we bring it front and center into awareness. Hold the presses!

Appreciate that normal waking consciousness is characterized by selective attention (p. 137). Many of the tasks we perform during the day have become automatic, and so we perform them without full awareness. Consider driving a car down an interstate highway. You drive perfectly well, but you are not attending to everything going on about you. Oops, watch out! There's an abandoned car on the shoulder up ahead. Suddenly your consciousness is engaged. There is a problem to be solved. You check your rearview mirror, put on your turn signal, and swing into the passing lane.

Psychologists point out that there are two ways in which we go about our normal waking activities (Logan, 1980). In **automatic processing,** we initiate an activity and simply carry it out. Tying shoes, locking a car door, or dialing a telephone are for most people examples of automatic processing. In **controlled processing,** we initiate an activity and then make a conscious effort to direct our behavior. Activities that are unusual, difficult, or important are often good examples of controlled processing. Remember the first time you used a typewriter or the first time you danced in public. You scrutinized every aspect of what you did as you did it.

The distinction between automatic and controlled processing is not always perfectly clear, because many of our activities represent a combination of the two. When you drive your old car in a new neighborhood, your use of the gas pedal and the brake represents automatic processing; the route you devise represents controlled processing. In many cases, automatic processing begins as controlled processing. As behaviors become familiar, their performance becomes automatized, allowing us to pay conscious attention to new demands made upon us.

Consciousness has both costs and benefits. When we are aware of our activities, we often can

- select particularly useful information for our attention,
- set priorities for our behavior,
- guide our actions,
- detect discrepancies in our experience, and
- resolve these discrepancies.

These important functions of consciousness suggest why human beings have evolved the capacity for awareness (Ornstein, 1973, 1977). Think of the selective advantage given to our ancestors who had this capacity over their contemporaries who lacked it.

automatic processing
the approach to normal waking activities in which we initiate an activity and carry it out without conscious direction

controlled processing
the approach to normal waking activities in which we initiate an activity and then make a conscious effort to direct our behavior

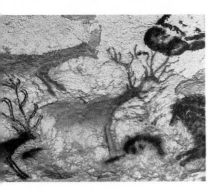

Cave paintings such as these reveal that prehistoric human beings had developed a keen awareness of their environment over 10,000 years ago.

At the same time, we have limits on our conscious attention. When we are conscious of one aspect of our behavior, we may be oblivious to others. Also, consciousness sometimes impairs our ongoing behavior, which means that as our capacity for consciousness evolved, so, too, did a corresponding capacity to turn it off. This is why automatic processing is just as important to our survival as controlled processing. In normal waking consciousness, we constantly switch between automatic and controlled processing.

In a provocative book, Julian Jaynes (1976) argues that consciousness as we currently use the term is a cultural invention, occurring about 3000 years ago. Before that time, our ancestors cruised the world on automatic pilot. On occasions of novelty or stress, they sometimes heard "voices" telling them what to do. They attributed these voices to the intervention of gods and goddesses, and it was only when people began to regard these voices as emanating from themselves that modern consciousness was born.

This argument is obviously speculative, although Jaynes supports it with historical research. References to consciousness only started to appear in the relatively recent past, perhaps suggesting that earlier people did not possess the concept. At any rate, the general point that normal wakefulness is only periodically and selectively visited by consciousness is an important one.

The Unconscious

Sigmund Freud theorized extensively about the mind and distinguished among three types of awareness. The first is what we have called normal waking consciousness, experiences front and center in our minds. The second type of awareness Freud identified is the **preconscious.** Here he refers to thoughts and memories not currently in awareness but readily available. What was the name of your first-grade teacher? When did you go to bed last night? Where is your car parked? You probably were not thinking about any of these questions as you read them, but you can answer each one readily. This material is therefore in your preconscious.

The third type of awareness about which Freud wrote is the **motivated unconscious**—thoughts actively kept out of awareness because they are threatening to the conscious mind. The key term here is *motivated;* according to Freud, we have a *need* to keep certain material out of our normal waking consciousness. Some psychologists have criticized the psychoanalytic notion of the unconscious because it leaves an important question unanswered: Just who or what is responsible for censorship? But note that the problem of a hypothesized executive within the mind plagues theories of sensation and perception as well. Who or what "has" sensations and perceptions? The psychodynamic unconscious is no more problematic on this score than other mentalistic concepts, and many psychologists therefore have no trouble accepting the notion (e.g., Erdelyi, 1985).

The idea of a perceptual set explains that our prevailing needs and drives may influence what we perceive (p. 147). We've all driven on the interstate highway and found ourselves in dire need of food, gasoline, or a bathroom. (I usually require all three.) We begin to see every roadsign as an announcement of whatever we want.

preconscious

material not in conscious awareness that is readily available

motivated unconscious

the psychoanalytic idea that memories threatening to one's conscious mind are actively kept out of awareness

perceptual defense

phenomenon of taking longer to recognize offensive or threatening stimuli than to recognize neutral stimuli

daydreaming

the state of consciousness in which people shift their attention inward, away from the external world

The opposite phenomenon may also occur. If people protect themselves against thoughts and impulses that are unacceptable to their conscious minds, then the motivated unconscious should lead us whenever possible to literally overlook nastiness in the world. Research shows that this does indeed happen. In one experiment, for example, research subjects were asked to identify words that were flashed for a fraction of a second on a screen (McGinnies, 1949). Some of the words were less than polite, like *whore* or *bitch*. Subjects took longer to recognize these words than innocuous words. This phenomenon, in which people protect themselves from offending stimuli, is called **perceptual defense.**

The concept of perceptual defense has proven controversial, and some psychologists have suggested alternative explanations. For instance, in the experiment just described, perhaps subjects indeed recognized the nasty words but hesitated to say them out loud. This possibility has been ruled out by first showing research subjects a list of all the words they might see, including the nasty ones, and asking them to say them all; when the experiment itself is conducted, perceptual defense is still evident. Other alternative explanations have also been ruled out, leading to the conclusion that perceptual defense indeed exists (e.g., Erdelyi, 1974, 1985; Peterson, 1988).

The motivated unconscious allows psychoanalytic theory to explain a host of otherwise puzzling aspects of people's behavior. Perhaps you have friends who rant and rave about certain habits of people they detest, while they themselves have the exact same habits. This self-deception makes sense in view of the unconscious. In their conscious minds, your friends know that they dislike people who are tardy or wasteful or immature; in their unconscious minds, they keep hidden from themselves the fact that they act in these ways as well. More generally, the unconscious plays a large role in psychoanalytic theorizing about personality (Chapter 11). According to Freud, our central needs and motives are not known to our conscious minds.

Daydreams

In one of his papers, Freud (1908) touched upon the phenomenon of **daydreaming,** and he proposed that only unhappy individuals engage in the practice of shifting their attention inward and away from the external world. But when Jerome L. Singer (1966, 1975, 1984) undertook systematic investigations of daydreaming, he found no evidence for equating daydreaming with unhappiness. Indeed, Singer finds that occasional daydreaming is an almost universal occurrence.

For most people, daydreaming begins in early childhood and lasts throughout their life. People do show considerable variation in the amount of time devoted to daydreaming (Lynn & Rhue, 1986). Some individuals may spend as many as half their waking hours engaged in daydreaming! Other individuals obviously spend much less time.

What specifically do people daydream about? Singer found that the following categories encompassed most daydreams:

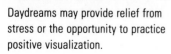

Daydreams may provide relief from stress or the opportunity to practice positive visualization.

- Self-recrimination—going back over what one should have said or done in actual situations
- Thoughtful planning—organizing and rehearsing future events

- Autistic—experiencing bizarre images like those in dreams
- Self-conscious—engaging in fantasy, imagining great adventures and triumphs

People show stable preferences for types of daydreaming and even for specific daydreams. Singer (1966) himself described several ongoing daydreams of his own that began years ago in his childhood. In one, he is a great athlete. In another, he is a statesman. And in a third daydream, he imagines himself to be a composer.

Those interested in daydreaming have proposed that it has several functions. One obvious role played by a daydream is an escape from stress or boredom. The person briefly turns off the external world in favor of an internal one; later returning to the task at hand, refreshed by the daydream. Daydreams also serve to alter our moods or to enhance our sexual excitement (Chapter 16).

Some types of daydreaming can specifically help us in everyday life. If we mentally rehearse what we might say during a conversation, or the route we will take on a vacation, or a different way to arrange our furniture, we may hit upon a useful course of action. Similarly, daydreaming can enhance our motivation to achieve certain goals. An example familiar to many of us starts out with "I'm going to show them" and ends with a plan that we put into action. In contrast to Freud's (1908) negative view of daydreaming, the research conducted by Singer and others shows that daydreaming has many adaptive possibilities.

Sleep and Dreams

On the average, we spend one third of our lives in the state of consciousness known as sleep. When we sleep, we experience a reduction in our alertness, awareness, and perception of ongoing events. While sleeping, we are not conscious of being asleep. At the same time, we know that sleep is a state of consciousness with special characteristics that mark it as different from normal waking consciousness. Most notably, we dream while we sleep.

Hobson (1988) points out that the experience of dreaming is marked by five characteristic features:

- Emotion so intense that it may terminate the dream
- Illogical content and organization
- Complex sensory impressions
- Uncritical acceptance of the dream as if it were part of everyday experience
- Difficulty in remembering a dream once it is over

Not all dreams have these five characteristics, but we are all familiar with these aspects of dreams.

All of us sleep, and all of us dream. Psychologists have studied sleep and dreams extensively, yet answers to some of the most basic questions remain elusive. For example, the functions served by sleeping are not clear. Neither is the significance of dreams. Researchers have made some progress in describing the basic nature of sleep and dreams. In this section, we discuss first the findings from this descriptive work. Then we will take a look at the range of theories proposed about the function and

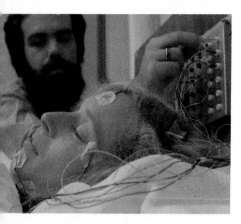

Researchers record eye movement (using the EOG) to track the particular stages of sleep a person experiences.

electroencephalogram (EEG)
device that measures and records electrical activity in the brain

electromyogram (EMG)
device that measures and records electrical activity of the muscles

electrooculogram (EOG)
device that measures and records eye movements

alpha waves
brain waves that cycle between 8 and 12 times per second, associated with relaxation

take a look at the range of theories proposed about the function and significance of sleep and dreams.

Sleep Research.   Despite the universality of sleep, and the sheer amount of time we spend in this state, only in the last few decades did scientists begin to regard sleep as a rewarding topic of investigation. Previously, sleep was regarded as inaccessible. A researcher could watch somebody sleep, and measure changes in pulse or respiration or body position, but these observations gave little insight into the essence of sleep (Borbely, 1986).

The scientific study of sleep became possible with the invention of the **electroencephalogram (EEG)**. As you remember from Chapter 2, the EEG is a device that measures electrical activity in the brain. Electrodes are attached to a person's skull, and electrical patterns are recorded over time. The EEG was first available in the 1920s, and in the following decade it was used to measure brain activity during sleep (Loomis, Harvey, & Hobart, 1937). Researchers discovered that the sleeping individual's brain waves changed in regular ways throughout the night. From the very beginning of EEG research, investigators suspected that sleep could be described as a sequence of stages.

Other devices soon became available for investigating changes during sleep. The **electromyogram (EMG)** is a device similar to the EEG, except that its electrodes are attached underneath one's chin, where they record electrical activity of the muscles. So, the EMG provides information about one's muscular tension or relaxation.

The **electrooculogram (EOG)** is yet another recording device, with electrodes attached near the outer corners of the eyes. The EOG measures movement of the eyes. As we will discuss shortly, eye movements during sleep are associated with a particular sleep stage.

Researchers typically study sleep in what is called a sleep laboratory, to which research subjects report at the end of a day. They prepare for bed just like you or I might, except that they additionally allow electrodes to be attached to their scalp and face. Free movement is still possible, and most individuals have no trouble relaxing and falling asleep. As a caution, though, many sleep researchers ask their subjects to sleep in the lab for several nights in a row, and use the first night simply to let the subject get used to the arrangements. On subsequent nights, various recordings are made over the duration of the subject's sleep.

Stages of Sleep.   What has been discovered from research in sleep laboratories? Sleep indeed is characterized by a series of stages (see Figure 4.11). Let's discuss these in the order they occur. When we first lie down before falling asleep, we are in a state of consciousness described as *relaxed wakefulness*. In this state, the EEG pattern indicates a type of brain activity known as **alpha waves,** which cycle between 8 and 12 times per second. As we mentioned in Chapter 2, alpha waves are associated with relaxation. To the degree that someone in this presleep state begins to think about problems or tasks, these alpha waves are disrupted. In relaxed wakefulness, both the EMG and the EOG show considerable activity, indicating muscular tension and movements of the eyes.

If the person stays relaxed, eventually he will fall asleep. We may speak about gradually falling asleep, but sleep researchers have found that peo-

Figure 4.11

Stages of Sleep. Shown here are the characteristic recordings of the EEG, EOG, and EMG for each of the different stages of sleep.

Source: Borbely, 1986.

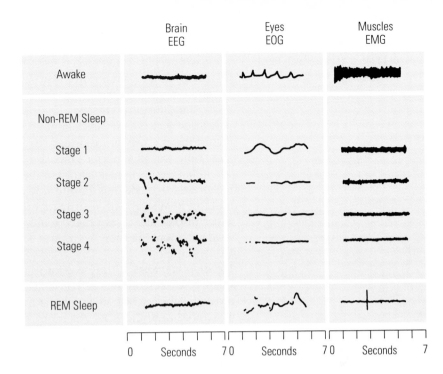

	Brain EEG	Eyes EOG	Muscles EMG
Awake			
Non-REM Sleep			
Stage 1			
Stage 2			
Stage 3			
Stage 4			
REM Sleep			

0　Seconds　7　0　Seconds　7　0　Seconds　7

theta waves

brain waves that cycle between 3 and 5 times per second, associated with Stage 1 sleep

sleep spindles

bursts of brain activity associated with Stage 2 sleep

delta waves

brain waves that cycle between .5 and 3 times per second, associated with Stage 3 and Stage 4 sleep

REM sleep

rapid eye movement sleep; period of sleep during which the eyes move rapidly beneath closed lids; particularly vivid dreaming occurs during REM sleep

ple enter sleep suddenly. The first stage of sleep is called *Stage 1 sleep,* and it lasts but a few minutes. In Stage 1 sleep, a pattern of brain activity known as **theta waves** is detected by the EEG; these cycle between 3 and 5 times per second. Our sleeper in Stage 1 sleep is easily awakened.

Next, the sleeper enters *Stage 2 sleep,* which is deeper and marked by bursts of brain activity called **sleep spindles.** These bursts of activity occur every 15 seconds or so. Muscular tension is now greatly reduced. The eyes do not move.

After about 20 minutes of Stage 2 sleep, the sleeper passes through 30 minutes of *Stage 3 sleep.* The EEG detects the presence of yet another type of brain activity known as **delta waves,** which cycle between .5 and 3 times per second. In Stage 3 sleep, other types of brain waves are present as well. A person's temperature, breathing, and pulse slow down. It is difficult to awaken him from Stage 3 sleep.

Stage 4 sleep follows next, and this is the deepest sleep we experience. The EEG shows delta waves almost exclusively. The sleeper's muscles are completely relaxed. The eyes do not move at all. From the time that our sleeper entered Stage 1 sleep and progressed to Stage 4 sleep, about 1 hour has passed. The sleeper will not stay in Stage 4 throughout the night, however, but will pass back through Stage 3 and into Stage 2 sleep. Then, the cycle repeats. In the course of a night, we all go through the different stages of sleep four or five times. The deep stages of sleep—Stages 3 and 4—occur most distinctly during the first two cycles.

One important part of the sleep cycle has so far been left out of our discussion. When someone has passed through the first cycle of sleep stages, and is back in Stage 2 sleep, yet another type of sleep becomes apparent. The sleeper's eyes begin to dart back and forth rapidly underneath closed eyelids. This is appropriately called the period of **REM** (rapid eye movement) **sleep.** REM sleep was first discovered in the 1950s (Aserinsky & Kleitman, 1953), and it has so intrigued sleep researchers that the other periods of sleep are called **non-REM sleep.**

Each period of REM sleep lasts about 10 minutes. During this time, our brain waves again become active, our heart rate and respiration speed up, and our genitals show signs of arousal. But we are also deeply asleep, and quite difficult to awaken. Soon we resume Stage 2 sleep, then pass into Stage 3 sleep, and the entire cycle is repeated. We've already noted that as these cycles are repeated, deep sleep becomes less likely. At the same time, our REM periods increase in length with each successive cycle.

REM sleep originally attracted the interest of researchers because of the presence of dreams during this period. A person awakened in the midst of REM sleep will usually report a vivid dream. Dreams can and do occur during all stages of sleep, but those in non-REM periods are less vivid and more jumbled.

The Nature of Dreams.   The close association between vivid dreams and REM sleep gives researchers a convenient way of studying the content of dreams. Subjects in a sleep laboratory are asked to fall asleep. They are monitored until the EOG detects movement of their eyes. Then they are awakened and questioned. Recall of dreams is very good in these circumstances. From research like this, we know that everyone dreams every night. People who report that they don't dream should really be saying that they don't remember their dreams, because they have occurred.

We also know that time in dreams corresponds fairly closely to time in waking life. In other words, when people are awakened early in an REM period, the dream they report is very brief, and when people are awakened late in an REM period, the dream they report is correspondingly longer.

By the way, the particular movement of eyes during REM sleep bears no relationship to the content of dreams. When REM sleep was first described, it was hypothesized that one's rapid eye movements corresponded to back-and-forth scanning of visual scenes in a dream (Dement, 1974). Subsequent research failed to support this intriguing possibility (Borbely, 1986).

Researchers have made extensive catalogs of the types of dreams that people report (e.g., Hall & Van de Castle, 1966). Many dreams are mundane, containing few bizarre or unusual elements. Perhaps strange dreams are easier to remember, which means we overestimate their frequency (Chapter 7). Almost all dreams contain at least one person familiar to the dreamer. Physical activity and movements usually occur without effort. Dreams with negative themes, like unhappiness and defeat, occur somewhat more frequently than dreams with positive themes.

A *nightmare* is simply a dream with frightening content, and it should be distinguished from what is called a *night terror,* in which we wake up suddenly in a state of great fright and confusion. Nightmares occur during REM sleep, usually in one of the periods toward the end of the night. We awaken with a start, and we know instantly that we have had a bad dream.

In contrast, night terrors occur during a period of non-REM sleep, usually Stage 3 or Stage 4. Again, we awaken with a start, but we are disoriented, perhaps for several minutes. We awaken in a panic, showing all the signs of the body's emergency reaction (Chapter 2). We do not know where we are or what we are doing. We have no memory of a

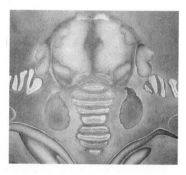

Dream imagery can be recorded in a number of ways—as an oral or written recollection of the dream or as a visual representation of it.

Figure 4.12

As we age, we spend less time sleeping and proportionately less time in REM sleep.

Source: Roffwarg, Muzio, & Dement, 1966.

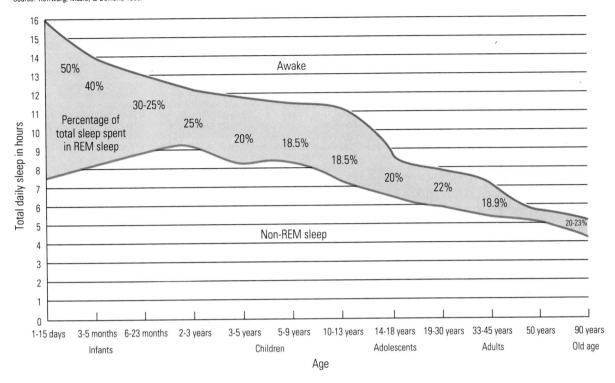

dream. According to Cohen (1979), night terrors may result from a blurring of states of consciousness. Our minds become suddenly aware that our bodies are asleep—that is, not moving—and the realization is a frightening one that creates a state of panic.

Sleep and Dreams Across the Lifespan. The nature of sleep and dreams changes as we grow older (see Figure 4.12). Infants sleep as many as 16 hours out of every 24, and half of this time is spent in REM sleep. Infants presumably dream, but only gradually learn to distinguish dreaming as a special state (Maurer & Maurer, 1988). Young adults sleep 7 or 8 hours a night, of which 20 percent is REM sleep.

People in their sixties or seventies usually sleep only 6 hours a night, and only 15 percent of this is REM sleep. Further, at about age sixty, a substantial number of adults begin to complain that they do not get a good night's sleep. They sleep not only fewer hours but also more fitfully. The deepest stages of sleep shorten dramatically. These patterns may provide clues about the functions of sleep and dreams, although theorists are still sifting through them for firm answers (Cartwright, 1978).

Functions of Sleep. People deprived of sleep obviously become tired and irritable. Prolonged sleep deprivation can result in marked decreases in the performance of skilled tasks and increases in hallucinations and delusions (Borbely, 1986). People who habitually sleep fewer than 7 hours per

Sleep deprivation—for 72 hours, in the case of these subjects—can have serious behavioral consequences, along with the physical effects seen here.

night do not live as long as people who usually get 7 or 8 hours of sleep (Kripke et al., 1979). (Interestingly, people who sleep *more* than 10 hours per night also tend to have a shortened life.)

On the whole, sleep appears to be associated with psychological and physical well-being. Why is this? Different theories suggest different answers. One possibility is that we sleep in order to restore our bodies. Whatever wear and tear accumulates during our waking lives is repaired while we sleep.

The function of sleep is probably more complicated than this simple theory suggests. Consider that individuals deprived of sleep for several days at a time usually require only a few extra hours of sleep to return to their normal cycle. In a celebrated case, a college student named Randy Gardner earned a place in the *Guiness Book of World Records* by staying awake for 264 hours and 11 minutes; that's 11 days (Gulevich, Dement, & Johnson, 1966)! He then slept for about 15 hours, woke up with no ill effects, and then resumed his regular habit of sleeping 8 hours per night. If sleeping did nothing but restore wear and tear, we would expect that Randy Gardner would have needed more than a single extended period of sleep to catch up to normal.

Other hypotheses about the functions of sleep propose more specific roles. Some studies suggest that we integrate newly acquired information during REM sleep (McGrath & Cohen, 1978). If research subjects are deprived of REM sleep in a laboratory, by waking them up every time their EOG shows eye movements, they show deficits in retaining material they have recently learned.

There is a relationship between sleeping and increased production of growth hormone (Oswald, 1980), but this is not a strong finding. And there are hints that the brain synthesizes complex compounds like neurotransmitters more readily when we are asleep than when we are awake. However, these possible functions of sleep have not yet been definitively established.

Other theorists take the provocative position that sleep has *no* inherent function. Instead, sleeping is an evolutionary by-product that no longer serves its original purpose, which was to keep our ancestors quiet and out of danger. Relatedly, sleep may allow us not to restore our body's resources but rather to conserve them (Webb, 1975).

Support for this evolutionary view of sleep comes from studies of the sleep patterns of different species. Mammals, birds, and reptiles all sleep, but they do so in characteristic ways, implying that sleep has become adapted to the niche of each type of creature (Borbely, 1986). For instance, rats sleep only 10 minutes at a time. Then they awaken for an equally short period. Cows continue to chew their cud while asleep. Dolphins sleep with only one cerebral hemisphere at a time, an intriguing pattern perhaps related to living in the water.

Functions of Dreams. Dreams are as fascinating as sleep itself, but again we don't have a complete understanding of their function. Freud (1900) proposed that people dream in order to preserve sleep. In our dreams, he hypothesized, we guard against threatening thoughts that might awaken us. So, if outside distractions occur, we can sometimes incorporate them into our dreams and keep on sleeping (e.g., Dement & Wolpert, 1958). And if reprehensible thoughts occur to us while dreaming, we disguise them.

Freud's theory explains why dreams are so incoherent—their confusing aspects constitute their disguise. He went on to distinguish the **manifest content** of dreams—the images and events of which the dreamer is aware—from their **latent content**—the underlying meaning and significance of them. The manifest content is not psychologically meaningful; rather, it is the latent content that reveals something important about the dreamer.

Here is an example from Freud (1916).

> A lady who, though she was still young, had been married for many years, had the following dream: She was at the theatre with her husband. One side [of the theatre] . . . was completely empty. Her husband told her that Elise L. and her fiance had wanted to go too, but only had been able to get bad seats . . . and of course they could not take those. She thought it would not really have done any harm if they had. (p. 122)

Using other information provided by the dreamer, Freud argued that the details in the dream all refer to being in a hurry. For example, the dreamer in actual life had recently attended a show. She had bought her tickets so early that she had to pay a booking fee. However, there had been no need to pay extra for the tickets because the theater was half empty for the show. Her friend Elise was the same age, but had waited 10 years longer than

manifest content
according to Freud, the images and events in dreams of which the dreamer is aware

latent content
according to Freud, the underlying meaning and significance of dreams

the dreamer to get married. Her fiance was an attractive man, showing again that there is no need to be in such a hurry. In sum, Freud concluded that the manifest content of this dream disguised the dreamer's wish *not* to have married so soon as well as her jealousy of her friend Elise.

According to Freud, we can understand people's unconscious motives if we can pierce the disguise of their dreams. Indeed, Freud labeled dreams the "royal road to the unconscious" and explicitly incorporated dream interpretation into psychoanalytic therapy (Chapter 13). As clients relate dreams, the psychoanalyst works with them to derive their meanings, bringing the conflicts supposedly at their basis to light.

Other theorists suggest that dreams are more than reactions to threatening stimuli. Instead, dreams represent an attempt to come to grips with unresolved challenges faced in waking life. In support of this idea is the fact that we often dream about ongoing business. Whether these dreams actually help solve problems from our waking life is not clear (Dement, 1974).

There are isolated examples of dreams that have provided good solutions to problems faced by a dreamer (Krippner & Hughes, 1970). For instance, Elias Howe, who invented the sewing machine, hit upon its design during a dream. He had been working for some time on the idea of a sewing machine, but was stymied by how to thread the needle. In his dream, he was taken captive by a savage tribe, and the tribe demanded that he create a workable sewing machine within 24 hours. He failed and so was to be put to death. The savages approached him with sharp spears *containing holes in their tips.* This provided the solution that Howe needed—putting the hole for the thread in the tip of the sewing machine needle. In discussing dreams like these that solve problems, Cohen (1979) speculated that dreams best lend themselves to problems that can be phrased in terms of visual imagery, as opposed to words or mathematics.

activation-synthesis theory
a theory of dreams proposing that a dream represents someone's interpretation of random activity of the cortex during sleep

Yet another explanation of dreams proposes that they are not intrinsically significant. The **activation-synthesis theory** of dreams proposes that a dream represents someone's interpretation of random activity of the cortex during sleep (Hobson & McCarley, 1977). By this view, dreaming is the same as any cognitive activity in which we use material stored in memory to make sense of incoming information (Chapter 7). Because the "information" interpreted in a dream is random, dreams themselves make little sense. Dreamers do the best job they can in making their experiences coherent, but they are handicapped by its essentially random nature.

Figure 4.13 contrasts the psychoanalytic explanation of dreams with the activation-synthesis theory. The two theories differ most clearly with respect to the presumed cause of dreams. Psychoanalytic theory regards dreams as unconscious wishes. The activation-synthesis theory explains them as by-products of brain activation. According to both theories, something is revealed about the dreamer by the nature of his or her dreams, although the theories differ in their reasons for this. Psychoanalytic theory tries to look beneath the manifest content of the dream to infer the motives underneath. And as already discussed, the activation-synthesis theory draws our attention to how someone interprets the dream (Foulkes, 1985). So, the manifest content is critical.

Let's wrap up this section on sleep and dreams by repeating that firm answers concerning the functions of sleep and dreams are still not at hand. However, as researchers devise better methods for studying sleep and

Figure 4.13

Comparison of the Psychoanalytic Theory of Dreams with the Activation-Synthesis Theory

The Psychoanalytic Theory

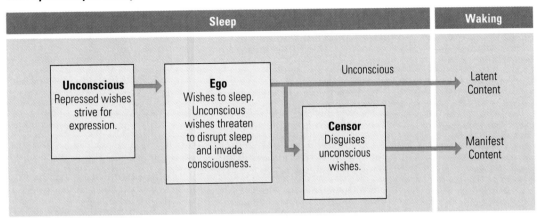

The Activation-Synthesis Hypothesis

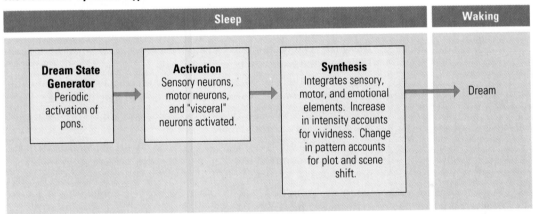

dreams, an increasing number of facts become available. We hope that greater knowledge will lead to greater understanding.

Deliberately Altered Consciousness

People have long found ways to deliberately alter consciousness, changing their perception, mood, and behaviors, leaving behind undesired states for those that give promise of being pleasurable, exciting, interesting, or profound. In this section, we will discuss three means for altering consciousness: meditation, hypnosis, and drugs.

meditation

a strategy for altering consciousness through relaxation and a refocusing of attention

Meditation. A form of altering consciousness long practiced by many groups, **meditation** combines a refocusing of attention with relaxation. Meditation sometimes involves repetitive activity, such as slow breathing or chanting. It can also involve reversing the automatization of thought through contemplation, becoming aware of stimuli we normally tune out, like the sound of our beating heart.

Though there are different procedures for meditating, most meditators experience a common result. A century ago, William James (1890) described it as a *mystical experience* combining these elements:

- a feeling of oneness
- a sense of truth
- an inability to express experience in mere words
- vividness and clarity of sensations and perceptions

More recently, researchers have documented that physiological changes indeed occur during meditation (Wallace & Benson, 1972). Alpha waves predominate in one's EEG. Remember that this pattern of brain activity is linked to relaxation. Breathing becomes deeper and slower. And the heart rate of a meditator usually slows down.

Other researchers have claimed long-term emotional and physical benefits of meditation, concluding that meditators are happier and healthier than their nonmeditating counterparts (Smith, 1975). However, this conclusion has been challenged by critics who argue that meditation is beneficial only because it leads someone to relax (e.g., Holmes, 1984). Whether or not someone experiences an alteration in consciousness is irrelevant, as long as relaxation is produced. Research continues.

hypnosis
a state of consciousness characterized by heightened suggestibility

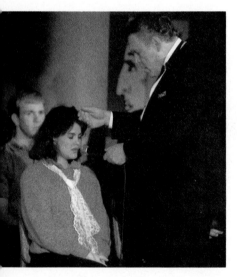

Hypnotic induction can be performed for various purposes in many different environments. Here Sam Vine hypnotizes members of a club audience.

Hypnosis.   Often defined as an altered state of consciousness characterized by heightened suggestibility, **hypnosis** is a condition in which a person appears greatly relaxed, but is not asleep. There is considerable debate as to whether hypnosis is an altogether different state than everyday wakefulness (Kihlstrom, 1985). Let's first discuss what we know about hypnotism, and then return to the debate over how best to think about it.

Hypnotic induction typically proceeds with the subject being asked to narrow her attention to what the hypnotist is saying, and then to follow his directions. The more suggestions that are followed by the individual, the more hypnotized she is said to be. Some people are more susceptible to hypnosis than others. One characteristic shared by those who can readily be hypnotized is an ability to engage freely in fantasy (Kihlstrom, 1985).

In one representative hypnotic induction, suggestions include the following (Hilgard, 1977):

- swaying while standing
- closing eyes
- lowering one's outstretched arm
- being unable to raise one's arm
- being unable to say one's name
- hallucinating a buzzing fly
- being unable to open one's eyes
- posthypnotic suggestion (following a command outside the hypnotized state)
- posthypnotic amnesia (failing to remember events outside the hypnotized state)

These are arranged in increasing order of difficulty. Someone who follows all of these suggestions is a good candidate for showing some of the striking phenomena of hypnosis.

For example, a hypnotized individual might show *age regression,* following the suggestion to act like a child of a given age. The person does

Figure 4.14

Normal versus Age-Regressed Handwriting

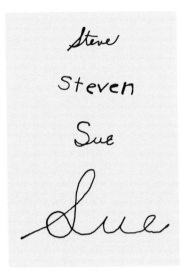

not become a child or even recreate her own childhood behaviors. Rather, she acts in a childish way. Figure 4.14 shows what happens when a hypnotized individual is asked to write her name. What results is an immature style, but not the exact style of a child. But this is amazing enough, because "regression" occurs without self-consciousness.

Over the years, there have been many provocative claims made about hypnosis. Research has usually qualified these claims, showing that the effects of hypnosis can be highly complex. For instance, does hypnosis allow otherwise forgotten memories to be recovered? Most of us have read stories about how witnesses to a crime were hypnotized and thereby able to recall obscure details like license plate numbers. This may tie up the loose ends of a crime story, but hypnosis provides no foolproof route to our forgotten experiences.

A study by Dywan and Bowers (1983) found that individuals could correctly remember more information to which they had been previously exposed when they were hypnotized than when they were not. However, hypnotized subjects also showed an increase in false recollections. Correct and incorrect recall went together; as one increased, so did the other. False memories under hypnosis outnumbered true memories two to one.

Other studies show that the recall of hypnotized individuals is particularly susceptible to bias by leading questions (e.g., Sheehan & Tilden, 1983). Further, false memories are reported with more confidence by subjects who are hypnotized than by subjects who are not (Laurence & Perry, 1983). Results like these imply that hypnosis has no simple effect on memory. Further, if hypnosis is used as an aid in criminal investigations, the potential for unintentional abuse must be kept clearly in mind (see Reiser & Nielson, 1980).

Does hypnosis allow individuals to tolerate pain that they otherwise would find unbearable? The answer to this question is yes (Hilgard & Hilgard, 1983). In one common research strategy, subjects immerse their hand in a bucket of ice water. (This hurts but is not dangerous.) When hypnotized and told that they are not feeling pain, they indeed do not. In fact, hypnotism can rival morphine, tranquilizers, and acupuncture as a means of reducing pain.

When endorphins (p. 59) were first discovered, some investigators wondered if hypnosis reduced pain by stimulating the production of these naturally occurring substances. They administered to subjects a drug that blocks the effects of endorphins, but found that hypnosis still was effective in reducing pain (Goldstein & Hilgard, 1975). This finding tells us that hypnosis does *not* work through endorphins. How it does work remains an open question.

Let's turn to the debate over the nature of hypnosis (Kihlstrom, 1985). Most psychologists agree that hypnosis involves a state in which the hypnotized individual allows another person, the hypnotist, to take over certain functions like being aware and determining what is real. From this point, explanations diverge, particularly concerning the special status of the hypnotic state.

Some psychologists explain hypnosis as simply a way of acting that is characterized by heightened suggestibility (Sarbin & Coe, 1972). Yes, the hypnotized individual obeys the commands of the hypnotist, but this is no different than what happens when a motorist obeys the commands of a traffic cop. Advocates of this view point to the fact that hypnotized individ-

The human species has a predilection for drug usage, as well as drug abuse.

uals cannot be induced to do something they would not ordinarily do. In other words, hypnosis does not rob people of their will and turn them into robots.

Other psychologists explain hypnosis as a special state of consciousness marked by **dissociation** (Hilgard, 1973, 1977). In this state, two conscious activities are carried out with little or no communication between the two. By this view, the hypnotized individual is thought to have a divided awareness. In the hypnotized state, one part of the subject yields to the suggestions of the hypnotist. The other part is sometimes called the *hidden observer,* because it is concealed from the hypnotized consciousness yet remains aware of what it is doing.

How might this hidden observer be revealed? One way is to give the hypnotized individual paper and pencil, and ask him to write on it but not to be aware that he is doing so. Some people follow this instruction, showing a "consciousness" of which they are unaware. Under the direction of the hidden observer, they write messages about which their hypnotized consciousness knows nothing.

Whether or not hypnosis is a special state of consciousness is a continuing debate. Regardless, hypnosis has practical applications. Therapists attempt through hypnotic suggestion to directly remove the symptoms of their patients. The use of hypnosis to relieve pain has already been mentioned. Hypnosis has also been used to reduce cravings for addictive substances like nicotine, to combat fear and anxiety, and to undo amnesia (Frankel, 1976). In reviewing these applications, Kihlstrom (1985) urged a cautious view, noting that carefully controlled investigations of the benefits claimed for hypnotherapy still need to be conducted.

Drugs. Probably the most common way of deliberately altering consciousness is through the ingestion of **psychoactive drugs.** These are chemicals that affect brain activity and thereby the nature of consciousness. To the degree that one regards the changed state of consciousness as desirable, one will use a given drug for this purpose. Abuse may follow.

Ours is a drug-using and drug-abusing society. Indeed, ours is a drug-using and drug-abusing species. People have long used psychoactive drugs for the purpose of altering their thoughts, feelings, and actions (Brecher et al., 1972).

- When the Bible tells us that "ointment and perfume rejoice the heart" (Proverbs 27:9), the reference is not to Old Spice or English Leather toiletries, but probably to psychoactive drugs.
- Ashes recovered from altars abandoned 2500 years ago on islands in the Mediterranean have been identified as marijuana.
- Native Americans used peyote and mescal (hallucinogens extracted from cactus).
- Over 3500 years ago, the Aztecs consumed magic mushrooms (psilocybin).
- The Incas chewed coca leaves (the source of contemporary cocaine and crack).
- In 1885, these leaves were added to John Pemberton's "sovereign remedy"—a product marketed under the name of Coca-Cola.
- The Victorians in Europe were great fans of nitrous oxide, camphor, ether, and chloroform.

- People in various cultures sniff, snort, smoke, and/or swallow substances like fungus, nutmeg, morning glory seeds, glue, oven spray, Sterno, Aqua Velva, and gasoline.

It sometimes seems as if there is a taboo in the popular media about acknowledging that drugs alter consciousness (Weil, 1972). Think of the millions of advertisements we see every year on television, which urge beer upon us because it tastes good . . . and/or is less filling. But we all know that neither the taste of beer nor its caloric content has much to do with why people drink. We consume alcohol because it makes us feel good, the result of a deliberate alteration of our consciousness. Similarly, why do people use narcotics? One of heroin's famous casualties, comedian John Belushi, proclaimed that using this drug was "like kissing God" (Woodward, 1985, p. 321).

The same is true of the other drugs we use and abuse. We call the alteration in consciousness following ingestion of a psychoactive drug **intoxication.** Depending on the specific drug, the effects of intoxication range from euphoria to depression. Another alteration in consciousness follows the cessation or reduction of drug use. This is **withdrawal.** Again, the specific nature of withdrawal depends on the drug in question, but withdrawal usually has the opposite effects of intoxication. It is invariably unpleasant. Common to psychoactive drugs is the phenomenon of **tolerance** with increased use—the need to take more and more of a drug in order to produce the same effect.

We will discuss substance abuse and its causes and treatments in Chapter 12. In the present section, you will find thumbnail sketches of the major types of psychoactive drugs, focusing on how they affect consciousness (see Table 4.1). **Stimulants** are drugs that stimulate the nervous system. They increase our arousal and spur on both mental and physical

intoxication
alteration in consciousness following ingestion of a psychoactive drug

withdrawal
alteration in consciousness following cessation or reduction of drug use

tolerance
the need to take more and more of a psychoactive drug to produce the same effect

stimulants
psychoactive drugs that increase an individual's alertness, such as caffeine, nicotine, and cocaine

Table 4.1
Psychoactive Drugs

Classification	Examples	Psychological Effects
Stimulants	Caffeine	Increased alertness, excitation, decreased fatigue
	Amphetamine	Increased alertness, excitation, decreased fatigue
	Cocaine	Euphoria, increased alertness, excitation, decreased fatigue
Depressants	Alcohol	Relaxation, reduced inhibitions
	Narcotics	Euphoria, analgesia, drowsiness, nausea
	Barbiturates	Relaxation, disorientation, sleep
Hallucinogens	LSD	Distortions, illusions, hallucinations, time disorientation
	Marijuana	Euphoria, relaxed inhibitions, increased sensory sensitivity, disorientation

activity. Stimulants also increase our alertness and elevate our mood. Sometimes stimulants produce agitation and insomnia.

The most widely used stimulant is caffeine, found in coffee, tea, chocolate, and many soft drinks. Another familiar stimulant is nicotine, the active ingredient in tobacco. Also classified as stimulants are amphetamine ("speed") and cocaine. The use of the derivative of cocaine known as crack is increasing rapidly and poses a serious threat to our country. And a derivative of amphetamine known as "ice" may soon join crack as a widely used and highly addictive drug.

In terms of their effects on consciousness, **depressants** are the opposite of stimulants. Depressants reduce awareness of external stimuli and slow down bodily functions. In small amounts, depressants create a relaxed state that makes the user feel free from anxiety and inhibition. In large amounts, they lead to sedation and sleep, even coma and death.

Alcohol is the most commonly used depressant. Indeed, at least in our culture, it is the most widely used of all the psychoactive drugs. It has been estimated that Americans spend tens of *billions* of dollars every year on alcohol. As will be explained in Chapter 12, alcohol takes an incredible toll on physical health.

Depressants include the opiates, also known as narcotics: opium, morphine, heroin, and methadone, to name a few. Opium is derived from juice in the seeds of the poppy plant. The other opiates are either derived from opium or synthesized in laboratories. As explained in Chapter 2, the opiates are highly effective painkillers.

Barbiturates ("downers") like phenobarbital are yet another type of depressant. They work by slowing down activity in our entire nervous system. Barbiturates have been used to aid sleep, and to combat anxiety and seizures. Despite these benefits, barbiturates are highly dangerous. If someone overdoses on them, it can be fatal, particularly if a person has mixed them with alcohol. And finally, withdrawing from barbiturates is not merely unpleasant but potentially life-threatening. A chronic user may experience convulsions if and when these drugs are suddenly stopped.

Hallucinogens are drugs that produce hallucinations. Most of the time, these are visual. The user sees things that are not present, or sees things in ways that other people do not. Other types of sensations and perceptions may be influenced as well, notably one's sense of time. Hallucinogens have widely varying effects on one's mood. In some cases, euphoria results. In other cases, the consequence is extreme fear. One possibility is that the hallucinogens exaggerate the user's present mood, for better or for worse.

One well-known hallucinogen is LSD (lysergic acid diethylamide). Its consciousness-altering effects were first discovered when a Swiss researcher named Albert Hofmann (1968) accidentally swallowed a small amount. He described the experience as follows:

> I had a great difficulty in speaking coherently, my field of vision swayed before me, and objects appeared distorted like images in curved mirrors. I had the impression of being unable to move from the spot. . . . The faces of those around me appeared as grotesque, colored masks. . . . Everything seemed to sway and the proportions were distorted like the reflections in the surface of moving water. Moreover, all objects appeared in unpleasant, constantly changing colors, the predominant shades being sickly green and

depressants
psychoactive drugs, such as alcohol, narcotics, and barbiturates, that reduce awareness of external stimuli and slow down bodily functions

hallucinogens
psychoactive drugs that produce hallucinations, including LSD, mescaline, and psilocybin

These self-portraits were painted by an individual under the influence of the hallucinogenic drug LSD.

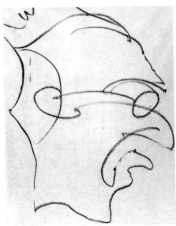

blue. When I closed my eyes, an unending series of colorful, very realistic and fantastic images surged in on me. (pp. 185–186)

Other hallucinogens include mescaline, psilocybin, and PCP (phencyclidine).

Marijuana can be classified as a hallucinogen, although some contest this designation because marijuana produces distortions of perception only in extremely high doses. The more typical effects of marijuana are mild euphoria and increased appetite ("munchies"). This drug is produced from the leaves and flowers of the hemp plant, long used as a source of rope.

Many psychoactive drugs are illegal in the United States, and among these illegal drugs, marijuana is one of the most widely used. There has been vigorous debate over the possible consequences of long-term use. Because marijuana is usually smoked, a user obviously is at risk for bronchitis and lung ailments. Other bad effects, both psychological and physical, are suspected but not agreed upon by all researchers. Part of the problem in evaluating the effects of marijuana is that people who use this drug differ in various ways from those who do not. It can be difficult to determine whether a supposed consequence is due to marijuana per se or to another characteristic of the user.

In all cases, we use psychoactive drugs to bring about a different state of consciousness. Sometimes this new state helps us get along better in our life, as when we banish needless worry and anxiety. But all too frequently, this new state leads us into deep trouble, as when we neglect our physical and social well-being in the pursuit of the altered state.

In the 1960s, some enthusiasts claimed that drugs like mescaline or LSD were mind-expanding or consciousness-raising (e.g., Leary, 1964). How have these claims fared in the ensuing years? On the one hand, there is a surface similarity between the mystical experience described earlier and the altered state of consciousness produced by hallucinogenic drugs (Huxley, 1954). On the other hand, there is no evidence that these drugs lead to any of the benefits documented for meditation. Creative performance is not enhanced. Long-term happiness and health are not served.

In this section, we have not labeled the various states of consciousness as higher or lower, expanded or compressed, because these terms muddle our understanding of consciousness more than they explain it. The different states are simply different; they don't fall along any obvious continuum. Perhaps because users of hallucinogenic drugs so enjoy the state thereby induced, they conclude that it must represent "more" than normal consciousness. But we should not treat consciousness as a physical thing.

In this chapter, we have discussed perception and consciousness. A common thread running through these topics is that people are not simply passive recipients of their experiences. Although one's biological makeup significantly affects these phenomena, so too do a person's personal and social characteristics. We will find further examples of the interplay between biological and psychological determinants of behavior in subsequent chapters.

Summary

Topics of Concern

- Perception is the process by which we organize and interpret sensory information. Consciousness can be defined as our awareness of our environment and our mental processes.
- Psychologists who study perception want to understand the organization that characterizes perception. Is it inherent in original sensations, or is it imposed only after we experience sensations? The answer appears complex; the organization of perception reflects both nature and nurture.
- Psychologists are also concerned with how sensation, perception, and consciousness differ from one another as well as how they are related. Currently popular is a view that describes mental activity in terms of the processing of information. By this view, firm distinctions among sensation, perception, and consciousness are hard to draw.

Perception

- Perception is sometimes used to refer to the process by which sensations are organized, and sometimes to refer to the product of this organization.
- Perception is selective, which means that we cannot attend simultaneously to all the stimuli occurring around us. The processes responsible for the selectivity of perception are called attention. Two theories of attention are popular: the bottleneck model, emphasizing biological limitations on the amount of sensory information we can notice; and the capacity model, emphasizing psychological limitations.
- Perception is coherent; our conscious experiences merge into a whole. The early gestalt psychologists described a number of organizational principles such as proximity, similarity, closure, and continuity which govern our perception of forms. These work to create good gestalts.
- An example of the coherence of perception is found in Gibson's ecological approach. He proposes that certain phenomena, like aspects of depth perception, are inborn. We do not need to learn to perceive the distance of an object from us. Instead, we automatically make use of the

clues that are provided by the texture of its background to perceive how far away it is.
- Perception is creative. We perceive not a literal version of reality but rather a creation that reflects external stimuli as well as the habits, tendencies, and styles we bring to bear on our sensations. Psychologists interested in the creativeness of perception study the visual constancies, in which our visual experience of size, shape, and brightness remains the same even when physical stimulation changes, and illusions, in which our perception of an object is at odds with its actual characteristics.
- Finally, perception is personal. We see the world from our own point of view, which means that perceptual styles and habits develop over time. Also, our prevailing psychological states influence what and how we perceive. For instance, a perceptual set is a predisposition to perceive a particular stimulus in a particular context, simply because we expect to see it there.

Consciousness

- We experience consciousness in different forms known as states of consciousness. Normal waking consciousness switches between automatic processing, in which we initiate an activity and simply carry it out, and controlled processing, in which we initiate an activity and then make a conscious effort to direct it.
- Sigmund Freud argued that people possess a motivated unconscious, material actively kept out of awareness because it is threatening. The notion of the motivated unconscious plays a major role in psychoanalytic theory, which proposes that our central needs and motives are not known to our conscious minds.
- Daydreaming occurs when we shift attention inward and away from the external world. Research shows daydreaming to be an almost universal occurrence. Various useful functions have been suggested for daydreaming, including tension relief, problem solution, and enhancement of motivation.
- We spend about one third of our lives in the state of consciousness known as sleep. Investigations of the psychology of sleep have been made

possible by devices like the electroencephalogram, electromyogram, and electrooculogram.

- Researchers have discovered that when we sleep, we cycle several times through various discrete stages characterized by differing amounts and patterns of brain activity, muscular tension, and eye movements.

- REM sleep is a particularly intriguing stage of sleep. Here our eyes move rapidly back and forth behind closed lids. Vivid dreams occur during REM sleep.

- Although sleep is apparently associated with physical and psychological well-being, its exact functions have not been determined.

- Similarly, psychologists do not agree on the significance of dreams. Freud proposed that they represent disguised wishes and motives. The activation-synthesis theory proposes that dreams are the interpretation of random brain activity.

- People deliberately alter their state of consciousness, using various techniques. Meditation combines a refocusing of attention with relaxation. During meditation, characteristic physiological changes occur. Some psychologists claim meditation offers long-term emotional and physical benefits, although this claim is disputed.

- Hypnosis is a state characterized by heightened suggestibility. There is a disagreement concerning whether or not hypnosis is a special state of consciousness. Although some claims about the special nature of hypnosis have proven exaggerations, other claims are supported by research. In particular, hypnosis allows individuals to tolerate pain they would otherwise find unbearable.

- One explanation of hypnosis suggests that it is a special state of consciousness known as dissociation, in which one's awareness is split in two. An alternative explanation proposes that hypnosis is not a special state of consciousness but rather a social role characterized by heightened suggestibility.

- Perhaps the most common way of altering consciousness is through the ingestion of psychoactive drugs which affect brain activity. Among the common categories of psychoactive drugs are stimulants like amphetamine and cocaine; depressants like alcohol, narcotics, and barbiturates; and hallucinogens like LSD, mescaline, and marijuana. Each produces characteristic alterations in consciousness, during intoxication and during withdrawal.

Important Terms and Names

What follows is a list of the core terms and names for this chapter. Your instructor may emphasize other terms as well. Throughout the chapter, glossary terms appear in **boldface** type. They are defined in the text, and each term, along with its definition, is repeated in the margin.

Topics of Concern

perception/134
consciousness/134
information processing/135

Perception

attention/136   James Gibson/140
figure-ground relationship/138
ecological approach/140
visual constancies/142
illusions/143
perceptual set/147

Consciousness

states of consciousness/   Julian Jaynes/149
   147   Sigmund Freud/149
automatic processing/148
controlled processing/148
preconscious/149
motivated unconscious/149
daydreaming/150
REM sleep/153
activation-synthesis theory of dreams/158
meditation/159
hypnosis/160
psychoactive drugs/162
intoxication/163
withdrawal/163
tolerance/163
stimulants/163
depressants/164
hallucinogens/164

Review Questions

1. The important implication of an information-processing approach to sensation, perception, and consciousness is that
   a. people are exactly like computers.
   b. the biological basis of mental activities can be ignored.
   c. we do not have to define these psychological states.
   d. we need not make rigid distinctions among these psychological states.
   The key idea of an information processing approach is that sensation, perception, and consciousness all entail the transformation or "processing" of information from the environment. Process means an ongoing sequence of mental activity which need not be divided into discrete stages./135

2. Gestalt organizational principles explain the _____ of forms.
   a. coherence
   b. diversity
   c. utility
   d. all of the above
   According to gestalt psychology, we inherently organize stimuli into coherent forms./139

3. Which saying best captures the significance of illusions for the psychology of perception?
   a. "Doctor, it's my eyes; tell me what is wrong."
   b. "The whole is not equal to the sum of the parts."
   c. "What you see is what you get."
   d. "You can't always get what you want."
   The study of illusions was particularly popular among gestalt psychologists, because they illustrated the basic gestalt truism that experience is not simply the sum of sensations./143

4. You have owned the same car for years. It has a manual transmission. The steps you go through in starting it every morning are probably best described as
   a. a mystical experience.
   b. automatic processing.
   c. controlled processing.
   d. manual processing.
   If your car is like mine, starting it on a cold morning may indeed be a magical and mystical experience. But most of the time, you start your car without any thought, by following a well-learned routine./148

5. Notable about Freud's version of the unconscious is that he regarded it as
   a. inherited from our ancestors.
   b. motivated.
   c. rational.
   d. unusual.
   Freud proposed that all people actively keep some thoughts out of awareness because these thoughts are threatening. The process is therefore motivated./149

6. Research on daydreaming suggests
   a. almost everyone daydreams.
   b. almost everyone daydreams, but only when unhappy.
   c. only creative people daydream.
   d. only mentally ill people daydream.
   Daydreaming is a virtually universal experience, and it serves many functions./150

7. Notable about REM sleep is the occurrence of
   a. cessation of brain activity.
   b. slowing down of respiration.
   c. vivid dreams.
   d. all of the above.
   Although dreams occur in other stages of sleep, those during REM sleep are usually particularly vivid. During REM sleep, brain activity and respiration increase, not decrease./154

8. Freud proposed that the psychological significance of dreams is to be found in their
   a. dissociative tendencies.
   b. gestalt organizational principles.
   c. latent content.
   d. manifest content.
   According to Freud, the meaning of dreams is to be found under their surface, in what he called their latent content./157

9. Much controversy accompanies the claim that hypnosis
   a. allows people to tolerate pain.
   b. exists.
   c. is a special state of consciousness.
   d. none of the above is controversial.
   Psychologists agree that there is a phenomenon we can call hypnosis that has characteristic effects on people, like allowing them to tolerate pain. Disagreement enters when psychologists try to determine whether hypnosis is a special state of consciousness or simply a form of suggestion./161

10. The most common way to deliberately alter one's consciousness is with
    a. drugs.
    b. hypnosis.
    c. meditation.
    d. Stanley Kaplan courses.
    Ours is a drug-using and drug-abusing species./162

Even the simplest examples of learning may reflect the influence of cognitive factors.

Chapter Five

Learning

Topics of Concern

I used to be a letter carrier for the postal service. You know, sleet, rain, snow, and all that stuff that never got in the way of mail delivery. But dogs did, particularly ferocious ones, and to a letter carrier, all dogs are ferocious. When I would deliver the mail to a home with a dog, the dog would dash out of the backyard and run at me, its collar jingling as the creature launched itself at my jugular. After this occurred a number of times, just the sound of the collar would make me cringe.

I had learned something. My behavior had changed because of what had happened to me. Before my experience as a letter carrier, jingling sounds had no emotional impact on me. After my experience, they produced fear. To this very day, I catch my breath and feel my heart accelerate when someone tosses a key chain on a table, resulting in a sound like that of Fido's collar.

Have some sympathy for me, please, but let's now take the perspective of the dog in this example. What did Fido learn when the mail was delivered? One obvious lesson is that when he barked and growled and acted like an NFL linebacker going after a quarterback, the letter carrier would make tracks. The next time the mail was delivered, Fido would attack again, with even more vigor. He, too, showed a change in behavior, and for all we know, he may still be attacking letter carriers today.

This story illustrates two instances of learning and thus leads into our discussion of the psychology of learning.

Both actors in this drama—mail carrier and dog—are displaying learned behavior.

When I first took introductory psychology, I looked forward to the section of the course devoted to learning. I was enthusiastic because I took seriously what I was trying to do at college—learn. I assumed that the psychology of learning would focus on the details of my everyday life as a student, like taking notes during a lecture, reading a textbook, mastering a new subject, choosing a career, and making distinctions between "none of the above" and "all of the above" on multiple-choice examinations.

These activities weren't specifically addressed in the learning section of my psychology course, however. Why not? I now know that I entertained a much too restricted definition of learning: that is, what took place in college courses. In contrast, psychologists opt for a much broader meaning that encompasses both how I learned to react to dogs when I was a letter carrier and how Fido learned to react to me. So, **learning** is any relatively permanent change in behavior resulting from experience. The qualification "relatively permanent" excludes temporary states like fatigue or illness or injury as part of learning.

We used to hunt and peck at a typewriter keyboard. Now we type without looking. We used to be indifferent to baseball games. Now our hearts pound in the bottom of the ninth. We used to get lost on the way across town. Now we take ever more efficient shortcuts. These changes in our behavior came about not through physical growth or maturation but through particular interactions with the world.

It is important to distinguish between learning and performance. *Learning* is what occurs as a result of experience, but it may or may not show itself in ways we can immediately see. You may have passed your cooking class with flying crullers, learning a lot about how to make gooey delicacies. But if you're not hungry, you probably will not display what you have learned. *Performance* refers to a person's observable behavior. Some changes in performance can be attributed to learning, like the desserts you can make now that you couldn't make before. But not all changes in performance reflect learning. Suppose you improve your grade from the first exam in a course to the second, but only because the teacher made the second test extremely easy. In this chapter, the term *learning* is used in a general sense, to refer to internal and external changes brought about by experience.

What Are the Basic Forms of Learning?

At one time, psychologists debated whether there was a basic form of learning. In the 1920s and 1930s, during psychology's era of great schools (Chapter 1), there was controversy over which was *the* basic type. Many contemporary psychologists acknowledge several types of learning, none more primary than others. **Habituation,** for example, is a very simple form of learning, in which we stop paying attention to an environmental stimulus that never changes, like the clock that ticks in our living room or the faucet that drips in the bathroom.

Conditioning is another simple form of learning, and refers to the acquisition of particular behaviors in the presence of particular environmental stimuli. Two types of conditioning will be discussed later in the chapter. First is *classical conditioning,* which involves learning associations between particular stimuli. When I learned to associate a jingling sound with a ferocious dog, this was classical conditioning. Second is *operant conditioning,* which involves learning associations between responses and stimuli that follow them. When the dog learned to associate its attack with my quick exit, this showed operant conditioning.

Another form of learning is **cognitive learning,** in which a person or animal comes to think differently about the relationships between behavior and environmental occurrences. Current research by learning psychologists implicates the role of cognition in even the most simple types of conditioning.

learning
a relatively permanent change in behavior resulting from experience

habituation
a simple form of learning in which the organism stops paying attention to environmental stimuli that never change

conditioning
the acquisition of particular behaviors in the presence of particular environmental stimuli

cognitive learning
learning that involves thinking about the relationship between behavior and environmental occurrences

contiguity
a principle of associative learning; associations are learned readily if they occur closely together in time

contingency
a principle of associative learning; associations are learned if two stimuli or a stimulus and a response predict each other

What Is Learned?

Psychologists are also concerned with knowing exactly what is learned when behavior changes. One answer has been that we learn an association, a link between two stimuli—as in the case of classical conditioning—or between a response and its effect—as in the case of operant conditioning. Several factors influence the strength of these links. One obvious determinant is their frequency. The more times I heard a jingling sound in the presence of a ferocious dog, the more established was my learned association between these two stimuli. The more times I ran away after the dog attacked me, the more established was its learned association between what it did and what ensued.

Another factor influencing associations is their **contiguity**—the degree to which two stimuli or a stimulus and response occur closely together in time. Classical conditioning occurs most readily when the one stimulus quickly follows the other. Suppose I heard a jingling sound, and then was attacked by a dog a few minutes or hours later. I would be much less likely to form any association. Similarly, operant conditioning occurs most readily when environmental stimuli immediately follow some behavior. Suppose that when the dog attacked me, I didn't run away for 20 minutes. Fido would be much less likely to learn any association.

In recent years, the idea that learning at its essence involves contiguity has been challenged, because contiguity alone may not guarantee that someone learns something.

Consider again my encounter with Fido and his noisy collar. Let's say that half of the time when his collar jingles, he attacks, and half of the time, he does not. Classical conditioning will not take place.

Note that in this case, there *is* contiguity (association in time) between the noise and the attack. What is missing is a unique association. This is called **contingency**. One current view holds that what we learn in classical or operant conditioning is a contingent association (Schwartz, 1984). According to the notion of contingency, what is learned is the predictability of a stimulus relative to the other stimuli present. Jingling sounds come to be linked to attacking dogs only when they are the best predictor of the attack.

How Is Learning Studied?

All psychologists, but particularly those interested in learning, seek to explain complex behavior in the simplest possible terms. For this reason, researchers have often operationalized "learning" in extremely stark terms. This strategy may seem strange to the uninitiated, but it makes perfect sense granted the goal of simple explanations. Let's therefore discuss how learning has been studied, keeping in mind the intent of researchers.

Studies of learning are usually experiments. Remember that the strength of the experimental method is its ability to identify causes—events in the environment that have effects on behavior (Chapter 1). Experiments are perfectly suited for studying conditioning, because they allow stimuli to be explicitly manipulated.

Both humans and animals are used as subjects. Why do researchers use animals in experimentation? Many theorists assume that learning occurs in much the same way among all species. If this is so, one might as well study forms of learning that are particularly simple, like learning by animals. Pigeons readily learn to peck at an object in order to acquire food. And rats readily learn to run through a maze in order to escape shock. These forms of learning— by assumption—are equivalent to forms of learning that are more difficult to study. So why not do what is simple? "Pigeon, rat, monkey, which is which? It doesn't matter. . . . Behavior shows astonishingly similar properties" (Skinner, 1956, pp. 230–231).

Also, animals allow the researcher to minimize extraneous variation on the one hand and maximize the impact of manipulations on the other. Learning researchers use animals that are specially bred to have minimal genetic variation. These animals are kept under uniform conditions in special colonies. If a researcher is interested in how an animal learns responses for food, for instance, she deprives it of food until it is at 80 percent of its normal weight. If a researcher is interested in punishment, she uses strong electric shocks.

Finally, researchers implement their experiments using specially constructed mechanical devices: A rat may be placed in a maze with food at its end; or a pigeon may be placed in a box with a button that can be pushed to produce a pellet of grain. These devices seem far removed from the natural environment of rats and pigeons, not to mention people.

What is the rationale for the use of such apparatus? The theoretical interest of learning researchers in the environment inspires them to create experimental situations in which relevant stimuli can be readily manipulated, while leaving out irrelevant stimuli. These situations represent extremely simple worlds, and this is intentional. Experiments need not provide realistic versions of the animal's natural environment. Indeed, they are deliberately pared down to the simplest possible terms. These devices are easy to manipulate in desired ways. With high tech innovations, everything can be automated, from the presentation of stimuli according to a programmed schedule, to the measurement of what the animal does and when it does it, to the analysis of the recorded data.

There is considerable disagreement among psychologists as to just how simple explanations of learning can become while still doing justice to their subject matter. Do we really learn nothing more than contiguous or contingent associations? Is learning so simple that one set of principles applies to worms, pigeons, cats, dogs, and people? Can a research strategy that deliberately makes learning as simple as possible produce results that apply to the seemingly complex accomplishments of people? There are no generally agreed upon answers to these questions, so just keep in mind that these are legitimate concerns.

Behaviorism and the Psychology of Learning

In 1913, John Watson published an influential paper, "Psychology as the Behaviorist Sees It," calling on psychologists to abandon their study of mental processes in favor of behavior. Watson thereby founded **behaviorism,** an approach that sees only overt behavior, not mental or physiological states, as the proper subject matter of psychology (Chapter 1). Behaviorists view learning as one of the most important psychological processes. Indeed, most influential behaviorists have proposed their own theories of learning. Their laboratory experiments, with animals as well as people, have become a preferred research method for investigating learning.

Behaviorism has profoundly shaped psychology as a whole, particularly in the United States, where its strong claims about the environment fit with this country's ideology of equality and freedom. Behavior is seen as determined by environmental stimuli, not as something due to inheritance. Watson himself made ample use of conditioning principles. His belief that the environment was of overriding importance is evident in his famous proclamation (Watson, 1930, p. 65).

Give me a dozen healthy infants, well-formed, and my own specified world to bring them up in, and I'll guarantee to take any one at random and train him to become any type of specialist I might select—doctor, lawyer, artist, merchant-chief, and yes, even beggar-man and thief, regardless of his talents, penchants, tendencies, activities, vocations and race of his ancestors.

Under the influence of Watson's message, psychology quite literally lost its mind. The study of "unobservables"

> **behaviorism**
> influential approach to psychology associated with Watson and Skinner that stresses the study of observable action, the importance of the environment, and the primary role of learning

became a taboo subject within many fields. Certainly, Watson was correct when he branded Wundt's method of introspection an unreliable research strategy. But in arguing that thoughts and beliefs are an inappropriate subject matter for science, the behaviorists perhaps went too far.

Their argument confuses *data* on the one hand with *explanations* on the other. Data of course need to be public and observable. That's what defines science, as stressed in the beginning of the book. But science is not just data. It is also explanations in terms of factors that themselves may or may not be observable. Consider gravity or atoms or natural selection or magnetism or any of a number of perfectly respectable scientific notions. We've never seen any of these things, but we still accept them as good explanations because they have many observable consequences.

What's the point for psychology? Well, you can't see thoughts, hopes, dreams, intentions, attitudes, memories, skills, or interests either, but you can see the consequences of these mental states and processes. If these unobservable notions help to explain the consequences, then they have a role in psychology. This idea is now accepted by many behaviorists, who find that one of the best ways to explain behavior is in terms of someone's thoughts and beliefs. These psychologists call themselves *cognitive behaviorists* and explain what people are all about by referring both to thoughts and to stimuli. Their research will be explained later in this chapter. For the time being, appreciate the great impact that Watson's behaviorism had on psychology in general and the psychology of learning in particular.

Let's now turn to a discussion of the important types of learning, starting with classical conditioning.

Classical Conditioning

classical conditioning

a basic form of learning in which an originally neutral stimulus, when paired with another stimulus capable of eliciting a reflexive response, comes to elicit that response in its own right; also called Pavlovian conditioning

Classical conditioning is learning that takes place when we come to associate two stimuli in the environment. One of these stimuli triggers a reflexive response. The second stimulus is originally neutral with respect to that response, but after it has been paired with the first stimulus, it comes to trigger the response in its own right. Remember the example that began the chapter. The ferocious dog automatically elicited fear from me. The sound of the dog's collar originally had no effect. But when I began to have the same response (fear) to the jingling sound as to the attacking dog, I had become classically conditioned.

Pavlov's Discovery

Classical conditioning was first described by the Russian scientist Ivan Pavlov (1849–1936), and thus it is sometimes called *Pavlovian conditioning*. Although Pavlov's place in the history of psychology is secure, he was not himself a psychologist. Rather, he had a medical degree and was particularly interested in the physiology of digestion. In fact, his work in physiology earned him a Nobel Prize in 1904.

Pavlov's research on digestion led him to discover the principles of classical conditioning. Using dogs as research subjects, he studied their salivation. If you know dogs, you know they are great at salivating. In particular, dogs salivate when food is placed in their mouths. This response is a **reflex,** an involuntary behavior requiring no learning (Chapter 2). However, dogs also start to salivate when presented with objects that have been associated with food. This observation could have been made by anyone who had ever been around dogs, but it took the genius of Pavlov to recognize that this was an interesting phenomenon. Objects originally neutral with regard to eliciting salivation, like a dish in which food is served or the research assistant who fills the dish with food, come to elicit salivation on their own. The crucial factor is that the neutral object be paired with food. As this association is repeatedly encountered, the animal begins to make a new response to the neutral stimulus; its behavior changes, and we can conclude that classical conditioning has occurred.

reflex

an involuntary behavior requiring no learning

unconditioned stimulus (UCS)

in classical conditioning, the stimulus that produces a response as a reflex

Pavlov called the food presented to the dogs the **unconditioned stimulus (UCS),** because it produced a response as a reflex, without

Pavlov's research on digestion led to his well-known classical conditioning experiments.

Figure 5.1

Example of Classical Conditioning. In Pavlov's famous experiment, a ringing bell came to elicit salivation after it had been paired with food.

Before Conditioning

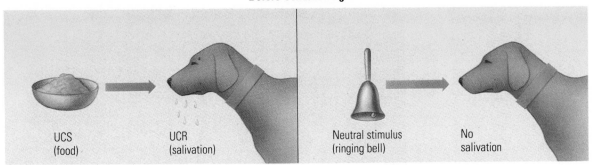

UCS
(food)

UCR
(salivation)

Neutral stimulus
(ringing bell)

No
salivation

An unconditioned stimulus (UCS) produces an unconditioned response (UCR). A neutral stimulus produces no response.

During Conditioning

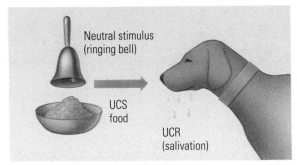

Neutral stimulus
(ringing bell)

UCS
food

UCR
(salivation)

The unconditioned stimulus is presented just after a neutral stimulus. The unconditioned stimulus continues to produce an unconditioned response.

After Conditioning

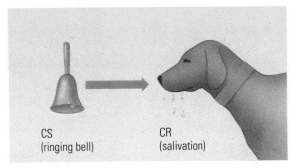

CS
(ringing bell)

CR
(salivation)

The neutral stimulus becomes a conditioned stimulus (CS), now producing a conditioned response (CR).

unconditioned response (UCR)
in classical conditioning, the response reflexively produced by a stimulus (the UCS)

conditioned stimulus (CS)
in classical conditioning, an originally neutral stimulus that produces the conditioned response after pairing with an unconditioned stimulus (UCS)

conditioned response (CR)
in classical conditioning, the response produced by pairing the conditioned stimulus (CS) with an unconditioned stimulus (UCS)

learning (see Figure 5.1). The dog's salivation in response to the food he called the **unconditioned response (UCR).** Note that when a UCS elicits a UCR no learning has taken place; the UCR is simply an innate reflex. The originally neutral stimulus that is paired with the unconditioned stimulus is called the **conditioned stimulus (CS).** The food dish and Pavlov's research assistant are both conditioned stimuli. Pavlov later used neutral stimuli like buzzers or bells that easily could be turned on and off. Finally, the response that the conditioned stimulus produces after being paired with the unconditioned stimulus is the **conditioned response (CR)** because it is learned. When the dog salivated to the food dish or the research assistant, it was showing a conditioned response.

Processes in Classical Conditioning

Pavlov soon developed a more controlled way of studying classical conditioning (see Figure 5.2). Continuing to use dogs as his subjects, he held them immobile in a harness. He fed them meat powder at precise times. A tube in their mouths collected saliva, allowing its quantity and rate of secretion to be exactly measured. Before giving the dogs food, Pavlov would sound a tone—a buzzer or bell. By using this procedure, Pavlov

Figure 5.2

Studying Pavlovian Conditioning. With this apparatus, classical conditioning can be precisely studied. The dog is held immobile in a harness, and its saliva is collected in a tube.

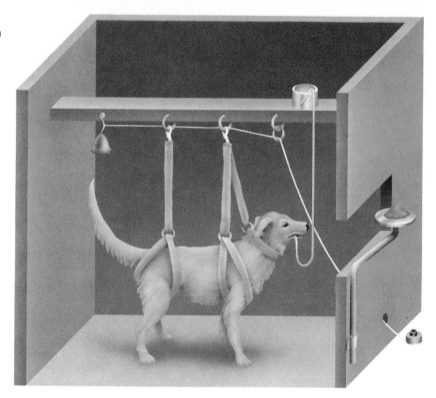

acquisition

in classical conditioning, the process in which the conditioned response becomes stronger through repeated pairings of the conditioned stimulus (CS) with the unconditioned stimulus (UCS)

and other researchers could study classical conditioning. In their experiments, they identified several important processes involved in classical conditioning.

Acquisition. The process in which the conditioned response becomes stronger through repeated pairings of the conditioned stimulus (CS—the tone) with the unconditioned stimulus (UCS—the food) is known as **acquisition.** As the number of pairings (or conditioning trials) increases, the dog begins to associate the CS and UCS. Soon the conditioned response (CR—salivation) will appear when the CS is presented alone. With more trials, the CR grows in magnitude or amplitude (i.e., the dog produces greater amounts of saliva) and decreases in latency (the dog salivates more quickly following the appearance of the CS). Eventually, as the number of pairings increases, the magnitude and latency of the CR reach leveling-off points (see Figure 5.3). The CR develops at various rates, which means that it takes different numbers of conditioning trials to reach these final points.

Researchers have carefully investigated the factors in the classical conditioning procedure that affect its magnitude, latency, and rate. The relationship in time between the UCS and the CS is often critical. We now know that classical conditioning occurs most readily when the CS precedes the UCS. This arrangement is known as **forward conditioning.** The exact time interval for optimal learning varies from response to response, but usually the briefer the interval, the more rapidly conditioning occurs.

forward conditioning

classical conditioning procedure in which the CS precedes the UCS in time

Figure 5.3

Processes in Classical Conditioning. During acquisition, the strength of a classically conditioned response grows. During extinction, it weakens. However, the response may appear again at a later time, showing spontaneous recovery.

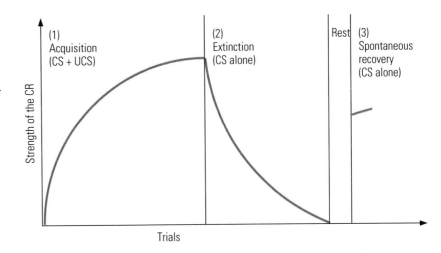

simultaneous conditioning

classical conditioning procedure in which the CS and the UCS occur at the same time

backward conditioning

classical conditioning procedure in which the UCS precedes the CS in time

What happens if the CS and UCS are presented at the same time, in a procedure called **simultaneous conditioning?** Conditioning is not as likely to occur as in forward conditioning. And what happens if the UCS precedes the CS, in what is referred to as **backward conditioning?** Conditioning takes place with great difficulty, if it takes place at all.

Note that the difficulty of conditioning responses with the simultaneous or backward procedure gives us reason to question that mere association in time is critical in classical conditioning. In all cases—forward, simultaneous, and backward conditioning—the CS and the UCS are equally associated in time, but only in the case of forward conditioning does the occurrence of the CS "tell" the person or animal anything. Obviously, contingency is important.

The CR isn't always the same response as the UCR. In many cases, the two indeed resemble each other, as in the example of Pavlov's salivating dogs, but in other cases the CR and UCR are altogether different responses. For instance, suppose a rat hears a tone for several seconds. Then the experimenter provides a pellet of food. Here we have the ingredients for classical conditioning: a CS (tone) and a UCS (food). How does the animal's behavior change in this situation? It becomes more active when the tone sounds—moving about and jerking its head (Holland, 1977, 1980). Note that this increased activity, the CR, does not at all resemble the UCR, the inherent response to food.

Pavlov's work, which secured his place in the history of science, has become a part of popular culture.

Extinction and Spontaneous Recovery. After an association between a conditioned stimulus and an unconditioned stimulus has been learned, the conditioned stimulus alone will elicit a response. However, what happens if the conditioned stimulus is repeatedly presented to the person or animal, yet no longer paired with the unconditioned stimulus? You might guess that the CS would eventually lose its power to elicit a response, and this is exactly what happens. This is the process of **extinction** (see again Figure 5.3). Extinction leads the organism to change its behavior when the associations in the world change, leading it to stop responding when responses are no longer appropriate. If Pavlov continued to present the tone alone to his dogs, no longer pairing it with meat powder, they eventually would stop salivating.

One interpretation of extinction is that it is *un*learning, the erasure of the association between CS and UCS that had been learned in the first place. But Pavlov viewed extinction differently. He thought that extinction involved new learning, in this case learning that the CS and the UCS did *not* go together. One effect of such learning is that the CS comes to inhibit a response akin to the one that the UCS reflexively elicits. Remember that the nervous system involves both excitation and inhibition (see Chapter 2). Learning can reflect both processes as well.

These ideas help explain the phenomenon of **spontaneous recovery,** in which a classically conditioned response that has been extinguished will sometimes reappear later (see again Figure 5.3). If extinction were simply unlearning, then spontaneous recovery would be difficult to explain. But if extinction involves new learning, then spontaneous recovery can be seen as due to a weakening of this new learning, so that the old learning resurfaces.

Generalization and Discrimination. Remember the earlier example of my learning to associate the jingling sound of a dog collar with an attacking dog? After I learned this association, I responded with a start to the sound of a jingling key chain. The sounds were similar but not identical. This illustrates another important phenomenon known as **generalization.** The more similar a new stimulus is to the conditioned stimulus, the more likely that stimulus is to elicit on its own the conditioned response.

Generalization is not rampant, however, because if a stimulus is too dissimilar, it will not elicit a response. The more dissimilar a new stimulus to the conditioned stimulus, the less likely that stimulus is to elicit on its own the conditioned response. This phenomenon is called **discrimination.** So, you develop an allergy to shrimp, and every time you eat shrimp, you become ill. You find yourself nauseated by just the taste of shrimp, and at first you have the same reaction to the taste of clams, oysters, and fish as well. But you eventually learn that you can eat these types of seafood with no problem. Your aversion to shrimp remains, and you have thus learned to discriminate.

Classical conditioning helps both people and animals live in the real world. Generalization is useful because we can apply our learning as stimuli change, without having to start all over again in every new situation. And discrimination is useful as well, because when situations change too much, we refrain from performing what we have learned in other settings.

extinction
in classical conditioning, the process by which a CS stops eliciting the CR, because the CS is no longer paired with the UCS

spontaneous recovery
in classical conditioning, the reappearance of a response some time after it has been extinguished

generalization
in classical conditioning, the process by which a new stimulus similar to the CS is able to elicit on its own the CR

discrimination
in classical conditioning, the process by which a new stimulus dissimilar to the CS does not elicit on its own the CR

Second-order Conditioning. We know that a conditioned stimulus, after pairing with an unconditioned stimulus, can elicit a response by itself. Now suppose we pair a third stimulus with the conditioned stimulus. Does further conditioning take place? In some cases, the answer is yes. This process of pairing a neutral stimulus with a conditioned stimulus is called **second-order** or **higher-order conditioning.** Second-order conditioning is not the same as generalization, because it depends on the pairing of stimuli with one another, not simply on their similarity. Schwartz (1984) gives the example of someone who starts out afraid of thunder, who then comes to fear lightning, and then rain, and then the outdoors—all through second-order conditioning. The significance of second-order conditioning is that it gives classical conditioning the potential to provide a quite broad explanation of learning, encompassing not just various conditioned stimuli but also all stimuli in turn associated with them.

Applications of Classical Conditioning

When Pavlov first described classical conditioning, psychologists saw it as an explanation for all behavior, human and animal (Watson, 1913). Current opinion is more modest about the applicability of classical conditioning to the behavior of people, although there are areas where classical conditioning fares particularly well as an explanation.

You may have noticed that many of the examples in this chapter involve stimuli that make the organism feel either good (like meat powder in the mouth of a hungry dog) or bad (like a ferocious animal or a booming thunderstorm). Psychologists distinguish between these two instances of classical conditioning, calling the former **appetitive conditioning,** because it involves pleasant stimuli, and the latter **aversive conditioning,** because it involves unpleasant stimuli. An emotional reaction is common to both. Basically, we learn to associate stimuli with emotions.

Conditioned Emotional Responses. We have now arrived at the area where classical conditioning most readily applies to human behavior—in the acquisition of emotional associations. Why do we like or dislike certain objects, events, or situations? Perhaps because they have been associated with pleasant or unpleasant stimuli. When in elementary school, I'd sometimes get the stomach flu and stay home. I'd sit on the couch and watch daytime television, all the time feeling dizzy and nauseated. Eventually, I was unable to watch these shows anymore, because they made me feel sick!

More complex behavior also reflects classical conditioning. For example, attitudes toward a social group or political issue entail an evaluation and hence an emotional response (Chapter 14). At least part of this emotional response is determined by classical conditioning. Did you ever notice that political candidates are frequently tall, handsome men with full heads of hair? Are we swayed to their platform because their good looks make us feel good?

In several experiments, William Scott (1957, 1959) showed that people are more likely to agree with a message if they hear it while eating. Do you see the Pavlovian point? The message is paired with food, and food makes us feel good. And so the message comes to make us feel good, as well, regardless of its content.

Advertisers are well aware of the power of classical conditioning, and it is common to see the most mundane products accompanied in advertisements by stimuli that are clever or impressive or sexy (Figure 5.4). Presumably, the consumer comes to associate lawn mowers or office furniture or fast food with these other stimuli, and ends up enthralled.

Classical conditioning can also be responsible for emotional disorders (Chapter 12). In a famous example, John Watson, in collaboration with Rosalie Rayner (1920), showed that fear could be established through classical conditioning. Their research subject was an infant named Albert. When initially presented with animals like a white rat, a rabbit, or a dog, he showed no negative reactions whatsoever.

Then Watson and Rayner again showed Albert the rat. Behind him the researchers made an extremely loud noise by striking a metal bar, which they knew from previous testing would upset the infant. CLANG! Albert jumped violently. The experience was repeated: first the rat, then the loud noise. CLANG! Albert started to whimper. After repeated pairings of the rat and the noise, what happened when the rat alone was shown to the child?

> The instant the rat was shown the baby began to cry. Almost instantly he turned sharply to the left, fell over on [his] left side, raised himself on all fours and began to crawl away so rapidly that he was caught with difficulty before reaching the edge of the table. (p. 5)

You can readily see that classical conditioning occurred. The white rat (CS) was initially paired with a loud noise (UCS) that reflexively produced a fear response (UCR). After just a few pairings of the rat and the noise, the rat elicited a fear response (CR) all by itself.

Several days later, Watson and Rayner demonstrated that Albert's fear of the rat had generalized to other white, furry things. He was presented with a dog, a rabbit, and even Watson wearing a Santa Claus mask. In each case, the infant whimpered and cried.

Figure 5.4
Sexy Advertisement. Advertisers make their mundane products attractive to consumers by pairing them with attractive stimuli, as in this ad.

Watson's 1919 film *Experimental Investigation of Babies* documents the series of classical conditioning experiments involving "Albert."

counterconditioning

therapy techniques based on classical conditioning principles in which undesirable responses to stimuli are replaced with desirable ones

Subsequent researchers have not always been able to replicate the results of Watson and Rayner, and ethical objections about the study's procedures can certainly be raised (Harris, 1979). Nonetheless, the Albert study remains a provocative demonstration of how classical conditioning can be involved in emotional disorders. Albert's fear response resembles a *phobia:* fear and avoidance of some object, event, or activity where no danger is actually posed (Chapter 12). Watson and Rayner's experiment gives us one way to think about phobias—as the result of classical conditioning. And it also raises an important question: If excessive fears can be acquired through learning, can they be removed in the same way? The answer is yes, through **counterconditioning,** which employs therapy techniques based on classical conditioning principles in which undesirable responses to stimuli are replaced with desirable ones.

Let's say we wish to "cure" Albert of his fear of white, furry things. We might engage him in some pleasurable activity, such as eating cookies or playing with his blocks. Then we would introduce the white rat. If this is done in a gradual fashion, starting at a distance and slowly moving it closer, he won't be overcome with fear. Instead, he will feel good and eventually come to like rats because he now has learned to associate them with something pleasurable.

An alternative procedure, again derived from classical conditioning, would be to expose Albert to the rat without letting him crawl away. Albert will not be happy about this at first, but eventually he will stop whimpering and crying. We are extinguishing the association between the rat and the noise. When this procedure is used in therapy, it is called *flooding,* a colorful metaphor that captures the basic strategy of allowing fear to flood over (and out of) the phobic individual. Spontaneous recovery of the fear response may occur, in which case flooding should be repeated.

Conditioning and Disease.   One of the most intriguing applications of classical conditioning is reported by Robert Ader and Nathan Cohen (1981), who found that they could condition the immune system of rats. Some drugs suppress the ability of the body to fight disease. What happens when researchers administer these drugs in conjunction with a stimulus (like a particular taste)? Learning occurs. The animal forms a link between the taste and poor immune functioning. When the animal later encounters the conditioned stimulus alone, its body less readily produces antibodies in response to foreign material.

Ader and Cohen's work extends even further the types of responses that can be classically conditioned. And their research suggests that certain stimuli can become associated with poor health, and thus contribute to illness in their own right. Conversely, if healthy immune functioning can be conditioned, perhaps disease can be countered not just by physicians but also by psychologists.

In his book *Anatomy of an Illness,* writer Norman Cousins (1981) offered a now famous account of how he mustered his body's psychological resources to combat a potentially fatal disease. One of his tactics was to check out of his hospital room and into a plush hotel (which proved less expensive than the hospital). And he watched funny movies. It is impossible to tell from this case study what was responsible for Cousins's successful battle with his disease, but perhaps classical conditioning was part of his journey to good health. He avoided stimuli which were associated with illness (the hospital) and sought out stimuli that were associated with health (fancy surroundings and humor). Perhaps he elicited good health from his body! Pavlov the physician might have been pleased with this turn of events.

Operant Conditioning

In classical conditioning, we learn how to react to stimuli in the environment. This is an important form of learning, and it helps people and animals alike adapt to the world (Rescorla, 1988). However, classical conditioning is limited to responses that unconditional stimuli reflexively trigger. Much of the behavior of people and animals is not triggered by particular stimuli; this behavior is better described as voluntary rather than elicited.

Psychologists use the term **operant** to describe any behavior that the person or animal emits spontaneously. An operant is *not* a specific reflex. Rather, it is a behavior that occurs at some frequency in the absence of any specific environmental triggers. Examples of operants include animals pressing bars or levers to produce food and/or avoid electric shock, basketball players shooting free throws, children playing tag, and scientists designing experiments.

We can further understand operants by remembering Fido's behavior described at the beginning of the chapter. When I delivered the mail, my presence did not trigger attacks in the way that meat powder would trigger salivation. In this case, barking and jumping are different sorts of behaviors than those explained by classical conditioning. Such behaviors are influenced by what follows from them, not by what precedes them. These and similar actions are termed operants because they "operate" on the environment, producing consequences for the person or animal.

So, another form of learning is **operant conditioning.** Here we learn to associate a behavior with its consequences. Depending on the consequences, this behavior will become more or less likely to occur in the future. What happened when Fido attacked me? I ran from the scene in terror. This consequence led the dog to attack with greater vigor the next time I ventured onto the scene. Other consequences might have reduced Fido's tendency to attack. For example, suppose I didn't leave when the dog attacked. Indeed, suppose that the more the dog jumped and barked, the longer I lingered. This consequence might well have led the dog to attack me with less ferocity the next time I delivered the mail.

Thorndike's Discovery

An American psychologist, Edward L. Thorndike (1874–1949), is credited with the first formal theory of operant conditioning, which he called **instrumental conditioning** to underscore his interest in responses that proved instrumental (useful) to the individual. He studied how cats solved problems, placing them in "puzzle boxes" (like the one in Figure 5.5), from which they attempted to escape. The puzzle box was built so that its door would spring open if the cat pushed against a particular lever.

Thorndike found that a cat so confined becomes very active. It claws and bites and struggles inside the box. After some period of time, it

operant
any behavior that is emitted spontaneously, occurring at some frequency in the absence of specific environmental triggers

operant conditioning
a basic form of learning in which a response is associated with its consequences; the response becomes more likely in the future if followed by a reinforcer and less likely if followed by a punisher; sometimes called instrumental conditioning

instrumental conditioning
another term for operant conditioning, to stress that responses are learned to the degree that they are instrumental (useful)

Edward L. Thorndike

Figure 5.5

Thorndike's Puzzle Box. To study learning, Thorndike placed cats in boxes like this one. To get out of the box, the cat had to move the lever, a response that occurred more and more rapidly over time.

eventually moves the lever that opens the door, and it bounds from its prison. The researcher then puts the cat back in the box. Again, the cat does all sorts of things, and eventually it again moves the lever and wins its freedom. Back in the box. More frantic movements. Back out of the box. Over time, the cat becomes more efficient in escaping. Irrelevant behaviors are no longer made. Instead, the cat in the box immediately moves the lever and escapes. Through trial and error, the cat has learned something: Moving the lever opens the door and allows it to escape.

Thorndike was struck by how the useful responses remained while the futile responses fell away. He concluded that reward stamped in these useful responses, and that lack of reward stamped out the useless ones. Thorndike (1911) named this process the **law of effect** and proposed this as a basic principle of learning. The law of effect was to become the foundation for what would later be called operant conditioning. If the effect of a behavior is to bring reward, then the behavior is more likely to occur. If the effect of a behavior is not to bring reward, then the behavior is less likely to occur.

law of effect

Thorndike's principle of learning: responses that lead to a reward are strengthened, and those that do not are weakened

Like Pavlov's discovery of classical conditioning, Thorndike's law of effect is important because it describes a form of learning, and his experiments provided researchers with a concrete procedure for research. Subsequent studies of operant conditioning use much the same methods as Thorndike. Various animal species continue to be used as research subjects, with rats and pigeons overtaking cats in popularity. These animals are placed in special devices where a simple response produces certain consequences.

Skinner's Approach

Pavlov, Thorndike, and Watson are the pioneers of learning theory. The most influential individual among the subsequent generation of learning theorists is Burrhus Frederick (B. F.) Skinner, whose approach to learning represents an extremely important statement within contemporary psychology. Skinner (1950) is a "radical" behaviorist, believing that psycholo-

B. F. Skinner

apparatus used to study operant conditioning; typically it has a lever or button to be pushed by the organism and a mechanism for delivering reinforcement (like food) or punishment (like shock); also called a Skinner box

gists should not concern themselves with unobservable (inner) states of the organism. Some behaviorists relax with regard to this stance, but not Skinner.

Skinner's work picks up where Thorndike's left off. He was particularly interested in how the consequences of behaviors affect their subsequent occurrence. Indeed, Skinner introduced the term *operant* to describe any behavior that the person or animal emits spontaneously. Remember that an operant is *not* a specific reflex but a behavior that occurs at some frequency in the absence of specific triggers. For instance, my operants include pulling on my nose, pulling on my socks, pulling on other people's legs, and pulling for the Chicago Bears to win.

If we know nothing else about Skinner's approach to psychology, we know that he gave the field the so-called Skinner box, or **operant chamber** (see Figure 5.6). Such a device provides a simple way to study operant conditioning. In one of its typical forms, an operant chamber consists of an enclosed box with a lever that can be pushed. There is a place where food pellets are delivered. The chamber may be equipped as well with various lights or buzzers.

All of the components of an operant chamber are under the control of the researcher, who varies their operation to see how an animal placed in the chamber behaves. The chamber might be programmed so that a food pellet appears whenever the lever is pushed once, or twice, or in whatever manner is of interest to the researcher. Things can be arranged so that lever pressing produces food only when a particular light is turned on, or only when another light is turned off. Favorite research subjects include pigeons or rats, but operant chambers have been designed for all sorts of creatures, from lizards to human beings to elephants!

Common to all operant chambers is that they allow a particular operant—pressing the lever—to be studied under various conditions. Usually

Figure 5.6
Operant Chamber

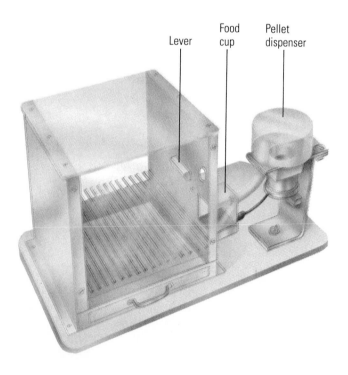

Lever   Food cup   Pellet dispenser

Figure 5.7

Cumulative Recorder. This device records the frequency of operants—like pressing a lever—in a given period of time. The pen moves every time a response is made, making a mark on the moving sheet of paper. The steeper the line, the more rapidly the operant occurs.

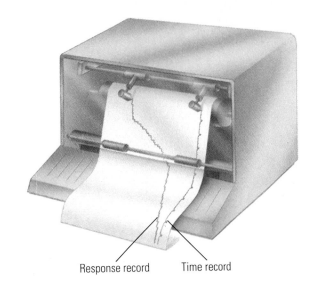

Response record   Time record

operant chambers are equipped with mechanical devices that automatically record how often the operant occurs in a given period of time (see Figure 5.7). Then when the researcher manipulates the consequences of the operant, it becomes possible to gauge the effects. Is the frequency of the operant increased, decreased, or unaffected?

Skinner does not use the term *reward,* because it refers to something that makes a person or animal feel good, and feeling good is an unobservable state. Skinner therefore speaks of reinforcers, defining them only in terms of their effects on behavior. **Reinforcers** are changes in the environment that follow some behavior and increase the probability that it will recur. **Reinforcement** is the process by which this occurs. We have no idea if a reinforcer makes someone feel good, bad, or ugly, and for Skinner, these feelings are irrelevant.

He further distinguishes between **positive reinforcement,** which involves a stimulus *presented* after a response, and **negative reinforcement,** which involves a stimulus that is *removed.* A positive reinforcer might be money given to a child for cleaning his or her room. A negative reinforcer might be the threat of a poor credit rating that someone avoids by paying a bill before it is due. A reinforcer is a reinforcer, whether positive or negative, and it increases the probability of a particular behavior.

Punishment is not the same thing as negative reinforcement (see Table 5.1). Rather, punishment is the process by which a stimulus follows a response and reduces the frequency of that response, and punishers are stimuli that decrease the frequency of a particular behavior. In *positive punishment,* an aversive stimulus that reduces the frequency of some response is presented. Getting a speeding ticket, for example, exemplifies positive punishment insofar as it reduces fast driving on your part in the future. In *negative punishment,* a reinforcer is removed, again with the effect of reducing the frequency of some response. Losing your salary bonus because you file reports late will lead you to decrease this tardy behavior, for example. From Skinner's perspective, we go too far when we ask if punishment is painful or unpleasant. We cannot observe the inner

reinforcers
changes in the environment that follow some behavior and increase the probability that it will recur

reinforcement
the process by which the frequency of behavior is increased because of changes in the environment that follow its occurrence

positive reinforcement
the process by which the presentation of a stimulus increases the frequency of some behavior that it follows

negative reinforcement
the process by which the removal of a stimulus increases the frequency of some behavior that it follows; *not* the same as punishment

punishment
the process by which a stimulus follows a response and reduces the future likelihood of that response; *not* the same as negative reinforcement

Table 5.1

Important Operant Conditioning Concepts

Process	Effect on Frequency of Behavior
Positive reinforcement	**Increases** frequency by presenting a stimulus
Negative reinforcement	**Increases** frequency by removing a stimulus
Punishment	**Decreases** frequency either by presenting an aversive stimulus or removing a reinforcer

states to which these words refer. All we can see is the effect of stimuli on an animal's or person's behavior.

To identify reinforcers and punishers, we must consider the individual case and look at how particular stimuli affect the behaviors of a given organism. We can make some good bets that food will reinforce and electric shock will punish, but this won't always be true. Identifying reinforcers and punishers by observing actual behavior and its consequences is what Skinner calls a **functional analysis** of behavior.

One finding from functional analyses is that we can be quite mistaken in our guesses about which stimuli will prove reinforcing or punishing. We might think, for instance, that a parent who spanks and scolds a child following some action is punishing the child, that is, reducing the frequency of that action. But in some cases, the child becomes more likely to behave in the way that leads to spankings and scoldings. We then conclude that these consequences are reinforcing for this child. If the parent wishes to reduce the frequency of the child's behavior, perhaps the wise course is to *withhold* the spankings and scoldings. Reinforcement and punishment are not always as simple as they first seem, and they will be discussed in greater detail later in the chapter.

Processes in Operant Conditioning

When Skinner and other researchers studied operant conditioning, they discovered a number of important processes that help explain exactly how this type of learning occurs.

Acquisition. As with classical conditioning, psychologists want to know the factors that determine the rate at which new responses are acquired. **Acquisition** is the process by which the frequency of operants increase. Several factors importantly influence acquisition. First is the degree to which reinforcement is contingent on a response, consistently following it and no other responses. Second is the immediacy of the reinforcement. All other things being equal, a reinforcer that follows a response quickly is more likely to affect learning than one that follows with some delay. Third is repetition. The more frequently a given consequence follows a particular behavior, the more likely the two are to become associated, and the more likely behavior is to be affected by that consequence.

functional analysis
the process of identifying reinforcers and punishers by observing actual behavior and its consequences

acquisition
in operant conditioning, the process by which the frequency of operants increases

How can you increase the rate at which you study for a particular course, like introductory psychology? Start with a reinforcer—perhaps a favorite snack or a television program. Then arrange your life so that you eat the snack or watch the television show only when you have studied your textbook for at least two hours. No exceptions. You don't eat the snack or watch the show under any other circumstances. This is what is meant by contingency. Now be sure that when you study this book for two hours, you toss it aside and immediately get your reward. Knock people over in the process! This is what is meant by immediacy. Finally, do this again and again. This is what is meant by repetition. (You may become overweight, unfortunately, or addled by reruns, but you'll know introductory psychology well!)

Shaping and Chaining.   Remember that an operant is a spontaneous behavior that occurs at some frequency. Only after an operant is emitted can it be influenced by reinforcement. If you think about this, you will see that operant conditioning seems highly limited as an explanation for complicated behaviors. For starters, we encounter difficulty explaining novel responses. How does someone learn to drive a car, or pilot an airplane, or make a cheese souffle if he must first "emit" these behaviors? Operant theorists have an answer: One does not learn to do these all in one piece. Instead, one gradually learns to perform complex behaviors by starting with simpler versions of them. This is the process of **shaping.** If the "standard" for reinforcement changes gradually over successive occasions, so that ever more complex versions of a response are followed by a reinforcer, then simple responses can eventually become complex ones.

Any of you who have trained a dog to do a trick like rolling over know that you can't wait for Rover to do this on his own. Instead, you first wait for him to list to one side. Then you give him a food treat. Then you wait for him to list even further. Another treat. Then you wait for him to fall over. (From too many prior treats?) Shaping explains how seemingly novel responses can be acquired through operant conditioning.

shaping
the process by which simple responses gradually become more complex through changing the standard of reinforcement on successive occasions

Positive reinforcement is the key to teaching animals complex behavior.

Another apparent limitation of operant conditioning is suggested by the fact that people or animals perform complicated sequences of behaviors over long periods of time with no reinforcement until the very end. For example, people buy airplane tickets, drive to the airport, check their luggage, get a boarding pass, find their seat, fly across the country, get off the plane, push through a crowd of people, and only then receive reinforcement—hugs and kisses from old friends.

What's going on? How do examples like these square with the notion that immediate reinforcement is a crucial factor in learning? Again theorists have an answer: A person or animal will readily learn a response that allows them to perform another response that brings a reward. And a third response will be readily learned, and so on, in a process known appropriately enough as **chaining.** Reinforcement need not occur following each response in a long series, as long as it follows the last behavior in the sequence. In chaining, the last response in the chain—the one immediately followed by the reinforcer—is learned first, then the second-to-last response, and so on.

Extinction and Spontaneous Recovery. Now, suppose you have learned a response that produces a reinforcing consequence. The rate at which you perform that response will increase. But suppose the world changes so that the response you have learned no longer produces a reinforcement. What happens now? Obviously, you perform the response less frequently. Its rate will eventually fall to whatever it was before reinforcement was first initiated. We can say that **extinction** has occurred—a decrease in the frequency of an operant behavior when reinforcers are withheld.

Clinical psychologists who work with children use extinction procedures to eliminate tantrums or profanity or disobedience. First, they identify the reinforcers that maintain these behaviors, let us say attention from parents, teachers, or peers. Then they ensure that when the child throws a tantrum or says a nasty word or disobeys a request, reinforcers do *not* follow. In plain English, the child is ignored. If this can be done consistently, then the undesirable behavior will decrease.

Needless to say, extinction procedures are easier to recommend in the abstract than to carry through in reality. One problem with carrying out extinction is that it is slow. Another problem is that behaviors may show a temporary increase in their rate before they start to fall off. Imagine calling a friend on the telephone. When there is no answer, you at first call more frequently.

There is still another problem with using extinction to decrease undesired behaviors. The child whose profanity has been consistently ignored by everyone and who now seems to have lost this nasty habit may start cursing again after a period of time. Parents and teachers may despair, and believe that extinction has been a failure, but the reappearance of an extinguished operant is not unusual. This is called **spontaneous recovery.** Extinction must again be undertaken. Indeed, many operant responses require several periods of extinction before they finally cease.

Generalization and Discrimination. Suppose your dog has learned to roll over because you have given him a treat every time he does so. When he sees you, he rolls over and opens his mouth. But when he is out cruising the streets alone, he never stops, rolls over, and opens his mouth. Why not?

chaining
the process by which a sequence of responses is learned through operant conditioning: first the last response is learned, then the next-to-last response, and so forth

extinction
in operant conditioning, the process by which the frequency of a response decreases because it is no longer followed by a reinforcer

spontaneous recovery
in operant conditioning, the reappearance of an operant some time after it has been extinguished

discriminative stimulus
a signal that reinforcement for a given response is (or is not) available in a particular situation

generalization
in operant conditioning, the process by which an organism behaves in a new situation as it did in an old situation because the discriminative stimuli in the two settings are similar

discrimination
in operant conditioning, the process by which an organism does not behave in a new situation as it did in an old situation because the discriminative stimuli in the two settings are dissimilar

primary reinforcers
stimuli that serve as reinforcers because of their inherent biological properties

secondary (conditioned) reinforcers
stimuli that serve as reinforcers because they have been previously associated with primary reinforcers; see primary reinforcers

In learning to exchange tokens for food, the chimps in this experiment came to "value" these secondary reinforcers for the reward they would bring.

Because you're not around. Rover has learned not only what responses lead to what consequences, but also the circumstances in which these contingencies hold true. To use a technical phrase, you are a **discriminative stimulus** for the treat that Rover gets for rolling over. Think of discriminative stimuli as signals that reinforcement is (or is not) available.

Discriminative stimuli affect the degree to which people or animals generalize responses learned through operant conditioning. If stimuli in a new situation are similar enough to those in a previous situation where responses led to reinforcers, then **generalization** has taken place. If the new stimuli are dissimilar, then learning is *not* generalized; rather, **discrimination** has taken place. Back to Rover. He has learned to roll over when you bend over him and say "please." When you bend down and say "fleas," he may also roll over. This is generalization. But if you say, "yuck, bugs," he doesn't roll over. This is discrimination.

Reinforcement

Let's now take a close look at the cornerstones of operant conditioning: first reinforcement, and then punishment. Psychologists interested in learning have investigated a number of basic questions about these important phenomena. What is their nature? What are their basic types? How do they influence the frequency of behavior?

Conditioned Reinforcement. Some stimuli are reinforcing because of their inherent biological properties. These are called **primary reinforcers.** Primary reinforcers include both positive and negative reinforcers, and obvious examples include food, water, and relief from pain. But as you go about your everyday life, few of the stimuli that affect your behavior are primary reinforcers. Instead, what reinforce you are stimuli like smiles and money and good grades and pats on the back. Why do these stimuli function as reinforcers?

A neutral stimulus can become a reinforcer if it is repeatedly paired with a primary reinforcer. Stimuli that derive their reinforcing nature from association with primary reinforcers are called **secondary** or **conditioned reinforcers.** Secondary reinforcers have the power to increase the rate of behavior because of learning. A whole host of stimuli can become conditioned reinforcers. Note how these reinforcers greatly extend the ability of operant conditioning to explain complex behavior. Even in situations where no primary reinforcers are to be found, we can use operant conditioning to explain behavior if we are able to specify existing conditioned reinforcers.

In several studies, chimpanzees were taught to perform particular responses for a food reward (e.g., Cowles, 1937; Wolfe, 1936). Along with the food, they were given "tokens" (like poker chips) that had no intrinsic meaning to them. However, the tokens could later be exchanged for food. After the link between tokens and food was established, the tokens themselves functioned as reinforcers. The chimps would learn a response in order to earn a token. Learning occurred even if there was a 1-hour delay between getting the token and exchanging it for food, as long as the chimp was allowed to hold on to the token. If more than one chimp became involved in the process, they began to beg and steal each other's tokens.

The parallels between the chimps' approach to poker chips and people's approach to money are obvious and intriguing.

What Is Reinforcing?   Some psychologists are content merely to note that particular stimuli are reinforcing. They inquire no further about the nature of these stimuli. But others are interested in what actually makes certain stimuli reinforcing. One possibility is that reinforcers "work" because they reduce biological needs (Bolles, 1967). In some cases, this is certainly a reasonable hypothesis. Food reinforces a hungry person because the hunger drive is reduced. Water reinforces a thirsty person because the thirst drive is reduced. In other cases, though, this drive reduction hypothesis doesn't really explain what is going on. For instance, animals will learn a response that does nothing other than turn on a light. Here there is reinforcement, but where is the drive reduction?

Another explanation of what makes stimuli reinforcing is known as the Premack principle, because it has been suggested by psychologist David Premack (1965). He proposes that more preferred activities can act as reinforcers for less preferred activities. Think of an activity you prefer (like watching television) and one you do not prefer (like dusting knick-knacks). If you arrange matters so that you will gain access to television if you first dust, then you will have a clean apartment. Television watching reinforces dusting. But reverse the contingency between these activities. Obviously, dusting will not reinforce television watching.

The Premack principle has considerable generality. For a hungry person, eating is a highly preferred activity that will reinforce almost any other activity. Further, the Premack principle helps the psychologist identify possible reinforcers without having to rely on trial and error. It also explains what is punishing: being forced to engage in a less preferred activity following performance of a more preferred one. Suppose you *had* to dust your apartment if you had watched television. According to Premack, your television watching would decrease.

The Premack principle has been challenged by some researchers, who argue that rigorous evidence in support of its predictions is scant (Knapp, 1974). A revision of the Premack principle has therefore been suggested: Access to activities is reinforcing when the person or animal has not been allowed to engage freely in these activities, but not otherwise (Timberlake & Allison, 1974). Regardless, an important implication of the Premack principle and its more recent modification is that reinforcement and punishment are not inherent properties of stimuli. No firm line divides reinforcers and punishers from other stimuli. What is reinforcing or punishing depends on the activity we wish to increase or decrease.

Schedules of Reinforcement.   In the discussion so far, reinforcement follows every response. But the world doesn't always work this way. Often reinforcement follows a particular behavior only some of the time. Someone who sells products over the telephone may have to make 101 phone calls before she makes a single sale.

Let's take a look at learning under circumstances where reinforcement does not always follow a response. Remember the distinction between learning and performance. In the process of acquiring some response, **continuous reinforcement** after every response speeds up learning.

continuous reinforcement
reinforcement that occurs after every response

Some people cannot resist the lure of a possible "jackpot."

intermittent reinforcement
reinforcement that occurs only after some (not all) responses

partial reinforcement effect
the tendency of responses that are reinforced intermittently to resist extinction

schedules of reinforcement
different patterns of delivering reinforcers following the desired response

But after a response has been learned, **intermittent reinforcement** has an important effect on its performance: The person or animal reinforced only once in a while keeps on responding vigorously in the absence of reinforcement. The response that has been learned resists extinction. This is known as the **partial reinforcement effect,** and it helps to explain what might otherwise seem like unusual persistence at a mostly futile endeavor.

Why does someone keep betting on football games? Because he wins every once in a while. Why does someone keep fishing? Because she catches a fish every once in a while. Why do adolescents keep playing a video game? Because they win every once in a while. Consider these activities—betting, fishing, and playing a video game—and the unlikely case where someone is reinforced every time he or she engages in them. What happens then if reinforcement ceases? Betting, fishing, and dropping quarters soon cease as well. These behaviors are extinguished. But take the more likely case where reinforcement is intermittent. Now what happens when there is a long dry spell, a period of no reinforcement? People keep responding.

Psychologists study intermittent reinforcement by manipulating **schedules of reinforcement:** different patterns of delivering a reward following the desired response. Several different schedules have been identified, each with characteristic effects on someone's performance.

When in high school, I had a summer job cleaning carpets in people's homes. I worked with the owner of the business, and his rule was that we would take a break only after we had cleaned three rooms. Once the carpet in the third room was cleaned, we stopped working and relaxed. This sort of schedule is called a *fixed ratio* (FR) *schedule,* because reinforcement (the break) came after a fixed number of responses (cleaning three carpets). When FR schedules are instituted in a Skinner box, their

Figure 5.8

Schedules of Reinforcement. Different patterns of reinforcement produce different patterns of response.

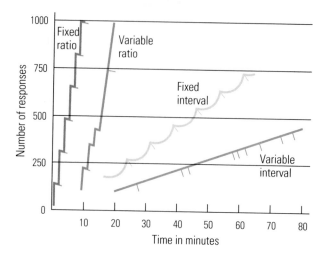

effect is to produce high rates of responding, with brief pauses following the reinforcement (see Figure 5.8).

The use of FR schedules in the workplace is called piecework. One is paid only for what one produces. These schedules indeed lead to high rates of productivity. They are popular with management but at the same time unpopular with workers. Salary from day to day and from week to week is inconsistent. Workers become reluctant to rest, go to the bathroom, or take a sick day, because it costs them to do so. Union contracts over the years have eliminated piecework in favor of hourly wages (Schwartz, 1984). Animals show the same aversion to FR schedules. Even though these schedules lead to high rates of responding, if given the opportunity to "escape" this schedule (that is, to turn it off momentarily), a pigeon will readily do so (Appel, 1963).

What happens when reinforcement is delivered only after a number of responses have been made, but this number varies? Here we have a *variable ratio* (VR) *schedule,* and this schedule leads to the highest rate of responding of all schedules that psychologists have studied (see Figure 5.8). There are no pauses following the reinforcement. Gambling is a frequently cited example of a VR schedule, because slot machines and other games of chance are specifically built to pay off on a variable ratio schedule. If you have visited Atlantic City or Las Vegas or similar places, you have seen the effect these VR schedules have on the patrons of casinos. They respond and respond and respond. . . .

In a *fixed interval* (FI) *schedule,* reinforcement occurs for the first response a person or animal makes, granted that a given interval of time has passed. Once the subject is reinforced, further responses have no effect until the interval of time passes again. Then the first response once more produces reinforcement. Suppose you have a newspaper delivered every day at the crack of dawn. When you go out in the morning, you find the paper and proceed to read it. If you go out again in the afternoon, however, you won't find a newspaper. You have to wait until the next morning.

FI schedules produce a characteristic rate of performance termed a scallop (see Figure 5.8). Immediately after reinforcement occurs, one's response rate is very low. One's rate increases slowly as the required time interval passes, though, so that when the interval is over, responding is high. Then it falls off again.

You should be able to puzzle out what a *variable interval* (VI) *schedule* involves. Basically, reinforcement occurs for the first response a person or animal makes, following some interval of time since the last reinforcer was given. The specific interval varies—sometimes one length, sometimes another. Think of when you've called a friend on the telephone with a message, only to find that the line is busy. You call back, knowing that eventually your friend will be off the phone. But you don't know when your friend will hang up. It might be seconds. It might be hours. What is the effect of this VI schedule on your redialing? If you are like the animals and people that psychologists study, you call back at a relatively low yet stable rate (see Figure 5.8). Responses reinforced on a variable interval schedule prove highly resistant to extinction.

Learned Helplessness—Learning No Contingency. When psychologists study schedules of reinforcement, they always arrange some contingency between responses and reinforcers. But sometimes people or animals may be exposed to a complete lack of contingency between responses and outcomes. Think of this situation as a schedule with *no* relationship between what the organism does and the delivery of rewards or punishments. Indeed something is learned: There is no link between what one does and what happens. What is interesting and important about this form of learning is that it may be generalized to a new situation. Even if responses and consequences are contingent in the new situation, the person or animal may not learn this association, because it has already learned to be helpless. We call this phenomenon (naturally) **learned helplessness.**

learned helplessness
learning that responses and outcomes are unrelated in one situation and generalizing this learning to a new situation, where passivity results

Learned helplessness was first observed in dogs, who were immobilized and given electric shocks on a prearranged schedule (Overmier & Seligman, 1967; Seligman & Maier, 1967). Regardless of what the dogs did or did not do, the shocks went on and off. Twenty-four hours later, these animals were placed in a shuttlebox, which is a long box with a barrier in the middle. Shock was periodically delivered through the floor of the box, and the dogs could turn it off if they "shuttled" from one end to the other, jumping or climbing over the barrier. Researchers found that animals previously exposed to uncontrollable shock acted passively when placed in a shuttle box. They sat there and endured the shocks. In contrast, animals without prior experience with noncontingent shocks had no difficulty learning to shuttle down the box to terminate the shocks.

Learned helplessness may help to explain a variety of failures of adaptation characterized by passivity. For instance, Seligman (1974, 1975) suggests that learned helplessness lies at the root of depression (Chapter 12). Other theorists suggest that people may fail in school or at work or in interpersonal relationships because they have learned in one situation that responses and outcomes are unrelated, and then have generalized this learning to a second situation. Although the second situation may be one in which behavior indeed produces reward and punishment, the person nonetheless acts passively, never learning that responses are instrumental. This passivity, so puzzling to an observer who doesn't know the person's prior history, makes perfect sense if we understand the original situation where helplessness was learned.

Punishment

Punishment has always been the principal means by which societies attempt to eradicate criminal behavior.

Punishment, like extinction, decreases the frequency of some behavior. However, extinction and punishment differ. We can make the difference clear by returning to our child who throws tantrums, curses, and/or disobeys. This undesirable behavior can be decreased through extinction, but it can also be decreased through punishment. We have to identify a stimulus that functions as a punisher. For our purposes, perhaps a loud NO! will suffice. Perhaps not. Regardless, if punishment is to be effective, it must be intense, consistent, and immediate. Then it will decrease the undesired behavior.

For several reasons, many psychologists recommend against the use of punishment as a means of decreasing behavior. They sometimes argue that it suppresses not just the targeted behavior but all operants by producing a host of disruptive emotional reactions. Research shows this argument to be invalid. Although punishment may temporarily disrupt a person's overall behavior, it is only the response contingently punished that is affected in the long run (Schwartz, 1984). The profane child may first respond to punishment of cursing by not talking at all, but eventually will show only a decrease in swearing.

Psychologists may also argue that punishment does not add anything to one's repertoire of available responses. Undesired behaviors are emitted in the first place because they win reward. If these are suppressed by punishment, then what is the person left with? This argument is obviously true. It is reasonable to recommend that we find an alternative and incompatible behavior to reinforce, rather than simply punish the target behavior. In the example of the child who uses nasty words to get attention, we might instead reward the child for talking politely.

Punishment is justified in circumstances where we cannot afford any delay in eliminating undesirable behavior. Here is a compelling example. Autism is a profound disturbance occasionally seen in young children. These children show marked impairment in language and social relationships. Autistic children may also perform self-damaging acts, like repeatedly pounding their heads against the wall, even to the point of fracturing their skulls and creating brain damage. One might deal with this problem behavior by ignoring it or by reinforcing alternative behaviors. Needless to say, these strategies may take too long, resulting in a seriously injured child.

Some therapists have therefore used punishment, like spankings or electric shock, to reduce such self-damaging acts. These procedures are effective (Lovaas, 1977) but have been controversial because they seem cruel. In a well-publicized case several years ago, Massachusetts barred such punishment procedures in a school for autistic children. The children at the school went back to self-destruction, and their parents went to court to get the ban overturned!

Applications of Operant Conditioning

Operant conditioning encompasses not just Thorndike's law of effect, but concepts like shaping, chaining, conditioned reinforcement, discriminative stimuli, and schedules of reinforcement as well. Taken together, these concepts provide a powerful explanation of people's behavior. In a section like this one, where we encounter "applications" of operant conditioning, it might almost be simpler to list those actions of a person *not* influenced by this form of learning, because almost everything we do (or don't do) is sensitive to the consequences.

Criteria for Good Applications. At the same time, we can specify particularly good applications, in situations where actions are (a) discrete, (b) observable, and (c) sensibly described in terms of the rate at which they occur. When what we do departs from these criteria, operant conditioning becomes a less satisfactory explanation.

A discrete action is a behavior that has a specifiable beginning and ending. Although it is possible to talk about one's career, one's identity, one's college career, or one's personality as "behavior," these designations are fuzzy because there are no particular responses to which these abstract notions refer.

An observable action is an overt response in the fashion of Watson and Skinner. Some theorists have tried to explain thinking in operant terms, rephrasing thoughts and beliefs as "covert behavior," but again this seems fuzzy, because "behavior" by definition cannot be unseen.

Finally, not everything that a person does is best described at the rate at which it occurs. Consider language. Some behaviorists have tried to include language within their general formula, but as we will see in Chapter 9, this hasn't been successful. Although reinforcers and punishers influence aspects of language, language itself is not learned through the trial and error process hypothesized by operant conditioning. And the essence of language—its meaning—is not explained at all by a theory that stresses the rate at which behaviors occur.

Operant Techniques in Therapy. Let's turn to therapy for some good examples of operant conditioning. Operant techniques systematically manipulate the consequences of behaviors in order to reduce the frequency of undesirable behaviors and increase the frequency of desired ones. For example, *time out* is an operant procedure recommended for decreasing disruptive behavior in children. When a child acts up, he is removed from the situation and placed in a quiet room where reinforcement is unavailable for a fixed period of time, say 5 or 10 minutes. This reduces the future likelihood of misconduct.

Social skills training involves learning how to do the things that produce reinforcement when interacting with others, like making eye contact, listening attentively, paying compliments, and so on. These may seem like obvious strategies for social interaction, but if you stop and think for a minute, you know that there are many people who seem not to know how to make others take an interest in them. Once these skills are imparted, reinforcement becomes more plentiful.

Behavioral contracting is a technique sometimes used in marital therapy, where a couple makes explicit their expectations for each other's behavior. Then they agree how each will respond to particular behaviors by their partner. Behavioral contracting in effect makes schedules of reinforcement clear and consistent.

A clinical psychologist is not needed to implement these techniques. You can carry them out yourself. Indeed, you can even do them *to* yourself, which puts you in the intriguing position of being your own behavior

Even the most obvious social skills— smiling, making eye contact—are learned through reinforcement.

modifier. You can use your knowledge of operant conditioning in a deliberate way to modify the world so that you end up acting in ways you desire. For example, I make use of the Premack principle in getting myself to do household chores. My example of dusting (yech!) and television viewing (yeah!) was not chosen at random.

Self-control.   When we talk about altering our environment and thereby influencing our own behavior, we are talking about self-control. The practical importance of self-control is obvious. The theoretical significance is in relation to the debate as to whether self-control itself is an example of operant conditioning, or whether it necessarily falls outside of it. Learning theories assume that what we do is determined by the environment. They assume that "inner" states are not important in explaining what we do. How then can we explain self-control? One answer from the viewpoint of traditional learning theory is that what looks like the deliberate initiation of action is really due to external rewards and punishments which we haven't yet identified.

Others argue that self-control puts a "strain" on the behavioral approach because it contradicts some of its basic premises (Catania, 1975; Goldiamond, 1976). Here we see the debate over the validity of simple explanations played out in a specific way. Some psychologists subsume self-control under operant conditioning. Others believe that self-control deserves a more complicated explanation, one that accords thoughts and beliefs a critical role.

Challenges to Traditional Theories

Classical and operant conditioning are both examples of simple forms of learning. In each case, the organism learns associations. But is all learning really this simple? Some psychologists argue that learning involves more than mere connections between stimuli and responses. Let's end this chapter by discussing several lines of work that question traditional views of classical and operant conditioning. In presenting these challenges, the intent is not to persuade you to dismiss the ideas presented so far in this chapter. These challenges do not invalidate the concepts and findings of traditional theories so much as they call for an expanded conception. This, after all, is the essence of science—changing theories in light of evidence.

Distinguishing Classical and Operant Conditioning

Up to now, our discussion makes it seem as if we can neatly divide instances of learned behavior into those produced by classical conditioning and those brought about by operant conditioning. Things are not always so neat. It was once believed that classical conditioning applied only to involuntary responses (i.e., reflexes or bodily processes), whereas operant conditioning applied only to voluntary responses. Subsequent research has shown this to be a false distinction.

"Involuntary" responses such as heart rate or blood pressure can be modified by altering their consequences (Schwartz, 1972, 1975). **Biofeedback,** for example, is a procedure for measuring and amplifying changes in bodily processes so that people can be aware of them. Once informa-

biofeedback
procedure for measuring and amplifying changes in bodily processes (like heart rate, skin temperature, or brain waves) so that people can be aware of them and thus modify them

tion about their biology is "fed back" to them, people know when their efforts to modify these processes are succeeding (Miller, 1978).

It is also possible for "voluntary" responses to be elicited. Consider a common response studied by psychologists interested in operant conditioning: a pigeon pecking at an object in order to get a kernel of grain. This pecking is regarded as an excellent example of operant learning, because the rate of pecking is strongly determined by the ensuing reward. However, pecking is also determined by classical conditioning. Pigeons tend to peck at stimuli associated with feeding, even when pecking has never produced food (Brown & Jenkins, 1968). This is called *autoshaping*, and illustrates the difficulty in distinguishing between classically conditioned responses and operantly conditioned ones, because the same response of pecking reflects both types of learning.

Perhaps classical and operant conditioning are involved in many types of behavior. Think of the example, one more time, from my letter-carrying days. It was used to illustrate classical conditioning, but it illustrates operant conditioning as well. I learned that the faster I delivered the mail to certain houses, the sooner I'd be away from a situation that scared me. The more general phenomenon here is called avoidance learning. First, through classical conditioning, one learns that certain situations are frightening. Second, through operant conditioning, one learns to reduce this fear by getting out of these situations.

Phenomena like biofeedback, autoshaping, and avoidance learning challenge traditional theories of learning by showing that the distinction between classical and operant conditioning can be a difficult one to make. In theory, these two types of learning are quite different, and we have discussed these differences in great detail. But in reality, a particular example of learning often and perhaps always reflects both types of conditioning.

Modeling

In classical or operant conditioning, the person or animal must literally do something in order for learning to occur. However, not all learning requires that we first go through the motions. Suppose you visit a new restaurant for the first time. You walk in and see a sign that invites you to seat yourself. You do so. But no one comes to take your order, and this surprises you. You've heard this is a great place, and how could service be so bad? Then you look around, and see that the other customers are walking back and forth from a counter at the end of the restaurant. Aha! They place orders with someone working there, and then pick up their food and drinks at the same counter a few minutes later.

What do you do? You get up and place your order. No big deal. However, from the viewpoint of traditional learning theory, this is a very big deal. You have demonstrated **observational learning,** or **modeling.** The fact that you have learned something simply through observing the behavior of others cannot be accommodated within the framework of either classical or operant conditioning.

modeling (observational learning)
learning by observing the behavior of others

Albert Bandura (1974) argues that modeling is the most typical way that human beings learn. We acquire our values, our attitudes, our characteristic patterns of behavior not in small parts through trial and error but in whole pieces by observing others. In a classic experiment, Bandura,

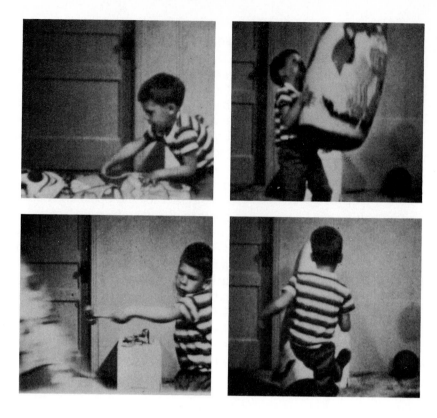

Ross, and Ross (1963) showed children a film in which an adult actor punched and kicked a large plastic Bobo Doll (see Figure 5.9). When the children later found themselves face-to-face with a Bobo Doll, they pummelled it! Children who had not previously seen the film were less likely to act aggressively towards the doll.

Research has identified a number of factors that influence the degree of observational learning (Bandura, 1986). Among these are characteristics of the model, the person who is observed. If she is liked, then someone is more likely to follow her example. The consequences of the model's actions also matter. If she is rewarded, then observational learning is encouraged. And finally, similarity between the model and the observer facilitates modeling.

Modeling may play a role in aggression (Chapter 15). People may act violently to the degree that they see others act violently. Models may come from one's family, one's peer group, or the mass media. The more attractive a model, and the more his or her violent actions result in reward rather than punishment, the more we expect an observer to follow suit.

If aggression may be learned through modeling, society must make some hard decisions about how violence is portrayed on television or in movies. Consider these facts. More American homes have a television set than have a telephone or a bathtub. The average television set in the United States is turned on 7 hours per day. Among prime time shows, eight out of ten contain violence, at rates ranging from five to twenty violent acts per hour. The highest rates are found on Saturday morning cartoons (Myers, 1987).

There is growing evidence that television provides models of aggressive behavior for children who watch it.

Documenting a link between violence in the media and subsequent violence by viewers has proven difficult. Popular attention centers on copy-cat crimes, where someone mimics an act of violence portrayed on a television show, but these are too infrequent to allow firm conclusions. A better research strategy is to undertake a survey in the population at large, correlating television viewing with measures of later aggression. Although confounds threaten this strategy, recent evidence suggests that children who watch violent shows on television while growing up are more likely to be convicted of serious crimes when adults than children whose television diet did not contain violence (Eron & Huesmann, 1984).

We will encounter modeling elsewhere in this book, because it provides a powerful explanation for a wide variety of behavior. But for now, you should recognize the challenge that observational learning poses to the traditional theories of learning: A person can learn different ways of behaving simply by watching other people.

Biological Constraints on Learning

In both classical and operant conditioning, we find the assumption that learning obeys general laws that hold regardless of the response or the species. From this assumption follows the position that all responses are equally able to be learned. This position is termed **equipotentiality.** The problem with equipotentiality, and hence with the assumption on which it is based, is that it is wrong. Not all responses are equally easy to learn. Recent research shows that an organism's biology puts constraints on what it can learn. Some responses are learned only with great difficulty. Other responses are learned readily.

equipotentiality
the assumption that all responses are equally able to be learned

taste aversion
the avoidance of a food because it was previously associated with illness

Taste Aversion.   For instance, if you drink too much alcohol, and then become violently ill, you may later avoid the type of drink in which you overindulged, because just the taste and smell of it suffice to make you queasy. This phenomenon is called **taste aversion,** on the face of it a simple example of classical conditioning. But examine this example carefully, and it makes no sense given the assumption of equipotentiality. How come the association you learned was between illness and the taste of alcohol, as opposed to an association between illness and ice cubes, or between illness and glasses, or between illness and the loud songs that played while you drank on and on?

You might say that of course you formed an aversion to the taste of alcohol, because that's what made you sick. But that's too easy a way out of the puzzle. Sometimes taste aversion occurs when the flu makes you sick. Even though lasagna, or orange soda, or chocolate chip cookies are not the "real" culprit, you later avoid these if they had been paired with being ill. Apparently, we are predisposed to form certain associations rather than others. In this example, we readily form an association between tastes and gastric upset. This bias has been confirmed in animal studies, along with an analogous bias in which research subjects link external pain more readily to visual stimuli than to tastes (e.g., Garcia & Koelling, 1966).

Preparedness.   A persuasive way to account for these biases is to place them in an evolutionary context. Think about our distant ancestors and the selection pressures to which they were exposed. The ability to learn—to modify behavior based on experience—is a tremendous advantage. Organisms capable of learning possess much greater fitness than organisms without this ability. But isn't a further step possible in ensuring the survival of an organism? How about being able to learn in an especially efficient fashion those associations that really exist in the world? Because upset stomachs often result when we eat or drink something foul, an organism predisposed to form this link will survive better than one that has to learn it by slow trial and error. Similarly, because things that are visible often can cause bodily harm, an organism predisposed to make this link has increased fitness.

Seligman (1970) concluded from such examples that there are three types of learning, each reflecting different influences of evolution. **Prepared learning** is learning that is biased by our evolutionary history. We can recognize it by several criteria.

- It occurs in one trial.
- It involves links over considerable periods of time.
- It is relatively permanent.

Think of how taste aversion satisfies these criteria. Some theorists speculate that people's phobias (irrational fears, such as fear of insects) and fetishes (inanimate sexual turn-ons, such as shoes or underwear) represent the operation of prepared learning. What is striking about phobias and fetishes is that they encompass a restricted range of objects, those that "sensibly" should be linked to fear or desire, respectively (see Chapters 12 and 16).

Contraprepared learning is learning that evolution has made difficult to acquire, if it can be acquired at all. For example, although it is easy to teach a cat to move toward something in order to be fed, it is difficult to teach a cat that if it moves away from something it will be fed. Think about the evolutionary story here. There is little advantage in learning that one can get what one wants by backing away from it.

Finally, there is **unprepared learning,** learning that is neither favored nor disfavored by evolutionary considerations. Perhaps the instances of classical and operant conditioning typically studied in experiments by learning psychologists represent unprepared learning.

Seligman's distinctions are not the only possible way to relate evolution to learning. He does maintain some universality in the principles that describe learning, in effect saying that there are three sets of learning principles: those governing prepared, contraprepared, and unprepared learning. But one can push this idea to the extreme, concluding that all "laws" of learning apply only to a particular species.

Instinctive Drift.   Breland and Breland (1961) described their tribulations in using operant conditioning techniques to teach tricks to various animals. Although successful after a fashion, these psychologists found that with time, animals approached the various tricks in ways characteristic of their particular species. The term for this is **instinctive drift.** So, through reinforcement with food, a raccoon can be taught to pick up a coin and deposit it in a bank. But it doesn't do this without first handling and rubbing the coin. And a pig can be taught the same trick, but it first throws

prepared learning
readily acquired learning presumably made easy by evolution

contraprepared learning
hard to acquire learning presumably made difficult by evolution

unprepared learning
learning presumably made neither easy nor hard by evolution

instinctive drift
the tendency of learned responses over time to take the form of an animal's instinctive behavior

the coin in the air, then pokes at it with its snout when it falls to the ground. If you know something about raccoons and pigs in their real worlds, this "misbehavior" (as the Brelands labeled it) is not at all strange. It's exactly how these creatures treat their food. The point is that in order to understand learning, we also have to appreciate the biological nature of the organism that is doing the learning.

The Role of Cognition

One more challenge to traditional theories of learning argues that mental processes influence behavior, including the simple responses learning theorists tend to study. Many statements of classical conditioning and operant conditioning make these forms of learning sound automatic. Indeed, some behaviorists seem to regard learning as something that one's body parts do.

But here is a problem with such a simple view. Suppose your hand is placed palm down on an electric grid. A bell goes off. Ring! Your hand gets a nasty shock. Argh! You raise your hand. As this procedure is repeated, you rapidly learn to raise your hand when you hear the bell. Now suppose you place your hand so that its *back* rests on the grid. The bell sounds. What happens? If learning is simply body movements, you should push your hand down against the electric grid. But this is not what you do. You pull your hand up and escape the shock. So what? Learning involves something more than just peripheral movement. If what you had learned was a particular movement, we would not expect you to make the novel but obviously effective response that you did. Learning must have a central—and presumably mental—representation.

cognitive map
a mental representation of a physical space

Cognitive Maps. E. C. Tolman (1948, 1959) was one of the first behaviorists to argue that cognition is important in learning. He studied rats that learned to traverse a maze in order to gain food at the end. If you're a rat, the pot at the end of the rainbow apparently contains food pellets rather than gold. Tolman's animals had no difficulty learning to get through the maze. Tolman then altered the maze. The food was still in the same location, but the old route wouldn't get the animal to it. If learning is only a series of particular responses, then the rats should have been stymied, because their previous responses wouldn't work. But the rats still found the food, and Tolman concluded that they had learned a **cognitive map**— a mental representation of the maze.

Wolfgang Köhler

Insight. Another example of cognitive factors in learning comes from Wolfgang Köhler's (1924) studies of problem solving among chimpanzees. He was marooned during World War I on one of the Canary Islands. Lacking access to human subjects, he did research with the chimp colony that lived on the island. In one of the problems Köhler posed, a chimp was placed in a cage that had a banana suspended on a string hanging from the ceiling, out of reach. Köhler had also placed in the cage a box and a stick. You probably see how the chimp could solve the problem of obtaining the banana. Hide in the box until the experimenter shows up, then threaten him with the stick until he turns over the banana!

The chimps in these photographs from Köhler's *The Mentality of Apes* (1925) exhibit problem-solving behavior based on "insight."

Well, not really. What the successful chimps did was move the box under the banana, climb onto it, and knock down the banana with the stick. Köhler called this form of learning **insight,** a sudden understanding of the relationship among the parts of a problem that leads to a solution. As you might guess granted this emphasis on the importance of seeing relationships, Köhler was a gestalt psychologist (Chapter 1).

An interesting follow-up to Köhler's studies is an experiment by Epstein, Kirshnit, Lanza, and Rubin (1984) using pigeons as research subjects. These investigators showed that pigeons could learn to solve the banana and box problem devised by Köhler, as long as the pigeons first learned the component behaviors: moving a box to a particular spot on the floor of the operant chamber, climbing on top of the box, and pecking at a button otherwise out of reach to produce a food pellet. This study shows how insight is made possible by previous learning that may be much more mundane. Remember the interest on the part of learning psychologists in explaining behavior in as simple a way as possible. In this study, "insight" is accounted for in terms of chaining (p. 190).

Information.   Yet one more demonstration of the role cognition plays in simple learning is the following example showing that the information provided by the CS is critical in producing conditioning. Suppose you can control the stimuli presented to a person. First, you sound a brief tone. Then, just a moment later, you turn on a brief light. And just another moment later, you deliver an electric shock to your subject's foot. You repeat this procedure a number of times.

What happens? You might expect that your research subject will learn to associate the light with the shock, and thus show some response when the light alone is turned on. Should conditioning take place with the tone?

Figure 5.10

Information and Classical Conditioning. During acquisition, a tone is sounded, then a light is turned on, and finally a shock occurs, which elicits a response. Later, when the light alone is turned on, no conditioned response occurs; when the tone alone is sounded, conditioning is evident. This demonstrates that conditioning occurs to stimuli that provide information about the unconditioned stimulus. No conditioning occurs to the light because it is redundant with the tone.

Acquisition

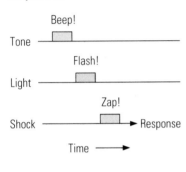

Test

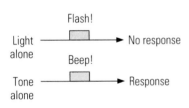

rules

abstract guidelines about how to behave in certain situations

Maybe, but this association will not be as strong as the link between the light and the shock, because it is not so close in time. However, when experiments like this are conducted (see Figure 5.10), exactly the opposite occurs (e.g., Kamin, 1969). The subject flinches in response to the tone and not at all to the light. Conditioning does not occur to the light because it is redundant with the tone, and thus provides no new information to the subject. Once we start talking about classical conditioning in terms of the information that the CS provides, the processes that underlie this apparently simple form of learning must be regarded as sophisticated and complex.

Rules.   Psychologists today increasingly hold that learning involves cognition. In fact, one currently popular way to describe learning is to say that people and animals learn **rules.** In contrast to an association, which is the simplest of links, a rule is an abstract guideline about how to act in certain situations; under these circumstances, a particular action leads to a particular outcome. If a person can phrase such a rule in words, then learning is made more efficient. However, we need not require that a rule be verbally represented to conclude that it is cognitive.

For example, animals can master the following task without benefit of words. Show them two shapes: squares, circles, triangles, whatever. Each shape has a lever underneath it. If the animal pushes the lever beneath the larger stimulus, it is given a food reward. Then another pair of shapes are shown. Again, pressing the lever beneath the larger of the pair results in reinforcement. After repeated trials, the animal consistently chooses the larger shape, showing that it has acquired the rule governing reward. We can also say that the animal shows a grasp of the "larger than" concept.

Other studies show that pigeons can learn to select slides based on whether or not they contain pictures of trees, vehicles, or even a particular person (e.g., Herrnstein, Loveland, & Cable, 1976). And they do more than learn particular responses to particular slides, because once a pigeon learns to make a distinction in one set of slides, it can apply this rule perfectly with an altogether different set of slides. Pigeons apparently understand abstract concepts. The importance of these studies is not what they tell us about pigeons, but what they imply about learning in people. If simple creatures like pigeons learn rules and acquire concepts, then we shouldn't hesitate in attributing this mode of learning to people.

In this chapter, we have seen how psychologists approach the study of learning. Among the basic forms of learning are classical conditioning and operant conditioning. A great deal of theory and research concerns itself with explaining the processes involved in such learning. We have also discussed several recent challenges to traditional views of learning that show that learning is more complicated than it may at first seem. Learning is a critically important psychological phenomenon, and we will see numerous applications of learning throughout the rest of the text.

Summary

Topics of Concern

- Learning refers to relatively permanent changes in behavior that result from interaction with the environment.
- Psychologists interested in learning have long been concerned with describing the basic types of learning.
- Another topic of concern to psychologists interested in learning is specifying exactly what is learned when behavior changes. One popular answer has been that we learn an association: a link between two stimuli or between a response and a stimulus. The strength of an association is influenced by the frequency with which these events occur, the degree to which they occur closely together in time (contiguity), and the uniqueness of their association (contingency).
- To study learning, researchers often employ animals as research subjects, conduct experiments, and use specially constructed mechanical devices that greatly simplify the environment of their subjects. This research approach stems from the goal of arriving at simple explanations of presumably general processes of learning.
- When John Watson founded behaviorism in 1913, he directed psychology's attention to processes of learning as an explanation of how overt behavior was determined.

Classical Conditioning

- One important form of learning is classical conditioning, in which organisms learn to associate two environmental stimuli. Classical conditioning was first described by the Russian Ivan Pavlov, who noticed that his laboratory dogs came to salivate in response to stimuli associated with food.
- Subsequent researchers have described in detail how associations formed by classical conditioning are acquired, generalized, discriminated, and extinguished following the undoing of the original association.
- Classical conditioning provides a good explanation of how people come to link various emotions—both positive and negative—to particular events and situations.

Operant Conditioning

- Another important form of learning is operant conditioning. Here, organisms learn the consequences of their responses—either reinforcers or punishers. This type of learning was first described by Edward Thorndike, who called it instrumental learning and studied how cats learned to escape from boxes.
- B. F. Skinner became the best-known behaviorist and learning theorist of his generation. His approach to learning picked up where Thorndike's left off. Skinner renamed instrumental learning operant conditioning. He carefully defined reinforcers as any stimuli that increase the likelihood of some response and punishers as any stimuli that decrease its likelihood.
- Researchers have studied various processes of operant conditioning, specifically how it is acquired; how complex behaviors are built up from simple ones; and how it is generalized, discriminated, and extinguished.
- Previously neutral stimuli can become reinforcers or punishers in their own right if they are associated with other reinforcers or punishers.
- Some theorists have tried to understand just what makes a stimulus reinforcing or punishing. According to David Premack, more preferred activities serve as reinforcers for less preferred activities, and vice versa for punishers.
- The particular pattern of reinforcement following a response can vary, and psychologists have extensively studied these so-called schedules of reinforcement. One important conclusion is that responses that are reinforced intermittently—not on every occasion—resist extinction.
- Some psychologists argue that punishment is not a good way to change behavior, because it adds nothing to an individual's repertoire of responses. However, punishment is probably justified in circumstances where no delay can be tolerated in eliminating undesirable behavior. Operant conditioning has wide applicability because so much of our behavior is sensitive to its consequences. Particularly good applications are to situations in which actions are discrete, observable, and sensibly described in terms of the rate at which they occur.

Challenges to Traditional Theories

- Recent years have seen several challenges to the traditional psychology of learning, suggesting that expanded theories are needed.
- For example, classical and operant conditioning prove far more difficult to distinguish in practice than in theory. Perhaps both forms of learning are involved in many instances of behavior.
- People need not actually perform responses in order to learn. Sometimes observation of others suffices to change our behavior. This is called modeling, and modeling may well be the way in which we acquire most of our complex behaviors and characteristics.
- Although traditional theories of learning assume that all associations are formed in the same way, research suggests that our biological inheritance influences the relative ease or difficulty with which we learn particular associations.
- One's thoughts and beliefs may be involved in even the simplest instances of learning, suggesting that all human learning involves cognitive processes.

Important Terms and Names

What follows is a list of the core terms and names for this chapter. Your instructor may emphasize other terms as well. Throughout the chapter, glossary terms appear in **boldface** type. They are defined in the text, and each term, along with its definition, is repeated in the margin.

Topics of Concern

learning/172
conditioning/173
contiguity/173
contingency/174
behaviorism/175

John Watson/175

Classical Conditioning

classical conditioning/176
acquisition/178
extinction/180
spontaneous recovery/180
generalization/180
discrimination/180
second-order
   conditioning/181
appetitive
   conditioning/181
aversive conditioning/181

Ivan Pavlov/176
John Watson and
   Rosalie Rayner/182

Operant Conditioning

operant/184
operant conditioning/184
law of effect/185
positive reinforcement/187
negative reinforcement/187
punishment/187
acquisition/188
shaping/189
chaining/190
extinction/190
spontaneous recovery/190
generalization/191
discrimination/191
secondary reinforcer/191
intermittent reinforcement/193
schedules of reinforcement/193
learned helplessness/195

Edward L. Thornike/184
B. F. Skinner/185
David Premack/192

Challenges to Traditional Theories

biofeedback/198
modeling/199
taste aversion/201
prepared learning/202
cognitive map/203
insight/204
rules/205

Albert Bandura/199
E. C. Tolman/203
Wolfgang Köhler/203

1. Learning is any change in behavior due to
   a. experience.
   b. maturation.
   c. physical constraint.
   d. all of the above.
   Behavior can change for a variety of reasons, but the term *learning* is reserved for changes due to experience./172

2. The current opinion among most psychologists is that
   a. habituation is the most basic form of learning.
   b. classical conditioning is the most basic form of learning.
   c. operant conditioning is the most basic form of learning.
   d. there are several basic forms of learning.
   After decades of wrangling over which form of learning was most basic, psychologists today acknowledge several basic forms./173

3. The hypothesis that the critical characteristic of a learned association is contingency has replaced an earlier notion emphasizing
   a. contiguity.
   b. frequency.
   c. intensity.
   d. proximity.
   Contiguity refers to a close association in time; contingency refers to a unique association. Recent thinking in the psychology of learning holds that contingency is more critical to the forming of an association than is contiguity./174

4. The psychology of learning was popularized in the United States by the approach to psychology known as
   a. behaviorism.
   b. functionalism.
   c. pragmatism.
   d. the cognitive revolution.
   When he founded behaviorism, John Watson directed the attention of psychology to overt behavior, to the importance of the environment, to processes of learning./175

5. Classical conditioning is a form of learning in which we come to associate
   a. operants and insights.
   b. responses with their consequences.
   c. stimuli in the environment.
   d. thoughts and feelings.
   In classical conditioning, originally neutral stimuli come to elicit responses through their association with other stimuli./176

6. Operant conditioning is a form of learning in which we come to associate
   a. physical illness with particular settings.
   b. responses with their consequences.
   c. stimuli in the environment.
   d. thoughts and feelings.
   The term *operant conditioning* was introduced by Skinner to emphasize that behavior "operates" on the environment, producing consequences that affect its likelihood of recurring./184

7. Negative reinforcement is a process by which the likelihood of behavior
   a. is decreased.
   b. is increased.
   c. stays the same.
   d. none of the above; it depends.
   Reinforcement is reinforcement is reinforcement! Whether positive or negative, it increases the likelihood of behavior./186

8. Intermittent reinforcement is associated with the _____ of operant responses.
   a. generalization
   b. rapid acquisition
   c. resistance to extinction
   d. vicarious reinforcement
   Operant responses are most readily acquired when reinforcement is continuous, but intermittent reinforcement results in responses that are highly resistant to extinction./192

9. People can learn behaviors by observing others. This process is called
   a. contingency learning.
   b. insight learning.
   c. modeling.
   d. plagiarism.
   Bandura argues that people typically learn by watching other people called models./199

10. In recent years, the psychology of learning has increasingly acknowledged the role of
   a. cognition.
   b. contiguity.
   c. emotion.
   d. species-specific characteristics.
   Traditional theories of learning have recently been challenged to take account on the one hand of the biological characteristics of particular species and on the other hand of cognitive factors./198

Whether or not human beings have instincts is a topic of
long-standing debate.

Chapter Six

Motivation, Emotion, and Stress

Topics of Concern
Classifying Motives and Emotions
Biological and Environmental Influences
The Role of Cognition / Stress

Approaches to Motivation
Motives as Instincts / Motives as Needs and Drives
Cognitive Approaches to Motivation

Studying Motivation
Animal Motivation / Human Motivation

Biological Motives
Thirst / Hunger / Sexual Motivation

Learned Motives
Aggression / Achievement Motivation
Power Motivation / Mastery

Approaches to Emotions
Evolutionary Approach: Darwin and Plutchik
Psychophysiological Approach: James and Lange
Neurological Approach: Cannon and Bard
Cognitive Approach: Schachter and Singer
Opponent-Process Approach: Solomon and Corbit
An Integrative Approach: Tomkins

Complex Emotions
Depression / Grief / Guilt
Humor / Love / Shyness

Stress and Coping
Conceptions of Stress and Coping
Cognition, Stress, and Coping

Topics of Concern

Method acting is an influential acting technique created by Konstantin Stanislavsky (1863–1938), a Russian actor and producer. He didn't intend to develop an acting style. All he wanted to do was devise a systematic way to teach people to be very good actors. He was tired of the classical teaching approach, which developed only the *external* talents of actors: diction, song, and dance. This approach to theater training didn't allow actors to be imaginative in their character portrayal. It didn't allow audience members to lose themselves in a character—they were always aware that they were watching an actor playing a part. So, Stanislavsky came up with a way to develop the *internal* resources of actors: their motivational and emotional abilities. Characters were to be portrayed by creating psychological states appropriate to the character being played.

By the 1920s, Stanislavsky's acting technique found its way to the United States, where today it's considered the basic building block of good acting (O'Malley, 1979). Among those who later studied method acting are Jane Fonda, Dustin Hoffman, Marlon Brando, Robert DeNiro, and Marilyn Monroe.

Strategies like improvisation, physical exercises, and relaxation are part of the typical training for any actor or actress who becomes the part that is played. Here are some representative exercises used in method acting:

- *Sense memory*—Actors try to remember their sensations, so they can bring them alive on stage. An exercise might involve an actor imagining a cup of hot coffee on a table next to him. He can smell the coffee's rich aroma. He imagines picking up the cup and feeling the warmth on his fingers. He then tastes the coffee, and feels it glide down his throat. The smell tickles his nostrils. The exercise ends with him putting the empty cup back on the table. Oops, a spill! No matter, nothing is real except the sensation.
- *Affective memory*—Actors try to remember key events from their past, and the emotions that accompanied them. Then they apply those feelings to the character they are portraying. The premise here is that a compelling character must have depth, including thoughts and feelings. The best way for an actor to add such depth to a character is to borrow it from his or her own past.

Marlon Brando is one of the most renowned practitioners of method acting, which stresses the development of the actor's internal resources: sense memory, affective memory, and concentration among them.

- *Concentration*—Actresses must relax on stage, but they must also concentrate. So, a typical exercise to aid concentration might involve the actress sitting in a chair with her eyes closed. Calling forth mental images, she starts to create a "sensory circle" around herself. She tries to keep her concentration within the boundaries of the circle—just thinking about the chair and floor. Once comfortable, the actress expands her circle of concentration to include a stage.
- *Animal exercises*—As you've seen already in this textbook, animal behavior can give us an insight into human behavior. Both method acting and psychology make this assumption. So, actors may go to the zoo and study animals, especially our close cousins, chimps and gorillas, to understand motivation and emotion and how they can be expressed.

Motivation and emotion—now so basic to acting, thanks to Stanislavsky—are important aspects of the human condition, and psychologists have long been interested in them. Both terms come from the same word: *motion.*

Motivation refers to the processes that arouse, direct, and maintain our behavior. In method acting, the actor must convey to the audience the particular motives of his character.

Emotion includes not only the subjective feelings that move through us in response to situations, but also patterns of physiological arousal, thought, and behavior. Again, in method acting, an actor must create the emotions appropriate to a part, which means a rich psychological and physical response.

If we wish to be precise in how we use the word, we should employ *emotion* not simply for particular feelings, but additionally for the accompanying physiological, cognitive, and behavioral reactions. In everyday language, *emotion* is often used to describe someone's subjective feelings, but *mood* is probably a more exact word in this case.

Motivation and emotion have something else in common besides their origin in the word *motion.* They both refer to the organization of behavior over time. In the case of motivation, we focus on the consequences of our motives. Thirst leads to drinking; hunger leads to eating; achievement motivation leads to all-nighters in the library. In the case of emotion, we focus on what precedes our emotions. Frustration leads to anger; disappointment leads to sadness; a clever bumper sticker leads to humor. The relationship between motivation and emotion can become quite complex, of course, because in many cases they mutually influence each other. Motivation and emotion form a bridge between the topics covered in Chapters 2 and 3, in which biological factors play a major role, and the topics covered in Chapters 4 and 5 as well as subsequent chapters, in which environmental factors take on central importance.

motivation
the processes that arouse, direct, and maintain our behavior

emotion
the subjective feelings we experience in response to situations, as well as patterns of accompanying physiological arousal, thoughts, and behaviors

primary motives
biologically based motives like hunger, thirst, and sex

acquired motives
learned motives like achievement, power, and mastery

Classifying Motives and Emotions

What are the basic motives and emotions? Psychologists have long attempted to answer this question by proposing a classification scheme, or typology. In method acting, for example, if one wishes to acquire a repertoire of basic motives and feelings, just what should be included? And what is the rationale for deciding that a motive or emotion is a basic one?

Many psychologists classify motives as either primary or acquired. **Primary motives** are biological in nature: hunger, thirst, and sex. **Acquired motives** are learned: achievement, power, and mastery, to name but a few. In this chapter, we will follow this classification of motives into primary and acquired categories. Note, however, that there is considerable debate regarding whether certain motives are primary or acquired, echoing again the nature-nurture controversy.

When we consider emotions and how they might be classified, we may find that the simplest way to describe them is in terms of those that are positive and those that are negative. Recent research suggests that people in different cultures readily recognize the same emotions—anger, fear, sadness, disgust, surprise, curiosity, acceptance, and joy, to name a few—giving us another way to classify emotions (Ekman, 1984). Perhaps these are basic emotions, inherent in our biological makeup. If so, emotions like guilt or love or humor are complex ones, formed by combining various basic emotions.

The fact that people tend to express and recognize emotions in the same way implies that these generally characterize our species. Studies of infants born without sight further support this possibility. They show the same facial expressions as children who can see (e.g., smiling, pouting, and crying), and these expressions appear in the same situations (Eibl-Eibesfeldt, 1970). These findings rule out imitation as an explanation of the universality of emotional expression, because blind infants quite obviously have never seen how others express emotions.

Biological and Environmental Influences

Psychologists who study motivation and emotion are also concerned with the interplay between the biological and environmental determinants of these phenomena. For example, hunger involves tissue needs and stomach contractions, but these can't account for why some hungry people seek out a Pepsi and a cheeseburger, whereas others look for tofu and sprouts. When someone steps on our foot, we feel angry because crushed toes hurt. But we need to take into account more than pain receptors to explain why anger goes away if the person who stepped on our foot is apologetic, while it escalates if he or she tells us to watch where we place our feet. Both biology and environmental factors are needed to explain many human motives and emotions.

The Role of Cognition

Theories of motivation and emotion first arose when people started to ask themselves or others, "Why did we act that way?" For instance, almost 2400 years ago the Greek philosopher Thrasymachus proposed that people are motivated solely by their desire to avoid pain and find pleasure. His contemporary, Socrates, argued differently. He felt that people are motivated by their beliefs about what is right and wrong.

Thrasymachus suggested that people are incapable of sympathy or altruism: "Go for it." But according to Socrates, people take into account what is right and wrong independently of selfish concerns. Indeed, Socrates held that a person is incapable of acting in a way that he or she knows to be wrong: "To know the good is to do the good." Here

stress
the complex reactions that take place when someone tries to adapt to the demands of external events

stressors
events that threaten or challenge the individual (produce stress)

we see the first phrasing of an important issue that still concerns contemporary psychologists, whether motivation and emotion should be linked to cognition or not. When the cognitive revolution swept through psychology in the 1960s and 1970s, the topics of motivation and emotion were included in its wake. And so we now have a number of cognitive theories that propose thoughts and beliefs as the cause of motives and emotions (Mineka & Henderson, 1985). Quite recently, however, there has been a backlash against this cognitive theorizing (e.g., Zajonc, 1980, 1984). Later in the chapter, we will look more closely at the connection between motivation and emotion on the one hand and cognition on the other.

Stress

Motivation and emotion can be separated for purposes of discussion, but they are found together in our actual behavior. The links between motivation and emotion are particularly obvious in one important area of psychological investigation, **stress**—the complex reactions that take place when someone tries to adapt to the demands of external events, called **stressors.** A variety of biological and psychological responses, including particular motives and emotions, directly result from stress.

Researchers have linked stress to psychological problems as well as to physical illnesses, and psychologists seek to understand the exact details of this link. Further, psychologists are interested in helping people respond better to stress, blunting the damage that might otherwise be caused. Some of the strategies devised by psychologists for this purpose resemble the method acting techniques of Stanislavsky. We'll discuss stress in detail later in the chapter, as well as the ways by which people cope with it.

Approaches to Motivation

How do we explain human motivation? Over the years, psychologists have approached this question from several different theoretical viewpoints. In this section, we will look at three of these approaches to motivation: motives explained in terms of instincts, motives explained in terms of needs and drives, and motives explained in terms of cognition.

Motives as Instincts

When we explain the behavior of animals, the concept of instincts can be quite persuasive, because in various species, complex behavior can appear without ever having been learned (remember Chapter 2). Consider sex and aggression in the stickleback fish, a popular research subject for the ethologists. During the spring, the male undergoes hormonal changes that prepare him for reproduction. His belly turns red, and he builds a nest. He begins to patrol the territory about the nest. If he encounters another male, recognizable by *its* red belly, he attacks him. If he encounters a female, recognizable by a swollen belly filled with eggs, he courts her. Then she may follow him to his nest, where she releases her eggs. He fertilizes and watches over them until they hatch.

Let's emphasize several aspects of this scenario. First, note the connection between sex and aggression, a connection which among sticklebacks has a biological basis. Indeed, in many species, including mammals, the same hormones that enhance the male sex drive also enhance aggressiveness. Second, the stickleback's behaviors (attack or courtship) are complex, unlearned sequences. Contrast these behaviors with those of interest to learning theorists (Chapter 5). Third, these sequences occur in response to particular environmental events called *releasing stimuli*. Red bellies elicit attack; swollen bellies elicit courtship. We can sensibly speak of the stickleback fish as showing instincts.

The courtship behavior of the male stickleback fish, on the left, is purely instinctive, the result of seasonal hormonal changes.

To what degree can we generalize from stickleback fish to people? Naturally, you're going to find considerable differences of opinion. In the nineteenth century and early in the twentieth century, explanations of human behavior in terms of instincts were quite popular (e.g., McDougall, 1908). Theorists proposed numerous human instincts, like sympathy, secretiveness, cleanliness, and modesty. In each case, they started with a behavior that needed an explanation. Then they suggested an instinctive motive for the behavior. Finally, they concluded that this motive proved useful, in the course of human evolution, and hence natural selection led to the current form of the behavior.

In Chapter 2, we saw how evolutionary explanations can invite circular reasoning. Here is some strong criticism of the entire endeavor:

> If a man seeks his fellows, it is the instinct of gregariousness; if he walks alone, it is the solitary instinct; if he twiddles his thumbs, it is the thumb-twiddling instinct; if he does not twiddle his thumbs, it the thumb-not-twiddling instinct. Thus everything is explained with the facility of magic—word magic. (Holt, 1931, p. 4)

Contemporary psychologists have heeded such criticism and refrain from telling just-so stories about human motivation. At the present, the prevailing view is that people's motives are less rigidly wired into the nervous system and therefore much more a function of our particular learning and culture.

Motives as Needs and Drives

By the 1940s, the view of motives as instincts gave way to theories that conceived motives as internal states that set behavior in motion (Hull, 1943). Two related concepts are important in this viewpoint. First is a **need,** which we may define as the lack of some biological essential, like food or water. Second is a **drive,** a state of tension or arousal that a need produces. When a person experiences a drive, he or she tries to reduce the tension, typically by satisfying the need that gives rise to the drive. Suppose we are thirsty. We are, so to speak, driven to ask for a glass of water, to stick our head under a faucet, or to melt an ice cube in our mouth. If one or more of these behaviors reduces our thirst, we are no longer motivated to seek out and drink liquid.

You are well aware that other motivational states exist besides thirst. To need-and-drive theorists, all such motives work in the same way:

a need occurs →
a corresponding drive is aroused →
goal-directed behavior takes place →
the goal is achieved →
the drive is reduced →

Note how this approach to motivation includes a crucial role for biological factors, because the drive is stimulated by physiological needs. However, the actual behaviors that reduce the drives may be learned.

Understanding the process of **homeostasis**—the maintenance of a stable or balanced state of physiological conditions—is an important idea if we are to understand most need-and-drive theories of motivation. Drives

need
the lack of some biological essential, like food or water

drive
a state of tension or arousal produced by a need

homeostasis
maintenance of a stable or balanced state of physiological conditions

are aroused when our internal state gets out of balance: for example, when we are too hungry or too thirsty. The goal of behavior caused by a drive is to return our system to a balanced state.

A common means of maintaining homeostasis is by using a feedback system, which produces changes in the environment which in turn affect the system's operation. Most of us live in houses or apartments with thermostats that turn the furnace on when the temperature falls too low and turn it off when the temperature rises too high. Thermostats keep the temperature within certain limits, just as needs and drives maintain the homeostasis of our bodies.

So far, in our discussion of drives, we have focused on primary motives, those based in physiological needs. However, motives themselves can be learned; psychologists speak of these motives as acquired drives. In Chapter 5, we saw how previously neutral stimuli can take on reinforcing or punishing properties through classical conditioning. Suppose a rat is placed in a cage with an electrified floor. A buzzer sounds, and a shock is administered a few seconds later. If the animal scrambles from one side of the cage to the other within these few seconds, the shock does not occur. The first few times this is played out, the rat gets shocked. But after a while, it starts moving when the buzzer sounds. Learning has occurred, because the rat now readily avoids shock. One way to look at this example is to say that the rat has learned to fear the buzzer. Fear then leads to avoidance (Mowrer, 1950). In this case, fear of the buzzer is an acquired drive that motivates attempts to reduce it.

The idea of acquired drives greatly extends the ability of need-and-drive theories to explain motivation. Nonetheless, the problem with this approach as an account of all motives is that some of our motives simply don't act as drives are supposed to. Take sexual and aggressive behavior as shown by human beings, rather than stickleback fish. Sex functions much more like a drive than does aggression, in that orgasms lead to a temporary waning of sexual activity, whereas an outburst of aggression

Running to stay warm is an example of behavior aimed at maintaining a balanced physiological state.

typically leads to even more aggression. Aggression among people cannot be explained as simply as aggression among animals, a point to which we will return later in this chapter, as well as in Chapter 15.

Cognitive Approaches to Motivation

Theories that explain human motivation in terms of instincts or needs and drives neglect the important role played by our interpretations. Even a biological motive such as hunger reflects thoughts and beliefs about how best to satisfy our desires. These cognitions are instilled in us by socialization. Gardner Murphy (1947) considers food preference an excellent example of how biological motives become entwined with social significance. Infants are generally hungry or not hungry. But as we grow older, "hunger" becomes specific and symbolic. We hunger not for generic food, but for baked potatoes, eggplant parmigiana, stir-fried vegetables, borscht, or tacos. Many of us would rather go hungry than eat certain foods. It should be obvious that other human motives, such as thirst or sex or aggression, also take on social significance.

Another example of the importance of cognition comes from the investigations of learned helplessness conducted by Maier and Seligman (1976). As explained in Chapter 5, these researchers exposed rats to electric shocks that could neither be avoided or escaped. Twenty-four hours later, these animals again were exposed to shock, but in a situation that would allow them to terminate it with a simple response. Their behavior was striking: They did nothing at all!

Even though the rats could escape the shocks, they made no attempt to do so. Why? Further studies showed that the rats were not traumatized by the original shocks. They were physically capable of responding. Maier and Seligman believe that the rats failed to initiate an escape because they lacked the motivation to do so. This lack of motivation was the result of what the rats learned when they first experienced shocks: Nothing they did mattered. In other words, the rats learned that they were helpless, and this learning took the form of an *expectation* that future responding would also be futile. A belief in their own helplessness produced a lack of motivation to escape shock, which is ironic given the fact that, in the second instance, they were able to do so.

Learned helplessness has intrigued a number of psychologists, who see the same process involved in various aspects of human passivity: depression, school failure, response to victimization, chronic unemployment, even dismal performance by athletic teams (Peterson, 1989). The point of the learned helplessness phenomenon illustrates how motivation can reflect cognition.

Recent years have seen an explosion of cognitive theories of motivation (Weiner, 1985). These theories share the notion that one's beliefs shape one's activities. Indeed, as in learned helplessness, beliefs can even determine whether activities are undertaken at all. Note that instinct theories and drive theories of motivation make no room for cognitions as causes of behavior.

intrinsic motivation
pursuit of activities when there is no external reward for doing so

The cognitive approach to motivation can be seen in one of the ways that we can undermine **intrinsic motivation**—our pursuit of activ-

This kayaker could be responding to intrinsic motivation—the thrill of the activity for its own sake; or extrinsic motivation—preparing for a competitive event.

extrinsic motivation
pursuit of activities because of external reward or punishment

ities when there is no external reward for doing so. Intrinsic motivation leads us to pursue activities for their own sake, because the activities themselves give us pleasure. In contrast, **extrinsic motivation** refers to motivation that is determined by external reward or punishment. Suppose we were to give someone who collects stamps a tangible reward for what she has been doing all along, say fifty cents for every stamp put in an album. After a period of time, we withdraw the reward. Our stamp collector is then less likely to engage in the activity! Her intrinsic motivation has been reduced by the offer of an extrinsic reward (Deci, 1975; Deci & Ryan, 1980).

We can readily explain these results in terms of the person's interpretation of her own motivation. If paid for collecting stamps, she may say to herself, "I must be collecting stamps because of the money." When the money is withheld, she then says, "I no longer have a reason to collect stamps." In other words, her particular cognitions about herself determine her motivation, and they change after she is paid.

Although a cognitive approach to motivation is currently popular, not all psychologists are convinced that cognitions are the most important determinants of motivation. What about biological processes, which are ignored in many cognitive explanations? The learned helplessness phenomenon, for instance, apparently reflects not just expectations but also physiology. Uncontrollable shock stimulates the secretion of endorphins, the chemicals our brain produces that reduce pain (Chapter 2). Thus subsequent shocks do not hurt a helpless animal as much (Maier & Jackson, 1979). Accordingly, its motivation to escape shock is decreased by both cognitive factors and physiological ones. Future theorists might someday propose a theory that integrates these various determinants of motivation.

Studying Motivation

Psychologists study the motivation of both animals and people. With animals, the focus has often been on biological motives that can be explained as instincts or drives. With people, the focus has often been on learned motives that involve goals that we strive toward. In either case, motives are conceived as states (physiological or cognitive or both) that direct behavior toward certain ends. Many different behaviors can achieve the same goal (Mook, 1987). A hungry animal will do whatever is needed to get food—run through a maze, jump through a hoop, or sit up and beg.

Because motivation is reflected in an incredible variety of behaviors, researchers use a corresponding diversity of techniques to study it. Here we'll look at a few of the ways that psychologists investigate motivation.

Animal Motivation

dual-center theory
biological theory of motivation which proposes that the hypothalamus contains two centers, one exciting behavior and the other inhibiting it; these two centers work together to maintain the body's homeostasis

When a researcher's interest lies in the physiological underpinnings of motivation, he relies on strategies like those described in Chapter 2 for studying the brain and nervous system (Whalen & Simon, 1984). His interest will often center on the hypothalamus. As you remember, the hypothalamus is located at the top of the brain stem, where it links the autonomic nervous system with the endocrine system. The autonomic nervous system and our glands work together to maintain homeostasis, and the hypothalamus serves as the "thermostat" for our biologically based motives. This has been repeatedly demonstrated in various lesion studies of animals.

As explained in Chapter 2, lesioning involves cutting or destroying tissue. Depending on the exact part of the hypothalamus that is destroyed, motives such as eating, drinking, sex, or aggression are affected. In each case, either too much or too little of the motivated behavior is produced. Figure 6.1 shows a striking example: A rat with a lesion in one part of its hypothalamus eats enthusiastically and endlessly, tripling its normal weight in a matter of weeks! A lesion in a slightly different area of the hypothalamus will cause a rat to stop eating.

Dual-center theory proposes that the hypothalamus contains two centers, one that excites behavior and the other that inhibits it (Stellar, 1954). Both centers respond to information—neural or hormonal—and thereby work in concert to maintain the body's homeostasis. If one center is destroyed, as by a lesion, the system is disrupted. Today, this theory is regarded as an oversimplification (Mook, 1987). For example, both the fat rat and the skinny rat previously mentioned may recover normal feeding patterns, even though the hypothalamus remains damaged. Other systems take over. Still, dual-center theory remains useful for perspective, reminding us that motivation involves not just turning on behavior but also turning it off.

Human Motivation

Remember that an important goal in the psychology of motivation is to specify the basic motives. Two of the major figures in this area are Henry

Figure 6.1
Rat with Lesion in Hypothalamus. Following the surgical destruction of part of its hypothalamus, this rat consumed enough food to triple its body weight.

Murray (1893–1988) and Abraham Maslow (1908–1970). Murray proposed a complete catalog of human needs. Maslow theorized about relationships among the different human needs.

Henry Murray. According to Murray (1938), we can recognize a particular need in terms of several criteria:

- attention to certain aspects of the environment rather than others
- reports of particular feelings
- repeated patterns of behavior
- satisfaction with attainment of these consequences, and dissatisfaction with failure to attain these consequences

Using these guidelines, Murray identified approximately twenty human needs (see Table 6.1).

For instance, the need for order might show itself as knowledge of dates and deadlines (selective attention), as pride and purpose while doing errands (particular feelings), as persistent emptying of garbage cans (repeated patterns of behavior), and as pleasure from an alphabetized spice rack (satisfaction with the attainment of order). Murray organizes needs along several dimensions: more or less biological, direct or indirect expression, and so on.

An interesting aspect of Murray's approach is his suggestion that people differ in the characteristic strength of their particular needs. For example, some individuals have a strong need for achievement and a weak need for play, whereas others show just the opposite pattern. Advertisers often use Murray's analysis of human needs (McNeal, 1982), sometimes making a product appeal to people who score high in need for achievement ("when you deserve the very best") and sometimes to people who score high in need for play ("it's a good time for the great taste"). Some advertisers even work both sides of the street ("oh yes, you can have it all").

Murray is remembered not only for cataloging human motives, but also for creating a means to measure their strength. Along with Christiana Morgan, Murray in 1935 devised the **Thematic Apperception Test (TAT),** which is still used today. Subjects, like the one in Figure 6.2 on page 223, are shown ambiguous pictures. Then they are asked to tell a story about what is going on in each picture.

The TAT is called a projective test because subjects "project" their own motives onto the characters in the story (Chapter 11). The picture itself doesn't provide any clues about what's going on. If a subject mentions achievement, play, or power, the researcher has good reason to believe these themes are coming from the subject and reflect the particular strength of his or her own motives. This is exactly how the TAT is scored. The more times a theme pertaining to a particular motive is mentioned, the higher the subject's score for that motive.

Abraham Maslow. One lesson from psychology's study of motivation is that a single person marches to a number of drummers. How can we make sense of all the motives that arouse and direct our actions? One important attempt to systematize human motives was proposed by psychologist Abra-

Thematic Apperception Test (TAT)
a set of ambiguous pictures about which research subjects tell stories, used to infer the strength of one's needs

Abraham Maslow

Table 6.1

Murray's Needs

Need	Characterization
Abasement	Need to submit to external forces, to comply, to accept punishment
Achievement	Need to accomplish, to overcome obstacles, to do something difficult
Affiliation	Need to form and maintain a friendship, to live with others, to cooperate, to love
Aggression	Need to overcome opposition, to assault or injure, to belittle or accuse another person
Autonomy	Need to be free of restraint, to resist influence, to defy authority
Counteraction	Need to make up for failure, to refuse defeat, to defend one's honor
Defendance	Need to defend self against criticism, to justify one's actions, to offer explanations and excuses
Deference	Need to admire a superior, to cooperate with a leader, to serve another
Dominance	Need to control one's environment, to persuade, to lead and direct
Exhibition	Need to make an impression, to attract attention to oneself, to excite others
Harmavoidance	Need to avoid physical harm, to escape danger, to take precautions
Infavoidance	Need to avoid humiliation, to avoid failure, to hide shame
Nurturance	Need to assist the helpless, to express sympathy, to nourish another
Order	Need to put things in order, to be tidy, to act precisely
Play	Need to have fun, to seek diversion, to laugh
Power	Need to have an impact on others, to be in charge of people and situations
Rejection	Need to snub, to reject, to be aloof
Sentience	Need to seek and enjoy sensuous feelings
Sex	Need to form and maintain an erotic relationship, to have sexual intercourse
Succorance	Need to have one's needs gratified by another, to seek aid, to be dependent
Understanding	Need to ask and answer questions, to analyze experience, to discriminate among ideas

Source: Murray, 1938.

Figure 6.2

Taking the TAT. This person's interpretation of the ambiguous subject matter of the TAT will reveal the strength and direction of his motives.

hierarchy of needs

Maslow's notion that human needs can be arranged along a single dimension in which basic needs such as hunger must be satisfied before "higher" needs such as love or self-esteem

self-actualization

the full use of one's talents and abilities

ham Maslow (1970). He suggested that all of our possible motives are arranged according to a **hierarchy of needs** (see Figure 6.3).

At the bottom are physiological needs, such as hunger and thirst. Obviously, we cannot leave these needs unsatisfied for too long, because our very lives hang in the balance. Only when physiological needs are met does the need to be free from threatened danger arise. Maslow calls this need one of safety, and he means not just physical safety but also psychological safety—our sense that the world is stable and coherent. Next in the hierarchy is the need to seek out other people, to love and to be loved.

If we successfully satisfy this need for attachment, then we need to feel esteemed, by ourselves and by others. Maslow groups our needs for knowledge, understanding, and novelty together as cognitive needs, and proposes that they are next in his hierarchy. Then we find esthetic needs: the desire for order and beauty.

According to Maslow, we must satisfy lower needs before we go on to seek satisfaction of higher needs. Near the very top of Maslow's hierarchy is **self-actualization,** "the full use and exploitation of talents, capacities, potentialities" (Maslow, 1970, p. 150). The need for self-actualization is difficult to achieve because it only becomes relevant when the other needs that fall below it have been addressed. Maslow was particularly interested in the self-actualized individual, to whom he attributed such characteristics as spontaneity, autonomy, sense of humor, and a capacity for deep interpersonal relations. At the very top of Maslow's hierarchy is the need for transcendence, which refers to spiritual and religious needs.

The particular order in which Maslow arranged the different needs can be criticized, but the general idea is sensible. Maslow's hierarchy does approximate the order in which people attend to their various needs. For example, hungry people tend not to pursue their esthetic needs until their stomachs are full. Keep in mind the most important idea inherent in Maslow's hierarchy of needs: that people's motives are interconnected and organized. Whether or not we try to satisfy a particular motive depends on the current state of our other motives.

Figure 6.3
Maslow's Hierarchy of Needs

Biological Motives

With a general idea about how psychologists approach the study of motivation, let's take a close look at several particular motives. We will start with biologically based motives and move on in the next section to learned motives.

Thirst

When our bodies are low on water, we experience thirst. We seek liquid, and we drink. Once we fill up, we stop drinking. Thirst, therefore, is a feedback system, and researchers have pretty well mapped out how this system works. Current opinion holds that two different mechanisms produce thirst. First, if the volume of fluid inside the cells of our body becomes too low, thirst occurs. Second, if the volume of fluid outside our cells becomes too low, thirst also occurs. So, the theory used to explain the causes of thirst is called the **double-depletion hypothesis,** because it specifies two different routes—intracellular *or* extracellular depletion of fluid—to thirst.

What happens in our bodies to signal that we have had enough to drink? The simplest way would be if a physiological "thermostat" kept track of the volume of fluid inside and outside of our cells, and then halted our experience of thirst when the volume of fluid was sufficient. If you

double-depletion hypothesis
theory of the causes of thirst which proposes that thirst results either from depletion of fluid within cells or outside cells

Thirst and the body's response to it form a feedback system that has been closely studied by researchers.

think about this, you'll see that it is not an ideal arrangement. As we drink, fluid is slowly absorbed into our body. Suppose we kept drinking until the volume of fluid in and around our cells was adequate. What then happens to the fluid we have swallowed but have not yet absorbed?

For this reason, feedback from our mouth (no longer feeling dry) and our stomach (no longer feeling empty) serves to inhibit thirst. In addition, we learn to keep track of the amount of fluid we drink so we don't overdo it. If you've been out exercising on a hot day, you become quite thirsty, but when you find a water fountain, you usually remember to sip slowly. Finally, as water begins to enter the cells of our body, our feelings of thirst are inhibited (Blass & Hall, 1976).

Sometimes we keep drinking past the point where our thirst is satisfied. This might happen, for instance, if we gulp down water faster than our body's feedback system can react to it and inhibit thirst. What results is a feeling of discomfort and in some cases a serious disruption of the body's functioning because there is too much fluid in and around our cells. This state is called water intoxication, and although rare, it can prove fatal (Mook, 1987)!

Hunger

The Hungry Fly sounds like a B-grade horror movie, but it is actually a book by Vincent Dethier (1976), which describes how flies respond when they are hungry. As you may have noticed, flies are skilled at finding stray spills containing sugar. This is because they have nerve cells in their feet that detect sugar. Suppose a fly is taking a stroll one day and happens to step with its right foot into a puddle of something sweet. The sugar detectors are then stimulated, and a message is sent to the brain. The brain in turn inhibits movement on the right side of the body.

The fly keeps on walking with its left legs, however, which means that it begins to pivot like a miniature basketball player about its right front foot. As the fly circles, its left foot eventually encounters the sugar solution as well. Again the nerve cells fire, and now movement on the left side is inhibited as well. What happens when movement on both sides of the fly's body stops? The fly automatically extends its proboscis and starts to eat. As the sugar is ingested, the fly eventually fills up, and the nerve cells in its digestive tract are stimulated. This cancels feeding and disinhibits movement. The fly is now free to leave.

This is a wonderfully simple biological reaction. Flies never eat and run, and, as we all know, they thrive. This example shows how a primary drive, in this case hunger, can be wired into the nervous system of an organism. It also illustrates the process of homeostasis. The fly eats when it encounters sugar, but only if its gut is sufficiently empty. The fly is thereby protected from starvation on the one hand and overeating on the other. The various parts of the fly (sugar receptors, brain, legs, and digestive system) are all coordinated to maintain homeostasis.

Finally, the example of the fly illustrates the operation of a feedback system (no pun intended). Hunger resembles thirst in that it is also a feedback system that can be stimulated in several ways and inhibited in several ways. For humans, the exact details are not well understood, but we have several likely candidates as stimuli to hunger, including:

- stomach contractions signifying that the stomach is empty
- a low concentration of glucose in the blood
- a low level of fat stored in the body

None of these factors by itself is critical in producing hunger. For example, people who have had their stomachs surgically removed still experience hunger, showing that stomach contractions don't tell the whole story. And people with diabetes—which leads to a high concentration of blood sugar—still experience hunger, showing that a low glucose level cannot be the sole stimulus to hunger. Finally, people with high levels of fat stored in the body still experience hunger, showing that one's fat level per se does not cause hunger.

The cautious conclusion is that these internal states influence hunger, in some yet-to-be-specified combination with one another. Also to be considered are external influences on hunger. As we all know, the aroma or taste or appearance of food may stimulate our desire to eat. Some restaurants show their customers a tray of desserts following a meal, rather than just referring them to the menu, perhaps to capitalize on this influence on hunger. Sometimes we eat when the clock on the wall tells us that it is time for lunch or dinner, or simply because other people in our vicinity happen to be eating. In sum, numerous events inside and outside our bodies may trigger hunger. The same conclusion applies to inhibition of hunger: There are many possible factors that may well work in combination with one another, such as feedback from the mouth, stomach, intestine, and blood.

Specific Hungers. The well-being of animals and people requires that they ingest not just miscellaneous foods but those containing fats, proteins, vitamins, and minerals. How do organisms manage to eat correctly? In some cases, Mother and Father tell us what to eat, but in other cases, there

The internal states that cause hunger in humans and the corresponding feedback system are not as well understood as those involved with thirst.

specific hungers
a desire for foods containing substances in which an organism is deficient

are **specific hungers:** motives to seek out and consume food containing particular substances. If organisms lack sodium, for instance, they experience a desire for salty foods. Research further suggests that some species, like rats, have specific hungers for protein and for carbohydrates (Rozin, 1968). It is not clear just how many specific hungers people have, but there are probably only a few.

Instead, we possess a general reflex that accomplishes the same thing as a host of specific hungers. When we feel sick to our stomach, we often start to avoid the particular foods we had been eating (Rozin & Kalat, 1971). Because of this aversion to recent tastes, we end up seeking new foods. This makes sense, because a diet deficient in some necessary substance usually makes us feel ill. As we try new foods in the wake of our illness, we might well encounter the substance we needed in the first place.

Of course, sometimes gastric upset has nothing to do with our diet, as when a bout with the flu coincides with guacomole. We may develop an aversion to avocadoes, and this is an unfortunate consequence of a usually helpful reflex (Chapter 5). However, we are mostly protected from such capricious consequences because taste aversion occurs most readily with novel foods. We tend not to avoid familiar foods, no matter how sick we may get.

Obesity may not indicate the failure of homeostasis, but rather its success, according to set-point theory.

set-point theory
the idea that our bodies work to maintain a certain level of body fat (the set point)

Obesity.   The physiological mechanisms responsible for hunger and thirst have considerable redundancy built into them. In other words, the body's homeostasis can be maintained in several ways. Nevertheless, problems can occur with these motives. In particular, the weight of several million people in the United States exceeds healthy limits. Obesity is commonly defined as 20 percent or more in excess of what is considered a "normal" weight. What causes this?

One current theory attributes obesity not to the failure of homeostasis but to its success (Keesey & Powley, 1986). **Set-point theory** proposes that our bodies work to maintain a certain level of body fat, called the set point. As we depart from our particular set point, higher or lower, processes are set in motion to counteract the departure. So, if our body fat increases, we may eat less frequently and increase our activity. And if our body fat decreases, we may eat more frequently and decrease our activity.

The problem with obese individuals may be that their set point is too high. If they eat less food, their bodies simply use it more efficiently. Contrary to our stereotypes, many studies show that obese people do not eat much more than people of normal weight (Spitzer & Rodin, 1981). Because their bodies resist the loss of fat, it takes very few calories to keep them overweight. The question remains as to why the set point is too high in some people. There's not much agreement here, although genetic influences and/or early eating habits are perhaps responsible. It is also not clear whether someone's set point can be changed, but habits like exercising or smoking may indeed alter someone's set point (Rodin & Wack, 1984).

Whether one's set point can be changed or not, set-point theory definitely does not imply that weight loss is impossible. However, it does have two implications that would-be dieters must heed. First, it is difficult to lose weight; the body resists it, even when weight loss is a healthy goal.

Our response to developing sexuality—whether serious or playful—is the result of the interplay of instinctive and learned behavior.

Second, dieting is not a once-in-a-lifetime experience. For people with a high set point, the struggle to stay thin must be ongoing.

It is important to realize that there are many causes of obesity, and set-point theory focuses on but one of them. Most generally, people become obese because they take in more calories than they use. So, overeating is one obvious cause of obesity, and so too is a sedentary life. Also contributing to obesity are genetic factors, eating habits established early in life, and the tendency to turn to food when anxious or depressed.

Sexual Motivation

In Chapter 16, we will consider human sexuality in detail. For our present purposes, let's discuss sex as a motive. It differs from other primary motives in several ways. First, sexual activity is not necessary for individual survival in the way that drinking and eating obviously are. Second, our sex drive does not lead us to reduce tension and arousal, but rather to increase it. Stated another way, homeostasis is not the goal of sexual activity. Third, unlike thirst and hunger, present in full force at birth, our sex drive develops as we become older.

Sexual motivation has been placed here in the section on biological motives, but it just as readily could have been located in the next section dealing with learned motives. This is because human sexual motivation reflects the interplay of both biological *and* learned factors. We can regard the sexual motives of people as primary and acquired (Feder, 1984).

With lower animals like rats or dogs or cats, there is a straightforward link between hormones and sex. Among females, sexual behavior is associated with the hormone estrogen, produced by the ovaries. Among males, sexual behavior is associated with the hormone testosterone, produced by the testes. However, with people, these links become more subtle and less important. Compared to other species, human sexuality depends less on hormones and more on experiences. Men and women who have had their sex glands surgically removed may show no loss of sexual interest. As we will see in Chapter 16, human sexuality has social significance, and the particular ways in which people satisfy their sexual drives reflect what they have learned while growing up in a given time and place.

Learned Motives

Sexual motivation, as emphasized, occupies a position between biological and learned motives. In this section, we will discuss some of the learned motives that psychologists have studied: aggression, achievement motivation, power motivation, and mastery. These are but a sample of the acquired motives that may drive human activity.

Aggression

aggression
intentionally destructive acts directed against individuals or groups

Psychologists define **aggression** as intentionally destructive acts directed against individuals or groups. Over the years, considerable debate has occurred over whether human aggression is a primary motive or an acquired motive (Chapter 15). Many psychologists are now of the opinion that aggression in people is an acquired motive, but let's consider the evidence on both sides, starting with the view that aggression is biologically based.

First, aggression can be influenced by internal states. We saw, for instance, how male sticklebacks are predisposed by hormonal changes to attack other males. Among most mammalian species, there is a similar link between male hormones and aggression. The hormones do not directly cause aggression, but they make the animal much more likely to respond aggressively when the appropriate provocations are present.

Second, among some species, aggression may be inhibited by built-in reflexes, showing again that biological factors can regulate aggression. When two males confront each other, the fight may end abruptly when the loser makes a submissive display, a ritualized behavior like lowering the head or baring the neck. These displays bring the fight to an end, because the winner no longer presses his advantage. Both live to fight another day.

What about people? One argument, advanced by ethologist Konrad Lorenz (1966), is that the impulse to act aggressively is inherent in humans just as it is in animals. However, because human technology makes it possible for people to aggress at a distance, with sticks and stones, bullets and bombs, we never developed submissive displays that were effective. So, human aggression has escalated throughout history.

Some have used the arguments of Lorenz to explain the patterns of child abuse that psychologists have observed. Very few parents physically attack their own children, perhaps because the very appearance of a young child inhibits attack, just as submissive displays among animals inhibit aggression (e.g., Southwick, Pal, & Siddiqui, 1972). But those parents who do abuse their children tend to have poor impulse control, suggesting that they are oblivious to the "inhibiting" effects of an infant's appearance (Parke & Collmer, 1975). Further, premature children are particularly apt to be abused, perhaps because they neither look nor sound like normal infants (Gill, 1970). Child abuse is not fully explained by these ideas, but the findings just discussed do support the case that Lorenz has made.

You might wonder if male sex hormones affect aggression in humans as they do in lower animals. Males throughout the world are much more likely than females to commit violent crimes. And some studies find a positive correlation between males' testosterone level and their tendency to act in hostile ways (e.g., Kreuz & Rose, 1972). Recent publicity about the psychological effects of steroids, which contain male sex hormones, further supports this argument, because excessive rage and violence apparently occur among some who abuse these drugs.

Let's now consider the arguments in favor of regarding human aggression as an acquired motive. For starters, unlike thirst and hunger, aggression does not work according to a feedback system. There is no homeostatic level of aggression that an organism needs to maintain. Indeed, human aggression occurs in response to some external event, such as frustration or pain, and it continues to occur if it leads to a desired consequence. Human aggression is therefore instrumental—that is, learned (Chapter 5). Further, a person's interpretation is critical in determining how he or she acts in a particular situation (Chapter 14). If someone trips us, for example, we may respond with aggression if we are playing hockey and with amusement if we are dancing.

What about the evidence just described that finds aggression more common in men than women? The role of socialization must be taken into account. Perhaps little boys are encouraged to be aggressive, whereas little girls are not. Bandura's (1965) studies of modeling, discussed in Chapter 5, show that with sufficient incentives, girls are just as capable as boys of performing the aggressive responses that a model has displayed.

Perhaps the apparent correlation between testosterone and hostility reflects the operation of some third factor, like physical appearance, that in turn influences hostility and violence. A young male with bulging muscles may "invite" others to treat him in an aggressive way; when he responds in turn, he establishes a link that appears to be biological, but is in fact social. This possibility is speculative, but so too are the arguments that human aggression is a primary motive. Until the final answer is known, we would do well to remember what psychologists already do know: Whatever the cause of aggression, people can learn *not* to act this way (Mook, 1987).

Achievement Motivation

achievement motivation
the need to accomplish something difficult in situations characterized by a standard of excellence

Some people throw themselves into their schoolwork or their job, wanting to do the very best they can. Others are quite indifferent. We can explain these very different approaches as due to variation in one's underlying motive to achieve. Henry Murray (1938) defined **achievement motivation** as the need to accomplish something difficult in situations that are characterized by a standard of excellence. Psychologists typically measure achievement motivation by looking at TAT responses. In contrast to many of the other motives so far mentioned, achievement motivation has no apparent biological component. It is solely due to socialization, produced by parents who encourage their children to be independent and successful (Weiner, 1978).

In a well-known study of achievement motivation, Atkinson and Litwin (1960) used the TAT to measure achievement motivation among research subjects, who attempted a task requiring them to toss rings over a peg. The subjects chose the distance they stood from the peg. Subjects high in the need to achieve chose an intermediate distance—neither too close nor too far—more frequently than subjects low in the need to achieve. Do you see why? Standing too close makes success almost automatic and hence a

The strength of a person's drive to achieve is the result of socialization.

poor way to satisfy the need to achieve. Standing too far away turns the task into a game of chance, again a poor way to satisfy achievement needs.

David McClelland (1961) has investigated societal differences in achievement motivation. With the TAT as a model, he devised ways of scoring an entire society for its level of achievement motivation. For instance, he examined grade school readers from different countries for the presence or absence of achievement themes. McClelland then correlated these achievement scores with the economic growth of that country one generation later, and found a positive relationship!

These findings do not prove a cause and effect relationship, because they are based on correlations (Chapter 1). However, McClelland wishes to conclude from them that achievement motivation was fostered in those children who read stories containing achievement themes and thwarted in those children whose stories lacked them. Several decades later, the achievement motivation produced presumably translated itself into actual behavior—as measured by dollars and cents.

One approach to understanding achievement motivation has been to break it up into smaller components (Atkinson, 1958). It is possible, for example, to distinguish between desire for success and fear of failure. For many, these are entwined, but imagine the person who wishes very much to be successful but cares little one way or the other about failures along the way. We would expect this person to be a risk-taker: "nothing ventured, nothing gained." Conversely, the person whose achievement motivation is dominated by fear of failure follows a cautious path: "better safe than sorry."

Analyses like these led Matina Horner (1972) to discover an intriguing phenomenon. She provided female research subjects with a brief sentence:

> After her first exam, Mary finds herself at the top of her medical school class.

The subjects were asked to write a story that followed from this beginning. Male subjects writing about a man at the top of his class invariably wrote about the wonderful things that will follow in his life, but Horner's female subjects writing about Mary detailed one horrible event after another. Mary would find herself without friends. She would be lonely and unfulfilled. Or, she would sabotage her career in order to find a husband. Fully 65 percent of the female subjects linked Mary's "success" to an unhappy outcome!

fear of success

the motive to avoid doing well because of the negative consequences that may follow

This finding was unanticipated and so striking that it has been given its own name: **fear of success.** Fear of success among women has been hotly debated. According to one argument, Horner discovered not a motive in her female subjects but rather a stereotype that many of them held (Chapter 14). And perhaps this stereotype contained a kernel of truth. "Success" for a woman may indeed bring bad consequences, which means that Horner's subjects feared not success per se but rather these consequences.

Further research supports this alternative interpretation. In Horner's original study, she had female subjects write about Mary and male subjects write about a man at the top of the medical school class. What happens if female subjects write about a male and male subjects write about a female? If fear of success is a motive that women possess, we would expect different results. Specifically, male subjects writing about Mary should *not* mention negative consequences for her. But it turns out that they do (Monohan, Kuhn, & Shaver, 1974). When subjects predict that Mary's success will lead to a bad outcome for her, they seem to be reflecting not their own fear of success but rather their belief about how the world works. However we interpret fear of success among women, more recent research implies that it is less prevalent nowadays than in the 1960s when Horner first documented the phenomenon (e.g., Terborg, 1977).

Power Motivation

power motivation

the need to have an impact on others, to be in charge of people and situations

Power motivation is another motive originally described by Murray (1938): the need to have an impact on others, to be in charge of people and situations. Again, the strength of this motive can be gauged by looking at TAT stories and counting the number of times social impact is mentioned.

Let's discuss two intriguing lines of research into power motivation. The first looks at the relationship between the need for power and leadership (Winter, 1988). Both men and women high in power motivation are more likely than those low in this motivation to hold elective office. They also are more likely to pursue careers in which influence of others is possible, such as teaching, psychotherapy, journalism, and business management.

Winter (1973) has scored the need for power among political leaders, treating their speeches as if they were TAT stories. Power motivation among presidents of the United States has varied greatly during the twentieth century. High scorers include Theodore Roosevelt, Franklin Roosevelt, Woodrow Wilson, John Kennedy, and Lyndon Johnson, and low scorers include Robert Taft, Herbert Hoover, and Dwight Eisenhower. Note the tendency for Democrats to be higher on the need for power than Republicans; note also that presidents in office when the United States entered a war tended to have high power motivation.

A second line of work looks at the relationship between power motivation and physical health. In his research, David McClelland (1975) found that a high level of this motivation, when coupled with excessive self-restraint, puts someone at risk for high blood pressure, respiratory illness, and immunological dysfunction. The specific physiological pathway by which these effects occur is not known at the present time, but perhaps the conflict between power motivation and its restraint puts a strain on the sympathetic nervous system, which in turn takes a toll on health (McClelland, 1982).

These findings are intriguing, but we must be cautious in interpreting them. All are correlational results (Chapter 1). Winter, McClelland, and other researchers do not have any control over which of their subjects are high or low in power motivation. They wish to conclude that power motivation leads directly to certain occupational and health outcomes, but other possibilities exist. Perhaps someone's health determines how he responds to a measure of power motivation. Perhaps someone's occupation determines her level of power motivation.

Researchers are not oblivious to these possibilities, and they try to rule them out. One obvious research strategy is to measure power motivation prior to the outcome of interest. Then it is not possible to argue that a supposed consequence of power motivation is really its cause. The problem of third variables, such as someone's socioeconomic status, still exists, and as we have discussed already (Chapter 1), researchers must anticipate and measure these as well.

Mastery

The **need for mastery** is the motivation to interact in a competent way with the environment. Mastery has been variously described as

> capability, capacity, efficiency, proficiency, and skill. It is therefore . . . suitable . . . to describe such things as grasping and exploring, crawling and walking, attention and perception, language and thinking, manipulating and changing the surroundings, all of which promote an effective—a competent—interaction with the environment. (White, 1959, p. 317)

In short, people experience intrinsic pleasure in doing things well (Pittman & Heller, 1987).

Remember the first time you mastered a bicycle, a typewriter, a video game, or a necktie. You felt good because you had just satisfied your need for mastery. The learned helplessness phenomenon described earlier in this chapter illustrates how the need for mastery can be thwarted. If a person or animal lives in a world that eludes control, helplessness and apathy, and perhaps even illness and death, eventually follow (Peterson & Seligman, 1987).

Some theorists extend the need for mastery to include the conceptual world, proposing that people are motivated to understand the coherence of things (Antonovsky, 1979). When we are faced with puzzling occurrences, we try to understand the possible reasons, not stopping until we find a satisfactory explanation. This may be why crossword puzzles, soap operas, and riddles intrigue us so much.

Small successes early in life bring with them the intrinsic pleasure of accomplishment.

Being able to control the environment is obviously an advantage, because this ability allows us to accomplish what is desirable and avoid what is not. But the need for mastery is not the same as simply getting what one wants. Rather, the need for mastery is satisfied when one acts *in a skillful manner,* whether or not desired goals are attained. For people high in this need, what matters is quite literally how they play the game.

Approaches to Emotions

Let's now turn from motives to emotions, keeping in mind that psychologists ask the same questions about both motivation and emotion. What are the basic types? What are their causes? What are their consequences? In short, psychologists interested in emotion want to know how and why we experience the particular feelings that we do: fear or loathing, love or hate, passion or apathy. Over the years, several different approaches to understanding emotions have appeared. These perspectives are different but not always at odds with one another. Rather, each takes as its special concern one particular aspect of our emotional life.

Evolutionary Approach: Darwin and Plutchik

The first theoretical viewpoint we will discuss is the evolutionary approach begun by Charles Darwin. In his 1872 book, *The Expression of Emotions in Man and Animals,* Darwin documented numerous parallels between lower animals and people in their reactions to events. For example, dogs, cats, and humans all bare their teeth when angry. Darwin suggested that emotions increase chances for survival because they represent appropriate reactions to emergencies. This approach leads one to seek the survival function of particular emotions.

A modern theorist who adheres to the evolutionary viewpoint is Robert Plutchik (1962, 1980, 1984), who proposes that we experience eight biologically given emotions: fear, surprise, sadness, disgust, anger, anticipation, joy, and acceptance. Plutchik links each of these eight emotions to an adaptive pattern of behavior (see Table 6.2). For example, the emotion of fear accompanies the avoidance of danger. It is obviously adaptive to be afraid when we are threatened, as opposed to indifferent, and thus the emotion of fear tends to occur in these circumstances.

Plutchik's model is based on the work of perception psychologists who study color vision (Chapter 3). The basic emotions are like primary colors, because both can be combined to produce innumerable variations. For example, we experience love when joy and acceptance are combined; we experience contempt from a combination of anger and disgust. Plutchik arranges the basic emotions in a circle reflecting their relative similarity and dissimilarity (Figure 6.4). The closer together two emotions, the more they are alike; the further apart, the more they are different.

Analogous to brightness is the intensity of an emotion, which Plutchik interprets as the degree of arousal that accompanies it. In other words, apprehension is a mild version of fear. Boredom is a mild version of disgust. And distraction is a mild version of surprise. Plutchik proposes that emotions become more difficult to distinguish at lower intensities, so that people must turn to their environment for clues about what they

Table 6.2

Patterns of Survival and Associated Emotions

Plutchik theorizes about how basic human emotions increase fitness. He starts by identifying what organisms must do in order to survive. He proposes eight patterns of behavior necessary for survival. Each has a corresponding basic emotion.

Pattern of survival	Emotion
Incorporation: ingestion of food or acceptance of beneficial stimuli from the world	Acceptance
Rejection: expulsion of material that has previously been incorporated	Disgust
Protection: avoidance of danger	Fear
Destruction: removal of a barrier that prevents an important need from being satisfied	Anger
Reproduction: passing on genetic material to offspring	Joy
Reintegration: reaction to the loss of something important that aims at regaining contact	Sadness
Orientation: reaction to novel situations	Surprise
Exploration: mapping of a given environment	Anticipation

Figure 6.4

Basic Emotions. According to Plutchik, there are eight basic emotions, shown here in the inner circle. Complex emotions, shown here in the outer circle, result from combinations of the basic emotions.

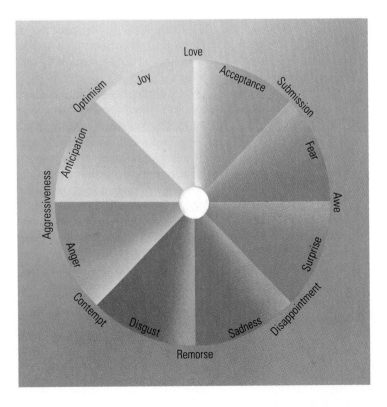

"must" be feeling. In the case of extreme anger, joy, or grief, people know exactly what they are experiencing. In less extreme cases, people may be genuinely confused by their emotions, so they must consider the circumstances that prompted these emotions.

Suppose you find yourself talking to someone you don't know too well. As your conversation continues, you experience an emotional reaction, but you're not quite sure if it is anger at what the person is saying, or interest in the topic, or physical attraction. You have to *infer* what you are feeling by thinking back over the details of the conversation and attaching the rise and fall of your emotions to these details.

Psychophysiological Approach: James and Lange

In contrast to the evolutionary approach, which is concerned with the functions of emotions, the psychophysiological approach looks at their causes. Specifically, this approach explains emotion as a psychological reaction to physiological occurrences. William James (1884, 1890) observed that the commonsense way of thinking about emotion is to assign it an intermediate position in the following sequence:

event → emotion → physiological response

To use a famous example from James, common sense proposes that we see a bear, experience fear, and then run. But James took issue with this view and proposed a different sequence:

event → physiological response → emotion

We see a bear, run, and only then do we experience fear. Indeed, to James, the perception of our body's physiological responses is the emotion. Because a Danish physiologist named Lange independently proposed the same idea, this account has come to be known as the **James-Lange theory of emotion.** It's an important theory because it encourages researchers to look at the relationship between what our body does and what we feel.

Psychologists today are still concerned with the role of physiological arousal in emotions. Their interest focuses on the nervous system and the endocrine system. As you remember from Chapter 2, the autonomic nervous system is divided into two parts. The parasympathetic nervous system maintains a relaxed and unemotional state. It controls digestion, keeps the heart rate steady, and directs our breathing.

The sympathetic nervous system, in contrast, produces arousal. Digestion is inhibited, the pupils dilate, the heart beats faster, the face becomes flushed, breathing speeds up, and the palms sweat. These physiological responses comprise the body's **emergency reaction,** which readies one to respond to threat. We are prepared to fight off whatever menaces us and/or to run away from it. Critical in this process are the adrenal glands, located on the kidneys (see Figure 2.10, p. 71). In response to threat, these glands secrete hormones that stimulate physiological arousal into the bloodstream.

There is considerable debate as to whether the different emotions we experience are associated with different patterns of arousal. If there are differences, they are probably quite small. It is therefore accurate to say that *all* emotions involve in some way the emergency reaction. This helps

James-Lange theory of emotion
the theory that people's perceptions of their physiological responses in a particular situation constitute emotion

emergency reaction
physiological response to threat, in which an organism prepares itself through internal reactions for defending itself (fight) or running away (flight)

Figure 6.5

Polygraph. A typical polygraph simultaneously records heart rate, blood pressure, respiration, and skin conductivity. Changes in these measures (shown by the arrow) indicate emotional arousal and thus the *possibility* of deceit.

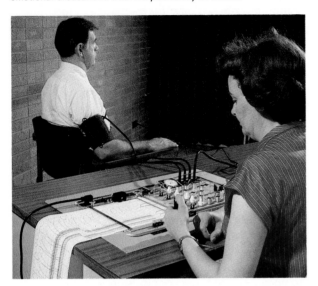 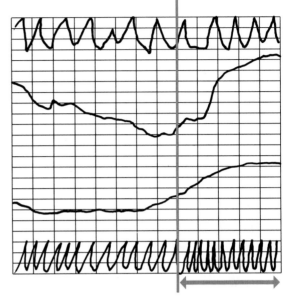

polygraph

lie detection device which actually measures physiological arousal

explain why a lie detection device, or **polygraph,** cannot directly sense falsehood. Rather, it measures arousal, which presumably accompanies the intent to deceive (Ekman, 1986). Although we don't need a polygraph to detect such obvious signs of arousal as sweating or blushing or swallowing too frequently, this device may help to detect more subtle signs of arousal: changes in blood pressure, skin conductivity, and skin temperature.

All of these can be recorded and measured with special sensors attached to the body. These "read" changes in the nervous system when an examiner asks the subject questions (Figure 6.5). "Did you steal $50 from Aunt Jessie yesterday?" Let's say the person says no, but that the sensors on his fingers show a sharp increase in perspiration, and those on his chest indicate that his heart rate just shot up. These dramatic increases in arousal may indicate that he is lying.

Or they may not. Too many problems surround polygraphs, as well as the way the tests are administered, to put great confidence in their results. Consider their use in a criminal investigation. Police officers may be biased against one of the subjects, making him anxious about the test. Indeed, any strong emotion, such as a subject's hostility, can make it difficult for the polygraph operator to interpret reactions to critical questions relative to reactions to noncritical questions. Finally, not all lies are accompanied by emotional arousal.

Neurological Approach: Cannon and Bard

Yet another theoretical tradition in the psychology of emotions is the neurological approach introduced by Walter Cannon (1929, 1939). The neurological approach also seeks to explain the causes of emotions. However, Cannon disagreed with James and Lange, arguing that the process hypothesized in the James-Lange theory was not plausible, granted the way the body actually works. According to Cannon, the physiological changes that take place during the body's emergency reaction do not differ greatly from emotion to emotion. If these changes are the basis of emotions, as James and Lange suggested, then where do distinctions come into the picture? Further, even if there are physiological differences, there is no good reason to believe that people are particularly sensitive to them. Cannon argued that some process other than the one suggested in the James-Lange theory must be responsible for our experience of emotions.

Cannon looked not at the body itself for an answer, but specifically at the brain. He proposed that in response to particular stimuli, the cortex produces both bodily changes *and* emotions. The emergency reaction and the experience of emotions do not occur one after the other, as James and Lange hypothesized, but rather simultaneously. Another physiologist named Philip Bard (1928) elaborated on Cannon's ideas, and now this position is called the **Cannon-Bard theory of emotion.**

Cannon-Bard theory of emotion the theory that the cortex simultaneously produces bodily changes and emotions in response to particular stimuli

The Cannon-Bard position leads researchers to look for the causes of emotions in the brain. As described in Chapter 2, researchers have conducted numerous lesion and stimulation studies to map the neurological basis of emotions. Results usually point to the importance of the limbic system, located in the center of the brain. A consistent conclusion from studies such as these is that higher parts of the brain can inhibit emotional expression. Here is Cannon's (1929, p. 246) description of a cat after its cerebral hemispheres were surgically removed:

> As soon as recovery from anesthesia was complete a remarkable group of activities appeared, such as usually seen in an infuriated animal—a sort of sham rage . . . lashing of the tail, arching of the trunk, thrusting and jerking of the restrained limbs, display of the claws and clawing motions, snarling and attempts to bite. . . . Besides these . . . were erection of the tail hairs, sweating of the toe pads, dilation of the pupils, micturition, a high blood pressure, a very rapid heart beat, an abundant outpouring of adrenalin, and an increase in blood sugar up to five times the normal concentration.

In other words, this reaction is usually held in check, but when inhibition is removed, by a lesion or an appropriate stimulus, it automatically occurs.

In contrast to the difficulty in showing that different emotions give rise to different patterns of bodily arousal, some recent research implies emotion-specific brain mechanisms (Leventhal & Tomarken, 1986). For example, Davidson (1984) proposes that the left hemisphere of the brain is responsible for positive emotions, whereas the right hemisphere is responsible for negative emotions. Accordingly, left brain damage results in depression, fear, and pessimism, and right brain damage produces indifference or even euphoria.

Cognitive Approach: Schachter and Singer

two-factor theory of emotion Schachter and Singer's theory that emotions result first from a state of general physiological arousal and second from a cognitive label placed on this arousal

Theorists Stanley Schachter and Jerome Singer (1962) proposed the **two-factor theory of emotion,** yet another influential account of the causes of emotions. The first factor is physiological arousal, and according to Schachter and Singer, all emotions have the same physiological underpinnings. Whether the emotion in question is fear or anger or love or disgust or joy, your physiology is the same—aroused. This echoes Cannon's criticism of the James-Lange theory. The second factor is the label we place on the particular instances of arousal. In some cases, we tag our arousal as anger, and in other cases as euphoria or fear or love. According to this theory, an infinite variety of emotions exist, limited only by available labels.

Schachter and Singer conducted an ingenious experiment that supports their two-factor theory. Research subjects were injected with adrenalin, creating a state of arousal for them. Some subjects were told what effects the injection would have. Other subjects were misled, told instead that the injection was a special vitamin. In particular, no reference to its arousing effects was made.

All subjects were put in a situation that would produce an emotional reaction. One experimental condition was designed to create anger in the subjects. For instance, they were asked to complete a questionnaire asking about their mother's sexual activity outside of her marriage! Another experimental condition was designed to create euphoria. The subjects here were joined by other people (who were actually working in conjunction with the researchers) who acted silly, folding questionnaires into airplanes and zooming them about the room.

Schachter and Singer then asked their subjects to report any emotions they were experiencing. The subjects in the "anger" condition reported feeling angry, whereas the subjects in the "euphoria" condition reported instead that they felt happy. These results occurred strongly only for the subjects who believed they had been injected with a vitamin. The subjects given accurate information about the arousing effects of the injection did not report the same strong emotions.

To explain these results, Schachter and Singer proposed that people who experience physiological arousal search for its source. In some cases, the cause is readily apparent—"oh, this must be the effect of the injection." In other cases, the cause may not be so obvious, and the person turns to his or her immediate environment for an answer. If something insulting is taking place, the person may attribute the arousal to anger. If something silly is going on, the person may instead attribute the arousal to euphoria.

Subsequent researchers have not always been able to repeat successfully the Schachter and Singer (1962) study just described. And critics point out that not all people in all situations are so easily misled about the actual source of their emotional reactions. Two-factor theory applies best when there is ambiguity about the actual causes of people's reactions. Perhaps children, who are in the process of learning how to label their emotions, are particularly well described by two-factor theory. Regardless, two-factor theory is important for introducing cognition into theories of emotion. Figure 6.6 contrasts two-factor theory with the James-Lange and Cannon-Bard positions.

Opponent-Process Approach: Solomon and Corbit

Both positive and negative emotions change over time. Indeed, one of the striking characteristics of emotions is how fleeting they may be. Richard Solomon and John Corbit (1974) use the concept of homeostasis to explain the waxing and waning of emotions over time. They start with some common observations. First, when we initially encounter a situation that produces a positive or negative emotion, we have an immediate and in-

Figure 6.6

Comparison of Emotion Theories. All theories of emotion specifically mention external stimuli, physiological reactions, and subjective feelings. They differ with respect to the specific relationships hypothesized to exist among these.

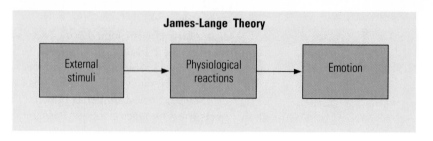

The James-Lange theory proposes that our emotions are the result of our perceptions of our physiological reactions to external stimuli.

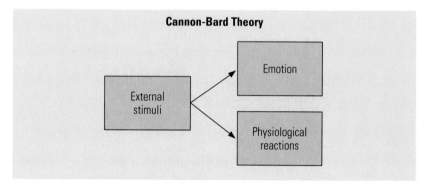

The Cannon-Bard theory proposes that both our emotions and physiological reactions to external stimuli occur simultaneously.

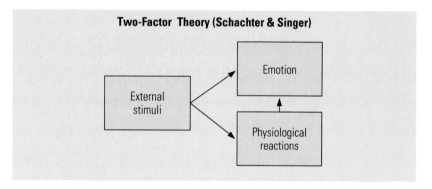

The two-factor theory of Schachter and Singer proposes that our emotions are jointly determined by our physiological reactions and external stimuli which suggest particular interpretations of these reactions.

tense reaction. Consider parachute jumping. The first few jumps are thoroughly terrifying. Subsequent encounters produce less intense reactions. With repeated jumps, the terror goes away.

Why does the emotion of terror in this example change over time? Solomon and Corbit propose that when we experience a particular emotion, the homeostasis of our bodies is disrupted. As a result, inherent physiological processes begin to counteract these feelings—to restore homeostasis. In the particular case of parachute jumping, the body strives to reduce the emotion of terror. In general, good feelings engender a process that works against feeling good, whereas bad feelings set off a process that works against feeling bad.

Because these processes oppose the initial feeling, Solomon and Corbit call their theory the **opponent-process theory.** The opponent process grows in strength over time. As we repeatedly experience a particular positive or negative feeling, its intensity decreases, because the opponent process increasingly cancels it out. Good things become not so good, and bad things become not so bad. The opponent-process theory suggests that moderation is not simply a virtue; it's the way our bodies work.

According to this theory, the opponent process does more than restore our feelings to where they were in the first place. As the opponent process grows in strength, it comes to produce an emotional reaction in its own right. This reaction is the opposite of the initial emotion, and it becomes increasingly intense.

Let's go back to parachute jumping. As people jump more and more, not only does their terror decrease, but they become increasingly relieved each time they hit the ground. Eventually, this relief grows until the aftermath of a jump feels exhilarating. These emotional changes are exactly what Solomon and Corbit would predict. The initial negative feeling (terror) sets off an opponent feeling (relief) which increases in intensity the more times it is set off. Eventually, the terror is counteracted by the opponent process, so much so that the parachutist experiences only a positive feeling (exhilaration).

Solomon and Corbit suggest that their explanation sheds some light on the dynamics of drug addiction. Someone who first tries alcohol or heroin or nicotine experiences pleasure. Over time, though, the pleasure inevitably decreases, because a process opposing pleasure begins to build. The individual must use ever greater quantities of the drug to attain the same emotional effect. Also over time, as the opponent process grows, the aftermath of using a drug—withdrawal—is experienced as increasingly unpleasant.

An Integrative Approach: Tomkins

So far we've seen how psychologists seek to understand various aspects of emotions: their functions, causes, and changes over time. The evolutionary, psychophysiological, neurological, cognitive, and opponent-process approaches disagree in places, but each has something important to say about a particular aspect of emotions. A theory that somehow combines these different perspectives would be highly valuable. Psychologist Silvan Tomkins (1962, 1963, 1982) has taken steps toward an integrative theory of emotions in his work, and we will end this section by considering his ideas.

Tomkins's theory spans body and mind, and it makes the connection between emotion and motivation explicit. He proposes that emotions serve to amplify the body's needs, thereby making one's motives obvious to oneself. He believes that psychologists have misinterpreted the psychological urgency that accompanies our motives. He believes that the urgency is not part of the motive itself, but rather the product of our emotions.

opponent-process theory
the theory that the experience of a positive or negative emotion sets off an opposing process, negative or positive, to restore homeostasis

Consider oxygen deprivation. If someone covers our nose and mouth so that we cannot breathe, we instantly thrash about to regain free breathing. It is tempting to attribute our behavior to a drive:

no oxygen → thrashing → breathing → oxygen

But here's an interesting fact. If a person is ever so slowly deprived of oxygen, panic does not develop. Instead, a state of euphoria ensues, and no attempt whatsoever is made to obtain more oxygen. This was discovered in a tragic way when airplanes first were able to climb to such altitudes that pilots needed to don oxygen masks. Because their ascent was gradual, some pilots did not experience the need for oxygen, ignored their masks, and thus perished.

Tomkins argues that emotions amplify our drives and therefore are the real causes of behavior. It is the emotion of panic, not the physiological need for oxygen, that makes us struggle to breathe when our nose and mouth are obstructed. Drives are important because they provide information, but emotions then take over to ensure that our bodies act on this information.

Tomkins (1984) proposes nine basic emotions, some positive (interest, joy, surprise) and some negative (distress, fear, shame, contempt, disgust, and rage). He believes they all have an innate physiological basis, specifically in the degree of neural activity associated with each and whether this activity is increasing, decreasing, or constant. So, interest, fear, and surprise are all characterized by increased patterns of neural firing. Surprise shows the most rapid increase, whereas interest shows the least.

According to Tomkins, the face is particularly important because it expresses our emotions and thus our motives. Human beings are obviously social, and many of our motives involve other people. There is great advantage to being able to communicate our wishes and desires to others, and facial expressions can serve this purpose (see Figure 6.7).

Tomkins's approach to emotion is a broad one, encompassing factors deemed important by the evolutionary, psychophysiological, and neurological approaches. Cognition also figures in his approach. According to Tomkins, socialization provides scripts that tell us which emotions are appropriate in which circumstances. When "should" we experience and express joy? When is anger the wrong emotion? Although we have to learn many of the circumstances of emotional expression, we don't have to learn the means of expression. Because of its breadth, Tomkins's theory has attracted growing interest and support in recent years.

Complex Emotions

Despite the existence of basic emotions, these feelings do not comprise the whole of our everyday emotional life. We also experience much more complex emotions as well. In this section, we'll take a brief look at several of these. In each case, note how physiological, psychological, and cultural factors entwine to influence our emotional experience and expression. Note the interplay between motivation and emotion. Finally, note how the psychoanalytic approach frequently proves useful in understanding emotions that involve conflict.

Figure 6.7

Expression of Basic Emotions. People in different cultures have no difficulty agreeing on the particular emotions expressed in these photographs.

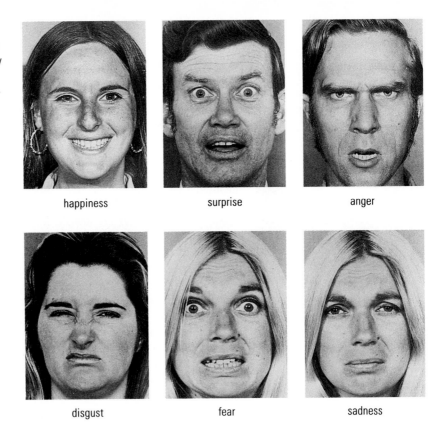

happiness   surprise   anger

disgust   fear   sadness

Depression

Depression is a broad term that includes transitory disappointment on one extreme and severe emotional disturbance on the other (Chapter 12). In all cases, though, depression refers to particular emotions: sadness, anxiety, and anger, among others (Izard, 1977). Psychologists are greatly interested in depression, perhaps because it is the most common emotional problem suffered by contemporary Americans. As many as 20 percent of the people in our country will see a psychotherapist at some point in their lives because of depression.

Severely depressed individuals often regard themselves as inadequate and morally deficient. Freud (1917) was so struck by the self-blame that accompanies depression that he regarded it as the critical factor. To explain this self-blame, Freud suggested that depression is brought about by anger that's been turned inward against the self. By this view, a depressive's suicide is literally a murder. The perpetrator and the victim are one and the same person.

Freud's theory is just one of many possible explanations. Indeed, researchers today point to an array of determinants of depression, from disordered biochemistry to stressful life events to idiosyncratic styles of thinking to fractured social relationships (Akiskal & McKinney, 1975). Running through these explanations is the theme of loss. Perhaps depression is a reaction to disappointment that forces us to take time out and regroup. Most depressions, even serious ones, lift on their own as time passes. (We'll return to depression in Chapter 12.)

Public expression of grief, in this case the dedication of a Vietnam War memorial, provide an outlet for a collective sense of loss.

Grief

Related to depression is the emotion of grief, the sorrow and agitation experienced when a loved one dies or any great loss is sustained. Grief blends sadness, anger, and worry together, although the particular proportions differ from culture to culture (cf. Block, 1957). Regardless, people in all societies show some form of grief, and psychologists have taken a close look at the individual and social functions of this emotion. Grief helps the individual work through and adjust to a loss. Negative emotions are dissipated, and the person can pay honor to the deceased. For the group, grief facilitates empathy and strengthens bonds among its members. Do you remember the memorial ceremony for the astronauts who perished in the space shuttle *Challenger*? Ronald Reagan's public grief, on behalf of the entire country, powerfully catalyzed our feelings.

Virtually all societies have a culturally provided means by which a person expresses grief: mourning. One study found that mourning includes crying in seventy-two out of seventy-three cultures (Rosenblatt, Walsh, & Jackson, 1976). Only in Bali was crying not part of the accepted ritual. (Apparently, the Balinese avoid crying not only while mourning but in other situations as well. When people might be tempted to cry, they instead smile or joke, thereby inhibiting their tears [Rosenblatt, Walsh, & Jackson, 1976].) Less frequent, but still present in a substantial number of cultures, are attempts at self-injury: scratching one's face, pulling one's hair, or slashing one's body.

Many cultures also have rituals that mark the end of grieving. In contemporary America, we do not have such final ceremonies, which effectively limit the period of grief. Instead, our funerals are best described as initial ceremonies. Grief often begins rather than ends with funerals (Gorer, 1965). This means that grief among Americans can be prolonged. Rosenblatt et al. (1976) compare individuals who have lost a spouse through divorce to those who have lost one through death. In our society, the divorced are much more likely to remarry than the widowed, even when age is taken into account. Perhaps this is because the widowed do not know when they should cease to grieve. Grief occurs in the wake of a divorce, to be sure, but the "divorce papers" play the role of a final ceremony, telling the person to get on with life.

Guilt

A person experiences guilt when he violates a code: religious, moral, or ethical. Guilt involves shame, worry, fear, and anger. It shows up on a person's face, in his posture, among his thoughts, and even in his dreams. Theorists suggest that guilt has substantial adaptive value for our species, holding in check waste and exploitation. The anticipation of guilt is enough to keep many of us on the straight and narrow.

Freud (1926) theorized extensively on guilt, particularly those cases where it oversteps its useful bounds and creates problems for the individual. Psychoanalytic theory suggests that guilt becomes possible when the conscience develops. The conscience is the internalization of societal dictates about what one should and should not do. The "should nots" tend to be exactly what people really want to do, at least in Freud's scheme of things, so there is an inevitable tension between one's conscience and one's motives. Strong guilt can thus be produced by a particularly strong impulse, a particularly harsh conscience, or a combination of the two.

The psychoanalytic account of guilt is not the only possibility. Some theorists derive guilt from fear (e.g., Mowrer, 1960). That is, people experience guilt because they are afraid they will be punished for some misdeed, such as telling a lie or spreading gossip. Other theorists propose that guilt occurs when a person fails to fulfill her own potential, what she knows she can do and be (e.g., Bugental, 1965). By this view, people experience guilt because they fall short of their own expectations for themselves. Note how these contrasting explanations play out that age-old debate between Thrasymachus and Socrates, mentioned earlier in the chapter. Guilt is linked to feelings in the first case and to beliefs in the latter.

Humor

Have you heard this one? Perhaps not, but you can guess that a joke is about to be told. If it's a good one, then you'll experience the complex emotion of humor, which combines joy and surprise, although anger, disgust, and contempt may sneak in as well. Humor is an excellent example of how biology and culture come together in defining emotion. On the one hand, a laugh is a biological response. Infants as young as 5 weeks old laugh, usually in situations presenting unexpected and incongruous stimuli, which at the same time are safe. So, peek-a-boo is a fun game, whereas doctor examinations are not. And on the other hand, a joke has meaning, and socialization must equip us to understand it. Not to know why everyone else is laughing is quite unpleasant.

Freud (1905a) wrote about humor, making a useful distinction between innocent jokes and nasty ones. In the case of innocent humor, incongruity and surprise predominate. Pleasure follows when we see the point of a joke. The psychic energy devoted to making sense of a complicated and confusing circumstance is released with the punch line, which makes the joke simple. This saving of energy is experienced as humor.

In the case of humor that is not innocent, the joke has a purpose: the indirect satisfaction of aggressive or sexual motives. "Dirty" jokes try to cloak sexuality in an acceptable way, and "practical" jokes do the same with aggression. In either case, a transparent disguise results in a joke that fails to be funny. No one is offended by an innocent joke. However, nasty humor that works is invariably more funny than innocent humor. Both types of jokes provide pleasure through technique, but only nasty jokes provide pleasure through the indirect satisfaction of unconscious motives.

Love

Besides making the world go around, the complex emotion of love keeps psychologists busy trying to understand it. In fact, they have cataloged numerous types of love (Clark & Reis, 1988). We have the love for a child by the parent. At the same time, there is the love for a parent by the child. Ethologists speculate that infants elicit caretaking from parents. In the case of birds, for example, the mechanism is clear. A gaping mouth elicits the shoving of a worm down Junior's throat. Perhaps something analogous occurs among people. Human infants are cute, which we can operationally define as having large eyes in a round head, chubby cheeks, and a button nose. "Cuteness" draws us to babies, as well as to cartoon characters, koala bears, and the California Raisins.

Passionate love is an intense and tumultuous emotion. When we speak of "falling" in love, we mean specifically passionate love. We become enveloped in the other person, sexually excited in his or her presence, and miserable if the person leaves the room for but a moment. Psychologists Ellen Berscheid and Elaine Walster (1974) suggest that the Schachter-Singer theory of emotions can explain aspects of passionate love. Passionate love occurs to the degree that someone is aroused and labels it as passion. The interesting twist here is that the arousal may not be due to one's romantic partner. The cause of the arousal is irrelevant, as long as the person believes the partner is responsible for it.

A study by Dutton and Aron (1974) substantiates this argument. An attractive female researcher approached individual men as they were crossing the Capilano River Bridge in British Columbia (Figure 6.8). This is a footbridge that soars 200 feet above rapids and rocks. She told them she was conducting a study on creativity. Would they tell her a brief story as they crossed the bridge? The same request was made of other men as they crossed a lower and much safer bridge. Sexual themes in the stories were assessed, and were found to be more common in the stories of those crossing the precarious bridge. The researchers interpreted these findings according to Schachter and Singer's two-factor theory. Crossing the high bridge created arousal, but the men interpreted their arousal as due to the attractive woman who accompanied them. Thus, their stories were more sexual in nature.

In contrast to passionate love, **companionate love** is a more sober emotion, characterized by concern and affection. Perhaps companionate love occurs as the "opponent process" of passion that grows in strength. Or perhaps companionate love is the mature version of passionate love, what happens when we choose to "stand" in love rather than fall (Fromm, 1956). Regardless, companionate love makes long-term relationships possible and probably deserves greater attention by psychologists than it has received to date.

Shyness

Shyness is a complex emotion that combines interest, shame, and fear, among other basic feelings. Psychologists, who have just recently started to study shyness, find that up to 80 percent of all Americans report being

Figure 6.8
Capilano River Bridge, British Columbia

uncomfortable in the presence of others at some point in their life. And 40 percent regard themselves as currently shy (Zimbardo & Radl, 1979).

Shyness expresses itself physiologically as the body's emergency reaction, although neither fight nor flight is an appropriate response to most situations that elicit shyness. Shyness is accompanied by beliefs such as the following:

- I'm not making a good impression.
- I can't think of anything to say.
- What must they be thinking of me?
- I'm going to do something dumb.
- Why do I have to be so shy?

Although a small degree of shyness can be appealing, in larger degrees it can be damaging and inhibiting to the individual. Shy people avoid eye contact, get derailed in their conversations, and experience difficulty establishing friendships. Loneliness, anxiety, and depression are among the few constant companions of shyness (Cheek & Busch, 1981).

The roots of shyness may paradoxically lie in the attachment process. Children begin to fear strangers at exactly the same time that they begin to form strong bonds with their caretakers (see Chapter 9). Hesitation in the presence of the unknown can be self-protective, but the shy child or adult carries this to an extreme. Psychologists are thus busy devising ways to help people overcome shyness.

One approach based on two-factor theory provides shy folks with alternative labels for their arousal. Brodt and Zimbardo (1981), for instance, placed shy subjects in an extremely noisy setting and told them that the noise would increase their heart and pulse rate. Compared to shy subjects who were not given this false information, these individuals were fluent and assertive during a subsequent interaction with a member of the opposite sex. The loud music presumably provided a reason for the arousal they experienced while making conversation. They didn't have to regard their nervousness as due to their own shyness, and so they were much more free than they otherwise might have been. Is this why adolescents blast music so loud?

Stress and Coping

Psychologists interested in stress and coping bring to bear theories and findings from their investigations of motivation and emotion. Accordingly, a historical view of stress and coping research shows the trends already discussed in this chapter. Let's briefly take such a view, noting how the general perspectives on motivation and emotion so far discussed help to explain the specific topics of stress and coping.

Conceptions of Stress and Coping

Some terms prove more difficult to define than others, and *stress* is one of these terms. Although there is general agreement that stress is what occurs when demands are made on someone, there is much less agreement when we try to be more precise. Sometimes we talk as if stress were a property of the environment: "That place was a pressure cooker; I couldn't wait to

Positive stress allows us the opportunity to exercise mastery; negative stress can lead to anxiety, depression, or worse.

leave." Sometimes stress is attributed to a particular societal role, like being an emergency room nurse, a police officer, or an air traffic controller. Other times stress refers to the bodily changes that result from environmental demands: "My back is tied up in knots, just like my life!" And sometimes stress means one's psychological response: "I'm all stressed out."

So what is stress? We have defined it as a complex transaction between a particular individual and a particular environment that ensues when the person is threatened or challenged. Sometimes these demands are experienced as positive, as when someone poses to us a challenge that we enjoy meeting: "Can you help me get the top off this peanut butter jar?" Positive stress—also called *eustress*—allows us the opportunity to satisfy our need for mastery. In contrast, negative stress—*distress*—disrupts our life, leading to anxiety and depression, poor health, and even death. Psychologists often use the term *stressor* to refer to the events that threaten or challenge the individual. They reserve *stress* for the biological and psychological consequences of exposing an individual to a stressor.

Individuals are not usually passive victims of the stressors they happen to encounter. They will often try to decrease stress by thinking, feeling, or acting in particular ways. That is, they cope. What makes coping an interesting topic for psychologists is that people cope in a variety of ways, some successful and some not. Being able to predict which way of coping someone chooses as well as the success of his or her choice has long been a goal of psychologists working in this area.

defense mechanism

according to psychoanalytic theory, an unconscious strategy for protecting the individual's conscious mind against threat

Defense Mechanisms. Psychoanalytic theory ushered in an influential perspective on coping by introducing the notion of **defense mechanisms.** These are unconscious strategies that we use to defend ourselves against threat. Freud and other psychoanalytic theorists described a variety of defense mechanisms that people may use, some familiar and some bizarre (see Table 6.3). In *projection,* for example, people attribute unacceptable characteristics of their own to other folks. Some types of prejudice involve projection (Chapter 14), as when sexually preoccupied individuals criticize the sexual behavior of other groups. In *repression,* we actively keep an upsetting memory out of our conscious minds. Repression is the process responsible for cases of amnesia that have a psychological basis (Chapter 12).

Defense mechanisms rank as one of the major contributions of psychoanalytic theory. Note how many of the defenses described in Table 6.3 have become part of everyday vocabulary. These coping strategies were there all along for someone to see, but it took the genius of Freud to recognize them and offer a single explanation.

Subsequent theorists have tinkered with how best to regard defense mechanisms. Some theorists suggest that defense mechanisms can be ranked from relatively immature defenses such as denial to relatively mature defenses such as sublimation, depending on the degree to which the individual using the defense distorts reality (e.g., Vaillant, 1977). And these ways of coping may not always be wholly unconscious, as Freud implied. Or they may not always be simply a reaction to threat; they may be undertaken forthrightly, in a show of initiative. The term *coping mechanism* is favored by some contemporary theorists because it has broader connotations than *defense* mechanism.

Table 6.3

Defense Mechanisms

Defense mechanism	Characterization and example
Compensation	Investing one's energies in some activity to offset difficulties in another area; for example, working out or studying after a disappointing date
Denial	Acting as if something bad did not happen; for example, continuing to attend classes after flunking out of school
Displacement	Directing one's impulses toward a substitute object or person; for instance, kicking the dog or yelling at the children after a difficult day at work
Fantasy	Engaging in wishful thinking or daydreaming when feeling stressed; for example, fantasizing about winning the lottery while taking final examinations
Intellectualization	Discussing a traumatic event without experiencing any emotions, as when a patient with a serious illness calmly discusses the chances of survival
Projection	Attributing one's own unacceptable characteristics to others; for example, a hostile person who sees everyone else as belligerent
Rationalization	Rewriting history after a disappointment, like the fox in Aesop's fables who decided that the grapes he couldn't have were probably sour anyway
Reaction formation	Replacing one impulse with its opposite; for example, acting hatefully toward a person one finds attractive
Regression	Acting like an infant or child in stressful circumstances; for example, throwing a tantrum during an argument
Repression	Forcing a threatening memory from awareness, as might happen when someone "forgets" the details of an assault
Sublimation	Channeling undesirable impulses into socially acceptable activities; for example, an aggressive individual might become a fire "fighter" or a police officer

The General Adaptation Syndrome.   Not only did psychologists in the psychoanalytic tradition address stress and coping, so too did those favoring a physiological approach. Their attention focused, naturally, on the changes that took place within the body when a challenge was posed. Remember the notion of the emergency reaction of the body, when physical changes take place preparing us for fight or flight. What happens, though, when fighting or fleeing cannot take place, or when they are unsuccessful in countering a challenge?

Hans Selye (1956) studied precisely this circumstance, arriving at an influential description of the body's response to stress. He found that

a sequence of physiological changes in response to continued stress: first an alarm reaction, then resistance, and finally exhaustion

regardless of the stressor, its continued presence leads to the same sequence of physiological reactions. He calls this sequence the **general adaptation syndrome (GAS).** It encompasses three stages.

In the *alarm reaction,* the organism mobilizes internal resources to restore homeostasis. For instance, in extreme heat or cold, his heart rate and respiration change to regulate the body's temperature. If the threat is psychological, he may use a defense mechanism to blunt its effect.

If stress is not reduced by the alarm reaction, then the second stage of the GAS is entered: *resistance.* Here the organism uses its resources to fight off the effects of the stressor. A struggle ensues. If a virus has entered the body, the immune system is called into play. If the individual is starving, her overall metabolism may slow down to conserve energy. If psychological threat continues, the person's use of defense mechanisms intensifies.

If resistance is unsuccessful, the organism's resources are eventually depleted and *exhaustion* ensues. The organism is now vulnerable to illnesses ranging from the common cold to heart disease. Death can result. The person may lose touch with reality, showing one or more of the severe emotional disorders (Chapter 12).

The general adaptation syndrome is helpful in explaining why different problems may occur together. In using bodily resources to resist one stressor, an individual is less likely to have these resources available to cope with other stressors. The course of a particular disease, for example, may be influenced by the presence or absence of other diseases.

psychosomatic medicine

a field of medicine concerned with how psychological states contribute to physical illnesses

Psychosomatic Medicine.   The psychoanalytic defense mechanisms explain coping in psychological terms, whereas the general adaptation syndrome takes a physiological approach. Still other perspectives try to grapple with both mind and body (Mandler, 1984). **Psychosomatic medicine,** pioneered by Franz Alexander (1950), is a well-known attempt to explain various illnesses as physiological reactions to specific psychological states. Suppose someone is always hostile and competitive. She thus experiences chronic excitation of her body's emergency response, and according to Alexander, she develops high blood pressure.

Alexander theorized as well about illnesses like asthma, arthritis, and colitis. According to him, each illness bears a symbolic as well as physiological relationship to an underlying conflict. Alexander's pronouncements proved influential for years. However, research fails to support many of these hypotheses (Weiner, 1977).

Alexander proposed links between specific emotional states and specific illnesses, but few of the details are correct. Current thinking in psychosomatic medicine now regards the overall relationship between emotional conflict and physical illness as nonspecific. In other words, negative emotions per se are believed to predispose poor health per se (Friedman & Booth-Kewley, 1987). Research shows that emotional states like anxiety, anger, hostility, and depression are associated with illnesses like heart disease, asthma, ulcers, and arthritis. On the whole, the association tends to be a general one; there are no specific links matching particular emotions with particular illnesses.

Type A Behavior Pattern.   Alexander was not completely wrong in proposing specific links between psychological states and particular illnesses. Recent work indeed supports his hypothesis that heart disease is related to chronic anger. So, the **Type A behavior pattern** is a set of behaviors marked by excessive time urgency, competitiveness, and hostility. The Type A personality is "aggressively involved in a chronic, incessant struggle to achieve more and more in less and less time, and if required to do so, against the opposing efforts of other things or other persons" (Friedman & Rosenman, 1974, p. 67). The opposite style of behavior is called Type B, and people of this sort are easygoing and cooperative. Compared to Type B personalities, Type A's are thought to be at increased risk for heart disease (Matthews, 1982).

The Type A behavior pattern is a mixed blessing. Although it can contribute to illness, it also is associated with perseverance in the face of frustration, academic achievement, career advancement, and high salaries (Glass, 1977). Professional football coach Mike Ditka, who suffered a well-publicized heart attack in 1988, illustrates the dilemma. Ditka has been an enormous success because of his impatient and combative style. He also may have weakened his heart.

The link between the Type A behavior pattern and heart disease is complex. Although many studies have supported the hypothesized association, some recent research finds no correlation between such behavior and heart disease (Wright, 1988). Other studies imply that it is not the entire behavior pattern that puts one at risk, but only the element of hostility (Barefoot, Dahlstrom, & Williams, 1983). And a recently reported investigation suggests that Type A individuals, once they suffer a heart attack, show a *better* recovery than Type B individuals following a heart attack (Ragland & Brand, 1988)!

More research is needed, but despite the complexity of this line of work, it would not be wise to ignore the possible contribution of behavior to heart disease. A person is able to change the Type A behavior pattern, learning to meet stress with relaxation rather than a full frontal attack (Levenkron, Cohen, Mueller, & Fisher, 1983). We can hope a Type A personality who begins to act like a Type B personality thereby reduces his or her risk for heart disease (Friedman et al., 1984).

Life Events and Hassles.   Another viewpoint in stress research looks at the role of environmental events in producing stress. Pioneering investigators Thomas Holmes and Richard Rahe (1967) created the Social Readjustment Rating Scale to gauge the *quantity* of stress a person had experienced in recent months. In responding to this scale, a research subject indicates which of forty-three major life events occurred in the past year (see Table 6.4). The more the event in question disrupts ongoing life and requires readjustment, as judged by research subjects, the higher the "life change unit" score assigned to the event. When total scores on the Social Readjustment Rating Scale are correlated with subsequent psychological and physical problems, a positive relationship is found. The more stressful life events you have recently experienced, the more likely you are to be depressed or anxious or sick.

It's not just major life events that create stress for us. Indeed, Kanner, Coyne, Schaefer, and Lazarus (1981) created a measure that parallels the Social Readjustment Rating Scale, except that it asks about hassles: small but annoying events in the course of daily life, such as losing one's car keys, being interrupted at dinner, making a mistake while balancing the checkbook, and having to take care of a pet. As hassles accumulate, so

Table 6.4

Major Life Events

Event	"Life Change Unit" Score
1. Death of spouse	100
2. Divorce	73
3. Marital separation	65
4. Jail term	63
5. Death of a close family member	63
6. Major personal injury or illness	53
7. Marriage	50
8. Being fired at work	47
9. Marital reconciliation	45
10. Retirement	45
11. Major change in health of family member	44
12. Pregnancy	40
13. Sexual difficulties	39
14. Gaining a new family member	39
15. Major business readjustment	39
16. Major change in financial state	38
17. Death of a close friend	37
18. Changing to a different line of work	36
19. Major change in number of arguments with spouse	35
20. Taking out a mortgage or loan for a major purchase	31
21. Foreclosure on a mortgage or loan	30
22. Major change in responsibilities at work	29
23. Son or daughter leaving home	29
24. Trouble with in-laws	29
25. Outstanding personal achievement	28
26. Spouse begins or ceases work outside the home	26
27. Beginning or ending school	26
28. Major change in living conditions	25
29. Revision of personal habits	24
30. Trouble with boss	23
31. Major change in working hours or conditions	20
32. Change in residence	20
33. Changing to a new school	20
34. Major change in usual type and/or amount of recreation	19
35. Major change in church activities	19
36. Major change in social activities	18
37. Taking out a mortgage or loan for a minor purchase	17
38. Major change in sleeping habits	16
39. Major change in number of family get-togethers	15
40. Major change in eating habits	15
41. Vacation	13
42. Christmas	12
43. Minor violations of the law	11

Source: Holmes & Rahe, 1967.

does stress, taking a toll on psychological and physical well-being. In their sheer numbers, hassles may be even more stressful than major life events (Weinberger, Hiner, & Tierney, 1987).

Cognition, Stress, and Coping

Cognitive perspectives now dominate the field of stress and coping. In this view, an event becomes stressful to the degree that one thinks about it in a particular way. Consider the person who makes catastrophes out of minor disappointments, as in the following sequence of thoughts (Beck, 1967):

- I had a bad time on my date.
- It seems I've always had bad times on dates.
- Plus my schoolwork doesn't go much better.
- I failed a midterm last year.
- I did lousy on the SATs the first time I took them.
- It took me three times to pass my driver's license test.
- My father said he was disappointed in me.

Needless to say, this fellow has worked himself into a dither by his way of thinking. Suppose he had said instead about his date, "She must have been tired—that's why we didn't have a great time"?

Researchers have discovered a number of ways of thinking that magnify the stressful effects of events. The more that one regards events as unpredictable and uncontrollable, the more stressful the events are (Mineka & Henderson, 1985). When one is experiencing conflicts about events, this causes stress (Dollard & Miller, 1950). When one blames oneself for bad events but feels powerless to change them, these events are stressful (Peterson & Seligman, 1984). In some cases, these beliefs about events reflect the reality of the situation, but in other cases, beliefs go beyond the facts of the matter and create unnecessary stress for the individual.

Attempts to cope also show the influence of cognitions. Think of a student who does poorly on an exam, but believes that she can do nothing to improve her grade on subsequent occasions. How does she cope? The answer is not at all (Peterson, 1989). This student's beliefs produce passivity. And passivity may well make things worse for her, as she enters a vicious circle of poor performance, poor coping, poor performance, and so on.

The best-known cognitive theorist in stress and coping is Richard Lazarus (1966, 1982; Lazarus & Folkman, 1984). He takes a strong position that the stressfulness of a particular situation depends entirely on how someone appraises the situation and her ability to meet the demands posed by it.

Primary appraisal refers to the individual's interpretation of what is at stake. Suppose you get a traffic ticket for failing to signal a turn. No one likes to get a ticket, of course, but your emotional reaction will vary greatly depending on whether you are required to go to court, how much you might be fined, whether your driving record is good or bad, and if your car insurance rates might be raised. A single event—being given a traffic ticket—takes on wholly different form depending on how you appraise its consequences for you.

Secondary appraisal is the individual's assessment of those resources that are available to cope with a stressful event. Some negative occurrences are perceived as easily resolved: by waiting them out, by talking to someone in charge, by regarding them as a joke and/or a good lesson. Distress following such events is minimal. Other negative occurrences are seen as not so easy to cope with, and considerable distress follows.

Psychologists make a basic distinction between coping strategies that are problem-focused and those that are emotion-focused. In problem-focused coping, one tries to change the world to remove the source of stress. A broken television set usually demands problem-focused coping. In emotion-focused coping, one tries to change how one is feeling about an event. A broken heart usually demands emotion-focused coping.

> . . . [G]ive us grace to accept with serenity the things that cannot be changed, courage to change the things which should be changed, and the wisdom to distinguish the one from the other.
> Reinhold Niebuhr (1892–1971)

Lazarus cautions that no coping strategy is best for all circumstances. The most effective coping depends on the person and on the particular stressor faced.

At the present time, we are seeing reactions against a strictly cognitive approach to stress and coping. Robert Zajonc (1980, 1984) questions whether cognitions invariably determine emotions. He studies what is known as the **mere exposure phenomenon.** Research subjects are shown various stimuli unfamiliar to them, like Chinese characters, for extremely brief periods of time. Exposure is so short that subjects cannot consciously recognize what they see. However, when subjects are later asked to state their preference for these stimuli, they report liking the ones they were more frequently exposed to.

Some years earlier, Littman and Manning (1954) reported a similar result. In a blind comparison, smokers were unable to identify their usual brand of cigarettes, but when asked to state their preference among cigarettes, they unknowingly chose their own brand! Zajonc (1980) summarizes these findings by suggesting that "preference need no inferences." In other words, emotion (preferences) and cognition (inferences) may be more independent than cognitive theorists believe. Events may be stressful regardless of how we think about them. Still, the cognitive approach is important for showing that ways of thinking about events can exacerbate or mitigate stress.

To sum up, please note that cognitive approaches to stress and coping resemble the method acting exercises described at the very beginning of the chapter. You should now understand why method acting is so successful in creating believable characters on the stage. Stanislavsky identified many of the important influences on motivation and emotion and devised exercises that brought these under the actor's control. The resulting character is believable precisely because the motives and emotions portrayed are genuine.

mere exposure phenomenon
the tendency to like stimuli the more one is exposed to them, even when conscious recognition does not take place

Summary

Topics of Concern

- Motivation refers to the basic causes of behavior, and emotion refers to the feelings we experience as we behave.
- Psychologists interested in motivation and emotion have long been interested in several issues.
- What are the basic human motives and emotions? One common distinction with regard to motives is between primary motives—those biological in nature—and acquired motives—those which are learned. Emotions are similarly classified into basic ones, evident in people from all cultures, and complex ones, resulting from a combination of basic emotions and reflecting socialization.
- How do biological and environmental factors interact to determine motivation and emotion?
- What role is played by our thoughts and beliefs? With the general popularity in psychology of biological approaches, cognitive theorizing has been influential.
- How do theories and findings from the study of motivation and emotion shed light on stress and how we cope with stress?

Approaches to Motivation

- Motivation theories have gone through several stages.
- At the turn of the century, explanations in terms of unlearned instincts were popular. These proved problematic when applied to human beings.
- Instinct explanations gave way in the 1940s to theories that looked at motives in terms of physiological needs and drives. A need is a lack of some biological essential, whereas a drive is a state of tension or arousal that a need produces in someone, moving him or her to reduce the need.
- Most recently, theorizing about motivation has stressed the individual's thoughts and beliefs. These theories stress the role played by someone's interpretation in defining particular motives.

Studying Motivation

- Psychologists use a variety of research methods to study motivation. When animals are the research subjects, techniques for investigating the brain and nervous system are often employed.
- When human beings are the research subjects, projective tests like the Thematic Apperception Test (TAT) may be used to gauge the presence and strength of particular motives. In these tests, people are asked to respond to ambiguous stimuli, thereby "projecting" their own needs onto what they see.
- Abraham Maslow has proposed an integrative theory of motivation, arguing that human needs exist in a hierarchy. Needs at the bottom—such as hunger and thirst—must be satisfied before needs at the top—such as love or self-esteem. One of the highest needs identified by Maslow is self-actualization: the need to use to the fullest one's talents and potentialities.

Biological Motives

- Among the important motives with a biological basis are thirst, hunger, and sex.
- These motives are reasonably described in terms of needs and drives, and researchers have mapped out the biological processes that underlie them.
- However, when we compare these motives in animals and human beings, we find that learning and experience play a much greater role for people.

Learned Motives

- Among the important motives that reflect socialization are aggression, achievement motivation, power motivation, and mastery.
- Psychologists often treat the strength of these motives as individual differences among people, and try to understand the causes and consequences of someone's particular level of motivation.

Approaches to Emotion

- Several perspectives on emotion have been popular. First is the evolutionary approach begun by Darwin and followed today by Plutchik. This approach looks at emotions in terms of their survival value.
- Another perspective of emotion is the neuropsychological approach of James and Lange, where emotions are regarded as one's psychological reaction to bodily sensations, particularly to emergency reaction, the set of physiological responses that readies one to respond to threat.
- A third approach to emotions is neurological and tries to link emotions to activity in the brain and nervous system. Cannon and Bard have made important contributions to the neurological approach, and the limbic system is regarded as critically important to emotion. It has also been clearly established that higher parts of the brain serve to inhibit emotional expression.
- Schachter and Singer proposed a cognitive theory of emotion, suggesting that the emotions we experience are due to the way we interpret our general arousal. By this view, it is only our interpretations that distinguish among different emotions.
- Solomon and Corbit's opponent-process theory of emotion uses the notion of homeostasis to explain why emotions change over time. Every time we experience particular emotions, biological processes that counter these feelings are set into operation.

- Tomkins has suggested an integrative theory of emotions, arguing that emotions serve to amplify our motives, making them clear to ourselves and others. Tomkins places great emphasis on the facial expressions associated with particular emotions, which cross-cultural research suggests may be innate.

Complex Emotions

- Although recent research implies that basic emotions exist, we should not overlook such complex emotions as depression, grief, guilt, humor, love, and shyness.
- To explain these, we need to take into account factors proposed by all the major theoretical approaches to emotion.

Stress and Coping

- Psychological approaches to motivation and emotion prove useful in understanding how people cope with stressful events. Both psychoanalytic and biological approaches have been popular, and now in vogue are cognitive approaches to stress and coping.
- According to these cognitive theories, events are stressful according to how individuals think about them and their ability to meet the challenges they pose.

Important Terms and Names

What follows is a list of the core terms and names for this chapter. Your instructor may emphasize other terms as well. Throughout the chapter, glossary terms appear in **boldface** type. They are defined in the text, and each term, along with its definition, is repeated in the margin.

Topics of Concern

motivation/213
emotion/213
primary motives/213
acquired motives/213
stress/214

Approaches to Motivation

need/216
drive/216
homeostasis/216

Studying Motivation

Thematic Apperception Test (TAT)/221
hierarchy of needs/222
self-actualization/223

Henry Murray/221
Abraham Maslow/221

Biological Motives

specific hungers/227
set-point theory/227

Learned Motives

aggression/229
achievement motivation/230
fear of success/231
power motivation/232
need for mastery/233

Konrad Lorenz/229
David McClelland/231
Matina Horner/231

Approaches to Emotion

James-Lange theory of emotion/235
emergency reaction/236
Cannon-Bard theory of emotion/238
two-factor theory of emotion/238
opponent-process theory/241

Robert Plutchik/234
Stanley Schachter and Jerome Singer/238
Richard Solomon and John Corbit/239
Silvan Tomkins/241

Stress and Coping

stressor/214
defense mechanism/248
general adaptation syndrome/250
psychosomatic medicine/250
Type A behavior pattern/251

Hans Selye/249
Franz Alexander/251
Richard Lazarus/253

Review Questions

1. Primary motives are to acquired motives as
   a. adaptive is to nonadaptive.
   b. biological is to learned.
   c. constant is to variable.
   d. simple is to complex.
   Primary motives are biological, whereas acquired motives are learned./213

2. Homeostasis is most closely associated with an explanation of motivation in terms of
   a. instincts.
   b. needs and drives.
   c. cognition.
   The idea of homeostasis is central to need-and-drive theories of motivation. Needs produce drives which trigger behaviors that reduce the drive, returning the person or animal to a balanced state./216

3. Maslow's hierarchy of motives explains
   a. the biological basis of motivation.
   b. the cognitive basis of motivation.
   c. a and b.
   d. the order in which people will attempt to satisfy different motives.
   e. why people have the motives that they do.
   According to Maslow, our motives can be arranged in a hierarchy according to the order in which we attempt to satisfy them. "Lower" needs like food and water must be satisfied before we are concerned with "higher" needs like self-actualization./222

4. Sexual motivation among people can be classified as a(n)
   a. primary motive.
   b. acquired motive.
   c. both a and b.
   d. neither a nor b.
   Human sexuality reflects both nature and nurture. Chapter 16 discusses at length the complexity of human sexuality./228

5. Is human aggression a drive?
   a. yes
   b. no
   c. not clear
   Some theorists have argued that aggression among humans is a drive, much as it appears to be among animals. Other theorists have argued that human aggression does not work according to a feedback system and instead is instrumental—that is, learned. What we have at present is a theoretical impasse./229

6. Darwin and Plutchik regard emotions as _____ for people.
   a. disruptive
   b. irrelevant
   c. nonexistent
   d. useful
   Over a century ago, Darwin argued that particular emotions have survival value. More recently, Plutchik has echoed this hypothesis./234

7. Schachter and Singer agree with _____ that the body's physical reactions do not differ greatly from emotion to emotion.
   a. Cannon and Bard
   b. Darwin and Plutchik
   c. James and Lange
   d. Solomon and Corbit
   e. Tomkins
   The Cannon and Bard approach to emotions began with the position that bodily changes taking place during the emergency reaction do not differ greatly from emotion to emotion. Cannon and Bard look to the cortex for the basis of different emotions, and Schachter and Singer look to someone's interpretations./238

8. The current view of how emotional conflict is related to physical illness regards this relationship as
   a. nonexistent.
   b. nonspecific.
   c. plausible but unestablished.
   d. specific.
   e. symbolic.
   Most psychologists today accept the existence of a relationship between emotional conflict and poor health, and they regard this relationship as nonspecific. In other words, conflict per se produces poor health per se./250

9. The "fatal" ingredient of the Type A behavior pattern is probably
   a. competitiveness.
   b. fatalism.
   c. hostility.
   d. time urgency.
   e. all of the above.
   By definition, the Type A behavior pattern is a complex of habits—competitiveness, hostility, and time urgency—but recent research implies that it is chiefly the hostility of the Type A individual that puts him or her at risk for coronary disease./251

10. Lazarus's approach to coping is thoroughly
    a. behavioral.
    b. ethological.
    c. cognitive.
    d. psychoanalytic.
    In stressing that people respond to events according to how they appraise them and their ability to meet the demands they pose, Lazarus provides very much a cognitive view of coping./253

The failure of memory—forgetting—has many determinants.

Chapter Seven

Memory and Cognition

Topics of Concern

In the summer of 1973, John Dean testified before a Senate committee investigating the Watergate incident. Dean's testimony was impressive, to say the least. Once transcribed, his opening statement alone occupied almost 250 pages. He recounted dozens of meetings with President Richard Nixon and top-ranking individuals in the White House. His testimony seemed to confirm that these high officials had conspired to cover up White House involvement in the original burglary of the Democratic party's offices in the Watergate complex.

Watergate and its subsequent investigation are among the most notable events in recent United States history, leading to the resignation of President Nixon and a host of social and political consequences still being felt today. John Dean figured prominently in Watergate and its aftermath, and you are probably not surprised to see him mentioned in a psychology textbook. But perhaps you will be intrigued when you realize that this particular chapter concerns itself not with power or politics, but with memory.

When psychologists investigate memory, they usually show their research subjects material to be memorized and then test them later for their recall. The researchers know the "right" answer, and so they can check the memories of their subjects. This is why John Dean and his testimony before the Senate are pertinent to our discussion of memory. President Nixon had secretly tape-recorded meetings in his office. This was not known at the time of Dean's testimony, but when these tapes became available, it was possible to check Dean's memory against what he was trying to remember, just as if he were a subject in a memory experiment.

Psychologist Ulric Neisser (1981) systematically compared Dean's testimony against the taped record, and we draw here on his intriguing case history. Was John Dean accurate or inaccurate in his recollection of conversations in the White House? This proves to be too simple a question. Instead, this case suggests that memory is a highly complex matter.

One of the important conclusions from this study is that John Dean's memory for specific conversations was on the whole atrocious. He reported statements that were never made and overlooked others that were made. Even when he correctly recounted actual exchanges, he located them in the wrong part of a conversation or even in the wrong con-

versation. Further, he repeatedly exaggerated his own role in the incidents he recalled.

On September 15, 1972, the Justice Department handed down the first indictments in the Watergate case. Dean was called to the Oval Office to meet with Nixon and Robert Haldeman (Nixon's Chief of Staff). Months later, when testifying, Dean recalled this meeting as follows:

The President asked me to sit down. Both men appeared to be in very good spirits and my reception was very warm and cordial. The President then told me that Bob—referring to Haldeman—had kept him posted on my handling of the Watergate case. The President told me I had done a good job and he appreciated how difficult it had been. . . . I responded that I could not take credit because others had done much more difficult things. . . . I also told him that there was a long way to go before this matter would end and that I certainly could make no assurances that the day would not come when this matter would start to unravel.

According to the tapes, Nixon did *not* ask Dean to sit down. He did *not* say that Haldeman had kept him posted. He did *not* tell Dean that he had done a good job. Dean did *not*

The accuracy of John Dean's memory was a central issue in the Congressional investigation of the Watergate scandal.

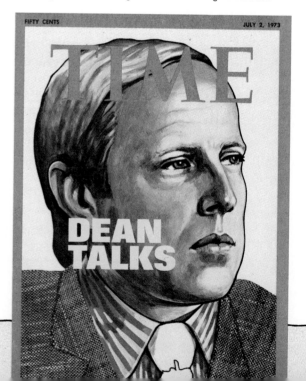

say he could take no credit. Dean did *not* give a warning that the event might yet unravel; indeed, he promised just the opposite.

Was John Dean therefore a liar? Neisser (1981) concludes that Dean did not attempt to deliberately mislead the Senate. Instead, he displayed a number of the striking characteristics of memory as psychologists have come to understand it. In everyday life, we may think of memories as if they were stored in a file drawer until we wish to inspect them. But a more reasonable way to characterize memories is to say that we *construct* our experiences as they occur and *reconstruct* them upon recall. Memories are thus subject to possible bias. As already mentioned, Nixon did not ask Dean to sit down when entering the Oval Office, but this is so typical that Dean sincerely believed that it had happened.

Although Dean was wrong about almost all the details of the conversations, he was correct with regard to their overall thrust; there most certainly had been a cover-up. What he apparently did was to abstract the common themes of many conversations and experiences. He incorporated these into his testimony, dramatically to be sure, and thus ended up being right in his overall testimony. Here is another important lesson about memory. Events may not be represented in one's mind as they literally occurred, but rather in terms of their general meaning. Memories may be colored by one's values, needs, and expectations.

There were several instances when Dean's testimony proved to be quite accurate. Statements repeated several times by Nixon or others went into his memory verbatim. And when he had previously planned and rehearsed what he wanted to say during a White House conversation, he recalled his own statements with high fidelity. This fact cautions us that sometimes recall can be literal. Perhaps there are several different processes we use to remember things.

Because of the issues it raises concerning how our minds work, the case of John Dean serves to introduce the present chapter. **Memory** can be defined as our mental representation of knowledge. **Cognition** encompasses the psy-

---

memory
our mental representation of knowledge

cognition
the psychological processes which transform and retain knowledge

cognitive psychology
the field of psychology that studies memory and cognition

---

chological processes that transform and retain this knowledge. Among our important cognitive processes are those responsible for judgment, decision making, and problem solving (Sternberg & Smith, 1988). The field of psychology that studies memory and cognition—mental representations and processes—is called **cognitive psychology.** Several general concerns cut across the whole field. Let us turn now to them.

The Importance of Memory and Cognition

Over the years, psychology has flip-flopped considerably with respect to the importance of mental representations and processes. As explained in Chapter 1, the very first psychologists defined psychology as the study of the mind. But as we then saw in Chapter 5, the influential approach known as behaviorism disavowed the importance of cognition and attempted to rid psychology of all mention of the mind.

Why is cognitive psychology alive and well today? The answer is that psychologists could not escape the fact that memory and cognition are important. It is all but impossible to speak about human beings without speaking of them in terms of their capacity for knowledge. A person shorn of cognitive representations and processes is no kind of person at all, a tough realization for those who tried to follow strictly the behaviorist agenda. We cannot fully explain even the simplest habits without reference to something mentalistic (Chapter 5). Cognition allows us to modify our behavior in light of our experience, letting us transcend immediate stimuli.

Memory and cognition underlie much of what we regard as uniquely human: language, learning, memory, personal identity, and culture. They help us cope with the demands of the world in the ways that we do (Chapter 6). Consider people in contrast to creatures who cannot sensibly be said to "know" very much, like moths or slugs or cockroaches.

Cognition returned to a legitimate place within psychology by the 1960s and has remained there ever since. But psychologists did not embrace cognition just because they couldn't live without it. Improved research methods made the return of cognition possible. From several disparate research traditions came methods for studying cognition that greatly improved upon the flawed practice of introspection, as practiced by the first psychologists. The availability of these methods gave new impetus to cognitive psychology, and the field rapidly began to take form. Many date the "official" arrival of the field as 1967, when Ulric Neisser pulled together the raw ingredients in his appropriately titled book *Cognitive Psychology*.

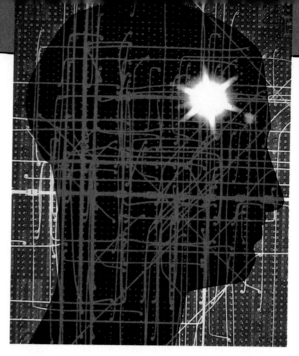

Because it is so hard to grasp, artists often depict the essence of the mind symbolically.

Thinking about Thinking

Probably the major concern of cognitive psychologists is how to capture the essence of the mind. They have typically turned to models in the hope that memory and cognition can be clarified. Indeed, more than most fields, cognitive psychology has seen a rich succession of models.

Why should this be so? One contributing factor is that the mind—its contents and processes—cannot literally be seen by a researcher. Introspectionists thought they were glimpsing the mind when they identified the elements of consciousness, but this was a different sort of "looking" than peering into the refrigerator and seeing if you have the ingredients for stew.

It is difficult to capture mental phenomena with the words we have available to us (Ryle, 1949). Most terms are drawn from a visual or spatial domain. We treat the mind *as if* it were a physical place and thoughts *as if* they were objects that occupy this space.

- I see what you mean.
- Things just became clear to me.
- Do you follow my logic?
- My thoughts are a jumble.
- It's on the tip of my tongue.
- Let me collect my thoughts.

When we use such expressions to talk about cognition, we are necessarily using a model. This is alright, except when

we forget that the mind is not a physical place and that our thoughts are not things.

Models for the mind often come from prevailing technology, probably because theorists have believed that the mind is so complicated that they need to have a complicated comparison in order to do it justice (Marshall, 1982). Over the years, theorists have likened the mind to a wax tablet, a piece of paper, a library, a plumbing system, a railroad terminal, a telephone switchboard, and a computer.

Let's take a step back from these models for some observations about cognitive theorizing. It is impossible to describe the mind without using comparisons. We simply don't have terms available to describe cognition that aren't borrowed from other domains. At the same time, no model will perfectly capture the mind, because that's the nature of a model . . . and the nature of scientific theories (Chapter 1). We should remember not to put all of our eggs in one metaphorical basket, because each new generation of theorists will discover a model that captures aspects of cognition that previous models had overlooked or neglected.

Cognitive psychologists propose many different models for the mind, and their sheer number can be overwhelming. However, we can look at the assumptions common to these different perspectives and see these as core ideas concerning cognition. All models acknowledge that cognition consists of both representations and processes. They assume that knowledge is structured, and has an organization of some kind. And all models try to be consistent with what we know about the brain and nervous system, under the assumption that cognition has a biological underpinning.

We can also look at how the models differ and learn about the yet to be resolved issues in cognition. One important issue is whether cognition is regarded as passive, something that inevitably is triggered granted certain stimuli; or whether it is active, something that the person can influence or direct granted his or her goals. Although many cognitive theorists feel that a passive view of the mind is not reasonable, they are not comfortable with where this conclusion leads them. To view the mind as active is to assume that there is something or someone "calling the shots" behind the scenes of cognition, and the identity of this presumed entity is elusive.

Basic Questions for Cognitive Psychology

Cognitive psychologists are interested not just in what we know but in how we acquire, transform, retain, and use knowledge. Different processes are therefore studied by cognitive psychologists, who approach them from the vantage of particular models of the mind, as just discussed (Sternberg & Smith, 1988). Regardless of which model is favored, certain basic questions must be addressed.

Is cognition rational or irrational? Our stereotype of the cognitive being—Mr. Spock of *Star Trek* fame—is an individual of thorough rationality. But psychologists are not so quick to accept this stereotype, and they have investigated the degree to which human cognition reflects the influence of one's emotions or motives (Chapter 6).

Is cognition general or specific? There are a number of cognitive processes: attention, categorization, and reasoning among them. Psychologists and others tend to regard these processes as highly general, operating in the same way regardless of their content. So, we describe people as having good memories, as being poor at deduction, as thinking quickly or slowly, and so on. A different point of view on the

matter suggests that cognitive processes are highly specific. The type of recall we use for recipes may entail a different process than the type we use for phone numbers. Both in turn may differ from the memory we use to recall physical skills like riding a bicycle.

How and why do people differ in their cognitive processes? Many cognitive psychologists pursue their research without worrying about variation among people, but others look at these differences with interest, seeking clues about how cognition originates and changes. These researchers make comparisons among different groups of people, say, between children and adults, or between novices and experts in a certain domain, or between people with brain damage that compromises cognitive processes and those with intact brains.

What is the biological basis of cognition? The brain and cognition obviously have something to do with each other. No brain means no cognition, so we can assume. At the same time, most cognitive psychologists carefully argue that their subject matter does not reduce to neurology (e.g., Glass & Holyoak, 1986). They point out that the same information can be represented in a variety of ways. A telephone number can be stored in a computer, written on a cocktail napkin, or somehow located in one's brain. What this means is that the information and its physical representation are conceptually different.

Regardless, the specific relationship between cognition and the brain remains a question of interest. As already discussed, cognitive psychologists study how memories might be represented in the brain. They also want to know whether different cognitive processes are located in different parts of the brain (Chapter 2), and if cognitive activity is inherent in the brain or learned. The question of this relationship revives the old debate between the empiricists and rationalists about the origin of knowledge (Chapter 3).

> Models for the mind often come from prevailing technology.
> • • •

Information Processing

Psychologists have been drawn to *information theory* as one possible way to understand memory and cognition. This approach originally surfaced in the field of engineering as a way to study radio and telephone communications. As you probably know, the transmission of messages through these (and other) channels is less than perfect. Some distortion always occurs, which means that the person at the receiving end of a radio faces the task of deciding the actual communication from among those that are possible.

Because of the current popularity of computers, we are all familiar with the term *bit,* short for *binary digit* (0 or 1). A bit is defined as the amount of information that reduces the possible alternatives in two. Remember the game Twenty Questions? The absolute minimum number of yes-no questions that you must pose in order to zero in on the "real" answer is the number of bits of information that the answer contains.

Strictly speaking, information is whatever reduces uncertainty. Many cognitive psychologists use the term as a synonym for knowledge. Information enters the body via the senses. To say that it is processed is to emphasize that people *do something* to the information. Cognition construed as information processing is necessarily dynamic—it moves.

Inherent in the notion of information processing is that cognition involves various stages defined by the different transformations taking place. First, the information is organized. Then it is represented in terms that are psychologically meaningful. Next, it is variously transformed or acted upon. Finally, it directs a person's subsequent actions. The model of the mind contained in the information-processing approach is a rich one, because we can readily distinguish among different ways of processing information, that is, among different ways of thinking.

Information-processing theory provides a model for psychologists studying memory and cognition.

Serial and Parallel Processing

serial processing
information processing of stimuli
one at a time

parallel processing
information processing of stimuli
simultaneously

In its simplest form, information processing following a particular stimulus proceeds along one direction at a time. This is called **serial processing.** Suppose you are cooking dinner. If you prepare one dish at a time, this is akin to serial processing. However, information processing may be more complex, just as actual cooking often is. One stimulus may give rise simultaneously to different processes: **parallel processing.** Reading is a good example, because it requires that we move our eyes, recognize words, abstract meanings, and so on. These are coordinated together, not done one after another. Actual cognition represents a mix of serial and parallel processes.

Bottom-up and Top-down Processing

**bottom-up information
processing**
information processing in which
simple aspects are not influenced by
more complex ones

In **bottom-up information processing,** simple aspects of thinking are not influenced by more complex ones. For example, consider one possible process by which we recognize that certain visual stimuli comprise the letters that spell out a word (Glass & Holyoak, 1986). We first discriminate between light and dark areas on a page where the word is contained. Then we "see" the letters as figure and the page as ground. Then we identify the individual letters. We finally put the letters together to form the word.

If each stage here is influenced only by what happened in the immediately preceding stages, then it is a bottom-up process. I recently had an experience much like this example. I bought an old radio at a flea market, and it was covered with years of grime. I wiped its front when all of a sudden my attention was captured by some markings there. As I stared at them, I saw first they were letters, and then I saw a word: *PHILCO,* the brand of the radio. The whole process took several seconds, and my gradual recognition indeed went through discrete stages.

Theorists fond of the bottom-up approach often use a computer as their metaphor for information processing. A typical computer cannot proceed other than bottom-up. Indeed, the common criticism of computers—"garbage in, garbage out"—reflects precisely the reliance of most computers on a bottom-up approach to processing information. Granted the first step, no matter how silly or flawed, the subsequent steps ensue.

It is no coincidence that information-processing approaches became popular in psychology precisely as computers became well known within the larger society. Computers provide a fertile vocabulary for depicting cognition. The central characteristics of cognition—representation and task solution—are exactly what computers do. The problem with the computer metaphor is that it cannot readily capture cognitive processes where later considerations affect earlier ones. Typical computers have no controlling "executive," who can modify early stages in light of later ones.

**top-down information
processing**
information processing in which
simple aspects are influenced by
more complex ones

The opposite of a bottom-up approach is, naturally, called **top-down information processing.** In this case, the simple aspects of information processing are influenced by the complex ones. Let's go back to the earlier example of the radio. Suppose the radio had not been so grimy. At a glance I would have seen that it had a brand name emblazoned on the front. I would have peered at it, trying to make out what it was. I would have known that there are only a few brands that it could possibly be, and I would compare what I saw with them: GENERAL ELECTRIC, ATWATER KENT, MOTOROLA, and so on. My recognition of the word *PHILCO* would have been influenced by the fact that I knew I was looking at the brand name of a radio. This example of cognition is therefore top-down processing. Here we have to discuss cognition in terms of higher mental functions, such as goals, intentions, and general knowledge, dominating and directing lower functions. In this example, my expectation sat on top of the hierarchy.

Critical in supporting the top-down approach to cognition were a series of studies by John Bransford and his colleagues showing that "general" knowledge affects even the simplest cognitive task. In one experiment, for instance, subjects were instructed to listen to sentences, including the following:

- The ants ate the jelly.
- The ants were in the kitchen.

When later questioned about sentences they did or did not hear, subjects reported that they had heard sentences like "The ants in the kitchen ate the jelly" (Bransford & Franks, 1971). This is a reasonable inference, you might say, but appreciate that it argues against bottom-up processing. Computers don't make inferences like this; they don't drag in other information, reasonable or otherwise (Bransford, 1979).

Depth of Processing

depth of processing

an approach to information processing that assumes people encode information in different ways, some simple (or shallow) and some elaborate (or deep)

Yet a different way to regard information processing, **depth of processing** (Craik & Lockhart, 1972), developed as the result of research like the Bransford study. The essence of this approach is the assumption that people can encode incoming information in various ways, some simple (or shallow) and some elaborate (or deep).

Suppose you have written a short story, and you have named your central character Bob. Then you decide that that's not a good name for the character, and you wish to change it to Norbert. You read over the pages you have written, on the lookout for "Bob" when it appears, so you can change it each time. This is a rather superficial way of accessing information because you focus only on what the words in your story look like.

In contrast, suppose you decide to change your characterization of Bob/Norbert from friendly to aloof. Again, you read over the pages, but now you are on the lookout for all possible synonyms for friendly. This is a deeper way of accessing information because you must focus on the meaning of the words in your story. When we learn material, the more deeply we process it, the easier it is on subsequent occasions to recall it. In the next section, you will see that information-processing approaches have been popular among cognitive psychologists trying to understand the nature of memory.

Memory

Let's start with a look at the cognitive processes that allow us to represent events that were previously experienced and then later recall or recognize them. The process by which we put information into memory is called

Human memories, like books on a library shelf, can be catalogued, stored, and retrieved.

encoding
the process by which we put information into our memory

storage
the process by which information is kept in our memory

retrieval
the process by which information is located in our memory and then used

forgetting
the failure of memory

nonsense syllables
sets of letters with no inherent meaning, used by psychologists to study memory

encoding. Once in our memory, we speak of the **storage** of information. And the process by which information is located in our memory and then used is called **retrieval.** Keeping in mind the metaphor implicit in these terms can help you grasp them: They liken memories to things that can be put away at one time and taken out at another.

On the other hand, we can also look at encoding, storage, and retrieval in terms of information processing, seeing them as aspects of the same basic process. Note that encoding, storage, and retrieval are terms that can be applied not only to human memory, but also to all other systems concerned with information, including computers, libraries, or your list of "things to do" during the day. In each case, there exist ways of acquiring information, retaining it, and then making it available for use.

Failure of memory—or **forgetting**—can be due to any of several problems. We may be unable to remember a particular item of information because we never encoded it in the first place, because we are unable to retrieve it given the way we have stored it, or because the memory has literally been lost.

Psychologists have long been interested in memory. Herman Ebbinghaus (1850–1909), a German philosopher and psychologist, was credited with the first systematic studies of memory. His procedures were simple, yet they produced reliable results with important implications for how the mind works. Even today, when contemporary cognitive psychologists bring to their subject matter sophisticated methods and theories, the work of Ebbinghaus continues to be influential, if only as an important point of departure.

To gain some appreciation of the significance of Ebbinghaus's (1885) pioneering investigations, consider that Ebbinghaus worked at a time when there were no other researchers in this field to provide him with theoretical or methodological precedents for the study of memory. Ebbinghaus had to make a number of important decisions about how to proceed with his investigations—not least of which was deciding what kind of material should be memorized—completely on his own. He created what have come to be known as **nonsense syllables,** sets of letters with no inherent meaning, such as ZPS, CER, ZAQ, or EEQ.

Herman Ebbinghaus

Figure 7.1
Serial Position Effect. When people are shown a list of words and then asked to recall them, they best recall the first few words—due to the primacy effect—and the last few words—due to the recency effect.

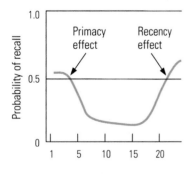

Why use a nonsense syllable? This technique allowed the researcher to study memory without having to worry about the meaning of the material being memorized. Because meaningfulness always influences memorization, by eliminating it Ebbinghaus thereby simplified matters greatly. We've already seen in previous chapters how simple versions of phenomena may prove enlightening precisely because they are simple. In particular, simplifications lend themselves to experimentation, and Ebbinghaus indeed studied memory experimentally. He used himself as his own research subject. He would study a list of nonsense syllables until he had memorized it. Then some time later he would test himself for recall.

Many other psychologists of the era believed that "higher" mental processes (as opposed to sensation) could not be expressed quantitatively and indeed could not be studied experimentally. Even Wilhelm Wundt, the first psychologist and certainly an advocate of the experimental method, did not bring such topics as memory into the laboratory (Chapter 1).

A number of reliable principles of memory emerged from the studies of Ebbinghaus, findings that are accepted even today. He showed that the more times a person rehearsed a list of syllables, the better it was committed to memory. He also showed that when we commit more than one list of syllables to memory, we will experience interference with our recall of each, particularly when specific syllables in them are similar.

The **serial position effect** refers to the fact that in a series of nonsense syllables, those at the beginning or ending of the series are better remembered than those in the middle (see Figure 7.1). Ebbinghaus was the first researcher to demonstrate this effect, which proved to be quite common. Most of us encounter it all the time when we meet a series of people at a party. We remember the faces and names of the first and last people more readily than those in the middle. The serial position effect describes what we remember from baseball games, movies, and even textbooks.

Ebbinghaus's approach fits with a particular view of the way the mind works, specifically the idea that learning consists of associations between items. According to this view, the associations we make with particular items determines our recall. Some associations help our recall because they lead to the item in question, whereas others inhibit it because they mislead us. Remember that we encountered associations in Chapter 5 as a common ingredient in many theories of learning. And so we see compatibility between the Ebbinghaus tradition of memory and the behavioral tradition of animal learning, which explains why studies of memory did not stop during the reign of behaviorism (Chapter 1).

Memory Systems

Following the example of Ebbinghaus and other psychologists who pioneered investigations of memory, subsequent cognitive psychologists studied memory extensively. One important discovery by the next generation of researchers was that we apparently can distinguish among three different types of memory, corresponding to the steps through which incoming information is processed as it is remembered (see Figure 7.2).

At one time, these types of memory were regarded as discrete stages in the encoding → storage process (Atkinson & Shiffrin, 1968; Waugh & Norman, 1965). This view is called the **multistore model of memory,** because it assumes that memories are represented ("stored") in several different ways. At the present time, however, there is skepticism about our ability to determine when one type of memory ends and another type begins. A different view is that there is only one type of memory, in which material is processed to varying depths (Craik & Lockhart, 1972). So, the supposed stages of memory represent different levels of information processing, and this approach is appropriately called the **levels of processing model of memory.**

In light of our previous discussion of models of the mind, we should not expect either view of memory to be literally true. What they share in common is the idea that memory is not a simple phenomenon. Different aspects of memory—whether we regard them as stages or levels—entail different processes. Let's turn to these aspects now, and learn about their distinctive characteristics.

Sensory Memory. Information processing was introduced in Chapter 4, where the point was made that sensation and perception blur into one another. A similar observation can be made about perception and cognition; it can sometimes be difficult to say when perception stops and cognition begins. This is particularly so with our **sensory memory,** which holds ever so briefly a relatively faithful version of our sensory experiences. A synonym for *sensory memory* is *sensory register,* which implies that this type of memory "registers" what we have perceived. The sensory memory is limited both in the amount of information it can hold as well as in how long it can hold it. The more intense the original stimulus, the longer it lingers in one's sensory memory. A scream stays in the sensory memory longer than a whisper.

levels of processing model of memory
theory of memory that assumes there is only one type of memory in which information is processed to varying depths

sensory memory
also called sensory register; the first stage of memory, a brief but faithful version of our sensory experiences

Figure 7.2
Memory Systems. One popular view of memory proposes that information passes through discrete stages: sensory memory, short-term memory, and long-term memory. Information can be lost or forgotten at every step in the process.

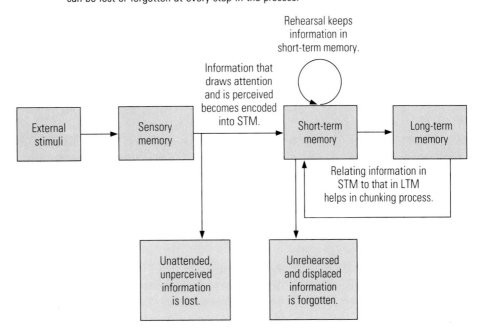

Figure 7.3

Sperling's (1960) Experiment. Subjects were presented with an array of letters for just a fraction of a second. A tone then sounded telling them which row of letters to recall: top, middle, or bottom. Subjects correctly reported the requested letters. However, they could not remember the entire array, showing that information is kept in sensory memory for only a brief period.

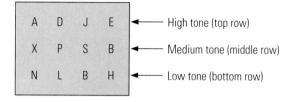

1. Subject is shown an array with a varying number of letters for 50 milliseconds.

2. Immediately following, a tone is sounded telling the subject which row to report.

3. The subject is asked to report the letters in the row indicated by the signal.

A	D	J	E	← High tone (top row)
X	P	S	B	← Medium tone (middle row)
N	L	B	H	← Low tone (bottom row)

?

icon

visual image that briefly lingers following the presentation of a stimulus

An **icon** is the visual image that briefly lingers following the presentation of a stimulus. A classic experiment by George Sperling (1960) helped establish the existence of icons and provide some clues about how they function. He showed research subjects an array of letters for but a fraction of a second (see Figure 7.3). The array had three rows. When the letter display was turned off, a tone was sounded that was high, medium, or low in pitch. If the tone was high, subjects were to recall the top row of letters. If it was medium, they were to report the middle row. And so on.

Sperling's subjects could recall the letters in the indicated row with no difficulty, even when each row contained four or five letters. The subjects at one time must have represented to themselves all the letters in the array—because the tone sounded *after* the display of letters was turned off. However, these representations were obviously fleeting, lasting no more than one-quarter of a second. When asked to recall all the letters, subjects failed, invariably coming up with only four or five. Other research suggests that icons are minimally transformed from the original sensation (Neisser, 1967). In other words, people can be said to "look at" their icons as much as to "remember" them. Icons are best placed somewhere between perception and cognition.

Icons are important because they make our visual experience continuous. Our eyes work by making little jumps (Chapter 3). From instant to instant, therefore, breaks occur in the flow of sensory information. Icons smooth out these breaks. Sometimes a valuable characteristic has limitations when carried to an extreme. One theory of the reading disorder *dyslexia,* in which letters are reversed and otherwise confused, points the finger at icons that linger too long (DiLollo, Hanson, & McIntyre, 1983).

echo

auditory image that briefly lingers following the presentation of a stimulus

Other sensations presumably have the equivalent of icons, although these have not been as frequently studied as icons. Sensory memory has been shown for touch (e.g., Bliss, Crane, Mansfield, & Townsend, 1966). It also has been shown for hearing, where the briefly lingering image is called an **echo.** It behaves much like an icon, except that it doesn't go away quite as rapidly. Echoes typically last up to several seconds.

short-term memory

the stage of memory into which information passes from the sensory memory, so named because information stays there for no more than 20 seconds

Short-term Memory.   The next step in the process of memory storage is called **short-term memory,** where a limited amount of information is held for a brief period of time, usually 15 to 20 seconds. Only some of the information from the sensory memory passes into short-term memory.

Interestingly "packaged" information—such as that found in popular magazines—is often most easily recalled.

chunking
grouping cognitive elements into larger wholes

Which aspects of the information move on? Obviously, the process of selective attention is involved (Chapter 4). Information that is bizarre often grabs our attention. And to the degree that particular information is familiar and/or meaningful, it passes into short-term memory as well. However, if the information is too familiar, we may tune it out. This process is more formally known as *habituation*. Finally, it's important to emphasize that the amount of information that we can represent at any given time in short-term memory is severely limited.

George Miller (1956) wrote a well-known paper on "the magic number seven, plus or minus two," in which he argued that the capacity of short-term memory is limited to between five and nine items ("bits") of information. In other words, the number of discrete items that we can represent at any one time is about seven. Some of you may be skeptical, because you know that you can hold on to more information than this. If you get a long-distance number from directory assistance, you usually do not need to write it down before you dial. And the area code and number together comprise ten digits. Doesn't this experience contradict the supposed limit of seven, plus or minus two?

The answer is no, because we can form clusters of the digits in phone numbers, grouping them into meaningful groups. Our tendency to group elements into larger wholes is called **chunking.** There are those of us who know that the area code for New York City is 212, for example, or that the area code for Chicago is 312. We thus can turn three items of information into one.

Or suppose your roommate asks you to pick up the following items at the grocery store: flour, baking powder, salt, butter, sugar, bananas, and walnuts. Will you remember all of these? Maybe, maybe not. But suppose you say to yourself, "Those are the ingredients for banana bread!" Then you will have no trouble remembering the specific items, because you have been able to chunk them into a meaningful—and tasty—whole. By consolidating information into chunks, we can greatly increase the capacity of short-term memory (Ericsson & Chase, 1982).

What happens to information when it passes into short-term memory? It tends not to be represented "deeply." Words are often stored in terms of how they sound rather than what they mean. How do we know this? Studies show that errors of recall for information in short-term memory often stem from our confusion between the *sounds* of letters and words, not their *meanings* (Conrad, 1963, 1964). If subjects are visually presented with single letters and then asked to recall what they have just seen, they confuse *E* with *G* or *V* or *B*. Interestingly *E*'s and *F*'s are not confused in short-term memory, even though they look alike. One conclusion from such studies is that short-term memory is a way of talking to ourselves.

Information does not stay too long in short-term memory. Estimates are that most information is lost after about 20 seconds (e.g., Peterson & Peterson, 1959). The amount of information stored in short-term memory and the length of time it stays there can be increased in several ways. You can *rehearse* the information. When I get a phone number from directory assistance, for instance, I repeat it out loud several times, which usually helps me hold on to it long enough to dial it.

You can also *elaborate* the information and make it more meaningful. Where I live, the first three digits of a telephone number reflect the approximate area where someone lives. This means I can remember a telephone number better if I stop and realize, "Yes, he lives on the Old West Side."

Finally, you can *chunk* the material, grouping it into meaningful wholes. As already discussed, chunking allows us to deal with the well-documented limits on short-term memory. We may only be able to entertain seven discrete items in our mind at any one time, but if these are chunks, we nonetheless can consider a great deal of information simultaneously.

long-term memory
the stage of memory into which information passes from the short-term memory, so named because information here represents our permanent storehouse of past experiences

Long-term Memory. The next and final step in the memory process is **long-term memory,** so named because information can be retained for an extremely long time. Further, its capacity is virtually unlimited. Information moves into long-term memory from short-term memory, and here we have our entire storehouse of past experiences: thoughts, feelings, and events. Our skills and abilities are also represented in long-term memory, along with our identity and personality. As in short-term memory, there is selectivity as to what information passes into it. Not everything makes it there. For instance, I know that yesterday I answered questions in class, but today I don't remember the specific questions or the specific students who asked them. That information is gone because it probably never made it into my long-term memory.

It is impossible to overestimate the importance of this aspect of memory. Consider what it would be like to be unable to add new information to long-term memory. Neurologist Oliver Sacks (1986) described the case of Jimmie G., a forty-nine-year-old man who could not recall any events during the last thirty years of his life. Because of brain damage brought about by alcoholism (Chapter 12), Jimmie G. was unable to hold on to ongoing experiences for more than about 10 seconds. In other words, new information never moved from his short-term memory to his long-term memory.

Whatever anyone said to him was promptly forgotten. Whatever he said or did or felt was promptly forgotten. Although he had been hospitalized in the same institution for years, every time he met a doctor or nurse, it was in effect for the first time. Current events baffled him. He had few interests other than crossword puzzles. Although he was charming and intelligent, he had no friends. Without long-term memory, his ability to function was obviously diminished, to say the least.

A popular research strategy for investigating long-term memory involves asking research subjects to memorize stories and later recall them. This tradition can be traced to Frederick Bartlett (1932), who had subjects read and later recall complex stories. His results were quite important. He found that recall was not literal. Instead, subjects abstract the major points of the story (as they see them) and represent the essence of the story in their memory. When later asked to recall the story, they elaborated on the gist of the story, sometimes departing considerably from the original material. As we discussed earlier, much of John Dean's testimony revealed the same tendencies.

Findings like these imply that long-term memory is an active process (e.g., Bransford, 1979; Kintsch, 1974; Neisser, 1967). Theorists sometimes say that memory is constructive. Memories are not reproductions of experiences stored somewhere in the mind but rather are created or built anew each time they are remembered. Notice that the terms *storage* and

A photo album can be more than a place to store photographs—it is often a key to our long-term memory.

retrieval can be misleading here, because they tempt us to treat memories as fixed things rather than constructions.

Typically, representation occurs "deeply" in long-term memory. The critical characteristic of most long-term memories is that the represented information is meaningful to the individual. Representations are therefore abstract, elaborate, and organized. Cognitive psychologists tend to agree on the following divisions of long-term memory (Tulving, 1985, 1986):

- procedural memory—knowledge of how to do something: bake bread, change a tire, or build a charcoal fire
- semantic memory—knowledge of particular facts about the world, like the name of the president, the location of the post office in town, and the meanings of words
- episodic memory—knowledge of events that one has experienced: for example, where one grew up, went to school, and worked during summers; one's autobiography, so to speak

Dividing lines between these aspects of long-term memory can blur, but the important point is that all contain information that is meaningful and organized.

Remembering

How do we retrieve information from our memory? The answer is not difficult with respect to sensory memory or short-term memory. Information is simply "there" in a persons' awareness, and there is no need to hunt for it. A person simply focuses his or her attention. The more interesting question concerns retrieval from long-term memory. Granted all the information we have represented in long-term memory, it is remarkable that we can get as much out of it in as rapid a fashion as we do.

We typically speak of two types of retrieval. **Recognition** is the realization that certain information presented to us looks familiar. "Do I need to turn left or right at Green Street to get to Fred's house?" In **recall,** we retrieve information from memory without being provided explicit clues. "How do I get to Fred's house?" Put another way, recognition corresponds to examinations with multiple-choice questions, whereas recall entails fill-in-the blank questions.

recognition
the realization that certain information presented to us looks familiar

recall
the retrieval of information from memory without being provided explicit clues

Recognition.   Let's start with recognition. Here a person is faced with a task. She must decide whether a presented stimulus matches a representation in memory. According to one explanation of recognition, the process is quite simple. Given the stimulus to be recognized, the person simply takes into account its central characteristics and compares these to her mental representations that have similar characteristics.

So, there's a dog playing in your front yard. Do you recognize this dog? It's a golden retriever. How many golden retrievers do you know? There's the one that your cousin just bought. This one's bigger. There's the one that your college roommate has. This one's smaller. There's the one that your new neighbor is taking care of for her parents. Yes, that's a match. This comparison process can take place within just a fraction of a second (e.g., Intraub, 1980).

The critical factor in recognition is the similarity between the stimulus in question and someone's mental representations. Because encoded representations may not exactly match the actual object to be identified, your recognition can be hampered. An interesting example of this comes from research asking subjects to recognize extremely familiar objects: United States coins (Nickerson & Adams, 1979). Most of us have considerable difficulty distinguishing actual coins from those that are similar, because our mental representations of the coins are not particularly detailed (see Figure 7.4).

Sometimes a person's expectations influence his memory. Psychologist Elizabeth Loftus (1979) has studied how eyewitnesses to a crime testify about what happened. Although eyewitness testimony is accorded great weight in our judicial system, her research consistently shows that it is subject to the same influences as any memory task. Consider a lineup where you have to pick out the suspect: "Yes, that's the man who robbed the bank!" This is a recognition task, and it can be distorted by one's expectations. For instance, suppose a witness believes that the criminal was a certain sex, or race, or age. This may lead the witness to focus only on this salient characteristic, perhaps resulting in a misidentification.

generate-and-recognize model theory of recall that proposes we generate possible answers to the memory task and then see if we recognize any of them

Recall.   Now let's turn to recall, a more complicated process than recognition. Here the person must undertake the initial step of generating possible answers to the memory task, and then undergo the comparison process already described for recognition. This process is dubbed the **generate-and-recognize model** of recall (Glass & Holyoak, 1986).

Figure 7.4
Actual versus False Coins. The coins on the left in each pair are actual American coins. Subjects frequently confuse these with the false coins shown on the right. Source: Rubin & Kontis, 1983.

Memory of the details of an event can be distorted by our preconceptions. In this case, misidentification by witnesses led to the conviction of one man (on the right) for crimes committed by another (on the left).

Researchers have extensively studied how the generation step takes place. Various *cues*—items of information that guide our recall—are used by the person to generate possible responses. The effectiveness of a given cue depends on how the person's long-term memory is organized. Suppose you have to come up with the names of all fifty states. You might generate the names by going through the states alphabetically. Or you might do it geographically. If for some reason you know area codes or zip codes, you might generate the names of states by running through these in numerical order.

A single cue eventually loses its effectiveness in suggesting potential responses, which means that a person who is able to use several strategies for generating cues will do better than someone who uses but one. Said another way, the more ways in which a person's long-term memory is organized, the better the recall.

What else do we know about recall? The more recently you have thought of an item of information, the easier it is to recall: "What did the last batter do?" Another important factor influencing recall is practice. If we have frequently generated a response in the past, we can readily generate it in the present. In college, for example, the identification number we placed on tests was our social security number. I wrote mine on so many tests that my social security number is now extremely easy for me to recall.

tip-of-the-tongue phenomenon the experience of knowing we have a given memory but being unable to retrieve it

Tip-of-the-Tongue Phenomenon.   Researchers investigating recall have documented several interesting aspects of it. One of these is the **tip-of-the-tongue phenomenon** (Brown & McNeill, 1966). We've all had the experience of knowing that we have a given memory but not being able to come up with it: "Where did I put that library book that's now overdue? . . . I know it must be here in my bedroom, but where?"

Psychologists have systematically studied this experience by giving their subjects dictionary definitions of somewhat obscure words (see Table 7.1). Some of the subjects "know" the word being defined but are unable to produce it. However, they can correctly specify the letter with which the

Table 7.1

Words on the Tip of One's Tongue

Brown and McNeill (1966) showed subjects definitions such as those in the list that follows. When subjects could not come up with the exact word, but reported that it was on the tip of their tongue, they were asked to specify the word's first letter, how many syllables it had, and other words that sounded like it. Often the subjects could correctly answer these questions.

1. Favoritism shown to a relative, such as giving him or her a job.
2. A projecting part of a church that is usually semicircular in shape and vaulted.
3. A waxy substance believed to originate in the intestines of whales and used in making perfumes.
4. A flat-bottomed Chinese boat.
5. A staff with two entwined snakes and two wings at the top.

(1. nepotism	2. apse	3. ambergris	4. sampan	5. caduceus)

word starts, the number of syllables in it, and so on. The tip-of-the-tongue phenomenon shows the importance of active processes in recall, because a person can deliberately use the information known about the word to come up with it.

Context-dependent Recall. Another interesting phenomenon is that we can more readily recall memories in the same setting in which we encoded them than in different settings. One dramatic demonstration of such **context-dependent recall** comes from an experiment by Godden and Baddeley (1975), who used divers as their research subjects. These individuals learned a list of words either on shore or 20 feet below the surface. Recall for "on shore" words was better when tested on shore than under water, whereas recall for "submerged" words showed the opposite pattern.

context-dependent recall
the tendency to recall information better when in the situation where it was originally encoded

State-dependent Recall. Related to context-dependent recall is **state-dependent recall.** If we initially encode information when in a given physiological state—like drunkenness or exhaustion—then we can more readily recall this information when we are in the same state (Eich, 1980). Recent extensions of this idea have examined how mood—happy or sad—influences recall (e.g., Blaney, 1986; Bower, 1981). For both context-dependent and state-dependent recall, the interpretation is straightforward: The context or state of the individual provides yet another cue for recall.

state-dependent recall
the tendency to recall information better when in the psychological or biological state during which it was originally encoded

Forgetting

One might simply regard forgetting as our failure to remember something, and be done with the subject. However, many cognitive psychologists have studied forgetting in its own right. We now know that forgetting has many determinants. Two prominent theories of forgetting emphasize the roles played by decay of the memory over time and by interference from other memories, respectively.

Decay. The term *decay* is used to describe forgetting due to the passage of time. In a strict sense, any information that fails to move from the sensory memory to short-term memory can be described as having decayed, as can information that fails to move from short-term memory to long-term memory.

Usually decay is used to describe storage loss in long-term memory. Showing decay from long-term memory can be difficult, because one must show that the memory is truly gone and not just unable to be retrieved. If you recall Penfield's studies described in Chapter 2, you know that seemingly lost memories can return when the appropriate part of the brain is stimulated. Still, decay from long-term memory seems plausible, particularly when the memory has been retrieved infrequently and when a great deal of time has passed (Loftus & Loftus, 1980).

proactive interference
a cause of forgetting, when previously learned material gets in the way of remembering subsequently learned material

retroactive interference
a cause of forgetting, when subsequently learned material gets in the way of remembering previously learned material

Interference. Another explanation of forgetting proposes that our recall for material we have learned is affected by the presence of other material in memory. As already mentioned, Ebbinghaus (1885) first documented the role of interference in the recall of word lists. Interference can occur for other types of information as well, particularly in short-term memory. We've all had the experience of being introduced to a roomful of people, and then not being able to remember a single person's name. This is due to interference.

When previously acquired material gets in the way of remembering subsequent material, it is called **proactive interference.** Suppose you learn List A, then List B, and finally are tested for memory of List B. If the fact that you first memorized List A impairs your recall, this is due to proactive interference (see Figure 7.5). And when learning a subsequent list makes it difficult to remember a previous list, it is called **retroactive interference.** Here you learn List A, then List B, and finally are tested on List A. If your recall for List A is poor, then retroactive interference has occurred (see Figure 7.5 again).

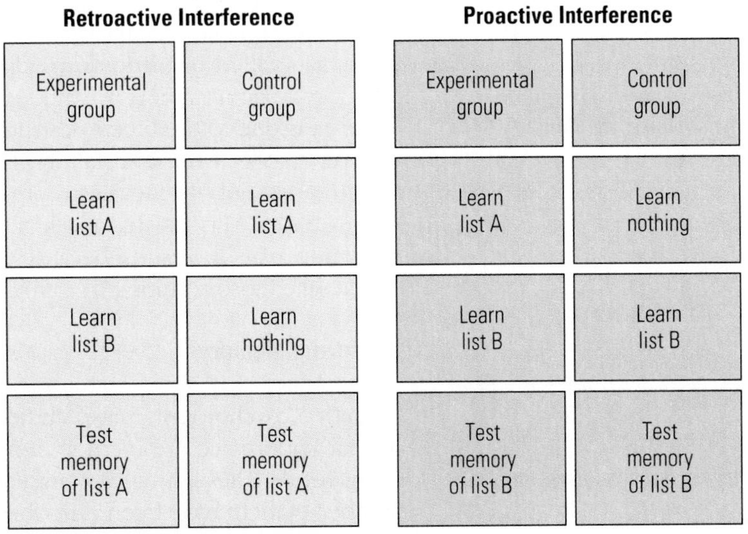

Figure 7.5

Proactive and Retroactive Interference. When previously remembered information interferes with the recall of subsequently learned information, this is proactive interference. When subsequently learned information interferes with the recall of previously learned information, this is retroactive interference. This figure shows how proactive and retroactive interference can be demonstrated in an experiment.

Retroactive Interference		Proactive Interference	
Experimental group	Control group	Experimental group	Control group
Learn list A	Learn list A	Learn list A	Learn nothing
Learn list B	Learn nothing	Learn list B	Learn list B
Test memory of list A	Test memory of list A	Test memory of list B	Test memory of list B

We can interpret interference in terms of competing associations among items in the lists. It is not an exotic phenomenon found only in the laboratory. Everyday life gives us plenty of examples, any time we have a series of things to remember, like errands or phone messages. As students, you dread having several examinations on the same day, at least in part because interference hampers your performance. Or consider learning to drive cars with different types of manual transmissions. Proactive and retroactive interference can readily take place, as you "shift" (so to speak) from a four-speed to a five-speed model.

Retrieval Failure. Sometimes we fail to remember material not because the memories are gone, but because we do not have the means to retrieve them. Our cues are inadequate. This is called retrieval failure. For instance, I recently attended the twentieth reunion of my high school class. I had seen very few of my classmates in the ensuing years, and on my way to the reunion, I tried to remember different friends and acquaintances who might be at the reunion. I wasn't too successful. However, once at the reunion, seeing my classmates with their name tags, I not only remembered everybody, but a number of other memories seemingly lost readily came to my mind.

A dramatic example of retrieval failure is **psychogenic amnesia:** a sudden inability to remember personal information following a psychological trauma (Chapter 12). A common interpretation of psychogenic amnesia comes from psychoanalytic theory, which proposes that memories may be repressed to the degree that someone finds them painful. For example, when working in a psychiatric hospital, I encountered a patient who had no clue about his personal identity or history. Eventually, we learned that his amnesia stemmed from a fight with his wife, during which she demanded a divorce. That event was so horrible to the patient that he repressed its occurrence, along with all other memories that might serve as a cue to its recall—almost everything personal in his memory.

Psychogenic amnesia represents a problem with retrieval, because the memories are stored, although not accessible. With time, most individuals with psychogenic amnesia recover their memory. Hypnosis, free association, and/or tranquilizing drugs can aid the process (Chapter 4).

When amnesia occurs due to physical damage or an injury to the brain, it is called **organic amnesia.** Table 7.2 contrasts organic amnesia with psychogenic amnesia. Although some information lost in organic amnesia is due to the literal destruction of memories, other lost information represents a retrieval failure, because memories are often regained with the passage of time. Cases of psychogenic amnesia and organic amnesia are rare. Very few instances of forgetting are due to amnesia. Instead, forgetting usually results because of more mundane difficulties in retrieval, like those resulting from interference.

Improving Memory

Cognitive psychologists have studied how we can improve memory. Of special importance are memory aids, strategies and techniques for facilitating recall. These strategies are sometimes called **mnemonics,** and a number of them have been described.

psychogenic amnesia
extensive memory loss following psychological trauma

organic amnesia
extensive memory loss following physical damage or an injury to the brain

mnemonics
strategies and techniques for facilitating memory

Table 7.2

Organic versus Psychogenic Amnesia

	Organic Amnesia	**Psychogenic Amnesia**
Typical cause	Blow to the head	Psychological trauma
Extent of memory loss	Recent and remote past	Recent past
Personal identity	Not lost	Lost
Loss of memory for events since onset of amnesia	Yes	No
Return of memory	Gradually if at all	Suddenly

One type of mnemonic entails associating new information with something familiar. For example, the *method of loci* (*loci* means places) dates to the ancient Greeks. Here the person thinks of a familiar scene, and remembers items of information by "placing" them in it.

> First, a person imagined a space, commonly a quiet building he already knew well. The space was never a purely abstract grid or set of pigeon holes . . . students [therefore] used to seek out large architectural spaces and commit them to memory. After selecting a space, one placed, mentally of course, associative images in this space. Each person filled his space with privately created pictures. Recall consisted of an imaginary stroll through this space. Although the action was imaginary, the experience was profoundly felt . . . [One] might imagine himself walking past a stairwell. At the landing he sees, through memory's eyes, a large image of a young man thrashing an older woman. Thus reminded, . . . [he] says, "I will not linger over the occasion in which this ruffian beat his mother-in-law," and—still in his mind—he walks past the stairs and notices another image, this time in an alcove. (Bolles, 1988, p. 6)

Figure 7.6 depicts yet another example of the method of loci.

More generally, people can use visual imagery to improve memory. Suppose you have a list of words in a foreign language that you need to remember, say for an examination or a trip abroad. Atkinson (1975) suggests that you come up with a visual association between the foreign word and its English equivalent. For instance, the French word for sea is *mer,* which sounds somewhat like our word *mare.* You might therefore create a visual image of a horse galloping through the surf. Atkinson calls this the *key word method* of study.

Let's not overlook the numerous external strategies that can serve as memory aids: lists, notes, timers, calendars, and so on (Harris, 1978). These approaches tend to be used more often than internal strategies such as the method of loci. For some reason, psychologists have not investigated external strategies nearly to the extent that they have studied internal strategies, but their importance is obvious (Neisser, 1982).

Some researchers have compiled the findings of cognitive psychologists to suggest the optimal way of studying material so that recall is served.

Figure 7.6

Method of Loci. This illustration dates to the sixteenth century (Romberch, 1553). The artist was a Dominican monk. On the left is his abbey and its surrounding buildings. On the right are the ideas he wishes to remember. He will take a mental walk through the grounds of the abbey, placing the ideas along his way.

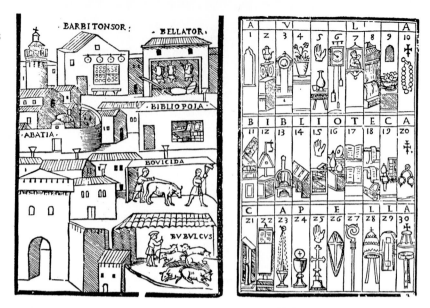

A representative approach is called the *PQ4R method* (Thomas & Robinson, 1972). The acronym comes from the suggested stages:

1. *Preview* the material to be remembered.
2. Make up *questions* about the material.
3. *Read* the material carefully.
4. *Reflect* on the material.
5. *Recite* the important points in the material.
6. *Review* the material in your mind.

This method and similar ones are of proven effectiveness in helping students remember course material (Anderson, 1985). You might try studying the chapters in this book with this method. Do you understand why it works as well as it does? Among other things, this method ensures that the material is structured in your memory, and that you have multiple cues for its access.

The Biological Basis of Memory

Studies of people with brain damage provide some clues about where memory might be stored in the brain. As described in Chapter 2, researchers have noted relationships between particular lesions and particular memory deficits. The initial encoding of knowledge seems to take place in the limbic system, and long-term memories appear to be stored in the cortex (Murray & Mishkin, 1985).

Is it possible to point to something specific in the brain that corresponds to our memories? The term **engram** has been coined to refer to the physical basis of memory (Lashley, 1950), which remains undiscovered (Thompson, 1976). Psychologists have considered various candidates (see Allport, 1986).

At one time, it was thought that memory might somehow be represented in RNA molecules. Psychologist James McConnell (1962, 1964) explored this possibility by classically conditioning a flatworm, pairing an electric shock with a flash of light so that eventually the worm responded

engram

the hypothesized physical basis of memory

(by tensing) to the light alone (Chapter 5). Then he ground up this worm and fed it to another flatworm, which then learned the classically conditioned response more rapidly. One interpretation of these findings is that information had somehow been transmitted via cannibalism.

McConnell's results have proven difficult to replicate, but they illustrate an interesting search for the engram. Other research programs started with the hypothesis that memory existed in the pattern of axons and dendrites. And still another attempt to find the engram was based on the premise that it was to be found in changed tendencies for the nerves to fire or not, that is, in the chemical makeup of individual nerve cells.

Currently of interest to psychologists trying to locate the biological basis of memory is the neurotransmitter *acetylcholine*. Deficits in acetylcholine appear to be related to memory problems seen in patients suffering from Alzheimer's disease (Chapter 10). This implies that the forgetfulness of Alzheimer patients might be reduced if somehow acetylcholine could be increased (Coyle, Price, & Delong, 1983). Drugs that increase brain levels of this neurotransmitter have been developed, and they are being tested with Alzheimer patients. Other researchers are looking at how these drugs affect memory in laboratory animals, and the day may come when people can routinely strengthen their memories with similar drugs!

We've discussed the basics of memory, the mental representation of knowledge. We will now consider how people use these representations in the course of everyday life. Memory is obviously important, in that few if any cognitive processes would be possible without it. More generally, human behavior as we ordinarily conceive it would be drastically changed without memory.

How to Investigate Cognition

How do psychologists study our cognitive representations and processes? I used to tease my students that the American Psychological Association should commission IBM to develop a cogniscope, a device linking a person's mind and a television monitor so that everything the person thought could be readily viewed. Needless to say, cogniscopes do not exist. But cognitive psychologists have shown plenty of ingenuity in devising methods that allow us to *infer* what and how a person is thinking.

Like any procedure that relies on inference, these methods are only as sound as the assumptions on which they are based. Cognitive psychologists thus hope that their assumptions are reasonable ones. For instance, they assume that people indeed have cognitions, and that cognitive activity takes place over time. Most of us probably accept these as plausible statements, but it is possible to argue against them. What's the point? Simply that the methods that cognitive psychologists use cannot prove the assumptions on which they are based. A strict behaviorist would not be swayed by findings from cognitive psychology investigations because she would not accept the unproven assumptions that make these investigations possible.

At the present time, cognitive psychologists have available a variety of research strategies. You'll see the results made possible by these methods throughout this chapter. Right now, let's briefly examine some of them.

Figure 7.7
Abacus. This abacus represents the
number 123,456,789.

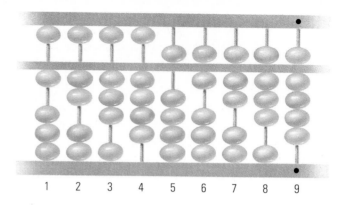

Reaction Times

Cognitive activity occurs over time. This is plausible inasmuch as cognition
must somehow be grounded in our brain activity—chemical and biological processes that do not take place instantaneously. From this assumption
comes the strategy of studying mental events by seeing how long it takes
people to perform tasks that we pose them. The longer one's *reaction
time,* the longer the person needed to carry out the mental activity underlying the task performance.

For example, researchers have studied how people use mental imagery to solve problems in their heads. What is the nature of these images?
One answer is that they are very much like "real" perceptions of actual
objects, which means that the amount of time it takes to solve a problem
in one's head should be analogous to the amount of time it takes to solve
the problem using external aids. Consider the abacus, a device for arithmetic calculations used in Asian cultures (see Figure 7.7). Expert users of
the abacus don't bother to actually move the beads. Instead, they visualize
the abacus and perform the calculations with their image. When asked to
report on the intermediate steps involved, their response times parallel
the respective steps that would take place if they were literally moving the
beads (Stigler, 1984).

Errors

When researchers ask subjects to do things, their performance is rarely
perfect. Errors need not always be the problem they might seem, because
the analysis of a subject's pattern of mistakes can be a powerful technique
for making inferences about cognition. Indeed, errors sometimes tell us
more than correct answers, as we saw in the case of John Dean's testimony.
Errors entailing either additions or deletions, that is, errors of commission
and omission, can be informative.

Suppose we show someone some words and ask him to memorize
them. We later test his memory. If his recall is perfect, we won't know what
transpired—just that something must have. But suppose his recall is
flawed, and that his errors are systematic. Then we have a clue about how
the original material must have been represented—that is, in a way that
would produce the observed pattern of mistakes. If his mistakes entail

The study of language development in young children has provided clues to the nature of cognitive activity, such as the importance of rules.

confusing the way words *sound* (remembering *sappy* as *happy*), that tells us something different about memory than if his mistakes involve the confusion of what words *mean* (remembering *rich* as *wealthy*).

Development

Cognitive psychologists sometimes study young children because they can thereby see the very beginnings of cognitive activity. Researchers have found the study of development particularly useful with respect to language (Chapter 9). For example, when children first begin to utter words and sentences, they overgeneralize what they know and make language more consistent than it actually is. All four-legged creatures are dogs. All past tense verbs end in *-ed:* "I throwed the ball." Findings like these suggest that when we learn language, we learn more than particular words and sentences. We also learn rules. And the exceptions to the rules can only be acquired once the rules are mastered.

Pathologies

Every field of psychology finds in abnormality a useful perspective on what is normal. Cognitive psychology is no exception. Some researchers pose tasks for subjects who have suffered various brain illnesses and injuries. Their observed performance provides clues about how knowledge is represented and transformed.

Consider memory loss following a blow to the head. Lynch and Yarnell (1973) watched football practices, on the lookout for collisions that dazed a player. When such collisions occurred, they quickly interviewed the player. What play was being run when the collision happened? Usually the answer was correct. But when the same players were asked the same question some minutes later, they often could not answer it.

What do these results show about memory? For starters, they support the notion that experiences must somehow be transformed before they can be committed to permanent memory. Although the players at first knew what had happened to them, their dazed condition got in the way of representing this experience in a way that could later be remembered.

Thinking Aloud Protocols

We have seen that introspection was an early method of cognitive research, since devalued by psychologists (Chapter 1). However, contemporary psychologists have found that a version of this old technique indeed can reveal something about the workings of the mind. The trick here is not to ask people to report on things they don't know, as the first psychologists did (see Nisbett & Wilson, 1977). But if you ask people to "think out loud" while solving a problem, their comments can provide valuable information about what and how they think (Ericcson & Simon, 1984). One finding from studies using this approach of *thinking aloud protocols* is that people jump around a lot in solving problems. They try and discard many possibilities before settling on a final route to solution (see Table 7.3).

Cognitive Representations

How is information represented in the mind? The difficulties encountered years ago by the structuralists imply that we cannot identify *the* basic mental elements, probably because there are none. Cognitive psychologists today have proposed a variety of cognitive representations.

These do not compete with each other. Theorists use different ways of describing the contents of thought in order to suit their particular purpose. The number of terms makes it seem that the mind is literally crowded, but remember that the mind is not a physical place but a metaphorical one. We can bring some order to the topic by arranging these representations in order from the most concrete to the most abstract.

Images

image
a cognitive representation much like perception except without an external stimulus

An **image** is a representation much like perception—except without an external stimulus. We can regard an image as a mental depiction of a sensation. When we speak of images, we usually mean visual ones, but images exist for all sensory modalities. For example, we can imagine the warm sun on our face, fine sand between our toes, and the smell of the ocean. We can imagine someone calling our name. All of these are images.

How Imagery Resembles Perception.   Researchers have found that the resemblance between imagery and perception goes beyond superficial similarity. For instance, images interfere with perception in the same sensory mode (Segal & Fusella, 1970). Someone with a visual image in mind is less likely to detect a visual stimulus. And someone with an auditory image is less likely to detect an auditory stimulus. This pattern of interference implies that imagery and perception use common mental operations.

Stephen Kosslyn (1980) and his colleagues have conducted studies on visual imagery that further support the similarity between imagery and perception. Research subjects are asked to form a visual image, and then to perform some task using the image, such as answering the question "How far is it between points A and B on an imagined map?" The researchers note how long it takes the subjects to respond. Their reaction times are the same as if subjects were looking at a literal picture (Figure 7.8).

Table 7.3

Example of a Talking Aloud Protocol

Lindsay and Norman (1972) present the following example of a talking aloud protocol. The problem is a sum presented in code. One must break the code and determine which letter stands for which number, knowing only that:

$$
\begin{array}{r}
\text{DONALD} \quad\quad D = 5 \\
+\,\text{GERALD} \\
\hline
\text{ROBERT}
\end{array}
$$

Each different letter represents a different digit. Following is a paraphrased version of the protocol provided by one subject, a college student, who attempted to solve this problem:

"Okay, each letter stands for only one number, right?

"With ten different letters, I've got all ten digits there.

"So, I can start with the two D's—each D is 5, which means that the T they add up to must be 0.

"Let me fill in the other D with 5. I guess there's no other T.

"Now I see that I have two A's and two L's. Oh yes, and I have three R's. But what else do I know? I guess that R must be an odd number, because it equals the two L's plus the 1 that was carried over. That means R can be 1 or 3 or 7 or 9. It can't be 5 because I already know what that is.

"Hmm. Because R is going to be an odd number, and because D is 5, then G has to be an even number. Oops, I forgot I might have to carry over 1 from the $E + O$.

"This is hard to figure out logically. Maybe the best way to solve the problem is just to try different solutions and see what works."

Figure 7.8

Imagery Task. Subjects were shown a picture of a motorboat. Then they were asked to look away and form a mental image of the boat and look in particular at its motor. When asked if the boat had a windshield, they answered more quickly than when asked if the boat had an anchor (Kosslyn, 1980). Note that the windshield is closer to the motor than is the anchor, implying that their quicker reaction time was due to their scanning of the visual image.

Long image scan

Short image scan

One of the interesting findings in this line of work is that subjects skilled at visual imagery are susceptible to visual illusions in their images, like those described in Chapter 4 (Wallace, 1984)! Subjects not skilled at imagery fail to experience illusions in their images. Again, these results point to the similarity between imagery and perception.

How Imagery Does Not Resemble Perception.   At the same time, many theorists are reluctant to propose that images are simply "pictures in the head" (e.g., Anderson, 1985; Pylyshyn, 1984). They point to differences between mental images and actual perceptions. Specifically, images are more malleable than perceptions, and can be distorted by general knowledge in a way that perceptions cannot (e.g., Carmichael, Hogan, & Walter, 1932). Another difference between images and perceptions is that the former are segmented—arranged in a hierarchy—whereas the latter are not.

Both of these differences can be illustrated with geographical images, so-called **mental maps.** Form an image of the United States in your head. Now answer the following questions about this image (Stevens & Coupe, 1978):

mental maps
cognitive representations of physical places

- Which is farther east: San Diego or Reno?
- Which is farther north: Seattle or Montreal?
- Which is farther west: the Atlantic or the Pacific entrance to the Panama Canal?

In each case, the first answer is the correct one, but most people choose the second one. These incorrect answers follow because most of us "know" that California is west of Nevada, that Canada is north of the United States, and that the Atlantic Ocean is east of the Pacific Ocean. Do you see the point? Mental images are an example of top-down processing because your general knowledge distorts your image. Your image is apparently represented at different levels (e.g., states versus cities), and the higher representation affects the lower one.

Linear Orderings

linear ordering
cognitive representation of elements structured in some order

Somewhat different than a mental image and a degree more abstract is a **linear ordering:** a representation of elements that is structured in some order. For example, we might remember the order in which we met three people: Tom, Dick, and Harry. We might represent the steps to go through in readying a personal computer for operation. Or we might recall the relative heights or weights of a group of individuals.

Here are some generalizations about linear orderings (Anderson, 1985). We can most readily recall those items on either end of the order. This is the serial position effect first described by Ebbinghaus (1885). It is one of the consistent findings from memory research. If we try to memorize a list of items, we tend to do well with the first and last item.

Relatedly, when we are asked to make judgments about two items in a linear ordering, we respond quickly when the items are far apart on the scale. Which president served the earlier term: Adams or Jefferson? Monroe or Nixon? Most people answer the latter question more readily than the former.

When the number of elements increases, we tend to group them into a hierarchy. In other words, we form small linear orderings among subsets of elements; these orderings in turn are placed in their own order. Anderson (1985) gives the example of the alphabet, which most of us have memorized to the tune "Twinkle, Twinkle, Little Star," where pauses in the song correspond to breaks among the subgroupings of letters: *ABCD EFG HIJK LMNOP QRS TUV WXYZ.* The twenty-six letters are therefore grouped into a smaller number of discrete orders.

Klahr, Chase, and Lovelace (1983) gave subjects a letter in the alphabet and asked them to come up with the next one as quickly as possible. The fastest reaction times occurred when subjects were given the first letter of a subgrouping, like *E* or *H* or *L.* Their reaction times slowed toward the end of subgroupings.

Concepts

concept
the classification of elements into a group

An even more abstract cognitive representation is the **concept,** any mental categorization of elements into a group. Categorization is one of the most central cognitive processes, because no other process would be possible if we did not make distinctions. When we consider all of the elements that people categorize, we should expect concepts to take many different forms. Indeed, there are various ways in which we represent concepts (Glass & Holyoak, 1986).

One way to represent a concept is simply by listing all of the elements that belong to it. For instance, consider the concept "American car," which we can represent by Ford, Chevrolet, Chrysler, and so on. When the number of elements in a concept are large, we may not be able to recall all of them, and so we rely on a rule to generate them.

These generative rules are an efficient way of representing what may be an infinite number of elements. Consider the rules for producing Roman numerals. They allow us to come up with these numbers without having to commit any but a handful of them to memory in the first place.

Another way to represent a concept is in terms of characteristics that its elements share in common. We can group together all entities containing DNA and call this the concept of living things. We can group together all entities on which we can sit and call this the concept of chairs. We may group together all entities to whom we speak when meeting and call this the concept of acquaintances.

Many concepts come with a verbal tag attached, and psychologists have labored mightily to understand the way in which the meaning of these verbal tags is represented in the mind. It is currently believed that meanings are represented in a network of associations. This is similar to how traditional learning theorists view the essence of learning (Chapter 5), except that the links in the network represent not temporal associations between stimuli and responses forged through contiguity or contingency, but rather logical relationships among words (e.g., Rumelhart, Lindsay, & Norman, 1972). These associations are termed a **propositional network** (see Figure 7.9). And we can think of these propositions as arranged in a hierarchy.

propositional network
a depiction of meaning in terms of logical relationships among words

In commenting on propositional networks, Anderson (1985) compares them to "a tangle of marbles connected by strings" (p. 116). More technically, the marbles are called *nodes,* and the strings that connect them are called *relations.* (This model gives new meaning to the expression "losing one's marbles"!) Mental activity occurs when part of the network

Figure 7.9

Propositional Network. Here are how John bought some candy because he was hungry (top) and John believed Russia would invade Poland might be represented in someone's propositional network (bottom).

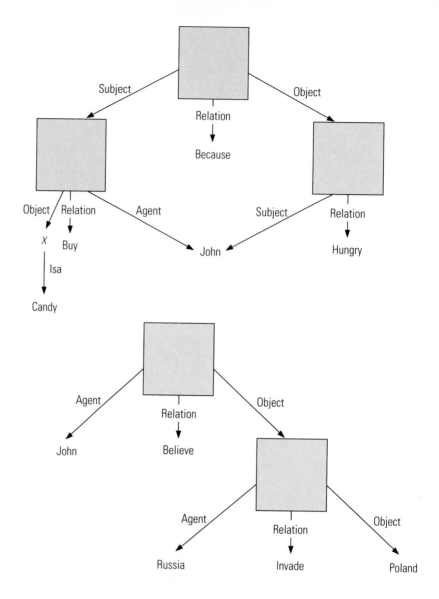

is activated. In other words, we "think" about an idea when the part of the network corresponding to it is metaphorically stimulated. For example, in Figure 7.9, we think about candy when the upper part of the network is activated, and about Russia when the bottom part of the network is activated. Network models explain how one thought can lead to another and still another by proposing that activation spreads throughout the network (Collins & Loftus, 1975).

One important type of propositional network is called a **schema,** defined as an organized set of information about some concept. The key word here is *organization.* A schema is not a heap of miscellaneous beliefs, but rather a representation of how these beliefs are related to one another. Anderson (1985, p. 124) uses *house* as an example of a schema. Here are some of the things many of us believe about a "house":

schema

an organized set of information about some concept

A schema helps us go from specifics to more generalized inferences about an object, from a "blue house" to the general category of "houses," as an example.

It belongs to the larger category of:	building
It is made of:	wood and/or brick
It contains:	rooms
It functions as:	human dwelling
It is shaped like:	rectangle
It costs:	arm and leg

Certainly, not all people have exactly the same schema for a house, but this one is representative.

A schema is not tied to a particular entity. It is necessarily abstract. Our schema for a house refers not to our house, or to the house next door, or to the White House, but rather to a generic house. A schema allows us to go beyond the immediate information we have available to make plausible inferences. Suppose someone you know says, "I'm so excited! I just bought a house!" You are probably safe in assuming that her house is a building, that it is made of wood or brick, that it has rooms, that she plans to live in it, and so forth. Of course, you can be wrong about some or all of these inferences. She may have bought a doll house, or a dog house, or a teepee, or an igloo. But regardless, your schema of house is packed with a lot of information, including how to recognize exceptions to it.

The existence of a schema affects a variety of cognitive processes. Many of us have schemas for people with given personality traits, for instance. If someone is introduced to us as an extravert, let us say, our interaction is accordingly influenced. We *attend* to some of his behaviors but not others, we *judge* him in certain ways but not others, and we *recall* particular aspects of our interaction with him but not others (e.g., Cantor & Mischel, 1977, 1979). Social psychologists have recently borrowed the notion of a schema to help explain stereotypes and their pervasive effects on our behavior (Chapter 14).

Artificial and Natural Concepts

For a long time, psychologists carried out research using concepts specially devised for their experiments (Bourne, 1966). Researchers created abstract stimuli that varied along different dimensions (see Figure 7.10). Subjects were asked to identify which stimuli were examples of a concept and which were not. They would choose one stimulus and were told if they were right or wrong. Over time, they would "acquire" the concept by learning which characteristics of the stimuli were associated with "right" answers (e.g., all red circles).

Two decades ago, the assumption that every concept was defined by necessary and sufficient characteristics was unquestioned. That is, psychologists assumed that for any concept there were critical properties that all examples of the given concept possess (*necessary characteristics*) and that only examples of that concept possess (*sufficient characteristics*). For example, "three-sidedness" is a necessary and sufficient condition for the concept "triangle." Concepts like these are now termed **artificial concepts** to emphasize that not all concepts are so defined. In particular, many of the concepts people use in their everyday life (like bird or dog

artificial concepts
concepts defined by necessary and sufficient conditions

Figure 7.10

Concept Identification Problem. Subjects are presented with pairs of abstract stimuli that vary along dimensions like color, size, and shape. They choose one member of each pair and are told "right" or "wrong." Over a series of trials, their task is to determine which characteristics of the stimuli define the concept.

(i)

(ii)

(iii)

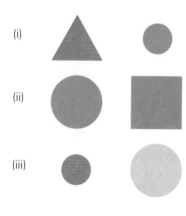

natural concepts
concepts without necessary and sufficient conditions

family resemblance
tendency of members of a natural concept to have a variety of characteristics in common, although none of these characteristics is necessary or sufficient to define the concept

prototype
typical member of a category

or illness) do not have necessary and sufficient conditions. These are therefore called **natural concepts.**

Here is an example originally devised by the philosopher Ludwig Wittgenstein (1953). What defines a game? We probably start to answer this question by thinking of properties that all games possess, and that nongames do not possess. But for each supposed property, we can cite a counterexample. Games require two people—but then there is solitaire. Games have winners and losers—but then there is Frisbee. Games are for fun—but then there is professional football. The concept of game is *not* characterized by necessary and sufficient conditions.

What this means is that conclusions from research on artificial concepts need not apply to natural concepts. So, a great deal of current theorizing and research has looked specifically at natural concepts. If these are not defined by critical elements, then what does define them? An answer to this question tells us how people cognitively represent concepts.

One possibility is that natural concepts are marked by a **family resemblance** among their elements (Rosch & Mervis, 1975). Just as members of a family tend to have a variety of characteristics in common, so too do natural concepts. But none of these characteristics in and of itself is critical. That's why you can recognize the child playing in the street as a member of the Smith family even though he doesn't have red hair like most of the Smiths. His other characteristics—skinny legs and a long nose—overlap with those of his family.

A related answer to what defines natural concepts is that they are defined by a **prototype** or typical member of the category in question (Attneave, 1957). By this view, people acquire natural concepts by abstracting from repeated instances of the concept an average member. The concept is mentally represented as this average. Then this prototype is used to categorize subsequent instances in terms of their resemblance to it. Our familiar social stereotypes are good examples of prototypes. Is someone a jock, a sorority member, or a movie star? Most of us can turn to a prototype for each of these concepts.

Yet another answer is that people define natural concepts in terms of remembered instances (Medin & Schaffer, 1978). Is he a basketball player or not? Yes, he must be, because he looks just like Herman, and Herman was certainly a player. Remembered instances are particular members of a concept, whereas a prototype is an average of particular members. The distinction can be a bit fuzzy, of course, and at present, cognitive psychologists are not certain how best to characterize natural concepts.

Let's draw out some of the broader implications of the notion of natural concepts. Most generally, natural concepts do not have fixed boundaries. Particular instances can "kind of" belong to a category, prompting some theorists to describe natural concepts as *fuzzy sets*. Traditional logic assumes that things either are or are not, and hence proves unwieldy in dealing with certain natural concepts.

Another point is that instances of a concept themselves vary from good to bad. This shouldn't be too surprising, because we all know that there are good examples and bad examples of almost all abstract notions. Research has repeatedly shown that people agree as to which examples of natural concepts are good and which are bad (e.g., Rosch, 1975).

So, an apple is a "good" example of the concept of fruit, just as a collie is a "good" dog and a robin is a "good" bird. We can call these good examples prototypes, and say that they possess many of the characteristics that define the family resemblance of the concept in question. (If you are curious, a kiwi is a "bad" example of a fruit, as well as a "bad" example of a bird. And a basenji is a "bad" dog, however well-behaved it might be.) The relevance for cognition in general is that good examples are more readily recognized by individuals as belonging to a concept, more easily distinguished from members of different categories, and more frequently recalled when committed to memory.

Basic Level Concepts

Eleanor Rosch and her colleagues (1976) suggest that people tend naturally to categorize the world at a level that maximizes the perceptual similarity among objects within a category and the perceptual dissimilarity between these objects and those in other categories. Consider this hierarchy:

- kitchen table
- table
- furniture

Their argument is that "table" represents the basic level at which people most easily categorize objects. "Kitchen table" is too concrete, whereas "furniture" is too abstract. Studies support this idea, showing that cognitive processes such as recognition proceed most efficiently when content is at the basic level. Also, when children start to name objects, they first use terms from the basic level. The notion of basic level concepts assumes a bottom-up approach because perception dominates abstract meaning, not vice versa.

An interesting line of research led to the hypothesis of basic level concepts. It began with the argument by linguist Benjamin Whorf (1956) that language literally shapes the way that a person perceives the world. The oft-cited example that Eskimoes have numerous words for varieties of snow seems to support Whorf's hypothesis. The availability of different words means that the person can recognize snow in a much more complex fashion than someone whose language does not provide such rich distinctions. This is a top-down view of cognition, because language dictates one's perception.

Whorf's hypothesis is difficult to investigate, but one way to do so is to compare the way that people in different cultures deal with color. As you recall from Chapter 3, the *sensation* of color depends on the wavelength of light. According to Whorf, the *perception* of color should depend on the words available to describe it. Because different cultures provide their members with a range of primary color words, from only two in the case of the Dani of New Guinea (white and black) to eleven in the case of the United States (white, black, red, green, yellow, blue, brown, purple, pink, orange, and gray) and twelve in the case of Russia (all of "our" terms plus *goluboy,* corresponding to light blue), we might expect substantial variation across cultures in the way colors are perceived (Berlin & Kay, 1969).

But this does not happen. Although people differ in where they draw the boundaries for colors, in accordance with their vocabulary, they otherwise deal with colors in identical ways. Regardless of their available vocabulary, they agree on the best examples of various color classes and remember these instances better than poor examples (Heider, 1972). These instances can be regarded as the "basic level" at which color categorization occurs. Most importantly, none of this depends on higher-order considerations like language.

Rules

Our discussion of cognitive representations has moved from images to increasingly abstract notions. By now you should understand why introspection as the first psychologists practiced it was bound to fail in identifying the basic elements of the mind (Chapter 1). The cognitive representations studied by contemporary psychologists cannot literally be seen. Instead, we can discern these mental representations only through inference. Granted that a person behaves in such and such a manner, what can plausibly be said about her cognition?

rules
cognitive representations that allow instances to be generated

This type of inference leads to our final cognitive representation: **rules.** We've already encountered generative rules as one way of representing a concept, but rules have relevance throughout all of cognitive psychology. Indeed, theorists frequently describe memory, problem solving, and language as rule-based.

Let's examine what this means with respect to language. What happens when we say a sentence? One answer might be that we search through the mental category of "all possible sentences" until we find the one we want. They we say it. But this answer fails upon examination. Many sentences we say are creative—we've never said them before (Chomsky, 1957, 1959). Sentences per se cannot have a cognitive representation.

grammar
the rules that allow language to be created and comprehended

Instead, theorists propose we cognitively represent rules that allow us to generate sentences. These are collectively termed the **grammar** of a language (Chapter 9). For example, one familiar rule is that we can usually create the plural of a word by adding an *s* at its end. Because we have grammar available, we can say an infinite number of creative sentences. Similarly, these rules allow us to understand sentences, including those we have never heard before. The grammar underlying language is not something speakers are aware of while speaking or listening. Rather, we know about grammar only indirectly, by observing how people use language.

We'll take a more detailed look at language in Chapter 9, when we discuss how children acquire the ability to create and understand sentences. In the present context, the point is that cognitive theorists use the term *grammar* not just for language but for the rules that underlie any complex behavior for which the particulars cannot possibly be represented in the mind. Consider making small talk while you wait with some friends for the elevator. How is this possible, this medley of questions and jokes and postures and facial expressions, exchanged and coordinated with one or more other people? Small talk is infinite. Indeed, one of its guiding principles is to avoid any exact repetition.

Small talk can be described, therefore, as having a grammar, because there are underlying rules used to generate and understand it. You certainly don't walk around with a store of witty comments represented in final form waiting to be unleashed on the world. (Ah, you say, that's what I've been doing wrong in my conversations!) A similar argument can be made for improvisational jazz, if you are highbrow, or for fast-break basketball, if you are like the rest of us.

Problem Solving

As we've stressed several times already, cognition is important because people *use* their knowledge in the course of everyday life. One important way in which people use knowledge is to solve problems, and we will now discuss what cognitive psychologists have learned about solving problems. Let's define a **problem** as a discrepancy between what we know and what we want to know. The process of reducing this discrepancy is what we do when we solve a problem.

Overview of Problem Solving

Many of life's demands can be construed as problems to be solved (Cantor & Kihlstrom, 1987), although we may not typically think about them in these terms. Because we know a lot about many of the tasks we perform, we usually can solve the problems they pose quite readily. Thus we overlook the fact that a problem confronted us in the first place.

Strong and Weak Methods. Suppose we wake up and want coffee. The "problem" is how to get coffee, but we usually stumble along without difficulty to its solution. In the jargon of cognitive psychology, we have **strong methods** available for many problems; we know exactly how to proceed. When we don't know exactly how to solve problems, we are said to have only **weak methods** available. For instance, suppose we find that our coffee maker isn't working. We don't know exactly how to get coffee, but we have some hunches. Maybe the next-door neighbor has brewed a pot. Maybe the convenience store down the street is open. These hunches represent weak methods for solving our problem, because we cannot be completely certain that they will provide a solution.

Problem-Space. In solving a problem, a person must first represent it cognitively. This representation is called a **problem-space,** and it consists of an initial state, a desired goal state, and the admissible operations or transformations that allow a person to get from the one to the other. The problem is solved when the initial state is transformed into the goal state.

Some problems are **well defined,** meaning that their initial states and goal states are clearly specified: "How much money did you spend today?" This is a well-defined problem, and you know how to proceed. Simply add up your credit card receipts and check stubs. Other problems are **ill defined** because their problem-space is characterized by vagueness. "Is your college major right for you?" This question poses an ill-defined problem. It may not even be clear how you would recognize a solution, even if it were staring you in the face. You have to decide what "right for you" means, and then proceed to evaluate your major against this criterion.

Metacognition.   Important in solving problems is our awareness of what we are doing. More formally, this is known as **metacognition:** awareness of oneself as a cognitive being. Someone skilled at metacognition knows what he knows and what he doesn't, and can monitor his ongoing cognitive processes (Flavell, 1979, 1981). Metacognition greatly aids in a person's solution of problems, because he can direct his own activity rather than just rely on trial and error.

metacognition
awareness of oneself as a cognitive being

Some of you may experience test anxiety, which means that you get worked up during a test, your mind goes blank, and you cannot think of answers that you actually know. One way to interpret test anxiety is in terms of anxiety interfering with your metacognition. It is not that your mind goes blank as much as it is that it becomes filled with extraneous thoughts and feelings that keep you from effectively monitoring your performance on the exam (e.g., Sarason, 1980).

Problem Representation

The initial representation of a problem is critical in determining its solution. Pitfalls abound. For example, a person may be distracted by extraneous information. Consider the following problem:

> A man buys a horse for $10, then sells it for $20. The next day he realizes that he wanted the horse after all, so he buys it back for $30. After a while he decides to sell it and does so for $40. What is the net profit or loss from this series of transactions?

Many people say that the man comes out even (Glucksberg, 1988). This is wrong, though, as you can see if you consider this problem:

> A man buys a horse for $10, then sells it for $20. The next day he buys a cow for $30 and after a while sells it for $40. What is the net profit or loss from this series of transactions?

Here most people say—correctly—that the man comes out $20 ahead. Do you see that the two problems are identical in form? Those who answer the first incorrectly may have become distracted by the irrelevant fact that the same horse has gone back and forth several times. They have framed the problem wrong, failing to separate the two transactions.

functional fixedness
the tendency to persist in representing problems in a particular way, perhaps precluding an appropriate solution

Functional fixedness refers to our tendency to persist in representing problems in a particular way, perhaps precluding an appropriate solution (Duncker, 1945). A well-known example is the two-string problem (see Figure 7.11). Two strings hang from the ceiling of a room, far enough apart that a person cannot grasp both at once. However, the task of the research subject is to tie the two strings together. There are various objects in the room, including a pair of pliers.

One good solution to the problem is to tie the pliers to one string and then start to swing it like a pendulum. The subject holds onto the other string and grasps the swinging string when it comes within reach.

Figure 7.11

The Two-String Problem. How can the subject tie together the two strings hanging from the ceiling when he cannot grasp both at the same time?

Not all subjects hit upon this solution, because they do not see that the pliers can be used to set the string in motion. Instead, they have "fixed" upon another "function" of the pliers, one quite irrelevant to the problem at hand.

Problem Solution

In framing a problem, we have already begun to solve it. If a strong method is available, we use it and are done. Otherwise, we use one or more weak methods. Here are several weak methods with general applicability (Lesgold, 1988):

- means-end analysis—procedures that narrow the distance between the initial state of the problem and the desired goal state
- working forward—procedures that begin with the initial state and transform it, in the hope of approaching the goal state
- working backward—procedures that begin with the goal state and transform it, in the hope of approaching the initial state
- generate and test—procedures that create many possible transformations of the initial state, checking each in turn against the desired goal state

Remember your first day at college. You peered at a map, needing to get from the point marked "you are here" to the other side of campus. How might you solve the problem of getting across campus by each of these weak methods?

With means-end analysis, you might break the problem into parts, and first get halfway across campus. Working forward, you trace a walkway on the map from where you stand to where you want to go. Working backward, you trace a path that begins with where you want to go. And with the generate and test method, surely familiar to lost freshmen everywhere, you walk in ever-widening circles, hoping eventually you arrive at your intended destination!

Algorithms. Sometimes the transformations that are available to you guarantee a solution to the problem at hand. In this case, they are called **algorithms.** For instance, suppose you are looking for a book of poetry on your shelf. If you start at one side of the shelf and deliberately read each title, then you are bound to come across the volume you seek (so long as it is there).

algorithms
methods for solving problems that guarantee a solution

Heuristics. Other times, though, we don't use transformations that guarantee a solution. Instead we employ **heuristics,** cognitive shortcuts that often prove efficient and effective, though not always. When I look for a book on my shelf, I usually start by remembering its color: orange or red or black or blue. I rapidly scan the volumes with that color, and I check just those that pass the test. This strategy is a heuristic rather than an algorithm because it sometimes fails, even if the book I seek is on the shelf. Why? Because over the years, the colors of some of my books have faded. If the red book I want has turned into a pink one, and I am unaware of the change, then I can't find it with this strategy. I must resort to the algorithm of reading each title.

heuristics
cognitive shortcuts for solving problems that often prove efficient and effective

In a series of important studies, Daniel Kahneman and Amos Tversky (1973) showed that people frequently use heuristics to solve problems. Such basic cognitive processes as prediction, judgment, and categorization are based largely on cognitive shortcuts. Often these shortcuts work, which is why our use of heuristics may go undetected. But Kahneman and Tversky devised problems that reveal people's use of heuristics.

For example, let's suppose you meet a fellow student. He is soft-spoken and wears glasses. He remarks that he doesn't like to be outdoors. Here's your task: decide if this student is majoring in classics or psychology. You will probably choose classics, but if your college is like most, you quite likely made a mistake. You haven't taken into account the fact that there are many more psychology majors than classics majors. In predicting

Our tendency to use heuristics can lead us to make certain assumptions about people, such as what type of student this individual might be.

what any given student is studying, you should take into account the relevant numbers in the student body as a whole. There are probably more soft-spoken, spectacled psychology majors who like to stay indoors than there are classics majors with these characteristics, simply because there are many more psychology majors to begin with.

People sometimes ignore the numbers and base judgments only on the degree to which the particular case resembles a general class. In doing so, they are using what Kahneman and Tversky call the **representativeness heuristic.** Let's take a second look at our soft-spoken student. He resembles our prototype of a classics major. So that's what we think him to be, even though it is unlikely.

Another cognitive shortcut we may use in making judgments is the **availability heuristic.** People often judge the frequency of events in terms of the ease with which they can be brought to mind. Because actual frequency determines ease of recall, this heuristic may prove accurate. Which type of word is more common in the English language: those that start with the letter *R* or those that have *R* as their third letter? Most people choose the first answer, even though the second one is correct, because it is easier for most of us (who are not crossword puzzle experts) to think of words that begin with a particular letter than words that have that letter embedded within them. Here the availability heuristic leads us astray.

You know that a host of factors influence our recall, and all of these factors can therefore influence our judgments when these are based on availability. For example, unusual occurrences often come readily to mind. This biases people's judgments about the likelihood of these occurrences. Or consider that people overestimate the chances of dying in a flood or tornado because these events tend to be given prominent coverage in the media; conversely, people underestimate the chances of dying from less memorable (but much more frequent) causes like diabetes and asthma (Fischhoff, 1988).

The existence of judgment heuristics is intriguing. They probably affect much of our thinking. Granted that we may be led to wrong conclusions, why do we employ heuristics? There are several reasons. For starters, heuristics often work. And when they do work, they take less time and effort than an algorithm that would accomplish the same end. Finally, we may use heuristics simply because appropriate algorithms do not exist for the problem at hand.

Rationality

Heuristics encourage us to think about the rationality of cognition (Gardner, 1985). They imply that human cognition is a mixture of rational and irrational processes. Although not strictly logical, heuristics often result in accurate judgments. Mr. Spock lives in all of us, but so too does Dr. McCoy. Indeed, the term **quasi-rational** has been used to describe the mixture of rationality and irrationality that characterizes most cognition.

Because we use cognition to adapt to situations, it cannot be too far removed from the way things are. But because cognition is used in the service of our adaptation, it is carried out from our own point of view, which means that it necessarily reflects our concerns. One's memory, for instance, is enhanced to the degree that the events to be recalled are personally relevant, recent, emotionally engaging, and/or consistent with

representativeness heuristic
basing judgments of likelihood on the degree to which the particular instance resembles a general class

availability heuristic
basing judgment of the frequency of events on the ease with which they can be brought to mind

quasi-rationality
the mixture of rationality and irrationality that characterizes cognition

one's prevailing beliefs. All of these influences can be characterized as irrational in one sense or another, but at the same time as highly functional.

How to Improve Problem Solving

The ability to find successful solutions to life's tasks underlies productive thinking and lies at the very heart of intelligence (Cantor & Kihlstrom, 1987). Is there something that we can do to improve our ability to solve problems? This question can be posed on two levels: specific and general. First, can we improve thinking with regard to given tasks? Here there is no doubt that practice leads to improvement. Experts differ from novices because they have spent thousands of hours performing the task of concern. Their experience leads to task-specific skills that let them better represent and solve problems (Lesgold, 1988).

People differ not only in terms of the content of their cognition but also in the ways they structure and use it (Chi, Feltovich, & Glaser, 1981). For example, chess experts have been extensively investigated (e.g., Simon & Gilmartin, 1973). Relative to novices, masters perceive chessboards in much more sophisticated ways. They don't see just a bunch of pieces. They see structured patterns and the moves these allow. Indeed, a master may be able to recognize as many as 50,000 different configurations of pieces, and he or she can recall what should be done in response to each. Chess masters respond to the whole of the chessboard, whereas novices respond only to parts.

Second, can we improve our ability to solve problems per se? Here there is disagreement as to whether general cognitive skills exist and, if so, whether they can be learned. One of the traditional rationales for education is that it improves thinking. Although classes necessarily have a particular content, whether history or algebra or language, many educators hope that the skills developed from the study of one topic will generalize to other areas of life.

As far back as the ancient Greeks, people have believed that the "formal discipline" learned in the study of language or logic or mathematics has broad generality. We hear former athletes testify that the lessons they learned on the playing field help them in today's business world or in government. In either case, training in specific fields presumably makes us think more logically, and this enhanced thinking presumably pays dividends elsewhere. Are these beliefs justified?

There is reason for doubt. People taught to solve a specific type of problem may still be unable to solve a highly similar problem phrased in different terms. And research subjects often show great difficulty in seeing how the abstract rules of formal logic apply in concrete situations (e.g., Wason, 1966). In other words, people who can solve logic problems using abstract symbols may not be able to solve the identical problems phrased in terms of everyday life. If most people can't apply the rules of logic, we can't very well argue that "formal discipline" imparts these rules.

Recent work shows, however, that some general forms of thinking can be taught. Lehman, Lembert, and Nisbett (1988) described a program of research showing a person's probabilistic thinking is improved if he or she receives instruction in statistics. Graduate students served as their subjects. They were chosen from fields in which statistics courses were

People differ in their ability to apply abstract concepts learned in a discipline to more general problem-solving situations.

required (e.g., psychology) and those in which they were not (e.g., chemistry). Problems like the following were posed to them at the beginning of their graduate work and again after several years:

> A manufacturer's representative whose job took her to many cities was also a gourmet. Whenever she ate an excellent meal in a restaurant she returned to the restaurant as often as possible. However, she was usually disappointed, because subsequent meals were rarely as good as the first. (Holyoak & Nisbett, 1988, p. 86)

Why is this the case? The reasonable answer in light of the information provided is a statistical one phrased in terms of regression to the mean (e.g., the more samples we take, in this case of meals, the more likely they are to approach an average value). In other words, an extremely good meal at a restaurant is probably a freak, and so it is likely to be followed by a meal that is less tasty. An extremely good anything is probably a freak and likely to be followed by something less spectacular, whether we're talking about meals, athletic performances, movies, kisses, or essays for your English class. It's simply a matter of probability.

Students with formal training in statistics offered this type of answer. In contrast, students without training in statistics gave less plausible answers that ignored probabilities: "Cooks change frequently," "Her expectations are too high," and so on. These results are important because they show that thinking indeed can be improved by formal training. Lehman et al. attributed the success of their research to the fact that they studied the types of tasks that people actually use in their everyday lives, not abstract problems based on formal logic. Thus, there is the possibility that problem solving skills of some generality can be taught to children (e.g., Vye, Delclos, Burns, & Bransford, 1988).

Figure 7.12
Tower of Hanoi Problem. One must move the rings from Peg A to Peg C, one at a time, removing a ring only when it is on the top of a peg and never placing a larger ring over a smaller one.

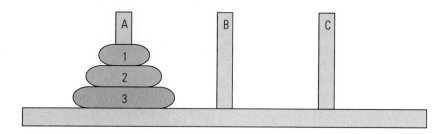

Cognitive Science and Artificial Intelligence

cognitive science
newly developing field that combines disciplines like cognitive psychology, linguistics, computer science, anthropology, and neuroscience and has the goal of understanding the what and how of human knowledge

artificial intelligence
the creation of computer programs that mimic the intelligent behavior of people

Cognitive science is a field just now developing through the combination of several more established disciplines, including cognitive psychology, linguistics, computer science, anthropology, and neuroscience (Gardner, 1985). It shares with cognitive psychology the goal of understanding the what and how of human knowledge, but it draws on a broader set of methods than those of psychology alone.

In particular, cognitive science lays great stock on the use of the computer to shed light on cognition in general and problem solving in particular. Here is where **artificial intelligence** often finds its home. You probably know about artificial intelligence chiefly through sensationalistic stories about computers taking the place of people (like the computer HAL did in the movie *2001*), but the real story of artificial intelligence is more mundane.

Researchers create computer programs that perform tasks similar to those that people perform. There are two types of such programs. The first is intended as a literal simulation, not just of the end product of human cognition but of the intermediate steps as well. The second makes no attempt to mimic the process; it only aims to achieve the end product. In either case, though, the results can provide information concerning how human cognition occurs and how we might improve it, because a computer program is necessarily explicit.

Early examples of artificial intelligence were open to criticism because their "expertise" was quite narrow. For example, consider the Tower of Hanoi problem shown in Figure 7.12. The task here is to move the rings on Peg A to Peg C, one at a time, under two restrictions. First, only the top ring on a peg can be moved. Second, when it is moved, a ring cannot be placed on top of a smaller one. It is possible to create a computer program to solve this problem, but a skeptic could ask "so what?" (Gardner, 1985). On the one hand, this is not a fair criticism of an approach to cognition that is obviously preliminary. On the other hand, it is legitimate to wonder just what the eventual yield of such efforts might be.

More recent examples of artificial intelligence are indeed impressive in terms of practical importance. One particularly interesting example of artificial intelligence is a program called MYCIN (Shortliffe, 1976). This was the first program to function at the level of experts in a particular domain, and is thus called an *expert system* (Davis, 1984).

What does MYCIN do? It diagnoses particular types of infectious illnesses. Attending physicians make use of MYCIN just as they would a consulting specialist. When they suspect the involvement of the diseases in which MYCIN is expert, they "call in" its help by booting up the program on a personal computer. The program asks for certain information, such as the patient's age and sex, the presence or absence of symptoms like headaches or dizziness, and the results of various laboratory tests. Depending on the information provided, different questions are posed, just as an actual diagnostician would pursue different lines of inquiry in light of particular answers. Eventually, MYCIN arrives at a diagnosis and makes a treatment recommendation.

MYCIN has been evaluated by comparing its diagnoses and recommendations against those of human specialists. As judged by a panel of experts blind to the source of the diagnoses and treatment recommendations, MYCIN consistently outperformed actual physicians. This may be surprising to you, but remember that as a computer program, MYCIN has a more extensive base of knowledge than any individual. It can also apply this knowledge in a more consistent and careful manner than any person. Needless to say, human beings created MYCIN, programming its rules in the form of if-then statements (e.g., if the test result is X, then ask about Y). But MYCIN is both interesting and practical. We can expect to see more programs like MYCIN in the future. Indeed, there are now programs that can recognize writing and speaking, forecast weather, offer tax advice, give airplane pilots directions for landing, and even judge wines.

This chapter has described what psychologists know about cognitive representations and processes. The entire field of psychology is today a cognitive endeavor. In subsequent chapters, we will see the cognitive influence in many areas: intelligence (Chapter 8), developmental psychology (Chapters 9 and 10), personality (Chapter 11), abnormal psychology and therapy (Chapters 12 and 13), and social psychology (Chapters 14 and 15). Even human sexuality is sensibly approached in terms of thoughts and beliefs (Chapter 16).

Summary

Topics of Concern

- Memory is our mental representation of knowledge. Cognition encompasses the psychological processes that transform and retain this knowledge. Cognitive psychology is the field that studies memory and cognition.
- With the rise of behaviorism, cognition ceased to be of central interest to many psychologists. However, the importance of cognition to a full explanation of human activity is undeniable, and cognition returned to a legitimate place within psychology by the 1960s.
- In their attempt to capture the essence of the mind, cognitive psychologists turn to concepts and comparisons drawn from other domains. We should not expect these models to be literally true—just useful in terms of clarifying memory and cognition.
- Regardless of the particular cognitive process in which they are interested or the model of the mind that they prefer, psychologists must address basic questions about cognition: Is it rational or irrational; is it general or specific to a particular content; how and why do people differ in their cognitive processes; and what is the biological basis of cognition?

Information Processing

- Many cognitive psychologists today conceive cognition in terms of information processing, of which several types can be distinguished.
- In bottom-up processing, simple aspects of cognition are not influenced by more complex aspects. Here the computer is a popular model.
- In top-down processing, complex aspects do influence simple ones. Cognitive psychologists interested in top-down processing describe cognition in terms of how "deeply" it is represented in the mind.

Memory

- The process by which we put information into memory is called encoding. Once in memory, we speak of the storage of information. The process by which information is located in our memory and then used is called retrieval. Failure of memory is termed forgetting.
- Memory researchers distinguish among three different types of memory, although they disagree regarding whether these correspond to discrete stages in the encoding of information or simply to the degree to which information is transformed as it is remembered.
- The sensory memory briefly holds a relatively faithful version of our sensory experiences. Icons are visual images that persist in the sensory memory after we see something. Echoes are auditory images that persist after we hear something. The sensory memory is limited both in the amount of information it can hold as well as in how long it can hold this information.
- From the sensory memory, some information passes into short-term memory, where it is held for up to 20 seconds. Short-term memory is limited in the amount of information it can contain—about seven discrete items of information. However, the capacity of short-term memory can be greatly increased if we group disparate information into meaningful groups, in a process known as chunking.
- From short-term memory, some information passes into long-term memory. In long-term memory resides our entire storehouse of past experiences, our skills and abilities, and our identity and personality. Long-term memory can be divided into memory of episodes, meanings, and procedures. Regardless, information in long-term memory is abstract, elaborate, and organized.
- There are two types of retrieval from long-term memory: recognition and recall.
- In recognition, we decide if certain information presented to us looks familiar. Recognition memory is explained by proposing that we compare stimuli with our mental representations.
- In recall, we retrieve information from memory without being provided explicit clues. Recall memory is explained by the generate-and-recognize model, which proposes that we create possible answers to the memory task, and then compare these answers with what is in our mem-

ory, as in recognition. The more ways we have to generate possible responses, the better our recall.

- The tip-of-the-tongue phenomenon refers to the experience of knowing we have a particular memory but being unable to come up with it. This phenomenon shows that recall is an active process, because we can deliberately use information at our disposal to facilitate remembering.
- Context-dependent recall refers to the finding that we can more readily recall information in the same setting in which we encoded it than in different settings. Similarly, state-dependent recall occurs when we better remember information when in the same physiological or psychological state in which we initially encoded it than in different states.
- Memory can be improved through internal strategies like the method of loci or through external strategies like lists or notes.
- Forgetting has several explanations. One explanation stresses decay, the loss of memories over time. Another explanation emphasizes interference due to the presence of other material in memory.
- Retrieval failure is an inability to retrieve information that is represented in memory. A dramatic example of retrieval failure is psychogenic amnesia, the sudden inability to remember personal information following a psychological trauma.
- In contrast to psychogenic amnesia is organic amnesia, the inability to remember that follows damage or injury to the brain.
- Psychologists want to know how memory is stored in the brain. The as-yet unidentified physical basis of memory, or *engram*, has proven elusive. One current candidate is the particular chemical makeup of individual nerve cells and their tendencies to fire or not.

How to Investigate Cognition

- Contemporary cognitive psychologists have available a host of research strategies that allow them to infer what and how a person is thinking. They assess the reaction times of subjects to tasks, the errors that are made, the course of development, the consequences of brain illness and injury, and what people say aloud while thinking.

Cognitive Representations

- Various cognitive representations can be distinguished, and they differ in their degree of concreteness or abstractness.
- An image is a cognitive representation that resembles perception in some but not all ways.
- A linear ordering is a cognitive representation of elements that are structured in some order.
- One of the most important cognitive representations is the concept, the categorization of elements into a group. Concepts are represented in several ways: by simple enumeration, rules, properties, and propositional networks.
- A propositional network is a set of logical associations among words. One type of propositional network is called a schema, an organized set of beliefs about some concept.
- Artificial concepts are defined by necessary and sufficient characteristics. Many of the concepts people use in everyday life are not so defined and are called natural categories. These tend to be fuzzily defined, in terms of so-called family resemblances among their elements, prototypes (typical members), and/or remembered instances.
- According to Eleanor Rosch, people tend naturally to categorize the world at a level that maximizes the perceptual similarity among objects within a category and the dissimilarity between these objects and those in other categories.
- When it is implausible that the particulars of cognition are represented, psychologists suggest that people instead possess rules that allow these particulars to be generated as necessary. Such rules are collectively called a grammar, and language is one familiar example of a cognitive activity possible only because people have a representation of its underlying grammar.

Problem Solving

- One of the important uses to which we put cognition is to solve problems. Most generally, a problem is a discrepancy between what we know and what we want to know.
- When we know exactly how to proceed in solving a problem, we are said to have a strong method of solution available. Otherwise, we only have weak methods available.

- To solve a problem, one must first represent it in terms of a starting point, a desired end state, and the admissable operations for getting from the beginning to the end. This representation is called a problem-space.
- The initial representation of a problem is critical in determining its solution. Functional fixedness refers to our tendency to persist in representing problems in a particular way, perhaps precluding an appropriate solution.
- Algorithms are procedures that guarantee a solution to a problem. Heuristics are procedures that sometimes lead to a solution to a problem, and sometimes do not.
- In everyday life, people frequently use heuristics to solve problems. The representativeness heuristic is a way of making judgments based only on the degree to which a particular instance resembles a general class. The availability heuristic is a way of making judgments based only on the ease with which a particular instance can be brought to mind.
- Most cognition is characterized by a mixture of rational and irrational aspects, in what is termed *quasi-rationality*.

- Practice at particular problems improves someone's performance at them. Although formal instruction does not improve "logical" thinking, recent research shows that coursework in statistics indeed improves one's ability to think in terms of probabilities.

Cognitive Science and Artificial Intelligence

- Cognitive science is an interdisciplinary field just now developing that shares with cognitive psychology the goal of understanding the mind. Cognitive science draws on a broader set of methods than those of psychology alone. In particular, cognitive science relies a great deal on computer simulations to shed light on cognition. Artificial intelligence refers to computer programs that perform the same types of tasks that people do.

Important Terms and Names

What follows is a list of the core terms and names for this chapter. Your instructor may emphasize other terms as well. Throughout the chapter, glossary terms appear in **boldface** type. They are defined in the text, and each term, along with its definition, is repeated in the margin.

Topics of Concern

memory/263
cognition/263
cognitive psychology/263

Ulric Neisser/262

Information Processing

serial and parallel
   processing/267
bottom-up and top-down
   processing/267
depth of processing/268

John Bransford/268

Memory

encoding/269
storage/269
retrieval/269
forgetting/269
sensory memory/271
icon/272
short-term memory/272
chunking/273
long-term memory/274
recognition/275
recall/275
proactive and retroactive
   interference/279
psychogenic and organic
   amnesia/280
mnemonics/280
engram/282

Herman Ebbinghaus/269
George Sperling/272
George Miller/273
Elizabeth Loftus/276

Cognitive Representations

image/287
linear ordering/288
concept/289
propositional network/
   289
schema/290
artificial and natural con-
   cepts/291
prototype/292
rule/294
grammar/294

Eleanor Rosch/293

Problem Solving

problem/295
strong and weak meth-
   ods/295
metacognition/296
functional fixedness/296
algorithm/298
heuristic/298
quasi-rationality/299

Daniel Kahneman and
   Amos Tversky/298

Cognitive Science and Artificial Intelligence

cognitive science/302
artificial intelligence/302

Review Questions

1. _____ refers to the content of knowledge, and _____ refers to the processes by which we transform and retain this knowledge.
   a. A heuristic; an algorithm
   b. Memory; cognition
   c. Semantic memory; episodic memory
   d. Short-term memory; long-term memory
   We can think of memory as the content of our minds, and cognition as what we do with this content./263

2. Describing cognition in terms of models and metaphors can at times be all of these except
   a. accurate.
   b. misleading.
   c. unnecessary.
   d. useful.
   Although the only way we have for conceiving cognition is by using terms borrowed from other domains, we should remain aware that cognitive models and metaphors are potentially misleading because they can never be strictly accurate. We hope, however, that they are useful./264

3. Memory can fail at the stage of _____ information.
   a. encoding
   b. storing
   c. retrieving
   d. all of the above
   e. none of the above
   We fail to remember information we have encountered for many reasons. Perhaps we did not encode the information; perhaps we did not store it; perhaps we cannot retrieve it./268

4. The intent of Ebbinghaus in using nonsense syllables to study memory was to remove _____ from his investigations.
   a. culture
   b. drama
   c. meaning
   d. simplicity
   Ebbinghaus wished to study memory of material without the confound of meaningfulness. He hoped that nonsense syllables would remove this factor from his investigations./269

5. Chunking is a way to increase the capacity of
   a. long-term memory.
   b. sensory memory.
   c. short-term memory.
   d. all of the above.
   e. none of the above.
   We can increase the amount of information we can hold in short-term memory by grouping different items into meaningful wholes called chunks./273

6. In which of these failures of memory is information permanently lost?
   a. decay
   b. proactive interference
   c. retroactive interference
   d. psychogenic amnesia
   Only in decay is information gone forever. In these other failures of memory, retrieval failure has occurred, although we can still regard memories as present./279

7. The engram refers to the as-yet undiscovered
   a. grammar for the English language.
   b. location of transfer from short-term to long-term memory.
   c. mechanism for selective attention.
   d. physical basis of memory.
   The physical basis of memory is not yet known, although it has long had a name: the engram./282

8. The serial position effect is an example of a(n)
   a. artificial concept.
   b. chunk.
   c. linear ordering.
   d. natural concept.
   e. rule.
   We often remember items best when we encounter them at the beginning or end of a series. This is called the serial position effect, and it illustrates a common property of linear orderings./270

9. Compared to algorithms, heuristics are often
   a. more efficient.
   b. more fallible.
   c. indistinguishable in terms of their end products.
   d. all of the above.
   Algorithms guarantee solutions to problems, but we often rely on heuristics instead. Although heuristics may fail, they often yield much more efficiently the same answer as do algorithms./298

10. An expert system is a
    a. computer program.
    b. how-to book written by a professional.
    c. set of algorithms for a domain of problem solving.
    d. set of heuristics for a domain of problem solving.
    e. transcript of the Oprah Winfrey show.
    Computer programs that function at the level of experts in a particular domain, like MYCIN, are called expert systems./302

Final page of the Medical Boards

Psychologists interested in measuring intelligence often distinguish between achievement tests and aptitude tests.

Chapter Eight

Intelligence

Topics of Concern

Alex Jones is a playground legend from New York. He plays basketball so well that his opponents sometimes forget to guard him. They just stop and marvel as his passes defy the laws of physics to find their destination, as his jump shots rain through the hoop, and as his dunks rattle the pavement all the way to the World Trade Center.

Alex comes from a rough neighborhood, and many of his friends from school have turned to drugs or crime or both. He has attended more funerals of teenagers than he cares to remember. But Alex has always had basketball to keep him on the straight and narrow, even as he flies through the air. He plays morning to night, during all seasons of the year. His parents sometimes wish he spent a bit more time at his studies, but at least he stayed in school and out of trouble. The family dream, rarely spoken but often thought, was that basketball could be a ticket for Alex out of the rough neighborhood. He could get a college scholarship and make something of himself.

So far, the story of Alex is a classic tale from the sports pages. What comes next? You can imagine: visits from college recruiters, deep conversations with the family, and the decision that Alex will attend school far from home on an athletic scholarship. His coach is a gruff but fair man. Under his tutelage, Alex will grow as a player, as a student, and as a person.

But this classic tale takes on a new wrinkle in light of recent guidelines by the National Collegiate Athletic Association (NCAA). Proposition 48 is a rule mandating minimum scores on the SAT college entrance exam if a player on scholarship is to participate in sports his first year at college. Alex takes the SAT exam, but falls short of the required score.

There is some question as to whether the scholarship offer to Alex will be honored. Indeed, Proposition 42 is an even more recent NCAA rule preventing schools from offering athletic scholarships to students who don't score highly enough on the SAT. If Alex cannot play basketball his first year in college, he will feel completely out of place. Other basketball players will progress while he stands still. And without a scholarship, he cannot attend college at all.

The story of Alex is a sad one, but it takes on added meaning once we know a bit more about the SAT exam on which Alex failed to score highly enough. It is one of many intelligence tests currently available. But just what is the "intelligence" that the SAT exam measures? Perhaps it doesn't get at the intelligence that Alex displays so well in athletics and his everyday life. Like any measure, the SAT exam falls short of perfect validity. Perhaps it is inadvertently biased against individuals from the lower class, like Alex. These and related questions have been of concern to psychologists ever since they first attempted to define and measure intelligence. Keeping Alex in mind, let's discuss these topics of concern.

Defining and Measuring Intelligence

We show our **intelligence** when we act in adaptive ways, confronting and surmounting the challenges that face us, and in purposive ways, pursuing a goal (Sternberg & Salter, 1982). There's no question that intelligence allows us flexibility, both individually and collectively. It gives us a great selection advantage. It explains the spread of the human species to all corners of the world and our achievements there. For these reasons, intelligence is one of the most valued human characteristics.

The definition of intelligence as adaptive and purposive behavior is quite abstract, and psychologists have necessarily made intelligence more concrete by devising measures of

Do standardized intelligence tests accurately measure the abilities of gifted, hard-working young athletes?

it. Particularly popular as an operationalization have been tests like the SAT. These presumably allow the psychologist to predict who will or will not show intelligent behavior, but the tests themselves have proved controversial. For example, they often yield but a single score for an individual, implying that intelligence is a continuum along which all people can be placed. Is this really true about intelligent behavior? Remember Alex. One could argue that he shows his intelligence in ways that the SAT doesn't measure. Currently of interest to psychologists are several theories that explicitly suggest that intelligence is plural, that is, composed of distinct abilities. By this view, people's intelligence is better described as a profile of scores than as a single number.

intelligence
the capacity to act in adaptive and purposive ways

first that many intelligence tests may have an unintended bias against members of minority groups, and second that blacks tend not to have access to the experiences that allow whites to score well.

Our story does not mention whether Alex is black or white, and his race doesn't matter to the story. But here is some information about how Proposition 48 differentially affects black and white athletes. Black freshmen are perhaps four or five times less likely than their white counterparts to meet the guidelines; traditionally black colleges have been hit particularly hard by the NCAA rule (*Jet*, 1986a, 1986b).

Related to the nature-nurture issue is whether intelligence can be changed. Those who favor a biological view of the causes of intelligence tend to regard it as fixed, whereas those who favor an environmental view are optimistic that appropriate interventions can boost intelligence.

The Causes of Intelligence

Throughout the chapters you've read so far in this book, you've seen the nature-nurture issue raised repeatedly. We encounter it again with regard to the causes of intelligence. At one extreme is the view that intelligence is largely a matter of genetic inheritance, and at the other extreme is the argument that intelligence is a product of particular experiences, notably opportunity for education. Alex comes from a poor neighborhood, and his parents did not finish high school. Why did he score poorly on the SAT exam? There are differences of opinion over the answer to this question.

This issue concerning the causes of intelligence becomes heated when it is extended to address race differences in intelligence. On tests like the SAT, black Americans on the average score lower than white Americans. Some suggest that this fact reflects an inherent difference between blacks and whites. Others disagree strongly, pointing out

Intelligence at the Extremes

Intelligence proves difficult to define and measure precisely, but it is somewhat easier to recognize intelligence at the extremes, as shown by people with great or modest talents. Although the extremes of intelligence are interesting in their own right, psychologists also focus on these because of what they imply about the intelligence of those of us in the middle. One important finding from these investigations is that intelligence is indeed plural. People talented in one area of achievement may not be talented in another. Alex Jones may be a genius on the basketball court, but there is no reason to expect him to excel in the classroom, or in music, or in any other domain.

A History of Intelligence Testing

Do you have a number two pencil? You know what follows this request. You're about to take a test. Sometimes it is a test for a class, where you are asked to recognize the definitions of various terms. Maybe it is a test of how you evaluate political or social issues. Or maybe it is a test of your abilities and intelligence.

Tests may seem a twentieth-century invention, but they have been around much longer. Indeed, tests to measure how people differ in terms of their fitness for various purposes have existed for at least 4000 years. In ancient China, those who aspired to civil service positions took a series of written examinations on the writings of Confucius. Only 5 out of 100,000 individuals thereby qualified for the high office of mandarin (DuBois, 1970).

By the most common operationalization of intelligence, you are considered intelligent if you score high on an intelligence test. And you are unintelligent if you score low. These labels, placed on people by their test performance, profoundly affect the lives they lead. What schools are open to them? What jobs? What promotions? This section presents the story of psychology's investigation of intelligence in terms of the various tests devised to measure this characteristic.

aptitude tests
tests that measure one's capacity for learning

achievement tests
tests that measure what one has already learned

Psychologists sometimes divide intelligence tests into **aptitude tests,** which attempt to measure one's capacity for learning, and **achievement tests,** which attempt to measure what one has already learned. The SAT, for instance, is an aptitude test, because it is used to predict how a student will do in college. A midterm exam in Art History, on the other hand, is an achievement test because it is used to ascertain how much a student has already learned.

The distinction between aptitude and achievement tests is often easier to make in theory than in practice, because aptitude tests necessarily reflect some learning on the part of the test taker (if only how to follow the test's instructions). Some prefer to describe only aptitude tests as true measures of intelligence, but because the practical distinction between aptitude and achievement can be so murky, this chapter will use "intelligence test" to refer to *both* aptitude and achievement tests.

Throughout our discussion of tests, keep in mind the important ideas of reliability and validity introduced in Chapter 1 (pp. 24–26). Intelligence tests tend to be quite reliable, yielding the same score for an individual on different occasions. However, the validity of intelligence tests—whether they actually measure what they purport to measure—is not so easily decided. Much of the controversy surrounding these tests can be described as disagreement about their validity.

Francis Galton's Approach to Intelligence

The modern era of intelligence testing is marked by the 1869 publication of the book *Hereditary Genius* by Sir Francis Galton (1822–1911), an interesting historical figure who left his characteristic stamp on the study of intelligence. Galton was an upper-class Englishman, a contemporary and half-cousin of Charles Darwin. Like other men of his class, Galton did

Sir Francis Galton

not work. Rather, he pursued various interests, which included science in general and human abilities in particular. The theory of evolution very much captivated science during Galton's era, and so he applied evolutionary ideas to his study of human abilities.

Galton was interested in how people differed from each other with respect to their abilities.

> I have no patience with the hypothesis occasionally expressed, and often implied, especially in tales written to teach children to be good, that babies are born pretty much alike, and that the sole agencies in creating differences between boy and boy, and man and man, are steady application and moral effort. It is in the most unqualified manner that I object to pretensions of natural equality. The experiences of the nursery, the school, the University, and of professional careers, are a chain of proofs to the contrary. (Galton, 1869, p. 12)

Note the contrast between Galton's sentiment and the feeling of John Watson, the American behaviorist, as expressed in Chapter 5 (p. 175). Watson was concerned with what people have in common—their capacity to learn, whereas what concerned Galton was how people differ from each other—in this case the limits of their capacities.

Galton believed that these differences were pervasive ones. A person's intellectual capacity is not linked to specific domains. Rather, intelligence is a general characteristic brought to bear in a variety of ways. Hence, he used the term *genius* to describe individuals—not their feats. However, geniuses could be recognized by their accomplishments.

> People lay too much stress on apparent specialties, thinking over-rashly because a man is devoted to some particular pursuit, he could not possibly have succeeded in anything else. . . . After a man of genius has selected his hobby, and adapted himself to it as to seem unfitted for any occupation in life, and to be possessed of but one special aptitude, I often notice, with admiration, how well he bears himself when circumstances suddenly thrust him into a strange position. (pp. 20–21)

Galton further believed that the differences in people's intelligence could be quantified. People not only differ, but they differ in degrees. Galton further suggested that these differences fall along a bell-shaped curve, with most people clustered in the middle. Moving further toward one extreme or the other (toward the more intelligent or the less intelligent), ever fewer people were represented.

> I propose . . . to range men according to their natural abilities, putting them in classes separated by equal degrees of merit, and to show the relative number of individuals included in the several classes. Perhaps some person might be inclined to make an offhand guess that the number of men included in the different classes would be pretty equal. If he thinks so, I can assure him he is most . . . mistaken. (p. 22)

He gave people letter grades that reflected their relative intelligence and hence their relative frequency in the population. "A" people were one in four, "B" were one in six, and so on (see Table 8.1).

Galton believed that differences in genius were inherited. As the title suggests, *Hereditary Genius* documented how talents and achievements run through families, a fact Galton used to support his thesis of inherited

Table 8.1
Galton's Frequency Distribution of Genius

According to Francis Galton, people differ in their intelligence, and these differences fall along a bell-shaped curve. The more extreme someone's degree of intelligence, either below or above average, the more infrequently it is found in the population.

Grades of Natural Ability		Numbers of People Comprised in the Several Grades of Mental Ability
Below average	Above average	Proportion: one in
a	A	4
b	B	6
c	C	16
d	D	64
e	E	413
f	F	4,300
g	G	79,000
x	X	1,000,000
Much below average	Much above average	

(Adapted from Galton, F., 1869. *Hereditary genius*. London: Macmillan)

genius. He showed that eminent men (like himself) had eminent relatives. In retrospect, we can see that a society like Galton's England is the last place in the world where we would want to argue that genius is hereditary. After all, in England, property and titles and influence and opportunities passed from grandfather to father to son.

We can see that Galton's data just as readily imply that accomplishments are a result of privilege and happenstance, not biology. He was aware of this alternative view, and was the first to explicitly phrase the nature-nurture issue. How many of a person's characteristics can be attributed to biology (nature) and how many to learning and socialization (nurture)? Galton argued that with respect to intelligence, the role of nurture was negligible. As already mentioned, this issue is still very much alive today.

Galton believed that people's potential for genius could be measured prior to any actual accomplishment. Starting with the assumption that information comes from our senses, he proposed that people with superior sensory and motor abilities must be more able. Hence, the earliest "intelligence" tests developed by Galton measured individual differences in the strength of people's grip, the rate at which they could tap their finger, the speed with which they reacted to sounds, the accuracy with which they could divide a line in two, and so on.

Finally, Galton founded the movement known as **eugenics**, which held that the human species could be improved through the systematic application of the theory of evolution (see Chapter 2). Biologically superior people should be encouraged to interbreed, and the less superior should be dealt out of the process altogether. This controversial position became repugnant to society as a whole during the rise of Nazism in

eugenics
a social movement based on the premise that the human species can and should be improved through the systematic application of the theory of evolution, for example, by encouraging biologically superior people to interbreed

Led by Adolf Hitler, the Nazis distorted the principles of eugenics in their effort to create a "master race."

Europe in the twentieth century. The Nazis expressed their hatred of other groups using the language of biological superiority and inferiority. Because eugenics has been associated with intelligence testing from the very start, it is obvious why its negative connotations often color the testing movement. Still, the idea of eugenics has not entirely disappeared. It is still apparent, for example, in the commonly held opinion that mentally retarded individuals should not be allowed to have children.

As we have already seen, Darwin's theory of evolution affected Galton's approach to intelligence. For instance, note the emphasis on a biologically based variation that determines how one gets along in the world. Indeed, because of Galton, the meaning of intelligence became entwined with Darwinian ideas of fitness (Gould, 1981). When Galton proposed that some people had more genius than others, he seemed to be saying that these people were more fit. A further leap was sometimes made from fitness to moral worth, an unfortunate equivalence that still seems to hold in the minds of some people today, who think the results of an intelligence test say all that is necessary to know about a person. But remember, as we discussed in Chapter 2, fitness merely means the capacity for reproduction, not intelligence or eminence or genius or worth or any of the other notions with which we may erroneously associate it.

Francis Galton's views are important for two reasons. First, modern approaches to intelligence very much stem from his pioneering work. Even when contemporary psychologists disagree with him, they tend to use his terminology and take positions on the issues that he first phrased. Second, his work shows that science is never undertaken in a vacuum. Theory and research reflect the larger social and historical setting where scientists work. Galton was a product of nineteenth-century England, and his assumptions about intelligence reflect that world.

Alfred Binet's Approach to Intelligence

Alfred Binet

We've seen that Galton developed an intelligence test based on motor and sensory functions. By his view, the more efficiently someone performed the tasks posed in these tests, the more intelligent he or she was. Other researchers followed this example, including American psychologist James McKeen Cattell (1860–1944), who at the turn of the century devised his own battery of sensory and motor tests. But when these tests were administered to university students, there were no correlations between these measures of "intelligence" and the grades that the students earned in school (Cattell & Farrand, 1896; Wissler, 1901).

So, if these tests indeed measured intelligence, then intelligence did not relate to school grades. Psychologists could accept this surprising conclusion, or they could question the validity of these particular measures of intelligence. They chose the latter course, leading to new ways of investigating intelligence.

The next era of intelligence testing thus began with the use of tests that relied on complex tasks. The central figure here was French psychologist Alfred Binet (1857–1911), who was interested not only in educational issues such as testing, but also states of consciousness (Chapter 4) and psychopathology (Chapter 12).

Binet's contributions to the measurement of intelligence were sparked when the French Minister of Public Instruction asked him to solve

Table 8.2
Items from Binet's Intelligence Test

Year 3
1. Point to eyes, nose, and mouth
2. Repeat two digits
3. Identify objects in a picture
4. Repeat a sentence of six syllables

Year 7
1. Show right hand and left ear
2. Describe a picture
3. Carry out three commands given simultaneously
4. Count the value of six coins

Year 15
1. Repeat seven digits
2. Find three rhymes for a given word in one minute
3. Repeat a sentence of twenty-six syllables
4. Interpret a set of given facts

a problem confronted by the schools. How could a teacher distinguish students unable to learn (i.e., the mentally retarded) from those unwilling to learn? If this distinction could be made, then those unable to profit from typical instruction could be sent to special schools where they might be helped. Perhaps a test could be devised to measure one's ability to learn. And so Binet, with the help of his colleague Theophile Simon, came up with a strategy to make this distinction. Their first intelligence test was published in 1905, and it proved so popular that it went through several rapid revisions (e.g., Binet & Simon, 1913).

Binet and Simon instituted a number of procedures in their tests that still characterize intelligence testing today. First, their tests posed complex tasks for subjects (see Table 8.2 for some examples). They compiled a myriad of test activities for students, trying to represent the range of activities actually involved in schoolwork. The test was administered to one student at a time, by an examiner who posed tasks and questions to the student. The process could take several hours. Initial items on the test were easy, and subsequent items became increasingly difficult. Testing proceeded until the student failed to give correct answers.

norms
descriptions of how large samples of individuals perform on a test

Second, Binet and Simon established extensive **norms** for test performance. In other words, they administered test items to large numbers of students to determine the average performance. A given student's performance could then be compared to these norms and interpreted as above, below, or at the average.

Third, Binet and Simon showed that their tests were valid, that they accomplished their intended purpose of identifying students unable to profit from typical instruction. They assembled a large variety of possible items which they administered to numerous children. Then they determined which items allowed them to predict good and poor performances in school. Only those items that successfully provided this distinction were kept for the final version of the test.

Recall the discussion of validity in Chapter 1. Validity refers to the accuracy of an operational definition; whether or not it truly captures what it intends to measure. There are various ways to judge validity. Binet and Simon established what is known as *criterion validity* for their test, judging it by how well it predicted the particular criterion of doing well in academic classes—that is, getting good grades on tests and papers. This remains a popular strategy for proving the validity of an intelligence test.

One of the rules of thumb concerning criterion validity is that when scores on the criterion variable are closely bunched together, it is increasingly difficult for a test to make sharp distinctions among them. Because Binet was concerned with the gross distinction between the mentally retarded and the mentally normal, his test could readily perform its intended function. But as intelligence tests have become increasingly popular, they are called upon to make ever finer discriminations, making them less dependable (see Figure 8.1).

A fourth innovation by Binet and Simon was the recognition that whatever they were measuring should reflect the student's chronological age, so they created different norms for individuals at each age. A student's score could then be described by referring to the average score of children at that particular age. This was the student's **mental age.** Suppose your test score matches the way an average eight-year-old child scores. Your mental age, regardless of your chronological age, is therefore eight.

Today you may hear people saying that sixth-grade classes are reading at an eighth-grade level (or vice versa). This reflects the Binet and Simon innovation of describing a test score in terms of the age group for which it is typical. If your mental age is higher than your chronological age, then you have above average intelligence. If your mental age is lower than your chronological age, then you have below average intelligence. If the two are the same, then you have average intelligence. Let's discuss some of the implications of this view.

Most importantly, intelligence is relative—in several ways. It is obviously relative to one's chronological age. Equal performance by two

mental age

the average intelligence test scores of children of a given age; if your mental age is eight, you score on a test the way an average eight-year-old child scores

Figure 8.1
Predicting the Criterion of Grades. Intelligence tests can be used to predict who will do relatively well or relatively poorly in school. However, it is easier to distinguish F students from A students than B students from A students.

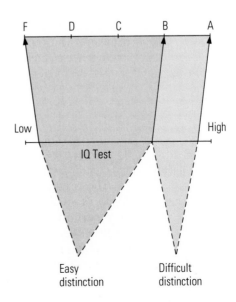

children of different ages means that they have different degrees of intelligence. Intelligence is also relative to the group on which the scores have been normed. Remember that mental age is determined by matching someone's performance to that of a larger group. Depending on who is in that group, one's mental age can vary. Intelligence is also relative to the particular questions posed on the test. Tests such as Binet's must be periodically updated. One place where revisions have to be made is in the section concerned with vocabulary. Words pass in and out of common use, and if we are to measure intelligence by assessing someone's vocabulary, we have to recognize the changes that occur in language over time.

Another implication is that rigid distinctions among people of different levels of intelligence are arbitrary. Although cutoffs are frequently used to identify the mentally retarded on the one hand and the geniuses on the other, the specific cutoff values are arbitrary. The population doesn't fall into three discrete clumps of people: the retarded, the geniuses, and the rest of us.

Lewis Terman's Contribution

Binet and Simon's tests were successful in that they distinguished between students who could and could not profit from traditional instruction. As noted, the tests went through several revisions, and were soon translated into other languages and imported to other countries, including the United States. Several individuals undertook the English translation, but the best-known was originally done in 1916 at Stanford University by Lewis M. Terman (1877–1956). Today we call this test the Stanford-Binet Intelligence Scale, to reflect its origins in Binet's work and its translation at Stanford.

The Stanford-Binet reflects an important innovation (originally suggested by William Stern in 1914): dividing one's mental age by his or her chronological age, then multiplying by 100 (to avoid decimal places). This quotient is called the **intelligence quotient,** abbreviated as **IQ:**

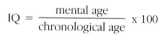

$$IQ = \frac{\text{mental age}}{\text{chronological age}} \times 100$$

You've heard about IQ your entire life, but did you know that this is what it means? The qualifications we discussed earlier about the relativity of intelligence as measured by these tests apply to IQ scores as well.

We no longer define IQ as the quotient of mental age and chronological age. Today we compare someone's score on the Stanford-Binet to the larger population of those the same age who have taken the test. An IQ of 100 is average, by definition. An IQ of 115 means that you score higher than 84 percent of people your age who have taken the test, whereas an IQ of 85 means that your score exceeds that of 16 percent of people your age (see Figure 8.2).

The original Binet test was intended to distinguish only within the group of students not doing well in school. Presumably, students who were performing satisfactorily in their schoolwork need never be tested, because their performance was proof that they had the ability to perform. Indeed, Binet was reportedly reluctant to regard his measure as a test of mental ability for all students. He feared that the results of his test would be used to restrict opportunities, not enhance them.

Lewis Terman

intelligence quotient (IQ)
the ratio of one's mental age to one's chronological age, multiplied by 100 to eliminate decimals

Figure 8.2

Distribution of IQ Scores on the Stanford-Binet Intelligence Scale. If a large number of people took this test, here is how their scores would look. The numbers at the top of the curve show the percentage of people who would score below the indicated score.

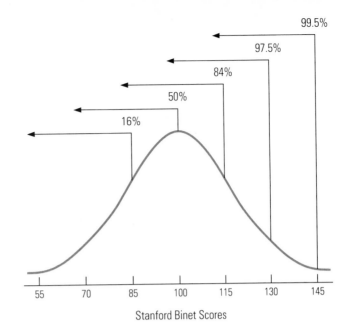

Stanford Binet Scores

Terman disagreed with this restricted use of intelligence tests, and advocated instead the testing of all students.

> What pupils should be tested? The answer is, all. If only selected children are tested, many of the cases most in need of adjustment will be over-looked. The purpose of the tests is to tell us what we do not already know, and it would be a mistake to test only those students who are recognized as obviously below or above average. Some of the biggest surprises are encountered in testing those who have been looked upon as close to average in ability. Universal testing is fully warranted. (Terman et al., 1923, p. 22)

Terman's call was heeded, particularly in the United States, where mass intelligence testing is now the rule.

Terman agreed with Galton that intelligence is principally a matter of biological inheritance. This view thus permeated the mass testing movement, resulting in the use of intelligence testing to decide who need not be given opportunities for further schooling, as well as to support pronouncements that different racial and ethnic groups varied in terms of their biological endowment.

The Wechsler Intelligence Scales

In 1939, David Wechsler developed his own test of intelligence, which improved on the Stanford-Binet in several ways. Wechsler wanted a test that could be used with adults, not just children. And he was bothered that people who came from non-English-speaking homes did not seem fairly tested by intelligence tests phrased exclusively in English.

Wechsler thus devised a test that had separate verbal and performance sections. The verbal sections test individuals' knowledge of general information ("What is a ruby?"), comprehension ("Why do people keep money

Wechsler's intelligence tests include both verbal and nonverbal tasks.

Figure 8.3
WAIS Block Design

Block arrangement
Arrange the blocks to create this design.

Figure 8.4
WAIS Picture Arrangement

Picture order
Put these pictures in the right order so that they tell a story.

in a bank?"), and the like. The performance sections require the manipulation of material without any verbal content. For example, the block design task asks people to reproduce the designs they see by using colored blocks (see Figure 8.3). Another task asks people to put pictures together to form a coherent story (see Figure 8.4). Once tested, each person ends up with a separate score for verbal intelligence and performance intelligence. Wechsler's tests are widely used today. The latest revision, published in 1981, is called the Wechsler Adult Intelligence Scale-Revised (WAIS-R).

There is also a parallel test for school-age children called the Wechsler Intelligence Scale for Children-Revised (WISC-R) that provides separate estimates of verbal and performance intelligence. The idea of breaking intelligence into components has been persuasive, so much so that the most recent version of the Stanford-Binet has been modified to yield not only an overall intelligence score, but also separate estimates of one's verbal, quantitative, reasoning, and memory abilities (Thorndike, Hagan, & Sattler, 1986).

Group Tests of Intelligence

The Stanford-Binet and the Wechsler scales require individual administration. The next chapter in the history of intelligence testing involved the development of group intelligence tests that did not need to be administered individually. World War I gave group testing its first big boost.

Army Alpha and Army Beta. Robert M. Yerkes (1876–1956) and other psychologists, including Terman, created an intelligence test that could be administered in written form to large numbers of individuals. The United States Army cooperated by giving this test to 1,750,000 army recruits between 1917 and 1919. There were two versions of the test. Army Alpha was a test for literate individuals. Army Beta was a test for the illiterate, relying on pictures rather than words (see Figure 8.5). The tests had two purposes: eliminating the unfit (those scoring low) and choosing candidates for officers (those scoring high).

Whether Army Alpha and Army Beta helped to win the war, as Yerkes believed, is unclear (Gould, 1981). What is clear is that intelligence testing was legitimized to a great extent by the existence of norms based on almost 2 million individuals. Once the results of the army testing became available, commercial testing businesses and educational institutions showed great interest in them. Indeed, society as a whole was greatly affected by the aftermath of the Army testing.

Strictly speaking, Army Alpha and Army Beta did not yield IQ scores. Rather, these tests assigned to men grades ranging from A, the highest grade, to E, the lowest. However, it was possible to translate these letter grades into IQ scores, and one of the conclusions that followed was that the average mental age of white Army recruits was thirteen. We know what this means—that the average recruit scored the same as an average group of thirteen-year-old children on the particular test. But the general public was shocked and dismayed by this result, because it seemed to be saying that we were a nation of adolescents. Those who favored eugenics pointed to this result as proof positive for the impending doom of our nation.

Figure 8.5

Examples from Army Alpha and Army Beta Intelligence Tests. Army Alpha was a test for those who could read and thus used written questions. Army Beta was a test for the illiterate and relied on pictures.

From the Alpha Test

Disarranged Sentence: property floods life and destroy (True or False)

If you save $7 a month for 4 months, how much will you save?

Revolvers are made by: Smith & Wesson   Armour & Co.   Ingersol.   Anheuser-Busch

Why is tennis good exercise?

The Battle of Gettysburg was fought in: 1863   1813   1778   1812

From the Beta Test

What is missing from the picture below?

From the Beta Test

Rearrange the three pictures below in the correct order:

Another result of the army testing was that the recruits were compared in terms of their country of origin. Recruits from southern and eastern European backgrounds typically scored lower than those from western and northern Europe. Because of these results, some lobbied for restrictions on immigration by certain groups and for screening of would-be immigrants by testing. To be fair, blatant prejudice against certain groups of immigrants was not the only motive operating here. Some people feared that large numbers of individuals with low intelligence would be detrimental to the country. Regardless, the result was the administration of intelligence tests to European immigrants at Ellis Island. Imagine these folks, newly arrived from a crowded and tiring boat trip, speaking no English, and not understanding what they were being asked to do. It's hardly surprising that they often scored in such a way as to appear feeble-minded (Goddard, 1917).

Finally, when blacks and other racial minorities were compared with whites, they tended to score lower on the Army intelligence tests, once again reinforcing stereotyped beliefs about the innate superiority of some groups over others. Here is what Terman (1916, pp. 91–92) said about racial minorities in the United States.

> Their dullness seems to be racial. . . . There is no possibility at present of convincing society that they should not be allowed to reproduce, although from a eugenic point of view, they constitute a grave problem because of their unusually prolific breeding.

Note the irony in complaining about the biological fitness of a group of people judged intellectually unfit! More generally, we see an issue still controversial today: what to make of the fact that blacks and whites in the United States on the average score differently on IQ tests. We've already seen this issue in relation to the NCAA's Proposition 48, and we'll see it again later in the chapter.

Modern Group Tests.   Today, the best-known descendant of Army Alpha is probably the Scholastic Aptitude Test (SAT), which you probably took to get into college. It is a group-administered test that presumably measures your aptitude for college work. There are other group tests that are used to select students for medical school, law school, business school, graduate school, and so on. Most of these tests are designed to measure aptitude, not achievement. There is considerable controversy as to what these tests actually measure, and whether this is best regarded as aptitude.

Many of you are aware of the private businesses that prepare students to score higher on these group tests than they might on their own. Extreme claims about the effectiveness of such coaching are sometimes made, but these are difficult to evaluate (e.g., Owen, 1985). Research does show that crash courses that teach test-taking strategies can result in modest gains on the SAT, perhaps enough to make a difference for a college applicant on the border between admission and rejection, or for a college athlete whose career is threatened by Proposition 48 (Kulik, Bangert-Drowns, & Kulik, 1984). These results should give pause to any who interpret the SAT as a valid measure of one's inherent aptitude for college work. Presumably, crash courses should have no effect on what we mean by aptitude.

Can Intelligence Tests Be Culture Fair?

Throughout the history of intelligence testing, many individuals have spoken of intelligence apart from a person's particular background. We see this in Galton's belief that genius would show itself wherever one happened to be. We see this in the dismissal of racism as an explanation of black-white differences in IQ. The opposite view argues that one cannot speak of intelligence apart from a particular context, specifically, someone's culture. If we wish to speak of intelligence, we must locate it in a particular time and place. At the beginning of the chapter, we defined intelligence as adaptive behavior. There is no such thing as adaptation in general. We can only adapt to particulars, whether the demands of Latin class, the requirements of trench warfare, or the rigors of high altitudes.

Undaunted by this view, psychologists have attempted to create what are called **culture-fair intelligence tests,** which are designed to measure abilities that are unaffected by one's particular background (Carroll, 1982). However, it has proven difficult if not impossible to devise a test that doesn't, in some way, rely on a particular culture for grounding.

Consider the questions in Table 8.3. When these questions were administered to children in both urban and rural settings, children from cities did better on Test A, whereas children from farms did better on Test B (Shimberg, 1929). What does this show? Intelligence tests necessarily reflect what one knows because one lives in a particular place.

culture-fair intelligence tests intelligence tests that attempt to measure abilities unaffected by one's particular background

Table 8.3

"Intelligence" Test Questions

Information Test A

1. What are the colors in the American flag?
2. Who is President of the United States?
3. What is the largest river in the United States?
4. How can banks afford to pay interest on the money you deposit?
5. What is the freezing point of water?
6. What is a referendum in government?

Information Test B

1. Of what is butter made?
2. Name a vegetable that grows above ground.
3. Why does seasoned wood burn more easily than green wood?
4. About how often do we have a full moon?
5. Who was President of the U.S. during the World War?
6. How can you locate the Pole star?

Source: Shimberg, M. E., 1929. An investigation into the validity of norms with special reference to urban and rural groups. *Archives of Psychology*, No. 104.

Or consider this item from Army Alpha: "Washington is to Adams as first is to _____." This is a reasonable enough question if one has studied American history and recognizes Washington and Adams as the names of the first two presidents of the United States. But all sorts of perfectly intelligent people might not know this. It seems unreasonable to regard correct answers to this particular question as indicating innate intelligence, but that is exactly how advocates of Army Alpha interpreted the test.

It is not only the content of test items that may favor one group over another, but also the way that items are phrased. Not everyone in the United States speaks the same version of the English language. Because many intelligence tests are phrased in the dialect of the white middle class, those from other backgrounds may be at a disadvantage because they don't understand the questions.

One test often cited as culture fair is the Raven (1948) Standard Progressive Matrices Test, which consists of sixty designs, each with a missing part (see Figure 8.6). The individual taking the test must choose the missing part from several possibilities presented. This test is thought by some psychologists to measure one's logical abilities and powers of discrimination independently of cultural background. This strong claim has been disputed by other psychologists.

Note that all of the arguments about culture-fair tests of intelligence should be carried out with the explicit acknowledgment that by "intelligence" we mean a particular level of performance measured by a particular kind of test. If debates were phrased in terms of whether scores on the 1987 revision of the So-and-So Test reflected nature or nurture, there probably wouldn't be so much controversy.

You should also know that IQ scores and school grades bear at best a moderate relationship to later success in life as measured by income or

Figure 8.6

Item from Raven Standard Progressive Matrices Test. Which lettered block best completes this pattern? Questions like these are believed by some psychologists to be culture-fair measures of one's intelligence.

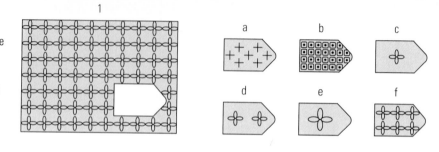

job status (e.g., Jencks et al., 1972; McClelland, 1973). Indeed, it appears that number of years of education is a much more important predictor of subsequent occupational status and achievement than IQ or grade point average. Some of the furor in the nature-nurture debate would fade if it was made clear that "intelligence" as measured by IQ scores indeed predicts grades, but that grades in turn predict very little except who graduates.

Throughout this chapter, intelligence tests have come in for some severe criticism. However, there are benefits to intelligence testing that deserve our explicit acknowledgment. Remember Binet's original purpose. The use of intelligence tests to aid instruction, matching educational approaches to characteristics of particular students, remains a laudable use of such tests. And if an intelligence test identifies a promising student who might otherwise have gone overlooked, this too is laudable. The common thread that runs through the criticisms of intelligence testing bemoans their use to restrict opportunity rather than to enhance it.

Heredity and the Environment in Intelligence

By the 1930s, criticisms of cultural bias in intelligence tests first raised with regard to Army Alpha and Army Beta were taken seriously by most psychologists (Hilgard, 1987). The advocates of a strict "nature" view, which carried with it the implication that some groups were inherently superior to others, called a truce with those who favored a "nurture" interpretation. Matters were calm for several decades, through much of the 1940s and 1950s. Intelligence testing continued, but it ceased being a focus of societal debate. However, this truce was not to hold indefinitely, and in the 1960s a new round of the nature-nurture debate, with all of its social policy implications, raged anew.

The debate began in 1969 with the publication of an article by educational psychologist Arthur Jensen entitled "How Much Can We Boost IQ and Scholastic Achievement?" Social events immediately prior to 1969 help explain the impact of his work. The 1950s and 1960s had seen a number of landmarks in the civil rights movement.

Martin Luther King, Jr., and other leaders of the civil rights movement emphasized the importance of a positive environment in the development of a person's intelligence.

- In 1954, the Supreme Court outlawed segregation in public schools.
- In 1956, Martin Luther King, Jr., started to campaign against segregation in public transportation.
- In 1957, Congress passed the Equal Rights Act.
- In 1963, King led his "March on Washington" and gave his famous "I have a dream" speech.

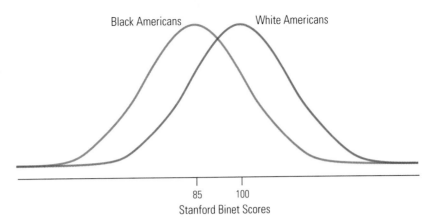

Figure 8.7

Black-White Differences in IQ. On the average, black Americans and white Americans score differently on intelligence tests.

Black Americans   White Americans

85   100
Stanford Binet Scores

- In 1964, Congress strengthened the Equal Rights Act.
- In 1965, President Johnson declared "war on poverty" and funds were made available for the Head Start program, which provided learning experiences for underprivileged children prior to their entering school, in an attempt to give them a head start on school.

These were times of growing hope and promise for blacks and whites alike, and then Jensen's article appeared, with implications to the contrary.

Jensen started with a well-established fact: Black Americans on the average score about 15 IQ points below white Americans. (Figure 8.7 shows what this difference means.) This fact was not itself controversial. What was controversial was Jensen's conclusion that blacks score lower than whites because of biological differences.

Thus, according to Jensen, compensatory education (like Head Start) could do very little to boost IQ and scholastic achievement, because one would have to push against inherent limitations. Although Jensen considered the possibility that this racial difference resulted from environmental factors, namely that blacks tend to have less access to the experiences and educational benefits that lead to good performance on conventional intelligence tests, he disagreed with this explanation and championed the "nature" view.

Other psychologists jumped into the fray and argued with Jensen's conclusions (e.g., Kamin, 1974). What are the views of psychologists today, some twenty years since this controversy began? Let's see what we have learned since then about the roles of heredity and the environment in determining intelligence (as measured by IQ tests) and how this pertains to racial differences.

The Role of Heredity

When we study the role of heredity, we rely on correlational methods (Chapter 1). In fact, Francis Galton invented the notion of correlation (which he called co-relation, meaning "relation with") precisely to quantify the degree to which the genius of fathers corresponded with the genius of their sons.

If, for example, intelligence reflects genetic inheritance, then we would expect that the IQ scores of relatives would show a positive corre-

Twin studies have contributed to psychologists' understanding of the role of heredity in intelligence.

twin studies

procedures for estimating the relative contributions of heredity and the environment to some characteristic; in studying intelligence, the resemblance in IQ's of identical twins is compared with the resemblance in IQ's of fraternal twins

lation with each other. The closer the relation, the higher this positive correlation should be. So, a parent and his or her children have in common 50 percent of their genes. And a grandparent and his or her grandchildren have in common 25 percent of their genes. The results of numerous studies show the pattern expected by hereditarians: the closer the biological relatedness, the higher the correlation between intelligence test scores. On the other hand, these correlations may show that the degree of similarity among people's environments is responsible for the agreement in their IQ scores.

A special case of family studies are **twin studies,** which compare the resemblance in IQs of identical twins (who have in common 100 percent of their genes) and fraternal twins (who are no more similar genetically than ordinary siblings—that is, 50 percent overlap). A further refinement is made when these twins are divided into those raised together (presumably in a similar environment) and those raised apart (presumably in dissimilar environments).

You can probably see what all of this is leading to. A true experiment to determine the relative influence of heredity and the environment is of course impossible, but a researcher can make use of the special characteristics of twins to carry out a study that looks very much like an experiment. The effects of nature and nurture can be separated by looking at the correlations between IQs of identical and fraternal twins, raised together and raised apart. Again, Galton was the first to sketch the logic of such comparisons among twins as a way of unraveling the contributions of heredity and the environment.

Of course, there are some heroic assumptions that must be made in the process. For example, we must assume that identical twins raised together experience the same environment, as do fraternal twins raised together. This cannot be strictly true. Surely the fact that one has an "other" is a unique experience not reflected in this assumption. How does being an identical twin affect the way parents, teachers, and peers treat you? How about the way you view yourself?

We must also assume that twins raised separately are placed randomly in orphanages or foster homes, so that their environments are not similar. Again, this assumption is not strictly true. In locating foster homes, agencies often try to match the background of the biological family. If this is done for both members of a set of twins, then "raised apart" may not really be all that different than "raised together."

Researchers are mindful of these possible confounds, and try their best to control them. The results of many studies converge to suggest that genetic factors contribute to intelligence (Plomin, 1987). In other words, the correlations between intelligence test scores of twins fall in the order we would expect from a hereditarian perspective (see Figure 8.8).

Some qualifications are necessary here. First, twin studies suggest that intelligence is heritable. As explained in Chapter 2, *heritable* is a technical term meaning the degree to which variation in a characteristic (like intelligence) reflects variation in genes. This does not mean that the characteristic itself is inherited as a whole. Rather, it means that a certain proportion of the differences in intelligence within a group of people has a genetic basis. Second, we do not know just what genes are involved in producing this variation in intelligence. Nor do we know the biological manifestation

Figure 8.8

Correlations of IQ scores from Various Family Studies. The closer the biological relatedness, the higher the correlation. Sources: Bouchard & McGue, 1981; Erlenmeyer-Kimling & Jarvik, 1963; Rowe & Plomin, 1981.

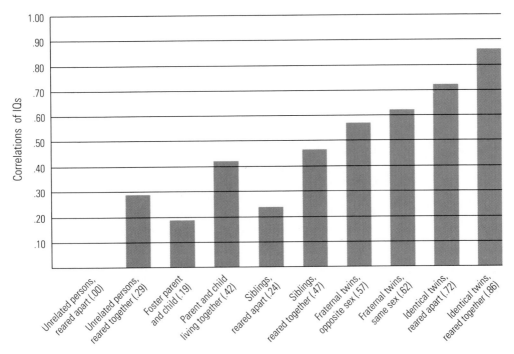

of the genes that produce the variation in intelligence. Third, the heritability estimates are not so high that we can conclude that genetics are all that matter.

The Role of the Environment

If something other than heredity also influences intelligence test scores, then it must be the environment. Other lines of research investigate this possibility, looking at how intelligence changes over the life span, and trying to determine which particular factors bring about these changes.

Prenatal events are important. Injury or illness to the mother while she is pregnant may adversely affect the child's intelligence (Chapter 9). Pregnant mothers should avoid smoking, drinking, physical trauma, poor nutrition, and illnesses like German measles. On the positive side, studies that intervene with pregnant women to improve their medical care and diet show demonstrable improvements in their children's IQs (e.g., Harrell, Woodyard, & Gates, 1956).

Difficulties in the process of birth itself may lower intelligence. A baby deprived of oxygen during birth, or suffering some trauma to the head, may be adversely affected.

Once a child is born, other experiences can raise or lower intelligence (Loehlin, Lindzey, & Spuhler, 1975; Vernon, 1979). Good nutrition and a stimulating environment are vital. There is a correlation between intelligence and socioeconomic status, particularly as children become older,

A stimulating early childhood environment is essential for intellectual development.

suggesting that all of the experiences made available by money and status affect intelligence for the better. Research has also shown that intelligence decreases as the number of children in a family increases, perhaps because parents cannot give as much attention to each child (Zajonc, 1976).

What about Head Start programs? Remember that Jensen criticized them for trying to overcome deficits entrenched in biology. There have been numerous attempts to evaluate the success of compensatory education programs, and the results are complicated and controversial (Hunt, 1982; Zigler & Berman, 1983). Head Start programs are difficult to evaluate because they are conducted in drastically different ways, some more successfully than others. Nevertheless, some early studies showed that IQ was boosted for those preschoolers who participated in Head Start. Later studies suggested that these gains in measured intelligence were not maintained as the children continued in school.

Note, though, that the goal of Head Start programs was *not* to boost IQ scores, but rather to boost academic performance of the participants once they got to school. And the evidence shows that this happened and, further, that these gains were maintained throughout school (Jordan, Grallo, Deutsch, & Deutsch, 1985). Judged on these grounds, Head Start programs were successful.

In evaluating the success or failure of these programs in terms of IQ scores, researchers sometimes betray a curious bias. The appropriate use of IQ scores is to predict academic performance. If it turns out that IQ scores and academic performance don't rise in lockstep for children in Head Start programs, this simply means that the intelligence tests don't work here. But many critics of Head Start programs end up treating the test as more real than the criterion against which it is validated.

Imagine taking a medical test that predicts your risk of heart disease from your cholesterol level. On the whole, there is a positive correlation here, but one that is less than perfect. Suppose the doctor says to you:

> You have a very high cholesterol level. Your heart and circulatory system seem completely healthy, but I'm a believer in the test. I've filled out your death certificate and called the coroner. We'll arrange your burial as soon as you tell me how you plan to pay for it.

This may sound silly, but it is exactly what happens when we treat IQ scores as more real than academic performance.

Labels based on IQ scores have considerable power in our society. Consider, for example, one of the most sobering studies ever conducted—Robert Rosenthal's investigation of teacher expectations about intelligence (Rosenthal & Jacobson, 1968). At the beginning of a school year, Rosenthal received permission from grade school teachers to administer a special IQ test to their students. Unlike typical tests, these new tests would predict someone's IQ in the future. There are no such tests; indeed, you know that there could never be such tests. But the teachers were not so enlightened, and they believed Rosenthal's instructions. Then he instituted a specific intervention. "Don't let this influence you," he said to particular teachers, "But I thought you'd find it of interest that in your classroom, John and Susan scored particularly high on the test. Their intellects will bloom in the coming year."

There was nothing special about John and Susan, except that their teachers expected them to show some sort of intellectual leap in the future. Indeed, John and Susan were chosen at random. Guess what? They leaped. By the end of the year, their grades greatly improved. And their performance on conventional intelligence tests improved as well, sometimes dramatically.

Presumably the teachers treated the Johns and Susans differently, perhaps taking more time with them, perhaps encouraging them, perhaps challenging them to do better. Whatever transpired as a result of the expectation planted by Rosenthal affected the academic performance of these students. And "intelligence" as measured by typical tests was affected as well. Faced with these results, it is hard to maintain that IQ reflects simply a biological inheritance. And there is an insidious implication here as well: If teacher expectations can affect academic performance and intelligence tests for the better, might they not as well be able to affect them for the worse?

To sum up this discussion of the environment and intelligence, we can conclude first that the environment matters (although we already knew this from the less-than-perfect role played by biology). Second, we don't know the exact mechanism that leads from particular experiences to intelligent behavior.

Taken together, research shows that both nature and nurture play a role in determining intelligence. These are not incompatible conclusions. Those who look at nature use correlations, which are concerned with the ordering of scores. Those concerned with nurture use mean scores, which are concerned with absolute levels. Of course we can show the influence of both nature and nurture. Biology is not destiny. As we saw in Chapter 2, genetics provide only a blueprint for development. The environment determines whether this blueprint is actualized or thwarted.

Race and Intelligence

What then can we conclude about racial differences in IQ? Is heredity solely responsible for the documented difference in IQ between blacks and whites? The answer favored here is no. Race is an important category in our society, one of the important ways in which we think about ourselves and others. However, race is properly viewed as a social category, not a biological one.

The term *race* has a particular biological meaning: a subgroup of a species that is geographically separated from other subgroups and hence not interbreeding with them. This has nothing to do with the so-called human races, particularly in the United States. Blacks and whites and other groups all live in the same place, and marriage among these groups obviously takes place. A large number of American "blacks" have rather immediate ancestors of European origin. And many American "whites" have rather immediate ancestors of African origin. It makes no sense to force people into neat categories of black or white—although society does so—and then to compound the awkward fit by saying that these fuzzy categories are really biological ones (but see Rushton, 1988).

Several important lines of research suggest that black-white differences in IQ have little to do with biological differences. One study looked at the IQs of children born to German mothers and American fathers following the United States occupation of Germany after World War II (Eyferth, 1961). There was no difference between the IQs of children with

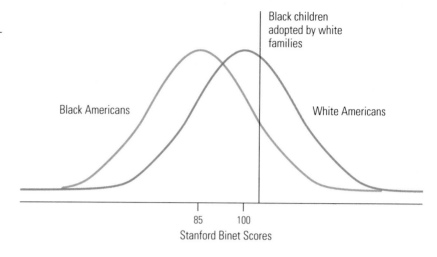

Figure 8.9
Black children adopted by white families had IQs that averaged 106, exceeding the national averages for blacks as well as whites. Source: Scarr & Weinberg, 1976.

white fathers and those with black fathers. Another study looked at the IQs of black children as a function of the relative mix of African and European ancestry (Loehlin, Willerman, & Horn, 1975). Again, no differences were found, meaning that the proportion of European genes bore no relationship to measured intelligence among black children. A third bit of evidence arguing against the interpretation of race differences in IQ as biologically based is Scarr and Weinberg's (1976) study. Their research subjects were black children adopted by white families. These adopted children—raised in a "white" environment—had IQs that averaged 106, exceeding the national average not only for blacks but also for whites (Figure 8.9). Taken together, these results make a strong case against the hereditarian hypothesis.

Ethnic minorities in the United States, particularly blacks, tend to be poor (Jaynes & Williams, 1989). Comparing blacks and whites means comparing groups of people with dramatically different histories and experiences. These differences seem much more important than any to be found in their chromosomes.

Sex and Intelligence

On the average, men and women do not differ in terms of their overall IQ scores. Why? Simply put, when intelligence tests were first developed, particular items that favored men over women, or women over men, were discarded. This strategy is still followed. As a result, the debates over racial differences in IQ have no real counterpart in the realm of sex differences.

However, when researchers have looked at sex differences in terms of specific factors of intelligence, they have found differences. In 1974, Maccoby and Jacklin published an important review of the state of knowledge at that time concerning the similarities and differences between men and women (Chapter 9). Here is what they reported.

- Females have greater verbal ability than males.
- Males excel in visual-spatial ability.
- Males have greater mathematical ability than females.

Recent research shows that many of the differences in male and female intelligence have disappeared over the last twenty years.

These differences correspond to common stereotypes about men and women in society: Women talk and men tinker. Theorists wonder about the reasons for these differences (see Deaux, 1985; Eccles, 1985), and some have proposed that they are neurologically based and make sense in terms of human evolution. Men with spatial and mathematical ability were better able to hunt, and women with verbal abilities were better able to raise children. Other theorists have disagreed, pointing to socialization as the reason for these sex differences. These theorists argue that males and females are encouraged to develop different abilities, and so, on the average, they do. And thus we have another version of the nature-nurture debate.

Something interesting has happened since 1974, when Maccoby and Jacklin published their review. In a 1988 article, Alan Feingold presented data showing that over the past two decades, many of the previously documented sex differences in specific intellectual abilities have disappeared. The only exception is male superiority at the upper end of mathematical ability.

Feingold's data do not explain why most of the differences have vanished, nor why the mathematics difference remains. We can only speculate about the impact of social movements like feminism, the new popularity of women's sports, the availability of different role models for youngsters, or changes in the elementary school curriculum.

It's important to note that some of these differences have disappeared. Consider the implications for psychology's approach to intelligence. First, the differences that have vanished cannot be biologically determined if they vanish in two decades. That's not how evolution works. Second, perhaps evidence bearing on other nature-nurture debates might be forthcoming if we continue to study changes in psychological characteristics over time. Third, Feingold's research suggests that psychology is indeed becoming a mature science, one in which knowledge accumulates and allows psychologists today to draw conclusions they could not draw just a generation ago. Might the future bring new information regarding racial differences? Stay tuned.

Extremes of Intelligence

In this section, we'll consider some of the extremes of intelligent behavior, from the mentally retarded on the one hand to prodigies, geniuses, and the highly creative on the other. We do not completely leave intelligence tests and IQ scores behind us, because they may enter into the definition of these extremes. However, what we know about these individuals necessarily goes beyond their test scores, because there is more to intelligence than IQ.

Mentally Retarded Individuals

mental retardation
below average intellectual functioning existing along with deficits in adaptive behavior and showing itself before age eighteen

According to the definition proposed by the American Association on Mental Retardation (Grossman, 1977), **mental retardation** is "significantly subaverage general intellectual functioning existing concurrently with deficits in adaptive behavior, and manifested during the developmental period" (i.e., before age eighteen). Earlier definitions of mental

Table 8.4

Levels and Characteristics of Mental Retardation

Level	Percent of Retarded Individuals	IQ Score	Characterization
Mild	75.0	55–69	Can develop social and communication skills; can do sixth grade work without special help; can perform semiskilled jobs
Moderate	20.0	40–54	Can talk; have difficulty learning social conventions; can do second grade work; can work in protected settings
Severe	3.5	25–39	Have difficulty learning to speak; show poor motor development
Profound	1.5	< 25	Unable to learn any but simple motor tasks; severe physical problems common; require custodial care

retardation relied solely on IQ scores, and cutoffs based on IQ are still used to distinguish degrees of retardation, from mild to moderate to severe to profound (see Table 8.4). Added to the modern definition is the inability to meet the demands of everyday life: achieving personal independence and social responsibility.

Mental retardation encompasses a wide variety of difficulties, both physical and mental.

> Retarded individuals vary widely in intellectual ability, from the profoundly retarded who may possess no speech and no testable IQ, and who must live vegetative lives under continual medical supervision, to the mildly retarded, many of whom appear to have perfectly normal intellectual ability until confronted by tasks of mathematics or reading. Some retarded individuals also have disabling physical handicaps, but many have none. Some have severe emotional problems, but others are remarkably well adjusted. Some will require protective care throughout their lives, but others will learn to live independently as adults. (Edgerton, 1979, pp. 2–3)

Nevertheless, we can make some generalizations. In the United States, about three out of one hundred children are retarded. Of these, about two out of every three are boys. Finally, pathological physical conditions or environmental influences can cause mental retardation.

Clinical Retardation. When mental retardation can be traced to specific illness, injury, or physiological dysfunction, it is called **clinical retardation.** Different factors may be responsible, including the following:

- infections of a mother while carrying her baby (like rubella)
- infections of the young child (like meningitis, mumps, or chicken pox)

clinical retardation

mental retardation caused by a specific illness, injury, or physiological dysfunction

Given the proper level of environmental stimulation and education, persons with Down's syndrome can lead rewarding lives.

- intoxication or poisoning (due to lead, alcohol, or other harmful substances)
- trauma to the head
- anoxia (lack of oxygen)
- malnutrition (of the pregnant mother or the young child)
- metabolic disorders (like Tay-Sachs disease or phenylketonuria)
- gross brain disease
- premature birth
- cranial malformation

Genetic anomalies can also produce clinical retardation. Here the best-known example is **Down's syndrome,** which stems from an extra chromosome. Approximately 25 percent of the clinically retarded have Down's syndrome, which is usually recognizable at birth. Characteristic signs include poor muscle tone, a small head, a small nose, slanting eyes, small ears, a protruding and fissured tongue, a short neck, small hands with short fingers, dry skin, and sparse, fine hair (Edgerton, 1979).

Most children with Down's syndrome have IQs that place them in the severely to moderately retarded range. However, those with Down's syndrome show considerable variation. Most have difficulty using language in complex and abstract ways. As adults, few live completely independently, but many carry on well with some supervision from a parent, friend, or other caregiver. Children raised in institutions tend to be less competent than those raised by their parents, presumably because parents provide a more stimulating environment. This in turn triggers the child's intellectual and social growth.

Down's syndrome cannot be "cured" in the sense of making it go away. However, with the appropriate education and experiences, individuals with Down's syndrome can successfully live outside institutions, hold jobs, and maintain social relationships. Again, no less so for the genetically abnormal than for the genetically normal, both nature and nurture are important in determining how a person turns out.

Down's syndrome
a common form of clinical retardation caused by an extra chromosome

sociocultural retardation
mental retardation not linked to specific physical causes but instead to social disadvantages

Sociocultural Retardation.   When mental retardation cannot be linked to specific physical causes, it is instead attributed to social disadvantages and is thus called **sociocultural retardation.** Children so labeled tend to come from social groups that are educationally and economically below average. Many come from broken homes. About 75 percent of the retarded are socioculturally retarded, and not surprisingly, poor children are ten times more likely to be represented than those from the population at large.

In all likelihood, a number of factors contribute to sociocultural retardation (Edgerton, 1979). Even if demonstrable physical injury does not take place, lead poisoning, poor nutrition, or lingering childhood disease (all more likely among the lower class) can chip away at a child's intellectual ability. An environment that provides no intellectual stimulation, such as that offered by books, can also negatively affect intelligence.

One of the striking facts concerning sociocultural retardation is that psychologists know very little about what happens to individuals given this label once they leave school. Most of these people are never again identified as retarded. Following school, they presumably get along perfectly well.

Edgerton (1979) uses the expression "six-hour retardation" to describe children with low IQs whose only difficulty in adaptation shows up in school. "Since the great majority of socioculturally retarded children are from poor and culturally different backgrounds, the possibility remains that . . . in reality they are simply unprepared—in terms of language, culture, or motivation—to cope effectively with the academic demands that schools place on them" (Edgerton, 1979, p. 73). Here we see an irony in the definition of mental retardation. Although we have seen attempts to broaden the definition beyond IQ scores to include failure at the demands of life, the fact remains that for school-age children, the most significant demands placed on them are by school. We already know that a low IQ foreshadows poor school performance, so the broadened definition ends up telling us what we already know by considering only IQ scores: that these children do not do well in school.

It's distressing to note that children referred to special classes for the mentally retarded are disproportionately ethnic minorities. Even when their tested IQs are the same, the minority child is more likely to be regarded as retarded than the majority child (Mercer, 1973). When white children have problems in school, they are considered to have a learning disability; analogous black children may be seen as retarded (Franks, 1971). Needless to say, learning disability and mental retardation are different. A learning disability entails a *particular* problem with reading or writing or speaking, whereas mental retardation is a *general* difficulty. These should be recognized correctly regardless of race.

There is a difference of opinion as to how retarded children are best served in school. One point of view, which harks all the way back to Binet, is that the mentally retarded should be separated from normal children and given special education tailored to their needs. The other point of view holds that the retarded should be educated with normal children, in a practice called mainstreaming. Mainstreaming is required by the law, if possible, but the issue is not resolved. Obviously, definitive research would be difficult. In comparing special education classes with mainstreaming, we end up comparing not simply alternative ways of educating our children, but possible confounds like social class or stigma or level of school funding.

Prodigies

A **prodigy** is a child who shows a special skill or talent advanced far beyond what is considered normal for his or her age. There are many well-documented cases of such children (Barlow, 1952):

- Zerah Colburn (b. 1804)—At age six, Colburn gave public exhibitions in which he calculated the products of three-digit numbers as rapidly as problems were posed to him.
- Jean Louis Cardiac (b. 1719)—When three months old, he could recite the alphabet; at age three he could read Latin; at age six, he could read French, English, Greek, and Hebrew.
- Christian Friedrich Heinecken (b. 1721)—At age two, Heinecken was well acquainted with the major events described in the Bible.
- John Stuart Mill (b. 1806)—By age three he knew Greek, and by age ten, he had studied all of Plato.
- Wolfgang Amadeus Mozart (b. 1756)—An accomplished composer and performer by age six, Mozart embarked at that age on a European tour that lasted several years.

prodigy

a child who shows a special skill or talent far advanced of those considered normal for his or her age

Mozart, here portrayed with his father and sister, was one of the most celebrated prodigies of all time.

Because of the extreme interest generated by such early displays of talents, popular newspapers and magazines regularly feature stories on prodigies in such domains as music, chess, mathematics, and language.

Prodigies by definition are so rare that psychologists know much less about them than we would like to. One developmental psychologist who has extensively studied them is David Feldman (1980). He is attracted to prodigies because they seem at odds with one of the principles of developmental psychology that you will encounter in Chapter 9: Psychological development proceeds in an orderly sequence. Put less elegantly, you have to crawl before you walk, and you have to walk before you run. Prodigies apparently challenge this truism, in effect running from the very start.

Feldman's investigations of six prodigies—two chess players, one violinist, a natural scientist, a writer, and a child not yet three years of age who could read adult-level books—suggest that prodigies are not the freaks they at first seem. One of Feldman's conclusions is that prodigies only appear in some fields of endeavor. Musical or mathematical or athletic prodigies are relatively common. Feldman calls these fields universal ones, because they tap perceptual and physiologically based abilities inherent in the human species. In other fields, prodigies do not exist. There are no reports of prodigious achievement within the social sciences, for instance. Feldman calls these fields cultural ones, because achievement within them less directly reflects inherent skills.

Another conclusion is that prodigious achievements are not spontaneous. They don't appear from nowhere, but rather develop through stages. The individual may go through these stages much more quickly than others, but nevertheless starts from the beginning. For example, Bobby Fisher, the former world champion of chess, could beat strong players when he was six years old, but not until he was a teenager could he compete with Grand Masters.

Feldman found that prodigies do not achieve their advanced levels without extensive instruction, usually of a formal nature. Without guidance through the stages involved in mastering a skill, their expert achievement does not occur. To use another chess example: 50 percent of the top players under age thirteen in the United States come from New York or California, simply because these are the only areas where instruction in chess is readily available.

Also, aside from their particular skill, prodigies are otherwise normal children. Feldman administered to his subjects the sorts of tests that developmental psychologists use to gauge physical and cognitive development, and the children invariably fell within the normal ranges. Perhaps our stereotype of a child prodigy is that of a miniature adult, but there is no evidence for this.

Finally, prodigies may or may not grow up to make noted contributions within their fields as adults. Feldman's own subjects have not yet matured, but history shows that some prodigies make it and some do not. In the list with which this section started, you may recognize the names of Mozart and Mill, who were hailed as geniuses when adults. It is much more common, however, for a child prodigy to fail to excel as an adult.

Concerning this final point, Feldman offers an interesting explanation as to why some prodigies become accomplished adults whereas others do not. He regards early prodigious achievement as a "coincidence"—a coming together of a specialized individual and a specialized environment. We

Like prodigies in other fields, chess prodigies must undergo rigorous training to achieve their extraordinary levels of skill.

are tempted to look solely within the child for a clue to his or her skill, but the environment is just as important. "Early prodigious achievement is a joint effort among dedicated individuals, of whom the prodigy is but one participant" (Feldman, 1980, p. 148). Parents are important; instructors are important; someone to pick up the bill is important, too. So, a continuing combination of individual promise and nurturance is crucial in determining whether a prodigy grows up to be a successful adult.

The advent of intelligence tests made possible another type of prodigy: a child with an extremely high IQ. Note that the "accomplishment" of the high IQ child is simply his or her performance on an intelligence test, not a remarkable feat in music or mathematics or language. However, granted the significance placed on IQ, there is considerable interest in these children.

Lewis Terman (1925) conducted one of the most extensive studies of children with high IQs. In the early 1920s, he located some 1500 children in the state of California with high scores on the Stanford-Binet (135 or above). These children were thoroughly studied over the years. Indeed, the research project is still going on at Stanford University. The original child subjects were followed through their teenage years, their early adulthood, and now their late adulthood.

When Terman began his research, the prevailing belief was that gifted children were tainted, both physically and emotionally. They were thought to be uncoordinated, sickly, and poorly adjusted. It was also thought that they did not measure up to their potential as adults. "Early bloom, early rot" summed up this belief. Those who show early signs of great intelligence presumably have nothing good in front of them. What Terman and his fellow researchers found challenged this dire prediction.

Terman showed that children with high IQs were *not* spindly neurotics. Instead, on the average, they exceeded their normal classmates in physical prowess, health, social adjustment, and emotional stability. A similar study by Leta Hollingworth (1942), which focused on children with Stanford-Binet IQ scores in excess of 180, yielded the same conclusions. Children with high IQs are for the most part physically and emotionally superior to their less gifted counterparts.

There is one exception in this research, though, in the substantial minority of these children who had difficulty adjusting to school. The practice in the early part of this century was to place a student in the grade where he or she could do the work. High IQ children tended to be placed several years ahead of where they would ordinarily find themselves. They thus were the youngest and smallest in their classes. Remember that prodigies, except for their particular skill, are otherwise children. You can see the potential problems for these children who were placed beyond their years—thrown in with adolescents. (It's tough enough for an adolescent to get along with other adolescents!) Interestingly, school systems today are much more reluctant to allow children to skip grades, precisely because of the problems associated with being a child among teenagers.

One more note about Terman's study before we move on. What happened to those children with high IQs? On the whole, his subjects grew up to be successful adults, as shown by various occupational and educational attainments. However, they were not uniformly the best and brightest members of their generation. High IQ does not guarantee subsequent success.

Geniuses

Psychologists are also quite interested in adults who are geniuses. This term is often used to describe individuals with high IQs, but we can define a **genius** as someone whose accomplishments exert a profound influence on contemporary and subsequent generations (Simonton, 1984). Researchers try to determine the factors that contribute to these profound accomplishments. What are the possible causes of genius?

One of the first studies of genius was conducted by Catherine Cox (1926), an associate of Terman. Cox began with a sample of 300 eminent historical figures and then worked backward through biographical material to find evidence for their intellectual precociousness. From this evidence, she could calculate IQ. One of her subjects was John Stuart Mill, whose early accomplishments we previously noted. She determined at what age he could read Greek, understand Plato, and master calculus and at what age the average person could do these things. Dividing the latter (mental age) by the former (chronological age) yields Mill's intelligence quotient—about 190. See Table 8.5 for some other examples.

Cox also arranged her sample from more to less eminent (although of course all the people were eminent), and reported that her intelligence

Table 8.5
Cox's Geniuses (1926)

Individual	Precocious Behavior	Estimated IQ
Jean Jacques Rousseau	"At age 6 the boy was so carried away by his reading that he shed tears in sympathy with the misfortunes of his romantic heroes."	130
Johann Kepler	"In the elementary schools the teachers praised Kepler for his fortunate gifts . . . [including] remarkable proficiency in the use of Latin."	140
René Descartes	"Before he was 8 years old, René was called by his father 'the little philosopher' because of his questions about reasons and causes."	150
William Pitt	"At age 7 he was writing letters to his father . . . even at this early age he had political aspirations."	160
Samuel Taylor Coleridge	"Coleridge talked for the first time before he was 2 years old, saying 'Nasty Doctor Young!' while his hand was being dressed for a burn. . . . [A]t 3 he could read a chapter in the Bible."	175

estimates positively correlated with rankings of eminence. This conclusion has been challenged because she did not take into account possible confounds (like reliability of the historical material) which might affect both ratings of intelligence and ratings of eminence. Nevertheless, her study shows how one might use historical material to investigate genius.

Dean Simonton (1984) is a contemporary psychologist who has followed this example in a methodologically sophisticated way, specifying ways of coding variables of interest from historical material—always on the alert for possible confounds. He has studied several samples of historically eminent individuals: political leaders, writers, artists, generals, composers, even famous psychologists. What does he conclude? Genius does not have a single determinant but rather reflects a complex of psychological, social, and historical factors. Being the first-born in a family is positively correlated with later attainment, as is intelligence, intellectual complexity, and a disposition toward dominance and extraversion. Also important is formal instruction and the presence of a role model. Finally, one must be in the right place at the right time for one's accomplishments to have an impact.

Creative Individuals

There is a theme running through the discussion of the extremes of intelligence. Those classified as retarded, prodigies, and geniuses are not simply types of people. They are people in particular situations where their intelligence or lack thereof shows itself. In speaking about the extremes, as well as when speaking about intelligence per se, we must ask ourselves "intelligent for what purpose?" If intelligence shows in behavior that is adaptive and purposeful, we must locate it in a context.

creativity
the capacity to act in adaptive, purposive, and novel ways

The same is true for a cousin of intelligence—creativity. Most psychologists distinguish creativity from intelligence, holding that **creativity** characterizes behavior that is adaptive and purposeful (i.e., intelligent) as well as novel. Creativity represents not only an appropriate solution to some problem of life, but a new one as well.

divergent thinking
the ability to think along many alternative paths

The story of psychology's approach to creativity is much the same as the story of its efforts to study intelligence. Many theorists and researchers regard creativity as a general characteristic that people possess to varying degrees. A common explanation of creativity proposes that it involves a cognitive style called **divergent thinking,** the ability to think along many alternative paths. Attempts to measure creativity embody this definition, and are exemplified by the so-called Unusual Uses Test, in which you are asked to think of all the things you can do with an ice cube and a screwdriver (or any such objects). The more uses you can think of in a given period of time, and the more unusual, the more creative you are said to be.

The trouble with such tests is that they do not relate to actual creative productivity (e.g., Wallach, 1985). The problem is not with the tests as much as with the conception that creativity is a characteristic of a person, as opposed to a product of that person. In forgetting this, psychologists take creative behavior out of its context.

Indeed, Robert Weisberg (1986) pursues this analysis a step further and has written extensively on what he calls the myths of creativity. His

Psychologists have not yet been able to determine the precise nature of the special intellectual abilities that creative individuals possess.

approach is a refreshing one. Here are some of the "myths" that Weisberg attacks, despite their acceptance by many psychologists and the general public:

- Creativity reflects the unconscious incubation of ideas.
- Creativity involves sudden leaps ("aha" experiences).
- Creativity results from special types of thinking.
- Creative individuals possess psychological characteristics that set them apart from other people.

Weisberg prefers what he calls an incremental approach to creativity. The person who does something creative is not different in kind from those who do not, but simply different in degree. Creative works, whether scientific, literary, or artistic, reflect a gradual process. Training is important, practice is important, and the help of other people is important.

Are creative individuals exactly like everyone else? There are skills that perhaps are necessary for someone to be creative, like a degree of intelligence (Anastasi, 1971), the ability to concentrate, and the ability to be productive. But these are not sufficient to explain creativity. And the skills that make for a creative artist are not the same as those that make for a creative scientist.

In an often-cited study, MacKinnon (1962) investigated the personality characteristics of the most highly creative architects in the United States, as judged by a panel of experts. When compared to a randomly chosen sample of architects, matched only by age, the creative architects differed in numerous ways. They were open to experience, unconventional, spontaneous, and flexible. (These results are usually the ones reported in textbooks.) However, MacKinnon also included a second comparison group that is more informative, one composed of architects who worked side by side with those judged creative. They shared many things in common with the creative group, except that they had not been judged creative. MacKinnon found that there were essentially no personality differences between these two groups. In short, there are no special traits uniquely associated with creative accomplishment in architecture.

Where does this leave us? Weisberg suggests that our judgments of creativity are best left to posterity. If we are to understand creativity, we should recognize that it exists in the eye of the beholder. Perhaps psychologists who study creativity should look less at the person who produces creative work and more at the people who will later be impressed by what he or she did. To repeat the theme of this chapter, the extremes of intelligence, like intelligence itself, must be examined within their larger social and historical context.

Savants

savants
individuals with a singular skill or ability in the context of general subnormality

Savants (once called idiot savants—i.e., learned fools) are individuals who, despite mediocre or even deficient skills in most domains, possess one extraordinarily developed ability (Treffert, 1989). They challenge psychologists to think more creatively about intelligence, because both extremes are contained in the same person.

Savants are found in various domains, usually the same as those in which prodigies exist (Gardner, 1976, 1983): music, art, and mathematics.

One common type can perform lightning calculations. These individuals can rapidly add up long lists of numbers, tell the day of the week on which any date in history happened to fall, and perform other similar feats (Smith, 1983). For example, in the 1960s, a set of identical twins came to the attention of the world because of their uncanny ability to tell on what day of the week various dates fell. Although they had IQs that placed them in the retarded range, their calculating abilities were phenomenal. One twin in particular was accurate with any date between 4,100 B.C. and A.D. 40,400 (Horwitz, Kestenbaum, Person, & Jarvik, 1965).

Or consider Nadia, a young girl who suffered from autism, a profound psychological disturbance (Chapter 5). She had an incredible talent for drawing (Selfe, 1977). Her sketches are remarkable for their skill and accuracy (see Figure 8.10). At the same time, Nadia was greatly impaired in what we would consider general intelligence. Her behavior was often counterproductive. Indeed, sometimes she drew right off the edge of a paper without noticing.

And then there is the memory expert that Luria (1987) described. This individual, S., literally could not forget anything. He made his living on stage, displaying his abilities. In the 1920s, S. came to the attention of Luria, who would give him long lists of words, numbers, or mathematical formulas to remember. S. could always remember, even when retested decades later.

The abilities of these savants and others are usually difficult if not impossible for us to explain (Gardner, 1983). Typically, they have not been

Figure 8.10

Drawing by Nadia. Although suffering from autism, this young girl could make highly skilled drawings like this one (done when she was five years old).

given formal instruction in their skill, although they do practice extensively. What else is responsible? In the case of S., he perceived the world differently from the rest of us, showing a phenomenon known as *synesthesia:* the tendency of one type of sensory impression to call up other types (Marks, 1975). To S., a word not only had a sound, but a taste, a feel, and a smell, as well. When he remembered words, he remembered all the sensory impressions associated with them.

Luria likened S.'s memory not to a cognitive process, but to a perceptual one. One of the strategies S. used in remembering a list of words involved taking a mental walk and placing the items to be remembered along a familiar street. When called upon to remember, he would simply walk down the street again and see (and smell and hear) what was stored. His infrequent mistakes were due not to forgetting, but to placing things where he overlooked them: "Oops, the streetlight was dim."

This is just not the way that most of us think (Chapter 7). Perhaps we should be grateful. S. also suffered because of the imagery that made his memory possible. He could not readily grasp abstractions, as in a poem, because he was so overwhelmed by his particular associations to the individual words. He readily confused inner and outer reality. Before he did something, he would imagine how it would be, and if his imaginary scene departed from reality, he became perplexed. For instance, he described going to court to press a minor case. He had rehearsed the case in his mind, but upon arriving in court, he found that the judge didn't look exactly as he had imagined. S. became so disoriented that he lost the case.

In sum, savants are interesting to psychologists because of what they imply about intelligence in general. One important implication is that intelligence is plural, not a unitary characteristic that allows us to place all people along the same line according to "how much" of it they possess. Modern society likes to rank everything and everybody. Witness the Top 40 countdown of records, Emmy Awards, Golden Globes, Pulitzer Prizes, grade point averages, batting averages, the *Fortune* 500 list, and Miss America contests. Some of these rankings are fun, and some are valid. However, ranking people by intelligence is neither.

Is Intelligence Unitary or Plural?

Binet's approach did not address one important issue in defining and measuring intelligence. Because he was originally asked to make an either-or decision (can the child learn in school or not), it was enough to conceive intelligence as a single entity or capacity. But other researchers have taken a look at the issue in its own right, and there is a variety of opinions regarding whether intelligence is one thing, several, or many.

Intelligence as Unitary

One point of view holds that intelligence is a general characteristic widely exhibited across different domains. Francis Galton championed this idea, as we already saw, and so did Charles Spearman (1863–1945), another early investigator of intelligence. Spearman was struck by the finding that when a group of people were given a set of disparate tests measuring abilities and aptitudes (e.g., tests of classics, mathematics, or French), all

general intelligence (g)
Spearman's term for whatever underlies the tendency of different intelligence tests to correlate with each other

specific intelligences (s)
Spearman's term for factors that influence performance on particular intelligence tests but not others

their test scores tended to correlate with each other. In other words, people who scored high on one test tended to score high on others, and people who scored low on one scored low on the others as well.

From findings like these, Spearman (1904) argued for the existence of what he called **general intelligence,** which is abbreviated as **g.** For Spearman, g is whatever underlies the fact that tests tend to correlate with each other; g is the factor common to all cases of intelligent performance.

However, different tests do not show perfect consistency. Spearman therefore concluded that besides g there are also **specific intelligences** that influence one's performance on particular tests. A specific intelligence is abbreviated as **s.** So people's performance on any given test reflects a combination of their general intelligence and their specific intelligence for whatever that test measures.

Spearman argued that if two different tests correlated, it was because they both reflected g. By definition, they could not reflect the same s. But this is not the only way to handle these data, and indeed, many disagree with Spearman. Two tests may correlate not only because they both reflect g, but also because they reflect the same s. It is a matter of judgment whether tests of French on the one hand and classics on the other do or do not reflect anything in common except general intelligence. Spearman's tests were not an infinite sampling of domains in which people performed—there is no way that they could be—so we should not be surprised that he was unable to convince everyone that intelligence was unitary.

Intelligence as Plural

What are the alternative views? To use Spearman's lingo, other psychologists prefer to emphasize s over g, suggesting that intelligence is composed of a set of abilities and capacities largely independent of each other. For instance, in 1938, L. L. Thurstone (1887–1955) suggested that intelligence was composed of a variety of distinct abilities (see Table 8.6).

Table 8.6
Thurstone's Abilities

Ability	Definition
Numerical	Ability to perform arithmetic operations
Word fluency	Ability to think of words rapidly
Verbal comprehension	Ability to define words
Spatial	Ability to recognize objects rotated in space
Memory	Ability to recall information
Inductive reasoning	Ability to derive general principles
Perceptual speed	Ability to rapidly compare visual patterns

(Adapted from Thurstone, L. L., & Thurstone, T. C., 1941. Factorial studies of intelligence. *Psychometric Monographs*, No. 2.)

crystallized intelligence
skills or knowledge developed
through education or practice

fluid intelligence
the ability to adapt to new situations

In addition, Raymond B. Cattell (no relation to James McKeen Cattell, whom we met earlier in this chapter) has made a distinction between two different types of intelligence. **Crystallized intelligence** refers to skills or knowledge that have been formed through education or practice, whereas **fluid intelligence** means the ability to adapt to new situations (Cattell, 1971; Horn, 1968). Cattell believes that crystallized intelligence reflects life experience and that fluid intelligence reflects inherent ability. This is a clever distinction; it allows him to argue that intelligence reflects either nature or nurture, depending on the aspect you look at.

A particularly influential example of intelligence as plural comes from David Wechsler (1974), who gave us the already described Wechsler intelligence scales. Remember that these tests yield separate scores for verbal intelligence and performance intelligence, which are, according to Wechsler, two distinct ways of acting adaptively and purposefully. And in the most recent revision of the Stanford-Binet test, we see explicit recognition that intelligence can be described in terms of different components (Thorndike, Hagan, & Sattler, 1986).

Yet another influential view of intelligence as plural was proposed by J. P. Guilford (1967), who argues that the number of discrete abilities and skills typically subsumed under "intelligence" may well exceed one hundred. His scheme is more than just a list of different abilities. He explains these abilities in information-processing terms. Each ability can be described as a mental operation performed on some informational input and resulting in some behavioral output:

information → mental operation → behavior

Guilford distinguishes among types of content (e.g., symbols or words), types of mental operations that can be applied to these contents (e.g., cognition, memory, or evaluation), and types of products resulting from these mental operations (e.g., transforming one product into another or drawing implications). The possible combinations multiply into a large number of discrete abilities.

How has the conception of intelligence as plural fared? Though many psychologists endorse the view that intelligence is plural, there is still debate over the exact issues raised by Galton a century ago (Modgil & Modgil, 1987). Intelligence as unitary is alive and well. Intelligence as a characteristic that transcends our background and leaps from our genes onto tests is alive and well. Even when intelligence tests yield several scores, we often lump them together into an overall score.

Remember the story that opened this chapter? As you know, the SAT that Alex took yields two scores, one for verbal ability and one for mathematical ability. But is it sensible to add these together, particularly in deciding if someone should be allowed to play basketball?

Perhaps one answer to all these issues and controversies is to start over again, putting tests aside and looking to intelligent behavior: actions that show adaptiveness and purposiveness. Indeed, the biggest problem with the conception of intelligence as plural has been the failure of investigators to develop useful measures of the supposedly separate factors. They may be stumbling over the earlier debate between g and s, and just how different two skills really need to be before they can be measured or predicted independently of one another.

At any rate, two of the most important contemporary investigators of intelligence apparently agree that it is necessary to look at behavior first, and then at tests. Their approaches to intelligent behavior will be discussed in the remainder of the chapter. Note that both regard intelligence as plural, and that both explicitly locate intelligence in the context where it is displayed.

Robert Sternberg's Triarchic Theory

One influential approach to intelligent behavior is that of Yale psychologist Robert Sternberg (1985, 1986), who argues that intelligence is best approached simultaneously from three different directions. He therefore calls his approach a **triarchic theory** ("ruled by three"), and presents his ideas in terms of three separate subtheories.

Subtheory One concerns itself with contextual intelligence. If intelligence is defined as adaptive and purposive, this definition must be specified relative to a particular environment. What is intelligent in one setting may be irrelevant in a second setting or even stupid in a third.

> The intelligence of an African pygmy could not legitimately be assessed by placing the pygmy into a North American culture and using North American tests, unless it were relevant to test the pygmy for survival in a North America culture. . . . Similarly, a North American's intelligence could not be assessed in terms of his or her adaptation to a pygmy society unless adaptation to that society were relevant or potentially relevant to the person's life. (Sternberg, 1985, pp. 47–48)

This subtheory is very much a relativistic one, because it holds that intelligent behavior necessarily changes across time and place and culture. Sternberg offers the intriguing observation that the advent of pocket calculators may well make "arithmetic ability"—considered so important by Binet, Thurstone, and others—irrelevant in the modern world.

Adaptation can take place in various ways. The person may try to achieve a good fit between herself and a particular environment. Or if this proves to be difficult or undesirable, she may modify the environment to make the fit possible. Or she may choose an alternative environment where she can satisfactorily adapt.

Consider someone who has rented an apartment, sight unseen, and has just moved into it. Adaptation consists of finding a place for everything, and putting everything in its place. Some people can readily do this. Other people might change the apartment—talk the landlord into knocking down a wall, let us say. Still others would see that the apartment across the hall, which is vacant, is a better place to live and arrange to move into that one. All of these people are intelligent, but notice that intelligence means something quite different from case to case.

Subtheory Two in Sternberg's approach focuses on experiential intelligence: Just what are the tasks that most readily show someone's intelligence? Sternberg suggests that two characteristics of tasks are important: They have to be somewhat novel, and they must lend themselves to becoming automatized. Both are involved in what is meant by adaptation—encountering some new demand in the environment (novelty) and learning to deal ever more efficiently with it (automatization). For many Americans, the task of driving a car through rush hour traffic in a strange

triarchic theory

Sternberg's theory of intelligence that stresses (a) the context of intelligent behavior, (b) the tasks that most readily show intelligence, and (c) the cognitive operations that lead to intelligent behavior

The intelligence of these African pygmys should be assessed only in terms of their success in adapting to their environment, according to Sternberg's triarchic theory.

city would be a reasonable way to assess intelligence. Note that encountering a novel demand and then automatizing one's response to it correspond to what Cattell means by fluid and crystallized intelligence, respectively.

This particular subtheory has several important implications. First, it tells the psychologist to measure intelligence by finding tasks relevant to a person's life that are somewhat novel and can become automatized. This avoids the circular definition that intelligence is whatever intelligence tests measure. Second, a variety of tasks may be used to measure intelligence. Third, someone may do well on a given task because he possesses skill at confronting novelty, skill at automatizing, or both. Finally, at different stages in performing a task, his skills may come into play in various ways.

Subtheory Three concerns itself with componential intelligence, the actual cognitive operations that underlie intelligent behavior. Componential intelligence involves analytic skills, being able to break down a task into its components. How does a person go about deciding which problems need to be solved? What strategy does she use once she chooses a problem? How does she judge potential solutions? How does she use external feedback? These mental steps can be given an ever more precise description, thereby wedding intelligent behavior to underlying information processing (Chapter 7).

Sternberg's emphasis on the components of intelligence is a notable improvement over previous approaches to intelligence because it leads him to focus on the underlying process that produces intelligent behavior. Contrast this with the traditional approaches to intelligence. In their concern with tests and performance, they never ask precisely what leads someone to act in an intelligent or unintelligent fashion. Sternberg grapples with this question by studying the ways that people go about solving problems.

Suppose you are given an analogy to solve: "Lawyer is to client as doctor is to _____." A typical approach to intelligence might be to simply look at your answer, score it right or wrong, and move on. But Sternberg studies the process that leads up to your answer. First you have to understand the task that has been posed. Then you solve the problem. Sternberg (1985) finds, for example, that when you take your time with the first step, you end up doing well with the second step.

What emerges from Sternberg's work and that of others who opt for a close look at the processes underlying intelligent behavior (e.g., Hunt, 1983; Vernon, 1983) is the conclusion that people can be intelligent in different ways. Different routes lead to intelligent action. Consider the different ways in which someone can excel.

With contextual intelligence, we select and shape real-world environments that are relevant to our lives. We colloquially call this being street smart. Sternberg (1986) cites an example of a retarded man who could not tell time, but didn't want to tell anyone that he could not. He solved his problem by wearing a watch that did not work. Then he could stop people and ask them what time it was.

With experiential intelligence, we adapt ourselves to novel situations. Can we meet demands? Can we add suggested solutions to our own repertoire? This is creativity.

Finally, with componential intelligence, we process standardized information. This is what traditional intelligence tests measure, and this type of intelligence is responsible for the acquisition of vocabulary, facts, and other such information. Sternberg thus does not dismiss the traditional intelligence testing as much as he suggests that it be supplemented with measures of other forms of intelligence. Most importantly, we should remember that intelligence is plural.

Howard Gardner's Theory of Multiple Intelligences

Harvard psychologist Howard Gardner (1983) has proposed another contemporary approach to intelligence. Like Sternberg, he opts for a pluralistic view of intelligence, and proceeds by looking at actual behavior and how it proves useful to people in their worlds. Here are the types of intelligence he distinguishes:

- linguistic—sensitivity to the meanings and functions of language
- logical-mathematical—competence at organizing ideas in abstract ways
- spatial—capacity for visual or spatial imagery, including the ability to transform images
- musical—ability to produce and organize sounds according to prescribed pitch and rhythm
- bodily-kinesthetic—mastery over body movements
- personal—ability to access one's own feelings and those of others

The first three types of intelligence are those measured with traditional tests, but Gardner feels that the other three types are just as important, despite their neglect by psychologists interested in intelligence.

To Gardner, intelligence is a set of problem-solving skills that allow the individual to resolve difficulties that he or she encounters. These skills are presumably biologically based and independent of each other. A person can be high or low in one type of intelligence yet low or high in another type.

How did Gardner go about identifying these six types of intelligence from the many possible candidates? He employed several criteria, including whether or not a particular set of skills is selectively isolated by brain damage. If damage to nervous tissue selectively attacks—or spares—a given competence, then one can argue that it has a biological basis (Chapter 2). Gardner also looked for a distinctive developmental history for a set of skills, an associated set of symbols that people use in exercising these particular skills, and the existence of prodigies who excel at them. When all these criteria point to the same discrete ability, Gardner labels it a basic intelligence.

Gardner's theoretical approach is exciting. It starts with a conception of intelligence, and specifies how one will know intelligence when one stumbles across it in the real world. Only when the criteria are met does Gardner suggest that a type of intelligence is present. Contrast this with the traditional approaches described earlier in the chapter, where intelligence tests preceded conceptions of intelligence, and subsequent work debated just what is meant by intelligence.

multiple intelligences
Gardner's idea that intelligence should be described as several sets of biologically based problem-solving skills

On the downside, Gardner's approach is speculative, something he readily admits. Indeed, he calls his approach the "idea" of **multiple intelligences,** so his readers will appreciate that he proposes a possibility and not an established fact. One might quarrel with his reliance on biology, but at least he makes his starting point clear.

Of course, psychologists need to devise measures of these intelligences and explore them further. For the time being, let's regard Gardner's theory of multiple intelligences as a bold stroke that goes far beyond previous conceptions. It redirects the attention of psychologists to the actual world where people live and the actual things that they do. Like Sternberg's theory, Gardner's approach makes it explicit that there are many ways to be intelligent. People possess multiple intelligences to varying degrees, allowing for a variety of ways in which they can be combined.

Let's review our progress through this chapter. We started with the story of a young student-athlete who possesses particular skills valued by the world but is not allowed to showcase them because he doesn't seem "intelligent" in a traditional academic sense. We ended with a theory suggesting that his skills *are* a form of intelligence. In between, we encountered numerous ideas about intelligence and in particular how to measure it. Out of these ideas come several conclusions.

1. Despite an ongoing debate, psychologists are increasingly inclined to view intelligence as plural—a set of abilities—rather than a single entity.
2. Intelligence must be defined in terms of particular contexts.
3. Intelligence is not simply a matter of biological inheritance.
4. Traditional intelligence tests have value mainly for their original purpose: distinguishing those who can profit from education from those who cannot.

Strong controversy has accompanied psychology's approach to intelligence. Interest in the topic is not likely to wane, however, particularly in light of the new directions sketched by Sternberg and Gardner.

Summary

Topics of Concern

- Intelligent behavior is adaptive and purposive, and intelligence is one of the most valued human characteristics. Of concern to psychologists interested in intelligence is how best to move from this abstract characterization of intelligence to more concrete definitions and measures.
- Also of interest are the causes of intelligence. There is considerable debate surrounding the nature-nurture issue as it pertains to intelligence.
- A final topic that concerns psychologists is explaining those who demonstrate extreme forms of intelligence. What do these individuals tell us about intelligence in general?

A History of Intelligence Testing

- Modern intelligence testing began with the work of Francis Galton, a cousin and contemporary of Darwin. Galton approached intelligence in evolutionary terms, regarding it as a biologically based capacity. Galton thought that intelligence could be measured with extremely simple tests of reaction time and sensory acuity, but this proved incorrect.
- Now it is recognized that intelligence is best measured with complex tasks, an approach pioneered in the early 1900s by the French psychologist Alfred Binet, who developed tests still used today.
- Lewis Terman popularized intelligence testing in the United States. World War I saw the development of tests that could be administered to groups of people, not just individuals. Various intelligence tests are currently available.

Heredity and the Environment in Intelligence

- What causes intelligence? One extreme view argues that intelligence is largely a matter of genetic inheritance.
- Another extreme view proposes instead that intelligence is determined mainly by particular experiences in a given environment.

- This debate is of social significance because black Americans on the average score lower on intelligence tests than do white Americans, and some psychologists have concluded that the racial difference has a biological basis.
- This view is disputed by several lines of evidence and argument, not the least of which is that the human "races" represent social categories, not biological ones.
- Relevant to the debate about race differences in intelligence is recent research showing that previously documented sex differences in aspects of intelligence have vanished altogether in recent decades.

Extremes of Intelligence

- Several groups of individuals have attracted the attention of psychologists interested in intelligence.
- Mentally retarded individuals show below average intelligence and deficits in adaptive behavior.
- Prodigies are children with special skills or talents far in advance of what we consider normal for their age.
- Geniuses are people whose intellectual capacity allows them to exert a profound influence on contemporary and subsequent generations.
- Creative individuals are people who devise appropriate *and* novel solutions to some problem in life.
- Finally, savants have mediocre or even deficient skills in most domains, yet possess one extraordinarily developed ability. Those at the extremes of intelligence show us that there exist a variety of ways to be intelligent.

Is Intelligence Unitary or Plural?

- Psychologists have long debated whether intelligence is a single capacity or a group of relatively distinct abilities.
- Two recent theories of intelligence, proposed by Robert Sternberg and Howard Gardner, opt for the conclusion that intelligence is plural. Notable about both these theories is their concern with the actual behavior through which people display their intelligence.

Important Terms and Names

What follows is a list of the core terms and names for this chapter. Your instructor may emphasize other terms as well. Throughout the chapter, glossary terms appear in **boldface** type. They are defined in the text, and each term, along with its definition, is repeated in the margin.

Topics of Concern

intelligence/312

A History of Intelligence Testing

aptitude test/314
achievement test/314
mental age/319
intelligence quotient (IQ)/320
culture-fair intelligence tests/324

Francis Galton/314
Alfred Binet/317
Lewis Terman/320
David Wechsler/321

Heredity and the Environment in Intelligence

twin studies/328

Arthur Jensen/326

Extremes of Intelligence

mental retardation/333
Down's syndrome/335
prodigy/336
genius/339
creativity/340
savant/341

Is Intelligence Unitary or Plural?

general intelligence/344
specific intelligence/344
crystallized intelligence/348
fluid intelligence/345
triarchic theory/346
multiple intelligences/348

Charles Spearman/343
Robert Sternberg/346
Howard Gardner/348

Review Questions

1. Intelligence is shown when we
   a. act in adaptive ways.
   b. earn an advanced degree.
   c. make a high salary.
   d. receive good grades in school.
   e. score well on an intelligence test.
   By definition, intelligence is shown in adaptive behavior. Intelligence has various connotations—see the other answers—but these are not necessary aspects of its definition./312

2. What is the correct chronological order?
   a. Binet → Galton → Terman → Jensen
   b. Binet → Terman → Galton → Jensen
   c. Galton → Binet → Terman → Jensen
   d. Galton → Terman → Jensen → Binet
   e. Jensen → Galton → Binet → Terman
   The modern era of intelligence testing began with the contributions of Galton. Binet then developed the first useful tests, which were translated into English by Terman. Jensen is a contemporary psychologist, known for his controversial position that racial differences in intelligence have a biological basis./314

3. Galton's approach to intelligence was influenced by
   a. Darwin.
   b. Freud.
   c. Sternberg.
   d. Watson.
   Galton's approach to intelligence was influenced in many ways by the theory of evolution proposed by his half-cousin Darwin./314

4. Binet and Simon's intelligence test was more successful than earlier tests because the tasks they posed
   a. did not use words.
   b. relied on sensory abilities.
   c. were culture fair.
   d. were difficult.
   e. were more complex.
   The intelligence test of Binet and Simon was successful because its tasks were complex, similar to those which schoolchildren must actually perform as students./318

5. The Wechsler Intelligence Scales provide separate scores for
   a. aptitude and achievement.
   b. deductive IQ and inductive IQ.
   c. reading and writing.
   d. verbal IQ and performance IQ.
   e. verbal performance and quantitative performance.
   The Wechsler Intelligence Scales have sections with and without verbal content, thereby providing separate verbal and performance scores./321

6. One's intelligence is influenced by
   a. nature.
   b. nurture.
   c. both a and b.
   d. neither a nor b.
   Despite the long-standing debate about the determinants of intelligence, research supports the importance of both biological and environmental influences./331

7. The most frequent form of mental retardation is due to
   a. genetic anomalies.
   b. illnesses.
   c. injuries to the brain.
   d. sociocultural factors.
   Retardation has many causes, but by far the most common form cannot be linked to specific physical factors. Instead, it is due to social disadvantages./335

8. In which of these domains of achievement do we *not* find prodigies?
   a. chess
   b. language
   c. mathematics
   d. music
   e. social sciences
   Early achievement is shown in all of these domains except social sciences./337

9. Prodigies and savants often excel
   a. at different ages.
   b. in different domains.
   c. in the same domains.
   d. without practice.
   Prodigies and savants usually excel in the same domains. Both show accomplishment early in life, but only with extensive practice./337

10. Which theorist does not belong with the others?
    a. Gardner
    b. Spearman
    c. Sternberg
    d. Wechsler
    Spearman championed the idea that intelligence is unitary. These other theorists have proposed that intelligence is plural, composed of two or more largely independent capacities./344

How nature and nurture influence development is a concern to many,
including psychologists.

Chapter Nine

Infant and Child Development

Topics of Concern

The thought that someone might treat a child as anything less than a precious gift is abhorrent. Yet cases of profound abuse directed against children by their own parents are reported with some frequency. For example, Curtiss (1977) describes the plight of a girl she named Genie—after the creatures of fantasy and myth who spend years cooped up in small bottles until called forth. Genie's story is chilling, but it highlights some important ideas about how people develop over their lives.

For the first twenty months of her life, the infant Genie was fed poorly and mostly ignored. Then things took a turn for the worse, when her father locked her in a room where she stayed for more than a dozen years. During the day, she was strapped naked onto a potty-chair. At night, she was strapped into a crib. She saw almost no one. She never heard language. She was beaten for making the slightest noise.

At age thirteen, Genie was rescued and taken from her family. She was physically and psychologically retarded. She did not speak at all. Because she had never eaten solid food, she did not know how to chew. She swallowed only with great difficulty. She could not stand up straight. She could not run or jump. Genie salivated all the time. Curtiss (1977, p. 9) characterizes Genie at the time of her rescue as "unsocialized, primitive, hardly human."

With extensive rehabilitation over a period of years, Genie became more socialized. She learned some language and self-control, and how to form rudimentary social relationships. Genie may never be what the rest of the world considers normal, but her development—granted the cruelty of her early life—is still miraculous.

It is difficult to hear the story of Genie without puzzling over the motives of her father. He eventually committed suicide, leaving a note reading "the world will never understand." We also may wonder why the rest of the family stood by while this outrage took place. Genie's mother was blind and in many ways a captive herself, although it was she who eventually fled with her child from the father.

developmental psychology
the field of psychology that studies the physical and psychological changes that take place throughout life—from conception to death

chronological age
one's age measured in months and years

developmental age
the age when most individuals show a particular characteristic indicative of development

Let's now look beyond the parents to see the questions that the case raises concerning the nature of development. How was Genie transformed from a normal infant into the pathetic creature she was as an early adolescent? And how is it that she progressed as well as she did during rehabilitation? How much of the damage done by her environment could be undone by a new environment (Skuse, 1984)? And how much could be undone simply because children are resilient and themselves able to overcome many of the barriers put in their way (Anthony & Cohler, 1987)? How far can Genie progress? If her deprivation occurred at a different point in life, how would subsequent development have been affected?

These and related questions guide the work within **developmental psychology,** the field of psychology concerned with the physical and psychological changes that take place throughout life, from conception to death. This broad definition is a recent one. For quite some time, the end of adolescence was considered the end of development. Adulthood was thought to be a time of great stability and little change. Today psychologists believe that people continue to develop throughout adulthood, and so developmental psychology studies the entire life span.

There is no general consensus about how to divide up someone's life. There is even debate as to whether the life span falls into separate periods or not. Regardless, Table 9.1 specifies one way that developmental psychologists have distinguished the various periods or times in someone's life. Each is identified with an approximate age range. But note that a person's **chronological age**—measured in months or years—although convenient to use because of its objectivity, may not match his or her **developmental age,** which is the age when a particular characteristic is usually demonstrated. For example, if most children walk at one year of age, a child of nine months who walks would be said to have a developmental age of one year (with respect to walking).

In this chapter, we'll focus on infancy and childhood. In Chapter 10, we'll pick up with adolescence and then move into adulthood. The division between these chapters is simply one of convenience. Together, they examine development from the perspective of a life span. Let's start by considering some of the issues of long-standing concern to developmental psychologists.

Nature versus Nurture

The very idea of development contains within it the implication that change occurs in the direction of some goal (Overton, 1984). This is obvious in the case of physical development. Infants become larger as they develop into children. Children become larger as they develop into adolescents. These changes occur in only one direction. Adolescents don't grow into children; children don't grow into infants. Is the same inherent direction of growth found for psychological development? Theorists such as Erik Erikson and Jean Piaget (who will be discussed a bit later in this chapter) believe that psychological development has an inherent goal. Other theorists are less willing to embrace all that "development" implies. For these theorists, it is more prudent to speak simply of change rather than development.

Whether or not development has an inherent direction echoes the debate we have previously encountered over nature versus nurture. The nature-nurture controversy is concerned with what drives development: heredity or experience. Is development one's inborn potential unfolding in a particular way? Or is development mainly influenced by specific learning and experiences (Lerner, 1984)? Consider the example of Genie. Her development was disrupted by the profound abuse she suffered. What was needed to get her back on course: simply removing the trauma and letting Genie develop "naturally" or explicitly intervening and providing particular training in social and language skills?

Few modern theorists take an extreme stance on the nature-nurture issue. The wise resolution is to say that nature and nurture interact to determine the course of development. The ultimate aim of developmental psychologists is to describe the details of this interaction, a continual give-and-take between heredity and environment.

Is Development Stable?

Of particular interest to developmental researchers is whether an individual's characteristics—physical, temperamental, intellectual, social, whatever—are stable throughout life or show considerable variation (Goldsmith, 1983). At one time, the prevailing belief was that early characteristics

Table 9.1
The Times in One's LIfe

Period	Chronological Age	Important Domains of Development
Prenatal period	Conception to birth	Physical growth
Infancy	Birth to 18 months	Motor development, attachment
Early childhood	18 months to 6 years	Language, gender identity
Late childhood	6 years to 13 years	Cognitive development
Adolescence	13 years to 20 years	Identity, independence, sexuality
Young adulthood	20 years to 40 years	Career, family
Middle adulthood	40 years to 60 years	Self-assessment
Later adulthood	60 years to death	Retirement

persisted, setting the stage for later ones: "As the twig is bent, so grows the tree." But developmental research challenges any simple idea of stability. Although many characteristics, including certain personality traits, exhibit a degree of stability, many studies have shown that change is possible and indeed occurs at all points throughout life (Brim & Kagan, 1980). Early experiences and characteristics are important, but they do *not* always tell the whole story concerning subsequent development. In other words, it is possible for Genie the adult to be at least in some ways a different person than Genie the abused child.

Developmental Stages

Another important issue is whether or not development should be thought of as a passage through discrete **developmental stages,** each marked by particular achievements (Fischer & Silvern, 1985). Developmental stages figure prominently in a number of theories. All these theories assume that development is *discontinuous*—occurring in leaps and bounds. Several other assumptions further characterize any stage theory:

- Stages represent altogether different psychological states. Infants and children and adults, according to stage theories, differ in their basic operating principles—they think, feel, and act in different ways.
- Movement from one stage to the next is abrupt (Hinde & Bateson, 1984).
- Different aspects of development should proceed in lockstep, that is, changes in one psychological domain should occur simultaneously with changes in other domains.
- Specific experiences will not affect a child's general level of development because capacities of characteristics appear only when the developing individual is ready to exhibit them.
- The stages are traversed in a fixed order. There are early stages and later stages, and we must get from the first to the last in the old-fashioned way, one step at a time.

developmental stages
discrete periods occurring in a fixed sequence in a person's life, each marked by particular physical, mental, or behavioral characteristics and achievements

critical periods
times during development when one is most ready to acquire a certain behavior if particular experiences occur

- Difficulties encountered at earlier stages interfere with functioning at later stages.
- Stages are universal, as apparent among children raised in African or Asian cultures as they are among those raised in European or American cultures.

Despite the prominence of stage theories, many of these assumptions have been challenged by researchers who argue that they are not supported by the evidence. What then can we turn to as an alternative? One possibility is represented by learning theories (Chapter 5), which do not assume a necessary direction to development or stages on the route to this nonexistent destination. A theory also can assume that development is progressive, but that differences across the life span are quantitative rather than qualitative. In other words, alternatives to stage theories see development as *continuous*—occurring in a slow and gradual process.

Stage theorists and their critics disagree specifically over the existence of **critical periods** of development, during which particular experiences must occur to avoid hindering subsequent development (Colombo, 1982). Stage theorists support the idea of critical periods, whereas their critics do not. What does the evidence support? Critical periods are obvious for physical development. At various stages before birth, the developing embryo is vulnerable to disruptions from maternal illness and stress, alcohol and drugs, radiation, and so on. Among mammals, normal visual experience must take place early in life for the brain to develop appropriately (e.g., Blake & Hirsch, 1975).

There is vigorous debate over the issue of critical periods for psychological development. According to some theorists, people have critical periods for intellectual development, language development, and social development. Genie, for instance, may be permanently disadvantaged because, as an infant and child, she missed out on particular experiences that are necessary for the development of normal intelligence, language, and social skills. The opposing view holds that Genie eventually can overcome the deprivations of her young life.

A Brief History of Developmental Psychology

The field of developmental psychology has itself developed over the years. In this section, we will look at the evolution of the study of development, beginning with some views that were popular before psychology even existed as a science (Chapter 1).

The Child as Adult

One of the intriguing facts that history reveals is that "childhood" is a recent invention (Aries, 1962). In fifteenth-century Europe, people certainly recognized the notion of infancy: newborns were small and helpless. But that did not mean they were treated with much tenderness. Babies were tightly swaddled and literally hung up on the wall while parents did their chores. If the babies were noisy, they were drugged with alcohol to keep them quiet. For all of these reasons, along with the general lack of medical sophistication, infant mortality was extremely high. And as many as one-third of all babies born were simply abandoned.

Infants were regarded as animals, and for the few who made it through infancy, parents undertook strict "training" to rid them of their animal characteristics. Crawling was disdained. Babbling was treated with impatience. As soon as children could stand, they were dressed in clothes reinforced with iron and whalebone, to hold them in "adult" postures. At about age six or seven, they were sent to work, where harsh treatment continued.

There was no discrete period marking the transition from infancy to adulthood. Aries (1962) illustrates this point well, telling us to look at how children were depicted in medieval art.

> An Ottonian miniature . . . provides us with a striking example of the deformation which an artist at that time would inflict on children's bodies. The subject is the scene in the Gospels in which Jesus asks that little children be allowed to come to Him. . . . The miniaturist has grouped around Jesus what are obviously eight men, without any of the characteristics of childhood; they have simply been depicted on a smaller scale. (p. 33)

Figure 9.1
Painting Showing Children as Adults

Some of you are probably thinking that children at that time *really* looked like little adults, but a better explanation is that the concept of childhood simply did not exist in this earlier culture and thus had no representation in its art (see Figure 9.1).

Today, we of course recognize a transition between infancy and adulthood, and we call it childhood. In contemporary America, childhood lasts until about age twelve, and it is a time when a young person is expected to be . . . well, simply a child.

Why were children in medieval Europe expected to be adults? The rationale was entwined with notions of salvation. The most important goal in life was to end up in heaven, not hell. Medieval life was severe, and happiness and even good health were not realistic goals. Stamping out sin was, and so children were treated harshly to rid them of their animal—that is, sinful—nature.

The Emerging Child

In Chapter 4, you encountered the philosopher John Locke (1632–1704). He championed the empiricist point of view, the notion that experience makes us what we are. Locke applied this idea to human development, and concluded that childhood was important because early experience could shape a person's later character and abilities. In several of his essays published in the late 1600s, he advised parents to encourage their children's curiosity and rationality (e.g., Locke, 1690). It is for this reason that Locke is important in the history of developmental psychology. He helped create the very notion of childhood, and he also emphasized the idea that prior experiences shape our subsequent actions.

Another important figure who continued Locke's attention to childhood was the French philosopher Jean-Jacques Rousseau (1712–1778). Rousseau took a different perspective on childhood than Locke, expounding the rationalist point of view (Chapter 3). He believed that children had an inherent nature, one that was good and noble (e.g., Rousseau, 1762). They became bad only because of how they were treated.

Further, Rousseau believed that children were qualitatively different than adults, that development consisted of a passage through discrete stages. These stages are not imposed on the child, but rather are part of the child's very nature. As noted earlier, stages play an important role in many contemporary theories of development.

Darwin's Influence on Developmental Psychology

Science first provided an explicit position on development with the introduction of Charles Darwin's (1859) theory of evolution, which, after all, is a theory of development. Darwin's concern was with the development of individual species, but we've been able to broadly apply his basic ideas. As we saw in Chapter 2, some theorists applied Darwinian ideas to the development of societies—these were the social Darwinists. And other thinkers applied the ideas to the development of the individual. These theorists were the first developmental psychologists.

Recall from Chapter 2 the idea that ontogeny recapitulates phylogeny: Individual development mirrors the development of one's species. Although this idea is not accepted at the present time as anything more than a rough description (Gould, 1977), it was quite influential at the turn of the century when developmental psychology first began. So, infants were seen as an extremely primitive version of human beings, children as somewhat more advanced, and so on.

A Darwinian view of development had two important implications. First, to understand development one had to approach it like a naturalist, by observing carefully the changes that occurred as an infant became a child and a child became an adult. Darwin (1877) pioneered the first explicit research technique in developmental psychology, the infant biography. This was a journal of daily observations of a given child's behavior. A number of these biographies were written and published, including Darwin's account of his own son, William Erasmus. The tradition of studying single infants still continues in developmental psychology. You will see later in this chapter that the influential Swiss researcher, Jean Piaget

G. Stanley Hall

maturation

inherent growth processes considered critical to a person's physical or psychological development

Arnold Gesell, shown here examining an infant, developed innovative research strategies, including the use of motion picture cameras to capture children's behavior.

(1926), undertook his important studies of cognitive development by observing a small number of children, including his own.

Second, psychological development was thought to parallel biological development, and like it, to pass through stages. An early American psychologist, G. Stanley Hall (1844–1924), for example, distinguished five stages in the life span: infancy, childhood, youth, adolescence, and adulthood (Hall, 1904). He is credited with the "invention" of adolescence, in the sense of describing it as a coherent developmental stage. Before Hall's theorizing, people were thought to move from childhood right into adulthood. Puberty was an event, not an extended episode. (Those of you who hated adolescence might now be satisfied knowing where to fix the blame!)

Influential Theorists

This brief history would not be complete without mentioning a handful of influential theorists. Much of the early research in developmental psychology was descriptive, simply charting what happened to infants and children as they grew. Although rough ideas about development guided this work by drawing attention to some characteristics rather than others, researchers did not propose hypotheses to be tested against the evidence.

John Watson.   Some early theorists *did* make specific predictions, and they did so from the vantage provided by explicit developmental theories. One of the first was behaviorist John Watson (Chapter 1), who started his career studying rats but then turned to babies. He was interested in their emotions (e.g., Watson & Morgan, 1917). The infant Albert, famous now for his conditioned fear of rats (Chapter 5), exemplifies this research tradition, which was guided by Watson's extreme behaviorism (Watson & Rayner, 1920).

According to Watson, an infant is born with but a small number of emotions: fear, rage, and love. All changes in these emotions are tied to specific learning. Albert illustrated how fear could become attached to a new object. Subsequent work by Watson's colleagues showed how such conditioned emotions could be removed, through an early form of behavior modification (e.g., Jones, 1924).

Because learning theories provide a general explanation of change, they have always been an important aspect of developmental psychology. Watson (1928) spread his view widely in his popular *Psychological Care of the Infant and Child,* which counseled parents on how best to raise their children. Some of his advice seems harsh, at least in retrospect. For instance, he advised against holding or cuddling a baby, because this would reinforce undesirable behaviors like crying.

Arnold Gesell.   In contrast to Watson's emphasis on change via learning was another influential theory proposed by one of his contemporaries, Arnold Gesell (1880–1961), a physician and psychologist at Yale University. Gesell (1925) stressed the importance of inherent growth processes in development, arguing that this **maturation** was critical in development. In other words, specific learning does not produce change unless the individual is ready for this change.

One of Gesell's research strategies was to start with a pair of identical twins. One twin would be taught a specific physical or cognitive task. The other twin would not be allowed to work at the task until some time later, but then would rapidly catch up to the first twin. This shows the importance of maturation by ruling out the influence of learning and practice. Although the two twins had different experiences, they ended up at the same level of ability.

Gesell pioneered research strategies allowing precise observations of infant behavior. He used motion picture cameras to capture frame by frame what infants actually did (Gesell & Thompson, 1934). He also wrote a popular version of his theories for parents (Gesell, 1928). It was widely read until supplanted a generation later by Benjamin Spock's (1946) famous book, *Baby and Child Care*. Gesell's books featured extensive tables specifying what a child should be able to do by a given age, reassuring some parents and no doubt driving others crazy.

Sigmund Freud. Yet another important theorist who influenced developmental psychology was Sigmund Freud (1856–1939). His approach to personality, normal and abnormal, was very much a developmental one. He laid great emphasis on early experiences in shaping subsequent actions. Freud believed that children developed through a series of **psychosexual stages** in which their instinctive needs were satisfied through stimulation of various parts of the body. The means of satisfaction defined the developmental stage. Freud proposed that all of us pass through the following stages (in order):

psychosexual stages
according to Freud, developmental stages in which a child's instinctive needs are satisfied through stimulation of different parts of the body

- oral stage (birth to age one)—here the child satisfies his needs through activities involving the mouth: nursing, chewing, biting, and so on
- anal stage (ages one to three)—gratification centers around elimination, either retaining or expelling feces
- phallic stage (ages three to five)—satisfaction is achieved through self-stimulation of the genitals: that is, masturbation
- latency period (age six to puberty)—a period of relative calm during which there is no particular focus for gratification
- genital stage (from puberty on)—marked by the onset of adolescence, satisfaction is achieved through sexual contact with others

We'll examine Freud's theory in more detail in Chapter 11, but here's what's important in regard to development. First, Freud strongly believed that the early conflicts and frustrations that center around the psychosexual stages shape our later personality via the solutions that we devise for the problems they pose. In other words, how we react to these psychosexual crises becomes our characteristic style.

Second, Freud suggested that if a particular conflict characterizing a given stage of development was not satisfactorily resolved, it would later affect our behavior. Here we see an example of one of the assumptions central to stage theories: If you don't make it through one stage, you will have trouble with subsequent ones. This prediction gave rise to numerous studies looking at the link between such childhood experiences as weaning or toilet training and later adult personality characteristics.

A third important aspect of Freud's theory is that development ends with the onset of adolescence. Our character is thought to be fixed by this time. Adulthood thus is regarded as a time of great stability.

Freud's ideas influenced the general public, particularly in the United States, where they were packaged in popular form by pediatrician Benjamin Spock (1946). His chatty *Baby and Child Care* is the best-selling paperback book of all time. He counseled against harshness, restriction, and coercion, because these produce conflicts for children and hamper their development. Therefore, children should be fed when hungry, not on a schedule. Toilet training should not be rushed. Parents should encourage and enjoy their children, and they should not punish them in severe ways.

Erik Erikson

Erik Erikson. Freud's follower Erik Erikson (b. 1902) is the next important theorist who deserves mention. Erikson (1963, 1968, 1982) both built upon and drastically changed Freud's theory of development. Like Freud, Erikson proposed that people pass through stages. At each stage, a particular conflict is central, and a satisfactory resolution must be reached if the individual is to progress well through subsequent stages. But unlike Freud, Erikson called his approach a theory of **psychosocial stages,** taking away the sexual emphasis of the stages and looking at their interpersonal nature. Where Freud saw toilet training as a conflict involving the gratification of sexuality, Erikson saw the events surrounding toilet training as a conflict between the child and his or her parents.

The second way in which Erikson changed Freud's view of development was by expanding it to include the entire life span. Following the onset of adolescence, individuals still confront important developmental tasks: forging an identity, merging one's self with another person, taking steps to help the next generation, and so on. Again, note the social nature of these stages. Erikson's theory will be discussed in detail later in this chapter as well as in the next chapter on adult development, because it has figured prominently in contemporary psychology's attempts to explain the whole of development.

Jean Piaget

Jean Piaget. Finally, we have Jean Piaget (1896–1980), the Swiss theorist, the most influential of all developmental thinkers. Originally trained as a biologist, and with a strong interest in philosophy, Piaget turned to the study of how children come to think about the world. Through extensive observation and questioning of children, Piaget devised a stage theory of cognitive development, proposing that children's thinking developed in an orderly way through discrete stages. According to this theory, the very principles underlying thought develop, so that young children quite literally think about the world differently than do older children or adults. It's not just the content of thought that changes, but the processes as well (Chapter 7).

Piaget's impact on developmental psychology in the United States has itself progressed through several stages. (Perhaps our thinking needed to develop before we could fully grasp what he was saying!) When his first books were translated from French into English, in the 1920s, they had a strong impact and earned Piaget (1926, 1928, 1929) a lofty reputation in the United States. Then interest in his work died off. Piaget continued to write, but no new English translations appeared until the 1950s.

Then his work had a second and much larger impact, perhaps because the times were right for the cognitive perspective Piaget (1950) presented. Indeed, he should be counted among the prime movers in psychology's cognitive revolution (Chapter 7). The second time around, Piaget became the world's leading developmental theorist.

In recent years, the field has seen an increasing number of research challenges to Piaget's specific findings and claims about cognitive development (e.g., Osherson, 1974). We'll look at these challenges later in this chapter, but appreciate that while they elaborate and modify his approach to studying development, they owe a great debt to the example he set.

Studying Development

As early as Locke and Rousseau, there was interest in improving the process of child development. It is therefore not surprising that once developmental psychology took form, the field forged links with education. For instance, kindergartens were started in Germany during the 1800s and transplanted to the United States in 1870. From the start, they were based on a developmental rationale. Their goal was to instill in children the foundations of knowledge and skill that would prove useful for their adult life. Nowadays, a variety of early education programs exist, including day care, nursery school, and Montessori schools. Each embodies an explicit philosophy phrased in developmental terms.

Developmental psychologists first advised educators about how to set up school curricula. These psychologists soon found that schools provided such a ready source of research subjects that they established their own schools. Starting in the 1920s, psychologists founded nursery schools at such universities as Columbia, Iowa, and Yale. They studied the children, mapping out the process of their physical and intellectual growth. Some researchers conducted laboratory experiments of the type described in earlier chapters. They investigated perception, learning, and cognition among infants and children.

Establishing Norms

norms

standards based on large samples of people that allow an individual to be compared to them

Developmental psychologists have been greatly concerned with establishing **norms:** standards based on large samples of people that allow an individual to be compared to them. What are the average ages at which most children begin to crawl or talk or walk or remember to put gasoline in the car? Throughout the twentieth century, an unending series of popular books on child rearing has appeared, replete with norms and advice on how to help the child stay even with or ahead of the game. Some contemporary critics suggest that we push our children too hard (e.g., Elkind, 1987). This may be true, but it's nothing new. Note the irony. We discussed earlier the revelation that children are not like adults, and now we see attempts to push our children as rapidly as possible through childhood!

Developmental psychologists use a variety of specific techniques in their investigations. To a large degree, these methods are drawn from the

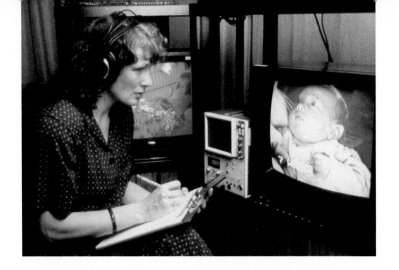

In the process of establishing measurable norms against which an individual can be compared, modern researchers make use of a variety of technologies.

specific content area of psychology in which the researchers are interested. If they are interested in development of the brain and nervous system, they use the techniques of researchers who investigate these topics (Chapter 2). If they are interested in perceptual development, they use strategies for studying sensation and perception (Chapters 3 and 4). Because infants don't understand language, researchers need to show considerable ingenuity in adapting research techniques that are usually implemented with verbal instructions.

Developmental psychologists face an additional task that other psychologists do not—describing and explaining change across the life span. They are interested in comparing and contrasting people of different ages, but they additionally want to understand how similarities and differences arise. Developmental researchers must take into account the variable of time, and there are two general strategies for doing so (see Figure 9.2). The first strategy undertakes **cross-sectional studies.** In these, individuals of different ages are simultaneously studied and then compared. The second strategy uses **longitudinal studies** that follow the same individuals over a considerable period of time. What are the pros and cons of these two types of studies?

cross-sectional studies

research strategies that simultaneously study and compare individuals of different ages

longitudinal studies

research strategies that study the same individuals over a long period of time

Cross-Sectional Research

The benefit of cross-sectional research is that it is usually simpler to conduct than longitudinal research, and many cross-sectional studies do clearly lay out the course of development. Suppose you are interested in the development of friendships among children. With a cross-sectional research strategy, you would obtain research subjects of different ages and study the types of friends they have. You can argue that any differences you find across your age groups reflect development.

There are some obvious problems to watch out for in cross-sectional research. For example, you must be careful to avoid confounds in choosing your various groups. Six-year-old children should not be chosen from a parochial school when eight-year-olds are chosen from a public school, or vice versa. Subjects must be matched closely on factors not of theoretical concern, so that these do not contaminate the conclusions.

Another problem is that cross-sectional studies may not reveal the *process* underlying development, because they provide snapshots only.

Figure 9.2

Cross-Sectional versus Longitudinal Research. In cross-sectional research (see top), subjects of different ages are compared. In longitudinal research (see bottom), subjects are studied at different points in time.

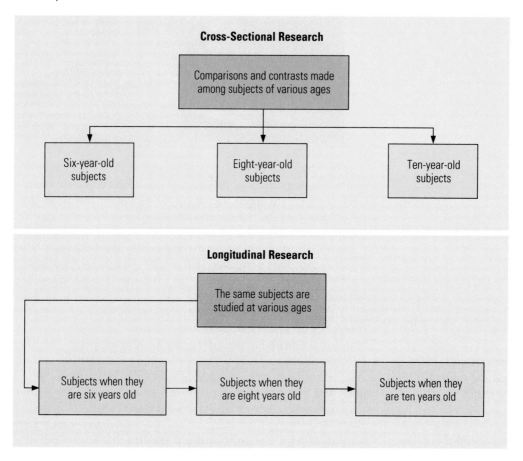

Age comparisons may suggest processes, but they cannot nail them down. Simply comparing six-year-olds and eight-year-olds does not tell you exactly what takes place as children become older. Also, it's impossible to perfectly match subjects of different ages. And certain questions, such as those concerning the continuity of development, are impossible to answer with a cross-sectional design, because these don't tell us what happens to specific individuals over time.

Life-span researchers in particular must be alert to **cohort effects,** the fact that people born at different points in time (into what we commonly call generations and what researchers call birth cohorts) may necessarily be different from each other by virtue of prevailing historical and social conditions. If there is a considerable spread in the ages of research subjects in a cross-sectional study, cohort differences may confound age comparisons.

People who were children during the Great Depression, for instance, are always going to differ from people who did not have this experience (Elder, 1974). Such folks are now our senior citizens, and we have to be careful in what we conclude from any study that includes this cohort as the "older" group. Perhaps characteristics we might first attribute to grow-

cohort effects

differences between various age groups, not because of their age, but because of the particular historical and social conditions that existed while they were growing up ing older, for instance, being cautious about financial matters, have nothing to do with aging per se but simply to experience with hard times.

Longitudinal Research

Cohort effects can obscure true developmental changes or be mistaken for them. For these reasons, cross-sectional studies must be cautiously evaluated. Then again, researchers can opt for longitudinal studies, which provide a much more valid view of the process of development. Although only a handful of such studies have lasted for several decades, those that did have provided invaluable information about life-span development. These findings have helped bring developmental psychology around to the life-span perspective, by showing that change is possible throughout one's life.

Longitudinal studies have problems, too, however. Chief among them is *attrition:* Research participants drop out for all the reasons, good and bad, that people drop out of any activity. In a longitudinal study, attrition is a nightmare from which the researcher cannot awake, being unable to go back in time and fix it.

Longitudinal research is constrained by the original choice of research subjects, techniques, and questions. For example, the Harvard Study of Adult Development is an investigation of several hundred Harvard students that began in the late 1930s and still follows the same individuals today (e.g., Vaillant, 1977). This study provides unique insights into the process of adult development, *but* there were no women students at Harvard in the 1930s. This exciting study tells us about men only, and there's no way to undue this limitation. And because the topics of concern to psychology rapidly change, a longitudinal study runs the risk of becoming irrelevant.

These studies are also expensive and laborious, eating up almost as many resources as a Defense Department contract. The major resource may well be time. Even if they have the other means with which to conduct a longitudinal study, many researchers are reluctant to wait for 20 or 30 years to see the outcome of their investigation. But bless those researchers who have surmounted the difficulties in conducting longitudinal studies. We have learned much from them.

Physical Development

Development takes place on many fronts, and development in one domain affects development in another. Developmental psychologists customarily distinguish among physical, social, cognitive, and moral development for convenience. These distinctions are followed in the remainder of this chapter, but don't forget that change goes on simultaneously in all these areas throughout one's life. Let's start with **physical development:** the processes of bodily change and growth in the developing individual.

physical development
the processes of bodily change and growth

Aspects of Prenatal Development

conception
the beginning of physical development: when a male's sperm cell fertilizes a female's ovum

Physical development begins at the moment of **conception,** when a male's sperm cell fertilizes a female's ovum, mixing together chromo-

zygote

the single cell created by the union of a sperm cell and ovum

embryo

the term used to describe the developing unborn child from about two weeks to two months after conception

somes from each parent into the particular genetic combination that serves as the individual's biological blueprint (Chapter 2). The drama of conception takes place on a microscopic stage. The ovum is smaller than the period that ends this sentence, yet it is still much larger than the sperm, which is only 1/500 of an inch long.

A typical pregnancy, from conception to birth, lasts about nine months. We commonly think of a woman's pregnancy as occurring in three trimesters: the first, middle, and last three-month periods. During the first trimester, the newly fertilized cell, called a **zygote,** rapidly divides and increases in size (see Figure 9.3). The zygote attaches itself to the wall of the mother's uterus, after which it is referred to as an **embryo.** Further growth occurs. At the beginning of the third month following conception, al-

Figure 9.3

Early Prenatal Development. These drawings show the progression from ovum to zygote to embryo in the first 38 weeks following conception.

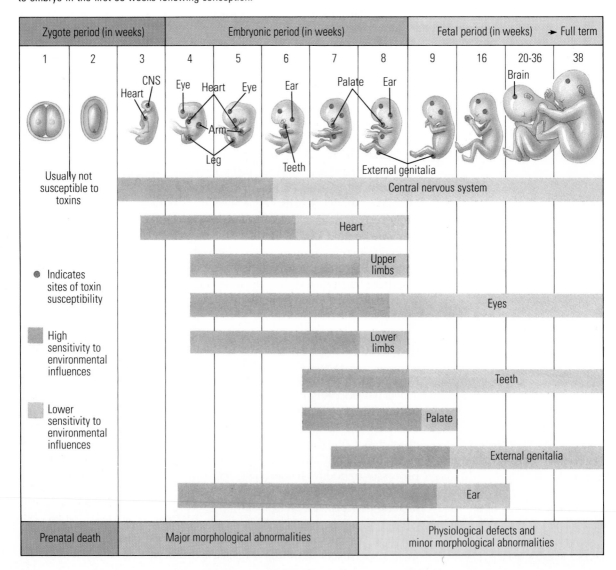

fetus
the term used to describe the developing unborn child from about the third month after conception until birth

fetal alcohol syndrome
a complex of deformities in the babies of alcoholic mothers

though not yet an inch long, the developing embryo has a discernible face, arms, and legs—even fingers and toes. From this point until birth, it is termed a **fetus.**

During the second trimester, the fetus begins to move in ways that the mother can feel, as it kicks against her abdominal wall. At first mechanical, these movements become smoother with further development. The fetus can make a fist, bend its wrist, open its mouth, and swallow. Male or female genitals take clear form. Characteristic fingerprints show up.

During the third trimester, the fetus develops the ability to breathe. Hiccups may even occur! Because it can breathe, a baby born as early as 23 or 24 weeks following conception has some chance of surviving. However, such extremely premature infants weigh little more than 1 pound and usually have immature lungs and digestive systems, all of which work against their survival.

The mother's uterus is quite literally the environment for the developing embryo/fetus. Changes in the uterus therefore affect its development. And though the uterus protects the developing fetus from much harm, researchers now know that a variety of factors can disrupt its development. Depending on the particular insult and exactly when it occurs during pregnancy, different consequences may follow.

Maternal malnutrition, for example, can result in a child that is small and weak and susceptible to disease. So too can smoking by a pregnant woman (Jacobson, 1984). And maternal drug use or alcohol consumption greatly increases the chances of a stillborn child or one with serious physical deformities. **Fetal alcohol syndrome** refers to a complex of characteristics seen in the children of alcoholic mothers: small size, mental retardation, distinctive facial features, and a variety of heart and limb defects (Aranson et al., 1985; Jones, Smith, Ulleland, & Streissguth, 1973). Even occasional drinking during pregnancy can cause damage because the liver of the fetus is not particularly effective at breaking down alcohol.

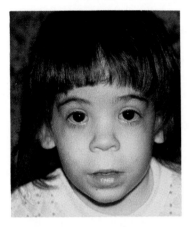

This child exhibits the tragic effects of fetal alcohol syndrome.

Sex Differences

The first thing we ask about a newborn baby is whether it is a boy or girl. From the moment of birth, a baby's gender influences our treatment of him or her. However, biologically based sex differences actually exist from the instant of conception. This means that development does not take place for a generic human being, but rather for a male or a female. Although the distinctions between males and females may seem simple and unambiguous, they can actually be quite complicated. Males and females are fuzzy categories, and these terms are used to encompass a number of more specific contrasts: physical, psychological, and social.

sex differences
physical differences between males and females

Physical differences between men and women are called **sex differences.** So, *chromosomes* determine a person's sex (Chapter 2). All eggs have an X chromosome. Biological sex is determined by whether the egg is fertilized by a sperm cell carrying an X chromosome or one carrying a Y chromosome. Males have one X chromosome and one Y chromosome (XY). Females have two X chromosomes (XX). Another contrast has to do with *sex glands.* Males have testes, which produce sperm cells. Females have ovaries, which produce eggs. Yet one more contrast concerns *sex organs.* Males have penises. Females have vaginas.

The developing male is much more vulnerable than the developing female, at every step in development (Verbrugge, 1989). Did you know that more males are conceived than females? Estimates range from 120 to 170 males conceived for every 100 females conceived. Once conceived, males are more at risk for spontaneous abortion, so that at birth, we find the male-female ratio to be approximately 106:100. Males are more likely to die in the first year of life than females. Indeed, males are more susceptible to death or damage or defect at *all* ages than are females. (So much for stereotypes about the weaker sex.)

We don't know the reason for this striking sex difference in physical hardiness. Explanations usually center on something about the XY chromosome pattern that is harmful (e.g., Ounsted & Taylor, 1972), or something about the XX chromosome pattern that is protective (e.g., Purtilo & Sullivan, 1979), or some combination of both. Regardless, this difference is well established in our species, and perhaps the overabundance of males at conception has been selected through evolution to compensate for the greater loss of males at all other points in life.

In the sixth week following conception, males and females start to follow different biological courses because of the effects of sex hormones on the developing embryo. The "basic model" of the human embryo is a female, and only when a male sex hormone—testosterone—is added does the embryo develop the physical characteristics of a male. What this means is that a chromosomally male individual will develop as a female in the absence of testosterone (Money & Ehrhardt, 1972).

Throughout much of childhood, girls and boys are about the same height and weight. With puberty, this changes, so that men on the average are larger than women. Males and females come out of puberty with marked physical differences: in size, shape, and strength. They have different hormonal systems, and any behavior influenced by these hormones may well reflect a biological difference between males and females.

For instance, in recent years, a lot of interest has centered on sex differences in the nervous system (MacLusky & Naftolin, 1981). Sex hormones affect the development of the brain and nervous system, and some speculate that they give rise to structural and/or functional differences between males and females (McGlone, 1980). This is one explanation for the fact that males, on the average, are superior to females in tasks involving spatial visualization (Chapter 8).

These interpretations have not been accepted by all psychologists (see Lowe & Hubbard, 1983), and work continues. Perhaps male superiority in spatial visualization is the result of experiences that males typically have and females typically do not, such as Little League baseball or shop class in school. Because girls as well as boys are now participating in these activities, the sex difference in visualization ability may no longer be found by future researchers if, indeed, it is based in experience.

Although biologically based differences between the sexes are obvious, so too are environmentally based differences, once we look for them. Developmental researchers have shown that parents respond differently to males than to females, from birth on (Berk, 1989). For example, parents perceive their sons as alert, strong, and hardy, and their daughters as soft, weak, and delicate—even when there are *no* objective differences between male and female infants (Condry & Condry, 1976; Rubin, Provenzano, & Luria, 1974). Parents play more roughly with sons than daughters. They interrupt their daughters but let their sons finish sentences. Accordingly, males and females develop within different social environments.

The Newborn's Reflexes

reflexes
automatic, coordinated responses to external stimuli

Although newborn infants are vulnerable creatures, they enter the world with a considerable repertoire of **reflexes:** automatic, coordinated responses to external stimuli. These reflexes aid in their survival. Consider the following examples, just some of the reflexes present early in life.

The *rooting reflex* is the tendency of the newborn to turn his mouth toward whatever touches his cheek. This helps the newborn find his mother's breast to be fed. And when something touches the infant's lips, the sucking reflex is elicited. So, once mother's breast is found, the infant automatically begins to nurse.

The *grasping reflex* leads the child to grab onto anything that touches his palm. This reflex is so strong that the infant can literally suspend his own weight for a brief period of time. Some speculate that this reflex can be traced back to our distant ancestors who lived in trees, where the ability to hang on for dear life proved highly useful.

The *Moro reflex* refers to the child's reaction to loud noises or the sudden loss of physical support. She throws her arms and legs outward. She spreads her fingers. Then she clenches her fists and pulls her arms and legs back together. Again, the survival value of this reflex is easy to specify. It leads the child to grab a nearby parent when threatened.

Adults do not have these particular reflexes. Infants make use of them early in their lives, and then they disappear. The ones just described go away after three or four months. If a newborn lacks one or more of these basic reflexes, this may indicate that something is wrong with his or her neurological development, and so pediatricians routinely test for them.

An infant's grasping reflex, which will disappear during the third to fifth month of life, is just one of a number of survival reflexes present in newborns.

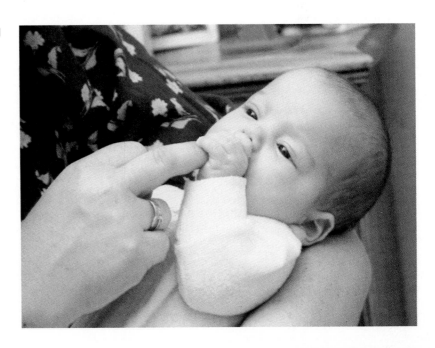

Growth and Motor Development

"My, haven't you grown?" Every child gets sick of hearing this from relatives, because they say it so often. And they say it often because growing—increasing height and weight—is one of the obvious things that children do. Here are some brief generalizations about physical growth:

1. Growth occurs at a greater rate earlier in life, although there is a spurt in adolescence.
2. The proportions of the body change as well as its overall size; after the first year of life, the head becomes proportionately smaller, whereas the limbs become proportionately longer (see Figure 9.4).
3. Growth is influenced by genetic factors, but such environmental influences as poor nutrition, disease, and neglect can hold down both the rate of growth as well as its overall attainment.

motor development

the process by which children become more skilled at using their bodies

Not only does the child's body become bigger, but the child becomes more skilled at using it. This process is called **motor development,** and it reflects the interplay of environmental and biological factors. The child's nervous system must mature, *and* the child must practice in order to perfect his movements.

At birth, the nervous system of the newborn infant is not fully formed. Not all nerve fibers are covered by the myelin sheath (Chapter 2), and so the infant must wait for this to occur before she can move all parts of her body skillfully. With myelination, the child shows a progression of movements she can control: first movement of the head and neck, then the shoulders, then the elbows and knees, and finally the fingers and toes. Motor development also proceeds from large actions like waving to small actions like picking up pennies.

Even the simple act of grasping a small object shows a characteristic developmental sequence. First, a baby holds an object in her palm with

Figure 9.4

Body Proportions across the Life Span. Note that as the child grows, the head becomes relatively smaller and the legs become relatively longer.

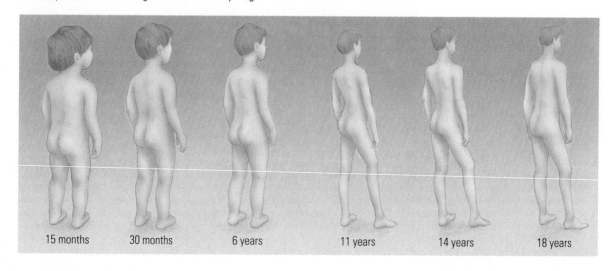

| 15 months | 30 months | 6 years | 11 years | 14 years | 18 years |

Figure 9.5

Sequence of Motor Development. Although there is considerable variation in the ages at which different children can perform particular behaviors, the sequence in which these behaviors occur is the same. In these drawings, the left end of each bar represents the age at which 25 percent of children perform the particular behavior; the right end of each bar corresponds to the age at which 90 percent of children show the behavior. Source: Frankenburg & Dodds, 1967.

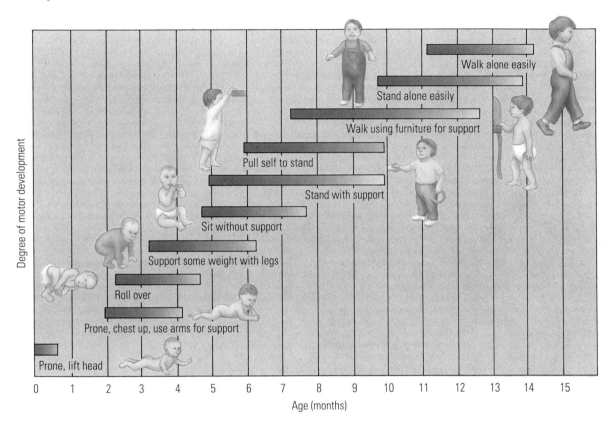

her fourth and fifth fingers. Later she uses the middle finger. Finally, around seven months of age, the thumb is brought into the process. At nine months, babies show the adult pattern of grasping small objects between the forefinger and thumb. Note the steady progression toward ever finer skill.

At what ages do babies show particular motor skills? Research results here show striking variability, perhaps as a result of cohort effects in nutrition, stimulation, and the like. Less controversial is the sequence in which different skills are first mastered, and Figure 9.5 shows when some important abilities show up early in life.

Temperament

temperament

a biologically based style of interacting with the world

One more aspect of physical development should be noted, because it concretely shows the interplay between nature and nurture. **Temperament** is a biologically based style of interacting with the world. The key word in this definition is *style*. It refers not to what a person does but to the way he or she goes about it. Psychologists have distinguished several dimensions of temperament, including emotionality, activity, and sociability (Buss & Plomin, 1975, 1984). These dimensions are reflected in the *frequency* of particular behaviors, their *duration,* and/or their *intensity.* Consider emotionality. One child cries frequently, loudly, and endlessly. Another child cries rarely, softly, and briefly. The former child quite obviously would be regarded as emotional, and the latter as placid.

Temperaments such as emotionality have a genetic basis, a conclusion that follows from twin studies comparing the resemblance of identical and fraternal twins (Chapter 8). On a theoretical level, this means we should consider temperament as a raw ingredient participating in physical development, because temperament is based in one's biology. On a practical level, this helps us understand why newborn infants may differ from each other. So-called difficult babies may simply be predisposed to be emotional (Thomas, Chess, & Korn, 1982).

However, temperament per se has no predictable effect on the sort of person the child becomes. Why is this? Because we must take into account the environment and how it interacts with a particular temperament (Kagan, Reznick, & Gibbons, 1989). Thomas and Chess (1977) cite the example of a child who is temperamentally active. In an urban environment, her high activity level leads her into danger, as she darts among cars on busy streets. Her parents worry about her and respond with severe prohibitions and punishments, which in turn will affect the woman she will be. Perhaps she will end up a cautious and resentful individual.

But suppose this same child and her boundless energy are placed in a rural environment. Danger is not courted by her style, and her parents encourage the wide exploration of the world that her temperament makes so easy. She becomes a bold, confident, and happy adult.

Social Development

social development
the process by which a child develops attitudes, values, and roles

The social behavior of infants differs drastically from the social behavior of children, adolescents, and adults. Developmental psychologists subsume differences in social behavior under the general category of **social development:** a child's development of characteristic attitudes, values, and roles. These psychologists try to describe and explain socialization, the process by which the social knowledge appropriate to a particular society is imparted to an individual. The child becomes not a generic social being but a particular type of social being. A personality is forged, one out of the infinite number that are possible. He or she develops certain attitudes and values and adopts certain roles, creating a unique identity.

Erikson's Theory: Infancy and Childhood

Before we get into the details of social development in early life, it will be helpful to look at the major social changes that occur between birth and adolescence. We can rely on Erikson's (1968) influential descriptions of these changes. As noted earlier, Erikson favors a stage approach. Each stage of development is defined by a particular social conflict that the individual must solve (see Table 9.2). For this reason, the conflicts are sometimes

Table 9.2

Erikson's Early Stages of Psychosocial Development

Chronological Age	Central Issue
First year	Trust versus mistrust
	Infants must learn to achieve a sense of safety, trusting caretakers to provide for their well-being.
Second year	Autonomy versus self-doubt
	Children must learn to make things happen, to choose, to exercise will.
Third to sixth year	Initiative versus guilt
	Children must learn to initiate their own activities, thereby gaining self-confidence.
Sixth year through puberty	Competence versus inferiority
	Children must learn to systematically explore their skills and abilities.

described as tasks. The developing individual must confront and resolve each task in order. According to Erikson, an issue that is successfully worked through leads the individual to develop a central characteristic that allows him or her to confront subsequent social tasks. If an issue is not satisfactorily resolved, the individual carries along the burden of this failure.

Erikson specifies eight different stages across the life span. Here we discuss the four that encompass infancy and childhood. In the next chapter, we will discuss the remaining stages that he proposed.

Trust versus Mistrust. The newborn infant must first achieve a sense of safety, trusting that his environment (in the form of caretakers) will provide for his well-being. If a child's needs for food, warmth, and physical contacts are met, then the child develops trust. If not, the child develops mistrust, which is shown as anxiety and insecurity.

Autonomy versus Self-doubt. At about eighteen months, when the child's physical development allows movement and exploration, she begins to confront the notion of her own self. She is someone who can make things happen or prevent them from happening. Central to this task is the control of her own body, and here is the social significance of toilet training. This can be an area of conflict between children and their parents. Who will prevail? If the child successfully resolves this stage, he or she achieves a sense of autonomy. Otherwise, children doubt their own ability to make things happen.

Initiative versus Guilt. The next stage takes place from about age three to six, when the child starts to initiate his own activities, intellectual and physical. Erikson regards this stage as critical in allowing the child to gain self-confidence. If thwarted by parents in these self-initiated activities, the child is likely to experience guilt and a lack of self-worth.

Competence versus Inferiority.   From age six to the onset of puberty, the child begins to systematically explore her skills and abilities. School begins, and she starts to interact with peers. A number of possible skills beckon: physical, intellectual, and social. Children take lessons in ballet or gymnastics, or throw themselves into art class or swimming pools or the intense study of dinosaurs. Successful resolution of this stage produces feelings of competence. Children who experience failure in mastering skills during this stage may suffer feelings of inferiority.

Erikson regards these as social stages because of the critical role played by other people in helping or hindering the child as she confronts each task. The child develops from a socially dependent creature into one who can act independently while interacting with others. This story continues in the next chapter, with the individual becoming a parent for his or her own children, helping or hindering their social development.

The Infant as Mimic

One of the intriguing things that infants do is to imitate adult facial gestures (Abravanel & Sigafoos, 1984). Kaye and Marcus (1978) showed that six-month-old infants who looked at an adult researcher opening and closing his mouth with a popping sound came quickly to repeat this sequence, including the sound (see Figure 9.6)! More controversial—because the results have been difficult to replicate—is a similar study that purported to show imitation of adult expressions like sticking out the tongue by infants as young as two weeks of age (Meltzoff & Moore, 1977).

Figure 9.6
Baby as Mimic. This infant is imitating the facial expression of the researcher, sticking out its tongue as he does!

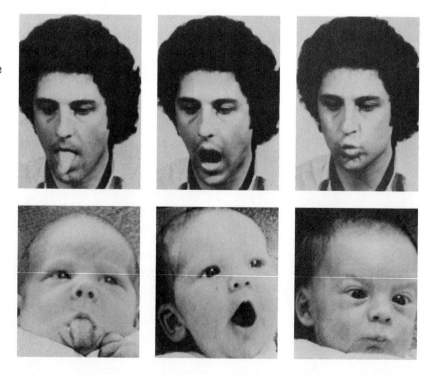

Appreciate the function served by imitation. Because people express their emotions through their facial expressions (Chapter 6), an infant who imitates these expressions ends up responding appropriately to the emotional state of the parent. The selective advantage for an infant who can "empathize" is obvious. By this view, even young babies are already social beings.

Attachment

The child's first social relationship is an emotional **attachment** with her caregiver, usually the mother (Bowlby, 1969). A question that has generated a great deal of interest within developmental psychology is whether there exists a critical period for the development of such an attachment. Animals may show such critical periods. For example, shortly after hatching, ducklings follow whatever moving object they first encounter, in a process called **imprinting** (Lorenz, 1937). Usually, this object is their mother, and imprinting gives an obvious selection advantage, keeping the vulnerable ducklings out of danger. Imprinting can be disrupted, though, if there is no moving object for them to follow.

Is there any parallel here with human development? Infants obviously don't start out life by following their mothers around, but some theorists suggest that a human newborn must form an attachment with a caretaker during a critical period within the first few years of life. This attachment sets up the child's subsequent approach to social relationships. If an attachment is not formed, or is formed poorly, then subsequent social development is, by this view, thwarted.

Stages of Infant Attachment. Observational studies show that a newborn's attachment goes through several stages. During the first few months of life, the child is socially responsive but not discriminating. The infant looks at everyone, and can be comforted by anyone. This period comes to an end when the child discriminates her primary caretakers from other people. Then the child responds differently to familiar people, smiling and vocalizing more in their presence, and being more easily comforted by them. After about six or seven months, a third period is entered, where the child shows a strong attachment to a single individual. This stage is marked by the infant actively seeking contact with this person. The child crawls after the person, calls out to him or her, and so on. Strangers elicit fear. This pattern may continue for the next several years of the child's life.

This third stage of attachment has been studied by observing how infants react when separated from their mothers. A popular way to study attachment among infants between twelve and eighteen months of age is with the strange situation test (Ainsworth & Wittig, 1969). The child, accompanied by his mother, comes to the researchers' laboratory, which is equipped with its own playroom. The playroom is filled with toys. A carefully scripted series of encounters take place, observed by researchers behind a one-way mirror.

- The mother puts the baby on the floor, some distance from the toys, and then takes a seat.
- A stranger enters the playroom and also sits down.
- The stranger talks to the mother, and then the stranger attempts to play with the baby.

Imprinting is a form of attachment found in some animal species. Here a group of ducklings follows Konrad Lorenz, a scientist well known for his study of animal behavior.

attachment
an emotional and social bond that forms between an infant and its primary caregiver(s)

imprinting
an attachment, formed by ducklings and the young of some other species, to whatever moving object they first encounter; it occurs only during a critical period

- Next the mother leaves her baby alone with the stranger for a few minutes; she returns shortly to be "reunited" with her infant.
- Then both the mother and stranger leave, again for a few minutes.
- The stranger returns first and attempts to play with the baby.
- Finally, the mother returns, and picks up her baby.

This procedure provides rich information about how the child reacts to separation. When the mother first leaves the room, about half the children cry before she comes back. More than three-quarters respond to her return by reaching to her in some way: smiling, touching, speaking. When the mother leaves the room again, the typical child becomes upset again. The stranger proves unsuccessful in soothing the child. When the mother returns, half the children keep on crying, and three-quarters of them climb into her arms.

Patterns of Attachment. This is the pattern shown by most children, but variation exists. Ainsworth describes three different patterns of attachment shown by responses of children in the strange situation. *Avoidant children* (about 20 percent of those tested) do not cry when their mother leaves, and either ignore her or turn away upon her return. *Securely attached children* (about 70 percent) show the pattern of seeking and maintaining contact with the mother. The third pattern, shown by only about 10 percent of children, is termed *ambivalent*. These kids cry when mother leaves but take no comfort from her return.

The strange situation test can be used to assess the effect of other factors on attachment. One obvious comparison yields the expected results. Children whose mothers are supportive and affectionate in dealing with them show the "securely attached" pattern; mothers who are critical and rejecting produce "avoidant" infants (Ainsworth, 1973).

Infant Attachment in the Modern World. The bond between an infant and her parent is obviously strong, and some people therefore worry that some of the changes we see in modern society, such as divorce, two-career families, day care, and nontraditional gender roles, may adversely affect the social development of the child. These issues have been hotly debated in both scientific journals and the popular media, with no firm answers available, much less agreed upon (cf. Zigler & Frank, 1988).

Let's focus on the debate over day care. Do parents who allow another person to care for their young child undercut the child's attachment to them? Do they preclude any sort of attachment? What are the long-term effects of a generation of children raised in day care? A review of the relevant research, by Clarke-Stewart and Fein (1983), found no cause for alarm. Indeed, day care struck these reviewers as beneficial for a child. When compared to children reared at home, day-care children still showed attachment to their mothers, going to them in distress. And day-care children evidenced *increased* social competence and independence. They also scored *higher* on tests of cognitive and intellectual development.

On the other hand, studies also suggest that day-care children may be less securely attached to their mothers, in that they are less disturbed by their absence, and do not stand as close to them in the strange situation test (Belsky, 1988). These findings may indeed show the lack of a secure relationship, or they may just mean that the day-care child is more independent and familiar with brief separations (Clarke-Stewart, 1989). The findings also may mean that the child has formed attachments to individuals in addition to the mother. Remember, the strange situation test is just one way to measure attachment, and it is not a foolproof operational definition. Research and theorizing here continue.

Deprivation and Its Reversal. Although it is clear that various deprivations and unusual experiences interfere with forming a secure attachment, this does not prove that attachment involves a critical period. We would need to show further that retardation of social development during the first years of life has irreparable consequences.

Needless to say, no researcher will experiment with human infants in this way, manipulating early attachments to see what happens. Sometimes unfortunate cases of abuse or neglect come to the attention of researchers, like poor Genie whose story began the chapter. However, in these cases there are so many possible confounds that conclusions are more tentative than we would like. For this reason, some researchers have studied attachment among our close primate cousins.

Pertinent here are Harry Harlow's (1958) well-known experiments with rhesus monkeys. Harlow wondered whether attachment was due simply to the fact that mothers satisfy the infant's need for food. He separated rhesus monkeys at birth from their mothers and raised each alone in a cage with two stationary models (see Figure 9.7). One figure was made of wire and the other of terry cloth. The wire "mother" had a nipple that provided milk, whereas the cloth "mother" did not. If attachment is the result of being fed, then the infant monkey should form an attachment to the model associated with food.

That's not what happened. The infant monkey preferred the cloth model. It sought out the wire model when hungry but otherwise stayed closer to the cloth one. And when the infant was frightened, by an unfamiliar sight or sound, it ran to the cloth mother and clung to it. Harlow deliberately used terry cloth because it has a pleasing texture, and he had suspected that infants are predisposed to form attachments with objects that are easy to cuddle. Blankets and teddy bears may be popular among human children for exactly the same reason. Harlow's research is important for showing that even among animals, emotional bonds reflect more than the satisfaction of hunger.

In a related line of research, Harlow (1965) raised rhesus monkeys in complete isolation. After a year without contact with other monkeys, these animals were fearful and withdrawn. Some of their common behaviors—like biting themselves—can only be described as bizarre. The isolated monkeys did not interact normally with other monkeys, and they proved notably inept when dealing with infants.

The possible parallels between these monkeys and human children raised in an abusive or deprived environment are obvious. The monkeys were not malnourished or physically traumatized, but because they did not have social contact with their kind, their social development was thwarted. These results converge with findings showing that insecurely

Figure 9.7
What Determines Attachment? The baby monkey is fed by a wire figure but prefers to spend its time with this cloth figure.

attached children are less sociable with peers at age two, less flexible and persistent at age four, and more likely to be depressed and withdrawn at age six (Clarke-Stewart, Friedman, & Koch, 1985).

Other studies show that such problems can be corrected if deprived monkeys are placed together with normally raised monkeys (e.g., Novak & Harlow, 1975). Eventually, the isolated monkeys learn to interact normally and show few effects of their earlier isolation. Similarly, studies with human children also show that many of the effects of early deprivation can be reversed if the child subsequently finds herself in a supportive environment (White, 1967). However, if the deprivation takes place for too long a time, it cannot be so easily reversed, suggesting at least a weak version of critical periods for social development. Remember that Genie caught up somewhat—but not completely—in her social development once she was removed from the abusive environment of her childhood.

Styles of Parenting

Developmental psychologists have also been interested in styles of parenting—how parents encourage behaviors they like in their children and discourage ones they don't like. Baumrind (1971) has found that in the United States, there are three major styles of parenting. **Authoritarian parenting** is firm, punitive, and emotionally cold. Such parents value obedience from their children and do not encourage their independence or involve them in decision making. **Permissive parenting** is loving but lax. Such parents exert little control over their children. Indeed, these children are given freedom and are allowed to make decisions, but they have little guidance. **Authoritative parenting** involves negotiating with children. Such parents set limits for a child, but explain why, and they encourage independence. As the child demonstrates responsibility, the parents provide more freedom. Decisions are arrived at through give-and-take.

How do these different styles of parenting affect the subsequent social development of children (Becker, 1964)? Authoritarian parents tend to produce children who are unhappy, dependent, and submissive. Permissive parents raise children who are likely to be outgoing and sociable, but also immature, impatient, and aggressive. The best approach appears to be that of authoritative parents, whose children tend to be friendly, cooperative, socially responsible, and self-reliant.

Parenting style is but one of the ingredients that goes into producing a social being. Just as important as the type of discipline is the affection that accompanies it. And we must also be alert to the possibility that findings like the ones just described do not just show a one-way influence from parent to child. Because children differ with respect to their temperaments, perhaps parents come to the method of discipline that their children "allow" them to.

Socialization of Gender Roles

The terms *male* and *female* refer not only to biological characteristics of people but to psychological and social characteristics as well. These psychological and social differences between men and women are often termed **gender differences.** They encompass several important con-

authoritarian parenting
style of raising children that is firm, punitive, and emotionally cold; authoritarian parents value obedience in their children and do not encourage their independence

permissive parenting
style of raising children that is loving but lax; permissive parents exert little control over their children

authoritative parenting
style of raising children that involves negotiating with them; authoritative parents set limits for their children but explain why, encouraging independence

gender differences
psychological and social differences between males and females

trasts. A person's *gender identity* refers to whether someone experiences the "self" as a male or female (Chapter 16). One's *gender role* refers to society's prescription of how people should behave granted that they are males or females.

Although in most cases people with XY chromosomes also have testes and penises, experience themselves as males, and fulfill male roles in society, there are exceptions. The same is true for the different senses in which the term *female* is used. People's chromosomes, genitals, gender identities, and gender roles may combine in all possible ways (e.g., Money & Ehrhardt, 1972).

For instance, the notion of *androgyny,* which refers to the blending of stereotypically masculine and feminine traits and interests, well illustrates the complexity of the language we use to describe males and females. In our society, many men like competitive sports, and many women like romantic novels. What do we make of someone, male or female, who likes both the Pittsburgh Steelers and Danielle Steel? We call this person androgynous, proving that it is impossible to classify all people with simple categories.

When we talk about males and females, their similarities and their differences, we must be specific about our level of discussion. Sex differences—which by definition are biological in nature (p. 369)—are apt to be much the same across time and place. Gender differences may vary greatly throughout history and from culture to culture.

Societies differ in terms of how distinctly gender roles are specified (Whiting & Child, 1953). One generalization from cross-cultural studies is that societies characterized by nuclear families (mother, father, and children under one roof) have less distinction between gender roles than those characterized by extended families (several families under one roof). Why does this difference occur? In a nuclear family, the absence of one adult means that the other adult, of the opposite sex, must be able to perform the relevant tasks. In an extended family, there are almost always other adults of the same sex to do the tasks of an absent individual. And so no one has to be conversant with the role of the other gender.

In their important book, *The Psychology of Sex Differences,* Eleanor Maccoby and Carol Jacklin (1974) summarized what researchers had discovered about psychological differences between the sexes. They presented their conclusions under three general categories: (a) well-established differences, (b) open questions, and (c) unfounded beliefs (see Table 9.3).

These conclusions deserve your scrutiny (see also Eagly, 1987; Hyde & Linn, 1986). First, there are very few clearly established psychological differences between males and females. Second, as you recall from Chapter 8, one of these differences—female superiority in verbal ability—appears to have declined in recent years. Third, many of the "unfounded beliefs" about gender differences are widely held stereotypes in our society.

Where do the handful of psychological differences originate? Biology may well play a role, particularly in aggression (Chapter 6). Males are more aggressive than females in almost all human cultures as well as most subhuman species. This may be due to testosterone levels, which have been linked to aggression. But of undeniable importance in producing male-female differences is socialization (Jacklin, 1989). As they grow, boys

Table 9.3
Sex Differences

Well-Established Sex Differences	1.	Females have greater verbal ability than males.
	2.	Males have greater visual-spatial ability than females.
	3.	Males have greater mathematical ability than females.
	4.	Males are more aggressive than females.
Open Questions about Sex Differences	1.	Tactile sensitivity?
	2.	Fear and anxiety?
	3.	Activity level?
	4.	Competitiveness?
	5.	Dominance?
	6.	Compliance?
	7.	Nurturance and "maternal" behavior?
Unfounded Beliefs about Sex Differences	1.	Females are more social than males.
	2.	Females are more suggestible than males.
	3.	Females have lower self-esteem than males.
	4.	Males are more analytic than females.
	5.	Females lack the motive to achieve.

Source: Maccoby & Jacklin, 1974.

and girls learn to become men and women. They imitate adults, and are reinforced for showing "appropriate" behavior for their sex. They forge an identity that revolves around a sense of maleness or femaleness.

Most of us have strong ideas about the characteristics of "real" men and "real" women—or "real" people, for that matter. These ideas not only affect our reaction to gender differences but may also create these differences. Surely the parents who greet the arrival of a new daughter with an explosion of pink end up raising a different child than the parents who buy their young daughter a doll and a baseball bat.

Whatever the biological differences between males and females, let us not forget that we *learn* particular gender roles (Etaugh, 1983). Indeed, there may be vast differences in the way one's culture prescribes roles for males and females. Developmental psychologists have taken a close look at how these prescriptions are transmitted to the developing child. Earlier in the chapter, we discussed the tendency of parents to perceive their sons and daughters differently. These differences may have no basis in the actual characteristics of the children. Instead, they reflect widely held stereotypes about the way boys and girls should be.

Throughout childhood, parents continue to treat their children in accordance with stereotypes. As early as the second year of life, children are rewarded for play and behavior "appropriate" to their gender, and punished for "inappropriate" actions (Fagot, 1978). Girls end up playing

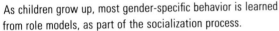
As children grow up, most gender-specific behavior is learned from role models, as part of the socialization process.

with dolls and helping around the house. Boys end up playing with blocks and hollering.

Not only do parents treat girls and boys differently, so too do their teachers once they begin school. Differential treatment again is in keeping with male and female stereotypes. For example, boys are rewarded with attention from their teachers for being assertive, whereas girls receive attention for being gentle (Fagot, Hagan, Leinbach, & Kronsberg, 1985).

One more way in which children develop gender roles is through the process of observational learning (Chapter 5). Boys and girls see male and female adults acting in characteristic ways, in actual life and in media portrayals. Children cannot help but come to the conclusion that there are "female" behaviors and "male" behaviors, and this conclusion encourages them to choose the gender role that seems appropriate to their sex (Raskin & Israel, 1981).

Society: The Context of Development

So far our discussion has focused on rather immediate factors influencing social development, such as the way in which parents encourage or discourage particular behaviors by their children. Many developmental psychologists prefer this close look. But the small world of the child is closely linked to larger worlds, each nested within one another: the community, the nation, and the world.

Urie Bronfenbrenner (1970) stresses that development occurs in the context of all these environments simultaneously. Each larger setting necessarily shapes the smaller settings within. Bronfenbrenner's own research involves comparing child development in different countries, such as the United States and the Soviet Union.

For instance, a pervasive difference between these two cultures, one inherent in the respective ideologies of capitalism and communism, is the relative emphasis placed on the individual as compared to the group. These emphases are reflected in the way children are raised. American children end up more competitive than their Soviet counterparts, while Soviet children are more cooperative. A common perception, in both the United States and the Soviet Union, is that the citizens in the other country are pretty much the same as folks at home. The facts suggest otherwise, because of the different values imparted during socialization. Social development cannot be fully understood until we place it in a societal context.

Consider the extent to which our own society is stratified by sex. Equal opportunity laws notwithstanding, males and females tend to take different jobs, and "female" jobs are devalued relative to "male" jobs, in that salaries are lower. It was not until 1921 that women could vote in the United States. Even today, few women hold high political office.

That women bear children is a biological fact. But women also end up raising children, which is *not* a biologically based phenomenon. Maccoby and Jacklin's (1974) review found no convincing evidence that women are more nurturant than men. This means that fathers can do just as good a job raising children as do mothers, except that it tends not to happen. Because the responsibilities of child-rearing fall to women, women are more likely than men to interrupt their careers because of a family, women are more likely than men to receive custody following a divorce, and so on. These tendencies produce differences between the sexes that are best described as socially based, and attention to the larger society helps us make sense of them.

Cognitive Development

cognitive development
the development of the processes of knowing, including perception, intelligence, memory, problem solving, and language

Cognitive development refers to how the processes of gaining knowledge change across the life span. Of specific importance here are changes in perception, intelligence, memory, problem solving, and language. The major theorist in cognitive development has been Jean Piaget, as mentioned earlier. In this section, we'll first discuss the stages that he described and then the challenges that have been raised concerning his approach. Then we'll briefly look at a remarkable area of cognitive development, the acquisition of language.

Piaget's Theory

scheme
Piaget's term for any organized mental structure that represents knowledge

operation
according to Piaget, one or more mental processes that transform and manipulate information

Like the cognitive theorists discussed in Chapter 7, Piaget was concerned with both mental representations and mental processes. He used the term **scheme** to refer to any mental structure that represented knowledge. A scheme could be as simple as the sucking reflex or as complex as language. Another important Piagetian concept is the **operation:** one or more mental processes used to transform and manipulate information. For example, addition and subtraction are operations that make arithmetic possible.

As we will shortly see, Piaget proposed that the key changes in cognitive development involve the child's available operations. The child's operations overall become more complex, more adaptive, and more independent of immediate stimuli. Said another way, cognitive development moves toward increasing abstractness, progressing from the concrete to the symbolic. Earlier operations provide the foundation on which later operations are built.

These changes take place through a child's interaction with the world, although they reflect biological maturation to a large degree. Piaget distinguished two general reactions of individuals to the new information they encounter. In **assimilation,** people modify or change new information to fit what they already know. In **accommodation,** people change what they know in order to fit the information.

Suppose a young child goes to a zoo and sees a camel for the first time (Berk, 1989). She might call it a horse, assimilating the camel to a scheme she already has—that of a horse. Or she might call the camel a lumpy horse, and accommodate her scheme to what she sees, recognizing that horses seem to come in two varieties—regular and lumpy. Assimilation and accommodation alternate in the course of cognitive development.

Piaget believed cognitive structures develop through four discrete stages (see Table 9.4). The exact times at which developing individuals enter or leave a given stage differ, but the sequence is regarded as invariant.

Sensorimotor Stage. The **sensorimotor stage** corresponds to the period from birth to about two years of age. Advances in the child's motor development allow him to explore his environment. He hits, shakes, touches, and tastes the objects that he encounters. Many of these activities are performed over and over again, like dropping a spoon from the high chair one million times during each meal. Piaget calls these repetitive behaviors

assimilation
according to Piaget, the modification of new information so that it fits what a person already knows

accommodation
according to Piaget, the modification of existing knowledge so that it fits new information that a person has just encountered

sensorimotor stage
Piaget's first stage of cognitive development, from birth to about two years of age, characterized by advances in motor development and object permanence

Table 9.4
Piaget's Stages of Cognitive Development

Chronological Age	Stage and Characteristics
Birth to second year	Sensorimotor stage Children explore the environment and build up schemes; they develop the notion of object permanence.
Second to sixth year	Preoperational stage Children think symbolically; they show egocentrism.
Seventh through eleventh year	Concrete operations stage Children think logically and coherently; they develop the ability to think of objects along more than one dimension at a time.
Twelfth year and over	Formal operations stage Children think abstractly; they can pose and answer hypothetical questions.

object permanence

in the sensorimotor stage of cognitive development, the knowledge that objects exist when out of one's sight

preoperational stage

Piaget's second stage of cognitive development, from two to six years of age, characterized by symbolic thinking and egocentrism

egocentric

able to see things only from one's own point of view and no one else's

The beginning of symbolic thought—expressing oneself in a simple drawing—can be a source of joy for the developing child.

circular reactions. Their purpose is to build up a scheme. They exemplify the general process of accommodation because the child thereby learns which of his actions are under his willful control (and which are not).

The notion of **object permanence** develops during the sensorimotor stage. This is the knowledge that objects exist even when out of one's sight. Here's a simple example. Let's say an infant is propped up so that she can see an interesting object in the researcher's hand. The researcher moves her hand, and the child's eyes follow along. What happens if the researcher's hand moves behind a screen, so that the infant can no longer see the object? In the first few months of life, once the hand and the object it holds are gone from sight, the child does not look for its reappearance. She acts as if the object does not exist anymore. An older infant continues to turn her head, expecting the object to appear on the other side of the screen. Piaget argues from such findings that the child must develop the notion of object permanence—that things continue to exist when they cannot be seen.

Preoperational Stage.　The **preoperational stage** takes place when the child is between two and six years of age. The paramount cognitive achievement during this stage is the beginning of symbolic thinking. Consider these behaviors, which first appear at this time:

- "making believe" that one object is another
- pretending to be mother or father
- starting to draw, intentionally representing objects on paper (or the wall, as sometimes happens!)
- reporting the occurrence of dreams
- beginning to count and understand the notion of "number"
- using language

With the ability to represent the world in symbolic terms, the child has at her disposal a host of new cognitive skills.

At the same time, the child does not think exactly like an adult. Children are notably **egocentric,** which means they can only see things from their own point of view. A classic demonstration devised by Piaget shows egocentrism at the preoperational stage. Children are shown a model of a mountain on a table, and are asked to walk around and inspect it from all sides (see Figure 9.8). Then the children are seated on one side of the mountain, and a doll is placed on the opposite side. The children are asked how the mountain looks to the doll. Early on, they don't appreciate that the doll would see things differently, and so believe that the doll sees the mountain as if from their own perspective. Toward the end of this stage, children understand that the doll would see the mountain differently but remain unable to specify just how.

Egocentrism occurs not just in this perceptual sense, but in other ways as well. If a child is asked what his mother or father might like for a present, the child will probably suggest something that he himself would like, such as a toy or a cookie. The child is not being selfish; he simply cannot grasp a perspective that is not his own.

Piaget characterizes the child's thinking during the preoperational stage as prelogical. Children don't recognize cause and effect links between events, or they misunderstand them (Piaget & Inhelder, 1969).

Figure 9.8

Demonstration of Egocentrism. When asked to describe what the doll sees, young children respond in terms of their own perspective.

The stars "were born when we were born," says a boy of six, "because before that there was no need of sunlight." (p. 110)

Children also evidence animism, believing that inanimate objects are living beings with intentions, consciousness, and feelings. Why do clouds drift slowly through the air? A child in the preoperational stage might explain that clouds don't have legs, and thus they must move ever so slowly, like a worm. Animism is an example of egocentrism, because the child assumes that everything in the world must be alive like she is.

concrete operations stage

Piaget's third stage of cognitive development, from seven to about eleven years of age, characterized by an understanding of conservation

conservation

the knowledge that characteristics of objects or substances—like number, length, or volume—stay the same even if their appearance changes

formal operations stage

Piaget's final stage of cognitive development, from age eleven through adulthood, characterized by the ability to think abstractly

Concrete Operations Stage.   Next we have the **concrete operations stage,** beginning at about age seven and lasting until about age eleven. The child's thinking during this stage becomes more logical and integrated. The child can now think of objects along more than one dimension at a time. He learns that objects can be transformed or manipulated in one way without being changed in other ways. Piaget studied a variety of examples of what is called **conservation:** the recognition that characteristics of objects or substances such as number, length, mass, area, and volume stay the same even if their appearance changes.

For example, a child can be shown a tall thin glass filled with milk. The same milk is then poured into a short wide glass. Which glass holds more milk? The tall one, says the child in the preoperational stage, because the level of milk is higher. Or a child might be shown a plate with five cookies bunched closely together. Then the researcher spreads them out. Which plate has more cookies? The second, because here the cookies occupy more space.

The ability to conserve means that the child can undertake mental operations that are reversible. Therefore, the child in the concrete operations stage recognizes that the milk poured into different glasses is the same, and that cookies spread around a plate remain the same. Logic becomes possible, and so does problem solving of the type sketched in Chapter 7. Note how the child's schemes become more abstract and more useful.

Formal Operations Stage.   The final stage of cognitive development appears about age twelve, and is called the **formal operations stage** because the

The inability to recognize that the two containers hold the same amount of liquid indicates that this child has not yet grasped the principle of conservation.

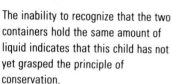

child's mental processes can now operate in the abstract. The child can now pose and answer hypothetical questions. Weighty topics such as the self, love, art, friendship, justice, and the meaning of life occupy the adolescent, able to think about these matters for the first time. The world is seen not just as it is, but as it might be . . . or should be . . . or can't be.

Criticisms of Piaget's Approach. Piaget's writings on cognitive development stimulated massive interest in the topic. Over the past decades, a considerable number of challenges have appeared, questioning Piagetian theory.

One criticism is that Piaget relied too much on verbal inquiries of the children. Not everything that someone "knows" can be put into words, and this is particularly true for young children. Schemes may exist that go undetected in verbal inquiry.

It has also been charged that Piaget's theory hinges on the particular tasks he posed for the children in his studies, and it places great emphasis on what children at a given age cannot do. It is hazardous to say "never" in science. There is always the possibility that another researcher can devise a procedure showing that a given accomplishment by a child is possible earlier than thought. This has happened repeatedly with regard to Piaget's pronouncements. Achievements like object permanence or conservation can be demonstrated much earlier than originally thought if the appropriate task is used (e.g., Bruner, 1964).

Such studies lead to a third criticism, namely that the stages do not cohere as neatly as Piaget proposed. If the skills showing concrete operations are apparent for a particular child on some tasks but not others, we cannot argue that these skills comprise discrete stages (Gelman & Baillargeon, 1983).

Studies show that specific training indeed helps children acquire skills earlier than Piaget believed possible (Brainerd, 1978). Gelman (1969), for example, showed that children could be taught conservation by learning not to be distracted by irrelevant cues. Further, training at one conservation task generalized to others.

There's a fourth problem with Piaget's theorizing. According to some researchers, only about half the adults tested seem to have achieved Piaget's final stage of formal operations (e.g., Neimark, 1982)! This is problematic, because our common sense tells us that most adults can think in abstract and hypothetical terms. As you can imagine, these findings cast doubt on the validity of Piaget's tasks.

Where does this leave us? Piaget remains an important figure because he first drew psychology's attention to the fact that the ways and means of an individual's cognition can and do change. And research suggests that changes in children's brains during development parallel changes in their level of cognitive development (Fischer, 1987). None of the contemporary criticisms of Piaget's work questions the general trend from concrete thinking to increasing complexity and abstractness. On the other hand, the details of his approach, particularly regarding stages, will be substantially revised in the years to come.

Language Development

At one time, psychologists assumed that people's use of language could be seen as just another example of behavior. Behaviorist John Watson (1925) argued that we should study language in terms of how movements of the tongue and larynx produce it. And B. F. Skinner (1957) continued this tradition in his book titled *Verbal Behavior,* in which he generalized from studies of animal learning to human language to conclude that people spoke as they did because they had been reinforced for doing so. Here is how he explained someone learning to read:

> If a child responds *cat* in the presence of the marks CAT and not otherwise, he receives approval; if he responds *dog* in the presence of the marks DOG and not otherwise, he also receives approval, and so on. (p. 66)

This seems alright as far as it goes, but it is in the "and so on" that a behaviorist interpretation of language falls apart.

Chomsky's Linguistic Theory. In 1959, linguist Noam Chomsky published a highly critical review of Skinner's book, in which he showed that language cannot possibly be learned one word at a time, as operant conditioning theories propose. His major argument was that language is creative, meaning that many of the sentences we speak and hear are completely novel, yet we have no trouble understanding what they convey. Skinner's approach, and others like his, cannot explain this important aspect of language.

Chomsky (1957) argued that language has a structure that must be acknowledged if we are to explain it. The *surface structure* of language refers to someone's actual utterances. In contrast, the *deep structure* of language refers to the underlying rules one possesses that generate language. By this view, we miss what is important about language if we focus only on the surface structure. Consider these two sentences:

1. Andrew threw the ball in the air.
2. The ball was thrown in the air by Andrew.

At the level of surface structure, these two sentences represent different utterances. But at the level of deep structure, they convey the same meaning. The fact that sentences like these two are frequently confused in recall supports the notion that their cognitive representations are the same.

Most psychologists now generally accept Chomsky's belief that language has a structure. But they find several of his other claims controversial, including his theory of **transformational grammar.** It proposes that people create sentences by performing particular operations, called trans-

transformational grammar
Chomsky's theory that language results from people transforming meanings represented in the deep structure of language

formations, on underlying meanings represented in deep structure. There are presumably a finite number of transformations, and one or more is performed every time a sentence is uttered and every time an uttered sentence is comprehended.

For instance, the two sentences described earlier concerning Andrew and the thrown ball both have the same meaning and thus the same representation in deep structure. Each sentence comes about when the speaker transforms it from the underlying meaning; each sentence is comprehended when the listener transforms it back to the underlying meaning. Transformational grammar has come in for its share of criticism on a number of grounds, not least of which is that theorists cannot agree on what the basic transformations might be.

Chomsky further believes that much of our capacity to acquire language is innate. He thus posited a yet-to-be-discovered neural mechanism dubbed a **language acquisition device (LAD).** It allows children to process the particular language to which they are exposed, abstract its rules, and then use them. Perhaps we should not regard the hypothesized LAD as an explanation of how language is acquired as much as a suggestion that the eventual explanation must take into account the nervous system as well as the environment.

Stages of Language Development. Chomsky's arguments are mainly "in principle" statements about what language can and cannot be. Developmental psychologists have studied children and how their capacity for language actually develops. Observational studies have given us a chronology (see Table 9.5).

At about four months of age, infants begin babbling, repeating the same sounds over and over. Some of these syllables will later be used in the language the child learns to speak, but not all. Indeed, infants around the world babble in exactly the same way, which implies that they are all

language acquisition device (LAD)

Chomsky's hypothesized neural mechanism that allows children to acquire language readily

Table 9.5
Stages of Language Development

Approximate Chronological Age	Accomplishment
Four months	Babbling, repeating the same sounds over and over
Nine months	Dropping sounds out of babbling repertoire not heard in the spoken language of others; using particular sounds in the same context
Twelve to eighteen months	Using single words
Eighteen to twenty-four months	Using two-word sentences
Thirty months	Using more complex sentences; rapidly expanding vocabulary

born with the capacity to speak any language (Jakobson, 1968; Rice, 1989). At about nine months of age, the sounds that the child doesn't hear in the language spoken around her start to fall out of her babbling repertoire.

Also at about nine months, the child starts to use particular sounds in the same context. These are not precisely words, but they seem to be the earliest versions. So, a child uses one expression (like "ooo") to indicate pleasure and another expression (like "uhh") to indicate displeasure. Some of these expressions are addressed to adults (like "dah") when the child wants something done.

Actual words begin to appear between the ages of twelve and eighteen months. Single words come first, usually accompanying some action. These tend to be words that are easy to pronounce, which is why children say "dada" and "mama" before they say father or mother. The child starts to comment on changes in the immediate environment, including the appearance of another person on the scene.

Language use consists of one word at a time until the child's vocabulary contains about fifty words, typically by the time he is between eighteen and twenty-four months of age. Then two-word sentences start to appear (Clark, 1978). These brief sentences, consisting of a noun and a verb, are called **telegraphic speech** because they are so compressed, but their meanings are usually clear to an adult listener:

- Daddy look
- Want cookie
- Kitty wet
- Give towel

At thirty months of age, language development is off and running for most children. They add new words and longer sentences to their vocabulary daily. And the word parents come to dread—NO!—becomes particularly popular. The general trend is that the child's language becomes increasingly less tied to her immediate surroundings. And the social uses of language are increasingly exploited.

A Critical Period for Language Development? How does this remarkable transformation from a babbling baby into a fully verbal person take place? You already know Chomsky's answer to this question: human nature. So long as a young child is exposed to some form of language, her language ability will develop. Only in an extremely unusual case does this not take place.

One infamous example is the child Genie, described earlier in this chapter. Among the abuses she suffered was never hearing language. When finally discovered and liberated, she could neither speak nor comprehend words. After six years of extensive instruction, Genie was able to speak, but only at the level of a two-year-old (Curtiss, 1977).

In light of the information gleaned from unfortunate individuals such as Genie, many psychologists believe that language acquisition occurs most readily during a critical period sometime between infancy and puberty, when the brain is "ready" to perform this function (Lenneberg, 1967). As discussed in Chapter 2, specific areas of the brain are involved in language. Damage to these areas prior to puberty is not nearly as disruptive to one's use of language as is damage after puberty, suggesting that during the critical period of language development, one part of the

telegraphic speech
brief sentences, consisting of a noun and verb only, that a child usually starts to say between eighteen and twenty-four months of age

brain can take over for another. Additional evidence for a critical period is the fact that most adults find it more difficult to learn a foreign language than do children.

Environmental Influences. Most parents spend a great deal of time talking to and with their young child. One interesting result from studies of this process is that the typical parents do not give their child explicit instruction in grammar (Hirsch-Pasek, Treiman, & Schneiderman, 1984). When parents correct their children's speech, it is often the content that is criticized, not the grammar (Brown & Hanlon, 1970). If a child says, "I eated the cookie," his father may say, "No, that was a cracker." If the child then says, "I eated the cracker," then his father says, "Good!" Parents often will provide the grammatically correct sentence for their child, but if the child is very young, he is not criticized for his poor grammar. These findings support Chomsky's argument that reinforcement per se cannot explain the whole of language use. Without ever being explicitly shaped, grammar eventually develops.

Children often imitate the speech of those around them. (And any parent will be able to tell you that they have an uncanny ability to pick up profanity.) But they only imitate grammatical forms they have already mastered. If the sentence to be mimicked is too complicated, the child says it more simply (McNeill, 1966, p. 69).

> Mother: Say "nobody likes me."
>
> Child: Nobody don't like me.
>
> . . . [after eight repetitions of the above exchange] . . .
>
> Mother: Listen carefully . . . "nobody likes me."
>
> Child: Oh! Nobody don't likes me.

Imitation is apparently used by children to practice language that they are in the process of acquiring (Slobin, 1979).

Language Use by Apes. Although language is a cherished human ability, there is debate as to whether language is unique to humans. As we mentioned in Chapter 1, in the 1960s and 1970s several independent research groups reported success in teaching a small number of apes to use language. The research reports make for fascinating reading and raise important questions about cognition in animals.

For example, in June 1966, Allen and Beatrice Gardner began to teach the infant chimp *Washoe* how to use the gestural language of the deaf known as American Sign Language. Although she was wild-born, Washoe quickly adjusted to her many human companions, playmates, and instructors. She was exposed to a wide variety of objects together with their appropriate signs. Eventually, Washoe started to sign for the objects. After four years of instruction, she could make 132 signs: asking for objects, posing questions about them, and answering others (Gardner & Gardner, 1969).

As she grew older, Washoe began to "talk" about her likes and dislikes, just as human children do. She loved to be tickled, to pick flowers, to play with dolls, and to go for rides in a car. She hated to brush her teeth, and she found barking dogs frightening.

The degree to which animals can master and understand language is the subject of some controversy. Koko, shown here with Dr. Francine Patterson, had a sign-language vocabulary of hundreds of words.

At about the same time, David Premack taught a five-year-old chimp named *Sarah* to communicate as well. Instead of learning to sign, Sarah learned to read and write, using variously shaped and variously colored pieces of plastic, each representing a word. Beginning with the word *banana*, Premack rewarded Sarah with a real banana whenever she placed the plastic symbol on a large board. She was then introduced to new fruits and new plastic words. Before long, Sarah could carry on conversations using the symbols for 130 words, including *apple, dish, green, give,* and *take* (Premack & Premack, 1972).

Finally there is *Koko,* the first gorilla to be instructed in sign language. After six years of instruction, Francine Patterson (1978) reported that Koko had a working vocabulary of about 375 signs, including those for belly button, airplane, and stethoscope! With this many words at her fingertips, so to speak, Koko expressed a variety of likes and dislikes. For example, she preferred men to women, and corn on the cob to olives or radishes. Arguing, trading insults, and relaxing with a book were some of her favorite pastimes.

Just what to conclude from these studies is a topic of hot debate. Skeptics argue that "true" language use by apes has not been demonstrated, because Washoe, Sarah, Koko, and others do not show the spontaneity and creativity that humans do when speaking. Perhaps the appropriate conclusion at this time is simply that these special animals learned to produce something like language that allows communication between them and us. This conclusion is certainly provocative enough.

Moral Development

moral development
the process by which one develops a system of judgments about the rightness or wrongness of acts

Morality is the system of judgments that underlies our sense of the rightness or wrongness of the acts performed by ourselves and others. **Moral development** therefore refers to the changes that take place in these judgments throughout a person's life span. Piaget (1932) proposed that people's level of moral development was tied to their level of cognitive development, showing the same progression from concrete to abstract. Lawrence Kohlberg (1981, 1984) elaborated Piaget's earlier ideas to become the best-known theorist in this area.

Kohlberg's Theory

moral dilemma
a situation requiring a person to make a moral decision and justify it

Following Piaget's example, Kohlberg studies the development of moral reasoning by posing to research subjects a task to be solved, a **moral dilemma** such as the following:

> In Europe, a woman was near death from a special kind of cancer. There was one drug that the doctors thought might save her. It was a form of radium that a druggist in the same town had recently discovered. The drug was expensive to make, but the druggist was charging ten times what the drug cost him to make. He paid $200 for the radium and charged $2000 for a small dose of the drug. The sick woman's husband, Heinz, went to everybody he knew to borrow the money, but could only get together about $1000, which was half of what it cost. He told the druggist that his wife was dying and asked him to sell it cheaper or let him pay later. But the druggist said, "No, I discovered the drug and I'm going to make money from it." So Heinz got desperate and considered breaking into the man's store to steal the drug for his wife. Should Heinz steal the radium? (Kohlberg & Gilligan, 1971, pp. 1072–1073)

A child is asked to decide if it would be right or wrong for Heinz to steal, and then to justify this decision. To Kohlberg, how one justifies the course of moral action is more important than the actual decision.

Kohlberg's theory of moral development, like Piaget's, strictly adheres to a stage interpretation. A particular individual either is at a given level of reasoning or is not. People pass through these levels in the proposed sequence only. And these stages are a universal aspect of human nature. Kohlberg distinguished three general levels of development, each divided into two stages, resulting in six different stages of moral development. Table 9.6 describes these stages. Overall, the progress of moral development is toward increasing abstractness. Less advanced moral judgments are tied to particular situations. More advanced moral judgments, in contrast, transcend the particular and use universal standards of justice, equality, and respect.

preconventional reasoning
Kohlberg's first stage of moral development, in which the child can take into account only rewards and punishments

Preconventional reasoning takes into account only rewards and punishments. Morality is placed outside the individual. A child at the level of preconventional morality would say that Heinz should not steal the drug because he'd be punished if he did.

conventional reasoning
Kohlberg's second stage of moral development, in which most adolescents and adults can justify moral actions in terms of society's rules or expectations

Conventional reasoning justifies moral action in terms of society's rules and conventions, hence the term Kohlberg uses to describe it. Most adolescents and adults seem to think in these terms, and their concern is with conformity. Someone at the level of conventional morality would say that Heinz should steal the drug because marriage entails an obligation to take care of your spouse.

postconventional reasoning
Kohlberg's third and last stage of moral development, in which the adult recognizes that society's rules may conflict with each other, and so he must apply his own abstract standards

Postconventional reasoning, shown by only 20 percent of the adult population, involves the application of one's own abstract standards.

Table 9.6
Kohlberg's Levels and Stages of Moral Development

Levels and Stages			Description
Preconventional reasoning	1.	Obedience and punishment orientation	Rules are obeyed to avoid punishment.
	2.	Instrumental orientation	Rules are obeyed to earn rewards.
Conventional reasoning	3.	Good boy/good girl orientation	Rules are obeyed to earn approval and avoid disapproval.
	4.	Authority-maintaining orientation	Rules are obeyed to show respect for authority.
Postconventional reasoning	5.	Contractual orientation	Morality reflects a social agreement to act in ways intended to serve the common good and to protect the rights of individuals.
	6.	Conscience orientation	Morality reflects internalized standards.

Those at this level recognize that laws and rules are useful but sometimes in conflict with one another. In resolving moral conflicts, people at this stage may try to judge the relative importance and intentions of different laws. Therefore, an answer to the dilemma of Heinz might be that he should steal the drug because respect for another's property must give way to respect for human life.

Criticisms of Kohlberg's Approach

Kohlberg's approach has been influential. Nonetheless, it has been criticized, on both theoretical and research grounds. His overall scheme may reflect his own value judgments. Specifically, according to the way he measures one's level of moral development, a political liberal would often score higher in moral reasoning than a political conservative. Do you see why? The law-and-order emphasis of many conservatives would come across as preconventional morality, but this makes it difficult to argue that Kohlberg's stages reflect something intrinsic about development.

Relatedly, Kohlberg's levels may not apply equally well in all cultures, particularly those without the formal institutions such as courts and schools that dominate our particular world (Simpson, 1974). Kohlberg takes issue with this charge, and to his credit has studied moral development in different cultures (e.g., Nisan & Kohlberg, 1982). The debate continues.

Some critics argue that the types of dilemmas Kohlberg poses in his research are not realistic ones, and hence his research results lack generality. And other critics observe that the scoring of responses to the dilemmas is not always highly reliable.

The highest stage of moral reasoning is rarely encountered using Kohlberg's research technique, leading Kohlberg himself to consider dropping it from his scheme (e.g., Colby, Kohlberg, Gibbs, & Lieberman, 1983). But is this consistent with common sense? Surely most adults understand morality in abstract terms. They may not always show postconventional morality in their judgments, but they do some of the time. Witness the societal dismay at various political scandals in recent decades, such as the marital infidelity of public figures. Although many of these scandals seemed not to involve any technical illegality (conventional morality), they flaunted higher principles (postconventional morality). The fact that many people regarded the behavior revealed in these scandals as wrong shows postconventional moral reasoning.

As we discussed earlier with respect to Piaget's stages, researchers find that instructing children in moral reasoning may accelerate their "passage" through Kohlberg's stages (e.g., Turiel, 1966). The relevant studies expose children to examples of moral reasoning at levels higher than their own, assessing the effect on moral development some time later. Findings here are inconsistent (e.g., Rest, 1983), but the occasional finding that short-term training affects someone's measured stage is not consistent with Kohlberg's view of moral development.

The relationship between moral reasoning and moral behavior is not clear. Research in the Kohlberg tradition often assumes that the former leads to the latter without explicitly showing that it does. A few studies show that people at the level of postconventional reasoning indeed are less likely than others to lie or cheat, but other investigations do not find the expected link (Clarke-Stewart, Friedman, & Koch, 1985).

Moral action has many determinants, of which moral reasoning is but one. For instance, in a study of Berkeley students staging a sit-in supposedly to support free speech, researchers found that some protesters justified their actions in abstract terms, whereas others explained what they did in self-centered and immature ways (Haan, Smith, & Block, 1968).

Kohlberg's approach has also been criticized for embodying a masculine view of morality; indeed, his original studies used only male research subjects. Carol Gilligan (1982) makes the provocative argument that there are two general approaches to moral reasoning. The first orientation concerns itself with rules and principles, taking justice as its bottom line. This is the morality studied by most developmental psychologists, from Piaget to Kohlberg. The second orientation reflects human relationships, and is a morality of caring.

By and large, Gilligan argues, men and women respectively speak in these different moral voices. In resolving moral dilemmas, men will speak of rights and obligations, phrasing them as costs and benefits: Heinz should steal the drug because the sentence won't be that heavy. Women speak of the need to preserve human relationships: Heinz should talk to the druggist and work out a way to buy the drug on installment. If the morality of justice is taken as the standard, then those who think in terms of human relationships are necessarily relegated to a lower level.

Some of Gilligan's specific arguments themselves elicit criticism. Her initial premise—that women score lower than men on Kohlberg's dilemmas when his scoring system is employed—may not itself be true; some studies have found that women and men score much the same (Walker, 1984). But her general point is still valid. There are different approaches to morality, and psychology should take a broad approach in studying its development.

Let's look back over the topics covered in this chapter. We started with a definition of developmental psychology and the issues that concern developmental psychologists. Then we discussed the early history of this field. With this background, we proceeded to cover what is known about the physical, social, cognitive, and moral development of infants and children. Remember that contemporary psychologists regard development as a process that continues throughout one's life, and so in the next chapter we continue our discussion, focusing on adolescents and adults.

Summary

Topics of Concern

- Developmental psychologists study people's physical and psychological changes across time. The first developmental psychologists focused on infancy and childhood, but contemporary theorists recognize that change can and does occur throughout one's entire life, including adulthood.
- Several questions are of great importance to developmental psychologists: (a) how do nature and nurture interact to determine development; (b) to what degree does stability characterize the process of development; and (c) as people develop, do they pass through discrete stages?

A Brief History of Developmental Psychology

- Developmental psychology was not possible until society marked off the discrete period of childhood, something that happened only within the last few hundred years.
- Darwin's theory of evolution explicitly drew the attention of science to the process of change.
- Influential theorists in developmental psychology include John Watson, Arnold Gesell, Sigmund Freud, Erik Erikson, and in particular Jean Piaget.

Studying Development

- Two general research strategies are used in developmental psychology: cross-sectional approaches that simultaneously study people of different ages, and longitudinal approaches that study the same people over time.

Physical Development

- Physical development reflects the interaction of biological and environmental factors. It includes prenatal development, as well as the physical changes occurring during infancy and childhood.

- Temperament is the individual's emotional style, and is a good example of how nature and nurture interact to determine behavior.
- Sex differences in development begin at the moment of conception and continue through life, influenced by the complex interplay of nature and nurture.

Social Development

- Social development refers to the person's development as a social being. The first social relationship is the infant's attachment to his or her mother, and this process has been extensively investigated by seeing how the young child reacts to brief separations from mother.
- Parents differ in their style of socializing their children, and these various styles are linked to subsequent social development, including the development of gender roles.

Cognitive Development

- Jean Piaget theorized extensively about cognitive development, and proposed that children's thinking progressed through several stages, becoming less concrete and more symbolic with each stage.
- The details of Piaget's theory of cognitive development have been criticized in recent years, but his general approach has made the entire field possible.
- Developmental psychologists also study the way that language use develops. Although psychologists at one time treated language as verbal behavior controlled by reinforcement, Chomsky's approach to language as having a structure of meaning proved more viable.
- Language develops in regular patterns, from babbling to single words to sentences, under the influence of both biological and environmental factors.

Moral Development

- Lawrence Kohlberg followed Piaget's example in studying moral development in terms of people's reasoning concerning moral dilemmas.
- Kohlberg proposed that people's moral reasoning is originally tied to external considerations but progresses to abstract principles such as justice and equality.
- Critics take issue with Kohlberg's approach, most notably by observing that Kohlberg focused on a moral system based on rules rather than the preservation of human relationships.

Important Terms and Names

What follows is a list of the core terms and names for this chapter. Your instructor may emphasize other terms as well. Throughout the chapter, glossary terms appear in **boldface** type. They are defined in the text, and each term, along with its definition, is repeated in the margin.

Topics of Concern

developmental psychology/356
developmental stages/358
critical period/358

A Brief History of Developmental Psychology

maturation/361
psychosexual stages/362
psychosocial stages/363

Charles Darwin/360
John Watson/361
Arnold Gesell/361
Sigmund Freud/362
Erik Erikson/363
Jean Piaget/363

Studying Development

cross-sectional studies/365
longitudinal studies/365

Physical Development

zygote/368
embryo/368
fetus/369
sex differences/369
temperament/373

Social Development

social development/374
attachment/377
imprinting/377
gender differences/380

Harry Harlow/379
Eleanor Maccoby and
    Carol Jacklin/381

Cognitive Development

assimilation/385
accommodation/385
sensorimotor stage/385
preoperational stage/386
concrete operations
    stage/387
formal operations stage/
    387
transformational grammar/389

Noam Chomsky/389

Moral Development

preconventional reasoning/394
conventional reasoning/394
postconventional reasoning/394

Lawrence Kohlberg/394
Carol Gilligan/396

Review Questions

1. Developmental psychologists concern themselves with changes from
   a. birth to death.
   b. childhood to adulthood.
   c. conception to death.
   d. infancy to childhood.
   Although developmental psychologists at one time focused on infancy and childhood, the field now encompasses the entire life span, from conception to death./356

2. To get at the *process* underlying development, _____ research is often necessary.
   a. case study
   b. cross-sectional
   c. experimental
   d. longitudinal
   In longitudinal research, the same individuals are studied over time. This may be the only way to get a good glimpse at the process underlying development./365

3. Which sex is more vulnerable to death, damage, and/or defect during development?
   a. females at all ages
   b. males at all ages
   c. younger females, older males
   d. younger males, older females
   Stereotypes to the contrary, males are more vulnerable than females at all ages./370

4. Temperament refers to a biologically based
   a. capacity for language.
   b. set of needs and drives.
   c. style of behaving.
   d. style of learning.
   By definition, temperament refers to one's style of behaving. Among the dimensions of temperament are emotionality, activity, and sociability./376

5. Erikson believes that stages of development are defined by
   a. available cognitive operations.
   b. characteristic defense mechanisms.
   c. social conflicts to be resolved.
   d. sources of sexual gratification.
   According to Erikson's theory of development, the individual at each stage must confront and solve a particular problem that involves relating to other people./374

6. The "strange situation test" is used by researchers to study
   a. attachment.
   b. creativity.
   c. curiosity.
   d. learning.
   e. moral development.
   The strange situation test is an operational definition of a child's attachment to his or her parent. How does the child respond when placed in a strange situation and then separated from his or her parent?/377

7. Harlow's research with monkeys points to the importance of _____ during development.
   a. environmental stimulation
   b. nutrition
   c. physical contact
   d. sibling rivalry
   Harlow showed that infant monkeys separated from their mothers prefer to cling to a "cuddly" wire model, even when they are fed elsewhere./379

8. According to Piaget, cognitive development occurs in the direction of increasing
   a. adaptiveness.
   b. complexity.
   c. independence from immediate stimuli.
   d. all of the above.
   Piaget's theory of cognitive development proposes that during development, changes occur in the child's available operations, so that her thinking increases in terms of its adaptiveness, complexity, and independence from the immediate setting./384

9. Children are notably egocentric during the
   _____ stage.
   a. sensorimotor
   b. preoperational
   c. concrete operations
   d. formal operations
   Children are quite egocentric during the preoperational stage of cognitive development because they quite literally cannot take the perspective of another person./386

10. In proposing his theory of moral development,
    Kohlberg was most importantly influenced by
    the ideas of
    a. Freud.
    b. Gesell.
    c. Piaget.
    d. Watson.
    Like Piaget, Kohlberg argues that moral develop-
    ment reflects the individual's passage through in-
    creasingly abstract stages of reasoning./394

Peer-group influence increases in adolescence.

Chapter Ten

Adolescent and Adult Development

Topics of Concern—One More Time

One of the central events in the 1955 movie *Rebel Without a Cause* is a test of nerve between two teenagers, Buz (played by Corey Allen) and Jim (played by James Dean). They play a game of chicken with their cars, driving them head-on at each other until one fellow "chickens out" and swerves away. In the course of this game, something goes awry. Buz catches his sleeve on the handle of his door and cannot escape when his car catches fire. Trapped inside, he dies in a burst of flames.

A shaken Jim returns to his home, telling his parents that something terrible has happened. A television set plays in the background, foreshadowing the apathy of his parents. His father acknowledges that an "accident" occurred. He heard it on the news. But Jim's parents deny the reality of his involvement, and they counsel Jim against going to the police.

Mother: I don't want him to go to the police. There were other people involved, and why should he be the only one. . . .

Jim: But I am involved! I was in a crime, Mom. A boy was killed! You don't get out of that by pretending it didn't happen.

Father: You know you did wrong. That's the main thing, isn't it?

Jim: No! It's nothing. Just nothing. . . .

Father: Son, this is all happening so fast. . . .

Jim: You better give me something, Dad. You better give me something fast . . . Dad? Are you going to stand up for me?

His father has no response. Jim grabs him by the neck and drags him down the stairs. His mother screams at him not to kill his father. Jim runs out of the house, forsaken by his father when he needed support from him.

In talking to a friend (played by Natalie Wood) later that night, Jim says, "I never figured I'd live to see eighteen. Isn't that dumb? . . . Each day I'd look in a mirror, and I'd say, 'What? You still here?' . . . Like even today, I woke up this morning, you know? And the sun was shining, and everything was nice. Then the first thing that happens is I

see you, and I thought this is going to be one terrific day so you better live it up, boy 'cause tomorrow maybe you'll be nothing."

Rebel Without a Cause remains a popular movie to this day, and its hero remains a symbol for teenagers disenchanted with the hypocrisy and shallowness that seem to mark the adult world they must so soon enter. But for all its appeal, is this movie an accurate depiction of what it means to be an adolescent? And for that matter, is it fair to the typical adult? More generally, *Rebel Without a Cause* draws our attention to adolescent and adult development.

The preceding chapter concluded with a child developing simultaneously as a physical, social, cognitive, and moral being. The story of this developing individual continues in the present chapter. **Adolescence** refers to the developmental period that begins with the onset of the physical changes that comprise puberty. It is a period marked by rapid physical and psychological growth. By current convention, adolescence ends at about age twenty with **adulthood,** when many people begin a career and start a family. Developmental psychologists increasingly regard adulthood as a period of great changes, and make distinctions among different periods within adulthood (see Table 9.1, p. 357).

A better title for this chapter might well be "Adolescent and Adult Development in the Here and How"—that is, in the United States in the late twentieth century. In the last chapter, we noted that it is impossible to discuss development without paying explicit attention to the cultural and historical context in which development occurs. This principle holds strongly for child development (Bronfenbrenner, 1970), and even more so for adolescent and adult development.

Consider these phenomena that profoundly shape who and what we are today:

- mandatory retirement
- universal schooling

> **adolescence**
> the developmental period that begins with puberty and ends at about age twenty, marked by rapid physical and psychological growth
>
> **adulthood**
> the developmental period that begins with the end of puberty, at about age twenty, and lasts until death

- working mothers
- high divorce rate
- life expectancy in excess of seventy years
- effective birth control
- television and the mass culture it creates

All of these are relatively recent arrivals on the historical scene.

Even the "here and now" is in itself far from a monolithic culture. Great diversity along racial, ethnic, and socioeconomic lines marks this country. Researchers do not always take these distinctions into account, which means that problems of generality—always an issue in psychology—are front and center when the focus is on adolescent and adult development. Cohort differences further complicate matters, as we discussed in the previous chapter. All these considerations combine to make the task of the developmental psychologist interested in adolescents and adults a difficult one, because theories and results must be regarded as highly tentative.

Recall the topics of concern to developmental psychologists covered in the previous chapter. These are central not just to the study of infant and child development, but also to the study of adolescent and adult development. Let's examine these topics again, this time with the emphasis on these next periods of the life span.

Nature versus Nurture

People change throughout their lives, reflecting a continual interaction between biological and environmental determinants of behavior. Developmentalists, whether interested in adults or children, seek to specify the exact ways in which this interaction takes place. Consider the teenagers in *Rebel Without a Cause*. Does their impulsivity and emotionality reflect the surge of hormones through their systems—a biological influence—or a reaction to life in the suburbs—an environmental influence? At the present time, there have not been enough longitudinal studies of adult development to make general statements about what actually happens. However, psychologists have begun to make progress with regard to understanding how nature and nurture affect specific aspects of adolescent and adult development, such as sexuality or aging.

James Dean's enduring popularity is in part a testament to the accuracy of his portrayal of a troubled adolescent in *Rebel Without a Cause*.

Is Development Stable?

The issue of stability can be raised with regard to adult development. Remember that the prevailing belief in psychology until relatively recently was that adulthood was a time of great stability and little change. Studies have challenged this position by showing that change occurs throughout the entire life span. But these studies do not necessarily mean that extreme discontinuity prevails.

Indeed, we should expect a complex resolution of this issue with regard to adolescent and adult development. The thrust of developmental research in recent years is to caution us against expecting single modes or directions in any developmental process, and there is no reason to suspect that adult development will prove any different. Were James Dean's character in *Rebel Without a Cause* to become an adult (and/or were James Dean himself to have lived past young adulthood), we would see some of his psychological characteristics persisting in much the same form. Other characteristics would be profoundly different.

Developmental Stages

As with child development, stage theories are often used to explain adolescent and adult development. The most influential account of adult development has been the psychosocial theory of Erik Erikson. We encountered this theory as it applies to children in the previous chapter, and we will discuss its application to adolescents and adults shortly. Erikson's description of psychosocial stages has inspired a host of similar stage theories of adult development, as well as explanations that take issue altogether with the idea that adults pass through discrete stages as they age.

Remember that one implication of the existence of developmental stages is that there should be critical periods in life, times during which particular experiences must occur to avoid hindering subsequent development. In the previous chapter, we saw two examples of critical periods in early development: language development and, more controversially, social development. Some theorists argue that analogous periods exist for adults as well, occurring within what we commonly call crises. A crisis is a period of transition marked by confusion, turmoil, and vulnerability. If you don't resolve a crisis in a satisfactory fashion, you are likely to carry the burden of that failure into subsequent periods of your life.

Popular belief has it that we experience two major crises in our lives, the first during adolescence and the second during middle adulthood. These crises seem to have provided the raw material for almost every other movie in recent years, as well as vintage films such as *Rebel Without a Cause*. One popular plot device has the adolescent and his parent switching places with comic effects, underscoring the similarity of the two crises.

In a "typical" family in the United States, where parents are 20–25 years older than their children, the crises of adolescence and middle adulthood are quite possibly going on simultaneously under the same roof. This raises the question of whether the two crises are really one larger crisis for the family. But many developmentalists doubt that any such crises exist at all.

Perspectives on Adolescent and Adult Development

In Chapter 9, we introduced Erikson's theory of psychosocial development. His is the most influential of the theories of development after childhood, and many more recent accounts represent variations on his approach. However, note as well that other contemporary theories sometimes take issue with Erikson's ideas. We'll discuss some of their criticisms in just a bit.

Erikson's Theory: Adolescents and Adults

In the previous chapter, we covered the earliest of Erikson's psychosocial stages, stopping just short of puberty when children grapple with the issue of competence versus inferiority. They develop self-confidence to the degree that their struggle is successful. What comes next (see Table 10.1)?

Identity versus Role Confusion.　In Erikson's scheme of things, the central issue of adolescence is the creation of an ideology—a set of personal values and goals by which to live. Such an ideology translates itself into a set of related identities, including an occupational identity, a gender identity, a sexual identity, a political identity, a religious identity, a social identity, and so on. The importance of these identities is that they orient adolescents to the future, determining not just who they are but who they will be. This identity can only be chosen once one has the cognitive skills to do so, in particular, the ability to think in hypothetical terms (Chapter 9).

While walking down Main Street in Ann Arbor, Michigan, past a place where the local teenagers congregate, I was thinking about writing this section of the chapter. So, I saw these young people in a different light.

Table 10.1
Erikson's Later Stages of Psychosocial Development

Chronological Age	Central Issue
Puberty to age 18	Identity versus role confusion
	Adolescents must create a set of personal values and goals by which to live, represented as a coherent identity.
Age 18 to 25	Intimacy versus isolation
	Young adults must learn to merge their identity with that of another person.
Age 25 to 50	Generativity versus stagnation
	Middle adults must learn to concern themselves with the world and the next generation.
Age 50 to death	Ego integrity versus despair
	Later adults must learn to be content with the way that they have resolved previous psychosocial issues.

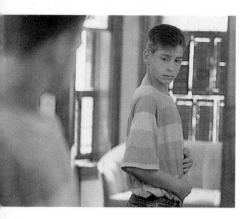

The physical and emotional changes experienced in adolescence trigger the individual's need to establish an identity.

generativity

according to Erik Erikson, concern for the next generation that is the focus of middle adulthood

ego integrity

according to Erik Erikson, acceptance of one's choices in life (those that led to triumphs as well as disappointments), and a sense that one's dilemmas have been well-resolved—the focus of later adulthood

Lots of them wore buttons with slogans: political, humorous, and/or obscene. It struck me that prepubescent children don't wear such buttons, and neither do adults. Perhaps buttons play some role in creating an identity. Once you know who you are, you need no longer caption yourself for the larger world. At any rate, those teenagers who fail to achieve an identity for themselves feel diffuse and undefined, a state that Erikson refers to as role confusion. "Who am I?" they ask, and there is no answer, neither on their buttons nor in their hearts.

Intimacy versus Isolation. For those who leave adolescence with an identity, the next task is to merge this identity with that of another individual—to achieve intimacy. By Erikson's view, people cannot find out who they are in a relationship. Just the contrary. Identity is a prerequisite for a relationship, or at least one to be characterized by shared feelings and closeness. Those who fail to achieve an intimate relationship with another person feel isolated.

Some suspect that Erikson's sequence of identity leading to intimacy better describes the course of development for men than for women (Sangiuliano, 1978). Even Erikson (1968) has wondered if women's identities are forged from the relationships, rather than vice versa. Note the similarity between this argument and that of Carol Gilligan (1982) mentioned in the last chapter: Women are oriented toward other people throughout their lives. Accordingly, women's identities are defined by other people, suggesting that their developmental sequence leads from intimacy to identity, not vice versa.

Generativity versus Stagnation. At any rate, when identity and intimacy are achieved, men and women enter Erikson's next psychosocial stage. Here the concern is with matters outside of oneself, with the world and the next generation. Erikson terms this concern **generativity.** An obvious way to resolve this issue is by raising one's own children. There are other ways as well, through an occupation such as teaching, or through one's support for causes like environmentalism or the elimination of nuclear weapons. These show concern for the future. According to Erikson, those who do not achieve generativity will feel stagnant and self-absorbed.

Ego Integrity versus Despair. The final stage proposed by Erikson comes at the end of one's life, as a person looks back over the issues faced over the years. If they have been resolved successfully, the person feels content, having achieved the state of **ego integrity.** To use Erikson's (1959, p. 104) own words:

> [Ego integrity] . . . is the acceptance of one's own and only life cycle and of the people who have become significant to it as something that had to be . . . an acceptance of the fact that one's life is one's own responsibility.

One leads but a single life, and integrity results from the conviction that one has led it well. If this is not the case, the person feels despair. Life has been too short, too unfair, too filled with failure.

Conclusions. We can look at Erikson's theory with varying degrees of skepticism. If we take a close look, we find legitimate shortcomings. Evidence for a strict stage approach to development is lacking. As already noted, the

According to Erikson's theory, many of the people in this crowd must have reached the developmental stage in which their attention shifts to problems related to their own—or their children's—futures.

theory is a better description for men than women, simply because women's career paths are more difficult to traverse. And similarly, the theory is culturally bound, relevant to contemporary life in the Western world but not to life in other times and places.

If we look at his approach more generally, however, there is much to commend in Erikson. First, his work reminds us that development is a continual process throughout one's life span. Second, it supports the notion that development involves biological and environmental influences. Third, it specifies the issues that confront a person throughout life, making explicit that these change with age. Adolescents worry about different things than young adults, and young adults worry about different things than middle-aged adults. Fourth, Erikson argues that the tasks that confront us are social ones. We do not develop in isolation from other people.

Cultures seem to recognize the social nature of people's conflicts, and provide their members with help to accomplish the tasks that confront them. For instance, consider the dating rituals institutionalized within our own society. They help young people achieve intimacy by bringing them together precisely when intimacy is their prevailing concern.

Vaillant's Theory: Adaptation to Life

A good example of a theorist strongly influenced by Erikson's stage approach is George Vaillant (1977). Influenced as well by other psychoanalytic writers, Vaillant regards development as the process of adapting oneself to the demands of life. One does not resolve all demands simultaneously, but rather takes them on in a given order: first defining one's own identity, next merging oneself with another person, then achieving a career, and so on.

Vaillant is interested in the particular ways in which a person adjusts and adapts to the demands of life, and he lays great stock in psychoanalytic **defense mechanisms.** As discussed in Chapter 6, these are unconscious strategies that people use to deal with their anxiety. Vaillant suggests that defense mechanisms can be arranged in a hierarchy, from less mature to mature (see Table 10.2).

defense mechanisms

unconscious strategies that people use to protect themselves against anxiety

An immature defense mechanism is a strategy such as *projection,* which grossly distorts reality. Put another way, you attribute your own unacceptable motives and characteristics to someone else. "Have you noticed how our new neighbors are preoccupied with sex? I know because I've been peeking through their windows!"

In contrast, a mature defense mechanism involves much less distortion and is exemplified by *sublimation.* Here you redirect your motives into socially acceptable actions. So, someone with aggressive impulses does not punch out people but, instead, gets a job demolishing buildings.

At any given point in life, a person uses a variety of defense mechanisms, some mature and some immature. However, Vaillant (1977) argues that the broad trend over life is for people to increasingly use mature rather than immature defenses; mature defenses allow people to cope better than immature defenses (Chapter 6). This change presumably represents the inherent direction in adult development. In fact, Vaillant has documented this trend toward maturity in defense mechanisms in the Harvard Study of Adult Development. (This is the longitudinal study mentioned in Chapter 9.) Those men who were more mature than their coun-

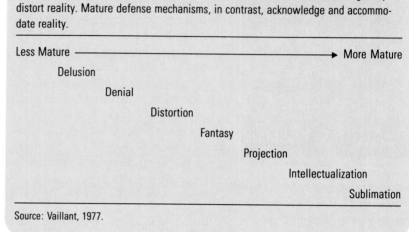

Table 10.2

Hierarchy of Defense Mechanisms

According to Vaillant, a person's characteristic defense mechanisms can be arranged along a hierarchy, from less to more mature. Immature defense mechanisms grossly distort reality. Mature defense mechanisms, in contrast, acknowledge and accommodate reality.

Less Mature ─────────────────────────────────➤ More Mature

　　　　Delusion
　　　　　　Denial
　　　　　　　　Distortion
　　　　　　　　　　Fantasy
　　　　　　　　　　　　Projection
　　　　　　　　　　　　　　Intellectualization
　　　　　　　　　　　　　　　　Sublimation

Source: Vaillant, 1977.

terparts experienced greater occupational, psychological, and social success. The mature individuals in this study were even physically healthier than the immature ones.

Vaillant's theory can be criticized because its major research support comes from investigations of men only. Further, these men come from a particular cohort and are far from representative of the population as a whole. Another problem in his approach to studying development is that he theorizes about discrete stages, but presents data that seem to lend themselves to a view of development as continuous, a slow and gradual maturing of one's defenses. Let us not be too harsh on Vaillant, though, because the evidence he cites is more abundant than that cited by most other developmentalists interested in changes through adulthood.

Gould's Theory: Transformations

Another stage theory of adolescent and adult development is proposed by Roger Gould (1978) in his popular book *Transformations*. Gould concerns himself specifically with the period between ages sixteen and forty-five. He argues that people in their early and middle adulthood go through a process of identifying "myths" about the world, trying to live by them, and finally giving them up. Here are the major myths that define the stages of adult development:

- ages 16–22: "I'll always belong to my parents."
- ages 22–28: "Following the rules will always bring results."
- ages 28–34: "My life is simple and controllable."
- ages 34–45: "There is nothing evil in the world."

According to Gould, the person who can successfully grasp that these are false beliefs is ready, at age forty-five, to achieve his or her full potential as an adult.

The general thrust of Gould's theory has appeal, but he provides little support for its details. Indeed, our common sense suggests that his stages are vastly simplified if not altogether incorrect. Is it reasonable to propose that the "there is nothing evil in the world" myth persists throughout middle age for most adults? Jim's father in *Rebel Without a Cause* seems to endorse this myth, but he is a tragic—and fictional—character. Remember Kohlberg's research on moral development among children that we discussed in the previous chapter. Children grapple with notions of good and evil, and some do so with much more sophistication than Gould grants to the typical adult.

Levinson's Theory: Life Structures

life structure
the unique way people combine the various roles they play (at work, at home, in the community) at any given time

In contrast to the views of Erikson, Vaillant, and Gould, Daniel Levinson (1978) proposes an adult development theory that disavows any inherent direction to the changes that people go through as they lead their lives. Levinson does, however, regard development as discontinuous. The key notion in his system is the **life structure:** a broad term referring to the way that people combine the various roles they play at any given time. These roles come from the workplace, from the family, from one's peer group, and so on. We each create a unique pattern from these roles, what is popularly called our life-style.

Changes occur with age inasmuch as our society is stratified this way. As we age, and different roles become available—or are thrust upon us!—we must create a new life structure. Adult development thus alternates between periods of relative stability (when a given life structure is in place and sensible) and periods of unrest (when we are making a transition from one type of life structure to another).

In early adulthood, we first enter the adult world of work and intimate relationships. Levinson argues that at this time many people create goals and then strive to reach them. This particular life structure cannot last forever. Some goals may be reached, and some are abandoned. At about age forty, many people experience a transition into middle adulthood, with their life structure rearranged so that it crystallizes around issues that concern the meaning of life. And then at about age sixty, many enter yet a new period. This is the time for confronting one's physical aging and the likelihood that one has already achieved everything possible in life.

Unlike Vaillant, Levinson does not imply that middle adulthood is any more advanced than early adulthood, or that late adulthood is any more advanced than middle adulthood. People may become more mature and wise as they age, or they may not. So, Levinson terms his view of adult development the "seasons of life." Seasons change, usually in predictable ways, but there is no inherent hierarchy to them.

Pearlin's Theory: Resources and Coping

Let's consider a theoretical alternative to a stage theory of development, one that posits change or even progress but not in terms of a series of discrete and inevitable steps. Sociologist Leonard Pearlin (1982) has studied the sources of distress in adults' lives. He acknowledges that the issues we confront change during our life and bear a relationship to our age. After all, you cannot face the fact of children leaving home until you first have children. But Pearlin feels there is nothing inherent in these occurrences or life changes that dictates our reaction to them. Rather, each of us reacts according to the resources we have available to us at the time.

Chief among these resources is information: the predictability of changes, or what Pearlin refers to as their schedule. We can anticipate those changes that occur on schedule. Usually, your spouse dies toward the end of your own life. That's expected. But what if he or she dies early, when you are unprepared—emotionally, financially, socially—for this change to occur? The impact here is great, much more so than if you have anticipated this event. Note how Pearlin's view stands in sharp contrast to stage theories of development. We experience changes during our life span, but they do not result from the unfolding of some inherent nature. Rather, they reflect our idiosyncratic adjustment to external happenings.

Taking Stock of These Theories

Figure 10.1 compares and contrasts these theories with respect to several of the important issues of concern to developmentalists. It is impossible to offer highly general conclusions about the comparative validity of these theories, but we can evaluate them with respect to particular points where they diverge. Let us focus on the notion of developmental crises. Some theories posit their existence during adolescence and adulthood. What does the research evidence show?

The Generation Gap. For years we have been hearing about a gap between parents and their adolescent children: profound differences in values and behaviors that lead to a lack of communication, mutual contempt, and outright conflict. This is the so-called **generation gap,** and it portrays the adolescent as a rebel: delinquent, alienated, and crazed by sex, drugs, and rock and roll.

The facts of the matter are much less dramatic. Adolescence indeed is a time when the developing individual becomes more autonomous, and spends more time with peers than with family members (Steinberg, 1981).

generation gap
the differences in beliefs and values that supposedly exist between adults and adolescents, leading to lack of communication, contempt, and conflict

Figure 10.1
Comparison of Theories of Adult Development. Life-span theories can be compared and contrasted in terms of whether or not they propose an inherent direction to development and whether or not they posit discrete stages.

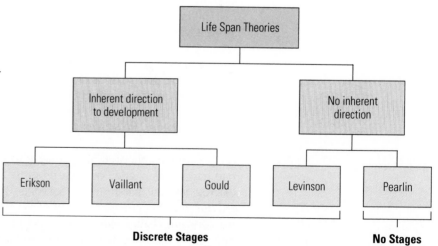

Although the image of the rebellious teenager is a popular one, research indicates that with respect to basic values, adolescents and their parents have much in common.

But this does not mean that teenagers have an across-the-board conflict with their parents. Research shows, for example, that the great majority of adolescents feel close to their parents and respect them (e.g., Offer, Ostrov, & Howard, 1981).

Other research shows that parents and their adolescent children tend to agree with respect to basic values, such as the importance (or unimportance) of religion, work, and education (Conger, 1977). Adolescents resemble their parents more than they resemble other adolescents as a whole. There is considerable variation among adolescents with respect to their values, of course, just as there is considerable variation among adults, prompting some to conclude that the generation gap is a myth, that adolescents are an incorrectly stereotyped group (Adelson, 1979). Although some conflicts between adolescent children and their parents do occur (Hill et al., 1985), perhaps a dramatic generation gap exists more in Hollywood's depictions of adolescence than in the facts. *Rebel Without a Cause* may be without a basis in reality.

Adolescents and adults do differ with regard to personal taste: styles of dress, music preferences, and leisure pursuits. These are precisely the areas where most families argue (Montemayor, 1982). But disagreements about the moral status of rock music or designer jeans are probably insufficient to warrant the term *generation gap*.

midlife crisis

a critical period of life, around age forty, marked by the confrontation of one's mortality and heightened concern regarding the meaning of one's identity and career and the significance of one's primary relationships

The Midlife Crisis.   Is the **midlife crisis** also a myth? According to popular lore (e.g., Sheehy, 1974), this critical period of life is marked by the simultaneous confrontation of one's own mortality, the meaning of one's identity and work, and the significance of one's primary relationships. Adults may respond by changing their job, changing their appearance, changing their spouse, or changing their residence.

However, there is not much evidence that most adults pass through a crisis at midlife. To be sure, adult life is marked by transitions, but those experienced at around age forty do not overwhelm a person's ability to cope, as the term *crisis* implies. Yes, many changes can occur at midlife, but these changes are not inevitable, and they hardly constitute any more of a crisis than do changes at other points in life. For instance, studies of the prevalence of suicide, divorce, and alcoholism do *not* find peaks at midlife (Brim, 1976), which we would expect if the transitions a person confronts constitute a special crisis.

Don't misunderstand the point here. Some people do fall apart during middle adulthood, and there is evidence that particular groups, such as college-educated males, may be more likely to do so than people in general (Tamir, 1982). But this is not a universal stage in adult development. Age-related role changes are probably the culprit, rather than an internal clock ticking away that sounds an alarm that all is unstable. To repeat, crises are not concentrated in middle adulthood any more than they are in adolescence.

The Multiplicity of Developmental Paths. Perhaps particular theories of adolescent and adult development are not wrong so much as they are bound to particular times and places. Remember Bronfenbrenner's (1970) reminder to locate child development in its cultural context. The same warning applies to adult development as well. Theorizing in adult development has been strongly influenced by Erikson's stage theory, which quite explicitly proposes a "right" way to pass through adulthood.

Many developmental psychologists, however, have become wary of such a notion, arguing that various routes traverse adulthood. Bee (1987), for example, suggests that we liken development to a mountain down which numerous criss-crossing gullies run (see Figure 10.2). As children, we stand atop the mountain. We come down the mountain in the course of development. At each point, we face numerous choices, although our previous path constrains us at each point. There are easier or harder ways

Figure 10.2
A Model of Development

to come down the mountain, to be sure, and we may end up in more or less desirable locations. But there is no one best way to make the trip.

Ponder the implications of this metaphor for development. Upon reading about theories of adult development, the initial reaction of many people—and certainly my own—is to feel out of step. Why are the stages or crises or accomplishments proposed by the theories not occurring to oneself on schedule, or in the right order, or even at all! What is ironic is that a majority of people may well be having these same reactions.

Adolescence

Let us now turn to what developmental psychologists know about adolescence. We may think of adolescence mainly in terms of the dramatic physical changes that mark puberty, but adolescence is just as importantly a psychological and social state (Petersen, 1988). Indeed, the physical, psychological, and social changes that characterize adolescence entwine to present the developing individual with a series of challenges to be resolved. As noted earlier in the chapter, many of these involve the adolescent's identity.

Physical Changes

puberty
the physical changes that accompany adolescence: maturation of the reproductive system, development of secondary sexual characteristics, and increases in height and weight

The term **puberty** comes from a Latin word meaning "to grow hair" and refers to the physical changes that accompany adolescence. These changes are of several types. Obviously, the reproductive system matures, so that males can father children and females can bear them. Secondary sexual characteristics also develop: for example, beards in men, breasts in women. There is a growth spurt (Chapter 9) and increased height and weight. Body composition changes—a person fills out. Strength and endurance increase. The voice changes, more so for males than females.

It is not just the absolute magnitude of these changes that make puberty a striking process. It is also the *rate* at which these changes take place. For instance, adolescent males on the average grow 3 to 5 inches in height during the first year of their growth spurt.

At the present time, the various physical changes associated with puberty start to occur around age ten or eleven for females, and around eleven or twelve for males. This age is lower than that of people 100 years ago, and we can attribute this difference to the better nutrition of today. In females, the first menstruation is called the **menarche.** Menarche is treated as a special event in many cultures, but in our society, we sometimes surround it with secrecy, so that a young female may be taken by surprise when she first begins to menstruate. Males do not have so dramatic a transition into physical adulthood, although we can certainly point to the first ejaculation as a notable event.

menarche
a female's first menstruation

Issues of Adolescent Development

What issues concern adolescents? Most basically, an adolescent needs to devise a theory of self, a process that may be fraught with difficulty. Adolescent sense of identity is often shaky, changing from day to day, and it may therefore be accompanied by low self-esteem (Simmons, Rosenberg,

& Rosenberg, 1973). All of this is compatible with Piaget's depiction of the cognitive characteristics of people at this age. To have one's own identity, one must be able to think abstractly. For an adolescent, this is a newly acquired skill that needs to be practiced.

Indeed, adolescents can be highly egocentric, particularly at the beginning of this developmental period. As you probably remember, adolescents often act as if the whole world is an audience for their coming of age, and this heightened self-consciousness can make the most trivial activities painful (Elkind, 1978a). Do my clothes look alright? Are my ears too big? Is my voice going to sound funny? Here we see the cognitive characteristics of adolescence (heightened self-awareness) combining with the physical characteristics (the changes that mark puberty) to affect the individual's self-esteem.

Because the most general psychological issue of adolescence involves identity formation, this issue is confronted simultaneously on many fronts by the young person. The various resolutions—good, bad, or ugly—are eventually integrated into the sense of self that the adolescent brings into adulthood.

Autonomy. One important ingredient in people's sense of self is a belief in their own independence and autonomy. Adolescents labor mightily with this specific concern. Many of the struggles that teenagers have with their parents or teachers should be seen as a struggle for independence, not really a battle over curfews or homework assignments in their own right (Smetana, 1987). If an adolescent pleads with her mother in the course of an argument that "you just don't understand," perhaps the point is that the stakes are different—and much higher—for the child than for the parent.

Friendship. Adolescents also must come to know they are capable of close relations with others (Douvan & Adelson, 1966). Although young children of course have friends, becoming an adolescent marks the beginning of personal friendships (Chapter 15). You want to know how your friends think and feel about things (Youniss & Smollar, 1985). You are more responsive to others, trying to anticipate and interpret their desires. And you worry for the first time that others are not returning your effort. "What does it mean? Don't they like me?" Such friendships require that you be able to take another's point of view, something young children cannot do because their level of cognitive development does not allow it (Chapter 9).

Much has been written about adolescent egocentrism. Nonetheless, personal friendships based on an awareness of and an interest in the feelings and opinions of others are first formed during adolescence.

Because of conflicting societal attitudes about sexuality, in general, and contraception, in particular, adolescent sexual activity often leads to the dilemma of an unwanted pregnancy.

Sexuality. The physical changes of puberty combine with societal expectations to place sexuality in the forefront among the issues that concern adolescents. In recent decades, the attitudes of young people toward sex have become much more liberal, following the larger social trends collectively called the *sexual revolution* (Chapter 16). For example, the majority of American teenagers believe that sex before marriage is appropriate if the partners are in love. Intercourse among adolescents also has become much more common than it once was. Surveys estimate that about 50 percent of contemporary high school students have had intercourse by the time they graduate (e.g., Dreyer, 1982). Many sexually active adolescents do not regularly use contraception, resulting in an alarming number of unplanned teenage pregnancies. Indeed, the United States has *double* the rate of teenage pregnancies found in other industrialized countries.

At first glance, these generalizations seem contradictory. If young people are becoming ever more liberal in their sexual attitudes and activities, why isn't there a corresponding increase in caution? The answer, at least in part, is that sexuality is still regarded with great ambivalence by many people in our society (Silbereisen & Noack, 1988). To take the steps necessary to use contraception is to acknowledge that one is planning to have intercourse, and this is a difficult admission for many youngsters to make—to themselves, to their partners, or to the person from whom they obtain the means of contraception (Cvetkovich, Grote, Bjorseth, & Sarkissian, 1975).

Achievement. Another adolescent concern reflecting the process of identity formation has to do with academic and occupational goals. Achievement is very much woven into the fabric of American culture, and throughout history, Americans have been greatly preoccupied with competition and success. Teenagers today are expected to follow in this tradition, but a dizzying array of choices confronts them in planning for their futures. How best to achieve? What course of studies to pursue in school? What occupation to choose? Which options to keep open? Under these pressures, some question the competitiveness and wonder if the goals to be strived for are worth it.

During adolescence, young people start to take such questions about achievement quite seriously (Simmons & Blyth, 1987). They begin to recognize the long-term consequences of success or failure in this area. Children express interest in jobs based on their fantasies; adolescents take into account reality—their skills, motives, and available opportunities.

Contexts of Adolescent Development

In sum, adolescence is a developmental period that young people traverse while they undergo the physical changes of puberty. They bring into adolescence certain raw abilities for abstract thinking, but these cognitive skills have yet to be fully honed. They grapple simultaneously with diverse issues concerning identity. These issues are not resolved independently of each other, nor are they confronted in isolation from other people. In his book *Adolescence,* Laurence Steinberg (1985) argues that the resolution of adolescent issues is best understood by examining them in terms of the different social contexts in which the young person confronts them: the family, the peer group, school, and work.

The Family.   Although some bemoan the waning of the American family in the late twentieth century, there is no reason to think the family will disappear. What is clear is that the family has changed drastically over the last few decades, following societal trends in work (women entering the labor force in unprecedented numbers), housing (people changing dwelling places much more frequently than ever before), values (growing importance of self-fulfillment rather than social obligation), and family composition (decreasing family size).

The net effect of these changes is to make the American family different than it used to be. Consider the stereotype of the "ideal" American family: father as wage earner, mother as housewife, and children. Only 25 percent of adolescents now live in such a family. Just as common for an adolescent is a single-parent household—headed usually by a working mother. Another common pattern in the modern world is a two-parent household in which only one parent is biologically related to the child.

A great deal of developmental research looks at how these changes in the family affect the adolescent's well-being. In particular, researchers have focused on the effects of divorce, absent fathers, and working mothers. Note the assumption here that deviations from the "ideal" family structure are potentially disruptive and thus worthy of investigation.

Steinberg (1985) concludes that one cannot offer broad generalizations about the effects of these variations. Instead, the actual effects on the adolescent are determined by other factors—such as the age of the child, the sex of the child, and how the parents respond to the change in question. Further, one must distinguish between short-term and long-term consequences. Finally, note that factors such as divorce, an absent father, and a working mother are not independent of one another. This creates great difficulties for the researcher trying to understand the specific consequences of one of these in isolation from the others. Confounds thus abound in studies of how family characteristics influence adolescent development. Conclusions become more tentative than we might like.

For example, a working mother may or may not disrupt the development of her child, depending on the degree to which she is happy to be working and enjoys the job she has (Hoffman, 1974, 1989). And this is just one of the many factors that needs to be taken into account. A father's absence may or may not be disruptive, depending on the sex and age of his children (Hetherington, Cox, & Cox, 1978). Furthermore, these particular findings may be highly specific to a particular time period. Remember Pearlin's idea that the predictability of life changes determines their impact on individuals. As the frequency of divorce and remarriage change, the exact nature of their impact on the people involved may change as well.

With these qualifications made explicit, we can now discuss what psychologists have learned from this type of research, focusing on the apparent impact of divorce on adolescents. As common sense suggests, the period immediately surrounding divorce is marked by heightened family conflict (Berk, 1989). Disputes over personal possessions, family finances, and child custody occur, and these naturally take a toll on the well-being of all family members, including the adolescent children.

To these difficulties can be added potentially stressful life events that may follow in the wake of separation and divorce: moving from a familiar home and neighborhood, changing friends and schools, having less in-

Parents' divorce threatens an adolescent's sense of identity, and can lead to feelings of anger, depression, and guilt.

come. Household routines may disintegrate (Wallerstein & Kelley, 1974). Disciplining of the children may become highly inconsistent (Hetherington, Cox, & Cox, 1982).

In the short run, then, the adolescent may respond to the divorce of his or her parents with anger, fear, depression, guilt, and divided loyalty (Hetherington, 1979). School performance may suffer. The adolescent child of divorce may turn increasingly to the peer group to escape the unpleasantness of home life, with truancy, drug use, and delinquency among the possible consequences (Dornbusch et al., 1985). Adolescent females may show an increase in their sexual activity.

We should emphasize that not all adolescents respond to divorce in these negative ways. Some children, particularly those who are the oldest in a family, may show enhanced maturity in the wake of divorce. And to the degree that an adolescent can understand the reasons behind divorce, damaging reactions are mitigated (Neal, 1983). In other words, the ability to think abstractly about other people aids an adolescent in navigating the aftermath of his or her parents' divorce.

The immediate response of adolescents to divorce is better understood than the eventual response, because research necessarily becomes more difficult to conduct over greater periods of time. Several longitudinal investigations of the long-term impact of divorce on children have recently been completed, so let us draw on their results to sketch what is known. Perhaps the most striking result is that the impact of divorce on children can be an enduring one, and contrary to earlier suggestions by researchers (e.g., Wallerstein & Kelley, 1974), adolescents may be particularly vulnerable to this impact.

Wallerstein and Blakeslee (1989) followed the members of sixty different families for ten years after divorce. Here is what they concluded:

- Adolescents are frightened by divorce because they end up without guidance through adolescence.
- They fear that they will repeat the failures of their parents.
- They feel rejected by their parents following the divorce, because the parents appear preoccupied with their own issues.
- They are disturbed to see their parents develop new sexual relationships, at precisely the time when they as adolescents are grappling with their own sexuality.

These conclusions make sense in light of the primary task of adolescence: forming an identity. Divorce can be harmful to adolescents if its lessons are harsh ones and they become incorporated into their sense of what they are all about. Other studies of the long-term effects of divorce caution us that these effects can be positive as well as negative, depending on a host of conditions (e.g., Emery, 1982; Hetherington & Arasteh, 1988).

The Peer Group. Peer groups provide yet another influence on adolescent identity formation. For the teenager struggling with identity issues, peer groups provide an answer. Actually, they provide many answers, and from these possibilities, the adolescent eventually chooses an identity that feels comfortable. The technical term for the group that provides one's identity is the **reference group,** because the individual refers to this group to define and evaluate the self.

reference group
the group of people that an individual uses to define and evaluate the self; the members are usually his or her age, social class, and race

Our society is extremely age segregated, that is, separated into social groups on the basis of chronological age. This phenomenon is relatively new on the historical scene. Only in the 1930s, when the majority of adolescents first began to attend high school, did it begin to occur. But nowadays, children and adolescents spend the majority of their time in contact with other people of the same age (Csikszentmihalyi, Larson, & Prescott, 1977).

Age segregation shows up in friendships, the vast majority of which are with age peers. Age segregation shows up in organized leisure activities, such as Little League, Girl Scouts, and church groups, all of which are grouped by age. And age segregation even shows itself at work. Adolescents are more likely to find themselves working side by side with other adolescents than with adults (Greenberger & Steinberg, 1981).

Once the peer group is constituted, it exerts powerful influence on the development of adolescents. Indeed, one of our societal "signs" that a child has become an adolescent is the development of these groups:

"Where are you going?"

"Out."

"What are you going to do?"

"Nothing."

"Who are you going to be with?"

"The guys."

"When will you be home?"

"Gee, do you have to know everything?"

If you were raised in the United States, I'm sure your high school was much like mine. Students congregated into discrete groups that dressed alike, acted alike, and thought alike. We had slang names for each group, which is no doubt still common. Whatever the specific labels, there has always been a group that mainly "did" sports, another that mainly "did" academics, and still another group that mainly "did" alcohol or drugs.

What determines the reference group that we choose during adolescence? Researchers who look at the formation of such groups find that they cohere around similarities—adolescents within a group are usually the same age, social class, and race. Similarities in attitudes, such as orientation to school or orientation to drug use, also affect the choice of reference groups. And once adolescents take a reference group as their own, they seek further similarity with their peers. Thus, the reference group's influence on an adolescent both precedes and follows the adolescent's decision to join the group.

peer pressure
the legitimization by one's peers of particular activities

Let us therefore place so-called **peer pressure** in perspective. Peer pressure has become the favorite explanation of all the ills that plague adolescents today, from drug and alcohol abuse to dropping out of school to unplanned pregnancy. However, a person's peers do not literally force one to engage in any of these things. A literal interpretation of peer pressure is wrong. Rather, peer pressure entails a legitimization of particular activities, so that a child who is interested will then try them. Legitimization is different from coercion. The practical implication of this view is clear. Parents who want their adolescent children to resist going along with the crowd have to do more than curtail contact with the peer group. However difficult it may be, they must additionally legitimize the alternative activities they favor.

Peer groups also help adolescents meet their need for intimacy. Consider the process mapped out in research by Dexter Dunphy (1963). As adolescence begins, children congregate in same-sex **cliques**—small groups of about six people. Different cliques are isolated from each other. But eventually, cliques of males and females start to come together. This precedes actual dating.

Boy-and-girl cliques start to attend parties together, though there may actually be little mixing between them at the parties. Next, the leaders of the cliques take an interest in dating, and they start to pair up. Other clique members soon follow. Mixed-sex cliques are now the rule. At the end of adolescence, cliques themselves dissolve, to be replaced by a loose association of couples. Does this sequence of events seem familiar to you?

Some argue that the adolescent peer group is so important that it literally provides a different culture for those who belong to it (Coleman, 1961). The effect of this alternative culture is to cut off adolescents from the adult culture which they must—willingly or unwillingly—eventually enter. For example, academic achievement is *not* the route to social success among adolescents; much more effective are good looks and athletic prowess (Eitzen, 1975). As a result, many adolescents devalue doing well in school. But it is usually difficult later on to spend adolescent currency in the adult world.

Others who comment on the adolescent peer group are not as alarmed, arguing that our modern world is so complex that socialization cannot be limited to one's family of origin (Mead, 1978). Adolescents' peers introduce them to the real world. Adolescents today confront issues altogether out of the realm of most parents—AIDS and crack, to mention but two. With a little help from one's friends, one learns how to think about these matters.

cliques
small groups of people who help each other fulfill their needs for intimacy

The peer group often legitimizes, rather than shapes, an adolescent's behavior.

School. As you well know, it is impossible to speak about adolescent development without placing it in the context of schools. Universal school attendance by adolescents has only occurred during the last 60 or so years (Tanner, 1972). And did you also know that the school year has steadily lengthened since that time, from 162 days in 1920 to 180 days at the present? Before you feel too put upon, though, appreciate that European school years may be as long as 220 days per year!

Compulsory education was brought about by a confluence of factors: industrialization, urbanization, and immigration. Schools were seen by the larger society as a way of socializing adolescents—Americanizing them and preparing them for life and work in a complex world. So, American education in the twentieth century has been the servant of many masters, creating a tension between academic rigor and societal relevance.

What did your high school present to you: traditional academic education, vocational training, or innovative electives? My high school, more than 20 years ago, offered choices among all of these programs, and most students were tracked into one to the exclusion of the others. Your course of studies then determined the cliques you joined. (And all of this had a lot to do with the socioeconomic status of our parents.)

Schools have been seen by many as a vehicle for social change. Desegregation, a laudable goal for all walks of life in America, has been carried out mainly in the schools—not in the workplace, not in the housing market, and not in leisure activities, except of course for beer commercials. More recently, schools have been the place where students formally learn about sexuality. And some people want adolescents to affirm their patriotism and/or their belief in God in school.

Developmental psychologists have studied how various characteristics of school influence the progress and well-being of students. School size, class size, age grouping, desegregation, and other factors have received considerable research attention. It is difficult to offer firm conclusions about most of these, because numerous variables lurk among them. School systems rarely assign students to different classes or programs on a random basis, which means that experimentation cannot be used to disentangle the confounds.

Research on the effects of school is therefore difficult to sift through. Some psychologists prefer to look not at larger school characteristics but at more immediate ones. How do students experience the atmosphere of their particular classroom, and what experiences are linked to good performance? Results here are clear-cut. Classrooms where the students experience warmth, high standards, and a moderate amount of teacher control bring out the best in the students, academically and psychologically (Rutter, 1983). Does this sound familiar? It is the academic equivalent of the authoritative parental style discussed in Chapter 9, which brings out the best in children.

Work. With the advent of child labor laws, the presence of adolescents in the workplace steadily declined throughout the early part of the twentieth century. By 1940, no more than 5 percent of high school students worked during the school year. However, in the last few decades, this has changed considerably. One reason is the growth of retail stores and fast-food restaurants that employ part-time workers at low wages. Here is a societal need that adolescents can best fill, and indeed they have done so. Another reason is the general inflation that has hit our society, particularly the adolescent world. It costs big bucks to be a teenager today, so economic necessity drives adolescents to work.

By some estimates, it is more common for a high school student to work during the school year than not. Those adolescents from the middle and upper-middle class are most likely to be employed, because they live in the suburban areas where the jobs are. Least likely to be employed are teenagers from the lower class.

There are several important implications of the level of adolescent employment found today in the United States. First, this is an American phenomenon. Teens in Europe, or Japan, or even Canada are not nearly as likely to work as are the American teenagers. This means that American adolescents don't have as much time to do schoolwork. Perhaps the tendency for grades to drop during adolescence (e.g., Schulenberg, Asp, & Petersen, 1984) makes perfect sense.

Second, the vast majority of jobs that teenagers fill are, simply put, boring. One wonders just what these jobs prepare someone to do. As noted earlier, teenage jobs are age segregated. An adolescent rarely works directly with adults, and perhaps as a result develops a cynical attitude toward employment (Steinberg, 1985).

Third, teenage work is often split between "boy" jobs (such as clearing tables, carrying newspapers, and doing lawn or construction work) and "girl" jobs (such as babysitting, waiting on tables, or working as a maid). Might this channel adult males and females into sex-stereotyped jobs? Or perhaps this sex-typing occurs before teenagers enter the workplace, as a result of socialization at home or in school, so that males and females choose jobs appropriate to their gender.

The evidence concerning working adolescents paints a bleak picture. Is there a positive side? Certainly, one can give a solid rationale for why teenagers should work. The lessons that one might learn at work—such as the importance of responsibility, foresight, and cooperation—can help consolidate an adolescent's identity. These lessons can help lay the foundation for one's subsequent development. However, research shows that the typical jobs filled by teenagers do not measure up to this rationale. The challenge we face as a country is to discover ways to increase the likelihood that adolescent work will benefit development rather than harm it.

Adulthood

Adolescence fades into adulthood as our teenage years end. The distinctions among the adult years were presented earlier in Table 9.1. From twenty to forty, we are in *young adulthood*. From forty to sixty, we are in *middle adulthood*. From sixty on, we are in *later adulthood*. In light of increased longevity, some theorists suggest further distinctions at the upper end of the life span, but we'll stick with these terms for the time being.

Let's look at two general concerns of researchers of adult development (Honzik, 1984). First is the way that adults confront various issues, including marriage, child-rearing, work, and retirement. Second is the changes in people's biological, social, and psychological characteristics from young to middle to later adulthood. How does physical prowess wax and wane across the life span? Do cognitive abilities increase, decrease, or stay the same from age twenty to death? Are friendships later in life similar to those earlier in life?

Obviously, these two concerns are interrelated, because the person who undertakes a particular task at a given age brings to bear on it his or her characteristics at that time. To the degree that these characteristics change over time, so too does someone's approach to a particular life task.

Issues of Adult Development

Adult development consists of alternating stable and unstable periods. Although we may think of adulthood as defined by the stable periods, such as an ongoing marriage or job, just as important psychologically is the way we bridge these stable periods. People make transitions with the resources available to them at the time. A person can better cope with the death of his spouse if he has previously established solid relationships with other people. He can retire with satisfaction if he has previously found leisure activities to pursue.

Marriage. One of the most profound transitions that most adults make is from the status of single person to that of married person. The vast majority make this transition during young adulthood. Marriage is one of the socially sanctioned ways of declaring that the psychosocial issue of intimacy has been resolved. But there is a lot more to marriage than simply this. Marriage involves a drastic change in the roles that people play.

Some of these changes are obvious—wedding bands, anniversaries, and joint income tax returns. But others are more subtle. Did you know that gender role differences between men and women tend to *increase* following marriage (Feldman & Aschenbrenner, 1983)? Particularly when children arrive on the scene, men become more concerned with work and finances, whereas women become more immersed in cooking, housework, and nurturance (Abrahams et al., 1978). This intensification of gender role differences may reflect our preparation for child-rearing, because it is seen in various cultures (Gutmann, 1975). Regardless, marriage creates quite a change for young adults, one they may not have fully anticipated.

The successful transition from single to married life often signals a resolution of the issue of intimacy.

Just how does the transition into marriage take place? Developmental psychologists describe the process as a series of steps. The most superficial step involves judging a prospective mate on such characteristics as appearance, social class, and behavior. The next involves looking a bit deeper at his or her beliefs and attitudes. Agreement here is important. Finally, prospective mates choose each other on the basis of how well their needs mesh. Two individuals with a need to dominate an interaction do not get along as well as a leader and a follower (Winch, 1958).

In the United States, about 95 percent of the population marries at some point. This overall figure has stayed much the same over recent decades, although the average age of first marriage has increased, particularly among women with professional careers. Here we have another example of how larger social trends influence the course of development. For various reasons, more women pursue careers today, which means they marry later . . . which means they have children later . . . which means their children have older parents . . . and so it goes.

At middle adulthood, there are hints that gender roles converge and perhaps even cross over (Rossi, 1980). Middle-aged women tend to become more autonomous, and middle-aged men tend to become more compassionate and nurturant. So far, this trend has only been shown with cross-sectional data, and it will be interesting to see if longitudinal data show the same pattern. One possibility is that gender role convergence during middle adulthood is a cohort effect, found among those born in the 1920s and thus reaching middle age at the time the women's movement began (Bee, 1987).

Researchers have extensively studied marital satisfaction, and find, not surprisingly, that satisfaction is high early in the marriage. It reaches a low point when a couple has adolescent children (Rollins & Feldman, 1970). (This finding was obtained even before the advent of MTV.) Among those who stay married for decades, marital satisfaction starts to rise again once the children have left home.

These are the trends, and we should *not* assume that time per se is the critical factor. Many other factors are linked with marital satisfaction—emotional security, respect, communication, sexual intimacy, and loyalty among them—and the way in which these factors combine to influence satisfaction depends on how long a couple has been together (Swensen, Eskew, & Kohlhepp, 1981). On the whole, men report greater satisfaction with marriage than do women (Veroff & Feld, 1970). Women tend to value their marriage more if they have children *or* if they work outside the home (Baruch, Barnett, & Rivers, 1983).

Many women today want to "have it all"—a family and a career. However, those committed to both their children and their work tend to experience decreased satisfaction with their marriage (Philliber & Hiller, 1983). The likely explanation is that their husbands more often than not fail to share equally in raising the children, and the women become greatly overextended.

An interesting fact is that married adults are physically and emotionally healthier than their single counterparts (Bee, 1987). There are various explanations for this. Perhaps the less robust do not get married in the first place. Perhaps the companionship that marriage affords buffers a person against poor health (cf. Cobb, 1976). Whatever the reasons, the benefits of marriage on health are greater for men than for women!

Alternatives to Marriage. In years past, you were either married or single. But more recently, "living together," or cohabitation, has become quite common in the United States. Perhaps as many as 2,300,000 couples live together without being married, implying that cohabitation is a significant social phenomenon. There is some debate as to whether it represents a true alternative to marriage, or simply an additional step in the process of courtship (e.g., Bower & Christopherson, 1977).

Among those couples living together who eventually get married, their marital satisfaction is *lower* than among couples who did not live together prior to marriage (DeMaris & Leslie, 1984). And divorce may be *more* likely (Browder, 1988). In making sense of these findings, we must keep in mind the possibility of confounds. People who live together before marrying are different in the first place than those who do not. For instance, men and women who live together before marriage tend to have slightly less education and are somewhat more likely to be employed than those who marry without first living together (Watson, 1983). Perhaps these differences—and not cohabitation per se—produce later marital satisfaction and stability.

Divorce. In the middle 1800s, only about 4 percent of marriages ended in divorce. By the 1970s, this figure had grown to more than 40 percent. At first glance, this seems an incredible crisis for the American family. A closer look, placing these figures in a historical context, gives us another perspective. There is the same proportion of intact marriages today as there was more than a century ago.

How is this possible? Because people on the average live so much longer today. Once upon a time, marriages ended with the untimely death of one partner or the other. Today, the same proportion of marriages end with divorce. Of course, the end of a marriage by death is different than the end of a marriage by divorce, but the fact remains that the proportion of intact American families has not changed at all throughout the twentieth century.

If we can speak of an "average" divorce, it occurs after six or seven years of marriage, when the partners are about thirty years old (Norton, 1983). But divorce can occur at any point during marriage. Surprisingly, marital dissatisfaction is *not* a strong predictor of divorce. Considerations like alternative mates, career decisions, and financial crises combine to create a divorce. The degree to which divorce is regarded as legitimate within a person's cultural group is another crucial factor. For an obvious example, among those whose religion proscribes divorce, divorce is less likely than among the general population.

Regardless of what causes divorce, it is a painful experience for those involved. During the immediate aftermath of a divorce, depression or alcohol abuse may occur, and there is an increased risk of physical illness (Perlmutter & Hall, 1985). These problems are accentuated when the couple has children. In the great majority of cases, mothers receive custody following a divorce, causing single mothers to be disproportionately burdened. None of these findings means that divorce is always harmful for individuals. Most make a satisfactory adjustment within 2 years following a divorce (Hetherington, Cox, & Cox, 1979).

Indeed, the majority of those who divorce remarry, particularly if they have divorced early in adulthood. A second marriage is necessarily different than a first marriage, but on the average, it is as satisfying (Huyck, 1982). By the way, the comparison here is to *all* first marriages, not just to those ending in divorce. Whether second marriages are more or less likely to end in divorce is not clear, because the comparison is confounded by age and hence the increased possibility of the death of one partner.

Parenthood. Another major adult transition is taking on the role of parent. Several recent trends here should be noted. First, except for the post–World War II burst between 1947 and 1957 that gave us the baby boom generation, the birth rate in the United States has steadily decreased throughout the twentieth century. In other words, families are becoming smaller. Second, because of effective birth control, adults are becoming parents later in life, on the average. Although most children are still born to women younger than thirty years of age, there is an increase in the birth rate among women over thirty. Third, the increase in divorce results in an increasingly large number of single-parent families. Fourth, remarriage following divorce is leading to a growing number of families that include stepparents.

Researchers consistently find that being a parent is both rewarding *and* stressful. The vast majority of parents report that if given the chance to start their life over, they would choose again to have children (Yankelovich, 1981). Nonetheless, the presence of children in a household profoundly changes the relationship between a husband and wife. Child-rearing responsibilities tend to fall to mothers, perhaps contributing to the low self-esteem and increased depression found among them (Brown & Harris, 1978). And following the birth of a child, the typical mother takes on more household chores, regardless of how she and her mate divided the tasks before (Cowan, Cowan, Coie, & Coie, 1978).

When children grow up and leave home, the roles of parents necessarily change. At one time, psychologists thought that parents, particularly mothers, were vulnerable to the so-called *empty nest syndrome*—a loss of purpose experienced when all the children have left home. But research fails to bear out this notion. If anything, just the opposite occurs: Mothers report the most satisfaction and the highest morale once their children leave home (Neugarten, 1970). And why not? On the one hand, life becomes less demanding. And on the other hand, the successful development of offspring from dependent children to autonomous adults means that a parent has done well.

Career. So far, we've touched on aspects of the family as major issues of adulthood. But work is also important in shaping adult development. An occupation does more than pay the bills; it consumes one-third to one-half of the average adult's waking hours. It provides one of our most central identities. "What do you do?" is a conversational gambit that could be answered in any of a number of ways, but most of us hear it as a question about our occupation.

Much of what psychologists know about work comes from studies of men, because men traditionally have filled the work force. This is now changing, of course, as women increasingly work outside the home. In recent years, there has been a great increase in the number of studies that investigate working women (e.g., Betz & Fitzgerald, 1987; Nieva & Gutek, 1981; Smith, 1979).

Choosing a job that is compatible with one's personality and basic values should result in high job satisfaction.

How do people go about choosing an occupation? First, it is important to know that most workers do not stay with a single type of job throughout their entire working life. Between five and ten significant job shifts occur throughout adulthood for the typical worker, meaning that the question of occupational choice is more complicated that it may first seem. Some theorists therefore prefer to speak of an individual's career path rather than his or her career per se.

Second, the range of careers to choose from is limited by factors such as gender-role socialization, family background, and education. For the young adult, some jobs represent legitimate careers, whereas others do not. Many sons follow the careers of their fathers, particularly in professional families (Mortimer, 1976).

Third, within the range of acceptable jobs, a worker tends to choose one that satisfies his or her basic values. Psychologist John Holland (1966, 1985) proposed an influential approach to occupational choice. He hypothesized six basic personality types, each with corresponding jobs (see Table 10.3). When a person's personality matches his job, his satisfaction is high, and his work goes well.

Studies of worker satisfaction find that it increases with age. Older workers like what they do better than younger workers, which is hardly a surprising result. Those who hate a particular job tend to leave it. Further, older workers usually have better jobs, with more influence and greater challenges. Finally, older workers—to a greater degree than younger ones—evaluate a job in terms of extrinsic characteristics such as salary, benefits, and security, which usually increase the longer they hold a job (Rabinowitz & Hall, 1981).

Retirement. Mandatory retirement was "invented" in nineteenth-century Europe by German politicians who wanted to be seen as doing something for citizens that really required no change in society (Woodruff-Pak, 1988). The age of retirement was first set at seventy, and later changed to sixty-five, precisely because so few people lived to be this old! The United States followed suit in the early twentieth century. Needless to say, retirement has since become much more than a cosmetic social institution.

In contemporary America, two opposing trends are very much in evidence. First, we see ever earlier retirement for the average worker. Second, we see mandatory retirement laws thrown out altogether except for those covering a handful of occupations. It is difficult to predict just what effect these trends will have on the composition of our future work force.

Most workers retire in their early sixties. Two types of men retire early: the affluent and the ill. Keep this in mind when interpreting the consistent finding that retired individuals have a higher mortality rate than workers of the same age. Here the likely direction of causality runs from poor health to retirement, not vice versa. Among those who retire because their financial situation allows them to do so, retirement is usually a time of good health, increased social activity, and high life satisfaction (Bee, 1987). Those who fare best in retirement are the same people who fared well when working, a striking example of consistency across the life span (Palmore, 1981).

Paralleling the increase in studies of working women is an increase in studies of retired women (Szinovacz, 1982). Like men, today's women are retiring at an increasingly earlier age (Hayward, Grady, & McLaughlin, 1988). However, the factors that influence one's decision to retire vary between men and women. As just mentioned, men's decisions to retire can be predicted by taking into account their health and financial status; these variables seem *not* to influence women's decisions (George, Fillenbaum, & Palmore, 1984). The meaning of this difference awaits further investigation.

Widowhood. One last issue of adult development which is usually confronted in later adulthood is widowhood. Women tend to marry men several years older than they are. And women on the average live about 7 years longer than men. These two facts combined mean that the loss of a spouse to death is much more common among women than men. By some estimates, there are more than ten times as many widows in the United States as widowers!

The transition to widowhood is stressful, particularly when this change is unexpectedly early in life (Ball, 1976–1977). When a person

A "successful" retirement often follows a successful working life, a clear indication of consistency across the life span.

Table 10.3
Personality Types

Type	Characterization	Job Example
Realistic	Prefers working with objects or tools	Mechanic
Investigative	Prefers observation and study	Scientist
Artistic	Prefers creative activities	Musician
Social	Prefers activities that aid other people	Social worker
Enterprising	Prefers economic gain	Salesperson
Conventional	Prefers manipulation of information	Accountant

Source: Holland, 1985.

loses a spouse, she loses not only a relationship with a loved one, but also the support and assistance of that person. Also gone is her own role as a spouse. Not surprisingly, both physical and mental difficulty may follow in the wake of widowhood (e.g., Balkwell, 1981; Stroebe & Stroebe, 1983). Close and supportive relationships with other people help to buffer her against the resulting stress. Interestingly, her friends are of more help in this regard than are her children, perhaps because friends are much more likely to have had firsthand experience with widowhood themselves (Ferraro, 1984).

Changes in Middle and Later Adulthood

Developmental psychologists take great interest in documenting changes that occur during the adult years, in physical, social, and cognitive domains. Many of the changes they investigate can be classified as *gains* or *declines,* that is, increases or decreases in skills or abilities. Popular stereotypes often depict aging as an across-the-board set of declines. Research shows that this view is false (Datan, Rodeheaver, & Hughes, 1987). Later adulthood is increasingly seen as a rewarding period of life.

Still, some declines inevitably occur, and part of anyone's path through the adult years entails an adjustment to them. Some people make a better adjustment than others, drawing on the coping strategies described in Chapter 6 (Lazarus & DeLongis, 1983). In an intriguing article, the behaviorist B. F. Skinner (1983) describes some of the adjustments he made to his old age. He starts with the provocative point that not only do people age, but so too do their environments. Some of the problems of old age can thus be combatted by changing the environment. If one is forgetful, one can leave reminders.

> Ten minutes before you leave your house for the day you hear a weather report: It will probably rain before you return. It occurs to you to take an umbrella . . . [but] ten minutes later you leave without the umbrella. You can solve that kind of problem by executing as much of the behavior as possible when it occurs to you. Hang the umbrella on the doorknob, or put it through the handle of your briefcase, or in some other way start the process of taking it with you. (p. 24)

Needless to say, not only the aged can benefit from this strategy for remembering (Chapter 7).

Skinner also notes that our particular society does not generously reinforce what older people do. Young people are often disinterested in their elders. It behooves the older individual to find a setting in which what he or she says and does will be valued. New interests may need to be pursued. New friends may need to be cultivated. New settings may need to be explored.

Physical Changes.   As we move through adulthood, our physical body ages, eventually changing over time for the worse. People vary greatly in the rate they show these declines, but the following are some representative examples (Woodruff-Pak, 1988):

- Among the elderly, atrophy of the brain occurs, and neural firing slows.

- The heart loses its capacity to compensate for stress.
- The respiratory system becomes less efficient.
- The gastrointestinal system loses strength, and the incidence of constipation increases.
- Bone mass decreases, particularly among women.
- The skin becomes less flexible: drying, wrinkling, and sagging.
- Muscles become smaller, weaker, and slower.

Our sensory and perceptual systems also age. The documented changes that take place during middle and later adulthood include:

- loss of sensitivity of touch after age fifty or so
- no loss in pain sensitivity, but a gain in pain tolerance
- loss of taste sensitivity
- hearing loss, particularly of higher frequency sounds
- decline in visual acuity and speed of adaptation to the dark

Also with age, people have a less efficient sense of balance, which produces dizziness and falls. Because our bones also become more brittle as we become older, broken legs, arms, and hips can be quite common among the aged.

One of the most pervasive changes with age is the speed with which we do things (Gottsdanker, 1982). On the average, older people take longer to perform a variety of behavior: walking, talking, and choosing. Despite the obviousness of this change, the exact mechanism producing slowness among the aged is not known. Changes in sensory acuity or the speed of neural conduction have been ruled out as explanations.

Why do some people age more rapidly than others, leading to a shorter life? Developmentalists have proposed a number of theories to explain the process of aging, but none has won general acceptance. For obvious reasons, this is a hot topic in the field of **gerontology,** an interdisciplinary approach to the study of aging that draws on psychology, biology, sociology, and other fields. All of us age, and we need no better reason to take a close look at how and why this happens.

Granted that physical changes occur with age, how do gerontologists explain them? Here are some of the theories proposed. First, physical decline may be programmed into our genes. Remember from Chapter 2 the notion of inclusive fitness. Organisms can sometimes further the survival of their own genes if they sacrifice themselves, so long as their death enhances the survival of their close relatives. Perhaps this argument applies to the human life span. Maybe it is adaptive for the elderly, who have already passed on their genes, to move out of the way and not use up resources that their offspring need. Accordingly, maximum life expectancy might well be part of our genetic inheritance.

What is the evidence for this argument? There is the compelling fact that each species appears to have a characteristic maximum life expectancy. Even under the most optimum conditions, dogs don't live past 25 years of age, and people don't live much past 110 years of age. Claims of extreme longevity among people, like yogurt-eaters living in the Caucasus Mountains of the Soviet Union, always prove exaggerated (Fry, 1985). Such claims persist because we so much want to believe in them, but the oldest documented age of a human being is the 120 years of the Japanese man Shigechiyo Izumi (Woodruff-Pak, 1988). In fact, some theorists believe that

gerontology

an interdisciplinary approach to the study of aging that draws on psychology, biology, sociology, and other fields *maximum life expectancy* (or life span) has not appreciably changed for centuries (Fries & Crapo, 1981). Our *average life expectancy* has of course increased, but it appears to have an upper limit.

However, there are other factors we need to consider. Aging may reflect accumulated mutations brought about by our exposure to random insults from the environment. Because these mutations necessarily increase over time, they eventually result in extremely abnormal chromosomes, which cause the body to simply stop working because its cells can no longer replicate themselves.

Other explanations of aging focus on larger physical systems within the body, places in which the wear and tear of everyday life takes its toll. In particular, the cardiovascular system is quite vulnerable to the effects of aging. Arteries become more brittle and less flexible as fatty acids (such as cholesterol) deposit themselves on vessel walls. As the blood vessels are compromised, so too is our circulation. And because circulation of blood is critical in maintaining our health, aging and death follow.

With age, the immune system becomes less able to recognize and fight off foreign organisms, such as viruses. Indeed, the body increasingly becomes confused and starts to treat its own cells as foreign material, fighting them and hence itself. This subversion of the immune system may be the fundamental cause of diseases such as rheumatoid arthritis.

At any rate, note how these explanations (taken as a whole) explain aging in terms of an interaction of biological and environmental factors. Recent work also suggests that psychological characteristics may directly influence physical well-being (Chapter 6). In a longitudinal investigation, Peterson, Seligman, and Vaillant (1988) showed that men at age twenty-five who viewed events optimistically were healthier at age sixty than their pessimistic counterparts. Notable about this study is that the most likely confound, level of health at age twenty-five, was taken into account and found *not* to influence the results.

Figure 10.3 depicts just some of the factors found to be associated with longer life (Woodruff-Pak, 1988). These factors have been identified using correlational investigations, which means that they may not be direct causes of long life but are simply linked to other, as yet undefined, factors responsible for longevity.

For example, completely abstaining from drinking alcohol has been associated with shorter life than has occasional drinking in small amounts. Does this mean that alcohol in small amounts is healthy? Well, perhaps, but just as plausible is the possibility that abstaining per se is irrelevant. Maybe abstinence correlates with other characteristics of a person that are critical.

If you wish to increase the length of your life, follow this advice. Match the profile of a long-lived person as best you can. It is difficult, I admit, to go back in time and pick your grandparents. But some of these factors are completely under your control. For example, people who smoke live on the average *twelve years fewer* than those who don't smoke. That's a correlational result worth treating as a causal one.

Let us end this section on physical changes during adulthood by discussing sexuality during the adult years. Remember that sexual behavior is a complex phenomenon with biological and psychological aspects (Chapter 16). Biological changes in sexuality take place as levels of circu-

Figure 10.3
Predictors of Longevity

Having grandparents who lived past the age of eighty
Having parents who lived past the age of eighty
Being the first-born in a family
Being "intelligent"
Not being overweight
Eating vegetables and fruits
Not eating fatty and sweet foods
Not smoking
Drinking alcohol moderately
Exercising
Sleeping between 6–8 hours every night
Having high socioeconomic status
Living in a rural area
Being married and living with one's spouse
Having at least two close friends

menopause

the cessation of menstruation and the ability to conceive, occurring in a woman's late forties or early fifties

lating sex hormones decrease. In their forties or fifties, women experience **menopause:** cessation of menstruation and the ability to conceive. Men show a less dramatic but nonetheless steady decline in fertility after age forty.

These biological changes must be distinguished from the psychological aspects of sexuality. Contrary to popular belief, sex is alive and well for most people throughout their entire adult lives. Sheer frequency of intercourse declines with age, due mostly to the male's decreased capacity. But sexual desire and satisfaction show no falling off as we age. Indeed, women who remain sexually active may actually show an increasing capacity for orgasm throughout middle and later adulthood (Woodruff-Pak, 1988).

Social Changes.   People show development in their personalities as well as in their social relationships as they move through middle and later adulthood. To understand personality stability and change, we must distinguish literal stability (which refers to some characteristic staying exactly the same over time) from relative stability (which refers to one's relative ranking on some characteristic staying the same, even if its overt manifestation changes). This distinction clarifies the mass of information about changes in our personality with age (McCrae & Costa, 1984; Neugarten, 1977). So, there are changes on the surface. Bee (1987, p. 266) summarizes some of these as follows:

An individual's basic outlook and the extent of that person's effort to enhance physical and emotional well-being can have a significant impact on the life span.

senility
the widespread loss of cognitive abilities, commonly caused by Alzheimer's disease

Alzheimer's disease
progressive and eventually fatal neurological condition marked by forgetfulness, confusion, and loss of ability to take care of oneself

The first change—which may occur gradually . . . from about age 30 to about age 50—seems to include . . . (1) an increase in "maturity" and in personality integration . . . (2) an increase in . . . achieving . . . doing . . . succeeding . . . (3) an increase in individuality and a decrease in dependence on others, perhaps particularly for men. . . . Information about a possible shift between midlife and old age is scarcer, but there are at least some hints . . . of increasing philosophical concern . . . greater introversion . . . and greater . . . integrity [of personality].

At the same time, an individual's standing relative to other people stays much the same for many characteristics. For instance, most of us become more introverted as we get older, but if you were a relatively extraverted adolescent, you are still going to be a relatively extraverted adult. The research thus supports both stability and change in personality as we age.

How does friendship change throughout adulthood? On the one hand, the determinants of friendship remain the same. We tend to become friends with people we see a lot, find attractive, and regard as similar to us (Chapter 15). On the other hand, we make fewer friends as we age, so that older adults report fewer close friends than do adolescents or younger adults.

Contrary to what these findings suggest, older adults are *not* particularly lonely. Indeed, the younger an adult, the more likely he or she is to report feeling lonely at least some of the time (Dickens & Perlman, 1981). This is not surprising when we consider Erikson's idea that intimacy is an important concern of early adulthood, and the young adult is less likely to have resolved this issue than someone who is older.

Because of widespread beliefs about differences between men and women in their approach to friendship, this has been a topic of frequent investigation. Some studies find that women's friendships are more personal, expressive, and emotional, whereas men's friendships are more circumscribed and reserved, revolving around shared activities more than self-disclosure. Other studies show few differences between the friendships of men and women.

The resolution of this contradiction seems to lie in the "conventionality" of the adults studied (Bell, 1981). Men and women with conservative attitudes and values show different patterns in their friendships. Men and women with a more liberal approach to life have similar friendships. Also, in contrast to conservative individuals, they are more likely to have friends of the opposite sex.

Cognitive Changes.   Finally, let's look at the cognitive changes occurring in middle and later adulthood. Many people fear that **senility**—the widespread loss of cognitive abilities—is an inevitable consequence of aging. Thankfully, this is a mistaken fear. Only a small number of the elderly, perhaps 5 percent, become senile, and among this group, the most common cause of senility is **Alzheimer's disease,** a progressive and eventually fatal disease characterized by forgetfulness, confusion, and loss of ability to care for oneself.

Even though Alzheimer's disease is relatively rare, it is becoming more prevalent simply because people are living long enough to become its victims. At the present, perhaps two million people in the United States have Alzheimer's disease. By one estimate, based on a projection of current longevity trends, there may be as many as five million Americans with Alzheimer's disease by the year 2020 (Woodruff-Pak, 1988).

Alzheimer's disease is neurological in nature; it has an underlying biological basis. However, its first signs are usually psychological. Specifically, the disease begins with a mild impairment of memory and knowledge of words. The individual is well aware of these changes, and often attempts to compensate for them, using mnemonic devices similar to those described in Chapter 7. The course of Alzheimer's disease is progressive, and the cognitive impairment becomes steadily worse. Because the person with Alzheimer's disease is initially conscious of his or her cognitive loss, depression and grief may accompany the disease.

The typical case of Alzheimer's disease results in death 5 to 7 years after its first appearance, but some individuals have survived as long as 15 years after the initial diagnosis. At the present time, there is no cure or treatment. However, medical researchers appear well on their way to unravelling the causes of Alzheimer's disease, looking at possible roles of viral infection, trace metal contamination, genetic predispositions, and/or neurotransmitter abnormalities (Gruetzner, 1988).

Cognitive changes less dramatic than those brought about by Alzheimer's disease also occur over the adult years. Classical conditioning declines. The ability to rapidly assimilate new information falls off. Recall memory appears to become less accurate, although this finding might reflect differences in initial acquisition.

Metacognitive abilities stay the same throughout adulthood, allowing the individual to compensate for other losses. Some studies suggest that thinking is more integrative among the elderly, subsuming larger chunks of information within typical categories of thought (Kramer & Woodruff, 1984). Developmentalists have also turned their attention to *wisdom,* which they define as the ability to combine thought and feeling so as to choose which tasks are worth pursuing (Clayton, 1982). It may be that wisdom, in this sense, is a characteristic that only older individuals possess. Work here is preliminary, but it promises to document cognitive gains with age.

Let's turn now to research that addresses changes in intelligence as we age. When intelligence tests were first made available (Chapter 8), researchers using cross-sectional designs found massive declines in intelligence with age. Later data from longitudinal studies contradicted these initial findings.

Intelligence does *not* decline with age once cohort effects (p. 366) are taken into account. Here's one reason why. Throughout the twentieth century, each successive generation has had more education; cross-sectional comparisons by age end up comparing people with differing amounts of schooling. Indeed, the importance of cohort effects (Chapter 9) was first documented clearly in studies of intelligence and aging (e.g., Baltes, 1968; Schaie, 1965).

We have covered a great deal of territory in these two chapters on development, moving from infancy to childhood to adolescence to early, middle, and then later adulthood. But our discussion of development is not quite complete, because we need to discuss death. Current thinking conceives death not as a discrete event, but rather as a process that unfolds over time. Some theorists therefore prefer to describe what happens to us at the end of our life as dying, to make explicit that this too is a developmental process.

Death and Dying

The most important theorist concerned with death and dying is Elizabeth Kübler-Ross (1969). Based on interviews she conducted with terminally ill individuals, both children and adults, Kübler-Ross proposed that the process of dying takes places in five stages, through which people pass in order.

- Denial—the first reaction is to refuse to believe that death is going to happen: "There must be a mistake here."
- Anger—the second stage in the process of dying is resentment: against those who remain healthy, against those taking care of the individual, against whatever circumstances put the person in this position.
- Bargaining—in the third stage of dying, the individual tries to "make a deal" with doctors, or nurses, or God: "If I get better, I'll devote my life to good deeds."
- Depression—bargaining then gives way to depression, which Kübler-Ross sees as a form of mourning—for oneself and for all the losses that death will bring.
- Acceptance—finally, the dying individual comes to accept and understand death as inevitable, and dies quietly, even serenely.

Like other stage theories of development, this theory assumes that each step is necessary for the subsequent ones to occur. For instance, the initial stage of denial allows the individual to muster his defenses to cope with his impending death. The bargaining stage allows him to keep going long enough to finish the important business in his life.

Although Kübler-Ross deserves praise for legitimizing the psychological study of yet another period of life, her particular theory has not been generally accepted. When other researchers look for her stages, they do not find that all dying individuals show the five hypothesized stages; even when present, the five stages do not necessarily appear in the order she proposes (e.g., Schulz & Aderman, 1974). A dying person's attitude toward death may change continuously. Though acceptance may come after periods of denial, anger, bargaining, and depression, any of these responses may reappear (Butler & Lewis, 1981). Dying is no more simple than life, and we should expect that there are various ways to go about it.

Nevertheless, Kübler-Ross is an extremely important theorist, as she was the first to call our attention to the psychological process of dying. As you surely know, social attitudes toward death in the United States can only be described as repressive. We do not witness death. We do not discuss death. We do not even acknowledge death. People "pass away" rather than die, and we are thus ill-equipped to deal with death, in ourselves or others. Kübler-Ross has helped to change these attitudes, and so death is now much more openly discussed than it once was.

For example, developmental psychologists have studied the attitudes that people have toward death and dying, with a focus on the fears they express about their own mortality. Where in the life span is someone most likely to fear death? Perhaps you will be surprised to find that studies point to middle adulthood as the time when people are most likely to voice explicit fear (e.g., Bengtson, Cuellar, & Ragan, 1977). With increasing age, adults become less frightened about death. At the same time, they are more likely to think and talk about death.

Researchers have also found that older adults who have achieved their goals in life fear death less than those who believe they have fallen short (Neimeyer & Chapman, 1980–1981). This finding is consistent with Erikson's hypothesis that the satisfactory resolution of one's major life tasks results in a sense of integrity in later adulthood. A belief in the significance of the life that one has led makes the end of life less frightening.

Another sign of psychology's increased interest in dying is recent attention to the ways that people prepare themselves for death. Notable here is the movement known as **hospice care**—a strategy for taking care of the terminally-ill individual that directly involves the individual and the family in making decisions and providing the hands-on care (Saunders, 1977). Hospice care may take place in a special ward of a hospital or, more typically, at home.

The hospice movement is based on the assumption that dying is an inherent part of life. It should be prepared for in the same way that one prepares for other important tasks—within the social context in which one lives. Hospice care allows the dying individual as well as the family to come to grips with death, facing and accepting its inevitability. Systematic investigations of hospice care are just now being conducted, but case studies suggest that it can be an enriching—yet difficult—experience for all involved (Bass, 1985).

Having discussed death and dying, we have now completed our examination of adult development. Remember the brief history of developmental psychology presented in Chapter 9. A major trend in this field has been the recognition that development occurs throughout the entire life span, literally from birth to grave.

Certain questions concern all developmental psychologists, regardless of the particular aspect of development in which they are interested. How do nature and nurture interact to determine development? Is development stable? Do people pass through discrete stages as they develop? If nothing else, the material we have discussed in Chapters 9 and 10 implies that answers to these questions are complex.

hospice care
strategy for taking care of the terminally ill by directly involving the individual and the family in making decisions and providing hands-on care

Summary

Topics of Concern—One More Time

- This chapter continues the story of development begun in the previous chapter. Our focus here is on adolescent and adult development, and we must be careful to locate individuals in their appropriate historical and social context, because larger cultural phenomena play such an important role in shaping their lives.
- The same issues that concern developmentalists studying children continue to be of interest when the focus is shifted to adolescents and adults. How do nature and nurture interact to determine development? To what degree does stability characterize the process of development? As people develop, do they pass through discrete stages?

Perspectives on Adolescent and Adult Development

- Erik Erikson's psychosocial theory has been the most influential account of development during adolescence and adulthood. This is a stage theory proposing an inherent direction to development, and it has inspired other theorists—including Vaillant and Gould—to propose similar accounts.
- According to Erikson, the stages of development are defined by particular psychosocial conflicts that people must confront. Only when a conflict is successfully resolved can the person go on to satisfactorily resolve subsequent conflicts.
- Erikson proposes that the central issue facing the adolescent is establishing an identity. As young adults, we face the task of intimacy: merging our identity with that of another person. Later as adults, our concern is generativity: nurturing the next generation. Finally, at the end of our lives, we confront the issue of ego integrity: has our life made sense to us?

- Still other developmental theories—such as those of Levinson and Pearlin—take issue with key assumptions made by Erikson. Here we see a disagreement with Erikson's beliefs that development proceeds through stages and has an inherent direction.
- Research can help us evaluate particular claims of developmental theories. Perhaps surprisingly, there is scant evidence for two widely proposed stressful aspects of development: the generation gap and the midlife crisis. One conclusion implied by these findings is that development can take a variety of paths through adolescence and adulthood.

Adolescence

- Adolescent development can be understood in terms of how the young person confronts such identity issues as autonomy, friendship, sexuality, and achievement.
- Adolescent development occurs within the contexts provided by the family, the peer group, school, and work.

Adulthood

- Developmental psychologists who study adults are interested in how people approach such major issues in life as marriage, divorce, children, widowhood, work, and retirement.
- Another concern of developmentalists who study adults is how the physical, social, and cognitive characteristics of people change over the adult years. Some skills and abilities decline, others stay the same, and still others improve with age.
- Developmentalists now include the process of dying within the scope of their work, extending their theories literally from birth to death.

Important Terms and Names

What follows is a list of the core terms and names for this chapter. Your instructor may emphasize other terms as well. Throughout the chapter, glossary terms appear in **boldface** type. They are defined in the text, and each term, along with its definition, is repeated in the margin.

Topics of Concern—One More Time

adolescence/404
adulthood/404

Perspectives on Adolescent and Adult Development

generativity/408
ego integrity/408
defense mechanism/409
life structure/411
generation gap/412
midlife crisis/413

Erik Erikson/407
George Vaillant/409
Roger Gould/410
Daniel Levinson/411
Leonard Pearlin/411

Adolescence

puberty/415
reference group/419
peer pressure/420

Adulthood

gerontology/431
menopause/433
senility/434
Alzheimer's disease/434
hospice care/437

Elizabeth Kübler-Ross/436

1. According to Erikson, the central task of adolescence is establishing a(n)
   a. career.
   b. identity.
   c. romantic relationship.
   d. sense of trust in others.
   "Who am I?" asks the adolescent. Erikson believes that the central issue that adolescents face is coming up with an answer to this question./407

2. Vaillant's theory of adult development emphasizes the maturity of someone's
   a. cognitive development.
   b. defense mechanisms.
   c. life structure.
   d. social relationships.
   Influenced by Erikson and other psychodynamic theorists, Vaillant describes adult development in terms of the defense mechanisms that one habitually uses. According to Vaillant, these become more mature as the individual ages./409

3. In contrast to Erikson's theory of adult development, the theory proposed by Levinson
   a. assumes no inherent direction to changes.
   b. assumes no stages.
   c. both a and b.
   d. neither a nor b.
   Levinson's theory of adult development emphasizes the "seasons of life" that one passes through. His is a stage theory that assumes no inherent ordering of the stages./411

4. Research calls into question the existence of the
   a. generation gap.
   b. midlife crisis.
   c. both a and b.
   d. neither a nor b.
   Both the generation gap and the midlife crisis are frequently discussed in the popular media, but actual research fails to document dramatic crises during adolescence or middle adulthood./413

5. The adolescent's peer group is often segregated along _____ lines.
   a. age
   b. racial
   c. socioeconomic
   d. all of the above
   Striking about adolescent peer groups is their homogeneity. Adolescents associate with other adolescents similar to themselves in many ways./420

6. Men who are _____ tend to retire early.
   a. affluent
   b. ill
   c. both a and b
   d. neither a nor b
   Two types of men retire early: those who can afford to do so and those who are unable to keep working./429

7. Which of these do not change during middle and later adulthood?
   a. pain sensitivity
   b. pain tolerance
   c. sensitivity to touch
   d. taste sensitivity
   e. visual acuity
   Pain tolerance increases with age. Touch, taste, and vision become less sensitive. The one characteristic listed here that does not change during middle and later adulthood is pain sensitivity./430

8. Why do people age? Explanations usually point to _____ causes.
   a. biological
   b. environmental
   c. both a and b
   d. neither a nor b
   No single explanation of aging is accepted. The theories currently suggested mention both biological and environmental determinants./431

9. Intelligence _____ with age.
   a. increases
   b. does not change
   c. decreases
   Older adults tend to be less educated than younger adults, and so they do not score as well on intelligence tests. However, once this cohort difference is taken into account, intelligence does not decrease with age./435

10. Research _____ support the sequence of stages hypothesized by Kübler-Ross.
   a. does
   b. does not
   Although a dying individual will often show all of the reactions described by Kübler-Ross, these tend not to occur in the exact sequence that she hypothesized./436

"Personality" includes the characteristics that make every person unique.

Chapter Eleven

Personality

Topics of Concern

Speculation about human nature has to be as old as human nature itself. One early view is contained in the writings of Theophrastus (372 –287 B.C.), a student of Aristotle. He viewed his fellow men and women the same way that many of us do: as members of discrete categories or types. This personality approach is called a **typology.** Here are paraphrased versions of some of his types (based on R.C. Jebb's 1870 translation):

- The *greedy man*—The greedy individual is one who, when he entertains, will not set enough bread on the table. He will borrow from a guest staying in his house. He will take his children to a play only when the theater has free admissions. If a friend is to be married, he will travel abroad a little while before in order to avoid giving a wedding present.
- The *gossip*—This person will sit down beside someone she does not know, and proceed to criticize her husband, then relate her dream of last night, then go through in detail what she had for dinner. Then, warming to the work, she will remark that the men of the present day are greatly inferior to those of the past, and how cheap wheat has become in the market, and what a number of foreign visitors are in town, and how hard it is to live, and that yesterday she felt sick. If she is tolerated, she will never leave you alone.
- The *patron of rascals*—She is one who will throw herself into the company of those who have been found guilty in criminal cases, believing that she will thereby become worldly and inspire awe. She is apt to become the champion of worthless persons, and to form conspiracies. In short, sympathy with rascality is akin to rascality itself.
- The *Little League coach*—He is one to be found in a T-shirt and dungarees, driving a station wagon filled with bats and balls and children. He imparts wisdom to the children, like the direction in which to run after balls have been thrown four times over one's head. He believes that boys and girls alike should play games in order to learn serious lessons about sportsmanship. He also believes that umpires are malicious and incompetent. He complains all the time and cannot imagine spending his Saturday afternoons doing anything else.

Some scholars doubt whether this last characterization really stems from Theophrastus. But the others certainly do, and we find them quite persuasive, more than 2300 years after their first appearance.

Do these characterizations capture the essence of each person? Indeed, what is someone's essence? Granted that the greedy man differs from the gossip in an obvious way, what other differences exist? What is the origin of these differences? The answers to such questions are often implicit in the particular approach that a psychologist chooses. It affects how she studies sensation, perception, learning, motivation, emotion, or development. In personality psychology, these assumptions are explicit. They not only influence the field; they literally *are* the field. The psychology of **personality** concerns itself with people in their entirety, including those aspects that are general, characteristic, enduring, integrated, and functional (Peterson, 1988).

To understand what "personality" means, let's briefly examine each of these aspects. A person's thoughts, deeds, and feelings qualify as personality if they are painted in broad strokes. This is why we define personality as someone's *general* aspects. Personality usually refers to behavior that shows up across different settings. Consider a thrifty individual. She acts thrifty whenever the opportunity presents itself: in restaurants and department stores, in locker rooms and libraries, at gas stations and garbage dumps. If she doesn't, then "thrift" is not part of her personality.

This Little League coach fits one of the common personality types that we use to categorize people who we casually observe.

To say that a quality is *characteristic* of a person is to stress how it distinguishes him from others. Perhaps you think of yourself as intelligent. (Indeed, studies show that most of us believe we are above average in intelligence!) So, you believe that you have more of this characteristic than other people. Ditto for a sense of humor. Sometimes a particular combination of qualities best characterizes your personality: wild *and* crazy, young *and* restless, dazed *and* confused.

Some of the things that people do are fleeting, whereas other thoughts and feelings and actions are consistent over time. Contrast a telephone number you remember just long enough to dial with the personal history that defines who you are (Chapter 7). Contrast a bad mood with chronic depression (Chapter 12). In other words, personality refers to *enduring* behaviors, those that are not tied to immediate circumstances and happenstance. Granted, personality can and does change throughout an individual's life, but this occurs gradually or in response to profound events.

Everyday people and psychologists alike often regard personality as a unitary aspect of a person, an *integration* of specific characteristics that may on the surface look inconsistent. Roosevelt ("Rosey") Grier was once a ferocious football player who now does needlepoint as a hobby. At first glance, these characteristics clash. But when we understand the rest of his personality—he is a gentle giant—then their combination makes sense. Consider the self, accorded a central role by many personality theories. The self is typically singular, and we believe that it holds the rest of us together. Our self is who we "really" are.

Finally, personality usually refers to how we meet the demands of the world. Therefore, it is either *functional* or it is not. Why do some people have no trouble earning straight *A's* while others go straight to jail? Answers to such questions may be found in someone's personality. Indeed, most of the major personality theorists have also been clinicians working with disturbed individuals. You've seen in other chapters how abnormality provides a window onto normality, so it should not be surprising to learn that many theories of personality are entwined with theories of psychopathology (Chapter 12).

Sometimes personality psychology is called **personology,** to stress that it concerns itself with the person as a whole. In this chapter, we'll discuss the major perspectives from which psychologists view the person. These broad strategies of understanding personality will recur throughout subsequent chapters. Let us now turn our attention to some of the topics that concern psychologists interested in personality.

typology

a personality classification scheme comprised of presumably basic and discrete types of people

personality

aspects of a person that are general, characteristic, enduring, integrated, and functional

personology

a term sometimes used to describe personality psychology, conveying the idea that the field concerns itself with the person as a whole

What Model for Human Nature?

Personality typologies such as that proposed by Theophrastus have been popular throughout the ages, but so too have criticisms of such attempts to pigeonhole people in such a simple way. Rival personality theories propose different ways to understand people, choosing various models or metaphors to capture the essence of human nature.

For example, the most influential theory of personality—that proposed by Sigmund Freud—likens people at their core to wild animals, best understood in terms of biology and instinct. His view of human nature might well have stepped out of the pages of Darwin's *The Origin of Species.* Freud believed that men and women are involved in a struggle for survival, motivated by instincts for sex and aggression. In the course of socialization, they learn to hold these instincts in check. But they still exist under the surface, waiting to erupt when circumstances allow.

What Theoretical Strategy?

Personality theories can be classified within several major strategies, each sharing its own model of human nature. Four strategies in particular are important (Peterson, 1988). Personality psychologists working within each approach go about their business in different ways: emphasizing different aspects of personality, favoring different research methods, and assuming different bottom lines regarding what makes for an adequate explanation.

Like the study of psychology as a whole, personality theory went through an era of great schools, in which theories and theorists were synonymous (Chapter 1). But unlike the discipline in general, the great schools are still very much a part of the study of the personality. Theories proposed decades ago still affect the research activities and applications that we undertake today, and particular theorists still command allegiance among contemporary psychologists. (This explains why there are so many names of note in this chapter.)

From one point of view, the continued influence of grand old masters reflects a lack of progress (Mendelsohn, 1983), but that's not the only point of view. Much of what are called personality theories are actually general orientations, not specific hypotheses that rise or fall on the results of a particular study. Different personality "theories" have different emphases, and because each of these emphases is plausible, we shouldn't expect any of them to go out of fashion.

Let's now take a quick look at the four major approaches to personality (soon to be discussed in detail). The *psychoanalytic approach* includes those theories proposed by Freud and his followers. It stresses psychological energy and how it motivates our behavior. Psychoanalytic theories explain personality in terms of how we transform energy into thoughts, feelings, or actions. To help understand how personality is shaped, a developmental perspective is often introduced. "Because of ambivalence toward her parents, she has been reluctant to marry and settle down. Instead, she's prolonging her adolescence, traveling around, and taking jobs as they appear."

The *trait approach* includes those theories that classify people, putting them in categories (reflecting their basic "type") or describing them along quantitative dimensions (according to "how much" of a particular quality they possess). Once people are classified, they are explained. "He's a vegetarian, a Sagittarian, short, and sweet."

The *phenomenological* (or *cognitive*) *approach* assumes that what is most important is how people think about themselves and their world. People are compared to scientists or to computers. What does Edward believe, and how and why does he believe it? "He has lofty ideals, and tends to judge himself and others harshly. At the same time, he is curious and an expert on many subjects."

Finally, the *social learning approach* stands apart from the other general strategies for studying personality. Instead of looking at characteristics within the person, social learning theories look to the environment for explanations. These theories appeared when psychologists began to apply learning theories to traditional personality topics. Consequently, they emphasize the give-and-take between individuals and their environment. In recent years, social learning theories have taken into account a person's thoughts and beliefs, but they still focus on the environment. "Appreciate what she's been through. She grew up in a poor neighborhood, and her father was an invalid. This woman never had any advantages, and she's been forced to fight every step along the way."

> Freud's . . . view of human nature might well have stepped out of the pages of Darwin's *The Origin of Species.*
> • • •

Individual Differences

Note that theories within each of these general approaches describe personality in different terms. Together, the ways that people are characteristically themselves and different from others—where they stand with respect to the factors deemed important by a strategy—are termed **individual differences.** Psychologist Gordon Allport (1961), one of the pioneers in the study of personality, regards the identification and description of individual differences as *the* fundamental issue in the field:

It is often said that personality is "far behind" other sciences because psychology cannot discover its fundamental units. . . . Something must account for the *recurrences* and *stabilities* in personal behavior. . . . [W]e do find that personality is relatively stable over time and in different situational fields. How can we account for this fact unless we search for some sort of structures? (pp. 311–312)

Allport believed that traits hold the most promise as the fundamental units of personality, but the field as a whole

individual differences
the ways that people are characteristically themselves (and different from others)

personality assessment
the measurement of individual differences in personality

has not agreed with him. Instead, we see different units championed within the different approaches.

Assessment

Personality psychologists have devised an array of measures to assess individual differences, and the process of using these measures is termed **personality assessment.** Intelligence testing (Chapter 8) represents the earliest attempt within psychology to measure how individuals differ, and so it has served as a model for a great deal of personality assessment, for better or worse. Accordingly, researchers often assume that individual differences in personality are highly stable and general, that they can be measured with a questionnaire, and that they bear a simple relation to one's behavior. Questionnaires are an important tool of personality assessment, but as will later become clear, other types of measures also exist.

The Psychoanalytic Approach

The first of the modern personality theories to take form grew out of Sigmund Freud's attempts to understand the disorder known in his time as hysteria (Chapter 1). He believed that sexual conflicts from childhood brought about the condition. When he proposed his theories at the turn of the century, he attracted numerous followers. Many ended up disagreeing with certain aspects of Freud's theory and proposed theories of their own, which nonetheless preserved many of Freud's major thrusts. Therefore, **psychoanalysis** refers to the whole family of theories by Freud and others. These theories make the following assumptions about human nature (Peterson, 1988):

- People possess psychological energy called **libido.** Our behavior is driven by this energy.
- Drives and instincts provide this energy and are thus part of people's biological inheritance. We are motivated to satisfy instinctive needs.
- There is often conflict between the individual and society, because a person's biological instincts do not always conform to social rules.
- The most important of a person's motives are unconscious, forcibly kept from awareness because they offend and threaten the conscious mind.
- Past events shape subsequent behavior. In particular, struggles and conflicts during childhood affect an adult's thoughts, feelings, and actions.
- Like Piaget's theory of cognitive development, psychoanalytic views of personality development assume that people must pass satisfactorily through early stages in order to negotiate later stages with success.

Not every psychoanalytic theory fully embraces all of these positions, but together they represent a generic version of this approach to human nature.

psychoanalysis

a strategy for explaining personality that stresses psychological energy and how it motivates our behavior

libido

in psychoanalytic theory, psychological energy that motivates behavior

Psychoanalysis involves a number of procedures, including free association and dream analysis, that help uncover conflicts buried in the unconscious.

Sigmund Freud

The best place to start our discussion of the psychoanalytic approach is with the creator of this perspective. Sigmund Freud (1856–1939) was a Viennese physician trained in neurology. While treating patients suffering from hysteria, he began to develop his theory of psychoanalysis. As noted earlier, hysteria involves puzzling physical symptoms, like the inability to move or to see, with no obvious physical basis (Chapter 1; see also Chapter 12). Freud first worked with another physician named Joseph Breuer. From Breuer he learned the technique of *catharsis,* the so-called talking cure. A hysterical patient who could be hypnotized and encouraged to talk about earlier events might, as she touched upon areas of conflict, experience an outpouring of emotion and a cessation of her symptoms.

Breuer and Freud (1895) interpreted hysteria and catharsis in terms of energy. Hysterical symptoms represented a restraining of energy (libido), and catharsis quite literally was the freeing of this energy. Because Freud did not like hypnosis, he developed another means of achieving catharsis, which he called *free association.* Patients were encouraged to say anything and everything that came into their minds, without censoring. Their train of associations often led back to a hidden conflict, and catharsis followed.

At first, Freud believed that the conflicts he unearthed in treating hysteria referred to actual childhood experiences of his patients. Accordingly, he suggested that childhood sexual abuse produced adult hysteria. He later modified this belief, suggesting instead that the memories of his patients represented sexual wishes on their part. These wishes had undergone **repression,** or exile to the unconscious. Nevertheless, these wishes still exerted a strong influence upon the patients decades later.

More recent evidence shows that the sexual abuse of children has been much more widespread than originally believed. Indeed, many of Freud's original patients might well have been accurately reporting what happened to them as children. If this is the case, important revisions of psychoanalytic theory may be needed. Psychoanalytic scholars are currently debating what to make of this new evidence (Masson, 1983).

Freud was a prolific writer who frequently revised his theories. His *Collected Works* occupy over twenty volumes, and it is therefore difficult to present a brief overview of his ideas. In the following sections, we will cover some of Freud's major ideas, notably the structure of personality and the central place of unconscious processes, the role of instincts in human behavior, and how personality develops.

repression
the process by which threatening thoughts and feelings are kept out of one's awareness

The Structure of Personality.   Freud proposed that the mind has three parts. The **conscious** is what we are aware of at a particular moment ("my favorite television show is about to start"). The **preconscious** is whatever we can voluntarily call into awareness, such as telephone numbers, birthdays, and definitions of psychoanalytic terms. The **unconscious** contains thoughts, feelings, and desires of which we are unaware.

The psychoanalytic unconscious is motivated, which means that its content is not the result of simple forgetfulness (Chapter 7). Rather, ideas become unconscious because they upset us. For instance, one of Freud's (1918) case histories concerns a troubled young man whose psychological difficulties stemmed in part from witnessing his parents make love (what

conscious
thoughts and feelings of which we are aware

preconscious
thoughts and feelings of which we can become aware voluntarily

unconscious
thoughts and feelings of which we cannot become aware because they are threatening to us in some way

Freud politely called "the primal scene"). Although this man did not consciously remember what he had seen years before, the memory resided in his unconscious and affected his later behavior. He was specifically afraid of wolves and other animals, presumably because they reminded him of how his father looked during the primal scene.

Later in Freud's career, he revised his view of the mind in several ways. He supplanted his division of mental functioning into the conscious, preconscious, and unconscious with a new set of distinctions (see Figure 11.1). The **id** (the German word for "it") is where our instincts reside and the *pleasure principle* rules. In other words, under the influence of the id, our thinking is dominated by wishes and impulses. We see the world as we would like it to be, not as it actually is. The id alone is present at birth, thus the newborn is nothing more than a bundle of instincts seeking immediate gratification.

As we develop, we become aware of external reality, and a second mental structure develops: the **ego.** The ego is practical and allows us to satisfy our needs and desires without courting disaster. The ego makes it possible for us to adapt to the world, and it operates according to what Freud called the *reality principle.* When influenced by the reality principle, our thinking is rational and logical.

Note that because the id is present prior to the ego, the pleasure principle is necessarily more basic to our functioning than the reality principle. Indeed, Freud termed thinking dominated by wishes and impulses *primary process,* whereas he called rational and logical thinking *secondary process,* to emphasize its derived and presumably fragile nature. Primary process is the language of dreams, fevers, drunken stupors, and lust. According to Freud, children think exclusively in terms of primary process. Only through socialization do logic and order—secondary process—enter the mental scene.

The last mental structure to develop is a person's moral sense, which Freud called the **superego.** The superego emerges at about age three or four, and represents the child's internalization of parental and societal

id

in psychoanalytic theory, that aspect of personality that is instinctive

ego

in psychoanalytic theory, that aspect of personality that makes adaptation to the world possible; the ego makes compromises between the id and the superego

superego

in psychoanalytic theory, that aspect of personality that represents the internalization of societal values; our conscience

Figure 11.1

The Structure of Personality. Freud described personality in two important ways: in terms of the conscious, preconscious, and unconscious; and in terms of the id, ego, and superego.

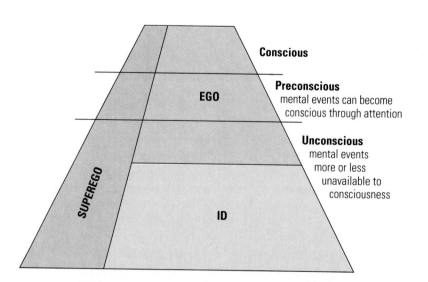

values. Freud conceives the id, ego, and superego as constantly interacting. All come to bear in a given situation, and their blending explains a particular personality.

The ego mediates between the impulses of the id and the prohibitions of the superego. Suppose your boss infuriates you. You want to punch him in the nose, but doing so would create great trouble for you. So, you tell a joke at his expense to your fellow workers. This provides not quite as intense a satisfaction as punching him, but neither does it get you in any trouble, even if he happens to overhear the joke. After all, you were just kidding.

At the disposal of the ego are the defense mechanisms discussed in Chapter 6. They represent various compromises that allow us to satisfy our instincts indirectly. Freud's description and explanation of defense mechanisms rank with his most notable and original contributions to psychology. In fact, his terms have become part of contemporary culture, used even in our casual conversations: "Goodness, isn't John horribly repressed?"

Instincts. From his very first psychoanalytic writings, Freud emphasized sexuality as the major human concern. Our psychological energy—libido—is channeled into sexual activity, direct and indirect. People are motivated by what Freud called the **life instinct** or **Eros** (after the Greek god of love). But toward the end of his life, Freud became convinced that Eros did not explain the whole of human motivation. He was struck by the tendency of some individuals to act out, again and again, painful episodes from their past.

This compulsion to repeat particular experiences cannot be explained if our only instinct is a desire for pleasure. So, Freud proposed a **death instinct,** called **Thanatos** by some psychoanalytic writers, after the Greek god of death. The death instinct motivates violence and aggression, against others as well as ourselves. It explains warfare and hatred, drug and alcohol abuse, murder and suicide. Psychologists are reluctant to explain human aggression in terms of instincts (Chapters 6 and 15), and Freud's death instinct has probably been the least accepted aspect of his theory.

The Development of Personality. One of Freud's best-known assumptions is that children are inherently sexual. *All* children entertain sexual wishes. Freud's (1905b) pronouncements on the universality of childhood sexuality created considerable controversy, as you might imagine. Let's see what he meant. When Freud says that children are sexual, he does *not* mean in the same way that adults are sexual. Rather, children and adults possess the same sexual instinct, desiring and seeking out physical pleasure as the id impels them to do. But the means by which their sexual instincts are satisfied changes throughout development. Indeed, Freud suggested that one key to understanding personality is in terms of psychosexual stages.

As explained in Chapter 9, each stage of psychosexual development is defined by the part of our body that gives us pleasure. During the *oral stage,* from birth to one year, the child's mouth is the source of gratification: sucking, biting, chewing, and crying. With weaning, the child enters the *anal stage,* from about one to three years, and elimination becomes the source of pleasure. Retaining feces and/or expelling them provides pleasure to the youngster (and aggravation to parents). The child encoun-

life instinct (Eros)
according to Freud, our instinct for self-preservation and sexual gratification

death instinct (Thanatos)
according to Freud, our instinct for violence and destruction

According to Freud, during the phallic stage, children feel sexual desire for opposite-sex parents.

ters external restraints during this stage, in the form of toilet training. The manner in which weaning and toilet training occur—harshly, permissively, whatever—is thought to affect adult personality.

Then comes the *phallic stage,* from about three to five years, when the child's source of pleasure first centers in his or her sexual organs. "Playing doctor" is popular. Children become interested in masturbation, and curious about just where babies come from. Some critical events occur during the phallic stage, and Freud uses the Greek myth of Oedipus as a metaphor for these events.

Oedipus was the tragic character who inadvertently and unknowingly killed his father and married his mother. Freud suggests that this myth taps a universal desire, what he calls the **Oedipus complex.** During the phallic stage, children feel sexual desire for the opposite-sex parent. The same-sex parent becomes the rival. Once in this triangle, children figure out that the same-sex parent will not bow out, gracefully or otherwise. They begin to fear that the same-sex parent will retaliate against them.

The Oedipus complex is resolved when children eventually realize that they will not win the opposite-sex parent for themselves. They therefore settle for the next best thing, which is to possess Mom or Dad indirectly and symbolically, by identifying with the other parent. This is how children acquire the behaviors, attitudes, and interests that they will have as adults.

After the phallic stage, at about six years, children enter what Freud calls a *latency period,* where sexual impulses are curbed. Other interests occupy the child, and development in other domains is most important (Chapter 9).

The *genital stage,* which coincides with the onset of puberty, is the last step in psychosexual development. During this stage, sexual impulses again emerge, only now pleasure is obtained through the genitals in the course of sexual activity with others.

Many of Freud's specific claims about psychosexual development are not supported by research (Peterson, 1988). Regardless, psychosexual development has been influential in personality psychology. Like other stage theories of development, Freud's theory proposes that we must pass through the stages in a particular order. If we do not pass successfully through a particular stage, either because we are frustrated by not enough satisfaction or indulged by too much, a **fixation** results. Psychic energy is left behind, and the concerns of that particular stage continue to dominate in adult personality.

The behavior of someone fixated at the oral stage, for example, will center around oral gratification, through excessive eating, drinking, smoking, or talking. Such individuals are also thought to be highly dependent on others, seeking nurturance from them. Someone fixated at the anal stage might symbolically express either the retention of feces, by relentlessly pursuing neatness and order, or their expulsion, by being unbelievably sloppy and wasteful. Felix and Oscar are hardly an odd couple when viewed in these terms, because they perfectly exemplify the two forms that anal fixation may take. Finally, someone fixated at the phallic stage shows an exaggerated concern with sexuality, which may be expressed in excessive vanity. The contemporary macho man, draped in gold chains and drenched in cologne, presumably acquired his excess baggage while passing through the phallic stage.

Oedipus complex

the psychoanalytic hypothesis that children experience sexual desire for their opposite-sex parent and resentment toward their same-sex parent

fixation

in psychoanalytic theory, the failure to resolve a particular stage of psychosexual development, so that the concerns of that particular stage continue to dominate in adult personality

Approaches After Freud

Psychoanalytic theory began with a focus on abnormality, but Freud went on to apply it broadly: to dreams, humor, creativity, religion, and even the origin and function of society. Psychoanalytic theory thus became an influential approach to the study of normal personality. As noted earlier, other theorists followed Freud's lead to propose their own version of psychoanalytic theory. These theorists all disagreed with Freud's strong emphasis on sexuality. Most preferred a more social explanation of personality, so again we return to the nature-nurture controversy, with Freud championing the biological perspective and those who followed him taking a more environmental view.

Alfred Adler.   Among Freud's first followers was another Viennese physician, Alfred Adler (1870–1937). At first enthusiastic about Freud's ideas, Adler soon came to disagree with the primacy Freud had assigned to sexuality. The disagreement resulted in a complete break between them, personally and professionally. Adler (1910) believed that conflict plays an important role in shaping our personality, but that it was social conflict, rather than sexual. He introduced the concept of the **inferiority complex,** suggesting that all people feel inadequate with respect to some aspect of their being, physical or psychological. Our development can be understood as our attempt to compensate for perceived inferiority. For example, Theodore Roosevelt is a famous example of a sickly and weak child who develops himself into a hearty and robust adult: "Speak softly but carry a big stick."

Another example of Adler's (1927) interest in the social determinants of personality is his theorizing about the child's position in the family while growing up. He believed that birth order dictates the way children are treated, and thus the way that their personalities develop (cf. Leman, 1985). So, the eldest child is the original center of attention in a family, acquiring a need for power and authority. The second child continually strives to overcome the older rival. The youngest may be spoiled and pampered on the one hand, or flexible and diverse on the other.

Birth order is a social phenomenon, not a biological one. Research bears out some of Adler's ideas about birth order. For instance, first-born individuals are more likely to become eminent. Among those men who have run for president, first-borns won more frequently than later-borns (Wagner & Schubert, 1977).

Carl Jung.   Another early follower of Freud was Carl Jung (1875–1961), a Swiss physician who first worked with schizophrenic patients. In their bizarre hallucinations and delusions, Jung (1907) detected a similarity to Freud's descriptions of the dreams of less troubled individuals. In either case, primary process thinking dominates.

Like Adler, Jung broke with Freud over the significance of sexual motivation. In going his own way, he became interested in symbols, studying mythology and anthropology extensively. He was struck by the degree to which particular images showed up in different times and places (see Figure 11.2), to him too much of a coincidence to be explained by cultural diffusion. Jung instead proposed that by virtue of belonging to the same species, all people share access to a **collective unconscious:** a reposi-

inferiority complex
Adler's concept that all people feel inadequate with respect to some aspect of their selves

collective unconscious
Jung's idea that all people have a common storehouse of experiences and memories inherited from our ancestors

Carl Jung

Figure 11.2

Mandala Symbolism. Certain symbols show up across diverse cultures. One such symbol is the mandala, or magic circle, symbol, which, according to Jung, stands for people's search for unity.

tory of ancestral experiences and memories, both human and prehuman. The collective unconscious represents tried and true ways of thinking about the business of life, and when people tap into it, they literally receive the wisdom of the ages. Jung further believed the collective unconscious to be a much more important aspect of personality than Freud's unconscious, which included only an individual's personal history.

Neo-Freudians. A second generation of psychoanalytic theorists followed the lead of Adler by stressing the social character of people over their instinctive, sexually motivated nature. The theorists who adopted this point of view became known as **neo-Freudians.** Karen Horney (1885–1952) dispensed with the Oedipus myth altogether to argue that people are motivated by basic anxiety: feelings of isolation and helplessness stemming from their disturbed relationships with other people. According to Horney, the primary human need is to feel safe and secure with others. Erich Fromm (1900–1980) integrated psychoanalytic ideas with sociological notions of alienation, proposing that people are driven to reduce their separateness from one another. Harry Stack Sullivan (1892–1949) articulated the most thoroughly "social" of the psychoanalytic theories by redefining personality as relationships between people. To Sullivan, an individual only becomes a person when he or she enters into a relationship with someone else.

neo-Freudians

psychoanalytic theorists who followed Freud and stressed the social character of people over their instinctive, sexually motivated nature

Erik Erikson. One final psychoanalytic theorist should be mentioned. We've already encountered Erik Erikson (1902–   ) in Chapters 9 and 10, where his ideas about life-span development were discussed. Unlike so many other psychoanalytic theorists, Erikson never formally broke with

Freud. Indeed, Erikson prefers to call himself a post-Freudian, one who follows Freud and builds on his earlier ideas. But Erikson could quite easily be classified with the neo-Freudians, because his developmental theory has an explicit social emphasis. Social dilemmas—such as trust versus mistrust and intimacy versus isolation—define the stages of life in his psychosocial theory of development (see Chapter 9, pp. 374–376; and Chapter 10, pp. 407–409).

Erikson also contributed to *psychohistory,* a field that uses psychological theories to shed light on historical figures and events. He has published studies of Adolph Hitler, Martin Luther, George Bernard Shaw, Gandhi, and Thomas Jefferson, among others. An important goal of psychohistory is to understand a person in the context of his or her particular era. To understand motives, we have to understand their meaning within a given time and place. This principle—carefully adhered to by Erikson—underscores his attempt to view personality in social terms.

Evaluating the Psychoanalytic Approach

The psychoanalytic approach represents the earliest attempt by psychologists to explain the whole of personality. The accounts of Freud, Adler, Jung, and others continue to be influential, although new personality theories have been proposed that challenge them on many grounds. Many critics find psychoanalytic theories so complicated that they cannot readily be tested. Nonetheless, two aspects of the psychoanalytic approach have strongly influenced modern thinking about personality. First is the idea that many of our important motives are unconscious. Second is the idea that early childhood events can affect our characteristic behavior decades later.

The Trait Approach

trait approach
a strategy for explaining personality that classifies people in terms of their stable and general individual differences

Like the psychoanalytic approach, the **trait approach** consists of a group of related theories that are united by common emphases. Most trait theories concern themselves with the following questions (Peterson, 1988):

- What are the fundamental ways in which people differ?
- How can these differences best be measured?
- How do individual differences lead to positive or negative functioning?
- What is the origin of a particular individual difference?

The trait approach, like psychoanalysis, can be traced to Darwin's theory of evolution. Note the emphasis on individual variation and how this determines adaptation. Also, trait theorists are often quite interested in whether or not personality characteristics are inherited, which leads them to consider the biological basis of traits.

Gordon Allport

Harvard psychologist Gordon Allport (1897–1967) set the agenda for trait strategies. His importance within the trait approach corresponds to that of Freud within the psychoanalytic tradition. Allport taught the first personality psychology course in the United States, and in 1937, he wrote one of the first personality textbooks. Even theorists who disagree with Allport's particular ideas use his terms and take positions on the issues he first stated.

Let's briefly contrast Allport's approach with the psychoanalytic approach. Where psychoanalysts began with an emphasis on abnormality and then generalized to normality, Allport from the start of his theorizing focused on normal individuals. Indeed, he felt that Freud's theories applied only to people with profound troubles. Instead of understanding people in terms of unconscious conflicts from their past, Allport believed that the key to personality was in someone's conscious and rational striving toward future goals.

Allport believed that traits are the appropriate units with which to understand personality. He defined a **trait** as:

> a neuropsychic structure having the capacity to render many stimuli functionally equivalent, and to initiate and guide equivalent (meaningfully consistent) forms of adaptive and expressive behavior. (1961, p. 347)

Let's clarify several terms in this definition. In calling a trait neuropsychic, Allport means that it has a biological as well as a psychological basis. By saying that a trait renders different stimuli functionally equivalent, he means that traits are associated with a consistent pattern of response across different situations. In proposing that a trait initiates and guides behavior, he means that traits cause us to think, feel, and act in certain ways. Finally, Allport defines traits as adaptive (meaning they aid survival) and expressive (meaning they show up in a person's style of behaving).

In one of Allport's well-known endeavors, he and a colleague read an entire dictionary and located 17,953 words describing personality traits (Allport & Odbert, 1936)! Not all of these traits sensibly apply to everyone. Indeed, Allport (1961) believed that each of us possesses only seven to ten traits. These particular qualities, termed **personal traits,** differ from person to person. So, for example, my personality might be described as cautious and humorous, because I consistently act in these ways. However, your personality might be poorly described with these traits. Sometimes you are cautious, and sometimes you are bold. And you might occasionally crack a joke, but otherwise you are somber. According to Allport, different traits are needed to describe your personality.

In contrast to personal traits are **common traits,** so named by Allport because they can be used to describe everyone. Consider the strength of one's needs, like those described in Chapter 6 (Murray, 1938). We can arrange all people from low to moderate to high on achievement motivation. Allport believed that common traits had limited usefulness in capturing someone's individuality, so he urged personality psychologists to focus on personal traits. This recommendation is appealing, but it makes conventional research difficult if not impossible. If different people require different traits to describe their personalities, how can a psychologist make any generalizations?

Allport argues that generalizations should not be the goal of personality psychology. According to him, psychology per se is a *nomothetic science,* striving to make valid statements about people in general. However, personality should be studied idiographically, recognizing that each

Gordon Allport

trait

a stable and pervasive individual difference with a biological and psychological basis that initiates and guides diverse behavior

personal traits

characteristics that sensibly describe only some people

common traits

characteristics that sensibly describe all people

person is a unique individual who needs his or her own explanation. Most trait theorists disagree with Allport's call for an *idiographic science,* because the methods required to achieve this don't seem to exist. Most trait researchers therefore study common traits.

Are Traits Inherited?

A major concern of trait theorists is whether individual differences in personality are inherited or instilled through experience. Certainly we can see resemblances within many families, but we know from our previous discussions, particularly of intelligence (Chapter 8), that these can reflect common nurture as well as common nature. Let's discuss several well-known approaches to this issue within the field of personality.

William Sheldon. One strategy for disentangling nature and nurture with respect to personality is to find an actual biological basis for individual differences. While this does not prove that traits are inherited—biological characteristics might after all be altered by experience—the argument is nonetheless strengthened. A well-known example of this approach is William Sheldon's (1899–1977) investigations of a person's physique (or body build) and how physique corresponds to personality.

Sheldon (1940, 1942) started with the observation that physiques could be described along three different dimensions:

- endomorphy—degree of roundness
- mesomorphy—degree of muscularity
- ectomorphy—degree of linearity

He devised ways of rating each of these dimensions with 7-point scales, from low (1) to high (7). Someone's profile of scores is called a *somatotype.* For example, a quite chubby person would be rated 7-1-1, whereas an extremely skinny person would be 1-1-7. Most of us, being average, would have a 4-4-4 somatotype.

Sheldon's theory is an account of personality because of his hypothesis that different physiques go with different personality styles. Endomorphs are easygoing and affectionate, mesomorphs are action oriented, and ectomorphs are sensitive and inhibited. Sheldon's original investigations of his theory have been criticized because he rated both the somatotypes and the personality characteristics of research subjects; unintended bias due to his expectations may have confounded the results.

However, more recent research in which ratings of physique are made independently of ratings of traits tends to support Sheldon's hypothesized links between physique and personality (Hendry & Gillies, 1978). The reasons for these links have yet to be discovered. Sheldon believed the links to be direct and inherent. Others point to the role of social stereotyping.

Twin Studies. A more contemporary approach in the spirit of Sheldon's biological theorizing investigates the genetic basis of individual differences. Recent research uses the twin method for separating nature and nurture to show that various personality traits are heritable. Tellegen et al. (1988) studied identical twins and fraternal twins, those raised together and those raised apart. On the average, 50 percent of the variation in personality test scores was due to genetic variation. As explained in Chapter 2, heritability estimates like these do not mean that complex characteristics are inherited as a whole, but rather that their *variation* across individuals has a genetic basis.

Factor Analytic Theories of Personality

Trait theorists are more concerned with measurement than are other personality psychologists. This concern reaches the height of sophistication in the work of researchers who use a statistical technique called **factor analysis** to identify the basic dimensions of personality. Factor analysis is a procedure for detecting patterns in a large set of correlations. Suppose research subjects complete dozens of personality questionnaires, each measuring a different trait. Factor analysis allows the researcher to identify those measures that go together and those that do not. Sets of characteristics found together in most people are thought to reflect an underlying dimension, or factor, of personality.

Factor analytic theorists of personality make a useful distinction between surface traits and source traits (Cattell, 1950). *Surface traits* are the characteristics of people that meet the eye, any of the thousands of individual differences that people display. *Source traits* are underlying individual differences that give rise to these surface traits. There are many more surface traits than source traits; the latter are necessarily more abstract and general. Surface traits such as moodiness, restlessness, and irritability may reflect a single underlying source trait—unhappiness, for example.

Factor analytic research proceeds by assessing numerous surface traits of various research subjects and then looking for basic patterns. The factors thereby identified are thought to be source traits. The two most influential factor analytic theorists are Raymond Cattell (1905–   ) and Hans Eysenck (1916–   ). Cattell identifies sixteen basic factors of personality, presented in Figure 11.3 (Cattell, 1950).

Eysenck (1947), in contrast, identifies but two factors (see Figure 11.4). The first is **introversion-extraversion,** which refers to the degree to which someone is inwardly or outwardly oriented. The second is **neuroticism,** the degree to which someone is moody, nervous, and unstable. Eysenck proposes a physiological interpretation for each of his factors, arguing that introversion-extraversion reflects the chronic level of cortical excitation and that neuroticism is based in the reactivity of the autonomic nervous system (Chapter 2).

At first glance, it seems that Cattell and Eysenck must disagree. However, Eysenck's scheme is compatible with Cattell's, differing chiefly at its level of abstraction (e.g., Guilford, 1975). In other words, if one were to factor analyze Cattell's sixteen factors, Eysenck's factors would emerge.

Both Eysenck and Cattell believe that personality traits are heritable, so they join with other trait theorists in regarding personality as having a genetic basis. Missing in their work to date is any detailed investigation of the biological mechanisms by which information on one's chromosomes is translated into complex behavior. However, Eysenck's physiological interpretations of the personality factors he identifies seem promising.

---

factor analysis

a statistical procedure for detecting patterns in a large set of correlations, used by personality researchers to identify the basic dimensions of personality

introversion-extraversion

according to Eysenck, a basic factor of personality that reflects whether one is generally oriented inward (introversion) or outward (extraversion)

neuroticism

according to Eysenck, a basic factor of personality that reflects the degree to which one is moody, nervous, and unstable

Figure 11.3

Cattell's Sixteen Personality Factors. Through factor analysis, Raymond Cattell has identified sixteen basic dimensions along which people differ.

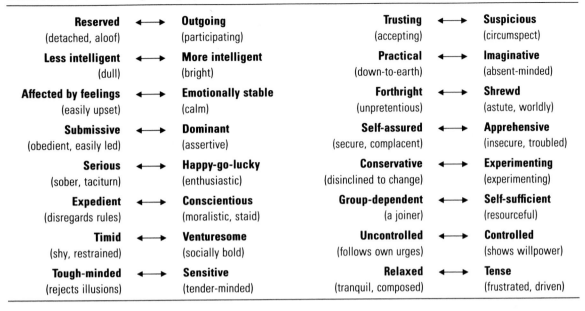

Reserved (detached, aloof)	←→	**Outgoing** (participating)		**Trusting** (accepting)	←→	**Suspicious** (circumspect)
Less intelligent (dull)	←→	**More intelligent** (bright)		**Practical** (down-to-earth)	←→	**Imaginative** (absent-minded)
Affected by feelings (easily upset)	←→	**Emotionally stable** (calm)		**Forthright** (unpretentious)	←→	**Shrewd** (astute, worldly)
Submissive (obedient, easily led)	←→	**Dominant** (assertive)		**Self-assured** (secure, complacent)	←→	**Apprehensive** (insecure, troubled)
Serious (sober, taciturn)	←→	**Happy-go-lucky** (enthusiastic)		**Conservative** (disinclined to change)	←→	**Experimenting** (experimenting)
Expedient (disregards rules)	←→	**Conscientious** (moralistic, staid)		**Group-dependent** (a joiner)	←→	**Self-sufficient** (resourceful)
Timid (shy, restrained)	←→	**Venturesome** (socially bold)		**Uncontrolled** (follows own urges)	←→	**Controlled** (shows willpower)
Tough-minded (rejects illusions)	←→	**Sensitive** (tender-minded)		**Relaxed** (tranquil, composed)	←→	**Tense** (frustrated, driven)

Figure 11.4

Eysenck's Personality Dimensions. Through factor analysis, Hans Eysenck has identified two basic dimensions along which people differ. Also shown in this figure are some of the surface traits related to these two source traits.

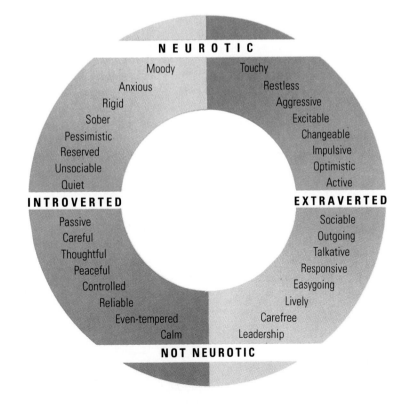

Evaluating the Trait Approach

The trait approach to personality has made its greatest contribution to the field by identifying the ways in which people differ and devising research procedures for assessing these basic differences. All personality researchers use the tests and measures devised by proponents of the trait approach. At the same time, the trait approach to personality can be criticized for neglecting the influence of the environment on behavior. Many trait theorists seem to assume that people act the same way—that is, consistently with their traits—regardless of where they find themselves. This assumption has been hotly debated, and at the end of the chapter, we'll discuss this issue in detail.

The Phenomenological Approach

phenomenological (cognitive) approach
a strategy for explaining personality that looks at the characteristic contents and processes of one's thinking

The basic premise of the **phenomenological** (or **cognitive**) **approach** to personality is that our personality is defined by what we think and how we think. *Phenomenological* refers to a person's awareness—one's thoughts and beliefs. The other personality theories so far described are cognitive in the sense that they acknowledge the importance of a person's mental life. However, phenomenological theories of personality are set apart by their assumption that thoughts and beliefs are the primary aspect of personality. How we feel and how we act are determined by how we think, not vice versa.

Phenomenological theories share the following assumptions (Peterson, 1988):

- Behavior occurs within a psychological reality, defined as how an individual perceives the world. Ghosts and demons are real to a person so long as he believes in them. Psychological reality may overlap perfectly, somewhat, or not at all with physical reality.
- People are like scientists in that they actively propose "theories" about themselves and the world, and then try to test out these theories.
- People inherently strive toward greater accuracy, precision, and/or consistency in their understanding.
- People's reports on their own thoughts and beliefs are taken seriously. To study personality, a researcher can start by asking research subjects what they think.

Phenomenological personality theories may be traced to gestalt psychology, particularly to Kurt Lewin's (1951) attempts to apply gestalt theory to our complex behavior (Chapter 1). A concern with how people structure their experiences unites gestalt approaches to perception and phenomenological personality theories. The two most influential phenomenological theories today are George Kelly's personal construct theory and Carl Rogers's self-theory, and so it is to their work that we now turn.

George Kelly

A self-taught clinical psychologist, George Kelly (1905–1967) developed a therapy approach that focused specifically on how a client interpreted events. Kelly (1955) believed that a variety of interpretations were always personal construct theory

Kelly's theory of personality that stresses how people think about events

possible, with some more useful to an individual than others. From this notion, he developed an approach to personality called **personal construct theory.** Kelly argued that the basic unit of personality is the personal construct. Personal constructs, quite simply, are the terms with which we interpret our experiences.

Kelly uses the term *personal* because cognitive activity belongs to the individual. His use of the term *construct* is based on his belief that people build (or construct) their personality with the ideas that they entertain. His theory is based on the assumption that people can revise or replace any of their interpretations. Because our interpretations literally are our personality, Kelly is proposing that personality need not be fixed. Contrast this with psychoanalytic or trait conceptions, which assume personality to be unchanging, across time and across situations.

Kelly developed a method for measuring personal constructs called the *Role Construct Repertory Test* (*REP Test*). A subject is given a list of twenty social roles (mother, father, friend, employer, and so forth) and asked to think of the person who fills each role in his life. Then he is presented with a set of three of these roles. How are two of them alike yet different from the third? He writes his answer down. Then another trio of roles is presented, along with the same question. Again, he writes down the basis of his comparison and contrast. This process is repeated dozens of times, always with different sets of three roles.

Patterns begin to emerge that reflect the person's habitual constructs. Suppose the subject always compares and contrasts people in terms of how much he likes them: "I love my mother and father, but I'm not so keen on my employer." Or suppose he always mentions their physical appearance: "Those two are good looking, but this one is a real dog." These two examples depict quite different worlds, the first a place awash with feelings, and the second a place where beauty holds sway.

Kelly wasn't just interested in the contents of personal constructs. He also investigated their more abstract properties. For example, constructs vary in their *range of convenience:* the set of events for which they work best. Remember your first day on a new job, where nothing made sense to you? Kelly would say that the constructs you brought with you through the front door were inadequate. Their range of convenience did not include the demands placed on you. You eventually devised new constructs, or expanded the ones already at your disposal, or quit the job.

Kelly also proposed that personal constructs are organized in a hierarchy. Some are more important than others, and so we use these to resolve conflicts among less important constructs. The superordinate construct differs from person to person. For some, it may be religion. For others, it may be politics. For still others, it may be family.

A construct system as a whole may be simple or complex, depending on how one uses constructs: redundantly or independently of each other. For instance, if a woman believes that all her friends are interesting and intelligent and that all her enemies are bloated and disgusting, she is really making one simple contrast. She uses constructs redundantly. Now consider a woman who believes that her friends have occasional flaws, just as her enemies have occasional virtues. She makes distinctions that the first woman does not, and thus uses constructs independently of each other. This individual difference is called *cognitive complexity* (Bieri, 1955). Here we have an important point about personal constructs: They are not identical to someone's vocabulary. The first woman may have a rich vocabulary, but she uses words in a simple way.

Just as people interpret their experiences using constructs, they also anticipate future events in the same terms. Sometimes these anticipations prove useful, in which case people keep using their constructs. At other times anticipations prove disastrous, and then they are revised. By Kelly's view, people can change their personality as readily as their eyeglasses, because personality resides solely in how we regard the events in our life. But change may be easier to understand than to accomplish.

We've seen, for example, that personal constructs are not the same as vocabulary. Words represent the simplest way to get at constructs, but there are some constructs with no verbal handles attached to them. These affect behavior but cannot be readily apprehended. Kelly developed a system of psychotherapy that targets personal constructs for change. One aspect of his therapy is role-playing techniques that encourage a person to try out different perspectives. We will discuss Kelly's approach to therapy further in Chapter 13.

Carl Rogers

Carl Rogers

Like Kelly, Carl Rogers (1902–1987) was a clinical psychologist whose personality theory grew out of his experiences in working with clients. Rogers (1942) first worked within a Freudian framework but became disenchanted, finding that "insight" imposed by the therapist rarely had beneficial effects on clients. If anything, the clients seemed to know better than the therapist what ailed them and what needed to be done. Rogers developed this notion into **self-theory,** an approach to personality that explains personality in terms of how people view themselves.

Central to Rogers's (1951) theory is a drive toward self-actualization, familiar to us from Abraham Maslow's work (discussed in Chapter 6). Both Rogers and Maslow assume that people strive to achieve their full potential, to become all that they can be, to increase their complexity, independence, and social responsibility. Further, people know what is good for them and how to achieve it. This is an upbeat and optimistic view of human nature, and both Rogers and Maslow are prominent figures in **humanism,** the school of psychology emphasizing that human beings are essentially good and motivated toward growth.

Still, not all people actualize themselves. Why is this? Rogers blames the environment, particularly experiences that give people distorted views of themselves. He makes a distinction between experience and awareness. *Experience* refers to everything that happens to a person. In contrast, that part of experience that a person thinks about in symbolic terms is *awareness.* If a person is to become self-actualized, awareness and experience must come together. When a discrepancy occurs, self-actualization is thwarted, and problems can follow.

According to Rogers, discrepancies result when we encounter **conditional regard:** acceptance contingent on particular ways of behaving. A parent, for example, may say, "I love you, but if you marry that person, then I never want to see you again." Such conditional regard, particularly from parents to young children, leads us to use other people's rules to define our own desires and needs. We no longer define ourselves, and

As Rogers would interpret it, these wheelchair athletes have overcome physical handicaps in their drive for self-actualization.

are thereby cut adrift to cope with experience, because our awareness is not useful to us.

Carl Rogers believes, however, that the casualties of conditional regard can be reclaimed by reversing the process. In other words, we should be given **unconditional regard:** acceptance regardless of what we think or feel or do. A parent may say, "I don't approve of your marrying that person, but I support your right to make that decision." Under these circumstances, we can again come to rely on personal definitions and interpretations. Awareness and experience come together, and self-actualization takes over as a motive.

Rogers's system of psychotherapy is called *client-centered therapy* because it quite literally centers on the client. The therapist creates a benign setting, characterized by unconditional regard, in which clients can devise their own solutions to their problems. In the course of client-centered therapy, one's perceived self and ideal self increasingly converge. The most successful therapy is conducted by clinicians who are warm, sincere, and accepting (e.g., Gurman, 1977). (We'll return to client-centered therapy in Chapter 13.)

unconditional regard
acceptance of people regardless of what they think or feel or do

Evaluating the Phenomenological Approach

The phenomenological approach to personality has grown in popularity during recent years, in part because it makes clear contact with the influential cognitive revolution that has swept through psychology as a whole. Phenomenological theories allow personality psychologists and cognitive psychologists to speak readily to one another, with benefits for both fields (Cantor & Kihlstrom, 1987). These theories have also led to successful psychotherapies that target thoughts and beliefs for change.

The shortcoming of the phenomenological approach is the drawback of cognitive psychology in general: an overemphasis on how people process information and too little attention to our irrational and emotional sides. Kelly, Rogers, and other cognitive theorists derive our feelings from our thoughts, but sometimes they seem not to do full justice to our emotions (Chapter 6).

The Social Learning Approach

social learning approach
a strategy for explaining personality that emphasizes the role of one's environment and learning

The last perspective on personality we will discuss is the **social learning approach:** a group of related theories that explain our complex behavior using principles of learning. Accordingly, the roots of the social learning approach are to be found in behaviorism, which we discussed in Chapter 5. Social learning theorists believe that the environment determines behavior, and further that the most important aspect of the environment is other people. Hence, the term *social* is used for emphasis. The following assumptions are common to most of these theories:

- The most important aspect of personality is observable behavior.
- Learning is the most important psychological process in personality.
- The most basic explanations of personality are phrased in terms of the environment.
- Behavioral change is possible through interventions that are guided by learning theory.

Although behavioral in origin, social learning theories freely introduce "unobservable" factors in their explanations, including drives and expectations. The most modern social learning theories somewhat resemble the phenomenological personality theories just discussed. However, in contrast to the theories of Kelly and Rogers, these theories explicitly tie cognitions to particular settings, thereby preserving an environmental emphasis.

John Dollard and Neal Miller

The first social learning theorists were John Dollard (1900–1980) and Neal Miller (1909–   ). Their influential book, *Personality and Psychotherapy,* published in 1950, took as its premise the belief that people learn behavior to reduce their physiological drives (Chapter 6). They noted the similarity between the drive reduction concept and the psychoanalytic hypothesis that people strive to satisfy their instincts. They therefore attempted to integrate learning theory and psychoanalysis, discussing in detail how Freudian phenomena could be explained in terms of mundane learning.

According to Dollard and Miller, repression results from reinforcement for "not thinking" about particular topics. Suppose a sexual encounter has left you feeling anxious. If and when you stop thinking about it, the anxiety stops. That's reinforcing, so you are likely to increasingly behave in this way—not thinking. The difference between the psychoanalytic unconscious and the social learning unconscious is that the former is a place to which thoughts are banished, whereas the latter is a behavioral deficit.

Also like Freud, Dollard and Miller view development in terms of the interplay between biological drives and the social environment. Conflicts surface if parents punish their children for attempting to satisfy drives, and these drives may involve hunger, elimination, sex, and aggression. In each case, a child may be driven to behave in ways that parents may not like.

approach-avoidance conflict
a situation that poses a conflict because it is simultaneously attractive and unattractive

Dollard and Miller introduced the idea of an **approach-avoidance conflict** to describe a course of activity both attractive (because it reduces drives) and unattractive (because it produces punishment). By this view, the issue at the center of each of Freud's psychosexual stages is an approach-avoidance conflict. For example, it is pleasurable for a child to masturbate, but it is not pleasurable to be punished for doing so.

Approach-avoidance conflicts are difficult to resolve. When the goal is distant, it looks attractive and so we pursue it. When the goal is close, it looks unattractive and so we avoid it. What results is literal oscillation, a back-and-forth movement in the vicinity of the goal. People may "resolve" such conflicts with repression: thinking about neither the anticipated drive reduction nor the threatened punishment. This is an unhealthy solution to the dilemma.

Julian Rotter

Dollard and Miller inspired subsequent theorists to explain personality using principles of learning. Julian Rotter (1916–   ) deserves special mention for showing how cognitive factors apply in accounts of personality based on learning theory. Rotter (1954, 1966) believes that learning occurs to the degree that particular responses produce reinforcement. However, reinforcement alone does not fully explain personality. In particular, reinforcement fails to explain how a person in a particular situation chooses among various actions (all previously reinforced).

To explain the specific behavior that an individual chooses, Rotter suggests we look to the person's *expectancy,* a belief that a specific behavior will result in a given outcome and that reinforcement will occur. For instance, someone who is hungry runs out to a fast-food restaurant if he expects that it will provide a tasty sandwich within 30 seconds. Different expectations lead to different courses of action.

What makes Rotter's theory an explanation of personality? It is his further suggestion that expectancies transcend given settings. He thereby accounts for the stability and consistency of a person's behavior. His theory is a "social" learning theory because of his belief that other people are a prime source of our expectancies.

locus of control
one's expectancy about where rewards originate, from within oneself (internal locus of control) or from without (external locus of control)

Rotter refers to one type of expectancy as **locus of control,** which means that people believe that reward is controlled either internally or externally (see Figure 11.5). People who believe that rewards come from their own actions and characteristics have an *internal locus* of control, whereas those who believe that rewards come from other people, circumstances, luck, or cosmic rays have an *external locus.*

Figure 11.5
Internal versus External Locus of Control. People with an internal locus of control believe that rewards come from their own actions and characteristics. People with an external locus of control believe that rewards come from outside themselves.

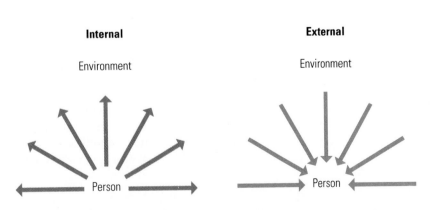

Locus of control is a frequently investigated individual characteristic. Researchers, in thousands of studies, have come to the general conclusion that internals are more vigorous and show greater perseverance than externals, across time and place. However, we must not conclude that internality is always functional. Rotter (1975) explicitly cautions that the responsiveness of someone's specific environment must be taken into account. Internal expectancies are useful only if the world really works that way. If life events are capricious, someone is better off with an external locus of control, which is more realistic.

Albert Bandura

Albert Bandura

In Chapter 5, we discussed the approach that Albert Bandura (1925–   ) takes to learning. He believes that people acquire complex behavior chiefly through modeling. We watch other people behave, and then act accordingly. If we see people act aggressively and get exactly what they want as a result, then we are more likely to act the same way. Bandura uses modeling as the cornerstone of his version of social learning theory. Here the adjective *social* is easy to understand, because the role that others play is so obviously important to what we learn.

In his most recent presentation of social learning theory, Bandura (1986) stresses *reciprocal determinism* as an important principle for understanding personality. This idea proposes that behavior, cognition, and the environment mutually influence each other. Consider the example of watching television. Your interests (cognition) determine the channel you select (behavior). If your television set is hooked to a Nielsen box, then your channel selection influences subsequent programming (environment). And what's available on television shapes your interests. Note that all possible directions of influence may occur. Learning explanations of human behavior are often regarded as highly simplistic, but Bandura's theory is not. Reciprocal determinism allows him to recognize the complexity of personality.

Walter Mischel

consistency controversy
the debate within personality psychology as to whether or not people act consistently across different situations

Next we discuss the social learning theorist Walter Mischel (1930–   ). He first forayed into personality psychology as a harsh critic of the premise that people behave consistently in different situations (Mischel, 1968). He stirred up the **consistency controversy** within personality, suggesting that people really don't act the same in different situations. We'll cover this controversy at the end of the chapter.

Mischel's (1973, 1986) more recent contributions involve his own substantive theory, which regards learning as the central process in human behavior. Like Rotter and Bandura, he assumes that learning involves a person's thoughts and beliefs. He specifies several cognitive factors he calls *person variables*. Although person variables are unique characteristics, they are not to be confused with traits, because a person variable is closely tied to a particular setting. Further, because person variables are learned styles, they are in flux to a much greater extent than traits. Among the variables that Mischel (1986) identifies are how we cognitively represent information, how we use information, what we believe about the consequences of our actions, and the values we assign to different outcomes.

Mischel is also interested in self-control as discussed in Chapter 5. He regards people's intentional changing of the environment as an important person variable. Although he continues to believe that situational factors affect behavior, he also suggests that when people alter the environment in deliberate ways, they thereby affect their own behavior.

One of Mischel's (1986) research topics that illustrates his social learning perspective is the phenomenon of *delay of gratification*. Where theorists within the other personality approaches might attribute the ability to postpone rewards to internal characteristics such as willpower or a strong ego, Mischel prefers to explain it in terms of the particular environment. Are there strategies that make delay of gratification possible? Yes. Here is a common experimental procedure. A child is shown a treat, such as a donut or marshmallow. She can have the treat right now, or she can wait for several minutes and get an even tastier reward. The catch is that she must wait alone in the same room with the treat. If the child stares at the treat, she probably will succumb to temptation. But if she turns her back, or thinks of the treat as something gross, then she successfully delays her gratification. She earns the more enjoyable reward and lives happily ever after.

Evaluating the Social Learning Approach

The social learning approach explicitly incorporates processes of learning and an emphasis on the social environment into an account of personality. Social learning theories thus direct the attention of the field of personality from factors within the person, that is, motives, traits, and thoughts, to the context in which the person behaves. Most exciting about the social learning approach are recent extensions by Bandura, Mischel, and others to include both internal and external determinants of personality. Perhaps a consensus view of human nature will someday emerge from such extensions (Peterson, 1988).

Assessing Individual Differences

Personality as a field of psychology did not take form until researchers began to measure personality characteristics, and that became possible little more than 100 years ago. These measures are concerned with differences among people (the characteristic aspect of personality). As noted earlier in the chapter, intelligence testing has served as a model for personality assessment. However, personality assessment and intelligence testing are not the same thing.

First, intelligence testing tries to assess someone's maximum performance. In contrast, personality assessment measures a person's typical performance. Second, and relatedly, intelligence tests have right answers (a, b, c, d, none of the above), and personality tests do not. Third, intelligence tests often have an explicit criterion against which they can be validated.

We saw in Chapter 8 how researchers check intelligence test results against their ability to predict someone's academic performance. Most personality tests, in contrast, do not have such a simple criterion available, because "personality" refers to many diverse aspects of a person's behavior.

Obviously, this difficulty with "validating" personality testing is another example of the by-now familiar statement that no measure is foolproof. All operationalizations, including those of individual differences in personality, are subject to confounds. The best that a researcher can do is to be on the lookout for these threats, and then try to eliminate the most obvious of these confounds.

The Basic Individual Differences

Are some traits more basic than others? Within physics, the consensus holds that time, mass, and space are the fundamental units of our physical universe. Which of the 17,000+ trait words found by Allport and Odbert are *the* fundamental ones? At the present, there is no agreement, although many candidates have been put forward.

One popular suggestion is the so-called *Big Five* proposed by psychologist Warren Norman (1963). According to Norman, the five personality traits that may capture the important ways in which people differ from each other are

- neuroticism (i.e., worried, nervous, emotional)
- extraversion (i.e., sociable, fun loving, active)
- openness (i.e., imaginative, creative, artistic)
- agreeableness (i.e., good-natured, soft-hearted, sympathetic)
- conscientiousness (i.e., reliable, hardworking, neat, punctual)

These are proposed as dimensions of personality along which all people fall. So, someone could be described as more or less neurotic, more or less agreeable, more or less conscientious, and so on. These dimensions are also independent of each other, which means that someone who falls on the extreme end of one of these may be high, medium, or low with respect to any of the others.

At first glance, trait theories of personality, such as the Big Five, seem limited. But in actuality, these theories can be quite sophisticated. For

What personality traits does this music teacher demonstrate? Extraversion, openness, and agreeableness might be important parts of his makeup.

Table 11.1

Some Frequently Studied Personality Dimensions

These individual differences are among the most frequently studied by personality researchers (Peterson, 1988). One or more measures of each characteristic is available, allowing investigations of how each originates and influences our adaptation to the world.

Achievement motivation—the degree to which one is driven to accomplish something difficult (Chapter 6)

Androgyny—the degree to which one blends together stereotypically masculine and feminine traits (Chapter 10)

Anxiety—the degree to which one responds to situations with apprehension and uneasiness (Chapter 12)

Authoritarianism—the degree to which one adheres to convention, submits gladly to authority, and degrades minority groups (Chapter 15)

Field dependence—the degree to which one uses external frames of reference to interpret the world

Repression-sensitization—the degree to which one avoids psychological threats (repression) or confronts them directly (sensitization)

Self-esteem—the degree to which one has regard for him- or herself

Type A coronary-prone behavior pattern—the degree to which one is time urgent, competitive, and hostile in the face of frustration or challenge (Chapter 6)

---

example, Norman's scheme predicts extreme variation among people. Suppose we make just three distinctions with respect to each of the basic dimensions: high, medium, and low. Because the traits are independent, a large number of different combinations of these traits are possible. For instance, one person may be high on the first trait, low on the second trait, medium on the third, high on the fourth, and high on the fifth. A second person may show a different pattern. With three distinctions per trait, we have 243 possible combinations (that is, $3 \times 3 \times 3 \times 3 \times 3$). Suppose we make five distinctions? That gives us 3,125 combinations. Seven distinctions will increase it to 16,807 combinations, and so on.

Research support for the Big Five comes from studies that use the statistical technique of factor analysis. McCrae and Costa (1987), for example, report several representative studies. They asked research subjects to describe themselves or other people in one of two ways: either by choosing appropriate adjectives or by rating the degree to which the different adjectives applied. In all cases, factor analysis showed the same five factors. In fact, identical results have been obtained in different countries, implying that the Big Five may be universal dimensions of personality (e.g., John, Goldberg, & Angleitner, 1984).

The five dimensions of personality captured by the Big Five are obviously broad individual differences. But theorists and researchers are often concerned with more specific personality characteristics. For a sampling of these, see Table 11.1, which describes some frequently studied dimensions of personality that are more specific than the Big Five (Peterson, 1988).

Assessment Strategies

After a researcher decides what types of individual differences she wishes to study, she must settle on the best strategy for doing so. To a considerable degree, the decision concerning basic units dictates investigative strategy. Psychoanalytic notions are readily investigated with case studies, and traits with questionnaires. Historically, these respective strategies have been preeminent.

Personological assessment is the attempt "to describe the particular person in as full, multifaceted, and multilevel a way as possible" (Korchin & Schuldberg, 1981, p. 1147). This strategy for assessing individual characteristics reflects an idiographic conception of personality psychology. The researcher studies her subjects in unconstrained situations, relying strongly on her own intuition about the subject's meanings, motives, and meanderings. Because personological assessment stresses rich details of a person's life, it is highly compatible with the psychoanalytic goal of providing a complex view of our behavior.

In contrast, *psychometric assessment* embodies a nomothetic view of personality psychology (Korchin & Schuldberg, 1981). Those who favor this strategy try to place people along carefully defined personality dimensions by using their responses on questionnaires. Comparisons and contrasts among people are inevitable. The goal of psychometric assessment is to maximize objectivity while minimizing judgment and inference. Test reliability and validity take on central importance here. This approach to assessment well serves the goals of personality psychologists favoring the trait approach.

The proponents of personological assessment have been known to skirmish frequently over the years with proponents of psychometric assessment. One debate in particular concerns which strategy of understanding personality allows for better predictions about the future behavior of an individual. If you are called upon to say how someone will think, act, or feel, are you better off knowing rich details about the person's life (as provided by personological assessment) or knowing his or her scores on objective personality tests (as provided by psychometric assessment)? Common sense perhaps leads you to favor personological assessment, but research shows that psychometric assessment yields more accurate predictions (Meehl, 1954).

There is practical significance to this debate. Personality psychologists work in a variety of real-life settings where they must make predictions about individuals: the clinic, the classroom, the armed forces, the government, business and industry, and others. Relying on hunches and gut feelings will lead to poor predictions. We would be better off if we used objective tests to make predictions. If you think about it, this isn't that surprising. Prediction is, after all, a statistical matter, an attempt to determine the most likely course of action granted certain conditions. Psychometric assessment is explicitly engineered to allow the researcher to predict the most likely behavior by an individual using a particular set of test scores. It *should* exceed personological assessment in its ability to forecast future behavior.

The value of personological assessment lies elsewhere, because prediction of someone's behavior is only one of several purposes of personality assessment. Indeed, personological assessment suggests to the researcher factors worthy of attention in the first place (Meehl, 1957), thus these two approaches to assessment might best be used in tandem.

More recently, personality psychology has seen the advent of *behavioral assessment,* a third approach to measuring individual differences. As you can guess from its name, behavioral assessment describes what a person actually does in particular circumstances.

Let me give you an example from a psychological clinic where I once worked. An eight-year-old girl was brought to our clinic by her father because her elementary school teacher said she had problems with discipline. The situation was potentially quite complicated. The family had recently moved to the United States from Eastern Europe, so that the father could attend graduate school. After just a few weeks, the mother returned to their home country to care for an ill relative, taking with her the two younger children in the family. This is when the girl began to have problems at school.

We could have spoken at length with the girl about her feelings of rejection and abandonment (personological assessment). We could have administered objective tests to see how she compared to her American peers with respect to intelligence, self-control, and social skills (psychometric assessment). But instead, we followed her to school and observed how she behaved and the consequences that followed her actions. Besides, we were not quite sure what "problems with discipline" really meant.

Behavioral assessment made matters clear, because we discovered that the little girl was excluded from games during recess because she did not know how to play them. She rarely talked to the other students because they made fun of her accent when she did. The only time anyone took her seriously during the entire school day was when the teacher noticed her fidgeting. In light of this information, we recommended that the school give her remedial instruction in schoolyard games as well as special help with her diction. The teacher caught the spirit of our suggestions and went one step further, devoting an entire week of class to life in other countries, which made our client the center of attention, this time because she had a positive contribution to make.

If you are keeping track, you see that these strategies of personality assessment each match up with a general approach to personality as identified earlier in the chapter.

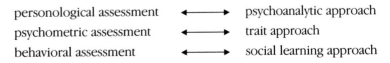

personological assessment	⟷	psychoanalytic approach
psychometric assessment	⟷	trait approach
behavioral assessment	⟷	social learning approach

Are you ready for a fourth assessment strategy? *Cognitive assessment* derives from the cognitive approach to personality. The goal of cognitive assessment is to ascertain a person's characteristic way of thinking about matters.

Sometimes cognitive assessment relies on questionnaires, asking research subjects to indicate which of several beliefs they usually entertain. Another technique of cognitive assessment is called *thought monitoring.*

It requires subjects to keep track of the thoughts that occur to them in particular situations. Figure 11.6 is an example of thought monitoring. An individual who frequently experiences negative emotions writes down the thoughts that accompany his feelings, and at the same time challenges the basis for these thoughts. This "Daily Record of Dysfunctional Thoughts" is an important part of cognitive therapy for depression (Beck, Rush, Shaw, & Emergy, 1979), which will be examined in Chapter 13.

Particular Measures of Individual Differences

In this section, we'll survey some of the popular measures that personality psychologists use as they go about their research. Most of these procedures can be placed readily within one of the four assessment traditions: personological, psychometric, behavioral, or cognitive.

projective techniques

measures that present people with ambiguous stimuli onto which they "project" their personality in responding

Projective Techniques.   Personality researchers, working in the personological assessment tradition, often use **projective techniques** that involve asking research subjects to respond to ambiguous stimuli. Because the stimuli themselves do not demand any particular reactions, anything and everything the subjects do in response to them reveal the workings of their personality. Therefore, projective tests allow the research subject to project his or her own drives and desires onto the test stimuli. In Chapter 6, we discussed Morgan and Murray's (1935) *Thematic Apperception Test (TAT)*, which is used to gauge individual differences in needs such as achievement and power. You can now see why the TAT is considered a projective technique, and why it is favored by researchers who attempt personological assessment.

Here is an example of a TAT story told in response to a picture of a boy sitting at a desk with a book in front of him.

> A boy in a classroom who is daydreaming about something. He is recalling a previously experienced incident that struck his mind to be more appealing than being in the classroom. He is thinking about the experience and is now imagining himself in the situation. He hopes to be there. He will probably get called on by the instructor to recite and will be embarrassed. (McClelland, 1961, p. 41)

What does this story suggest about the subject's need for achievement? About his attitude toward education? About his fears concerning books, teachers, and bricks in the wall? We can assume that he is low in the need to achieve, at least in traditional academic domains. As you can see, a person's responses to projective tests provide rich and revealing information about him, some of which may touch on areas of which he is unaware.

Hermann Rorschach's (1942) inkblots, known as the *Rorschach Inkblot Test,* represent another well-known projective procedure. This test presents subjects with a series of symmetric inkblots (see Figure 11.7), asking them what each blot looks like and why. Their responses are scored in terms of what they see as well as their explanations. Did you know that some of the inkblots are printed in brilliant colors? The way that someone responds to the color cards is usually interpreted in terms of his or her characteristic response to emotion. Someone who ignores the colors in responding to the inkblot may also ignore the feelings that color everyday experience.

Figure 11.6

Example of Thought Monitoring: The Daily Record of Dysfunctional Thoughts

Date	Situation Describe: 1. Actual event leading to unpleasant emotion, or 2. Stream of thoughts, daydream, or recollection, leading to unpleasant emotion.	Emotions 1. Specify sad/anxious/angry, etc. 2. Rate degree of emotion, 1-100.	Automatic Thought(s) 1. Write automatic thought(s) that preceded emotion(s). 2. Rate belief in automatic thought(s), 0-100%.	Rational Response 1. Write rational response to automatic thought(s). 2. Rate belief in rational response, 0-100%.	Outcome 1. Re-rate belief in automatic thought(s), 0-100%. 2. Specify and rate subsequent emotions, 0-100.
Early in therapy	Felt overweight	Depressed 50	I'm out of control I'm unattractive 99%	Cut out sweets 50%	50% depressed 2
	Couldn't complete project	Anxious 60	I'll get in trouble I'll get fired 80%	It's alright to be late - most people are 60%	20% anxious 10
Later in therapy	Felt overweight	Depressed 10	I don't look as good as I should 60%	Cut out sweets 90%	10% depressed 0
	Couldn't complete project	Anxious 20	I'll disappoint my boss 50%	It's alright to be late - most people are 100%	5% anxious 0

EXPLANATION: When you experience an unpleasant emotion, note the situation that seemed to stimulate the emotion. (If the emotion occurred while you were thinking, daydreaming, etc., please note this.) Then note the automatic thought associated with the emotion. Record the degree to which you believe this thought: 0% = not at all; 100% = completely. In rating degree of emotion: 1 = a trace; 100 = the most intense possible.

Figure 11.7
Example of a Rorschach Card

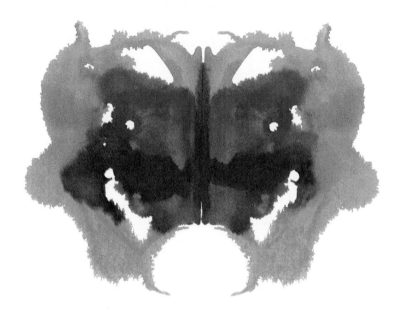

Projective techniques are frequently criticized on grounds of reliability and validity. Poor reliability occurs when two psychologists interpreting the same set of responses arrive at different conclusions. Poor validity occurs, even when responses can be reliably scored, if scores do not relate well to other aspects of the subject's behavior. To some degree, this criticism is to be expected, because it uses criteria from the psychometric tradition of assessment to evaluate methods within the personological tradition. Projective techniques are best used to gain an overall understanding of a subject and *not* to make specific predictions about future behavior.

Objective Tests.   If, on the other hand, a personality psychologist wants to make predictions, then objective tests are the appropriate procedure. **Objective tests** belong in the psychometric tradition of personality assessment, and are any measure of an individual characteristic in which the scores are assigned according to explicit rules. The scoring of a projective test (like the Rorschach) requires judgment on the part of the psychologist. In contrast, the scoring of objective tests requires little judgment. Consider a questionnaire measure of a trait such as introversion-extraversion. Subjects agree or disagree with various statements, some reflecting introversion ("I like to spend time alone") and others reflecting extraversion ("I like to go to crowded parties"). A person receives a high score on introversion or extraversion to the degree that she agrees with the appropriate statements. She receives a low score to the degree that she disagrees with them. There is no ambiguity here, so this is an objective test.

The "objective" in objective tests refers only to the method by which the psychologist uses them to describe someone's personality. This does not imply that they are foolproof, because an objective test can be flawed in several ways. First, it may fail to be reliable. Two types of reliability are usually of concern. **Test-retest reliability** refers to whether the test gives the same scores to an individual on repeated occasions. Suppose we give William and Oliver a test of moral development. William scores high, and

objective tests
measures from which personality scores are assigned according to explicit rules

test-retest reliability
the degree to which a test gives the same score to an individual on different occasions

internal reliability (consistency)

the degree to which different items on the same test yield the same scores for an individual

Oliver scores low. Six months later, we give both of them the same test again, expecting—if our measure has test-retest reliability—that William will continue to score high and that Oliver will continue to score low.

The second type of reliability is called **internal reliability** (or **consistency**). It refers to whether or not different items on the same test give the same scores to an individual at the same point in time. Let's go back to moral development. Suppose our measure contains ten different items. If it is consistent, then William should score high on most of the items, and Oliver should score low. No test is perfectly reliable, in either the test-retest sense or the internal sense, but researchers within the psychometric tradition continually strive to increase the reliability of their measures. Poor reliability limits predictability. Imagine using a broken thermometer to decide whether to wear long underwear or bikini briefs.

Objective tests may also fail because they lack validity, that is, they do not measure what they purport to measure. As noted in Chapter 1, validity is not as simple a notion as reliability. There are different criteria of validity, particularly with respect to objective tests of individual characteristics. Table 11.2 defines some of the important ways in which the validity of objective personality tests is evaluated, along with examples.

Like projective techniques, objective tests of personality have been frequently criticized on grounds of poor validity. But as with all operationalizations within psychology, perfect measures do not exist. Rather, the value of any measure depends on the purpose for which it is used.

personality inventory

a set of objective tests that measures a range of individual differences

Personality Inventories.   A **personality inventory** is a set of objective tests that attempts to measure the range of important individual differences. There are two important qualifications concerning inventories. First, no one ever claims that a particular inventory reveals every way in which people differ from each other. Rather, the goal is to measure major individual differences. Second, as we saw earlier, there is a difference of opinion

---

Table 11.2

Types of Validity

Face validity—does the test look like it measures what it is supposed to measure? (e.g., exit interviews outside voting booths that ask about political preferences)

Content validity—does the test contain a sample of the behavior of interest? (e.g., a typing test to measure secretarial skills)

Criterion validity—does the test predict some behavior of interest? (e.g., a test of introversion that correlates with the pursuit of solitary hobbies)

Known-groups validity—does the test distinguish between groups of people known to differ on the characteristic of concern? (e.g., a measure of locus of control that distinguishes between convicts [external locus of control] and people not in prison [internal locus of control])

Construct validity—does the test relate to other tests as some theory predicts? (e.g., a measure of creativity that correlates with a measure of divergent thinking [Chapter 8])

---

as to what constitutes these "major" individual differences. For example, remember that Raymond Cattell believes there are sixteen factors of personality (see Figure 11.3). His *Sixteen Personality Factor Inventory* measures all of these factors (Cattell, Eber, & Tatsuoka, 1970). In contrast, Hans Eysenck opts for a much smaller number of major individual differences, and the personality inventory he favors includes a correspondingly smaller number of measures (Eysenck & Eysenck, 1975). Proponents of the Big Five approach to individual differences use inventories composed of five subtests.

Perhaps the best known personality inventory is the *Minnesota Multiphasic Personality Inventory (MMPI)*, created in the 1940s at the University of Minnesota (Hathaway & McKinley, 1943). The original intent of the MMPI was to aid psychiatric diagnoses. Hundreds of items were assembled, all of which were to be answered *true* or *false*. Here are some examples:

- I seldom worry about my health.
- Evil spirits possess me at times.
- I go to church almost every week.
- I sweat very easily even on cool days.
- Lightning is one of my fears.
- I think Lincoln was greater than Washington.

Numerous individuals with known psychiatric diagnoses (given by clinicians) answered these questions, and researchers looked to see which patterns of responses successfully distinguished respondents with a particular diagnosis from those without that diagnosis.

Over the decades, hundreds of thousands of individuals have taken the MMPI, and it's been highly successful in identifying patients who warrant particular diagnoses. Many diagnosticians therefore routinely administer the MMPI to their clients. Although one does not make a diagnosis solely on the basis of MMPI scores, a diagnostician takes these scores quite seriously, and goes against their recommendation only when given a good reason for doing so.

Note that the MMPI was developed solely by the known-groups method of ascertaining validity (see Table 11.2). In other words, items were chosen for MMPI subscales if responses to them successfully distinguished between respondents in two groups known to differ with respect to whatever characteristic the scale intended to measure, such as depression or anxiety. The items have no necessary face validity, meaning that it is difficult to look at a particular question and decide what it is measuring. (Indeed, I deliberately chose the examples above to illustrate this point.) Note also that the MMPI does not have a fixed number of subscales, because researchers are continually coming up with new configurations to predict characteristics not envisioned by those who originally devised it. However, by convention, there is a set of characteristics typically scored from MMPI responses, as shown in Table 11.3.

The MMPI has also been used to study "normal" individuals. Someone's personality can be described in terms of where he falls along the dimensions measured by the conventional subtests. Consider the view of human nature embedded here: The basic individual differences are those dimensions that distinguish among different forms of abnormality. We've seen throughout the book how abnormality provides a window on normality; here is just one more example.

Table 11.3

MMPI Subscales

Hypochondriasis—reflects the degree to which someone exaggerates concerns about physical well-being

Depression—measures feelings of sadness, worthlessness, and pessimism

Hysteria—reflects somatic complaints stemming from psychological causes

Psychopathic deviance—indicates one's disregard for social and moral standards

Masculinity/femininity—measures one's adherence to traditional "masculine" or "feminine" values

Paranoia—reflects the degree to which someone is suspicious and feels persecuted

Psychasthenia—indicates the degree of irrational fears and nervous compulsions

Schizophrenia—measures the degree to which someone shows bizarre thoughts or actions

Hypomania—reflects emotional excitability and excess activity

Social introversion—measures the degree to which someone is socially withdrawn

Observations and Ratings by Judges. Sometimes personality researchers study people by asking those who know them to make judgments. In some cases, these judges provided direct ratings of someone's traits: "Is this person thrifty, reverent, courteous, and brave?" In other cases, they offer judgments concerning someone's particular behaviors: "How many times in the last week did he help elderly women across the street?" The rationale is the same in either case. Questionnaires that require a person to describe his own characteristics or behaviors may give too restricted a view. People often present themselves in the best possible light, which means that their self-descriptions can be skewed in a flattering direction. The majority of people, for instance, regard themselves as "above average" in characteristics like sense of humor, intelligence, and popularity (e.g., Lewinsohn, Mischel, Chaplin, & Barton, 1980).

Another drawback to self-report is that people may be unable to report on individual characteristics of interest to the personality psychologist. One obvious example of this is when research subjects are young children who cannot describe themselves using the typical questionnaire formats. A less obvious example is when the characteristic of concern (by definition) eludes someone's awareness, as in defense mechanisms such as repression or projection.

For these reasons, researchers turn to other people who know the research participants well to make a judgment about their personalities. Studies of temperament among children often ask parents to rate the activity, emotionality, and sociability of their offspring (e.g., Plomin, 1986). Similarly, studies of emotional disturbance among children often rely on teacher ratings of such characteristics as aggression and withdrawal (e.g., Achenbach, 1986).

Like other research techniques, ratings by judges are not foolproof. One problem in particular plagues them. Judges may let their opinion on one aspect of a subject's personality color their opinion elsewhere. This so-called *halo effect* introduces a confound when employers try to rate the performance of their employees. Employees usually get rated high or low on all characteristics because it is difficult for the judge to make finer distinctions. A partial solution to the problem posed by halo effects is to define the characteristics of concern narrowly and explicitly, typically in terms of overt behaviors. "The employee arrives at work on time every Monday" is less susceptible to rating bias than "This employee is conscientious."

Experience Sampling.   The newest way to study personality is thoroughly high tech. Popularly called the beeper method, this procedure is more formally known as **experience sampling** (Hormuth, 1986). Here's how it works. Research subjects are given an electronic device not much larger than a pack of cigarettes. They carry it around with them, and at randomly determined intervals, it gives off a signal (Beep!). Subjects interrupt what they are doing to complete a questionnaire, asking them where they are, what they are doing, how they are feeling, what they are thinking, and so on. The most modern version of experience sampling allows subjects to answer the questions by entering responses on a tiny keyboard, but a pencil and paper usually suffice.

Do you see the benefits of this procedure? Assuming that subjects indeed answer questions on the spot, any problems with memory are avoided. Subjects need not think about what they "usually" do; they need only say what's going on at the present time. This allows the researcher to make conclusions about their everyday thoughts, feelings, and actions. Another benefit of experience sampling is that it allows the researcher to take the subject's immediate surroundings into account. Current thinking in personality psychology accords great importance to the setting in which our behavior occurs. Beepers give the researcher a glimpse at the subject's environment, although Hormuth (1986) reports that they don't work too well in swimming pools, discos, or churches! And a sad commentary on today's society is that some research subjects now refuse to carry beepers because they look like the pagers popular among drug pushers.

Tying It Together and Studying Lives.   Where other psychologists quite contentedly study some part of the person, personality psychologists want to understand the whole person. The difficulty in achieving this goal is that the methods for studying personality at best capture only aspects of personality. How is the researcher to put these different aspects together?

This has always concerned the clinician, of course, because a therapist treats the whole person, not his or her parts. Recently, personality psychologists show renewed interest in combining small items of information into a bigger picture. One way to integrate findings is by remembering that people lead lives that unfold over time (e.g., Bandura, 1982; Runyan, 1982; White, 1966).

Psychiatrist George Vaillant (1977) likens personality research to natural history, proposing that we study people just like the natural historian studies glaciers, wild flowers, or coyotes: by gathering as much information as possible over time about subjects in their actual environments. To this end, a whole range of research procedures become legitimate. As researchers weave together the findings from different methods, Allport's goal of a personality psychology that speaks to individuals is approached.

experience sampling
a research technique in which subjects carry a beeper that gives a signal at randomly determined intervals; when the signal goes off, subjects interrupt what they are doing and complete a questionnaire given to them by the researcher

The Consistency Controversy

Do people act consistently in different situations? For most personality theories (particularly psychoanalytic and trait accounts), cross-situational consistency is a bedrock assumption. The very language we use to describe individual characteristics presupposes consistency. Someone who is gregarious should seek out others in a variety of circumstances. That's what *gregarious* means.

As mentioned earlier, Walter Mischel challenged the assumption of personality consistency in his 1968 book *Personality and Assessment*. He surveyed research dealing with consistency and found little evidence to support this widespread assumption. He then suggested that psychoanalytic and trait approaches to personality were simply wrong and should be replaced with social learning theory. Social learning theorists expect lack of consistency across various situations, because people respond to the rewards and punishments present in each setting. We might think that the opposite of consistent is inconsistent, which has connotations of randomness and chaos. But this is not what Mischel implies when he proposes that people do not act the same in different settings. Instead, he claims that "personality" resides in particular situations. Behavior remains sensible and orderly, but its coherence stems not from psychological states and traits but from the environment.

Mischel's book created a storm within personality psychology, stimulating researchers to test more rigorously the consistency hypothesis. We'll get to the details of this research shortly, but first let's understand that a resolution of the matter appears to have been reached. Yes, people act consistently, but not in any simple way. Mischel's original criticism is now regarded as a much-needed kick in the pants for personality psychology (West, 1983). Ouch—we needed that.

Mischel's Argument

Personality and Assessment started out as a textbook, a survey of different approaches to personality. But when Walter Mischel studied the available research literature, the textbook took a backseat. Much to his surprise, he found little evidence that people acted consistently in different situations. Remember that psychoanalytic, trait, and cognitive theories all assume that individual differences are manifestations of highly general characteristics, shown in a variety of settings. Spuds McKenzie, the original party animal, is the life of the party in every circumstance he encounters: a beach, a bar, a cruise ship, or a maternity ward. Alas, for the rest of us, the major personality theories predict that regardless of the party, we will never be its life.

There are many different measures of individual differences. In order to test the assumption of personality consistency, we could assemble various measures of a particular individual difference and administer them to the same people in a range of settings. Do the measures correlate positively? If so, then we know that the same people are consistently high, consistently low, or consistently in between on the trait of concern. This would support the assumption of personality consistency.

Yet Mischel's review did not so neatly support such an assumption. One such investigation was Hartshorne and May's (1928) study of children's moral conduct. These investigators wanted to know if there is a general trait of honesty or dishonesty. Concretely, when school children are given different opportunities to transgress, do the same kids always step over the line? Hartshorne and May (1928) thought of many different situations in which someone might lie or cheat or steal. Settings included the home, the classroom, and the playground. Findings showed that moral conduct is not particularly consistent. Although correlations across situations were usually positive, they were not of great magnitude, suggesting that "honesty" is not the general trait that most theories (and most people) believe it to be.

Personality and Assessment similarly described investigations of such individual characteristics as attitudes toward others, sexual identification, dependency, aggression, rigidity, avoidance, and conditionability. In no case was there strong evidence that these were general characteristics, shown similarly in different situations. Note that this is not an arbitrary list of characteristics. These individual characteristics occupy central places in the major personality theories. In addition, the major approaches to psychopathology (Chapter 12) and clinical psychology (Chapter 13) presuppose consistency, *particularly* in characteristics such as these.

Needless to say, in attacking the idea of consistency, Mischel attacked the very field of personality. Some read his book as claiming that people have no personality, at least as the word is typically used. Personality psychologists might as well take their place in the unemployment line along with alchemists, astrologers, and those who sold Edsels, Nehru jackets, Herb t-shirts, and Gary Hart campaign buttons. Further, a profound statement about human nature lurks in Mischel's message. Psychologists and everyday people alike make a mistake, he suggests, by looking solely within the person in seeking to understand the person. Better to look at the situation if we wish to know what someone is all about.

This is the core of Mischel's argument, although he needed to tie up two loose ends. First, if there is little consistency in how people behave, why do so many of us believe in pervasive traits? He answers by suggesting that people construct consistency out of very little raw material, relying mainly on cognitive biases. Traits exist not in the person we observe so much as in our ways of looking at that person.

Second, if traits do not sensibly describe how people behave, then what have personality psychologists been investigating over the years with their tests of individual characteristics? Mischel contends that personality research all too rarely looks at people's actual behavior. Instead, investigators concern themselves with how people respond to personality tests. This kind of research is subject to a host of confounds yielding a false view of consistency.

Before we look at some of the reactions that *Personality and Assessment* stimulated, let's make some qualifications that somewhat blunt the implications of this book. First, Mischel did find that some personality traits display impressive consistency across situations. Second, he did not say that people show zero consistency. Correlations across situations are almost always positive. What Mischel said is that many correlations are too low to be impressive. However, the magnitude of a correlation cannot always be interpreted in absolute terms, and perhaps those typical of personality coefficient research should not be dismissed so glibly (see the

Mike Ditka is as famous for his personality as he is for his coaching success. The high-pressure environment of professional football apparently brings out the best—and worst—in Ditka's personality.

Appendix following Chapter 1). Third, his book is completely silent on the biological and genetic basis of individual differences. As we have seen, research shows that some individual differences have a biological underpinning. It is difficult to interpret positive correlations between the traits of twins as due to a questionnaire confound.

These qualifications notwithstanding, Mischel's criticisms hit a target. Personality researchers had failed to substantiate one of the central claims of their field. Eventually, his work evoked several lines of research much more sophisticated than prior investigations. These lines of research, taken together, give us a much better understanding of consistency and hence of personality. We will now look at several of them.

Aggregation

Psychologist Seymour Epstein (1979) observed that personality researchers tend not to be careful when they measure behaviors supposedly reflecting a particular trait. Within a given setting, there is rarely more than a single behavior measured on more than one occasion. How much confidence would we place in an intelligence test that consisted of but a single item? Suppose a college transcript had only one grade recorded? Could we judge a football team that ran only one play? What about a personality test that posed but one question?

Needless to say, we recognize these as inadequate measures, and we know that, in each case, the way to improve matters is to include more items, more grades, more plays, or more questions. Epstein advises researchers interested in cross-situational consistency to look at behaviors in a particular setting on repeated occasions. He calls this strategy *multiple assessment aggregation,* and he shows that aggregated measures of behavior appear much more consistent than single measures, regularly exceeding the limits cited by Mischel.

Interaction

Another research reaction to Mischel's critique of consistency integrates trait and situational approaches to personality. Does it make sense to talk of people independently of particular situations? Does it make sense to talk of situations independently of people? The answer to both of these questions is clearly no, but the debate that Mischel stimulated has sometimes transpired in such stark terms. The more reasonable position is that the *interaction* between a person's traits and his world best explains his personality.

The term *interaction* has a particular meaning here: We can only understand the effects of one factor (trait or environment) by knowing the other factor. Suppose we have two people, an introvert and an extravert, as well as two settings, a raucous rock concert and an isolated art museum. Let us concern ourselves with happiness. Who is happier—the introvert or the extravert? We can't say unless we know *where* these people are. And where is a person happier—the rock concert or the art museum? Again, we can't say unless we know just *who* is in these places. This is what interaction means, and personality theorists now recognize that we should take greater account of trait-environment interactions than researchers did in the past (Bowers, 1973; Ekehammar, 1974; Endler & Magnusson, 1976).

Predicting Some of the People Some of the Time

Do you remember Gordon Allport's dictum that different people possess different traits? If at all reasonable, this idea means that personality consistency should not be approached in the fashion of Hartshorne and May (1928) or any other researcher who measures the same characteristics for all people. According to the notion of personal traits, consistencies differ from Tom to Dick to Harry. The problem with Allport's idea is how to test it. For years, no one, including Allport himself, was able to devise an adequate means of investigating personality consistency from the vantage point of personal traits.

Daryl Bem and Andrea Allen (1974) solved the dilemma by adopting a modified version of Allport's idiographic approach to personality. Rather than assuming that each person's personal traits are unique, as Allport proposed, Bem and Allen argued that for any particular trait, there are some people who can be described as mostly consistent and other people who can be described as mostly inconsistent. What happens if these people are all lumped together in a study of trait consistency? On the average, we should see a moderate but not overwhelming degree of consistency— exactly what Mischel found in his review.

What if we can distinguish between these two groups of people? If Allport is correct, then the "consistent" group should act the same across situations, whereas the "inconsistent" group should not. Bem and Allen tested this line of reasoning in an investigation of sixty-four college students, who were asked, "How much do you vary from one situation to another in terms of how friendly and outgoing you are?" The same subjects were also asked to rate their consistency with respect to conscientiousness.

Then, the researchers ascertained friendly (or unfriendly) behavior in several settings, as well as conscientious (or unconscientious) behavior. After combining the results for all subjects, a moderate degree of consistency emerged. But when subjects were split into consistent and inconsistent groups (by dividing them at the midpoint of their own ratings), the researchers found high consistency among the former subjects and low consistency among the latter subjects, for both friendliness and conscientiousness. Bem and Allen concluded that perhaps the best a personality psychologist can do with personality traits is to predict some of the people some of the time, but this still is a more positive conclusion than the one Mischel offered in *Personality and Assessment*.

Self-monitoring

Let's take one more perspective on the consistency controversy. This one comes from research into an individual difference known as *self-monitoring* (Snyder, 1983). People high in self-monitoring attend closely to situations and guide their behavior according to the feedback they receive. High self-monitors are socially adept, veritable chameleons in their ability to modify their actions to fit particular circumstances. Low self-monitors attend not to situational demands, but rather to their own inner states and feelings. To their own selves they are true.

Granted these characterizations, we shouldn't be surprised that high self-monitors act differently across different situations and that low self-monitors act the same (e.g., Snyder & Gangestad, 1982). The high self-monitors are not inconsistent, because in their responsivity to differing environmental demands, they indeed show consistency. Their consistency resides at a different level than the consistency of the low self-monitors. In other words, the particular way in which a person acts consistently is itself an individual difference.

A Resolution to the Consistency Controversy

Do people act consistently across different situations or not? The answer is a highly qualified yes. Personality researchers can demonstrate consistency by aggregating observations of behavior, by taking into account interactions between traits and environments, by distinguishing consistent from inconsistent individuals, and/or by looking for consistency at different levels of personality. No single research project has simultaneously included all of these refinements, but I suspect that if there were one, the researchers would find striking consistency.

Walter Mischel (1968) was for the most part correct when he concluded that little evidence existed in support of the assumption of personality consistency. However, in the two decades since *Personality and Assessment* appeared, the evidence has been gathered. Without the stimulus provided by Mischel, personality psychology would not approach individual differences and their assessment with nearly as much sophistication.

Personality psychologists attempt to study people in their entirety. To this end, they draw on broad perspectives, specifically, psychoanalytic, trait, phenomenological, and/or social learning approaches. We are not yet finished with these major approaches to personality. In the next chapter, which concerns itself with psychopathology, and in Chapter 13, which focuses on clinical psychology, we will see how these approaches to the whole of a person influence the way that problems are conceived by psychologists and how they are treated.

Summary

Topics of Concern

- Personality psychologists are interested in people in their entirety.
- Personality psychology has traditionally concerned itself with several issues: what model of human nature to endorse, which strategy for explaining personality to follow, what individual differences are important, and how should these be assessed.

The Psychoanalytic Approach

- Personality theories can be placed into several discrete groups. Psychoanalytic theories stress motivation as the key to understanding personality.
- The central theorist here is Sigmund Freud. Other influential psychodynamic theorists include Alfred Adler, Carl Jung, the neo-Freudians, and Erik Erikson.

The Trait Approach

- Trait theories approach personality by describing people, placing them in basic categories, or along dimensions that reflect how much of a particular characteristic they possess. Gordon Allport first stated the issues that concern trait theorists.
- Raymond Cattell and Hans Eysenck are two contemporary theorists who use the statistical technique of factor analysis to identify people's traits.

The Phenomenological Approach

- Phenomenological (or cognitive) theories focus on the way that people think about themselves and the world.
- George Kelly's personal construct theory and Carl Rogers's self-theory are two important statements within this tradition.

The Social Learning Approach

- Social learning theories approach personality in terms of situations and thus emphasize processes of learning. Central importance is accorded the role of other people in one's environment, hence the use of the term *social* to describe these accounts of personality.
- Social learning theories have been proposed by a number of theorists including John Dollard and Neal Miller, Julian Rotter, Albert Bandura, and Walter Mischel.

Assessing Individual Differences

- The ways in which people are characteristically themselves are termed individual differences. Personality assessment is the business of measuring these individual differences.
- Several traditions of personality assessment can be distinguished, each corresponding to one of the major theoretical approaches to personality.
- Personality researchers may use projective techniques, objective tests, personality inventories, judgments by others, and/or experience sampling.

The Consistency Controversy

- In recent decades, the most significant controversy in personality research stemmed from Walter Mischel's (1968) argument that people do not act consistently across situations.
- Research reactions to Mischel's proposal successfully demonstrated consistency, but these required a much greater sophistication than past research into the issue.

Important Terms and Names

What follows is a list of the core terms and names for this chapter. Your instructor may emphasize other terms as well. Throughout the chapter, glossary terms appear in **boldface** type. They are defined in the text, and each term, along with its definition, is repeated in the margin.

Topics of Concern

personality/444
individual differences/447
personality assessment/447

The Psychoanalytic Approach

psychoanalysis/448
conscious, preconscious, and unconscious/449
id, ego, and superego/450
Oedipus complex/452
inferiority complex/453
collective unconscious/453
neo-Freudians/454

Sigmund Freud/449
Alfred Adler/453
Carl Jung/453
Erik Erikson/454

The Trait Approach

trait approach/455
trait/456
factor analysis/458

Gordon Allport/455
William Sheldon/457
Raymond Cattell/458
Hans Eysenck/458

The Phenomenological Approach

phenomenological (cognitive) approach/460
personal construct theory/461
self-theory/462
humanism/462

George Kelly/460
Carl Rogers/462

The Social Learning Approach

social learning approach/464
locus of control/465
consistency controversy/466

John Dollard and Neal Miller/464
Julian Rotter/465
Albert Bandura/466
Walter Mischel/466

Assessing Individual Differences

projective techniques/472
objective tests/474
personality inventories/475
experience sampling/478

The Consistency Controversy

Walter Mischel/479

1. Personality refers to the aspects of people that are
   a. general.
   b. characteristic.
   c. enduring.
   d. integrated.
   e. functional.
   The psychology of personality is concerned with people in their entirety, particularly those aspects that are general across situation, characteristic, enduring over time, integrated, and functional./444

2. The _____ approach to personality emphasizes psychological energy and how it motivates our behavior.
   a. psychoanalytic
   b. trait
   c. phenomenological
   d. social learning
   Psychoanalytic theory describes people's behavior in terms of how psychological energy—libido—is transformed and used./446

3. The _____ approach to personality classifies people into categories or along quantitative dimensions.
   a. psychoanalytic
   b. trait
   c. phenomenological
   d. social learning
   Classification of people is the hallmark of the trait approach./446

4. The _____ approach to personality assumes that what is most important about people is how they think about themselves and their world.
   a. psychoanalytic
   b. trait
   c. phenomenological
   d. social learning
   The phenomenological approach to personality is also known as the cognitive approach, and it emphasizes how and what one thinks./446

5. The _____ approach to personality looks to the environment for explanations.
   a. psychoanalytic
   b. trait
   c. phenomenological
   d. social learning
   Social learning theories apply principles of learning and thus emphasize the role played by rewards and punishments found in the environment./446

6. _____ set the agenda for the trait approach to personality.
   a. Gordon Allport
   b. Sigmund Freud
   c. George Kelly
   d. Carl Rogers
   e. Julian Rotter
   Harvard psychologist Gordon Allport was the founding father of the trait approach to personality. He introduced terms and phrased issues still important today./455

7. Factor analysis is a statistical technique used chiefly by personality researchers who favor the _____ approach.
   a. psychoanalytic
   b. trait
   c. phenomenological
   d. social learning
   Factor analysis has been used by researchers interested in identifying people's basic traits./458

8. The theories of Carl Rogers and Abraham Maslow share in common an emphasis on
   a. libido.
   b. personality assessment.
   c. phenomenology.
   d. self-actualization.
   e. traits.
   Both Rogers and Maslow believed that people strive to achieve their full potential./462

9. The Big Five refers to
   a. a large-print version of the MMPI.
   b. Freud's most loyal disciples.
   c. presumably fundamental individual differences.
   d. the age at which the Oedipus complex usually appears.
   e. the most frequently used set of objective personality tests.

   One popular suggestion concerning basic individual differences is the Big Five: traits of neuroticism, extraversion, openness, agreeableness, and conscientiousness./468

10. In *Personality and Assessment,* Walter Mischel argued that
    a. people do not act consistently across different situations.
    b. psychoanalytic theories of personality had never been fairly investigated.
    c. researchers should make greater use of personological assessment.
    d. social learning theory should replace other approaches to personality.
    e. the study of lives was the proper subject of personality psychology.

    Mischel argued in *Personality and Assessment* that people do not act consistently across different situations. Trait and psychoanalytic approaches ignore the situation and thus are inadequate accounts of personality. Mischel proposed that the social learning approach is much more satisfactory./479

Psychological abnormality must be defined before it can be explained.

Chapter Twelve

Abnormal Psychology

Topics of Concern

David Rosenhan of Stanford University described one of the most famous studies in the whole of psychology in his article entitled "Being Sane in Insane Places" (1973). Rosenhan and seven other researchers each got themselves admitted to mental hospitals, by telling the examining physician that they heard voices saying "empty, dull, and thud." Based on this one symptom, they were given the diagnosis of schizophrenia, meaning that the physician believed each to be suffering from a serious form of psychological difficulty.

Length of hospitalization varied from 7 to 52 days, with an average stay of 19 days. Only in one case was the presence of one of these so-called pseudopatients known in advance to hospital administrators. In the other cases, the pseudopatients were told that they were on their own. Their task—which they had accepted—was to win discharge from the hospital by convincing the staff that they were sane.

Thus, they acted in a perfectly normal fashion following their admission to the hospital ward, and not in a single case did a member of the professional staff suspect that they were anything other than what the initial diagnosis said. In fact, the label was used to interpret what the pseudopatients did. For example, Rosenhan and the others took notes while on the ward. At first, they disguised what they were doing, fearing that they'd be detected. Then they realized that they could take notes openly because the nurses and doctors just saw it as another manifestation of their presumed illness. One nurse duly recorded in a chart, "Patient engages in writing behavior."

Do you see how this description strips away the meaning of what the person was actually doing? When you take notes in class, are you "engaged in writing behavior"? Of course not. You're taking notes, a meaningful activity freely chosen by a healthy individual. But if you're diagnosed as schizophrenic, then the same activity becomes just another sign of your illness.

Two more points about the study are important. First, the other patients on the ward often detected the sanity of the pseudopatients, asking them if they were journalists or professors. Second, when the pseudopatients were eventually discharged, they were given a diagnosis at that time of schizophrenia *in remission*—which means that the physi-

The diagnosis and treatment of mental illness is often a lengthy, complex, and uncertain process.

cian still believed that the mental illness of schizophrenia was present within them, although not currently active.

Rosenhan's pseudopatient study can be criticized for putting staff members of mental hospitals in an impossible position (Spitzer, 1975). Just because sanity may sometimes not be identified does not mean that it is always overlooked. Nonetheless, this study remains important because it is so provocative, and it serves to introduce the subject matter of the present chapter: **abnormal psychology.** This is the field within psychology that studies people's emotional, cognitive, and/or behavioral problems. Such problems are sometimes called psychopathology, to stress their presumed psychological origins. What is the nature of psychopathology? How can a condition that creates misery and even death in literally millions of individuals be confused with perfectly normal behavior? Psychologists who study psychopathology have two paramount concerns: defining psychological abnormality and explaining it.

Defining Abnormality

It is difficult to precisely define psychological abnormality. Nevertheless, we can characterize psychopathology in approximate terms. When was the last time you said, "Hey, that's outrageous! Something ought to be done about it." Maybe those weren't your exact words, but we commonly make such statements. Perhaps it was when you heard about a parent abusing a child, a woman attempting suicide, or a man standing in the middle of a busy street cursing at the cars.

Any statement about abnormality, by you or a professional, entails three related judgments: an *assertion* that something is amiss in a person's thoughts, feelings, or actions (Hey!); a *label* placed on this state of affairs (outrageous); and a *recommendation* that somehow matters be made right (something ought to be done about it).

Abnormality is one of those natural concepts explained in Chapter 7 (Cantor, Smith, French, & Mezzich, 1980). In other words, there are no critical elements that necessarily and sufficiently define it. Rather, there is a set of pertinent characteristics that fuzzily capture the meaning of **abnormality,** including suffering, maladaptiveness, loss of control, unconventionality, and the production of discomfort among observers (Rosenhan & Seligman, 1989). None of these criteria by itself defines abnormality, but the more of them that are present, and the more intense they are, the more likely we are to say that psychopathology exists.

abnormal psychology
the field within psychology that studies people's emotional, cognitive, and/or behavioral problems

abnormality
feelings, thoughts, and behaviors characterized by such attributes as suffering, maladaptiveness, loss of control, and unconventionality that produce discomfort among observers

biomedical model
approach that explains abnormality as due to organic injury or illness

The position that abnormality is a vague concept inherently involving social judgment is a reasonable but not fully satisfying one, because it makes the subject matter of abnormal psychology seem somewhat arbitrary. However, we can easily recognize and agree upon extreme examples of abnormality. And the particular instances of abnormality discussed in this chapter are extreme examples. Although there is often disagreement as to the best way to explain them, there is no question that they constitute problems.

Explaining Abnormality

There are currently three popular explanations of abnormal behavior: the biomedical model, the psychoanalytic model, and the cognitive-behavioral model. Each model of abnormality is a set of interrelated assumptions about human nature, the way that problems can develop, and how problems can be solved or prevented in the first place. Psychologists often align themselves with only one model, meaning that their entire approach to abnormality centers around a particular model.

Biomedical Model. Let's look at the **biomedical model** first. Psychologists who adopt this approach view people as physical systems: products of evolution and seekers of homeostasis. They regard abnormal behavior as a disease—as mental illness—because it presumably has organic causes. These illnesses may have a genetic predisposition. According to the biomedical model, people are susceptible to injury, breakdown, or malfunction. Injuries and tumors of the nervous system, for example, can produce abnormal thoughts, feelings, and actions (Chapter 2). And therapy from this perspective involves physical interventions that include drugs or surgery.

Psychoanalytic Model. According to psychoanalytic theory, people are energy systems (Chapter 11). Problems result when psychic energy is tied up in a particular symptom and therefore not available for more productive activities. Why is energy so poorly invested? The **psychoanalytic model** argues that the person behaving abnormally suffers unconscious conflicts often rooted in childhood experiences. These conflicts are too threatening to acknowledge, and only through an active expenditure of energy can the conflict be kept out of consciousness. One way of doing this is by using defense mechanisms, which we discussed in Chapters 6 and 10. When taken to an extreme, a defense mechanism results in abnormality. The paranoid individual, for instance, who believes that everyone else in the world is out to get him, might really be projecting his own hostility.

Cognitive-Behavioral Model.   Finally, psychologists who favor the **cognitive-behavioral model** regard people as information-processing systems, best understood in terms of their give-and-take with the world (Chapter 5). By this view, particular thoughts and behaviors are the causes of abnormality, and these have been learned. People try to predict and understand the events that occur to them in order to maximize their positive feelings and minimize their negative ones. In other words, the cognitive-behavioral model views people as thinking pleasure-seekers (or pleasure-seeking thinkers, if you prefer).

As psychological beings, we are prone to ignorance, error, or confusion, and abnormality therefore reflects our faulty learning. A depressed person, for example, may have learned to regard herself in inappropriately harsh terms. Her depression makes perfect sense once her habitual thoughts are revealed. Therapy is a process of unlearning problematic habits and replacing them with more useful ones. Indeed, therapists who work within this framework often liken therapy to education.

> The position that abnormality is a vague concept inherently involving social judgment is a reasonable but not fully satisfying one. . . .

Evaluation of the Models.   Sometimes the proponents of the different models of abnormality enter into heated debate with one another. For example, the biomedical model has often been criticized for promoting the notion that the problems of everyday life are really diseases. Thomas Szasz (1961) calls this the **myth of mental illness,** and argues that psychological problems such as depression, anxiety, and schizophrenia are not illnesses in the sense that pneumonia, chicken pox, and malaria are diseases.

Indeed, Szasz believes that when we mistakenly regard these problems as illnesses, we absolve the person from any responsibility in trying to solve them. This argument is a powerful one. Examine it with respect to alcoholism, for example. Does an alcoholic have a disease in the same way that someone with measles has a disease? The counter-argument is that when we hold people responsible for solving their problems, we come perilously close to blaming them for having problems in the first place, and that is neither enlightened nor productive.

The psychoanalytic model and cognitive-behavioral model come in for their share of criticism as well. Both neglect biological considerations. In view of recent research showing genetic links for a large number of psychopathologies, this is a serious oversight. As one critic of Szasz quips, if mental illness is a myth, it is a myth with a strong genetic component (Kety, 1974).

Another problem with both the psychoanalytic and cognitive-behavioral models is that they assume that people basically strive to feel good, whether through discharging their drives or gaining reinforcement. But abnormality often involves doing things that explicitly cause the individual to suffer. How can this self-destruction be explained? Psychoanalytic theorists speak of the *death instinct:* a supposed drive that impels us to doom and destruction (Chapter 11). Cognitive-behavioral theorists similarly invoke the *neurotic paradox:* the tendency of people with problems to turn their small problems into large ones. But these are merely labels for baffling human behavior. They don't really explain why people sometimes make their problems worse.

These approaches to understanding abnormality represent profoundly different ways of explaining and thus treating people's problems. Students sometimes become impatient with the multiplicity of models in the field of abnormal psychology, particularly because each approach has merits (and shortcomings).

Can't the models be combined? Not in a simple way, because they often contradict each other. Consider the biomedical model versus the cognitive-behavioral model as they might be applied to excessive fears and worries. In the former case, abnormality is attributed to biochemistry (and nothing else). In the latter case, the culprit is the environment (and nothing else). If you combine these views, either nothing causes anxiety or everything does!

Actually, some theorists do concern themselves with integrating the different models. One reasonable attempt along

psychoanalytic model
approach that explains abnormality as due to unconscious conflicts often rooted in childhood experiences

cognitive-behavioral model
approach that explains abnormality as due to learned ways of thinking or acting

myth of mental illness
the argument by Thomas Szasz that psychopathology represents not a disease but rather a problem in living

diathesis-stress model
integrative approach that explains abnormality as due to a biological weakness (diathesis) coupled with certain environmental conditions (stress)

these lines is called the **diathesis-stress model** of abnormality. It proposes that people develop disorders if they have a biological weakness (diathesis) that predisposes them to the disorder when certain environmental conditions (stress) are encountered. We are familiar with the diathesis-stress approach because it is often used to explain the development of some forms of cancer: a biological predisposition coupled with certain environmental conditions. As we will discuss later, the diathesis-stress model may be equally useful in helping us to understand the causes of schizophrenia, which appear to include both biological and environmental factors.

Additional integrative models of abnormality must await further developments in the field. At present, the best psychologists can do is to make sure the model that they entertain works well for the specific problem they are addressing. The pitfall of the current models, of course, is that they can blind practitioners. As we will see in this chapter, different approaches seem to be best suited for treating different types of abnormality. A psychologist must consider various perspectives as the need arises.

A Brief History of Abnormality

A historical view of abnormality will shed light on the current complexity of the subject, so let's sketch some history for you. Psychologists usually distinguish three major eras with regard to how abnormality has been conceived. By the way, do not confuse these three eras with the three models just discussed. They do not interconnect in any simple way. It is a historical coincidence that the field of abnormal psychology has three currently popular models of explanation and that its history falls into three eras.

The Supernatural Era

The earliest era can be called the **supernatural era,** during which abnormality was viewed in terms of beliefs about magic, including the following (Frazer, 1922):

1. There exist immaterial forces in nature that can be directed by divine intervention or liberated by special arts.
2. These forces determine what people think, feel, and do.
3. The techniques of magic include certain words (or spells), substances, and symbols.
4. People and their environment are continuous.
5. People can influence each other through telepathy.
6. The future can be predicted.

Such beliefs led people to explain unusual or bizarre behavior as due to possession by a spirit, the casting of a spell, or the influence of some unseen part of the world.

You may know from your study of mythology that the ancient Greeks and Romans attributed abnormal behavior to the influence of various gods and goddesses: "Those who the gods would destroy, they first make mad." In the *Iliad* by Homer, for example, heroes on the battlefield show dramatic changes in behavior, due to the influence of a god or goddess. Similar notions can be found in the Bible. When King Saul did not follow the commandment of God, "an evil spirit from the Lord tormented him" until he repented (1 Samuel 16:14).

An interesting illustration of the supernatural approach to abnormality comes from skulls found in a number of different parts of the world, including Africa, Europe, and South America, and dating as far back as 3000 B.C. These skulls had holes bored in them and portions of bone removed (see Figure 12.1). The popular interpretation of this procedure, called *trephining,* is that it was undertaken to liberate evil spirits residing within a person's head (Mora, 1980). Apparently many people survived this procedure, at least long enough for the skull to begin to grow back.

In the Middle Ages, when Christianity dominated, people equated abnormality with being possessed by the devil. People so "afflicted" were often tortured in order to drive the devil out of their bodies, and failing this, were burned at the stake in order to make their bodies inhospitable for Satan. Driving away the devil saved the person's immortal soul, and it was simply an unfortunate side effect that the person's body was burned to a crisp in the process!

Figure 12.1
Trephined Skull. This skull had holes drilled in it, presumably to let evil spirits trapped within escape.

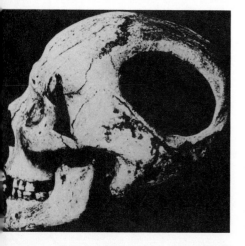

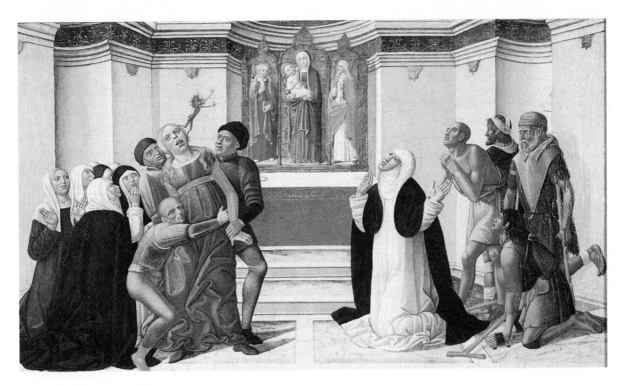

In the Middle Ages, mental illness was often "diagnosed" as Satanic possession. Exorcism—which at times involved attacking the devil's pride, insulting him—was the treatment of choice.

We may glibly dismiss such practices as ignorant or inhumane, but such dismissals miss an important point. People confronted with abnormality are impelled to explain it and to do something about it. In their efforts, they necessarily draw on the beliefs they hold. When these beliefs involve the supernatural, then abnormality can only be viewed in supernatural terms.

The Illness Era

illness era

historical period during which psychopathology was interpreted as injury, illness, or defects within the body

The next stage in conceiving abnormality developed in the 1800s. During this **illness era** abnormality was attributed to injury, illness, or defects within the body. This interpretation became possible only with the realization that illness is caused by tiny organisms called germs. We are so familiar with the idea that germs cause illness that you may be surprised to learn that the world had printing presses, bicycles, eyeglasses, soccer, and the *New York Times* before it had the notion that one should cover one's mouth while coughing.

The first mental disorder to be explained in illness terms was general paresis. At one time, this was a common disorder, responsible for as many as 20 percent of all admissions to mental hospitals in the United States (Dale, 1980). Specifically, general paresis involves progressive paralysis and loss of one's intellectual ability.

Individuals tend to be unmannerly, tactless, unconcerned with their appearance, and unethical in their behavior. Memory defects . . . become more obvious. Afflicted individuals may be unable to remember what they did just a short time ago—for example, they may ask when dinner will be served only a few minutes after they have finished eating it. This memory impairment extends to less immediate events, and memory losses are made up for by various fabrications. (Carson, Butcher, & Coleman, 1988, p. 457)

During the late 1800s, William Krafft-Ebing established a definitive link between the sexually transmitted disease syphilis and general paresis by injecting several patients who suffered from general paresis with pus from syphilitic sores. None of the patients developed syphilis, suggesting—according to the logic of the germ theory of illness—that they had already been exposed to the infection. (Note that research ethics at the present would preclude such an experiment.) The study is considered a landmark, as it showed that a physical illness (syphilis) can produce psychological abnormality (general paresis) decades later.

The success of Krafft-Ebing's demonstration inspired subsequent researchers to further the search for the causes of abnormality within a person's body: in someone's hormones, genes, brain function, biorhythms, nutrition, and so on. Collectively, this approach is the biomedical model which we discussed earlier: "Whenever you see mental illness, look to biology" (Bursten, 1979, p. 662).

You may recall that Sigmund Freud was originally trained as a neurologist. Neurology developed as a separate speciality within medicine during the early 1800s. It was a time when researchers learned enough about the nervous system to speculate about how damage to it might produce abnormal thoughts, feelings, and actions. Freud's emphasis on energy, on processes of inhibition and excitation, and on the far-reaching effects of early trauma all stem directly from neurology (Chapter 2). Although psychoanalytic theory is phrased in psychological language, its roots clearly stretch back to the illness era (Sulloway, 1979).

The Psychological Era

psychological era
historical period during which psychopathology was interpreted as learned behavior

A third way of interpreting abnormality, as a psychological phenomenon, has dominated the twentieth century—the **psychological era.** The cognitive-behavioral model of abnormality is the current statement of this view. Because abnormality is regarded as a psychological phenomenon, abnormality and normality are therefore not intrinsically different, because both are subject to the same psychological laws and principles.

Let's contrast the psychological era with its predecessors. In the supernatural era, it was assumed that abnormal behavior is something imposed on a person by an outside force. In the illness era, we see the assumption that abnormal behavior results from a malfunction within the body. In the psychological era, abnormal behavior is understood as something that a person learns to do.

No single event ushered in the psychological era, but there were several noteworthy occurrences. Freud's interpretation of hysteria in terms of unconscious conflicts legitimized psychological explanations of abnormality. And when Freud's pronouncements about the inevitable determinants of abnormality were challenged by anthropological evidence, there was further reason to examine the psychological basis of abnormality. Margaret Mead (1928), for instance, reported in her book *Coming of Age in Samoa* that early sex play among Samoan children did not produce adult abnormality. If anything, just the opposite occurred. Thus, theorists must pay attention to someone's cultural setting when explaining what does and does not produce problems in living. Remember the neo-Freudian theorists who revised psychoanalytic theory explicitly to incorporate social and cultural considerations (Chapter 11).

Also, experimental psychologists created in their laboratory bizarre behavior in animals by manipulating their environment. These instances of "abnormality" have come to be known as **experimental neuroses.** For instance, Pavlov (1927) taught dogs to discriminate between circles and ellipses. Then he slowly blurred the distinction, making the circles more elliptical and the ellipses more circular. The dogs reacted by squealing, squirming, and barking. Another researcher, Jules Masserman (1943), punished cats for obtaining food, producing excessive arousal and trembling. And H. S. Liddell (1944) presented sheep with difficult discrimination problems (as Pavlov did for dogs) and wound up with, if you can imagine, irritable sheep!

Don't misunderstand the intent of these demonstrations. No researcher proposes that "abnormal" behavior on the part of animals is strictly analogous to human abnormality. Rather, the researchers intend to be provocative. What would you think if all you saw was the aftermaths of their procedures: the squealing dog, the trembling cat, or the restless sheep? You might well conclude that the animal was profoundly damaged by an illness or injury. But when the researcher tells you that he produced these strange behaviors by a mundane manipulation of the animal's environment, you would undoubtedly say, "Think of what that implies for human abnormality. Maybe the environment is responsible as well."

Another important event marking the beginning of the psychological era was the experiment, already described in Chapter 5, in which John Watson and Rosalie Rayner (1920) conditioned a fear response in the infant known to history as Albert. This study is important because it demonstrates how abnormality (a phobia in this case) can result from simple

experimental neuroses
various types of abnormal behavior produced in laboratory animals by the manipulation of environmental conditions

Anthropological evidence, such as that provided by Margaret Mead (center) in *Coming of Age in Somoa,* emphasizes the need to consider cultural influences when defining what is or is not abnormal behavior.

learning. We need not invoke more elaborate explanations. Just as Krafft-Ebing's study encouraged researchers to seek further examples of abnormality as an illness, Watson and Rayner's study encouraged researchers to search for further examples of abnormality as a psychological phenomenon.

Psychopathology is a complex field because the different conceptions of abnormality still compete with each other. Although a supernatural perspective is mainly behind us, the other perspectives remain popular. Some mental health professionals embrace a psychological perspective, whereas others endorse an illness perspective. Both points of view have much support even though they usually stand in opposition to one another. An integrated perspective is a worthy goal that we have yet to fully achieve.

diagnosis
identifying a person's psychological disorder according to a particular set of signs and symptoms

Diagnosing Abnormality

Misdiagnosed as being mentally retarded, Gladys Barr was institutionalized for 42 years, despite the fact that IQ tests showed her to be of normal intelligence. She was released in 1978 and received a court-ordered financial settlement.

People do not have general problems. They instead have particular problems that take widely different forms. Different problems presumably reflect different causes and demand different treatments. Psychologists interested in abnormal behavior therefore devote much time and effort to describing the various types of psychological difficulties. Their overall goal is to bring order to the subject of psychopathology. They hope that valid diagnoses can aid in the planning of successful treatment.

To diagnose means literally to distinguish or differentiate. As applied to people's physical or psychological problems, **diagnosis** usually means placing people in categories in accordance with the particular signs or symptoms of their difficulties. In order to undertake diagnosis, one must have available a set of diagnostic categories and rules for assigning people to these categories.

The ideal set of categories satisfies several requirements. The categories available to the diagnostician should not overlap. They should encompass the range of problems that people actually experience. And they should lend themselves to all-or-nothing decisions. No diagnostic scheme used to describe psychological abnormality perfectly measures up to this ideal. The question of concern is how close any actual system is to the ideal.

DSM-III-R

DSM-III-R (*Diagnostic and Statistical Manual of Mental Disorders-Third Edition-Revised*)
the 1987 diagnostic scheme of the American Psychiatric Association, currently used to diagnose mental disorders in the United States

The system of classifying mental disorders most widely used in the United States today is one proposed by the American Psychiatric Association (1987) and contained in a book with a long title: *Diagnostic and Statistical Manual of Mental Disorders-Third Edition-Revised,* usually referred to as **DSM-III-R.** (By the way, the word *statistical* refers merely to the fact that each type of abnormality listed in DSM-III-R has an associated code number, allowing the particular abnormality to be briefly identified, like on an insurance reimbursement claim. These numbers need not concern us.) DSM-III-R describes disorders in five different domains called axes. A full DSM-III-R diagnosis contains information on each axis. Clinicians typically gather information by interviewing patients or administering various tests, as described in the previous chapter.

Axis I describes someone's **clinical syndrome:** an acute problem that brings a person into therapy. Clinical syndromes include such familiar difficulties as alcohol abuse, depression, phobia, schizophrenia, and the like.

Two types of diagnoses are made on Axis II. First, problems are noted that occur in the context of development, such as difficulties with the acquisition of cognitive, language, or motor skills. Such developmental disorders may be pervasive, like mental retardation, or they may be specific, like difficulties with recognizing words. The other problems found on Axis II are personality disorders: pervasive styles of behaving that can make a clinical syndrome worse as well as create difficulties in their own right.

On Axis III, the diagnostician notes any physical illnesses or conditions pertinent to the individual's clinical syndrome. Suppose someone has thyroid disease. Among the possible consequences of such a condition are mood changes, and one would certainly want to take this into account in judging whether or not this person warrants an Axis I diagnosis of depression.

As the cognitive-behavioral model proposes, abnormal behavior should be explained by taking into account the setting where it occurs. Axis IV of DSM-III-R captures one important situational characteristic: the severity of existing stressors, such as unemployment or divorce (Chapter 6).

Finally, Axis V is a global assessment of how well or poorly a person functions in social and occupational spheres, both at the present time and during the prior year. It is important to know how a person got along before his clinical syndrome developed, because this provides a plausible goal for therapy. Remember the old joke:

Patient: Will I be able to play the piano after my operation?

Doctor: Of course you'll be able to play the piano.

Patient: That's funny, I couldn't play before.

It's not that a therapist should have minimal expectations; it's just that the expectations must be grounded somewhere. One's level of optimal functioning in the past provides a reasonable clue about one's optimal level in the future.

As stated, a full DSM-III-R diagnosis describes someone's problems in terms of all five axes. Table 12.1 gives an example of what such a diagnosis actually looks like. The person described is an actual patient that I treated for depression some years ago.

Pros and Cons of Diagnosis

Diagnosing psychological abnormality is a controversial business. On the positive side, diagnoses can facilitate communication. Professionals know the types of problems that fall within various diagnostic categories, and hence diagnoses can serve as a convenient shorthand. If one clinician says to another, "Mr. Smith experiences panic disorder, without agoraphobia," they both know that Mr. Smith suffers intense attacks of apprehension, but that he does not avoid situations from which he cannot readily flee. They both know Mr. Smith's problems probably began in his late twenties, that

Table 12.1

Example of a DSM-III-R Diagnosis

While working as a therapist some years ago, I treated a thirty-five-year-old man for depression. This is a full DSM-III-R diagnosis of this individual.

Axis I	Major depressive episode, chronic; alcohol dependence
Axis II	Dependent personality disorder
Axis III	Physical disorders and conditions: none
Axis IV	Psychosocial stressors: severe—unemployment and marital discord
Axis V	Global assessment of functioning: at present—serious impairment; during past year—mild to moderate impairment

he is apt to be depressed, and that he frequently broods about the possibility of having a panic attack.

A second advantage is that diagnoses can provide clues about the presumed cause of a disorder—its *etiology*—based on previous research with other individuals who have the same diagnosis. Bipolar disorder, for example, in which periods of extreme (and inappropriate) sadness alternate with periods of extreme (and inappropriate) elation, probably has a genetic basis.

Third, diagnoses allow for educated predictions about the likely outcome of a disorder—its *prognosis*. It has been established, for example, that individuals with the type of schizophrenia characterized by paranoid beliefs usually fare better than other schizophrenic individuals.

And fourth, diagnoses can suggest effective forms of treatment. Let's return to Mr. Smith with the panic disorder. He will probably respond favorably to antidepressant medication. A therapist will recommend this treatment if a patient warrants this particular diagnosis. Without the diagnosis, there would be no reason to explore this nonobvious form of therapy.

Diagnostic schemes, however, pose several problems. First, they are not theoretically neutral. For instance, DSM-III-R in many ways embodies the biomedical model of abnormality (Persons, 1986). This presents obvious difficulties for psychologists who advocate other approaches.

Second, diagnosis in effect assumes discontinuity between abnormality and normality. By the logic of DSM-III-R and similar diagnostic schemes, people either warrant a diagnosis or do not. Although many disorders fall along a continuum of severity, most diagnostic systems treat problems as present or absent. Again, this may be objectionable to some psychologists.

Third, although DSM-III-R is a more reliable diagnostic system than its previous versions, reliability is still a problem, at least for some disorders. In other words, two diagnosticians assessing the same individual may arrive at altogether different diagnoses. All the virtues just enumerated for diagnosis go right out the window if these diagnoses fail to be reliable.

Finally, diagnostic labels may take on a life of their own and create problems for patients above and beyond the actual difficulties that originally warranted the label. Remember what happened to Rosenhan and the other pseudopatients in his study. Once diagnosed, the label stuck to them and altered how others viewed them. The more general argument against the diagnosis of abnormality is that particular diagnoses have social significance. Negative attitudes often accompany labels such as "mental illness" or "psychological disorder." Diagnoses may create a stigma about an individual that compounds whatever problems he or she had in the first place. This stigma may persist even when the individual's problems no longer exist.

There is no easy resolution of the difficulties surrounding diagnosis. Psychologists are in an awkward position here. The reality of the mental health system dictates that DSM-III-R be used to describe people's psychological problems, even if this diagnostic scheme conflicts with certain psychological theories and assumptions. Because DSM-III-R is *the* diagnostic system in use in the United States, the major disorders in this chapter are described with respect to DSM-III-R criteria. But keep in mind that this is not an ideal classification scheme.

Typology of Disorders

DSM-III-R lists several disorders on Axes I and II (see Table 12.2). The question thus arises: Why these problems and not others? A car breaks down in a finite number of ways that can be specified by someone who

Table 12.2
The Major Disorders Described in DSM-III-R

Major Category	Specific Example
Disorders of infancy, child, or adolescence	Mental retardation
Organic mental disorders	Alzheimer's disease
Substance-use disorders	Alcohol dependence
Schizophrenia	Paranoid schizophrenia
Mood disorders	Bipolar disorder
Anxiety disorders	Generalized anxiety disorder
Somatoform disorders	Hypochondriasis
Dissociative disorders	Psychogenic amnesia
Sexual disorders	Transsexualism
Sleep disorders	Insomnia
Factitious disorders	Feigned illness
Impulse control disorders	Pathological gambling
Adjustment disorders	Stress-related anxiety
Psychological factors affecting physical condition	Stress-related hypertension (high blood pressure)
Personality disorders	Antisocial personality disorder

Reprinted with permission from the *Diagnostic and Statistical Manual of Mental Disorders, Third Edition, Revised.* Copyright © 1987 American Psychiatric Association.

knows the structure and function of cars. Can the same be said about people and their problems? There have been attempts to organize the various forms of abnormality into an overall system.

One way to systematize disorders is by providing overarching categories, along with a rationale for this organization. So, psychopathologists have frequently distinguished between two types of problems. **Psychotic disorders** are those in which a person is considered out of touch with reality. Schizophrenia, which is marked by hallucinations and delusions, is one such disorder. **Neurotic disorders,** on the other hand, include problems such as anxiety and depression, which do not impair reality testing. (Some writers cleverly comment that neurotic behavior is *too* much in touch with reality.)

The distinction between psychotic and neurotic can be interpreted in psychoanalytic terms as the relative success of someone's defenses against unacceptable impulses. In the case of psychosis, impulses overwhelm a person's capacity to deal with them, resulting in bizarre behavior that takes him out of the world. In the case of neurosis, the defenses win out, although the individual still pays a price, staying in the world but unhappy about it.

The psychotic-neurotic distinction is not currently used in DSM-III-R, although it figured prominently in earlier editions. Dividing the disorders this way just didn't prove accurate. People with psychotic disorders are often oriented to the real world, and those with neurotic disorders often entertain thoughts and beliefs at odds with the facts. At any rate, the terms still have utility as adjectives, if not as nouns.

Not all psychologists believe that an overall scheme of disorders is possible. Many who endorse the cognitive-behavioral model of abnormality believe that behavior (normal and abnormal) is produced by specific rewards and punishments. People have no inherent weaknesses; disorders are only what they learn or fail to learn. Along these same lines, historical and cross-cultural studies of abnormality document disorders tied to given times and places. If one's particular social setting determines the very types of abnormality possible, there is no overall scheme—simply historical happenstance.

The debate continues over how best to explain why people develop particular psychological problems instead of others. There is much less controversy over the continued use of diagnosis in abnormal psychology. The benefits of placing individuals in categories according to the symptoms they show outweigh the drawbacks, although attempts to improve particular diagnostic systems are ongoing. DSM-III-R will soon be replaced by an updated version—DSM-IV—that is already in the works.

Types of Disorders

In the remainder of this chapter, we will discuss some of the psychological disorders listed in DSM-III-R. It is important to keep in mind the following points regarding this material. First, the study of psychopathology by psychologists is a subset of general psychology, thus it should be approached with a scientific attitude. Because psychopathology is so interesting in its own right, we can lose track of psychology's goal of explaining how disorders come about and devising means of preventing and treating them.

psychotic disorders
disorders in which the person is considered out of touch with reality, e.g., schizophrenia

neurotic disorders
disorders in which the person's reality testing is not impaired, e.g., phobia

Second, there is a tendency to distance ourselves from people with problems. We can sometimes see ourselves in them and their problems, and this makes us uncomfortable. When you are tempted to think of people with problems as "those kind of people," keep in mind that in reality all people, with and without psychological difficulties, share much in common.

Third, there is, at the same time, a tendency to romanticize abnormality, to think that people with strange problems are charismatic and creative, that they march to a different drummer somehow more true than our own. Not exactly. Different drummers exist, and they should be heeded by those fortunate enough and brave enough to hear them. But choice has little to do with the major disorders. The people described in this chapter are not to be envied. By definition, they have problems with life. They are socially estranged. They are not happy. We should try to understand them and reach out to them, but we should not make them heroes.

Fourth, many of our problems exist in degrees, meaning that you shouldn't panic simply because part of what you experience in your life is similar to the striking cases of abnormality described here. Indeed, sadness and worry, obstinacy and error, confusion and hurt are all part of the human experience. If you are a well-rounded enough person to occasionally experience a symptom of some disorder, that itself is normal. Don't waste a lot of time diagnosing yourself or your friends, worrying if someone "really" has a problem. Real problems make themselves known in unmistakable fashion.

Having made these qualifications and appeals, let's now get about the business of presenting and explaining the major disorders. For each disorder, you will find a description as well as a sketch of what is known about its causes and consequences. In passing, we'll note the treatment currently believed most effective for a particular disorder, although a detailed view of therapy is postponed until Chapter 13.

We start with a discussion of disorders characterized by excessive fear and anxiety. We end with schizophrenia and personality disorders. In between, we discuss a variety of other disorders listed in DSM-III-R (remember Table 12.2).

Fear and Anxiety Disorders

Fear was first discussed in Chapter 6. It is a basic emotion with associated physiological characteristics (the body's emergency reaction), expectations of harm in the future, and behaviors ("fight or flight"). **Anxiety** shares much in common with fear—the same feelings of apprehension and uneasiness, the same emergency reaction, and the same "fight or flight" behavioral response. Anxiety differs from fear in that its associated expectations are more diffuse. The anxious individual feels threatened, but the sense of danger is not a specific one.

Fear and anxiety are part of everyday experience, but when pervasive or severe, they become problems. Indeed, there are several related difficulties in which fear and anxiety predominate. When dread or apprehension are linked to specific objects or situations, we call these **fear disorders.** When expectations of harm are more general, we call these **anxiety disorders.** In either case, people feel uneasy, show the bodily

anxiety
feelings of apprehension and uneasiness accompanied by the body's emergency reaction, a "fight or flight" response, and diffuse expectations of harm

fear disorders
disorders characterized by dread or apprehension linked to specific objects or situations, e.g., phobia

anxiety disorders
disorders characterized by general expectations of harm, e.g., generalized anxiety disorder

emergency reaction, and expect harm to befall them. They feel inadequate, and avoid problems instead of trying to solve them.

How might we conceptualize the causes of these disorders? We can turn to each of the three models of abnormality for a possible answer. The biomedical model calls our attention to possible physiological predispositions. For example, the tendency of people to experience anxiety in the face of threat may be an individual difference with a genetic basis. We would thus expect fear and anxiety disorders to run through families, a hypothesis confirmed by family studies (e.g., Carey, 1982).

Psychoanalytic theorists view anxiety in terms of underlying conflicts. Freud theorized extensively about anxiety, distinguishing three types:

- realistic anxiety—legitimate fear of things in the world
- neurotic anxiety—fear of one's own impulses
- moral anxiety—fear of one's own conscience

By the psychoanalytic view, anxiety is not a disorder in its own right, but a process that can produce a variety of disorders, depending on how the individual defends against it. Anxiety disorders can reflect any or all of the three types of fear that Freud specified.

The cognitive-behavioral model leads us to interpret anxiety in terms of learning. How do we come to associate the response of anxiety to various objects or situations? Anxiety can be classically conditioned. Fear is viewed as an unlearned response to a threat. If other stimuli are paired with whatever arouses fear, then the originally neutral stimulus comes to arouse fear (anxiety) in its own right. We saw this process, for instance, in the case of Albert.

Why doesn't anxiety as a conditioned response extinguish itself? You know from Chapter 5 that conditioned responses can be readily extinguished by exposing the person to the conditioned stimulus without the accompanying unconditioned stimulus. This seems at odds with the persistence of many anxiety disorders. Outside the laboratory, however, people with conditioned anxiety do not stand still long enough for extinction to take place. Indeed, a person fleeing an anxiety-provoking situation is reinforced, because her flight decreases the fear.

With the cognitive revolution legitimizing explanations in terms of thoughts and beliefs, fear and anxiety disorders become even easier for psychologists to explain. Kelly (1955) approaches anxiety from the vantage point of his personal construct theory (Chapter 11), seeing it as the emotion that accompanies the realization that events lie outside one's ability to make sense of them. This accounts well for the anxiety that may follow in the wake of an event such as an auto accident or an assault. What has happened to the person may be beyond understanding.

Similarly, Beck and Emery (1985) explain anxiety disorders in terms of people's exaggerated beliefs about their own fragility. The anxious individual assumes that catastrophe waits around every corner. If you believe that you are particularly vulnerable and inadequate, you may end up behaving that way. Thus fear and anxiety disorders may involve a vicious circle—anxious thoughts incite anxious behavior which leads to more anxious thoughts.

Let's now discuss particular disorders, beginning with two fear disorders—phobias and post-traumatic stress disorders—in which people's uneasiness revolves around specific objects or situations. Then we will discuss problems characterized by more diffuse anxiety, such as generalized anxiety disorder, panic disorder and agoraphobia, and obsessive-compulsive disorder.

phobia
a fear disorder marked by persistent avoidance of some object or situation

Phobia.   Someone who shows persistent fear and avoidance of some specific object or situation has a **phobia.** We can distinguish two types of phobias. First are *simple phobias,* in which a person shows excessive fear of a particular object or event. The most common of the simple phobias include fears of animals (e.g., spiders, snakes, insects, rats, mice), blood, enclosed spaces, heights, and air travel. There are more exotic types as well (Table 12.3).

The second type is phobia is called a *social phobia* because the individual is afraid of particular situations where she might be scrutinized by others. Her fears revolve around the presumed humiliation that will occur if she somehow fails to adequately perform some act. DSM-III-R lists the common fears of a social phobic:

- becoming tongue-tied while speaking in public
- choking on food while eating in public
- blushing while in public
- trembling while writing in public
- not being able to urinate in a public bathroom

These fears of course interfere with the performance of these behaviors, making one's social phobia worse.

The social phobic avoids situations in which embarrassment might occur, often going to great lengths to do so. Note that this phobia is not

Table 12.3
Some Exotic Phobias

Name	Definition
Ailurophobia	Fear of cats
Arachibutyrophobia	Fear of peanut butter sticking to the roof of one's mouth
Belonophobia	Fear of pins and needles
Erythrophobia	Fear of blushing
Haphephobia	Fear of being touched
Pnigophobia	Fear of choking
Scopophobia	Fear of being stared at
Taphophobia	Fear of being buried alive
Triskedekaphobia	Fear of the number 13

simply a concern with what other people think. That's part of the human condition. Rather, social phobia qualifies as an instance of abnormality precisely to the degree that it interferes with one's life. Alcohol and drug abuse may accompany social phobias, as people try to "medicate" their worries. What begins as one problem may soon become two or more.

People with phobias are quite aware of their fear. They experience immediate anxiety in the presence of the object or situation, go to great lengths to avoid it, yet at the same time acknowledge that their fear is out of proportion to the actual danger posed. Phobias can greatly disrupt one's everyday life.

Because phobias can be circumscribed, people who experience them do not necessarily seek treatment. They may be able to avoid the object of their fears. It is therefore difficult to get a handle on the prevalence of phobias, but estimates suggest that 1 percent of our population has one or more of them (Nemiah, 1980). Women are more likely than men to have these problems, and it is interesting that this sex difference becomes apparent only with the onset of puberty. Also interesting is the fact that these phobias often run in families. Note that the sex difference and the family pattern admit to either a biomedical interpretation, a social one, or both.

Proponents of each model of abnormality have attempted to explain phobias. Attempts to find specific physiological differences between phobics and nonphobics have not been successful, so biomedical theorists remain largely silent.

As we saw in Freud's discussion of Little Hans (Chapter 1), psychoanalytic theorists see a phobia as symbolizing some underlying conflict. It can be a sexual conflict, but other types of conflicts also can be implicated, as the following example shows. Prince (1924) described a woman's fear of church bells. Years earlier, the woman's mother had gone through a lengthy illness before she died. The woman frequently went to a church to pray for her mother's health, always accompanied by the ringing of the church bells. On one occasion she neglected to pray, and her mother died shortly thereafter. The subsequent phobia symbolized her guilt.

Learning theories point to traumatic events as the cause of phobias. Weighing against this explanation is the fact that many phobics can recall no particular event involving the phobic object or situation. Indeed, some phobias involve objects never encountered by a person, such as giant snakes. Perhaps modeling is a better explanation than classical conditioning, because we can thereby explain how a phobia can be acquired without the phobic having direct experience with the object or situation.

The explanation of phobias is more complicated than their name implies. Simplicity returns, though, when we address the issue of therapy. It is clear that behavior modification can effectively eliminate many phobias. Regardless of the cause of a phobia, the person can be taught not to fear the object or situation.

Post-Traumatic Stress Disorder. Phobias entail fear out of proportion to the objective circumstances. The next fear disorder we discuss is different because it follows a distressing event sufficient to upset anyone, such as the following:

- military combat
- civilian disaster
- imprisonment in a prisoner of war camp
- imprisonment in a concentration camp
- rape or assault
- accident or injury
- torture

Following these experiences, all people show an immediate reaction, but some people show a long-term reaction.

post-traumatic stress disorder
a fear disorder characterized by the reexperiencing of a traumatic event, avoidance of reminders of the original trauma, diminished interest in activities, and various signs of anxiety

The defining characteristic of **post-traumatic stress disorder** is that the person reexperiences the original traumatic event. This may take the form of recurrent memories that cannot be banished from one's mind. As a therapist, I worked with a Vietnam veteran who saw his best friend blown to pieces. One of the friend's limbs landed in his lap! Years after this horrible occurrence, the memory remained a vivid part of his everyday waking life.

Sometimes the person dreams repeatedly of the traumatic event. For example, I know a woman who was raped over a decade ago. During the day, she goes about her business and rarely thinks of the rape. But almost every night, she dreams about it, awakening in terror.

Finally, someone with post-traumatic stress disorder may reexperience the event by acting and feeling as if the event is literally recurring. Another Vietnam veteran I knew experienced flashbacks every couple of days, believing himself in the jungle, walking the point and leading the group into an ambush. He would crouch in the middle of the room and scan its corners with such apprehension that every onlooker followed his gaze, expecting to see snipers hidden somewhere.

People with post-traumatic stress disorder try to avoid reminders of the trauma. At the same time, they show diminished interest in other activities, social estrangement, blunted feelings, and a sense of hopelessness about the future. A variety of anxiety symptoms also mark post-traumatic stress disorder: sleep difficulty, irritability, concentration problems, and an exaggerated startle response.

What causes post-traumatic stress disorder? By definition, a trauma must be present, but this cannot bear the entire load of explanation, because not all who experience a trauma have a long-term negative reaction. A host of additional factors bring about post-traumatic stress in some individuals while precluding it in others. Among the factors that make post-traumatic stress *more* likely are physical disability caused by the original event (Strom, 1980), lack of immediate counseling (Ludwig & Ranson, 1947), and a prior history of problems (Andreasen, 1984).

Another risk factor for post-traumatic stress disorder is the person's inability to find any meaning in the traumatic experience. This may explain why the Vietnam War appears to have produced more than its share of post-traumatic stress disorders. The war was not conducted in a way that made it easy for the participating soldiers to make sense of what they witnessed. Vietnam was not a war over territory, which is tangible, but a war over body counts, which are abstract. GIs served in Vietnam not until the war was won, but for twelve months. They were shipped over not with friends from their hometown, but with strangers chosen randomly by a computer.

Even though post-traumatic stress disorders can persist for decades, treatment is possible. Talking about the trauma in a supportive context is a common ingredient in successful therapies. Why should this be an effective therapy tactic? Perhaps when people talk about traumatic events, they release deep conflicts and thereby experience emotional relief. Perhaps they extinguish their fear. Or perhaps as they talk about the traumatic events, they come to think about them differently and experience a sense of mastery. Note that these explanations stem from different theories about abnormality and its treatment—psychoanalytic, behavioral, and cognitive, respectively.

Generalized Anxiety Disorder.   Disorders involving anxiety that is diffuse and pervasive are referred to as **generalized anxiety disorders.** Remember Chicken Little, the storybook character who was afraid that the sky would fall on her head? She serves as an apt example of this disorder, because the sky is everywhere, and so too is the anxiety about its imminent fall. More formally, according to DSM-III-R, the diagnostician should look for a person worrying excessively and inappropriately about two or more domains of life—such as family, job, or health.

People with generalized anxiety disorder show a full range of anxiety responses. They tremble and twitch; they feel tired and tense. They are chronically aroused, with rapid breathing, racing pulse, clammy hands, recurrent diarrhea, frequent urination, and a lump in their throat. They have difficulty concentrating because they are so easily distracted. They are easy to startle: "What was that?!"

What causes generalized anxiety disorder? Again, all three models of abnormality can contribute to an understanding. Generalized anxiety involves the body, of course, particularly the autonomic nervous system. Perhaps inherited individual differences in reactivity predispose someone to an anxiety disorder. Twin studies suggest a genetic basis to anxiety, although the specific mechanism is unknown at the present time (Andreasen, 1984).

generalized anxiety disorders
disorders characterized by diffuse and pervasive symptoms of anxiety

Psychoanalytic theorists use the term *free-floating anxiety* to refer to highly general symptoms of anxiety that the person is unable to connect to a particular context because it would be too threatening to do so. By this view, a generalized anxiety disorder defends against a more specific fear. Nemiah (1980, p. 1487) describes the case of a man who

> reported that, for several days before he had to go away on a trip . . . began to feel increasingly anxious. . . . A sense of uneasy tension was constantly present in his stomach, and he often felt mildly flushed and unable to think as clearly as he wished. . . . These [symptoms] . . . totally destroyed any pleasurable anticipations about his journey.

Other details suggest that our unhappy traveler was really afraid of being separated from his loved ones because as an infant he had felt abandoned by his mother. He repressed these particular feelings, because they were entwined with hostility, substituting instead a general state of uneasiness.

Cognitive-behavioral theorists trace anxiety to particular learning which is generalized in the way that any learning can be generalized (Chapter 5). In other words, anxiety aroused in a specific situation can spread to other situations if they are sufficiently similar. Cognitive psychologists stress the role of exaggerated beliefs in bringing about this generalization of anxiety (Beck, 1976). Suppose you encounter difficulties in one sphere of life, and you become anxious. If you say to yourself, "I'm the sort of person who always has these disasters happen," then you are apt to feel anxious in other areas of your life as well, even though absolutely nothing has gone amiss in them.

Treatment of generalized anxiety disorder takes different forms. Tranquilizing medicine (such as Librium or Valium) may be used to control the person's bodily symptoms. Psychotherapy is another avenue. It allows a person to talk about the anxiety, achieving insight or reassurance or both. Behavior therapists teach anxious clients how to relax.

Panic Disorder and Agoraphobia. We have all experienced momentary panic: discrete periods of intense anxiety. Usually panic accompanies a life-threatening situation, such as merging onto a busy highway, walking down a dark alley, or completing an income tax form. But some of us experience panic attacks in the absence of any objective danger, with sufficient frequency and disruption to constitute a major problem in our daily lives.

DSM-III-R suggests that four panic attacks within a 4-week period qualify a person for the diagnosis of **panic disorder.** Attacks occur suddenly and without warning. They usually last only a couple of minutes, but are nonetheless highly aversive, arousing intense discomfort and fear. Victims of panic attacks feel like they are choking or smothering. They are dizzy, nauseous, and shaky; they fear that they are going out of control; they may even think they are about to die. A panic attack is a particularly intense version of the fight-or-flight response, except that there is no apparent external threat. After several panic attacks, people start to fear the onset of yet another one, and so become generally apprehensive.

Agoraphobia, fear of being in a situation from which escape is difficult or embarrassing, is a phobia that frequently accompanies panic disorder. It manifests itself as avoidance of activities such as traveling, shopping, standing in line, and attending movies. In extreme cases, someone with agoraphobia may become completely housebound, not going

panic disorder
an anxiety disorder marked by the recurrence of sudden and extreme attacks of anxiety

agoraphobia
fear of being in a situation from which escape is difficult or embarrassing, usually resulting in the avoidance of public places

out for years or even decades. The link between panic disorder and agoraphobia is direct: Someone prone to panic attacks may be afraid of having one in a public setting and thus avoids going out. However, an individual may have panic attacks without agoraphobia or agoraphobia without panic attacks.

Taken as a whole, agoraphobia and panic disorders affect as many as 7 percent of the population. Women are more likely than men to have these difficulties. Onset is usually in the late twenties, and without treatment, these disorders may last an extremely long time.

Recent research suggests that both the biomedical and cognitive-behavioral models of abnormality can help explain the causes of panic disorders. Let's consider the evidence for a biological basis. First, twin studies show that agoraphobia and panic disorders are to some degree inherited (Torgersen, 1983). Second, panic attacks can be created chemically, with infusions of sodium lactate, a chemical that builds up in the body during exercise (Liebowitz et al., 1985). Further, if an individual has a history of panic attacks, then a smaller dose of sodium lactate can induce a panic attack, suggesting that people prone to panic attacks have an excess of sodium lactate. Third, these disorders often respond well to medication that directly targets panic symptoms.

Beck and Emery (1985) propose further that the physiological aspects of agoraphobia and panic disorders only become problems for people if they interpret them catastrophically. To understand these problems, we must look not just at a person's biology but also at that person's thoughts and beliefs. An interesting therapy emerges from the cognitive model: encouraging people with these problems to reinterpret the "disorder" in innocuous terms, say as a harmless consequence of hyperventilation. This strategy reduces the frequency of panic attacks, as well as the other anxiety symptoms that accompany them.

obsessions
recurring and persistent thoughts that one finds upsetting

compulsions
repetitive acts that one is impelled to carry out to prevent some dreaded event, even though these acts bear no realistic connection to the event

obsessive-compulsive disorder
an anxiety disorder characterized by obsessions and compulsions

Obsessive-Compulsive Disorder. **Obsessions** are recurring thoughts that a person finds upsetting. Attempts to ignore or suppress these obsessive thoughts are not successful. Several themes predominate here:

- violence—e.g., losing control and striking one's child
- contamination—e.g., getting AIDS from shaking hands
- blasphemy—e.g., having sexual fantasies while praying
- doubt—e.g., wondering if an already-mailed check was signed

Compulsions are the behavioral equivalent of obsessions: repetitive actions carried out to prevent some dreaded event, even though the actions bear no realistic connection to the event. They are recognized as excessive and unreasonable, but the person cannot resist performing them, because great anxiety ensues when a compulsion is interrupted.

Obsessions and compulsions often accompany each other, and so the term **obsessive-compulsive disorder** describes both. As many as 1.5 percent of our population suffers with this disorder, with women more likely to have the problem than men (National Institute of Mental Health, 1985). If extreme, obsessive-compulsive disorders can inordinately disrupt life (Rapoport, 1989). Imagine what you would *not* be doing if you washed your hands 350 times a day, if you recited the Lord's Prayer every 25 seconds, or if you peered into every passing car on the lookout for a terrorist (see Figure 12.2).

Figure 12.2

A few basic themes characterize most obsessive-compulsive disorders. This suggests that the psychoanalytic model provides a ready explanation, because it is the only approach that allows the psychologist to grapple readily with the meaning of symptoms. Indeed, Freud's explanation still proves influential. According to Freud (1909b), obsessive-compulsive disorders represent ambivalence surrounding events during the anal stage. In short, obsessions and compulsions symbolize the struggles of toilet training.

Cognitive-behavioral psychologists can explain the persistence of obsessions and compulsions, if not their content. Repetitive thoughts and actions reduce anxiety because they distract people from whatever is distressing them (Rachman & Hodgson, 1980). Accordingly, these thoughts and deeds are reinforced. And whatever created the initial distress is left unchanged, which means that the obsessions and compulsions escalate. By employing obsessions and compulsions as a "coping" strategy, one risks becoming the psychological equivalent of a runaway locomotive.

These disorders are difficult to treat. Therapists have tried drugs, psychoanalytic therapy, and behavior modification with only modest success (Carson, Butcher, & Coleman, 1988). Some therapists therefore try to combine strategies with obsessive-compulsive clients, under the reasonable (but unproven) assumption that the benefits will be cumulative.

Somatoform Disorders

somatoform disorders

disorders characterized by physical symptoms that have no basis in physiology

conversion disorder

a somatoform disorder in which there is a loss of physical functioning without a physical cause; formerly called hysteria

Some cases of psychological abnormality involve physical symptoms but have no actual basis in physiology. These are called **somatoform disorders,** and there are several common types. The best-known somatoform disorder is **conversion disorder,** familiar to us from Chapter 11 by its former name, hysteria. This disorder manifests itself as a loss of physical functioning without a physical cause: for example, hysterical blindness, deafness, or paralysis (see Figure 12.3).

When I worked as a psychologist in a general medical hospital, I encountered a striking example of conversion disorder. A man woke up one morning, suddenly unable to see. His family rushed him to the hospital, where he was examined by eye specialists. They couldn't find anything wrong with his eyes, so they called in neurology experts, thinking that his blindness stemmed from damage to his brain. The neurologists couldn't find anything wrong with his brain, so they called in psychiatrists and psychologists, who diagnosed his difficulty as a conversion disorder.

The symptoms displayed by the women accused of witchcraft in Salem, as displayed in this period painting, may have been the result of somatoform disorders.

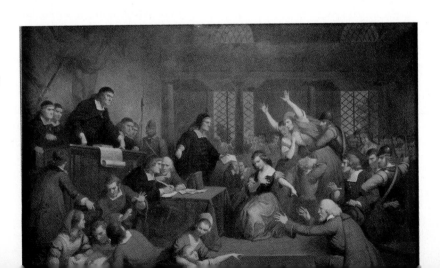

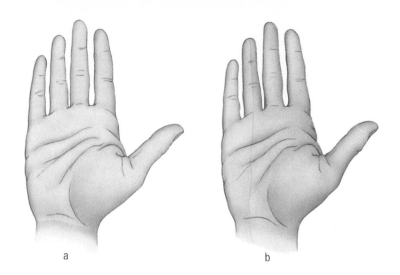

Figure 12.3

Glove Anesthesia. In one form of conversion disorder, a person loses all feeling in areas of the hand that would be covered by a glove (a). However, the actual nerves in the hand are *not* distributed this way. If there were a loss of feeling due to actual physical causes, it would show a different pattern (b).

a   b

DSM-III-R provides several criteria for diagnosing conversion disorder. First, the individual must show a loss or alteration of physical functioning. Second, a biological basis for the physical symptoms must be ruled out. Third, these symptoms cannot be under the individual's voluntary control. There is a temptation, perhaps, when considering cases of conversion disorder, to think that the symptoms are somehow not "real" or that the individual is deliberately faking. Both suspicions are wrong. Those with conversion disorders indeed cannot see or hear or move, and they are quite sincere about it. Fourth, the onset of symptoms must bear some psychological relationship to conflicts or needs. The patient just described became blind following an argument with his wife the night before over changes in her personal appearance, which he found unattractive.

hypochondriasis

a somatoform disorder characterized by a preoccupation with having one or more serious illnesses, when all medical evidence is to the contrary

Another well-known somatoform disorder is **hypochondriasis:** a preoccupation with having one or more serious illnesses, when all medical evidence is to the contrary. Someone with hypochondriasis is overly concerned with particular bodily functions, such as sweating or the beating of the heart, and interprets small injuries or illnesses as signs of impending physical doom. As in conversion disorder, the hypochondriacal individual is neither malingering nor faking. He or she may visit numerous doctors, never feeling that the medical care received is adequate.

Somatoform disorders often begin in one's teens or twenties, persist for some time, and impair everyday life to varying degrees—from mild to moderate to severe. On the whole, somatoform disorders appear more common among women than men, but accurate estimates of overall prevalence seem to elude researchers. These disorders are often confused with actual physical illnesses.

It was his work with hysterics that led Freud to develop psychoanalysis (Chapter 1), and psychoanalytic theorists still have much to say about somatoform disorders. The physical symptom is thought to symbolize an underlying conflict that the person keeps from consciousness by metaphorically converting it into a physical difficulty. Remember the example of the "blind" patient. He was strongly ambivalent about his wife's appear-

dissociative disorders
disorders marked by lack of integration of a person's identity, memory, or consciousness

psychogenic amnesia
a dissociative disorder in which a sudden inability to recall important personal information follows a psychological trauma

This victim of psychogenic amnesia was found near death in Florida. The national exposure given to "Jane Doe" led a couple in Roselle, Illinois, to identify her as their daughter.

ance. He resolved his conflict, so to speak, by becoming blind. Then he didn't have to look at her.

Cognitive-behavioral theorists believe that physical symptoms allow the individual to gain some reward, such as the attention of others, and/or to shirk unwanted responsibilities. Needless to say, neither conversion disorder nor hypochondriasis represents a reasonable long-term solution to life's problems. Treatment proceeds with this recognition. The ostensible physical symptoms are not directly attacked. Instead, the therapist identifies a person's conflicts and helps resolve them and/or encourages the person to find less extreme means of gaining what he wants from the world.

Dissociative Disorders

We learned in Chapter 11 that people typically regard the self as integrated. At the same time, variation occurs within ourselves and others. We (and they) think different thoughts, feel different emotions, and perform different behaviors. When this variation becomes so extreme that we can no longer sensibly speak of people as integrated wholes because they show marked divisions within identity, memory, or consciousness, then we are talking about the **dissociative disorders.** We can make certain generalizations about the dissociative disorders.

- By definition, none of the dissociative disorders can be caused by a physical problem.
- Advocates of the biomedical model (not surprisingly) have been unable to find physiological predispositions to these disorders.
- Because the dissociative disorders involve states of consciousness, the psychoanalytic model provides the most useful explanation.
- According to the psychoanalytic account, the symptoms of dissociative disorders let the person defend against underlying anxiety.

There are three well-known dissociative disorders: psychogenic amnesia, psychogenic fugue, and multiple personality disorder.

Psychogenic Amnesia. As mentioned in Chapter 7, a person suffering from **psychogenic amnesia** experiences a sudden inability to recall important personal information. First and foremost, this memory loss must be distinguished from that caused by physical trauma. In the latter case, the person is often unaware that any memories are missing, and other cognitive difficulties accompany memory loss. But in psychogenic amnesia, the person knows that he does not know and shows no impairment of attention, language, and the like.

This disorder usually follows a highly stressful event and therefore is most common in wartime and during natural disasters. If an event so upsets a person that he cannot accommodate it within his conscious mind, he will repress the event, along with whatever other memories are linked to it.

How is psychogenic amnesia treated? The therapist helps the individual recapture threads of the lost memories with hypnosis or free association. So-called truth serum (e.g., sodium amytal) can also help, not because it magically unleashes the truth, but because it is a potent tranquilizer, stripping away the anxiety that inhibits recall. Once the person begins to grasp his memories, his recovery is rapid. At this point, the person's underlying problems can be attacked.

Psychogenic Fugue.   Another dissociative disorder in which one's memory of the past is partially or completely lost for psychological reasons is **psychogenic fugue.** But in fugue, the person leaves home, moves to a new locale, and establishes a different identity. In some cases, this new identity is complex and coherent, and the person lives a new life for an indefinite period of time. In other cases, the person's new identity is incomplete, and she doesn't establish a wholly "different" life. Regardless, the explanation and treatment of psychogenic fugue proceed much the same as they do for psychogenic amnesia.

Multiple Personality Disorder.   This is one of the most exotic forms of psychopathology. At one time it was believed to be virtually extinct, but recent case studies show that this disorder is alive and well, although still exceedingly rare. We may have trouble conceptualizing multiple personality disorders because the very words we have to describe people and their problems don't lend themselves to this disorder.

DSM-III-R defines **multiple personality disorder** as the existence within the same individual of two or more distinct personalities, each of which at a given time takes control of the person's thoughts, feelings, and actions. The transition from one personality to the other is abrupt, and there may be barriers of amnesia between personalities. In other words, the left hand may quite literally not know what the right hand is doing. The celebrated cases of Eve (with her three personalities) and Sybil (with her seventeen) illustrate how individuals with multiple personality disorders take on and discard their different selves in response to stressful situations (see Figure 12.4).

What causes multiple personality disorder? The precise answer is not known, although Eugene Bliss (1980) offered an intriguing theory after he studied fourteen cases of this disorder. From interviews with his patients, Bliss identified three common factors: (a) the creation of an imaginary playmate between the ages of four and six, (b) skill at self-hypnosis, and (c) use of the imaginary playmate to cope with stress. You can see how these factors might predispose multiple personality disorder. Further, we

Figure 12.4
Multiple Personality Disorder. Joanne Woodward starred in the film *The Three Faces of Eve,* based on the well-known case of an actual woman with multiple personality disorder. Here she is shown portraying the three distinct personalities of this woman.

can readily interpret this disorder as a defense against intolerable situations. Current research documents sexual abuse during childhood as a frequent precursor to multiple personality disorder.

Therapy can be difficult. People with multiple personality disorder may not be aware of the full range of their problem, and they may be unwilling to confront it. Treatment is successful when the person takes control of the different personalities, regarding them all as part of himself (Rosenhan & Seligman, 1989).

Mood Disorders

mood disorders
problems marked primarily by disturbances of one's emotions

depressive disorder
a mood disorder marked by excessive and inappropriate sadness

bipolar disorder
a mood disorder marked by alternating periods of excessive and inappropriate sadness (depression) and periods of excessive and inappropriate elation (mania); formerly called manic-depression

Mood disorders are problems in which disturbances of one's emotions are the primary symptoms. These are among the most common psychological difficulties in the late twentieth century. Indeed, depression appears on the increase in contemporary society, which may seem ironic given the societal emphasis on feeling good. Maybe this isn't so paradoxical after all. If it were easy to feel good, we wouldn't have pop psychology books, bumper stickers, and fortune cookies urging us to be happy.

At any rate, there are two major types of mood disorder. In **depressive disorder,** or depression, the person experiences excessive and inappropriate sadness. In **bipolar disorder** (formerly called manic-depression), periods of depression alternate with periods of excessive and inappropriate elation (mania). There are cases of pure elation, but they are rare. We will therefore limit our attention to depressive disorder and bipolar disorder.

Depressive Disorder.   There are few better examples of the difficulty in drawing a line between normality and abnormality than the case of depression. It refers to a transient mood—an appropriate reaction to disappointment—as well as a chronic disorder. When does "normal" depression become abnormality? There is probably no clear boundary between the two. There are a number of signs and symptoms of depression, and the more that are present, the more severe the disorder.

People display depression with a variety of symptoms, as shown in Table 12.4. A depressed mood is obviously salient in depression, but note that depressive symptoms may involve all psychological spheres.

Suicide as a depressive symptom deserves special mention. Although not all suicidal individuals are depressed, and not all depressed people are suicidal, there is a strong link between depression and suicide in our country. Of the 200,000 or more known suicide attempts each year in the United States, perhaps 80 percent are carried out by seriously depressed individuals. Depression is potentially a lethal disorder that should be taken seriously. Table 12.5 describes some common myths about suicide. (If you want to know more about suicide, in general or in particular, please see your instructor or contact your college health center.)

Here are some epidemiological facts about depression. First, one's chance of becoming depressed enough to warrant a diagnosis and clinical intervention at some period in one's lifetime is now estimated as somewhere between 8 percent and 23 percent. Because of its frequency, depression has been dubbed the common cold of psychopathology (Seligman, 1973). Second, depression occurs much more frequently among women than men, at least twice as much and maybe eight times as much. Numer-

Table 12.4

Symptoms of Depression

Depressed mood (which can be expressed as feeling sad, down, blue, in the dumps, empty, or irritable)

Loss of interest in pleasurable activities

Significant increase *or* decrease in appetite, resulting in weight gain or loss

Increase *or* decrease in sleep

Increase *or* decrease in physical activity, resulting in feelings of restlessness or sluggishness

Fatigue

Self-reproach: a belief that one is worthless, wicked, or stupid

Diminished ability to concentrate or make decisions

Thoughts of death and suicide; suicide plans; suicide attempts

Source: American Psychiatric Association, 1987, p. 222.

ous explanations of the sex difference have been proposed, but none seems fully adequate (Nolen-Hoeksema, 1987). Third, the prevalence of depression among adults is largely independent of social class and race. Fourth, the younger an adult, the more likely he or she is to be depressed.

Let's first take a look at how theorists explain depression in terms of a biological dysfunction. What is the evidence for biological causes? For starters, family studies show that individuals with a depressed biological relative are much more likely to become depressed than those who do not have such a relative. This is not true of individuals with an adoptive relative who is depressed. Also, the bodily symptoms of depression, which occur in pairs, imply that the disorder is biological, as we would expect if one's physical system were somehow out of balance: agitation *or* lethargy, too much sleep *or* too little, weight loss *or* weight gain. Another bit of support for a biological role in depression is that some physical illnesses cause depression. Similarly, some medications produce depression as a side effect. Finally, depression can be successfully treated by a variety of biomedical interventions: drugs, electroconvulsive shock, and aerobic exercise (Chapter 13).

Biomedical theorists posit low levels of neurotransmitters, particularly norepinephrine and serotonin, as the cause of the disorder (Chapter 2). According to these theories, interventions succeed to the degree that they increase the level of these neurotransmitters. Research methods are not yet sophisticated enough to directly measure norepinephrine and serotonin in the brains of depressed individuals, but the indirect evidence is strong. Nevertheless, the other models of abnormality also contribute to our understanding of depression, explaining certain aspects of the disorder more fully than does the biomedical model.

Psychoanalytic theorists view depression in terms of the unconscious. Freud (1917) introduced an influential formulation in his paper "Mourning and Melancholia," in which he contrasted mourning (i.e., grief) with

Table 12.5

Myths about Suicide

1. People who talk about suicide won't do it.
2. Suicide has no warning.
3. Suicide rates are increasing steadily.
4. Only a certain class of people commit suicide.
5. Those in "good circumstances" do not commit suicide.
6. Suicide is explained fully by sociological considerations.
7. The motives of those who commit suicide are easily established.
8. Suicide only occurs among the depressed.
9. All suicides have the same cause.
10. Terminally ill individuals will not commit suicide.
11. Those who attempt suicide are insane.
12. Suicide is inherited.
13. Suicide is related to the weather.
14. Suicide is related to the phase of the moon.
15. When a suicidal individual feels better, the risk of suicide is past.
16. Those under a doctor's care, in or out of a hospital, are not at risk for suicide.
17. Only mental health professionals can prevent suicide.

Source: Pokorny, 1968.

melancholia (i.e., depression). The striking difference is that in grief, people are simply sad, whereas in depression, people are sad *and* believe they are worthless. Why do people have negative beliefs about themselves? Freud suggests we consider the reason why we have negative beliefs about anyone—because we are angry at them. So, Freud proposed that depression is anger turned against the self. This view explains why suicide so frequently accompanies depression. Suicide is murder perpetrated against the self.

The depressive's anger stems from childhood, argues Freud, the period when the child's sense of self is created by internalizing images of his or her parents. If the parents frequently disappoint the child by acting inconsistently, then the child internalizes an ambivalent image. A readiness to be depressed (angry) in the face of disappointment is thereby created. Not all of these dynamics are easy to investigate, but general support for the psychoanalytic model comes from studies showing that childhood losses are particularly common among adult depressives, at least for females (McLeod, 1987), and that disappointments and failures can trigger depressive episodes (Lloyd, 1980).

The cognitive-behavioral approach contributes several theories of depressive disorder. *Reinforcement theories* attribute depression to low levels of reward in someone's environment (Lewinsohn, 1974). This is a simple theory:

not enough goodies → depression

Things become more complicated when you realize that there are two ways by which people can find themselves in an impoverished world. One is to be somewhere that is objectively boring. Second is to lack the skills needed to get reinforcement that potentially exists in a particular setting. If you don't have a can opener, it doesn't matter how many canned goods are stashed in your cupboard. You're still going to starve to death. Ditto for social skills and rewards. If you don't have any social skills, you are not likely to have any friends. Therapy from the reinforcement point of view thus takes two forms as well: either change the person's world so that reinforcement is more plentiful, or impart skills to the person so that he can win reinforcement.

Seligman's (1974, 1975) *learned helplessness theory* proposes that depression is a person's inevitable reaction to uncontrollable events. Just as dogs and rats exposed to uncontrollable shocks become listless, so too do people when they cannot influence events in their lives (Chapter 5). Studies show that uncontrollable events precede depressive episodes (Paykel, 1974).

To strengthen helplessness theory's explanation of individual differences in response to uncontrollable events, Abramson, Seligman, and Teasdale (1978) revised it to include the person's interpretation of the cause of the original events. By this reformulated theory, depression follows uncontrollability to the degree that someone explains the event with causes that are internal ("it's me"), stable ("it's going to last forever"), and global ("it's going to undermine everything I do"). *Explanatory style* refers to the causal explanations that people habitually offer for negative events. Research shows that causal explanations and explanatory style relate to depression as proposed by helplessness theory (Peterson & Seligman, 1984).

A final account of depression is Aaron Beck's (1967, 1976) *cognitive theory.* He contends that depression is not so much a disorder of mood as one of thought: The depressed person thinks about herself, her world, and her future in negative terms. Everything is bleak and grim. Presumably, the depressed individual sees things as worse than they are. Why is this worldview maintained? Why don't events to the contrary challenge depressive beliefs? Beck provides two answers to this.

First, the depressed person is prone to automatic thoughts: unbidden and habitual ways of thinking that continually put her down. Suppose you're at a party, and you see an attractive person that you met a few weeks before. You might walk across the room to strike up a conversation. Then again, automatic thoughts might freeze you midstep.

- He won't remember who I am.
- He's probably waiting for his girlfriend.
- I'll say something stupid.
- Gee, do I look ugly tonight!
- I have nothing to say to him anyway.
- I should have known—he's ignoring me already.
- I hate parties.
- I'm the only one not having fun.
- I'm going to die old and lonely.

And if automatic thoughts like these are not depressing enough, Beck argues that depression is further maintained by errors in logic, slipshod ways of thinking that keep one's self-deprecating beliefs immune to reality. For example, a depressed person selectively attends to negative events while overlooking positive ones. On the way to pick up your Nobel Prize, let us suppose, you get a traffic ticket, and the ticket is all that you can think about for the rest of the week! Or a depressed person may overly personalize the petty hassles of everyday life. Waiting in a slow checkout line at the grocery store is proof positive that *you* are a loser, for picking this time to go shopping, for choosing that particular line, for offending the cashier, for living and breathing and needing to eat.

Beck's cognitive theory is influential because it accurately captures the way depressed people think and because it gives rise to an effective treatment of depression: **cognitive therapy.** In this approach, the therapist works with the depressed client to challenge his negative beliefs. These must first be made explicit, because automatic thoughts can be so ingrained that he pays little attention to them, only to their depressing consequences. Once on center, he can compare the automatic thoughts against the evidence and presumably find little justification.

Not that many decades ago, the outlook for depression was as bleak as the disorder itself. Little could be done for the depressive except to keep him from killing himself until his depression passed, usually (but not always) in three to six months. But now there's good news. Many successful treatments have been developed: antidepressant medication, electroconvulsive shock, social skills training, and talking therapies—notably Beck's approach.

Bipolar Disorder. In bipolar disorder, depressed episodes alternate with manic episodes. We already know the signs of depression. How about **mania**? In many ways, it is just the opposite of depression, as the symptoms listed in Table 12.6 show. Bipolar disorder affects about 1 percent of the population, with its onset usually between the ages of twenty and thirty.

cognitive therapy

treatment for depression developed by Aaron Beck that challenges one's negative beliefs about oneself

mania

excessive and inappropriate elation, an expansive mood, inflated self-esteem, talkativeness, increased activity, and agitation

Table 12.6

Symptoms of Mania

Elevated, expansive, or irritable mood

Inflated self-esteem

Decreased need for sleep

Much more talkative than usual

Racing thoughts

Distractibility

Increased activity and agitation

Excessive involvement in pleasurable but risky activities, such as buying sprees, sexual indiscretions, and foolish business investments

Impairment in social or occupational functioning

Source: American Psychiatric Association, 1987, p. 217.

Women seem to outnumber men, but the sex difference is not nearly as pronounced as it is for depressive disorder.

Recent research shows that bipolar disorder is very much a biological phenomenon. Psychologists have long known that the problem runs in families, which suggests a genetic predisposition but does not prove it. However, two research groups—one working with extended families in Pennsylvania and the other with extended families in Jerusalem—have definitively linked specific chromosomes to bipolar depression, by showing that the disorder co-occurs with inherited physical conditions such as color-blindness (Lyon & Gorner, 1987). These are important findings, supporting the biomedical model of abnormality as strongly as any research since Krafft-Ebing's work (p. 496) of long ago. Although a number of psychopathologies appear to be genetically predisposed, these studies of bipolar depression are the first to zero in on the actual chromosomes involved.

There are some complications here. First, the Pennsylvania research group and the Jerusalem research group found different chromosomes involved in bipolar depression. This must mean that bipolar disorder, although genetically based, cannot be located on a single gene. Second, not everyone at risk for bipolar depression (because of the chromosome) ends up with the disorder. About 60 percent do. Thus additional factors—presumably environmental conditions—must combine with genetic inheritance to produce bipolar depression. Third, along the same lines, stressful life events may precipitate particular depressive or manic episodes. A diathesis-stress conception is apparently demanded, although no theorist has yet fleshed out how biological predispositions interact with environmental events to produce bipolar disorder.

The treatment of choice for bipolar disorder is *lithium*—a naturally occurring salt that dampens a person's mood. The physical mechanism of lithium is unclear, but its effects are not. It stabilizes the bipolar individual, preventing manic *and* depressive episodes. It does not cure bipolar disorder in the sense that penicillin cures pneumonia. Rather, lithium treats the symptoms, and a person must stay on lithium even when feeling and acting normally. Getting people to comply with this treatment can sometimes be a problem, though. Lithium has undesirable side effects, including kidney and liver damage, dry mouth, and skin irritation.

Eating Disorders

anorexia nervosa
an eating disorder characterized by a deliberate restriction of the intake of calories, extreme weight loss, and a distorted body image

Another category of disorders recently on the increase in our society is the eating disorders, of which two are particularly well known. **Anorexia nervosa** refers to a problem in which a deliberate restriction of calories results in extreme weight loss. People with anorexia also have a distorted image of their own body size and shape. They believe they look fat, even as they are starving to death. Anorexia leads to serious physical problems associated with malnutrition, and it proves fatal in as many as 18 percent of cases.

The onset of anorexia is usually during adolescence, and in the overwhelming majority of cases—about 95 percent—its victims are females. Anorexia is more common among individuals in the middle and upper socioeconomic classes than among individuals in the lower class. Esti-

The death of pop music star Karen Carpenter focused national attention on eating disorders such as anexoria nervosa.

mates of the prevalence among teenage females range from .1 to 1 percent.

No single answer as to the causes of anorexia is generally agreed upon. Biomedical theorists speculate about dysfunctions of the hypothalamus. Psychoanalytic theorists speculate that the anorexic individual is afraid of sexuality, and in starving herself, alters her body so that she ends up looking prepubescent. Cognitive-behavioral theorists wonder about the role played by the family in anorexia. Perhaps anorexia involves a struggle for control between parents and their child, one with life and death consequences. All of these possible explanations must be considered in conjunction with our cultural preoccupation with being thin.

Treatment of anorexia is difficult, in large part because the disorder involves the insistence that nothing is wrong (Crisp, 1980). In cases of extreme weight loss, aggressive medical intervention is demanded to restore the person's nutritional state to normal. This may take the form of involuntary hospitalization and forced feeding. Behavior modification is thought to be helpful in the treatment of anorexia. So too is family therapy.

Bulimia is defined as an alteration between binging (ingesting thousands of calories of food in a short period of time) and purging (ridding oneself of these calories through vomiting, taking laxatives, fasting, or exercising). The person with bulimia is usually of normal weight, but is nonetheless preoccupied with the fear of becoming fat. Although not as dangerous as anorexia, bulimia does have a variety of negative consequences. People who frequently vomit may erode their teeth (because digestive juices from their stomach attack tooth enamel), suffer dehydration, and create electrolyte imbalance. Bulimia is often accompanied by depression, and the sheer amount of time needed to binge and purge means that the person has limited time for other activities.

The typical individual with bulimia is a female from the middle or upper class, as with anorexia. Onset is often in the early twenties. Estimates of the prevalence of bulimia vary greatly, depending on the particular criteria used to define its presence (Schotte & Stunkard, 1987). So, some studies report that almost 20 percent of college women are bulimic, while other studies give a figure as low as 1 percent. Regardless, bulimia is probably more common than anorexia, and is certainly on the rise.

bulimia
an eating disorder in which someone alternates between binging and purging

There is no generally agreed upon cause of bulimia, nor have effective treatments been developed. Because of its association with depression, some therapists treat bulimia with the various strategies available for helping people with depressive disorder. Also, only tentative support for behavior modification and family therapy has been reported (Schlesier-Stropp, 1984).

Substance Use Disorders

Controversy surrounds almost all attempts to explain the cause of a particular psychological disorder. An important exception is disorders stemming from a physical dysfunction of the brain brought about by tumors, lesions, infections, or toxins. There are numerous such problems, reflecting the range of possible causes of brain dysfunction. In Chapter 10, for instance, we discussed Alzheimer's disease, which results in psychological consequences such as dementia.

Other types of disorders related to brain dysfunction are linked to use of psychoactive drugs. DSM-III-R distinguishes between *psychoactive substance-induced organic mental disorders,* the characteristic symptoms of intoxication or withdrawal from drugs, and *psychoactive substance use disorders,* the problems that reflect and result from the loss of control over drug use and the continuation of use despite adverse consequences. Obviously, these two classes of problems involving psychoactive substances go hand in hand, so let us discuss them together.

Definition of Substance Abuse.   As emphasized in Chapter 4, ours is a drug-using and drug-abusing society. Substance use and abuse illustrate all of the issues raised earlier in the chapter. In particular, definition is problematic. When does drug or alcohol use become abuse? By all accounts, cases of substance use fall along a continuum. People are not either completely abstinent or hopelessly addicted, whether the drug is alcohol, tobacco, cocaine, or PCP. Some people use none, some use a lot, and many fall in between.

DSM-III-R regards substance use as abnormal when a person becomes dependent on the substance. The essential feature of **psychoactive substance dependence,** to use the technical term, is "a cluster of cognitive, behavioral, and physiological symptoms that indicate that the person has impaired control . . . and continues use . . . despite adverse consequences" (American Psychiatric Association, 1987, p. 166). Dependence may include the physiological signs of *tolerance,* meaning the person needs increasing amounts of the substance to produce the same psychological effects, or *withdrawal,* during which the person experiences the cessation of substance use as highly aversive and craves the substance. However, these signs are not critical to the definition. Rather, dependence is inferred from actions such as those listed in Table 12.7.

psychoactive substance dependence
a cluster of cognitive, behavioral, and physiological symptoms that indicate impaired control over drug use

---

Table 12.7
Signs of Substance Dependence

A person is dependent on a psychoactive substance to the degree that he or she shows
a persistent desire for the substance
an inability to control the use of the substance, as when "just one drink" leads to an all-night bender
an inability to cut down or cease substance use
an inordinate amount of time and energy devoted to pursuit of the substance
intoxication or withdrawal in the face of social or work obligations
a curtailing of other activities in order to use drugs
continued use of the substance despite knowledge of its harmful effects

Source: American Psychiatric Association, 1987, pp. 167–168.

Explanations of Substance Abuse.   How can we explain substance abuse? Here are brief sketches of the explanations suggested by each of the different models of abnormality. A biomedical explanation focuses on a person's bodily processes, interpreting substance abuse as an illness and treating it with physical means, such as *detoxification*—letting the substance clear the person's body—and the administration of *antagonists*—drugs that block the effect of the abused substance.

Psychoanalysts, in contrast, view substance abuse as a symptom of some underlying problem. Indeed, the substance one abuses is thought to symbolize the particular conflict causing the abuse. Alcoholics, for example, presumably have a problem with excessive neediness, stemming from fixations at the oral stage. They therefore "suck down" one drink after another. Treatment consists of having the substance dependent person achieve insight into his or her motives for drug abuse.

Finally, a cognitive-behavioral explanation of substance abuse is that it is something that a person learns to do because of reinforcement. Drugs make a person feel good, either because of their direct chemical effects or because their use leads to social approval. Alcohol, for instance, may reduce someone's feelings of anxiety, at least in the short run. Bars provide an opportunity to meet and interact with other people. Treatment from a cognitive-behavioral perspective would encourage the person to learn other ways of behaving in order to gain such rewards.

We know very little about the relative merits of these viewpoints as they apply to substance dependence, for several reasons. First, many of the drugs on which people become dependent are illegal. Researchers do not have an open door to study those who use them. The notable exception, of course, is alcohol, which we will soon discuss in detail. Second, even when researchers do gain access to drug dependent subjects, it is usually after the problem has developed. Reconstructing the antecedents of substance abuse is difficult, for the same reasons that any retrospective research is difficult. And it's compounded by the delirium, dementia, delusions, and hallucinations produced by prolonged use. A researcher is hard pressed to understand the causes of substance abuse by interviewing someone who has done so much damage to his brain over the years that a simple conversation is virtually impossible.

Alcohol Abuse.   The substance that we know the most about is alcohol. Alcohol is legal in most places in the United States, it is relatively inexpensive compared to other drugs, and it is accepted and even encouraged in many circles. These factors conspire to make alcohol the number one drug problem in the United States, if not the entire world. Indeed, some believe that the competition between the United States and the Soviet Union will be resolved not in the Middle East, not in Eastern Europe, not in outer space, but in the livers of our respective citizens. In both nations, alcohol abuse takes an incredible toll on well-being, productivity, and resources.

Let's take a look at what happens when we drink alcohol. It's absorbed mainly through the small intestine. Once in the blood, it is metabolized: broken down into water and carbon dioxide. The rate of alcohol metabolism is fixed, and can readily be exceeded by one's rate of ingestion, which means that alcohol circulates in our blood until it can be broken down.

Hence, one's *blood alcohol content* (*BAC*) is a more exact index of the degree of intoxication than the amount of alcohol consumed. Most states define legal intoxication as a BAC of .10 percent or higher—roughly four drinks in an hour—although one's body size determines the precise number. There is essentially the same amount of alcohol in a can of beer, a glass of wine, and a cocktail! If you drink them at the same rate, all will have the exact same effect on you.

Alcohol depresses the functioning of the nervous system, but because it initially affects brain centers that are inhibitory, people may experience alcohol intoxication as stimulating (Chapter 2). As time passes and more alcohol is consumed and metabolized, the person begins to have difficulty thinking, speaking, walking, and/or seeing. He or she might become withdrawn and sullen. In larger amounts, alcohol induces sleep. In still larger amounts, coma and death may follow.

The long-term effects of alcohol are ubiquitous. A person comes to tolerate alcohol and to depend on it. Lesions in the brain develop, producing dementia and amnesia. Risk of heart failure increases. Hypertension is common, as is capillary rupture (which is why chronic alcohol abusers have red noses). Alcohol contains calories but no nutrients, and so an abuser is malnourished because he or she doesn't want food. Liver tissue is destroyed as cirrhosis develops. Curtailing alcohol ingestion may bring on seizure. In Chapter 9, we discussed how alcohol use during pregnancy can harm the developing fetus.

When does alcohol use become alcohol abuse? Remember the discussion concerning the fuzziness inherent in defining abnormality with which this chapter began. You may read assertions that two drinks per day is normal, and more than two drinks is abnormal. Or that drinking with other people is all right, whereas drinking alone signifies a problem. Such "rules" are too simple, and alcohol use slides into alcohol abuse in no precisely defined manner. However, the more ways in which people show dependence on alcohol (see Table 12.7), the more confidently we can say that they are alcohol abusers.

Cases of severe alcohol abuse occur and are easily identified, thus the question arises: Why do people do this to themselves? Let's turn to research reported by psychiatrist George Vaillant (1983) in his book *The Natural History of Alcoholism*. Vaillant conducted a virtually unprecedented investigation: a prospective study of alcohol use and abuse among more than 600 men. He started with research subjects before they had any problems with alcohol, and he followed them through time to see how and why alcohol abuse developed. Note the methodological improvement represented here, in comparison to the typical retrospective study, which starts with a group of alcohol abusers and works backward to uncover possible causes.

Vaillant's findings call into question the ability of any given model of abnormality to fully explain the development of alcohol abuse. For starters, he found that particular people may go in and out of the "abuse" category, not what we would expect if alcoholism is a disease with an insidious progression. He also found that problems and conflicts follow alcohol abuse more frequently than they precede it, not what we would expect if alcoholism is a symptom of underlying difficulties. And he found that alcohol abusers are anxious and estranged, not what we would expect if alcohol use is reinforcing.

Vaillant calls for an integrated model to explain alcohol abuse. He quotes a Japanese proverb:

First the man takes a drink;
Then the drink takes a drink;
And finally the drink takes the man.

In other words, at different stages in alcohol use/abuse, different factors intervene. Taken together, the popular models of abnormality suggest the range of factors that must be included in an explanation. Obviously alcohol abuse involves the body, and so the biomedical model has a role in explaining it. Obviously the alcohol user has motives and problems, and so the psychoanalytic model has a place. And obviously the person who drinks is affected by the immediate environment, including other people, and so the cognitive-behavioral model must be heeded as well.

A final aspect of Vaillant's findings deserves a special note: *None of the conventional treatments for alcohol abuse work.* Granted that a person has developed a drinking problem at Time One, whether he still has the problem at Time Two is completely unrelated to whether or not he has received treatment suggested by the biomedical model, the psychoanalytic model, and/or the cognitive-behavioral model. This conclusion raises hackles among mental health professionals. Things become even more provocative when Vaillant concludes that there is a "treatment" that is effective: Alcoholics Anonymous.

Alcoholics Anonymous (AA) is a self-help group founded over 50 years ago by recovering alcohol abusers. AA chapters are found in most cities in the United States and in 100 other countries. They hold frequent meetings, at which members tell their stories and hear the stories of others. AA's official stance is that members remain alcoholics for life, even if they haven't had a drink in years. Its goal is to prevent a relapse, and so members seek out meetings and each other when they are tempted to drink.

Why is AA effective? It requires a lifetime commitment and thus a lifestyle change. And it provides its members with an explicit belief system (see Table 12.8) and a social group with which to commune. AA is not for everyone, and early dropout rates can approach 80 percent (e.g., Edwards,

Alcoholics Anonymous (AA)
a self-help group for recovering alcoholics

Using the approach pioneered by Alcoholics Anonymous, twelve-step programs have become an increasingly popular means of arresting self-destructive behavior.

Table 12.8

The Twelve Steps of Alcoholics Anonymous

1. We admitted that we were powerless over alcohol . . . that our lives had become unmanageable.

2. Came to believe that a Power greater than ourselves could restore us to sanity.

3. Made a decision to turn our will and our lives over to the care of God as we understood him.

4. Made a searching and fearless moral inventory of ourselves.

5. Admitted to God, to ourselves, and to another human being the exact nature of our wrongs.

6. Were entirely ready to have God remove all these defects of character.

7. Humbly asked Him to remove our shortcomings.

8. Made a list of all persons we had harmed and became willing to make amends to them all.

9. Made direct amends to such people wherever possible, except when to do so would injure them or others.

10. Continued to take personal inventory and when we were wrong, promptly admitted it.

11. Sought through prayer and meditation to improve our conscious contact with God as we understood Him, praying only for a knowledge of His will for us and the power to carry that out.

12. Having had a spiritual awakening as the result of these steps, we tried to carry this message to alcoholics, and to practice these principles in all our affairs.

The Twelve Steps are reprinted and adapted with permission of Alcoholics Anonymous World Services, Inc. Permission to reprint and adapt the Twelve Steps does not mean that AA has reviewed or approved the content of this publication, nor that AA agrees with the views expressed herein. AA is a program of recovery from alcoholism. Use of the Twelve Steps in connection with programs and activities which are patterned after AA but which address other problems does not imply otherwise.

Hensman, Hawker, & Williamson, 1967). Therefore, Vaillant's conclusions about the effectiveness of AA must be taken with a grain of salt. Still, for those people who stay with the AA program, alcohol abuse ceases.

Schizophrenia

Schizophrenia seems to be an almost perfect example of psychological abnormality. However, good examples need not mean lack of controversy, and no disorder described in this chapter is as controversial as schizophrenia. Before we get into the controversy, though, let's look at the DSM-III-R picture of **schizophrenia.** The presence of psychotic symptoms is essential for diagnosis: that is, loss of contact with reality, as shown by delusions, hallucinations, inappropriate emotions, and unusual thinking. The person's social or occupational functioning must also be impaired.

DSM-III-R further proposes a subclassification of schizophrenia. Someone satisfying the general criteria for schizophrenia who also shows

schizophrenia
a disorder characterized by psychotic symptoms such as delusions, hallucinations, inappropriate emotions, and unusual thinking, and accompanied by impaired social or occupational functioning

bizarre motor movements is described as *catatonic*. A schizophrenic patient who has complicated delusions of persecution and/or grandiosity is said to be *paranoid*. If someone with schizophrenia is frequently incoherent and shows inappropriate emotions such as constant giggling, he or she is classified as *disorganized*. A schizophrenic individual who fits none of these categories is described as *undifferentiated*. Finally, the term *residual* schizophrenia is used to describe individuals who once warranted a diagnosis of schizophrenia, do not do so at the present time, yet still show peculiarities in their behavior.

Let's take a close look at some of the symptoms of schizophrenia. **Delusions** are not simply eccentric beliefs, but bizarre and unsettling ideas that are completely implausible. Someone might believe that his thoughts are being stolen from his head, that the government has hidden a nuclear device in his backyard, or that he is six million years old. **Hallucinations** are sensations and perceptions with no basis in reality. They most frequently are auditory, usually voices conveying insults and threats. For example, a patient with whom I worked had been a cook in the army and was tormented by a voice that urged him to jump into the 50-gallon vat of scalding soup that he prepared every evening. When he finally attempted to follow these directions, he was hospitalized.

When emotional disturbance is present in schizophrenia, it usually takes the form of *flat affect*. This means that the person shows no signs of emotion, speaks in a monotone, and has an immobile face. Sometimes the individual will say that she no longer has any feelings. And sometimes her emotions are expressed, but in a completely inappropriate manner. Another patient I knew was told that his mother died, and hearing that, he gave a hearty laugh.

Schizophrenia is often described as a thought disorder, because the person's style of thinking is abnormal. Quite common are abrupt shifts from one topic to another, with only the wispiest of transitions. A person's speech may be impoverished, conveying no information despite many words. Someone may make up her own words, and these are termed *neologisms* (Lehmann, 1980, p. 1161):

> A schizophrenic woman who had been hospitalized for several years kept repeating, in an otherwise quite rational conversation, the word "polamolalittersjitterstittersleelitla." Her psychiatrist asked her to spell it out, and she then proceeded to explain to him the meaning of the various components, which she insisted were to be used as one word. "Polamolalitters" was intended to recall the disease poliomyelitis. . . . The component "litters" stood for untidiness and messiness, the way she felt inside. . . . [and so on]

By the way, this example contains another sign of schizophrenic thought disorder—*clang associations,* or the stringing together of words that sound alike (*litters, jitters, titters*).

Schizophrenia certainly refers to strange ways of behaving. So where's the controversy? No one disagrees that diagnosticians are on to something abnormal when they apply the label of schizophrenia. Indeed, symptoms like those just described occur in about 1 percent of people in almost all cultures. The controversy revolves around how to conceive schizophrenic behaviors. Should they be viewed as a physical illness, or are they better regarded as problems in living brought about by environmental stress

delusions
bizarre and unsettling beliefs that others do not find plausible

hallucinations
sensations and perceptions with no basis in reality

Scientists who favor a biological explanation of schizophrenia cite the case of the Genain quadruplets, all of whom have suffered from schizophrenic disorders.

and trauma? This is not an idle debate, because prevention and treatment necessarily take different forms depending on what schizophrenia "really" is.

Numerous theorists disagree vehemently with the notion that schizophrenia is a discrete disease, suggesting instead that it is

- a myth (Szasz, 1961)
- a moral verdict (Sarbin & Mancuso, 1980)
- a product of society (Scheff, 1966)
- a role forced upon an individual (Goffman, 1961)
- a sane reaction to an insane world (Laing, 1967)

These theorists criticize those who regard schizophrenia as a disease for overlooking the social context in which schizophrenia occurs and the psychological meaning of symptoms. Laing (1965), in particular, stresses that even the most bizarre "symptoms" mean something to the schizophrenic individual. In contrast, sore throats and runny noses do not contain levels of meaning for the individual with a cold.

Let's review the evidence that bears on this debate. When researchers argue that schizophrenia is a biologically based illness, they point to

- family and twin studies showing that schizophrenia tends to be inherited; for instance, if one identical twin is diagnosed schizophrenic, odds are 40 percent that the other twin also carries the diagnosis; concordance is much lower for fraternal twins, about 10 percent (Gottesman & Shields, 1972)
- PET scans (discussed in Chapter 2) comparing the brains of schizophrenic individuals with the brains of normal individuals that show differences in activity (see Figure 12.5)
- the fact that chronic amphetamine use can produce a syndrome indistinguishable from "naturally occurring" schizophrenia
- the successful treatment of schizophrenic symptoms with drugs such as Thorazine and Haldol
- an interesting relationship between Parkinson's disease (known to be biological) and schizophrenia: the drugs respectively used to treat each disorder produce as side effects symptoms like that of the other disorder

dopamine hypothesis
an explanation of schizophrenia proposing that excess amounts of the neurotransmitter dopamine cause this disorder

A popular explanation of findings like these is that schizophrenia results from an excess of the neurotransmitter dopamine (Chapter 2). The so-called **dopamine hypothesis** makes sense of the findings just de-

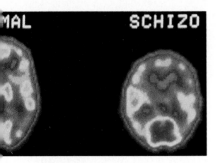

Figure 12.5
PET Scan of a Schizophrenic's Brain. Different colors show different levels of brain activity. Note that the schizophrenic's brain—on the right—shows a different pattern of activity than the normal individual's brain—on the left—which suggests a biological basis for schizophrenia.

double-bind hypothesis
a hypothesis proposing that schizophrenia is created when families present their children with unresolvable conflicts

scribed (Matthysse, 1977). Chronic amphetamine use, for example, is thought to increase levels of dopamine in one's brain. Thorazine and Haldol work by decreasing levels of dopamine. Parkinson's disease is known to be characterized by insufficient dopamine, implying that schizophrenia is marked by excessive dopamine. And recent studies that examined the brains of schizophrenic patients following death found an increased number of dopamine receptors, again supporting the dopamine hypothesis (Mackay, 1980).

On the other hand, when researchers argue that schizophrenia is a socially produced phenomenon, they point to

- the lack of perfect correlation in twin studies of schizophrenia
- the fact that traumatic events may precipitate a schizophrenic episode
- the preponderance of schizophrenia among members of the lower class
- findings that family dynamics influence the course of schizophrenia

These various findings can be explained by theorizing that schizophrenia is an extreme and maladaptive response to a confusing and contradictory world.

Just such an explanation of schizophrenia is the **double-bind hypothesis** of Bateson, Jackson, Haley, and Weakland (1956). Parents sometimes place their children in a no-win situation from which they cannot escape. Consider this scenario. A father says to his child, "Come give me a kiss, Junior." When the child approaches, his father looks horrified. "Ugh, your hands are so dirty. Are you going to touch me with those hands?" So the child retreats, and the father then asks, "What about my kiss?" According to the double-bind hypothesis, when such interactions take place repeatedly, schizophrenia results. Schizophrenia may be the one way a child can meet such contradictory demands, by making his behavior fully as bizarre as the world where he lives. The problem with the double-bind hypothesis and similar theories is that many schizophrenic individuals are not raised in pathological families. And inconsistent parents do not always produce schizophrenic children (Anthony & Cohler, 1987). Still, stress and contradiction cannot be dismissed as causes of schizophrenia.

Although the debate concerning the nature of schizophrenia still rages in some quarters, there is a possible intermediate position: the diathesis-stress approach that was introduced earlier in the chapter (p. 493). This can accommodate the evidence that schizophrenia is a biological disorder as well as the evidence that it is a social disorder. Suppose that someone inherits a tendency to produce excess dopamine. Suppose that under stress, this tendency becomes an actuality. The excess dopamine affects the person's perceptual experience, producing understandably great anxiety. In response to unsettling experiences, the person develops bizarre beliefs, unusual emotions, and idiosyncratic ways of thinking. While all of this is going on, the demands of everyday life are necessarily neglected.

This is just one possible chain of events that fits the evidence. No one has mapped out the natural history of schizophrenia in this (or any) specific way. The point is merely to show that a diathesis-stress conception is a potentially powerful way of integrating what we know about schizophrenia.

How is schizophrenia treated? In the 1950s, it was discovered that particular drugs—called *neuroleptics*—effectively curtail the flagrant symptoms of schizophrenia. These drugs created a major revolution in the mental health professions, because the number of hospitalized schizophrenics was reduced by almost 75 percent in the two decades following their introduction. Despite this success in reducing the number and length of psychiatric hospitalizations for schizophrenia, neuroleptics leave much to be desired.

First, neuroleptics only treat the so-called *positive symptoms* of schizophrenia: the delusions and hallucinations that DSM-III-R explicitly lists as hallmarks of this disorder. Neuroleptics do not affect the *negative symptoms,* the psychological deficiencies that also play a part. When we examine this disorder from the inside, from the viewpoint of the schizophrenic individual, we find someone who feels unreal, uncommitted, empty, depressed, and evil (Bernheim & Lewine, 1979). Neuroleptics don't change these feelings in the least.

Second, the drugs currently available produce a host of aversive side effects, including oversedation, decreased spontaneity, motor restlessness, involuntary movements of the head and mouth, susceptibility to sunburn, constipation, low blood pressure, jaundice, and impotence. As you can imagine, compliance with the medication is a continual problem.

What can we do for individuals with schizophrenia? Most therapists agree that medication is an important part of their treatment but that it must be supplemented with additional interventions. Individual therapy, family therapy, and group therapy are all used in conjunction with neuroleptics. We can be cautiously optimistic. At one time, it was believed that someone who experienced an episode of schizophrenia inevitably worsened. This conclusion is no longer justified. Some individuals continue to be troubled throughout their lives, but others get on with things quite satisfactorily, putting schizophrenia behind them.

Personality Disorders

personality disorders
pervasive styles of behaving that can both exacerbate a clinical syndrome and create difficulties in their own right

Personality disorders are pervasive styles of behaving that exacerbate the sorts of disorders described in this chapter while also creating difficulties in their own right (p. 499). DSM-III-R distinguishes eleven different personality disorders, and these are briefly described in Table 12.9.

These eleven disorders are sometimes classified into three larger groups or clusters (Millon, 1981). Cluster One consists of paranoid, schizoid, and schizotypal disorders—styles of behaving that are odd or eccentric. Cluster Two includes antisocial, borderline, histrionic, and narcissistic disorders. People with these personality disorders are dramatic, erratic, and/or emotional. Finally, Cluster Three encompasses disorders involving anxiety and timidity: avoidant, dependent, obsessive-compulsive, and passive-aggressive personality disorders.

Personality disorders stir up considerable debate, particularly among those psychologists who question the very notion of personality types. If people's characteristic behavior is very much determined by the situation in which they find themselves, then it is highly misleading to regard someone's "personality" as disordered. Problems should be considered in terms of the person's environment.

Not surprisingly, then, many of the personality disorders are not reliably diagnosed. And the common assumption that certain personality disorders make certain clinical syndromes more likely is not always

Table 12.9
DSM-III-R Personality Disorders

Type	Description
Paranoid	Pervasive tendency to interpret the actions of people as threatening
Schizoid	Pervasive tendency to be indifferent to social relationships and to show restricted emotions
Schizotypal	Pervasive tendency to be peculiar in thoughts, appearance, and behavior and to be socially inept
Antisocial	Pervasive tendency to act irresponsibly toward others: lying, cheating, stealing, fighting, and so on
Borderline	Pervasive tendency to be erratic in mood, self-image, and social relationships
Histrionic	Pervasive tendency to seek attention and express excessive emotion
Narcissistic	Pervasive tendency to be grandiose
Avoidant	Pervasive tendency to feel discomfort in the presence of others, to fear evaluation, and to be timid
Dependent	Pervasive tendency to depend on others to make decisions
Obsessive-compulsive	Pervasive tendency to be perfectionistic and inflexible
Passive-aggressive	Pervasive tendency to resist social demands by acting passively in response to them

Reprinted with permission from the *Diagnostic and Statistical Manual of Mental Disorders, Third Edition, Revised.* Copyright © 1987 American Psychiatric Association.

supported by research. Obsessive-compulsive personality disorder, for instance, proves *not* to be a risk factor for obsessive-compulsive disorder (Rachman & Hodgson, 1980).

On the other hand, particular personality disorders—notably antisocial personality disorder—can be reliably diagnosed, and have clear causes and consequences. The general concept of personality disorders can be quite useful, reminding us that people's problems may reside in their very style of life. In treating one's problems, a therapist must look beyond specific symptoms to the person experiencing the symptoms.

We have completed our discussion of the major psychological disorders. In the next chapter, we will take a detailed look at what psychologists do to help people who suffer from such problems. The models of psychopathology remain important, because treatment of psychological difficulties is never theoretically neutral. And keep in mind how the models derive from views of human nature such as those presented in Chapter 11. It is not simply a coincidence that so many of the influential personality theorists were also clinicians: Freud, Adler, Jung, Kelly, and Rogers, to name just a few.

Summary

Topics of Concern

- Psychological abnormality is difficult to define precisely. One possible definition regards abnormality as a fuzzy category characterized by such attributes as suffering, maladaptiveness, loss of control, and unconventionality.
- At the present time, abnormality is explained with three competing sets of theories: the biomedical model, which sees people as physical systems susceptible to breakdown or malfunction; the psychoanalytic model, which sees people as energy systems at risk for overload or short circuit; and the cognitive-behavioral model, which sees people as information-processing systems prone to ignorance or error.

A Brief History of Abnormality

- Throughout history, abnormality has been viewed from three different vantage points, in terms of supernatural, illness, and psychological considerations.
- Each of these perspectives makes certain assumptions about the causes and treatments for particular problems.
- Although the supernatural perspective no longer has a legitimate place, the illness and psychological perspectives are both alive and well today.

Diagnosing Abnormality

- Diagnosis is the placement of a person into a category according to his or her problems. The American Psychiatric Association's DSM-III-R is currently popular as a diagnostic scheme. It describes people's problems in terms of five areas: acute disorders; underlying personality styles that exacerbate these disorders or create problems in their own right; physical disorders; severity of stressors in the environment; and the level of highest functioning in the past.
- Diagnosis is controversial, and reasons for and against it can be cited.
- On the positive side, diagnosis can facilitate communication, provide clues about the presumed cause of a disorder, allow educated pre-dictions about the likely outcomes of a disorder, and suggest effective forms of treatment.
- On the negative side, diagnosis is never theoretically neutral; it presupposes a particular model of abnormality, and this can be limiting. Also, traditional diagnosis assumes discontinuity between abnormality and normality. The reliability of diagnosis is a continuing problem, particularly because diagnostic labels may take on a life of their own and create problems for individuals above and beyond any actual difficulties they had prior to receiving a label.
- Some theorists try to explain the particular disorders that exist in terms of an overall system of disorders, whereas others believe that no overall structure exists.

Types of Disorders

- Different problems demand different models of abnormality to explain them. In some cases, no single model suffices.
- The fear and anxiety disorders are problems characterized by excessive apprehension and avoidance: phobia, post-traumatic stress disorder, generalized anxiety disorder, and obsessive-compulsive disorder.
- Somatoform disorders are physical symptoms with no physical cause, such as conversion disorder or hypochondriasis.
- Dissociative disorders include psychogenic amnesia, psychogenic fugue, and multiple personality disorder.
- Mood disorders are marked by excessive and inappropriate emotions. In depressive disorder, sadness predominates, whereas in bipolar disorder, periods of sadness alternate with periods of elation.
- Substance use disorders are difficulties in everyday life brought about by the ingestion of psychoactive drugs.
- Schizophrenia is a thought disorder characterized by delusions, hallucinations, unusual styles of thinking, and deteriorated functioning.
- Finally, personality disorders are pervasive styles of behaving that exacerbate other types of disorders while creating problems in their own right.

Important Terms and Names

What follows is a list of the core terms and names for this chapter. Your instructor may emphasize other terms as well. Throughout the chapter, glossary terms appear in **boldface** type. They are defined in the text, and each term, along with its definition, is repeated in the margin.

Topics of Concern

abnormal psychology/490
abnormality/491
biomedical model/491
psychoanalytic model/492
cognitive-behavioral
    model/492
diathesis-stress model/
    493

David Rosenhan/490
Thomas Szasz/492

A Brief History of Abnormality

supernatural era/494
illness era/495
psychological era/496

William Krafft-Ebing/496

Diagnosing Abnormality

diagnosis/498
DSM-III-R/498
clinical syndrome/499
psychotic disorder/502
neurotic disorder/502

Types of Disorders

fear disorder/503
anxiety disorder/503
phobia/505
post-traumatic stress
    disorder/507
generalized anxiety
    disorder/508
panic disorder/509
agoraphobia/509
obsessive-compulsive
    disorder/510
somatoform disorder/511
conversion disorder/511
hypochondriasis/512
dissociative disorder/513
psychogenic amnesia/513
psychogenic fugue/514
multiple personality
    disorder/514
depressive disorder/515
bipolar disorder/515
anorexia nervosa/520
bulimia/521
organic mental syn-
    drome/522
organic disorder/522
psychoactive substance
    dependence/522
schizophrenia/526
personality disorder/530

George Vaillant/524
Aaron Beck/518

Review Questions

1. Rosenhan's "pseudopatient" study is important because it shows how difficult it may be to recognize
   a. brain damage.
   b. medical illness.
   c. racism.
   d. sanity.
   In Rosenhan's study, the sanity of perfectly normal individuals was not detected once they had been admitted to mental hospitals./490

2. Which model of abnormality views people as energy systems?
   a. biomedical
   b. psychoanalytic
   c. cognitive-behavioral
   d. all of the above
   e. none of the above
   The psychoanalytic model assumes that people are energy systems and that their problems can be described in terms of the tying up of psychic energy in particular symptoms./491

3. The diathesis-stress model explains abnormality in terms of a combination of _____ and _____ factors.
   a. biological; environmental
   b. conscious; unconscious
   c. innate; learned
   d. rational; irrational
   The diathesis-stress model proposes that abnormality results from a biological weakness (diathesis) coupled with environmental events (stress)./493

4. DSM-III-R describes people in _____ different domains called axes.
   a. two
   b. three
   c. five
   d. seven
   e. ten
   DSM-III-R distinguishes five different axes./498

5. The difference between fear and anxiety disorders lies in the specific nature of people's
   a. behavior.
   b. expectations.
   c. feelings.
   d. physiology.
   In both fear and anxiety disorders, people expect harm. However, in fear disorders, these expectations are specific, whereas in anxiety disorders, they are more diffuse./503

6. Simple phobias are best treated in terms of the _____ model of abnormality.
   a. biomedical
   b. psychoanalytic
   c. cognitive-behavioral
   d. all of the above
   e. none of the above
   Although the causes of simple phobias are still debated, there is no doubt that behavior modification provides the most satisfactory treatment of these problems./507

7. Recent research suggests that the _____ model of abnormality can help explain panic disorders.
   a. biomedical
   b. psychoanalytic
   c. cognitive-behavioral
   d. a and b
   e. a and c
   Recent research implicates both biological and cognitive factors in the etiology of panic disorder./510

8. The content of obsessive-compulsive disorders is readily explained by the _____ model.
   a. biomedical
   b. psychoanalytic
   c. cognitive-behavioral
   d. all of the above
   e. none of the above
   The content of obsessive-compulsive disorders is usually limited to only a few themes, which are fully explained in psychoanalytic terms./511

9. The most common form of abnormality is
   a. bipolar disorder.
   b. depressive disorder.
   c. psychogenic fugue.
   d. schizophrenia.
   e. simple phobia.
   Depressive disorder has been called the common cold of psychopathology. It is by far the most common form of abnormality seen today./515

10. Recent research has documented particular _____ associated with bipolar disorder.
    a. brain structures
    b. chromosomes
    c. hormones
    d. neurotransmitters
    Two different research groups have identified particular chromosomes linked to bipolar disorder./520

THE FAR SIDE By GARY LARSON

© 1986 Universal Press Syndicate

Professor Gallagher and his controversial technique of simultaneously confronting the fear of heights, snakes, and the dark.

Behavior modification is one of the major achievements of psychology in the twentieth century.

Chapter Thirteen

Therapy

Topics of Concern

There is no such thing as a theoretically neutral therapist. A therapist's theories profoundly influence his or her work by determining goals for therapy, techniques to be employed to reach these goals, and judgments concerning whether these goals have been met. Embedded here are prior decisions about what is meant by abnormality and health.

In the last chapter, we encountered popular approaches to explaining abnormality. These approaches also represent popular approaches to the treatment of problems. Let's consider a hypothetical individual, Mr. Johnson, a thirty-one-year-old man with an exceedingly strong interest in betting on horse races. According to DSM-III-R, Mr. Johnson has an *impulse control disorder,* and his inability to restrain himself from gambling has created great trouble for him. He embezzled thousands of dollars from his employer in order to pay gambling debts. He was caught, charged, and convicted. However, the judge has suspended his sentence if he will seek therapy for his problem.

Mr. Johnson has found his way to a clinic that allows potential clients simply to walk in without a prior appointment. He stands in the lobby of this clinic. There are three doors on which he might knock. Behind each is a therapist.

If Mr. Johnson knocks on the first door, he will find a mental health professional who strongly advocates a biomedical approach to psychopathology. Of course there is no "anti-gambling" drug available, but that doesn't mean that biomedical treatment has nothing to offer. Mr. Johnson's problems may stem directly from an undiagnosed problem, such as bipolar disorder, which we know to be biologically predisposed. Gambling may be one of the reckless activities characterizing a manic episode. Assuming that other signs of bipolar disorder are present, perhaps lithium could be prescribed.

Or perhaps Mr. Johnson has an underlying anxiety or depressive disorder. Gambling allows him to feel less anxious or depressed, because it distracts him. The problem is that he runs up large debts in the course of his attempts to "medicate" himself, and he gives himself even more cause to feel anxious or depressed. The therapist might be able to help Mr. Johnson by giving him medications that reduce his anxiety or depression, thus precluding his impulse to gamble.

Some of you are probably not satisfied that Mr. Johnson's problem can be so readily solved. You may acknowledge that these biomedical treatments may help in the short run, but can we assume that he will not gamble in the future? What else is going on in his life that has made gambling so attractive? What about his job and his family?

For most people, betting on horse races can be fun, but for some individuals it is symptomatic of serious problems that can only be alleviated through therapy.

These are all legitimate questions, of course, and they illustrate the point that one's theoretical bent defines one's conception of the goal of therapy. Therapists working with the biomedical model see their clients as physical systems needing a return to equilibrium. If you work within another framework, this seems incomplete, perhaps even shallow and naive.

There is a second door on which Mr. Johnson might knock. Behind this door is a therapist with a psychoanalytic point of view. Her conception of beneficial change in therapy is a different ball game altogether. Her goal with Mr. Johnson is to bring about a long-term alteration of his personality. Personality from this perspective means the mesh of all the various processes and structures that Freud and his followers stress (Chapter 11). People like Mr. Johnson have problems because their psychic energy is tied up in symptoms. To cure someone, therefore, is to free up this energy for more productive use.

How would the psychoanalytic therapist react to Mr. Johnson? She would want to understand the conflicts that led him to gamble in the first place. She would use various techniques for discerning these conflicts: free association, dream interpretation, and the like. And then she would try to change his basic personality so that these conflicts no longer exist. This process might take years, and it might never succeed. Those who lack patience do not make good psychoanalytic patients.

Now, again, some of you might be shaking your head at this. What a waste of a person's time, energy, and money! This man is ruining his life, gambling away money he doesn't have, and the therapist wants to talk about his dreams and early memories from his childhood, all with no guarantee that this type of therapy will work for him. Suppose incarceration takes place before insight? Again, these are legitimate questions that stem from a different orientation to the nature of psychological problems and their solutions.

Let's suppose that Mr. Johnson knocks instead on the door of the third therapist, who is enamored of the cognitive-behavioral approach and thus believes that abnormality is the result of learning. This therapist would want to know exactly what Mr. Johnson does when he gambles so recklessly. He would try to specify the prevailing rewards and punishments that make these behaviors on the part of Mr. Johnson more likely than others, such as reading a book, planting a garden, or baking cookies for his kids. Perhaps the local racetrack is the only place where Mr. Johnson isn't criticized and made to feel inadequate. At home and at work, everybody yells at him. Gambling becomes an attractive alternative, despite all the grief that it brings in its wake.

> **W**hat a waste of a person's time, energy, and money! This man is ruining his life . . . and the therapist wants to talk about his dreams and early memories from his childhood.

The cognitive-behavioral therapist might arrange matters so that Mr. Johnson's betting is punished and his nonbetting rewarded. He might ask his client to put up a $100 deposit. If he bets more than $2 per race, the deposit will be donated to some local organization that Mr. Johnson finds reprehensible. That's punishing. At the same time, he tells Mr. Johnson to join a backpacking club that stays away from racetracks and instead takes vigorous hikes every weekend. That's rewarding . . . we think.

Some of you are no doubt reacting negatively to *this* form of therapy. How utterly superficial, you think, to treat the symptom of a problem but not its source. Maybe betting on horses is, for Mr. Johnson, a relatively harmless reaction to his real problems. If this outlet is closed off, who knows what will happen to him? The cognitive-behavioral therapist will disagree with your criticisms, though, and assert that betting *is* the problem. Why obscure the obvious fact that gambling creates difficulties for the person? But you remain unconvinced, and what you have is a theoretical impasse.

The subject of this chapter is **therapy:** the treatment of people with psychological disorders by psychologists and other mental health professionals. Therapy is theoretically motivated, as we saw in the case of the hypothetical Mr. Johnson. Depending on their view of the nature of problems, different therapists take altogether different approaches to treatment. **Biomedical therapies** treat problems by intervening biologically, for example, with drugs or surgery. **Psychological therapies,** also known as **psychotherapies,** treat problems with psychological means. Talking is often an important ingredient in psychotherapy, as is encouraging insight into one's problems. Psychological therapies may also involve changing someone's environment, or how they interact with others, or the skills and resources they have available.

"Talking" therapies entail more than just having conversations with people about their problems. Otherwise, bartenders, tax lawyers, cab drivers, and hair stylists would be considered therapists, and they're not. Unlike others who listen to people talk about their problems, therapists deliberately use the facts and theories of general psychology to solve someone's difficulties. This often involves talking, but the talking is special. It has a purpose, and follows a deliberate strategy, which the therapist believes will benefit the client.

As mentioned earlier, psychologists and other professionals may function as therapists (see Table 13.1). So, clinical and counseling psychologists are trained in psychology and undertake therapy from a psychological perspective. And psychiatrists are trained in medicine, and often take a biomedical approach. Although many therapists fit the common stereotype—carrying out therapy as one-on-one interaction between an expert and someone with a problem—this is just one form therapy may take.

therapy
the treatment of people who have psychological disorders by psychologists and other mental health professionals

biomedical therapies
techniques and strategies for therapy that intervene biologically, for example, with drugs or surgery

psychological therapies (psychotherapies)
techniques and strategies for therapy that intervene psychologically

eclectic therapy
an approach to therapy that draws on techniques and rationales from a variety of theoretical strategies

As in previous chapters, we'll first discuss questions of concern to all therapists. Then we'll move on to what is known about therapists and clients. The next part of the chapter considers specific types of therapy. Finally, we'll discuss how researchers have attacked the central question concerning therapy: Does it work? The answer is yes, but perhaps your appetite will be whetted a bit when you hear that this is a relatively recent conclusion. In other words, the legitimacy of therapy has been questioned frequently over the years.

The Vision of Psychological Health

The case of Mr. Johnson and his three therapists is an oversimplification, because few therapists are so narrowly single-minded. But therapists nonetheless have rationales for why someone has a particular difficulty and for how this problem can best be solved. Many practice what is called **eclectic therapy,** meaning that they draw on a variety of techniques in their work. But eclectic does not mean they have no theories. Indeed, eclectic therapists rely on numerous theories, choosing different models for different problems.

You saw in Chapter 12 that one's theories dictate a particular conception of psychological abnormality. One's theories similarly provide a particular vision of psychological well-being. The notion of health is of great concern to those who study abnormality, because abnormality can only be judged against the particular ideal of well-being that one holds. These ideals provide the goals for psychotherapy. How else can a therapist be certain that the solution to a client's problems has been achieved?

Psychological health can be as fuzzy a concept as abnormality, although again we can specify some pertinent characteristics. The more of the following attributes present, the more likely we are to say that people have their act together, that they live optimally (Rosenhan & Seligman, 1989):

- positive attitude toward the self
- continual growth and development as a person
- autonomy
- accurate perception of the world
- competent interaction with the environment
- positive relationships with others

Proponents of the different models of abnormality may place different emphasis on the various criteria of psychological well-being. A biomedically oriented psychologist regards health in terms of the individual's robustness in the face of insult and injury. One's ability to keep on with the business of life is most important, and the business of life is captured by the biological notion of fitness (Chapter 2).

In contrast, a psychoanalytic theorist stresses the degree to which a person successfully channels his instinctive energy into socially valued activities. The healthy person is one who can work and love, creating problems neither for himself nor for others (Vaillant, 1977).

Finally, the cognitive-behavioral model visualizes health in terms of the preponderance of pleasure over pain (Wallach & Wallach, 1983). Cognitive and behavioral habits that lead nowhere have been avoided or changed. To the cognitive-behavioral therapist, psychological health means that reinforcement is plentiful in the individual's world and that he or she can do what is needed to produce it.

Table 13.1
Mental Health Professionals

Clinical psychologist	Individual with advanced graduate work in psychology, usually leading to a Ph.D. (Doctor of Philosophy) or Psy.D. (Doctor of Psychology) degree, who provides therapy to people suffering from psychological difficulties
Counseling psychologist	Individual with advanced graduate work in psychology, usually leading to a Ph.D. (Doctor of Philosophy) or Psy.D. (Doctor of Psychology) degree, who helps clients use already existing skills to achieve academic, vocational, or personal goals
Psychiatrist	Individual with a medical degree who has completed a residency in a mental health setting; unlike other mental health professionals, this individual can prescribe medication and administer electroconvulsive shock
Social worker	Individual with an M.S.W. (Master of Social Work) degree, who provides therapy to individuals or groups
Psychoanalyst	Individual with training in a mental health profession (such as psychology, psychiatry, or social work) who has additionally received instruction in performing psychoanalytic therapy

An extremely healthy person is easy to recognize, because the different visions of health ultimately converge. But more typically, we can imagine people—including ourselves—who exemplify one form of psychological well-being but not others. An intriguing individual difference is whether we value the type of health we possess. Or is the grass greener elsewhere?

The Inevitability of Disorder

Another issue of concern to those who treat psychological disorders involves the possibility of a world without abnormality. Is it possible to eradicate all forms of psychological disorder, or are some human beings always going to be less than what they might be? No definitive answer is presently available, of course, but an incredible array of opinions on the subject can be found.

Behaviorist B. F. Skinner believes that utopia is possible, if society would only use what is already known about reinforcement to shape desired behavior and wipe out undesired behavior. His novel *Walden Two* details one form that happiness for all might take: An enlightened group of leaders arranges reinforcements in the world so that people learn to be unfailingly pleasant and productive (Skinner, 1948). His book *Beyond Freedom and Dignity* presents the same argument in more theoretical language (Skinner, 1971):

[My] . . . analysis shifts the determination of behavior from autonomous man to the environment—an environment responsible both for the evolution of the species and for the repertoire acquired by each member. . . . Is man then "abolished"? Certainly not as an individual or as an individual achiever. It is the autonomous inner man who is abolished, and that is a step forward. . . . A scientific view of man offers exciting possibilities. We have not yet seen what man can make of man. (pp.214–215)

This optimistic view is shared by many behavioral therapists. They are joined in their optimism by their more cognitively-oriented colleagues. Cognitive therapists believe that most if not all psychological problems can be solved, once the cognitions that produce needless anxiety or depression are changed. Similarly, those who take a biomedical approach to therapy are also hopeful that the prevalence of disorders can be drastically reduced. We may have to wait for medical breakthroughs to provide the most effective treatments, but, in principle, these should someday exist.

For a different view of the inevitability of abnormality, we need merely turn to Sigmund Freud (1930), who gives us quite a pessimistic perspective. So long as people live in society, he argues, the best they can hope for is to be neurotic. Why? Society requires us to compromise our instinctive behavior, and such compromise inevitably produces abnormality. Still other psychoanalytic theorists suggest we can have our cake and eat it too, because technology can liberate us from the compromises forced upon us by our earlier socialization (e.g., Brown, 1959; Marcuse, 1962). Stay tuned.

Let's look at one more perspective on the possibility of psychological utopia. It's a pessimistic notion. Consider that more people now die from cancer than ever before. One reason for this is simply that the other diseases which once plagued human beings have been conquered, allowing us to live longer and hence be at risk for cancer. Perhaps when cancer is vanquished, something else will take over as a leading cause of death.

Is there a possible parallel here with psychological abnormality? We know, for instance, that hysteria is much less common today than it was at the turn of the century, when hysterics formed the majority of Freud's caseload. We also know that depression is much more common today than it once was. Is this because individuals who might once have developed hysterical symptoms avoided doing so only to become depressed? This is speculation, of course, but epidemiological studies in the future may provide some pertinent evidence. If the prevalence of depression can be decreased through biomedical and psychological therapy, we can then see if another disorder rises up to take its place.

This debate as to the inevitability of disorder is not an idle one. It affects the approach that therapists take in trying to help their clients. An optimistic therapist is apt to treat her clients' problems aggressively and to expect treatment to be brief. A pessimistic therapist may take a more

Opinions on whether either individual or group therapy is effective have varied over the years. Currently, psychologists see the therapy process as efficacious, while seeking to understand the reasons for its success.

leisurely approach to treatment. More basically, these attitudes translate themselves into a concern—or a lack of concern—with social programs that try to prevent psychological problems from arising in the first place.

Does Therapy Work?

The previous issues raised in this section are obviously important ones. But the overarching question in the entire field of therapy is whether it works. If clients don't benefit, then all other concerns become moot. We can identify several

discrete opinions about the effectiveness of therapy, which have predominated at one time or another. First there was an attitude of unquestioned acceptance, eventually followed by a period of considerable skepticism. For example, when I took introductory psychology in 1970, it was flatly asserted in class that people did not benefit from therapy at all. This conclusion was then challenged, as researchers obtained relevant evidence showing that therapy does indeed work. The psychologists of today accept the effectiveness of therapy, but search for the specific reasons for its success. The last section of this chapter considers in detail issues concerning the effectiveness of therapy.

Therapists and Clients

Therapy works, but far from 100 percent of the time, so there is obvious interest in fine-tuning the process so that it successfully serves as many people as possible. Indeed, a great deal of research has attempted to identify the ingredients that make for successful therapy. In this section, we will discuss what is required of the therapist, the client, and the relationship between the two for therapy to be effective.

The Therapist

All who comment on therapy remark that part of its effectiveness stems from the therapist's role. Mental health professionals are not simply friends to those with problems. They have a socially recognized and sanctioned role as experts on thoughts, feelings, actions, and relationships, and the general public is understandably impressed.

Education versus Training. An important question is how best to prepare someone to be a good therapist. James Eaton (1980) makes a useful distinction between training and education. *Training* emphasizes imitation, repetition, and discipline, whereas *education* stresses creativity, initiative, and freedom. Training imparts particular skills; education gives the person the ability to acquire new skills.

Sketched this way, education is necessarily more valuable than training. The issue becomes controversial, however, when specific educational material is considered. Perhaps an "educational" program is too permissive, and what passes as creativity is just blowing smoke. Emphasis on education per se overlooks the fact that therapists need to know particular things. Paul Meehl (1977, pp. 278–280), a noted clinical psychologist, relates the following story, a conversation between himself and a student therapist:

> Meehl: You look kind of low today.
>
> Student: Well, I should be—one of my therapy cases blew his brains out over the weekend. . . .
>
> Meehl: Did you see this man when he first came into the hospital?
>
> Student: Yes . . . he was very depressed at that time.
>
> Meehl: Well, was he psychotically depressed?
>
> Student: I don't know. . . .
>
> Meehl: Tell me some of the ways he was "very depressed" at the time he came into the hospital.
>
> Student: . . . He was mute.
>
> Meehl: If he was literally mute . . . then you have the diagnosis right away . . . psychotic depression.
>
> Student: I guess I didn't know that.
>
> Meehl: Why was he sent out on pass?
>
> Student: Well . . . his depression was lifting considerably.
>
> Meehl: . . . When does a patient with psychotic depression have the greatest risk of suicide?

Student: I don't know.

Meehl: Well, what do the textbooks of psychiatry and abnormal psychology say about the time of greatest suicide risk for a patient with psychotic depression?

Student: I don't know.

Meehl: You mean you have never read, or heard in a lecture, or been told by your supervisors, that the time when a psychotically depressed patient is most likely to kill himself is when his depression is "lifting"?

Student: No, I never heard that.

Meehl: Well you have heard it now. You better read a couple of old books, and maybe next time you will be able to save somebody's life.

This exchange illustrates the importance of the training/education issue. The student therapist was no doubt educated, at least in some sense, but he certainly had not been trained. A therapist must know specifics, and thus training should not be dismissed glibly.

Boards and agencies that give official approval to graduate programs in clinical psychology are currently focusing on this issue. So, the American Psychological Association certifies some graduate programs but not others. In recent years, it has certified programs only if they require particular courses of their students: statistics, assessment, psychopathology, therapy, and so on. The required courses have steadily become more numerous, so much so that little time is left for other graduate school activities. A backlash has therefore occurred at some universities, where faculty members feel that mandated training is smothering education.

Mystique.   Considerable mystique adheres to the role of the therapist. Therapists are sometimes seen as people with mysterious power, able to "analyze" people with a single glance and devise solutions to all of their problems. In fact, some writers suggest that therapists play the role of priest in our modern society. We nowadays refrain from using words such as *good* and *bad* to describe someone's actions, substituting instead terms such as *adjusted* and *maladjusted* or *normal* and *abnormal*—thus giving therapists final judgment on these matters. Confession of one's "sins" (i.e., neuroses) becomes quite complicated because someone may not even know what they are! Thus, people need an expert to tell them if they are bad (abnormal) and what to do about it if they are.

Certainly, therapists have special skills. But is therapy entirely a matter of mystique? On one side of this issue is the opinion that the role of the therapist is the most important tool that he or she has. To diminish the role would be to diminish the effectiveness of therapy. Some therapists, for instance, deliberately remove all clues of their personal life from their office: no family pictures, no knickknacks, no books. They become quite unlike their clients, and all the more impressive as a result.

On the other side of the issue is the opinion that therapists are effective to the degree that they know of particular strategies for bringing about change. Here the role per se is de-emphasized, with the stress falling instead on a particular medication, or technique for resolving disputes, or way to effect an environmental change. The therapist wants to be thought of as an expert in his particular domain, of course, but he really is like the rest of us in other ways.

To illustrate this issue, we've looked at extremes here. But the emphasis on therapist mystique is a real issue. Individual therapists place themselves somewhere along the dimension emphasizing mystique on the one hand and technique on the other. Students seem drawn to the study of therapy for one of two reasons, either because it allows them to be seen as particularly skilled at human relations—mystique—or because it allows them to apply psychological science—techniques (Kimble, 1984).

Characteristics of the Good Therapist. "Oh, you're so good with people. Have you thought about a career in psychology?" Many of you may have had this said to you, and perhaps that's why you've enrolled in this course. What characteristics make for a good therapist? When students are admitted into graduate school in clinical psychology, they are expected to be good students, as judged by grades and standardized test scores. But no program goes strictly by these numerical criteria. Admissions committees additionally try to choose a certain type of person.

Carl Rogers (1951), the noted humanistic psychologist and founder of client-centered therapy (to be discussed later in the chapter), theorizes extensively on the type of person who makes the best therapist: someone well adjusted, empathic, warm, and supportive. Although these attributes have particular meaning within Rogers's system, therapists in general accept that these characteristics facilitate effective therapy. The problem that results, though, is how best to assess them (cf. Chinsky & Rappaport, 1970).

One thing that researchers have *not* been able to do is to map general personality characteristics, such as those discussed in Chapter 11, into the more specific attributes of the effective therapist. In a recent review, Beutler, Crago, and Arizmendi (1986, p. 271) conclude that "the influence of therapist's personality on psychotherapy is inconclusive . . . [but] it is unlikely that any single dimension of personality . . . is a major facilitator or inhibitor of therapy benefit."

Studies also have looked at how such therapist characteristics as age, experience, gender, ethnicity, and theoretical orientation affect therapy. Ambiguity is invited, of course, by the fact that these attributes are not handed out randomly in our society. Investigations of age or gender or race end up as investigations of everything else that might be correlated with them—including education and income. Disentangling the confounds is difficult, to say the least. Most therapists are white and from the middle or upper class, which means that the full range of people is not well represented among the ranks of therapists.

Nevertheless, let us consider the conclusions offered by Beutler et al. (1986) following their extensive review of the relevant research on therapist characteristics. They found that age per se shows little relation to successful treatment. Younger therapists are somewhat more effective with younger clients, though, in that therapy is less apt to end prematurely with this particular matchup. Experience per se also shows little relationship to the outcome of therapy, although more experienced therapists are more adept when dealing with particularly severe or complex problems.

What about gender? According to Beutler et al. (1986), women tend to be more effective therapists than men. This is a newly reported result, and perhaps should be regarded as tentative. There is agreement that therapy proceeds better when therapists and clients are of the same gender. Perhaps these results can be explained by hypothesizing that a client

The personality of the therapist can be a key factor in the effectiveness of therapy.

responds particularly well to an egalitarian attitude on the part of the therapist (Beutler et al., 1986). Female therapists in general, and any therapist who is the same gender as his or her client, may better be able to achieve and act on an egalitarian stance.

As for the effect of therapist ethnicity, it is unclear. Abramowitz and Murray (1983) surveyed different reviews of relevant research and concluded that one tends to see the results according to one's race! White reviewers minimize any differences that are found, whereas minority reviewers place great weight on differences. A cautious conclusion is that ethnic similarity is beneficial in the earliest stages of therapy, because it can prevent premature termination. When a therapist and client are of different races, and therapy gets off on the wrong foot, the problem is not because of skin color itself but insensitivity to differences (Beutler et al., 1986). Neither therapists nor clients can change their race, of course, but both can become aware of what it means to stand in another's shoes. That's what Rogers means by empathy.

Throughout the last few chapters, we've stressed that all the models of human nature convey something important. Don't be surprised, then, that the theoretical orientation of a therapist (the model to which he or she ascribes) does not relate to therapy outcome across the board. In other words, *there is no best therapy.* This conclusion is pretty well accepted by now, and therapists are thus taking a more refined view, wondering if particular therapies are best suited for particular problems.

John Hinckley, who attempted to assassinate President Reagan, was found not guilty by reason of insanity and confined to St. Elizabeth's Hospital rather than a federal prison.

insanity plea

a legal defense that one is not guilty of a crime because of psychological abnormality at the time the crime was committed

Whom Does the Therapist Serve?   Therapists have a complex relationship with society at large. Although many therapists attribute the problems their clients experience to social conditions such as poverty and blocked opportunities, therapy is inherently a conservative endeavor. In many ways, it is the business of helping the individual fit into the world, even if the world is sometimes crazy, cruel, or contradictory. This characterization should not surprise you. Remember the disorders described in Chapter 12, which are problems that can be readily located within the individual. Societal problems such as genocide, nuclear proliferation, and homelessness are not usually considered psychopathological, despite the suffering and maladaptiveness they clearly exemplify.

Whom does the therapist serve? On one level, the answer is the client. But few clients directly pay their therapist. Instead, the therapist is reimbursed by an institution (a school or business, for example), a governmental agency, or an insurance company. So on another level, the therapist also serves society. Recent legislation requires that therapists report suspected cases of child abuse, even if the information is obtained in an ostensibly confidential conversation between therapist and client. As you can see, the therapist must perform a balancing act.

Therapists may also get involved in the legal system. As experts on human behavior, they are asked to testify in court on a variety of matters. Are certain people fit parents? Do they understand the criminal charges filed against them? What was their state of mind when a crime was committed? Consider the example of the **insanity plea,** the legal defense that one is not guilty of a crime because of psychological abnormality at the time the crime was committed. Insanity is a controversial social issue, and there is even controversy over whether psychologists have anything useful to say on the matter (Coleman, 1984). After all, insanity is a legal term, not a psychological one (recall the discussion of this matter in Chapter 1). There are no specific conclusions offered here, just the comment that clinical psychology is much more than a purely academic discipline.

The Client

The therapist is only half of the equation in therapy. Clients are the other half. A great deal of the therapist's attention goes toward understanding characteristics of the client that predispose successful or unsuccessful therapy. Let's discuss some of what is known about clients and how they fare in therapy by drawing on Garfield's (1986) review of the topic.

We can begin with the following question: Who goes into therapy in the first place? There are several routes into therapy. People can refer themselves. Someone else—a teacher, friend, relative, or employer—can suggest that they seek help. Or they can be required by a court order to see a therapist. As explained in Chapter 11, different problems dictate the route one is likely to take into therapy, or even whether the journey is begun.

One out of every five Americans will seek out therapy at some point in life (Rosenhan & Seligman, 1989), but not everyone with a problem turns to a therapist. A critical factor pushing someone into therapy seems to be demoralization. In other words, a person seeks out therapy because he or she feels helpless in the wake of some problem. Common sense suggests, however, that demoralization in the extreme will keep a person out of therapy. Why bother?

Another issue is the kinds of therapy administered to different clients. Research resolves any ambiguity concerning this issue. Individuals from the lower socioeconomic class tend to receive biomedical treatment, whereas those from the middle and upper classes tend to receive psychological treatment (Hollingshead & Redlich, 1958). This pattern has been evident for decades, still holding true today (Garfield, 1986).

This treatment pattern may reflect the different types of problems experienced by people of different socioeconomic classes. Poverty is clearly associated with increased rates of various disorders, including schizophrenia (Dohrenwend & Dohrenwend, 1981). Perhaps the disorders of those from the lower class on the one hand and the middle and upper classes on the other differ so that drugs and psychotherapy are respectively appropriate treatments. This interpretation can be criticized, though, because social class differences in disorders are not as pronounced as social class differences in treatment. Further, we don't always know enough to say whether biomedical or psychological therapy is the preferred approach in a particular case. Indeed, one contemporary opinion is that biomedical treatment and psychological treatment need not compete; they can be profitably combined.

The data on the relationship between social class and type of treatment may instead show bias in the delivery of mental health services. This certainly does not mean intentional prejudice on the part of the individual therapist. Rather, considerations such as the cost of different forms of therapy play an important role. Psychological therapy is often much more expensive than biomedical therapy, because of the time required of the therapist. Let us not be naive; therapists do not work for free, and the client's ability to pay for therapy determines what type of treatment is offered. At any rate, therapists are increasingly recognizing the need to make psychological treatment available to all segments of our population (Lorion & Felner, 1986).

Ideally, a client continues in therapy until his original problem is solved or at least alleviated. In practice, termination before satisfactory change occurs is frequent, with estimates over 60 percent commonly cited (e.g., Taube, Burns, & Kessler, 1984). Who does stay in therapy until the end? Again, social class is a strong predictor here. Clients from the lower class leave therapy earlier than those from the middle and upper classes. Education also can be used to predict continuation; the more educated a client, the longer he or she stays in therapy. *Not* consistently related to continuation in therapy are client characteristics such as sex, age, race, and type of problem.

One critical ingredient that determines continuation is whether a client's expectations for therapy are being met. A conflict here often provides a simple rationale for why lower class and/or less educated people don't stay in therapy. Their expectations for therapy—its procedures and goals—are at odds with those of their therapists, who are typically from the middle or upper class and of necessity highly educated. A useful strategy here is to precede therapy with a "training" interview in which a potential client is told exactly what to expect (Orne & Wender, 1968).

Finally, psychologists have been interested in who improves the most in therapy. Researchers have not isolated specific personality characteristics of the successful client, but the acronym *YAVIS* captures what many therapists believe to be an ideal candidate for therapy, someone who is young, attractive, verbal, intelligent, and successful (Schofield, 1964). People with these attributes have abundant resources, and their problems are apt to be less severe in the first place.

In Chapter 12, we discussed the importance of seeing abnormality in its social context. The same is true of therapy, and the conclusions summarized in this section reveal as much about our society as they do about the particular people who seek help for psychological problems. One of the thorniest matters in clinical psychology is how best to serve the psychological needs of people from different backgrounds.

The Therapist-Client Relationship

The discussion so far artificially separates therapists and clients. Let's bring them together now, as they are joined in therapy. Whatever else therapy might be, it is always a human interaction. We know that such interactions are not simply the sum of the two (or more) people involved.

Freud was the first to direct explicit attention to the relationship between the therapist and client. **Transference** is the term he gave to the tendency of a client to relate to his therapist as he relates to other important individuals in his life, such as a parent or spouse. "Working through" the transference is an important aspect of psychoanalytic therapy. This means that the person comes to separate current styles of thinking, feeling, and acting from past styles. Note that transference, although occurring within the client, actually reflects the relationship between the client and the therapist.

Freud and other psychoanalytic therapists recommend that the therapist act so that transference will readily occur and hence be easy to rec-

transference
the tendency of a client to relate to his therapist as he has related to other important individuals in his life

ognize and resolve. This usually means that the therapist should set aside his or her reactions to the client's behavior. Thus the therapist allows the client to project attitudes and feelings carried over from a prior relationship. Research shows that successful therapy in fact is accompanied by a resolution of transference issues (Luborsky, Crits-Christoph, & Mellon, 1986).

Another approach to the therapist-client relationship assumes that different therapists excel in different situations. As suggested by interactionist approaches to personality (Chapter 11), perhaps therapists with certain personalities do best when matched with certain types of clients. Much research has been guided by the **matching model hypothesis:** the idea that therapists and clients work best together when they possess the same personality characteristics.

In one study testing this notion, basic dimensions of personality were separately determined by factor analysis (p. 458) for both therapists and their clients at the beginning of therapy (Berzins, 1977). According to the matching hypothesis, the therapists and clients who were most similar with respect to their underlying factors of personality would embark on the most successful treatment. Mismatched therapists and clients would not be as successful. But at the end of therapy, there was little evidence for the matching hypothesis. If anything, the results suggested that complementary personalities were important. For example, dependent clients fared best with autonomous therapists, whereas autonomous clients improved most with dependent therapists.

Yet another view concerning the relationship between therapist and client focuses on their shared expectations for therapy (Frank, 1978). To the degree that both parties believe that therapy will be helpful, it is helpful. This so-called **helping alliance** between therapist and client is so important that some theorists propose it as a necessary condition for successful therapy. Regardless of the particular techniques and strategies of a therapist, if these are not carried out within an empathic, warm, and genuine relationship between therapist and client, nothing will happen. *"There is little or no evidence for . . . the effectiveness of . . . [any] . . . methods or approaches to psychotherapy in the absence of these conditions"* (Patterson, 1986, p. 562, emphases in original).

Types of Therapy

There are many different types of therapy, with the number growing all the time (Garfield & Bergin, 1986). In the 1960s, we could identify approximately 60 versions of therapy. In the early 1970s, this number had increased to 130. By the late 1970s, 250 different techniques could be distinguished. In the mid-1980s, there were more than 400 different therapies. By the time you read this paragraph, who knows how many therapies will exist!

It is impossible to describe even a fraction of the existing therapies in a chapter such as this. What we will do, instead, is look at the major types of therapy. We'll start with biomedical approaches to the treatment of abnormality, particularly the use of drugs. Technically speaking, these are not psychological treatments, because they must be administered by a medical doctor, usually a psychiatrist (see Table 13.1, p. 541). But psychol-

matching model hypothesis
the idea that therapists and clients work best together when they possess the same personality characteristics

helping alliance
the shared expectations of therapist and client that therapy will be helpful

ogists may work in conjunction with psychiatrists in treating clients. Then we'll consider full-fledged psychological therapies: psychoanalysis, cognitive therapy, behavior modification, family therapy, group therapy, and others.

The details of these are fascinating, but try to see the overall picture. Most importantly, appreciate that each form of therapy presupposes one of the three models of abnormality introduced in Chapter 12. The model gives the rationale for the particular approach. We can also classify therapies along various dimensions, including:

- the identity of the client—individual, couple, family, group, or community
- whether the therapy goals are global or specific
- how directive the therapist is
- whether the therapy emphasizes client insight or client action
- whether the therapy is time-limited or open-ended

Biomedical Therapies

Biomedical treatments of abnormality focus on the body, under the assumption that people's problems reflect physical malfunctioning. The most prevalent biomedical therapies involve the use of drugs, but surgery and shock treatments are also used. The common factor among these treatments is that they change someone's physical functioning, presumably in a beneficial way.

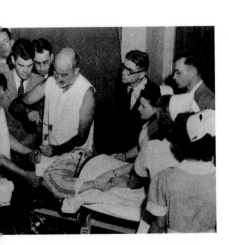

Dr. Freeman (shown here) often performed lobotomies on patients using only a local anesthetic. He toured the country demonstrating his surgical technique.

Psychosurgery. Surgery undertaken on the brain in an attempt to treat psychological disorders is called **psychosurgery.** A *lobotomy* is a well-known example of psychosurgery. In this operation, fibers connecting parts of the brain are severed, with the goal of helping patients with depression or schizophrenia. In 1935, a Portuguese neurologist named Eges Moniz cut through the top of a mental patient's skull. With a specially designed instrument, Moniz then severed the nerve fibers linking the frontal lobes of the brain to the thalamus. He believed that by destroying the pathway between these two areas, presumably the respective centers of thought and emotion, he would thereby lessen the negative effects of feelings on thinking. The patient not only lived, but he seemed better off as a result of the operation. Moniz published his results.

The medical community was greatly excited about his work. For years, psychopathologies such as depression and schizophrenia had resisted treatment. When Moniz pioneered his surgical treatment, he was hailed as a genius. The lobotomy was considered a major medical breakthrough for which Moniz was awarded the Nobel Prize in 1949 (Valenstein, 1986).

Soon, different physicians devised their own versions of Moniz's brain operation, looking for a better method. Two American doctors, Walter Freeman and James Watts, came up with an alternative in which the surgeon entered the patient's brain not through the top of the skull but through its sides. They administered only local anesthesia for this procedure.

At first, there was little organized criticism of lobotomies in the United States. Skepticism was occasionally expressed, but Freeman and Watts kept positive media attention focused on the operation. They toured the country giving lectures and performing hundreds and hundreds of lobotomies at mental hospitals. They also wrote a popular book on the procedure. In 1942, only 300 lobotomies had been performed in the United States. By 1951, the number exceeded 18,000, many performed personally by Freeman and Watts.

In the late 1940s, Freeman broke away from Watts and introduced yet another refinement: entering the brain through the eye socket, pushing the eyeball aside and using an ice pick to sever brain tissue—because standard surgical scalpels proved too fragile and kept breaking off in a patient's brain! He toured the country, demonstrating how to perform his version of a lobotomy.

Widespread criticism of lobotomies began to surface by the mid-1950s, when the medical community realized that there was really no good evidence that these operations actually benefited mental patients. In fact, a close look showed that lobotomies left most patients worse off than ever. Among the serious consequences were apathy, withdrawal, seizures, hyperactivity, impaired learning, and death.

By the 1960s, the operation was no longer being performed, and a rather amazing episode in the treatment of psychological abnormality thus came to an end. However, psychosurgery as a treatment of abnormality may still be reasonable in cases where a specific problem in someone's brain, such as a tumor or lesion, produces difficulties. The objection to lobotomies is not that they involved surgery but that they were undertaken indiscriminately, in cases where no demonstrable problems with brain tissue existed.

Electroconvulsive Therapy. Another biomedical therapy entails briefly passing electric current through the brain of a patient, thereby inducing a seizure (see Figure 13.1). This procedure, known as **electroconvulsive therapy (ECT)**, effectively treats unipolar depression. And it is not as barbaric as it sounds. The patient is given a general anesthetic before receiving any shock. No pain is experienced. Fatalities are exceedingly rare, occurring in perhaps .003 percent of patients. For comparison, the mortality rate due to anti-depressant drugs is considerably higher (Kalinowsky, 1980).

How did therapists ever arrive at the idea of ECT as a treatment for depression? It had been observed that patients with schizophrenia who also had epilepsy showed less psychotic behavior following a seizure (Kalinowsky, 1980). This suggested the hypothesis that convulsions were

electroconvulsive therapy (ECT) a treatment for depression in which an electric current is briefly passed through the brain of a patient, inducing a seizure

Figure 13.1
Electroconvulsive Therapy. This patient is being prepared for ECT. Note the precaution taken so that she does not swallow or bite her tongue.

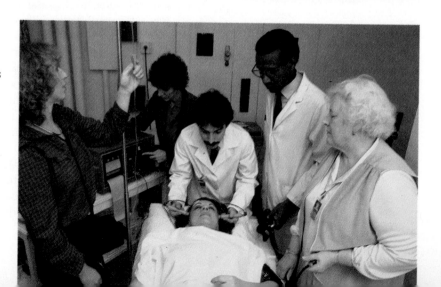

somehow psychologically beneficial, and so therapists induced them, first with drugs and later with electric current. Through trial and error, researchers learned that people with depression were the most likely to be helped by induced convulsions. Granted this history, it may be misleading to refer to ECT as "shock" therapy, because the critical ingredient is the convulsion and not the shock.

Despite its usefulness as a treatment for depression, there are drawbacks to ECT. A common occurrence is memory loss for events surrounding the course of treatment (usually a dozen shocks over a 2-week period). Some researchers suspect loss of distant memories as well, although studies are contradictory on this point. What is clear is that when ECT succeeds, it alleviates depression much more quickly than drugs or talking therapies. For this reason, ECT is often recommended for acutely suicidal individuals, for whom any delay in improvement might prove fatal. Similarly, people in the public eye who become depressed may opt for ECT because it rapidly gets them back into the swing of things.

Why ECT works is not so clear. Psychologists have proposed various theories, but none have been widely accepted. Psychoanalytic theorists suggest, for instance, that ECT satisfies a depressed patient's wish for punishment. Or perhaps ECT wipes out unpleasant memories. Biomedical theorists have more promising explanations in terms of chemical changes in the brain, but because the effects of shock on the brain are numerous and diffuse, it has so far been impossible to pinpoint just why ECT effectively treats depression.

Drug Therapy. In Chapter 12, which presented the major disorders, we alluded to various drugs prescribed by psychiatrists. There are three major categories of drugs that combat psychological problems, each targeting one of the major categories of disorders: anxiety, depression, and psychotic disorders such as schizophrenia. Table 13.2 lists the most important of these and the specific problems they are used to treat. Also noted are the side effects and dangers of each medication.

anti-anxiety medications
drugs such as the minor tranquilizers used to treat anxiety disorders

Anti-anxiety medications include such well-known minor tranquilizers as Valium and Librium. These are among the most frequently prescribed medications in the United States, with over seventy million prescriptions written each year (Rickels, 1981). The minor tranquilizers reduce anxiety and may be particularly effective for people with generalized anxiety disorders who do not additionally experience panic attacks or have severe phobias (Willerman & Cohen, 1990). The exact way in which minor tranquilizers work is not clear, but presumably they interfere with chemical processes in the brain that underlie fear and anxiety.

anti-depressant medications
drugs such as tricyclics and MAO-inhibitors used to treat depression

Anti-depressant medications are of two types: tricyclics and MAO-inhibitors. Both medications effectively treat unipolar depression and may also prevent or delay subsequent depressive episodes. Although the mode of action is different for tricyclics and MAO-inhibitors, both presumably work by increasing the availability of the neurotransmitters norepinephrine and serotonin. The overall effectiveness of the two classes of anti-depressant medication is much the same, and tricyclics are usually preferred because they have fewer possible side effects.

anti-psychotic medications
drugs such as the neuroleptics and lithium used to treat psychotic symptoms

Anti-psychotic medications include the neuroleptics, used to treat schizophrenia, and lithium, the treatment of choice for bipolar disorder. Although these medications have brought relief to literally millions of

Table 13.2

Psychiatric Drugs

	Type of Drug	Common Brands	Usually Used to Treat	Possible Side Effects
Anti-anxiety medication	Minor tranquilizers	Valium Librium	Anxiety disorders	Drowsiness Lethargy Dependence
Anti-depressant medication	Tricyclics	Aventyl Elavil	Depression	Dry mouth Dizziness Constipation Heart palpitations
	MAO-inhibitors	Parnate Marplan	Depression	Same as tricyclics Possibly lethal interactions with some foods (such as cheese or avocados)
Anti-psychotic medication	Neuroleptics	Thorazine Haldol	Schizophrenia	Dry mouth Blurry vision Grogginess Low blood pressure Constipation Restlessness Tremors Uncontrollable muscular movements
	Lithium carbonate	Lithonate Lithane	Bipolar disorder	Kidney and liver damage Dry mouth Skin irritation

patients, they do not constitute cures in the literal sense. They control many of the flagrant symptoms of schizophrenia or bipolar disorder, but they do not eradicate these disorders. The neuroleptics and lithium both have severe side effects. As mentioned in Chapter 12, the mechanism by which lithium works is not known. The neuroleptics are thought to work by affecting the availability of the neurotransmitter dopamine in the brain.

The use of drugs to treat psychological problems has aroused sharp debate both in and out of the mental health professions. We will take a moderate approach here that acknowledges both pros and cons.

The evidence for the effectiveness of the drugs listed in Table 13.2 cannot be denied. Medications can and do help people with psychological disorders, and it is shortsighted to categorically dismiss the use of drugs in the treatment of psychological abnormality. However, these drugs rarely hold the entire answer to an individual's problem. They invariably treat symptoms as opposed to curing problems. Sometimes symptom relief is all that one desires, but other times these "antidotes" for anxiety or sleeplessness encourage people to turn their backs on the real source of their difficulties. Some people become addicted to psychiatric medication, particularly the minor tranquilizers. They start with one problem and end up with two or more.

Drug therapy does have undesirable side effects, but high blood pressure medicine, cold tablets, antibiotics, and virtually all other drugs also create undesirable consequences for people who take them. In this sense, there are no miracle drugs, and a physician's decision to prescribe medication is always a compromise, in which it is hoped that the benefits will outweigh the costs.

In sum, the use of drugs to treat psychological disorders can be effective, so long as we do not forget that psychological therapies also have an important role to play. Nowhere is it written that drug treatment cannot be combined with psychotherapy (Klerman, 1986). For problems such as schizophrenia, this is probably the most reasonable course to take.

Other Biomedical Treatments.   Our bodies can be affected by more than just drugs, ECT, and surgery. Biomedically oriented therapists have left few procedures untried in their attempt to bring relief to people with problems. In the 1800s, patients were spun around, blindfolded, hosed with water, and physically immobilized (see Figure 13.2). These "therapies" were thought to correct whatever was wrong with someone's body, and hence they qualify as biomedical treatments.

Figure 13.2
Early Physical Treatments of Abnormality. History has seen varied—and sometimes bizarre—attempts to treat abnormality by doing things to someone's body.

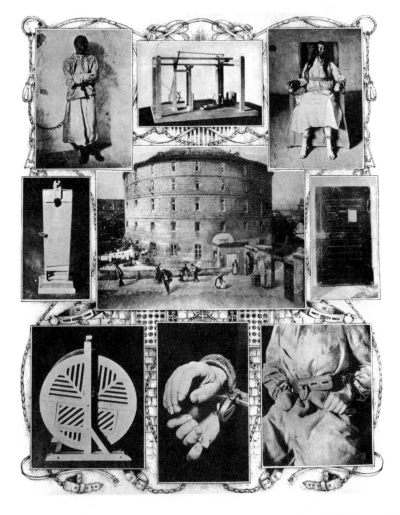

In some cases, aerobic exercises can be an effective means of relieving depression.

seasonal affective disorder
recurrent episodes of depression that worsen in the fall and improve in the spring, thought to be due to the amount of light to which one is exposed

Some people experience seasonal depressions that seem to be triggered by a decreased number of daylight hours.

More contemporary treatments with the same rationale include quite a variety of procedures:

- the induction of comas
- forced sleep via drugs, such as barbiturates
- sleep deprivation
- deep muscle massage
- purification of blood with hemodialysis
- inhalation of carbon dioxide
- acupuncture
- macrobiotic diets
- vitamin supplements

Psychiatrists have even used hyperbaric oxygen chambers (made famous by Michael Jackson) to treat delirium and dementia (and being bad, as it were).

Two contemporary biomedical treatments are particularly intriguing. The first one is aerobic exercise. Studies show that a program of running or dancing decreases one's depression (e.g., McCann & Holmes, 1984). One obvious explanation for this is that physical activity increases neurotransmitters, such as norepinephrine and serotonin. However, this explanation has not been nailed down. Subsequent research may well show that this apparently biological treatment works not through physiological pathways but through psychological ones. For example, people who exercise usually develop a sense of mastery, and perhaps enhanced self-efficacy decreases depression (Chapter 11).

The second contemporary treatment of note is light. **Seasonal affective disorder** is a recently described phenomenon: recurrent episodes of depression that worsen in the fall and improve in the spring. In an intriguing study, Rosenthal et al. (1984) advertised in the *Washington Post* for people whose mood swings showed this pattern, obtaining twenty-nine individuals who consented to be studied. These people were then observed into the winter, when indeed they became depressed. The amount of sunlight they experienced seemed critical, because if they happened to travel north or south (from Washington), their moods respectively became more or less depressed.

Rosenthal et al. then treated eleven of these individuals by exposing them to bright white light (three hours in the morning and three hours in the afternoon). They improved in most cases, experiencing a relapse when the lights were removed. This is hardly definitive evidence; a skeptic would have a field day pointing out alternative explanations. Nevertheless, theorists already have a tentative explanation for why this treatment improves the mood of people with seasonal affective disorder: Light stimulates melatonin (a hormone) that in turn affects one's biological rhythms that in turn elevate mood. (For the time being, you at least have a good excuse for going south during the winter.)

It's much too soon to evaluate these procedures, because many are in their most preliminary stages. But here are some lessons from history. First, only a handful of these biomedical therapies will stand the test of time. Second, even for those therapies that prove useful, explanations for their effectiveness will prove elusive.

Individual "Talking" Therapies

psychoanalysis

approach to therapy based on psychoanalytic theory that attempts to identify one's unconscious conflicts and free up the psychological energy invested in them

free association

a psychoanalytic technique for revealing unconscious conflicts by asking the patient to say whatever comes to mind, without attempting to censor it

dream interpretation

a psychoanalytic technique for revealing unconscious conflicts in which the patient describes dreams, free associates to them, and works with the therapist to interpret their underlying meaning and significance

resistance

according to psychoanalytic theory, the tendency of a client in therapy to resist the progress of therapy because unconscious conflicts are too painful to confront

Psychoanalysis is the grandparent of all psychotherapies that depend on talking. Even when subsequent therapies embrace a drastically different rationale than does psychoanalysis, many of their specific procedures explicitly evolve from the strategies Sigmund Freud and his followers developed. Let's therefore start this section with psychoanalytic therapy.

Psychoanalysis.   Remember that psychoanalysts define cure as the freeing of a person's psychic energy from symptoms so it can be put to more productive use elsewhere. And this is exactly what they aim to achieve through **psychoanalysis.** Therapists try to identify the unconscious conflicts that tie up this energy. To do this, they use several techniques. One such technique is **free association,** which involves the patient saying whatever comes to mind, without attempting to censor it; his or her train of associations leads to areas of unconscious conflict (Chapter 11). Another technique is **dream interpretation,** in which the patient describes dreams, free associates to their surface content, and works with the therapist to interpret their underlying meaning and significance (Chapter 4). With the technique known as *analysis of transference,* the patient gains insight into past feelings and relationships by seeing how these have been transferred to the present relationship with the therapist (p. 549). Accompanying all of these techniques is **resistance** on the part of the client, an unwillingness to accept what the techniques reveal about areas of conflict. Patients do not easily relinquish their problems.

What actually happens in psychoanalysis? The popular stereotype involves a bearded fellow tossing out obscure interpretations to a dazzled client. The truth is that the psychoanalyst does a lot more listening than talking. The only way that unconscious material can be made conscious is if the client unearths it for himself. Accordingly, the major task of the analyst is to facilitate this process.

An important part of psychoanalysis involves teaching the individual to be a good psychoanalytic client who observes the "fundamental rule" of free association and reports everything that comes to mind. During free association, the client reclines on a couch. The therapist sits at the head of the couch out of the client's direct line of sight (see Figure 13.3). The client talks, and the analyst interjects interpretive comments only occasionally. Interpretations are valid to the degree that they catalyze a change in the client.

Luborsky (1984) identified three active ingredients in psychoanalytic therapy, all of which have been incorporated into the other talking therapies. First is the importance of self-understanding. Different types of therapy define "understanding" in various ways consistent with their underlying views of human nature, but all agree that the client must come to an appreciation of the reasons for her actions. Next is the establishment of a good working relationship between the therapist and the client. As stated earlier, some theorists believe that this helping alliance is a prerequisite for therapeutic benefit. Third is a stress on maintaining progress made in therapy once it ends. Backsliding threatens all therapies, and psychoanalysts try to combat this problem by explicitly discussing with their clients the significance of termination and the anxiety it arouses.

Figure 13.3
Psychoanalytic Therapy

When Freud developed psychoanalytic therapy, he recommended it for intelligent people at least fifty years of age who functioned relatively well in the world. Therapy sessions lasted 1 hour each and occurred 6 days a week, for at least 6 months and perhaps for several years. Interestingly, Freud likened psychoanalysis to a chess game. Both have stages: a beginning, a middle, and an end. There is an ultimate goal throughout, but the means to this end differ across the stages.

In its contemporary versions, psychoanalysis is used with a wider range of clients, although it still is far from suitable for all. Therapy takes place from two to four times a week; the psychoanalytic hour has now shrunk to 50 minutes. The process continues to take a long time, usually from 2 to 5 years.

Who benefits most from psychoanalysis? All of the difficulties in determining therapy effectiveness become compounded in psychoanalysis because the treatment lasts so long and embodies a subtle criterion for cure. Nevertheless, Luborsky and Spence (1978) tentatively concluded that psychoanalysis is best indicated for well-educated people who experience strong anxiety but no severe problems in living. Because the more circumscribed anxiety disorders, such as simple phobia, can be treated effectively in ways other than psychoanalytic therapy, we should add the additional qualification that psychoanalysis is best reserved for people with diffuse fears or anxieties.

Psychoanalysis as a therapy is less popular today than it once was. Its place in the history of clinical psychology is secure, but an ever decreasing number of individuals undertake training to be psychoanalysts. Fewer people with problems seek out psychoanalytic treatment. Insurance companies are less willing to pay for this type of therapy. What has been responsible for this waning of interest? For one thing, the effectiveness of psychoanalysis has not been firmly established, particularly in comparison to more contemporary therapies. In addition, these newer therapies are almost always quicker and less expensive than psychoanalysis.

Client-Centered Therapy. One of the first alternatives to psychoanalytic therapy was developed by Carl Rogers (1942, 1951), whose personality theory was discussed in Chapter 11. Rogers believed that people develop problems when their experience is at odds with their awareness. Conditional regard from other people produces these discrepancies, which in turn produce psychological problems.

According to Rogers, the solution is to reverse the process and create a benign environment for the person: a place where her inherent drive toward actualization can operate without restriction. This is the premise of **client-centered therapy** (also called **person-centered therapy**). The therapist creates this atmosphere with several specific techniques (Prochaska, 1984) including:

- a nondirective stance, which allows the client to devise her own solutions to problems
- a good therapeutic relationship characterized by sincerity and concern
- accurate empathic understanding of the client's inner world
- unconditional positive regard, i.e., acceptance of the client as a person with worth and dignity

Under these circumstances, clients come to think more highly of themselves, and their problems become resolved.

Therapists often reflect back to the client his particular thoughts and feelings:

Client: I feel discouraged about life these days.

Therapist: It sounds like things have been rough.

Client: Yeah . . . work is a drag, and all my wife and I do is fight. When I wake up in the morning, the only thing I look forward to during the whole day is going to sleep again that night!

Therapist: And that's the way you feel now.

It is easy to caricature client-centered therapy as a process of simply agreeing with what a client says, but this is unfair. All of us know the difference between someone who actively listens and tries to understand our experience and someone who nods his head with his thoughts elsewhere.

It is difficult to characterize "typical" client-centered therapy. It may take the form of one-on-one therapy, conducted once a week for months, or it may be a single marathon session with a large number of people. Rogers (1970) pioneered **encounter groups,** which bring together individuals in conflict, such as labor and management, blacks and whites, students and teachers, or Protestants and Catholics, under conditions where they can understand each other better. Encounter groups sometimes lead to confrontation, but they are thought to be worthwhile because interchanges between their participants are open and honest. Encounter groups are no longer as popular as they once were, perhaps because people are more concerned with themselves these days.

One thing is certain: Client-centered therapy effectively promotes change for many people with problems. It is probably not a good idea for those whose problems are solidly based in a grim reality rather than in their perceptions of reality. Here we would be better off trying to change this reality. Also, client-centered therapy is probably not a good idea for those who would benefit from specific suggestions about how to behave (Shilling, 1984).

irrational beliefs

according to Albert Ellis, the rigid beliefs entertained by people that produce difficulties for them

rational-emotive therapy

an approach to therapy pioneered by Albert Ellis in which the client's irrational beliefs are actively disputed

cognitive therapy

approach to therapy developed by Aaron Beck that identifies a client's automatic thoughts and errors in logic and then tries to change these by evaluating them against the evidence of the world

Rational-Emotive Therapy.   Another alternative to psychoanalysis is rational-emotive therapy, which was created by psychologist Albert Ellis (1962). This is a thoroughly cognitive approach to people and their problems. According to Ellis, the manner in which people think about things can be the source of their problems. People tend to entertain **irrational beliefs** that necessarily make them anxious or depressed or otherwise troubled. Consider the following:

- I *must* do well at everything I try.
- I *must* be loved and respected by everyone I know.
- I *must* be completely happy all the time.
- I *must* get my way with other people.

Ellis calls this tendency "musturbation" and argues that rigid beliefs provide a poor road map for navigating the world.

In **rational-emotive therapy**, the therapist actively disputes the client's irrational beliefs. Therapy is therefore quite directive. On the face of it, the therapist seems argumentative when he challenges his client, but the ensuing arguments occur in the context of an accepting relationship. The therapist disputes beliefs, not his client:

Client: I feel discouraged about life these days.

Therapist: It sounds like you think no one should be discouraged.

Client: Well, being discouraged is a drag. I can't stand it.

Therapist: I'd agree that discouragement is no fun, but don't confuse your wants with your needs. Why do you say you can't stand discouragement? You've survived pretty well so far.

Client: But when I wake up in the morning, the only thing I look forward to during the whole day is going to sleep that night!

Therapist: Do you really mean that?

Research shows that rational-emotive therapy helps people with pervasive anxiety disorders, although there is disagreement over the effectiveness of argument per se (Shilling, 1984). In other words, rational-emotive therapy may work because the therapist obviously cares about his clients—not because he disputes their beliefs (Patterson, 1986).

Cognitive Therapy.   A final individual therapy, also thoroughly cognitive, is the one developed by psychiatrist Aaron Beck (1976; Beck & Emery, 1985; Beck, Rush, Shaw, & Emery, 1979). It's appropriately called **cognitive therapy.** Like other cognitive approaches to therapy, Beck's tries to change particular thoughts, under the assumption that if you modify someone's thinking, it will reduce her depression and anxiety. Beck describes cognitive therapy as "collaborative empiricism" to emphasize that the therapist and client work together (collaborate) to check the client's beliefs against the facts of the matter (empiricism).

The first step in cognitive therapy is to identify the client's automatic thoughts, habitual put-downs that flash through her mind in the course of her everyday activity (Chapter 12). She begins to pay attention to these thoughts, and not just to the emotional damage they do. And she writes them down, along with the feelings they produce. Then she challenges her automatic thoughts by asking what evidence she has for believing them, as in the following example:

Aaron Beck's approach—cognitive therapy—emphasizes a restructuring of clients' negative assumptions about themselves and their futures.

I got depressed at work when the boss walked by me without saying hello. My thoughts were that I did a lousy job on my last project, that he was mad at me, and that I was probably going to be fired.

But when I think further about that incident, I guess I can see that my boss was probably preoccupied. His son has been ill. Plus I've done projects like that before, with good results. And I got a good raise just two months ago.

The process of cognitive therapy is a lot more difficult than this example conveys. Automatic thoughts are not simply errors, like mistaken telephone numbers, that can be readily corrected once you attend to them. Rather, these thoughts are deeply ingrained, and, therefore, clients challenge them only with great reluctance. Cognitive therapists often devise experiments to aid belief change on the part of their clients.

"You think you're a social loser? Maybe yes, maybe no. Why don't you find out by asking ten different people to have a cup of coffee with you? Keep track of how many people say yes. And tell me before you start how many people would have to accept your invitation for you *not* to be a loser." Needless to say, the therapist must use some common sense in these assignments and not send an accountant off to party with the Hell's Angels. But maladaptive beliefs can be effectively challenged by appropriately chosen experiences.

Usually, cognitive therapy involves 10 to 15 weekly sessions. Research shows that the procedure effectively alleviates depression as well as various anxiety disorders (Hollon & Beck, 1986). It also holds promise for people who suffer from chronic pain, obesity, marital strife, and eating disorders.

Behavior Modification

behavior modification
an approach to therapy based on theories of learning through which people can rid themselves of undesired habits and replace them with desired ones

If people can learn to behave in an "abnormal" fashion, then they can also learn to behave in a "normal" way. This rationale underlies the approach to therapy known as **behavior modification:** techniques for helping a client rid himself of undesired habits and replace them with desired ones. The psychology of learning suggests specific behavior modification strategies (Chapter 5).

Through systematic desensitization, Joseph Wolpe (pictured here with client) helped patients confront anxiety-producing objects or situation.

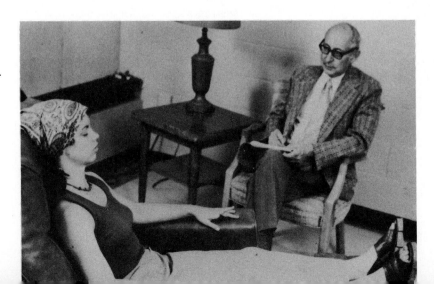

Table 13.3

Example of Systematic Desensitization

In systematic desensitization, an individual relaxes and imagines objects or situations that cause fear and anxiety. The client starts with less frightening images and gradually moves to more frightening ones. Here is an example of the images used by a client who was afraid of death.

1. Seeing an ambulance.
2. Seeing a hospital.
3. Being inside a hospital.
4. Reading an obituary notice of an old person.
5. Passing a funeral home.
6. Seeing a funeral.
7. Driving past a cemetery.
8. Reading an obituary notice of a young person dying of a heart attack.
9. Seeing a burial assemblage from afar.
10. Attending a burial.
11. Seeing first husband in his coffin.

Source: Wolpe, 1958.

systematic desensitization
behavior modification strategy that teaches a client to relax and then to imagine a feared object or situation, thus reducing anxiety

flooding
behavior modification strategy that exposes a client to a feared object or situation; the fear presumably extinguishes

Classical conditioning procedures are used to change someone's emotional associations to particular stimuli. In **systematic desensitization,** a person is taught to relax and then to imagine feared objects or situations, starting with mildly upsetting images and moving gradually to images that are quite frightening (see Table 13.3). Joseph Wolpe developed this classical conditioning therapy in 1958, and since then, it has become the treatment of choice for circumscribed fears and phobias. It's effective more than 80 percent of the time (Rachman & Wilson, 1980).

According to learning theory, phobias persist because people flee from the objects they fear, thereby reducing anxiety and reinforcing their avoidance (Chapter 6). What happens if someone doesn't flee? Presumably, they learn that the snake or the bug or the social interaction does not bring them harm. Their fear extinguishes. This leads us to another classical conditioning treatment for anxiety disorders called **flooding.** Someone with agoraphobia, for instance, may be taken to a shopping center and not allowed to leave. The first hour is frightening, sometimes unpleasantly so, but eventually her fear subsides. Flooding brings relief to as many as 75 percent of individuals with phobias, and the benefits remain years later (e.g., Emmelkamp & Kuipers, 1979).

Note that flooding involves a hazard. If a client flees from the anxiety-provoking situation before her anxiety has had time to dissipate, her escape response will be reinforced. Then, she will be even less likely to confront the situation in the future.

Operant conditioning procedures that change a person's behavior by manipulating its consequences also fall within this type of therapy. Bad habits can be eliminated by punishing these particular behaviors. Good habits can be increased by reinforcing these behaviors. Note that this approach intervenes in the person's environment. The therapist changes the rules of the game (i.e., the prevailing pattern of punishments and rewards), thereby modifying the client's behavior.

Consider **aversion therapy,** in which an aversive stimulus is associated with some behavior that is deemed undesirable, in the hope that the client will learn to link the behavior with its new consequences and thereby refrain from performing it. For example, alcohol might be mixed with a drug that produces nausea. Or someone with a deviant sexual impulse—such as one that involves children—might have his inappropriate sexual responses followed by electric shock (Chapter 16).

For another example of an operant approach to therapy, let's start with a child who never shares with other children, never follows his parent's suggestions, never does his homework, and never walks the dog. A behavior therapist wouldn't look to the child for an explanation of these actions, but rather to the child's environment. Perhaps the parents inadvertently reward precisely those behaviors that so upset them by paying a lot of attention to their son when he acts negatively. When he happens to behave himself, once in a blue moon, his parents ignore him or—even worse—heap unpleasant demands on him.

One solution here is **parent training:** teaching the parents how to respond to their child. They should reward him for behaviors they wish to increase and not reward him for behaviors they wish to decrease. Now, all of this may strike you as obvious. Are there really any parents out there who don't know that they can catch more flies with honey than with vinegar? The answer is that there are thousands if not millions of such parents. If you don't believe this, just go to a crowded store some weekend and watch how parents respond to their children. Keep in mind Thorndike's law of effect: Behaviors that are rewarded will recur. You will be horrified. Before your very eyes, you will see the creation of an entire generation of monsters! At any rate, parent training and similar procedures prove highly effective in changing someone's behavior (Ollendick, 1986).

Behavior modifiers also use techniques derived from Albert Bandura's (1986) notion of observational learning. In other words, problems can be solved by having clients watch models, either on film or in person, who successfully cope with whatever overwhelms them. Fears and phobias can be eliminated this way, providing the best justification ever for Grade B horror flicks. None of us fear swamp creatures or space aliens after seeing thousands of them wiped out by movie heroes or heroines. More seriously, another use of modeling is to reduce people's fears about entering hospitals for surgery. If shown a file of a patient who goes through a surgical procedure without fear, a person experiences less apprehension about doing so himself (e.g., King, Hamilton, & Murphy, 1983).

There is a considerable body of mythology surrounding behavior modification. Let's dispel a few of the false beliefs. First, some believe that behavior modification is an all-powerful strategy for making anyone do anything the behavior therapist wishes. This is inaccurate. Behavior modification has its share of failures, particularly as a treatment for substance abuse (Miller, 1983). Second, some believe that behavior modification

Therapists use various approaches—developmental, communications, behavioral—to address problems that threaten the marital relationship.

marital therapy
a form of therapy in which a married couple is treated as a unit because of problems in the relationship

family therapy
therapy in which a family as a whole is treated because of problems in the family relationship

doesn't work at all. This too is inaccurate, as we've seen in this section. Third, some believe that behavior therapy is dehumanizing. Perhaps brief descriptions of the procedures, like the ones presented above, are responsible for this misconception. Out of context, the techniques seem cold and mechanical. But behavior therapists are not technicians. They are first and foremost therapists, which means they deploy their strategies within a therapeutic relationship. The helping alliance is just as important in behavior modification as it is in other forms of therapy.

As stated several times in this book, behavior modification is one of the most notable achievements of psychology in the twentieth century. It has revolutionized the treatment of fears and phobias. And the therapists using this approach were the first to demonstrate how to assess the effectiveness of therapy. Mythology aside, the world is much better off for its existence.

Marital, Family, and Group Therapy

DSM-III-R assumes that problems exist within a person. But this is not always true. Some problems reside in the relationships between and among people. Therapy cannot proceed simply by treating the parts of the relationship. Instead, the relationship itself must become the client.

In **marital therapy,** the "client" quite obviously is the married couple. One of the goals of marital therapy is to encourage wives and husbands to solve their problems as a couple. Deciding who is right or wrong in squabbles is often counterproductive, and so one common strategy is to teach the couple how to fight. Rather than telling each other what wretched human beings you are, the emphasis is on saying what specifically annoys you and what would make you happy. This sounds like good advice for all of us, whether or not we are married.

There are three types of marital therapy: developmental approaches, communications approaches, and behavioral approaches (Sundberg, Taplin, & Tyler, 1983). With *developmental approaches,* the couple is urged to see that their marriage evolves and changes. What was comfortable at one stage in a marriage may be awkward at another. Many marriages break up soon after the honeymoon ends, simply because the couple doesn't appreciate that honeymoons *do* end.

With *communications approaches* to marital therapy, husbands and wives are helped both to send and to receive messages more skillfully. Too many couples believe they can read each other's minds, but they never test this assumption by directly asking their partner about things.

Finally, with *behavioral approaches,* the therapist has married individuals make their contract with each other explicit. What does each want from the other, and what is each willing to give in return? This may sound a bit crass, but it's better than divorce (remember the discussion of divorce in Chapter 10). But marital therapy does not always save marriages. Sometimes the explicit goal is to dissolve a relationship in a way that leaves survivors.

In **family therapy,** the "client" is the family as a whole: the parents, children, and anyone else who shares the same roof with them (see Figure 13.4). The rationale underlying family therapy is that there are no individ-

Figure 13.4
Family Therapy. In this therapy session, all the members of a family participate.

ual problems, only manifestations of disturbed family relationships. One member of a family, often a child, may be the identified patient in that he shows psychopathology, but the cause is not within him.

Suppose a child becomes a problem at school after several years of model behavior. A family therapist would look for recent changes within the family. Maybe Mom and Dad are contemplating divorce. Maybe a grandparent has moved into the house, and the child now has to share a bedroom with a younger sibling. Family therapy is usually explained from the vantage point of **systems theory,** which regards families as complex wholes. Changes in one part inevitably affect all other parts.

The goal of this kind of therapy is to encourage healthier interactions among family members before pathological symptoms appear. To this end, family therapists may use various exercises to reveal to the family their modes of relating. For example, a therapist might ask family members to switch places and act out each other's roles. Or family members may be encouraged to exaggerate the things they do to annoy each other. Once the insights are gained, the therapist can try to bring about change.

Group therapy shares the same rationale as marital therapy and family therapy: that problems are best conceived and treated in a social context. However, in this form of treatment, the therapy group is composed of individuals who do not know each other prior to treatment. Usually, the members of a group have similar problems, such as a particular diagnosis (e.g., schizophrenia), or a life transition to be surmounted (e.g., divorce).

Yalom (1970, 1975) argues that participation in group therapy helps people in a number of ways:

- by instilling hope in the members
- by letting them know they are not the only ones with problems
- by imparting useful solutions
- by allowing members to help one another
- by developing social skills
- by seeing the impact one has on others
- by creating bonds with a group

From this view, the group therapist tries to facilitate these changes by leading group discussions. Comments on the group process (the patterns of interaction rather than its content) are of critical importance here. "Does everyone notice how you gang up on James?" The hope in group therapy is that its participants will gain insight into how they relate to one another, and then use these insights in other spheres of life to create more harmonious relationships.

Community Psychology

community psychology
the use of psychological theories and findings to change social conditions so that the future likelihood of problems is reduced

We noted earlier that therapy is inherently conservative: trying to fit the person to the world, not vice versa. There is an exception to this generalization, however, and it is **community psychology.** Some therapists do not wait for people to develop problems before trying to help. Instead, they try to avoid problems in the first place by changing the larger community. If they can eliminate or minimize the preconditions for disorders, then they can reduce the prevalence of psychological problems.

Community psychology takes as its role model the field of public health, which combats disease not with antibiotics but with prevention. What is the psychological equivalent of draining swamps? We can identify several. In *primary prevention,* community psychologists literally try to undo possible causes of problems before they can have an impact (see Figure 13-5). For example, Head Start programs give youngsters from low-income families an educational boost prior to first grade, in hopes of staving off the problems that occur later in life when schooling goes awry (Chapter 8).

In *consultation,* community psychologists make their expertise available to community groups who want advice. For instance, they may give lectures on depression and suicide to community groups. They may be interviewed for magazines or newspapers or even radio and television. They may be hired by businesses to give advice on the treatment or prevention of problems such as drug and alcohol use among workers.

In *rehabilitation,* community psychologists help people who have been institutionalized for various reasons make a smooth transition back to everyday life. This is a particular problem for individuals leaving psy-

Figure 13.5
Community Psychology. Community psychologists try to establish programs that will prevent problems from occuring.

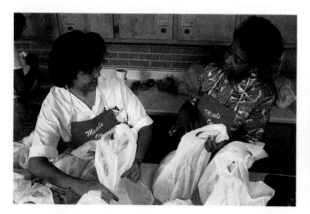

Beginning with Freud, therapists used techniques such as hypnosis to relieve patients' symptoms. Here Jean Charcot is shown lecturing on hypnosis.

chiatric hospitals. As you know, many homeless individuals in our large cities are former psychiatric patients who haven't fared well since leaving hospitals.

In *social advocacy,* community psychologists roll up their sleeves and delve into the political process, urging passage of legislation that will further benefit the psychological well-being of our citizens. Psychologists throughout the years have taken stances with respect to desegregation, gun control, welfare, mandatory seat belts in automobiles, the 55-mile-per-hour speed limit, and so on. The line between psychology and society is nowhere more fuzzy than in the work of community psychologists.

The effectiveness of community psychology is not clear, and the field is still very much in its infancy (Cowen, 1977). It is fair to say that there is less enthusiasm about community psychology today than several decades ago. Different reasons for this situation may be cited. On the one hand, perhaps too few of society's resources have so far been invested in community psychology projects, thereby decreasing the chance for success of those projects. On the other hand, perhaps certain problems are inevitable and cannot be prevented or minimized, regardless of the effort made. The success or failure of the recently declared "war on drugs" may shed some light on the ongoing debate over community psychology.

Evaluating Therapy Effectiveness

When Freud and others first began to treat patients using psychological methods, it was obvious when therapy was effective. Remember that these first psychotherapy patients were hysterics, with bizarre alterations in physical functioning. They were blind or deaf. They could not feel or walk or swallow. Following an intervention such as hypnosis, their symptoms vanished. There was no ambiguity about the cure, because both the therapist and the patient observed a change that was sudden, dramatic, and unlikely to have occurred without the intervention. The evidence was too compelling to question whether therapy worked.

As psychoanalysts began to treat an ever greater number and variety of patients, and as other forms of psychotherapy began to develop, the issue of effectiveness still did not arise. Therapists and patients alike continued to believe that beneficial change took place. Note, though, that the factors originally compelling a belief in therapy effectiveness fell away with the rise and spread of psychotherapy. Patients were typically "neurotic"— defined not by overt symptoms but by presumed underlying processes. How can we tell that change occurs if symptoms are not critical? Further, change for most patients is gradual. And therapy may take years, during which any number of things could transpire that might better explain any change that does occur.

As the profession of psychotherapy grew and grew, there was less and less reason to believe that clients were benefiting. Criticisms of the effectiveness of therapy eventually were raised. These criticisms in turn led psychology researchers to carefully examine the issue of therapy effectiveness. In this section, we will discuss therapy research, starting with the criticisms that inspired close scrutiny of the effectiveness of psychotherapy.

Eysenck: No, Therapy Doesn't Work

The popularity of psychotherapy combined with the lack of hard evidence of its effectiveness almost demanded that someone come along and stick a skeptical pin into the therapy balloon. And that's what Hans Eysenck did. In 1952, he published a highly critical attack on the entire business of psychotherapy. Does therapy work? Typically, the question was answered by pointing to an improvement in the patient's condition over the course of therapy. Eysenck argued, reasonably, that the results of particular case studies do not really answer the question, because a person may well have improved without the therapist's intervention. This improvement is called *spontaneous remission.*

The more useful comparison is therefore between those who receive therapy and those who do not. You'll recognize this as the simplest form of an experiment, where "therapy or not" is the independent variable and patient improvement is the dependent variable (Chapter 1).

Eysenck did not conduct his own study. Instead, he assembled data from different investigations. From five studies of the effect of psychoanalytic therapy, he calculated an average figure of 44 percent of neurotic patients showing improvement (as judged by their therapist). Nineteen studies of eclectic therapy yielded a 64 percent average of neurotic patients showing improvement (again, as judged by their therapist).

Next Eysenck needed to know how many people with problems similar to those of therapy clients improved without therapy. He chose two such comparison groups: the proportion of patients with anxiety or depressive disorders discharged from state mental hospitals because they improved (even though they received only custodial help); and the proportion of individuals who filed disability claims for psychological reasons with insurance companies and then returned to work within a 2-year period. In both cases, the figure was 72 percent, exceeding the average improvement rate following psychotherapy!

Although he pointed out that further research would be a good idea, Eysenck (1952, pp. 322–323) nonetheless drew some strong conclusions from his comparisons:

> . . . [T]hese data . . . fail to prove that psychotherapy, Freudian or otherwise, facilitates the recovery of neurotic patients. They show that roughly two-thirds of a group of neurotic patients will recover or improve to a marked extent within about two years of the onset of their illness, whether they are treated by means of psychotherapy or not. This figure appears to be remarkably stable from one investigation to another, regardless of type of patient treated, standard of recovery employed, or method of therapy used. From the point of the neurotic, these figures are encouraging; from the point of view of the psychotherapist, they can hardly be called very favorable to his claims. . . .
>
> These results and conclusions will no doubt contradict the strong feeling of usefulness and therapeutic success which many psychiatrists and clinical psychologists hold. While it is true that subjective feelings of this type have no place in science, they are likely to prevent an easy acceptance of the general argument presented here.

(By the way, these are very strong words for a professional article.)

Eysenck's challenge demanded attention. It did not convince all readers, because his data were not as compelling as he thought them to be. Patients were not randomly assigned to receive therapy or not, and unknown factors may have confounded his comparisons. Further, as you may have noticed, different criteria were used to ascertain improvement: therapist judgment on the one hand and hospital discharge or returning to work on the other. Nevertheless, his conclusions forcefully reminded psychologists that proof of their endeavor was not readily available.

Difficulties in Evaluating Therapy

Eysenck highlighted the problem of spontaneous remission (benefit without intervention), but other problems also make it difficult to decide whether therapy works. For example, what *criterion of improvement* should be used? As we saw earlier in the chapter, psychologists with allegiance to the different models conceive therapeutic change in drastically different ways, making it difficult to compare across types of therapy.

A related issue is the *operationalization of improvement* that the researcher chooses. Early studies of therapy effectiveness relied almost exclusively on the therapist's judgment on the matter. You can see why this operationalization is less than ideal. Therapists are not immune to the human tendency to present oneself in a positive light. Asking the client about the effectiveness of therapy may be somewhat more objective than asking the therapist, but again the skeptic would not be convinced that this is a rigorous measure. Clients, just like their therapists, strongly wish to believe that treatment has been worthwhile. Consider the investment of time, money, and energy demanded of those in psychotherapy.

Therapy research is plagued by *heterogeneity of clients*. To the degree that clients receiving therapy are quite different from one another, extraneous variables can cloud one's conclusions. The same can be said about *heterogeneity of therapists*. To the degree that therapists take drastically different approaches with their clients, still other confounds enter the picture. No one conducts therapy per se, but rather this form or that form of therapy. A question of great interest is whether a particular form of therapy is useful, but research shows that not all therapists who espouse a given approach really deliver that form of therapy (e.g., Fiedler, 1950, 1951).

Next is the problem posed by *placebo cures*. In medicine, a placebo is a drug that benefits a person not because of its inherent chemical properties but because the individual expects to feel better. In psychotherapy, therefore, a placebo cure is one brought about by expectations on the part of the client, and not because the therapist did anything that was specifically helpful. Presumably, such benefits in therapy are short-lived, but they nonetheless confound any attempt to evaluate the effectiveness of therapy.

It was mentioned earlier that a large number of individuals who start out in therapy drop out before it is finished. This *attrition* makes research terribly difficult. Imagine 60 percent of the white rats in a learning experiment deciding that running a maze is a poor use of their time. How much confidence would we have in the data yielded by those who remain? Remember, those who drop out of therapy are not a random group of clients. We can suppose that the clients who stay in therapy are those who are improving the most. All we gain by studying these people is the ability to offer the circular conclusion that "therapy is beneficial for clients who improve."

Yet another problem in doing research on the effects of psychotherapy is that of *relapse:* someone's problem returning after a period of time. For instance, people with substance use disorders, depression, or schizophrenia may solve their problems in the course of therapy, only to encounter the same difficulty some months or years later. Was therapy a success or failure for these individuals? A simple answer eludes us, because we need to know the time period involved, the circumstances surrounding the return of the problem, and so on. Regardless, many researchers try to follow therapy clients not only through therapy but for months or even years beyond.

One last problem worth noting is that of the *appropriate comparison group* in therapy research. We can easily imagine the ideal comparison. We start with a group of individuals, each having the exact same problem. We randomly divide them into two groups. One group receives therapy, and the other group does not. But it's hard to get people to stand still and stay in such a comparison group, particularly if they have a serious problem and particularly if therapy (for the other research subjects) takes months or years. Random assignment also raises ethical questions about withholding treatment, which is a lot easier to justify in the abstract ("for the good of humankind") than in the concrete ("we're sorry, Mrs. Jones, but your child will not receive the treatment that might help her; she's in the control group").

By now you may be thinking that the effectiveness of therapy is impossible to ascertain, but that's far from the consensus. In the decades since Eysenck's (1952) broadside attack on therapy effectiveness, researchers have devised reasonable solutions to all of these difficulties. The solutions are not foolproof, of course, but as sophisticated consumers of psychology research, we know that no field of psychology has perfect research methods.

Trends Making Therapy Research Possible

Here are some recent trends that make it possible to have better studies of therapy effectiveness:

- Behavioral therapies have become increasingly popular, which means that change is defined in terms of unambiguous criteria; for example, someone with agoraphobia is improved to the degree that she goes to crowded stores.
- There is a growing tendency to use "hard" measures of improvement such as observation of actual behaviors, as opposed to " soft" measures such as therapist or client opinions; for example, the effectiveness of therapy for simple phobias is measured by asking the client to touch a snake or lizard or whatever.
- Time limits are being set on therapy—often, 10 or 15 weekly sessions.
- Relatedly, individuals on a waiting list to receive therapy are being used as the comparison group; "Well, Mrs. Jones, your child will start therapy in 2 months; in the meantime, we'd like to ask her some questions."
- Particularly stringent criteria for including subjects in studies, called *research diagnoses,* are now being used, ensuring that subjects receiving therapy are homogeneous with respect to their problem; for instance, subjects included in a study of therapy for depression should unambiguously be depressed and at the same time have no other disorder.
- There is growing use of *therapy manuals,* explicit descriptions of what a therapist should do in particular sessions (Luborsky & DeRubeis, 1984); these ensure that all clients receive the same intervention.
- "Attention" control groups are now used. These are made up of individuals who meet with a professional to discuss problems but are not given active therapy; this procedure begins to control for placebo effects.
- There is now greater acceptance of *analogue research:* studying people with circumscribed and specific problems (such as test anxiety); it is recognized that these problems are not as profound as those of most individuals in therapy, but they are thought to resemble them in relevant ways.

These innovations, separately and together, strengthen therapy research.

Let's look closely at an exemplary investigation of the effectiveness of therapy: Gordon Paul's (1966) study of the treatment of public speaking anxiety. Indeed, this particular study is widely regarded as the first solid demonstration that it is possible to research the effectiveness of therapy.

Paul used an analogue approach, obtaining research subjects from public speaking classes at the University of Illinois. Anxiety about giving speeches in front of others is not by itself a DSM-III-R disorder, although it is a possible symptom of several disorders—notably social phobia. Regardless, public speaking anxiety is a problem for those who experience it, overlapping in important ways with more pervasive anxiety disorders.

Of the 710 students enrolled in these classes, Paul chose the 96 who were most anxious about speaking in public (and were willing to participate and were not in therapy elsewhere). "Anxiety" was ascertained by responses to a questionnaire that all public speaking students completed. The questionnaire posed questions such as the following (pp. 107–108):

true   false   1. I am in constant fear of forgetting my speech.

true   false   2. My thoughts become confused and jumbled when I speak before an audience.

true   false   3. I always avoid speaking in public if possible.

true   false   4. It is difficult for me to calmly search my mind for the right words to express my thoughts.

Once chosen for the research, and prior to therapy, the subjects completed a practice speech that allowed Paul to obtain a number of "objective" measures of their anxiety about speaking, including their pulse rate and degree of perspiration right before they began speaking. During the speech, four observers independently tallied the presence or absence of such behavioral manifestations of anxiety as pacing, swaying, grimacing, knees trembling, throat clearing, voice quivering, and stammering.

Then the subjects were randomly assigned to one of five conditions (see Table 13.4). Group One received insight-oriented psychotherapy, meaning that their therapy followed a psychoanalytic direction. In short, it encouraged individuals to understand why they experienced anxiety about speaking in public.

Group Two was treated with systematic desensitization. They were taught to relax, and while in a relaxed state, they were encouraged to imagine speaking in public. As you know, classical conditioning provides the rationale for this technique, because the person learns to associate speaking not with anxiety but with relaxation.

Group Three received an attention placebo. They met with a therapist who gave them a "fast-acting tranquilizer" (really made of baking soda) that supposedly would build their tolerance for stress. To prove the effec-

Table 13.4

Design of Paul's (1966) Study

Group One	Subjects received insight-oriented therapy.
Group Two	Subjects were treated with systematic desensitization.
Group Three	Subjects were given a "fast-acting tranquilizer"—in actuality a placebo made of baking soda—to encourage the expectation of change.
Group Four	Subjects were treated like those in Groups One, Two, and Three, except with no therapy.
Group Five	Subjects were never contacted about participation in the study until its end.

tiveness of this tranquilizer, these subjects participated in the supposedly stressful task of detecting sonar signals from an audiotape. The task was actually not at all stressful. It usually produced drowsiness. So, Paul did all he could in this condition to encourage subjects to expect some kind of benefit.

These three groups were the therapy conditions. Five experienced therapists administered the respective treatments to individual subjects in all of these groups. Note that the procedure of having the same therapist deliver different therapies cancels out confounds that would otherwise be introduced if the given therapists were assigned to only one therapy condition. In each case, the therapists were told that a reduction in anxiety symptoms was their goal. They spent 5 hours with each client over a 6-week period. And the therapy sessions were tape-recorded to ensure that the required form of therapy was undertaken and not another.

The two other groups in Paul's experiment were a no-treatment classroom control, made up of individuals who were just like the subjects in the therapy conditions but did not receive individual therapy; and a no-contact classroom control, made up of individuals who scored "anxious" on the original questionnaire but were never contacted about participating in the research. These subjects did *not* give the practice speech. Paul needed these comparison groups to see if subjects experience a reduction in anxiety without therapy or anything that resembles it.

Once the therapy sessions were over, all subjects completed questionnaires measuring their speaking anxiety. Subjects in the three therapy groups gave another practice speech, as did those in the no-treatment classroom control. The physiological measures were again taken, and observers again tallied manifestations of anxiety during their speeches.

Paul's results were clear and impressive. In terms of the questionnaire measures as well as the behavioral observations, subjects in all three therapy groups improved relative to the control subjects. Anxiety was therefore reduced, and the conclusion follows that therapy works. Those in the systematic desensitization group improved most of all and were the only subjects who showed a reduction in the physiological measures of anxiety. Ratings by therapists and clients corroborated these findings, which is important. Perhaps "soft" measures of therapy effectiveness are not so capricious after all. Finally, the benefits of therapy were still present when the subjects were again tested 2 years later (Paul, 1967).

Smith and Glass: Yes, Therapy Works

Paul's study shows how therapy effectiveness can be investigated. Researchers heeded this example well, and in the subsequent decades literally hundreds of similar investigations were conducted. In 1977, an extremely important review of this literature was reported by Mary Smith and Gene Glass.

They surveyed 375 separate studies of therapy outcome, representing some 25,000 subjects. But the sheer magnitude of the research summarized is not why this literature review is noteworthy. Instead, Smith and Glass (1977) surmounted a problem faced by all scholars who try to summarize the thrust of disparate investigations. What do you say when some studies point to one conclusion, other studies to the opposite conclusion, and still other studies to no conclusion at all?

Figure 13.6

The Effects of Psychotherapy. Here is a summary of the hundreds of studies investigating the effectiveness of psychotherapy (Smith, Glass, & Miller, 1980). The length of each line shows the percentage of clients receiving a particular treatment who improved relative to similar individuals who did not receive treatment. So, the average client in client-centered therapy did better than about 73 percent of individuals not treated.

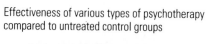

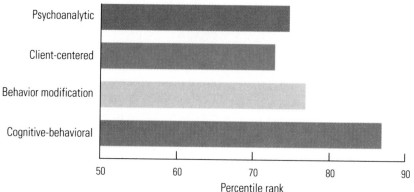

Effectiveness of various types of psychotherapy compared to untreated control groups

meta-analysis

a statistical technique for combining the results of separate studies and arriving at an overall conclusion about the magnitude of an experimental effect

Smith and Glass provided us with one answer using the statistical technique known as **meta-analysis.** This procedure takes the results of separate experimental studies and then combines them to yield an overall estimate of the magnitude of an experimental effect (in this case therapy). Specifically, they used meta-analysis to answer two questions. First, is therapy more effective than no therapy? Second, are some forms of therapy more effective than others?

> The results . . . demonstrate the beneficial effects of counseling and psychotherapy. Despite volumes devoted to the theoretical differences among different schools of psychotherapy, the results of research demonstrate negligible differences in the effects produced by different therapy types. Unconditional judgments of superiority of one type of therapy or another, and all that these claims imply about treatment and training policy, are unjustified. (Smith & Glass, 1977, p. 760)

In other words, therapy works . . . but all forms work with the same effectiveness (see Figure 13.6). It appears that "everyone has won and all must have prizes" (Luborsky, Singer, & Luborsky 1975).

This is good news to the consumer looking for therapy, but confusing to therapists. Right now, research takes a more detailed look at psychotherapy. Granted that skepticism concerning therapy effectiveness has been laid to rest, investigators are asking more specific questions, such as what is common to different forms of successful therapy? Can specific ingredients that are responsible for change be isolated? Is it possible to match particular therapies to particular problems? How can long-term relapse be prevented? Therapists hope that answers to these questions will allow them to devise and conduct forms of psychotherapy that are even more effective.

In this chapter, we have discussed how psychological disorders are treated. There are many different approaches to therapy that can be broadly classified as biomedical or psychological. Despite previous skepticism concerning the effectiveness of therapy, psychologists can now conclude with confidence that psychotherapy works.

Postscript: What Can a Friend Do?

Whenever I teach a psychology course, I am approached by at least one student, who waits after class until just the two of us remain. I know what she's going to say. She always starts with "I have a friend . . . " and proceeds to describe someone who sounds like a person who is really hurting. Maybe it's a problem with depression or bulimia or alcohol or sexuality. Regardless, the person apparently doesn't acknowledge that anything is wrong, even though the friend who is talking to me is convinced that this person is suffering from a major disorder.

"What can a friend do?" is ultimately what my students want to know. There are several answers here, and perhaps they will be useful to you if you are ever close to someone with a serious problem. On the "somebody ought to do something" level (Chapter 12), there is nothing you can legally undertake unless your friend poses an immediate danger to himself or others. No one can be forced to start therapy, and there is no magic formula to make someone want to be helped.

On the "I want to tell his or her parents" level, I urge you to think this through carefully. There may be little that parents can do except get angry or worried. And then your friend will have another problem.

On the "is it okay to talk directly to my friend?" level, I say sure, so long as you talk as a friend does. Say you're worried; say you'd like to help; say that you're a friend. Don't play diagnostician or therapist. The best thing a friend can do is to be a friend, and that's really pretty significant, friend.

Summary

Topics of Concern

- Psychotherapists use the facts and theories of general psychology to help solve someone's problems in living.
- One of the important topics concerning psychotherapists is defining what is meant by psychological health. As with defining psychological abnormality, the explanatory model to which one subscribes—biomedical, psychoanalytic, or cognitive-behavioral—determines exactly what vision of health is preferred.
- Another topic of concern to psychotherapists is whether psychopathology among at least some individuals is inevitable.
- Finally, regardless of a therapist's approach, he or she wants to know how and why therapy is effective.

Therapists and Clients

- Although a variety of therapies exist, all have in common a person with a problem (the client) working with another person who is an expert in change (the therapist) to solve that problem.
- Psychologists have extensively studied therapists, clients, and their working relationships in an attempt to specify the factors that contribute to successful therapy.
- Therapist characteristics—age, experience, gender, ethnicity, and theoretical orientation, for example—bear no consistent relationship to the success of therapy. More important are characteristics such as warmth, empathy, and supportiveness on the part of the therapist; these facilitate effective therapy regardless of the particular approach that is followed.
- Therapists have a sometimes complex relationship with society as a whole, because it is not always clear just who they serve: the individual client or the larger social group.
- As many as one out of five Americans will seek therapy at some point in their lives. Demoralization in the face of a problem seems to determine who seeks out therapy and who does not. Many people who begin therapy drop out before it is over because their expectations are not being met. Clients who stay in therapy and improve the most tend to be those who have abundant resources and less severe problems in the first place.
- The relationship between client and therapist is obviously important to the success of therapy. To the degree that clients and therapist can form a successful working relationship, therapy is successful.

Types of Therapy

- Biomedical therapies include drugs, electroconvulsive shock, and psychosurgery.
- Individual "talking" therapies include psychoanalysis (developed by Freud), client-centered therapy (Rogers), rational-emotive therapy (Ellis), and cognitive therapy (Beck).
- Behavior modification uses principles of learning to change an individual's behavior. Particular techniques are based on classical conditioning, operant conditioning, and modeling.
- Marital therapy, family therapy, and group therapy embody the assumption that problems reside not in the individual but between and among people. Treatment must therefore be social as well.
- Community psychology is the only approach to therapy that is not conservative, because it tries to change societal conditions to make problems less likely.

Evaluating Therapy Effectiveness

- Whether or not therapy works has been the most hotly contested issue in the entire field of clinical psychology. Numerous difficulties confront the researcher who wishes to investigate the effectiveness of therapy.
- When these difficulties are surmounted, however, the conclusion is clear that therapy is effective.
- At the present, no form of therapy seems more effective than any other form.

Important Terms and Names

What follows is a list of the core terms and names for this chapter. Your instructor may emphasize other terms as well. Throughout the chapter, glossary terms appear in **boldface** type. They are defined in the text, and each term, along with its definition, is repeated in the margin.

Topics of Concern

biomedical therapies/539
psychotherapies/539

Therapists and Clients

transference/549
matching model hypothesis/550
helping alliance/550

Types of Therapy

psychosurgery/551
electroconvulsive therapy (ECT)/552
anti-anxiety medication/553
anti-depressant medication/553
anti-psychotic medication/553
psychoanalysis/556
client-centered therapy/559
rational-emotive therapy/560
cognitive therapy/560
behavior modification/561
marital therapy/564
family therapy/564
group therapy/565
community psychology/566

Sigmund Freud/557
Carl Rogers/558
Albert Ellis/560
Aaron Beck/560

Evaluating Therapy Effectiveness

meta-analysis/574

Hans Eysenck/568
Gordon Paul/571
Mary Smith and Gene Glass/573

1. Which model of abnormality views psychological health as a preponderance of pleasure over pain?
   a. biomedical
   b. psychoanalytic
   c. cognitive-behavioral
   d. all of the above
   e. none of the above
   According to the cognitive-behavioral view, psychologically healthy people maximize good feelings while minimizing bad ones./541

2. A critical factor pushing someone into therapy is
   a. demoralization.
   b. manic symptoms.
   c. poverty.
   d. suicidal thoughts.
   People enter therapy when they have begun to give up hope in the wake of some problem in living./548

3. According to the matching model hypothesis, therapists and clients work best together when they
   a. are both extraverts.
   b. are both introverts.
   c. form a good working relationship.
   d. possess complementary personality characteristics.
   e. possess the same personality characteristics.
   The matching model hypothesis proposes that therapists and clients with similar personality characteristics work best together. Support for this hypothesis has not been found./549

4. The crucial factor in electroconvulsive therapy is the
   a. induction of a convulsion.
   b. loss of consciousness.
   c. loss of memory.
   d. use of electric shock.
   The induction of a convulsion is the crucial factor that makes ECT an effective treatment for depression. The forerunners of ECT induced convulsions chemically./553

5. The original "talking" therapy was
   a. client-centered therapy.
   b. cognitive therapy.
   c. psychoanalysis.
   d. rational-emotive therapy.
   Freud's psychoanalytic therapy was the first "talking" treatment, the one from which all others were derived./557

6. Carl Rogers developed
   a. client-centered therapy.
   b. cognitive therapy.
   c. psychoanalysis.
   d. rational-emotive therapy.
   Rogers based client-centered therapy on his self-theory of personality (Chapter 11)./559

7. _____ therapy is based on the premise that problems reside in the relationships between and among people.
   a. Family
   b. Group
   c. Marital
   d. All of the above
   e. None of the above
   In all of these therapies, problems are conceptualized as interpersonal, and treatment is accordingly social./564

8. Therapy tends to be inherently conservative, with the exception of
   a. behavior modification.
   b. cognitive therapy.
   c. community psychology.
   d. psychoanalysis.
   e. rational-emotive therapy.
   Because community psychology tries to change social conditions to make problems less likely, it is not a conservative endeavor./566

9. All of these trends made possible research into the effectiveness of therapy except
   a. "hard" measures of improvement.
   b. research diagnoses.
   c. the advent of psychoanalysis.
   d. therapy manuals.
   e. wait-list comparisons.

   The popularity of psychoanalysis made therapy research difficult because of the ambiguity of its terms. It was the advent of behavioral treatments that led to research into the effectiveness of therapy./570

10. According to Mary Smith and Gene Glass, therapy
   a. works.
   b. does not work.

   In their 1977 article, Smith and Glass surveyed research that conclusively pointed to the effectiveness of therapy./573

Our everyday social interaction is influenced by our tendency to classify
people according to stereotypes.

Chapter Fourteen

Social Cognition

Topics of Concern

November 23, 1951, was a Saturday, and on this day, the Dartmouth football team played the Princeton team in what proved to be a rough and controversial game. Both teams were frequently penalized. There were injuries to key players on both sides. Princeton's star quarterback, All-American Dick Kazmaier, left the game early with a broken nose. Not long after, two players from Dartmouth, Jim Miller and Gene Howard, suffered severe leg injuries.

Princeton ended up winning the game, but fans at both schools continued to talk about the violence that plagued the contest. Indeed, the student newspaper at each college editorialized about the questionable tactics of the other school's team. On November 27, the *Daily Princetonian* reported:

This observer has never seen quite such a disgusting exhibition . . . the blame must be laid primarily on Dartmouth's doorstep. Princeton, obviously the better team, had no reason to rough up Dartmouth. Looking at the situation rationally, we don't see why the . . . [Dartmouth team] should make a deliberate attempt to cripple Dick Kazmaier or any other Princeton player. The Dartmouth psychology, however, is not rational itself.

The Dartmouth paper also ran a story about the game, arguing that the Princeton coach had incited the violence by unjustly accusing the Dartmouth team of trying deliberately to injure his star player. Although the first injury had been inadvertent, argued the paper, the subsequent injuries were directly attributable to the fact the Princeton coach had:

. . . instilled the old see-what-they-did-go-get-them attitude into his players. His talk got results . . . one bad leg and one leg broken. The game was rough . . . yet most of the roughing penalties were called against Princeton while Dartmouth received more of the illegal-use-of-the-hand variety.

Although this game occurred decades ago, its aftermath is familiar to sports fans today. Roughness by our team is simply hard-nosed football, the way the game is meant to be played. Roughness by the opponent is obviously dirty, the result of intentional attempts to hurt our players.

In 1951, Albert H. Hastorf was teaching at Dartmouth, and Hadley Cantril was teaching at Princeton. These two psychologists were so struck by reactions of their respective schools to this football game that they decided to investigate systematically people's perceptions of the game. They con-

ducted two studies. In the first, they asked Dartmouth and Princeton students to answer a questionnaire about the football game. Was the game a dirty one? Who started the roughness? What were the intentions of the players on the two teams? In the second study, they showed Dartmouth and Princeton students a film of the game, asking them to keep track of the instances of rough play that they saw.

Both studies pointed to the same conclusion. The students "saw" the game according to their allegiances. Princeton students saw the Dartmouth team committing more infractions than the Princeton team. They believed that the Dartmouth team started the incidents and that the injury to Princeton's star player was intentional. And Dartmouth students answered in the opposite way.

Hastorf and Cantril (1954) added an interesting postscript to the report of their studies that underscores the major conclusion. A Dartmouth alumni group was sent a film of the game. No one in the group had seen the game previously, but the viewers were well aware of the controversy that surrounded it. When they watched the film, they

Princeton students were outraged when their All-American quarterback, Dick Kazmaier, featured here on the cover of *Time* magazine, was injured in a 1951 game against Dartmouth. Dartmouth students were not as concerned about the game's "excessive violence." Would an injury to the star player on your school's team affect your opinion of the way the game was played?

became confused, because they didn't see *any* of the infractions supposedly committed by the Dartmouth team. The alumni group concluded that the film must have been edited, although in fact it had not been. They requested that the complete film be sent to them!

This football game serves to introduce the present chapter, which looks at how people make sense of social events. Notice that the fans of the two teams didn't see the events of the game in a dispassionate way. Instead, they brought to bear on their perceptions a host of prior values and attitudes. They made evaluations and judgments. Their views fit together in a harmonious fashion. We can interpret all these tendencies by keeping in mind that each fan belonged to a larger social group; his or her group membership obviously dictated how the game was seen.

The field of psychology that is concerned with people as social beings is **social psychology.** Social psychology has been defined as "an attempt to understand and explain how the thought, feeling, and behavior of individuals are influenced by the actual, imagined, or implied presence of others" (Allport, 1968, p. 3). In other words, social psychology studies how we are affected by other people, whether they are in our immediate vicinity or not. People influence what we do even when we just think about them.

Social psychology is caught between the two larger disciplines of psychology and sociology. It's not unusual to find social psychologists working in both psychology and sociology departments. And if you've wandered through your school bookstore or thumbed through your college catalog, you know that social psychology books and courses reside in both departments as well. Overlap is substantial but not complete.

We'll discuss psychological social psychology here and in the next chapter, but you should be aware of the sociological approach as well. What distinguishes the two? Psychological approaches emphasize the individual, whereas sociological approaches concern themselves more with groups than with individuals. Things can become complicated in social psychology, because we are all "others" to

social psychology
the field of psychology that studies people as social beings, in particular, how the thoughts, feelings, and actions of individuals are influenced by the presence of others

social cognition
the cognitive representations and processes that people use in making sense of the social world

everyone else in the world. Nevertheless, psychological social psychologists keep things somewhat simple by usually focusing on one individual at a time.

The major assumption of social psychology is that each person is a social being whose behavior is shaped by his or her relationships with others. Accordingly, social psychologists study how factors outside people—the social situations in which they find themselves—determine their behavior.

At the same time, social situations do not have an automatic effect on how someone acts. It is only when the person makes sense of social situations, perceiving them and interpreting them in a given way, that there is any influence. This is the important point regarding the Dartmouth-Princeton football game. A particular social event, the game, had an effect on those who were there. Many fans became enraged. Some wrote editorials for their school papers. Strong feelings lingered for days. But the specific nature of these reactions depended on how the fans saw the game: Their initial allegiance shaped their interpretations.

Stated another way, social psychology is inherently cognitive (Manis, 1977). We interact with the social environment in terms of how we think about it. Social psychologists have extensively studied how our interpretations of the social world determine our social behavior.

Social cognition is the general term used to describe the cognitive representations and processes that people use in making sense of the social world. The present chapter takes a detailed look at social cognition. How have social psychologists studied the topic? What are the most important types of social cognition? How do these originate and change?

Social cognition is not of interest to social psychologists solely in its own right. Rather, one's thoughts and beliefs are deemed important because they are critical determinants of social behavior. Keep in mind that social cognition thus flows naturally into the topic of the next chapter, social influence itself: all the ways that people may affect the social behavior of one another.

Is Social Cognition Special?

The relationship between social psychology's approach to cognition and that of general psychology (Chapter 7) deserves examination. As you read this chapter, you will encounter a number of concepts already familiar to you, such as schemas and prototypes. Social psychologists acknowledge a considerable debt to other psychologists, because many concepts useful in explaining social cognition have been directly appropriated from other fields.

The influence has not just been one way. Remember that many psychologists abandoned mentalistic approaches throughout much of the twentieth century (Chapter 5), leaving social psychologists to keep the cognitive torch burning. When social psychologists borrow particular concepts from other psychologists, these are often concepts that were themselves borrowed from social psychologists in the first place!

Despite this frequent sharing of cognitive notions, we can still ask if it is justified. Do theories and findings concerning general cognition (Chapter 7) apply in particular to social cognition? Or is social cognition somehow a special form of thinking?

The processes that transform and maintain our social beliefs certainly look very much like those that transform and maintain knowledge in general. But the cognition studied by social psychologists often differs from that studied by other psychologists because of the respective *topics* of thought. Social psychologists are specifically interested in studying how people think about themselves and others. Other psychologists may instead study the way people think about objects per se. There are important differences between people and objects, and hence between our cognitions concerning them (Heider, 1944, 1958):

- People intentionally influence the environment; objects do not.
- People perceive back; an important aspect of what we think about others is what they think about us.
- Social "stimuli" change under our scrutiny; knowing that you are the object of someone's thinking may well change the way you act; objects are oblivious (except for automobiles, which often stop rattling when you try to have them examined by an expensive mechanic).
- Social cognition cannot be judged as accurate (or inaccurate) as readily as we can judge generic cognition.
- People are much more complex than objects.
- The complexity of people produces in us a need not just to describe but to explain; both people and teacups may be brittle, but we feel more impelled to explain the fragility of the former than the latter.

"For these reasons, social cognitive psychology will never be a literal translation of cognitive psychology" (Fiske & Taylor, 1984, p. 17). Social cognition is more complicated, more concerned with content, and more entwined with emotion.

Without a doubt, the aspect of social cognition most frequently studied by social psychologists over the years has been the **attitude,** defined as a stable and general disposition, encompassing beliefs, feelings, and behaviors. The subject of an attitude may be a social group, such as Asian-Americans, Republicans, or the elderly, or it may be a social issue, such as abortion, gun control, or affirmative action. We can also speak of attitudes toward such entities as commercial products or leisure activities. Regardless, attitudes are complex, precisely because they directly or indirectly concern other people, who in turn have their own attitudes. We will discuss attitudes in depth later in the chapter.

> **attitude**
> a stable and general disposition toward some object, encompassing beliefs, feelings, and behaviors

How Do We Structure Social Cognition?

Like cognition in general, social cognition can be described in terms of its contents and processes (Chapter 7). There is an understandable concern with enumerating the basic ways in which we represent social knowledge and with explaining how our beliefs originate and change. One of the most striking aspects of social cognition is that our social knowledge is structured.

Human interaction—the means by which we negotiate with one another and accomplish our objectives—is of great interest to the social psychologist.

Social psychologists thus concern themselves as well with how people put the parts of social cognition together. Different styles of organizing thoughts have been hypothesized. These styles reflect different views of human nature. Just as personality and clinical psychologists subscribe to various models or metaphors (Chapters 11–13), so too do social psychologists who study social cognition. Let us examine three common views of the social thinker (Taylor, 1981). What does each of them tell us about social thinkers, such as the fans at the Princeton-Dartmouth football game?

People as Consistency Seekers. A very influential approach to social cognition proposes that people are motivated to establish consistency among their thoughts and feelings. Fritz Heider's (1946) discussion of the importance of balance among an individual's cognitions led in the 1950s and 1960s to a proliferation of social cognition theories emphasizing consistency (Abelson et al., 1968). Common to these theories are two assumptions. First, when a person perceives an inconsistency among his thoughts, he experiences a negative feeling. Second, this aversive state motivates him to resolve the inconsistency in some way.

Remember the Dartmouth fans. They noticed the roughness of their own team, to be sure, but this was in-

consistent with their view of the team as "a bunch of good guys." So, they decided that their players were only defending themselves against the dirty play of a team aroused by a troublemaking coach. Consistency was served, and any negative feelings due to the initial discrepancy they experienced were reduced.

Consistency theories gave rise to a considerable amount of research showing the irrational lengths to which people will go to maintain a balance among their beliefs. For example, Festinger, Riecken, and Schachter (1956) studied members of a doomsday cult who predicted that the world would end on a particular date. As true believers, the cult members would be spirited away on a flying saucer by omnipotent space aliens and taken to the planet Clarion. This did not happen on the appointed day, as you may have noticed, but the cult members did not relinquish their beliefs. Just the opposite happened, as they decided that because of their sincerity, the world had been temporarily spared. They renewed their efforts to recruit new members.

People as Scientists. A different view arrived on the social cognition scene with the growing popularity of the person-as-scientist metaphor (Chapter 11). Consistency was no longer considered the overarching principle organizing our thoughts. Rather, theorists proposed that everyday people were much like scientists in their attempt to predict and control events in the world (Kelly, 1955). The theories proposed during the 1970s emphasized the rationality of social cognition rather than its irrationality. And accuracy rather than harmony was viewed as the goal of the social thinker.

According to this view, the tendency of the respective football fans to see the game as they did was not due to a need to be consistent, but rather to an attempt to explain in rational terms what they saw. Why then did they arrive at such drastically different interpretations? One possibility suggested by the scientist comparison is that they started with different information available to them.

In other words, Dartmouth fans knew a lot about Dartmouth players. They had seen them play previous games. They may have mingled with them on campus, in the dormitory, or in the classroom. They "knew" that their players were not dirty or malicious, because they had seen them in many circumstances in which they did not act this way. When an altercation took place between one of their players and a player from the other team, they were faced with the task of apportioning the blame. Based on what they knew, their player could not be guilty. It must be the other guy's fault, because the Dartmouth fans had no knowledge to the contrary. They didn't know these "other guys" at all. The same argument applies to the opposite case as well, explaining how a Princeton fan might decide—based on the information available to him—that Dartmouth players were dirty.

These one-sided views arise in a rational way, even though we as third parties can see them as incomplete. This does not invalidate the person-as-scientist comparison, because no one should expect scientists to be correct all of the time. All that a scientist can do is weigh the information available and make sense of it as best he or she can (Chapter 1). If we decide that our football fans were doing the same thing, then the scientist comparison is a good one.

People as Misers.   Research indeed shows that the scientist comparison is useful in capturing part of social cognition, but it also points to several weaknesses (Ross, 1977). There are instances in which people do not think like scientists. Because social psychologists did not want to characterize social cognition in terms of what it is not, they developed a third approach that tries to describe how people actually think about themselves and others (as opposed to what they should do if they are to be considered rational). Taylor (1981) summarized the findings of this approach by likening social thinkers to misers. In other words, people have limits in their ability to take all the available information into account, and so they take shortcuts wherever possible by simplifying the cognitive tasks they face (March & Simon, 1958).

In Chapter 7, we discussed Kahneman and Tversky's (1973) research on judgment heuristics, cognitive shortcuts used by people in making decisions and judgments. Social psychologists in the 1960s have found these ideas extremely useful, and an avalanche of recent research has documented the use of these strategies in social cognition. For example, the *vividness bias* refers to the tendency of people to base judgments not on sober generalizations, but on striking examples (Borgida & Nisbett, 1977).

Suppose you plan to buy a new car. You're thinking about a Ford Escort. An article in *Consumer Reports* summarizes the repair record for thousands of Escorts, and these results reflect well on the car. But your good friend once owned a beige 1982 Escort that was always in the shop, and she tells you in gory detail about one fuel pump transplant after another. What do you pay attention to? You know full well what you would do. Rationality be damned!

Or remember the *availability heuristic* described by Kahneman and Tversky, which we discussed in Chapter 7. According to this idea, we judge the frequency of events according to how readily we can bring examples of them to mind. Was it a dirty football game? Certainly, say the Princeton fans, because their All-American quarterback left the game with an injury. Let's slow down and examine this answer. Dick Kazmaier was a star, which meant that all eyes were on him. Indeed, he had just been featured on the cover of *Time* magazine. His injury was memorable and thus highly available. An injury to another player in a less glorified role would have been less memorable, less available to memory, and perhaps less likely to lead fans to decide that the game was a dirty one.

In sum, social psychologists rely on different perspectives to explain how people organize their thoughts and beliefs concerning the social world. Perhaps each perspective captures a bit of what people actually do. An item on the future agenda of social psychologists might be to establish where and when each perspective best applies.

Kurt Lewin: Father of Modern Social Psychology

No introduction to social psychology would be complete without mention of Kurt Lewin (1890–1947), the father of the modern discipline. Lewin was a German Jew, and like many of his fellows, he fled to the United States during the rise of Hitler. He brought with him the orientation of a gestalt psychologist and a keen interest in social problems (Chapter 1). In combining these two, Lewin (1951) stamped social psychology with the character it still possesses.

Let's review what we know about gestalt psychology, because it is important in understanding Lewin's contributions. Remember from Chapter 1 that two basic emphases define the gestalt approach:

- the idea that psychological phenomena are best described in terms of relationships among elements; these relationships are termed gestalts (meaning in German whole, pattern, configuration)
- the assumption that some relationships are more psychologically fundamental than others; these are called good gestalts

field theory

the idea that people are self-regulating, dynamic systems that naturally seek out balance and harmony

lifespace

according to Lewin, the total of all forces acting upon a person at a given time

Lewin phrased his ideas in terms of **field theory;** the notion that people are self-regulating, dynamic systems that naturally seek out balance and harmony within themselves as well as between themselves and the world. In other words, people tend toward good gestalts.

The first gestalt psychologists concerned themselves with topics such as perception (Chapter 4) and learning (Chapter 5), but those who followed applied the gestalt perspective to personality, clinical, and social psychology. Here is where Kurt Lewin fits in. His theorizing began with the stance that behavior is best understood in terms of the psychological "field" in which it takes place. He called this field the **lifespace,** the total of all forces acting on a person at a given time. These forces include internal biological needs as well as external social pressures. Lewin was fond of diagramming lifespaces in pictures (such as the one in Figure 14.1).

Lifespaces look a lot like thought bubbles in cartoons, and this is not as flip an analogy as you might at first suppose. Lewin defined a lifespace as the individual's construction of his or her relationship with the environment. The key term here is *construction,* which means that the lifespace is a psychological reality phrased in cognitive terms. Like Snoopy in *Peanuts* cartoons, the individual "lives" not in a physical world but in a psychological one. Lewin's approach is a thoroughly cognitive one.

Of course, the physical world bears on the psychological world, because many of our constructions (and even some of Snoopy's) have a basis in reality. Nevertheless, psychologists should concern themselves not with "stimuli" but with someone's interpretations of them. Lewin and other social psychologists believe that we must acknowledge perceived reality. As already stressed, people only behave in terms of how they take the world to be. Ghosts, demons, and the necessity of keeping one's options open are "real" because individuals treat them as such.

Lewin believed that the lifespace was divided into regions, each of which was positive or negative for the individual, according to the forces operating at that particular moment. Sometimes these regions come into

Figure 14.1

Sample Lifespace. Here is a representation of the lifespace of someone who needs money. This person (P) sees two routes toward this goal. Playing the lottery is a desirable route, so it is marked with a + sign in this diagram. Getting a job is an undesirable route, and so it is designated with a – sign. As other forces affect this person, his lifespace will change.

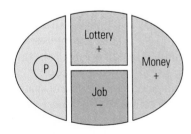

conflict, and one is left in a state of disequilibrium. Within the lifespace, processes then are automatically set into motion to restore one's equilibrium.

Lewin described the lifespace and its response to disequilibrium with complicated terms such as *forces* and *vectors* that never won much acceptance among his fellow psychologists. Nevertheless, his general statement that people strive to make their thoughts and feelings harmonious has been widely influential in social psychology. His approach was the forerunner of the consistency theories already mentioned.

Let's return one more time to the Dartmouth-Princeton football game on November 23, 1951, and perhaps we can better appreciate Lewin's approach to social cognition. Both the Dartmouth fans and the Princeton fans happened to share the same physical environment—Palmer Stadium, to be specific—but if we want to understand their social behavior, we have to look into their psychological environments. Each fan "lives" within his or her respective lifespace. At the time of the game, the lifespace of a fan contains not only the game being played but also the self and its characteristic attitudes and beliefs. As external events such as penalties and injuries impinged on them, the fans responded, each according to the contents of their particular lifespace. When Princeton was penalized by a referee's call, Princeton fans disparaged it. Dartmouth was of course helped by the same call, and thus Dartmouth fans praised the officiating.

Nowadays, theorists don't speak explicitly of lifespaces, but social psychologists nonetheless approach social cognition exactly in terms of the issues first phrased by Lewin: seeking to describe the way people view themselves and others, and to explain the way people maintain and/or restore the balance among their thoughts and feelings following some disturbance.

Before we move on, let's note two other aspects of Kurt Lewin's approach to social psychology. First, he believed that complex social behavior could be brought into the psychology laboratory and studied by systematically manipulating variables and assessing the consequences. For instance, one of his best-known studies was an investigation of leadership styles (Lewin, Lippett, & White, 1939). Where other researchers might study leadership by observing what happens within naturally occurring groups, Lewin created these groups himself, gave them tasks to perform, and instructed the respective leaders to act in different ways.

Democratic leaders took into account the wishes of the majority. *Authoritarian* leaders made unilateral decisions. *Laissez-faire* leaders simply let things happen, without exerting any real influence. Lewin found that democratic leadership most often led to greater satisfaction among group members. However, leadership styles did not make much difference in terms of group productivity, one way or another.

Second, Kurt Lewin was strongly committed to the use of psychology to address social problems. Science is divided by many into "pure" and "applied" research. Pure research addresses questions that are interesting or intriguing to the individual scientist. Applied research is practical, concerned with providing useful solutions or answers to pressing needs.

Lewin disagreed strongly with this distinction, feeling instead that a particular investigation could serve both theoretical and practical pur-

Kurt Lewin's best-known study was on the nature of leadership. Although democratic leadership (top right photo) resulted in greater satisfaction than did autocratic (left) or laissez-faire (bottom right) leadership, Lewin concluded that leadership style did not significantly affect group productivity.

action research
the attempt to make one's scientific investigations pertinent to larger social concerns

poses. This approach to social psychology is reflected in the phrase **action research:** the explicit attempt to make one's scientific investigations pertinent to larger social issues, including leadership style, group process, prejudice, aggression, and physical health.

It bears repeating that contemporary social psychology is very much Kurt Lewin's legacy: a cognitive endeavor that uses experiments in an attempt to shed light on socially relevant issues. Now that you've met the father of the field, let us turn to a discussion of the ways that social psychologists investigate social cognition.

Investigating Social Cognition

Like other researchers, social psychologists employ a variety of tactics, many already familiar to you from previous chapters. However, two of the major research methods that social psychologists use are sufficiently unique that an explicit discussion of them seems appropriate. Let's therefore take a look at deception experiments and survey research, both of which have broad applicability within social psychology. These methods are used to study social cognition as well as the other topics that comprise the field (Chapter 15). Deception experiments and surveys respectively represent experimental and correlational approaches to research (Chapter 1), but there is much more to them than these labels would seem to imply.

Deception Experiments

deception experiment

a study, usually by a social psychology investigator, in which research participants are deliberately misled about the true purpose of the study in order to avoid influencing how subjects might behave

When an experimenter deceives her research subjects about the true purpose of her investigation, she is conducting a **deception experiment.** Although many of the experiments performed by social psychologists do not entail deception, this strategy has nonetheless proven invaluable to social psychology research over the years. Why is this? Social psychologists are not intrinsically sneaky individuals. Rather, the particular topics that they study often make it impossible to tell subjects exactly what is going on. Consider the phenomena that interest social psychologists: prejudice, aggression, altruism, conformity, and obedience (Chapter 15). All of these are value-laden; that's why they're interesting.

Imagine telling a research subject, "This study is concerned with prejudice toward the elderly. We will ask you to observe older people or younger people performing a task. Their performances will be identical, but we will ask you to evaluate how well they do, and look to see if their age affects your evaluation." Wouldn't this influence what the subject did? What could we conclude about prejudice against the elderly if we conducted studies this way?

For reasons such as this, deception experiments may be undertaken in social psychology. Let's distinguish two types. In *active deceptions,* subjects are told something wrong concerning the purpose or procedures of the experiment. In *passive deceptions,* they are told nothing. Regardless, the social psychologist uses deception in experimentation to avoid influencing the subjects' "spontaneous" behavior. Deception prevents subjects from being overly mindful while they are being studied.

There is another reason for using deception. In an influential discussion of experimentation in social psychology, Aronson and Carlsmith (1969, p. 22) introduced the term *experimental realism,* which exists only if the experimental "situation is realistic to the subject, if it involves him, if he is forced to take it seriously, if it has impact on him." Experimental realism is an essential feature of social psychology experiments, because it allows them to capture the engagement of people in everyday social interactions. Paradoxically, deception furthers the goal of experimental realism.

Suppose a social psychologist wants to study how people respond to an emergency. She could ask her research subjects to imagine an emergency and to check off on a questionnaire the responses they would make if the emergency were to occur. Or the researcher could arrange things so that smoke pours under the door of the laboratory, alarms and buzzers begin to sound, and people scream. And then she could see what the research subjects do. Note that the first strategy uses no deception, whereas the second strategy is thoroughly misleading. But which is more realistic?

As you have come to expect, at this point we can now observe that no research approach is foolproof—including deception experiments. This strategy has been debated, not just on ethical grounds, but on scientific grounds as well. Some critics believe that a deception experiment creates a credibility gap between the researcher and the subject (Forward, Canter, & Kirsch, 1976). Although research participants may be deceived about the specific purpose of the study they are participating in, they are not deceived that it is a deception experiment. Whatever else is going on in a social psychology experiment, the subjects are suspicious, perhaps anxious, and even hostile (Weber & Cook, 1972). On the other hand, the vast majority of research subjects who participate in deception experiments do not seem to resent the experience; indeed, they seem to find it more interesting than participating in nondeception experiments (Smith & Richardson, 1983)!

Remember the basic premise of social cognition: People represent events in the world in terms that make sense to them. The possibility that one is a subject in a deception experiment is a likely possibility to many subjects. If a researcher overlooks this fact, then her study is at peril. Deception experiments are neither intrinsically valid nor intrinsically invalid. However, their special nature must be recognized as we make sense of the results they give us. Social psychology experiments are instances of social interaction (Orne, 1962).

Survey Research

survey
a study that chooses people at random from some larger group and poses them questions; their answers are considered representative of the responses of the larger group (e.g., political polls)

A quite different approach to social psychology research uses neither deception nor experimental manipulations. In a **survey,** research subjects are selected at random from some larger group and asked questions—sometimes face-to-face, sometimes over the phone, sometimes using a written questionnaire. Of interest, naturally, are the particular answers people give (e.g., 43 percent of Americans hate to fly) and how these answers relate to other characteristics of the respondents (e.g., the more infrequently Americans fly, the more they hate to do so). These answers are treated as more-or-less accurate representations of the sentiments of the larger group.

You are no doubt familiar with the famous polls conducted by George Gallup (1972) and others regarding political preferences. You know that such polls are strikingly accurate, almost always predicting with success the outcome of elections, and the reason for their accuracy is the care with which respondents are sampled. If people are selected randomly from the larger population—i.e., if every person has an equal chance of being selected in the final sample—no more than 1500 individuals are needed to estimate within 3 percent the opinions of the close to 300,000,000 people who live in the United States. Randomization guarantees this. If you stir the soup before you sample it, you can be pretty confident that the spoonful you taste represents the whole pot. Ditto for surveys.

Social psychologists find surveys quite useful for answering theoretical questions. Investigators interested in attitudes, values, and norms have used survey methods to understand marriage, income, sexual behavior, unemployment, and politics. The strength of the survey approach is that researchers can offer conclusions about the thoughts and feelings of people in general, as opposed to college students who happen to participate in psychology experiments.

There are several drawbacks to surveys, however. These include the generic problems with correlational research, notably the inability to discern causes and effects (Chapter 1). Other problems are unique to surveys. If representative sampling does not take place, then the whole endeavor is flawed. You may know of the most famous foul-up in survey research

Figure 14.2

Harry Truman with Newspaper. In 1948, the major political polls failed to predict the outcome of the presidential election. Here the newly elected President Truman holds aloft a newspaper that incorrectly forecasts his opponent as the victor.

history, which occurred in 1948, when Thomas Dewey, the Republican candidate for president, was projected as the winner over Democrat Harry Truman (see Figure 14.2).

The problem was that people were polled over the phone, and back then, not everyone had a phone. Those who did tended to be more affluent than those who did not, and they tended to prefer Dewey. The problem was not with polling, as some conclude from this example, but with the way that the polling was done. Nevertheless, a perfectly representative sample is an ideal that can only be approached.

In addition, survey researchers are usually limited in the types of questions they can ask subjects (Cannell & Kahn, 1969). Time poses one constraint. Subjects will not sit still for an infinite number of questions. Complicated queries cannot be posed, particularly over the telephone. Intimate topics must be avoided. Plus, the researcher must keep in mind the tendency for respondents to present themselves in a desirable light (Chapter 11). This means they can't ask loaded questions. If one were to judge only by the results of contemporary polls, prejudice has been eradicated in the United States, because so few will admit to it when asked. Needless to say, researchers nowadays need more subtle means than a survey to study prejudice. Yet surveys remain valuable for the investigation of less sensitive topics.

Social Perception

"I want to hear all about your new friend." From time to time, we may have said this to someone, and what we usually mean is that we would like answers to several related questions. What is this new friend like? We want to know his important characteristics. Here our interests can range from physical appearance to habits to personality traits to social attributes. Why does this person behave as he does? We want to understand the causes of his actions, the personal or situational determinants that impel him to act. And finally, where does this person stand with respect to our standards of right and wrong? We may evaluate the way he dresses, the goals for which he strives, or his basic philosophy of life.

Social psychologists describe the way we come to know about people as **social perception.** We also pose the same questions about ourselves, and so this includes as well the process of self-knowledge. Social perception is an important aspect of social cognition, and theorists have described it in detail. Indeed, social psychology is currently undergoing an explosion of cognitive theorizing, and many different cognitive representations have been distinguished (Fiske & Taylor, 1984; Markus & Zajonc, 1985). In this section, we will discuss how social psychologists approach social perception, touching on how we describe, explain, and evaluate other people and ourselves.

Social Description

We do not think about people in a vacuum. As we learn about someone's characteristics, we inevitably relate this new information to beliefs we already have. Social psychologists find the notion of a schema useful in explaining how we assimilate new information. Remember that a **schema** is an organized set of beliefs about the world that one uses to go beyond the information given (Chapter 7).

Applied to social perception, a schema leads us to fill in the blanks of social interaction. Suppose you are told that someone's new friend is a young man who belongs to a fraternity. All at once, you know a lot about him, as you draw on your "fraternity schema" to make sense of him.

Like other aspects of social cognition, a schema may be accurate or inaccurate in any particular case. Think of the fraternity member and how your schema could be right on the money in some ways and completely in outer space in other ways. Perhaps we should best regard a schema as a theory about the social world (Markus & Zajonc, 1985). Like any theory, it works well in some cases and poorly in others.

Fiske and Taylor (1984) enumerate the types of schemas that interest social psychologists:

- person schema—someone's "theory" about what personality traits and characteristics go together
- self-schema—someone's "theory" about their own characteristics
- role schema—someone's "theory" about appropriate and inappropriate behaviors for a given social role
- event schema—someone's "theory" about the standard sequence of events for social occasions

The schema notion is quite powerful theoretically. It allows us to describe much of social cognition in the same general terms.

Prototypes.   Some social psychologists have taken a close look at the way that schemas are cognitively represented, suggesting that many of them are defined in terms of typical or average members of a social group (Cantor, 1980). As you may recall from Chapter 7, these typical examples are called **prototypes.**

social perception
the way we come to know about other people and ourselves

schema
an organized set of beliefs about the world

prototypes
typical members of some category

Prototypes are useful only insofar as they do not prevent us from seeing the differences among members of each social group.

stereotype

a rigid and overly simple belief about members of a social group

Consider college professors. What are the central features of this group of people? Many answer this question by listing such characteristics as old, tweedy, and male. Now consider the following scenario (Fiske & Taylor, 1984, p. 139):

> A young woman, casually dressed, walked over to the campus bookstore's requisition desk. "I'd like to order the books for a course," she said. The older woman behind the desk said, "The books aren't in for the fall semester." "I know," the first woman replied. "I'd like to *order* the books for the course." "Oh, certainly. Well, what books does the professor want?" asked the other, helpfully. "I *am* the professor," was the frustrated reply.

Accurate or inaccurate, prototypes provide assumptions which we use to navigate the social world.

Granted that you hold a particular prototype, you perceive, judge, and remember events accordingly (Cantor & Mischel, 1977, 1979). As you hear about someone's new friends, for example, you may think about them according to particular prototypes, which means that you make sense of them in light of your previous beliefs.

Consider the number of stereotypes you hold dear. What opinions do the words *housewife, police officer,* or *minister* stir up? What do you know about the Shriners?

Stereotypes.   A special case of a prototype is a **stereotype,** defined as a rigid and overly simple set of beliefs about members of a social group (Lippmann, 1922). Stereotypes are widespread yet unjustified (Brigham, 1971), and we are familiar with "consensual" beliefs about blacks or Jews or lawyers or Presbyterians or preachers or feminists or athletes. What we may not be so aware of is how stereotypes impact on the way we think, feel, and act toward members of these groups.

Stereotypes often go hand in hand with prejudice because these beliefs are not simply idle ones. Rather, they accompany strong feelings. And further, stereotypes provide a ready rationale for prejudiced attitudes, because they allow people to fend off contrary evidence. "That's just the way they are, those types of people."

Social Explanation

Social description inevitably slides into social explanation. Bernard Weiner (1986, p. 1) illustrated the universality of people's concern with explaining *why* social events happen by first quoting Miyamoto Musashi, a samurai warrior who wrote the following in 1645:

> When I reached thirty I looked back on my past. The previous victories were not due to my having mastered strategy. Perhaps it was natural ability, or the order of heaven, or that other schools' strategy was inferior.

Then Weiner quoted a *Los Angeles Times* sports commentator who wrote in 1982:

> Here it is Thanksgiving week, and the Los Angeles Rams are looking like the biggest turkeys in town. Coach Ray Malavasi has eliminated bad luck, biorhythms, and sunspots as the reasons why his football team has lost 9 of its last 10 games. Now he's considering the unthinkable possibilities that: a) he has lousy players or b) they aren't really trying.

He might as well have quoted stories about political campaigns, crimes, accidents, or Hollywood premieres, because all of these contain explanations as well. If people separated by thousands of miles, hundreds of years, and the myriad of cultural differences between feudal Japan and modern Los Angeles are equally concerned with explaining why events take place, then we have good reason to suspect that these explanations are important aspects of social cognition.

causal attribution
a belief about the cause of some event

attribution theory
explanation of how causal attributions play a role in social behavior

Attribution Theory.   A **causal attribution** is a belief about the cause of some event. The term *attribution* is used by social psychologists to make it clear that a particular explanation may or may not be factually correct. What matters from the social psychological perspective is that the person regards his or her causal attributions as true, and then acts accordingly:

"I failed the examination because it was unfair."

"We broke up because we fought too much."

"You were offered the job because of your past experience."

The attempt to explain the role played by causal attributions in social behavior is called **attribution theory,** of which several versions exist.

The first attribution theory emerged from psychologist Fritz Heider's (1958) descriptions of how people explain events. According to Heider, causal attributions represent a person's "natural" way of making sense of others (Chapter 1). Why did they do what they did? Critical here is the judgment that a particular action was intentional or was not. And important in judging intentionality is whether people's behavior reflects their inner characteristics or the situational demands (Jones & Davis, 1965). In the former case, we speak of internal attributions; in the latter case, external attributions.

Another version of attribution theory is Harold Kelley's (1973) account of how people arrive at a particular causal attribution for some event (see Figure 14.3). Kelley's attribution theory is an example of a *normative model* of social cognition, because it prescribes how a "reasonable" person interested in the truth should think. Kelley suggested that people proceed exactly as a scientist would, by gathering information about how

Figure 14.3

Kelley's Attribution Theory. To explain how we arrive at particular attributions, Kelley suggests that we pay particular attention to three criteria. Suppose our friend Joan laughs uproariously at a movie. Is this because of something about Joan or something about this particular movie? We ask how *distinctive* Joan's response is; we ask how *consistent* it is; and we ask about the *consensus* evident in other people's responses to the movie. Depending on the pattern of answers to these questions, we offer the attribution for Joan's laughter that makes the most sense.

High distinctiveness		High consistency		High consensus		External attribution
Joan laughs just at this movie.	+	Joan usually laughs at this movie.	+	Many other people laugh at this movie.	=	The movie is funny.

Low distinctiveness		High consistency		Low consensus		Internal attribution
Joan laughs often.	+	Joan usually laughs at this movie.	+	Few people laugh at this movie.	=	Joan is easy to amuse.

different factors relate to the event in question. To the degree that the presence or absence of a factor is associated with the subsequent occurrence or nonoccurrence of the event, then it is a likely cause.

If you are trying to explain why you performed poorly on a midterm exam, you think of all the factors that might have influenced your performance. You figure out that the only factor that consistently distinguishes your good performances from your bad performances is the amount of time you devote to reviewing course material. *That* becomes your causal attribution, and the process is clearly a rational one.

A recent attribution theory is Denis Hilton's (1990) attempt to put the process of offering explanations into its social context. Hilton reminds us that when we explain events, we typically convey our explanations to another person. Accordingly, there are important influences on attributions that go beyond those enumerated by Heider and Kelley. For instance, in conversations we usually stick to the matter at hand, and our causal attributions are correspondingly to the point. A student may ask me why she received a particular grade on a paper. I could explain her grade in terms of her early experiences in school or in terms of the emphasis which her family did or did not place on writing, but such explanations—even if correct—are digressions from our conversation. I would be much more likely to explain her grade in terms of the ideas in the paper and its style.

Causal attributions affect how individuals respond to events. For example, motivation is influenced by how one explains events (Weiner, 1986). Suppose you get a D– on your midterm examination in Spanish. You might attribute this outcome to a stable characteristic within yourself, for example, "I have no ability at language." Or you might explain your poor grade with an unstable cause, saying, "I didn't study enough." In the latter case, you expect to do better on the final exam and thus work hard to prepare for it. In the former case, you expect no change in your performance, and you don't bother studying at all.

As we have already noted, causal attributions may or may not be accurate. Social psychologists must be careful not to assume that performance is solely under the sway of these attributions. Nevertheless, all other things being equal (and even sometimes when they are not), the way people explain their successes and failures determines the likelihood of their subsequent successes and failures (e.g., Wilson & Linville, 1982, 1985).

Our emotional reaction to events is also influenced by how we explain them. In general, successes make us glad, whereas failures make us sad. But within these general emotional reactions, attributions shape our particular feelings (Weiner, 1986). To the degree that we explain a success in terms of ability and effort, we feel pride. To the degree that we explain a failure in terms of task difficulty or bad luck, we preserve our self-esteem. This tendency to take credit for success but not failure is so widespread that social psychologists give it a name: the **self-serving bias.**

To call this tendency "self-serving" is to imply that people are motivated to enhance their self-esteem, but it is possible to explain this bias solely in terms of the information available to a person. When people undertake some activity at which they believe themselves to be competent, they expect to succeed. When they do succeed, explaining it in terms of their own characteristics makes a lot of sense. In contrast, when they fail, they look outside themselves and thus explain it in terms of external factors. Motivation is *not* responsible for the difference in how we explain our successes and failures—this difference results because we pay attention to different information in the respective cases.

There are other attributional tendencies as well. One pervasive phenomenon documented by social psychologists is our tendency to explain other people's actions in terms of their internal characteristics: needs, drives, and traits. "Look at him carrying on over there! *He must have no inhibitions.*" We overlook the possibility that situational forces may be influencing his behavior. This tendency is called the **fundamental attribution error** (Ross, 1977). Do you see how the fundamental attribution error provides a ready explanation for some of the most crass stereotypes people hold about others?

When asked to explain our own behaviors, we more readily refer to environmental demands and influences. "I really carried on! *The music*

In explaining our failures and successes to ourselves and to others, we often exhibit a tendency known as the self-serving bias.

actor-observer effect
someone's belief concerning whether or not he can exert control over events in his world

personal contol
someone's belief concerning whether or not he can exert control over events in his world

was so loud that it put everyone in a great mood." The difference between how we explain our own behavior and how we explain the behavior of other people we observe is called the **actor-observer effect,** and it is a widespread phenomenon.

Fritz Heider (1944, 1958) explained the actor-observer effect in perceptual terms. What do we see when we observe someone else behaving? Obviously, we see a person in a setting, but because people are so noticeable, we really don't pay attention to the environment. We see only the person and therefore explain what he is doing in terms of his characteristics. What do we see when we observe ourselves? We mainly see the environment that surrounds us. When making sense of ourselves, we take into account mainly our setting.

A somewhat different interpretation of the actor-observer effect was suggested by Ann McGill (1989). According to her, people explain events by placing them in a particular context and then looking for what is unique about the events relative to the context. As the context changes, so too do the attributions that people make. Suppose you are asked to explain why you chose your college major. If the question is, "Why did *you* choose this course of study?" then your attribution will be internal because your context is you as opposed to other people. If instead the question is, "Why did you choose *this course of study?*" then your attribution will be external because the context is the major you chose as compared to other majors. The actor-observer effect may result, therefore, from the fact that actors and observers often place events in different contexts.

Personal Control.   Closely related to the notion of causal attribution is the idea of **personal control:** people's beliefs about whether or not they can exert control over events in the world. A sense of personal control is related to one's perception of what brings about personally relevant outcomes—factors internal or external to the self. We've already seen one form of this belief in Rotter's (1966) *locus of control* concept: whether rewards are seen as coming from inside or outside the person (Chapter 11). Another version is Bandura's (1986) concept of *self-efficacy:* whether a person believes that she can perform behaviors that win reward or avoid punishment (Chapter 11). Yet another incarnation of this idea can be found in Seligman's (1975) *learned helplessness* theory: the hypothesis that uncontrollable events can make a person passive and ineffectual (Chapter 5). Common to all these personal control ideas is the assumption that such beliefs are an important aspect of social cognition.

Like causal attributions, one's perception of control may or may not be accurate. What is interesting and important about personal control is that it influences our behavior whether or not it is accurate (Bandura, 1986). In general, a sense of personal control helps a person cope with stress, in the short run as well as in the long run.

For instance, Rodin, Solomon, and Metcalf (1978) found that passengers in an elevator felt less crowded and anxious to the degree that they stood near the panel of buttons that controlled the elevator. What a striking example of the distinction between objective reality and perceived reality! The person near the "control" panel is just as crushed by the presence of others as the person far away, but the belief that control is possible alleviates the stress of crowding.

The level of stress that passengers in a crowded elevator experience depends on their position relative to the button panel, that is, their degree of personal control.

Another example of the importance of control is a study that looked at the impact of enhanced personal control on the well-being of residents in a nursing home. Ellen Langer and Judith Rodin (1976) assigned half of the elderly residents of a nursing home to an experimental condition in which they were given various choices to make: when to see movies, how to decorate their rooms, and so on. They assigned the other half of the residents to a comparison condition, where they were treated pleasantly but given no special experiences to underscore the control they had over the details of their lives.

Several weeks later, when subjects in the two groups were compared, those with enhanced control were healthier, happier, and more alert, even though no differences originally existed. And 18 months later, the researchers found that 15 percent of the subjects with enhanced control had died, as compared to 30 percent of the comparison subjects (Rodin & Langer, 1977).

Studies like these showing personal control associated with vigor and health underscore the emphasis placed by psychologists on social cognition. People's beliefs influence not only their moods and behaviors, but also their physical well-being. In the field of health psychology (see Appendix), we therefore see great interest in changing people's beliefs as a strategy for enhancing their health (Peterson & Stunkard, 1989).

Social Evaluation

The earlier description of the Princeton-Dartmouth football game showed that social perception entails more than just description and explanation. It also includes evaluation of the appropriateness of social behavior. Like other aspects of social cognition, social evaluations—once made—influence how we subsequently behave. In making judgments about events in the social world, we base our evaluations on several sets of criteria.

norms

shared expectations about appropriate and inappropriate behavior for some role

Norms. One important evaluation recognizes the fact that people enact different roles in their social lives. Each role serves a certain function within some larger group, and part of every role is a set of expectations about appropriate and inappropriate behavior. These expectations are called **norms,** and people typically behave in accordance with them. When norms are violated, people find themselves the object of social scorn or worse.

Norms exist at different levels. Purely local norms are those that describe how you and your roommates believe food in the common refrigerator should be treated. Butter and bread can be used by any and all, regardless of who purchased them. Hot dogs and eggs can mostly be used by everyone, except that only the purchaser can take the last one. Dove Bars are sacred; no one but the purchaser is allowed even to think about consuming them!

Norms are also held by larger groups. For example, among psychologists, it is almost a universally held belief that clinicians and their clients should not be "friends" during the course of therapy (Chapter 13). Lawyers and doctors and tax accountants have different norms about mixing professional and personal relationships. These individuals often don't think twice about befriending those to whom they offer professional services.

Finally, societies as a whole have certain norms. I recently had an enlightening conversation with a graduate student who just moved to the United States from Holland. He explained his embarrassment that he hadn't known that a "five page paper" in the United States means one that is double-spaced. Back home in Holland, students type their pages single-spaced. It had taken him twice as long as his classmates to write his first paper, plus the teacher criticized him for leaving no room for comments. (Adding insult to injury!) This is a small example, but it suggests that at least one reason cultures come into conflict is because people hold different beliefs as to what is appropriate behavior.

Scripts.   We also judge people according to how they go about acting in social settings. Most social events unfold over time, and there is usually an accepted sequence of events to be followed. Schank and Abelson (1977) introduced the term **script** to capture this aspect of social cognition. People believe that there is a "right" way to order a meal, catch a plane, or ask a favor. For instance, if you start a meal in a fancy restaurant with dessert, you will attract considerable attention. Indeed, when someone departs from an accepted script, people take special notice (e.g., Bower, Black, & Turner, 1979). Those who do not follow scripts run the risk of being judged socially inept, morally wrong, or psychologically abnormal (Chapter 12).

Many of the scripts that govern everyday social life have become automatized, so much so that we don't think much about them as we follow their dictates. Ellen Langer (1978, 1989) described the state of **mindlessness** as one in which individuals rely so much on familiar scripts that they no longer attend to the actual details of social interaction. Content is overlooked. You may have a friend who calls on the phone and talks excessively. As this routine goes on evening after evening, you may fall into the mindless habit of saying "yes" whenever there is a pause in the conversation. Then your friend asks, "Should I find a bridge and hurl myself over its railing?"

Langer, Blank, and Chanowitz (1978) demonstrated mindlessness in a study of people waiting in line to use a Xerox machine (a good place to find numb people). A researcher burst on the scene, saying one of three things:

- "Excuse me, may I use the Xerox machine?"
- "Excuse me, may I use the Xerox machine, because I'm in a rush."
- "Excuse me, may I use the Xerox machine, because I want to make copies."

The first request does not follow the right script for asking a favor of strangers, because he gave no reason. The second request gives a legitimate reason. The third request is an interesting one, because it has the *form* of legitimacy (request with reason) but not the *content* (the "reason" explains nothing).

Guess what? When the researcher wished to make only a few copies, the third request was just as effective as the second request, presumably because the people in line didn't attend to its content. When the re-

script
beliefs about the appropriate sequence of social events

mindlessness
one's reliance on social scripts to such an extent that the details of social interaction escape notice

value

an enduring belief about the desirability of a particular goal

searcher wanted to make many copies, the people in line were jarred from their mindless state, listened to the content of the request, and said no (or worse). This study shows that the form of social behavior can sometimes be more important than its content, and that as long as one follows what seems to be an appropriate script, negative evaluations do not ensue.

Values. We evaluate not only other people but ourselves. A **value** is an enduring belief that certain personal goals are preferable to others (Rokeach, 1973). It is a truism that people differ in their values, and social psychologists have found that if they attend to values it helps them explain how and why people pursue their lives as they do.

Gordon Allport (1937) described one influential typology of values:

- religious (seeking to understand the universe as a whole)
- esthetic (finding fulfillment in beauty and harmony)
- theoretical (trying to discover truth)
- economic (emphasizing those things that are useful and practical)
- social (treating other people as ends in themselves)
- political (seeking power, influence, and renown)

Individual or group values may lead people to choose a life-style outside the mainstream of their society.

Allport also developed a widely used questionnaire measure that assesses the relative importance of these values to a person (Allport, Vernon, & Lindzey, 1960). Someone responding to this questionnaire is shown statements that express these different values and asked to indicate how much he endorses each.

Scores on this questionnaire prove to be related to how people choose to pursue their lives. For example, values assessed in this way predict the course of studies one elects at college (Newcomb, 1943). What types of majors do you think are most apt to satisfy people with these different values?

Religious Beliefs

One of the curious things about recent psychology is the almost complete absence of interest in religion (cf. Shaver, 1973). The first important book on psychology and religion, *The Varieties of Religious Experience,* was written in 1902 by William James. This is almost the last important book on the subject as well.

If all we knew about human beings was what we read or heard in the typical psychology textbook or course, we wouldn't have an inkling that the vast majority of the world's citizens—past, present, and presumably future—subscribe to a particular religion. We wouldn't have an inkling that the tenets of their respective religions pervade their thoughts, feelings, and actions. We wouldn't have an inkling that religions provide people with a vantage point from which to understand and judge themselves and others. We wouldn't have an inkling that profoundly influential thinkers such as Lao-Tsu, Mohammed, Moses, the Buddha, and Jesus were religious figures. We wouldn't have an inkling that religions have played perhaps the prime role throughout history in shaping social events.

That's a lot of inklings not to have. What explains this lack of interest? One reason is that psychology and religion provide different worldviews. Witness the disagreements between evolutionary biologists and creation-ists over how to account for the origin of humankind. There is no way that one side will ever convince the other to change, because they start with such drastically different assumptions and use altogether different standards to recognize relevant facts and to evaluate evidence. The desire to avoid such wrangling has probably led psychologists to shield themselves from the study of religion.

However, the psychological investigation of religion does not involve endorsing particular beliefs—just studying them. Where do they originate? How do they change? What are their consequences? As Lewin proposed, psychologists must study what is real to their subjects. The psychologist need not (and cannot, at least in the role of a psychologist) take a position on the ultimate validity of these topics.

Another reason for psychology's lack of interest in religion is that when psychologists have studied religion, they have tended to do so in terms of church attendance. In other words, researchers often operationalize a person's "religiousness" as how frequently he or she attends church. Then they investigate what correlates with religiousness measured in this way. What has resulted from these investigations isn't very interesting.

Such studies miss the point that religion has an internal as well as an external manifestation (Allport, 1954), and surely the inside aspect of religion (thoughts and feelings) is significant, while the outside aspect of religion (church attendance) pales in comparison (Gorsuch, 1988). A potentially productive way for psychologists to study religious beliefs would be from a social psychological perspective. In particular, a person's religious beliefs could be seen as a form of social cognition. Indeed, there

The central place of religion in various cultures and the universality of religious symbols indicate that religion is in some way important to the psychological well-being of humankind.

are recent signs that psychology is beginning to approach religion in terms of the thoughts and beliefs of participants (e.g., Spilka, Shaver, & Kirkpatrick, 1985).

An intriguing example along these lines is Rothbaum, Weisz, and Snyder's (1982) theory. They concern themselves with what people do when they confront events that elude their control. We've reviewed a number of theories that predict that people in these circumstances become listless and apathetic. Sometimes this happens, but sometimes it doesn't. Rothbaum et al. address the latter case, suggesting that the ability to find meaning and significance in uncontrollable events helps us cope with their aftermath. They call this ability **interpretive control,** and they cite religious beliefs as a common way for people to make sense of their lives.

I'm conducting a study at the present time that takes as its point of departure the theory proposed by Rothbaum and his colleagues. Available to me are first-person narratives gathered in the 1930s from individuals who had lived as slaves during the nineteenth century in the American South (Yetman, 1970). When they told their stories, all of these individuals were quite old—some in excess of 100 years of age! One thing common to all these narratives, in which these individuals vividly described life as a slave, was their ample use of interpretive control. Somehow each had been able to make sense of what had been a horrendous situation.

When I look at other narratives from people who lived under less trying circumstances than slavery, I find much less evidence of interpretive control, perhaps because my comparison subjects didn't need to draw so deeply on their beliefs in order to cope. I hasten to add that these results don't prove that interpretive control leads to better coping and thus to longevity, but they raise an intriguing possibility (Antonovsky, 1988).

Let's conclude this section on social perception by remembering that when we think about ourselves and others, we simultaneously describe, explain, and evaluate what we perceive. Our different thoughts and beliefs are structured in a particular way. Theorists variously propose that considerations of consistency, accuracy, and/or efficiency govern the particular structure we impose on our social beliefs. Regardless, social cognition influences how we behave. In the next section we consider at length the role that our attitudes play in social interaction.

interpretive control
the ability to find meaning and significance in uncontrollable events in order to buffer the negative consequences of these events

Attitudes

We've already defined an attitude as a stable and general disposition toward some object. Attitudes can be complex, encompassing beliefs, feelings, and behaviors. Your attitude toward young children, for example, consists of characteristic beliefs about them (you believe that they represent the future of the world), characteristic emotions concerning them (you find them adorable), and characteristic behaviors (you bend over and talk to them in shopping malls).

The object of an attitude is often a social group or issue. Social psychologists aren't much interested in how we evaluate our left earlobes, last night's pizza, or tomorrow's weather forecast. Instead, they focus on our attitudes toward ethnic groups, political parties, and pending legislation.

When social psychologists study attitudes, they often look in particular at how we *evaluate* social groups. Indeed, some define an attitude solely

Attitudes have been extensively investigated by social psychologists. For example, given the nature—and history—of race relations in this country, racial attitudes would be of particular interest.

as an evaluation (e.g., Thurstone, 1946). This means that, despite the general definition of an attitude as including beliefs, feelings, and behaviors, one can nonetheless ask if these different components actually go together. Social psychologists have frequently examined how our evaluations relate to our behavior. As we will discuss shortly, the relationship between evaluative attitudes and overt behavior is not as simple as social psychologists once hoped.

Of all the characteristics of social cognition, attitudes have been the most extensively investigated. And the particular attitudes about which we know the most are racial attitudes, those held by white Americans about black Americans. Social psychology experienced great growth as a field in the 1950s and 1960s, coinciding with the integration of public schools in the United States and intense societal scrutiny of race relations. Social psychologists turned their attention to the highly salient problems of racial prejudice and discrimination, and they found the notion of attitudes useful in explaining what they found.

Many Americans, white and black, would like to believe that discrimination is a thing of the past, that civil rights legislation, affirmative action, and black political involvement have led at last to an integrated society. These hopes are not mirrored in reality, however, according to a recent examination of black-white relations in the United States (Jaynes & Williams, 1989). Discrimination against blacks persists, and prejudiced attitudes held by whites are in large part responsible for this discrimination.

It seems that social psychologists will be busy for the foreseeable future studying racial attitudes. For this reason we will frequently use these types of attitudes to illustrate the general points made in this section. Needless to say, other attitudes exist and also have great societal importance. Attitudes may be held about any social group, and discrimination can be discerned in many quarters (Chapter 15). We would hope that what is known about racial attitudes applies as well to attitudes about other social groups.

Formation of Attitudes

Where do attitudes originate? Social psychologists have documented numerous determinants of how people feel and think. Some of these determinants may be inherent in our nervous system. Recall the mere exposure effect from Chapter 6: the tendency to like those things that are familiar (Zajonc, 1980). This is not something we learn to do. It's simply the way we are constituted. Perhaps evolution worked in such a way that we come to respond favorably to objects in the environment the more frequently we encounter them.

It is not surprising that we often have favorable attitudes toward familiar objects and negative attitudes toward the less familiar. Gould and White (1974), for instance, conducted research asking Americans to evaluate different parts of the country. Everyone considers their own region a particularly desirable place to live. And everyone considers unfamiliar regions a good place to locate toxic waste dumps and nuclear missile silos!

The possibility that attitudes are in some way biologically predisposed is intriguing, but let's not forget that the major determinants of social cognition are undoubtedly found in our environment. Even if the form of social cognition is inherent, the details must be fleshed out through our experience. People learn particular attitudes (Chapter 5). When these change, learning is responsible as well.

What do we know about the origin of racial attitudes? We can start with the observation that our society is stratified so that blacks and whites often come into contact with one another only in limited ways: directly through occupational roles and symbolically through the media. This is where attitudes must be formed. To the degree that these interactions are associated with unpleasant feelings, we form negative attitudes through classical conditioning. To the degree that these interactions produce aversive consequences, we form negative attitudes through instrumental conditioning. To the degree that we see others expressing prejudiced attitudes, we form negative attitudes through modeling.

Although interracial couples are now more common than they once were in the United States, most contact between the races still takes place in highly formalized situations—work-related contact being the most obvious.

Watching Others. Weigel, Loomis, and Soja (1980) videotaped several hundred hours of prime-time television and then analyzed the depiction of interracial contact. Other researchers have documented a steady rise in the frequency with which black actors and actresses appear on television shows, but head counts are not the whole picture. It's also important to look at what the actors and actresses are doing, and for how long they do it. Here are some of the results:

> Blacks appeared in 52% of the situation comedies and 59% of the drama shows . . . [but] . . . cross-racial interactions accounted for only 2% of the human appearance time . . . [T]here is no reason to get excited about the socialization potential of vicarious exposure to cross-racial relationships. . . . Television broadcasting is no longer an exclusively white domain, but it is compartmentalized into program units in which blacks and whites rarely encounter one another. (pp. 888–889)

Of the few depictions of blacks and whites interacting with one another, fully 90 percent were work-related (versus 10 percent "voluntary" friendships). When these figures take into account male-female interaction between blacks and whites, they become 100 percent work-related versus 0 percent voluntary!

Certainly these percentages have changed since the time when this research was originally conducted. But the general point remains. Many Americans of different races come into contact with each other only in formalized ways. We don't see blacks and whites as friends. We don't see them doing anything other than their jobs. No wonder racial stereotypes and their associated feelings take on a momentum of their own.

James Michener (1976), in his book *Sports in America,* argues that these processes take an insidious turn. He discusses what he calls a widespread myth: A professional athletic career represents the way out of the ghetto for poor blacks. Why is this a myth? Simple examination of the hard facts reveals that an extremely small number of individuals ever succeed in professional sports. Even those who do succeed have a short career. But a rags-to-riches story is a compelling one (remember Alex Jones from the beginning of Chapter 8), and the sports media present these tales about sports rather than the hard facts. A professional career in sports *seems* right around the corner for hundreds of thousands of young men.

> Even the highly successful black athlete runs the risk of establishing himself as a destructive behavior-pattern for younger blacks who cannot hope to emulate him. This may be the greatest problem of all. If the entire black

community surrenders itself to the dream of a life in sports, while the white community is aspiring to a full-fledged body of options, the black community not only restricts itself to one of the most ephemeral life goals, but it denigrates itself, limits its talented youth, and appears juvenile in the eyes of others. It is as if a large portion of the black community had consciously set for itself the goal of providing gladiators for the white arenas, and that seems immoral. (Michener, 1976, p. 195)

Of course, factors other than social cognition create this state of affairs (Edwards, 1973), but our characteristic ways of thinking certainly contribute by creating and then maintaining stereotypes that rationalize what we observe.

self-perception theory
hypothesis proposed by Daryl Bem that we infer our attitudes from watching our own behavior

Watching Ourselves. In an intriguing hypothesis known as **self-perception theory,** Daryl Bem (1972) argues that we arrive at our attitudes not only through observing other people (on television, for example), but also from observing our own behavior. Bem argues that people behave in particular ways for various reasons that may have nothing to do with their initial attitudes. However, they may later take a look at how they have been acting and infer that they "must" have an attitude that has led to their behavior. And so an attitude is created through the process of perceiving one's own self behave in particular ways. This attitude may then influence subsequent behavior.

For example, students may take physics or chemistry not because they like these courses, but because their college requires them to elect some work in the natural sciences. And someone may eat pepperoni pizza from Domino's not because he likes this brand of pizza, but because it's the only place that delivers food quickly. A person may be abrupt with individuals of other races not because she dislikes them, but because she only sees these individuals when she is hurrying to and from work.

But all of these people at some time may reflect on their attitudes toward physics or chemistry, or Domino's pizza, or folks of different races. And they may infer from their own actions that they have negative attitudes, somewhat like the fundamental attribution error turned against oneself. This won't happen when the "real" reason for one's actions remains obvious, and of course there are numerous instances when a person is well aware of why he is acting as he is. But in those other cases where the actual cause of someone's behavior is obscure, we have yet another determinant of attitudes.

To conclude, attitudes may be learned in a variety of ways. Modeling is clearly one of the most important. Once established, attitudes may be maintained by the same cognitive processes that give consistency to any of our thoughts and beliefs.

Attitudes and Behavior

One of the reasons that social psychologists have been interested in attitudes is that—by definition—attitudes are shown in our overt behavior. By this view, people act in prejudiced ways *because* they have prejudiced attitudes. But when social psychologists split off the evaluative component of attitudes and examined it in its own right, it became possible to investigate just how well this definition squared with the facts.

For several decades, a controversy raged in social psychology over whether the evaluative aspects of attitudes really did predict overt behavior. More generally, the issue here was whether or not thoughts and actions were consistent with each other. (This debate is akin to the one described in Chapter 11 within personality psychology: whether "traits" predict subsequent behavior.) In this section, we'll discuss this debate and how it has been resolved.

Evidence for Inconsistency. Richard LaPiere (1934) reported one of the most famous demonstrations of attitude-behavior inconsistency. He was a white male. For 3 months, he took an automobile trip with a Chinese-American couple, twice across the United States and up and down the West Coast. The three of them stopped at 251 different hotels and restaurants and were only once refused service. Later, LaPiere wrote every one of these 251 establishments and asked if they would accept Chinese patrons. About 50 percent wrote back, and of these 90 percent indicated that they would not.

So, we have evidence of prejudiced attitudes held by the people who ran hotels and restaurants in the United States during the 1930s. But we also know that these attitudes did not translate themselves into prejudiced behavior, because these establishments were precisely the ones that had recently rendered service to LaPiere and his traveling companions. One conclusion suggested by this discrepancy is that attitudes and behaviors are not related.

The LaPiere (1934) investigation is intriguing but perhaps not rigorous enough to convince us that attitudes and behaviors are inconsistent. But a more carefully controlled investigation in the 1950s yielded the same results (Kutner, Wilkins, & Yarrow, 1952). One black female and two white females visited eleven restaurants in the northeast United States. In each case, they were given exemplary service. However, when letters were sent to each of these restaurants requesting reservations for an integrated party, no responses were received. Follow-up phone calls to these eleven restaurants requesting reservations for an integrated party yielded six refusals. In a comparison condition, reservation requests that did not mention the racial composition of the group were honored by all eleven restaurants.

Findings like these continued to accumulate until a crisis in social psychology occurred with regard to the issue. Some of the leading social psychologists despaired:

> Studies suggest that it is considerably more likely that attitudes will be unrelated to or only slightly related to overt behaviors than that attitudes will be closely related to actions. (Wicker, 1969, p. 65)

Some theorists even suggested that the entire idea of attitudes be abandoned (e.g., Abelson, 1972; Wicker, 1971).

Evidence for Consistency. At the same time that some social psychologists were showing that attitudes and behaviors were inconsistent, other researchers documented cases in which attitudes and behaviors proved to be highly consistent, such as the following:

- Among voters, attitudes toward political candidates predict actual voting for or against them.
- Among soldiers, attitudes toward combat predict actual performance under fire.
- Among whites, attitudes toward blacks predict participation in civil rights activities.
- Attitudes toward organ transplants predict the granting of permission to remove one's organs after death.
- Attitudes toward movies predict one's attendance at them.

Perhaps the real task of the social psychologist is to explain when attitudes and behaviors are consistent and when they are not. Researchers have made great strides in this regard.

Resolution. Several factors not taken into account in earlier studies of attitudes and behavior now are seen as important in explaining the relationship between them. Let's look at these factors (see Table 14.1), and note in turn how each sheds light on LaPiere's findings.

First are the circumstances under which someone originally acquires a particular attitude. Attitudes stemming from direct experience are more consistent with our behavior than those acquired secondhand. Perhaps in the 1930s few of the hotel or restaurant proprietors had ever met a Chinese-American.

Second is the degree to which an attitude helps define a person's self-image. If your identity is tied up in your evaluations of a particular group or object, then you act quite consistently. Again, perhaps the subjects studied by LaPiere had little investment in their feelings about Chinese-Americans.

Third is whether the person is self-conscious while she is behaving. Sometimes a person needs to reflect on her attitudes before her behavior shows consistency with them. People who are not thinking about the meaning of their actions, those who are "mindlessly" enacting social scripts as described earlier (p. 600), tend to behave inconsistently. Saying

Table 14.1

Factors Influencing Attitude-Behavior Consistency

A number of factors determine whether evaluative attitudes are consistent with overt behavior. To the degree that the questions shown here can be answered yes, we would expect attitudes and behaviors to be consistent with one another.

	Was the attitude acquired through direct experience?
	Does the attitude define one's self-image?
	Is the person self-conscious while behaving?
Attitude ⟶	Does the person regard the behavior as desirable? ⟶ **Behavior**
	Is the attitude specific with regard to the behavior?
	Is the behavior of sufficiently broad scope?

Wartime propaganda vividly reflects the prejudices each nation holds regarding its adversaries.

no in a letter is a more automatic (and much easier) task than doing so face-to-face.

Fourth is a person's evaluation of the particular behavior supposedly reflecting her attitude. If there is a strong norm for (or against) acting in a particular way, her attitude exerts little influence on her behavior. Here the individual is not inconsistent (with her attitudes) so much as consistent (with the expectations of others). Perhaps the people who ran the hotels and restaurants felt obliged to serve all who showed up at their door, even if they didn't like them.

Fifth is the generality of the attitude with regard to the behavior that's being predicted. Highly general attitudes toward the environment, for instance, do not predict particular behaviors such as returning aluminum cans, as well as more specific attitudes toward recycling. And one's attitudes toward "Chinese" people in general may have little bearing on how one treats particular individuals. Haven't we all been in a group when someone expressed a negative attitude about some social category (whites, Catholics, males, New Yorkers) to which one of the group members belongs, oblivious to the fact that his good friend is one of those wretched folks?

Sixth is the scope of the behavior relevant to the attitude. The correlations between how one feels and how one acts can be boosted considerably if one's behavior is measured in various ways on various occasions. In LaPiere's study, only a single behavior was ascertained (serving the Chinese-American couple). Perhaps a wider range of observations would have turned up behaviors consistent with the expressed attitudes of the hotel and restaurant proprietors.

Do our evaluations of social groups predict our overt behavior toward them? The answer is clearly yes, although the relationship is hardly as simple as social psychologists originally expected. A host of factors above and beyond our evaluations determines how we act. And these factors may be constrained by norms and prevailing situational demands. Here we have a good example of the nature of science; a theory is proposed, then tested, and then modified in light of the evidence (Chapter 1).

Attitude Change

Granted that our attitudes bear a relationship to our overt behavior, when and how might they change? Underlying this question is an important issue: whether or not people are motivated to entertain particular attitudes. Prejudiced attitudes may reflect a person's basic needs and drives. People who have just failed at some task evaluate others more harshly (Cialdini & Richardson, 1980). A lifetime of failure is a breeding ground for prejudice, as people boost their own sagging self-esteem by derogating other groups (Grube, Kleinhesselink, & Kearney, 1982). Indeed, psychoanalytic theorists regard prejudice as *scapegoating,* which means that people project precisely their own disappointments and conflicts onto others (Adorno et al., 1950). What is striking about the propaganda that nations circulate during wartime is that all the groups depict the enemy in exactly the same—disgusting—terms (Keen, 1986).

The person as scientist metaphor we discussed earlier takes the opposite stance, leading us to explain prejudice in strictly "rational" terms with no mention of needs or drives (e.g., Hamilton & Gifford, 1976).

Granted that someone has particular beliefs, these "logically" give rise to other beliefs, which may be quite prejudiced. Suppose you happen to believe, for whatever reason, that young males from the lower class are loud and rude. This theory you hold predisposes you to notice instances where it is confirmed and to overlook cases where it is disconfirmed. Motivational explanations are superfluous when it comes to your prejudice.

Whether or not motivation plays a role in the holding of attitudes has practical implications. Suppose a social psychologist is trying to change attitudes. In order to do so, she must know whether the intervention she plans is pushing against beliefs that are merely mistaken or against those that satisfy someone's basic needs and motives. Different strategies are indicated depending on whether or not motivational factors are at the root of the attitudes targeted for change. With this issue in mind, social psychologists have devised specific ways to remove old attitudes and encourage new ones in their place. Let's consider a couple of the popular approaches to attitude change.

Persuasive Communications. Attitude change through messages explicitly designed for this purpose is called **persuasive communications.** Hundreds of studies have looked at the process by which a person is (or is not) persuaded to change her attitude by hearing a message urging this change (e.g., Hovland, Janis, & Kelley, 1953). Researchers break the process of persuasion into three parts: the source of the persuasive message, the message itself, and the audience.

Change takes place to the degree that the source is credible, and credibility is served by expertise and trustworthiness (Brigham, 1986). You can look at advertisements as persuasive communications. Popular in ads today are celebrities regarded by the general public as experts with respect to the product they advocate. When Bo Jackson, the multitalented baseball and football star, urges the general public to buy certain athletic shoes, we may be duly impressed.

Public service announcements can also be seen as persuasive communications, attempts to change people's attitudes toward dangerous habits such as drug use. Popular in such announcements are celebrities regarded by the general public as experts with respect to the hazards of the fast lane. When a rock star or a raucous comedian urges us to "just say no" to drugs, we are inclined to listen.

Next is the message itself. Should you advocate an extreme position to produce maximum attitude change? The answer here is yes up to a point, after which extremity boomerangs and works against attitude change (Sherif & Hovland, 1961). Imagine that you want to create an effective message urging people to engage in "safe sex" so as to halt the spread of the AIDS epidemic. The safest sex of all is complete abstinence, but this would be heard as an extreme recommendation by most individuals outside a monastery. Accordingly, a message that urged abstinence would probably be ineffective in changing the attitudes and behaviors of the typical person who heard it.

Should you present arguments for and against the suggestion? Here the answer is no when the audience is already in general agreement but yes when the audience is initially skeptical (Lumsdaine & Janis, 1953). In the 1960s, we saw the consequences of a failure to heed this advice concerning how to create a persuasive communication. Public service announcements about the hazards of marijuana use were extremely one-sided, although many people in the general public knew from their own observations that mental breakdowns were far from a common reaction to this drug. The result was a tendency on the part of some to dismiss subsequent messages about drug use, even when these were on target.

Should you appeal to someone's fear if you are trying to change his or her attitude? At one time, social psychologists believed that the arousal of moderate fear was more effective in changing an attitude than the arousal of strong fear. But more recent research suggests that attitude change indeed can be brought about most effectively by a strong fear appeal, so long as the persuasive communication provides specific recommendations for how one can then go about reducing this fear (Sutton, 1982). A message about AIDS should stress that this is a deadly disease with no known cure; this message should also explain that AIDS is readily preventable by simple changes in one's sexual behavior.

Finally we have the message's audience: the person or persons to be persuaded. The persuader has less control over the target than over the other elements of the process of persuasion, because people usually exercise considerable discrimination in choosing the persuasive messages to which they expose themselves. As you might imagine (and as consistency theories would predict), people usually pay attention only to messages they agree with. Take campaign speeches by politicians. They quite obviously intend to change someone's attitude (and thus their voting), but, for the most part, speeches by particular candidates attract the attention of voters already committed to them.

Attempts to change attitudes through persuasive communications may fail because they bump up against people's tendency to maintain cognitive consistency. For example, recent years have seen numerous mass media campaigns calling on people to change their attitudes and behaviors so as to promote their health. These campaigns have been less than successful (Alcalay, 1983), perhaps because most people have inappropriately optimistic expectations concerning their chances of falling ill (Taylor & Brown, 1988; Weinstein, 1982). If I see myself as invulnerable to disease, why should I be persuaded by messages that start with the premise that I am not?

Social psychology researchers have investigated how the self-esteem and intelligence of audience members predisposes attitude change following a persuasive communication. High self-esteem apparently works against easy attitude change (Cook, 1970). The effect of intelligence appears to be more complicated. On the one hand, a degree of intelligence is needed to comprehend a message. But after a point, intelligence makes a person less likely to be persuaded (McGuire, 1968).

The effects of persuasive communications are numerous and complicated. One of my social psychologist friends calls this area of work "it depends" research, because this phrase captures the prevailing wisdom with regard to most lines of investigation. Nevertheless, some theorists have attempted a larger view of persuasive communications.

Let's note Richard Petty and John Cacioppo's (1986) work. They believe that persuasive communications change our attitudes through two means. What they call the *central route* is change that results from people thinking actively about an issue. The *peripheral route* is change through

The effectiveness of persuasive communications can be the deciding factor in consumers' buying decisions.

cognitive dissonance theory
Festinger's hypothesis that inconsistency between one's thoughts and actions is aversive and motivates one to somehow resolve the inconsistency

conceptually irrelevant means, for example, because the source of a message is funny or cute.

Petty and Cacioppo further say that attitude change through the central route is usually more enduring. In contrast, attitude change through the peripheral route is usually easier to accomplish, at least in the short run. Does this explain the recent trend toward advertisements that dwell on trivial details of whatever is being pushed upon the public, whether hamburgers, beer, or political candidates?

One of the interesting implications of the approach taken by Petty and Cacioppo is that the type of persuasive message we choose should take into account whether or not someone will be thinking deeply when he or she hears the message. If we suspect that someone will be listening intently to our message, we should concentrate on bolstering its arguments, because any attitude change that it produces will be through the central route. In contrast, if we suspect that our audience will be disinterested or distracted, we should embellish its form.

Cognitive Dissonance Theory. A different approach to attitude change comes from consistency theories. The best known of the consistency approaches is Leon Festinger's (1957) **cognitive dissonance theory.** This theory concerns itself specifically with the case in which a person perceives an inconsistency between her attitude toward some object and her behavior toward it. In such an event, an unpleasant feeling called dissonance results, and she casts about for a way to reduce it. An obvious way to reduce dissonance is to attribute her apparent inconsistency to external pressure, but if this fails, another strategy is to change her original attitude. Therefore, if a person has a particular attitude and can be induced to behave contrary to that attitude, then a state of dissonance should arise which might be reduced through attitude change.

One of the classic experiments in social psychology tested this hypothesized process. Festinger and Carlsmith (1959) recruited college students as subjects to perform an incredibly boring task: to stack spools on a tray, take them off, restack them, and so on for an hour. Each subject was then dismissed, but on his way out, the experimenter said, "Whoops, it looks like my assistant didn't show up. I need some help. I need someone to tell the next subject what an interesting task this will be. Will you help me out? I'll be able to pay you."

The subject said yes, unaware that he was still participating in the experiment. The researcher then told the subject either that the payment would be one dollar (small) or twenty dollars (large). The subject then spoke to the next person, after which he was again dismissed. But one more step. The subject, still an unaware participant in the experiment, was interviewed by another researcher who asked him to rate how interesting the original task had been.

Did you follow the procedure (see Figure 14.4)? In essence, subjects were paid either a small amount or large amount for telling a lie about how interesting the task was. Then they were given the opportunity to change their minds. According to dissonance theory, which type of subject should subsequently have reported a favorable evaluation of the task (i.e., an attitude change)? Puzzle this through by remembering that attitude change is proportional to the dissonance aroused. Would you feel greater inconsistency if paid one dollar to say a boring task was interesting, or if

Figure 14.4
Design of Festinger and Carlsmith's (1959) Study

Hypothesis: The amount of attitude change following counter-attitudinal behavior is *inversely* proportional to the incentive.

Subjects were college students assigned to two groups:

				Independent variable	Dependent variable
(Group One)	Boring task →	Apparent end of study →	Whoops, please help →	$1 →	Measure attitude toward task
				or	
(Group Two)	Boring task →	Apparent end of study →	Whoops, please help →	$20 →	Measure attitude toward task

paid twenty dollars? Most people experience greater dissonance with the smaller reward, because it provides no decent rationale for the lie. And this is precisely what Festinger and Carlsmith (1959) found: more positive attitudes for subjects paid one dollar as opposed to those paid twenty dollars.

Daryl Bem's (1972) self-perception theory, which we discussed earlier (p. 606), was originally proposed as an alternative account of findings such as those reported by Festinger and Carlsmith (1959). According to Bem, greater attitude change occurs when subjects are paid one dollar (as opposed to twenty dollars) because they observe themselves telling a lie with little justification. They conclude, therefore, that their attitude toward the task must be positive. Bem makes no reference to the motivational state of dissonance.

However we choose to interpret these findings, they show that one possible route to attitude change is through inducing a person to display counter-attitudinal behaviors. We will then bring our attitudes into line with the behavior we have already performed. There is an interesting implication here as well. The smaller the inducement, so long as it is successful, the more attitude change should be produced. Have you noticed that individuals who solicit for religious groups in airports and on street corners often press a "free" book or flower into your hand before they begin their pitch? Because you have accepted something from the person, you stand and listen to what they say; not to do so would clash with your belief that you should be polite to people who give you gifts.

attitude-value confrontation technique

attitude change technique in which people are encouraged to make their attitudes consistent with their more general values

Attitude-Value Confrontation. An intriguing version of the consistency approach to attitude change has been explicitly deployed by Milton Rokeach (1971, 1979) in what is called the **attitude-value confrontation technique.** By definition, values are more general than attitudes, so Rokeach tries to highlight inconsistencies between people's attitudes and values. He asks people to rank the importance of values, including freedom and equality. Among whites prejudiced against blacks, freedom is usually regarded as more important than equality, but in a simple intervention, Rokeach points out to these individuals that freedom and equality must go hand in hand; one way to serve freedom is to serve equality. Prejudiced individuals exposed to this intervention indeed show a tendency to change their attitudes toward civil rights as well as their behavior.

Group Contact.   Yet another approach to attitude change arranges matters so that people of different races interact in ways that produce positive thoughts and feelings. This work stemmed from an earlier notion called the **contact hypothesis,** which proposed that mere contact between different groups would suffice to decrease prejudice. Subsequent research showed this to be an oversimplification. However, if the contact takes a particular form, then prejudice can be effectively combated. In a series of important studies of actual work groups composed of whites and blacks, psychologist Stuart Cook (1970) delineated a number of the critical factors:

contact hypothesis
the notion that mere contact between different groups suffices to decrease prejudice

- people getting to know one another as individuals (not simply as folks who fill roles)
- equal status
- norm of friendliness
- cooperative reward structure (rather than a competitive one)
- personal characteristics of group members that are at odds with stereotypes

In their 1954 *Brown vs. Board of Education of Topeka* decision, the Supreme Court ruled against deliberately segregated public schools, and a profound social change began in our country. Part of the evidence considered by the Court was a statement from prominent social scientists detailing some of the negative consequences of desegregation, including racial prejudice (Cook, 1984). The suggestion was further made that integration would decrease prejudice so long as it was carried out in a way that created conditions similar to those just described.

We began this section on attitudes by referring to a recent report lamenting the state of race relations in this country. However, some progress has been made in decreasing prejudice and discrimination:

> The status of black Americans today can be characterized as a glass that is half full—if measured by progress since 1939—or as a glass that is half empty—if measured by the persisting disparities between black and white Americans since the early 1970s. (Jaynes & Williams, 1989, p. 4)

We have seen that social psychologists know a great deal concerning how attitudes relate to overt behavior, as well as how to go about changing attitudes. Perhaps this knowledge can be used more systematically than it has been to improve the status of black Americans by removing for them the very real barriers represented by prejudiced attitudes.

Let's review what we've covered in the present chapter. We started with the important point that social behavior is inherently meaningful to participants. To understand ourselves as social beings, we need to appreciate the thoughts and beliefs that lie behind our reactions to one another. Social psychologists study the cognition inherent in social behavior under the general topic of social cognition, and have theorized extensively about the contents and processes of social cognition. As noted earlier, the bottom line of this theorizing is the light that it sheds on actual social behavior, and so we turn to this in the next chapter.

Summary

Topics of Concern

- Social psychology studies people as social beings, in particular how individuals are influenced by the presence of others. The major assumption of social psychology is that each person's behavior is shaped by his or her social relationships. This influence does not take place automatically, but only in terms of how the individual perceives and interprets social situations.
- The term *social cognition* is used to describe the cognitive representations and processes that people use in making sense of the social world.
- Is social cognition a special type of thinking? The processes that transform and maintain our social beliefs seem very much like those that transform and maintain knowledge in general. But social cognition is often more complex than cognition in general because the topic of social cognition is other people, who themselves are social thinkers.
- The aspect of social cognition most studied over the years has been the attitude, defined as a stable and general disposition toward some object, usually a social group.
- Social cognition is structured in a particular way, and different theories propose particular principles that dictate this organization.

Kurt Lewin: Father of Modern Social Psychology

- The founder of modern social psychology was Kurt Lewin, who brought to the study of social problems the perspectives of a gestalt psychologist. Because of Lewin's influence, the contemporary study of social cognition is particularly interested in how a person's different thoughts relate to one another and how inconsistencies are resolved.

Investigating Social Cognition

- Social psychologists use a variety of research strategies, but two in particular deserve special mention. Deception experiments are studies in which the researcher deliberately conceals the purpose of the investigation from the research participants, under the assumption that knowledge of a study's goal would lead subjects to behave differently than they might otherwise.
- Surveys, in contrast, are extremely straightforward investigations in which the researcher chooses a sample of individuals representative of some larger group and asks them about their thoughts and feelings concerning any of a number of topics.

Social Perception

- Social perception describes how we go about knowing other people and ourselves. This process involves description, explanation, and evaluation.
- When we learn about someone's characteristics, we relate this new information to beliefs we already have. Social psychologists use the term *schema* to describe the organized set of beliefs to which we assimilate new knowledge. A schema allows us to fill in the blanks of social interaction. A schema may be represented as a prototype—a typical member of some social group.
- One type of schema in which social psychologists are particularly interested is a stereotype, defined as a rigid and overly simple view of a social group. Stereotypes often accompany prejudiced attitudes because they provide a rationalization for them.
- An important aspect of social perception is deciding why social events occur. Attribution theory concerns itself with how we arrive at causal explanations for the behavior of others as well as ourselves. The particular explanations we choose exert considerable influence on our subsequent motivation and emotion.
- Related to the notion of causal attribution is the idea of personal control: people's beliefs about whether or not they can exert control over events in the world. On the whole, a sense of control over events is associated with vigor and health, even when this perception is not strictly accurate.

- When we evaluate the appropriateness of social behavior, we use several sets of criteria. Norms are expectations about the behaviors which should be displayed by those filling particular social roles. Scripts refer to accepted sequences of action for a social event. Sometimes people following a script do not pay much attention to the details of social interaction, and so they can be characterized as mindless. Values are enduring beliefs that certain goals are preferable to others.
- Despite the importance and universality of religious beliefs, psychologists have tended not to study them. There are current signs that this neglect is ending, and perhaps the vantage point of social cognition is a good place from which we can start to understand the psychological significance of religion.

Attitudes

- The origin of attitudes has been a topic of great interest to social psychologists. Attitudes no doubt stem from our experience with the world, specifically observation of other people in everyday life or in media portrayals. Self-perception theory additionally proposes that we may infer our attitudes from observing our own behavior. If we happen to act in a certain way toward a social group, for whatever reason, we may decide that we have an attitude responsible for this behavior.
- To what degree do our evaluations of social groups predict our behavior toward them? For several decades, there was a raging controversy concerning the correspondence between evaluative attitudes and overt behavior. This controversy has been resolved with the realization that the attitude-behavior link is not a simple one, but rather depends on many factors not originally considered by researchers.
- Social psychologists disagree about the extent to which our needs and drives influence attitudes. For example, some explain prejudiced attitudes as due to frustrations and conflicts. Others suggest that prejudice may stem from the "logical" use of incorrect beliefs.
- There are several ways in which attitudes can change. One might hear persuasive communications and change how one thinks about matters. A great deal of research has studied the effects on attitude change of particular characteristics of the source of a persuasive message, the message itself, and those who hear it.
- Petty and Cacioppo argue that attitude change via persuasive communications takes place in two ways. The central route refers to change that results from people thinking actively about an issue. The peripheral route is change through conceptually irrelevant means, for example, when a message is funny.
- According to Festinger's cognitive dissonance theory, people who see an inconsistency between their attitudes and behaviors are motivated to reduce the discrepancy, and one way to do so is by changing their original attitude.
- A version of Festinger's approach is to encourage people to examine their attitudes in relation to the values they hold. If they perceive an inconsistency between a particular attitude and a more general value, they may change the attitude.
- A final way in which attitude change occurs is through contact with actual members of the relevant social group. If this contact takes place under certain circumstances, more favorable attitudes will be encouraged.

Important Terms and Names

What follows is a list of the core terms and names for this chapter. Your instructor may emphasize other terms as well. Throughout the chapter, glossary terms appear in **boldface** type. They are defined in the text, and each term, along with its definition, is repeated in the margin.

Topics of Concern

social psychology/583
social cognition/583
attitude/584

Kurt Lewin: Father of Modern Social Psychology

field theory/587   Kurt Lewin/587
lifespace/587
action research/589

Investigating Social Cognition

deception experiment/
    590
survey/591

Social Perception

social perception/593   Fritz Heider/595
schema/593   Harold Kelley/595
prototype/593   Denis Hilton/596
stereotype/594   Ellen Langer and
attribution theory/595   Judith Rodin/599
fundamental attribution   Gordon Allport/601
    error/597
personal control/598
norm/599
script/600
mindlessness/600
value/601
interpretive control/603

Attitudes

self-perception theory/   Daryl Bem/606
    606   Richard LaPiere/607
persuasive communica-   Richard Petty and
    tions/610   John Cacioppo/611
cognitive dissonance   Leon Festinger/612
    theory/612   Milton Rokeach/613
attitude-value confronta-   Stuart Cook/614
    tion technique/613
contact hypothesis/614

Review Questions

1. Social psychology studies the impact that the _____ presence of others has on individuals.
   a. actual
   b. imagined
   c. implied
   d. all of the above
   People need not be physically present for them to influence our behavior. People influence what we do even when we just think about them./583

2. The basic premise of contemporary social psychology is that social influence takes place
   a. automatically.
   b. because of biological factors.
   c. mainly in large groups.
   d. only for people with low self-esteem.
   e. through social cognition.
   Social cognition is important because social influence takes place only when the person makes sense of social situations, perceiving them and interpreting them in a given way./583

3. The founding father of modern social psychology was
   a. Fritz Heider.
   b. Gordon Allport.
   c. Kurt Lewin.
   d. Leon Festinger.
   e. Sigmund Freud.
   Although all of these individuals made important contributions to psychology, Kurt Lewin is the one honored as the founding father of modern social psychology./587

4. One of the best ways for a researcher to achieve experimental realism is by using
   a. case studies.
   b. correlational procedures.
   c. deception experiments.
   d. surveys.
   One of the reasons why social psychologists use deception experiments is to encourage experimental subjects to treat the research situation as if it were real./590

5. When we overlook the situational forces that may influence behavior, we are showing
   a. personal control.
   b. scapegoating.
   c. the fundamental attribution error.
   d. the self-serving bias in attribution.
   The fundamental attribution entails explaining behavior in terms of someone's dispositions and ignoring the possible influence of situational pressures and demands./597

6. The state of mindlessness results from
   a. familiarity with scripts.
   b. learned helplessness.
   c. norms to be polite.
   d. physiological arousal.
   Ellen Langer proposes that people behave mindlessly when following familiar scripts for interaction./600

7. Most frequently studied by social psychologists over the years have been people's attitudes toward
   a. gun control.
   b. racial groups.
   c. the elderly.
   d. women.
   Racial attitudes have been most frequently studied by social psychologists./604

8. According to Daryl Bem's self-perception theory, we arrive at our attitudes by
   a. introspection.
   b. observing others behave.
   c. observing ourselves behave.
   d. reliance on abstract schemas.
   Self-perception theory proposes that people infer their attitudes from observing their own behavior./606

9. According to Petty and Cacioppo, attitude change through the _____ route is usually the most long lasting.
   a. central
   b. peripheral
   c. group contact
   d. counter-attitudinal behavior

Petty and Cacioppo distinguished between the central and peripheral routes of attitude change. The central route, which entails people thinking actively about an issue, produces attitude change that is more enduring. Although attitudes can also be changed by group contact or through counter-attitudinal behavior, these are not part of Petty and Cacioppo's theory./611

10. According to cognitive dissonance theory, we are motivated to change our attitudes when we find them _____ our behavior.
    a. ideologically derived from
    b. inconsistent with
    c. instrumental with respect to
    d. irrelevant to

Cognitive dissonance results when someone realizes that her attitudes are inconsistent with her behavior. In an attempt to reduce the unpleasant state of dissonance, she may change her attitudes./612

Members of a group tend to act in similar ways.

Chapter Fifteen

Social Influence

Topics of Concern

Right before a concert in Hill Auditorium on the University of Michigan campus, two fellows in front of me started to stare at the ceiling. Other people began to crane their necks in the same direction. I did, too. Pretty soon it seemed as if all 4000 people in attendance were staring up in that direction. The dimming of the lights and the appearance of the emcee brought our attention to the stage and the beginning of the entertainment. I never did know what we had been staring at.

This is an innocuous example of how people can influence one another's behavior. Social psychologists call this particular type of influence *behavioral contagion:* some particular action sweeping over a group of people. It shows how immediately susceptible individuals can be to the actions of others, and so fits well the definition of social psychology offered in Chapter 14. As you recall, social psychology is the field of psychology that studies how the thoughts, feelings, and actions of individuals are influenced by the presence of others (p. 583).

Sometimes behavioral contagion creates tragedy in the form of panic. One person starts to run, followed by another, and another, and suddenly a disaster is at hand. In a 1979 Cincinnati concert given by The Who, eleven people died as a result of behavioral contagion. Here's what happened (Cocks, 1979). A large number of concertgoers had general admission tickets. While in line waiting to get into the Riverfront Coliseum, some folks mistakenly thought the show was beginning. They surged forward. Thousands of people behind them followed, and so did death, because the doors were locked.

For yet another look at behavioral contagion, let's turn back the clock even further to two of the earliest social psychologists: French theorists Gabriele Tarde (1843–1904) and Gustav Le Bon (1841–1931). Both concerned themselves with the behavior of people in crowds, and neither was impressed. Tarde (1903, p. 74) asserted that "society is imitation," and he likened imitation to a dream state. Le Bon (1895, pp. 34–35) went even further when he wrote that the person in a crowd

. . . may be brought into such a condition that, having entirely lost his conscious personality, he obeys all the suggestions of the operator who has deprived him of it, and commits acts in utter contradiction with his character and habits. . . . Certain

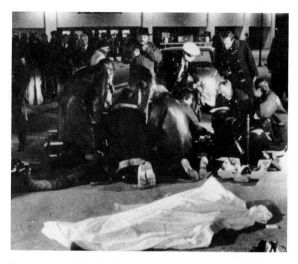

The behavior of the individuals in a crowd can lead to tragedy, as at this 1979 Who concert in Cincinnati.

faculties are destroyed . . . he will undertake the accomplishment of certain acts with irresistible impetuosity.

Again, we see the strong implication that the presence of other people exerts an influence, sometimes subtle and sometimes blatant, on what we think, feel, and do.

Let us now introduce the topic of the present chapter. **Social influence** encompasses all the ways that other people may affect the social behavior of an individual. As emphasized in Chapter 14, social psychologists explain an individual's social behavior in terms of other people. Rather than looking within a person to understand what she does, they look to those in her environment. Sometimes this is a difficult perspective to grasp, because it is at odds with the fundamental attribution error described in the previous chapter.

In Chapter 1, we discussed the Milgram experiment, which investigated obedience. Research subjects followed the commands of an experimenter to deliver increasingly painful electric shocks to another person, despite his apparent pain. You should not conclude that the research subjects who obeyed were sadistic or cruel or sick or weak. Rather, the point of this study was that people obey orders because an authority figure tells them to do so. Most anyone in that social situation would act the same way.

Social behavior takes a dazzling variety of forms, which means that social psychologists must impose some order on the topic. One way to do this is in terms of basic concerns that cut across particular types of social interaction. As you take a look at these questions, keep in mind that they recur throughout social psychology.

social influence
all the ways that other people may affect the social behavior of an individual

social support
the providing of interpersonal resources to those in need of them

presumably because they are thinking the same. One of the potent determinants of how and what we think is the presence of others, and so people in a group tend to act similarly. This is why we spent so much time with social cognition in the previous chapter. Theory and research in social cognition provide explanations for precisely how social influence takes place. Topics such as conformity, obedience, and prejudice are considered later in this chapter, and as you will see, each lends itself to explanations in terms of one's thoughts and beliefs.

How Does Social Influence Occur?

Other people don't just magically influence our behavior. There is necessarily some process by which this influence occurs, and social psychologists try to explain it. To account for the fact that people in a group show common ways of thinking, feeling, and acting, early theorists proposed the existence of a *group mind,* an entity above and beyond the minds of individual people:

[The] social aggregate has a collective mental life, which is not merely the sum of the mental lives of its units. . . . A society not only enjoys a collective mental life but also a collective mind, or, as some prefer to say, a collective soul. (McDougall, 1920, p. 10)

By this view, culture, language, religion, class consciousness, Hoosier hysteria, and *Late Night with David Letterman* represent forces that the group mind imposes upon the individual. These provide compelling experiences, and it isn't surprising that theorists feel a need to explain them.

The group mind eventually fell from favor because its advocates seemed to imply that it was an objective thing, like acid rain or the Goodyear Blimp. This struck other social psychologists as nonsensical, and so they vehemently criticized it (e.g., F. H. Allport, 1924). Today, we view the group mind not as a concrete reality but as an abstraction, a way to describe thoughts, feelings, or actions common to a group of individuals.

Yet social psychologists still need to explain these commonalities, which they do nowadays by using the concepts of social cognition. In responding to others, we respond to our mental representations of them, via principles described in Chapter 14. When people in a group act the same, it is

What's Good and Bad about Groups?

Social psychologists and everyday people alike often wonder if groups have a positive or negative influence on people. That's a tough call because things are rarely so simple. Groups have a variety of influences, some for better and some for worse. Let's start by considering some of the benefits of groups.

Social psychologists point out that only through participation in group life can we become truly human. Remember Maslow's notion of the self-actualized individual who pursues goals that are impossible without other people: love, art, and beauty (Chapter 6). And recall that psychoanalytic theorists propose that people are similarly at their best when using the defense mechanism of sublimation: channeling their sexual and aggressive drives into socially valued activities (Chapter 10).

Research has shown that individuals in close relationships with others benefit in numerous ways, as compared to those who are socially estranged (Cohen & Syme, 1985). They are happier; they are able to tolerate stress better; they even seem to be healthier and live longer (Cobb, 1976). What is so special about relationships with other people? Psychologists explain the benefits in terms of **social support:** the provision of interpersonal resources to those in need.

Consider what can be included here: love, services, information, status, goods, and money (Foa & Foa, 1975).

These are the very substance of life, and we can only receive them from one another. Because social support tends to be reciprocated, participating in group life is good for us and good for our fellows. Those standing on the outside benefit neither themselves nor others.

In contrast to these positive views, there is abundant evidence that "other people" can be hazardous to our well-being (Buys, 1978). We started this section with examples of behavioral contagion showing how groups can exert a negative influence on people. Or consider such historical events as lynchings and the rise of Nazism in Europe. Processes of social influence undoubtedly played a role in these occurrences. From the viewpoint of social psychology, participants in these heinous activities were carried along by each other.

Social Psychology and Society

One cannot simply conclude that groups are always good in their influence or that groups are always bad. What is indisputable is that other people profoundly affect what we think and feel and do, sometimes for the better and sometimes for the worse. Social psychologists also look for ways to arrange matters so that on the whole, good social influence outweighs the bad (see Appendix).

Lewin's call for social psychologists to pursue action research (Chapter 14) has been widely answered. Many research programs within social psychology explicitly address current societal needs. Indeed, some of these programs have become discrete fields of applied psychology, which we will discuss in the Appendix.

It is not surprising that social psychologists are usually concerned with *their* particular society. Theory and research often mirror specific societal events and issues. Remember that the events leading to World War II brought Lewin and other social scientists to the United States (Chapter 1). These researchers concerned themselves with social topics

> onsider such historical events as lynchings and the rise of Nazism in Europe. Processes of social influence undoubtedly played a role in these occurrences.
>
> • • •

demanding explanation: leadership, obedience, conformity, and aggression. Their work obviously mirrored societal concerns. For example, the rise of Nazism in Europe led to an interest in destructive obedience. The massive mobilization of people required by World War II led to an interest in group dynamics.

A good example of how research can mirror larger concerns in the society comes from an investigation of war bond drives during World War II (Merton, 1946). Bonds were sold to raise money in support of the war effort. One drive in particular was highly successful. Why? Interviews revealed that people were moved by singer Kate Smith, the spokesperson of the drive. She was seen as highly credible—indeed, the embodiment of American ideals. If she told people to buy bonds, then buy them they would (Chapter 14).

Another example comes from the court-ordered integration of public schools in the 1950s. School integration forced the attention of the larger society onto the attitudes held by people of different races toward each other. Social psychologists followed the lead of the larger society and extensively investigated prejudice. How could people's prejudiced attitudes—and prejudiced behaviors—be changed? Persuasive communications and other ways of changing attitudes became interesting not only on theoretical grounds, but on practical ones as well.

We began Chapter 7 with the story of John Dean's testimony related to the Watergate scandal, and saw that it illustrated some important points about the psychology of memory. Social psychologists have also found Watergate to be intriguing, although their interest centers on the processes of social influence that led the original burglars to break into the Watergate complex in an attempt to steal documents from the Democratic National Committee.

The men who perpetrated this crime and the subsequent cover-up defended their actions on the grounds of national security. Members of the press, in contrast, tended to view the Watergate affair as moral bankruptcy on the part of all those involved. One way to account for this difference in interpretation is to attribute it to differences between the conservative and liberal perspectives on government. But social psychologists wondered if it was not simply a case of the fundamental attribution error (Chapter 14).

So, a study was undertaken (West, Gunn, & Chernicky, 1975). Subjects were randomly assigned to various conditions. In one condition, they were asked to commit industrial espionage under the auspices of the Internal Revenue Service. They were promised immunity from prosecution; this parallels the Watergate situation as seen by its perpetrators. Fully 45 percent of the subjects consented to participate.

The study itself stopped at this point. Both consenting subjects and "observer" subjects were asked to explain why people would go along with the proposed plan. The basic Watergate effect was found—those involved in the crime justified it on the grounds of situational demands. Those who heard about the crime explained it in terms of the degeneracy of those involved. Whether subjects were liberal or conservative was quite superfluous in producing these differences.

Even more recent examples of how social psychology mirrors societal issues can be cited. Concern with our physical environment leads social psychologists to contribute to environmental psychology. Concern with our physical well-being leads social psychologists to the field of health psychology. Predicting the future is difficult, to be sure, but one safe bet about the decades to come is that research will continue to mirror the larger concerns of our society, whatever these might be.

As already mentioned, social psychologists study innumerable topics. However, some topics are more captivating than others. You should have an idea about what motivates interest: the fact that certain topics highlight theoretical issues of concern (such as how the group influences the individual) and the fact that contemporary social events and issues force attention on some phenomena rather than others. In this chapter we'll discuss representative theories and research, after briefly examining some of the important issues involved in social influence research.

Investigating Social Influence

The task of the social psychology researcher can be made difficult by the value-laden nature of the topics she investigates. Conformity, aggression, prejudice, obedience, and other areas of concern to social psychology can be difficult to study because research participants feel that they are being evaluated and thereby act differently than they might without the scrutiny of the social psychologist. For this reason, as discussed in Chapter 14, deception experiments are often undertaken.

Another factor that can make social psychology research difficult is the complexity of social influence. Social psychology researchers are well aware of the many determinants of our social behavior. They have tried to cut through this complexity in several ways. Let's discuss a particular research strategy used by social psychologists to grapple with the complexity of their subject matter.

Deception experiments direct the attention of research subjects away from the actual purpose of investigations. To what should the subjects be attending? Most importantly, they should be paying attention to the social situation that experimentalists create around them. The term **social analogue** describes this social situation, because researchers try to capture only the essential characteristics of some social phenomenon.

social analogue
a social psychology research technique that creates in the experimental laboratory a simple version of a complex social phenomenon

You encountered the notion of analogue research in Chapter 13, where we discussed approaches to research in psychotherapy. Although acknowledged as not identical to the major anxiety disorders, public speaking anxiety is still thought to be similar enough that it provides a convenient way to learn how to treat more complex disorders. The various social analogues that social psychologists devise are similarly acknowledged as not identical to social behavior outside the laboratory, but still similar enough to conformity or obedience or other social behavior to give the researcher a means of studying these topics in the laboratory. At its best, a social analogue is a paradigm case of social behavior: a pure form or prototype (Chapter 7). As a simplification, it lends itself to experimental manipulation, allowing the researcher to draw conclusions about causes and effects.

Solomon Asch's (1946) approach to social perception is an example of social psychology's use of a social analogue. He wanted to know how we combine different items of information about a person we meet into a coherent whole. This topic could be tackled in a number of ways. Certainly, an obvious—if difficult—strategy would require research subjects to meet different people, who would reveal different aspects of themselves according to the experimenter's instructions. After each interaction, the research subject would voice her overall impression of the person she had just met. But Asch took a simpler route. He gave subjects a list of personality traits and asked them what they would think of a person with these particular characteristics.

Do you see why this procedure qualifies as a social analogue? The list of traits is treated as analogous to an actual person. Here we can see both the benefits and drawbacks of this research approach. On the plus side, social analogues make research simple. If a brief list of traits really can stand in for another human being for the purposes of studying social perception, then a social psychologist can study how an individual forms dozens of impressions in a matter of minutes. Indeed, because this particular social analogue can be implemented on sheets of paper, dozens of subjects can be studied simultaneously.

On the negative side, social analogues can be strained. We know from the start that these are not identical to "real" social phenomena. But some are better analogues than others. Think of the difference between so-called paper people (like those studied by Asch) and honest-to-goodness people. Are these differences fatal to the validity of this social analogue? The answer probably depends on the researcher's purpose. A procedure like this might well capture the essence of what we go through as we scan the passengers in a train car to decide who we might sit next to. We check out a few characteristics of the passengers—such as the presence or absence of weapons, communicable diseases, and cigars—and then make a rapid decision. But paper people procedures fall short of capturing what we do when we choose a roommate, a spouse, or an employee.

Many social psychologists believe that social analogues have more benefits than costs, and so we see their frequent use to investigate social influence. The Milgram study of obedience, for instance, used a social analogue. Other important investigations of social influence, to be described later in this chapter, similarly have proceeded by creating simpler versions of the phenomenon of interest.

Identity

Contemporary America celebrates the individual—witness the American Dream, rugged individualism, the Me Generation, and our societal obsession with being Number One. Even social psychologists focus on the individual person. Thus an important question arises: How is a person's sense of self—his or her identity—shaped by other people? Well, the answer varies, and there are different types of influence—negative and positive.

Whether it is the extended family, a neighborhood gang, or a peer group, an individual's sense of self is, in part, influenced by other people.

Deindividuation

deindividuation

the process of submerging oneself in a group and feeling anonymous

One way in which other people influence our identity for the worse is shown in the phenomenon of **deindividuation:** when a person finds himself submerged in a group and feels anonymous. His inner restraints are relaxed (Festinger, Pepitone, & Newcomb, 1952). He may perpetrate outrages against others. Cross-cultural investigations find that the degree to which warriors costume themselves, thereby achieving anonymity, predicts their aggressiveness in battle (Watson, 1973). And research right here in the United States finds that Halloween trick-or-treaters are more likely to "trick" when wearing an impenetrable costume than when not (Diener et al., 1976).

A well-known demonstration of deindividuation is Philip Zimbardo's (1972) investigation of a mock prison, which he constructed in the basement of the psychology department at Stanford University. He recruited students to play the roles of either a prison guard or a prisoner. The particular role each played was determined by a flip of a coin.

The subjects were given uniforms appropriate to their role and encouraged to act out their parts. Guards were given billy clubs and whistles and the task of enforcing rules. Prisoners were locked in barren cells. In less than a day of playing out their respective roles, the guards and prisoners became lost in the anonymity provided by their respective uniforms and the roles. They ceased "playing" at their respective parts and began to take them seriously (see Figure 15.1).

The guards humiliated the prisoners; the prisoners rebelled against the guards. After 6 days, the study was stopped, leaving us with a powerful example of social influence. Indeed, the identities of the subjects in this study of a mock prison were profoundly influenced by roles they played for less than 1 week. Imagine the impact of social roles that are followed for years or a lifetime. In Zimbardo's own words, here are the important implications of this study:

Figure 15.1

Stanford Prison Study. In this well-known investigation of deindividuation, college students randomly assigned to play the roles of prison guards and prisoners lost their identities in their respective roles and began to take them seriously.

We preselected normal people, people we felt were similar to intelligent citizens, lawmakers, law enforcers, and prison staff members. When such people were randomly assigned as prisoners or guards, the power of the situation overwhelmed their prior socialization, values, and personality traits. And that's the message—the corrupting power of the prison situation—that we've taken to prison officials, judges, lawyers, and committees of the U.S. Senate and House. (Myers, 1987, p. 197)

Person-Role Merger

In deindividuation, a person's identity is thwarted by the influence of others. At the other extreme is the case of a person who fully takes on the identity and purpose of a social group. Here's a personal example. Some years ago, I took a job teaching at a small college. One of my colleagues kept confusing me because she never used the word *I* but only the word *we*. I knew she wasn't the Queen of England. And I knew she didn't mean just her and me. At first, I though she meant her family, but a lot of her sentences didn't make sense that way. Finally, I figured out that she meant the college at which we both worked. She had completely embraced the identity of the school: She and the library and the Board of Trustees and the English Department were all "we" in her mind. In Lewinian terms, her group had become her lifespace (Chapter 14).

This process is sometimes called **person-role merger** (Turner, 1978). In the extreme case, a person identifies so strongly with his assigned role in some group that he literally becomes that role. A "company man" is someone who lives and dies for the place he works. A "gunger" (as in one who is gung ho) is a Naval Academy plebe who has merged his identity with the United States Navy. From the entertainment industry, we have actors such as John Wayne and Sylvester Stallone, who are so famous for playing movie war heroes that the general public thinks of them as "real" heroes. And along these same lines, think of the advertisement in which the soap opera actor known for playing a physician encourages you to use a particular health care product.

What leads to person-role merger? Turner (1978) discusses some of its determinants. It is likely to occur when the number of people who play a given role is limited, when the role is a powerful one and highly conspicuous, and when particular people play the role well. Consider such roles as professional football coach, military commander, or member of the United States Senate. People who once filled these roles may still be addressed as Coach, Colonel, or Senator long after they have moved on to other occupations. They have merged with their earlier roles, not only in their own minds but also in the view of the general public.

Reference Groups

Deindividuation and person-role merger are extreme views of how an individual's identity can be affected by other people. In less extreme fashion, all of us experience a similar influence. In a famous study conducted in the 1930s at Bennington College, Theodore Newcomb (1943) showed that college students tend to take on the political attitudes of those around them. When they started college, Bennington students were for the most part conservative Republicans, like their well-to-do parents. As they were exposed to the more liberal views of the faculty, most became liberal Democrats, an identity these women still had decades later (Newcomb, Koenig, Flacks, & Warwick, 1967). In other words, their **reference group** changed, from family to teachers. Think of the attitude change processes described in Chapter 14, such as persuasive communications, attitude-value confrontation, and group contact. Might not these help to explain what happened to these young women during college?

John Wayne's public image, a direct result of his heroic movie roles, serves as a classic example of person-role merger.

person-role merger
the process of identifying with the role assigned in some group so strongly that one literally becomes that role

reference group
the group of individuals to which one compares one's values, attitudes, and beliefs

Let's move from the ways that an individual's identity is influenced by other people to several related topics that look at how interactions between and among people can be influenced by the social context in which they find themselves. We will start with a discussion of conformity and obedience.

Conformity and Obedience

conformity

changing one's behavior to be consistent with the behavior of others

People in groups often come to think, feel, and act in similar ways. The term **conformity** refers to this phenomenon of people changing their behavior to be consistent with the behavior of others. Is conformity good or bad? This is too simple a question, because conformity can have either negative or positive effects. On the downside, conformity is a threat to individuality in a society such as our own that values independent thinking. But conformity can also be good and useful, as when automobile drivers stay on the same side of the road at the same speed. Regardless of the value we place on conformity, it is a pervasive social process. Let's discuss two well-known studies that show how powerful conformity can be.

Sherif's Study of Conformity

Muzafer Sherif (1937) wanted to study the formation of norms in the experimental laboratory. He capitalized on the autokinetic effect: a perceptual phenomenon in which a point of light in an otherwise dark room appears to jump around. It's actually our eyeballs that are jumping, but against the black background, we attribute the movement to the light (Chapter 4).

At any rate, Sherif recruited several subjects to sit in a dark room and watch a light appear. The subjects were instructed to call out the distance and direction that they saw it move. Two inches to the left. Eight inches up. An so on. As this process was repeated, the subjects started to agree with each other about the movement of the light, which was really not moving at all. In other words, a norm had been formed. This norm had no basis in reality whatsoever. When subjects were reconvened a year later, they still ahered to the group norm!

The generality of Sherif's findings can be questioned because the experimental situation was genuinely ambiguous. Maybe studies of the autokinetic effect tell us little about conformity in other domains of life. Let's therefore consider a second investigation conducted by Solomon Asch (1956).

Asch's Study of Conformity

In Asch's study, about half a dozen subjects were seated around a table, all facing one another. The experimenter explained that the study concerned itself with people's ability to make perceptual judgments. The task of each subject, therefore, was to choose the one line from a group of several that matched a standard line (see Figure 15.2). The experimenter showed each set of lines to the group, and then asked each subject to say which line matched.

Figure 15.2

Line Matching Task. In Asch's study of conformity, subjects were asked to state which line matched the standard. Although there was a clearly correct answer, up to 40 percent of subjects conformed to the incorrect responses of individuals who previously answered.

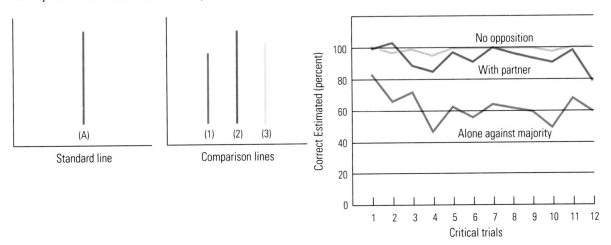

Unlike the task faced by Sherif's subjects, this one had an unambiguously right answer. Now suppose you were one of the subjects in the experiment. All of you were asked to make your judgment out loud. You go in order, and you just happen to be the last subject. You hear each of the other people before you give the same answer: one that seems quite wrong to you.

In actuality, the "subjects" who went before you were in cahoots with Asch. You don't know that, of course, and when it comes to your turn, what are you going to do? Almost 40 percent of the time, you'll go along with what the other people said. This is a striking result. But things get even more intriguing. When later interviewed, some of you who conformed seem unaware that you had gone against the evidence provided by your senses.

Subsequent research by Asch showed that conformity increased with the number of preceding people giving incorrect judgments, although a leveling-off point was reached. If at least one person in the group dissented from the majority, conformity on the part of the real research subject was dramatically decreased. In other words, although conformity is quite obviously an example of social influence, so too is resistance to conformity.

Social psychologists are not interested in lights and lines for their own sake. Rather, the point of the Sherif and Asch studies is that other people profoundly influence what we do. If we go along with others in situations like these, where there is no explicit pressure to conform, what does this say about the likelihood of being swayed in more complex areas of life?

We saw in Chapter 14, for example, that people may hold prejudiced attitudes toward members of groups with which they have never had any contact. The critical determinant is often simply the proximity of other prejudiced people. One begins to conform to their beliefs and evaluations, and the studies of Sherif and Asch imply that this would happen to most people placed in such circumstances. Later in this chapter, we will discuss prejudice and discrimination as products of social influence.

Milgram's Study of Obedience

obedience

complying with the explicit instructions of someone in a position of authority

Although conformity and obedience are both examples of social influence, we can readily distinguish between the two. Conformity entails behaving like one's peers are behaving, and people typically deny that conformity is behind their actions. In contrast, **obedience** is doing what a person in authority tells one to do. People who obey readily acknowledge the influence that has led to their particular actions. "I just work here." "I'm just following orders." "Those are the rules."

Stanley Milgram's (1963) study of obedience is the epitome of social psychological work. Milgram addressed a pressing social concern (obedience) by using a compelling social analogue. He made it abundantly clear that he intended to shed light on events such as the Holocaust:

> It has been reliably estimated that from 1933 to 1945 millions of innocent people were systematically slaughtered on command. Gas chambers were built, death camps were guarded, daily quotas of corpses were produced with the same efficiency as the manufacture of appliances. These inhumane policies may have originated in the mind of a single person, but they could only have been carried out on a massive scale if a very large number of people obeyed orders. (Milgram, 1974, p. 1)

His results strikingly illustrated the fundamental premise of social psychology: People do what they do because of the social situation in which they find themselves.

The major finding of Milgram's study was that when instructed by a researcher to deliver electric shocks to another person, two-thirds of the research subjects obeyed, even when their victim banged on the wall and complained about his heart condition. Strictly speaking, Milgram's basic study was not an experiment, because there was only the one condition (Chapter 1). He didn't *vary* anything. What makes his study so intriguing is that the two-thirds figure defies commonsense. We must conclude that obedience to authority is a much more potent and widespread phenomenon than we might at first believe.

In subsequent studies using much the same social analogue, Milgram (1974) systematically varied aspects of it to see how the rate of obedience would be affected. These studies qualify as true experiments, and their results flesh out our understanding of obedience and its determinants. Table 15.1 summarizes some of his findings.

We know that obedience occurs and is influenced by the social situation. But why does it occur? Milgram (1974) observed that obedience is a fundamental element of social life. Whenever people come together in an organized group, a chain of command is forged. In many ways, obedience is beneficial. We can be relieved, for example, that restaurants obey laws about cleanliness and that airplane pilots obey the commands from the control tower.

However, like conformity, obedience is so engrained within us that it can readily be harnessed to evil purposes. The person who obeys enters a psychological state in which he allows an authority figure to define reality for him. He lets this figure accept ultimate responsibility for what is occurring. "A substantial proportion of people do what they are told to do, irrespective of the content of the act and without limitations of conscience,

Table 15.1
Results of Obedience Experiments

Manipulated Factor	Effect on Obedience
Physical closeness of victim to subject	Reduced
Physical closeness of authority figure to subject	Increased
Salience of injury to victim	No effect
Prestige of university where research was conducted	No effect
Tidiness of laboratory	No effect
Allowing subject to choose shock levels	Painful shocks not given
Two authority figures in conflict	Reduced
Victim has peer who rebels	Reduced
Subject designated the "assistant" to authority figure	Increased

Source: Milgram, 1974.

so long as they perceive that the command comes from a legitimate authority" (Milgram, 1974, p. 189).

Milgram terms the embracing of this psychological state during obedience the *agentic shift,* meaning that the person ceases to be an agent in charge of initiating his or her own actions. The authority figure is accorded the power to do so. The similarity between the agentic shift and hypnotism as described in Chapter 4 is intriguing. Indeed, the early social psychologists Tarde and Le Bon (p. 622) explicitly compared social influence to hypnotism.

A related explanation of why obedience occurs makes use of Langer's notion of mindlessness (Chapter 14). People become mindless when ordered to do something by a legitimate authority because they are accustomed to following a social script in which this is the appropriate action. In sum, there are no ready solutions to the problems of destructive obedience. Perhaps wisdom is to be found in Milgram's (1974) comment that skepticism and freedom must go hand in hand.

Aggression

aggression
intentionally destructive acts directed against individuals or groups

Yet another pressing societal concern that reflects social influence is **aggression,** which we can define as intentionally destructive acts directed against individuals or groups. Just in case you need to be convinced of the degree to which aggression impinges on our daily lives, let's run through a simple exercise using a *Time* magazine. It is the January 30, 1989, issue, but a similar point can be made with any newspaper or newsmagazine. The exercise involves reading through the issue until you find a section *without* a story that features aggression. Unfortunately, you can usually get pretty far before this happens.

So, in the "Nation" section of this issue, the lead story concerns the riots that swept through Miami's Overtown section on the nights immediately following the celebration of the birthday of Martin Luther King, Jr., and immediately preceding Super Bowl XXIII. You may remember what happened. A policeman shot and killed a black motorcyclist. A passenger on the motorcycle died in the ensuing crash. This incident triggered several nights of arson, looting, and shooting. One looter was killed, another twenty-two wounded, and $1 million in property damage was reported.

The second story in this section concerns the mass shooting perpetrated by Patrick Purdy. Which one was he, you may be wondering, because there seems to be an epidemic of these incidents. He was the young man who donned combat fatigues and armed himself with a semiautomatic rifle. He then stalked school children at lunch recess in Stockton, California. In a 4 minute shooting spree, he killed five children, and left another twenty-nine individuals wounded. Then he killed himself with a pistol.

The third article is a collection of brief notes, and some of these also concern aggression. For example, consider the attempt of the New York City health commissioner to obtain mug shots of all the pit bulls within city limits. The objection to pit bulls, of course, is that drug dealers train them to be vicious attack dogs. Their ability to clamp their jaws powerfully on a person's arm or leg is legendary.

In the "World" section of this issue of *Time,* we find that the lead article focuses on how the Israeli Army is treating Palestinians on the West Bank. Here are some quotes from soldiers:

> I find myself acting violently toward people to make them afraid of me.
> The only thing they understand is an iron fist.
> We must be brutally violent to innocent people.
> We hate those P.L.O. people because they make us kill Arab children.

Other stories in this section address the manufacture of chemical weapons in Libya, a heavy-handed police attack against a peaceful demonstration in Czechoslovakia, a report of genocide in southeast Asia, a series of political assassinations in El Salvador, and fear of germ warfare on the part of Iraq.

The rest of this issue was less violent, but we needed to reach page 46 (out of a total of 82) before our exercise was complete. Granted the widespread examples of aggression, we shouldn't be surprised that psychologists from a variety of fields have tried to explain why people act this way. What can be done to prevent or at least minimize aggression?

Aggression as an Innate Urge

One perspective on aggression regards it as a biologically based instinct. Here sociobiologists (Chapter 2) and psychoanalysts (Chapter 11) agree that the human tendency to be aggressive is born within us. An evolutionary argument explaining why this should be so is easy to provide. An aggressive animal is more likely than its passive contemporaries to win scant resources: food, shelter, and access to mates. The tendency to be aggressive thus contributes importantly to one's fitness, and when natural selection takes its course, this tendency is passed on to subsequent generations.

In animal species studied by ethologists, fighting takes a ritualized form, suggesting an instinctive basis (Chapter 6). Certain stimuli prompt the animal to attack, whereas others inhibit an attack. Some theorists are reluctant to identify fighting among animals as aggression, because the

It is hard to determine whether the behavior of these male bighorn rams is genuine aggression—intending harm—or ritualized fighting.

"intent" of animals is difficult to ascertain, if not downright meaningless. They can certainly do considerable damage to one another, but it is not clear if damage per se is their goal.

At any rate, the link between male hormones and fighting is well established in many species. As noted in Chapter 6, male hormones do not directly cause aggression, but rather change the likelihood of attack following provocation. Whether these results generalize to people—human males—is a subject of much controversy that we will take up in Chapter 16.

Psychoanalysts argue that aggression is an instinctive drive that acts just like our sex drive, building up within us and demanding eventual release. An important implication of this view is that acts of aggression should be cathartic. If one "lets off steam" at one point in time, either directly or symbolically, then he should be less likely to feel the need to do so at a second point in time. The aggression is supposedly "out of his system" for at least a while. As we will see shortly, social psychology researchers who take a different view on aggression have carefully examined whether aggression really is cathartic, and they conclude that it is not.

Aggression as a Reaction to Frustration

frustration-aggression hypothesis
a theory proposing that all aggression is a reaction to frustration: the failure to attain a desired goal

In contrast to purely biological theories of aggression, some theorists look to the environment for an explanation. An influential theory is the **frustration-aggression hypothesis** of Dollard, Doob, Miller, Mowrer, and Sears (1939). In its simplest form, this hypothesis attributes all aggression to frustration: the failure to attain a desired goal. Aggression is regarded as a reflex, and without the trigger of frustration, no one would ever lash out at another person.

Descriptively, the frustration-aggression hypothesis accounts for many instances of aggression. Do we curse a vending machine or kick at it when it delivers the product we want? Of course not. Historical research suggests that riots and revolutions are most likely to occur when people's hopes have been raised but then dashed. One interpretation of the 1989 riots in Miami (as well as earlier riots there in 1980) is that black residents believed their lot in life to be improving until the influx of new immigrants from Cuba and South America occurred. They compared themselves to these new groups and felt that they were not getting a fair shake.

When the frustration-aggression hypothesis is examined more closely, it becomes apparent that we need to make some qualifications. For example, perhaps only frustrations that threaten one's sense of self trigger aggression. Perhaps aggression ensues only when ongoing behavior directed toward a goal is interrupted. We also know that under some circumstances, frustration leads not to aggression but rather to renewed efforts to achieve one's goals (Brehm, 1966). Under still other circumstances, frustration leads to passivity (Seligman, 1975). Even when the frustration-aggression link exists, it may not represent a reflex so much as a learned habit. We kick uncooperative vending machines more frequently than we kick personal computers that don't do what we want. Vending machines sometimes deliver when threatened. Computers just break.

Acknowledging these qualifications, Leonard Berkowitz (1981) proposes a modified version of the frustration-aggression hypothesis. According to his version of this theory, frustration results in a *readiness* to act aggressively. However, we only follow through on this readiness when we encounter discriminative stimuli (Chapter 5) associated with past aggression. This modified theory gives us two ways to head off aggression: either prevent frustration or remove cues to violence. When I discussed the Patrick Purdy mass shooting with a friend, I was intrigued by her suggestion that to prevent future tragedies like this, we should ban the sale not of guns but of combat fatigues.

Aggression as a Learned Response

Yet another perspective on aggression makes no mention whatsoever of biology or frustration; rather, it regards aggression simply as learned behavior. We act aggressively (or passively) because of prevailing rewards and punishments. This point of view is championed by many social psychologists, who emphasize in particular the role of the social environment in encouraging or discouraging aggression.

Remember Bandura's idea of modeling first introduced in Chapter 5. His initial demonstration of how we learn by watching others explicitly involved the vicarious learning of aggression (Bandura, Ross, & Ross, 1963). Children who see a model act aggressively then act the same way themselves. One need not invoke instincts or frustrations for an explanation, just modeling. Laboratory experiments show that aggression indeed is sensitive to reinforcers and punishers.

This explanation of aggression clearly disagrees with the psychoanalytic explanation with respect to catharsis. If aggression is simply learned, we would expect that the expression of aggression would not be cathartic. Indeed, through modeling, we would expect just the opposite: aggression begets aggression. Studies clearly support the learning prediction, thus contradicting psychoanalytic theory on this score (e.g., Bandura, 1973). The practical implication is clear. Aggression can be combated by altering situations where aggression proves of value and by removing reminders of such situations. At present, though, this "practical" implication is not realistic. As our *Time* magazine exercise showed, aggression is so widespread that it cannot be wiped out entirely.

To conclude, we can note that several perspectives have been used to explain the societal problem of aggression. One of the most persuasive points of view on aggression regards it as socially produced. And thus the interest in aggression by psychologists makes sense. Let us turn next to yet another important topic that social psychologists have studied.

Prejudice and Discrimination

The organized struggle against various forms of discrimination—racism, sexism, ageism—has long been part of our social and political environment.

Prejudice refers to the prejudgment of a person based solely on the group to which that person belongs. **Discrimination** describes what happens when someone acts on this prejudgment. In other words, prejudice involves attitudes, whereas discrimination involves behaviors. Contemporary society gives us all too many examples of both. Here are some familiar forms that interest social psychologists (Brigham, 1986).

Racism encompasses prejudice and discrimination directed at people by virtue of the ethnic group to which they belong. A racist may be prejudiced against blacks, for instance, or people of Asian ancestry, or native Americans, or eastern Europeans.

Sexism is prejudice and discrimination directed at people by virtue of their gender. A sexist may believe that women should not work, or that men should never be awarded custody of a child following divorce, or that restaurants and clubs should be allowed to bar men or women from entering.

Ageism is prejudice and discrimination directed at people because of their age. An ageist may harbor negative feelings about older people. "We only want youthful employees around here." Or an ageist may be prejudiced against younger individuals. "Never trust anyone under thirty."

Racism, sexism, and ageism have attracted the most attention from social psychologists, but these are not the only "isms" found in the modern world. Prejudice and discrimination may be directed at groups of people defined by

- sexual orientation
- the region of the country where they live
- physical appearance
- weight
- political leanings
- profession
- religion

And so on.

Television's Archie Bunker from *All in the Family* is a classic example of a blatantly prejudiced person. Many of us can compare our thoughts, feelings, and actions against Archie's, and come to the conclusion that, relatively speaking, we harbor little ill will toward any group. But prejudice comes in various forms, some more subtle than others.

Old-fashioned prejudice is what Archie represents: unambiguous expression of negative feelings about particular groups. Surveys suggest that old-fashioned prejudice is on the wane in this country. Fifty years ago, for example, few white Americans supported the idea of integrated schools. Today, there is little overt opposition to school integration.

prejudice
prejudging a person solely on the basis of the group to which that person belongs

discrimination
acting in accordance with one's prejudices

Yet old-fashioned prejudice may just have gone underground, replaced by what is termed *aversive prejudice:* negative feelings and opinions that someone doesn't publicly express. Aversive prejudice shows itself indirectly. For example, a person says that she favors school integration, *but* she disagrees with all possible strategies for achieving this goal. Or she says that men and women should be equally considered for political office, *but* there are just not enough qualified women.

An interesting example of how old-fashioned prejudice has been replaced by aversive prejudice comes from the 1989 election of Douglas Wilder as Governor of Virginia. Wilder is a black man, and polls forecast that he would easily win. However, the actual election was extremely close. The discrepancy resulted from reluctance on the part of white voters to say to a pollster that they would vote against a black candidate (Shapiro, 1989). But indeed many of them did vote against Wilder.

Modern prejudice is someone's belief that prejudice and discrimination used to exist in the world but do not any more. And thus society need no longer concern itself with them. Minority group members should simply stop complaining. "What do they want? Look at how much money Eddie Murphy and Michael Jackson make!"

Institutional prejudice is present when the practices of an organization end up discriminating against a particular group of people, even though no member of the organization necessarily harbors negative feelings. Here's a common example. Most businesses follow the rule that when they must cut back their labor force, the last people hired are the first to be fired. Okay. But suppose—for whatever reasons—that the newest employees are predominantly young, or female, or black. The company rule in effect discriminates against these people. The owners might feel horrible about this. But what is their choice? If they lay off the senior employees, then they are in effect discriminating against old, male, and/or white individuals.

In Chapter 14, we noted that prejudice and discrimination can be explained in terms of attitudes. But these are complicated phenomena, and we should expect that other determinants exist as well. Indeed they do. Let's look at a few of these, from cognitive factors to economic ones.

Prejudice from Categorizing

You know from Chapter 7 that people are natural categorizers. We can't go through life without using categories. Among the most frequently used social categories are precisely those in which prejudice shows up: race, gender, and age. Granted that we make distinctions along these lines, certain negative consequences may be inevitable (Crocker & Schwartz, 1985).

Members of a category seem more similar than those of different categories: "They all look alike." Category membership "explains" the actions of individuals: "They have natural rhythm." We generalize widely from one member of a category to all other members: "Well, I have a friend who is Jewish, and let me tell you about Jews." Our social categories even affect our perception and memory: "Did you notice that foreign guy at the party?" On purely cognitive grounds, stereotypes have a life of their own. Categories in and of themselves may not necessarily create discrimination, but they certainly are one of the raw ingredients.

Economic competition from Japan—in such areas as automobile manufacturing—has been the impetus for prejudiced behavior toward Asian-Americans by their fellow citizens.

People tend to value the groups they belong to. The other side of the coin is their tendency to devalue other groups (Tajfel, 1981, 1982). School pride becomes school rivalry. Patriotism becomes chauvinism. Ethnic pride becomes ethnic prejudice. What's the point? If we stratify and segregate our society, along any grounds, we shouldn't be surprised that prejudice follows.

Prejudice from Scapegoating

Another view points the finger at anger and frustration. People kick others to satisfy needs within themselves: to feel superior, to respond to pain, to overlook their own shortcomings and difficulties (Allport, 1954). This is the phenomenon of scapegoating discussed in Chapter 14.

People may vary in their need to scapegoat others. Consider the personality dimension of *authoritarianism* (Adorno et al, 1950). People high in this trait strictly adhere to conventionality and gladly submit to authority. Authoritarians are preoccupied with power, toughness, and the sexual activity of others. They project their issues onto other groups. Prejudice can result from this process. Indeed, research shows that those high in authoritarianism are more likely than those low to hold prejudiced attitudes toward a variety of minority groups, to belong to restrictive groups, and to show susceptibility to propaganda (Dillehay, 1978).

The slander spread by hate groups concerning their chosen targets is remarkably similar. For example, sexual promiscuity is often attributed to minority groups. This is what Nazis say about Jews. This is what white supremacists say about blacks. This is what male sexists say about feminists. If we understand that slander reveals more about the person who spreads it than it does about its target, then this convergence in stereotypes about obviously disparate social groups should not surprise us. And we should not be surprised to learn that people who are prejudiced toward one social group often tend to be prejudiced against other groups as well (Bierly, 1985).

Particular social conditions can also lead to prejudice and discrimination by creating frustrating conditions for people. For instance, the frequency with which white mobs in the South lynched blacks in any particular year between 1880 and 1930 reflected the prevailing price of cotton (Hovland & Sears, 1940)! The cheaper the cotton, the more lynchings. We can presume that the low prices frustrated the white cotton farmers, who in turn took it out on their black neighbors.

A more contemporary example is an incident that occurred in the Detroit area several years ago, when domestic car companies were being hit particularly hard by the competition of foreign imports. An Asian-American man was killed by a white man, who was an unemployed auto worker. The two men did not know each other; there had been no precipitating incident between them. The only explanation offered by the white man was his frustration with Japanese cars.

Prejudice from Economic Competition

Prejudice is particularly likely to occur when different groups are thrown into competition with each other for scarce resources (Sherif, 1966). The groups typically found by survey research to be most opposed to blacks

At the beginning of World War II many Americans of Japanese ancestry were relocated to camps throughout the country, experiencing personal and economic losses.

or women or Asian immigrants are precisely those groups that stand to lose out in competition with these people for jobs. Prejudice and discrimination in such cases become no less distasteful, but they do become easy to understand.

When World War II broke out, 110,000 Americans of Japanese ancestry were forcibly placed in "relocation centers" scattered across the country. The stated reason was fear of sabotage, although in point of fact, not a single instance of Japanese-American sabotage occurred during World War II. It seems more likely that the actual cause of internment was economic. The flames of prejudice and fear were fanned by those who stood to gain once Japanese-American businesses and workers were out of the picture. Indeed, property was confiscated, and many Japanese-Americans never did recoup their losses.

A more recent example of how economic competition can fuel resentment among groups is the defeat of the Equal Rights Amendment (ERA), the proposed change to the Constitution forbidding different treatment of men and women because of their sex. Although debate over the ERA often seemed to focus on trivial matters such as unisex toilets, some observers feel that the real issue was the fact that women in the United States, on the average, are paid 60 percent of the salaries that men are paid (Smith & Ward, 1989). Whatever else the ERA would have done, it would have forced the legal system to attend to this discrepancy. So, opposition to the ERA was entwined with opposition to equal salaries for men and women.

Prejudice as Normative Behavior

Let's not overlook one more determinant of prejudice, mundane yet powerful: business as usual in certain sectors of society (Pettigrew, 1961). Many of us grow up seeing everyone else acting in prejudiced ways. It's simply the norm. Don't befriend people of different races or religions. Don't question stereotypes about "real" men and women. Go along with the agenda. Win reward. Avoid punishment. If nothing else, this chapter should convince you that other people exert incredible influences upon us. If those around us are prejudiced, then it is hard for us not to follow suit.

Helping

The previous discussions of aggression and prejudice seem to suggest that all social behavior is ugly. These behaviors notwithstanding, people do help each other out. Social psychologists place "helping" within the general category of **prosocial behavior:** acts that benefit other people while having no obvious benefits for the person carrying them out.

prosocial behavior
actions associated with people helping one another

What causes us to help others? Theorists provide various answers to this question. Sociobiologists provide an interesting perspective with their notion of inclusive fitness: the fitness of an individual plus the influence of the individual on the fitness of its kin (p. 84). In Chapter 2, we discussed examples of how an animal that lays down its life for close relatives in effect passes on its own genes. Helping may thus have a biological basis.

In support of the biological explanation of helping is a substantial amount of evidence that we help our relatives more readily than we help individuals unrelated to us. When a natural disaster strikes, for example, family members are given help first, followed by friends and neighbors, and strangers last of all (Form & Nosow, 1958). "Blood is thicker than water," particularly when it is flowing.

Yet biological explanations of helping are difficult to nail down, if doing so means ruling out psychological factors. Of course we help people not related to us! A dramatic example of such help comes from the Christians in Europe who rescued Jews during World War II (Oliner & Oliner, 1988). If and when their assistance was discovered by Nazis, these rescuers were sent to concentration camps, often to perish. Even so, some people still helped.

Social psychologists interested in the phenomenon of helping provide a long list of psychological determinants, such as the following:

- guilt
- empathy
- good moods
- personal values favoring helping
- social norms encouraging helping

The more of these factors present, and the stronger they are, the more likely a person is to help others (e.g., Batson et al., 1988). Naturally, the absence of these factors works against helping.

Research interest in the determinants of helping received a boost some years ago from a well-publicized *failure* of individuals to help someone in need. In 1964, a young woman named Kitty Genovese was murdered in New York City . . . over a 35-minute period. Thirty-eight of her neighbors overheard her screams. Some even watched the assault through their windows. Yet no one intervened. No one even called the police.

When this horrible incident was reported in the news, two social psychologists, John Darley and Bibb Latané (1968), were stimulated to look more generally at conditions that make bystanders to an emergency unresponsive. As Darley recounted:

Figure 15.3

Bystander Intervention. According to Darley and Latané's (1968) research, the *more* people present during an emergency, the *less likely* any given individual is to help.

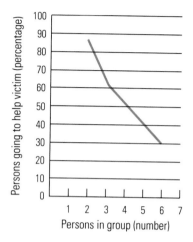

Because we were social psychologists, we thought about not how people are different nor about the personality flaws of the 'apathetic' individuals who failed to act that night, but rather about how people are the same and how anyone in that situation might react as did these people. (Myers, 1987, p. 456)

According to Darley and Latané, her neighbors did not help the struggling Kitty Genovese precisely because they knew others were present. They assumed that someone else was getting involved! Ironically, had only one individual heard her screams—as opposed to the thirty-eight people who actually did—the outcome might have been different.

Darley and Latané (1968) began to study the phenomenon of **bystander intervention:** individuals helping out in an emergency they happen to observe. These researchers systematically created their own emergencies. They dropped coins in an elevator. They blew smoke under the door of a room. They simulated injuries and seizures. For every emergency that was simulated, they noted the number of people present and how long it took someone to offer help. These researchers consistently found that the more people present, the greater the hesitation of any given individual to get involved (see Figure 15.3).

Their explanation examines the decisions that a would-be helper must make:

- Is this really an emergency?
- Am I responsible for helping?
- What are the costs of helping?
- Do I know what to do?

bystander intervention

individuals helping out in an emergency they happen to observe

pluralistic ignorance

a reason why bystanders may fail to intervene in an emergency: everyone uses each other's inaction as a clue that it is not an emergency

diffusion of responsibility

a reason why bystanders may fail to intervene in an emergency: the belief on the part of each individual that someone else is responsible

To the degree that ambiguity enters into any of these questions, the individual looks at what other people are doing. They, of course, are looking at him or her as well.

Failure to intervene may result from two different processes. In **pluralistic ignorance,** everyone uses each other's inaction as a clue that this is not an emergency. Cialdini (1985, p. 113) provides a somber illustration of pluralistic ignorance by quoting this UPI news release from Chicago:

A university coed was beaten and strangled in daylight hours near one of the most popular tourist attractions in the city, police said Saturday.

The nude body of Lee Alexis Wilson, 23, was found Friday in dense shrubbery alongside the wall of the Art Institute. . . .

Police theorized she may have been sitting or standing by a fountain in the Art Institute's south plaza when she was attacked. The assailant apparently then dragged her into the bushes. . . .

Police said thousands of persons must have passed the site, and one man told them he heard a scream about 2 P.M. but did not investigate because no one else seemed to be paying attention.

In **diffusion of responsibility,** the nature of the emergency is recognized, as in the murder of Kitty Genovese, but the fact that no one is doing anything suggests to each individual that someone else is responsible. In either case, we see that social influence can impede helping.

The good news is that social influence can also lead one to help others. When we observe someone else acting in a helpful way, we become more likely to do so ourselves when given the opportunity. Bryan and Test (1967) demonstrated the importance of modeling in a study conducted along a Los Angeles highway. They staged automobile breakdowns at two points along the road, one quarter mile apart. If they arranged it so that someone could be seen helping the driver of the first car change a flat tire, then drivers were more likely to stop a minute later to help the driver of the second car.

Research also shows that the failure of bystanders to intervene in an emergency occurs mainly when the victim is a stranger. Rutkowski, Gruder, and Romer (1983) repeated some of Darley and Latané's original investigations, with one important modification. Before staging an emergency, these investigators had some of their previously unacquainted subjects briefly interact in small groups. They discussed their likes and dislikes with one another and tried to discover ways in which they were similar. As you might imagine, these exercises increased the cohesiveness of the group.

After this exercise, an emergency was staged. One of the subjects—actually someone working with the experimenters—went into another room. A crash and scream were then heard. Subjects who had participated in the group discussion were more likely to help than subjects without this experience. Further, the larger the group size, the more likely were subjects to help, which completely reverses the finding of Darley and Latané that group size inhibits bystander intervention. In subsequent research, Rutkowski et al. (1983) showed that the group exercises created a norm for social responsibility among group members; the larger the group, the better established was this norm.

So far in this chapter we have focused on relationships between groups and individuals. Let's turn next to a discussion of relationships between two people.

Attraction

A relationship between two people can take many different forms. Norms prescribe innumerable types of relationships, both formal and informal. And among our freely chosen ways of relating to others, we can make various distinctions (cf. Rubin, 1973). In *affiliation,* the people involved simply want to be associated with some other person. In *liking,* the people involved have a positive attitude toward each other. When liking is coupled with a mutual perception of similarity, we call it *friendship.* And when a relationship is characterized by exclusiveness and absorption, predispositions to help one another, and mutual dependence, we call it—at least in our culture—*love.* Table 15.2 presents some items from questionnaires devised by social psychologists to measure the degree to which we like or love another person.

Theorists disagree as to whether these types of freely chosen relationships do or do not fall along a single dimension. If we focus just on the intensity of feelings, we can create a hierarchy from least to most intense:

affiliation → liking → friendship → love

But at the same time, love entails more than just intense friendship, friendship more than just intense liking, and so on. Social psychologists have

Table 15.2

Liking and Loving: How to Count the Ways

To measure the degree of one's liking or loving for another, social psychologists ask respondents how much they agree with statements such as these.

Liking Items	1.	I think that _____ is unusually well adjusted.
	2.	Most people would react very favorably to _____ after a brief acquaintance.
	3.	_____ is the sort of person who I myself would like to be.
Loving Items	1.	If I could never be with _____, I would feel miserable.
	2.	I would forgive _____ for practically anything.
	3.	When I am with _____, I spend a great deal of time just looking at him (her).

Source: Rubin, 1973.

concluded that each of these relationships should be studied in its own right. Let's see what has been learned about them.

Affiliation

affiliation
our tendency to seek out other people

social comparison
our tendency to evaluate our own skills, attitudes, values, and so on by comparing them to those of others, usually people similar to ourselves

Affiliation refers to our tendency to seek out other people. This is such a natural tendency for most of us that we may never question just why we choose to place ourselves in the company of others. Once we ask this question, though, we can turn to social psychologists for several answers.

Social Comparison. Leon Festinger's (1954) notion of **social comparison** provides a motive for affiliation. In order to evaluate our skills, aptitudes, attitudes, and values, we compare them to those of others. We can't do this without associating with other people. In short, affiliation helps us evaluate ourselves.

Shelley Taylor (1985) discovered an interesting use of social comparison in a study of how women coped with the aftermath of breast cancer. Her original intent was to discern factors predicting positive or negative adjustment. But she found that all of the patients she studied were doing well psychologically. Their physical conditions varied widely, but each woman engaged in what can be termed downward social comparison. Despite her particular problem, each woman was able to think of someone she knew whose troubles were greater. "Well, I'm doing okay. After all, I could be like so-and-so." Interestingly, if a patient's condition worsened, she simply changed the target of her social comparison. Because it was almost always possible to find someone who was worse off than they were, the women were able to feel good and to cope well (Chapter 6).

Does Misery Love Company? Another line of research that documents the role that affiliation can play in one's life is Stanley Schachter's (1959) investigations of the maxim "misery loves company." He recruited psychology students as research subjects and told them that they were to receive a series of electric shocks, painful but not harmful. A control group of subjects was not told this. For both groups, there was a 10-minute delay while someone set up the experimental equipment. The subjects could wait alone or with others. Which did they choose? Compared to the subjects not expecting to be shocked, those in the experimental group preferred to pass the 10 minutes in the company of others. We thus seek out others when we are anxious, presumably because other people decrease our worries.

Again, social comparison processes may be at work. Other people may provide clues about how we should act and feel in an ambiguous situation. Further research by Schachter clarifies this phenomenon. When given a further choice, anxious people prefer to associate with other anxious individuals, as opposed to those who are cool and calm. Misery loves miserable company!

Finally, when Schachter divided his subjects on the basis of their birth order, he found that the links between anxiety and affiliation occurred most strongly among first-borns and only children. Those born later into their families showed no increased tendency to seek out others when worried. These results support Alfred Adler's (1927) general proposals concerning the importance of birth order in shaping personality and thus social tendencies (Chapter 11).

Liking

Psychologists who study relationships have tried to identify factors responsible for the initiation and maintenance of satisfying friendships. To the degree that these factors can be identified, they can presumably be made more likely. The following is a grocery list of research findings about the factors that predict our liking for someone (Byrne, 1971):

- Proximity—other things being equal, we like those who live close to us.
- Similarity—other things being equal, we like those whose personality traits, values, and beliefs are similar to our own.
- Complementarity of needs—other things being equal, we like those who satisfy our needs.
- High ability—other things being equal, we like those who are competent.
- Attractiveness—other things being equal, we like those who are physically pleasing.
- Reciprocity—other things being equal, we like those who like us.

None of these findings is earth-shattering. But think about how they might be used by enlightened social engineers. Suppose you were put in charge of creating a dormitory where friendships would abound. How would you go about this in light of these findings?

The finding that people are attracted to those with good looks deserves further mention, because attractiveness is a potent aspect of social influence. Research shows that there are widely held stereotypes concerning physically attractive people; they are seen as happier, more intelligent, more successful, and better adjusted than their less attractive counterparts (Hatfield & Sprecher, 1986). Needless to say, these stereotypes do not

The stereotype of attractive people as happy, intelligent, and successful can give them greater social influence than that enjoyed by less attractive but equally able individuals.

equity theory
an explanation of relationships proposing that they persist when both people involved feel they are receiving in proportion to what they are giving

matching phenomenon
the tendency for husbands and wives to be of comparable attractiveness

always reflect reality. We can see them instead as one more example of the tendency to create balance among our thoughts, in this case equating what is beautiful with what is good.

This stereotype has widespread consequences (Cialdini, 1985). Consider that attractive individuals are more likely to win elections than their less attractive opponents, to be offered help when in distress, and to receive favorable treatment from the judicial system. In an intriguing experiment based on these findings, prisoners were given plastic surgery to correct facial disfigurement (Kurtzburg, Safar, & Cavior, 1968). When compared to a group of prisoners whose appearance had not been improved, they were less likely to return to jail following release. Do these findings mean that they had been rehabilitated by their surgery and thus were less likely to commit crimes, or do they merely show that good-looking criminals avoid subsequent punishment?

Friendship and Love

After the first spark of interest, what leads to lasting friendship and love? Social psychologists have explored several perspectives on enduring relationships. One influential approach emphasizes *social exchange,* explaining social relationships in terms of what the people involved give to each other (Kelley & Thibaut, 1978). Another important approach generalizes theories of *emotional attachment,* originally introduced to explain the bonds between parents and infants (Chapter 9), to relationships between adults. Let's examine these two approaches.

Equity Theory.   One example of a social exchange approach is **equity theory,** which suggests that relationships persist to the degree that both people involved feel that what they are getting out of the relationship is proportional to what they are putting into it (Walster, Walster, & Berscheid, 1978). Equitable relationships last, and inequitable ones break up (Gray-Little & Burks, 1983). Surely we have all been friends with people who never seem to remember our birthday, or return our phone calls, or defend us against gossip, although we do all these things for them. This is an unstable relationship—a bad gestalt, as it were. Something has to change. Our friends need to do more, or we need to do less, or there is no future.

Equity theory is an economic view of social behavior, assuming that people calculate the costs and benefits involved in interacting with others. A number of studies support its general predictions. For instance, equity theory suggests that people in a romance bring with them comparable degrees of physical attractiveness. Do you see the reasoning? "Good looks" in a romantic partner are highly desirable and thus constitute a considerable benefit offered by such a relationship. And one of the simplest ways of achieving equity with a heartthrob is to be good looking oneself. This is exactly what happens: Men and women often pair up according to looks (e.g., McKillip & Riedel, 1983). The tendency for husbands and wives to be of comparable attractiveness is widespread enough that social psychologists have given it a name: the **matching phenomenon** (Murstein, 1976).

Equity theory also predicts that when people in a relationship are mismatched on one dimension, such as physical attractiveness, then there

Partners in a romantic relationship tend to be of equal attractiveness, as equity theory would predict.

must be a compensating mismatch on another dimension, such as occupational success. Research bears this out. For example, highly attractive women are more likely than less attractive women to marry rich men (Elder, 1969). We can lament that physical attractiveness is a commodity in the social world, but it is a fact that social psychologists repeatedly discover.

Equity in the here and now is not the only influence on whether long-term relationships continue. Social psychologists have also documented other factors that determine who stays together and who parts company. A couple is less likely to break up if they are satisfied with their relationship, if no suitable alternatives are present, and if each has invested a great deal of time and effort in their relationship (Rusbult, 1980; Rusbult, Zembrodt, & Gunn, 1982).

Perhaps you will be relieved to know that equity theory has limits in its ability to explain friendships and romances. Here's why. Interpersonal relationships exist on two levels (Kelley & Thibaut, 1978). First, there are the specific actions and characteristics of the people involved. These more or less line up in terms of equity. Second, however, there are the various ways in which people interpret their relationships. They're best friends, true bluers, working things out, confused, whatever.

People's interpretations cannot be greatly at odds with their specific behaviors. A relationship that is strictly a mutual exchange of goodies can only be thought of as a business deal, and that's unsatisfactory. To preclude this crass interpretation, individuals in a friendship or romance must sacrifice some of their own rewards for the good of their partner. Then the relationship can be interpreted as a "genuine" one. What's the point? A purely equitable relationship can't work, because no one thinks of their friendship or romance in these terms.

Attachment Theory. The more intimate a relationship between two people becomes, the less satisfactory is the explanation provided by equity theory. Accordingly, social psychologists have explored other perspectives on lasting relationships. One intriguing example starts with research into social development among infants. In Chapter 9, we discussed the attachment between a child and her caregiver. This is a deep emotional bond that appears early in life. Attachment develops through stages, and it shows itself in different patterns.

Applied to romantic relationships between adults, these ideas are known as **attachment theory** (Hazan & Shaver, 1987). According to attachment theory, adults approach romantic relationships in accordance with their attachment history. In other words, if they were secure in their attachments as infants, they will be secure in their romances. And if they were avoidant or ambivalent infants, they will be avoidant or ambivalent lovers.

In an initial attempt to test attachment theory, Hazan and Shaver (1987) placed a "love quiz" in a newspaper. Within 1 week, they received more than 1000 replies. Their quiz was actually a questionnaire containing several parts. First, they asked respondents to characterize their attachment style by choosing the one description from the following that best described their approach to relationships:

Secure: I find it relatively easy to get close to others and I am comfortable depending on them and having them depend on me. I don't often worry about being abandoned or about someone getting too close to me.

Avoidant: I am somewhat uncomfortable being close to others; I find it difficult to trust them completely, difficult to allow myself to depend on them. I am nervous when anyone gets too close, and often, love partners want me to be more intimate than I feel comfortable being.

Ambivalent: I find that others are reluctant to get as close as I would like. I often worry that my partner doesn't really love me or won't want to stay with me. I want to merge completely with another person, and this desire sometimes scares people away.

The proportions of people endorsing these descriptions were 56 percent, 25 percent, and 19 percent, respectively, which are approximately the same as the known proportions of secure, avoidant, and ambivalent infants. These findings are consistent with the hypothesis that infant attachment styles are carried into adulthood, because the proportions stay about the same.

Also supporting this hypothesis were retrospective reports of subjects about their parents. Secure subjects reported warmer relationships between themselves and each parent as well as between their parents. Avoidant subjects were most likely to describe their parents as cold and rejecting. Finally, ambivalent subjects saw their fathers—but not their mothers—as unfair.

Respondents were also asked to describe their most important romance. Secure lovers used terms such as *happy, friendly,* and *loving,* whereas avoidant lovers expressed fear of intimacy and a great deal of jealousy. Ambivalent lovers described love as an obsession and reported great highs and great lows in their romances. Although respondents in the three groups were all on the average thirty-six years of age, the individuals with a secure attachment style reported that their most significant romance had lasted ten years, about twice as long as the romances reported by those with avoidant or ambivalent styles.

The findings of Hazan and Shaver (1987) have recently been replicated by Feeney and Noller (1990), and research into attachment theory

attachment theory
the idea that adults approach romantic relationships in accordance with their attachment history

continues. Let's conclude here by contrasting attachment theory with equity theory. In equity theory, we see an emphasis on the calculation of costs and benefits in a relationship. We can describe equity theory as a cognitive approach to friendship and love. In contrast, attachment theory emphasizes one's feelings; it explains relationships in emotional terms. The tension between thoughts and feelings is an enduring issue in psychology, as we have seen (Chapter 1). But someday we may find a way to integrate these perspectives, to view relationships as dependent on how we think about one another as well as how we feel.

Perhaps useful is the distinction by Clark and Mills (1979) between exchange relationships and communal relationships. In *exchange relationships,* people give benefits to one another with the expectation that comparable benefits will soon be repaid. These relationships are fully explained by equity theory, and they tend to occur between people who do not know each other very well or who have no reason for relating outside of business. In contrast, *communal relationships* are those in which people feel a special responsibility for the needs of one another. Benefits are provided because there is a need for them and a desire to show concern. However, specific debts are not incurred, which means that communal relationships are poorly explained by equity theory. Attachment theory may account for communal relationships, which we tend to have with our family members, friends, and romantic partners.

Group Processes

Obviously, social interactions take place between and among specific people. But can we explain the characteristics of social interaction simply in terms of the characteristics of the individual members? In the language of gestalt psychology, when is the whole the same as its parts and when is it different (Chapter 1)? Almost all social psychologists acknowledge that social interactions are usually *not* just the sum of their members. This explains why Kurt Lewin, with his background in gestalt psychology, was so influential when he turned his attention to social psychology (Chapter 14). He brought with him a point of view that allowed him to appreciate that social interactions have an organization not readily derived from the characteristics of their individual members.

aggregation
an assembly of individuals physically congregated in the same place

collectivity
a social category: two or more people who can be discussed as a whole

To introduce this next section let us note some distinctions that social psychologists make among interactions that take place among three or more people. They use the term **aggregation** to describe an assembly of individuals physically congregated in the same place. They may have nothing more to do with each other than the fact that they are in the same place at the same time, such as Christmas shoppers in K mart, pedestrians hurrying along Fifth Avenue at lunchtime, or joggers on a high school track.

A **collectivity** is simply a social category: two or more folks who can be discussed as a whole (Brown, 1954). All aggregations are collectivities, by definition, but not all collectivities are aggregations, because people in a collectivity don't have to be gathered in the same place at the same time: for example, voters over sixty-five years of age, newlyweds in Reno, people with unlisted telephone numbers, basketball players with green eyes, jugglers, and employees of the United States Postal Service.

This jazz band is a good example of a group, as it is defined by social psychologists.

group
interacting individuals who mutually influence each other

organization
an enduring and organized group

audience effects
the effects of the mere presence of others on one's performance of a task

coaction effects
the effects of others doing the same thing on one's performance of a task

collective effects
the effects of interacting with others on one's performance of a task

A **group** is a set of interacting individuals who mutually influence each other (Shaw, 1981). The "group" in group therapy (Chapter 14) is a good example, as are families, athletic teams, dance bands, and juries.

Finally, an **organization** is an enduring and organized group. Usually an organization has a body of traditions and customs. Its members think of the organization as a whole, and their roles are differentiated and specialized. By this definition, many work groups qualify as organizations. Consider IBM or the lunch shift at the local McDonald's. Social groups such as the Boy Scouts, political groups such as the Democratic National Committee, and special interest groups such as the National Rifle Association are also good examples of organizations.

One way to distinguish organizations from other groups is to ask whether particular members are dispensable. Regardless of who is coaching, playing, ailing, or holding out, National Football League teams go on. Thus, they are organizations. In contrast, most families wouldn't have much of an existence without Mom and Dad and the kids. They are not organizations.

Group Influences on Performance

The effect other people have on an individual's performance at some task has obvious practical implications—in school, in industry, or in entertainment. Psychologists study three types of influence: **audience effects, coaction effects,** and **collective effects.** Let's discuss in turn each of these types of social influence.

Audience Effects.   Does the presence of an audience help or hinder one's performance? Results here are contradictory. In some circumstances, the individual performs better. This even occurs among ants, who reportedly excavate more sand when in the presence of other ants than when alone (Chen, 1937)! But in other circumstances, audiences inhibit performance. Haven't we all pleaded with others "don't watch me" while we attempted some challenge, such as threading a needle, breaking an egg, or putting the batteries into a toy?

Happily, there is an elegant resolution to these contrary findings, one proposed by Robert Zajonc (1965). Studies finding that an audience facilitated performance were those that asked subjects to perform a task that was simple or well learned. When subjects were asked to perform complex or poorly learned tasks, an audience disrupted their performance (see Guerin, 1986). In other words, people (or ants, as the case may be) create physiological arousal in performing individuals, and this arousal improves the performance of previously acquired skills but disrupts the process of acquiring them. Anyone who has performed in front of others knows what this means. If you have your song or dance or speech down pat, an audience brings out the best in you. If you are winging it, the presence of an audience makes that abundantly clear.

Coaction Effects. Let's turn to coaction effects, which occur when two or more individuals perform the same task. Among the very first experiments in social psychology were Norman Triplett's (1898) investigations of bicycling, alone or with others. He found that a cyclist, when paced by another rider, could save more than 30 seconds per mile when compared with a lone rider. But studies using other tasks found that coaction interfered with performance.

The determinants of coaction effects are more complex than those of audience effects (Davis, 1969). On one level, arousal exerts an influence. But competition might also enter into it, complicating matters. Coactors distract each other, on the one hand, and provide each other with useful information, on the other. Coaction may increase morale and cohesion, or it may decrease them. Think about studying in a crowded library, where your fellow students are hitting the books as well. Coaction should facilitate your studying when you have enough time to overcome the delays created by distraction, and it should hinder it when time is precious.

Collective Effects. When interaction among individuals is inherent in the task, matters become even more complicated. Sometimes interacting with others improves a person's performance above and beyond what she would have been capable of by herself. Reasons for this are easy to find. A group of individuals has more information at hand than any one individual. Labor can be divided. Social support can be given. And so on. But sometimes performance can suffer because of a group.

social loafing
our tendency to work less hard when in a group than when alone

Social loafing refers to the finding that people in a group sometimes don't work as hard as people alone (Latané, Williams, & Harkins, 1979). It has been found in groups engaged in physical tasks (such as clapping) as well as intellectual tasks (such as problem solving). If social loafing is to result, it is critical that an individual's contributions to the group's outcome cannot be identified. Some theorists see broad applicability of this concept, using it to explain failures of typing pools, unions, and Russian collective farms (Myers, 1987). Arguing against such generality are findings that social loafing vanishes when the task is attractive, when the group is

The concept of groupthink can be used to explain decisions such as those made by Reagan administration officials leading up to the Iran-Contra affair.

highly cohesive, or when individuals are accountable (e.g., Zaccaro, 1984). Nevertheless, the fact that social loafing exists at all supports the charge that other people can have a negative effect on us.

Groupthink. Let's now discuss several further instances of collective effects on group performance. In reviewing recent U.S. history, social psychologist Irving Janis (1982) was struck that certain events could only be described as colossal blunders. Consider, for example, the failure to prepare for Japan's attack on Pearl Harbor in 1941, the decision to mount the Bay of Pigs invasion of Cuba in 1961, and the escalation of the Vietnam War from 1964 to 1967. Noteworthy about these blunders is that they were all products of supposedly careful group consideration by the brightest political and military leaders available.

To account for such disastrous group decisions, Janis proposed that in certain groups, processes are set into motion that suppress criticism and preclude considering alternatives. Collectively, these processes are termed **groupthink;** its "symptoms" are

groupthink
the tendency of groups to suppress criticism and not consider alternatives, thus ending up with poor decisions

- an illusion that the group is invulnerable to any harm
- rationalization of past errors
- unquestioned belief in the group's moral correctness ("we are good")
- stereotyped view of the opponent ("they are bad . . . and stupid")
- pressure to conform
- self-censorship
- the mistaken belief that all the group members are in agreement
- mindguards (i.e., members who protect leaders from criticism)

These factors conspire to produce a group in which dissent never takes place. And further, the members are not even aware that their group suppresses open discussion, thus leaving themselves at risk for bad decisions. What they see is a harmonious and confident group.

The idea of groupthink is intriguing. Theorists have applied it to events both mundane and sublime: for example, strikes by professional athletes, the Iran-Contra affair, and the fatal decision to launch the space shuttle Challenger. Think of other examples of bad group decisions. Do they fit the groupthink formula?

Group Polarization. Yet another example of how groups can impair the performance of individuals comes from studies of decision making. Conventional widsom tells us that the best way to make an important decision is to discuss it with others. This is why companies have boards of directors, why the legal system has juries, why the president has a cabinet, and why universities have trustees. Groups are said to "deliberate" over their decisions, presumably arriving at a more careful conclusion than individuals would have. But here's the punchline. Social psychologists have shown that under some circumstances, groups make more extreme decisions than individuals. This phenomenon is called **group polarization.**

Group polarization shows up in numerous experiments (e.g., Stoner, 1961). In a typical study, individuals are given brief descriptions of someone facing a dilemma. One choice might bring great happiness and reward, but it has a risk involved. It could lead to disaster. The other choice promises fewer benefits but carries no risk. What are the minimal odds of success for the first choice that should impel a person to go for it? Individual subjects make an estimate: 10 percent, 35 percent, 90 percent, whatever. Then they come together in a small group to discuss the same dilemmas and again arrive at estimates of the minimal odds. As you would expect, their estimates converge—but typically around a value more extreme than the average of the individual estimates.

Sometimes the group decision is more risky than those of individuals, and sometimes it is more cautious. The contemporary explanation is that groups polarize the initial inclinations of group members (Myers & Lamm, 1976). If this is what typically happens in group discussions, we have reason to be critical of the influence that others have on us.

What exactly produces group polarization? One explanation is that dilemmas—by definition—do not have an obvious solution. Individuals might be quite uncertain about the course of action they tentatively entertain. When exposed to the opinions of other people, they compare their own opinions in order to evaluate them (and themselves). Because people want to have the "right" opinion or attitude, they shift in accordance with the general thrust of others, sometimes doing them one better in the process.

Combating Process Loss. In any group, an inevitable inefficiency—called **process loss**—results, and it is a constant concern to social psychologists. How can they minimize inefficiency? Thousands of studies have compared the performance of different groups in an attempt to isolate factors that make groups more or less productive (Hare, 1976). The following are some of the helpful factors:

- small size
- high cohesiveness
- good communication
- frequent feedback about performance
- skilled leadership
- experience
- ample time

Another consistent research finding is that high productivity is *not* necessarily accompanied by member satisfaction. Here is an important lesson about groups. They have multiple purposes. Groups meet emo-

group polarization
the tendency of groups to polarize the initial inclinations of individuals, resulting in more extreme decisions than those reached by individuals alone

process loss
the inevitable inefficiency of groups

Although successful leaders seem to share certain personality traits, effective leadership is the result of the complex interaction of leader and group.

tional needs as well as performance goals, but we shouldn't expect them always to go hand in hand. In college, I coached an intramural sports team. Making sure everyone played in a game made all the players happy, but it certainly didn't help us win.

Leadership

With group influences on performance behind us, we now turn to a discussion of leadership. One of the most common ways in which groups are structured is in terms of leaders and followers. Let's focus now on leaders and the questions social psychologists wish to answer about them. What is a leader? What kind of person is the most effective leader? What kind of leadership style produces the best results?

Great Men and Women. Although these questions regarding leadership have remained central within social psychology for years, we can see drastic changes in the particular ways they have been pursued (House & Singh, 1987). Early attempts to understand leadership focused on great men or great women who put their stamp on others and on history. This view suggests that some people are leaders, and some are not, with particular personality traits characterizing each group. For example, we can set Indira Gandhi, Abraham Lincoln, Margaret Thatcher, and Mikhail Gorbachev apart from others because of their personalities. They would be leaders in any and all situations. They happen to have made their mark as heads of state, but they could have just as easily led social movements, armies, fast food franchises, or labor unions.

This is a commonsense view of leadership. However, it has a serious flaw. Research has not been able to identify "leadership" traits (Chapter 11)! Literally hundreds of studies have compared the personality traits of leaders and followers, and reviews concluded that the yield of this research was meager (e.g., Bass, 1960; Bird, 1940; Gibb, 1969; Mann, 1959; Stodgill, 1948).

The Leader and the Group. By the 1950s, the great man or woman theory of leadership was abandoned in favor of a view that looked at the functions of leadership (e.g., Bales, 1950; Hemphill, 1950; Stodgill, 1969). In other words, what is it that leaders do? One of the effects of this type of scrutiny was an emphasis on how various leaders differ from each other.

Two dimensions are critical (Bales, 1953). First is *task orientation:* the degree to which a leader is concerned with achieving her group's goals. Second is *group maintenance:* the degree to which the leader tries to boost morale and cohesiveness among her group's members. Research showed that these dimensions are largely independent, meaning that a particular leader can be high on one but not on the other. Further, it is difficult to talk about "leadership" as if it were unitary—precisely because leaders are not necessarily talented at both aspects of leadership.

In judging leadership effectiveness, one must also know the goals of the group. A group such as a bridge club, whose only purpose is to have fun every other Thursday evening, is not well served by a task-oriented leader who neglects group maintenance. The converse would be true for a crew of mechanics whose only job is to change tires of race cars as rapidly as possible. Of course, many groups are more complex than these examples, and need attention to both task performance and group harmony. In these cases, leaders who excel at both functions are obviously quite effective (e.g., Hemphill, 1955).

In more general terms, social psychology's view of leadership expanded to include both the leader and the group. A popular theory that embraces this expanded conception is Fred Fiedler's (1971) **contingency theory.** The term *contingency* captures the central premise: The best leader for a group depends on the nature of the group to be led (the use of this term in learning theories is described in Chapter 5). Like previous theorists, Fiedler categorized leaders as either task oriented or maintenance oriented. These characteristics interact with such attributes of the group as

- the degree to which the members trust the leader
- the explicitness with which group goals and tasks are specified
- the power that the leader has over the followers

Studies support Fiedler's claim that effective leadership is jointly determined by characteristics of the leader and her group (Strube & Garcia, 1981).

Great Men and Women Again. In recent years, there has been a renewed interest in traits associated with leadership. Kenny and Zaccaro (1983) studied research subjects participating in a variety of small groups. Regardless of the group, the same people tended to emerge as leaders, implying that these people have certain characteristics that make them leaders.

And what might these characteristics be? We have seen that previous reviews of the research literature were unsuccessful in identifying leadership traits, so we seem to face a dilemma. Two resolutions are likely. First, the previous literature reviews were wrong in their conclusions. When the studies they surveyed are summarized quantitatively using the statistical technique of meta-analysis (Chapter 13), relationships between leadership on the one hand and intelligence, dominance, and masculinity on the

contingency theory (of leadership)
Fred Fiedler's hypothesis that the most effective leader for a group depends on the nature of the group

other indeed emerge (Lord, De Vader, & Alliger, 1986). These relationships are modest in size but consistent.

Second, new studies show that leaders tend to be more flexible than followers (Ellis, 1988). Stated another way, leaders show more varied behavior than followers, as they adapt themselves to the particular needs of the group at the moment. When past studies tried to characterize leaders in terms of invariant traits, researchers missed the important fact that their behavior varies.

The renewed interest in leadership traits does not invalidate Fiedler's contingency theory and related formulations. Although characteristics of leaders indeed set them apart from followers, it remains an open question whether these characteristics are in turn related to the effectiveness of leaders. Here we would do well to remember the premise of contingency theory, that the effectiveness of a leader depends not only on his or her characteristics but also on the purpose of the group being led.

The next chapter is the final one in the textbook. Its topic is human sexuality. You will find the social psychological perspective important in understanding this topic, because sexuality is inherently social. Our thoughts, feelings, and actions in the sexual sphere reflect social influence just as clearly as does our behavior in so many other domains.

Summary

Topics of Concern

- When social psychologists explain phenomena such as conformity, obedience, and aggression, they do so in terms of social influence, explaining what someone does in terms of the presence of others.
- Certain basic concerns cut across the topics studied by social psychologists. One such concern is explaining exactly how social influence takes place. At the present, theorists use concepts of social cognition. When we respond to others, we respond to our mental representations of them.
- Groups can have both positive and negative influences on people.
- Social psychology research topics often mirror the current needs and issues of the larger society. As society changes, so too do the topics that interest social psychologists.

Investigating Social Influence

- Social psychologists often investigate social influence with social analogues: the creation in the laboratory of a simplified version of the particular social behavior in which they are interested. As a simplification, a social analogue lends itself to experimental manipulation.

Identity

- Several lines of social psychological research investigate how one's identity is shaped by other people.
- Deindividuation occurs when a person finds himself submerged in a group and feels anonymous. A person who is deindividuated may perpetrate outrages against others as a result.
- In person-role merger, a person identifies so strongly with an assigned role in some group that he or she literally becomes that role.
- One's reference group is the set of individuals to which one compares one's values, attitudes, and beliefs.

Conformity and Obedience

- When they conform, people change their behavior to be consistent with the behavior of those around them. Conformity is very much a social product, as shown in classic experiments by Sherif and Asch. People will act like other people act, even when conformity involves going against the evidence provided by their senses.
- Conformity entails acting like one's peers, whereas obedience is doing what a person in authority tells one to do. Milgram's study of obedience is a well-known example of people's tendency to obey, in this case, by delivering electric shock to another person when told to do so by a researcher.

Aggression

- Intentionally aggressive acts directed against individuals or groups constitute aggression. Aggression is obviously a pressing societal concern.
- Several perspectives have been used to explain aggression. One view sees it as an instinctive urge. Another view explains aggression as an inevitable response to frustration.
- Social psychologists often favor a third explanation that regards aggression as a learned response, one particularly sensitive to the social setting. The idea of modeling suggests that people act aggressively to the degree that they see others act aggressively.

Prejudice and Discrimination

- When we prejudge people solely in terms of the group to which they belong, we are displaying prejudice. When we act on these prejudgments, we show discrimination.
- There are different types of prejudice, subtle and blatant, that can be directed at a variety of social groups.

- Prejudice may stem from the simple act of making distinctions among social groups. Once these distinctions are made, we tend to value the groups to which we belong while devaluing other groups.
- Other determinants of prejudice include scapegoating, economic competition, and norms.

Helping

- Not all social behavior is ugly. "Helping" is one example of what social psychologists call prosocial behavior: acts that benefit other people while having no obvious benefits for the person who carries them out.
- Sociobiologists explain helping in terms of inclusive fitness; we aid people who share genes in common with us.
- There also are psychological influences on helping, including feelings of guilt or sympathy and values in favor of helping.
- Darley and Latane have studied the tendency of bystanders to help in an emergency, documenting a surprising result: The more people present in an emergency, the less likely any particular individual is to help. People use each other's inactivity as signs either that this is not really an emergency or that someone else is responsible.

Attraction

- Affiliation refers to our tendency to seek out other people. People have various motives for affiliation, including social comparison and the reduction of anxiety.
- Most of the factors that lead to initial attraction between people are commonsensical, such as similarity and attractiveness.
- Lasting relationships can be explained by equity theory, which proposes that relationships persist to the degree that both people involved feel that what they are getting out of the relationship is proportional to what they are putting into it.

- Another explanation of lasting relationships is attachment theory, which suggests that relationships between adults are similar to and derived from the types of relationships that infants have with their caretakers.

Group Processes

- An aggregation is simply an assembly of individuals in the same place. A collectivity is any social category. A group is a set of interacting individuals. An organization is a group that is enduring and organized, with a body of traditions and customs.
- Social psychologists have long studied how the presence of others affects the individual's performance at some task. Sometimes the presence of others facilitates performance, and sometimes it is disruptive.
- In groupthink, processes of social influence may suppress criticism and preclude the considering of alternatives, resulting in disastrous group decisions.
- Another phenomenon studied by social psychologists is group polarization, the tendency of group discussion to polarize the initial inclinations of its members. What this means is that groups may make more extreme decisions than individuals alone.
- Social psychologists have tried to combat the inefficiency of groups by determining factors that make groups more or less productive.
- Early studies of leadership attempted to discover traits that set leaders apart from followers. These attempts proved unsuccessful, and leadership is now seen as more complex. The best leader for a group often depends on the nature of the group to be led. Nonetheless, recent studies have shown that some characteristics do distinguish leaders from followers.

Important Terms and Names

What follows is a list of the core terms and names for this chapter. Your instructor may emphasize other terms as well. Throughout the chapter, glossary terms appear in **boldface** type. They are defined in the text, and each term, along with its definition, is repeated in the margin.

Topics of Concern

social influence/622
social support/623

Gabriel Tarde/622
Gustav LeBon/622

Investigating Social Influence

social analogue/626

Identity

deindividuation/628
person-role merger/629
reference group/629

Phillip Zimbardo/628
Theodore Newcomb/629

Conformity and Obedience

conformity/630
obedience/632

Muzafer Sherif/630
Solomon Asch/630
Stanley Milgram/632

Aggression

aggression/633
frustration-aggression
    hypothesis/635

Prejudice and Discrimination

prejudice/637
discrimination/637

Helping

prosocial behavior/641

John Darley and
    Bibb Latané/641

Attraction

social comparison/644
equity theory/646
attachment theory/648

Stanley Schachter/644

Group Processes

aggregation/649
collectivity/649
group/650
organization/650
social loafing/651
groupthink/652
group polarization/653
contingency theory
    (of leadership)/655

Irving Janis/652
Fred Fiedler/655

Review Questions

1. Social psychologists explain an individual's social behavior in terms of
   a. drives.
   b. other people.
   c. personality traits.
   d. the brain and nervous system.
   The fundamental premise of social psychology is that other people influence how we behave./622

2. Social analogues are
   a. blind dates.
   b. computer simulations of social behavior.
   c. naturally occurring social interactions among animals.
   d. simplified social phenomena.
   Social psychology researchers study social phenomena in the laboratory by creating simplified versions called social analogues./626

3. For the sake of this question, assume that professional wrestling is real. Now consider a wrestler who wears a mask in the rink and breaks the "rules" much more frequently than do other wrestlers. This is an example of the effects of
   a. conformity.
   b. deindividuation.
   c. frustration-aggression.
   d. obedience.
   e. person-role merger.
   Because our masked marvel is anonymous, his dastardly deeds exemplify deindividuation./628

4. According to Milgram, the agentic shift is the psychological state that accompanies
   a. aggression.
   b. conformity.
   c. deindividuation.
   d. obedience.
   e. prejudice.
   Milgram believed that people follow the commands of an authority figure when they cease to regard themselves as agents in charge of initiating their own actions./633

5. Berkowitz modified the frustration-aggression hypothesis by proposing that
   a. aggression is due solely to instincts.
   b. aggression is due solely to learning.
   c. aggression produces frustration.
   d. frustration inhibits aggression.
   e. frustration produces only a readiness to act aggressively.
   Although frustration often produces aggression, it does not do so inevitably, prompting Berkowitz to suggest that frustration produces a readiness to be aggressive. Whether or not someone then acts aggressively depends on other factors./636

6. Prejudice and discrimination may result from
   a. categorizing.
   b. scapegoating.
   c. economic competition.
   d. norms.
   e. all of the above.
   Prejudice and discrimination have numerous determinants, including all the factors listed here./638

7. Research by Darley and Latané suggests that the more bystanders present during an emergency
   a. the less likely any individual is to help.
   b. the less likely is a lawsuit.
   c. the more carelessly help is given.
   d. the more likely any individual is to feel responsible.
   According to Darley and Latané, the more people present during an emergency, the less likely is any bystander to intervene./641

8. Stanley Schachter's investigations of affiliation support which of these sayings?
   a. All you need is love.
   b. Misery loves company.
   c. Out of sight, out of mind.
   d. Turn the other cheek.
   e. What goes around comes around.
   Schachter showed that people about to undergo a frightening experience prefer to wait in the company of others as opposed to being alone./644

9. According to attachment theory, the individuals most secure in their romances are those who were
   a. most secure as infants.
   b. most spoiled as children.
   c. not allowed to date during high school.
   d. only children.
   e. physically attractive as adolescents.
   Attachment theory assumes continuity between the attachment style of infants and adults. So, secure infants grow up to be secure lovers./648

10. The presence of an audience _____ performance of well-learned tasks and _____ performance of poorly learned tasks.
    a. disrupts; disrupts
    b. disrupts; improves
    c. improves; disrupts
    d. improves; improves
    An audience produces arousal in an individual, which improves her performance at a task she know well but disrupts her performance at a task that is less familiar./651

Sexuality is symbolic as much as it is biological.

Chapter Sixteen

Human Sexuality

Topics of Concern

The *Left Hand of Darkness* is a science fiction novel by Ursula K. Le Guin (1969). Like any science fiction novel, it starts with a scientific premise not true in the mundane world of its readers and tells a story in the context of this premise. Like any great science fiction novel, its premise provides its readers with an important perspective on their own lives.

This novel is set on the planet called Gethen, where a man from Earth named Genly Ai visits the native inhabitants for the purpose of forging a treaty. These inhabitants are very much like people from our planet, with one difference. Their gender is not fixed. Sometimes they are men, and sometimes they are women. At regular intervals, they pass through a transition period called kemmering and change from one sex to the other.

What this means is that the inhabitants of Gethen experience life as both men and women. They can be either a father or a mother. Sex roles are not handed out the way they are on our planet. Indeed, there are *no* sex roles.

Genly Ai is disconcerted by his travels across Gethen in the company of one of the natives. For starters, Genly Ai is regarded as abnormal because he is "only" of one sex, unable ever to be a member of the other sex. Further, Genly finds himself attracted to his traveling companion and has difficulty acknowledging this love and understanding what it means.

Yet perhaps the most difficult thing for this character to accept is that the world of Gethen does not view people in terms of their gender. In one of the book's most striking passages, he proclaims:

Yet you cannot think of a Gethenian as "it." They are not neuters. They are potentials. . . . On [Gethen] . . . one is respected and judged only as a human being. It is an appalling experience.
(pp. 94–95)

By the end of the book, Genly has come to accept the Gethenian way of life and even to appreciate it. His traveling companion perishes on their long trip across the planet, but Genly Ai comes away with an appreciation not of the man or woman that his companion variously was, but of the person.

Keeping the premise of *The Left Hand of Darkness* in mind, let's begin the last chapter of this book. There is a good reason for saving the important topic of human sexual-

ity until the end. All of us are interested in sexuality, and many of us have very strong ideas and opinions about the matter. However, the theme running through this chapter is that the topic is quite complex. If we are to understand the psychology of human sexuality, then we must understand the whole of psychology. Hence the placement of this chapter.

Indeed, human sexuality as a psychological phenomenon finds itself wedged between biological considerations on the one hand and cultural considerations on the other. All of these entwine to influence our sexuality. This is clearly illustrated in *The Left Hand of Darkness*. Among the Gethenians, the transition from male to female and back had a biological basis. But the ramifications of this extended deeply into psychological and sociological realms, which in turn affected the way that sexuality was experienced and expressed. The same is no less true for sexuality in our species. We need to call forth much sophistication in order to distinguish what we know from what we don't know, to separate facts from theories—and both from myths, and to keep our value judgments explicit.

What do psychologists want to know about human sexuality? Well, there are a variety of topics that have concerned theorists and researchers ever since sexuality was first scrutinized with a scientific eye. Let's briefly mention some of these concerns, borrowing here from Katchadourian's (1985) discussion of "fundamental questions about human sexuality."

Why Do We Behave Sexually?

What lies behind people's sexual activity? At a biological level, this question has several obvious answers. One is that we behave sexually in order to reproduce. Seen in this way, sex is a deeply rooted human characteristic. We are driven to engage in sexual activity because it is our nature, and our nature has been shaped by the forces of evolution (Chapter 2). If any of us had but a single ancestor who didn't feel like pursuing sexual activity, then we wouldn't be here. It's that simple.

Another obvious answer is that we engage in sexual activity because it makes us feel good. Just a fraction of our sexual activity is channeled into reproduction. What determines the rest of it? Clearly, it gives us intense pleasure.

In *The Left Hand of Darkness,* Ursula Le Guin describes an extraterrestrial society without defined sex roles.

Note that these two biological motives for sex—reproduction and pleasure—are not incompatible. One need not make an either-or choice between them. We can tell a just-so story about the evolution of sexuality in people, and we would probably say that natural selection conspired to make sex feel good precisely so we would do it for the larger purpose of reproduction. This is the distinction made in Chapter 2 between the evolutionary function of a behavior and the specific mechanism by which this behavior comes about.

But there are other motives for human sexuality. Sexuality, at least in our culture, is a way of expressing love for another person (Chapter 15). And part of the identity we form during our teenage years is sexual (Chapter 10). Thus sexuality also serves the motive of self-expression. For most of us, it is tied into our self-esteem. Note how we have just moved from biologically based motives for sexuality (reproduction and pleasure) to psychological ones (expression and identity). So, one more time, we have encountered our familiar issue: the nature versus nurture controversy (Chapter 1).

How Do We Behave Sexually?

Psychologists are interested in how best to explain behavior, and you have encountered innumerable theories and controversies throughout this book. But these theories do not exist in a vacuum. They are explanations of what people do, and so another important concern of psychologists is to catalog the thoughts, feelings, and actions of people. Only when we have a notion of *how* people behave can we set about explaining *why* they do what they do; this of course includes their sexual behavior.

The "facts" of human sexuality are sometimes more obscure than the facts in other domains of human activity. Much of sexuality is a private matter. This means that a great deal of research in the sexuality field has been descriptive, to fill in these gaps concerning the specifics of sexual behavior.

As will be explained shortly, the pioneers of sex research include Alfred Kinsey, whose surveys gave us some of the facts about the range of sexual activity; and William Masters and Virginia Johnson, who gave us some of the facts about the mechanics of sexual activity. In both cases, the information provided by research had been previously unavailable and thus challenged widely held views of sexuality.

How Should We Behave Sexually?

Yes, there is a "should" involved in this question. Psychology, because it deals with people, cannot help but stray into matters of right and wrong. Our field cannot avoid value judgments, and in the case of human sexuality, many of these judgments end up front and center.

One of the thorny questions about human sexuality has to do with deciding what is normal and what is abnormal. On the one hand, this is the same issue faced in our study of psychopathology, deciding where to draw the line across an admittedly fuzzy terrain (Chapter 12). Things can get even more complicated with regard to sexual normality and abnormality, though, because we now encounter the additional considerations of legal versus illegal and moral versus immoral. If you talk to yourself, you might be considered abnormal, perhaps even schizophrenic (Chapter 12). But under most circumstances, talking to yourself is not illegal, and few ethical teachings would brand it as immoral. This is not the case for abnormal sexuality.

Cross-cultural and historical studies show that a great range of activities pass for normal, but the fact remains that in any given time and place, people feel strongly that certain sexual practices are abnormal, illegal, and immoral. Consider the special indignation with which our present society greets the person who engages in sexual activity with prepubescent children. Most of us are in agreement that this sexual practice is wrong. But what about activities that cannot be clearly designated as moral or immoral?

One method that psychologists use to determine whether a sexual practice is normal or abnormal is to study its consequences. What activities are harmful, either physically or psychologically? Perhaps these should be judged as abnormal. At one time, masturbation was thought to turn people into blithering idiots. This is no longer believed, and psychology, if not giving its blessing to masturbation, has at least moved it out of the "hazardous to one's health" category. Although masturbation creates difficulties for the person to the degree that he or she feels guilty about it (e.g., Arafat & Cotton, 1974), the same can be said of any activity.

Other changes have occurred with respect to, for example, intercourse with a woman having her menstrual period. Not dangerous. Or intercourse during pregnancy. Again, not dangerous. On the other hand, we now know that certain behaviors put us at risk for sexually transmitted diseases such as AIDS, and these behaviors—for example, having intercourse without a condom and with an HIV infected individual—are seen as imprudent, to say the least.

What about homosexuality? This has long been associated with mental illness. Indeed, until rather recently, homosexuality was considered by the American Psychiatric Association (1968) as a bona fide mental illness in its own right. This is no longer the case, because researchers have consistently found that homosexuals do not differ from their heterosexual counterparts on any criterion of mental or physical well-being.

> At one time, masturbation was thought to turn people into blithering idiots.
>
> • • •

Today there is a great hue and cry concerning the pros and cons of sex education—instructing students about sexual activity. The issue seems to break down pretty cleanly along conservative and liberal lines. The one side fears that knowledge will stimulate action, by legitimizing sexual activity, whereas the other side fears that lack of knowledge will have harmful consequences, such as unintended pregnancies or sexually transmitted diseases, particularly among young people who are going to engage in sexual activity whether or not they have a sex education course. Perhaps not surprisingly, research has not yet indicated which side is right, because sex education classes are embedded in a larger society, which is increasingly liberal with regard to sexual matters, as well as within a smaller school community, which may be liberal or conservative.

As noted in Chapter 10, teenage pregnancy and sexually transmitted diseases are among the most serious problems facing our country. The majority of sexually active teenagers fail to use contraception consistently (Zelnik & Kantner, 1977). We don't know if sex education is the cause or the cure, or a little bit of both and/or a whole lot of neither.

All sides seem to agree, though, that sex education is not carried out in an optimal way. Abstract facts about the mechanics of reproduction are not as important as concrete instruction in the realities of what it means to be a sexual being, whether this entails contraception and abortion on the one hand or pregnancy and child-rearing on the other.

In conclusion, psychologists interested in human sexuality have three related concerns: the description, explanation, and evaluation of sexual behavior. In the remainder of this chapter, we will discuss some of the particulars of the psychology of human sexuality. We will start with a brief history of sexuality, then move to the biological aspects of human sexuality, and next to a discussion of sexual behavior. We will conclude this chapter by considering sexual dysfunctions and disorders.

The History of Human Sexuality

You know by now that setting the stage for a topic in this book involves discussing its historical roots. But it is hard to know where to begin now that the topic is human sexuality. We could, of course, begin with the very first instance of sex by going back to the dawn of life. Very early on, single-celled organisms began to combine their chromosomes in the process of creating offspring (Chapter 2). Exciting stuff, to be sure, but we'll start our history by skipping ahead a few millenia.

Early History

Let's start around 35,000 B.C., when people made the earliest-known drawings on the walls of European caves (see Figure 16.1). What is important about these pictures is that they contain explicit sexual themes. Copulating animals are depicted in these paintings, along with human beings with genitals of exaggerated size. We can think of these cave paintings as the forerunners of *Playboy* or *Playgirl,* as it were, with a little bit of *Field & Stream* thrown in for good measure.

The specific meaning of these early paintings is not known, although the artists obviously did not choose random subjects. Sexual activity was depicted because it meant something to our distant ancestors. Human sexuality has never been simply unbridled passion. Although sexual activity among people involves bodies and biology, so it also involves meaning. *Sexuality is symbolic just as much as it is biological.* This was true tens of thousands of years ago, and it is just as true today. We cannot fully understand human sexuality until we acknowledge that it has meaning, both to individuals and society at large.

Keep the symbolic nature of sex in mind as we jump ahead to the attitudes of the early Jews and Christians. Those of us in the modern Western world have inherited their attitudes. As a result, we recognize sexuality as a powerful and basic force, but we fear it on these very

Figure 16.1
Cave Paintings. Some of the earliest paintings have obvious sexual themes. Source: Maringer & Bandi, 1953.

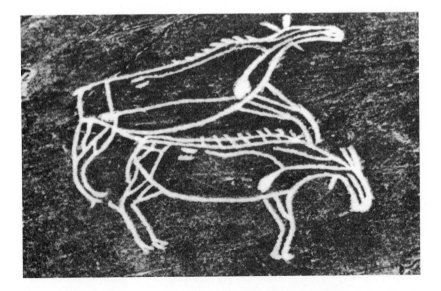

Even under a moral code as repressive as that of the Victorian period, human sexuality cannot be denied, as evidenced by the expression of this streetcar passenger.

grounds. We regard many aspects of sexuality as sinful. Indeed, lust represents the epitome of temptation. Also, the early Jews and Christians regarded virginity and celibacy as the most glorified of states. They frowned upon homosexuality, contraception, and sexual activity outside of marriage.

Victorianism

As you know, Christianity began as a faith, but developed over the centuries into a prime determinant of social institutions, including those responsible for education, business, and government. Judeo-Christian attitudes and values pervaded all activities, carrying with them particular beliefs about human sexuality. This is nowhere better seen than in nineteenth-century England, where sexuality became cloaked in a mass of prohibitions and restrictions we now refer to as *Victorianism* (after Queen Victoria of England, 1837–1901). The central thesis of Victorianism, insofar as it applied to sexuality, was the repression and denial of all sexual drives and feelings. Note that this takes the earlier distrust of sexuality one step further. It's one thing to say that sexuality is sinful. It's yet another to say that sexuality does not exist.

Societal Prohibitions. This thesis permeated the society's entire moral code, leading to practices that today look a bit peculiar. According to the Victorians, the ideal woman experienced no sexual feelings. However, she could be corrupted by outside forces—meaning men, who did experience sexual feelings. Luckily (?), men could be held in check if their temptations could be kept at a minimum.

So, to keep men minimally tempted, all reminders and mentions of sex were kept out of sight. Any of you who fancy antiques knows that pianos from this era had little skirts around the legs. Why? Because the legs might look like a woman's ankle, and a man who saw such a sight might be turned on, and he might seek out a real woman and seduce her.

Granted the power of pianos, actual women had to be disguised even more so, and thus they wore massive petticoats that obscured their shapes.

Read a novel from Victorian Europe. Notice that women did not have legs. Instead, they had limbs. Nor did they have breasts. They had bosoms. And you'll find references to people feasting on chicken necks. This will seem strange, because we all know that chickens have necks as scrawny as that of Frank Perdue. Why would anybody feast on a chicken neck? The answer is that the Victorians referred to chicken breasts as necks. It's not clear what they called chicken necks.

Naturally, written material was severely censored to remove all sexual references. Shakespeare's plays and sonnets were sanitized. Even the Bible was rewritten to be sex-fee. This took some doing, because the Bible proves quite an earthy document in places (see, for instance, Matthew 9: 20–22). One of those who helped rewrite the Bible was Noah Webster of dictionary fame.

Scientific journals dealing with sexual matters were kept from the general public. Gray's *Anatomy,* the classic textbook of its time, was considered so racy because of its pictures of genitals that only medical doctors were allowed to see it. For decades Gray's *Anatomy* was famous as the place where one first encountered pictures of naked folks, a role that *National Geographic* supplanted in the beginning of the twentieth century and MTV at its end.

Medical practice showed the influence of Victorianism as well. Women were examined with their clothes on. Gynecological exams did not take place at all, and indeed, gynecology as a medical speciality did not exist. Physicians did worry a great deal about masturbation, which during the Victorian era was believed to result in dire consequences, including fits, fever, decay of the spinal cord, blindness, impotence, insanity, and acne! Chastity belts were common for both males and females (see Figure 16.2). Little boys who persisted in their masturbation were sometimes castrated. Like-minded little girls had their clitoris surgically removed. We may conclude that Victorianism was serious business.

Figure 16.2
Chastity Belts for Men and Women
Source: Gay, 1984.

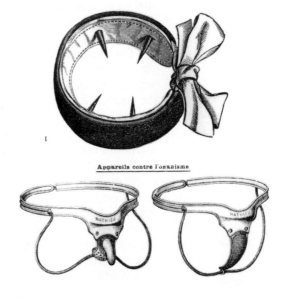

Appareils contre l'onanisme

Needless to say, the Victorians did engage in sex. Queen Victoria herself had nine children, and when her husband died at an early age, she was accused of wearing him out with her lust! Prostitution, pornography, and venereal disease flourished in Europe at this time. What this means is that Victorian sexuality was highly complex *and* inconsistent.

Sigmund Freud. At the turn of the century, societal attitudes began to change, largely due to the influence of Sigmund Freud. As his ideas about the central importance of instincts gained general currency, Europeans rediscovered sex and again acknowledged it as a primal force. People were regarded as inherently sexual. And the repression of sexuality—the essence of Victorianism—came to be regarded as the cause of mental distress.

Think back over the previous chapters, in which Freud's ideas were discussed, and then try to appreciate the splash he made when he published his books at the turn of the century, in the heyday of Victorianism. Perhaps earlier statements that his ideas were unpopular and met resistance in some quarters now register as a profound comment.

Recent History

Following Freud, other researchers took a close look at sexuality, and the twentieth century has seen a number of advances in our understanding. At the same time, people's sexual attitudes have become increasingly liberal, legitimizing further scrutiny of the topic.

Alfred Kinsey. Let's note in particular the contribution of Indiana University researcher Alfred Kinsey, who undertook the first surveys of "normal" sexuality in the 1940s. Kinsey and his fellow researchers interviewed thousands of males and females in the United States about their sexual practices (Kinsey, Pomeroy, & Martin, 1948; Kinsey, Pomeroy, Martin, & Gebhard, 1953). Who did what with whom, how often, and under what circumstances? Kinsey's books brim with tables, showing us repeatedly that there is much greater variety in sexual practice than in social codes. And when we take these numbers into account, the lines dividing normal from abnormal sexuality prove exceedingly difficult to draw.

For example, Kinsey asked men whether they had ever engaged in sex with men or women. He found that at least some degree of sexual activity with other men was rather common among his subjects: "37% of the total male population has at least some overt homosexual experience to the point of orgasm between adolescence and old age" (Kinsey et al., 1948, p. 650). Further, people's sexual activity placed them along a continuum from exclusive homosexuality to exclusive heterosexuality, implying that homosexuality and heterosexuality do not represent a dichotomy, but rather endpoints of a dimension.

These findings challenge the way that many think about our sexual orientation. The history of psychology has been filled with pronouncements on the nature of homosexuality (Bayer, 1987). But, following Kinsey, any pronouncement must take into account the information that he provided regarding the vague boundaries of homosexuality and the numbers of people in, outside, and across the category.

Of course, Kinsey's research can be criticized on the basis of a nonrepresentative sample. Surely people who are willing to speak to survey researchers about their sexual activity will differ systematically from those who prefer to keep such matters to themselves. Perhaps Kinsey's findings were exaggerated.

It is still common to criticize sexual surveys on the grounds of a nonrandom sample. A recent example is found in the response to Shere Hite's (1987) best-selling "report" concluding that women in the United States are not in the least impressed with their lovers or husbands. But the importance of Kinsey's work, and subsequent surveys such as Hite's, perhaps lies not in the exact figures they report, 22 percent versus 27 percent versus whatever, but in the undeniable *variety* of attitudes and actions they document.

Birth Control Pills and the Sexual Revolution. In 1956, birth control pills became commercially available in the United States, marking the first time that reliable birth control (other than abstinence) was ever available, from 35,000 B.C. on! Many of you reading this book have grown up in an era in which birth control has always been possible, so it may be difficult for you to appreciate a world where this was not an option, where pregnancy was a very real consequence of every act of intercourse around ovulation.

Birth control and other social factors conspired over the next two decades to usher in a **sexual revolution,** a widespread societal change in attitudes and behaviors surrounding sex. The sexual revolution was never a matter of people coupling wildly in the streets with strangers. But undeniable changes took place. Attitudes toward premarital sex, contraception, abortion, and homosexuality became increasingly liberal, and people were ever more willing to engage in these activities.

William Masters

Masters and Johnson. Part of the liberalized approach to sexuality was an increased willingness to study it scientifically. William Masters and Virginia Johnson (1966) brought human sexual activity into the laboratory, where they systematically investigated what was involved in the physical activity of intercourse. They literally watched volunteer research subjects engage in sexual activity with one another while hooked up to various instruments that measured their physiological reactions. The findings of this research program gave us much insight into what took place when men and women became aroused, engaged in intercourse, and experienced orgasm. Masters and Johnson's account of the human sexual response is the most detailed description yet provided by researchers, and we will rely on it when discussing sexual behavior later in the chapter.

Remember the earlier point that sexuality research often provides information previously unknown. One important example comes from Masters and Johnson's (1966) laboratory studies. They documented that the female's vagina was for the most part insensitive to erotic stimulation and that clitoral stimulation leads to orgasm much more readily than vaginal stimulation.

Some history here is important. The prevailing belief throughout much of this century was the one championed by Freud: women had two kinds of orgasms—one resulting from stimulation of the clitoris and the other from stimulation of the vagina. The clitoral orgasm was regarded by

Virginia Johnson

Freud and his followers as "immature" and thus not as satisfying to the woman as a vaginal one. (That a male was regarded as *the* expert on female orgasms may strike you as a bit odd, but this is historical fact.)

Freud's distinction undoubtedly affected the lives of many women, who would read what he had to say about their orgasms, take these ideas as truth, and then wonder why their own sex lives didn't work this way. Although no figures are available, we can suppose that many women went through psychotherapy because they could only have an orgasm in the "immature" way—via stimulation of the clitoris.

Masters and Johnson proved that Freud was wrong. The clitoral orgasm *is* the orgasm that women experience. To avoid stimulating the clitoris during sexual activity is not the way to go about things, at least if pleasure is one's goal. This fact is incredibly important, therefore, not just in terms of its impact on theories of female sexuality, but also in terms of how people conduct their daily lives.

Another area of research carried out by Masters and Johnson (1970) was aimed at developing techniques for treating the difficulties people have in performing sexually. Their sex therapy program has been both successful and controversial, particularly the strategy of supplying a sexual partner—a sexual surrogate, to use the technical term—for clients without a partner of their own. We will discuss the sex therapy program of Masters and Johnson in greater detail later in the chapter.

Sexuality in Modern Society

So far, so good. Our history recounts a gradual loosening of the restraints placed on our sexuality by our ancestors. Sexuality has not become simple, however, and nowadays it lies at the center of many crucial societal issues with deep psychological implications. Nowhere is this more obvious than in the social crisis brought about by AIDS.

AIDS has stirred up a wide variety of emotional responses among those stricken with the disease as well as the general public.

AIDS.   In 1981, the first case of **acquired immune deficiency syndrome (AIDS)** was diagnosed in the United States, and the history of sexuality took yet another turn. AIDS is a fatal disease caused by a virus that enters the body through contact with the bodily fluids from an individual infected with the virus. AIDS can thus be transmitted sexually, that is, by having sex with someone carrying the virus. AIDS can also be transmitted by sharing needles and syringes with an infected individual. In some few cases, people have developed AIDS following a transfusion of infected blood. And babies born to mothers who carry the virus are at risk as well.

The good news, if there is any, is that AIDS is not easily transmitted (U.S. Department of Health and Human Services, 1988). Despite scare stories that have appeared in the sensationalistic media, someone cannot get AIDS from kissing, from casual contact with infected individuals, from mosquito bites, from swimming pools, from telephones, or from toilet seats. AIDS is only passed on through certain bodily fluids. Blood, semen, and vaginal secretions can be dangerous; tears, sweat, saliva, urine, and feces are *not* dangerous.

AIDS is a particularly insidious disease because it attacks the body's immune system, thus destroying a person's ability to fight off other diseases. Forms of cancer or pneumonia that otherwise are exceedingly rare occur with much greater frequency among individuals with AIDS, precisely because they have lost the ability to resist these diseases. AIDS also creates symptoms in its own right, and some of these include psychological difficulties. The AIDS virus often attacks the central nervous system (Chapter 2), resulting in cognitive impairment ranging from forgetfulness to profound dementia.

At the present time, there are no ways to immunize a person against AIDS or to cure an infected individual. The virus may stay inactive within someone's body for a long period of time—exact estimates vary greatly—but if and when AIDS develops, the majority of people die within several years. Drugs that slow the progress of AIDS, such as AZT, are now available, but they are expensive and have side effects that make them unsuitable for some individuals. AIDS was first diagnosed in this country among homosexual males, but we now know that AIDS honors no barriers. Indeed, it threatens to become a worldwide scourge of a magnitude not seen since the plagues of the Middle Ages.

For several reasons, AIDS has attracted the attention of psychologists. First, this disease has psychological consequences (U.S. Department of Health and Human Services, 1986, p. 1):

- Seventy percent of all people with AIDS die within 2 years of diagnosis.
- To date, all but a small minority of AIDS patients [in the United States] are homosexual and bisexual men or intravenous drug abusers—individuals who already may be stigmatized and subject to social and job-related discrimination. Such problems multiply with a diagnosis of AIDS.
- Ninety percent of all adults with AIDS are . . . between the ages of 20 and 49—when people are not commonly prepared to deal psychologically with imminent death.
- The infections and malignancies that accompany AIDS can diminish and disfigure the body. . . .
- The course of AIDS is marked by a series of life-threatening episodes. . . .
- Few other diseases produce as many losses—loss of physical strength, mental acuity, ability to work, self-sufficiency, social roles, income and savings, housing, and the emotional support of loved ones. Often, self-esteem also fades in the wake of catastrophic losses.
- The physical weakness and pain resulting from AIDS-related diseases diminish the patient's ability to cope with psychological and social stress.
- Treatments for AIDS-related diseases . . . may themselves cause psychological symptoms, such as listlessness, depression, and anxiety.

Psychologists have devised interventions to help infected individuals cope (Chapter 13) and to change social attitudes so as to reduce prejudice and discrimination against these individuals (Chapter 15). Work here continues (Backer, Batchelor, Jones, & Mays, 1988).

A second reason why psychologists are interested in AIDS is that the spread of this disease can be halted if people change their behavior, eliminating the practices that put themselves and others at risk for infection.

This effort on the part of psychologists to reduce high risk behavior is simply an example of health psychologists' more general goal of encouraging "healthy" ways of behaving, as discussed in the Appendix.

A key element in health promotion is making the facts about reasonable and unreasonable ways to behave available to the general public (see Table 16.1). However, information alone may not be sufficient to encourage people to change their behavior. This is particularly true in the case of AIDS because of its link to sexuality. Whatever gains people have made in increasing tolerance and openness about sexuality were probably not deep-rooted, because the reaction to the AIDS epidemic has not been consistently liberated.

Many people in the United States at first managed to ignore or shrug off AIDS because the vast majority of those suffering from the disease were homosexuals. Attempts to spread information about the disease were at first resisted, although we are fortunate that the tide has now turned (e.g., U.S. Department of Health and Human Services, 1988). But even now, there are signs of a heterosexual backlash: people's wrong-headed belief—again—that heterosexuals cannot get AIDS.

sexually transmitted diseases (STDs)

diseases spread mainly through sexual contact, such as gonorrhea, syphilis, and genital herpes

Sexually Transmitted Diseases.   AIDS is but one of several diseases spread mainly through sexual contact. These **sexually transmitted diseases (STDs)** were formerly called venereal diseases, after Venus, the goddess of love. They often affect the sex organs, but by no means does this suggest

---

Table 16.1

What Behavior Puts You at Risk for Aids?

You are at risk of being infected with the AIDS virus if you have sex with someone who is infected, or if you share drug needles and syringes with someone who is infected.

Since you can't be sure who is infected, your chances of coming into contact with the virus increases with the number of sex partners you have. Any exchange of infected blood, semen, or vaginal fluids can spread the virus and place you at great risk.

The following behaviors are risky when performed with an infected person. You can't tell by looking if a person is infected.

Risky Behavior	Sharing drug needles and syringes.
	Anal sex, with or without a condom.
	Vaginal or oral sex with someone who shoots drugs or engages in anal sex.
	Sex with someone you don't know well (a pickup or prostitute) or with someone you know has several sex partners.
	Unprotected sex (without a condom) with an infected person.
Safe Behavior	Not having sex.
	Sex with one mutually faithful, uninfected partner.
	Not shooting drugs.

Source: U.S. Department of Health and Human Services, 1988, p. 3.

Advertisements have long been used in the effort to control the spread of sexually transmitted diseases.

that these are localized ailments. More than ten million cases of STDs are diagnosed every year in the United States, the majority among individuals between fifteen and twenty-nine years of age (Katchadourian, 1985). The prevalence of STDs is on the rise, in lockstep with societal increases in sexual activity. Let's take a look at some of these diseases.

Gonorrhea is an infection caused by a bacteria. It is transmitted through contact with the mucous membranes of an infected individual. Among men, the primary site of infection is the urethra, and the most noticeable symptoms are a yellow discharge from the tip of the penis and burning sensations during urination. Among women, gonorrhea often affects the cervix. A discharge from the vagina may also be present, but gonorrhea is more difficult for an infected woman to notice than an infected man. This disease usually responds well to penicillin and other antibiotics.

Pelvic inflammatory disease is an inflammation of the fallopian tubes or lining of the uterus due to a variety of causes, most often gonorrhea. This is a relatively common condition, affecting as many as one million women every year in the United States. Adolescent and young adult women are most at risk, perhaps because their immune systems are not sufficiently mature (Katchadourian, 1989). If untreated, pelvic inflammatory disease may result in infertility.

Syphilis is another type of bacterial infection usually transmitted by intimate contact. This is a serious disease. If untreated, it can eventually prove fatal. Syphilis shows up in several stages. The first stage is marked by a skin lesion appearing 2 to 4 weeks following infection at the site where the bacteria originally entered the body—usually somewhere on the genitals. During this stage, syphilis can readily be eradicated with antibiotics. If untreated, it enters its second stage, several weeks or months later. An infected individual develops a skin rash, fever, and various aches and pains. A person with syphilis is most infectious during its first two stages.

Even if treatment is not undertaken, overt symptoms of syphilis appear to go away. However, the disease lingers, invading the person's blood vessels, bones, and central nervous system. Two to twenty years may pass, and then the infected individual may suffer heart disease and neurological impairment. Even during this last stage of the disease, successful treatment with penicillin can be effective.

Genital herpes is a disease marked by painful blisters or sores on or near the genitals. These usually clear up within several weeks, but then recur at highly variable intervals—from once or twice a month to once a decade. Genital herpes is caused by a virus similar to the one that causes cold sores. Although it was not an unknown disease, it did not become prevalent in the United States until the 1970s, when it showed a 100-fold increase! Perhaps as many as one out of every five American adults has genital herpes (Katchadourian, 1985).

This disease is transmitted through contact with infected areas of the body. It is believed that the risk of infection is nil when the person shows no overt symptoms. At the present time, someone with genital herpes cannot be cured. However, the drug acyclovir can alleviate the symptoms and shorten the time that blisters and sores are present. Herpes can be painful and unpleasant, but it is not otherwise a threat to one's health.

There are a number of other types of STDs in addition to AIDS, gonorrhea, syphilis, and genital herpes. It's important for us all to understand the details of these diseases, but the important point here is the special significance we attach to sexuality. "Sexually transmitted diseases" represent a curious category of illness. We don't have a special category for diseases spread by shaking hands, or one for diseases spread by breathing germs in the air. But sexuality is so imbued with significance that the diseases spread through sexual activity are given special status.

We as a society still show vestiges of the early Judeo-Christian attitudes, and those of the Victorians as well. Witness the fact that we are responding ever so sluggishly to the threat posed by sexually transmitted diseases. Many people will not ask their potential sexual partners about their current practices and past history. Or they won't use condoms for protection. The sexual revolution may have liberated our genitals, but it didn't fully liberate our minds, because STDs are still a taboo subject in many circles.

Abortion.   Sexuality is at the heart of many important social issues today, not just AIDS. One of the most divisive political and moral issues of our time involves abortion on demand: whether a pregnant woman should be allowed to terminate her pregnancy. Like all topics involving human sexuality, the issue of abortion cannot be examined outside its social context. Abortion has been practiced throughout history and across almost all cultures. And as many as 50 million abortions are now performed worldwide every year.

The political, social, and moral implications of abortion on demand have become the central issues in the struggle over women's reproductive rights.

Depending on the time and place, abortion has been criticized—or defended, as the case may be—on medical, moral, and religious grounds. The legal system may become involved as well. In the 1970s, the Supreme Court of the United States affirmed state rulings allowing abortion in the first trimester of pregnancy, on the grounds of the pregnant woman's right to privacy. In 1989, the Supreme Court modified this earlier ruling, and put the question of abortion's legality back into the hands of individual states.

Although polls consistently show that the majority of Americans support a woman's right to abortion, the issue has nonetheless become a hot political topic breaking down largely along liberal and conservative lines, just like the issue of sex education we discussed earlier (p. 666). One way the abortion debate is currently fought out in this country is in terms of who should pay for abortions. The liberal position is that society should pick up the medical costs for an abortion if a woman is poor. The conservative position is just the opposite.

We can surmise that people's positions on abortion, pro or con, are based on more than just political or moral rhetoric. Deep-seated and perhaps unacknowledged attitudes toward sexuality and the family influence one's specific attitudes toward this issue (Luker, 1986). How else to make sense of the survey result that the same people who oppose abortion favor the death sentence but not gun control, and vice versa (Petchesky, 1985)? On a strictly surface level, these positions should not line up as they do; something else must be going on to create these attitude constellations.

Infertility. One of life's sad ironies is that our country is filled not only with women who become pregnant against their wishes but also with women who very much wish to become pregnant but cannot. Perhaps as many as four million couples in the United States are childless but wish they were not. Many of these people seek out help to understand the causes of their infertility. The vast majority are given an answer, and of these couples, about 50 percent go on to have children (Menning, 1977).

Various physical conditions of the woman or man are responsible for infertility. These include genetic disorders, hormonal problems, injuries or defects in the reproductive system, aging, drug use, and a host of miscellaneous medical problems, not the least of which are sexually transmitted diseases. If these conditions can be alleviated, then pregnancy will occur.

Modern technology has made available still other solutions to infertility. Consider **artificial insemination,** which involves introducing previously obtained and frozen sperm into a woman's vagina when she is ovulating. Obviously, artificial insemination is undertaken when the male of the couple is infertile. The sperm may come from another male, or it may be accumulated from the male in question—a strategy that works when he suffers from a low sperm count.

In **surrogate motherhood,** another woman conceives, bears, and delivers the child of a fertile man. She then relinquishes the child. Obviously, again, surrogate motherhood is undertaken when the female of the couple is infertile.

You have no doubt read about so-called test-tube babies, who are the tangible proof of yet another high tech treatment of infertility. With **in vitro fertilization,** conception takes place outside of the womb. An egg cell and a sperm cell are obtained from a woman and a man, joined together in a test tube, and then the fertilized embryo is transferred to the woman's uterus.

Permutations of these and other treatments of infertility are increasingly becoming possible. Let me offer two comments consistent with the theme of this chapter. First, these procedures raise difficult ethical issues, and all have a direct psychological impact for those involved. In recent years, there have been several widely reported cases in which a surrogate mother does not want to give up the baby she has delivered, a situation that rapidly turns into a psychological minefield. Second, the status of being a parent is imbued with great significance in this and any culture (Chapter 10). Many people will go to great lengths to become parents because of the symbolic value of this role. As Houseknecht (1986, p. 513) expresses it, "children . . . [are] economically worthless but emotionally priceless."

Research to date does not give us a clear picture of the effects on a couple of not being able to have children. Studies have compared childless couples and those with children with respect to marital satisfaction, finding no difference (e.g., Glenn & McLanahan, 1981). However, such studies have not been fine-grained, and they did not distinguish between couples who were voluntarily childless and those who wished to have children but were unsuccessful (Bee, 1987).

Rape.   In the crime of **rape,** someone perpetrates a sexual act against an unwilling victim. Like all topics involving human sexuality, rape must be looked at in terms of its larger social meaning. It is important to emphasize that rape is a crime of violence more than a crime of lust (Brownmiller, 1975). The typical rapist does *not* feel sexually frustrated so much as he feels angry and inadequate concerning his lot in life (Delin, 1978). The act of rape is often carried out so as to humiliate or degrade the victim.

Classifying rape as a form of violence is at odds with common stereotypes emphasizing its sexual aspects, but most who study the topic stress that rape is surrounded by many myths that bear no relation to the actual facts. Here are some of the most common *false beliefs* about rape (Brownmiller, 1975):

artificial insemination
procedure in which previously obtained and frozen sperm is introduced into a woman's vagina when she is ovulating

surrogate motherhood
a woman conceiving, bearing, and delivering the child of a fertile man, then relinquishing the child to the man and his wife

in vitro fertilization
conception outside the womb; an egg cell and a sperm cell are obtained from a woman and a man, joined together in a test tube, and then the fertilized egg is transferred to the woman's uterus

rape
the perpetration of a sexual act against an unwilling victim

- The victim usually is young and attractive.
- The victim usually precipitates the assault.
- The rapist usually is a total stranger to his victim.

Nonetheless, these beliefs are widely held. They can result in a tragic state of affairs in which the victim of rape is assigned more blame than the rapist. Consider that most accused rapists are not arrested. Consider that most accused rapists who are arrested are then not brought to trial. Consider that most accused rapists who are arrested and brought to trial are acquitted or dismissed. What this means is that only 4 percent of rapes result in a conviction!

Rape victims have traditionally been viewed with suspicion by the police and judicial system, as well as the general public. They may be seen as lying or exaggerating, or even as precipitating the attack because of how they looked or acted. One of the reasons that rapists rarely come to trial is that their victims are often reluctant to put themselves in the position of having to prove that they indeed were assaulted.

Thinking on this matter is now changing, at least in some quarters. The general public has had its consciousness raised about coercive sexual attacks. And studies show that rape victims—when compared to victims of other crimes—are much *less* likely to have had anything to do with placing themselves in the situation in which the crime occurred (Katchadourian, 1985).

A recent survey suggests, however, that both male and female teenagers still tend to believe that there are circumstances in which males can legitimately force females to have sex (Katchadourian, 1985)! For example, if an adolescent female has any sexual experience, wears tight jeans, and/or attends drinking parties, she is seen by other teenagers as "inviting" a sexual attack. Perhaps this illogical reasoning on the part of adolescents reflects their failure to attain the highest stages of cognitive and moral development (Chapter 9). Regardless, *date rape* is now recognized as an all too common occurrence (e.g., Flynn, 1987; Kanin, 1984).

As already implied, the aftermath of rape can sometimes be as troublesome for the victim as the crime itself. Burgess and Holmstrom (1974) describe what follows rape as the **rape trauma syndrome.** The acute phase of this syndrome lasts for several weeks following the assault, and here the victim is either excessively emotional or excessively subdued. In the long-term phase, she struggles to come to grips with the assault. She may change her job or her residence. She may avoid reminders of the crime. She may experience anxiety and depression.

Note that the long-term reaction to rape is an example of the post-traumatic stress disorder described in Chapter 12. So, we can make sense of the rape trauma syndrome in terms of the general explanations already available for post-traumatic stress disorder. The victim of rape can be seen as struggling with an experience that is both traumatic and senseless. To the degree that she meets with indifference or suspicion on the part of others, she is apt to be even more distressed. Talking about the rape in a supportive context is probably an effective way to combat her trauma.

rape trauma syndrome
a typical victim's reaction to rape, characterized by an acute reaction involving excessive emotionality or excessive numbness and a long-term post-traumatic stress reaction (Chapter 12)

erotica
sexually arousing pictures or stories

Pornography. People can be sexually aroused by a variety of stimuli, including pictures or stories depicting or implying sexual activity. The generic term for such sexually arousing stimuli is **erotica,** and here we have

Although the distinction between erotica and pornography is hard to draw,
psychologists agree that hardcore
pornography usually portrays sex in a
violent or degrading manner.

another important societal issue revolving around sexuality. When does erotica become **pornography:** sexually oriented material that both arouses and offends? And what are the effects on a person of exposure to pornography?

Determining the line between erotica and pornography is not a task that psychologists are uniquely equipped to perform. This is a moral and social judgment to be made by each and every citizen. Psychologists can provide information regarding the effects of pornography, and perhaps people should take this information into account in making their judgments.

Another distinction we may wish to make is between soft-core and hard-core pornography. Again, precise definitions prove elusive (Katcha-dourian, 1989). According to one view, soft-core pornography suggests sexual activity, whereas hard-core pornography graphically displays it. Another possible contrast is that soft-core pornography depicts sexual activity between willing adults who function as equals, whereas hard-core pornography portrays sexual activity that is violent or humiliating. In this sense, hard-core pornography involves people forcing sexual acts upon others. Rape is thus a common theme. Children may be the victims. Because the vast majority of those who consume hard-core pornography are men, it is perhaps unsurprising that it frequently presents a degrading view of women.

Two opposite arguments have prevailed in the discussions of the effects of pornography. According to one argument, people who read or look at pornographic material are stimulated to sexual or violent crimes. According to the other argument, pornography functions as a safety valve, providing a symbolic outlet for sexual drives and thereby reducing crimes.

Relevant to this debate are several social psychology laboratory studies in which male college students viewed pornographic movies depicting violence against women (e.g., Donnerstein, 1980; Donnerstein & Berkowitz, 1981). Compared to subjects who had seen a non-pornographic movie or a soft-core movie, these men were *more likely* later to act aggressively against women when given the opportunity to do so in a supposedly unrelated experiment. These results are extremely sobering, implying as they do that exposure to violent pornography may distort men's attitudes toward women and lead to criminal behavior.

Do these laboratory findings generalize to the larger world? Here the answer is not clear, and studies that attempt to link the prevalence of violent pornography in a region to the incidence of sexual crimes reported there are contradictory. Some studies find a positive correlation. For instance, Baron and Straus (1984) found that the rate of sales of sexually explicit magazines in a state was positively correlated with the rate of rapes in that state. Other studies using different operationalizations have not found these results (e.g., Kutchinsky, 1973).

There are obviously innumerable confounds that threaten this type of study. Granted that we have one state or country that allows hard-core pornography to be available to its citizens and another state or country that does not, how can we ever equate them on all other factors that might then influence crime rates? Whatever the answer to this important question might be, let us not forget that it is not sexuality alone that characterizes hard-core pornography, but rather the violent or degrading way in which sexual acts are carried out.

Investigating Human Sexuality

Because human sexuality encompasses such a wide range of activities and topics, the methods researchers use are correspondingly diverse as well. All of the general research strategies are represented—case studies, correlational studies, and experiments (Chapter 1). Within each strategy, various techniques are employed. We'll discuss some of these techniques shortly, but first let's look at the special problems associated with sexuality research.

The Special Problems of Sexuality Research

Researchers interested in human sexuality face a particular problem that other researchers of psychological phenomena do not so frequently confront, and that is the problem of obtaining research participants typical of people as a whole. Representative samples are important if one is to generalize one's findings to the larger population of human beings. A perfectly representative sample is the ideal, one that is never achieved in practice. Those closest to this ideal are certain polls that randomly sample households, or telephone numbers, or precincts within the country (Chapter 14). For the most part, psychologists get the subjects they can get, hoping that their sample does not differ in any systematic way from the population as a whole.

So, if you are interested in perception, you study college students drawn from an advanced class in psychophysics, let us say, without even considering that these students might have unusual perceptual systems. But the problem of representative samples is not so easily solved in the case of sexuality research. As already noted, you cannot assume that people willing to participate in your research are representative of the general population.

Interviews and Questionnaires

Suppose a researcher is interested in the frequency of sexual practices, such as masturbation, or sex before marriage, or sex outside of marriage. She proceeds by asking people to participate in her study. Professional ethics dictate that she sketch the general purpose of the research when she requests the participation of volunteers (Chapter 1). "Would you talk to me about your sexual behavior?" Right off the bat, some people will say no, and there is every reason in the world to suspect that this is *not* a randomly made decision. Or perhaps a person gets into an interview, or halfway through a questionnaire, and then decides that this is not the sort of thing he wishes to pursue. Again ethics dictate that the person be allowed to stop.

Shere Hite's (1981) best-seller, *The Hite Report on Male Sexuality,* is an example of the problems inherent in obtaining a representative sample for sex research. She used a questionnaire procedure. Of the 119,000 questionnaires distributed, only 7239 were returned—only 6 percent of the total. These people were not typical of the population as a whole. On the average, for example, they were much more educated. And many of the respondents encountered the original questionnaire in magazines such as *Penthouse,* and again, the readers of these "men's" magazines are not a random sample of the population.

The issue is not whether biases in samples exist. They inevitably do. The concern is whether we expect these biases to slant the topic under scrutiny. In the case of research into sex, the answer seems to be yes. We know that people differ in the liberalness of their sexual activities, which includes their willingness to talk about sexuality. We know that educational attainment is related to differences in sexual activity, and so on.

Further, once in a study, there is no guarantee that the person will be completely candid in what he or she says. We've seen this already as a problem in personality research (Chapter 11) as well as in attitude assessment in social psychology (Chapter 14). In both cases, people are tempted to present themselves in a socially desirable light. This is a very real possibility any time the questions being asked have a social value. The more charged the question—and questions about sexuality are certainly loaded—the more likely someone is to shade an answer. So, one respondent might think it desirable to have many sexual partners, and accordingly inflate answers about this matter. Another might think masturbation is shameful, and so underestimate the frequency of this activity. The point is that we must take answers to questionnaires and interviews with a grain of salt.

Laboratory Studies

As mentioned earlier, laboratory studies of sexual activity were pioneered by Masters and Johnson (1966). A variety of high-tech devices are available to monitor and measure the physiological responses taking place during sexual activity. For instance, male genital response can be measured by a device called a *penile plethysmograph,* which fits over the penis and measures changes in its circumference.

The corresponding device for measuring genital response among females is the *vaginal photoplethysmograph,* which is a clear cylinder that is inserted in a woman's vagina. It contains a photocell that records color changes reflecting the blood volume in vaginal tissues and thus the degree of a woman's arousal.

These are just two examples of devices used in the laboratory, and researchers acknowledge that they do not reveal the whole of the sexual experience—just the genital response. But again, let us think about the possible differences among people who are willing to have their genitals wired up in a lab under the scrutiny of researchers and those who opt out of this experience. Is this a random decision? Probably not. Is this a decision that separates people into groups that differ with respect to their sexuality? Perhaps so. When Masters and Johnson (1966) began their laboratory investigations of the sexual response, they first used prostitutes as their research subjects. As word of the research spread, other individuals volunteered. The final sample of subjects was on the average better educated and of higher intelligence than the general population. Almost all of the subjects were white. Many were divorced.

Although this is a skeptical view, sexuality research is not impossible. Difficult, but not impossible. There is much worthwhile research in the field precisely because investigators are aware of the limitations of particular research strategies. We should also be aware of these limitations if we are to intelligently evaluate this research.

Biological Aspects of Human Sexuality

In this section, we'll distinguish between sexual anatomy and sexual response. This distinction is analogous to the one we made in Chapter 2 between the structure and function of the nervous system. Here we distinguish between sexual anatomy and sexual response for ease of presentation. Human sexuality obviously entails an entwining of both.

Male and Female Anatomy

gonads
reproductive glands: testes in the male and ovaries in the female

testes
a male's gonads, which secrete sex hormones and produce sperm

testosterone
male sex hormone

ovaries
a female's gonads, which secrete sex hormones and produce eggs

estrogen
female sex hormone

puberty
the physical changes that accompany adolescence, specifically, the maturation of one's reproductive system and the development of one's secondary sexual characteristics

menopause
the cessation of menstruation in midlife

ova
female eggs, produced in the ovaries

fallopian tubes
the tubes through which a female's eggs pass from her ovaries to her uterus

Remember from Chapter 9 that the fertilized egg is either male or female, depending on whether it contains XY chromosomes or XX chromosomes, respectively. The fetus begins to differentiate as a male or female as early as the sixth week following conception, when sex hormones trigger the appropriate changes. At this point, the fetus has two generic **gonads** (sex organs) connected to a common opening shared with the urinary tract. The rudiments of external genitals are also present.

When sexual differentiation begins, the gonads that will become the male sex organs—the **testes**—are influenced by the Y chromosome to develop their characteristic structures. As they take form, they begin to produce **testosterone,** the male sex hormone, which further influences the development of the sex organs and the external genitals. As explained in Chapter 9, in the absence of a sufficient amount of testosterone, the fetal gonads develop into the female sex organs—the **ovaries**—which produce **estrogen,** the female sex hormone. And the external genitals of a female ensue.

Male and female children have different sexual organs and genitals, but they are not yet the mature characteristics of an adult. This development takes place during adolescence, when the body increases its production of sex hormones. The term **puberty** refers to the physical changes that accompany adolescence (Chapter 10). The reproductive system matures. Secondary sexual characteristics develop. There is a growth spurt. Body composition changes.

At the present time, the various physical changes associated with puberty start to occur at around age ten or eleven for females, and around eleven or twelve for males. This age is lower than that of people 100 years ago, and we can attribute this difference to the better nutrition of today (Tanner, 1978). A female, on the average, first starts her menstrual cycle at about age thirteen. Thereafter, every 28 days until menstruation ceases in midlife (at **menopause**), her body undergoes a cycle in preparation for possible fertilization and pregnancy (Chapter 10).

What are the parts of the mature female sexual system? We can start with the ovaries, which produce eggs and secrete hormones, including estrogen. The ovaries are located in the pelvic cavity (see Figure 16.3). The **ova**, or eggs, are found near the surface of the ovary. Females start life with 500,000 to 700,000 eggs. However, no more than 400 or 500 are released during her life. The **fallopian tubes** connect the ovaries to the

Figure 16.3
Female Sexual Anatomy (internal)

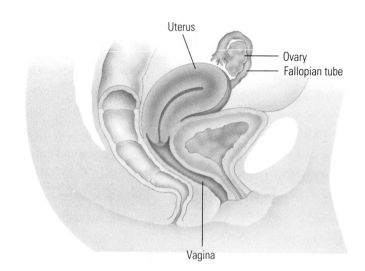

uterus

a hollow, muscular organ in a woman's abdomen where the fetus develops until birth

vagina

the lower part of the uterus, through which menstrual discharge occurs, children are born, and a penis is accommodated during intercourse

vulva

a collective term for the external genitals of the female

labia

the folds of skin that surround a female's urethral and vaginal openings

clitoris

the erotically sensitive structure of the female genitals

penis

the cylindrically shaped male organ through which semen and urine are secreted

glans

the erotically sensitive end of the penis

uterus. A released egg travels down the fallopian tube during ovulation until it reaches the uterus. The uterus has thick, muscular walls. This is where the fertilized egg develops, and the muscles here are responsible for contracting the uterus during childbirth. These muscles are also the source of the cramps that some women experience during menstruation.

The lower end of the uterus is connected to the **vagina,** the passageway that leads to the external opening in the **vulva:** the external genitals of the female. These include the vaginal opening, folds of skin called **labia,** and the erotically sensitive **clitoris** (see Figure 16.4).

What about the sexual system of the mature male? Start by looking at Figure 16.5. Each male has two testes, which produce sperm and sex hormones, notably testosterone. (By the way, the word *testes* comes from the Latin word meaning "to testify," because the early Roman practice was to take an oath while holding onto the testicles—not covering the heart as we do in the modern world!) Also present are several glands that produce semen, the liquid in which sperm cells are ejaculated. The **penis** is the cylindrically shaped organ that sends semen and sperm to the outside world. The end of the penis is called the **glans,** which is particularly sensitive to erotic stimulation. The glans is partly covered by the foreskin, which is removed in the operation known as circumcision.

Human Sexual Response

One of the interesting results of Masters and Johnson's (1966) research is that for all the anatomical differences between men and women, the same physiological changes take place during sexual activity. It is therefore possible to describe human sexual response in the same way for both men and women. In this section, we'll describe the four stages in human sexual response, as distinguished by Masters and Johnson.

Excitement.   The excitement stage involves physiological arousal in response to various stimuli, internal or external. The specific stimuli for sexual arousal will be discussed later in the chapter. Breathing, heart rate,

Figure 16.4
Female Sexual Anatomy (external)

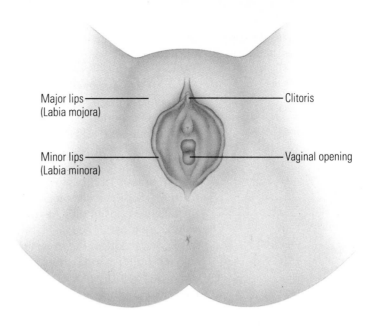

Major lips (Labia mojora)

Clitoris

Minor lips (Labia minora)

Vaginal opening

and muscular tension increase. Blood flow to the genitals increases. The male's penis becomes erect. The female's clitoris swells, and the walls of her vagina moisten.

Plateau. Arousal continues to increase during the plateau stage of sexual response. The man's penis becomes more erect and secretes a few drops of fluid, which may contain sperm. The woman's vagina becomes more lubricated, and it increases in size to accommodate the man's penis. The

Figure 16.5
Male Sexual Anatomy

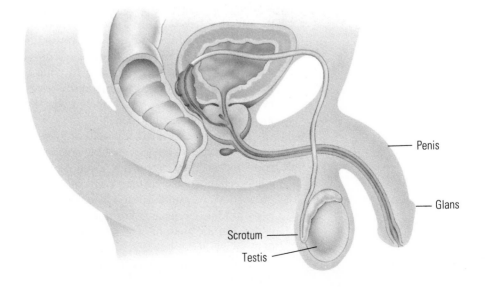

Penis

Glans

Scrotum

Testis

refractory period
interval following an orgasm during which another orgasm by the male is not possible

clitoris retracts. For both men and women, blood pressure and heart rate increase, breathing becomes shallow and rapid, and the skin becomes flushed.

Orgasm. Let's assume that our male and female begin to have intercourse. The penis is inserted in the vagina. Further stimulation takes place. An orgasm is experienced as intense pleasure, and a study in which males and females were asked to describe their psychological experiences during orgasm reveal *no difference* between the sexes (Vance & Wagner, 1976).

An orgasm occurs physiologically as a series of rhythmic muscle contractions. For the male, the muscles are those in and around his penis, and they are responsible for his ejaculation. For the female, the muscles involved are those of her vaginal walls and uterus. Both the male and female have contractions at the same rate—every .8 seconds—although they typically go on for a longer time for the woman (10 to 30 seconds) than for the male (5 to 10 seconds). During an orgasm, other muscles in the body contract as well.

Resolution. An orgasm is followed by the resolution stage, an immediate relaxation of muscle tension. Heart rate and respiration gradually return to normal. Males usually enter the **refractory period,** during which another orgasm is not possible for a while. Females are more capable of a series of orgasms, one after another, before the resolution phase is entered. The greater capacity of females to have multiple orgasms appears to be the only significant difference between the sexes in sexual response.

The period after orgasm—the resolution stage—can be one of warmth and relaxation.

Nature and Nurture. What role do our sex hormones play in sexual response? Common sense suggests that hormones have something to do with our sex drive—our need to have sexual activity *now*—but things are a bit more complicated than a one-to-one relationship between hormones and behavior. Certainly, sex functions as a drive (Chapter 6). The need for sexual release builds up within us. It is diminished after sexual activity that results in an orgasm. But what is behind this—nature or nurture? Among people, the answer seems to be both.

Almost all of the body's hormones influence our sexuality (Chapter 2), but those with the most obvious effects—testosterone and estrogen—are produced by our sex organs. To complicate matters a bit, although testosterone is produced mainly in the testes of men, it is also produced in the adrenal cortex, which means that women's bodies contain both male and female sex hormones.

As already explained, the sex hormones prove critical in determining physical development and creating anatomical differences between males and females. They trigger the onset of puberty, which turns children into adults capable of having their own children. Among women, menstruation, pregnancy, and childbirth follow a course influenced by complex interactions among circulating hormones. Among men, we do not find such cycles, but the amount of testosterone in their bodies influences the level of their sex drive.

However, hormones do not tell the whole story of human sexuality. Research has not shown that levels of estrogen influence a female's sex drive (Persky, 1983). And males who have been castrated as adults (i.e., had their testes removed) often show no loss of sexual interest, despite a drastic decrease in the level of testosterone in their bodies. What else is going on? Obviously psychological factors influence our sex drive, sometimes overriding biological influences.

Sexual Behavior

"Sexual behavior" encompasses a great deal. How can we bring some order to the topic? One common distinction that psychologists make is between the sheer frequency of sexual activity and where this activity is directed. The more interesting aspect of sexuality is its direction, so let's mention frequency just briefly before taking a detailed look at direction.

Granted an interest in the frequency of sexual behavior, just what do we count? Kinsey's surveys placed particular emphasis on an orgasm—a dramatic and significant aspect of sexual activity, to be sure. So, Kinsey gauged the total sexual outlet of a person by tallying orgasms from whatever source within a given period of time. Needless to say, an orgasm as an operational definition of sexual behavior is far from perfect. No one would wish to argue that an orgasm, or even behavior that culminates in one, is the whole of human sexual behavior.

Still, research using this operationalization allows us to offer some general statements about the frequency of sexual behavior among people in our society (Katchadourian, 1985).

- Over their lifetime, men have more orgasms than women; however, women as a group show a greater range than men in the frequency of total sexual outlet.
- For men, the frequency of orgasm is at its highest point during adolescence; it declines thereafter, particularly after age thirty.
- For women, the frequency of orgasm increases from adolescence until age thirty, and then stays constant for the next ten years, finally declining.

Now let's talk about where sexual activity is directed.

Sexual Objects and Sexual Aims

sexual object
a person or thing that one finds sexually attractive

sexual aim
what one wishes to do with a sexual object

autosexuals
individuals who direct the sex drive toward the self, as in masturbation

heterosexuals
individuals who direct the sex drive toward members of the opposite sex

homosexuals
individuals who direct the sex drive toward members of the same sex

bisexuals
individuals who direct the sex drive toward members of the same or the opposite sex

Freud made a useful distinction between the concepts of **sexual object,** a person or thing that one finds sexually attractive, and **sexual aim,** what one wishes to do with a sexual object. The use of the term *object* to include people may seem strange when you first hear it, but the intent behind the term is to encompass the entire range of what one may find attractive.

Many theorists divide people into four categories based on their orientation to sexual objects. **Autosexuals** direct the sex drive toward themselves as in masturbation. **Heterosexuals** direct the sex drive toward members of the opposite sex. **Homosexuals** direct the sex drive toward members of the same sex. **Bisexuals** direct the sex drive toward members of the same or the opposite sex. These categories may be at the wrong level of abstraction, because many people—perhaps all people—define the object of their sexual drive in much more specific and elaborate and personal ways. Consider what Stoller (1985, pp. 176–177) has to say about so-called heterosexuality among males:

Here, in males, are some of the heterosexual realities . . . preference for women in jodhpurs, excitement with other men's wives but not one's own . . . preference for fat women, thin women, tall women, short women, blonde women, red-headed women, . . . big-busted women, small-busted women, black women, white women, Italian women, Jewish women, Gabonese women, Thai women, . . . ladies, actresses, policewomen, poetesses, and women who are jet copilots. . . . What did you say was the definition of . . . heterosexual?

Sexual aims are obviously as varied and detailed as sexual objects. Later in the chapter we'll discuss objects and aims that attract the attention of clinical psychologists and psychiatrists, and sometimes the legal system as well, because they strike us as unusual, abnormal, wrong, or all of the above.

The term **sexual orientation** is sometimes used to indicate the sexual object and aim of a particular person—whatever turns one on, so to speak. Psychologists' interest in sexual orientation is two-fold. First, they want to catalog the sexual orientations of people, in the manner of Kinsey and other researchers in his tradition. Second, they want to explain particular orientations. So, let's look at both concerns.

Sources of Sexual Arousal

In explaining sexual orientation, some psychologists take a close look at the specific stimuli that arouse people sexually. All of us have experienced sexual arousal, so these findings may not be particularly surprising, but nonetheless let's run through some of what has been documented. The general point here is that *all* of our senses can be involved in sexual arousal.

Touch.   Touch is obviously important. Our bodies—particularly our genitals—contain many receptors sensitive to pressure (Chapter 3). Sometimes this pressure is experienced as sexually pleasurable. The areas with a rich concentration of such receptors are called **erogenous zones.** These include the clitoris or penis, of course, but also the mouth, ears, buttocks, inner surface of the thighs, soles of the feet, and toes.

Smell.   Smell can also be involved in human sexual arousal, although there is debate as to whether this is an inherent aspect of sexual response or something that some people learn. Among animals, many species secrete chemicals known as **pheromones** that attract potential mates. Female moths, for example, produce pheromones that can be detected by male moths miles and miles away. Male dogs urinate to mark off their territory, secreting pheromones in the process that tell female dogs to approach and other male dogs to keep their distance (Chapter 6).

Certainly, human beings secrete chemicals during sexual activity, and certainly, these have a characteristic smell. But it is not clear if these smells are turn-ons for all people or not. Some say yes, but many individuals purport to find these and other strong bodily odors disgusting. Of course, this protest is irrelevant in deciding if there really are human pheromones.

sexual orientation
one's sexual object and sexual aim together

erogenous zones
parts of the body that contain a rich concentration of receptors that provide sexual pleasure

pheromones
chemicals secreted by animals (and possibly humans) for communication with other members of their species

Every society has its sexual icons—people who become objects of fantasy for an entire generation of men or women. In our society, Marilyn Monroe was certainly such a figure.

Vision. Human beings are quite sensitive to visual cues as a stimulus to sexual arousal. Note that pornography is often nothing but visual, yet can still function as a strong sexual stimulus for many. No one questions that "looking" can be a turn-on, for men and for women. However, there is disagreement regarding the degree to which we learn that certain sights are sexually arousing. Some theorists argue that there are inherently attractive visual cues—such as clear skin or full lips or sleek muscles (Buss, 1989). Others would say that these are sexually attractive only because we are taught to think of them in these terms.

Fantasy. Sexual arousal is not simply a matter of having one's sensory receptors tickled. We are also cognitive creatures (Chapter 7), which means that our thoughts can also be an important source of sexual arousal. Sexual fantasies start in adolescence, and for many people continue throughout their adulthood, although the sheer amount of time spent in sexual reverie decreases with age. These fantasies are strongly defined and detailed. For most people who have sexual daydreams, they are the central character, with other aspects of the fantasies changing (Chapter 4).

What are the functions of sexual fantasies? For one thing, they allow us to pass the time in a pleasant way. But they are also an integral part of sexual activity itself. Masturbation, for instance, is rarely undertaken with a blank mind. People evoke past sexual experiences or create new ones while stimulating their own genitals. There is an interesting sex difference in masturbation fantasies (Katchadourian, 1985). Among men, 72 percent *always* fantasize while masturbating, but among women, the figure falls to 50 percent. The significance of this difference is not clear, although it appears to run contrary to the stereotype that women are less interested than men in the purely physical aspects of sexuality. Fantasy also plays a role in sexual intercourse with an actual partner. Some people report that they fantasize while engaging in intercourse—imagining sex with another partner, being in a different place, and so on.

Researchers are particularly interested in the content of sexual fantasies. One line of work looks at how men's and women's fantasies differ. Research shows that men are more likely than women to fantasize about forcing someone to have sex, whereas women are more likely than men to fantasize about being forced (Hunt, 1974). What is the significance of this fantasized violence? With psychoanalytic theory as his starting point, Robert Stoller (1979) firmly takes the position that hostility is inherent in all sexual excitement, and it thus shows up in fantasies. Other theorists suggest instead that sexual fantasies involving violence reflect prevailing societal attitudes about the relationships between men and women (e.g., Brownmiller, 1975).

Although it seems difficult to test these notions definitively, they are provocative—perhaps even disturbing. But maybe sexual fantasies, even those involving violence, serve a benign purpose, letting us momentarily free ourselves from societal sanctions and prohibitions surrounding sexuality. Perhaps these fantasies thereby enhance our sexual pleasure. Most people appreciate that there is a difference between fantasy and reality. And many share their fantasies with a sexual partner, increasing arousal for both (e.g., Barbach & Levine, 1980).

"A kiss is just a kiss . . ." and in some cultures less than that. Kissing—so much a source of sexual arousal in our culture—was not practiced in traditional Japanese or Chinese society, for example.

aphrodisiacs
substances believed to create or enhance sexual arousal

The Example of Kissing.   In the course of sexual activity, the various sources of arousal collectively come into play. Take kissing, for example. In this activity, which people in our culture find sexually arousing, we stimulate the senses of touch and taste and smell and—if we keep our eyes open!—vision as well. Fantasies flit through our minds. And because kissing involves nibbling and biting, perhaps Stoller's ingredient of hostility—held in check, we would hope—enters the picture as well.

Did you know that kissing is *not* a universal part of the world's sexual repertoire? Some cultures do it, and some do not (Ford & Beach, 1951). For instance, people in traditional Chinese or Japanese society did not kiss. This is an interesting reminder that sexuality must be placed in a larger social context.

Aphrodisiacs.   Substances believed to create or enhance sexual arousal are called **aphrodisiacs** (named after the Greek goddess of love, Aphrodite, a.k.a. Venus). Various cultures have championed as aphrodisiacs such items as powdered rhinoceros horn, mandrake root, bee wings, olives, vitamin E, and Rocky Mountain oysters (i.e., bull testicles). Do these work in the proposed way? It is difficult to tell, because the role of expectation cannot be easily ruled out.

If a male suffers from low levels of testosterone, and his sex drive is thereby decreased, then supplements can enhance his sexual functioning. Anecdotal reports of excess steroid use include enhanced sexual arousal and functioning (steroids contain male sex hormones). Some substances touted as aphrodisiacs, such as so-called Spanish fly, irritate the urinary tract, making it more sensitive during sexual activity and thus for some people increasing their sense of pleasure. But this is a dangerous drug, and it doesn't affect arousal per se.

It is easier to demonstrate that some substances readily depress our arousal and sexual performance. For such commonly abused drugs as alcohol, barbiturates, marijuana, and narcotics (Chapters 4 and 12), the effect of large doses is to decrease our sexual desire. That's not controversial.

Let's close by restating that we cannot explain sexuality solely in terms of chemicals, those produced inside the body or those superimposed from without. Aphrodisiacs might well exist and play some role in influencing our arousal, but they will never be the sole factor in this process. It is a testimony to human nature that the quest for such magical substances is apparently unending.

Explanations of Sexual Orientation

So, why does someone respond sexually to one object as opposed to another? At present, there is no generally accepted explanation as to how one is sexually attracted to a particular person or stimulus. All would agree that this process involves some interaction between biological and environmental factors, but controversy enters when we try to place greater emphasis on one influence or another.

Needless to say, theories of sexual orientation are only as reasonable as the facts that are available for them to explain. We've already mentioned the importance of Kinsey's "fact" concerning the indistinct demarcation between heterosexual and homosexual behavior. The same is true for the distinction between unusual sexual turn-ons and the more mundane. If we do not have such facts available, and for a long period of time we simply did not, then of course theories are not going to be very informative, because they account for what isn't the case.

Psychologists have proposed various theories to explain homosexuality, many dating to the time when it was assumed that homosexuality represented a neat and discrete category of people. Psychology has undoubtedly seen more theories of homosexuality than heterosexuality, and the reason is easy to specify. If these are two discrete orientations, then heterosexuality is simply the way it is "supposed to be" and needs no further explanation. It becomes simply the inherent consequence of normal development. What we need to explain are departures from this normal development, such as homosexuality. Adding to the apparent need to "explain" homosexuality but not heterosexuality is **homophobia**—the irrational fear and prejudice that some people have concerning homosexuality.

Now things are much more complicated, however. Psychology does not need a theory of specific sexual orientations so much as it needs a theory of sexual orientation in general, which applies to all the specifics. What are the ingredients that would need to go into such a general theory?

Sexual Development. A sound theory would have to explain the following aspects about sexual development. For starters, the capacity to be sexually aroused is present at birth. Newborn baby boys have erections, sometimes as many as forty per day (e.g., Conn & Kanner, 1940). Vaginal lubrication has been observed in newborn baby girls. And ultrasound studies even show erections by male fetuses (Masters, 1980)! These signs of sexual responsiveness have the nature of reflexes, because they are often triggered by external events, such as feeding or defecation. However, they also seem to have a sensual component, because even very young children smile and coo during genital stimulation.

The capacity to show a physical response to sexual stimulation is probably built deeply into us, and a link to pleasure is part of its inherent character. Nonetheless, infant and child sexuality differs from that of adults because it is more general and diffuse. In the course of development a sexual orientation is created: The sexual drive and response become attached to certain objects and situations but not others.

Both infants and children masturbate, which means that autoeroticism is an early manifestation of sexuality for many. And some proportion of preadolescent children engage in sex play with brothers or sisters or peers. I hesitate to specify exact percentages here because there is considerable variation, from place to place and time to time. At least in the United States, boys seem more likely to masturbate and to engage in sex play than their female counterparts.

While all of this is going on, the child is becoming a truly social being (Chapter 9). The attitudes of parents and society at large are communicated to him or her. Social learning gives children various models of how a sexual being acts and thinks and feels. Our sexual identity becomes entwined with other aspects of our identity, but the process is not the same for all of us. Sexual orientation should not be confused with gender identity (Chapter 9).

homophobia
irrational fear and prejudice that some people have concerning homosexuality

Development of a sexual identity is part of the socialization process. Children often act out the attitudes of their parents or of the community at large.

Katchadourian (1985) argues that in the United States at least, very little sexual socialization takes place in an overt way. Rather, parents give children brief messages without explanations ("that's not a nice thing to do"), or the wrong explanations ("if you keep touching yourself there it will fall off"), or a host of nonverbal messages that associate sexual behavior with shame or guilt. This approach to socialization is the historical consequence of events and trends described earlier in the chapter, particularly Christianity and Victorianism.

Some children learn about sexuality by being approached by an adult seeking to make them a sexual partner. Child sexual abuse is now recognized as all too common, and it may have long-term negative effects on the psychological development of the child. Remember the discussion of attachment between children and caretakers in Chapter 9, and recognize how this might be disrupted if a caretaker turns the child into a sexual partner.

Sexual orientation becomes more specialized and elaborate at the onset of adolescence (Chapter 10). The influx of sexual hormones at puberty accompanies an upsurge in a teenager's sexual drive, although we should note again that there is no necessary link between the two. In other words, sex drive is not simply hormone levels, as shown by the fact that interest in sex often does not wane with age, despite decreases in hormone levels (Chapter 10).

A Psychological Explanation of Sexual Orientation. For the majority of people, the first sexual experiences that include an orgasm occur during adolescence. Many theorists regard the circumstances of these early experiences as crucial in determining subsequent sexual orientation. One such theory has been proposed by Michael Storms (1981), who suggests that learning combined with the timing of puberty creates sexual orientation.

The onset of puberty means the ready ability to have orgasms. When people have orgasms, the stimuli associated with them—such as particular sights, sounds, smells, and tastes—may become a turn-on in their own right. This is simply classical conditioning (Chapter 5). The person then seeks out these stimuli, associates them further with pleasure, and thereby strengthens his or her particular sexual orientation.

At different times in life, people find themselves in different social circumstances. Recall the discussion in Chapter 10 of how your peer group changes through childhood and adolescence. According to Storms, if you experience an early puberty, then you are more likely to be surrounded by same-sex peers when orgasms first begin to occur. And your sexual orientation is thereby predisposed to homosexuality. If your puberty starts later, then you are likely to be surrounded by opposite-sex peers when orgasms first take place. Heterosexual orientation results.

What is the support for Storms's ideas? For starters, there is a correlation between the age at which someone's puberty begins and the tendency to prefer homosexual or heterosexual activity (Saghir & Robins, 1973). And the incidence of homosexuality among athletes apparently exceeds that found in the general population (Garner & Smith, 1977). Why? Perhaps because athletes are apt to spend their adolescence in the company of same-sex peers, in locker rooms and on playing fields.

Yet this theory is not perfect. The correlations cited by Storms are not particularly robust. Although they describe trends, they don't apply to all individuals. This poses a problem for the theory. And alternative explanations are certainly possible. Onset of puberty is doubtlessly confounded with many social and/or biological factors that might themselves influence sexual orientation. And even Storms (1981) acknowledges that the finding of increased homosexuality among athletes may merely mean that this group of people is more open than people in general about performing or admitting homosexual acts.

Finally, sexual orientation—once established—often proves remarkably stable. It doesn't change much for most people, and this puts a strain on any theory arguing that simple classical conditioning is responsible for sexual orientation. One would think that something learned would be easier to change than is sexual orientation. Perhaps sexual orientation represents a form of prepared learning, associations particularly apt to occur granted the evolutionary history of our species (Chapter 5). Or perhaps sexual orientation is learned early in life as just one aspect of a complex of characteristics (e.g., Green, 1987). To change one's sexual orientation would necessitate changing so many other things about a person that this cannot readily take place.

Neither psychological nor biological explanations of sexual orientation—homosexual or heterosexual—have been widely accepted as definitive.

Biological Explanations of Sexual Orientation. Other theories of sexual orientation place much greater emphasis on biological determinants, and here the focus is often on predispositions to homosexuality. A reading of the literature finds many suggestions, some hints in research data, but little firm evidence that sexual orientation is mainly a matter of biology (Brown, 1986).

Regardless, some posit a genetic basis to homosexuality—and thus by implication to heterosexuality (e.g., Pillard et al., 1982). Other theories point to the role of sex hormones, proposing that male homosexuals have lower levels of testosterone and female homosexuals have higher levels (Money, 1980). Some studies find these differences, but others do not. Yet another biological explanation puts emphasis on centers in the hypothalamus that dictate "male" or "female" patterns of sexual behavior (Dorner, 1976). If development proceeds in a normal fashion, then a person becomes a heterosexual. If something goes amiss during fetal development, when brain structure takes form, then an alternative orientation shows up.

Among nonhumans, sexual behavior can certainly be described as biologically based, but the problem with generalizing these notions to people is explaining the mechanism involved. Even if biological differences in genes or hormones or brains exist—and it is important to emphasize that these differences have *not* been documented—what is the specific pathway that leads from these to actual behavior? We are not born with images of Whitney Houston or Tom Cruise (or other prototypic females and males) coded onto our chromosomes. Much more work needs to be done here before the notion of sexual orientation is fully explained.

Sexual Dysfunctions and Disorders

In Chapter 12, we discussed general ideas about psychopathology: matters of definition, explanation, and the like. These ideas are pertinent in understanding how psychologists account for problems that people have in the course of their lives as sexual beings. In this section, we will discuss specific sexual difficulties.

DSM-III-R specifies three major types of sexual problems, and this usage will be followed here. First are difficulties with sexual performance: problems in experiencing arousal, excitement, or an orgasm. Second are unusual sexual orientations. Here there is no difficulty with the "mechanics" of sexuality, but rather one's object and/or aim is deemed abnormal. Third is gender identity disorder, in which people's psychological identities as males or females are at odds with their biological sex. We'll discuss each in order.

Sexual Dysfunctions

sexual dysfunction

a problem that takes place during the sequence of a person's sexual response

The term **sexual dysfunction** is reserved for problems that appear during a person's sexual response. These difficulties represent an interruption in business as usual. They may occur with respect to initial sexual desire. In *hypoactive sexual desire disorder,* the individual persistently experiences an absence of sexual fantasy or desire. (Needless to say, this is a difficult social judgment, because one must take into account a host of contextual factors in deciding what constitutes "too little" sexual desire.) In *sexual aversion disorder,* the person experiences actual sexual activity as unpleasant and therefore avoids it.

Desire may be present, but excitement may not translate itself into genital response or pleasure. Among females, this condition is known as *female sexual arousal disorder,* which means that the vagina does not lubricate or swell during sexual activity. Among males, the counterpart is *erectile disorder*—or impotence—a failure to achieve or maintain an erection sufficient for sexual activity.

Desire may be present, and physiological arousal may occur, but an individual may have problems achieving an orgasm. For women, we call this dysfunction *inhibited orgasm:* delay or absence of an orgasm despite sexual activity judged "adequate" in terms of its focus, intensity, and duration. Similarly, men may show this problem, but much more common is *premature ejaculation:* ejaculation before satisfactory sexual activity is complete.

Once again, please note the fuzziness in the definitions of these disorders. Some clinicians provide numerical guidelines, for example, proposing that less than X amount of time means premature ejaculation but that more than X means that everything is okay. Masters and Johnson's (1970) approach is preferable. They define problems from the vantage point of the sexual partners involved. *We* have a problem if *we* think *we* do, and not if a stopwatch tells us otherwise.

It is also important to note that all people occasionally experience difficulties with sexual desire, arousal, and orgasm. Sexual activity that is occasionally less than optimal does not mean that a couple has a sexual dysfunction. Unfortunately, because many of us have exaggerated ideas about what it means to be a sexual being, we may turn trifling incidents into a great worry. And excessive anxiety indeed can cause sexual dysfunction, because it interferes with enjoyment and performance at every step during the sexual response cycle.

Explanation. While excess anxiety may lie at the root of many sexual dysfunctions, a host of other causes are possible as well. Here the therapist's task becomes difficult. DSM-III-R reserves its particular terms for cases in which the "organic factor" has been ruled out, meaning that an illness or injury of the body is not producing the problem. It is well known that sexual activity can be impaired by circulatory problems, neurological conditions (brain injury, epilepsy, and multiple sclerosis, for instance), hormonal imbalances, advanced cancer, genital diseases (such as herpes), and urinary infections (Kaplan, 1974, 1979). And a variety of drugs, both medical and recreational, produce sexual dysfunctions (Chapter 4). Alcohol is a prime villain here, both in the short term and the long term.

Ruling out the "organic factor" to leave only psychological causes is a lot easier said than done, however, because biology and psychology are so entwined in human sexual activity. Nonetheless, the therapist embarking on the psychological treatment of sexual dysfunctions should know as much as she can about the physical condition of her clients, because psychological treatment will not work when there is an unambiguous physical cause.

What are the psychological causes of sexual dysfunction? We have already mentioned that excess anxiety surrounding sexual activity is a prime determinant, but so too are stress, conflict, other psychological disorders, guilt, and lack of sexual knowledge. Keep in mind the point stressed throughout this chapter, that human sexuality must be placed in its social context. The great significance attached to sexual activity becomes involved in one's attempts to act sexually, often with disastrous consequences.

Treatment. Granted that someone experiences a sexual dysfunction, what can be done to help? We've already alluded to the sex therapy program developed by Masters and Johnson (1970). Let's look at a few more details. Problems are thought to reside in the sexually interacting couple, not in one partner or the other. Treatment is therefore undertaken in pairs.

Suppose someone does not have a partner? Then the sex therapist provides one—a sexual surrogate, as they are called. Sexual surrogates are *not* recruited from the ranks of prostitutes. Instead, most hold jobs in addition to the one as sexual surrogate. The typical surrogate is divorced and currently without a spouse. Many have had personal experience with sexually unsatisfactory relationships.

Masters and Johnson believe that excess anxiety is usually the immediate cause of sexual dysfunction. Therefore, their preferred treatment aims at reducing the anxiety. One strategy for reducing anxiety is the technique of **sensate focus:** The couple is admonished not to attempt intercourse, but rather in their lovemaking to concentrate on giving each other pleasure by touching and stroking.

The logic here is to get people thinking about pleasure—not intercourse and orgasms—as the purpose of sexual activity. Many people with sexual dysfunctions regard sexual activity as a performance, something to be carried out in a particular way, with a particular end, with a particular evaluation to follow. Needless to say, none of this is conducive to relaxation and pleasure. Partners are further encouraged to talk to each other, making requests of their partner to do or not to do certain things. All the time, the focus is kept on sensual pleasure.

sensate focus
sex therapy technique in which sexual partners concentrate on giving each other pleasure and not on intercourse

As this form of sex therapy unfolds over time, it very much resembles the form of behavior modification we encountered earlier as systematic desensitization (Chapter 13). The idea is to pair a stimulus (sexual behavior, in this case) with a good feeling (sensual pleasure) as opposed to a bad one (anxiety). People "work up" a hierarchy, all the time holding anxiety in check, until they can have intercourse and an orgasm without difficulty.

Masters and Johnson report that their procedures eliminate sexual dysfunctions in up to 80 percent of their clients, a success rate as high as any known to clinical psychology (Chapter 13). Some observers are skeptical of this high rate, because Masters and Johnson tend not to use a "no treatment" comparison group against which to measure the success of their therapy (Zilbergeld & Evans, 1980). Nonetheless, it is clear that sex therapy provides help for many people who otherwise would muddle along poorly in their sexual lives.

Paraphilias

It is ironic that some people are deemed abnormal because they can't experience sexual arousal, whereas other people are abnormal because of an opposite problem: the experience of arousal to "inappropriate" sexual objects and aims. These problems are called **paraphilias,** and here is how DSM-III-R describes them:

paraphilias
"inappropriate" sexual objects or sexual aims

> Intense sexual urges and sexually arousing fantasies generally involving either (1) nonhuman objects, (2) the suffering or humiliation of oneself or one's partner . . ., (3) children or other nonconsenting partners. The diagnosis is made only if the person has acted on these urges, or is markedly distressed by them. (American Psychiatric Association, 1987, p. 279)

A variety of paraphilias exist, as shown in Table 16.2. Note that rape is not considered to be a paraphilia. As already described, rape is a crime of violence. Those who rape have motives that differ from those who show one of the paraphilias.

Paraphilias become a particular problem for people when they are the exclusive and preferred means of attaining sexual gratification. One's social and sexual relationships with other people thereby suffer. For example, Stekel (1930) described the case of Mr. P., a thirty-two-year-old man who became sexually aroused when a woman would walk upon him while he was lying on his back. When she would step on his erect penis, he would have an orgasm. Mr. P. reported that he had engaged in this sort of sexual experience with about 100 different partners, but few would go along with it more than once. He suspected that his partners initially complied with his request that they "walk all over him" because they did not fully appreciate the sexual nature of his request. Once it was obvious, they wished not to see him again. Mr. P.'s ability to establish a long-term relationship with a woman was hampered by his particular paraphilia.

When a paraphilia involves a nonconsenting partner, as in pedophilia or exhibitionism or voyeurism, the objectionable nature of paraphilias becomes obvious. However, it is important to keep in mind that the line separating normal from abnormal sexuality can sometimes be a difficult one to draw.

Table 16.2

Paraphilias

Name	Description
Exhibitionism	Exposing one's genitals to an unsuspecting stranger
Fetishism	Using an inanimate object as one's sexual object
Frotteurism	Touching or rubbing oneself against a nonconsenting partner
Klismaphilia	Being given an enema as one's sexual aim
Masochism	Being humiliated or beaten by another person as one's sexual aim
Pedophilia	Using a prepubescent child as one's sexual object
Sadism	Humiliating or beating another person as one's sexual aim
Telephone scatologia	Having obscene telephone conversations
Transvestism	Dressing one's self in the clothes of the opposite sex
Voyeurism	Observing unsuspecting people in the process of disrobing or engaging in sexual activity
Zoophilia	Using an animal as one's sexual object

Suppose you prefer a sexual partner with green eyes and yellow hair, or vice versa. Is this a paraphilia? Suppose you can only experience sexual pleasure with your partner when using a single sexual position. Is this a paraphilia? Certainly some of the bizarre paraphilias that involve psychological or physical damage to other people are unambiguously objectionable and deserve to be called abnormal. But we must use caution concerning other sexual practices that are uncommon but not harmful.

Explanation.   There are two strategies for explaining paraphilias. In the first, psychologists explain one's orientation to the unusual as a special case of general sexual orientation. People come to be turned on by lace panties or enemas the same way they come to be turned on by members of the opposite sex: through a process of classical conditioning like that described earlier as an explanation of one's general sexual orientation (Storms, 1981). Particular experiences dictate the details of one's orientation, but the underlying process is thought to be identical (Rachman, 1966).

The second way of explaining paraphilias stresses their pathology and regards them as different in kind from "normal" sexual orientations. Freud and other psychoanalytic theorists regarded the paraphilias as immature, for instance, and argued that they represent the lingering of childhood fantasies that most of us give up as we grow up (Fenichel, 1945). Consider someone like Mr. P., discussed earlier, who is sexually aroused by feet. According to psychoanalytic thought, the foot is a phallic symbol that stands in (no pun intended) for the penis that children supposedly believe their mothers to possess. By this view, a paraphilia involving feet represents an extremely poor resolution of the Oedipus complex (Chapter 11).

A fully accepted explanation of paraphilias has not yet been developed. Any theory must explain several well-established facts about these sexual orientations. First, the overwhelming majority—perhaps 100 percent—of individuals with paraphilias are males. Second, someone with one paraphilia usually has several others as well (Willerman & Cohen, 1990). In other words, the different paraphilias in Table 16.2 tend to be seen in the same people. This fact seems to strain any simple account of paraphilias in terms of classical conditioning. Third, not all objects or aims we can imagine are equally represented among the paraphilias. Certain paraphilias, for example, involve objects with characteristic textures that may be reminiscent of human skin: leather or rubber or lace. Does this represent the working of some version of prepared learning, as suggested earlier for sexual orientations in general?

Treatment. Paraphilias are highly stable throughout one's life. Indeed, these disorders prove notoriously difficult to treat (Kilmann et al., 1982). The full range of therapy approaches has been tried, with notably little success in the majority of cases. One frequently used intervention has been aversion therapy, in which pain or other discomfort is paired with the stimuli that sexually excite someone, such as pictures of nude children. You probably recognize this technique as derived from classical conditioning (Chapter 13). Perhaps a more promising strategy in changing paraphilias is one that tries not to rid someone of their unusual sexual orientation, but instead to instill a more acceptable one (Barlow & Abel, 1976).

Gender Identity Disorder

The final sexual disorder we will discuss involves a gender identity at odds with one's biological sex (Chapter 9). Someone with a **gender identity disorder,** also called **transsexualism,** feels like a man trapped in a woman's body, or a woman trapped in a man's body. More specifically, DSM-III-R proposes these criteria for gender identity disorder:

gender identity disorder (transsexualism)
a disorder in which an individual's gender identity is at odds with his or her biological sex

- persistent discomfort and sense of inappropriateness about one's biological sex
- persistent preoccupation to be rid of one's primary and secondary sexual characteristics
- desire to acquire the sexual characteristics of the opposite sex

Transsexualism is rare, and apparently more common among biological males than females, occurring at the rate of about 1 per 30,000 males versus 1 per 100,000 females. Although DSM-III-R reserves the diagnosis of gender identity disorder for those who have attained puberty, almost all people who report this problem recall it as existing for as long as they have been alive.

Transsexualism is not to be confused with transvestism (Table 16.3), which involves dressing as the opposite sex to achieve sexual pleasure. The transvestite, despite his unusual way of getting aroused, has nothing unusual about his gender identity. He knows he is a male. Nor should transsexualism be confused with schizophrenia (Chapter 12). And

Gender reassignment surgery is, in some cases, the only solution to the transsexual's sense of discomfort. Shown here are half sisters who were once half brothers; they underwent the surgical procedure within 6 months of one another.

gender reassignment surgery
sex-change operation, used as a treatment of transsexualism

transsexualism and homosexuality are different matters altogether. All of these are distinct.

Explanation.   Quite simply stated, psychologists don't know why some people grow up transsexual. Some theorists suggest biological determinants (e.g., Pauly, 1974), but research has found no consistent physical differences between transsexuals and nontranssexuals. Even if these were to be found, the problem of explaining the mechanism leading from these characteristics to gender identity would be daunting. Other theorists propose an environmental basis to this disorder, for example, parental styles of early child-rearing (e.g., Stoller, 1972). Again, research bearing on these hypotheses has failed to provide consistent support for them.

Treatment.   Psychological therapies do not seem to alter the transsexual's sense of discomfort and inappropriateness about the body with which he or she was born. Accordingly, the treatment that has been undertaken is a biomedical one: **gender reassignment surgery.** That is, one's original genitals are surgically removed, and new ones are fashioned. Secondary sexual characteristics appropriate to one's gender identity are encouraged through surgery, hormone treatments, and so on.

These sex-change operations, as they have come to be known, are controversial. At a very basic level, they fly in the face of many people's deeply held beliefs about the primacy of biological sex. Critics find these operations somehow unnatural, even immoral (e.g., Starr, 1978). But if one's psychological characteristics are accorded equal status with one's biological characteristics, this condemnation makes no sense.

Regardless, a pragmatic question can be raised: Does a sex-change operation make the transsexual happier? Results here are unclear (Meyer & Reter, 1979). Perhaps we should expect a straightforward answer to be elusive. After all, despite all the attention society directs to these operations, relatively few have actually been performed. And possible confounds abound, threatening our attempts to interpret the psychological aftermath of a sex-change operation. For instance, the more unhappy a transsexual is in the first place, the more likely he or she is to pursue gender reassignment surgery. What then can we conclude if transsexuals are still distressed following surgery?

This chapter has considered the topic of human sexuality. Its placement at the end of the book was deliberate, because human sexuality is such a complex matter. To understand the psychology of sexuality requires an appreciation of the whole of psychology, from its biological to its social aspects. Let us close with one of the ideas stressed throughout this chapter and indeed throughout the entire book: Human behavior must be considered in its social and historical context. Although the focus of psychology is often on the individual, the individual never exists in isolation from others.

Thank you, and good night.

Summary

Topics of Concern

- The psychology of human sexuality is exceedingly complex, representing biological determinants on the one hand and cultural determinants on the other.
- Among the larger topics of enduring concern to psychologists are these questions: Why do we behave sexually? How do we behave sexually? How should we behave sexually?

The History of Human Sexuality

- A historical view of human sexuality shows that people have always endowed the topic with great significance. The modern Western world has inherited early Judeo-Christian attitudes that link sexuality with sin and shame.
- During the Victorian era, all mention of sexuality was repressed and denied.
- Throughout the twentieth century, sexual attitudes and behaviors have become more liberal.
- Our willingness to study human sexuality scientifically has also increased throughout this century, and pioneering contributions were made by Alfred Kinsey in his surveys of sexual practice and by William Masters and Virginia Johnson in their laboratory studies of sexual response.
- Sexuality continues to be a focus of modern society, as shown by the importance we attach to AIDS and other sexually transmitted diseases, abortion, infertility, rape, and pornography.

Investigating Human Sexuality

- Whether they use surveys or laboratory experiments, human sexuality researchers must confront the daunting problem of obtaining willing research subjects who are representative of the population as a whole.

Biological Aspects of Human Sexuality

- Differences in the sexual anatomy of males and females begin during prenatal development, but become most strikingly distinct with the onset of puberty.
- The male sex glands are the testes, which produce testosterone, the male sex hormone. The female sex glands are the ovaries, which produce estrogen, the female sex hormone.
- Both men and women show the same stages in their sexual response: excitement, plateau, orgasm, and resolution.
- Although one's sex hormones influence sexual behavior, they do not tell the whole story. Psychological factors influence the sex drive, sometimes overriding purely biological considerations.

Sexual Behavior

- Sexual behavior can be described in terms of its sheer frequency or in terms of where sexual activity is directed.
- The direction of sexual activity involves a favored object (person or thing one finds attractive) and a favored aim (what one wishes to do with the object). Together, one's object and aim are called sexual orientation.
- All of our senses can be involved in sexual arousal, along with our thoughts.
- No generally accepted theory of sexual orientation yet exists, although it seems that both biology and learning somehow combine to determine the manner in which one's sexual orientation develops.

Sexual Dysfunctions and Disorders

- Sexual dysfunctions are people's problems with the mechanics of sexual activity. These can be treated successfully with the sex therapy program developed by Masters and Johnson.
- Paraphilias are unusual sexual objects or aims. No good explanation of their origin has yet been proposed, and we do not know how to reliably alter them.
- Gender identity disorder (or transsexualism) is a rare difficulty in which someone's gender identity is at odds with his or her biological sex; sex-change operations are undertaken as a treatment.

Important Terms and Names

What follows is a list of the core terms and names for this chapter. Your instructor may emphasize other terms as well. Throughout the chapter, glossary terms appear in **boldface** type. They are defined in the text, and each term, along with its definition, is repeated in the margin.

The History of Human Sexuality

sexual revolution/671
AIDS/672
sexually transmitted
   diseases/674
rape/678
pornography/680

Sigmund Freud/670
Alfred Kinsey/670
William Masters and
   Virginia Johnson/671

Investigating Human Sexuality

William Masters and
   Virginia Johnson/682

Biological Aspects of Human Sexuality

testes/683
testosterone/683
ovaries/683
estrogen/683
puberty/683
uterus/684
vagina/684
clitoris/684
penis/684

Sexual Behavior

sexual object/687
sexual aim/687
sexual orientation/688
erogenous zones/688

Michael Storms/692

Sexual Dysfunctions and Disorders

sexual dysfunction/694
sensate focus/695
paraphilia/696
gender identity disorder/698

1. Human sexuality is a _____ phenomenon.
   a. biological
   b. historical
   c. psychological
   d. social
   The central idea in the chapter is that sexuality is a complex phenomenon that must be examined in biological, psychological, social, and historical terms./665

2. Perhaps the most striking aspect of the Kinsey surveys is what they reveal about the _____ sexual activity.
   a. moral right and wrong of
   b. motivation behind
   c. physiological mechanisms responsible for
   d. range of
   When Kinsey and his colleagues cataloged sexual practices of men and women in the United States, they found much greater variety in practice than in social codes./671

3. The Victorians _____ sexuality.
   a. celebrated
   b. denied
   c. did not engage in
   d. feared
   e. worshipped
   Although they were unsuccessful in so doing, the Victorians attempted to deny the existence of sexuality./668

4. A person can contract AIDS from
   a. casual contact with an infected individual.
   b. kissing.
   c. mosquito bites.
   d. swimming pools.
   e. none of the above.
   AIDS is spread through the exchange of certain bodily fluids—blood, semen, and vaginal secretions—with an infected individual. Nothing on this list is a way in which AIDS is spread./672

5. The textbook describes rape as a form of
   a. abnormality.
   b. paraphilia.
   c. sexual orientation.
   d. violence.
   Current thinking on rape classifies it as a crime of violence./678

6. Sexuality research is plagued by the problem of obtaining
   a. federal funding.
   b. interested investigators.
   c. reliable measures.
   d. representative research participants.
   e. valid measures.
   It has always been difficult for sexuality researchers to find research subjects similar to people in the general population./681

7. Sexual "objects" are _____ one finds sexually attractive.
   a. people
   b. things
   c. both a and b
   d. neither a nor b
   As used by psychologists, sexual "objects" are both people and things./687

8. According to Storms, one's orientation as heterosexual or homosexual depends most directly upon
   a. genetics.
   b. modeling.
   c. prenatal hormones.
   d. the timing of puberty.
   The sexual orientation theory proposed by Storms emphasizes the timing of a person's puberty./692

9. Masters and Johnson "locate" sexual dysfunctions within the
   a. individual.
   b. couple.
   c. society.
   According to Masters and Johnson, couples have sexual problems, individuals do not./695

10. The overwhelming majority of cases of _____ are observed among males.
   a. paraphilia
   b. sexual dysfunction
   c. transsexualism
   d. none of the above
   The most striking sex difference is with respect to paraphilia; perhaps 95 percent of all cases occur among males./698

Appendix: Applied Psychology

John B. Watson, the founder of behaviorism (Chapter 5), was a full professor at Johns Hopkins University before he was thirty years old. His research and his papers led to this early acclaim, and as you saw in the text, he is still honored for his pioneering contributions to psychology. However, Watson's career was not without blemish. In 1920, a well-publicized scandal involving an affair and a divorce led to his dismissal from Johns Hopkins.

Although he continued to lecture and supervise the research of graduate students, Watson never again held a regular academic appointment. But his career as a psychologist was not over. He accepted a job with one of the first national advertising agencies, J. Walter Thompson. This agency was interested in the possible contribution that the new field of psychology could make to the equally new field of advertising. Could psychological theories and findings be used to help sell products to the consuming public?

Watson's career in advertising was a great success, so much so that virtually every advertising agency today has psychologists on its staff. Indeed, an entire field of psychology, called consumer psychology, is concerned solely with explaining, predicting, and, most importantly, altering the process by which a member of the public decides to buy one product rather than another.

What follows is a discussion of Watson's contributions to the field of advertising (Goldstein & Krasner, 1987). Some of these are now so ingrained in standard practice that you may be surprised that they can be traced to one individual. Watson may not have been the very first person to recommend each of these practices, but he was the first to derive them from psychological theory and to explain, from his behavioral perspective, exactly how and why they were successful.

- *Placing candy and magazines near the checkout stand of supermarkets.* Candy and magazines are called impulse products, in that people do not usually go to a store to buy the *National Enquirer* or a Nestlé's Crunch candy bar. Consumers buy them when they see them and the impulse hits. What better way to guarantee that they are seen than to put these products near the checkout stand where every customer must walk by them? Further, granted the pileup at a checkout line, most every customer has to stand in front of these products for several minutes or longer, looking at them and smelling them (the candy, silly reader, not the tabloids). Finally, consider that people stand in front of these products with money already in their hands! An idea such as this follows straightforwardly from Watson's view of human beings as creatures responsive to the stimuli in their environment and his view of learning as a product of repeated associations.

- *The arousal of fear.* One of the clients of J. Walter Thompson was Johnson & Johnson, of baby powder fame. Using survey data, Watson determined that the likely consumers of Johnson & Johnson Baby Powder were young, upwardly mobile middle-class mothers expecting their first child. Watson assumed that these mothers would be particularly worried about disease and infection, and so Johnson & Johnson Baby Powder was advertised as a means of preventing calamity. Unstated but quite obvious was the message that if you did not buy this product and sprinkle it liberally on your child, you were courting disaster. You were a bad mother! Remember the importance attached to being a parent (Chapter 10).

To this day, advertisers strike at the insecurity of parents, even going so far as to arouse fear where none previously existed, in order to sell products. A current favorite along these lines is the series of television ads run by Michelin Tire Company, which picture little babies crawling among tires while voices offscreen talk about the merits of saving a few dollars by buying tires from "another" company. I don't know about you, but these ads really have an effect on me. I usually promise myself that I will buy Michelin tires the very next day, to safeguard my own children. Then I remember I don't have any children. Oh well.

- *Endorsements.* One more innovation of Watson's was to hire supposed experts to endorse products. So, a Dr. Holt—a forerunner of Dr. Spock and pediatrician of the Rockefeller family—was hired to extol the virtues of Johnson & Johnson Baby Powder. And Pond's Cold Cream greatly increased in popularity when Watson arranged endorsements by the Queen of Spain as well as the Queen of Romania!

The United States must not have changed very much over the years. We are still fascinated by royalty. Imagine the impact that Princess Di would have if she endorsed a product! In her absence, we have Michael Jordan, Willard Scott, and Arnold Palmer hawking products. And even Paul McCartney of Beatle fame has been endorsing products on television.

- *Pop psychology.* Finally, John Watson was one of the first examples in this country of what we now call pop psychologists: individuals who present to the general public a popularized version of scientific psychology (Starker, 1989). He wrote a variety of articles for popular magazines, including *McCall's, Harper's,* and *Cosmopolitan.* Watson dispensed his advice, all in chatty fashion, reflecting his behaviorist ideas, telling readers how to live happier and more fulfilling lives. Nowadays, Dr. Ruth, Joyce Brothers, Scott Peck, Leo Buscaglia, and Bernie Siegel are simply following Watson's example in applying psychological ideas to concrete problems in the contemporary world.

Defining Applied Psychology

The topic of this Appendix is applied psychology, so let's remember how applied psychology has been discussed throughout the book. In Chapter 1, we drew a distinction between basic and applied fields of psychology. To repeat the general definitions offered there, **basic psychologists** propose theories and conduct studies for the purpose of better understanding our behavior and mental processes. **Applied psychologists** use the theories and findings of basic research to help solve people's practical problems.

This distinction is not always a clean one, because so much of psychology is a practical endeavor. The way in which basic psychologists go about their business cannot help but shed light on practical problems. Similarly, the way applied psychologists do what they do also leads to an understanding of basic questions about human nature.

Consider some of the particular topics discussed in the previous chapters of this textbook, such as the control of pain (Chapter 4), stress and coping (Chapter 6), eyewitness testimony (Chapter 7), intellectual assessment (Chapter 8), psychotherapy (Chapter 13), and attitude change (Chapter 14). One cannot easily say where the basic aspects of these areas of work stop and the applied aspects begin, or vice versa.

Another way of defining applied psychology, as opposed to the rest of psychology, is in terms of *where* the psychologist does his or her work. The basic psychologist typically works in a university setting, doing research in a laboratory, often with introductory psychology students like you as research subjects. In contrast, the applied psychologist usually works outside the university, in a business or industrial setting, in a hospital, in a school, on a playing field, or in a courtroom.

Many applied psychologists find most definitions of their field to be too simple. Applied psychology is *not* the automatic application of a basic science called psychology. As we have seen, psychology itself is a highly diverse field. One does not—because one cannot—apply the whole of psychology. Rather, one applies a particular subfield of psychology and, within this subfield, a particular theory or result.

Another point to emphasize about applied psychology is that one uses particular techniques to carry out one's application. We can classify given applications as we did in Chapter 1, as embodying a case study, correlational, or experimental approach, but as has become clear throughout the book, one does not simply carry out a case study or an experiment or a correlational study. One conducts a particular type of study, and these

basic psychologists
psychologists who propose theories and conduct research for the purpose of better understanding our behavior and mental processes

applied psychologists
psychologists who use theories and research for the purpose of solving people's practical problems

require particular skills and techniques. One must know the specific requirements for each application; there are many instances of naive psychologists taking techniques out of their laboratory and into the real world, only to find that they might as well have taken these techniques into another galaxy, so inappropriate are they in the new setting.

For example, questionnaires devised for use with college students may not work well with other research subjects. College students are quite familiar with questionnaires and usually do not need to have directions spelled out for them. Research subjects who have never before encountered a questionnaire may not know what to do with it.

My favorite illustration of this point, which may or may not have really happened, has to do with a researcher who administered a questionnaire that included an item reading simply "sex _____." The researcher wanted to know if the respondent was a male or female, but among the answers to this question were phone numbers, frequency estimates, and particular times and places. (Contrary to what you may be thinking, the Kinsey surveys did *not* start out this way.)

Yet one more way of defining applied psychology proceeds by taking a historical look at the field. As described throughout the book, psychology has become increasingly specialized and diverse in the century of its existence. There was a time when all psychologists knew one another, when they could (and did) have meetings at which everyone was present, where everyone had read everyone else's books and papers. Taking this historical view, we can see the very beginnings of applied psychology, and how these beginnings developed into the contemporary fields that are usually included today under the umbrella term.

Applied psychology received its biggest boost in the United States, with the approach to psychology known as functionalism. As we discussed in Chapter 1, functionalists such as William James and John Dewey proposed that psychology concern itself with mind in use, with the consequences of one's mental processes. This interest in the functions of mind resulted in a field that was highly pragmatic, leading inevitably to the application of psychological theory and research to human concerns outside the laboratory.

Among the very first of these practical efforts were applications to business. In 1903, Walter Dill Scott published *The Theory of Advertising,* in which he explained how the new science of psychology generated numerous suggestions about how to influence the buying behavior of the general public. Scott frequently cited William James in this book, echoing in particular the idea of James that people are defined by their habits. Advertisers must try to make the buying of their particular products a habit. To this end, slogans should be associated with products because these provide a cognitive basis to the habit that an advertiser is trying to cultivate (Chapter 5).

Another boost to applied psychology came from American involvement in World War I. We noted in Chapter 8 how intelligence testing first came into widespread use during World War I, in an attempt to pick the right people for military positions. Whether or not this had any direct effect on the war effort is debatable, but the immediate aftermath of this mass testing cannot be denied. Immediately after World War I, written tests became a widely used means of hiring and placing people in industry. Personnel selection, now a thriving concern of applied psychology, therefore had its beginnings in the intelligence tests administered to recruits during World War I.

To sum up this discussion, we can note that applied psychology can be characterized most generally as the attempt to apply theory and research to practical problems. However, we must add some qualifications and elaborations. First, the distinction between applied and basic psychology is quite vague, particularly as the two fields have developed in the United States, because American psychology—due to functionalism—is inherently a practical endeavor. Second, some psychologists use a very simple strategy to decide whether or not psychology is applied: They look at where the psychologist in question works. If it is in a university laboratory, then it is basic psychology; if elsewhere, it is applied psychology. Third, one does not apply psychology per se, but rather one subfield of psychology. One uses particular techniques to go about the application, so much so that it is misleading to speak about applied psychology as a singular entity. Rather, it is a grouping of different approaches, reflecting the applications of diverse aspects of psychology, itself a varied field.

In the rest of this Appendix we will cover some of the speciality fields of applied psychology. The subfields selected here, consistent with our discussion so far, represent but one way to slice the pie of applied psychology. Our approach is simply to get a flavor of each subfield, noting the area of basic psychology with which it starts and then giving some examples of the types of practical uses to which it has been put. More complete discussions of the subfields of applied psychology can be found in books devoted to these subjects (e.g., Anastasi, 1979; Goldstein & Krasner, 1987; Gregory & Burroughs, 1989). And your college probably has one or more advanced courses in the curriculum that cover these subfields.

Engineering Psychology

Every day of your life you confront the products of engineering psychology, although you may never have heard the name of this subfield. **Engineering psychology** can be defined as the use of psychological theories and research to design environmental settings—usually machines—to be safe, efficient, and/or pleasurable (Martin, 1989). Have you driven a car recently? The controls and the lights on the dashboard have been arranged in such a way that they are easy to see and not confusing. The research that suggests the optimal way of designing instrument panels is the work of engineering psychologists.

Have you driven your car down the street? Different street signs compete for your attention, and one of the topics to which engineering psychologists devote their efforts is how best to convey information in a symbol that will be glimpsed but briefly. They wish to minimize any ambiguity, so you don't confuse the meaning of one sign with that of another (see Figure A.1).

Do you use a personal computer with a word-processing program? Many such programs have menus—commands at the bottom of the screen. Engineering psychologists design these commands to be easy to understand and use. For example, when complex commands are abbreviated as single letters, these should be letters with which the full command begins:

Figure A.1

Symbols for Public Information. Different symbols have been used to convey information to the public. Above each symbol is a number representing its relative efficiency: a composite of the accuracy with which it can be recognized when seen but briefly, the distance from which it can be recognized, the correctness with which it can be interpreted, and the correspondence between it and its meaning. The higher the number, the better the symbol. Source: Mackett-Stout & Dewar, 1981.

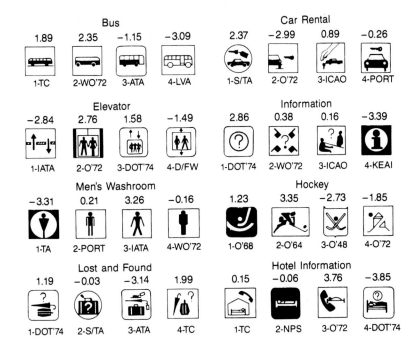

P for print, *S* for save, and the like. When we speak of a computer as user-friendly, we don't mean that it uses amusing graphics that bring a smile to our face. Instead, we mean that its design is psychologically informed; the computer works in a way congruent with the way that we work.

Have you sat in a chair, or taken a shower, or used a light switch? The dimensions of these devices have been chosen, in most cases, to fall within limits judged comfortable for the range of typical people. Engineering psychologists are well versed in people's dimensions, and the speciality field that specifically studies these is called *anthropometry*. Thanks to these psychologists, we know the average reach of Americans, their eye height when sitting, and how high their knees are from the ground. One of the reasons why the Armed Forces have height requirements is to ensure that recruits can use the devices that the military provides, whether shoes or hats or weapons or beds.

Engineering psychologists have learned that there is really no such thing as an average person with respect to all possible bodily dimensions. For instance, Daniels (1952) studied 4000 pilots, measuring ten relevant dimensions of their bodies. *Not a single person* out of the 4000 fell between the top and bottom third on all ten dimensions.

Most of you are not pilots, but you wear clothing, and so you know that there is some item of clothing that is always difficult for you to get to fit, whether it be shoes, shirts, or pants. Is it any comfort to know that this is the typical state of affairs? Engineering psychologists therefore try to design devices not for the nonexistent "average" person, but rather for a range of people, typically those who fall between the 5th and 95th percentiles.

What kinds of methods do engineering psychologists use? Obviously they rely on surveys of bodily parts. They also must be familiar with basic findings regarding sensation (Chapter 3), perception (Chapter 4), and cognition (Chapter 7). If they design products for people of different ages, they must know about developmental changes (Chapters 9 and 10).

How bright must a display be in a cockpit in order to be visible but not distracting? How should emergencies be signaled—with a buzzer, bell, or spoken voice? Should switches move up or down or sideways?

Analogue switches are frequently used. With these switches, the amount the switch is changed or the direction it moves is analogous to changes in whatever the switch is controlling. On a stove, the switches for the burners are usually arranged similarly to the way the burners are arranged. Other times, conventions are purely arbitrary, but then these conventions tend to become standardized within a culture. So, North American light switches are turned on by moving them up; in Australia, the opposite convention is followed. And in Japanese and American cars, volume controls for radios are usually on the opposite sides.

Industrial-Organizational Psychology

industrial-organizational (IO) psychology
the subfield of applied psychology that uses theories and research to improve the functioning of complex work organizations

job analysis
a detailed description of the skills and abilities needed to perform successfully at a given job

Industrial-organizational (IO) psychology concerns itself with improving the functioning of complex work organizations. IO psychologists are interested in fitting the person to the job and vice versa. They proceed by applying theory and research to the topic of work.

Several speciality areas within IO psychology can be distinguished (Dorfman, 1989). It is common to split the *I* in IO psychology off from the *O*, at least approximately. So, industrial psychology, sometimes called *personnel psychology,* focuses on selecting, training, and evaluating people in an organization. This orientation to personnel gives industrial psychology a strong interest in individual differences, and in many ways we can look at personnel psychology as applied personality (Chapter 11). Devising and administering tests for selection and evaluation are among the most typical activities of personnel psychologists.

Organizational psychology, the *O* of IO, focuses instead on the process by which workers adjust to one another and their work organization. Here we see interest in workers' attitudes, motivation, job satisfaction, and leader-follower relationships. Given these interests, organizational psychology is very much the application of social psychological ideas, as discussed in Chapters 14 and 15. Let's take a closer look now at the *I* and the *O* of IO psychology.

Industrial Psychology

Industrial psychologists help organizations devise explicit descriptions of what people are expected to do at their jobs. This often requires them to undertake what is known as a **job analysis,** a detailed description of the skills and abilities needed to perform successfully at a given job.

There are several standard procedures for performing a job analysis. Personnel psychologists may start by observing people on the job, then interviewing them and their supervisors. They may undertake a survey, using questionnaires to assess the opinions of a variety of people about the requisite skills.

Sometimes the best way to conduct a job analysis is for the personnel psychologist to do the job herself. As you know from your own efforts in the workplace, a job title may not tell you much about what really goes on. There may be no substitute for getting firsthand experience.

Industrial psychologists have drawn the attention of employers to so-called **critical incidents,** specific occurrences that distinguish satisfactory workers from unsatisfactory ones (Flanagan, 1954). They recommend that jobs be characterized in terms of critical incidents, because these really are of greatest interest to employers. Table A.1 provides examples of critical incidents for college administrators (Hodinko & Whitley, 1971).

Another activity of personnel psychologists is recruiting people for jobs. Which is a better strategy for finding employees: hiring from within or going outside? Are employee referrals better or worse than newspaper ads or employment agencies? Needless to say, no simple answer suffices across the board, but it seems as if employee referrals are good because they reduce turnover, yet bad because they breed homogeneity in the workforce (Dorfman, 1989). These conclusions make sense in terms of the social psychological findings about the similarities of friends discussed in Chapter 15.

How should a job be portrayed to a potential applicant? Currently popular is a technique known as a **realistic job preview** (Wanous, 1980),

critical incidents

specific occurrences that distinguish satisfactory workers from unsatisfactory ones

realistic job preview

job interview procedure in which the applicant is given a realistic view of what a job entails

---

TABLE A.1

Critical Incidents for College Administrator

Hodinko and Whitley (1971) are college administrators who drew on their own experiences to compile a list of critical incidents that confront people in their role. Here are some of the incidents they describe. How should an administrator respond? Although this list is two decades old, it is still current, suggesting that the demands of college administration have not changed all that much over recent years.

Campus Parking	A community college is soon to open in a confining urban area. Planners have allowed for 1000 parking spaces, but a survey you have just completed shows that more than 3000 individuals will need to park on campus daily.
Building Takeover	A student with a list of demands plans to take over a college building.
Drug Use	You are told by campus police that known drug dealers have been seen in the student union and other campus gathering places.
Censorship of Student Publications	The faculty sponsor of the student "humor" magazine calls you in a panic, worried that some articles planned for the next issue might strike some readers as obscene. Should she forbid their publication?
Contraception	Students ask that birth control be made available upon demand in the campus health center, but the college board of regents is opposed.

in which the applicant is given a realistic view of a job, warts and all, rather than a rosy view that will only be dashed once work begins. Research suggests that realistic job previews reduce turnover by about 10 percent, which results in considerable savings of time and money that would otherwise be spent in recruitment and training (McEvoy & Cascio, 1985).

Notice the parallel between realistic job previews and the "training" interview described in Chapter 13 as a way to give psychotherapy clients realistic views of what awaits them in therapy. We can take a step back from both procedures and see that they share the goal of molding expectations so that they are congruent with subsequent experiences. Disappointment is thereby blunted.

Many jobs will have more than one applicant, and the personnel psychologist will also be involved in choosing which one will get the nod. Virtually every major organization in the United States uses an interview as a way to select employees. Face-to-face meetings with several people in the organization take place, after which these people pool their impressions and make a decision. Research by personnel psychologists is uniform in concluding that the validity of interviews as a way to assess someone's ability—that is, to predict how well they will do at the job—is essentially nil (Arvey & Campion, 1982).

Psychological principles discussed throughout the text help explain why (Chapters 7 and 14). First, different interviewers often disagree; their conclusions are not reliable because what they think about the applicant is more likely to reflect their own thoughts and beliefs than the actual characteristics of the applicant. Relatedly, all sorts of biases formed early in the interview influence how the interviewer perceives and evaluates the rest of the interview. The interviewer has his own stereotype of a good employee, and so he tries to match applicants to it. As we know, stereotypes are simplifications at best and downright wrong at worst.

Jobs that rarely include women or minorities may stay that way because of the self-fulfilling nature of an interviewer's stereotypes. For example, look at the hesitation of professional sports teams in hiring black coaches, despite the large number of black athletes. The reason for not hiring black coaches seems simply to be that there have never been any before, and so the owners of teams have trouble recognizing what one might look like.

Besides interviews, selection also relies on written tests. As mentioned earlier in this Appendix, work organizations started using questionnaires to select workers shortly after World War I. The debate over proper and improper uses of intelligence tests, detailed in Chapter 8, has a parallel in the use of personnel selection tests. Indeed, recent years have seen legal challenges and rulings that more explicitly limit such tests.

The logic behind such tests is straightforward, and it is easy in principle to specify what would be a good test. People presumably differ in characteristics that will lead to good or bad job performance. If we wish to have the best workers on a job, then we would like to know what the characteristics leading to good performance might be and how we can assess them before the job begins. If we can do all of this, then we need merely give a test and choose those who score high.

So far so good, but the debate revolves around the validity of such tests. Do they do what they purport to do? This is really two questions. What skills are necessary for a job? And does a test measure these skills and not irrelevant factors? The best way to answer these questions is to give a variety of people a test, hire them all, assess their performance, and then see whether the test performs well or not in distinguishing good and bad workers. In some cases, this whole process may be impossible, because you might want to hire only a few people in the first place. You never get a chance to know how everyone else will do.

An alternative strategy is to give tests to people already working in the organization and see which questions discriminate between workers you judge as good or bad. But this strategy is not strictly identical to choosing people before the fact. It parallels the difference between cross-sectional and longitudinal designs, as discussed in Chapter 9. Maybe workers who are doing less well than others come to answer tests in certain ways, but they would not have before they started.

General personality tests typically are poor predictors of job success, perhaps because they are simply that: general personality tests, measures of broad traits (Chapter 11). Traits by definition are abstract and general characteristics of people, and it is implausible to assume—let us say—that an introvert is always going to be a better worker than an extravert, or vice versa. Chances are that introverts and extraverts will approach a job in different ways, but they can still both excel (or fail to).

work-sample tests
job selection procedure in which prospective workers are asked to perform tasks similar to those involved in the actual job

More useful are **work-sample tests,** in which prospective workers are asked to perform tasks similar to what the actual job entails. Prospective auto mechanics repair a car. Prospective typists type a letter. Prospective teachers conduct a class. These tests echo the point of social learning theorists such as Bandura and Mischel that, in assessing people's personalities, you must locate them in a given setting. In terms of terminology introduced earlier (see Table 11.2), work-sample tests have content validity, because they explicitly sample what they try to predict.

Organizational Psychology

Let's begin our discussion of organizational psychology with a look at one of the very first organizational psychology investigations, which was actually several investigations now known as the "Hawthorne studies," because they were conducted at the Hawthorne Works of the Western Electric Company outside Chicago. These studies began in 1924 and lasted for years (Mayo, 1933). Their original intent was to investigate the effects of "objective" factors, for example, illumination and length of work periods, on productivity, but a consistent finding derailed this original goal. Regardless of the conditions imposed on workers, those in the experimental groups did better than those in comparison conditions.

Hawthorne effect
the effect on one's behavior of knowingly participating in an experiment, above and beyond any particular experimental manipulations

We call this phenomenon the **Hawthorne effect.** It refers to the fact that participation in an experiment can change someone's behavior, above and beyond particular experimental manipulations. Being in an "experimental" group enhances subjects' self-esteem and status and hence their willingness to work hard. Although the original Hawthorne studies are now regarded as methodologically flawed, they are still important. They sparked concern with the *social* context of work and, therefore, the entire field of organizational psychology. Not surprisingly, this approach to understanding how people work in organizations is sometimes called *human relations.*

At present, organizational psychologists study the effects on productivity of such factors as worker opinions and attitudes, job satisfaction, worker motivation, communication, and modes of conflict resolution (Anastasi, 1979). Researchers rarely find simple results. Various factors usually combine and mingle to affect productivity, and thus these psychologists regard organizations as complex psychological fields (Chapter 14).

The good news about this complexity is that it gives the organizational psychologist multiple targets for intervention. For example, a topic that has been frequently investigated is the effect of a worker's goals on his or her productivity. Goals per se neither help nor hinder. What is important with regard to productivity is the type of goal that one sets.

We can offer two generalizations about the types of goals that improve a worker's performance (Locke, Shaw, Saari, & Latham, 1981). First, her goals must be difficult but at the same time realistic. Second, her goals must be specific. Organizational psychologists regard "do your best" goals as too vague to provide useful information about satisfactory or unsatisfactory performance. By the way, students similarly do their best work when they set difficult and specific goals for the school year (Peterson & Barrett, 1987). Optimal goals can be provided to workers through processes of social influence, such as those described in Chapter 15.

Another example of how organizational psychology applies basic ideas from social psychology comes from studies of the determinants of worker satisfaction. In order to be pleased with what they are doing, workers must believe that they are justly rewarded for their efforts (Vroom, 1964). Salaries and benefits need to be in keeping with those earned by fellow workers who perform similar jobs. Here equity theory can be used to predict accurately the conditions that will produce happy or unhappy workers (Middlemist & Peterson, 1976). Equity theory also suggests how unhappy workers can be made into happy ones: by making the relationship between their work and their compensation more equitable.

Consumer Psychology

In discussing John Watson's work in applied psychology at the beginning of the Appendix, we introduced the subfield of **consumer psychology,** which we can now define explicitly as the application of psychological theory and research to the acquisition and consumption of goods and services (Mowen, 1989). Consumer psychology, although it is focused on one particular domain of behavior—buying and using things—nonetheless is an extremely broad area. It borrows from all areas of psychology. Indeed, one of my colleagues, who saw the table of contents for this book, made a wry comment when he saw Chapter 16, devoted to human sexuality. "You know," he said, "sex is important, but it seems that I spend a lot more time at shopping malls than I do making love. Maybe you should have a chapter on the psychology of shopping malls."

His comment was humorous, I think, but the point is not all that silly, granted the complexity of consumer behavior. Remember the point we made about human sexuality: We must know a great deal about the whole of psychology to understand sexuality. Ditto for consumerism, in or out of shopping malls.

As many as 95 percent of the studies currently conducted by consumer psychologists look at the factors that influence the buying of particular products, and many of these studies look in particular at advertisements (Mowen, 1989). Many psychological factors conspire to influence the impact of advertising, from needs and motives to memory and decision making to social influence. Let's briefly look at some of these factors, and representative research by consumer psychologists.

The decision to buy a product is multiply determined. Let us say you need a beverage or a laundry detergent or a soap or a meal. There are innumerable choices you might make within each of these categories. What determines exactly which product you choose? In some cases, the intrinsic characteristics of a particular product dictate your choice. But advertisers do not rely on products to sell themselves; instead they attempt to link their goods to needs and motives you may have.

Look at the way that automobiles are advertised. A car is not simply something that gets you to work or to the country on weekends. According to advertisements, automobiles provide a way to express and actualize your true self. Why do so many men walk around wearing hats or T-shirts displaying the brand names of the vehicles they drive? Car and truck advertisements have been highly successful in their campaign to make Chevy or Ford part of someone's sense of self.

Henry Murray's catalog of needs (Chapter 6) has been useful to advertisers as a reminder of the range of needs that products might satisfy. For instance, beer advertisements typically appeal either to one's need to play or to one's need to achieve (McNeal, 1982). Watch television commercials for beer, and see if the depicted actors are simply having a good time (e.g., Miller Lite) or celebrating a notable accomplishment (e.g., Lowenbrau).

Beers have changed their image over the years. If you are old enough, you may remember that Miller was once sold as the "champagne of bottled beer" and Michelob was urged on someone "for special occasions." Formerly achievement beers, these are now play beers.

In general, advertisements pair products with powerful images, and we come to associate them with one another, through classical conditioning as well as more cognitive processes (Chapter 5). McDonald's, for example, seems like the absolute most fun place in the entire world, to judge by the commercials. Employees and customers alike appear wide-eyed and bushy-tailed, attractive and glib.

We can speculate that if Carl Jung were alive today he would look for evidence of archetypes not in myths but in advertisements (Chapter 11). So many of the images popular in ads today seem primal and potentially universal. Currently seen in a variety of commercials are men and women cavorting in splashing water. Is it farfetched to conclude that this image has a sexual aspect?

As we noted earlier, at the beginning of the century, Walter Scott (1903) discussed the psychology of advertising. He proposed that ads are successful to the degree that they are remembered, and that basic principles of memory therefore help to explain which ads are the most effective. He enumerated three key factors, all of which are well supported in the recent research literature (Chapter 7). For example, *repetition* is important. Ads should be repeated over and over. There is a new trend in television advertising in which the same ad, or a series of related ads, are run back-to-back-to-back. For instance, did you ever see the commercial for batteries in which the battery-powered toy rabbit marches tirelessly through what appear to be other commercials?

Another factor is *association*. Can the product be linked to other ideas or stimuli in the environment? Here we see a rationale for trademarks, slogans, and endorsements. Why do advertisers spend so much money sponsoring sporting events? One answer is that they thereby associate their product with the event in question. Virginia Slims has for years underwritten women's tennis. Budweiser sponsors a variety of racing events. And so on. Never mind the fact that most tennis players don't smoke cigarettes or that most racing car drivers don't drink. We think of particular products whenever we think of the sporting event that they sponsor (see Table A.2).

Table A.2
Product Endorsements by Sports Figures

In 1989, corporate America paid athletes more than $600 million to endorse products and to make special appearances on behalf of particular companies. Here is one listing of the top athletes in terms of their earnings, not from playing sports, but from endorsing products. Of the top fifteen athletes, only two—Michael Jordan and Wayne Gretzky—play a team sport. Jordan is the only black athlete represented in this group. More than half of these athletes are *not* American citizens.

Rank	Athlete	Sport	1989 Earnings in Millions of Dollars
1.	* Arnold Palmer	golf	9
2.	Greg Norman	golf	8
3.	* Jack Nicklaus	golf	7
4.	* Michael Jordan	basketball	4
5.	* Jimmy Connors	tennis	3
6.	* Curtis Strange	golf	3
7.	Bernhard Langer	golf	3
8.	* Lee Trevino	golf	2.7
9.	Seve Ballesteros	golf	2.5
10.	Ayako Okamoto	golf	2.5
11.	Nick Faldo	golf	2.5
12.	Sandy Lyle	golf	2.5
13.	* Chris Evert	tennis	2.2
14.	Wayne Gretzky	hockey	2
15.	Ivan Lendl	tennis	1.5

Source: Comte, 1990.
*American citizen

Yet another key factor in advertising that Scott distinguished is what he called *ingenuity,* meaning the ease with which something comes to mind. As explained in Chapter 7, items are easier to recall when they have multiple cues. Scott argued therefore that advertisements should link products with slogans that are ridiculous or clever or otherwise memorable. In recent years, we have such examples of ingenuity as Wendy's ("Where's the beef?"), Nike athletic shoes ("Bo knows . . ."), and Clint Eastwood movies ("Go ahead, make my day").

Health Psychology

health psychology
the subfield of applied psychology concerned with health and illness

Psychological studies of stress and coping (Chapter 6) have led recently to the creation of a new subfield: **health psychology** (Genest & Genest, 1987; Krantz, Grunberg, & Baum, 1985). Health psychologists are concerned with the psychological aspects of health and illness. More specifically, they address two important questions that parallel the topics of stress and coping.

First, what links behavior and disease? We no longer think of germs as necessary and sufficient causes of poor health. People's thoughts, feelings, and actions enter into the equation that describes physical well-being. In Chapter 6 we discussed the examples of the relation between negative emotions and poor health and of the Type A behavior pattern. Habits such as smoking, drinking, and lack of exercise contribute significantly to poor health (Belloc, 1973; Belloc & Breslow, 1972).

Second, what can be done to modify the links between behavior and disease? We may be entering an era in which psychologists have as much to contribute to good health as do physicians, because so many risk factors for contemporary illnesses are behavioral (Taylor, Denham, & Ureda, 1982). If psychologists can help people to change unhealthy habits, or better yet, to avoid developing them in the first place, then the health of our entire society can be improved (Peterson & Stunkard, 1989). Perhaps clinical psychologists in the next generation will treat not just anxiety and depression (Chapter 13) but physical illnesses as well.

There are many ways to promote people's health. Several altogether different strategies can be readily distinguished. One approach, for example, derives from Bandura's notions of observational learning (Chapter 5). People are encouraged to act in more healthy ways by being shown models who do so. To the degree that models are attractive and meet with reward, then those who observe them will undertake their own efforts to improve their health. The Stanford Five City Heart Project, for instance, is an ambitious program aimed at promoting cardiac health by encouraging people to cut back on salt and cholesterol. It is explicitly based on Bandura's ideas and carried out on a community-wide basis, via public service announcements on radio, television, and other media (e.g., Farquhar et al., 1977).

Another way to promote people's health comes out of social psychology's concern with cognition (Chapter 14), specifically the attempt to boost people's sense of perceived control. Remember that people's sense of control is a potent determinant of their robustness in the face of stress. One of the best-known studies in the whole of psychology was Langer and

Rodin's (1976) investigation of the elderly residents of a nursing home. They conducted an experiment, giving some of the nursing home residents choice and control over the mundane events in their life. The other residents received the typical care and concern but no intervention to boost their sense of control. As discussed in Chapter 14, the effect of the intervention for the residents in the experimental condition was to improve their health and to increase their life span relative to those in the control group (Rodin & Langer, 1977).

Here is yet another example of an approach that has a beneficial impact on people's health. Spiegel et al. (1989) worked with women with serious cases of breast cancer. Some of the women were assigned to group therapy sessions, which met once a week for a year. The group was problem-focused in its orientation, discussing the fears and concerns of the members and attempting to devise solutions for them (Chapter 13). The group members also provided a great deal of social support for one another (Chapter 15). The other women were not assigned to this particular type of group. All received state of the art medical care. Long-term follow-up revealed that the women in the therapy groups outlived the other women, almost twice as long!

In general, health psychologists help people "manage" stress by instructing them in a variety of strategies that reduce the negative impact of life events and hassles. Here are some of the approaches they suggest:

- Relax in the face of stress; breathe deeply and regularly.
- Get in good physical condition.
- Think about things differently; remember past triumphs.
- Give yourself occasional pats on the back.
- Take breaks and vacations.
- Turn to other people for advice and support.

None of these suggestions is profound advice—unless you decide to follow it! These *stress management* techniques are designed to make you feel better. Each technique targets for change a particular determinant of motivation or emotion—biological, psychological, or social.

You do not need to wait for stressors in order to cope with them. It is possible to anticipate stress and head it off at the pass. Psychologists have developed programs of *stress inoculation* that impart to a person skills and strategies for coping with stress before it occurs (Kendall & Turk, 1984). These programs usually have three parts.

In the first part, the person is encouraged to become aware of the relationship between how he thinks about events and how he then reacts to them. Said another way, he is instructed in the basics of the cognitive approach to motivation and emotion. Then he is invited to try out different ways of thinking about potentially stressful events. Suppose he is about to undergo surgery, and the goal of stress inoculation is to help him reduce his anxiety. Psychologists help him to regard the surgery not as something that may end his life, but instead as something that will soon allow him to do new things. Where before he may have felt completely helpless in the face of surgery, he now feels instead that he can exert at least some control over its outcome by following recommended procedures before and after the operation.

In the second part, the person is shown specifically how to cope. It is silly to tell someone "just don't worry" if he does not know *how* to put a lid on his anxiety. Psychologists have developed a variety of behavioral and cognitive techniques that successfully reduce negative emotions by removing their antecedents (Chapter 13). The person is instructed in how to use these.

In the third part of stress inoculation, the person practices his newly acquired skills. In our example of the man about to undergo surgery, he might visit the hospital prior to his surgery. As he tours the ward where he will stay, he probably will experience some anxiety, which he then can combat with the strategies he has learned, such as breathing deeply or distracting himself. If he is unsuccessful, then it is back to the second part of stress inoculation for more instruction. Stress inoculation programs such as the one just described prove highly successful in helping people meet challenges (e.g., Kendall et al., 1979; Langer, Janis, & Wolfer, 1975).

Sports Psychology

Sports psychology is the application of psychological theory and research to physical performance, usually in the context of competitive athletics. Only in recent years has the subfield of sports psychology received national recognition, but it dates to at least the 1920s, when psychologist Coleman Roberts Griffith at the University of Illinois studied football stars such as Red Grange (Wiggins, 1984). In 1977, the United States Olympic Committee appointed its first sports psychologist, and in subsequent years, the USOC has increasingly involved psychologists in the training of the nation's elite athletes.

Although the specific applications of sports psychology may vary from sport to sport, depending on whether it is a team or individual sport and on the particular physical skills demanded, certain concerns cut across this subfield of applied psychology. Researchers start with the general premise that athletic performance is a function of the athlete, the coach, and the particular setting (i.e., the opponent, spectators, and the physical environment). They look at how these factors lead to good or bad performance, and they try to intervene as possible to improve the athlete's performance.

Let's consider briefly characteristics of the athlete. One of the consistent findings is that her performance is enhanced to the degree that athletic skills are routinized, practiced over and over so that they are performed automatically, without conscious thought. This is just one more example of the distinction between automatic and controlled processing made in Chapter 4. For example, the practice habits of basketball player Larry Bird are legendary. His goal is to master particular shots and passes to such a degree that he can perform them in a game without conscious thought.

Common opinion has it that certain personality types are more conducive to success in sports, but research has failed to support this idea. Personality inventories such as the MMPI (Chapter 11) do *not* predict which athletes will succeed or fail (Fisher, 1977). Even measures of individual differences that seem explicitly relevant to athletic success—such as drive, aggressiveness, determination, and mental toughness—have proved to be of little use (Martens, 1975).

Some small differences between the personalities of successful and unsuccessful athletes can be found in need for achievement, for example, but even here it is not clear whether these are a cause of performance differences or a result. For instance, hockey and football players tolerate pain better than golfers or bowlers (Ryan & Kovacic, 1966), but this may simply be the result of frequent pain and the stimulation of endorphins (Chapter 2). Work here continues, but for the present, it looks as if all types of people—personality-wise—can and do succeed at sports.

As mentioned earlier, sports psychologists propose and investigate different strategies for improving performance. Both cognitive and behavioral techniques like those discussed in Chapter 13 have proven useful (Goldstein & Krasner, 1987). *Mental imagery*—in which the person rehearses in his mind how to swing a golf club or throw a football—improves actual performance. *Thought stopping*—a technique for banishing anxiety-producing cognitions—helps rid the athlete of disruptive emotions. And *goal setting,* which pays dividends at work (p. 714), is just as helpful in the sports domain.

Sports psychology is still casting about for an identity, and there is the legitimate worry that the field's focus is too much on the highly skilled athlete. Indeed, this criticism is a general one that can be made about sports per se in our society. While the elite athletes of our country attain ever more impressive performances and win ever more acclaim and reward, the average fitness of our citizens is declining.

We know that physical exercise is healthy for all people, both physically and emotionally (Chapter 13). Perhaps sports psychologists need to additionally include the average citizen, those of us residing on couches throughout the land, in their attempts to motivate and involve people in physical activity. Here their efforts would entwine with those of clinical and health psychologists.

Environmental Psychology

The emphasis that social psychologists place on social cognition does *not* mean that our social world is a hallucination (Chapter 14). Although we know "objective" reality only in terms of how we think and feel about it, our thoughts and feelings nonetheless concern the real world. Amid all their attention to thoughts and feelings, cognitively oriented social psychologists may risk losing sight of the real world and the importance of objective reality in determining a person's thoughts and beliefs. This obviously would be a mistake.

environmental psychology
the subfield of applied psychology concerned with the impact of the physical environment on people

One subfield of applied psychology where reality is always on focus is **environmental psychology.** Here psychologists concern themselves with how the general physical environment affects the thoughts, feelings, and behaviors of people. This subfield draws on several areas of psychology, including in particular social psychology.

Environmental psychologists have several concerns. One is clearly social psychological in nature: How do individuals use physical space to regulate their interactions with others (Hall, 1966; Sommer, 1969)? You probably know that people differ in how closely they stand next to someone else during a conversation, and that their cultural group is a determinant here. Those from Middle Eastern cultures stand much closer than many Americans or Europeans (see Figure A.2).

Figure A.2
Personal Space During Conversations. Different cultures vary in terms of the distance regarded as appropriate to maintain when talking.

cognitive map

one's mental representation of a physical place

Another concern of environmental psychologists is cognitive: How do people think about the physical environment? Psychologists have introduced the notion of a **cognitive map,** a direct descendant of the lifespace (see Figure A.3). Cognitive maps are schemas: organized (and simplified) representations of the real world.

Steve Kaplan and Rachel Kaplan (1982) stress the importance of landmarks in cognitive maps. When we think of the city where we live, we do so in terms of its landmarks: particular buildings, streets, monuments, whatever. Landmarks denote choice points (where we turn to go to the grocery store or do not). They are regarded as prominent in size and distinctiveness, even if this is not entirely accurate. They are used to estimate distance. If Point A and Point B have no landmarks in between, the distance is seen as shorter than that between Point C and Point D, which have numerous landmarks in between, even if they are actually the same distance.

If landmarks are removed or altered, a person can become disoriented. For instance, I fell into the habit of finding my way to a friend's house by turning right immediately after a large orange MEN AT WORK sign, posted for months (while, of course, no one ever worked). One day the sign was removed, and I sailed right by my turn and drove for several miles before I realized that something was wrong.

A third concern of environmental psychologists is the effects of environmental stressors on people. Although events such as crowding, noise, and pollution of course have direct physical consequences, their psychological impact is also influenced by one's sense of personal control (pp. 598–99). We experience little discomfort when surrounded by many people so long as we have chosen to be in this situation and believe that we are free to leave. Contrast a rock and roll concert with O'Hare Airport at Christmas. In both cases, we are crushed by other people, but stress is much more likely in the latter situation than the former.

Here is an intriguing lesson from environmental psychology, one that brings us back to social cognition. As we attend to the physical environment, we are led to the conclusion that how and what we think is important. This, of course, is the premise of those psychologists who study social cognition (Chapter 14).

Figure A.3
Cognitive Map of Los Angeles. This picture is not a literal map of Los Angeles but rather a psychological one. The person who holds this view of the city includes only those parts that play an important role in his life.

Source: Gould & White, 1974.

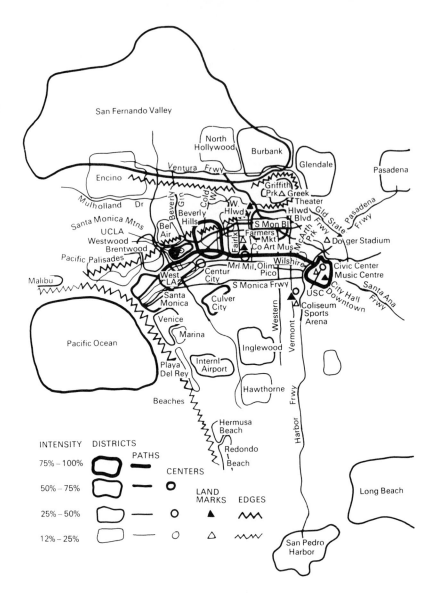

Psychology and Law

We saw in Chapter 7 how cognitive psychologists have been useful to the legal system in providing consultation concerning the pitfalls of eyewitness testimony. Clinical psychologists (Chapter 13) become involved in legal matters when they are asked to provide expert testimony regarding such matters as whether people will be violent: dangerous to themselves or others; whether a defendant was suffering from a problem at the time of a crime to the degree that he or she did not understand the consequences of what was done; or whether a defendant is currently able to understand legal proceedings. As mentioned in Chapter 1, these decisions are difficult ones, and much controversy accompanies psychologists' attempts to be helpful with regard to them (Coleman, 1984).

Social psychologists also have their day in court, and they have made several important contributions to our understanding of the legal process. For example, studies show that stereotypes can introduce bias into decisions to convict or acquit defendants (Chapter 14). Physical attractiveness of defendants can inspire leniency on the part of jurors (e.g., Stewart, 1980). However, if attractiveness seemed to play a role in the crime itself, as when someone capitalizes on good looks to pull off a swindle, then jurors are more harsh (Sigall & Ostrove, 1975). In either case, justice is not necessarily blind.

Social psychologists also study what transpires during jury deliberation (Hastie, Penrod, & Pennington, 1983). After all, juries are small groups convened in order to make a decision, and they are hardly immune to the processes that take place within other small groups. Most juries do not begin deliberation in agreement, although 95 percent eventually agree on a verdict (Kalven & Zeisel, 1966). Apparently, some process unfolds. Here are some representative findings:

- Most juries arrive at the verdict initially favored by the majority of the jurors.
- When individuals in the minority prove influential, they are usually of high socioeconomic status.
- Group polarization—toward harshness or leniency—occurs.

Do you see how these findings are consistent with theories and studies described in Chapter 15? That juries end up with the verdict initially favored by the majority illustrates conformity in action, or even groupthink! That some jurors exert more influence than others makes sense in light of research on attractiveness and social influence. That juries show group polarization is simply a special case of the more general tendency of group interaction to intensify initial opinions.

Perhaps the most tangible effect of social psychological research on the legal system was in response to the decisions in some states to depart from the traditional twelve-person jury (Myers, 1987). According to these decisions, smaller juries, some as small as five people, were deemed acceptable, because there was no reason to suppose that the decisions reached by a small group would be different than those reached by a larger group.

Actually, there is plenty of reason, supplied by social psychology's investigations of conformity. Our legal system is based on the premise that one is innocent until proven guilty. This places a great deal of importance on a juror who is not convinced by the evidence. In a twelve-person jury, someone in dissent is more likely to find an ally and hence to be able to resist the majority. In a smaller jury, dissenters are less likely to find an ally, which makes them more likely to be swayed by social forces. Citing social psychological research, the Supreme Court ended up explicitly rejecting five-person juries. This shows that research results can indeed have an appreciable influence.

Psychology and Peace

peace psychology
the subfield of applied psychology concerned with reducing international conflict and encouraging peace

Yet another subfield of applied social psychology is **peace psychology**: the use of theories and research to reduce international conflict and encourage peace. Social psychology provides some ideas that world leaders might find worth exploring. Let's consider a classic study with important implications: Muzafer Sherif's (1966) investigation of cooperation and competition among boys at a summer camp. Actually, several related studies were conducted, and what is presented here is a composite.

Twenty eleven-year-old boys from Oklahoma arrived at a 3-week summer camp. None of them knew each other previously. They were divided into two groups and kept apart for a week. During that week, each group cooperated in the various activities of summer camp: building fires, camping out, and telling gross stories. Each group became unified, and the boys even came up with names for their groups: the Rattlers and the Eagles.

During the second week of camp, the two groups were brought together in a tournament featuring competition between Rattlers and Eagles. In no time at all, the boys in each group became openly hostile to those in the other group. They called each other names, pelted each other with garbage, ransacked each other's cabins, and started fistfights.

The boys had been randomly assigned to the groups. There was no historical precedent for their mutual antagonism. Merely placing an individual into one group was enough to cause him to devalue a second group. Ostensibly friendly competition only made things worse. The evidence of recent Olympic competition makes this result unsurprising. Even when Sherif called off the competitions, the kids remained hostile.

The story does not end here. Sherif knew that a particular arrangement of social circumstances had created the difficulties. Perhaps a different arrangement might solve them. He set up a supposed emergency using a whoops technique as described in Chapter 14: "Whoops, boys, I've got some bad news. Our truck broke down. All of you have to pull together to get it started." By creating this and other **superordinate goals,** Sherif indeed reduced the fighting. The more the Rattlers and the Eagles worked together, the better they got along. Is it naive to think that the future of the world might be served by finding a superordinate goal for all nations?

Another way in which social psychologists attempt to further peace among nations is by making clear what can go amiss in complex decision making. The susceptibility of all people—even world leaders—to social phenomena such as groupthink is extremely useful information to publicize. It may be simply a coincidence, but a magazine article describing how President George Bush goes about making important decisions makes it sound as though he explicitly tries to avoid falling victim to the hazards of groupthink (Duffy, 1989).

When President Bush confronts a crisis, he tends to avoid snap decisions, regard almost all matters as negotiable, find compromises, seek out advice not only from his personal advisors but from other world leaders as well (this has been dubbed Rolodex diplomacy, because Bush so readily reaches for the phone), and encourage his top advisors to argue issues in front of him. This decision-making strategy minimizes the potentially dangerous effects of social influence on the process.

How *You* Can Apply Psychology

Psychology is one of the most popular college majors, and it has been for several decades. My students often ask me, "What can one do with a degree in psychology?" I tell them sincerely, "Anything you want to do." A back-

superordinate goals
goals shared by two groups; when pursued together, they reduce conflict between the groups

ground in psychology is a great springboard into business and sales, law, medicine, social service, government work, and many other fields. And obviously, a background in psychology is a great springboard into psychology itself, whether you wish to pursue a career in teaching and research, or therapy, or any of the subfields of applied psychology which we have discussed in this Appendix. Psychology—as has been made abundantly clear in this book—is indeed a broad discipline. An education in psychology is necessarily a broad education.

Whatever you do with your life, you will be applying psychology, theories and research, because you are a product of what you have learned. How will you be different for having studied psychology? For starters, you will ask the types of questions that psychologists ask, those that relate to the general concerns with which we began each chapter. You will rely on evidence to answer your questions, and you will be skeptical and cautious, realizing that evidence is never perfect, that theories are hypotheses, and that a person must always consider the possibility that he or she can be wrong. You will hope that better explanations await us in the future.

You will be a different type of person as well, what psychologists refer to as psychologically minded. You will be aware that people have reasons for what they do, whether you call these motives, drives, interests, or attitudes. You will be aware that people have a mental life, replete with thoughts and dreams, hopes and wishes, passions and dreads. You will also be aware that someone's overt behavior does not correspond perfectly to his or her mental life. You will know that people have conflicts and ambivalences, and indeed that sometimes their very motives may be unavailable to their conscious minds.

You will know that people are at times rational, but that there are limits to this rationality. You will appreciate that people are influenced mightily by the social setting in which they find themselves. You will be aware that people are complex, at once biological and social creatures, products of nature and nurture. You will know that people are minds and bodies. You will know that people are the same in many ways and different in others. However, the differences are not necessarily fixed for life.

You will believe that at least some aspects of the human condition can be changed for the better. You will be aware that people bring their own perspectives to bear on life, that you see the world from where you stand, and that others do the same. Ours is a unique historical era in terms of the emphasis that contemporary individuals place on contemplation and introspection. Psychology is the field of study that best mirrors this aspect of the era in which we live. How might you apply psychology? It will be impossible for you not to do so.

Glossary

ablation destruction or removal of part of the brain/73

abnormal psychology the field within psychology that studies people's emotional, cognitive, and/or behavioral problems/490

abnormality feelings, thoughts, and behaviors characterized by such attributes as suffering, maladaptiveness, loss of control, and unconventionality that produce discomfort among observers/491

absolute threshold the minimal amount of energy needed to create a psychological experience/103

accommodation according to Piaget, the modification of existing knowledge so that it fits new information that a person has just encountered/385

achievement motivation the need to accomplish something difficult in situations characterized by a standard of excellence/230

achievement tests tests that measure what one has already learned/314

acquired immune deficiency syndrome (AIDS) a fatal condition in which the body loses its ability to fight off disease, caused by a virus transmitted through the exchange of bodily fluids, such as semen and blood/672

acquired motives learned motives like achievement, power, and mastery/213

acquisition in classical conditioning, the process in which the conditioned response becomes stronger through repeated pairings of the conditioned stimulus (CS) with the unconditioned stimulus (UCS); in operant conditioning, the process by which the frequency of operants increase/178, 188

action potential electrical and chemical changes that take place when a neuron fires/58

action research the attempt to make one's scientific investigations pertinent to larger social concerns/589

activation-synthesis theory a theory of dreams proposing that a dream represents someone's interpretation of random activity of the cortex during sleep/158

actor-observer effect our attributional tendency to explain our own behavior in terms of the situation while explaining the behavior of people we observe in terms of their presumed dispositions/598

acuity the ability to make fine visual discriminations among stimuli/113

adaptation process by which a sensory system becomes more or less sensitive to stimuli/114

adaptation level theory an approach to scaling that takes into account not just the stimuli being judged but also other stimuli that we have experienced in the past/108

adolescence the developmental period that begins with puberty and ends at about age twenty, marked by rapid physical and psychological growth/404

adrenal glands endocrine glands located on top of the kidneys that control the body's reaction to threat and danger/72

adulthood the developmental period that begins with the end of puberty, at about age twenty, and lasts until death/404

affiliation our tendency to seek out other people/644

aggregation an assembly of individuals physically congregated in the same place/649

aggression intentionally destructive acts directed against individuals or groups/229, 633

agoraphobia fear of being in a situation from which escape is difficult or embarrassing, usually resulting in the avoidance of public places/509

Alcoholics Anonymous (AA) a self-help group for recovering alcoholics/525

algorithms methods for solving problems that guarantee a solution/298

all-or-none principle   the idea that neurons either fire totally or not at all/59

alpha waves   brain waves that cycle between 8 and 12 times per second, associated with relaxation/152

Alzheimer's disease   progressive and eventually fatal neurological condition marked by forgetfulness, confusion, and loss of ability to take care of one's self/434

amplitude   the height of a wave of light/109

amygdala   part of the limbic system that seems to produce rage and aggression/64

anorexia nervosa   an eating disorder characterized by a deliberate restriction of the intake of calories, extreme weight loss, and a distorted body image/520

anti-anxiety medications   drugs such as the minor tranquilizers used to treat anxiety disorders/553

anti-depressant medications   drugs such as tricyclics and MAO-inhibitors used to treat depression/553

anti-psychotic medications   drugs such as the neuroleptics and lithium used to treat psychotic symptoms/553

anxiety   feelings of apprehension and uneasiness accompanied by the body's emergency reaction, a "fight or flight" response, and diffuse expectations of harm/503

anxiety disorders   disorders characterized by general expectations of harm, e.g., generalized anxiety disorder/503

aphrodisiacs   substances believed to create or enhance sexual arousal/690

appetitive conditioning   classical conditioning that involves pleasant stimuli, such as food/181

applied psychology   psychological theories and research for the purpose of solving people's practical problems/706

approach-avoidance conflict   a situation that poses a conflict because it is simultaneously attractive and unattractive/464

aptitude tests   tests that measure one's capacity for learning/314

artificial concepts   concepts defined by necessary and sufficient conditions/291

artificial insemination   procedure in which previously obtained and frozen sperm is introduced into a woman's vagina when she is ovulating/678

artificial intelligence   the creation of computer programs that mimic the intelligent behavior of people/302

assimilation   according to Piaget, the modification of new information so that it fits what a person already knows/385

association areas   locations in the cortex once thought to link sensory and motor projection areas and now believed to be where higher mental activities take place/68

attachment   an emotional and social bond that forms between an infant and its primary caregiver(s)/377

attachment theory   the idea that adults approach romantic relationships in accordance with their attachment history/377, 648

attention   processes responsible for the selectiveness of perception/136

attitude   a stable and general disposition toward some object, encompassing beliefs, feelings, and behaviors/584

attitude-value confrontation technique   attitude change technique in which people are encouraged to make their attitudes consistent with their more general values/613

attribution theory   explanation of how causal attributions play a role in social behavior/595

audience effects   the effects of the mere presence of others on one's performance of a task/560

auditory canal   connection between the outer ear and the middle ear/119

auditory nerve   nerve that runs from the inner ear to the brain/120

authoritarian parenting   style of raising children that is firm, punitive, and emotionally cold; authoritarian parents value obedience in their children and do not encourage their independence/380

authoritative parenting   style of raising children that involves negotiating with them; authoritative parents set limits for their children but explain why, encouraging independence/380

automatic processing   the approach to normal waking activities in which we initiate an activity and carry it out without conscious direction/148

autonomic nervous system   the part of the peripheral nervous system that controls our heart, lungs, and digestive organs/55

autosexuals   individuals who direct the sex drive toward the self, as in masturbation/687

availability heuristic   basing judgment of the frequency of events on the ease with which they can be brought to mind/299

aversion therapy behavior modification strategy that associates an aversive stimulus with an undesirable behavior/563

aversive conditioning classical conditioning that involves unpleasant stimuli, such as electric shock/181

axon the part of a neuron that sends messages to other neurons/57

backward conditioning classical conditioning procedure in which the UCS precedes the CS in time/179

basic psychology psychological theories and research for the purpose of better understanding our behavior and mental processes/706

basilar membrane structure which runs the length of the cochlea, which when moved by the cochlea's fluid, triggers the movement of hair cells on its surface/120

behavior actions and reactions of a person or animal that can be observed by others and measured/2

behavior genetics field that studies how genetic differences within a species are related to behavior differences/90

behavior modification an approach to therapy based on theories of learning through which people can rid themselves of undesired habits and replace them with desired ones/561

behaviorism an influential approach to psychology associated with Watson and Skinner that stresses the study of observable action, the importance of the environment, and the primary role of learning/14, 175

biofeedback procedure for measuring and amplifying changes in bodily processes (like heart rate, skin temperature, or brain waves) so that people can be aware of them and thus modify them/198

biomedical model approach that explains abnormality as due to organic injury or illness/491

biomedical therapies techniques and strategies for therapy that intervene biologically, for example, with drugs or surgery/540

bipolar disorder a mood disorder marked by alternating periods of excessive and inappropriate sadness (depression) and periods of excessive and inappropriate elation (mania); formerly called manic-depression/515

bisexuals individuals who direct the sex drive toward members of the same or the opposite sex/687

blind spot the part of the retina through which the optic nerve passes; because there are no photoreceptors in the blind spot, it is incapable of vision/113

bottleneck model theory of attention that proposes a biological restriction on the amount of sensory stimulation that can be noticed/137

bottom-up information processing information processing in which simple aspects are not influenced by more complex ones/267

brightness the psychological experience of the intensity of light/109

bulimia an eating disorder in which someone alternates between binging and purging/521

bystander intervention individuals helping out in an emergency they happen to observe/642

Cannon-Bard theory of emotion the theory that the cortex simultaneously produces bodily changes and emotions in response to particular stimuli/238

capacity model theory of attention that proposes a psychological limit, determined by available effort, on the amount of sensory stimulation that can be noticed/137

case study a research strategy in which a single individual or group is studied intensively/27

CAT scan (computerized axial tomography) a technique for forming an image of the brain by taking many X rays and then assembling them into a three-dimensional picture by computer/77

causal attribution a belief about the cause of some event/595

cell body the neuron's largest concentration of mass, containing the nucleus of the cell/57

central nervous system (CNS) all the neurons in the brain and spinal cord/55

central tendency the mean or average value of a variable/45

cerebellum the part of the hindbrain that is involved in maintaining coordination and balance/62

cerebral cortex outer layer of the forebrain, responsible for organizing information and initiating responses/64

cerebral hemispheres the symmetric halves of the forebrain/64

chaining the process by which a sequence of responses is learned through operant conditioning: first the last response is learned, then the next-to-last response, and so forth/190

chemical sense sensory system that is stimulated chemically, like taste or smell/120

chromosomes sets of genes contained in each cell of the body/82

chronological age one's age measured in months and years/356

chunking grouping cognitive elements into larger wholes/272

classical conditioning a basic form of learning in which an originally neutral stimulus, when paired with another stimulus capable of eliciting a reflexive response, comes to elicit that response in its own right; also called Pavlovian conditioning/176

client-centered therapy (person-centered therapy) approach to therapy pioneered by Carl Rogers that provides the client with an accepting and empathic environment in which the client has the opportunity to devise his or her own solutions to problems/559

clinical retardation mental retardation caused by a specific illness, injury, or physiological dysfunction/334

clinical syndrome an acute disorder that is described on Axis I of DSM-III-R/499

cliques small groups of people who help each other fulfill their needs for intimacy/421

clitoris the erotically sensitive structure of the female genitals/684

coaction effects the effects of others doing the same thing on one's performance of a task/651

cochlea fluid-filled canals in the inner ear/126

cognition the various mental processes responsible for how we "know" the world, including perceiving, thinking, and remembering/19, 263

cognitive development the development of the processes of knowing, including perception, intelligence, memory, problem solving, and language/384

cognitive dissonance theory Festinger's hypothesis that inconsistency between one's thoughts and actions is aversive and motivates one to somehow resolve the inconsistency/612

cognitive learning learning that involves thinking about the relationship between behavior and environmental occurrences/173

cognitive map a mental representation of a physical space/203

cognitive psychology the field of psychology that studies memory and cognition/263

cognitive science newly developing field that combines disciplines like cognitive psychology, linguistics, computer science, anthropology, and neuroscience and has the goal of understanding the what and how of human knowledge/302

cognitive therapy approach to therapy developed by Aaron Beck that identifies a client's automatic thoughts and errors in logic and then tries to change these by evaluating them against the evidence of the world/519, 560

cognitive-behavioral model approach that explains abnormality as due to learned ways of thinking or acting/492

cohort effects differences between various age groups, not because of their age, but because of the particular historical and social conditions that existed while they were growing up/364

collective effects the effects of interacting with others on one's performance of a task/650

collective unconscious Jung's idea that all people have a common storehouse of experiences and memories inherited from our ancestors/453

collectivity a social category: two or more people who can be discussed as a whole/649

common traits characteristics that sensibly describe all people/456

community psychology the use of psychological theories and findings to change social conditions so that the future likelihood of problems is reduced/566

companionate love sober love for another, in which we feel concern and affection for the other person/246

comparative psychology the study of behavioral similarities and differences among animal species, usually with the goal of discerning their evolutionary history/88

compulsions repetitive acts that one is impelled to carry out to prevent some dreaded event, even though these acts bear no realistic connection to the event/510

concept the classification of elements into a group/289

conception the beginning of physical development: when a male's sperm cell fertilizes a female's ovum/367

concrete operations stage Piaget's third stage of cognitive development, from seven to about eleven years of age, characterized by an understanding of conservation/387

conditional regard acceptance of people that is contingent on a particular way of behaving/462

conditioned response (CR) in classical conditioning, the response produced by pairing the

conditioned stimulus (CS) with an unconditioned stimulus (UCS)/177

conditioned stimulus (CS) in classical conditioning, an originally neutral stimulus that produces the conditioned response after pairing with an unconditioned stimulus (UCS)/177

conditioning the acquisition of particular behaviors in the presence of particular environmental stimuli/173

cones photoreceptors with a tapered shape responsible for vision in bright light and sensations with color/111

conformity changing one's behavior to be consistent with the behavior of others/630

confound an irrelevant factor that distorts an operational definition/23

conscious thoughts and feelings of which we are aware/449

consciousness our awareness of our environment and our mental processes/134

conservation the knowledge that characteristics of objects or substances—like number, length, or volume—stay the same even if their appearance changes/387

consistency controversy the debate within personality psychology as to whether or not people act consistently across different situations/466

consumer psychology the subfield of applied psychology concerned with the acquisition and consumption of goods and services/714

contact hypothesis the notion that mere contact between different groups suffices to decrease prejudice/614

context-dependent recall the tendency to recall information better when in the situation where it was originally encoded/278

contiguity a principle of associative learning; associations are learned readily if they occur closely together in time/173

contingency a principle of associative learning: associations are learned if two stimuli or a stimulus and a response predict each other/174

contingency theory (of leadership) Fred Fiedler's hypothesis that the most effective leader for a group depends on the nature of the group/655

continuous reinforcement reinforcement that occurs after every response/192

contraprepared learning hard to acquire learning presumably made difficult by evolution/202

control group in experiments, the group of subjects not exposed to the independent variable/33

controlled processing the approach to normal waking activities in which we initiate an activity and then make a conscious effort to direct our behavior/148

conventional reasoning Kohlberg's second stage of moral development, in which most adolescents and adults can justify moral actions in terms of society's rules or expectations/394

conversion disorder a somatoform disorder in which there is a loss of physical functioning without a physical cause; formerly called hysteria/511

cornea the transparent, protective outer covering of the eye/111

corpus callosum the bundle of neurons that connects the cerebral hemispheres/64

correlation coefficient a number between −1.00 and 1.00 reflecting the degree to which two variables are correlated with one another; the further the number is from 0.00, the stronger the correlation—negative or positive, as the case may be/47

correlational investigation a study that ascertains the degree of relationship between two variables/29

counterconditioning therapy techniques based on classical conditioning principles in which undesirable responses to stimuli are replaced with desirable ones/182

creativity the capacity to act in adaptive, purposive, and novel ways/340

critical incidents specific occurrences that distinguish satisfactory workers from unsatisfactory ones/711

critical periods times during development when one is most ready to acquire a certain behavior if particular experiences occur/359

cross-sectional studies research strategies that simultaneously study and compare individuals of different ages/362

crystallized intelligence skills or knowledge developed through education or practice/345

culture-fair intelligence tests intelligence tests that attempt to measure abilities unaffected by one's particular background/324

cutaneous senses the sensory systems that respond to touch and temperature/123

data facts obtained through measurement or observation in a scientific study/5

daydreaming the state of consciousness in which people shift their attention inward, away from the external world/150

death instinct (Thanatos) according to Freud, our instinct for violence and destruction/451

deception experiment a study, usually by a social psychology investigator, in which research participants are deliberately misled about the true purpose of the study in order to avoid influencing how subjects might behave/590

defense mechanism according to psychoanalytic theory, an unconscious strategy for protecting the individual's conscious mind against threat/248, 409

deindividuation the process of submerging oneself in a group and feeling anonymous/628

delta waves brain waves that cycle between .5 and 3 times per second, associated with Stage 3 and Stage 4 sleep/153

delusions bizarre and unsettling beliefs that others do not find plausible/527

dendrites the parts of a neuron that receive messages from other neurons/57

dependent variable in experiments, the factor assessed by the researcher following a particular manipulation/32

depressants psychoactive drugs, such as alcohol, narcotics, and barbiturates, that reduce awareness of external stimuli and slow down bodily functions/164

depressive disorder a mood disorder marked by excessive and inappropriate sadness/515

depth of processing an approach to information processing that assumes people encode information in different ways, some simple (or shallow) and some elaborate (or deep)/268

descriptive statistics statistics that describe the patterns within data/45

determinism the philosophical assumption, held by psychologists, that all behaviors have causes/6

developmental age the age when most individuals show a particular characteristic indicative of development/356

developmental psychology the field of psychology that studies the physical and psychological changes that take place throughout life—from conception to death/356

developmental stages discrete periods occurring in a fixed sequence in a person's life, each marked by particular physical, mental, or behavioral characteristics and achievements/358

diagnosis identifying a person's psychological disorder according to a particular set of signs and symptoms/498

diathesis-stress model integrative approach that explains abnormality as due to a biological weakness (diathesis) coupled with certain environmental conditions (stress)/494

difference threshold the minimal (physical) distinction between two stimuli that can be discriminated/105

diffusion of responsibility a reason why bystanders may fail to intervene in an emergency: the belief on the part of each individual that someone else is responsible/642

discrimination acting in accordance with one's prejudices/637

discrimination in classical conditioning, the process by which a new stimulus dissimilar to the CS does not elicit on its own the CR; in operant conditioning, the process by which an organism does not behave in a new situation as it did in an old situation because the discriminatve stimuli in the two settings are dissimilar/180, 191

discriminative stimulus a signal that reinforcement for a given response is (or is not) available in a particular situation/191

dissociation a state of consciousness in which two conscious activities are carried out with little or no communication between the two/162

dissociative disorders disorders marked by lack of integration of a person's identity, memory, or consciousness/513

divergent thinking the ability to think along many alternative paths/340

divided attention ability to attend to different stimuli at the same time/136

dominant gene the member of a pair of genes that determines one's phenotype/82

dopamine hypothesis an explanation of schizophrenia proposing that excess amounts of the neurotransmitter dopamine cause this disorder/528

double-bind hypothesis a hypothesis proposing that schizophrenia is created when families present their children with unresolvable conflicts/529

double-depletion hypothesis theory of the causes of thirst which proposes that thirst results either from depletion of fluid within cells or outside cells/224

Down's syndrome a common form of clinical retardation caused by an extra chromosome/335

dream interpretation a psychoanalytic technique for revealing unconscious conflicts in which the patient describes dreams, free associates to them, and works with the therapist to interpret their underlying meaning and significance/557

drive a state of tension or arousal produced by a need/216

DSM-III-R (Diagnostic and Statistical Manual of Mental Disorders-Third Edition-Revised) the 1987 diagnostic scheme of the American Psychiatric Association, currently used to diagnose mental disorders in the United States/498

dual-center theory biological theory of motivation which proposes that the hypothalamus contains two centers, one exciting behavior and the other inhibiting it; these two centers work together to maintain the body's homeostasis/220

eardrum membrane between the auditory canal and the middle ear that vibrates when sound waves push against it/120

echo auditory image that briefly lingers following the presentation of a stimulus/272

eclectic therapy an approach to therapy that draws on techniques and rationales from a variety of theoretical strategies/540

ecological approach Gibson's theory of visual perception that stresses the role of the actual environment in determining what is seen/140

effector neuron that initiates some response toward the environment/60

ego in psychoanalytic theory, that aspect of personality that makes adaptation to the world possible; the ego makes compromises between the id and the superego/450

ego integrity according to Erik Erikson, acceptance of one's choices in life (those that led to triumphs as well as disappointments), and a sense that one's dilemmas have been well-resolved—the focus of later adulthood/408

egocentric able to see things only from one's own point of view and no one else's/386

electroconvulsive therapy (ECT) a treatment for depression in which an electric current is briefly passed through the brain of a patient, inducing a seizure/552

electroencephalogram (EEG) device that measures and records electrical activity in the brain/76, 152

electromyogram (EMG) device that measures and records electrical activity of the muscles/152

electrooculogram (EOG) device that measures and records eye movements/152

embryo the term used to describe the developing unborn child from about two weeks to two months after conception/368

emergency reaction physiological response to threat, in which an organism prepares itself through internal reactions for defending itself (fight) or running away (flight)/236

emotion the subjective feelings we experience in response to situations, as well as patterns of accompanying physiological arousal, thoughts, and behaviors/213

empiricism philosophical doctrine that knowledge is acquired through experience/101

encoding the process by which we put information into our memory/268

encounter groups small groups of people in conflict who are brought together with arranged conditions so that they can understand each other better through an open and honest exchange of their thoughts and feelings/559

endocrine system the set of glands that secrete hormones into the bloodstream/71

endorphins pain-reducing chemicals similar to narcotics but produced in the brain/59

engineering psychology the subfield of applied psychology that uses theories and research to design environmental settings—usually machines—to be safe, efficient, and/or pleasurable/708

engram the hypothesized physical basis of memory/282

environmental psychology the subfield of applied psychology concerned with the impact of the physical environment on people/720

equipotentiality the assumption that all responses are equally able to be learned/201

equity theory an explanation of relationships proposing that they persist when both people involved feel they are receiving in proportion to what they are giving/646

erogenous zones parts of the body that contain a rich concentration of receptors that provide sexual pleasure/688

erotica sexually arousing pictures or stories/679

estrogen female sex hormone/683

ethology field that studies animal behavior from a biological perspective, usually stressing instincts/88

eugenics a social movement based on the premise that the human species can and should be improved through the systematic application of the theory of evolution, for example, by encouraging biologically superior people to interbreed/316

evolution the changes that take place over time in the characteristics of a species/54

excitation   process by which one neuron induces a second neuron to fire/58

experience sampling   a research technique in which subjects carry a beeper that gives a signal at randomly determined intervals; when the signal goes off, subjects interrupt what they are doing and complete a questionnaire given to them by the researcher/478

experiment   a research strategy in which the researcher manipulates certain events and measures the effects of these manipulations on other events/32

experimental group   in experiments, the group of subjects exposed to the independent variable/33

experimental neurosis   abnormal behavior in animals produced in the laboratory by the manipulation of environmental conditions/497

extinction   in classical conditioning, the process by which a CS stops eliciting the CR, because the CS is no longer paired with the USC; in operant conditioning, the process by which the frequency of a response decreases because it is no longer followed by a reinforcer/180, 190

extrinsic motivation   pursuit of activities because of external reward or punishment/219

factor analysis   a statistical procedure for detecting patterns in a large set of correlations, used by personality researchers to identify the basic dimensions of personality/458

fallopian tubes   the tubes through which a female's eggs pass from her ovaries to her uterus/683

family resemblance   tendency of members of a natural concept to have a variety of characteristics in common, although none of these characteristics is necessary or sufficient to define the concept/292

family therapy   therapy in which a family as a whole is treated because of problems in the family relationship/565

fear disorders   disorders characterized by dread or apprehension linked to specific objects or situations, e.g., phobia/503

fear of success   the motive to avoid doing well because of the negative consequences that may follow/231

Fechner's Law   changes in sensation intensity are a function of changes in stimulus intensity, divided by the magnitude of the stimulus already present/108

fetal alcohol syndrome   a complex of deformities in the babies of alcoholic mothers/369

fetus   the term used to describe the developing unborn child from about the third month after conception until birth/369

field theory   the idea that people are self-regulating, dynamic systems that naturally seek out balance and harmony/587

figure-ground relationship   the tendency to organize perception in terms of a coherent object—the figure—within a context—the ground/138

fitness   the ability to reproduce successfully/83

fixation   in psychoanalytic theory, the failure to resolve a particular stage of psychosexual development, so that the concerns of that particular stage continue to dominate in adult personality/452

fixed-action patterns (instincts)   unlearned behaviors, common to an entire species, that occur in the presence of certain stimuli/88

flooding   behavior modification strategy that exposes a client to a feared object or situation; the fear presumably extinguishes/562

fluid intelligence   the ability to adapt to new situations/345

forebrain   the highest and newest layer of our brain/62

forgetting   the failure of memory/269

formal operations stage   Piaget's final stage of cognitive development, from age eleven through adulthood, characterized by the ability to think abstractly/387

forward conditioning   classical conditioning procedure in which the CS precedes the UCS in time/178

fovea   the central point in the retina where an image is focused, containing the densest arrangement of nerve cells/113

free association   a psychoanalytic technique for revealing unconscious conflicts by asking the patient to say whatever comes to mind, without attempting to censor it/557

frequency   the number of times that sound waves repeat themselves in a given period of time/117

frequency theory   theory of hearing proposing that sound waves of different frequencies cause neurons in the ear to fire at different frequencies/120

frontal lobe   cerebral hemisphere region located right behind the forehead/64

frustration-aggression hypothesis   a theory proposing that all aggression is a reaction to frustration: the failure to attain a desired goal/635

functional analysis the process of identifying reinforcers and punishers by observing actual behavior and its consequences/188

functional fixedness the tendency to persist in representing problems in a particular way, perhaps precluding an appropriate solution/296

functionalism an approach to psychology which emphasizes the function of thought: how one's mental abilities aid adaptation to the environment/12

fundamental attribution error our tendency when explaining someone's behavior to overlook the role played by situational factors/597

gate-control theory theory of pain proposing that we experience pain only when hypothesized gates in the spinal cord allow sensory signals to pass to the brain/125

gender differences psychological and social differences between males and females/380

gender identity disorder (transsexualism) a disorder in which an individual's gender identity is at odds with his or her biological sex/698

gender reassignment surgery sex-change operation, used as a treatment of transsexualism/699

gene the microscopic mechanism of inheritance, composed of DNA molecules, passed from parents to offspring/82

general adaptation syndrome (GAS) a sequence of physiological changes in response to continued stress: first an alarm reaction, then resistance, and finally exhaustion/250

general intelligence (g) Spearman's term for whatever underlies the tendency of different intelligence tests to correlate with each other/344

generalization (of learning) in classical conditioning, the process by which a new stimulus similar to the CS is able to elicit on its own the CR; in operant conditioning, the process by which an organism behaves in a new situation as it did in an old situation because the discriminative stimuli in the two settings are similar/180, 191

generalization (of research findings) the degree to which the findings from a given study apply to animals or people in general/26

generalized anxiety disorder diffuse and pervasive symptoms of anxiety/508

generate-and-recognize model theory of recall that proposes we generate possible answers to the memory task and then see if we recognize any of them/276

generation gap the differences in beliefs and values that supposedly exist between adults and adolescents, leading to lack of communication, contempt, and conflict/412

generativity according to Erik Erikson, concern for the next generation that is the focus of middle adulthood/408

genius an individual whose accomplishments exert a profound influence on contemporary and subsequent generations/339

genotype an individual's genetic inheritance; the blueprint for development provided by the genes/82

germ cell cell involved in reproduction—egg or sperm—that contains only one pair of chromosomes/82

gerontology an interdisciplinary approach to the study of aging that draws on psychology, biology, sociology, and other fields/431

gestalt organizational principles various ways of describing how we organize stimuli into coherent forms, first proposed by gestalt psychologists/139

gestalt psychology the psychological approach which suggests that our experiences are best described by focusing on the relationships among the elements of our consciousness, rather than the elements themselves/11

glans the erotically sensitive end of the penis/684

gonads reproductive glands: testes in the male and ovaries in the female/683

grammar the rules that allow language to be created and comprehended/294

group interacting individuals who mutually influence each other/650

group polarization the tendency of groups to polarize the initial inclinations of individuals, resulting in more extreme decisions than those reached by individuals alone/653

group therapy a form of therapy in which people with similar problems meet together with a therapist in order to facilitate change/565

groupthink the tendency of groups to suppress criticism and not consider alternatives, thus ending up with poor decisions/651

habituation a simple form of learning in which the organism stops paying attention to environmental stimuli that never change/173

hair cells cells in the cochlea which send neural impulses to the brain/120

hallucinations   sensations and perceptions with no basis in reality/527

hallucinogens   psychoactive drugs that produce hallucinations, including LSD, mescaline, and psilocybin/164

Hawthorne effect   the effect on one's behavior of knowingly participating in an experiment, above and beyond any particular experimental manipulations/713

health psychology   the subfield of applied psychology concerned with health and illness/717

helping alliance   the shared expectations of therapist and client that therapy will be helpful/550

heritability   the proportion of a trait's variation due to genetic factors/90

heterosexuals   individuals who direct the sex drive toward members of the opposite sex/687

heuristic   cognitive shortcut for solving a problem that often proves efficient and effective/298

hierarchy of needs   Maslow's notion that human needs can be arranged along a single dimension in which basic needs such as hunger must be satisfied before "higher" needs such as love or self-esteem/222

hindbrain   the lowest and oldest layer of our brain, consisting of most of the brain stem/62

homeostasis   maintenance of a stable or balanced state of physiological conditions/216

homophobia   irrational fear and prejudice that some people have concerning homosexuality/691

homosexuals   individuals who direct the sex drive toward members of the same sex/687

hormones   chemicals secreted by endocrine glands that are carried through the bloodstream to affect various bodily organs/71

hospice care   strategy for taking care of the terminally ill by directly involving the individual and the family in making decisions and providing hands-on care/437

hue   the psychological experience of the wavelength of light/110

humanism   a school of psychology emphasizing that people are inherently good and motivated toward growth/462

hypnosis   a state of consciousness characterized by heightened suggestibility/160

hypochondriasis   a somatoform disorder characterized by a preoccupation with having one or more serious illnesses, when all medical evidence is to the contrary/512

hypothalamus   part of the limbic system that links the autonomic nervous system and the endocrine system/64

hypotheses   tentative predictions that can be tested against observable evidence/2

icon   visual image that briefly lingers following the presentation of a stimulus/272

id   in psychoanalytic theory, that aspect of personality that is instinctive/450

ill-defined problems   problems with problem-spaces characterized by vagueness, without clearly specified initial and goal states/295

illness era   historical period during which psychopathology was interpreted as injury, illness, or defects within the body/495

illusions   phenomena in which our perceptions of objects are at odds with their actual characteristics/143

image   a cognitive representation much like perception except without an external stimulus/287

imprinting   an attachment, formed by ducklings and the young of some other species, to whatever moving object they first encounter; it occurs only during a critical period/377

in vitro fertilization   conception outside the womb; an egg cell and a sperm cell are obtained from a woman and a man, joined together in a test tube, and then the fertilized egg is transferred to the woman's uterus/678

inclusive fitness   the fitness of an individual plus the influence of the individual on relatives that share genes in common/84

independent variable   in experiments, the factor manipulated by the researcher/32

individual differences   the ways that people are characteristically themselves (and different from others)/447

industrial-organizational (IO) psychology   the subfield of applied psychology that uses theories and research to improve the functioning of complex work organizations/710

inferential statistics   statistics that allow conclusions beyond the immediate results of a particular study, specifically, whether or not results arose by chance/48

inferiority complex   Adler's concept that all people feel inadequate with respect to some aspect of their selves/453

information-processing   an approach to sensation, perception, and consciousness that stresses the sequence by which information is transformed ("processed") from environmental stimuli into psychological terms/135

inhibition process by which one neuron induces another neuron not to fire/58

insanity plea a legal defense that one is not guilty of a crime because of psychological abnormality at the time the crime was committed/547

insight a sudden understanding of the relationship among the parts of a problem, leading to a solution/204

instinctive drift the tendency of learned responses over time to take the form of an animal's instinctive behavior/202

instrumental conditioning another term for operant conditioning, to stress that responses are learned to the degree that they are instrumental (useful)/184

intelligence the capacity to act in adaptive and purposive ways/312

intelligence quotient (IQ) the ratio of one's mental age to one's chronological age, multiplied by 100 to eliminate decimals/320

intermittent reinforcement reinforcement that occurs only after some (not all) responses/193

internal reliability (consistency) the degree to which different items on the same test yield the same scores for an individual/475

interpretive control the ability to find meaning and significance in uncontrollable events in order to buffer the negative consequences of these events/603

intoxication alteration in consciousness following ingestion of a psychoactive drug/163

intrinsic motivation pursuit of activities when there is no external reward for doing so/218

introspection a method of identifying the contents of thought through the precise reporting of one's mental experiences/10

introversion-extraversion according to Eysenck, a basic factor of personality that reflects whether one is generally oriented inward (introversion) or outward (extraversion)/458

iris the colored band around the pupil that responds reflexively to light levels, changing the size of the pupil/111

irrational beliefs according to Albert Ellis, the rigid beliefs entertained by people that produce difficulties for them/560

James-Lange theory of emotion the theory that people's perceptions of their physiological re-

sponses in a particular situation constitute emotion/235

job analysis a detailed description of the skills and abilities needed to perform successfully at a given job/710

just noticeable difference (jnd) unit used for comparing difference thresholds; for a given sensory system, one jnd is the same as the difference threshold/105

kinesthetic sense the sensory system that responds to the position and movement of body parts relative to each other/126

labia the folds of skin that surround a female's urethral and vaginal openings/684

language acquisition device (LAD) Chomsky's hypothesized neural mechanism that allows children to acquire language readily/390

latent content according to Freud, the underlying meaning and significance of dreams/157

lateralization the organization of the brain on a left-right basis/66

law of effect Thorndike's principle of learning: responses that lead to a reward are strengthened, and those that do not are weakened/185

learned helplessness learning that responses and outcomes are unrelated in one situation and generalizing this learning to a new situation, where passivity results/195

learning a relatively permanent change in behavior resulting from experience/172

lens the structure in the eye directly behind the iris that changes its shape in order to focus images/111

lesion a cut or incision in the brain/72

levels of processing model of memory theory of memory that assumes there is only one type of memory in which information is processed to varying depths/271

libido in psychoanalytic theory, psychological energy that motivates behavior/448

life instinct (Eros) according to Freud, our instinct for self-preservation and sexual gratification/451

lifespace according to Lewin, the total of all forces acting upon a person at a given time/588

life-structure the unique way people combine the various roles they play (at work, at home, in the community) at any given time/411

light radiant energy that travels in an oscillating pattern of waves/109

limbic system a collection of small structures in the brain, including the amygdala, septum, and hippocampus/63

linear ordering cognitive representation of elements structured in some order/288

localization of function doctrine that particular capacities, like memory or language, are located within specific parts of the brain/66

lock-and-key theory theory of smell which proposes that different sites on smell receptors have characteristic shapes into which only certain molecules fit, thereby triggering appropriate smells/123

locus of control one's expectancy about where rewards originate, from within oneself (internal locus of control) or from without (external locus of control)/465

long-term memory the stage of memory into which information passes from the short-term memory, so named because information here represents our permanent storehouse of past experiences/274

longitudinal studies research strategies that study the same individuals over a long period of time/362

loudness the psychological experience of the intensity of sound/117

malleus, incus, and stapes (hammer, anvil, and stirrup) three small bones in the middle ear that transmit vibrations from the eardrum to the oval window/120

mania excessive and inappropriate elation, an expansive mood, inflated self-esteem, talkativeness, increased activity, and agitation/519

manifest content according to Freud, the images and events in dreams of which the dreamer is aware/157

marital therapy a form of therapy in which a married couple is treated as a unit because of problems in the relationship/564

mass action doctrine that opposes localization of function, holding that the brain acts as a whole/68

matching model hypothesis the idea that therapists and clients work best together when they possess the same personality characteristics/550

matching phenomenon the tendency for husbands and wives to be of comparable attractiveness/646

maturation inherent growth processes considered critical to a person's physical or psychological development/361

medial forebrain bundle (MFB) group of neurons connecting the midbrain and the forebrain, involved in pleasure and reward/75

meditation a strategy for altering consciousness through relaxation and a refocusing of attention/159

medulla the part of the brain stem directly connected to the spinal cord that controls respiration and cardiac function/62

memory our mental representation of knowledge/263

menarche a female's first menstruation/415

menopause the cessation of menstruation and the ability to conceive, occurring in a woman's late forties or early fifties/433, 683

mental age the average intelligence test scores of children of a given age; if your mental age is eight, you score on a test the way an average eight-year-old child scores/319

mental maps cognitive representations of physical place/288

mental processes occurrences within someone's mind, like hopes and dreams, thoughts and beliefs, wishes and fears, that are not observable by others/2

mental retardation below average intellectual functioning existing along with deficits in adaptive behavior and showing itself before age eighteen/333

mere exposure phenomenon the tendency to like stimuli the more one is exposed to them, even when conscious recognition does not take place/254

meta-analysis a statistical technique for combining the results of separate studies and arriving at an overall conclusion about the magnitude of an experimental effect/574

metacognition awareness of oneself as a cognitive being/296

midbrain the middle layer of our brain, consisting of the upper part of the brain stem/62

midlife crisis a critical period of life, around age forty, marked by the confrontation of one's mortality, and heightened concern regarding the meaning of one's identity and career and the significance of one's primary relationships/413

mindlessness one's reliance on social scripts to such an extent that the details of social interaction escape notice/600

mnemonics strategies and techniques for facilitating memory/280

modeling (observational learning) learning by observing the behavior of others/199

mood disorders problems marked primarily by disturbances of one's emotions/515

moral development the process by which one develops a system of judgments about the rightness or wrongness of acts/393

moral dilemma a situation requiring a person to make a moral decision and justify it/394

motivated unconscious the psychoanalytic idea that memories threatening to one's conscious mind are actively kept out of awareness/149

motivation the processes that arouse, direct, and maintain our behavior/213

motor development the process by which children become more skilled at using their bodies/372

multiple intelligences Gardner's idea that intelligence should be described as several sets of biologically based problem-solving skills/348

multiple personality disorder a dissociative disorder in which a person experiences two or more distinct personalities, each of which takes control of a person's thoughts, feelings, and actions at a given time/514

multistore model of memory theory of memory that assumes memories are represented (stored) in several different ways/270

myelin a white fatty substance that covers some axons, protecting them and allowing them to send their messages more rapidly/57

myth of mental illness the argument by Thomas Szasz that psychopathology represents not a disease but rather a problem in living/492

natural concepts concepts without necessary and sufficient conditions/291

natural selection Charles Darwin's theory of evolution: species change in the direction of characteristics that lead to successful reproduction/81

nature-nurture controversy a long-standing debate central to the field of psychology that concerns whether our development is due to biological inheritance (nature) or learning and experience (nurture)/4

need the lack of some biological essential, like food or water/216

need for mastery the need to interact in a competent way with the environment/233

negative afterimage perceptual phenomenon in which one stares at an object of one color, quickly looks away, and sees an image of the "opposite" color/116

negative reinforcement the process by which the removal of a stimulus increases the frequency of some behavior that it follows; *not* the same as punishment/187

neo-Freudians psychoanalytic theorists who followed Freud and stressed the social character of people over their instinctive, sexually motivated nature/454

neurons the basic units of the nervous system, individual nerve cells/54

neurotic disorders disorders in which the person's reality testing is not impaired, e.g., phobia/502

neuroticism according to Eysenck, a basic factor of personality that reflects the degree to which one is moody, nervous, and unstable/458

neurotransmitter chemical secreted by a neuron that affects other neurons/58

NMR (nuclear magnetic resonance scanning) a technique for forming an image of the brain by detecting magnetic patterns/78

non-REM sleep stages of sleep during which rapid eye movements do not occur/153

nonfalsifiable explanation an explanation that cannot be proven wrong by any evidence/7

nonsense syllables sets of letters with no inherent meaning, used by psychologists to study memory/269

norm a shared expectation about appropriate and inappropriate behavior for some role/599

norms standards based on large samples of people that allow an individual to be compared to them/318, 361

obedience complying with the explicit instructions of someone in a position of authority/632

object permanence in the sensorimotor stage of cognitive development, the knowledge that objects exist when out of one's sight/386

objective tests measures from which personality scores are assigned according to explicit rules/474

obsessions recurring and persistent thoughts that one finds upsetting/510

obsessive-compulsive disorder an anxiety disorder characterized by obsessions and compulsions/510

occipital lobe cerebral hemisphere region located at the rear of the brain/64

Oedipus complex the psychoanalytic hypothesis that children experience sexual desire for their opposite-sex parent and resentment toward their same-sex parent/452

ontogeny changes that take place within the lifetime of an individual/85

operant any behavior that is emitted spontaneously, occurring at some frequency in the absence of specific environmental triggers/184

operant chamber apparatus used to study operant conditioning; typically it has a lever or button to be pushed by the organism and a mechanism for delivering reinforcement (like food) or punishment (like shock); also called a Skinner box/186

operant conditioning a basic form of learning in which a response is associated with its consequences; the response becomes more likely in the future if followed by a reinforcer and less likely if followed by a punisher; sometimes called instrumental conditioning/184

operation according to Piaget, one or more mental processes that transform and manipulate information/384

operational definition a concrete measure of an abstract concept/22

opponent-process color theory theory that proposes two systems for color vision, each composed of a pair of colors that "oppose" each other/116

opponent-process theory the theory that the experience of a positive or negative emotion sets off an opposing process, negative or positive, to restore homeostasis/241

optic nerve the nerve leading from the eye directly to the brain/113

organic amnesia extensive memory loss following physical damage or an injury to the brain/280

organization an enduring and organized group/650

orientation the process by which we position our sense organs so that they can best receive stimulation/136

ova female eggs, produced in the ovaries/683

oval window membrane that focuses sound waves and makes the fluid in the cochlea move/120

ovaries a female's gonads, which secrete sex hormones and produce eggs/683

pacinian corpuscle specialized receptor in the skin sensitive to touch/123

pain aversive sensation associated with overstimulation of any sensory system/125

panic disorder an anxiety disorder marked by the recurrence of sudden and extreme attacks of anxiety/509

parallel processing information processing of stimuli simultaneously/267

paraphilias "inappropriate" sexual objects or sexual aims/696

parasympathetic nervous system the part of the autonomic nervous system that serves an inhibitory role/56

parent training behavior modification strategy in which parents are explicitly instructed how to respond to their children to encourage desired behaviors and discourage undesired behaviors/563

parietal lobe cerebral hemisphere region found behind the frontal lobe and in front of the occipital lobe/64

partial reinforcement effect the tendency of responses that are reinforced intermittently to resist extinction/193

passionate love intense and tumultuous love for another, in which we become enveloped in the other person, sexually excited in his or her presence, and miserable in his or her absence/246

peace psychology the subfield of applied psychology concerned with reducing international conflict and encouraging peace/723

peer pressure the legitimization by one's peers of particular activities/420

penis the cylindrically shaped male organ through which semen and urine are secreted/684

perception the transformation of sensory information into psychological terms meaningful to the observer/101, 134

perceptual defense phenomenon of taking longer to recognize offensive or threatening stimuli than to recognize neutral stimuli/150

perceptual set (mental set) a predisposition to perceive a particular stimulus in a particular context/147

peripheral nervous system the part of the nervous system that links the CNS to our senses, glands, and muscles/55

permissive parenting style of raising children that is loving but lax; permissive parents exert little control over their children/380

person-role merger the process of identifying with the role assigned in some group so strongly that one literally becomes that role/629

personal construct theory Kelly's theory of personality that stresses how people think about events/461

personal control someone's belief concerning whether or not he can exert control over events in his world/598

personal traits characteristics that sensibly describe only some people/456

personality aspects of a person that are general, characteristic, enduring, integrated, and functional/444

personality assessment the measurement of individual differences in personality/447

personality disorders pervasive styles of behaving that can both exacerbate a clinical syndrome and create difficulties in their own right/530

personality inventory a set of objective tests that measures a range of individual differences/475

personology a term sometimes used to describe personality psychology, conveying the idea that the field concerns itself with the person as a whole/444

persuasive communications messages explicitly designed to change attitudes/610

PET scan (positron emission tomography) a technique for forming an image of the brain by ascertaining levels of metabolic activity/77

phenomenological (cognitive) approach a strategy for explaining personality that looks at the characteristic contents and processes of one's thinking/460

phenotype an individual's actual characteristics, produced by one's genotype in combination with the environment/182

pheromones chemicals secreted by animals (and possibly humans) for communication with other members of their species/688

phobia a fear disorder marked by persistent avoidance of some object or situation/505

photoreceptors the nerve cells contained in the retina that are sensitive to light/111

phylogenetic scale arrangement of species from primitive to advanced; not sensible when the species in question are contemporaries/85

phylogeny changes that take place within the evolution of a species/85

physical development the processes of bodily change and growth/367

pinna the outer ear/119

pitch the psychological experience of the frequency of sound/117

pituitary gland endocrine gland located at the base of the brain that controls the secretions of many other glands/72

place theory theory of hearing proposing that sound waves of different frequencies affect different locations along the basilar membrane/120

pluralistic ignorance a reason why bystanders may fail to intervene in an emergency: everyone uses each other's inaction as a clue that it is not an emergency/642

polygenic inheritance the determination of characteristics by several genes working in combination; for people, polygenic inheritance is the rule rather than the exception/83

polygraph lie detection device which actually measures physiological arousal/237

pons link between the hindbrain and the rest of the brain, thought to be involved in sleep and arousal/62

population the larger group to which a researcher wishes to generalize from a study of a particular sample/26

pornography sexually oriented material that both arouses and offends/680

positive reinforcement the process by which the presentation of a stimulus increases the frequency of some behavior that it follows/187

postconventional reasoning Kohlberg's third and last stage of moral development, in which the adult recognizes that society's rules may conflict with each other, and so he must apply his own abstract standards/394

post-traumatic stress disorder a fear disorder characterized by the reexperiencing of a traumatic event, avoidance of reminders of the original trauma, diminished interest in activities, and various signs of anxiety/507

power motivation the need to have an impact on others, to be in charge of people and situations/232

preconscious material not in conscious awareness that is readily available/149

preconscious thoughts and feelings of which we can become aware voluntarily/449

preconventional reasoning Kohlberg's first stage of moral development, in which the child can take into account only rewards and punishments/394

prejudice prejudging a person solely on the basis of the group to which that person belongs/637

preoperational stage Piaget's second stage of cognitive development, from two to six years of age, characterized by symbolic thinking and egocentrism/386

prepared learning readily acquired learning presumably made easy by evolution/202

primary colors red, green, and blue; lights of these colors can be combined to produce all other colors/115

primary motives biologically based motives like hunger, thirst, and sex/213

primary reinforcers stimuli that serve as reinforcers because of their inherent biological properties/191

proactive interference a cause of forgetting, when previously learned material gets in the way of remembering subsequently learned material/279

problem a discrepancy between what we know and what we want to know/295

problem-space cognitive representation of a problem, consisting of an initial state, a desired goal state, and the admissible steps that allow the problem-solver to get from the one to the other/295

process loss the inevitable inefficiency of groups/653

prodigy a child who shows a special skill or talent far advanced of those considered normal for his or her age/336

projective techniques measures that present people with ambiguous stimuli onto which they "project" their personality in responding/472

propositional network a depiction of meaning in terms of logical relationships among words/289

prosocial behavior actions associated with people helping one another/641

prototype a typical member of some category/292, 593

proximate causation the direct mechanism bringing about a biological phenomenon/84

psychoactive drugs chemicals that alter consciousness through changes in brain activity/162

psychoactive substance dependence a cluster of cognitive, behavioral, and physiological symptoms that indicate impaired control over drug use/522

psychoanalysis an approach to psychology, introduced by Sigmund Freud, that stresses the role of unconscious conflict in human behavior; also, a strategy for explaining personality that stresses psychological energy and how it motivates our behavior; and finally, an approach to therapy that attempts to identify one's unconscious conflicts and free up the psychological energy invested in them/15, 557

psychoanalytic model approach that explains abnormality as due to unconscious conflicts often rooted in childhood experiences/492

psychogenic amnesia a dissociative disorder in which a sudden inability to recall important personal information follows a psychological trauma/513

psychogenic fugue a dissociative disorder in which a partial or total loss of one's memory is accompanied by leaving home and establishing a new identity/514

psychological era historical period during which psychopathology was interpreted as learned behavior/496

psychological therapies (psychotherapies) techniques and strategies for therapy that intervene psychologically/540

psychology the scientific study of behavior and mental processes/2

psychophysics the field of psychology concerned with the relationship between physical stimuli and psychological experience/102

psychosexual stages according to Freud, developmental stages in which a child's instinctive needs are satisfied through stimulation of different parts of the body/362

psychosocial stages according to Erikson, distinct stages in life that are marked by a particular social conflict; each conflict must be satisfactorily resolved in order for a person to progress through subsequent stages/363

psychosomatic medicine a field of medicine concerned with how psychological states contribute to physical illnesses/250

psychosurgery surgery undertaken on the brain in an attempt to treat psychological problems/551

psychotic disorders disorders in which the person is considered out of touch with reality, e.g., schizophrenia/502

puberty the physical changes that accompany adolescence, specifically, the maturation of one's reproductive system and the development of one's secondary sexual characteristics/683

punishment the process by which a stimulus follows a response and reduces the future likelihood of that response; *not* the same as negative reinforcement/187

pupil opening in the iris that changes size in relation to the amount of available light/111

purity the degree to which light is dominated by a single wavelength/111

quasi-rationality the mixture of rationality and irrationality that characterizes cognition/299

random assignment in experiments, the process of assigning research subjects to different groups on a random basis, so that all subjects have an equal chance to be exposed to the different conditions created by the experimenter/33

rape   the perpetration of a sexual act against an unwilling victim/678

rape trauma syndrome   a typical victim's reaction to rape, characterized by an acute reaction involving excessive emotionality or excessive numbness and a long-term post-traumatic stress reaction/679

rational-emotive therapy   an approach to therapy pioneered by Albert Ellis in which the client's irrational beliefs are actively disputed/560

rationalism   philosophical doctrine that knowledge is inborn/101

realistic job preview   job interview procedure in which the applicant is given a realistic view of what a job entails/711

recall   the retrieval of information from memory without being provided explicit clues/275

receptor   neuron that receives stimulation from the environment/60

recessive gene   the member of a pair of genes that does not determine one's phenotype when a dominant gene is present/82

recognition   the realization that certain information presented to us looks familiar/275

reference group   the group of individuals to which one compares one's values, attitudes, and beliefs/419, 629

reflexes   automatic, coordinated, and unlearned reactions in which an external event leads to a response/60, 176, 371

refractory period (with respect to neural firing)   interval following the firing of a neuron during which it cannot fire again/58

refractory period (with respect to sexuality)   interval following an orgasm during which another orgasm by the male is not possible/686

reinforcement   the process by which the frequency of behavior is increased because of changes in the environment that follow its occurrence/187

reinforcers   changes in the environment that follow some behavior and increase the probability that it will recur/187

reliability   consistency in research results: on each occasion that particular measures are used, they yield the same results/24

REM sleep   rapid eye movement sleep; period of sleep during which the eyes move rapidly beneath closed lids; particularly vivid dreaming occurs during REM sleep/154

representativeness heuristic   basing judgments of likelihood on the degree to which the particular instance resembles a general class/299

repression   the process by which threatening thoughts and feelings are kept out of one's awareness/449

resistance   according to psychoanalytic theory, the tendency of a client in therapy to resist the progress of therapy because unconscious conflicts are too painful to confront/557

resting potential   the difference in electrical charge between the inside and outside of a neuron at rest/279

reticular formation   the core of the brain stem; it controls one's general level of arousal and mode of consciousness/63

retina   the structure at the back of the eye which is lined with nerve cells/111

retrieval   the process by which information is located in our memory and then used/269

retroactive interference   a cause of forgetting, when subsequently learned material gets in the way of remembering previously learned material/279

rods   cylinder-shaped photoreceptors responsible for vision in dim light and sensations without color/111

rule   a cognitive representation that allows instances to be generated/294

rules   abstract guidelines about how to behave in certain situations/205

sample   the actual group of research subjects investigated in a study/26

saturation   the psychological experience of the purity of light/111

savants   individuals with a singular skill or ability in the context of general subnormality/342

schedules of reinforcement   different patterns of delivering reinforcers following the desired response/193

schema   an organized set of information about some concept/290, 593

scheme   Piaget's term for any organized mental structure that represents knowledge/385

schizophrenia   a disorder characterized by psychotic symptoms such as delusions, hallucinations, inappropriate emotions, and unusual thinking, and accompanied by impaired social or occupational functioning/526

scientific method   the systematic procedures used by scientists to check explanations against evidence/3

script beliefs about the appropriate sequence of social events/600

seasonal affective disorder recurrent episodes of depression that worsen in the fall and improve in the spring, thought to be due to the amount of light to which one is exposed/556

second-order (higher-order) conditioning pairing of a neutral stimulus with a conditioned stimulus so that the neutral stimulus becomes a conditioned stimulus in its own right/181

secondary (conditioned) reinforcers stimuli that serve as reinforcers because they have been previously associated with primary reinforcers; see primary reinforcers/191

selective attention ignoring some information while paying attention to other information/137

self-actualization the full use of one's talents and abilities/223

self-perception theory hypothesis proposed by Daryl Bem that we infer our attitudes from watching our own behavior/606

self-serving bias our attributional tendency to take credit for successes but not failures/597

self-theory Carl Rogers's explanation of personality in terms of how people view themselves/462

senility the widespread loss of cognitive abilities, commonly caused by Alzheimer's disease/434

sensate focus sex therapy technique in which sexual partners concentrate on giving each other pleasure and not on intercourse/695

sensation the transformation of environmental stimulation into neural impulses/101

sensorimotor stage Piaget's first stage of cognitive development, from birth to about two years of age, characterized by advances in motor development and object permanence/385

sensory memory also called sensory register; the first stage of memory, a brief but faithful version of our sensory experiences/271

septum part of the limbic system that seems to lessen responses of rage and aggression/64

serial position effect when a series of items has been memorized, one's tendency to remember items from the beginning and end of the series better than items in the middle/270

serial processing information processing of stimuli one at a time/267

set-point theory the idea that our bodies work to maintain a certain level of body fat (the set point)/227

sex differences physical differences between males and females/369

sexual aim what one wishes to do with a sexual object/687

sexual dysfunction a problem that takes place during the sequence of a person's sexual response/694

sexual object a person or thing that one finds sexually attractive/687

sexual orientation one's sexual object and sexual aim together/686

sexual revolution the time in the 1960s and 1970s when American society took an extremely liberal stance concerning sexuality/671

sexually transmitted diseases (STD) diseases spread mainly through sexual contact, such as gonorrhea, syphilis, and genital herpes/674

shaping the process by which simple responses gradually become more complex through changing the standard of reinforcement on successive occasions/189

short-term memory the stage of memory into which information passes from the sensory memory, so named because information stays there for no more than 20 seconds/272

signal detection theory theory which assumes that people detect stimuli through a process of decision making in which they attempt to separate a stimulus (or signal) from background noise/106

simultaneous conditioning classical conditioning procedure in which the CS and the UCS occur at the same time/179

sleep spindles bursts of brain activity associated with Stage 2 sleep/153

social analogue a social psychology research technique that creates in the experimental laboratory a simple version of a complex social phenomenon/626

social cognition the cognitive representations and processes that people use in making sense of the social world/583

social comparison our tendency to evaluate our own skills, attitudes, values, and so on by comparing them to those of others, usually people similar to ourselves/644

social Darwinism the application of the theory of natural selection to human societies as a whole/88

social development the process by which a child develops attitudes, values, and roles/374

social influence all the ways that other people may affect the social behavior of an individual/622

social learning approach   a strategy for explaining personality that emphasizes the role of one's environment and learning/464

social loafing   our tendency to work less hard when in a group than when alone/651

social perception   the way we come to know about other people and ourselves/593

social psychology   the field of psychology that studies people as social beings, in particular, how the thoughts, feelings, and actions of individuals are influenced by the presence of others/583

social support   the providing of interpersonal resources to those in need of them/623

sociobiology   the application of modern evolutionary theory, particularly the notion of inclusive fitness, to social behavior/90

sociocultural retardation   mental retardation not linked to specific physical causes but instead to social disadvantages/335

somatic nervous system   the part of the peripheral nervous system that controls our skeletal muscles and sense organs/55

somatoform disorders   disorders characterized by physical symptoms that have no basis in physiology/511

specific hungers   a desire for foods containing substances in which an organism is deficient/227

specific intelligence (s)   Spearman's term for factors that influence performance on particular intelligence tests but not others/344

split-brain patients   individuals who have had the connections between the two cerebral hemispheres surgically severed in an attempt to reduce epileptic seizures/66

spontaneous recovery   in classical conditioning, the reappearance of a response some time after it has been extinguished; in operant conditioning, the reappearance of an operant some time after it has been extinguished/180, 190

sports psychology   the subfield of applied psychology concerned with physical performance, usually in the context of competitive athletics/718

state-dependent recall   the tendency to recall information better when in the psychological or biological state during which it was originally encoded/278

states of consciousness   forms of consciousness experienced as qualitatively different from one another/147

statistically significant results   a pattern of findings unlikely to have occurred by chance/48

stereotype   a rigid and overly simple belief about members of a social group/594

stimulants   psychoactive drugs that increase an individual's alertness, such as caffeine, nicotine, and cocaine/163

stimulus   any environmental event that produces a response in an organism/101

storage   the process by which information is kept in our memory/269

stress   the complex reactions that take place when someone tries to adapt to the demands of external events/214

stressors   events that threaten or challenge the individual (produce stress)/214

strong methods   approaches to solving problems in which a person knows exactly how to proceed/295

structuralism   the psychological approach which proposes that psychology is the science of consciousness, and experience its subject matter/10

superego   in psychoanalytic theory, that aspect of personality that represents the internalization of societal values; our conscience/450

supernatural era   historical period during which psychopathology was interpreted according to beliefs about magic/494

superordinate goal   a goal shared by two groups; when pursued together, it reduces conflict between the groups/724

surrogate motherhood   a woman conceiving, bearing, and delivering the child of a fertile man, then relinquishing the child to the man and his wife/678

survey   a study that chooses people at random from some larger group and poses them questions; their answers are considered representative of the responses of the larger group (e.g., political polls)/591

sympathetic nervous system   the part of the autonomic nervous system that serves an excitatory role/56

synapse   the gap between the axon of one neuron and the dendrite of another into which neurotransmitters are secreted/58

systematic desensitization   behavior modification strategy that teaches a client to relax and then to imagine a feared object or situation, thus reducing anxiety/562

systems theory   an approach to understanding families and other social groups that regards them as complex and interdependent wholes/565

taste aversion the avoidance of a food because it was previously associated with illness/201

taste buds receptors located on the tongue and elsewhere in the mouth that are responsible for taste/121

telegraphic speech brief sentences, consisting of a noun and verb only, that a child usually starts to say between eighteen and twenty-four months of age/391

temperament a biologically based style of interacting with the world/373

temporal lobe cerebral hemisphere region near the temple/64

terminal buttons the end of an axon where chemicals are secreted that influence other neurons/57

test-retest reliability the degree to which a test gives the same score to an individual on different occasions/474

testes a male's gonads, which secrete sex hormones and produce sperm/683

testosterone male sex hormone/683

thalamus part of the forebrain that relays input from the senses to higher structures/64

Thematic Apperception Test (TAT) A set of ambiguous pictures about which research subjects tell stories, used to infer the strength of one's needs/221

theories general explanations from which hypotheses are derived/2

therapy the treatment of people who have psychological disorders by psychologists and other mental health professionals/540

theta waves brain waves that cycle between 3 and 5 times per second, associated with Stage 1 sleep/153

timbre the sharpness or clarity of a tone; its quality/119

tip-of-the-tongue phenomenon the experience of knowing we have a given memory but being unable to retrieve it/277

tolerance the need to take more and more of a psychoactive drug to produce the same effect/163

top-down information processing information processing in which simple aspects are influenced by more complex ones/267

trait a stable and pervasive individual difference with a biological and psychological basis that initiates and guides diverse behavior/456

trait approach a strategy for explaining personality that classifies people in terms of their stable and general individual differences/455

transduction the process by which external energy produces a neural impulse in a sensory receptor/102

transference the tendency of a client to relate to his therapist as he has related to other important individuals in his life/549

transformational grammar Chomsky's theory that language results from people transforming meanings represented in the deep structure of language/389

triarchic theory Sternberg's theory of intelligence that stresses (a) the context of intelligent behavior, (b) the tasks that most readily show intelligence, and (c) the cognitive operations that lead to intelligent behavior/346

trichromatic color theory theory of color vision that proposes there are three types of cones, sensitive respectively to red, green, and blue wavelengths/115

twin studies procedures for estimating the relative contributions of heredity and the environment to some characteristic; in studying intelligence, the resemblance in IQ's of identical twins is compared with the resemblance in IQ's of fraternal twins/328

two-factor theory of emotion Schacter and Singer's theory that emotions result first from a state of general physiological arousal and second from a cognitive label placed on this arousal/238

Type A behavior pattern a set of behaviors characterized by time urgency, competitiveness, and hostility, linked to increased risk for heart disease/251

typology a personality classification scheme comprised of presumably basic and discrete types of people/444

ultimate causation the contribution of a biological phenomenon to fitness/84

unconditional regard acceptance of people regardless of what they think or feel or do/463

unconditioned response (UCR) in classical conditioning, the response reflexively produced by a stimulus (the UCS)/177

unconditioned stimulus (UCS) in classical conditioning, the stimulus that produces a response as a reflex/176

unconscious thoughts and feelings of which we cannot become aware because they are threatening to us in some way/449

unprepared learning learning presumably made neither easy nor hard by evolution/202

uterus a hollow, muscular organ in a woman's abdomen where the fetus develops until birth/684

vagina the lower part of the uterus, through which menstrual discharge occurs, children are born, and a penis is accommodated during intercourse/684

validity the degree to which a research study measures what it purports to measure/25

value an enduring belief about the desirability of a particular goal/601

variability the variation in a particular variable/46

vestibular sense the sensory system that responds to the position of the body relative to gravity, and is thus responsible for balance/126

vigilance deployment of attention to the same stimuli for long periods of time/107

visual constancies the tendencies for our perception of the size, shape, and brightness of objects to stay the same even as the moment-to-moment stimulation from the environment changes/142

visual pigments the chemicals in photoreceptors that change when exposed to light/113

vitreous humor the fluid contained in the eyeball/111

vulva a collective term for the external genitals of the female/684

wavelength the distance between peaks of two successive waves of light/110

weak methods approaches to solving problems in which a person does not know exactly how to procceed/295

Weber's law mathematical formula expressing the idea that the larger the standard stimulus, the more another stimulus must differ from it in order for this difference to be detectable/105

well-defined problems problems with clearly specified initial and goal states/295

withdrawal alteration in consciousness following cessation or reduction of drug use/163

work-sample tests job selection procedure in which prospective workers are asked to perform tasks similar to those involved in the actual job/713

zygote the single cell created by the union of a sperm cell and ovum/368

References

Abelson, R. P. (1972). Are attitudes necessary? In B. T. King & E. McGinnies (Eds.), *Attitudes, conflict, and social change.* New York: Academic Press.

Abelson, R. P., Aronson, E., McGuire, W. J., Nemcomb, T. M., Rosenberg, M. J., & Tannenbaum, P. H. (1968). *Theories of cognitive consistency: A sourcebook.* Chicago: Rand McNally.

Abrahams, J. P., et al. (1978). Sex role self-concept and sex role attitudes: Enduring personality characteristics or adaptations to changing life situations? *Developmental Psychology, 14,* 393–400.

Abramowitz, S. I., & Murray, J. (1983). Race effects in psychotherapy. In J. Murray & P. R. Abramson (Eds.), *Bias in psychotherapy.* New York: Praeger.

Abramson, L. Y., Seligman, M. E. P., & Teasdale, J. D. (1978). Learned helplessness in humans: Critique and reformulation. *Journal of Abnormal Psychology, 87,* 49–74.

Abravanel, E., & Sigafoos, A. D. (1984). Exploring the presence of imitation during early infancy. *Child Development, 55,* 381–392.

Achenbach, T. M. (1986). Developmental perspectives on psychotherapy and behavior change. In S. L. Garfield & A. E. Bergin (Eds.), *Handbook of psychotherapy and behavior change* (3rd ed.). New York: Wiley.

Adelson, J. (1979). Adolescence and the generalization gap. *Psychology Today, 12*(9), 33–37.

Ader, R., & Cohen, N. (1981). Conditioned immunopharmacological responses. In R. Ader (Ed.), *Psychoneuroimmunology.* New York: Academic Press.

Adler, A. (1910). Inferiority feeling and defiance and obedience. In H. L. Ansbacher & R. R. Ansbacher (1964) (Eds.), *The individual psychology of Aldred Adler.* New York: Harper.

Adler, A. (1927). *The practice and theory of individual psychology.* New York: Harcourt, Brace, & World.

Adorno, T. W., Frenkel-Brunswik, E., Levinson, D., & Sanford, N. (1950). *The authoritarian personality.* New York: Harper.

Ainsworth, M. D. S. (1973). The development of infant-mother attachment. In B. M. Caldwell & H. N. Ricciuti (Eds.), *Review of child development research* (Vol. 3). Chicago: University of Chicago Press.

Ainsworth, M. D. S., & Wittig, B. A. (1969). Attachment and exploratory behavior of one-year-olds in a strange situation. In B. M. Foss (Ed.), *Determinants of infant behavior* (Vol. 4). London: Methuen.

Akiskal, H. S., & McKinney, W. T. (1975). Overview of recent research in depression. *Archives of General Psychiatry, 32,* 285–305.

Albert, D. J., & Walsh, M. L. (1984). Neural systems and the inhibitory modulation of agonistic behavior: A comparison of mammalian species. *Neuroscience and Biobehavioral Reviews, 8,* 5–24.

Alcalay, R. (1983). The impact of mass communication campaigns in the health field. *Social Science and Medicine, 17,* 87–94.

Alexander, F. (1950). *Psychosomatic medicine: Its principles and applications.* New York: Norton.

Alexander, R. D. (1979). *Darwinism and human affairs.* Seattle: University of Washington Press.

Allport, F. H. (1924). *Social Psychology.* Boston: Houghton Mifflin.

Allport, G. W. (1937). *Personality: A psychological interpretation.* New York: Holt.

Allport, G. W. (1942). *The use of personal documents in psychological science.* New York: Social Science Research Council.

Allport, G. W. (1954). *The nature of prejudice.* Cambridge, MA: Addison-Wesley.

Allport, G. W. (1961). *Pattern and growth in personality.* New York: Holt, Rinehart, & Winston.

Allport, G. W. (1968). The historical background of modern social psychology. In G. Lindzey & E. Aronson (Eds.), *The handbook of social psychology* (2nd ed., Vol. 1). Reading, MA: Addison-Wesley.

Allport, G. W., & Odbert, H. S. (1936). Trait-names: A psycho-lexical study. *Psychological Monographs, 47* (Whole No. 211), 171–220.

Allport, G. W., Vernon, P. E., & Lindzey, G. (1960). *A study of values* (Rev. ed.). Boston: Houghton Mifflin.

Allport, S. (1986). *Explorers of the black box: The search for the cellular basis of memory.* New York: Norton.

American Psychiatric Association. (1968). *Diagnostic and statistical manual of mental disorders* (2nd ed.). Washington, D.C.: author.

American Psychiatric Association. (1987). *Diagnostic and statistical manual of mental disorders* (3rd ed., Rev.). Washington, D.C.: author.

American Psychological Association. (1981). *Ethical principles of psychologists.* Washington, D.C.: author.

Ames, A. (1951). Visual perception. *Psychological Monographs, 65*(14, Whole No. 324).

Amoore, J. E. (1964). Current status of the steric theory of odor. *Annals of the New York Academy of Science, 116,* 457–476.

Anastasi, A. (1971). Note on the concepts of creativity and intelligence. *Journal of Creative Behavior, 5,* 113–116.

Anastasi, A. (1979). *Fields of applied psychology* (2nd ed.). New York: McGraw Hill.

Anderson, C. A., & Anderson, D. C. (1984). Ambient temperature and violent crime: Tests of the linear and curvilinear hypothesis. *Journal of Personality and Social Psychology, 46,* 91–97.

Anderson, J. R. (1985). *Cognitive psychology and its implications* (2nd ed.). New York: Freeman.

Andreasen, N. C. (1984). *The broken brain: The biological revolution in psychiatry.* New York: Harper & Row.

Anthony, E. J., & Cohler, B. J. (Eds.) (1987). *The invulnerable child.* New York: Guilford.

Antonovsky, A. (1979). *Health, stress, and coping.* San Francisco: Jossey-Bass.

Antonovsky, A. (1988). *Unraveling the mystery of health.* San Francisco: Jossey-Bass.

Appel, J. (1963). Aversive effects of a schedule of positive reinforcement. *Journal of the Experimental Analysis of Behavior, 6,* 423–428.

Arafat, I. S., & Cotton, W. L. (1974). Masturbation practices of males and females. *Journal of Sex Research, 10,* 293–307.

Aranson, M., et al. (1985). Children of alcoholic mothers. *Acta Paediatrica Scandanavia, 74,* 27–35.

Aries, P. (1962). *Centuries of childhood: A social history of family life.* New York: Vintage.

Aronson, E., & Carlsmith, J. M. (1969). Experimentation in social psychology. In G. Lindzey & E. Aronson (Eds.), *The handbook of social psychology* (Vol. 2, 2nd ed.). Reading, MA: Addison-Wesley.

Arvey, R. D., & Campion, J. E. (1982). The employment interview: A summary and review of recent research. *Personnel Psychology, 35,* 281–322.

Asch, S. E. (1946). Forming impressions of personality. *Journal of Abnormal and Social Psychology, 41,* 258–290.

Asch, S. E. (1956). Studies of independence and conformity: A minority of one against a unanimous majority. *Psychological Monographs, 70*(9, Whole No. 416).

Aserinsky, E., & Kleitman, N. (1953). Regularly occurring periods of eye motility and concurrent phenomena during sleep. *Science, 118,* 273–274.

Aslin, R. N., & Smith, L. B. (1988). Perceptual development. *Annual Review of Psychology, 39,* 435–473.

Atkinson, J. W. (1958). *Motives in fantasy, action, and society.* Princeton, NJ: Van Nostrand.

Atkinson, J. W., & Litwin, G. H. (1960). Achievement motive and test anxiety conceived as motive to approach success and motive to avoid failure. *Journal of Abnormal and Social Psychology, 60,* 52–63.

Atkinson, R. C. (1975). Mnemotechnics in second-language learning. *American Psychologist, 30,* 821–828.

Atkinson, R. C., & Shiffrin, R. M. (1968). Human memory: A proposed system and its control processes. In K. W. Spence & J. T. Spence (Eds.), *The psychology of learning and motivation* (Vol. 2). New York: Academic Press.

Attneave, A. (1957). Transfer of experience with a class schema to identification learning of patterns and shapes. *Journal of Experimental Psychology, 54,* 81–88.

Backer, T. E., Batchelor, W. F., Jones, J. M., & Mays, V. M. (Eds.) (1988). Special issue: Psychology and AIDS. *American Psychologist, 43,* 835–987.

Bales, R. F. (1950). *Interaction process analysis: A method for the study of small groups.* Reading, MA: Addison-Wesley.

Bales, R. F. (1953). The equilibrium problem in small groups. In T. Parsons, R. F. Bales, & E. A. Shils (Eds.), *Working papers in the theory of action.* Glencoe, IL: Free Press.

Balkwell, C. (1981). Transition to widowhood: A review of the literature. *Family Relations, 30,* 117–128.

Ball, J. F. (1976–1977). Widow's grief: The impact of age and mode of death. *Omega, 7,* 307–333.

Baltes, P. B. (1968). Longitudinal and cross-sectional sequences in the study of age and generation effects. *Human Development, 11,* 145–171.

Bandura, A. (1965). Influence of models' reinforcement contingencies on the acquisition of imitative responses. *Journal of Personality and Social Psychology, 1,* 589–595.

Bandura, A. (1973). *Aggression: A social learning analysis.* Englewood Cliffs, NJ: Prentice-Hall.

Bandura, A. (1974). Behavior theories and the models of man. *American Psychologist, 29,* 859–869.

Bandura, A. (1982). The psychology of chance encounters and life paths. *American Psychologist, 37,* 747–755.

Bandura, A. (1986). *Social foundations of thought and action.* Englewood Cliffs, NJ: Prentice-Hall.

Bandura, A., Ross, D., & Ross, S. A. (1963). Imitation of film-mediated aggressive models. *Journal of Abnormal and Social Psychology, 66,* 3–11.

Bannister, R. C. (1979). *Social Darwinism: Science and myth in Anglo-American social thought.* Philadelphia: Temple University Press.

Barash, D. P. (1982). *Sociobiology and behavior* (2nd ed.). New York: Elsevier.

Barbach, L. G., & Levine, L. (1980). *Shared intimacies: Women's sexual experiences.* New York: Anchor.

Bard, P. A. (1928). A diencephalic mechanism for the expression of rage with special reference to the sympathetic nervous system. *American Journal of Physiology, 84,* 490–515.

Barefoot, J. D., Dahlstrom, W. G., & Williams, R. B. (1983). Hostility, CHD incidence, and total mortality: A 25-year follow-up study of 255 physicians. *Psychosomatic Medicine, 45,* 559–570.

Barlow, D. H., & Abel, G. G. (1976). Sexual deviation. In W. E. Craighead, A. E. Kazdin, & M. J. Mahoney (Eds.), *Behavior modification: Principles, issues, and applications.* Boston: Houghton Mifflin.

Barlow, F. (1952). *Mental prodigies.* New York: Philosophical Library.

Baron, L., & Straus, M. A. (1984). Sexual stratification, pornography, and rape in the United States. In N. M. Malamuth & E. Donnerstein (Eds.), *Pornography and sexual aggression.* New York: Academic Press.

Bartlett, F. C. (1932). *Remembering: A study in experimental and social psychology.* London: Cambridge University Press.

Baruch, G., Barnett, R., & Rivers, C. (1983). *Life prints: New patterns of love and work for today's woman.* New York: McGraw-Hill.

Basbaum, A. I., & Fields, H. L. (1984). Endogenous pain control systems: Brainstem spinal pathways and endorphin circuitry. *Annual Review of Neuroscience, 7,* 309–338.

Bass, B. M. (1960). *Leadership, psychology, and organizational psychology.* New York: Harper & Row.

Bass, D. M. (1985). The hospice ideology and success of hospice care. *Research on Aging, 7,* 307–328.

Bateson, G., Jackson, D. D., Haley, J., & Weakland, J. (1956). Toward a theory of schizophrenia. *Behavioral Science, 1,* 251–264.

Batson, C. D., et al. (1988). Five studies testing two new egoistic alternatives to the empathy-altruism hypothesis. *Journal of Personality and Social Psychology, 55,* 52–77.

Baumrind, D. (1964). Some thoughts on the ethics of research: After reading Milgram's "Behavioral study of obedience." *American Psychologist, 19,* 421–423.

Baumrind, D. (1971). Current patterns of parental authority. *Developmental Psychology Monographs, 4*(1, Part 2).

Bayer, R. (1987). *Homosexuality and American psychiatry: The politics of diagnosis.* Princeton: Princeton University Press.

Beck, A. T. (1967). *Depression: Clinical, experimental, and theoretical aspects.* New York: Hoeber.

Beck, A. T. (1976). *Cognitive therapy and the emotional disorders.* New York: International University Press.

Beck, A. T., & Emery, G. (1985). *Anxiety disorders and phobias: A cognitive perspective.* New York: Basic Books.

Beck, A. T., Rush, A. J., Shaw, B. F., & Emery, G. (1979). *Cognitive therapy of depression.* New York: Guilford.

Becker, W. C. (1964). Consequences of different types of parental discipline. In M. L. Hoffman & L. W. Hoffman (Eds.), *Review of child development research* (Vol. 1). New York: Russell Sage Foundation.

Bee, H. L. (1987). *The journey of adulthood.* New York: Macmillan.

Bekesy, G. V. (1947). The variation of phase along the basilar membrane with sinusoidal vibration. *Journal of the Acoustical Society of America, 19,* 452–460.

Bell, R. R. (1981). Friendships of women and men. *Psychology of Women Quarterly, 5,* 402–417.

Belloc, N. B. (1973). Relationship of health practices and mortality. *Preventive Medicine 2,* 67–81.

Belloc, N. B., & Breslow, L. (1972). Relationship of physical health status and family practices. *Preventive Medicine, 1,* 409–421.

Belsky, J. (1988). The "effects" of infant day care reconsidered. *Early Childhood Research Quarterly, 3,* 235–272.

Bem, D. J. (1972). Self-perception theory. In L. Berkowitz (Ed.), *Advances in experimental social psychology* (Vol. 6). New York: Academic Press.

Bem., D. J., & Allen, A. (1974). On predicting some of the people some of the time: The search for cross-situational consistencies in behavior. *Psychological Review, 81,* 506–520.

Bengston, V. L., Cuellar, J. B., & Ragan, P. K. (1977). Stratum contrasts and similarities in attitudes toward death. *Journal of Gerontology, 32,* 76–88.

Berk, L. E. (1989). *Child development.* Boston: Allyn & Bacon.

Berkowitz, L. (1981). Aversive conditions as stimuli for aggression. In L. Berkowitz (Ed.), *Advances in experimental social psychology* (Vol. 15). New York: Academic Press.

Berlin, B., & Kay, P. (1969). *Basic color terms: Their universality and evolution.* Berkeley and Los Angeles: University of California Press.

Bernheim, K. F., & Lewine, R. R. J. (1979). *Schizophrenia.* New York: Norton.

Berscheid, E., & Walster, E. (1974). A little bit about love. In T. L. Huston (Ed.), *Foundations of interpersonal attraction.* New York: Academic Press.

Berzins, J. I. (1977). Therapist-patient matching. In A. S. Gurman & A. M. Razin (Eds.), *Effective psychotherapy: A handbook of research.* New York: Pergamon.

Betz, N. E., & Fitzgerald, L. F. (1987). *The career psychology of women.* Orlando, FL: Academic Press.

Beutler, L. E., Crago, M., & Arizmendi, T. G. (1986). Research on therapist variables in psychotherapy. In S. L. Garfield & A. E. Bergin (Eds.), *Handbook of psychotherapy and behavior change* (3rd ed.). New York: Wiley.

Bieri, J. (1955). Cognitive complexity-simplicity and predictive behavior. *Journal of Abnormal and Social Psychology, 51,* 263–268.

Bierly, M. M. (1985). Prejudice toward contemporary outgroups as a generalized attitude. *Journal of Applied Social Psychology, 15,* 189–199.

Bigelow, H. J. (1850). Dr. Harlow's case of recovery from the passage of an iron bar through the head. *American Journal of Medical Science, 20,* 13–22.

Binet, A., & Simon, T. (1913). *A method of measuring the development of the intelligence of young children* (3rd ed.). Chicago: Chicago Medical Book.

Bird, C. (1940). *Social psychology.* New York: Appleton-Century-Crofts.

Bitterman, M. E. (1965). Phyletic differences in learning. *American Psychologist, 20,* 396–410.

Blake, R., & Hirsch, H. V. B. (1975). Deficits in binocular depth perception in cats after altering monocular deprivation. *Science, 190,* 1114–1116.

Blaney, P. H. (1986). Affect and memory: A review. *Psychological Bulletin, 99,* 229–246.

Blass, E. M., & Hall, W. G. (1976). Drinking termination: Interactions among hydrational, orogastric, and behavioral control in rats. *Psychological Review, 83,* 356–374.

Bliss, E. L. (1980). Multiple personalities: Report of fourteen cases with implications for schizophrenia and hysteria. *Archives of General Psychiatry, 37,* 1388–1397.

Bliss, J. C., Crane, H. D., Mansfield, P. K., & Townsend, J. T. (1966). Information available in brief tactile presentations. *Perception and Psychophysics, 1,* 273–283.

Block, J. (1957). Studies in the phenomenology of emotions. *Journal of Abnormal and Social Psychology, 54,* 358–363.

Bolles, E. B. (1988). *Remembering and forgetting: Inquiries into the nature of memory.* New York: Walker.

Bolles, R. C. (1967). *Theory of motivation.* New York: Harper & Row.

Borbely, A. (1986). *Secrets of sleep.* New York: Basic Books.

Borgida, E., & Nisbett, R. E. (1977). The differential impact of abstract versus concrete information on decisions. *Journal of Applied Social Psychology, 7,* 258–271.

Boring, E. G. (1950). *A history of experimental psychology* (2nd ed.). New York: Appleton-Century-Crofts.

Bouchard, T. J., & McGue, M. (1981). Familial studies of intelligence: A review. *Science, 212,* 1055–1059.

Bourne, L. E. (1966). *Human conceptual behavior.* Boston: Allyn & Bacon.

Bower, D. W., & Christopherson, V. A. (1977). University student cohabitation: A regional comparison of selected attitudes and behavior. *Journal of Marriage and the family, 39,* 447–453.

Bower, G. H. (1981). Mood and memory. *American Psychologist, 36,* 129–148.

Bower, G. H., Black, J. B., & Turner, T. J. (1979). Scripts in memory for text. *Cognitive Psychology, 11,* 177–220.

Bowers, K. S. (1973). Situationism in psychology: An analysis and critique. *Psychological Review, 80,* 307–336.

Bowlby, J. (1969). *Attachment and loss* (Vol. 1) *Attachment.* New York: Basic Books.

Bowmaker, J. K., & Dartnall, H. M. A. (1980). Visual pigments of rods and cones in a human retina. *Journal of Physiology, 298,* 501–511.

Boyle, R. H., & Ames, W. (1983, April 11). Too many punches, too little concern. *Sports Illustrated,* pp. 44–67.

Brainerd, C. J. (1978). *Piaget's theory of intelligence.* Englewood Cliffs, NJ: Prentice-Hall.

Bransford, J. D. (1979). *Human cognition: Learning, understanding, and remembering.* Belmont, CA: Wadsworth.

Bransford, J. D., & Franks, J. J. (1971). The abstraction of linguistic ideas. *Cognitive Psychology, 2,* 331–350.

Brecher, E. M., & the Editors of *Consumer Reports* (1972). *Licit and illicit drugs.* Mount Vernon, NY: Consumers Union.

Brehm, J. (1966). *A theory of psychological reactance.* New York: Academic Press.

Breland, K., & Breland, M. (1961). The misbehavior of organisms. *American Psychologist, 16,* 681–684.

Breuer, J., & Freud, S. (1895). Studies on hysteria. *Standard edition* (Vol. II). London: Hogarth.

Brigham, J. C. (1971). Ethnic stereotypes. *Psychological Bulletin, 76,* 15–38.

Brigham, J. C. (1986). *Social psychology.* Boston: Little, Brown.

Brim, O. G. (1976). Theories of the male mid-life crisis. *The Counseling Psychologist, 6,* 2–9.

Brim, O. G., & Kagan, J. (Eds.) (1980). *Constancy and change in human development.* Cambridge, MA: Harvard University Press.

Broadbent, D. E. (1958). *Perception and communication.* London: Pergamon.

Broadbent, D. E., & Gregory, M. (1963). Vigilance considered as a statistical decision. *British Journal of Psychology, 54,* 309–323.

Broadbent, D. E., & Gregory, M. (1965). Effects of noise and of signal rate upon vigilance analyzed by means of decision theory. *Human Factors, 7,* 155–162.

Broca, P. (1861). Remarques sur le siege de la faculte du langage articule, suives d'une observation d'aphemie (perte de la parole). *Bulletin de la Societe Anatomique, 36,* 330–357.

Brodt, S. E., & Zimbardo, P. G. (1981). Modifying shyness-related social behavior through symptom misattribution. *Journal of Personality and Social Psychology, 41,* 437–449.

Bronfenbrenner, U. (1970). *Two worlds of childhood: U.S. and U.S.S.R.* New York: Pocket Books.

Browder, S. (1988, June). Is living together such a good idea? *New Woman,* pp. 120–124.

Brown, G. W., & Harris, T. O. (1978). *Social origins of depression.* New York: Free Press.

Brown, N. O. (1959). *Life against death.* Baltimore: Penguin.

Brown, P., & Jenkins, H. M. (1968). Autoshaping of the pigeon's keypecking. *Journal of the Experimental Analysis of Behavior, 11,* 1–8.

Brown, R. (1954). Mass phenomena. In G. Lindzey (Ed.), *Handbook of social psychology* (Vol. 2). Cambridge, MA: Addison-Wesley.

Brown, R. (1986). *Social psychology, the second edition.* New York: Free Press.

Brown, R., & Hanlon, C. (1970). Derivational complexity and order of acquisition. In J. R. Hayes (Ed.), *Cognition and the development of language.* New York: Wiley.

Brown, R., & McNeill, D. (1966). The "tip of the tongue" phenomenon. *Journal of Verbal Learning and Verbal Behavior, 5,* 325–337.

Brown, T. S. (1975). General biology of sensory systems. In B. Scharf (Ed.), *Experimental sensory psychology.* Glenview, IL: Scott, Foresman.

Brown v. Board of Education of Topeka, 347 U.S. 483 (1954).

Brownmiller, S. (1975). *Against our will: Men, women, and rape.* New York: Simon & Schuster.

Bruner, J. S. (1964). The course of cognitive growth. *American Psychologist, 19,* 1–15.

Bryan, J. H., & Test, M. A. (1967). Models and helping: Naturalistic studies in aiding behavior. *Journal of Personality and Social Psychology, 6,* 400–407.

Bugental, J. F. I. (1965). *The search for authenticity.* New York: Holt, Rinehart, & Winston.

Burgess, A. W., & Holmstrom, L. L. (1974). *Rape: Victims of crisis.* Bowie, MD: Brady.

Bursten, B. (1979). Psychiatry and the rhetoric of models. *American Journal of Psychiatry, 136,* 661–666.

Buss, A. H., & Plomin, R. (1975). *A temperament theory of personality.* New York: Wiley.

Buss, A. H., & Plomin, R. (1984). *Temperament: Early developing personality traits.* Hillsdale, N.J. Erlbaum.

Buss, D. M. (1984a). Evolutionary biology and personality psychology: Toward a conception of human nature and individual differences. *American Psychologist, 39,* 1135–1147.

Buss, D. M. (1984b). Toward a psychology of person-environment (PE) correlation: The role of spouse selection. *Journal of Personality and Social Psychology, 47,* 361–377.

Buss, D. M. (1988). The evolution of human intrasexual competition: Tactics of mate attraction. *Journal of Personality and Social Psychology, 54,* 616–628.

Buss, D. M. (1989). Sex differences in human mate preferences: Evolutionary hypotheses tested in 37 cultures. *Behavioral and Brain Sciences, 12,* 1–14.

Butler, R., & Lewis, M. (1981). *Aging and mental health.* St. Louis: Mosby.

Buys, C. J. (1978). Humans would do better without groups? *Personality and Social Psychology Bulletin, 4,* 123–125.

Byrne, D. (1971). *The attraction paradigm.* New York: Academic Press.

Cannell, C. F., & Kahn, R. L. (1969). Interviewing. In G. Lindzey & E. Aronson (Eds.), *The handbook of social psychology* (Vol. 2, 2nd ed.). Reading, MA: Addison-Wesley.

Cannon, W. B. (1929). *Bodily changes in pain, hunger, fear, and rage.* New York: Appleton.

Cannon, W. B. (1939). *The wisdom of the body.* New York: Norton.

Cantor, N. (1980). Perceptions of situations: Situation prototypes and person-situation prototypes. In D. Magnusson (Ed.), *The situation: An interactional perspective.* Hillsdale, NJ: Erlbaum.

Cantor, N., & Kihlstrom, J. F. (1987). *Personality and social intelligence.* Englewood Cliffs, NJ: Prentice-Hall.

Cantor, N., & Mischel, W. (1977). Traits as prototypes: Effects on recognition memory. *Journal of Personality and Social Psychology, 37,* 337–344.

Cantor, N., & Mischel, W. (1979). Prototypes in person perception. In L. Berkowitz (Ed.), *Advances in ex-perimental social psychology* (Vol. 12). New York: Academic Press.

Cantor, N., Smith, E. E., French, R. deS., & Mezzich, J. (1980). Psychiatric diagnosis as prototype categorization. *Journal of Abnormal Psychology, 89,* 181–193.

Carey, G. (1982). Genetic influences on anxiety neurosis and agoraphobia. In R. J. Mathew (Ed.), *Biology of anxiety.* New York: Brunner-Mazel.

Carlson, N. R. (1986). *Physiology of behavior* (3rd ed.). Boston: Allyn & Bacon.

Carmichael, L., Hogan, H. P., & Walter, A. A. (1932). An experimental study of the effect of language on the reproduction of visually perceived form. *Journal of Experimental Psychology, 15,* 73–86.

Carroll, J. B. (1982). The measurement of intelligence. In R. J. Sternberg (Ed.), *Handbook of human intelligence.* Cambridge: Cambridge University Press.

Carson, R. C., Butcher, J. N., & Coleman, J. C. (1988). *Abnormal psychology and modern life* (8th ed.). Glenview, IL: Scott, Foresman.

Cartwright, R. D. (1978). *A primer on sleep and dreaming.* Reading, MA: Addison-Wesley.

Catania, A. C. (1975). The myth of self-reinforcement. *Behaviorism, 3,* 192–199.

Cattell, J. M., & Farrand, L. (1896). Physical and mental measurements of the students of Columbia University. *Psychological Review, 3,* 618–648.

Cattell, R. B. (1950). *Personality: A systematic, theoretical, and factual study.* New York: McGraw-Hill.

Cattell, R. B. (1971). *Abilities: Their structure, growth, and action.* Boston: Houghton Mifflin.

Cattell, R. B., Eber, H. W., & Tatsuoka, M. (1970). *The handbook for the Sixteen Personality Factor Questionnaire.* Champaign, IL: Institute for Personality and Ability Testing.

Chapman, C. R., Wilson, M. E., & Gehrig, J. D. (1976). Comparative effects of acupuncture and transcutaneous stimulation of the perception of painful dental stimuli. *Pain, 2,* 265–283.

Cheek, J. M., & Busch, C. M. (1981). The influence of shyness on loneliness in a new situation. *Personality and Social Psychology Bulletin, 7,* 572–577.

Chen, S. C. (1937). Social modification of the activity of ants in nest-building. *Physiological Zoology, 10,* 420–436.

Cherry, E. C. (1953). Some experiments on the recognition of speech, with one and with two ears. *Journal of the Acoustical Society of America, 25,* 975–979.

Chi, M. T. H., Feltovich, P. J., & Glaser, R. (1981). Categorization and representation of physics problems by experts and novices. *Cognitive Science, 5,* 121–152.

Chinsky, J. M., & Rappaport, J. (1970). Brief critique of the meaning and reliability of "accurate empathy" ratings. *Psychological Bulletin, 73,* 379–382.

Chomsky, N. (1957). *Syntactic structures.* The Hague: Mouton.

Chomsky, N. (1959). A review of B. F. Skinner's *Verbal behavior. Language, 35,* 26–58.

Cialdini, R. B. (1985). *Influence: Science and practice.* Glenview, IL: Scott, Foresman.

Cialdini, R. B., & Richardson, K. D. (1980). Two indirect tactics of image management: Basking and blasting. *Journal of Personality and Social Psychology, 39,* 406–415.

Clark, E. (1978). Strategies for communicating. *Child Development, 49,* 953–959.

Clark, M. S., & Mills, J. (1979). Interpersonal attraction in exchange and communal relationships. *Journal of Personality and Social Psychology, 37,* 12–24.

Clark, M. S., & Reis, H. T. (1988). Interpersonal processes in close relationships. *Annual Review of Psychology, 39,* 609–672.

Clarke-Stewart, K. A. (1989). Infant day care: Maligned or malignant? *American Psychologist, 44,* 266–273.

Clarke-Stewart, K. A., & Fein, G. G. (1983). Early childhood programs. In P. H. Mussen (Ed.), *Handbook of child psychology* (Vol. 2). New York: Wiley.

Clarke-Stewart, K. A., Friedman, S., & Koch, J. (1985). *Child development: A topical approach.* New York: Wiley.

Clayton, V. (1982). Wisdom and intelligence: The nature and function of knowledge in the later years. *International Journal of Aging and Human Development, 15,* 315–321.

Cobb, S. (1976). Social support as a moderator of life stress. *Psychosomatic Medicine, 38,* 300–314.

Cocks, J. (1979, December 17). Rock's outer limits. *Time,* pp. 86–94.

Cohen, D. B. (1979). *Sleep and dreaming: Origins, nature, and functions.* Oxford: Pergamon.

Cohen, S., & Syme, S. L. (1985). *Social support and health.* Orlando, FL: Academic Press.

Colby, A., Kohlberg, L., Gibbs, J., & Lieberman, M. (1983). A longitudinal study of moral development. *Monographs of the Society for Research in Child Development, 48,* (Serial No. 200).

Coleman, J. (1961). *The adolescent society.* Glencoe, IL: Free Press.

Coleman, L. (1984). *The reign of error: Psychiatry, authority, and law.* Boston: Beacon.

Collins, A. M., & Loftus, E. F. (1975). A spreading-activation theory of semantic processing. *Psychological Review, 82,* 407–428.

Colombo, J. (1982). The critical period concept: Research, methodology, and theoretical issues. *Psychological Bulletin, 91,* 260–275.

Comte, E. (1989, January 15). How they rank in endorsements. *The Sporting News,* p. 46.

Condry, J., & Condry, S. (1976) Sex differences: A study of the eye of the beholder. *Child Development, 47,* 812–819.

Conger, J. (1977). Parent-child relationships, social change, and adolescent vulnerability. *Journal of Pediatric Psychology, 32,* 513–531.

Conn, J., & Kanner, L. (1940). Spontaneous erections in childhood. *Journal of Pediatrics, 16,* 337–340.

Conrad, R. (1963). Acoustic confusions and memory span for words. *Nature, 197,* 1029–1030.

Conrad, R. (1964). Acoustic confusions in immediate memory. *British Journal of Psychology, 55,* 75–84.

Cook, S. W. (1970). Motives in a conceptual analysis of attitude-related behaviors. In W. J. Arnold & D. Levine (Eds.), *Nebraska symposium on motivation* (Vol. 17). Lincoln, NE: University of Nebraska Press.

Cook, S. W. (1984). The 1954 social science statement and school desegregation: A reply to Gerard. *American Psychologist, 39,* 819–832.

Cooper, J. R., Bloom, F. E., & Roth, R. H. (1986). *The biochemical basis of neuropharmacology* (5th ed.). New York: Oxford.

Coren, S., Porac, C., & Ward, L. M. (1984). *Sensation and perception* (2rd ed.). Orlando, FL: Academic Press.

Corso, J. E. (1959). Age and sex differences in thresholds. *Journal of the Acoustical Society of America, 31,* 498–509.

Cousins, N. (1981). *The anatomy of an illness.* New York: Norton.

Cowan, P., Cowan, C., Coie, J., & Coie, L. (1978). In L. Newman & W. Miller (Eds.), *The first child and family formation.* Durham, NC: University of North Carolina Press.

Cowen, E. L. (1977). Baby steps toward primary prevention. *American Journal of Community Psychology, 5,* 1–22.

Cowles, J. T. (1937). Food-tokens as incentive for learning by chimpanzees. *Comparative Psychology Monographs, 14* (No. 5).

Cox, C. M. (1926). *Genetic studies of genius. Vol. II: The early mental traits of three hundred geniuses.* Stanford, CA: Stanford University Press.

Coyle, J. T., Price, D. L., & Delong, M. H. (1983). Alzheimer's disease: A disorder of central cholinergic innervation. *Science, 219,* 1184–1189.

Craik, F. I. M., & Lockhart, R. S. (1972). Levels of processing: A framework for memory research. *Journal of Verbal Learning and Verbal Behavior, 11,* 671–684.

Crisp, A. H. (1980). *Anorexia nervosa—Let me be.* London: Plenum.

Crocker, J., & Schwartz, I. (1985). Prejudice and in-group favoritism in a minimal intergroup situation: Effects of self-esteem. *Personality and Social Psychology Bulletin, 11,* 379–386.

Csikszentmihalyi, M., Larson, R., & Prescott, S. (1977). The ecology of adolescent activity and experience. *Journal of Youth and Adolescence, 6,* 281–294.

Curtiss, S. (1977). *Genie: A psycholinguistic study of a modern-day wild child.* New York: Academic Press.

Cutting, J. E. (1987). Perception and information. *Annual Review of Psychology, 38,* 61–90.

Cvetkovich, G., Grote, B., Bjorseth, A., & Sarkissian, J. (1975). On the psychology of adolescents' use of contraceptives. *Journal of Sex Research, 11,* 256–270.

Dale, A. J. D. (1980). Organic mental disorders associated with infections. In H. I. Kaplan, A. M. Freedman, & B. J. Sadock (Eds.), *Comprehensive textbook of psychiatry* (Vol. 2, 3rd ed.). Baltimore: Williams & Wilkins.

Dallenbach, K. M. (1927). The temperature spots and end-organs. *American Journal of Psychology, 39,* 402–427.

Daly, M., & Wilson, M. (1978). *Sex, evolution, and behavior.* North Scituate, MA: Duxbury Press.

Daly, M., & Wilson, M. (1983). *Sex, evolution, and human behavior* (2nd ed.). Boston: Willard Grant.

Daniels, G. S. (1952). *The "average man?"* (Technical Note WCRD 53-7). Wright-Patterson Air Force Base, OH: Wright Air Development Center, USAF.

Darley, J. M., & Latané, B. (1968). Bystander intervention in emergencies: Diffusion of responsibility. *Journal of Personality and Social Psychology, 8,* 377–383.

Darwin, C. (1859). *The origin of species.* London: Murray.

Darwin, C. (1859/1979). *The illustrated origin of species* (abridged by Richard E. Leakey). New York: Hill & Wang.

Darwin, C. (1871). *The descent of man and selection in relation to sex.* New York: Appleton.

Darwin, C. (1872). *The expression of the emotions in man and animals.* London: Murray.

Darwin, C. (1877). A biographical sketch of an infant. *Mind, 2,* 285–294.

Datan, N., Rodeheaver, D., & Hughes, F. (1987). Adult development and aging. *Annual Review of Psychology, 38,* 153–180.

Davidson, R. J. (1984). Hemispheric asymmetry and emotion. In K. R. Scherer & P. Ekman (Eds.), *Approaches to emotion.* Hillsdale, NJ: Erlbaum.

Davis, J. (1984). *Endorphins: New waves in brain chemistry.* Garden City, NY: Dial.

Davis, J. H. (1969). *Group performance.* Reading, MA: Addison-Wesley.

Davis, R. (1984). Expert systems: Where are we and where do we go from here? In P. Winston & K. Prendergast (Eds.), *The AI business.* Reading, MA: Addison-Wesley.

Deaux, K. (1985). Sex and gender. *Annual Review of Psychology, 36,* 49–81.

Deci, E. L. (1975). *Intrinsic motivation.* New York: Plenum.

Deci, E. L., & Ryan, R. M. (1980). The empirical exploration of intrinsic motivational processes. In L. Berkowitz (Ed.), *Advances in experimental social psychology* (Vol. 13). New York: Academic Press.

Delgado, J. M. R. (1969). *Physical control of the mind: Toward a psychocivilized society.* New York: Harper & Row.

Delin, B. (1978). *The sex offender.* Boston: Beacon.

DeMaris, A., & Leslie, G. R. (1984). Cohabitation with the future spouse: Its influence upon marital satisfaction and communication. *Journal of Marriage and the Family, 46,* 77–84.

Dement, W. C. (1974). *Some must watch while some must sleep.* San Francisco: Freeman.

Dement, W. C., & Wolpert, E. (1958). The relation of eye movements, bodily motility, and external stimuli to dream content. *Journal of Experimental Psychology, 55,* 543–553.

Dethier, V. G. (1976). *The hungry fly.* Cambridge, MA: Harvard University Press.

Dickens, W. J., & Perlman, D. (1981). Friendship over the life-cycle. In S. Duck & R. Gilmour (Eds.),

Personal relationships: 2. Developing personal relationships. New York: Academic Press.

Diener, E., Fraser, S. C., Beaman, A. L., & Kelem, R. T. (1976). Effects of deindividuation variables on stealing among Halloween trick-or-treaters. *Journal of Personality and Social Psychology, 33,* 178–183.

Dillehay, R. C. (1978). Authoritarianism. In H. London & J. E. Exner (Eds.), *Dimensions of personality.* New York: Wiley.

DiLollo, V., Hanson, D., & McIntyre, J. S. (1983). Initial stages of visual information processing in dyslexia. *Journal of Experimental Psychology: Human Perception and Performance, 9,* 923–935.

Dohrenwend, B. S., & Dohrenwend, B. P. (1981). Hypotheses about stress processes linking social class to various types of psychopathology. *American Journal of Community Psychology, 9,* 145–159.

Dollard, J., Doob, L. W., Miller, N. E., Mowrer, O. H., & Sears, R. R. (1939). *Frustration and aggression.* New Haven: Yale University Press.

Dollard, J., & Miller, N. E. (1950). *Personality and psychotherapy: An analysis in terms of learning, thinking, and culture.* New York: McGraw-Hill.

Donnerstein, E. (1980). Aggressive erotica and violence against women. *Journal of Personality and Social Psychology, 39,* 269–277.

Donnerstein, E., & Berkowitz, L. (1981). Victim reactions in aggressive erotic films as a factor in violence against women. *Journal of Personality and Social Psychology, 41,* 710–724.

Dorfman, P. (1989). Industrial and organizational psychology. In W. L. Gregory & W. J. Burroughs (Eds.), *Introduction to applied psychology.* Glenview, IL: Scott, Foresman.

Dornbusch, S. M., Carlsmith, J. M., Bushwall, S. J., Ritter, P. L., Leiderman, H., Hastorf, A. H., & Gross, R. T. (1985). Single parents, extended households, and the control of adolescents. *Child Development, 56,* 326–341.

Dorner, G. (1976). *Hormones and brain differentiation.* Amsterdam: Elsevier.

Douvan, E., & Adelson, J. (1966). *The adolescent experience.* New York: Wiley.

Dreyer, P. (1982). Sexuality during adolescence. In B. Wolman (Ed.), *Handbook of developmental psychology.* Englewood Cliffs, NJ: Prentice-Hall.

Dubois, P. H. (1970). *A history of psychological testing.* Boston: Allyn & Bacon.

Duffy, M. (1989, August 21). Mr. Consensus. *Time,* pp. 16–22.

Duncker, K. (1945). On problem solving. *Psychological Monographs, 58* (Whole No. 270).

Dunphy, D. (1963). The social structure of urban adolescent peer groups. *Sociometry, 26,* 230–246.

Dutton, D. G., & Aron, A. P. (1974). Some evidence for heightened sexual attraction under conditions of high anxiety. *Journal of Personality and Social Psychology, 30,* 510–517.

Dywan, J., & Bowers, K. S. (1983). The use of hypnosis to enhance recall. *Science, 222,* 184–185.

Eagly, A. H. (1987). *Sex differences in social behavior: A social role explanation.* Hillsdale, NJ: Erlbaum.

Eaton, J. S. (1980). The psychiatrist and psychiatric education. In H. I. Kaplan, A. M. Freedman, & B. J. Sadock (Eds.), *Comprehensive textbook of psychiatry* (Vol. 3, 3rd ed.). Baltimore: Williams & Wilkins.

Ebbinghaus, H. (1885/1913). *Memory: A contribution to experimental psychology.* New York: Columbia University Press.

Eccles, J. S. (1985). Why doesn't Jane run? Sex differences in educational and occupational patterns. In F. D. Horowitz & M. O'Brien (Eds.), *The gifted and talented: Developmental perspectives.* Washington, D.C.: American Psychological Association.

Edgerton, R. E. (1979). *Mental retardation.* Cambridge, MA: Harvard University Press.

Edwards, G., Hensman, C., Hawker, A., & Williamson, V. (1967). Alcoholics anonymous: The anatomy of a self-help group. *Social Psychiatry, 1,* 195–204.

Edwards, H. (1973). *Sociology of sport.* Homewood, IL: Dorsey Press.

Eibl-Eibesfeldt, I. (1970). *Ethology: The biology of behavior.* New York: Holt, Rinehart, & Winston.

Eich, J. E. (1980). The cue-dependent nature of state dependent retrieval. *Memory and Cognition, 8,* 157–173.

Eitzen, D. (1975). Athletics in the status system of male adolescents. *Adolescence, 10,* 267–276.

Ekehammar, B. (1974). Interactionism in psychology from a historical perspective. *Psychological Bulletin, 81,* 1026–1048.

Ekman, P. (1984). Expression and the nature of emotion. In K. Scherer & P. Ekman (Eds.), *Approaches to emotion.* Hillsdale, NJ: Erlbaum.

Ekman, P. (1986). *Telling lies.* New York: Berkley.

Elder, G. H. (1969). Appearance and education in marriage mobility. *American Sociological Review, 34,* 519–533.

Elder, G. H. (1974). *Children of the great depression.* Chicago: University of Chicago Press.

Eldredge, N., & Gould, S. J. (1972). Punctuated equilibria: An alternative to phyletic gradualism. In T. J. M. Schopf (Ed.), *Models in paleobiology.* San Francisco: Freeman.

Elkind, D. (1978a). Understanding the young adolescent. *Adolescence, 13,* 127–134.

Elkind, D. (1978b). *The child's reality: Three developmental themes.* Hillsdale, NJ: Erlbaum.

Elkind, D. (1987). *Miseducation: Preschoolers at risk.* New York: Knopf.

Ellis, A. (1962). *Reason and emotion in psychotherapy.* New York: Stuart.

Ellis, R. E. (1988). Self-monitoring and leadership emergence in groups. *Personality and Social Psychology Bulletin, 14,* 681–693.

Emery, R. E. (1982). Interparental conflict and the children of discord and divorce. *Psychological Bulletin, 92,* 310–330.

Emmelkamp, P. M. G., & Kuipers, A. (1979). Agoraphobia: A follow-up study four years after treatment. *British Journal of Psychiatry, 134,* 352–355.

Endler, N. S., & Magnusson, D. (1976). Toward an interactional theory of personality. *Psychological Bulletin, 83,* 956–974.

Epstein, R., Kirshnit, C. E., Lanza, R. P., & Rubin, L. C. (1984). "Insight" in the pigeon: Antecedents and determinants of an intelligent performance. *Nature, 308,* 61–62.

Epstein, S. (1979). The stability of behavior: I. On predicting most of the people much of the time. *Journal of Personality and Social Psychology, 37,* 1097–1126.

Erdelyi, M. H. (1974). A new look at the New Look: Perceptual defense and vigilance. *Psychological Review, 81,* 1–25.

Erdelyi, M. H. (1985). *Psychoanalysis: Freud's cognitive psychology.* New York: Freeman.

Ericsson, K. A., & Chase, W. G. (1982). Exceptional memory. *American Scientist, 70,* 607–615.

Ericsson, K. A. & Simon, H. A. (1984). *Protocol analysis: Verbal reports as data.* Cambridge, MA: MIT Press.

Erikson, E. (1959). *Identity and the life cycle.* New York: International Universities Press.

Erikson, E. (1963). *Childhood and society* (2nd ed.). New York: Norton.

Erikson, E. (1968). *Identity: Youth and crisis.* New York: Norton.

Erikson, E. (1982). *The life cycle completed.* New York: Norton.

Erlenmeyer-Kimling, L., & Jarvik, L. F. (1963). Genetics and intelligence: A review. *Science, 142,* 1477–1479.

Eron, L. D., & Huesmann, L. R. (1984). The control of aggressive behavior by changes in attitudes, values, and the conditions of learning. In R. J. Blanchard & C. Blancard (Eds.), *Advances in the study of aggression* (Vol. 1). Orlando, FL: Academic Press.

Etaugh, C. (1983). The influence of environmental factors in sex differences in children's play. In M. Liss (Ed.), *Social and cognitive skills: Sex roles and children's play.* New York: Academic Press.

Eyferth, K. (1961). Leistungen verschiedener Gruppen von Besatzungskindern in Hamburg-Wechsler Intelligenztest fur kinder (HAWIK). *Archiv fur die gesamte Psychdogie, 113,* 222–241.

Eysenck, H. J. (1947). *Dimensions of personality.* London: Routledge and Kegan Paul.

Eysenck, H. J. (1952). The effects of psychotherapy: An evaluation. *Journal of Consulting Psychology, 16,* 319–324.

Eysenck, H. J. (1967). *The biological basis of personality.* Springfield, IL: Thomas.

Eysenck, H. J., & Eysenck, S. B. G. (1975). *Manual of the Eysenck Personality Questionnaire.* San Diego: EdITS.

Fagot, B. I. (1978). The influence of sex of child on parental reactions to toddler children. *Child Development, 49,* 459–465.

Fagot, B. I., Hagan, R., Leinbach, M. D., & Kronsberg, S. (1985). Differential reactions to assertive and communicative acts of toddler boys and girls. *Child Development, 56,* 1499–1505.

Farley, J., & Alkon, D. L. (1985). Cellular mechanisms of learning, memory, and information storage. *Annual Review of Psychology, 36,* 419–494.

Farquhar, J., et al. (1977). Community education of cardiovascular health. *Lancet, 97,* 1192–1195.

Feder, H. H. (1984). Hormones and sexual behavior. *Annual Review of Psychology, 35,* 165–200.

Feeney, J. A., & Noller, P. (1990). Attachment style as a predictor of adult romantic relationships. *Journal of Personality and Social Psychology, 58,* 281–291.

Feingold, A. (1988). Cognitive gender differences are disappearing. *American Psychologist, 43,* 95–103.

Feldman, D. H. (1980). *Beyond universals in cognitive development.* Norwood, NJ: Ablex.

Feldman, S. S., & Aschenbrenner, B. (1983). Impact of parenthood on various aspects of masculinity and femininity. *Developmental Psychology, 19,* 278–279.

Fenichel, O. (1945). *The psychoanalytic theory of neurosis.* New York: Norton.

Ferraro, K. R. (1984). Widowhood and social participation in later life: Isolation or compensation? *Research on Aging, 6,* 451–468.

Festinger, L. (1954). A theory of social comparison processes. *Human Relations, 7,* 117–140.

Festinger, L. (1957). *A theory of cognitive dissonance.* Evanston: Row, Peterson.

Festinger, L., & Carlsmith, J. M. (1959). Cognitive consequences of forced compliance. *Journal of Abnormal and Social Psychology, 68,* 359–366.

Festinger, L., Pepitone, A., & Newcomb, T. M. (1952). Some consequences of deindividuation in a group. *Journal of Abnormal and Social Psychology, 47,* 382–389.

Festinger, L., Riecken, H., & Schachter, S. (1956). *When prophecy fails.* Minneapolis: University of Minnesota Press.

Fiedler, F. E. (1950). A comparison of therapeutic relationships in psychoanalytic, non-directive, and Adlerian therapy. *Journal of Consulting Psychology, 14,* 436–445.

Fiedler, F. E. (1951). Factor analysis of psychoanalytic, non-directive, and Adlerian therapeutic relationships. *Journal of Consulting Psychology, 15,* 32–38.

Fiedler, F. E. (1971). Validation and extension of the contingency model of leadership effectiveness: A review of empirical findings. *Psychological Bulletin, 76,* 128–148.

Fischer, K. W. (1987). Relations between brain and cognitive development. *Child Development, 58,* 623–632.

Fischer, K. W., & Silvern, L. (1985). Stages and individual differences in cognitive development. *Annual Review of Psychology, 36,* 613–648.

Fischhoff, B. (1988). Judgment and decision making. In R. J. Sternberg & E. E. Smith (Eds.), *The psychology of human thought.* Cambridge: Cambridge University Press.

Fisher, A. C. (1977). Sport personality assessment: Facts, fallacies, and perspectives. *Motor Skills: Theory into Practice, 1,* 87–97.

Fiske, S. T., & Taylor, S. E. (1984). *Social cognition.* Reading, MA: Addison-Wesley.

Flanagan, J. C. (1954). The critical incident technique. *Psychological Bulletin, 51,* 327–358.

Flavell, J. H. (1979). Metacognition and cognitive monitoring: A new area of cognitive-developmental inquiry. *American Psychologist, 34,* 906–911.

Flavell, J. H. (1981). Cognitive monitoring. In W. P. Dickson (Ed.), *Children's oral communication skills.* New York: Academic Press.

Flynn, C. P. (1987). Relationship violence: A model for family professionals. *Family Relations, 36,* 295–299.

Foa, U. G., & Foa, E. B. (1975). *Resource theory of social exchange.* Morristown, NJ: General Learning Press.

Ford, C. S., & Beach, F. A. (1951). *Patterns of sexual behavior.* New York: Harper & Row.

Form, W. H., & Nosow, S. (1958). *Community in disaster.* New York: Harper.

Forward, J., Canter, R., & Kirsch, N. (1976). Role-enactment and deception: Alternative paradigms? *American Psychologist, 31,* 595–604.

Foulkes, D. (1985). *Dreaming: A cognitive-psychological analysis.* Hillsdale, NJ: Erlbaum.

Frank, J. D. (1978). *Psychotherapy and the human predicament: A psychosocial approach.* New York: Schocken Books.

Frankel, F. H. (1976). *Hypnosis: Trance as a coping mechanism.* New York: Plenum.

Frankenburg, W. K., & Dodds, J. B. (1967). The Denver Developmental Screening Test. *Journal of Pediatrics, 71,* 181–191.

Franks, D. J. (1971). Ethnic and social status characteristics of children in EMR and LD classes. *Exceptional Children, 37,* 537–538.

Frazer, J. G. (1922). *The golden bough: A study in magic and religion.* New York: Macmillan.

Freedman, D. G. (1979). *Human sociobiology: A holistic approach.* New York: Free Press.

Freud, S. (1900). The interpretation of dreams. *Standard edition* (Vol. IV). London: Hogarth.

Freud, S. (1905a). Humor and its relation to the unconscious. *Standard edition* (Vol. VIII). London: Hogarth.

Freud, S. (1905b). Three essays on the theory of sexuality. *Standard edition* (Vol. VII). London: Hogarth.

Freud, S. (1908). Creative writers and daydreaming. *Standard edition* (Vol. IX). London: Hogarth.

Freud, S. (1909a). Analysis of a phobia in a five-year-old boy. *Standard edition* (Vol. X). London: Hogarth.

Freud, S. (1909b). Notes upon a case of obsessional neurosis. *Standard edition* (Vol. X). London: Hogarth.

Freud, S. (1916). Introductory lectures on psychoanalysis. *Standard edition* (Vol. XV). London: Hogarth.

Freud, S. (1917). Mourning and melancholia. *Standard edition* (Vol. XIV). London: Hogarth.

Freud, S. (1918). From the history of an infantile neurosis. *Standard edition* (Vol. XVII). London: Hogarth.

Freud, S. (1926). Inhibitions, symptoms, and anxiety. *Standard edition* (Vol. XX). London: Hogarth.

Freud, S. (1930). Civilization and its discontents. *Standard edition* (Vol. XXI). London: Hogarth.

Friedman, H. S., & Booth-Kewley, S. (1987). The "disease-prone personality": A meta-analytic view of the construct. *American Psychologist, 42,* 539–555.

Friedman, M., et al. (1984). Alteration of Type A behavior and reduction in cardiac recurrences in post myocardial infarction patients. *American Heart Journal, 108,* 237–248.

Friedman, M., & Rosenman, R. H. (1974). *Type A behavior and your heart.* New York: Knopf.

Fries, J. F., & Crapo, L. M. (1981). *Vitality and aging.* San Francisco: Freeman.

Fromm, E. (1956). *The art of loving.* New York: Harper & Row.

Fry, C. L. (1985). Culture, behavior, and aging in the comparative perspective. In J. E. Birren & K. W. Schaie (Eds.), *Handbook of the psychology of aging* (2nd ed.). New York: Van Nostrand.

Galanter, E. (1962). Contemporary psychophysics. In R. Brown et al. (Eds.), *New directions in psychology.* New York: Holt, Rinehart, & Winston.

Gallistel, C. R. (1980). *The organization of action.* Hillsdale, NJ: Erlbaum.

Gallup, G. (1972). *The sophisticated poll watcher's guide.* Princeton, NJ: Princeton Opinion Press.

Gallup, G. G., & Suarez, S. D. (1985). Alternatives to the use of animals in psychological research. *American Psychologist, 40,* 1104–1111.

Galton, F. (1869). *Hereditary genius.* London: Macmillan.

Galton, F. (1888). Co-relations and their measurement. *Proceedings of the Royal Society, 45,* 135–145.

Garcia, J., & Koelling, R. A. (1966). The relation of cue to consequence in avoidance learning. *Psychonomic Science, 4,* 123–124.

Gardner, H. (1976). *The shattered mind.* New York: Vintage Books.

Gardner, H. (1983). *Frames of mind: The theory of multiple intelligences.* New York: Basic Books.

Gardner, H. (1985). *The mind's new science: A history of the cognitive revolution.* New York: Basic Books.

Gardner, R. A., & Gardner, B. T. (1969). Teaching sign language to a chimpanzee. *Science, 165,* 664–672.

Garfield, S. L. (1986). Research on client variables in psychotherapy. In S. L. Garfield & A. E. Bergin (Eds.), *Handbook of psychotherapy and behavior change* (3rd ed.). New York: Wiley.

Garfield, S. L., & Bergin, A. E. (1986). Introduction and historical overview. In S. L. Garfield & A. E. Bergin (Eds.), *Handbook of psychotherapy and behavior change* (3rd ed.). New York: Wiley.

Garfinkel, H. (1967). *Studies in ethnomethodology.* Englewood Cliffs, NJ: Prentice-Hall.

Garner, B., & Smith, R. W. (1977). Are there really any gay male athletes? An empirical survey. *Journal of Sex Research, 13,* 22–24.

Gay, P. (1984). *The bourgeois experience: Victoria to Freud* (Vol. 1) *The education of the senses.* New York: Oxford.

Gelman, R. (1969). Conservation acquisition: A problem of learning to attend to relevant attributes. *Journal of Experimental Child Psychology, 7,* 167–178.

Gelman, R., & Baillargeon, R. A. (1983). A review of some Piagetian concepts. In P. H. Mussen (Ed.), *Handbook of child psychology* (Vol. 3). New York: Wiley.

Genest, M., & Genest, S. (1987). *Psychology and health.* Champaign, IL: Research Press.

George, L. K., Fillenbaum, G. G., & Palmore, E. (1984). Sex differences in the antecedents and consequences of retirement. *Journal of Gerontology, 39,* 364–371.

Gescheider, G. A. (1988). Psychophysiological scaling. *Annual Review of Psychology, 39,* 169–200.

Gesell, A. (1925). *The mental growth of the preschool child.* New York: Macmillan.

Gesell, A. (1928). *Infancy and human growth.* New York: Macmillan.

Gesell, A., & Thompson, H. (1934). *Infant behavior: Its genesis and growth.* New York: McGraw-Hill.

Gibb, C. A. (1969). Leadership. In G. Lindzey & E. Aronson (Eds.), *The handbook of social psychology* (Vol. 4, 2nd ed.). Reading, MA: Addison-Wesley.

Gibson, E. J. (1988). Exploratory behavior in the development of perceiving, acting, and the acquiring of knowledge. *Annual Review of Psychology, 39,* 1–41.

Gibson, E. J., & Walk, R. D. (1960, September). The "visual cliff." *Scientific American*, pp. 64–71.

Gibson, J. J. (1979). *The ecological approach to visual perception*. Boston: Houghton Mifflin.

Gilgen, A. R. (1982). *American psychology since World War II*. Westport, CT: Greenwood.

Gill, K. G. (1970). *Violence against children*. Cambridge, MA: Harvard University Press.

Gilligan, C. (1982). *In a different voice*. Cambridge, MA: Harvard University Press.

Glantz, K., & Pearce, J. K. (1989). *Exiles from Eden: Psychotherapy from an evolutionary perspective*. New York: Norton.

Glass, A. L., & Holyoak, K. J. (1986). *Cognition* (2nd ed.). New York: Random House.

Glass, D. C. (1977). *Behavior patterns, stress, and coronary disease*. Hillsdale, NJ: Erlbaum.

Glenn, N. D., & McLanahan, S. (1981). The effects of offspring on the psychological well-being of older adults. *Journal of Marriage and the Family, 43*, 409–421.

Glucksberg, S. (1988). Language and thought. In R. J. Sternberg & E. E. Smith (Eds.), *The psychology of human thought*. Cambridge: Cambridge University Press.

Goddard, H. H. (1917). Mental tests and the immigrant. *Journal of Delinquency, 2*, 243–277.

Godden, D. R., & Baddeley, A. D. (1975). Context-dependent memory in two natural environments: On land and underwater. *British Journal of Psychology, 65*, 325–332.

Goffman, E. (1961). *Asylums*. Garden City, NJ: Anchor.

Goldiamond, I. (1976). Self reinforcement. *Journal of Applied Behavior Analysis, 9*, 509–514.

Goldsmith, H. H. (1983). Genetic influences on personality from infancy to childhood. *Child Development, 54*, 331–355.

Goldstein, A., & Hilgard, E. R. (1975). Lack of influence of the morphine antagonist naloxone on hypnotic analgesia. *Proceedings of the National Academy of Sciences, 72*, 2041–2043.

Goldstein, A. P., & Krasner, L. (1987). *Modern applied psychology*. New York: Pergamon.

Gorer, G. (1965). *Death, grief, and mourning*. New York: Doubleday.

Gorsuch, R. L. (1988). Psychology of religion. *Annual Review of Psychology, 39*, 201–221.

Gottesman, I. I., & Shields, J. (1972). *Schizophrenia and genetics: A twin study vantage point*. New York: Academic Press.

Gottsdanker, R. (1982). Age and simple reaction time. *Journal of Gerontology, 37*, 342–348.

Gould, J. L. (1986). The biology of learning. *Annual Review of Psychology, 37*, 163–192.

Gould, P., & White, R. (1974). *Mental maps*. New York: Penguin.

Gould, R. L. (1978). *Transformations: Growth and change in adult life*. New York: Touchstone.

Gould, S. J. (1977). *Ontogeny and phylogeny*. Cambridge, MA: Harvard University Press.

Gould, S. J. (1981). *The mismeasure of man*. New York: Norton.

Gray-Little, B., & Burks, N. (1983). Power and satisfaction in marriage: A review and critique. *Psychological Bulletin, 93*, 513–538.

Green, D. G., & Powers, M. K. (1982). Mechanisms of light adaptation in the rat retina. *Vision Research, 22*, 209–216.

Green, D. M., & Swets, J. A. (1966). *Signal detection theory and psychophysics*. New York: Wiley.

Green, R. (1987). *The "sissy boy syndrome" and the development of homosexuality*. New Haven, CT: Yale University Press.

Greenberger, E., & Steinberg, L. (1981). The workplace as a context for the socialization of youth. *Journal of Youth and Adolescence, 10*, 185–210.

Gregory, R. L. (1966). *Eye and brain: The psychology of seeing*. New York: McGraw-Hill.

Gregory, R. L. (1986). *Odd perceptions*. London: Methuen.

Gregory, W. L., & Burroughs, W. J. (Eds.) (1989). *Introduction to applied psychology*. Glenview, IL: Scott, Foresman.

Grossman, H. J. (1977). *A manual on terminology and classification in mental retardation*. Washington, D.C.: American Association on Mental Deficiency.

Grube, J. W., Kleinhesselink, R. R., & Kearney, K. A. (1982). Male self-acceptance and attraction toward women. *Personality and Social Psychology Bulletin, 8*, 107–112.

Gruetzner, H. (1988). *Alzheimer's: A caregiver's guide and sourcebook*. New York: Wiley.

Guerin, B. (1986). Mere presence effects in humans: A review. *Journal of Personality and Social Psychology, 22*, 38–77.

Guilford, J. P. (1967). *The nature of human intelligence*. New York: McGraw-Hill.

Guilford, J. P. (1975). Factors and factors of personality. *Psychological Bulletin, 82*, 802–814.

Gulevich, G., Dement, W. C., & Johnson, L. (1966). Psychiatric and EEG observations on a case of prolonged (264-hour) wakefulness. *Archives of General Psychiatry, 15*, 29–35.

Gurman, A. S. (1977). The patient's perception of the therapeutic relationship. In A. S. Gurman & A. M. Razin (Eds.), *Effective psychotherapy: A handbook of research*. New York: Pergamon.

Gutmann, D. (1975). Parenthood: A key to the comparative study of the life cycle. In N. Datan & L. H. Ginsberg (Eds.), *Life-span developmental psychology: Normative life crises*. New York: Academic Press.

Haan, N., Smith, M. B., & Block, J. (1968). Moral reasoning of young adults: Political-social behavior, family background, and personality correlates. *Journal of Personality and Social Psychology, 10*, 183–201.

Hall, C., & Van de Castle, R. L. (1966). *The content analysis of dreams*. East Norwalk, CT: Appleton-Century-Crofts.

Hall, E. T. (1966). *The hidden dimension*. Garden City, NY: Doubleday.

Hall, G. (1983). *Behaviour: An introduction to psychology as a biological science*. London: Academic Press.

Hall, G. S. (1904). *Adolescence* (Vol. 1). New York: Appleton.

Hamilton, D. L., & Gifford, R. K. (1976). Illusory correlation in interpersonal perception: A cognitive basis of stereotypic judgments. *Journal of Experimental Social Psychology, 12*, 392–407.

Hamilton, W. D. (1964). The genetical evolution of social behaviour. *Journal of Theoretical Biology, 12*, 12–45.

Hare, A. P. (1976). *Handbook of small group research* (2nd ed.). New York: Free Press.

Harkins, S. W., & Chapman, C. R. (1977). The perception of induced dental pain in young and elderly women. *Journal of Gerontology, 32*, 428–435.

Harlow, H. F. (1958). The nature of love. *American Psychologist, 13*, 673–685.

Harlow, H. F. (1965). Sexual behavior in the rhesus monkey. In F. Beach (Ed.), *Sex and behavior*. New York: Wiley.

Harrell, R. F., Woodyard, E. R., & Gates, A. I. (1956). The influence of vitamin supplementation of the diets of pregnant and lactating women on the intelligence of their offspring. *Metabolism, 5*, 555–562.

Harris, B. (1979). What ever happened to Little Albert? *American Psychologist, 34*, 151–160.

Harris, J. E. (1978). External memory aids. In M. M. Gruneberg, P. E. Morris, & R. N. Sykes (Eds.), *Practical aspects of memory*. London: Academic Press.

Hartshorne, H., & May, M. A. (1928). *Studies in deceit*. New York: Macmillan.

Hastie, R., Penrod, S. D., & Pennington, N. (1983). *Inside the jury*. Cambridge, MA: Harvard University Press.

Hastorf, A. H., & Cantril, H. (1954). They saw a game: A case study. *Journal of Abnormal and Social Psychology, 49*, 129–134.

Hatfield, E., & Sprecher, S. (1986). *Mirror, mirror: The importance of looks in everyday life*. Albany, NY: SUNY Press.

Hathaway, S. R., & McKinley, J. C. (1943). *The Minnesota Multiphasic Personality Inventory*. Minneapolis: University of Minnesota Press.

Hayward, M. D., Grady, W. R., & McLaughlin, S. D. (1988). The retirement process among older women in the United States: Changes in the 1970s. *Research on Aging, 10*, 358–382.

Hazan, C. C., & Shaver, P. (1987). Romantic love conceptualized as an attachment process. *Journal of Personality and Social Psychology, 52*, 511–524.

Heider, E. R. (1972). Universals in color naming and memory. *Journal of Experimental Psychology, 93*, 10–20.

Heider, F. (1944). Social perception and phenomenal causality. *Psychological Review, 51*, 358–374.

Heider, F. (1946). Attitude and cognitive organization. *Journal of Psychology, 21*, 107–112.

Heider, F. (1958). *The psychology of interpersonal relations*. New York: Wiley.

Heim, A. W. (1954). *The appraisal of intelligence*. London: Methuen.

Helson, H. (1964). *Adaptation level theory*. New York: Harper & Row.

Hemphill, J. K. (1950). *Leader behavior description*. Columbus: Ohio State University Personnel Research Board.

Hemphill, J. K. (1955). Leadership behavior associated with the administrative reputation of college departments. *Journal of Educational Psychology, 46*, 385–401.

Hendry, L. B., & Gillies, P. (1978). Body type, body esteem, school, and leisure: A study of overweight, average, and underweight adolescents. *Journal of Youth and Adolescence, 7*, 181–194.

Herrnstein, R. J., Loveland, D. H., & Cable, C. (1976). Natural concepts in pigeons. *Journal of Experimental Psychology: Animal Behavior Processes, 2*, 285–302.

Hetherington, E. M. (1979). Divorce: A child's perspective. *American Psychologist, 34*, 851–858.

Hetherington, E. M., & Arasteh, J. D. (1988). *Impact of divorce, single-parenting, and stepparenting in children.* Hillsdale, NJ: Erlbaum.

Hetherington, E. M., Cox, M., & Cox, R. (1978). The aftermath of divorce. In J. Stevens & M. Mathews (Eds.), *Mother-child, father-child relations.* Washington, D.C.: National Association for the Education of Young Children.

Hetherington, E. M., Cox., M., & Cox, R. (1979). Stress and coping in divorce: A focus on women. In J. E. Gullahorn (Ed.), *Psychology and women: In transition.* New York: Wiley.

Hetherington, E. M., Cox., M., & Cox, R. (1982). Effects of divorce on parents and children. In M. E. Lamb (Ed.), *Nontraditional families: Parenting and child development.* Hillsdale, NJ: Erlbaum.

Hilgard, E. R. (1973). A neodissociation interpretation of pain reduction in hypnosis. *Psychological Review, 80,* 396–411.

Hilgard, E. R. (1977). *Divided consciousness: Multiple controls in human thought and action.* New York: Wiley.

Hilgard, E. R. (1987). *Psychology in America: A historical survey.* San Diego: Harcourt Brace Jovanovich.

Hilgard, E. R., & Hilgard, J. R. (1983). *Hypnosis in the relief of pain.* Los Altos, CA: Kaufmann.

Hill, J., et al. (1985). Menarcheal status and parent-child relations in families of 7th-grade girls. *Journal of Youth and Adolescence, 14,* 301–316.

Hilton, D. J. (1990). Conversational processes and causal explanation. *Psychological Bulletin, 107,* 65–81.

Hinde, R. A., & Bateson, P. (1984). Discontinuities versus continuities in behavioral development and the neglect of process. *International Journal of Behavioral Development, 7,* 129–143.

Hirsch, J. (Ed.) (1967). *Behavior-genetic analysis.* New York: McGraw-Hill.

Hirsch-Pasek, K., Treiman, R., & Schneiderman, M. (1984). Brown and Hanlon revisited: Mothers' sensitivity to ungrammatical forms. *Journal of Child Language, 11,* 81–88.

Hite, S. (1981). *The Hite report on male sexuality.* New York: Ballantine.

Hite, S. (1987). *Women and sexuality.* New York: St. Martin's.

Hobson, J. A. (1988). *The dreaming brain.* New York: Basic Books.

Hobson, J. A., & McCarley, R. W. (1977). The brain as a dream state generator: An activation-synthesis hypothesis of the dream process. *American Journal of Psychiatry, 134,* 1335–1348.

Hodinko, B. A., & Whitley, S. D. (1971). *Student personnel administration: A critical incident approach.* Washington, D.C.: College Guidance Associates.

Hoffman, L. (1974). Effects of maternal employment on the child: A review of the research. *Developmental Psychology, 10,* 204–228.

Hoffman, L. (1989). Effects of maternal employment in the two-parent family. *American Psychologist, 44,* 283–292.

Hofmann, A. (1968). Psychotomimetic agents. In A. Burger (Ed.), *Drugs affecting the central nervous system* (Vol. 2). New York: Marcel Dekker.

Holland, J. L. (1966). *The psychology of vocational choice: A theory of personality types and model environments.* Waltham, MA: Blaisdell.

Holland, J. L. (1985). *Making vocational choices: A theory of vocational personalities and work environments* (2nd ed.). Englewood Cliffs, NJ: Prentice-Hall.

Holland, P. C. (1977). Conditioned stimulus as a determinant of the form for the Pavlovian conditioned response. *Journal of Experimental Psychology: Animal Behavior Processes, 3,* 77–104.

Holland, P. C. (1980). Influence of visual conditioned stimulus characteristics on the form of Pavlovian appetitive conditioned responding in rats. *Journal of Experimental Psychology: Animal Behavior Processes, 6,* 81–97.

Hollingshead, A. B., & Redlich, F. C. (1958). *Social class and mental illness: A community study.* New York: Wiley.

Hollingworth, L. S. (1942). *Children above 180 IQ.* New York: World Book.

Hollon, S., & Beck, A. T. (1986). Research on cognitive therapies. In S. L. Garfield & A. E. Bergin (Eds.), *Handbook of psychotherapy and behavior change* (3rd ed.). New York: Wiley.

Holmes, D. S. (1984). Meditation and somatic arousal reduction: A review of the experimental evidence. *American Psychologist, 39,* 1–10.

Holmes, T. H., & Rahe, R. H. (1967). The social readjustment rating scale. *Journal of Psychosomatic Research, 11,* 213–218.

Holt, E. B. (1931). *Animal drive and the learning process.* New York: Holt.

Holyoak, K. J., & Nisbett, R. E. (1988). Induction. In R. J. Sternberg & E. E. Smith (Eds.), *The psychology of human thought.* Cambridge: Cambridge University Press.

Honzik, M. P. (1984). Life-span development. *Annual Review of Psychology, 35,* 309–331.

Hormuth, S. E. (1986). The sampling of experiences *in situ. Journal of Personality, 54,* 262–293.

Horn, J. M. (1968). Organization of abilities and the development of intelligence. *Psychological Review, 75,* 242–259.

Horner, M. (1972). Toward an understanding of achievement-related conflicts in women. *Journal of Social Issues, 28,* 157–176.

Horwitz, W. A., Kestenbaum, C., Person, E., & Jarvik, L. F. (1965). Identical twins—"idiot savants"—calendar calculators. *American Journal of Psychiatry, 121,* 1075–1079.

House, R. J., & Singh, J. V. (1987). Organizational behavior: Some new directions for I/O psychology. *Annual Review of Psychology, 38,* 669–718.

Houseknecht, S. K. (1986). Voluntary childlessness: Toward a theoretical integration. In A. S. Skolnick & J. H. Skolnick (Eds.), *Family in transition* (5th ed.). Boston: Little, Brown.

Hovland, C. I., Janis, I. L., & Kelley, H. H. (1953). *Communication and persuasion.* New Haven, CT: Yale University Press.

Hovland, C. I., & Sears, R. R. (1940). Minor studies in aggression. VI: Correlation of lynchings with economic indices. *Journal of Personality, 9,* 301–310.

Hubel, D. H. (1979). The brain. *Scientific American, 241,* 45–53.

Hubel, D. H., & Wiesel, T. N. (1962). Receptive fields, binocular interaction and functional architecture in the cat's visual cortex. *Journal of Physiology, 160,* 106–154.

Hubel, D. H., & Wiesel, T. N. (1979). Brain mechanisms of vision. *Scientific American, 241,* 150–162.

Hughes, J., et al. (1975). Identification of two related pentapeptides from the brain with potent opiate agonist activity. *Nature, 258,* 577–579.

Hull, C. L. (1943). *Principles of behavior.* New York: Appleton-Century-Crofts.

Hunt, E. (1983). On the nature of intelligence. *Science, 219,* 141–146.

Hunt, J. M. (1982). Toward equalizing the developmental opportunities of infants and preschool children. *Journal of Social Issues, 38*(4), 163–191.

Hunt, M. (1974). *Sexual behavior in the 1970s.* Chicago: Playboy Press.

Hurvich, L. M., & Jameson, D. (1974). Opponent processes as a model of neural organization. *American Psychologist, 29,* 88–102.

Huxley, A. (1954). *The doors of perception.* New York: Harper & Row.

Huyck, M. H. (1982). From gregariousness to intimacy: Marriage and friendship over the adult years. In T. M. Field et al. (Eds.), *Review of human development.* New York: Wiley.

Hyde, J. S., & Linn, M. C. (1986). *The psychology of gender: Advances through meta-analysis.* Baltimore: The Johns Hopkins University Press.

Intraub, H. (1980). Presentation rate and the representation of briefly glimpsed pictures in memory. *Journal of Experimental Psychology: Human Learning and Memory, 6,* 1–12.

Izard, C. E. (1977). *Human Emotions.* New York: Plenum.

Jacklin, C. N. (1989). Female and male: Issues of gender. *American Psychologist, 44,* 127–133.

Jacobson, D. S. (1984). Neonatal correlates of prenatal exposure to smoking, caffeine, and alcohol. *Infant Behavior and Development, 7,* 253–265.

Jakobson, R. (1968). *Child language, aphasia, and phonological universals.* The Hague: Mouton.

James, W. (1884). What is emotion? *Mind, 4,* 188–204.

James, W. (1890). *Principles of psychology* (2 vols.). New York: Holt.

James, W. (1902). *The varieties of religious experience.* New York: Longmans, Green.

Janis, I. L. (1982). *Victims of groupthink.* Boston: Houghton Mifflin.

Jaynes, G. D., & Williams, R. M. (Eds.) (1989). *A common destiny: Blacks and American society.* Washington, D.C.: National Academy Press.

Jaynes, J. (1976). *The origins of consciousness in the breakdown of the bicameral mind.* Boston: Houghton Mifflin.

Jebb, R. C. (1870). *The characters of Theophrastus.* London: Macmillan

Jencks, C., et al. (1972). *Inequity: A reassessment of the effect of family and schooling in America.* New York: Basic Books.

Jensen, A. R. (1969). How much can we boost IQ and scholastic achievement? *Harvard Educational Review, 39,* 1–123.

Jerison, H. J. (1973). *Evolution of the brain and intelligence.* New York: Academic Press.

Jet (1986, September 8). Black college athletes hit hard by NCAA's new ruling. p. 49.

Jet (1986, February 3). Black college presidents vow to continue fight over NCAA's new Rule 48. p. 47.

John, O. P., Goldberg, L. R., & Angleitner, A. (1984). Better than the alphabet: Taxonomies of personality-descriptive terms in English, Dutch, and German. In H. J. C. Bonarius, G. L. M. van Heck, & N. G. Smid (Eds.), *Personality psychology in Europe*. Lisse, Switzerland: Swets & Zeitlinger.

Johnston, W. A., & Dark, V. J. (1986). Selective attention. *Annual Review of Psychology, 37,* 43–75.

Jones, E. E., & Davis, K. E. (1965). A theory of correspondent inferences: From acts to dispositions. In L. Berkowitz (Ed.), *Advances in experimental and social psychology* (Vol. 2). New York: Academic Press.

Jones, K. L., Smith, D. W., Ulleland, C. N., & Streissguth, A. P. (1973). Pattern of malformation in offspring of chronic alcoholic mothers. *Lancet, 1,* 1267–1271.

Jones, M. C. (1924). A laboratory study of fear: The case of Peter. *Journal of Genetic Psychology, 31,* 308–315.

Jordan, T. G., Grallo, R., Deutsch, M., & Deutsch, C. P. (1985). Long-term effects of enrichment: A 20-year perspective on persistence and change. *American Journal of Community Psychology, 13,* 393–414.

Jung, C. G. (1907). The psychology of dementia praecox. *Collected works* (Vol. 3). New York: Pantheon.

Kaas, J. H. (1987). The organization of neocortex in mammals: Implications for theories of brain function. *Annual Review of Psychology, 38,* 129–151.

Kagan, J., Reznick, J. S., & Gibbons, J. (1989). Inhibited and uninhibited types of children. *Child Development, 60,* 838–845.

Kahneman, D. (1973). *Attention and effort*. Englewood Cliffs, NJ: Prentice-Hall.

Kahneman, D., & Tversky, A. (1973). On the psychology of prediction. *Psychological Review, 80,* 237–251.

Kalinowsky, L. B. (1980). Convulsive therapies. In H. I. Kaplan, A. M. Freedman, & B. J. Sadock (Eds.), *Comprehensive textbook of psychiatry* (Vol. 3, 3rd ed.). Baltimore: Williams & Wilkins.

Kalven, H., & Zeisel, H. (1966). *The American jury*. Boston: Little, Brown.

Kamin, L. J. (1969). Predictability, surprise, attention, and conditioning. In B. A. Campbell & R. M. Church (Eds.), *Punishment and aversive behavior*. New York: Appleton-Century-Crofts.

Kamin, L. J. (1974). *The science and politics of IQ*. Potomac, MD: Erlbaum.

Kandel, E. R., & Schwartz, J. H. (1982). Molecular biology of learning: Modulation of transmitter release. *Science, 218,* 433–443.

Kanin, E. J. (1984). Date rape: Unofficial criminals and victims. *Victimology, 9,* 95–108.

Kanner, A. D., Coyne, J. C., Schaefer, C., & Lazarus, R. S. (1981). Comparison of two modes of stress measurement: Daily hassles and uplifts versus major life events. *Journal of Behavioral Medicine, 4,* 1–39.

Kaplan, H. S. (1974). *The new sex therapy*. New York: Bruner/Mazel.

Kaplan, H. S. (1979). *Disorders of desire*. New York: Bruner/Mazel.

Kaplan, S., & Kaplan, R. (1982). *Cognition and environment: Functioning in an uncertain world*. New York: Praeger.

Katchadourian, H. A. (1985). *Fundamentals of human sexuality* (4th ed.). New York: Holt, Rinehart, & Winston.

Katchadourian, H. A. (1989). *Fundamentals of human sexuality* (5th ed.). Fort Worth, TX: Holt, Rinehart, & Winston.

Kaye, K., & Marcus, J. (1978). Imitation over a series of trials without feedback: Age six months. *Infant Behavior and Development, 1,* 141–155.

Keen, S. (1986). *Faces of the enemy: Reflections of the hostile imagination*. New York: Harper & Row.

Keesey, R. E., & Powley, T. L. (1986). The regulation of body weight. *Annual Review of Psychology, 37,* 109–133.

Kelley, H. H. (1973). The process of causal attribution. *American Psychologist, 28,* 107–128.

Kelley, H. H., & Thibaut, J. W. (1978). *Interpersonal relations: A theory of interdependence*. New York: Wiley.

Kelly, G. A. (1955). *The psychology of personal constructs*. New York: Norton.

Kendall, P. C., et al. (1979). Cognitive-behavioral and patient education interventions in cardiac catheterization procedures: The Palo Alto medical psychology project. *Journal of Consulting and Clinical Psychology, 47,* 49–58.

Kendall, P. C., & Turk, D. C. (1984). Cognitive-behavioral strategies and health enhancement. In J. D. Matarazzo et al. (Eds.), *Behavioral health: A handbook of health enhancement and disease prevention*. New York: Wiley.

Kennedy, G. (1984). *Invitation to statistics.* Oxford: Basil Blackwell.

Kenny, D. A., & Zaccaro, S. J. (1983). An estimate of variance due to traits in leadership. *Journal of Applied Psychology, 68,* 678–685.

Kenshalo, D. R. (Ed.) (1968). *The skin senses.* Springfield, IL: Thomas.

Kety, S. S. (1974). From rationalization to reason. *American Journal of Psychiatry, 131,* 957–963.

Kihlstrom, J. F. (1985). Hypnosis. *Annual Review of Psychology, 36,* 385–418.

Kilmann, P., et al. (1982). The treatment of sexual paraphilias: A review of the outcome research. *The Journal of Sex Research, 18,* 193–252.

Kimble, G. A. (1984). Psychology's two cultures. *American Psychologist, 39,* 833–839.

King, N. J., Hamilton, D. I., & Murphy, G. C. (1983). The prevention of children's maladaptive fears. *Child and Family Behavior Therapy, 5,* 43–57.

Kinsey, A. C., Pomeroy, W. D., & Martin, C. E. (1948). *Sexual behavior in the human male.* Philadelphia: Saunders.

Kinsey, A. C., Pomeroy, W. D., Martin, C. E., & Gebhard, P. H. (1953). *Sexual behavior in the human female.* Philadelphia: Saunders.

Kintsch, W. (1974). *The representation of meaning in memory.* Hillsdale, NJ: Erlbaum.

Klahr, D., Chase, W. G., & Lovelace, E. A. (1983). Structure and process in alphabetic retrieval. *Journal of Experimental Psychology: Learning, Memory, and Cognition, 9,* 462–477.

Klerman, G. L. (1986). Drugs and psychotherapy. In S. L. Garfield & A. E. Bergin (Eds.), *Handbook of psychotherapy and behavior change* (3rd ed.). New York: Wiley.

Knapp, T. J. (1974). The Premack Principle in human experimental and applied settings. *Behaviour Research and Therapy, 14,* 133–147.

Knapp, T. J. (1986). The emergence of cognitive psychology in the latter half of the twentieth century. In T. J. Knapp & L. C. Robertson (Eds.), *Approaches to cognition: Contrasts and controversies.* Hillsdale, NJ: Erlbaum.

Kohlberg, L. (1981). *Essays on moral development* (Vol. 1) *The philosophy of moral development.* New York: Harper & Row.

Kohlberg, L. (1984). *Essays on moral development* (Vol. 2) *The nature and validity of moral stages.* San Francisco: Harper & Row.

Kohlberg, L., & Gilligan, C. (1971). The adolescent as a philosopher: The discovery of the self in a postconventional world. *Daedalus, 100,* 1051–1086.

Köhler, W. (1924). *The mentality of apes.* London: Kegan Paul.

Korchin, S. J., & Schuldberg, D. (1981). The future of clinical assessment. *American Psychologist, 36,* 1147–1158.

Kosslyn, S. M. (1980). *Image and mind.* Cambridge, MA: Harvard University Press.

Kramer, D. A., & Woodruff, D. S. (1984). Categorization and metaphoric processing in young and older adults. *Research on Aging, 6,* 271–286.

Krantz, D. S., Grunberg, N. E., & Baum, A. (1985). Health psychology. *Annual Review of Psychology, 36,* 349–383.

Kreuz, L. E., & Rose, R. M. (1972). Assessment of aggressive behavior and plasma testosterone in a young criminal population. *Psychosomatic Medicine, 34,* 321–332.

Kripke, D. F., et al. (1979). Short and long sleep and sleeping pills: Is increased mortality associated? *Archives of General Psychiatry, 36,* 103–116.

Krippner, S., & Hughes, W. (1970). Dreams and human potential. *Journal of Humanistic Psychology, 10,* 1–20.

Kübler-Ross, E. (1969). *On death and dying.* New York: Macmillan

Kuhn, T. S. (1970). *The structure of scientific revolutions* (2nd ed.). Chicago: University of Chicago Press.

Kulik, J. A., Bangert-Drowns, R. L., & Kulik, C. C. (1984). Effectiveness of coaching for aptitude tests. *Psychological Bulletin, 95,* 179–188.

Kurtzburg, R. L., Safar, H., & Cavior, N. (1968). Surgical and social rehabilitation of adult offenders. *Proceedings of the 76th Annual Convention of the American Psychological Association, 3,* 649–650.

Kutchinsky, B. (1973). The effect of easy availability of pornography on the incidence of sex crimes: The Danish experience. *Journal of Social Issues, 29,* 163–182.

Kutner, B., Wilkins, C., & Yarrow, P. R. (1952). Verbal attitudes and overt behavior involving racial prejudice. *Journal of Abnormal and Social Psychology, 47,* 649–652.

Laing, R. D. (1965). *The divided self.* Baltimore: Penguin.

Laing, R. D. (1967). *The politics of experience.* New York: Pantheon.

Langer, E. J. (1978). Rethinking the role of social interaction. In J. H. Harvey, W. J. Ickes, & R. F. Kidd

(Eds.), *New directions in attribution research* (Vol. 2). Hillsdale, NJ: Erlbaum.

Langer, E. J. (1989). *Mindfulness*. Reading, MA: Addison-Wesley.

Langer, E. J., Blank, A., & Chanowitz, B. (1978). The mindlessness of ostensibly thoughtful actions: The role of placebic information in interpersonal interaction. *Journal of Personality and Social Psychology, 36,* 635–642.

Langer, E. J., Janis, I. L., & Wolfer, J. (1975). Reduction of psychological stress in surgical patients. *Journal of Experimental Social Psychology, 11,* 155–165.

Langer, E. J., & Rodin, J. (1976). The effects of choice and enhanced personal responsibility for the aged: A field experiment in an institutional setting. *Journal of Personality and Social Psychology, 34,* 191–198.

LaPiere, R. T. (1934). Attitudes and actions. *Social Forces, 13,* 230–237.

Lashley, K. S. (1929). *Brain mechanisms and intelligence.* Chicago: University of Chicago Press.

Lashley, K. S. (1950). In search of the engram. *Symposium of the Society for Experimental Biology, 4,* 454–482.

Latané, B., Williams, K., & Harkins, S. (1979). Many hands make light the work: The causes and consequences of social loafing. *Journal of Personality and Social Psychology, 37,* 822–832.

Laurence, J. R., & Perry, C. (1983). Hypnotically created memory among highly hypnotizable subjects. *Science, 222,* 523–524.

Lazarus, R. S. (1966). *Psychological stress and the coping process.* New York: McGraw-Hill.

Lazarus, R. S. (1982). Thoughts on the relations between emotion and cognition. *American Psychologist, 37,* 1019–1024.

Lazarus, R. S., & DeLongis, A. (1983). Psychological stress and coping in aging. *American Psychologist, 38,* 245–254.

Lazarus, R. S., & Folkman, S. (1984). *Stress, appraisal, and coping.* New York: Springer.

Leakey, R. E. (1979). Introduction. In C. Darwin, *The illustrated origin of species.* New York: Hill & Wang.

Leary, T. (1964). The religious experience: Its production and interpretation. *Psychedelic Review, 1,* 324–346.

LeBon, G. (1895/1960). *The crowd: A study of the popular mind.* New York: Viking.

Le Guin, U. K. (1969). *The left hand of darkness.* New York: Ace Books.

Lehman, D. R., Lembert, R. O., & Nisbett, R. E. (1988). The effect of graduate training on reasoning: Formal discipline and thinking about everyday-life events. *American Psychologist, 43,* 431–442.

Lehmann, H. E. (1980). Schizophrenia: Clinical features. In H. I. Kaplan, A. M. Freedman, & B. J. Sadock (Eds.), *Comprehensive textbook of psychiatry* (Vol. 2, 3rd ed.). Baltimore: Williams & Wilkins.

Leman, K. (1985). *The birth order book: Why you are the way you are.* New York: Dell.

Lenneberg, E. H. (1967). *Biological foundations of language.* New York: Wiley.

Lerner, R. M. (1984). *On the nature of human plasticity.* New York: Cambridge University Press.

Lesgold, A. (1988). Problem solving. In R. J. Sternberg & E. E. Smith (Eds.), *The psychology of human thought.* Cambridge: Cambridge University Press.

Levenkron, J. C., Cohen, J. D., Mueller, H. S., & Fisher, E. B. (1983). Modifying the Type A coronary-prone behavior pattern. *Journal of Consulting and Clinical Psychology, 51,* 192–204.

Leventhal, H., & Tomarken, A. J. (1986). Emotion: Today's problems. *Annual Review of Psychology, 37,* 565–610.

Levinson, D. J. (1978). *The seasons of a man's life.* New York: Knopf.

Lewin, K. (1951). *Field theory in social science: Selected theoretical papers.* New York: Harper.

Lewin, K., Lippett, R., & White, R. K. (1939). Patterns of aggressive behavior in experimentally created "social climates." *Journal of Social Psychology, 10,* 271–299.

Lewinsohn, P. M. (1974). A behavioral approach to depression. In R. J. Friedman & M. M. Katz (Eds.), *The psychology of depression: Contemporary theory and research.* Washington, D.C.: Winston-Wiley.

Lewinsohn, P. M., Mischel, W., Chaplin, W., & Barton, R. (1980). Social competence and depression: The role of illusory self-perceptions. *Journal of Abnormal Psychology, 89,* 203–212.

Lezak, M. D. (1976). *Neuropsychological assessment.* New York: Oxford.

Liddell, H. S. (1944). Conditioned reflex method and experimental neurosis. In J. McV. Hunt (Ed.), *Personality and the behavior disorders* (Vol. 1). New York: Ronald Press.

Liebowitz, M. R., et al. (1985). Lactate provocation of panic attacks: II. Biochemical and physiological findings. *Archives of General Psychiatry, 42,* 709–719.

Lindsay, P. H., & Norman, D. A. (1972). *Human information processing: An introduction to psychology.* New York: Academic Press.

Lippmann, W. (1922). *Public opinion.* New York: Harcourt, Brace.

Littman, R. A., & Manning, H. M. (1954). A methodological study of cigarette brand discrimination. *Journal of Applied Psychology, 38,* 185–190.

Lloyd, C. (1980). Life events and depressive disorder reviewed: I. Events as predisposing factors: II. Events as precipitation factors. *Archives of General Psychiatry, 37,* 529–548.

Locke, E. A., Shaw, K. N., Saari, L. M., & Latham, G. (1981). Goal setting and task performance: 1969–1980. *Psychological Bulletin, 90,* 124–152.

Locke, J. (1690/1961). *An essay concerning human understanding* (Vols. 1–2). New York: Dutton.

Loehlin, J. C., Lindzey, G., & Spuhler, J. N. (1975). *Race differences in intelligence.* San Francisco: Freeman.

Loehlin, J. C., Willerman, L., & Horn, J. M. (1988). Human behavior genetics. *Annual Review of Psychology, 39,* 101–133.

Loftus, E. F. (1979). *Eyewitness testimony.* Cambridge, MA: Harvard University Press.

Loftus, E. F., & Loftus, G. R. (1980). On the permanence of stored information in the human brain. *American Psychologist, 35,* 409–420.

Logan, G. D. (1980). Attention and automaticity in stroop and primary tasks: Theory and data. *Cognitive Psychology, 12,* 523–553.

Loomis, A. L., Harvey, E. N., & Hobart, G. A. (1937). Cerebral states during sleep as studied by human brain potentials. *Journal of Experimental Psychology, 21,* 127–144.

Lord, R. G., De Vader, C. L., & Alliger, G. M. (1986). A meta-analysis of the relation between personality traits and leadership perceptions: An application of validity generalization procedures. *Journal of Applied Psychology, 71,* 402–410.

Lorenz, K. (1937). The companion in the bird's world. *Auk, 54,* 245–273.

Lorenz, K. (1965). *Evolution and modification of behavior.* Chicago: University of Chicago Press.

Lorenz, K. (1966). *On aggression.* New York: Harcourt Brace Jovanovich.

Lorion, R. P., & Felner, R. D. (1986). Research on mental health interventions with the disadvantaged. In S. L. Garfield & A. E. Bergin (Eds.), *Handbook of psychotherapy and behavior change* (3rd ed.). New York: Wiley.

Lovaas, O. I. (1977). *The autistic child: Language development through behavior modification.* New York: Halsted.

Lowe, M., & Hubbard, R. (Eds.) (1983). *Woman's nature: Rationalization through inequity.* New York: Pergamon.

Luborsky, L. (1970). New directions in research on neurotic and psychosomatic symptoms. *American Scientist, 58,* 661–668.

Luborsky, L. (1984). *Principles of psychoanalytic psychotherapy.* New York: Basic Books.

Luborsky, L., Crits-Christoph, P., & Mellon, J. (1986). Advent of objective measures of the transference concept. *Journal of Consulting and Clinical Psychology, 54,* 39–47.

Luborsky, L., & DeRubeis, R. J. (1984). The use of psychotherapy treatment manuals—a small revolution in psychotherapy research style. *Clinical Psychology Review, 4,* 5–14.

Luborsky, L., & Spence, D. P. (1978). Quantitative research on psychoanalytic therapy. In S. L. Garfield & A. E. Bergin (Eds.), *Handbook of psychotherapy and behavior change* (2nd ed.). New York: Wiley.

Luborsky, L., Singer, B., & Luborsky, L. (1975). Comparative studies of psychotherapies. Is it true that "Everyone has won and all must have prizes"? *Archives of General Psychiatry, 32,* 995–1007.

Ludwig, A. O., & Ranson, S. W. (1947). A statistical followup of treatment of combat-induced psychiatric casualties. *Military Surgeon, 100,* 51–62; 169–175.

Luker, K. (1986). Motherhood and morality in America. In A. S. Skolnick & J. H. Skolnick (Eds.), *Family in transition* (5th ed.). Boston: Little, Brown.

Lumsdaine, A. A., & Janis, I. L. (1953). Resistance to "counter-propaganda" produced by one-sided and two-sided "propaganda" presentations. *Public Opinion Quarterly, 17,* 311–318.

Lumsden, C. J., & Wilson, E. O. (1981). *Genes, mind, and culture: The coevolutionary process.* Cambridge, MA: Harvard University Press.

Luria, A. R. (1987). *The mind of a mnemonist: A little book about a vast memory.* Cambridge, MA: Harvard University Press.

Lynch, S., & Yarnell, P. R. (1973). Retrograde amnesia: Delayed forgetting after concussion. *American Journal of Psychology, 86,* 643–645.

Lynn, S. J., & Ruhe, J. W. (1986). The fantasy-prone person: Hypnosis, imagination, and creativity. *Journal of Personality and Social Psychology, 51,* 404–408.

Lyon, J., & Gorner, P. (1987, July 19). There's hope for the hopeless. *Chicago Tribune,* pp. 5–10.

Maccoby, E. E., & Jacklin, C. N. (1974). *The psychology of sex differences.* Palo Alto, CA: Stanford University Press.

Mackay, A. V. P. (1980). Positive and negative schizophrenic symptoms and the role of dopamine. *British Journal of Psychiatry, 137,* 379–386.

Mackett-Stout, J., & Dewar, R. (1981). Evaluation of symbolic public information signs. *Human Factors, 23,* 129–151.

MacKinnon, D. W. (1962). The personality correlates of creativity: A study of American architects. In G. S. Nielsen (Ed.), *Proceedings of the 14th International Congress of Applied Psychology* (Vol. 2). Copenhagen: Munksgaard.

Maclean, C. (1977). *The wolf children.* New York: Hill & Wang.

MacLusky, N. J., & Naftolin, F. (1981). Sexual differentiation of the central nervous system. *Science, 211,* 1294–1303.

Maier, S. F., & Jackson, R. L. (1979). Learned helplessness: all of us were right (and wrong)—inescapable shock has multiple effects. In G. H. Bower (Ed.), *The psychology of learning and motivation* (Vol. 13). New York: Academic Press.

Maier, S. F., & Seligman, M. E. P. (1976). Learned helplessness: Theory and evidence. *Journal of Experimental Psychology: General, 105,* 3–46.

Mair, R. G., Bouffard, J. A., Engen, T., & Morton, T. (1978). Olfactory sensitivity during the menstrual cycle. *Sensory Processes, 2,* 90–98.

Mandler, G. (1984). *Mind and body: The psychology of emotion and stress.* New York: Norton.

Manis, M. (1977). Cognitive social psychology. *Personality and Social Psychology Bulletin, 3,* 550–556.

Mann, R. D. (1959). A review of the relationships between personality and performance in small groups. *Psychological Bulletin, 56,* 241–270.

March, J. G., & Simon, H. A. (1958). *Organizations.* New York: Wiley.

Marcuse, H. (1962). *Eros and civilization.* New York: Vintage.

Maringer, J., & Bandi, H-G. (1953). *Art in the ice age.* New York: Praeger.

Marks, L. E. (1975). On colored-hearing synesthesia: Cross-modal translations of sensory dimensions. *Psychological Bulletin, 82,* 303–331.

Markus, H., & Zajonc, R. B. (1985). The cognitive perspective in social psychology. In G. Lindzey & E. Aronson (Eds.), *Handbook of social psychology* (Vol. 1, 3rd ed.). New York: Random House.

Marshall, J. C. (1982). Models of the mind in health and disease. In A. W. Ellis (Eds.), *Normality and pathology in cognitive functions.* London: Academic Press.

Martens, R. (1975). *Social psychology and physical activity.* New York: Harper & Row.

Martin, D. (1989). Engineering psychology. In W. L. Gregory & W. J. Burroughs (Eds.), *Introduction to applied psychology.* Glenview, IL: Scott, Foresman.

Maslow, A. H. (1970). *Motivation and personality* (2nd ed.). New York: Harper & Row.

Masserman, J. H. (1943). *Behavior and neurosis.* Chicago: University of Chicago Press.

Masson, J. M. (1983). *Assault on the truth: Freud's suppression of the seduction theory.* New York: Farrar, Straus, & Giroux.

Masters, W. H. (1980). Update on sexual physiology. Unpublished paper quoted in H. A. Katchadourian (1985). *Fundamentals of human sexuality.* New York: Holt, Rinehart, & Winston.

Masters, W. H., & Johnson, V. E. (1966). *Human sexual response.* Boston: Little, Brown.

Masters, W. H., & Johnson, V. E. (1970). *Human sexual inadequacy.* Boston: Little, Brown.

Matin, L., & MacKinnon, G. E. (1964). Autokinetic movement: Selective manipulation of directional components by image stabilization. *Science, 143,* 147–148.

Matlin, M. W. (1988). *Sensation and perception* (2nd ed.). Boston: Allyn & Bacon.

Matthews, K. A. (1982). Psychological perspectives on the Type A behavior pattern. *Psychological Bulletin, 91,* 293–323.

Matthies, H. (1989). Neurobiological aspects of learning and memory. *Annual Review of Psychology, 40,* 381–404.

Matthysse, S. (1977). The role of dopamine in schizophrenia. In E. Usdin, D. A. Hamburg, & J. D. Barkus (Eds.), *Neuroregulators and psychiatric disorders.* New York: Oxford.

Maugh, T. H. (1988, January). Mexican medicine to change your mind. *Discover,* pp. 39–40.

Maurer, D., & Maurer, C. (1988). *The world of the newborn.* New York: Basic Books.

Maurer, D., & Salapatek, P. (1976). Developmental changes in the scanning of faces by young infants. *Child Development, 47,* 523–527.

Mayo, E. (1933). *The human problems of an industrial civilization.* New York: Macmillan.

McArdle, J. (1984, Spring). Psychological experimentation on animals: Not necessary, not valid. *The Humane Society News*, pp. 1–3.

McCann, I. L., & Holmes, D. S. (1984). Influence of aerobic exercise on depression. *Journal of Personality and Social Psychology, 46*, 1142–1147.

McClelland, D. C. (1961). *The achieving society.* Princeton, NJ: Van Nostrand.

McClelland, D. C. (1973). Testing for competence rather than "intelligence." *American Psychologist, 28*, 1–14.

McClelland, D. C. (1975). *Power: The inner experience.* New York: Wiley.

McClelland, D. C. (1982). The need for power, sympathetic activation, and illness. *Motivation and Emotion, 6*, 31–41.

McConnell, J. V. (1962). Memory transfer through cannibalism in planarians. *Journal of Neuropsychiatry Supplement 1, 3*, 542–548.

McConnell, J. V. (1964). Cannibalism and memory in flatworms. *New Scientist, 21*, 465–468.

McCrae, R. R., & Costa, P. T. (1984). *Emerging lives, enduring dispositions: Personality in adulthood.* Boston: Little, Brown.

McCrae, R. R., & Costa, P. T. (1987). Validation of the five-factor model of personality across instruments and observers. *Journal of Personality and Social Psychology, 52*, 81–90.

McDougall, W. (1908). *An introduction to social psychology.* London: Methuen.

McDougall, W. (1920). *The group mind.* New York: Putnam.

McEvoy, G. M., & Cascio, W. F. (1985). Strategies for reducing employee turnover: A meta-analysis. *Journal of Applied Psychology, 70*, 342–353.

McGill, A. L. (1989). Context effects in judgments of causation. *Journal of Personality and Social Psychology, 57*, 189–200.

McGinnies, E. (1949). Emotionality and perceptual defense. *Psychological Review, 56*, 244–251.

McGlone, J. (1980). Sex differences in human brain asymmetry: A critical survey. *Behavioral and Brain Sciences, 3*, 215–263.

McGrath, M. J., & Cohen, D. B. (1978). REM sleep facilitation of adaptive waking behavior: A review of the literature. *Psychological Bulletin, 85*, 24–57.

McGuire, W. J. (1968). Personality and susceptibility to social influence. In E. F. Borgatta & W. W. Lambert (Eds.), *Handbook of personality theory and research.* Chicago: Rand McNally.

McKillip, J., & Riedel, S. L. (1983). External validity of matching on physical attractiveness for same and opposite sex couples. *Journal of Applied Social Psychology, 13*, 328–337.

McLeod, J. D. (1987). *Childhood parental loss and adult depression.* Unpublished dissertation, University of Michigan.

McNeal, J. U. (1982). *Consumer behavior: An integrative approach.* Boston: Little, Brown.

McNeill, D. (1966). Developmental psycholinguistics. In F. Smith & G. A. Miller (Eds.), *The genesis of language: A psycholinguistic approach.* Cambridge, MA: MIT Press.

Mead, M. (1928). *Coming of age in Samoa.* New York: Morrow.

Mead, M. (1978). *Culture and commitment.* Garden City, NY: Anchor.

Medin, D. L., & Schaffer, M. M. (1978). A context theory of classification. *Psychological Review, 85*, 207–238.

Meehl, P. E. (1954). *Clinical versus statistical prediction.* Minneapolis: University of Minnesota Press.

Meehl, P. E. (1957). When shall we use our heads instead of the formula? *Journal of Counseling Psychology, 4*, 268–273.

Meehl, P. E. (1977). Why I do not attend case conferences. In *Psychodiagnosis.* New York: Norton.

Meltzoff, A. N., & Moore, M. K. (1977). Imitation of facial and manual gestures by human neonates. *Science, 198*, 75–78.

Melzack, R. (1973). *The puzzle of pain.* London: Penguin.

Mendelsohn, G. A. (1983). What should we tell students about theories of personality? *Contemporary Psychology, 28*, 435–437.

Menning, B. (1977). *Infertility: A guide for childless couples.* Englewood Cliffs, NJ: Prentice-Hall.

Mercer, J. R. (1973). *Labeling the retarded.* Berkeley: University of California Press.

Merton, R. K. (1946). *Mass persuasion.* New York: Harper.

Meyer, J. K., & Reter, D. J. (1979). Sex reassignment. *Archives of General Psychiatry, 36*, 1010–1015.

Michener, J. A. (1976). *Sports in America.* New York: Random House.

Middlemist, R. D., & Peterson, R. B. (1976). Test of equity theory by controlling for comparison of workers' efforts. *Organizational Behavior and Human Performance, 15*, 335–354.

Milgram, S. (1963). Behavioral study of obedience. *Journal of Abnormal and Social Psychology, 67*, 371–378.

Milgram, S. (1974). *Obedience to authority.* New York: Harper & Row.

Miller, G. A. (1956). The magical number seven, plus or minus two: Some limits on our capacity for processing information. *Psychological Review, 63,* 81–97.

Miller, N. E. (1978). Biofeedback and visceral learning. *Annual Review of Psychology, 29,* 373–404.

Miller, N. E. (1985). The value of behavioral research on animals. *American Psychologist, 40,* 423–440.

Miller, W. R. (1983). Controlled drinking: A history and a clinical review. *Journal of Studies on Alcohol, 44,* 68–83.

Millon, T. (1981). *Disorders of personality.* New York: Wiley.

Mineka, S., & Henderson, R. W. (1985). Controllability and predictability in acquired motivation. *Annual Review of Psychology, 36,* 495–529.

Mischel, W. (1968). *Personality and assessment.* New York: Wiley.

Mischel, W. (1973). Toward a cognitive social learning reconceptualization of personality. *Psychological Review, 80,* 252–283.

Mischel, W. (1986). *Introduction to personality* (4th ed.). New York: Holt.

Modgil, S., & Modgil, C. (1987). *Arthur Jensen: Consensus and controversy.* New York: Falmer.

Money, J. (1965). Psychosexual differentiation. In J. Money (Ed.), *Sex research: New directions.* New York: Holt, Rinehart, & Winston.

Money, J. (1980). Genetic and chromosomal aspects of homosexual etiology. In J. L. Marmour (Ed.), *Homosexual behavior.* New York: Basic Books.

Money, J., & Ehrhardt, A. A. (1972). *Man and woman, boy and girl.* Baltimore: The Johns Hopkins University Press.

Monohan, L., Kuhn, D., & Shaver, P. (1974). Intrapsychic versus cultural explanations of the "fear of success" motive. *Journal of Personality and Social Psychology, 29,* 60–64.

Montemayor, R. (1982). The relationship between parent-adolescent conflict and the amount of time adolescents spend alone and with parents and peers. *Child Development, 53,* 1512–1519.

Mook, D. G. (1987). *Motivation: The organization of action.* New York: Norton.

Mora, G. (1980). Historical and theoretical trends in psychiatry. In H. I. Kaplan, A. M. Freedman, & B. J. Sadock (Eds.), *Comprehensive textbook of psychiatry* (Vol. 1, 3rd ed.). Baltimore: Williams & Wilkins.

Moray, N. (1959). Attention in dichotic listening: Affective cues and the influence of instructions. *Quarterly Journal of Experimental Psychology, 11,* 56–60.

Morgan, C. D., & Murray, H. A. (1935). A method for investigating fantasies. *Archives of Neurology and Psychiatry, 34,* 289–306.

Morris, D. (1967). *The naked ape.* London: Jonathan Cape.

Mortimer, J. T. (1976). Social class, work, and family: Some implications of the father's occupation for family relationships and son's career decisions. *Journal of Marriage and the Family, 38,* 241–256.

Mowen, J. C. (1989). Consumer psychology. In W. L. Gregory and W. J. Burroughs (Eds.), *Introduction to applied psychology.* Glenview, IL: Scott, Foresman.

Mowrer, O. H. (1950). *Learning theory and personality dynamics.* New York: Ronald Press.

Mowrer, O. H. (1960). *Learning theory and behavior.* New York: Wiley.

Murphy, G. (1947). *Personality: A biosocial approach to origins and structure.* New York: Harper.

Murray, E. A., & Mishkin, M. (1985). Amygdalectomy impairs cross-modal associations in monkeys. *Science, 228,* 604–606.

Murray, H. A. (1938). *Explorations in personality.* New York: Oxford.

Murstein, B. I. (1976). *Who will marry whom.* New York: Springer.

Myers, D. G. (1987). *Social psychology* (2nd ed.). New York: McGraw-Hill.

Myers, D. G., & Lamm, H. (1976). The group polarization phenomenon. *Psychological Bulletin, 83,* 602–627.

National Institute of Mental Health (1985). *Mental health, United States, 1985.* Washington, D.C.: U.S. Government Printing Office.

Neal, J. H. (1983). Children's understanding of their parents' divorces. In L. A. Kurdek (Ed.), *New directions for child development* (No. 19). San Francisco: Jossey-Bass.

Neimark, E. D. (1982). Adolescent thought: Transition to formal operations. In B. B. Wolman & G. Strickler (Eds.), *Handbook of developmental psychology.* Englewood Cliffs, NJ: Prentice-Hall.

Neimeyer, R. A., & Chapman, K. M. (1980–1981). Self/ideal discrepancy and fear of death: The test of an existential hypothesis. *Omega, 11,* 233–239.

Neisser, U. (1967). *Cognitive psychology.* Englewood Cliffs, NJ: Prentice-Hall.

Neisser, U. (1981). John Dean's memory: A case study. *Cognition, 9,* 1–22.

Neisser, U. (1982). *Memory observed: Remembering in natural contexts.* New York: Freeman.

Nemiah, J. C. (1980). Phobic disorder (phobic neurosis). In H. I. Kaplan, A. M. Freedman, & B. J. Sadock (Eds.), *Comprehensive textbook of psychiatry* (Vol. 2, 3rd ed.). Baltimore: Williams & Wilkins.

Neugarten, B. L. (1970). Adaptation and the life cycle. *Journal of Geriatric Psychiatry, 4,* 71–87.

Neugarten, B. L. (1977). Personality and aging. In J. E. Birren & K. W. Schaie (Eds.), *Handbook of the psychology of aging.* New York: Van Nostrand Reinhold.

Newcomb, T. M. (1943). *Personality and social change: Attitude change in a social community.* New York: Holt.

Newcomb, T. M., Koenig, K. E., Flacks, R., & Warwick, D. P. (1967). *Persistence and change: Bennington College and its students after 25 years.* New York: Wiley.

Nickerson, R. A., & Adams, M. J. (1979). Long-term memory for a common object. *Cognitive Psychology, 11,* 287–307.

Nieva, V. F., & Gutek, B. A. (1981). *Women and work: A psychological perspective.* New York: Praeger.

Nisan, M., & Kohlberg, L. (1982). Universality and variation in moral judgment: A longitudinal and cross-sectional study in Turkey. *Child Development, 53,* 865–876.

Nisbett, R. E., & Wilson, T. D. (1977). Telling more than we can know: Verbal reports on mental processes. *Psychological Review, 84,* 231–259.

Nolen-Hoeksema, S. (1987). Sex differences in unipolar depression: Theory and evidence. *Psychological Bulletin, 101,* 259–282.

Norman, W. T. (1963). Toward an adequate taxonomy of personality attributes: Replicated factor structure in peer nomination personality ratings. *Journal of Abnormal and Social Psychology, 66,* 574–583.

Norton, A. J. (1983). Family life cycle: 1980. *Journal of Marriage and the Family, 45,* 267–275.

Novak, M. A., & Harlow, H. F. (1975). Social recovery of monkeys isolated for the first year of life: I. *Developmental Psychology, 11,* 453–465.

Offer, D., Ostrov, E., & Howard, K. (1981). *The adolescent: A psychological self-portrait.* New York: Basic Books.

Olds, J., & Milner, P. (1954). Positive reinforcement produced by electrical stimulation of septal area and other regions of rat brain. *Journal of Comparative and Physiological Psychology, 47,* 419–427.

Oliner, S. P., & Oliner, P. M. (1988). *The altruistic personality: Rescuers of Jews in Nazi Europe.* New York: Free Press.

Ollendick, T. H. (1986). Behavior therapy with children and adolescents. In S. L. Garfield & A. E. Bergin (Eds.), *Handbook of psychotherapy and behavior change* (3rd ed.). New York: Wiley.

O'Malley, S. (1979, October 7). Can the method survive the madness? *New York Times Magazine,* pp. 32–34+.

Orne, M. T. (1962). On the social psychology of the psychological experiment: With particular reference to demand characteristics and their implications. *American Psychologist, 17,* 776–783.

Orne, M. T., & Wender, P. H. (1968). Anticipatory socialization for psychotherapy. *American Journal of Psychiatry, 124,* 1202–1211.

Ornstein, R. E. (Ed.) (1973). *Nature of human consciousness.* San Francisco: Freeman.

Ornstein, R. E. (1977). *The psychology of consciousness* (2nd ed.). New York: Harcourt Brace Jovanovich.

Ornstein, R. E. (1988). *Psychology: The study of human experience* (2nd ed.). San Diego: Harcourt Brace Jovanovich.

Ornstein, R. E., & Thompson, R. (1984). *The amazing brain.* Boston: Houghton Mifflin.

Osherson, D. N. (1974). *Logical abilities in children* (Vol. 1). *Organization of length and class concepts: Empirical consequences of a Piagetian formalism.* Hillsdale, NJ: Erlbaum.

Oswald, I. (1980). Sleep as a restorative process: Human clues. In P. S. McConnell et al. (Eds.), *Adaptive capabilities of the nervous system.* Amsterdam: Elsevier.

Ounsted, C., & Taylor, D. C. (1972). *Gender differences: Their ontology and significance.* London: Churchill, Livingston.

Overmier, J. B., & Seligman, M. E. P. (1967). Effects of inescapable shock upon subsequent escape and avoidance learning. *Journal of Comparative and Physiological Psychology, 63,* 23–33.

Overton, W. F. (1984). World views and their influence on psychological theory and research: Kuhn-Lakatos-Laudan. In H. W. Reese (Ed.), *Advances in child development and behavior.* New York: Academic Press.

Owen, D. (1985). *None of the above.* Boston: Houghton-Mifflin.

Palmore, E. (1981). *Social patterns in normal aging.* Durham, NC: Duke University Press.

Panksepp, J. (1986). The neurochemistry of behavior. *Annual Review of Psychology, 37,* 77–107.

Parisi, T. (1987). Why Freud failed: Some implications for neurophysiology and sociobiology. *American Psychologist, 42,* 235–245.

Parke, R. D., & Collmer, W. C. (1978). Child abuse: An interdisciplinary analysis. In E. M. Hetherington (Ed.), *Review of child development research* (Vol. 5). Chicago: University of Chicago Press.

Patterson, C. H. (1986). *Theories of counseling and psychotherapy* (4th ed.). New York: Harper & Row.

Patterson, F. (1978). Conversations with a gorilla. *National Geographic, 154,* 438–465.

Paul, G. L. (1966). *Insight versus desensitization in psychotherapy: An experiment in anxiety reduction.* Stanford, CA: Stanford University Press.

Paul, G. L. (1967). Insight vs. desensitization in psychotherapy two years after termination. *Journal of Counseling Psychology, 31,* 333–348.

Pauly, I. B. (1974). Female transsexualism: Part I & II. *Archives of Sexual Behavior, 3,* 487–507; 509–526.

Pavlov, I. (1927). *Conditioned reflexes.* Oxford: Oxford University Press.

Paykel, E. (1974). Life stress and psychiatric disorder: Applications of the clinical approach. In P. S. Dowrenwend & B. P. Dowrenwend (Eds.), *Stressful life events: Their nature and effects.* New York: Wiley.

Payne, K. (1989). Elephant talk. *National Geographic, 176,* 264–277.

Pearlin, L. I. (1982). The social contexts of stress. In L. Goldberger & S. Breznitz (Eds.), *Handbook of stress: Theoretical and clinical aspects.* New York: Free Press.

Penfield, W., & Jasper, H. (1954). *Epilepsy and the functional anatomy of the human brain.* Boston: Little, Brown.

Penfield, W., & Rasmussen, T. (1952). *The cerebral cortex of man.* New York: Macmillan.

Perlmutter, M., & Hall, E. (1985). *Adult development and aging.* New York: Wiley.

Persky, H. (1983). Psychosexual effects of hormones. *Medical Aspects of Human Sexuality, 17,* 74–101.

Persons, J. B. (1986). The advantages of studying psychological phenomena rather than psychiatric diagnoses. *American Psychologist, 41,* 1252–1260.

Petchesky, R. P. (1985). *Abortion and woman's choice.* Boston: Northeastern University Press.

Petersen, A. C. (1988). Adolescent development. *Annual Review of Psychology, 39,* 583–607.

Peterson, C. (1988). *Personality.* San Diego: Harcourt Brace Jovanovich.

Peterson, C. (1989). Explanatory style in the classroom and on the playing field. In S. Graham & V. S. Folkes (Eds.), *Advances in applied social psychology* (Vol. 5). Hillsdale, NJ: Erlbaum.

Peterson, C., & Barrett, L. C. (1987). Explanatory style and academic performance among university freshmen. *Journal of Personality and Social Psychology, 53,* 603–607.

Peterson, C., & Seligman, M. E. P. (1984). Causal explanations as a risk factor for depression: Theory and evidence. *Psychological Review, 91,* 347–374.

Peterson, C., & Seligman, M. E. P. (1987). Explanatory style and illness. *Journal of Personality, 55,* 237–265.

Peterson, C., Seligman, M. E. P., & Vaillant, G. E. (1988). Pessimistic explanatory style is a risk factor for physical illness: A thirty-five year longitudinal study. *Journal of Personality and Social Psychology, 55,* 23–27.

Peterson, C., & Stunkard, A. J. (1989). Personal control and health promotion. *Social Science and Medicine, 28,* 819–828.

Peterson, L. R., & Peterson, M. J. (1959). Short-term retention of individual items. *Journal of Experimental Psychology, 58,* 193–198.

Pettigrew, T. F. (1961). Social psychology and desegregation research. *American Psychologist, 16,* 105–112.

Petty, R. E., & Cacioppo, J. T. (1986). *Central and peripheral routes to persuasion: Theory and research.* New York: Springer-Verlag.

Philliber, W. W., & Hiller, D. V. (1983). Relative occupational attainments of spouses and later changes in marriage and wife's work experience. *Journal of Marriage and the Family, 46,* 161–170.

Phillips, D. P., & Brugge, J. F. (1985). Progress in neurophysiology of sound localization. *Annual Review of Psychology, 36,* 245–274.

Piaget, J. (1926). *The language and thought of the child.* New York: Harcourt, Brace.

Piaget, J. (1928). *Judgment and reasoning in the child.* New York: Harcourt, Brace.

Piaget, J. (1929). *The child's conception of the world.* New York: Harcourt, Brace.

Piaget, J. (1932). *Moral judgment of the child.* New York: Harcourt, Brace.

Piaget, J. (1950). *The psychology of intelligence.* New York: Harcourt, Brace.

Piaget, J., & Inhelder, B. (1969). *The origin of the idea of chance in children.* New York: Norton.

Pillard, R. C., Poumadere, J., & Carretta, R. A. (1982). A family study of sexual orientation. *Archives of Sexual Behavior, 11,* 511–520.

Pittman, T. S., & Heller, J. F. (1987). Social motivation. *Annual Review of Psychology, 38,* 461–489.

Plomin, R. (1986). Behavioral genetic methods. *Journal of Personality, 54,* 226–261.

Plomin, R. (1987). Genetics of intelligence. In S. Modgil & C. Modgil (Eds.), *Arthur Jensen: Consensus and controversy.* New York: Falmer.

Plutchik, R. (1962). *The emotions: Facts, theories, and a new model.* New York: Random House.

Plutchik, R. (1980). *Emotion: A psychoevolutionary synthesis.* New York: Harper & Row.

Plutchik, R. (1984). Emotions: A general psychoevolutionary theory. In K. R. Scherer & P. Ekman (Eds.), *Approaches to emotion.* Hillsdale, NJ: Erlbaum.

Pohl, F. (1984). *The years of the city.* New York: Pocket Books.

Pokorny, A. D. (1968). Myths about suicide. In H. L. P. Resnik (Ed.), *Suicidal behaviors.* Boston: Little, Brown.

Posner, M. I. (1978). *Chronometric explorations of mind.* Hillsdale, NJ: Erlbaum.

Premack, A. J., & Premack, D. (1972). Teaching language to an ape. *Scientific American, 277,* 92–99.

Premack, D. (1965). Reinforcement theory. In D. Levine (Ed.), *Nebraska symposium on motivation.* Lincoln: University of Nebraska Press.

Prince, M. (1924). *The unconscious.* New York: Macmillan.

Prochaska, J. O. (1984). *Systems of psychotherapy: A transtheoretical analysis* (2nd ed.). Homewood, IL: Dorsey.

Purtilo, D. T., & Sullivan, J. L. (1979). Immunological bases for superior survival of females. *American Journal of Diseases of Children, 133,* 1251–1253.

Pylyshyn, Z. W. (1984). *Computation and cognition: Toward a foundation for cognitive science.* Cambridge, MA: MIT Press.

Rabinowitz, S., & Hall, D. T. (1981). Changing correlates of job involvement in three career stages. *Journal of Vocational Behavior, 18,* 138–144.

Rachman, S. J. (1966). Sexual fetishism: An experimental analogue. *Psychological Record, 16,* 293–295.

Rachman, S. J., & Hodgson, R. J. (1980). *Obsessions and compulsions.* Englewood Cliffs, NJ: Prentice-Hall.

Rachman, S. J., & Wilson, G. T. (1980). *The effects of psychological therapy* (2nd ed.). New York: Pergamon.

Ragland, D. R., & Brand, R. J. (1988). Type A behavior and mortality from coronary heart disease. *The New England Journal of Medicine, 318,* 65–69.

Rapoport, J. (1989). *The boy who couldn't stop washing: The experience and treatment of obsessive-compulsive disorders.* New York: Dutton.

Raskin, P., & Israel, A. (1981). Sex role imitation in children: Effects of sex of child, sex of model, and sex-role appropriateness of modeled behavior. *Sex Roles, 7,* 1067–1076.

Raven, J. C. (1948). The comparative assessment of intellectual ability. *British Journal of Psychology, 39,* 12–19.

Reiser, M., & Nielson, M. (1980). Investigative hypnosis: A developing specialty. *American Journal of Clinical Hypnosis, 23,* 75–83.

Rescorla, R. A. (1988). Pavlovian conditioning: It's not what you think it is. *American Psychologist, 43,* 151–160.

Rest, J. R. (1983). Morality. In P. H. Mussen (Ed.), *Handbook of child psychology* (Vol. 3). New York: Wiley.

Rice, M. L. (1989). Children's language acquisition. *American Psychologist, 44,* 149–156.

Rickels, K. (1981). Benzodiazepines: Use and misuse. In D. F. Klein & J. Rabkin (Eds.), *Anxiety: New research and changing concepts.* New York: Raven.

Ring, K. (1967). Experimental social psychology: Some sober questions about some frivolous values. *Journal of Experimental Social Psychology, 3,* 113–123.

Robinson, J. O. (1972). *The psychology of visual illusion.* London: Hutchinson.

Rodin, J., & Langer, E. J. (1977). Long-term effects of a control-relevant intervention with the institutionalized aged. *Journal of Personality and Social Psychology, 35,* 897–902.

Rodin, J., Solomon, S., & Metcalf, J. (1978). Role of control in mediating perceptions of density. *Journal of Personality and Social Psychology, 36,* 988–999.

Rodin, J., & Wack, J. T. (1984). The relationship between cigarette smoking and body weight: A health promotion dilemma? In J. D. Matarazzo et al. (Eds.), *Behavioral health: A handbook of health enhancement and disease prevention.* New York: Wiley.

Roffwarg, H. P., Muzio, J. N., & Dement, W. C. (1966). Ontogenetic development of the human sleep-dream cycle. *Science, 37,* 604–619.

Rogers, C. R. (1942). *Counseling and psychotherapy: Newer concepts in practice.* Boston: Houghton Mifflin.

Rogers, C. R. (1951). *Client-centered therapy: Its current practice, implications, and theory.* Boston: Houghton Mifflin.

Rogers, C. R. (1970). *Carl Rogers on encounter groups.* New York: Harper & Row.

Rokeach, M. (1971). Long-range experimental modification of values, attitudes, and behavior. *American Psychologist, 26,* 453–459.

Rokeach, M. (1973). *The nature of human values.* New York: Free Press.

Rokeach, M. (1979). *Understanding human values: Individual and social.* New York: Free Press.

Rollins, P. C., & Feldman, H. (1970). Marital satisfaction over the life cycle. *Journal of Marriage and the Family, 32,* 20–28.

Romanes, G. J. (1882). *Animal intelligence.* London: Kegan Paul.

Romberch, J. (1553). *Congestorium artificia memoriae.* Venice.

Rorschach, H. (1942). *Psychodiagnostics: A diagnostic test based on perception.* Berne: Huber.

Rosch, E. (1975). Cognitive representations of semantic categories. *Journal of Experimental Psychology: General, 104,* 192–233.

Rosch, E., & Mervis, C. B. (1975). Family resemblances: Studies in the internal structure of categories. *Cognitive Psychology, 7,* 573–605.

Rosch, E., Mervis, C. B., Gray, W., Johnson, D., & Boyes-Braem, P. (1976). Basic objects in natural categories. *Cognitive Psychology, 8,* 382–439.

Rosenblatt, P. C., Walsh, R. P., & Jackson, D. A. (1976). *Grief and mourning in cross-cultural perspective.* New Haven, CT: HRAF Press.

Rosenhan, D. L. (1973). On being sane in insane places. *Science, 179,* 250–258.

Rosenhan, D. L., & Seligman, M. E. P. (1989). *Abnormal psychology* (2nd ed.). New York: Norton.

Rosenthal, N. E., et al. (1984). Seasonal affective disorder: A description of the syndrome and preliminary findings with light therapy. *Archives of General Psychiatry, 41,* 72–80.

Rosenthal, R. R., & Jacobson, L. (1968). *Pygmalion in the classroom.* New York: Holt, Rinehart, & Winston.

Rosenzweig, M. R. (1984). Experience, memory, and the brain. *American Psychologist, 39,* 365–376.

Ross, L. (1977). The intuitive psychologist and his shortcomings: Distortions in the attribution process. In L. Berkowitz (Ed.), *Advances in experimental social psychology* (Vol. 10). New York: Academic Press.

Rossi, A. S. (1980). Life-span theories and women's lives. *Signs: Journal of Women in Culture and Society, 6,* 4–32.

Rothbaum, F., Weisz, J. R., & Snyder, S. S. (1982). Changing the world and changing the self: A two-process model of perceived control. *Journal of Personality and Social Psychology, 42,* 5–37.

Rotter, J. B. (1954). *Social learning and clinical psychology.* Englewood Cliffs, NJ: Prentice-Hall.

Rotter, J. B. (1966). Generalized expectancies for internal versus external control of reinforcement. *Psychological Monographs, 81*(1, Whole No. 609).

Rotter, J. B. (1975). Some problems and misconceptions related to the construct of internal versus external reinforcement. *Journal of Consulting and Clinical Psychology, 43,* 56–67.

Rousseau, J. J. (1762/1979). *Emile: Or, on education.* New York: Basic Books.

Rowe, D. C., & Plomin, R. (1981). The Burt controversy: A comparison of Burt's data on IQ with data from other studies. *Behavior Genetics, 8,* 81–84.

Rozin, P. (1968). Are carbohydrate and protein intakes separately regulated? *Journal of Comparative and Physiological Psychology, 65,* 23–29.

Rozin, P. (1984). Disorders of the nervous system. In D. L. Rosenhan & M. E. P. Seligman, *Abnormal psychology.* New York: Norton.

Rozin, P., & Kalat, J. W. (1971). Specific hungers and poison avoidance as adaptive specializations of learning. *Psychological Review, 78,* 459–486.

Rubin, D. C., & Kontis, T. S. (1983). A schema for common cents. *Memory and Cognition, 11,* 335–341.

Rubin, J., Provenzano, F., & Luria, Z. (1974). The eye of the beholder: Parents' views on sex of newborns. *American Journal of Orthopsychiatry, 44,* 512–519.

Rubin, Z. (1973). *Liking and loving: An invitation to social psychology.* New York: Holt, Rinehart, & Winston.

Rumelhart, D. E., Lindsay, P. H., & Norman, D. A. (1972). A process model for long-term memory. In E. Tulving & W. Donaldson (Eds.), *Organization of memory.* New York: Academic Press.

Runyan, W. M. (1981). Why did Van Gogh cut off his ear? The problem of alternative explanations in psychobiology. *Journal of Personality and Social Psychology, 40,* 1070–1077.

Runyan, W. M. (1982). *Life histories and psychobiography: Explorations in theory and method*. New York: Oxford.

Rusbult, C. E. (1980). Commitment and satisfaction in romantic associations: A test of the investment model. *Journal of Experimental Social Psychology, 16,* 172–186.

Rusbult, C. E., Zembrodt, I. M., & Gunn, L. K. (1982). Exit, voice, loyalty, and neglect: Responses to dissatisfaction in romantic relationships. *Journal of Personality and Social Psychology, 43,* 1230–1242.

Rushton, J. P. (1985). Differential K theory: The sociobiology of individual and group differences. *Personality and Individual Differences, 6,* 441–452.

Rushton, J. P. (1988). Race differences in behaviour: A review and evolutionary analysis. *Personality and Individual Differences, 9,* 1009–1024.

Rutkowski, G. K., Gruder, C. L., & Romer, D. (1983). Group cohesiveness, social norms, and bystander intervention. *Journal of Personality and Social Psychology, 44,* 545–552.

Rutter, M. (1983). School effects on pupil progress: Research findings and policy implications. *Child Development, 54,* 1–29.

Ryan, E. D., & Kovacic, C. R. (1966). Pain tolerance and athletic participation. *Journal of Personality and Social Psychology, 2,* 383–390.

Ryle, G. (1949). *The concept of mind*. London: Hutchinson.

Sacks, O. (1984). *A leg to stand on*. New York: Harper & Row.

Sacks, O. (1986). *The man who mistook his wife for a hat*. New York: Simon & Schuster.

Saghir, M. T., & Robins, E. (1973). *Male and female homosexuality*. Baltimore: Williams & Wilkins.

Sanguiliano, I. (1978). *In her time*. New York: William Morrow.

Sarason, I. G. (Ed.) (1980). *Test anxiety: Theory, research, and applications*. Hillsdale, NJ: Erlbaum.

Sarbin, T. R., & Coe, W. C. (1972). *Hypnosis: A social psychological analysis of influence communication*. New York: Holt, Rinehart, & Winston.

Sarbin, T. R., & Mancuso, J. C. (1980). *Schizophrenia: Medical diagnosis or moral verdict?* New York: Pergamon.

Saunders, C. (1977). Dying they live: St. Christopher's Hospice. In H. Feifel (Ed), *New meanings of death*. New York: McGraw-Hill.

Scarr, S., & Weinberg, R. A. (1976). IQ test performance of black children adopted by white families. *American Psychologist, 31,* 726–739.

Schachter, S. (1959). *The psychology of affiliation*. Stanford, CA: Stanford University Press.

Schachter, S., & Singer, J. E. (1962). Cognitive, social, and physiological determinants of emotional state. *Psychological Review, 65,* 379–399.

Schaie, K. W. (1965). A general model for the study of developmental problems. *Psychological Bulletin, 64,* 92–107.

Schank, R. C., & Abelson, R. P. (1977). *Scripts, plans, goals, and understanding*. Hillsdale, NJ: Erlbaum.

Schechter, A. (1987, February 9). Eyeing ways to improve performance. *Sports Illustrated*, pp. 15, 18.

Scheff, T. J. (1966). *Being mentally ill: A sociological theory*. Chicago: Aldine.

Schiffman, S. S. (1977). Food recognition by the elderly. *Journal of Gerontology, 32,* 586–592.

Schlesier-Stropp, B. (1984). Bulimia: A review of the literature. *Psychological Bulletin, 95,* 247–257.

Schofield, W. (1964). *Psychotherapy: The purchase of friendship*. Englewood Cliffs, NJ: Prentice-Hall.

Schotte, D. E., & Stunkard, A. J. (1987). Bulimia vs bulimic behaviors on a college campus. *JAMA, 258,* 1213–1215.

Schulenberg, J. E., Asp, C. E., & Petersen, A. C. (1984). School from the young adolescent's perspective: A descriptive report. *Journal of Early Adolescence, 4,* 107–130.

Schulz, R., & Aderman, D. (1974). Clinical research and the stages of dying. *Omega, 5,* 137–143.

Schwartz, B. (1984). *Psychology of learning and behavior* (2nd ed.). New York: Norton.

Schwartz, G. E. (1972). Voluntary control of human cardiovascular integration and differentiation through feedback and reward. *Science, 175,* 90–93.

Schwartz, G. E. (1975). Biofeedback, self-regulation, and the patterning of physiological processes. *American Scientist, 63,* 314–324.

Scott, J. P., & Fuller, J. L. (1965). *Genetics and the social behavior of the dog*. Chicago: University of Chicago Press.

Scott, W. A. (1957). Attitude change through reward of verbal behavior. *Journal of Abnormal and Social Psychology, 55,* 72–75.

Scott, W. A. (1959). Attitude acquisition by response reinforcement: Replication and extension. *Sociometry, 22,* 328–335.

Scott, W. D. (1903). *The theory of advertising*. Boston: Small & Maynard.

Segal, S. J., & Fusella, V. (1970). Influence of imaged pictures and sounds in detection of visual and auditory signals. *Journal of Experimental Psychology, 83,* 458–474.

Selfe, L. (1977). *Nadia: A case of extraordinary drawing ability in an autistic child.* London: Academic Press.

Seligman, M. E. P. (1970). On the generality of the laws of learning. *Psychological Review, 77,* 406–418.

Seligman, M. E. P. (1973). Fall into hopelessness. *Psychology Today, 7*(1), 43–48.

Seligman, M. E. P. (1974). Depression and learned helplessness. In R. J. Friedman & M. M. Katz (Eds.), *The psychology of depression: Contemporary theory and research.* Washington, D. C.: Winston.

Seligman, M. E. P. (1975). *Helplessness: On depression, development, and death.* San Francisco: Freeman.

Seligman, M. E. P., & Maier, S. F. (1967). Failure to escape traumatic shock. *Journal of Experimental Psychology, 74,* 1–9.

Selye, H. (1956). *The stress of life.* New York: McGraw-Hill.

Shapiro, W. (1989). White lies, bad polls. *Time,* November 20, p. 56.

Shaver, P. (1973). Religious attitudes. In J. Robinson & P. Shaver (Eds.), *Measures of social psychological attitudes.* Ann Arbor, MI: Institute for Social Research.

Shaw, M. E. (1981). *Group dynamics: The psychology of small group behavior.* New York: McGraw-Hill.

Sheehan, P. W., & Tilden, J. (1983). Effects of suggestibility and hypnosis on accurate and distorted retrieval from memory. *Journal of Experimental Psychology: Learning, Memory, and Cognition, 9,* 283–293.

Sheehy, G. (1974). *Passages.* New York: Dutton.

Sheldon, W. H. (1940). *The varieties of human physique.* New York: Harper.

Sheldon, W. H. (1942). *The varieties of temperament.* New York: Harper.

Sherif, M. (1937). An experimental approach to the study of attitudes. *Sociometry, 1,* 90–98.

Sherif, M. (1966). *In common predicament: Social psychology of intergroup conflict and cooperation.* Boston: Houghton Mifflin.

Sherif, M., & Hovland, C. I. (1961). *Social judgment: Assimilation and contrast effects in communication and attitude change.* New Haven, CT: Yale University Press.

Shilling, L. E. (1984). *Perspectives on counseling theories.* Englewood Cliffs, NJ: Prentice-Hall.

Shimberg, M. E. (1929). An investigation into the validity of norms with special reference to urban and rural groups. *Archives of Psychology,* No. 104.

Shortliffe, E. H. (1976). *Computer-based medical consultations: MYCIN.* New York: American Elsevier.

Shostak, M. (1981). *Nisa: The life and words of a !Kung woman.* Cambridge: Harvard University Press.

Sigall, H., & Ostrove, N. (1975). Beautiful but dangerous: Effects of offender attractiveness and nature of the crime on juridic judgment. *Journal of Personality and Social Psychology, 31,* 410–414.

Silbereisen, R. K., & Noack, P. (1988). On the constructive role of problem behavior in adolescence. In N. Bolger et al. (Eds.), *Person and context: Developmental processes.* Cambridge: Cambridge University Press.

Simmons, R. G., & Blyth, D. A. (1987). *Moving into adolescence: The impact of pubertal change and school context.* New York: Aldine.

Simmons, R. G., Rosenberg, F., & Rosenberg, M. (1973). Disturbance in the self-image at adolescence. *American Sociological Review, 38,* 553–568.

Simon, H. A., & Gilmartin, K. (1973). A simulation of memory for chess positions. *Cognitive Psychology, 5,* 29–46.

Simonton, D. K. (1984). *Genius, creativity, and leadership: Historiometric methods.* Cambridge, MA: Harvard University Press.

Simpson, E. (1974). Moral development research: A case study of scientific cultural bias. *Human Development, 17,* 81–105.

Singer, J. L. (1966). *Daydreaming.* New York: Random House.

Singer, J. L. (1975). *The inner world of daydreaming.* New York: Harper & Row.

Singer, J. L. (1984). *The human personality.* San Diego: Harcourt Brace Jovanovich.

Skinner, B. F. (1948). *Walden two.* New York: Macmillan.

Skinner, B. F. (1950). Are theories of learning necessary? *Psychological Review, 57,* 193–216.

Skinner, B. F. (1956). A case history in scientific method. *American Psychologist, 11,* 221–233.

Skinner, B. F. (1957). *Verbal behavior.* New York: Appleton-Century-Crofts.

Skinner, B. F. (1971). *Beyond freedom and dignity.* New York: Knopf.

Skinner, B. F. (1983). Intellectual self-management in old age. *American Psychologist, 38,* 239–244.

Skuse, D. H. (1984). Extreme deprivation in early childhood. I. Diverse outcomes for three siblings from an extraordinary family. *Journal of Child Psychiatry and Psychology, 25,* 523–541.

Slobin, D. I. (1979). *Psycholinguistics* (2nd ed.). Glenview, IL: Scott, Foresman.

Smetana, J. G. (1987). Adolescent-parent conflict: Reasoning about hypothetical and actual family conflict. In M. R. Gunnar (Ed.), *21st Minnesota Symposium on Child Psychology.* Hillsdale, NJ: Erlbaum.

Smith, J. C. (1975). Meditation on psychotherapy: A review of the literature. *Psychological Bulletin, 82,* 558–564.

Smith, J. P., & Ward, M. (1989). Women in the labor market and in the family. *Journal of Economic Perspectives, 3,* 9–23.

Smith, M. L., & Glass, G. V. (1977). The meta-analysis of psychotherapy outcome studies. *American Psychologist, 32,* 752–760.

Smith, M. L., Glass, G. V., & Miller, T. I. (1980). *The benefits of psychotherapy.* Baltimore: Johns Hopkins Press.

Smith, R. E. (Ed.) (1979). *The subtle revolution: Women at work.* Washington, D. C.: The Urban Institute.

Smith, S. B. (1983). *The great mental calculators.* New York: Columbia University Press.

Smith, S. S., & Richardson, D. (1983). Amelioration of deception and harm in psychological research: The important role of debriefing. *Journal of Personality and Social Psychology, 45,* 1075–1082.

Smuts, B. (1985). *Sex and friendship in baboons.* New York: Aldine.

Snyder, M. (1983). The influence of individuals on situations: Implications for understanding the links between personality and social behavior. *Journal of Personality, 51,* 497–516.

Snyder, M., & Gangestad, S. (1982). Choosing social situations: Two investigations of self-monitoring processes. *Journal of Personality and Social Psychology, 43,* 123–135.

Sochurek, H. (1987). Medicine's new vision. *National Geographic, 171,* 2–41.

Solomon, R. L., & Corbit, J. D. (1974). An opponent process theory of motivation. I. The temporal dynamics of affect. *Psychological Review, 81,* 119–145.

Sommer, R. (1969). *Personal space.* Englewood Cliffs, NJ: Prentice-Hall.

Southwick, C. H., Pal, B. C., & Siddiqui, M. F. (1972). Experimental studies of social intolerance in wild rhesus monkeys. *American Zoologist, 12,* 651–652.

Spearman, C. (1904). "General intelligence" objectively determined and measured. *American Journal of Psychology, 15,* 201–292.

Spencer, H. (1864). *Social statics.* New York: Appleton.

Sperling, G. (1960). The information available in brief visual presentations. *Psychological Monographs, 74,* 1–29.

Spiegel, D., et al. (1989). Effect of psychosocial treatment on survival of patients with metastatic breast cancer. *Lancet, 109,* 888–891.

Spilka, B., Shaver, P., & Kirkpatrick, L. A. (1985). A general attribution theory for the psychology of religion. *Journal for the Scientific Study of Religion, 24,* 1–20.

Spitzer, L., & Rodin, J. (1981). Human eating behavior: A critical review of studies in normal weight and overweight individuals. *Appetite, 2,* 293–329.

Spitzer, R. L. (1975). On pseudoscience in science, logic in remission, and psychiatric diagnosis. *Journal of Abnormal Psychology, 84,* 442–452.

Spock, B. (1946). *Common sense book of baby and child care.* New York: Duell, Sloane, & Pearce.

Springer, S. P., & Deutsch, G. (1985). *Left brain, right brain* (Rev. ed.). New York: Freeman.

Starker, S. (1989). *Oracle at the supermarket: The American preoccupation with self-help books.* New Brunswick, NJ: Transaction Publishers.

Starr, R. (1978). Cutting the ties that bind. *Harper's Magazine, 256,* 48–56.

Stebbins, W. C. (1980). The evolution of hearing in the mammals. In A. N. Pupper & R. R. Fay (Eds.), *Comparative studies of hearing in vertebrates.* New York: Springer-Verlag.

Steinberg, L. (1981). Transformations in family relations at puberty. *Developmental Psychology, 17,* 833–840.

Steinberg, L. (1985). *Adolescence.* New York: Knopf.

Stekel, W. (1930). *Sexual aberrations: The phenomena of fetishism in relation to sex.* New York: Liveright.

Stellar, E. (1954). The physiology of motivation. *Psychological Review, 61,* 5–22.

Stern, W. (1914). *The psychological methods of testing intelligence.* Baltimore: Warwick & York.

Sternberg, R. J. (1985). *Beyond IQ: A triarchic theory of human intelligence.* Cambridge: Cambridge University Press.

Sternberg, R. J. (1986). *Intelligence applied.* San Diego, CA: Harcourt Brace Jovanovich.

Sternberg, R. J., & Salter, W. (1982). Conceptions of intelligence. In R. J. Sternberg (Ed.), *Handbook of human intelligence*. Cambridge: Cambridge University Press.

Sternberg, R. J., & Smith, E. E. (Eds.) (1988). *The psychology of human thought*. Cambridge: Cambridge University Press.

Stevens, A., & Coupe, P. (1978). Distortions in judged spatial relations. *Cognitive Psychology, 10,* 422–437.

Stewart, J. E. (1980). Defendant's attractiveness as a factor in the outcome of criminal trials: An observational study. *Journal of Applied Social Psychology, 10,* 348–361.

Stigler, J. W. (1984). "Mental abacus": The effect of abacus training on Chinese children's mental calculation. *Cognitive Psychology, 16,* 145–176.

Stodgill, R. M. (1948). Personal factors associated with leadership. *Journal of Psychology, 23,* 1–14.

Stodgill, R. M. (1969). Validity of leader behavior descriptions. *Personnel Psychology, 22,* 153–158.

Stoller, R. J. (1972). Etiological factors in female transsexualism: A first approximation. *Archives of Sexual Behavior, 2,* 47–64.

Stoller, R. J. (1979). *Sexual excitement*. New York: Pantheon.

Stoller, R. J. (1985). *Observing the erotic imagination*. New Haven, CT: Yale University Press.

Stoner, J. A. F. (1961). *A comparison of individual and group decisions involving risk*. Unpublished master's thesis, Massachusetts Institute of Technology.

Storms, M. D. (1981). A theory of erotic orientation development. *Psychological Review, 88,* 340–353.

Stroebe, M. S., & Stroebe, W. (1983). Who suffers more? Sex differences in health risks of the widowed. *Psychological Bulletin, 93,* 279–301.

Strom, A. (1980). *Norwegian concentration camp survivors*. New York: Humanities Press.

Strube, M. J., & Garcia, J. E. (1981). A meta-analytical investigation of Fiedler's contingency model of leadership effectiveness. *Psychological Bulletin, 90,* 307–321.

Sulloway, F. J. (1979). *Freud, biologist of the mind*. New York: Basic Books.

Sundberg, N. D., Taplin, J. R., & Tyler, L. E. (1983). *Introduction to clinical psychology*. Englewood Cliffs, NJ: Prentice-Hall.

Sutton, S. R. (1982). Fear-arousing communications: A critical examination of theory and research. In J. R. Eiser (Ed.), *Social psychology and behavioral medicine*. Chichester: Wiley.

Swensen, C. H., Eskew, R. W., & Kohlhepp, K. A. (1981). Stage of family life cycle, ego development, and the marriage relationship. *Journal of Marriage and the Family, 43,* 841–853.

Szasz, T. S. (1961). *The myth of mental illness*. New York: Hoeber.

Szinovacz, M. (Ed.) (1982). *Women's retirement: Policy implications of recent research*. Beverly Hills, CA: Sage.

Tajfel, H. (1981). *Human groups and social categories: Studies in social psychology*. London: Cambridge University Press.

Tajfel, H. (1982). Social psychology of intergroup relations. *Annual Review of Psychology, 33,* 1–39.

Tamir, L. M. (1982). *Men in their forties: A transition to middle age*. New York: Springer.

Tankard, J. W. (1984). *The statistical pioneers*. Cambridge, MA: Schenkman.

Tanner, D. (1972). *Secondary education*. New York: Macmillan.

Tanner, J. M. (1978). *Fetus to man*. Cambridge, MA: Harvard University Press.

Tarde, G. (1903). *The laws of imitation*. New York: Holt.

Taube, C. A., Burns, B. J., & Kessler, L. (1984). Patients of psychiatrists and psychologists in office-based practice: 1980. *American Psychologist, 39,* 1435–1447.

Taylor, R. B., Denham, J. R., & Ureda, J. W. (1982). *Health promotion: Principles and clinical applications*. Norwalk, CT: Appleton-Century-Crofts.

Taylor, S. E. (1981). The interface of cognitive and social psychology. In J. Harvey (Ed.), *Cognition, social behavior, and the environment*. Hillsdale, NJ: Erlbaum.

Taylor, S. E. (1985). Adjustments to threatening events: A theory of cognitive adaptation. *American Psychologist, 38,* 1161–1173.

Taylor, S. E., & Brown, J. D. (1988). Illusion and well-being: A social psychological perspective on mental health. *Psychological Bulletin, 103,* 193–210.

Tellegen, A., et al. (1988). Personality similarity in twins reared apart and together. *Journal of Personality and Social Psychology, 54,* 1031–1039.

Terborg, J. R. (1977). Women in management: A research review. *Journal of Applied Psychology, 62,* 647–664.

Terman, L. M. (1916). *The measurement of intelligence*. Boston: Houghton Mifflin.

Terman, L. M. (1925). *Genetic studies of genius* (Vol. 1) *Mental and physical traits of a thousand gifted children*. Stanford, CA: Stanford University Press.

Terman, L. M., et al. (1923). *Intelligence tests and school reorganization.* Yonkers, NY: World Book.

Thomas, A., & Chess, S. (1977). *Temperament and development.* New York: Bruner/Mazel.

Thomas, A., Chess, S., Korn, S. J. (1982). The reality of difficult temperament. *Merrill Palmer Quarterly, 28,* 1–20.

Thomas, E. L., & Robinson, H. A. (1972). *Improving reading in every class: A sourcebook for teachers.* Boston: Allyn & Bacon.

Thompson, R. F. (1976). The search for the engram. *American Psychologist, 31,* 209–227.

Thorndike, E. L. (1911). *Animal intelligence: Experimental studies.* New York: Macmillan.

Thorndike, R. L., Hagan, E., & Sattler, J. (1986). *Stanford-Binet* (4th ed.). Chicago: Riverside.

Thurstone, L. L. (1938). Primary mental abilities. *Psychometric Monographs* (No. 1).

Thurstone, L. L. (1946). Comment. *American Journal of Sociology, 52,* 39–40.

Thurstone, L. L., & Thurstone, T. C. (1941). Factorial studies of intelligence. *Psychometric Monographs* (No. 2).

Timberlake, W., & Allison, J. (1974). Response deprivation: An empirical approach to instrumental performance. *Psychological Review, 81,* 146–164.

Tinbergen, N. (1951). *The study of instinct.* Oxford: Clarendon.

Tinbergen, N. (1968). On war and peace in animals and man. *Science, 160,* 1411–1418.

Tolman, E. C. (1948). Cognitive maps in rats and men. *Psychological Review, 55,* 189–208.

Tolman, E. C. (1959). Principles of purposive behavior. In S. Koch (Ed.), *Psychology: A study of a science* (Vol. 2). New York: McGraw-Hill.

Tomkins, S. S. (1962). *Affect, imagery, consciousness* (Vol. 1). New York: Springer.

Tomkins, S. S. (1963). *Affect, imagery, consciousness* (Vol. 2). New York: Springer.

Tomkins, S. S. (1982). *Affect, imagery, consciousness* (Vol. 3). New York: Springer.

Tomkins, S. S. (1984). Affect theory. In K. S. Scherer & P. Ekman (Eds.), *Approaches to emotion.* Hillsdale, NJ: Erlbaum.

Torgersen, S. (1983). Genetic factors in anxiety disorders. *Archives of General Psychiatry, 43,* 222–226.

Treffert, D. A. (1989). *Extraordinary people: Understanding "idiot savants".* New York: Harper & Row.

Triplett, N. E. (1898). The dynamogenic factors in pacemaking and competition. *American Journal of Psychology, 9,* 507–533.

Tryon, R. C. (1940). Genetic differences in maze learning in rats. *Yearbook of the National Society for Studies in Education, 39,* 111–119.

Tulving, E. (1985). How many memory systems are there? *American Psychologist, 40,* 385–398.

Tulving, E. (1986). What kind of hypothesis is the distinction between episodic and semantic memory? *Journal of Experimental Psychology: Learning, Memory, and Cognition, 12,* 307–311.

Turiel, E. (1966). An experimental test of the sequentiality of developmental stages in the child's moral judgments. *Journal of Personality and Social Psychology, 3,* 611–618.

Turnbull, C. (1962). *The forest people.* New York: Simon & Schuster.

Turner, R. H. (1978). The role and the person. *American Journal of Sociology, 84,* 1–23.

U.S. Department of Health and Human Services (1986). *Coping with AIDS.* DHHS Publication No. (ADM) HHS-85-1432. Washington, D.C.: U.S. Government Printing Office.

U.S. Department of Health and Human Services (1988). *Understanding AIDS.* DHHS Publication No. (CDC) HHS-88-8404. Washington, D.C.: U.S. Government Printing Office.

Vaillant, G. E. (1977). *Adaptation to life.* Boston: Little, Brown.

Vaillant, G. E. (1983). *The natural history of alcoholism.* Cambridge, MA: Harvard University Press.

Valenstein, E. S. (1973). *Brain control.* New York: Wiley.

Valenstein, E. S. (1986). *Great and desperate cures.* New York: Basic Books.

Vance, E. B., & Wagner, N. N. (1976). Written descriptions of orgasms: A study of sex differences. *Archives of Sexual Behavior, 5,* 87–98.

Verbrugge, L. M. (1989). Recent, present, and future health of American adults. In L. Breslow, J. E. Fielding, & L. B. Lave (Eds.), *Annual review of public health* (Vol. 10). Palo Alto, CA: Annual Reviews.

Vernon, P. A. (1983). Speed of information processing and general intelligence. *Intelligence, 7,* 53–70.

Vernon, P. E. (1979). *Intelligence: Heredity and environment.* San Francisco: Freeman.

Veroff, J., & Feld, S. (1970). *Marriage and work in America: A study of motives and roles.* New York: Van Nostrand Reinhold.

Vining, D. R. (1986). Social versus reproductive success: The central theoretical problem of human sociobiology. *Behavioral and Brain Sciences, 9,* 167–216.

Vroom, V. (1964). *Work and motivation*. New York: Wiley.

Vye, N. J., Delclos, V. R., Burns, M. S., & Bransford, J. D. (1988). Teaching thinking and problem solving: Illustrations and issues. In R. J. Sternberg & E. E. Smith (Eds.), *The psychology of human thought*. Cambridge: Cambridge University Press.

Wagner, M. E., & Schubert, H. J. P. (1977). Sibship variables and United States presidents. *Journal of Individual Psychology, 33,* 78–85.

Walker, L. J. (1984). Sex differences in the development of moral reasoning: A critical review. *Child Development, 55,* 677–691.

Wallace, B. (1984). Apparent equivalence between perception and imagery in the production of various visual illusions. *Memory and Cognition, 12,* 156–162.

Wallace, R. K., & Benson, H. (1972). The physiology of meditation. *Scientific American, 226,* 85–90.

Wallach, H. (1987). Perceiving a stable environment when one moves. *Annual Review of Psychology, 38,* 1–27.

Wallach, M. A. (1985). Creativity testing and giftedness. In F. D. Horowitz & M. O'Brien (Eds.), *The gifted and talented: Developmental perspectives*. Washington, D.C.: American Psychological Association.

Wallach, M. A., & Wallach, L. (1983). *Psychology's sanction for selfishness: The error of egoism in theory and therapy*. San Francisco: Freeman.

Wallerstein, J. S., & Blakeslee, S. (1989). *Second chances: Men, women, and children a decade after divorce*. New York: Ticknor & Fields.

Wallerstein, J. S., & Kelley, J. (1974). The effects of parental divorce: The adolescent experience. In E. Anthony & A. Koupernik (Eds.), *The child in his family: Children as a psychiatric risk* (Vol. 3). New York: Wiley.

Walster, E., Walster, G. W., & Berscheid, E. (1978). *Equity: Theory and research*. Boston: Allyn & Bacon.

Wanous, J. P. (1980). *Organizational entry: Recruitment, selection, and socialization of newcomers*. Reading, MA: Addison-Wesley.

Wason, P. C. (1966). Reasoning. In B. M. Foss (Ed.), *New horizons in psychology*. Harmondsworth: Penguin.

Watson, J. B. (1913). Psychology as the behaviorist views it. *Psychological Review, 20,* 158–177.

Watson, J. B. (1925). *Behaviorism*. New York: Norton.

Watson, J. B. (1928). *Psychological care of infant and child*. New York: Norton.

Watson, J. B. (1930). *Behaviorism* (Rev. ed.). New York: Norton.

Watson, J. B., & Morgan, J. J. B. (1917). Emotional reactions and psychological experimentation. *American Journal of Psychology, 28,* 163–174.

Watson, J. B., & Rayner, R. (1920). Conditioned emotional reactions. *Journal of Experimental Psychology, 3,* 1–14.

Watson, R. E. L. (1983). Premarital cohabitation versus traditional courtship: Their effects on subsequent marital adjustment. *Family Relations, 32,* 139–147.

Watson, R. I. (1973). Investigation into deindividuation using a cross-cultural survey technique. *Journal of Personality and Social Psychology, 25,* 342–345.

Waugh, N. C., & Norman, D. A. (1965). Primary memory. *Psychological Review, 72,* 89–104.

Webb, W. B. (1975). *Sleep, the gentle tyrant*. Englewood Cliffs, NJ: Prentice-Hall.

Weber, S. J., & Cook, T. D. (1972). Subject effects in laboratory research: An examination of subject roles, demand characteristics, and valid inference. *Psychological Bulletin, 77,* 273–295.

Wechsler, D. (1939). *The measurement of adult intelligence*. Baltimore: Williams & Wilkins.

Wechsler, D. (1974). *Wechsler Intelligence Scale for Children-Revised*. New York: Psychological Corporation.

Weigel, R. H., Loomis, J. W., & Soja, M. J. (1980). Race relations on prime time television. *Journal of Personality and Social Psychology, 39,* 884–893.

Weil, A. (1972). *The natural mind: A new way of looking at drugs and the higher consciousness*. Boston: Houghton Mifflin.

Weinberger, M., Hiner, S. L., & Tierney, W. M. (1987). In support of hassles as a measure of stress in predicting health outcomes. *Journal of Behavioral Medicine, 10,* 19–31.

Weiner, B. (1978). Achievement strivings. In H. London & J. E. Exner (Eds.), *Dimensions of personality*. New York: Wiley.

Weiner, B. (1985). *Human motivation*. New York: Springer-Verlag.

Weiner, B. (1986). *An attributional theory of motivation and emotion*. New York: Springer-Verlag.

Weiner, H. (1977). *Psychobiology and human disease*. New York: Elsevier.

Weinstein, N. D. (1982). Unrealistic optimism about susceptibility to health problems. *Journal of Behavioral Medicine, 5,* 441–460.

Weinstein, S., & Sersen, E. A. (1961). Tactual sensitivity as a function of handedness and laterality. *Jour-*

nal of Comparative and Physiological Psychology, 54, 665–669.

Weisberg, R. W. (1986). *Creativity: Genius and other myths.* New York: Freeman.

Wernicke, C. (1874). *Der aphsiche symptomenkomplex.* Breslau, Poland: Cohn & Weigert.

Wertheimer, M. (1912). Experimentelle Studien uber das Sehen von Bewegung. *Zeitschrift fur Psychologie, 60,* 321–378.

Wertheimer, M. (1972). *Fundamental issues in psychology.* New York: Holt, Rinehart, & Winston.

Wertheimer, M. (1979). *A brief history of psychology* (Rev. ed.). New York: Holt, Rinehart, & Winston.

West, S. G. (1983). Personality and prediction: An introduction. *Journal of Personality, 51,* 275–285.

West, S. G., Gunn, S. P., & Chernicky, P. (1975). Ubiquitous Watergate: An attributional analysis. *Journal of Personality and Social Psychology, 32,* 55–65.

Wever, E. G. (1949). *Theory of hearing.* New York: Wiley.

Whalen, R. E., & Simon, N. G. (1984). Biological motivation. *Annual Review of Psychology, 35,* 257–276.

White, B. L. (1967). An experimental approach to the effects of experience on early human behaviors. In J. P. Hill (Ed.), *Minnesota symposium on child psychology* (Vol. 1). Minneapolis: University of Minnesota Press.

White, B. W., et al. (1970). Seeing with the skin. *Perception and Psychophysics, 7,* 23–27.

White, R. W. (1959). Motivation reconsidered: The concept of competence. *Psychological Review, 66,* 297–333.

White, R. W. (1966). *Lives in progress* (2nd ed.). New York: Holt.

Whiting, J. W. M., & Child, I. L. (1953). *Child training and personality: A cross-cultural study.* New Haven: Yale University Press.

Whorf, B. L. (1956). *Language, thought, and reality.* Cambridge, MA: MIT Press.

Wicker, A. W. (1969). Attitudes versus actions: The relationship of verbal and overt behavioral responses to attitude objects. *Journal of Social Issues, 25*(4), 41–78.

Wicker, A. W. (1971). An examination of the "other variables" explanation of attitude-behavior inconsistency. *Journal of Personality and Social Psychology, 19,* 18–30.

Wiggins, D. K. (1984). The history of sport psychology in North America. In J. M. Silva & R. S. Weinberg (Eds.), *Psychological foundations of sport.* Champaign, IL: Human Kinetics.

Willerman, L., & Cohen, D. B. (1990). *Psychopathology.* New York: McGraw-Hill.

Wilson, E. O. (1975). *Sociobiology: The new synthesis.* Cambridge, MA: Harvard University Press.

Wilson, E. O. (1978). *On human nature.* Cambridge, MA: Harvard University Press.

Wilson, T. D., & Linville, P. W. (1982). Improving the academic performance of college freshmen: Attribution therapy revisited. *Journal of Personality and Social Psychology, 42,* 367–376.

Wilson, T. D., & Linville, P. W. (1985). Improving the performance of college freshmen with attributional techniques. *Journal of Personality and Social Psychology, 49,* 287–293.

Wimer, R. E., & Wimer, C. C. (1985). Animal behavior genetics: A search for the biological foundations of behavior. *Annual Review of Psychology, 36,* 171–218.

Winch, R. F. (1958). *Mate selection: A study of complementary needs.* New York: Harper & Row.

Winter, D. G. (1973). *The power motive.* New York: Free Press.

Winter, D. G. (1988). The power motive in women— and men. *Journal of Personality and Social Psychology, 54,* 510–519.

Wissler, C. L. (1901). The correlation of mental and physical tests. *Psychology Review Monograph Supplement, 3*(6).

Wittgenstein, L. (1953). *Philosophical investigations.* New York: Macmillan.

Wolfe, J. B. (1936). Effectiveness of token-rewards for chimpanzees. *Comparative Psychology Monographs, 12*(No. 60).

Wolpe, J. (1958). *Psychotherapy by reciprocal inhibition.* Stanford: Stanford University Press.

Wolpe, J., & Rachman, S. (1960). Psychoanalytic "evidence": A critique based on Freud's case of Little Hans. *Journal of Nervous and Mental Disease, 131,* 135–147.

Woodruff-Pak, D. (1988). *Psychology and aging.* Englewood Cliffs, NJ: Prentice-Hall.

Woodward, B. (1985). *Wired: The short life and fast times of John Belushi.* New York: Pocket Books.

Woody, C. D. (1986). Understanding the cellular basis of memory and learning. *Annual Review of Psychology, 37,* 433–493.

Wright, L. (1988). The Type A behavior pattern and coronary artery disease. *American Psychologist, 43,* 2–14.

Yalom, I. D. (1970). *The theory and practice of group psychotherapy.* New York: Basic Books.

Yalom, I. D. (1975). *The theory and practice of group psychotherapy* (2nd ed.). New York: Basic Books.

Yankelovich, D. (1981). *New rules.* New York: Random House.

Yetman, N. R. (1970). *Voices from slavery.* New York: Holt, Rinehart, & Winston.

Youniss, J., & Smollar, J. (1985). *Adolescent relations with mothers, fathers, and friends.* Chicago: University of Chicago Press.

Zaccaro, S. J. (1984). Social loafing: The role of task attractiveness. *Personality and Social Psychology Bulletin, 10,* 99–106.

Zajonc, R. B. (1965). Social facilitation. *Science, 149,* 269–274.

Zajonc, R. B. (1976). Family configuration and intelligence. *Science, 192,* 227–229.

Zajonc, R. B. (1980). Feeling and thinking: Preferences need no inferences. *American Psychologist 35,* 151–175.

Zajonc, R. B. (1984). On primacy of affect. In U. R. Scherer & P. Ekman (Eds.), *Approaches to emotion.* Hillsdale, NJ: Erlbaum.

Zelnik, M., & Kantner, J. F. (1977). Sexual and contraceptive experience of young unmarried women in the United States, 1976 and 1971. *Family Planning Perspectives, 9,* 55–71.

Zigler, E. F., & Berman, W. (1983). Discerning the future of early childhood intervention. *American Psychologist, 38,* 894–906.

Zigler, E. F., & Frank, M. (Eds.) (1988). *The parental leave crisis.* New Haven, CT: Yale University Press.

Zilbergeld, B., & Evans, M. (1980). The inadequacy of Masters and Johnson. *Psychology Today, 14,* 28–43.

Zimbardo, P. G. (1972). *The Stanford prison experiment: A slide/tape presentation.* Stanford, CA: author.

Zimbardo, P. G. (1988). *Psychology and life* (12th ed.). Glenview, IL: Scott, Foresman.

Zimbardo, P. G., & Radl, S. L. (1979). *The shyness workbook.* New York: A & W Visual Library.

Zuckerman, M. (1974). The sensation seeking motive. In B. A. Maher (Ed.), *Progress in experimental personality research* (Vol. 7). New York: Academic Press.

Zuckerman, M., & Brody, N. (1988). Oysters, rabbits, and people: A critique of "Race differences in behaviour" by J. P. Rushton, *Personality and Individual Differences, 9,* 1025–1033.

Name Index

Subject Index

Acknowledgments

Illustration Credits

Proof Positive/Farrowlyne Associates, Inc.: Figures 1.1, 1.2, 1.3, 1.4, 2.1, 2.13, 3.1, 3.2, 3.6, 3.7, 3.9, 4.2, 4.6, 4.7A, 4.8A, 4.9, 4.10, 4.11, 4.12, 4.13, 4.14, 5.3, 5.8, 5.10, 6.3, 6.4, 6.5B, 6.6, 7.1, 7.2, 7.3, 7.4, 7.5, 7.9, 7.10, 7.12, 8.1, 8.2, 8.6, 8.7, 8.8, 8.9, 9.2, 9.8, 10.1, 11.1, 11.4, 11.5, 11.6, 13.6, 14.1, 14.3, 15.2, 15.3

Rolin Graphics Inc.: Figures 5.1, 5.5, 5.6, 5.7, 7.7, 7.8, 8.3, 8.4, 9.4, 9.5, 10.2, 10.3

Sarah Forbes Woodward: Figures 2.4, 2.5, 2.6, 2.7, 2.9, 2.10, 3.4, 3.10, 3.11, 3.12, 3.13, 3.14, 4.3, 12.3, 16.3, 16.4, 16.5

Hans Zander: Cover illustration

Literary Credits

p. 10 Fig. 1.1 From *Psychology in America: A Historical Survey* by Ernest R. Hilgard. Copyright © 1987 by Harcourt Brace Jovanovich, Inc. Reprinted by permission of the publisher. **p. 20** Table 1.2 APA Division List. Copyright © 1990 by the American Psychological Association. Reprinted by permission. **p. 55** Fig. 2.1 From *Psychology and Life*, 12th Edition by Philip G. Zimbardo, Copyright © 1988 by Philip G. Zimbardo. Scott, Foresman and Company. **pp. 109, 110, 118** Fig. 3.2, 3.3, 3.9 From *Psychology: An Introduction*. 2nd Edition by Josh R. Gerow. Copyright © 1989 by Scott, Foresman and Company. **p. 145** Fig. 4.9 From L. S. Penrose and R. Penrose, "Impossible objects: a special type of visual illustration," *British Journal of Psychology* (1958) 49, 31-33. Reprinted by permission of The British Psychological Society. **p. 146** Fig. 4.10 From *Sensation and Perception*, Second Editon by Stanley Coren, et al. Copyright © 1984 by Harcourt Brace Jovanovich, Inc. Reprinted by permission of the publisher. **p. 153** Fig. 4.11 From *Secrets of Sleep* by Alexander Borbely. English translation, copyright © 1986 by Basic Books, Inc. Reprinted by permission of Basic Books, Inc., Publishers, New York. **p. 155** Fig. 4.12 From *Secrets of Sleep* by Alexander Borbely. English translation, copyright © 1986 by Basic Books, Inc. Reprinted by permission of Basic Books, Inc., Publishers, New York. **p. 159** Fig. 4.13 Adapted from "The Brain as a Dream State Generator" by Allan Hobson and Robert McCarley, *The American Journal of Psychiatry*, December 1977. Copyright © 1977 by the American Psychiatric Association. Reprinted by permission. **p. 161** Fig. 4.14 From *Hypnotic Susceptibility* by Ernest R. Hilgard (Orlando, FL: Harcourt Brace Jovanovich, Inc., 1965). Reprinted by permission of the author. **p. 179** Fig. 5.3 From *Psychology*, 3rd Edition by Andrew B. Crider, et al. Copyright © 1989 by Andrew B. Crider, George R. Goethals, Robert D. Kavanaugh, and Paul R. Solomon. Scott, Foresman and Company. **p. 194**

Fig. 5.8 Adapted from "Teaching Machines" by B. F. Skinner, *Scientific American*, November 1961. Copyright © 1961 by Scientific American, Inc. All rights reserved. Reprinted by permission. **p. 200** Fig. 5.9 From "Imitation of film-mediated aggressive models" by Albert Bandura, et al., *Journal of Abnormal and Social Psychology*, 66, 3-11, 1963. Copyright © 1963 by the American Psychological Association. Reprinted by permission of the author. **p. 235** Fig. 6.4 From "A Language for the Emotions" by Robert Plutchik. Reprinted with permission from *Psychology Today*, February 1980. Copyright © 1980 (PT Partners, L.P.). **p. 252** Table 6.4 "The Social Readjustment Rating Scale" by T. H. Holmes and R. H. Rahe. Reprinted with permission from *The Journal of Psychosomatic Research*, 11:213-218, 1967. Copyright © 1967 by Pergamon Press plc. **p. 270** Fig. 7.1 From "Two Storage Mechanisms in Free Recall" by M. Glanzer and A. M. Cunaz, *Journal of Verbal Learning and Verbal Behavior*, 1966, 5, 351-360. Reprinted by permission of Academic Press, Inc. and Murray Glanzer. **p. 272** Fig. 7.3 From *Human Memory: The Processing of Information* by G. R. Loftus and E. F. Loftus. Copyright © 1976 by Lawrence Erlbaum Associates. Reprinted by permission of Lawrence Erlbaum Associates and G. R. Loftus. **p. 276** Fig. 7.4 From "A schema for common cents" by D. C. Rubin and T. S. Kontis, *Memory and Cognition*, 11, 335-341, 1983. Reprinted by permission of Psychonomic Society, Inc. and David C. Rubin. **p. 287** Fig. 7.8 From "Scanning Visual Images: Some Structural Implications" by Stephen Michael Kosslyn, *Perception and Psychophysics*, Vol. 14, No. 1, 1973. Reprinted by permission of Psychonomic Society, Inc. and the author. **p. 290** Fig. 7.9 From *Cognitive Psychology*, Second Edition, by John R. Anderson. Copyright © 1980, 1985 by W. H. Freeman and Company. Reprinted with permission. **p. 302** Fig. 7.12 From *Cognition* by Andrew Lewis Glass, Keith James Holyoak, and John Lester Santa. Copyright © 1979 by McGraw-Hill, Inc. Reprinted by permission. **p. 326** Fig. 8.6 From the Raven *Standard Progressive Matrices*. Reprinted by permission of J. C. Raven Limited. **p. 329** Fig. 8.8 Adapted from "Genetics and Intelligence: A Review" by L. Erlenmeyer-Kimling and L. F. Jarvik, *Science*, Vol. 142, pp. 1477-1479, December 1963. Copyright © 1963 by the American Association for the Advancement of Science. Reprinted by permission of the American Association for the Advancement of Sciences and L. Erlenmeyer-Kimling. **p. 342** Fig. 8.10 From *Nadia: Case of Extraordinary Drawing Ability in an Autistic Child* by Lorna Selfe. Copyright © 1978 by Harcourt Brace Jovanovich, Inc. Reprinted by permission of the publisher. **p. 372** Fig. 9.4 Adapted from "Individual patterns of development" by N. Bayley, *Child Development*, 27, 1956, pp. 45-47. Copyright © 1956 by The Society for Research in Child Development, Inc. Reprinted by permission. **p. 373** Fig. 9.5 From *The First Two Years* by Mary M. Shirley. Copyright 1933, 1960 by University of Minnesota Press. Reprinted by permission. **p. 450** Fig. 11.1 From *Personality—Strategies and Issues*, 4th Edition, by Robert

M. Liebert and Michael D. Spiegler. Copyright © 1982 by Brooks/Cole Publishing. Reprinted by permission. **p. 459** Fig. 11.3 From *Psychology: An Introduction*, 2nd Edition by Josh R. Gerow. Copyright © 1989 by Scott, Foresman and Company. **p. 465** Fig. 11.5 From *Psychology*, 3rd Edition by Andrew B. Crider, et al. Copyright © 1989 by Andrew B. Crider, George R. Goethals, Robert D. Kavanaugh, and Paul R. Solomon. Scott, Foresman and Company. **p. 473** Fig. 11.6 "Daily Record of Dysfunctional Thoughts" is reprinted by permission of Aaron T. Beck, the Center for Cognitive Therapy, University of Pennsylvania. **p. 562** Table 13.3 Reprinted from *Psychotherapy by Reciprocal Inhibition* by Joseph Wolpe, M.D. with the permission of the publishers, Stanford University Press. Copyright © 1958 by The Board of Trustees of the Leland Stanford Junior University. **p. 574** Fig. 13.6 From *The Benefits of Psychotherapy* by Mary Lee Smith, Gene V. Gloss, and Thomas I. Miller. Copyright © 1980 by Johns Hopkins University Press. Reprinted by permission. **p. 596** Fig. 14.3 From *Psychology*, 3rd Edition by Andrew B. Crider, et al. Copyright © 1989 by Andrew B. Crider, George R. Goethals, Robert D. Kavanaugh, and Paul R. Solomon. Scott, Foresman and Company. **p. 631** Fig. 15.2 Adapted from "Opinions and Social Pressure" by S. E. Asch, *Scientific American*, November 1955. Copyright 1955 by Scientific American, Inc. All rights reserved. Reprinted by permission. **p. 644** Table 15.2 From *Liking and Loving: An Invitation to Social Psychology* by Zick Rubin. Copyright © 1973 by Holt, Rinehart and Winston, Inc. Reprinted by permission of the publisher. **p. 642** Fig. 15.4 From "Bystander intervention in emergencies: Diffusion of responsibility" by J. M. Darley and B. Latane, *Journal of Personality and Social Psychology*, 8, 377-383, 1968. Copyright © 1968 by the American Psychological Association. Reprinted by permission of John McConnon Darley. **pp. 684, 685** Fig. 16.3, 16.4, 16.5 From Dienhart, *Basic Human Anatomy and Physiology*, 1979. Reprinted by permission of W. B. Saunders Co. and Charlotte M. Dienhart. **p. 709** Fig. A.1 From "Evaluation of Symbolic Information Signs" by J. Mackett-Stout and R. Dewar, *Human Factors*, Vol. 23, No. 2, 1981. Copyright © 1981 by The Human Factors Society, Inc. Reprinted by permission. **p. 716** Table A.2 From "How they rank in endorsements" by E. Comte, *The Sporting News*, January 15, 1989, p. 46. Reprinted by permission of The Sporting News Publishing Company. **p. 722** Fig. A.3 From *Mental Maps* by Peter Gould and Rodney White (New York: Viking Penguin, 1974). Reprinted by permission of Peter Gould.

Photo Credits

All photos not credited are the property of Scott, Foresman and Company. Positions of photographs are shown in abbreviated form as follows: top (t), bottom (b), center (c).

Table of Contents

Chapter 1

Chapter 2

Chapter 3

Chapter 4

Chapter 5

Chapter 6

Chapter 7

Donald Dietz/Stock, Boston **275** Elizabeth Crews/The Image Works **277** Wide World Photos **282** From *Congrestorium Artificia Memoriae* by Johannes Romberch, Venice, 1553 **285** Cary Wolinsky/Stock, Boston **298** Bob Daemmrich/The Image Works **301** Courtesy Conrac Corporation

Chapter 8
312 Ron Wyatt/Sportschrome, Inc. **315** National Portrait Gallery, London **317 (t)** U.S. Army **317 (b)** Historical Pictures Service, Chicago **320** Stanford University **321** Schleichkorn/Custom Medical Stock Photo **323** From Memoirs National Academy of Sciences, Psychological Examining in U.S. Army **326** Bob Adelman **329** Robert Brenner/PhotoEdit **336** Giraudon/Art Resource, NY **337** Owen Franken/Stock, Boston **342** From *Nadia: A Case of Extraordinary Drawing Ability in an Autistic Child.* Lorna Selfe. Academic Press, 1977 **346** Shostal Associates/Superstock

Chapter 9
359 Courtesy Connecticut Historical Society **361 (t)** Clark University Archives **361 (b)** Gesell Institute **363 (t)** Jon Erikson **363 (b)** Wide World Photos **365** Sharon Beals for *Insight* magazine **369** Courtesy Sterling K. Clarren, M.D. **371** Julie O'Neil/The Picture Cube **376** Andrew N. Meltzoff, Ph.D. **377** Thomas McAvoy. *Life* © Time Inc. **379** Martin Rogers/TSW/Click/Chicago **383 (l)** Myrleen Ferguson/PhotoEdit **383 (r)** Brian Vikander/West Light **386** Bill Ross/West Light **388** Marcia Weinstein **393** © Dr. Ronald H. Cohn/The Gorilla Foundation

Chapter 10
405 The Museum of Modern Art/Film Stills Archive **408** Don Smetzer/TSW/Click/Chicago **409** Mark Antman/The Image Works **413** Stacy Pick/Stock, Boston **416** Don Smetzer/TSW/Click/Chicago **417** Gale Zucker/Stock, Boston **419** Tony Freeman/PhotoEdit **421** Richard Hutchings/InfoEdit **424** Brent Jones **429** Gerry Souter/TSW/Click/Chicago **434** Bob Daemmrich/The Image Works

Chapter 11
444 Addison Geary/Stock, Boston **448** Paul Merideth/TSW/Click/Chicago **452** Myrleen Ferguson/PhotoEdit **453** The Bettmann Archive **454** Collection of the Newark Museum **456** Harvard University **462** The Bettmann Archive **463** Bob Daemmrich/Stock, Boston **466** Courtesy Dr. Albert Bandura **468** Larry Kolvoord/The Image Works **481** Bill Smith/*Sports Illustrated*

Chapter 12
490 Courtesy The American Mental Health Fund **494** The Bettmann Archive **495** Denver Art Museum, Samuel H. Kress collection **497** Library of Congress **498** Wide World Photos **511 (t)** UPI/Bettmann Newsphotos **511 (b)** Courtesy Essex Institute, Salem, MA **513** Susan Greenwood/Gamma-Liaison **514** The Museum of Modern Art/Film Stills Archive **521** Steve Schapiro/Gamma-Liaison **525** Bob Daemmrich/TSW/Click/Chicago **528** NIMH **529** Brookhaven National Laboratory & New York University Medical Center

Chapter 13
538 David Jennings/The Image Works **543** Rick Browne/Stock, Boston **547** Wide World Photos **551** UPI/Bettmann Newsphotos **552** Andy Freeberg **555** The Hulton Picture Company **556 (t)** Miro Vintoniv/The Picture Cube **556 (b)** Jocelyn Boutin/The Picture Cube **558** Ann Chwatsky/The Picture Cube **560** Photograph by Susan T. McElhinney **561** Courtesy Dr. Wolpe **564** Stacy Pickerell/TSW/Click/Chicago **565** Bob Daemmrich/Stock, Boston **566 (l)** Bob Daemmrich/The Image Works **566 (r)** Rob Nelson/Stock, Boston **567** The Bettmann Archive

Chapter 14
582 Copyright 1951 Time Inc. Reprinted by permission **585** Bob Daemmrich/The Image Works **589** Courtesy Dr. Ronald Lippitt **592** UPI/Bettmann Newsphotos **594 (t)** Beringer/Dratch/The Image Works **594 (b)** Herb Snitzer/Stock, Boston **592 (l)** David Austen/Stock, Boston **597 (r)** Bob Daemmrich/Stock, Boston **599** John Griffin/The Image Works **601** Jim Whitmer **604** Anna Flynn/Stock, Boston **605** Willie Hill/The Image Works **609** *Life,* July 25, 1915 **612** Walter Hodges/West Light

Chapter 15
622 Gamma-Liaison **628** Dr. Philip G. Zimbardo **629** Culver Pictures **635** *Animals Animals*/Brian Milne **639** Superstock **640 (l)** Photograph by Dorothea Lange. War Relocaton Authority in The National Archives **640 (r)** UPI/Bettmann Newsphotos **646** Henley & Savage/TSW/Click/Chicago **647** Bob Daemmrich/The Image Works **650** Charles Gupton/Stock, Boston **652** Wide World Photos **654** Dave Valdez/The White House

Chapter 16
665 Don Dixon **667** Historisk Museum, Universitetet I Bergen (From the book *Art in the Ice Age*, Frederick A. Praeger, New York © 1953) **668** UPI/Bettman Newphotos **669 (t)** 4-pointed urethral ring from J. L. Milton, *Pathology and Treatment of Spermatorrhoea* (London, 1887) **669 (b)** Apparatus against onanism from Maison Mathieu catalogue, 1904 **671** Scott F. Johnson **672** Brent Jones **675 (l)** American Society for Social Hygiene, 1926 **675 (r)** Courtesy Maryland Department of Health & Mental Hygiene **677 (l)** Barbara Alper/Stock, Boston **677 (r)** Joe Sohm/Stock, Boston **680** Charles Gatewood/The Image Works **686** Willie L. Hill Jr./Stock, Boston **689** Kobal Collection/Superstock **690** Dion Ogust/The Image Works **692** Alan Carey/The Image Works **693** Catherine Allport/The Image Works **699** Wide World Photos

Appendix
709 From "Evaluation of Symbolic Information Signs" by J. Mackett-Stout and R. Dewar, 1981, *Human Factors*, 23 (2), p. 142 **721 (r)** Jane Lewis/TSW/Click/Chicago **722** From *Mental Maps* by Peter Gould and Rodney White, 1974, Penguin Books Inc.